Sam Goldstein • Robert B. Brooks
Editors

Handbook of
Resilience in Children

Second Edition

 Springer

Editors
Sam Goldstein
Neurology, Learning
   and Behavior Center
Salt Lake City, UT 84102, USA

Robert B. Brooks
Department of Psychology
McLean Hospital and Harvard
   Medical School
Belmont, MA 02498, USA

ISBN 978-1-4614-3660-7 (Hardcover)   ISBN 978-1-4614-3661-4 (eBook)
ISBN 978-1-4899-7556-0 (Softcover)
DOI 10.1007/978-1-4614-3661-4
Springer New York Heidelberg Dordrecht London

Library of Congress Control Number: 2012940932

Printed on acid-free paper

Springer is part of Springer Science+Business Media (www.springer.com)

This work is dedicated with love to my partner Sherrie. You never really know you're unhappy until you are finally happy.

Sam Goldstein

With love and appreciation to my wife Marilyn, my sons Rich and Doug, my daughters-in-law Cybèle and Suzanne, and my grandchildren Maya, Teddy, Sophie, and Lyla, all of whom are a source of joy in my life.

Robert B. Brooks

This volume is also dedicated to the memory of Dr. Howard Kaplan, a distinguished contributor to both editions of our Handbook. At the time of his passing he was a Distinguished Professor of Sociology at Texas A&M University, the Mary Thomas Marshall Professor of Liberal Arts, a Regents' Professor, and Director of the Laboratory of the Studies of Social Deviance of the Department of Sociology. Among his accomplishments, Howard spent the last 37 years following the outcome of a group of seventh graders he began studying in 1971. His contribution to the field will be remembered and his wit and wisdom will be missed.

Robert B. Brooks
Sam Goldstein

Preface

A 5-year-old child watched helplessly as his younger brother drowned. In the same year, glaucoma began to darken his world. His family was too poor to provide the medical help that might have saved his sight. His parents died during his teens. Eventually he found himself in a state institution for the blind. As an African American, he was not permitted to access many activities within the institution, including music. Given the obstacles he faced, one would not have easily predicted that he would someday become a world renowned musician.

This man's name is Ray Charles. His life story, similar to many other individuals who faced great emotional, physical, and environmental adversities, exemplifies that some can and do survive and in fact thrive. Yet, many others who encounter similar patterns of problems struggle to transition successfully into their adult lives, often finding themselves adrift in poverty, despair, and psychiatric problems.

A comparison of individuals who overcome numerous obstacles with those who do not invites several intriguing questions. What exactly do the survivors do that enable them to succeed? How do they think? What kinds of experiences do they have that may be absent in the lives of those who are not successful? Are some of these experiences unique to surviving in the face of adversity? How much of their survival can be predicted by genetics, parenting, education, mentoring, temperament, and/or mental health? In a world in which stress and adversity appear to multiply almost exponentially from one generation to the next, the answers to these and related questions have become increasingly important. This edited volume reflects our efforts to address these questions.

We met by chance at a national conference almost 20 years ago. The first author was speaking about childhood disorders, including attention-deficit hyperactivity disorder and learning disabilities. The second was discussing his increasing focus on the qualities that appeared to help children at risk overcome adversity. There was an instant connection as we realized after a combined 50 years of clinical practice that the best predictors of children's functional outcome into adulthood lay not in relief of their symptoms, but rather in an understanding, appreciation, and nurturance of their strengths and assets.

In the past 20 years, our initial connection has evolved into a very close professional and personal friendship. We have spent countless hours elaborating ideas about the importance of a strength-based approach in our work and our lives. We have coauthored five books focusing on the process of resilience across the life span, a school consultation text built on our resilience model, three texts incorporating the resilience model to help parents of children with problems such as anxiety, learning disability, and anger, and numerous trade and professional articles as well as the first edition of this volume. We have developed a parenting curriculum for nurturing resilience in children and created an award-winning documentary. Throughout this work, we have come to realize the importance of thinking, feeling, and behaving in certain ways as a means of successfully and happily negotiating life.

Increasingly these qualities of success have found themselves under an umbrella of resilience. A resilient mindset, the ability to cope with and overcome adversity is not a luxury or a blessing possessed by some, but increasingly an essential component for all. This emerging field of study, which once focused only upon those who confronted and overcame adversity, has found universal appeal as researchers and clinicians examine how the qualities of resilience may be applied to all individuals, even those who have not experienced significant adversity.

What we have learned and still must learn from studying children who have overcome great hardships can be applied to enhance the lives of all children. It is not difficult to understand and accept that helping individuals develop such characteristics of resilience as dealing effectively with stress and pressure, coping with everyday challenges, bouncing back from disappointments, adversity, and trauma, developing clear and realistic goals, solving problems, relating comfortably with others, and treating oneself and others with respect are important ingredients to a satisfying life. As this second edition volume will attest, numerous scientific studies of children facing great adversity in their lives support the basic premise that resilience is an important and powerful force, worthy of the attention it is receiving. Resilience appears to explain why some children overcome overwhelming obstacles, sometimes clawing and scrapping their way to successful adulthood, while others become victims of their early experiences and environments. Yet as you will read, there is still much to be understood about the processes that mediate and shape resilience.

As we have written elsewhere, our belief as well as the belief of others in the significance of resilience emerged slowly. This slow recognition resulted in many children and their families not being helped as effectively as they might have had a strength-based model been in place. Reflecting on our years of clinical practice, we realize that many children suffered because well-meaning parents and professionals expended time and energy to fix deficits rather than giving at least equal weight to building assets. The focus of parents, clinicians, and educators on fixing children's problems is not difficult to understand. As professionals, we came by this bias honestly. It is how we were trained. We were taught to identify that which is different in a negative way and prescribe interventions to reduce symptoms or problems.

The professional field has come to increasingly realize that this "deficit model" is fine for identifying how and why individuals are different, even for prescribing strategies to improve those differences. However, we now believe and are setting out to scientifically demonstrate that our highest goal, namely, to improve the future of all children, is best accomplished by identifying and harnessing their strengths and shaping resilient qualities. The deficit model has fallen far short in helping to achieve this goal. Symptom relief has simply not been found to be robustly synonymous with changing long-term outcome. We have come to appreciate that the qualities of resilience examined scientifically in this volume can in fact protect and insulate not only children at risk, but all of us.

We are extremely pleased and honored about the success of the first edition of this volume and the opportunity to create an expanded and revised second edition. As with the first volume, we are pleased by the interest and willingness of our authors to share their knowledge and insight. This second edition has added seven new chapters, multiple new authors, and expanded and revised past chapters. Our contributors represent a great diversity of backgrounds and research interests, but share a vision of the importance of understanding and harnessing the power of resilience. As with the first edition, Part I begins with a number of background chapters. We offer a basic overview of resilience and reasons why resilience should be studied. Other authors describe resilient processes, the basic concept of resilience, and the processes of resilience differentially between genders. Drs. Margaret Wright and Ann Masten provide a comprehensive review of the study of resilience and its advancement through three major waves of research over the past 3 decades. Dr. Kirby Deater-Deckard and colleagues offer an integrated review of the resilience literature from a biopsychosocial perspective. This theme is exemplified in a translational framework in Chap. 13 as Drs. Shadi Houshyar and Joan Kaufman provide an overview of resilience in the maltreated child. We are exceptionally pleased that Dr. Emmy Werner, one of the earliest and most renowned researchers in the area of resilience, provides a revised overview of what we have learned from large scale, longitudinal studies about resilience. Dr. Jack Naglieri brings his expertise in assessment and offers a review of the current science in measuring resilience and the prospective future of evaluating resilience in clinical practice.

Part II continues with a section on environmental issues, including poverty, domestic violence and mental illness in parents, families as contexts for children's adaptation, and children as victims. Part III applies resilience as a phenomenon in more traditionally defined clinical disorders, including delinquency and other disruptive disorders, depression as it relates to learned helplessness, learning disability, and youth with impaired self-control. Drs. Jane Gilliam, Karen Reivich, Tara Chaplin, and Martin Seligman discuss their work at the University of Pennsylvania and the increasing focus on resilience as a means of creating an optimistic mindset and effective functioning in the face of stress.

Part IV dealing with assessment offers three new chapters to this volume. An overview of efforts to measure resilience and resilience-related processes are discussed as well as a number of promising new assessment tools. Part V focuses on resilience in clinical and school settings, offering a blend of revised and new chapters. These chapters represent our efforts at the beginning to create an applied psychology of resilience. A number of authors focus on the ways in which resilience theory can be used to enhance parenting, build self-esteem, provide educational opportunity, reduce schoolwide violence, and improve effective thinking. New to this edition are chapters by Dr. Beth Doll and Dr. Jonathan Cohen focusing on resilience processes in the classroom and school environment and Dr. David Crenshaw illuminating the treatment of traumatized children from a resilience framework.

Part VI includes four revised chapters focusing on resilience theory to shape the future of children and adults, including public health and developmental theories. Drs. Emily Winslow, Irwin Sandler, and Charlene Wolchik describe a program to build resilience in all children through a public health approach. Drs. Maurice Elias, Sarah Parker, and Jennifer Rosenblatt describe a model to facilitate educational opportunity as a means of strengthening resilience. Drs. Jennifer Taub and Melissa Pearrow describe schoolwide violence prevention programs as a means of strengthening resilient outcomes.

This second edition volume will again address which and by what processes variables within the child, immediate family, and extended community interact to offset the negative effects of adversity, thereby increasing the probability of positive development rather than dysfunction. Some of these processes likely reflect genetically inherent phenomena. Others involve the interaction of genetics and immediate environment, while still others reflect the impact of the extended environment. Some of these processes may serve to protect against the negative effects of stressors, while others may simply act to enhance development independent of the presence of stress.

It is our intent that this is the second edition of many volumes to change the foundation of applied psychology. It is our hope that this volume will provide readers with new ideas and theories and a more precise way of understanding and helping children. As we wrote in our first jointly authored text, *Raising Resilient Children* (2001), our worries for our children and their future are well founded. Yet there is reason to be optimistic about counteracting the negative influences in their lives. While advances in technology are taking place at an incredible pace, we believe strongly the future lies not in technology but in our children, children instilled by their parents, teachers, educators, and other adults with the resilient qualities necessary to help them shape a future with satisfaction and confidence.

Salt Lake City, UT, USA   Sam Goldstein, Ph.D
Needham, MA, USA   Robert B. Brooks, Ph.D

Bibliography

Brooks, R. & Goldstein, S. (2001). *Raising resilient children*. New York, NY: McGraw-Hill.

Happiness is not the absence of problems but the ability to deal with them.

H. Jackson Brown

I have been sustained throughout my life by three saving graces—my family, my friends, and a faith in the power of resilience and hope. These graces have carried me through difficult times and they have brought more joy to the good times than I ever could have imagined.

Elizabeth Edwards

Promise me you'll always remember: You're braver than you believe, and stronger than you seem, and smarter than you think.

Christopher Robin to Pooh (by A. A. Milne)

Acknowledgments

We would like to express our appreciation to Judy Jones for her confidence that we could create a second edition of this volume better than the first. Thanks also to the many professionals worldwide willing to share their exceptional theories, research, and ideas. Finally, thanks always to Ms. Kathy Gardner for coordination of authors and exceptional preparation of this manuscript.

Robert B. Brooks
Sam Goldstein

Contents

Contributors

Bonnie Aberson, Psy.D., ABN. Joe Dimaggio Children's Hospital, Hollywood, FL, USA

Jennifer P. Agans, M.A. Tufts University, Medford, MA, USA

Miriam R. Arbeit, M.A. Tufts University, Medford, MA, USA

Robert B. Brooks, Ph.D. Department of Psychology, McLean Hospital and Harvard Medical School, Needham, MA, USA

Colleen Carr Department of Psychology, Arizona State University, Tempe, AZ, USA

Tara M. Chaplin, Ph.D. University of Pennsylvania, Pennsylvania, PA, USA

Paul A. Chase Tufts University, Medford, MA, USA

Wai Chen, Ph.D. Ashurst Hospital, Lyndhurst Road, Southampton, MRC SGD, Institute of Psychiatry, King's College London, UK

Jonathan Cohen, Ph.D. National School Climate Center, New York, NY, USA

Michael J. Coutts, M.Ed. University of Nebraska, Lincoln, NE, USA

David A. Crenshaw, Ph.D., ABPP. Children's Home of Poughkeepsie, Poughkeepsie, NY, USA

Kirby Deater-Deckard, Ph.D. Department of Psychology, Virginia Polytechnic Institute and State University, Blacksburg, VA, USA

Melissa DeVries Neurology, Learning and Behavior Center, Salt Lake City, UT, USA

Beth Doll, Ph.D. Educational Psychology, College of Education and Human Sciences, University of Nebraska, Lincoln, 238 Mabel, Lee Hall Lincoln, NE, USA

Maurice J. Elias, Ph.D. Department of Psychology, Rutgers, The State University of New Jersey, Piscataway, NJ, USA

Robert D. Felner University of Louisville, Louisville, KY, USA

Jennifer L. Fleming, Ph.D. Department of Psychology, Devereux Center for Resilient Children, Villanova, PA, USA

Jane E. Gillham, Ph.D. Department of Psychology, Swarthmore College, Swarthmore, PA, USA

Andrea Gold, Department of Psychology, Yale University, New Haven, CT, USA

Sam Goldstein, Ph.D. Neurology, Learning and Behavior Center, Salt Lake City, UT, USA

Shadi Houshyar, Ph.D. Yale University School of Medicine, New Haven, CT, USA

Sara R. Jaffee, Ph.D. Institute of Psychiatry, Kings College London, London, UK

Judith V. Jordan, Ph.D. Jean Baker Miller Training Institute and Harvard Medical School, Lexington, MA, USA

Howard B. Kaplan, Ph.D. Department of Sociology, Texas A&M University, College Station, TX, USA

Paul A. LeBuffe Devereux Center for Resilient Children, Villanova, PA, USA

Richard M. Lerner, Ph.D. Tufts University, Medford, MA, USA

Mary Mackrain, M.Ed. Devereux Center for Resilient Children, Villanova, PA, USA

Marc Mannes, Ph.D. Booz Allen Hamilton, Minneapolis, MN, USA

Ann S. Masten, Ph.D. University of Minnesota, Minneapolis, MN, USA

Nancy Mather, Ph.D. University of Arizona, Tucson, AZ, USA

Jack A. Naglieri, Ph.D. University of Virginia, Charlottesville, VA, USA

Angela J. Narayan University of Minnesota, Minneapolis, MN, USA

Nicole Ofiesh, Ph.D. Stanford University, Stanford, CA, USA

Sarah J. Parker, Ph.D. Department of Psychiatry, Columbia University, New York, NY, USA

Melissa Pearrow, M.S. University of Massachusetts Boston, Boston, MA, USA

Sandra Prince-Embury, M.S. The Resiliency Institute of Allenhurst, LLC, West Allenhurst, NJ, USA

Karen Reivich, Ph.D. University of Pennsylvania, Pennsylvania, PA, USA

Jazmin A. Reyes Department of Psychology, Rutgers, The State University of New Jersey, Piscataway, NJ, USA

Richard Rider, Ph.D. Bellin Psychiatric Center, Green Bay, WI, USA

Jennifer L. Rosenblatt, Ph.D. New York University Child Study Center, New York, NY, USA

Katherine M. Ross, B.S. Devereux Center for Resilient Children, Villanova, PA, USA

Irwin N. Sandler, Ph.D. Department of Psychology, Arizona State University, Tempe, AZ, USA

Peter C. Scales, Ph.D. Search Institute, Minneapolis, MN, USA

Kristina L. Schmid Tufts University, Medford, MA, USA

Martin E.P. Seligman, Ph.D. University of Pennsylvania, Pennsylvania, PA, USA

Arturo Sesma Jr., Ph.D. St. Catherine University, St. Paul, MN, USA

Valerie B. Shapiro, Ph.D. University of California, Berkeley, CA, USA

Susan M. Sheridan, Ph.D. University of Nebraskan, Lincoln, NE, USA

Myrna B. Shure, Ph.D. Drexel University, Philadelphia, PA, USA

Tara M. Sjuts, M.A. University of Nebraska, Lincoln, NE, USA

Jennifer Taub, Ph.D. Boston Chinatown Neighborhood Center, Inc., Boston, MA, USA

Eric Taylor, Ph.D. MRC SGDP, Institute of Psychiatry, King's College London, UK

Zhe Wang Department of Psychology, Virginia Polytechnic Institute and State University, Blacksburg, VA, USA

Amy Eva Alberts Warren, Ph.D. Tufts University, Medford, MA, USA

Michelle B. Weiner Tufts University, Medford, MA, USA

Emmy E. Werner, Ph.D. University of California, Davis, CA, USA

Emily B. Winslow, Ph.D. Department of Psychology, Arizona State University, Tempe, AZ, USA

Sharlene A. Wolchik, Ph.D. Department of Psychology, Arizona State University, Tempe, AZ, USA

Margaret O'Dougherty Wright, Ph.D. Miami University, Oxford, OH, USA

Part I
Overview

Why Study Resilience?

Sam Goldstein and Robert B. Brooks

The study of resilience traces its roots back a scant 50 years. Early on, the field of study was not extensive and the number of researchers devoting their careers to the examination of this phenomenon was fairly small. The field, as Michael Rutter noted in 1987, reflected not so much a search for factual phenomena but "for the developmental and situational mechanisms involved in protective processes" (p. 2). The interest was and is not just on what factors insulate and protect, but how they went about exerting their influence. Resilience studies were reserved for high-risk populations with a particular focus on those youth demonstrating resilience or the ability to overcome the emotional, developmental, economic, and environmental challenges they faced growing up (Rutter, 1987).

The study of resilience has expanded significantly over the last 20 years. It is with a greater sense of urgency that resilience research has accelerated. There are a number of reasons for this phenomenon. First, as the technological complexity of the late twentieth century increased, the number of youth facing adversity and the number of adversities they faced appears to be increasing. More youth are at risk. Second, there has been an accelerated interest in not only understanding risk and protective factors and their operation, but in determining whether this information can be distilled into clinically relevant interventions (e.g., Fava & Tomba, 2009; Wolchik, Schenck, & Sandler, 2009) that may not only increase positive outcome for those youth facing risk, but also can be applied to the population of children in general in an effort to create, as Brooks and Goldstein (2001) point out, a "resilient mindset" in all youth.

The importance of such a mindset goes hand in hand with the perception that no child is immune from pressure in our current, fast-paced, stress-filled environment, an environment we have created to prepare children to become functional adults. Even children fortunate to not face significant adversity or trauma, or to be burdened by intense stress or anxiety, experience the pressures around them and the expectations placed upon them. Thus, the field has increasingly focused on identifying those variables that predict resilience in the face of adversity and developing models for effective application (Rutter, 2006). The belief then is that every child capable of developing a resilient mindset will be able to deal more effectively with stress and pressure, to cope with everyday challenges, to bounce back from disappointments, adversity, and trauma, to develop clear and realistic goals, to solve problems, to relate comfortably with others, and to treat oneself and others with respect.

S. Goldstein (✉)
Neurology, Learning and Behavior Center,
Salt Lake City, UT 84102, USA
e-mail: info@samgoldstein.com

R.B. Brooks
Department of Psychology, McLean Hospital
and Harvard Medical School, 60 Oak Knoll Terrace,
Needham, MA 02478, USA
e-mail: contact@drrobertbrooks.com

S. Goldstein and R.B. Brooks (eds.), *Handbook of Resilience in Children*,
DOI 10.1007/978-1-4614-3661-4_1, © Springer Science+Business Media New York 2013

A number of longitudinal studies over the past few decades have set out to develop an understanding of these processes, in particular the complex interaction of protective and risk factors with the goal of developing a model to apply this knowledge in clinical practice (Donnellan, Coner, McAdams, & Neppl, 2009; Garmezy, Masten, & Tellegen, 1984; Luthar, 1991; Rutter, Cox, Tupling, Berger, and Yule, 1975; Rutter and Quinton, 1984; Werner and Smith, 1982, 1992, 2001). These studies have made major contributions in two ways. First, they have identified resources across children's lives that predicted successful adjustment for those exposed to adversity, and second, they began the process of clarifying models of how these protective factors promote adaptation (Wyman, Sandler, Wolchik, and Nelson, 2000).

Whether these processes can be applied to all youth in anticipation of facing adversity remains to be demonstrated (Ungar, 2008). Masten (2001) suggests that the best recent evidence indicates that resilience processes are not only effective but can be applied, as demonstrated in the recovery to near-normal functioning found in children adopted away from institutional settings, characterized by deprivation. The positive outcome for many Romania adoptees appears to reflect this process (Beckett, et al., 2006; Kreppner, et al., 2007; Masten, 2001). Aames (1997), as cited in Rutter and the English and Romania Adoptees Study Team (1998), documents a significant degree of developmental catch up cognitively and physically in many of these children.

The process of creating a clinical psychology of resilience must begin with an understanding of the relevant variables and an appreciation and acknowledgement of certain key phenomena. The process of resilience first and foremost, for example, represents a biopsychosocial process. Such a process takes into account a range of biological, psychological, and social factors each with multidirectional influence in contributing to adequate functioning over time (Sameroff, 1995; Sroufe, 1997). Such a model must also begin with a basic foundation examining and appreciating the concept of wellness. In 1991 Emery Cowen, writing on the concept of wellness in children, suggested that a comprehensive approach to the promotion of wellness included four basic concepts: competence, resilience, social system modification, and empowerment. Cowen suggested that although wellness at the time continued to reflect an abstract concept, the pursuit of research in each of these four areas held promise in developing a scientific, reasoned, and reasonable model to ensure psychological health. In 1994, elaborating further on the concept of wellness, Cowen again emphasized the importance of resilience within the broader concept of wellness. For Cowen a wellness framework assumes the development of healthy personal environmental systems leading to the promotion of positive well-being and the reduction of dysfunction. A wellness framework emphasizes the interaction of the child in the family, academic setting, with adults outside of the home and with peers. Clearly, Cowen suggests a person–environmental interaction, one that ultimately predicts the strength and power of an individual's resilience in the face of adversity (Cowen, 1991).

Additionally, the absence of pathology does not necessarily equate with psychological wellness. This concept continues to represent a challenge for many mental health disciplines (Lorion, 2000). Mental health professionals are trained to collect data through a variety of means to measure symptoms. Such symptoms are equated with poor adaptation, inadequate adjustment, distress, and life problems. Emphasis on the negative equates with the perception that symptom relief will ultimately lead to positive long-term outcome. In fact, the accepted nosology of the mental health system is a model that reflects assessment of symptoms and severity packaged into what at this point are weakly factor-analyzed frameworks (American Psychiatric, 2000). Still unavailable, however, is a nosology and system to measure adaptation, stress hardiness, and the qualities necessary to deal successfully with and overcome adversity. Yet in clinical practice, it is increasingly recognized that it is these phenomena rather than relief of symptoms or the absence of certain risk factors that best predicts adaptation, stress hardiness, and positive adult adjustment.

As Cowen pointed out in 1994, mental health as a discipline must expand beyond symptom-driven treatment interventions if the tide of increasing stress and mental health problems in children are to be averted. There must be an increased focus on ways of developing an understanding of those factors within individuals, in the immediate environment, and in the extended environment that insulate and prevent emotional and behavioral disorders. Understanding these phenomena are as important as developing "an understanding of the mechanisms and processes defining the etiological path by which disorders evolve and a theory of the solution, conceptual and empirically supported or supportable intervention that alters those mechanisms and processes in ways which normalize the underlying developmental trajectory" (Cowen, 1994, p. 172).

Meta-analytic studies of preventive intervention effectiveness have generated increasing evidence of the ability to reduce the numbers of youth with certain emotional and psychiatric problems through an understanding of the forces that shape life outcome. As Emmy Werner has pointed out, "beating the odds" is an attainable goal. Researchers have made an effort to address the complex biopsychosocial phenomena that influence the incidence and prevalence of emotional and behavioral problems in youth with an eye towards developing a "science of prevention" (Coie et al., 1993).

Resilience is suggested as but one of a number of constructs that protect or reduce vulnerability. Lösel, Bliesener, and Köferl (1989) suggested that other protective factors include hardiness, adaptation, adjustment, mastery, good fit between the child and environment, and buffering of the environment by important adults in the child's life. As Sameroff (2000) points out, a transactional view of development suggests that a combination of factors within the child and environment are mutually interactive over time. With appropriate responsive and adequate care taking and environment in which mutual adaptations can occur, the odds favor good outcome (Campbell, 2002). In such a model, development is assumed to be discontinuous, characterized by qualitative change and reorganization. Children are viewed as active organizers of their experiences and their interactions with others are viewed as bidirectional. Children's responses to

adult behavior further influence that behavior. This model is consistent with artificial intelligence researcher, Gary Drescher's observation, suggesting that human beings are "choice-machines." That is, they act partly in response to genetically driven imperatives but generate reasons for acting as they do. These reasons are not hard wired but are responsive and modifiable to the environment and help guide future behavior (Dennett, 2003).

Finally, with a strong genetic influence, children consistently move towards attempting to develop normal homeostasis. In this model, a single potential traumatic experience would not be expected to lead to a chronically poor outcome. Instead it would be the cumulative, persistent, and pervasive presentation of stressors that promote risk. Within this type of conceptualization, risk falls within three dimensions: (1) external risk as opposed to protection, (2) vulnerability as opposed to invulnerability, and (3) lack of resilience as opposed to resilience (Greenbaum & Auerbach, 1992). Within such a model, a number of assumptions are made. These include: (1) early nurturing and age-relevant stimulation that provides protection by decreasing vulnerability (Bakermans-Kranenburg, van Ijzendoor, Pijlman, Mesman, & Juffer, 2008) and (2) risk-protection factors that are interactive. That is, factors within the child will interact and augment factors within the environment. This is likely true for risk factors as well; (3) vulnerability can be reduced and resilience increased by the introduction of additional protective factors; (4) risk and protective factors interact with a number of variables such as length of exposure, time of exposure, contributing to outcome; and (5) limited exposure to risk may in fact increase but not guarantee stress hardiness. Within these theoretical models, all of which will be discussed and reviewed in this text, the concept of resilience appears to play a major role. Within a wellness model, therefore, it is deserving of an identity and field of study.

The concept of resilience is fairly straightforward if one accepts the possibility of developing an understanding of the means by which children develop well emotionally, behaviorally, academically, and interpersonally either in the face of risk and adversity, or not. Such a model would offer valuable insight into those qualities that likely insulate and protect in the face of wide and varied types of adversities, including children experiencing medical problems (Brown and Harris, 1989), family risks (Beardslee, 1989; Beardslee & Podorefsky, 1988; Hammen, 1997; Worsham, Compas, & Ey, 1997), psychological problems (Hammen, 1997; Hauser, Allen, & Golden, 2006), divorce (Sandler, Tein, & West, 1994), loss of a parent (Lutzke, Ayers, Sandler, & Barr, 1999), as well as school problems (Skinner & Wellborn, 1994). Competent, appropriate parenting, for example, that which provides a democratic or authoritative model, parental availability, monitoring, and support, are powerful protective factors reducing the risk of antisocial behavior (Dubow, Edwards, & Ippolito, 1997; Masten et al., 1999). In fact, it appears to be the case that youth functioning well in adulthood, regardless of whether they faced adversity or not, may share many of the same characteristics in regards to stress hardiness, communication skills, problem solving, self-discipline, and connections to others. Though the earliest studies of resilience suggested the role of "exceptional characteristics" within the child that led to "invulnerability" (Garmezy & Nuechterlein, 1972), it may well be that resilience reflects very ordinary development processes to explain adaptation (Masten, 2001; Masten & Coatsworth, 1998). Though, as noted, a focus on symptoms and symptom relief, that is one assessing risk alone, may be satisfactory for identification of immediate needs and diagnoses within a psychopathology model, such data are necessary though not sufficient to improve future functioning. It has been well documented that not all children facing significant risk and adversity develop serious adolescent and adult psychiatric, lifestyle, and academic problems. Risk factors also do not appear to be specific to particular outcomes but relate to more broad developmental phenomena. It is likely, as noted, that there is a complex, multidimensional interaction between risk factors, biological functioning, environmental issues,

and protective factors that combines to predict outcome (e.g., Kim-Cohen & Gold, 2009).

Within this framework, resilience can be defined as a child's achievement of positive developmental outcomes and avoidance of maladaptive outcomes under adverse conditions (Rutter, 2006; Wyman et al., 1999). Within a clinical framework, a resilient mindset may be defined as the product of providing children with opportunities to develop the skills necessary to fare well in the face of adversity that may or may not lie in the path to adulthood for that individual. The study of resilience has overturned many negative assumptions in deficit-focused models about "the development of children growing up under the threat of disadvantage and adversity" (Masten, 2001, p. 227).

Finally, within the broader framework, the incorporation of resilience research into clinical practice may be based on four key assumptions as described by Benard, Burgoa, and Whealdon (1994). First, resilience helps to build communities that support human development based upon caring relationships. Second, resilience meets youth's needs for belonging and stability. Third, resilience is supported in the lives of practitioners as well. Fourth, resilience validates the wisdom of the heart or an intuitive, innate set of practices to guide clinical intervention.

A Cascade of Risk

Though children by their very nature have been vulnerable to a variety of risks throughout recorded history, perhaps advanced technological societies create new and different risks for children. Poverty, for example, has likely been a risk factor for children throughout history, yet the manner in which it impacts children may be different as times change. Beginning with the work of Pavenstedt (1965), examining children reared in poverty and well articulated by Garmezy and Nuechterlein (1972), researchers have questioned the processes by which individuals at risk for psychiatric conditions might be buffered or insulated developing these conditions or experiencing them to a greater degree of severity should they present. Epstein (1979) wrote of children exposed to trauma in the Holocaust, examining the variables that helped some survive. In many of these studies, positive, yet unexpected outcomes were considered interesting anomalies but not necessarily important data. Over time came growing recognition and acceptance that the ability to remain competent under adversity is not a random occurrence but one that can be investigated, understood, and instilled in others (Garmezy & Rutter, 1983).

Researchers have identified two distinct types of risk factors facing youth. The first kind reflects the at-risk status of the general population such as a child raised in a family with a depressed mother or absent father. The second kind of risk includes those factors that distinguish more or less positive outcomes among either groups with specified risks or those with seemingly little risk. In every case, each risk factor must be studied, understood, and then placed within a context of other risk and protective variables. It is for this reason that the scientific research of resilience is so complex. This too is perhaps a consequence of a complex, technologically advanced culture. A quick review of multiple risk statistics makes a strong case for developing a clinical psychology of resilience.

According to the Center for Disease Control (2002), at least 12% of students have considered suicide, with suicide being the third leading cause of death between the ages of 15 and 24, rare but increasing between the ages of 10 and 14. Three million teenagers struggle at any given time with depression. Only one-third receive mental health services.

According to the Center for Disease Control and Prevention and the Substance Abuse and Mental Health Services Administration (2002), one half of motor vehicle accidents in teens are associated with alcohol and drugs. Thirty percent of adolescent suicides are associated with alcohol and drugs. Further, children and teens who abuse alcohol and drugs engage in a variety of risk-taking behaviors at a significantly higher rate than the general population.

According to the National Center for Children of Poverty (2002), 37% of children in the United States live in low-income families. This comprises 27 million children. Forty percent of children under the age of six live in homes with an income below $27,000 per year for a family of four. Sixteen percent of children or over 11 million live in homes that are below the federal poverty level. Six percent of children or five million live in extreme poverty. Finally, the poverty rate is highest among African Americans (30%) and Latinos (28%).

According to the Center for Disease Control and Prevention National Household Survey of Drug Abuse, homicide is the second-leading cause of death for all 15–24-year-olds. It is the leading cause of death for adolescent African Americans and the second-leading cause of death for Hispanic youth. More than 400,000 youth in 2000 between the ages of 10 and 19 were injured as a result of violence. Over 800,000 children were documented victims of child abuse nationwide.

According to the Children's Defense Fund (2002), an American child was reported abused and neglected every 11 s. Over a half million children in the United States are in foster care. An American child is born without health insurance every minute. Millions of children are reported to lack safe, affordable, quality child care and early childhood education while their parents are at work. Seven and one-half million children are at home alone without supervision after school and almost 80% of children living at or below the poverty level are in working households (U.S. Census, 2000).

The Committee for Children at the National School Safety Center (2002) reports that one out of every seven children reports being bullied at school. In an average classroom there are at least three to four victims or bullies. Many victims report self-imposed isolation in response to bullying.

According to Children's Defense (2002) and the Youth Risk Behavior Surveillance System at the Centers for Disease Control (2002), births to girls ages 15–19 have steadily declined in the past decade, but sexually transmitted diseases among teenagers have increased. These statistics, only a sample of an emerging trend, make a strong case of the need to develop a clinical psychology of resilience.

Towards Defining a Clinical Psychology of Resilience

Within the materials sciences, resilience is defined as the ability of a material to resume its original shape or position after being spent, stretched, or compressed. In part resilience within this framework is defined by those properties that contribute to the speed and amount of possible recovery after exposure to stress. As previously discussed, the initial application of resilience into the clinical field focused on the absence of clinical diagnoses or psychiatric problems over time in the face of stress and adversity (Radke-Yarrow & Brown, 1993). Rutter (1990) suggested that within the clinical realm resilience and vulnerability may be at the opposite ends of a continuum, reflecting susceptibility to adverse consequences at one end and neutral or positive consequences upon exposure to risks at the others. This concept was further echoed by Anthony (1987). As Masten (2001) notes, "Early images of resilience in both scholarly work and mass media implied there was something remarkable or special about these children, often described by words such as invulnerable or invincible." One of the first popular press articles dealing with resilience appeared in the Washington Post on March 7, 1976. The headline read, "Troubles a Bubble for Some Kids." Thus, within the clinical realm, the idea of resilience reflected a process that was not necessarily facilitated through traditional psychotherapeutic or related intervention but rather was reflective of children who faced great adversity and in some internal way were special or remarkable, possessing extraordinary strength to overcome adversity. The belief was that these internalized qualities were somehow absent in others. Yet as Masten notes, resilience may be a common phenomenon resulting in most cases from the operation of "basic human adaptational systems." When these operate, development is successful even in the face of adversity. If these systems are impaired, children struggle.

Masten and Coatsworth (1998) suggest that resilience within a clinical realm requires two major judgments. The first addresses threat.

Individuals are not considered resilient if they have not faced and overcome significant adversity considered to impair normal development. The second assumption involves an inference about how one assesses good or adequate outcome in the face of adversity. This continues to be a complex issue that is just now being addressed empirically (Masten, 1999). It continues to be the case that most clinical practitioners define resilience on the basis of a child meeting the major requirements of childhood successfully (e.g., school, friends, family) despite facing significant life stress. Yet one must also consider that a child facing multiple developmental adversities who does not develop significant psychopathology but who may not demonstrate academic or social achievements may be resilient as well (Conrad & Hammen, 1993; Tiet et al., 1998).

Bronfenbrenner and Crouter (1983) describe a functional model for understanding the process of resilience that may lend itself well to building a foundation for the clinical psychology of resilience. Their model contains four domains of influence and two transactional points between domains. The four domains reflect: (1) the acute stressor or challenge, (2) the environmental context, (3) an individual's characteristics, and (4) the outcome. Points of interaction reflect the confluence between the environment and the individual as well as the individual and choice of outcome. These authors raise questions as to the exact mechanisms by which stressors or challenges interact with the environment, the internal set of characteristics, both genetic and acquired, of the individual, and the short-term processes individuals use to cope with stress and adversity. Interestingly, these processes most likely reflect skills learned by the individual through gradual exposure to increasing challenges or stressors. This "stress inoculation model" (Richardson, Neiger, Jensen, & Kumpfer, 1990) reflects Brooks and Goldstein (2001, 2003) concept of building stress hardiness by helping children develop a "resilient mindset."

Within clinical populations, three types of protective factors emerge as recurrent themes in most studies (Werner & Johnson, 1999). The first reflects dispositional attributes of the individual that elicit predominantly positive responses from the environment (e.g., easy temperament of the child within a family facing significant stress). The second reflects socialization practices within the family that encourage trust, autonomy, initiative, and connections to others. The third reflects the external support systems in the neighborhood and community that reinforce self-esteem and self-efficacy. Werner and Smith (1993) point out from their longitudinal work the large number of variables, such as age, birth order, ages of siblings, family size, and gender of the child that must be taken into account when assessing the relative vulnerability or resilience of an individual growing up in a family context of psychopathology or other risk. Such protective factors "moderate against the effects of a stressful or stress situation so that the individual is able to adapt more successfully than they would have had the protective factor not been present" (Conrad & Hammen, 1993, p. 594). Protective factors thus represent the opposite pole of vulnerability factors.

As discussed, the concept of resilience has not traditionally encompassed the potential of individuals to survive risks should they arise. Anthony (1987), Brooks and Goldstein (2001), and Rutter (2006) suggest that some individuals may appear resilient because they have not faced significant vulnerability, while others can be assessed for their potential to be resilient were they to face adversity. Defining risks and protective factors is not a simple process. They are likely variable in their presentation and in their impact on specific individuals. Cicchetti and Garmezy (1993) point out that it is difficult at times to distinguish between factors that place an individual at risk and factors that happen to distinguish between good or poor outcome but have no clear causal significance. These authors caution, for example, that "a child with a mother who has been depressed will not necessarily experience poor quality of care giving" (p. 500). Competent youth differ from those lacking competence, regardless of the level of adversity faced. Thus, even though resilient and maladaptive groups may experience similar life histories of severe negative life experience, outcome for those who are resilient appears more similar to those who have not faced adversity (Masten et al., 1999).

Youth demonstrating high competence despite facing strong adversity, when compared to youth equally competent facing low adversity, as well as groups of youth with low competence facing equal adversity, reflect this process. Competent, low adversity as well as resilient youth appear to possess average or better academic outcome, conduct, and social histories. They appear to possess very similar psychosocial resources, including better intellectual functioning, parent mental health, parental availability, and more positive self-concepts. Though a heatedly debated phenomenon, strong intellect has been found to be a protective factor (Hernstein & Murray, 1995). Intellectual aptitude appears to represent an important protective factor against the development of conduct problems for children growing up in highly disadvantaged settings or with high exposure to adverse life events (Masten et al., 1999; White, Moffitt, & Silva, 1989). However, there is no consensus on what defines intellectual ability (Masten, 2001). A strong performance on tests of intellectual functioning could reflect related neuropsychological factors, such as attention, memory, executive functioning, or, for that matter, motivation. Strong performance on intellectual and many of which are highly loaded on achievement tests, are also contributed to by the quality of the child-rearing environment.

A clinical psychology of resilience must also be capable of defining and understanding the multiple pathways by which outcome is achieved. Cicchetti and Rogosch (1996) describe this process through the concepts of equifinality and multifinality. Children may reach the same end point, in this case pathology or survival by different routes. Children with apparently similar risks and histories can have different outcomes. As Rutter (1994) pointed out in 1994, outcome is determined in part by the relative balance and interaction of risk and protective factors. The more risk factors present, the more likely the outcome will be adverse (Greenberg, Lengua, Coie, & Pinderhughes, 1999). It remains unclear, however, whether risk factors are equally potent in their adversity or protective factors equally stress resistant in their presentation (Shaw & Vondra, 1993). We have yet to develop a science to explain the manner by which biological factors such as stress during pregnancy, premature birth, and genetic variations leading to learning or related problems interact with family risk factors such as neglectful or harsh parenting and inconsistent child care, with physical phenomena such as poor nutrition and educational and community experiences. It has yet to be truly understood the means by which a child growing up with learning disability in a poverty stricken home, in a high-risk neighborhood, with parents exhibiting mental illness can and does overcome these adversities and transitions successfully into adult life.

On a basic level it is still debated as to how nature and nurture interact. How do genes and environment influence each other? How might a child's genetically driven temperament influence parent behavior, thus, in part, forming the basis for a child's attachment and ultimately affecting parental behavior? Whether a continuous or discontinuous process, children's development is impacted by a host of phenomena. The study of a clinical psychology of resilience will allow for the examination of the means by which biological, environmental, and related factors interact. For example, children who are active or irritable temperamentally may be more likely to continue to respond maladaptively in the face of ineffective parental behavior than children who do not demonstrate these patterns of temperament. Such children may be more sensitive to environmental risk factors (Belsky, Woodworth, & Crnic, 1996).

Finally, a clinical psychology of resilience must incorporate an understanding of the process of human development. Many of the great developmental theorists have assumed that human growth is in part driven by a need to cope, adapt, and develop a health homeostasis (Lorion, 2000). Across theoretical models resilience as encompassed within a wellness model is characteristic of positive adaptation. Thus, the absence of symptoms should not be equated with resilience or for that matter good functioning (Luthar & Brown, 2007). Studies of youth capable of overcoming a variety of unfavorable environmental phenomena are confirmatory that resilience in fact operates for some but not for others. Some youth are in

fact insulated or protected, seemingly invulnerable from risks likely to overcome most others. It may be that these resilience qualities are the best predictors of positive adult outcome (Brodsky, 1996; Masten & Coatsworth, 1998).

The Synthesis of a Model

In a review of successful prevention programs, Schorr (1988) suggests that effective programs for youth at risk are child centered and based upon the establishment of relationships with adults who are caring and respectful and who build trust. In writing about single mothers and their children, Polakow (1993) suggests that ultimately connections to people, interests, and to life itself may represent the key component in resilient processes. This phenomenon is well articulated by Hallowell (2001). As Michael Rutter has pointed out, "Development is a question of linkages that happen within you as a person and also in the environment in which you live" (as cited in Pines, 1984, p. 62). "The complexity of risk and resilience processes operating in multiple embedded systems of development in diverse contexts calls for the expertise of more than one discipline whether the goal is to advance empirical knowledge or to change the course of development through intervention" (Masten, 1999, p. 254).

Yet, if challenges are too severe normal processes break down (Baldwin et al., 1993). Baldwin et al. describe resilience as "a name for the capacity of the child to meet a challenge and to use it for psychological growth" (p. 743). In their description of an applied resiliency model, stressors are life challenges that if not balanced by external protective processes or resiliency factors within the individual lead to a disruption in functioning. Flach (1988) suggests that this process is not unidirectional but individuals can recover and function better as risks reduce and protective factors are introduced. It may well be, as Tarter (1988) noted, that vulnerability is "a characteristic that predisposes an individual to a negative outcome" (p. 78). Thus, a particular factor creates vulnerability but does not necessarily define the level of vulnerability experienced by a particular individual. Shared and nonshared environments likely also play moderating roles in determining risk and protective factors for particular individuals. Resilience perhaps is best understood as a product of phenotype–environment interaction (Tarter & Vanyukov, 1994). This phenomenon, referred to as epigenesis, likely offers the best understanding of the individual effects risk and protective factors have in shaping resilience. Such a phenomenon must be understood if it is to be applied effectively in a clinical framework.

Given the complexity of the human species and the culture we have created, there is a need to view the accomplishment of wellness and resilience from a multifaceted developmental and dynamic perspective (Masten & Coatsworth, 1998). The behavioral and emotional problems of children, the nature of our culture, risks such as emotional or physical abuse all present as significant challenges. None have single or simple etiologies or solutions. All appear to arise from a complex interaction of biological, environmental, and cognitive influences. All of these influences to some extent are idiosyncratic to the individual.

Many risk factors such as poverty or neighborhood adversity cannot easily be ameliorated. Though the process of resilience may reflect "the power of the ordinary" (Masten, 2001), there must be an increasing focus on understanding the protective variables that allow some children to function well in these environments and continue to function well in the future. Just as risk factors are not specific to particular adverse outcomes, protective factors may also not be equally specific. The "ordinary magic" that Ann Masten so eloquently writes about becomes an elusive phenomenon in the face of these risks. Masten (2001) notes that resilience does not appear to arise from rare or special qualities but from "the everyday magic of ordinary, normative human resources in the minds, brains and bodies of children in their families and relationships and in their communities" (p. 235).

In 1993, Coie et al. provided a list of generic risk factors including those of family conflict and poverty. These researchers and others have noted a diverse set of protective factors that often relate to close relationships with prosocial and caring adults (Masten, Best, & Garmezy, 1990). Finally, there is increasing research reflecting primarily genetic-driven phenomena that either predispose individuals to stress hardiness or risk in the face of adversity. These types of cumulative risk and protection models form the basis of what is hoped to be the future state of clinical psychology of resilience and treatment for youth at risk (Yoshikawa, 1994).

This volume addresses which and by what processes variables within the child, immediate family, and extended community interact to offset the negative effects of adversity, thereby increasing the probability of positive development rather than dysfunction. Some of these processes may serve to protect the negative effects of other stressors while others simply act to enhance development regardless of the presence of stress. As Seligman has pointed out (1998a, 1998b), attending to those issues that are preventative and that create a resilient mindset and wellness will require a significant paradigm shift in mental health professionals and the community at large. Seligman has suggested the shift will not be easy to make. While professionals may be "ill-equipped to do effective prevention" (1998a, p. 2) at this time the development of a clinical psychology of resilience would appear to offer the best hope of forming a cornerstone for the development of a "positive social science."

References

American Psychiatric Association. (2000). *Diagnostic and statistical manual of mental disorders* (4th ed., text revision). Washington, DC: Author.

Anthony, E. J. (1987). Risk, vulnerability and resilience: An overview. In E. J. Anthony & B. Cohler (Eds.), *The invulnerable child* (pp. 3–48). New York, NY: Guilford.

Bakermans-Kranenburg, M. J., van Ijzendoor, M. H., Pijlman, F. T. A., Mesman, J., & Juffer, F. (2008). Experimental evidence for differential susceptibility: Dopamine D4 receptor polymorphism (DRD4 VNTR) moderates intervention effects on toddlers' externalizing behavior in a randomized controlled trial. *Developmental Psychology, 44*, 293–300.

Baldwin, A. L., Baldwin, C. P., Kasser, T., Zax, M., Sameroff, A., & Seifer, R. (1993). Contextual risk and resiliency during late adolescence. *Development and Psychopathology, 5*, 741–761.

Beardslee, W. R. (1989). The role of self-understanding in resilient individuals. *The American Journal of Orthopsychiatry, 59*, 266–278.

Beardslee, W. R., & Podorefsky, D. (1988). Resilient adolescents whose parents have serious affective and other psychiatric disorders: Importance of self-understanding and relationships. *The American Journal of Psychiatry, 145*, 63–69.

Beckett, C., Maughan, B., Rutter, M., Castle, J., Colvert, E., Groothues, C., et al. (2006). Do the effects of early severe deprivation on cognition persist into early adolescence? Findings from the English and Romanian Adoptees study. *Child Development, 77*, 696–711.

Belsky, J., Woodworth, S., & Crnic, K. (1996). Trouble in the second year: Three questions about family interaction. *Child Development, 67*, 556–568.

Benard, B., Burgoa, C., & Whealdon, K. (1994). *Fostering resiliency in kids: Protective factors in the school (training of trainers)*. San Francisco: Far West Laboratory.

Brodsky, A. E. (1996). Resilient single mothers in risky neighborhoods: Negative psychological sense of community. *Journal of Community Psychology, 24*, 347–364.

Bronfenbrenner, U., & Crouter, A. C. (1983). The evolution of environmental models in developmental research. In P. H. Mussen (Ed.), *Handbook of Child Psychology* (4th ed.). New York, NY: Wiley.

Brooks, R., & Goldstein, S. (2001). *Raising resilient children: Fostering strength, hope and optimism in our children*. New York, NY: McGraw-Hill.

Brooks, R., & Goldstein, S. (2003). *Nurturing resilience in our children: Answers to the most important parenting questions*. New York, NY: McGraw-Hill.

Brown, G. W., & Harris, T. O. (1989). *Life events and illness*. New York: Guilford.

Campbell, S. B. (2002). *Behavior problems in preschool children* (2nd ed.). New York, NY: Guilford.

Center for Disease Control. (2002). Youth risk behavior surveillance system. Retrieved December 15, 2011, from www.cdc.gov

Children's Defense Fund. (2002). Health and safety trends in children. Retrieved December 15, 2011, from www.childrensdefensefund.org

Cicchetti, D., & Garmezy, N. (1993). Prospects and promises in the study of resilience. *Development and Psychopathology, 5*, 497–502.

Cicchetti, D., & Rogosch, F. (1996). Equifinality and multifinality in developmental psychopathology. *Development and Psychopathology, 8*, 597–600.

Coie, J. D., Watt, N. F., West, S. G., Hawkins, J. D., Asaranow, J. R., Markman, H. J., Ramey, S. L., Shure, M. B., & Long, M. B. (1993). The science of prevention: A conceptual framework and some directions for a national research program. *American Psychologist, 48*, 1013–1022.

Conrad, M., & Hammen, C. (1993). Protective and resource factors in high- and low-risk children: A comparison of children with unipolar, bipolar, medically ill, and normal mothers. *Developmental and Psychopathology, 5*, 593–607.

Cowen, E. L. (1991). In pursuit of wellness. *American Psychologist, 46*, 404–408.

Cowen, E. L. (1994). The enhancement of psychological wellness: Challenges and opportunities. *American Journal of Community Psychology, 22*, 149–179.

Dennett, D. C. (2003). *Freedom evolves*. New York, NY: Viking.

Donnellan, M. B., Coner, K. J., McAdams, K. K., & Neppl, T. K. (2009). Personal characteristics and resilience to economic hardship and its consequences: Conceptual issues and empirical illustrations. *Journal of Personality, 77*, 1645–1676.

Dubow, E. F., Edwards, S., & Ippolito, M. F. (1997). Life stressors, neighborhood disadvantage, and resources: A focus on inner-city children's adjustment. *Journal of Clinical Child Psychology, 26*, 130–144.

Epstein, H. (1979). *Children of the holocaust*. New York, NY: Penguin Books.

Fava, G. A., & Tomba, E. (2009). Increasing psychological well-being and resilience by psychotherapeutic methods. *Journal of Personality, 77*, 11903–11934.

Flach, F. F. (1988). *Resilience: Discovering new strength at times of stress*. New York, NY: Ballantine Books.

Garmezy, N., Masten, A. S., & Tellegen, A. (1984). The study of stress and competence in children: A building block for developmental psychopathology. *Child Development, 55*, 97–111.

Garmezy, N., & Nuechterlein, K. (1972). Invulnerable children: The fact and fiction of competence and disadvantage. *The American Journal of Orthopsychiatry, 42*, 328–329.

Garmezy, N., & Rutter, M. (1983). *Stress, coping, and development in children*. New York, NY: McGraw-Hill.

Greenbaum, C. W., & Auerbach, J. G. (1992). The conceptualization of risk, vulnerability, and resilience in psychological development. In C. W. Greenbaum & J. G. Auerbach (Eds.), *Longitudinal studies of children at psychological risk: Cross-national perspectives* (pp. 9–28). Norwood, NJ: Ablex.

Greenberg, M. T., Lengua, L. J., Coie, J. D., & Pinderhughes, E. E. (1999). Predicting developmental outcomes at school entry using a multiple risk model: Four American communities. *Developmental Psychology, 35*, 403–417.

Hallowell, E. M. (2001). *Connect: 12 Vital ties that open your heart, lengthen your life and deepen your soul*. New York, NY: Pocket Books.

Hammen, C. (1997). Children of depressed parents: The stress context. In S. A. Wolchik & I. N. Sandler (Eds.), *Handbook of children's coping: Linking theory and intervention* (pp. 131–159). New York, NY: Plenum.

Hauser, S., Allen, J., & Golden, E. (2006). *Out of the woods: Tales of resilient teens*. Cambridge, MA: Harvard University Press.

Hernstein, R. J., & Murray, C. (1995). *The bell curve: Intelligence and class structure in American life*. New York, NY: Simon & Schuster.

Kim-Cohen, J., & Gold, A. L. (2009). Measured gene-environment interactions and mechanisms promoting resilient development. *Current Directions in Psychological Science, 18*, 138–142.

Kreppner, J. M., Rutter, M., Beckett, C., Castle, J., Colvert, E., Groothues, C., et al. (2007). Normality and impairment following profound early institutional deprivation: A longitudinal follow-up into early adolescence. *Developmental Psychology, 43*, 931–946.

Lorion, R. P. (2000). Theoretical and evaluation issues in the promotion of wellness and the protection of "well enough". In D. Cicchetti, J. Rappaport, I. Sandler, & R. Weissberg (Eds.), *The promotion of wellness in children and adolescents*. Washington, DC: CWLA.

Lösel, F., Bliesener, T., & Köferl, P. (1989). On the concept of invulnerability: Evaluation and first results of the Bielefeld project. In M. Brambring, F. Losel, & H. Skowronek (Eds.), *Children at risk: Assessment, longitudinal research, and intervention* (pp. 186–219). New York, NY: Walter de Gruyter.

Luthar, S. S. (1991). Vulnerability and resilience: A study of high-risk adolescents. *Child Development, 62*, 600–616.

Luthar, S. S., & Brown, P. J. (2007). Maximizing resilience through diverse levels of inquiry: Prevailing paradigms, possibilities, and priorities for the future. *Development and Psychopathology, 19*, 931–955.

Lutzke, J. R., Ayers, T. S., Sandler, I. N., & Barr, A. (1999). Risks and interventions for the parentally bereaved child. In S. A. Wolchik & I. N. Sandler (Eds.), *Handbook of children's coping: Linking theory and intervention* (pp. 215–245). New York, NY: Plenum.

Masten, A. S. (1999). Resilience comes of age: Reflections on the past and outlook for the next generation of research. In M. D. Glantz, J. Johnson, & L. Huffman (Eds.), *Resilience and development: Positive life adaptations* (pp. 282–296). New York, NY: Plenum.

Masten, A. S. (2001). Ordinary magic: Resilience processes and development. *American Psychologist, 56*, 227–238.

Masten, A. S., Best, K. M., & Garmezy, N. (1990). Resilience and development: Contributions from the study of children who overcome adversity. *Development and Psychopathology, 2*, 425–444.

Masten, A. S., & Coatsworth, J. D. (1998). The development of competence in favorable and unfavorable environments: Lessons from research on successful children. *American Psychologist, 53*, 205–220.

Masten, A. S., Hubbard, J. J., Gest, S. D., Tellegen, A., Garmezy, N., & Ramirez, M. (1999). Competence in the context of adversity: Pathways to resilience and maladaptation from childhood to late adolescence. *Development and Psychopathology, 11*, 143–169.

Substance Abuse and Mental Health Services Administration. (2002). Drug abuse statistics. Retrieved December 15, 2011, from www.drugabusestatistics.samsha.gov

National Center for Children of Poverty. (2002). Poverty statistics. Retrieved December 15, 2011, from www.nccp.org

Pavenstedt, E. (1965). A comparison of the childrearing environment of upper-lower and very low-lower class families. *The American Journal of Orthopsychiatry, 35*, 89–98.

Pines, M. (1984). Resilient children: Interview with Michael Rutter. *Psychology Today, 18*, 56–57.

Polakow, V. (1993). *Lives on the edge: Single mothers and their children in the other America*. Chicago: University of Chicago Press.

Radke-Yarrow, M., & Brown, E. (1993). Resilience and vulnerability in children of multiple risk families. *Development and Psychopathology, 5*, 518–592.

Richardson, G. E., Neiger, B. L., Jensen, S., & Kumpfer, K. (1990). The resiliency model. *Health Education, 21*(6), 33–39.

Rutter, M. (1987). *Psychosocial resilience and protective mechanisms*. New York, NY: Irvington.

Rutter, M. (1990). Psychosocial resilience and protective mechanisms. In J. Rolf, A. S. Masten, D. Cicchetti, K. H. Nuechterlein, & S. Weintraub (Eds.), *Risk and protective factors in the development of psychopathology* (Vol. 9, pp. 181–214). New York, NY: Cambridge University Press.

Rutter, M. (1994). Beyond longitudinal data: Causes, consequences, changes and continuity. *Journal of Consulting and Clinical Psychology, 62*, 928–940.

Rutter, M. (2006). Implications of resilience concepts for scientific understanding. *Annals of the New York Academy of Sciences, 1094*, 1–12.

Rutter, M., Cox, A., Tupling, C., Berger, M., & Yule, W. (1975). Attainment and adjustment in two geographical areas: I. He prevalence of psychiatric disorder. *The British Journal of Psychiatry, 126*, 493–509.

Rutter, M., & the English and Romanian Adoptees (ERA) Study Team. (1998). Developmental catch-up and deficit, following adoption after severe global early privation. *Journal of Child Psychology and Psychiatry, 39*, 465–476.

Rutter, M., & Quinton, D. (1984). Long-term follow-up of women institutionalized in childhood: Factors promoting good functioning in adult life. *British Journal of Developmental Psychology, 18*, 225–234.

Sameroff, A. J. (1995). General systems theories and developmental psychopathology. In D. Cicchetti & D. Cohens (Eds.), *Developmental psychopathology* (Theory and methods, Vol. 1, pp. 659–695). New York, NY: Wiley.

Sameroff, A. J. (2000). Dialectical processes in developmental psychopathology. In A. J. Sameroff, M. Lewis, & S. Miller (Eds.), *Handbook of developmental psychopathology* (2nd ed., pp. 23–40). New York, NY: Plenum.

Sandler, I. N., Tein, J., & West, S. G. (1994). Coping, stress and psychological symptoms of children of divorce: A cross-sectional and longitudinal study. *Child Development, 65*, 1744–1763.

Schorr, L. (1988). *Within our reach: Breaking the cycle of disadvantage*. New York, NY: Doubleday.

Seligman, M. E. P. (1998a). Building human strength: Psychology's forgotten mission. *APA Monitor, 29*(1), 2.

Seligman, M. E. P. (1998b). Building human strength: Psychology's forgotten mission. *APA monitor, 29*(#4), 2.

Shaw, D. S., & Vondra, J. L. (1993). Chronic family adversity and infant attachment security. *Journal of Child Psychology and Psychiatry, 34*, 1205–1215.

Skinner, E. A., & Wellborn, J. G. (1994). Coping during childhood and adolescence: A motivational perspective. In D. R. Lerner & M. Perlmutter (Eds.), *Life-span development and behavior* (pp. 91–123). Hillsdale, NJ: Erlbaum.

Sroufe, L. A. (1997). Psychopathology as an outcome of development. *Development and Psychopathology, 9*, 251–268.

Tarter, R. E. (1988). The high-risk paradigm in alcohol and drug abuse research. In R. W. Pickens & D. S. Svikis (Eds.), *Biological vulnerability to drug abuse* (NIDA Research Monograph, Vol. 89, pp. 73–86). Washington, DC: U.S. Government Printing Office.

Tarter, R., & Vanyukov, M. (1994). Alcoholism: A developmental disorder. *Journal of Consulting and Clinical Psychology, 62*, 1096–1107.

Tiet, Q. Q., Bird, H. R., Davies, M., Hoven, C., Cohen, P., Jensen, P. S., & Goodman, S. (1998). Adverse life events and resilience. *Journal of the American Academy of Child and Adolescent Psychiatry, 37*, 1191–1200.

Ungar, M. (2008). Resilience across cultures. *British Journal of Social Work, 38*, 218–235.

U.S. Census. (2000). Retrieved December 15, 2011, from www.censusus.gov

Werner, E. E., & Johnson, J. L. (1999). Can we apply resilience? (pp. 259-268). In M. D. Glantz & J. L. Johnson (Eds.), *Resilience in development: Positive life adaptations*. New York, NY: Kluwer/Academic/Plenum.

Werner, E. E., & Smith, R. S. (1982). *Vulnerable but invincible: A study of resilient children*. New York, NY: McGraw Hill.

Werner, E. E., & Smith, R. S. (1992). *Overcoming the odds: High risk children from birth to adulthood*. Ithaca, NY: Cornell University Press.

Werner, E. E., & Smith, R. S. (1993). *Overcoming the odds: High risk children from birth to adulthood*. Ithaca, New York: Cornell University Press.

Werner, E. E., & Smith, R. S. (2001). *Journeys from childhood to mid-life: Risk, resilience and recovery*. Ithaca, NY: Cornell University Press.

White, J. L., Moffitt, T. E., & Silva, P. A. (1989). A prospective replication of the protective effects of I.Q. in subjects at high risk for juvenile delinquency. *Journal of Consulting and Clinical Psychology, 57*, 719–724.

Wolchik, S. A., Schenck, C. E., & Sandler, I. N. (2009). Promoting resilience in youth from divorced families: Lessons learned from experimental trials of the New Beginnings program. *Journal of Personality, 77*, 1833–1868.

Worsham, N. L., Compas, B. E., & Ey, S. (1997). Children's coping with parental illness. In S. A. Wolchik & I. N. Sandler (Eds.), *Handbook of children's coping: Linking theory and intervention* (pp. 195–215). New York, NY: Plenum.

Wyman, P. A., Cowen, E. L., Work, W. C., Hoyt-Meyers, L. A., Magnus, K. B., & Fagen, D. B. (1999). Caregiving and developmental factors differentiating young at-risk urban children showing resilient versus stress-affected outcomes: A replication and extension. *Child Development, 709*, 645–659.

Wyman, P. A., Sandler, I., Wolchik, S., & Nelson, K. (2000). Resilience as cumulative competence promotion and stress protection: Theory and intervention. In D. Cicchetti, J. Rappaport, I. Sandler, & R. Weissberg (Eds.), *The promotion of wellness in children and adolescents*. Washington, DC: CWLA.

Yoshikawa, H. (1994). Prevention as cumulative protection: Effects of early family support and education on chronic delinquency and its risks. *Psychological Bulletin, 115*, 28–54.

Youth Risk Behavior Surveillance System. (2002). Statistics on risk factors in youth. Retrieved December 15, 2011, from www.cdc.gov/nccdphp/dash/yrbs/index.htm

Resilience Processes in Development: Four Waves of Research on Positive Adaptation in the Context of Adversity

Margaret O'Dougherty Wright, Ann S. Masten, and Angela J. Narayan

How do children and adolescents "make it" when their development is threatened by poverty, neglect, maltreatment, war, violence, or exposure to oppression, racism, and discrimination? What protects them when their parents are disabled by substance abuse, mental illness, or serious physical illness? How do we explain the phenomenon of resilience—children succeeding in spite of serious challenges to their development—and put this knowledge to work for the benefit of children and society? The scientific study of resilience emerged around 1970 when a group of pioneering researchers began to notice the phenomenon of positive adaptation among subgroups of children who were considered "at risk" for developing later psychopathology (Masten, 2001, 2012).

The resilience research pioneers led a revolution in thinking about the origins and treatment of psychopathology. The primary focus of earlier clinical research on children at high risk for psychopathology had been either to observe the consequences of adversity or the unfolding of risk processes accounting for the etiology of disorders. Research efforts were directed towards understanding pathology and deficits, rather than on how problems were averted, resolved, or transcended. The field of mental health at the time was dominated by psychoanalytic theory and a disease-oriented biomedical model that located the source of illness within the individual. However, the first investigators to explore the phenomenon of resilience realized that models based primarily on predicting psychopathology were limited in scope and usefulness, providing little understanding of how good outcomes were achieved by many of the children identified as "at risk." Such information was vital to the goal of intervening to improve the odds of good developmental outcomes among children at risk. One of the great contributions of the early investigators was their recognition and championing of the idea that understanding positive developmental pathways in the context of adversity is fundamentally important for preventing and treating problems, particularly among children at risk for psychopathology.

The study of resilience has advanced in four major waves of research. In this chapter we highlight the concepts and findings resulting from these waves to date, as they have shaped an emerging resilience framework for research and practice. The first wave of work yielded good descriptions of resilience phenomena, along with basic concepts and methodologies, and focused on the individual. The second wave yielded a more dynamic accounting of resilience, adopting a developmental systems approach to theory and research on positive adaptation in the context of adversity or risk, and focused on the transactions among individuals and the many systems in which their development is embedded. The third wave focused on creating resilience by intervention

M. O'Dougherty Wright (✉)
Miami University, Oxford, OH, USA
e-mail: wrightmo@muohio.edu

A.S. Masten • A.J. Narayan
University of Minnesota, Minneapolis, MN, USA

S. Goldstein and R.B. Brooks (eds.), *Handbook of Resilience in Children*,
DOI 10.1007/978-1-4614-3661-4_2, © Springer Science+Business Media New York 2013

directed at changing developmental pathways. The fourth wave, now rising, is focused on understanding and integrating resilience across multiple levels of analysis, with growing attention to epigenetic and neurobiological processes, brain development, and the ways that systems interact to shape development.

The First Wave: Identifying Individual Resilience and Factors that Make a Difference

Initial research in this area was dominated by a strong cultural ethos in the United States that glorified rugged individualism—that Horatio Alger ability to "pick oneself up by one's own bootstraps" and succeed solely through one's own efforts. Early on, investigators as well as journalists referred to children who functioned well despite the odds as "invulnerable" (Anthony, 1974; Pines, 1975) and tended to focus on their personal traits and characteristics. Such children were thought to be impervious to stress because of their inner fortitude or character armor. As research extended across time and across types of trauma endured, the term of "invulnerability" was replaced by more qualified and dynamic terms such as stress-resistance and resilience. These concepts were thought to more appropriately capture the interplay of risk and protective processes occurring over time and involving individual, family, and larger sociocultural influences (Masten, Best, & Garmezy, 1990; Rutter, 1987; Werner & Smith, 1982, 1992).

Key Concepts

During the first generation of research on resilience in development, these phenomena were studied in a variety of different contexts throughout the world (Glantz & Johnson, 1999; Luthar, 2006; Masten, 2012; Masten, Best, and Garmezy, 1990). A consensus emerged on key concepts, though controversies continue to this day and there have been changes in emphasis over the years. For example, in early work, *resilience*

typically referred to a pattern of positive adaptation in the context of past or present adversity. Later definitions have become broader and more dynamic, in keeping with efforts to integrate the concept across levels of analysis and across disciplines (Masten, 2007, 2012). An example of a systems-oriented definition of resilience follows:

> The capacity of a dynamic system to withstand or recover from significant challenges that threaten its stability, viability, or development (Masten, 2011).

Resilience was also recognized as an inferential concept that involved two distinct judgments (Luthar & Cicchetti, 2000; Masten & Coatsworth, 1998). First, one judges by some criteria that there has been a significant threat to the development or adaptation of the individual or system of interest. Second, one judges that, despite this threat or risk exposure, the current or eventual adaptation or adjustment of the individual or system is satisfactory, again by some selected set of criteria.

There has been considerable confusion throughout the past four decades on the precise meaning of many terms used by resilience researchers (Luthar, Cicchetti, & Becker, 2000; Masten, 2001, 2012; Rutter, 2000). Nonetheless, there is some consensus on a working vocabulary for this domain of inquiry, as presented in Table 2.1. Much of that vocabulary (e.g., adversity, life events, risks, and vulnerability) was already familiar from studies of psychopathology. Resilience studies, however, underscored some concepts that had been omitted or underemphasized in earlier work, most particularly the concepts of assets, compensatory (promotive) factors, protective factors, and competence or developmental tasks.

Resilience definitions always consider the threats to good adaptation (or perturbations in a system), conceptualized in terms like *risk, adversity, and negative life events*. As illustrated in Table 2.1, *risk* most basically signifies an *elevated probability* of a negative outcome. It is a group or population term, in that a risk factor does not identify which individual or individuals in a group considered at risk will eventually display difficulties in adaptation, but rather that the group of people with this risk factor is less

Table 2.1 Definition and illustration of key concepts

Term	Definition	Examples
Adversity	Disturbances to the function or viability of a system; experiences that threaten adaptation or development	Poverty; homelessness; child maltreatment; political conflict; disaster
Resilience	Positive adaptation in the face of risk or adversity; capacity of a dynamic system to withstand or recover from disturbance	Child from violent family does well in school, has friends, behaves well, and gets along well with the teacher; earthquake survivor recovers to normal function and development
Risk	An elevated probability of an undesirable outcome	The odds of developing schizophrenia are higher in groups of people who have a biological parent with this disorder
Risk factor	A measurable characteristic in a group of individuals or their situation that predicts a negative outcome on a specific outcome criteria	Premature birth; parental divorce; poverty; parental mental illness; child maltreatment
Cumulative risk	Increased risk due to: (a) the presence of multiple risk factors; (b) multiple occurrences of the same risk factor; or (c) the accumulating effects of ongoing adversity	Children in homeless families often have many risk factors for developmental problems, including a single parent who hasn't graduated from high school, a history of poor health care, poor schooling, inadequate nutrition, and exposure to many negative events, such as family or community violence
Vulnerability	Individual (or system) susceptibility to undesirable outcomes; the diathesis in diathesis-stressor models of psychopathology	Anxious children find school transitions more stressful; compromised immune function increases susceptibility to infectious diseases
Proximal risk	Risk factors experienced directly by the child	Witnessing violence; associating with delinquent peers
Distal risk	Risk arising from a child's ecological context but mediated through more proximal processes	High community crime rate; inaccessible health care; recession
Asset, resource, on compensatory or promotive factor	A measurable characteristic in a group of individuals or their situation that predicts a positive or desirable outcome, similarly for low and high levels of risk	Cognitive skills; competent parenting; high social class
Protective factor	A predictor of better outcomes *particularly* in situations of risk or adversity	Airbags in automobiles; 911 services; neonatal intensive care; health insurance
Cumulative protection	The presence of multiple protective factors in an individual's life	A child in a poor neighborhood has attentive parents, a safe home, supportive kin, a school tutor, and connections to prosocial peers or community organizations
Psychosocial competence	Effectiveness or capabilities in the adaptive use of personal and contextual resources to accomplish age-appropriate developmental tasks	Active engagement of intellectual ability and positive relationships with teachers results in school success
Developmental tasks	Psychosocial milestones or accomplishments expected for people of different ages in a given historical or cultural context, often serving as criteria for judging how well a person is doing in life	Walking; talking; learning to read; developing friendships; following rules; taking care of one's children

likely overall to do well in some regard. There is often a lack of precision regarding risk factors, related to their complex and cumulative nature (Obradović, Shaffer, & Masten, 2012). Many broad risk indicators or "markers" encompass great heterogeneity in outcome within the group. For example, children born prematurely vary greatly in circumstances, birth weight, accompanying complications, family socioeconomic situation, and access to medical care. A closer analysis often provides clues to the processes accounting for the overall risk of the group. In the case of prematurity, knowing details about intracranial bleeding or delivery complications may not only improve prediction about outcomes but also lead to better understanding of the actual processes producing the risk (O'Dougherty & Wright, 1990).

It soon became apparent that risk factors rarely occur in isolation. More typically, children with high risk are exposed to multiple adversities extending over time, sometimes for very long periods of their lives (Dong et al., 2004; Finkelhor, Ormrod, Turner, & Holt, 2009; Masten & Wright, 1998; Obradović et al., 2012). Outcomes generally worsen as risk factors pile up in children's lives, and concomitantly, resilience becomes less common. Thus, it has become critical to examine *cumulative risk factors* in order to more accurately predict and understand developmental outcomes (Sameroff, Gutman, & Peck, 2003). Divorce, for example, has been a commonly studied stressor but research has revealed considerable heterogeneity in outcome for children whose parents have divorced. The concept of cumulative risk helps to clarify this diversity in outcome. Divorce is not a single, time limited risk factor or stressor, but rather an often lengthy process of multiple stressors and life changes. The extent and duration of these stressors vary considerably from family to family, and can occur before, during, and after the divorce itself. Finally, some forms of adversity are so chronic and massive that no child can be expected to be resilient until a safe and more normative environment for development is restored. Thus, in cases of catastrophic trauma, such as those resulting from war or torture, resilience typically refers to good recovery after the trauma

has ended (Masten & Obradović, 2008; Wright, Masten, Northwood, & Hubbard, 1997).

Risk terminology has undergone significant refinement in recent years, inspired by a series of influential articles by Helena Kraemer and colleagues (Kraemer et al., 1997; Kraemer, Stice, Kazdin, Offord, & Kupfer, 2001; Kraemer, Wilson, Fairburn, & Agras, 2002). Their work underscored the importance of distinguishing correlates of poor outcomes from risk factors that clearly predate the onset of the problem from causal risk factors that can be shown (perhaps through experimental manipulation) to contribute to the bad outcome of interest. This work not only has led to greater specificity in risk terminology but also provided a conceptual framework for research needed to identify a causal risk factor (see decision tree in Kraemer et al., 1997) and to test hypothesized mediating and moderating influences through experimental intervention designs (Kraemer et al., 2002).

The second key aspect of judging resilience in the lives of individuals involves decisions about how well a person is doing in life or, in other words, the quality of their adaptation or development. A variety of criteria have been utilized to judge positive adaptation in the literature, including criteria focused on the absence of pathology, successes in age-salient developmental tasks, subjective well-being, or all of these (see Table 2.1 for examples). In the developmental literature, many investigators have defined good outcomes on the basis of the child's observed or reported *competence* in meeting the expectations for children of a given age and gender in their particular sociocultural and historical context. Competence is typically assessed by how well the child has met, and continues to meet, the expectations explicitly or implicitly set in the society for children as they grow up. This is often referred to as the child's track record of success in meeting *developmental tasks,* age-related standards of behavior across a variety of domains, such as physical, emotional, cognitive, moral, behavioral, and social areas of achievement or function (McCormick, Kuo, & Masten, 2011). While these may vary from culture to culture, they typically refer to broad tasks that guide the development and socialization of children (see Table 2.1 for examples). Children judged to show resilience have typically negotiated these developmental tasks with reasonable success despite exposure to significant risks and adversities.

During the first wave of research, controversies emerged about how to define resilience and many of these debates concerned the criteria for adaptation by which resilience would be judged (see Masten & Reed, 2002 or Luthar et al., 2000 for overviews of these debates). There was debate, for example, about whether a child who was adapting well in terms of observable social behavior (academic achievement, work, relationships, etc.) but suffering internal symptoms of distress was showing resilience. There were debates about not only the "inside" vs. "outside" picture on adaptation but also on *how many* domains should be considered and *when* to assess "outcome." We would argue, for example, that resilience does not necessarily mean that one is unaffected or untouched by the trauma one has endured nor does it mean that one always functions well. It is also possible that a child may show resilience at one point in life and not at another, or in one domain and not another. Such debates linger in the literature (see Masten, 2012). Nonetheless, it is clear that the criteria by which resilience is judged in a population and how comprehensively it is assessed across domains of functioning will impact the prevalence of resilience in high-risk groups and the nature of the processes identified as relevant to resilience.

One of the most important emerging domains of study concerns the linkage among multiple domains of adaptation, positive and negative, and what this may mean for understanding resilience and psychopathology. Internal and external symptoms are related over time, as is adaptive functioning across different domains of competence and symptoms (Masten, Burt, & Coatsworth, 2006; Masten & Curtis, 2000). Symptoms can contribute to problems negotiating developmental tasks, and failure in such tasks can lead to symptoms, with snowballing consequences that have been referred to as *developmental cascades* (Masten, 2001; Masten, Burt, et al., 2006; Masten

& Cicchetti, 2010; Masten, Obradović, & Burt, 2006). In developmental theory, good functioning in developmental tasks provides a platform on which future success is built. It is becoming more evident that promoting such competence may be crucial to preventing some kinds of problem outcomes among high-risk populations of children (see section "The Third Wave: Intervening to Foster Resilience").

The first wave of resilience studies focused on identifying the correlates or predictors of positive adaptation against a background of risk or adversity. Thus, these investigators were also interested in assessing individual or situational differences that might account for differential outcomes among children sharing similar adversities or risk factors. Two major kinds of correlates were considered: (1) positive factors associated with better adaptation at all levels of risk, including high-risk levels, which were often termed *assets* or *compensatory factors* (e.g., Garmezy, Masten, & Tellegen, 1984; see also Benson, Scales, Leffert, & Roehlkepartain, 1999), and more recently, *promotive factors* (Sameroff, 1999); and (2) factors that seemed to have particular importance for positive adaptation at high levels of risk or adversity, which were typically termed *protective* factors (e.g., Rutter, 1979). The key difference in the two types of concepts was whether the factor played a special kind of role under hazardous conditions.

When a positive predictor is designated a *protective factor*, some type of shielding from the effects of risk or adversity is implied. Thus, protective factors are assets that particularly matter or only matter when risk or adversity is high. For example, airbags in automobiles or antibodies to specific disease agents are viewed as protective factors because they operate to protect individuals from the dangers of accidents or infections. Protective factors *moderate* the impact of adversity on adaptation. The examples of airbags and antibodies are causal protective factors in that they provide demonstrable and explainable protection to a living system in the course of an unfolding experience. Similarly, a parent who jumps in front of a child to take the brunt of a physical assault clearly is protective in the sense of shielding the child from worse harm. Yet many presumed protective factors in studies of resilience are far less easy to specify.

It has proven to be quite difficult to distinguish assets from protective factors in human development because many of the most important correlates of good adaptation are themselves complex systems or relationships that serve multiple functions. Parents, who could be viewed as "Mother Nature's Protective Factor," clearly comprise a protective system of immense complexity for child development. One finding that has emerged and been re-confirmed time and time again is that resilient adaptation rests on good family (or surrogate family) relationships. For very young children, early relationships with caregivers provide the foundation for developing secure attachments to others (Bowlby, 1988; Sroufe, Carlson, Levy, & Egeland, 1999). If this early infant-caregiver relationship is warm, attentive, and responsive, the child develops confidence that his or her needs will be met, learns positive ways of relating to others, becomes more able to regulate emotions, and develops feelings that the self is worthy and valued. Thus, a responsive, caring, and competent caregiver is a very powerful asset for fostering the child's healthy growth and development in any context. In the face of significant adversity, such parents also know how to respond effectively to threat and are able to adaptively shift their responses to provide protective modes of behavior. Similarly, the human brain is capable of many functions and responds to life situations in a multitude of adaptive ways. Thus it is not surprising to learn that IQ scores, a general estimate of adaptive problem solving abilities, predict a multitude of good outcomes regardless of risk or adversity level (meeting the definition of asset) and also have been shown to function as moderators of risk or adversity, mattering even more under threatening circumstances (Masten et al., 1999).

There has been considerable debate over the years about labeling a continuous variable that correlates with adaptation as a risk factor or an asset or compensatory factor, when it could be viewed as either or both. Often these constructs are composed of bipolar opposites that exist on the same continuum. That is, the attribute or variable in question is associated with poor adaptation at one end of the range and good adaptation at the other end. For example, when poverty is present it is identified as a risk factor for negative outcome whereas high socioeconomic status is observed to be a compensatory or promotive factor associated with positive outcomes. Eventually, we may learn "where the action is" for a particular attribute or factor, but in many cases, we may learn once again that adaptation arises from complex processes not easily labeled. Certainly, it is conceivable to think about a pure "risk factor" that has a clear negative influence on development when it occurs (e.g., foot amputated in an accident) but no influence when it does not occur. It is also conceivable to think about pure "asset" factors that have a positive influence when they occur (e.g., musical talent) but have little impact on development in their absence. But most factors currently studied as potential causal predictors of adaptation or good vs. poor development reflect continuously distributed variables that may operate in many ways at many levels (e.g., poor attentional skills vs. good attentional skills).

Developmental Perspectives

Resilience studies quickly revealed that children might have different vulnerabilities and protective systems at different times in the course of their development (Masten et al., 1990; Wright & Masten, 1997). Infants, because of their total dependence on caregivers, are highly vulnerable to the consequences of loss of their parents or mistreatment by caregivers. Yet infants are more protected from experiencing the full impact associated with war or natural disasters because they lack understanding of what is happening. As children mature, their school milieu and neighborhood can increasingly contribute to their exposure to traumatic events. Older children engage in more unsupervised activities and their involvement with peers can be protective or risk enhancing. Thus, while older children are much more capable of coping in the world on their own, their independence from the protection of their caregivers can also contribute to their trauma exposure. Adolescents are also vulnerable to a different type of loss or betrayal, such as loss or devastation concerning friends, faith, schools, and governments. They understand what these losses mean for their future, a realization well beyond the understanding of young children.

The "Short List" of Resilience Correlates

The first wave of research on resilience included both person-focused and variable-focused approaches. Person-focused approaches identified resilient individuals in an effort to determine how they differed from other individuals facing similar adversities or risks who were not faring as well. Variable-focused approaches, in contrast, examined the linkages among characteristics of individuals and their environments that contributed to good outcome when risk or adversity was high. This method focused on variables that cut across large, heterogeneous samples, and drew heavily on multivariate statistics. Across many studies from each of these perspectives and across widely divergent methodologies, the first wave of research revealed a striking degree of consistency in findings, implicating a common set of broad correlates of better adaptation among children at risk for diverse reasons. This consistency was noted early by Garmezy (1985), and has been corroborated repeatedly over the years. Masten (2001, 2007) has referred to these correlates as "the short list" (see Table 2.2) and argued that they may reflect the fundamental adaptive systems supporting human development. As investigators began to consider the *processes* that might account for why these correlates are repeatedly found, the second wave of resilience work began. While the first wave produced many ideas, constructs, methods, and findings about correlates of resilience (as well as many controversies), it was soon evident that more sophisticated models were needed to consider the complex processes that were implicated by the initial findings (see Glantz & Johnson, 1999).

Table 2.2 Examples of promotive and protective factors

Child characteristics
Social and adaptable temperament in infancy
Good cognitive abilities, problem solving skills, and executive functions
Ability to form and maintain positive peer relationships
Effective emotional and behavioral regulation strategies
Positive view of self (self-confidence, high self-esteem, self-efficacy)
Positive outlook on life (hopefulness)
Faith and a sense of meaning in life
Characteristics valued by society and self (talents, sense of humor, attractiveness to others)
Family characteristics
Stable and supportive home environment
Harmonious interparental relationship
Close relationship to sensitive and responsive caregiver
Authoritative parenting style (high on warmth, structure/monitoring, and expectations)
Positive sibling relationships
Supportive connections with extended family members
Parents involved in child's education
Parents have individual qualities listed above as protective for child
Socioeconomic advantages
Postsecondary education of parent
Faith and religious affiliations
Community characteristics
High neighborhood quality
Safe neighborhood
Low level of community violence
Affordable housing
Access to recreational centers
Clean air and water
Effective schools
Well-trained and well-compensated teachers
After-school programs
School recreation resources (e.g., sports, music, art)
Employment opportunities for parents and teens
Good public health care
Access to emergency services (police, fire, medical)
Connections to caring adult mentors and prosocial peers
Cultural or societal characteristics
Protective child policies (child labor, child health, and welfare)
Value and resources directed at education
Prevention of and protection from oppression or political violence
Low acceptance of physical violence

The Second Wave: Embedding Resilience in Developmental and Ecological Systems, with a Focus on Processes

Early studies delineated a number of important *factors* that were associated with later resilience, but did not provide an integrative understanding of the *processes* leading to resilience in development. As noted in a review of the first wave of work, "it is the task of future investigators to portray resilience in research questions that shift from the "what" questions of description to the "how" questions of underlying processes that influence adaptation" (Masten et al., 1990, p. 439). Subsequent research and theory has focused more specifically on understanding the complex, systemic interactions that shape both pathological and positive outcomes, emphasizing resilience as a phenomenon arising from many processes (Cicchetti, 2010; Egeland, Carlson, & Sroufe, 1993; Masten, 1999, 2007; Yates, Egeland & Sroufe, 2003). Wyman, for example, described resilience in the following way: "Resilience reflects a diverse set of processes that alter children's transactions with adverse life conditions to reduce negative effects and promote mastery of normative developmental tasks" (Wyman, 2003, p. 308).

The second wave of resilience work reflects a broader transformation occurring in the sciences concerned with normative and pathological development that has accompanied the emergence of *developmental psychopathology* (Cicchetti, 1990, 2006; Masten, 2006, 2007; Sroufe & Rutter, 1984). Resilience research over the past decade increasingly has focused on contextual issues and more dynamic models of change, explicitly recognizing the role of developmental systems in causal explanations (Cicchetti, 2010; Cicchetti & Curtis, 2007; Masten, 2007, 2011). This has led to greater emphasis on the role of relationships and systems beyond the family, and attempts to consider and integrate biological, social, and cultural processes into models and studies of resilience (Charney, 2004; Cicchetti, 2010; Cicchetti & Curtis, 2007;

Luthar, 2006; Masten, 2001, 2007, 2011, 2012). As a result, studies of resilience are more contextualized in multiple ways, including both how the individual interacts with many other systems at many levels throughout life and greater care about generalizing conclusions about risk and protective factors from one context to another or one period of development to another. The early pioneers certainly recognized the complex, dynamic nature of naturally occurring resilience (see Masten et al., 1990 for this history), but the basic descriptive data of the initial wave of studies was a necessary empirical first step before research could begin to address the complexity of the phenomena.

The fact that many of the promotive and protective factors that were identified in the first wave appeared to facilitate development in both high and low risk conditions suggested the importance of fundamental, universal human adaptation systems; these systems keep development on course and also facilitate recovery from adversity (Masten, 2001, 2007). Examples of these adaptive systems include the development of attachment relationships; moral and ethical development; self-regulatory systems for modulating emotion, arousal, and behavior; mastery and motivational systems; and neurobehavioral and information processing systems. Other systems involve the broader cultural context and consist of extended family networks, religious organizations, and other social systems in the society that offer adaptive advantages. These systems are versatile and responsive to a wide range of challenges, both normative and non-normative. If the major threats to children's adaptation are stressors that undermine the development of these basic protective systems, then it follows that children's ability to recover and to be resilient will be highly dependent on these systems being restored.

The influence of developmental systems theory (DST) is also evident in the multicausal and dynamic models of resilience characteristic of the second wave of work. Second wave theory and research often encompasses the language of DST, with concepts such as *equifinality* and *multifinality*, developmental *pathways* and *trajectories* that capture the dynamic, interactional, reciprocal, multicausal, and multiple-level models typical of DST (Bronfenbrenner, 1979; Cicchetti & Rogosch, 1996; Ford & Lerner, 1992). The focus of many second wave studies has been on the processes that may lead to resilience. Studies have attempted to explore moderating processes that would explain protective effects that seem to work only for some people under some conditions as well as mediating processes that explain how risk or protection actually works to undermine or enhance adaptation.

An ecological, transactional systems approach to understanding resilience marks a dramatic shift from a traditional focus on the individual to a broader focus encompassing family and community relational networks (Cowen, 2000; Cummings, Davies, & Campbell, 2000; Masten & Obradović, 2008; Walsh, 1998). Developmental outcome is determined by complex patterns of interaction and transaction. Wave two research studies incorporate design and analytic techniques and strategies that allow for detection of such multilevel influences. This dynamic approach emphasizes the need to formulate different research questions in order to understand the process of positive or negative adaptation following stress. Rather than asking questions about why a child is resilient, questions are asked about bidirectional connections between the child and his or her context. These child–context relationships and interactions become the focus of study. Such an approach fosters research designs that more adequately reflect individual differences in developmental pathways and contextual variation within families, communities, societies, cultures, and historical periods. Wave two research studies also provided a more complex assessment of family and environmental influences. Parents do not respond in identical ways to each of their own children, nor is the family environment experienced in an identical way by different children in the family (Plomin, Asbury, & Dunn, 2001). Even when there is significant conflict and disharmony within a family, the negativity expressed by the parents may focus more on one child than on another and the children themselves may be differentially reactive to and affected by such conflict. A transactional model of influence captures this dynamic pattern and highlights the importance of examining reciprocal patterns of interaction that shape development over time (Sameroff, 2000).

Finally, the impact of the social context on the child is mediated in part through the child's perception and interpretation of his or her experiences (Boyce et al., 1998), and some investigators have focused on such internal processes (Compas, Connor-Smith, Saltzman, Thomsen, & Wadsworth, 2001). Although important, such assessments are inherently difficult to obtain, particularly in very young children who lack the verbal skills and conceptual framework needed to describe the impact of their traumatic experiences. There are likely to be significant changes in the meaning the child assigns to different experiences at different ages and thus the meaning and the impact of a traumatic experience can change considerably over time. For example, some victims of childhood sexual abuse are so young at the time of the initial abuse that they do not understand the full meaning of the perpetrator's actions. However, when they become older, the extent of betrayal and the shame and humiliation they experience can intensify and significantly enhance the stressfulness of the experience (Wright, Crawford, & Sebastian, 2007). While children's subjective experience and other internal cognitive and affective coping responses to traumatic experiences are still sparsely researched areas, these may be critical areas to pursue in order to fully understand individual variability in response to traumatic stress (Park & Folkman, 1997).

Contextual Specificity of Protective Processes

With closer attention to processes that might account for resilience, second wave investigators also began to note that protective processes could be contextually specific. This research highlighted the importance of paying careful attention to the ways in which specific groups exposed to diverse stressors differentially adapt, and also to exploring which factors were protective for which individuals in these contexts. Cicchetti and Rogosch (1997), in their follow-up study of maltreated children, provide intriguing evidence in this regard. Whereas many studies of high-risk children have found that close interpersonal relationships and social support predict better long-term outcome, Cicchetti and Rogosch found that the maltreated children in their study who displayed positive long-term adjustment actually drew on *fewer* relational resources and displayed more restrictive emotional self-regulation styles than did comparison controls who were not maltreated. In a similar vein, both Werner and Smith (1992) and Wyman (2003) found that interpersonal and affective distancing and low expectations for parental involvement were related to later resilience, not poor adjustment. Expanding upon this, Werner and Smith reported that later in life many of their resilient adults detached themselves from parents and siblings, perhaps to prevent being overwhelmed by their families' emotional problems. These results highlight the distinctive challenges faced by children who come from highly dysfunctional families and emphasize the importance of avoiding premature conclusions about what constitutes positive coping.

The Rochester Child Resilience Project (Wyman, 2003; Wyman, Cowen, Work, & Kerley, 1993) has shed additional light on the issues of context-specific adaptation and the processes underlying resilience. In their follow-up study of urban children growing up in the context of adversity (high rates of poverty, violence, family discord, and substance use problems), factors considered to be "protective" differed in their effect, depending on additional characteristics of the child and the context. For example, although positive future expectations and perceptions of personal competence have often been found to be protective, this positive effect was only evident among participants in their study when these perceptions were realistic. If the adolescent had an unrealistic perception of his or her competence, this was associated with an elevated risk of serious conduct problems. Furthermore, in their sample, positive future expectations were actually associated with academic disengagement among those participants who also displayed conduct problems. Overall, these findings suggest that individual child characteristics such as high self-esteem or positive future expectations may be associated with resilience for some children but not for others. It may be quite important to pay attention to whether the child's beliefs and expectations are congruent with his or her ability to reach the goals set.

Stability and Change in Resilient Adaptation

As resilience research developed, more nuanced perspectives emerged. It was clear that the same child could be diagnosed "resilient" at one point in development but not another, that a child might be adaptive in one context but not another at the same point in development, and that children were often adaptive in some aspects of their life but not others. Moreover, wave two research gave far more consideration to multiple levels of context interacting to produce resilience. Consequently, the most complex models of resilience focus on healthy vs. maladaptive *pathways* of development in the lives of children exposed to adversity over time. These models provide an opportunity to attend specifically to turning points in individual's lives, and to consider the complex, holistic interactions of a changing person and context (Masten, 2012; Masten & Reed, 2002; Rutter, 2000).

To date, much of the discussion of developmental pathways has been drawn from case examples and composite data obtained in longitudinal studies (e.g., Cairns, & Cairns, 1994; Furstenberg, Brooks-Gunn, & Morgan, 1987; Hawkins et al., 2003; Masten et al., 2004; Masten, Obradović, & Burt, 2006; Rutter & Quinton, 1984; Sampson & Laub, 1993; Werner & Smith, 1992, 2001). This longitudinal data allows us to examine changes within-individuals over time rather than focusing on between-individual analyses. Such data speak to the enduring capacity for change that exists throughout development, and also provide valuable insight into the possible processes that may operate to produce either stability or change in functioning. For example, studies identifying and attempting to account for desistance trajectories in delinquency and criminal behavior based on longitudinal data (e.g., Hawkins et al., 2003; Mulvey et al., 2010; Sampson & Laub, 1993) suggest that complex interactions of youth with parents, peers, and other adults in the home, neighborhood, schools, and workplace contribute to positive and negative trajectories across the transitions from childhood to adolescence and early adulthood. Such studies also suggest that there are critical turning points in response to specific developmental challenges (such as entering school or the transition to adolescence) that may shape the nature and course of future adaptation.

Three studies that have followed a high-risk sample well into adulthood provide some very encouraging information about the potential for recovery. Werner and Smith (1992) report that *the majority* of their high-risk youths with serious coping problems in adolescence had recovered by the time they reached their 30s, and this was particularly true for the women in their sample. Only one in six troubled high-risk teens became a troubled adult. Furstenberg and colleagues (1987) found a similar pattern of later recovery among their sample of black adolescent teenage mothers. Also, among antisocial youth, large scale desistance is reported over time, so that by mid-life, the majority of antisocial youth have desisted (Sampson & Laub, 1993). Across all three studies, strong ties to work and to one's spouse were associated with eventual positive adaptation and strongly implicated in "turn around" cases. Activities which facilitated these ends, such as developing personal resources, obtaining further education, marrying an accepting and supportive spouse, joining the armed forces to gain vocational skills, and subsequent fertility control and family planning, were critical components promoting positive within-individual changes over time. For other high-risk individuals, supportive extended family and friendship networks or becoming a member of a church facilitated positive change. Follow-up studies of children adopted away from institutional rearing

characterized by extreme deprivation (Rutter & the English and Romanian Adoptees (ERA) study team, 1998), child soldiers (e.g., Betancourt et al., 2010) and refugees exposed to massive war trauma (Wright et al., 1997) also suggest a remarkable capacity for developmental recovery when normative rearing conditions are restored. All of these studies reveal the critical importance of turning points in the lives of those exposed to severe adversity. These turning points, often occurring in conjunction with substantial changes in status or context (e.g., adoption, immigration, postsecondary education, rescue, securing stable employment, successful marriage), may indicate lasting alterations in an individual's developmental pathway. Laub, Nagin, and Sampson (1998) have described these phenomena in terms of "knifing off" in the long-term follow-up of the Glueck and Glueck cohort of antisocial youth, and there are many anecdotal accounts of such dramatic turns in the life course.

The impressive recovery patterns observed in many individuals later in life, however, do not mean that all children will recover. A significant percentage of the children from the Romanian orphanages as well as from the refugee studies have serious and chronic emotional, behavioral, and/or cognitive problems that appear to be lasting effects of their experiences (Gunnar, 2001; Masten & Hubbard, 2003; Rutter & the ERA team, 1998; Wright et al., 1997; Zeanah, Smyke, & Settles, 2006). Both Werner and Smith's (1992) and Sampson and Laub's (1993) longitudinal studies (Laub & Sampson, 2002) revealed that if there were several problem areas at an early age, such as school failure, serious mental health problems, and repeated problems with delinquency, the pattern of maladjustment and deviant behavior was more stable. This finding sheds light on a pattern replicated by other longitudinal studies that there is stronger support for developmental continuity of poor adaptation when multiple areas of competence have been compromised. Compounding or cascading problems may explain why intervention becomes more challenging as individuals advance further along pathways of maladaptation, or problems show cascading effects, spreading across domains

(Masten & Cicchetti, 2010; Masten & Powell, 2003; Yates et al., 2003).

Another important consideration is the possibility that the effects of early adversity might not be evident immediately, but might emerge much later in development (a kind of "sleeper effect"). Some types of early adversity, such as living with a depressed mother (Goodman, 2007) or experiencing neglect or abuse (DiLillo & Damashek, 2003), might impair the child's later ability to function successfully in intimate family roles. For example, female survivors of child sexual abuse can display a wide range of later interpersonal problems, including problems with intimate partner relationships, disturbed sexual functioning, and difficulties in parenting (DiLillo, 2001). Longitudinal data on interpersonal functioning over time is particularly needed to understand the influence of early traumatic relationship experiences on later attachments and to explore the timing and types of subsequent interpersonal experiences that can counteract adverse effects (Egeland, Weinfield, Bosquet, & Cheng, 2000).

Understanding resilience in terms of processes that alter children's transactions with adverse life conditions, enabling them to reduce the negative effects of such experiences, and fostering mastery also avoids the type of damaging labeling that sometimes occurs when resilience is referred to as an individual outcome. Children who experience adversity, particularly severe and long lasting trauma, should be expected to have distress symptoms of some sort. For this reason it is particularly helpful to think of a "continuum of resilience" as well as a "continuum of vulnerability" across multiple domains (physical, psychological, interpersonal, and occupational) and to be alert to the ever changing dynamic of the child's functioning over time.

There are potentially damaging consequences of viewing resilience as an individual *trait* (Masten, 2012). Foremost among these is the tendency to view those children who do not adapt successfully as somehow lacking the "right stuff" and somehow personally to blame for not being able to surmount the obstacles they have faced. This focus minimizes the overwhelming social stressors and chronic adversities that many children face and also underplays the extensive role of context in individual resilience. Because adaptation is embedded within a context of multiple systems of interactions, including the family, school, neighborhood, community, and culture, a child's resilience is very dependent upon other people and other systems of influence (Masten & Obradović, 2008; Riley & Masten, 2005). The processes that foster resilience or vulnerability need to be understood within this holistic context. Children who do not "make it" often lack the basic support, protection, and respect they need for successful development, whereas children who succeed typically have sufficient external support to continue forward. The same forces that may constrain the child's development—poverty, discrimination, inadequate medical care, or exposure to community violence—also often impact and constrain the entire family. Economically impoverished families, or parents ravaged by their own struggles with alcoholism or mental illness, are often poorly equipped to provide the necessary resources and basic protections their children need. All individuals need the support and assistance of the society in which they live. The degree of success one has in surmounting these obstacles is a complex combination of personal strengths and vulnerabilities, as well as ongoing transactions with one's family and community network (Cowen, 2000; Riley & Masten, 2005; Walsh, 1998).

Cultural Influences on Resilience

Another critical component in understanding processes in resilience is the role of culture. Just as biological evolution has equipped human individuals with many adaptive systems, cultural evolution has produced a host of protective systems. Protective factors are often rooted in culture. Cultural traditions, religious rituals and ceremonies, and community support services undoubtedly provide a wide variety of protective functions, though these have not been studied as extensively in resilience research. Moreover, there may well be culturally specific traditions, beliefs, or support systems that function to protect individuals, families, and community functioning in the context of adversity within those cultures. Specific healing, blessing, or purification ceremonies, such as those found among American Indian tribal cultures (Gone, 2009; LaFromboise, Oliver & Hoyt, 2006a, 2006b), as well as in many cultures and religions around the world (Crawford, Wright, & Masten, 2006), may serve to counteract or ameliorate the impact of devastating experiences among people in a culture. Similarly, among minority groups in society, factors such as strength of ethnic identity, competence and comfort in relating to members of different groups, and racial socialization are particularly important in dealing with challenges that arise due to experiences of oppression and discrimination within the context in which they live (Szalacha et al., 2003; Wright & Littleford, 2002). To date there has been surprisingly limited systematic investigation of culturally based protective processes (Luthar, 2006, Masten & Wright, 2010). The movement away from an individually based conceptualization of resilience and towards a contextually situated framework has been a welcome one from the perspective of many cross-cultural researchers (Aponte, 1994; Boyd-Franklin & Bry, 2000; Hill, 1999). Whereas some of the factors and processes that have been identified as fostering resilience focus on individual functioning (such as good cognitive skills, socioemotional sensitivity, ability to self-regulate), the shape and function of these processes may be culturally influenced or may interact with cultural demands and expectations in ways that are poorly understood. Moreover, many other factors have been identified within the collective network of the family and the community. As the study of resilience continues, it will be critical to explore the extent to which factors found to promote resilience in one group will also be replicated across cultural groups and also how the same factor found across multiple groups may function differently in different cultural contexts. For example, for various cultural/ethnic groups there can be a great deal of difference in the relative importance placed on individualism, collectivism, and familism, and

these dimensions might mediate resilience in different ways for different groups (Gaines et al., 1997; Kim, Triandis, Kagitcibasi, Choi, & Yoon, 1994). Our intervention efforts might be significantly enhanced by consideration of these and of other cultural dimensions.

The Third Wave: Intervening to Foster Resilience

From inception, a compelling rationale for the systematic study of naturally occurring resilience was to inform practice, prevention, and policy efforts directed towards *creating resilience* when it was not likely to occur naturally. The second wave focused on a better understanding of mediating and moderating processes that might explain the links between adversity and developmental competence, as an intermediate step toward the ultimate goal of intervening to promote resilience and positive development. Research on such processes continues to be important. However, using lessons from the first two waves, investigators of the third wave began to translate the basic science of resilience that was emerging into actions intended to promote resilience. These investigators recognized that experiments to promote positive adaptation and prevent problems among individuals at high risk for developing problems represented a powerful strategy for testing resilience theory and hypothesized adaptive processes that were targeted in the theory or logic model of the experimental intervention. Initially, this work took the form of theory-driven intervention designs and subsequently, with growing frequency, third-wave research has taken the form of experiments with randomized control or comparison groups with explicit models of change. Such experiments represent the "gold standard" of evidence about change processes.

Historically, the third wave represented a confluence of goals, models, and methods from prevention science and studies of naturally occurring resilience (Cicchetti, Rappaport, Sandler, & Weissberg, 2000; Coie et al., 1993; Cowen & Durlak, 2000; Masten, 2007; Masten & Coatsworth, 1998; Weissberg & Kumpfer, 2003;

Yoshikawa, 1994). Multifaceted intervention studies designed to prevent or reduce risky behaviors, delinquency, and other problems in children (e.g., FAST Track or the Seattle Social Development Project) and also early childhood interventions developed to improve the odds of children growing up in poverty or disadvantage (e.g., Abecedarian, Head Start, Perry Preschool Project, Chicago Longitudinal Study) encompassed multiple strategies designed to promote success in developmental tasks at the same time they reduced risk for problem behaviors (Ramey & Ramey, 1998; Reynolds & Ou, 2003; Weissberg & Greenberg, 1998). As the data on assets, promotive, and protective factors began to accumulate in natural resilience studies, data was mounting in prevention science based on randomized clinical trials that promoting competence was a key element of programs that worked and the mediators and moderators of change bore a striking resemblance to the processes implicated by the "short list" in resilience research (Cicchetti et al., 2000; Luthar & Cicchetti, 2000; Masten, 2001, 2007; Masten, Burt, et al., 2006; Masten & Coatsworth, 1998; Masten, Obradović, et al., 2006; Reynolds & Ou, 2003).

Over the past decade, there has been a profound change in the models for intervention, particularly in prevention models, that likely reflects the growing influence of resilience theory and research (Masten, 2011). Numerous strength-based models and resilience frameworks for practice and policy have been articulated (e.g., Cicchetti et al., 2000; Galassi & Akos, 2007 Luthar & Cicchetti, 2000; Masten, 2001, 2006, 2011; Nation et al., 2003). In the prevention science field, intervention models are routinely described in terms of protective processes to promote resilient development (McLain et al., 2010; Patterson, Forgatch, & DeGarmo, 2010; Toth, Pianta, & Erickson, 2011; Weissberg, Kumpfer, & Seligman, 2003; Wyman, 2003; Wyman, Sandler, Wolchik, & Nelson, 2000). Intervening to alter the life course of a child potentially at risk for psychopathology or other problems, whether by reducing risk or adversity exposure, boosting resources, nurturing relationships, or mobilizing other protective systems, can be viewed as a protective process.

Strategic timing of intervention also holds great interest for third wave research because evidence suggests that there are windows of opportunity for changing the course of development, when systems may be more malleable or there is a higher likelihood of potentiating a positive cascade (Cicchetti, 2010; Masten & Cicchetti, 2010; Masten, Burt, et al., 2006, Masten, Obradović, et al. 2006, Masten, Long, Kuo, McCormick, & Desjardins, 2009; Steinberg, Dahl, Keating, Kupfer, Masten, & Pine, 2006). Timing an intervention well may lead to more lasting effects, broader effects, and/or higher returns on investment (Heckman, 2006; Masten et al., 2009; Masten & Cicchetti, 2010; Reynolds & Temple, 2006; Shonkoff, Boyce, & McEwen, 2009). For example, during a developmental transition or turning point, targeted interventions can be critically important in activating developmental cascades (i.e., progressive effects) that enhance multiple domains of functioning or deterring negative cascades of maladaptive behavior that could undermine adjustment (Masten, Burt, et al., 2006; Masten & Cicchetti, 2010; Masten, Obradović, et al. 2006). For example, the long-term effects of the Parent-Management Training-Oregon (PMTO) model to promote parents' positive involvement and deter coercive aggression included cascading pathways of adaptive development for both parents and children. A follow-up study revealed a higher standard of living and healthier social interactions 9 years after the intervention (Patterson et al., 2010).

Experimental intervention designs can provide a powerful test of hypotheses about how resilience occurs, particularly when the process of change is specified (e.g., parenting or attributional style), the intervention is tailored for specific needs and targets changes in this process, and the change processes affect subsequent change in the targeted behavior of an individual or system. For example, possessing the executive functioning capacity of strong inhibitory skills was demonstrated to be centrally important for school achievement in homeless children (Obradović, 2010). Also important was high quality parenting to buffer these children from further adversity and to serve as a mediator of risk and achievement (Herbers et al., 2011). These studies emphasize the need to promote competence as well as to reduce risk. Boosting fundamental skills for learning and school success and nurturing parent–child relationships are also promising pathways to adaptive development for young, disadvantaged children (Diamond, Barnett, Thomas, & Munro 2007; Masten & Gewirtz, 2006).

Kraemer et al. (2002) provided an illustration of how experimental intervention designs can test such mediating and moderating effects, with the intervention serving as the hoped-for moderator of the hypothesized mediating process. Experimental designs are also particularly well suited for identifying who benefits most from what aspect of treatment, mediated by which changes, thereby testing additional moderating and mediating effects. The Seattle Social Development Project provides an excellent example of an experiment designed to test whether and how an intervention worked to reduce problem behaviors (see Hawkins, Catalano, Kosterman, Abbott, & Hill, 1999; Hawkins et al., 2003). For example, a comprehensive intervention package (delivered to a group of children in schools serving high crime neighborhoods when they were in elementary school) produced demonstrable change in school bonding which was associated with better outcomes in the secondary school years, assessed by less antisocial behavior and better high school grades. Another excellent example is provided by Sandler, Wolchik, Davis, Haine, and Ayers (2003), who designed a preventive intervention for families going through a divorce, with the goal of moderating a key mediator in the child's life, the parent's behavior. Six-year follow-up data for this randomized prevention trial elucidated multiple cascading pathways to adaptation in adolescence. Mothers' more positive relationships with children and use of effective discipline activated positive trajectories of less internalizing problems leading to higher self-esteem, and less externalizing problems and substance use leading to higher academic achievement (McLain et al., 2010). Such studies offer compelling evidence both for the effectiveness of a particular intervention (the manualized program for

mothers in this case) and for the role of parental functioning in causal processes related to child outcomes during the course of negotiating adversity. The dynamic capacities afforded by close relationships to foster development and protect individuals and social groups in the face of adversity has led many to conclude that relationships are the most critical protective factor for young people at risk (e.g., Luthar, 2006). The children of parents who already function well during adversity or parents who mobilize what is needed to protect their children as a result of personal change, enlisting help, or other adaptive processes fare better during and following adversity in many situations studied around the globe.

Research on interventions to create resilience is gaining momentum as evidence builds from basic research and experimental data that resilience processes can be identified and changed, and that intervention methods are vital for testing resilience theory (Masten, 2011). It is still the case, as noted by Weissberg and Kumpfer (2003) some time ago, that much work remains to be done to understand resilience processes (e.g., mediating, moderating, promoting, compensating, and cascading processes) well enough to manipulate them most effectively and efficiently to benefit children and society. However, the evidence base is growing and a good case can also be made that progress would be accelerated by concerted efforts to span the translational divide through collaborative translational research that engages basic researchers and community partners in intervention trials that reflect current knowledge but also explicitly focus on testing theories of change (see Masten, 2011; Toth et al., 2011). These are ongoing tasks of third wave resilience research. Only by identifying the multifaceted processes underlying successful adaptation under adverse conditions will we find ways to intervene successfully in the lives of those who remain vulnerable.

Analyses of current preventive programs that work for children underscore the importance of theory-driven approaches that embrace a developmental, ecological systems approach and capitalize on windows of opportunity in development. Salient features of successful prevention programs include many of the factors that have been described in this chapter. These include a focus on strategically timed, culturally relevant, comprehensive programs across multiple settings, programs that are of sufficient length and depth to address the magnitude of the problem, and strive to maximize positive resources and the benefit-to-cost ratio of implementation. Additionally, because the effects of interventions might be delayed, unexpected, or indirect, it is important to consider more complex models of change and monitor outcome appropriately, over time, in multiple domains and possibly at multiple-system levels. Such comprehensive prevention approaches acknowledge the multiplicity of risks and the cumulative trauma that many children face and emphasize the importance of promoting competence and building protection across multiple domains in order to achieve a positive outcome.

The Fourth Wave: Resilience Research on Multiple-Systems Levels, Epigenetic Processes, and Neurobiological Processes

The fourth wave in resilience research is focused on multilevel dynamics and the many processes linking genes, neurobiological adaptation, brain development, behavior, and context at multiple levels. It is predicated on the idea that development arises from probabilistic epigenesis, involving many processes of interaction across multiple levels of function, with gene–environment interplay and co-action playing key roles (Gottlieb, 2007) and explicit recognition that adaptation is inherently multilevel (Masten, 2007). This wave began to rise as new methods for research became more widely available to study these processes, including the assessment of genes, gene expression, brain structure and function, social interaction, and statistics for modeling growth, change, and interactions in complex systems (Charney, 2004; Cicchetti, 2010; Cicchetti & Curtis, 2006, 2007; Feder, Nestler, & Charney, 2009; Masten et al., 2004, Masten, 2007, 2012; Masten & Obradović, 2008). There had been many calls for greater attention

to resilience at other levels of analysis (e.g., Curtis & Cicchetti, 2003), but earlier waves of resilience research were dominated by psychosocial studies emphasizing individual behavior and development, with some attention to other levels, such as relationships, families, peers, and schools or other community systems (Cicchetti, 2010; Luthar, 2006; Masten, 2007).

Over the past decade, research aiming to elucidate the biology or neuroscience of resilience has burgeoned (Cicchetti, 2010; Feder et al., 2009). At the same time, once independent and disparate fields of research on resilience at different levels in different disciplines (e.g., ecology, engineering, public health, management, emergency services) are coming together in response to urgent national and global threats that require integrative solutions, such as natural disasters, terrorism, global warming, and flu pandemic (Masten & Obradović, 2008; Masten & Osofsky, 2010; Norris, Steven, Pfefferbaum, Wyche, & Pfefferbaum, 2008).

Fully describing the exciting and interdisciplinary directions in the fourth wave of resilience research is beyond the scope of this chapter. However, as examples, there is considerable activity and interest in the following research areas:

- Gene X environment moderating effects including intervention moderating effects (for illustration see Kim-Cohen & Gold, 2009; Brody, Beach, Chen, & Murry, 2009).
- Programming, biological sensitivity to context, differential susceptibility, bidirectional influences, and calibration of adaptive systems crucial for adaptive response to adversity (see Boyce & Ellis, 2005; Del Giudice, Ellis, & Shirtcliff, 2011; Meaney, 2010).
- Reprogramming and interventions to normalize poorly regulated adaptive systems in the organism, such as stress or immune function, executive function skills, and emotion regulation (see Dozier, Peloso, Lewis, Laurenceau, & Levine, 2008; Fisher, Van Ryzin, & Gunnar, 2011; Meaney, 2010; Yehuda, Flory, Southwick, & Charney, 2006).
- Assessment of biomarkers, gene expression, or neural function in intervention studies to tailor the intervention or assess its effectiveness

(see Blair, 2010; Brody et al., 2009; Cicchetti, 2010).

- Integrating models and research on resilience in ecosystems, social systems, and individual biology or neural systems (see Longstaff, 2009; Masten & Obradović, 2008; Norris et al., 2008).

This wave of resilience research is just beginning but it promises to transform the science and the application of resilience.

Conclusion

In conclusion, the past 40 years of research on resilience have shed much light on the fundamental adaptive systems supporting human development and on identifying complex, multisystemic interactions that might shape both positive and pathological outcomes following adversity. A strong knowledge base has accrued on the processes implicated in resilience, particularly on factors that increase vulnerability and those that afford protection. However, much remains to be done, and as evident in the rising fourth wave of research, there is much uncharted territory. It will take time to unravel and understand these multiple levels of influence and build a stronger bridge between science and practice. It is essential at this juncture not to lose sight of the goals for this work—to enhance understanding of key mechanisms leading to risk reduction, to determine the key ingredients of successful interventions, and to apply what we are learning in prevention and intervention efforts to foster resilience among vulnerable children and their families. Clinical interventions and primary preventions with known effectiveness currently exist and need to be made accessible in more diverse community settings and evaluated. This will allow for critical exploration of factors that promote or interfere with resilient processes in different cultural contexts. Collaborative work across diverse contexts is urgently needed to refine resilience-based models of intervention and change, and also to inform the design of primary prevention and social policy programs. Past work in this area has focused very productively on the psychological and interpersonal arenas, but efforts to include biological and cultural levels of analysis are just beginning. The thrust of future research needs to attend more directly and explicitly to context and transactional, bidirectional analyses over time, clarifying the conditions under which interventions may and may not work, identifying the most strategic and cost-effective targets and timing for interventions, and exploring natural reparative processes. Although there is clear evidence that resilience in young people is highly dependent on other people and multiple systems of influence, there is limited knowledge of how these multiple levels of influence operate synergistically and how best to incorporate the biological, psychological, interpersonal, and cultural levels of analysis into our research and models for clinical intervention. Integrative approaches, spanning levels and disciplines, are needed to apply the expanding knowledge based on resilience in human development with efficiency and effectiveness to foster positive adaptation among the most vulnerable children, youth, and families in our communities.

Acknowledgments The work of the authors on resilience has been supported over the years by grants from the National Institute of Mental Health, the National Science Foundation (NSF), the William T. Grant Foundation, the University of Minnesota, and the Ohio Department of Mental Health. Preparation of this chapter was supported in part by a grant to Ann Masten from NSF (No. 0745643) and a predoctoral fellowship to Angela Narayan from the National Institute of Mental Health (NIMH; 5T32MH015755). The first two authors also express their deep and abiding appreciation for the wonderful mentorship of Norman Garmezy. Any opinions, conclusions, or recommendations expressed in this chapter are those of the authors.

References

Anthony, E. J. (1974). The syndrome of the psychologically invulnerable child. In E. J. Anthony & C. Koupernik (Eds.), *The child and his family* (Children at psychiatric risk, Vol. 3, pp. 529–544). New York, NY: Wiley.

Aponte, H. (1994). *Bread and spirit: Therapy with the new poor*. New York, NY: Morton.

Benson, P. L., Scales, P. C., Leffert, N., & Roehlkepartain, E. C. (1999). *A fragile foundation: The state of developmental assets among American youth*. Minneapolis, MN: Search Institute.

Betancourt, T. S., Borisova, I. I., Williams, T. P., Brennan, R. T., Whitfield, T. H., de la Soudiere, M., Williamson, J., & Gilman, S. E. (2010). Sierra Leone's former child soldiers: A follow-up study of psychosocial adjustment and community reintegration. *Child Development, 81*, 1076–1094.

Blair, C. (2010). Stress and the development of self-regulation in context. *Child Development Perspectives, 4*, 181–188.

Bowlby, J. (1988). *A secure base: Clinical applications of attachment theory*. London: Routledge.

Boyce, W. T., & Ellis, B. J. (2005). Biological sensitivity to context: I. An evolutionary-developmental theory of the origins and functions of stress reactivity. *Development and Psychopathology, 17*, 271–301.

Boyce, W. T., Frank, E., Jensen, P. S., Kessler, R. C., Nelson, C. A., Steinberg, L., & The MacArthur Foundation Research Network on Psychopathology and Development. (1998). Social context in developmental psychopathology: Recommendations for future research from the MacArthur network on psychopathology and development. *Development and Psychopathology, 10*, 143–164.

Boyd-Franklin, N., & Bry, B. H. (2000). *Reaching out in family therapy: Home-based, school and community interventions*. New York, NY: Guilford.

Brody, G. H., Beach, S. R., Chen, Y. F., & Murry, V. M. (2009). Prevention effects moderate the association of 5-HTTLPR and youth risk behavior initiation: Gene x environment hypotheses tested via a randomized prevention design. *Child Development, 80*(3), 645–661.

Bronfenbrenner, U. (1979). *The ecology of human development: Experiments by nature and design*. Cambridge, MA: Harvard University Press.

Cairns, R. B., & Cairns, B. (1994). *Lifelines and risks: Pathways of youth in our time*. New York, NY: Cambridge University Press.

Charney, D. (2004). Psychobiological mechanisms of resilience and vulnerability: implications for successful adaptation to extreme stress. *American Journal of Psychiatry, 161*, 195–216.

Cicchetti, D. (1990). An historical perspective on the discipline of developmental psychopathology. In J. Rolf, A. S. Masten, D. Cicchetti, K. H. Nuechterlein, & S. Weintraub (Eds.), *Risk and protective factors in the development of psychopathology* (pp. 2–28). New York, NY: Cambridge University Press.

Cicchetti, D. (2006). Development and psychopathology. In D. Cicchetti & D. J. Cohen (Eds.), *Developmental psychopathology: Vol. 1 Theory and method* (2nd ed., pp. 1–23). Hoboken, NJ: Wiley.

Cicchetti, D. (2010). Resilience under conditions of extreme stress: A multilevel perspective. *World Psychiatry, 9*(3), 145–154.

Cicchetti, D., & Curtis, W. J. (2006). The developing brain ad neural plasticity: Implications for normality, psychopathology, and resilience. In D. Cicchetti & D. Cohen (Eds.), *Developmental psychopathology* (Developmental neuroscience 2nd ed., Vol. 2, pp. 1–64). Hoboken, NJ: Wiley.

Cicchetti, D., & Curtis, W. J. (2007). Special issue: A multi-level approach to resilience. *Development and Psychopathology, 19*(3), 627–955.

Cicchetti, D., Rappaport, J., Sandler, I., & Weissberg, R. P. (Eds.). (2000). *The promotion of wellness in children and adolescents*. Washington, DC: CWLA.

Cicchetti, D., & Rogosch, F. A. (1996). Equifinality and multifinality in developmental psychopathology. *Development and Psychopathology, 8*, 597–600.

Cicchetti, D., & Rogosch, F. A. (1997). The role of self-organization in the promotion of resilience in maltreated children. *Development and Psychopathology, 9*, 797–815.

Coie, J. D., Watt, N. F., West, S. G., Hawkins, J. D., Asarnow, J. R., Markman, H. J., Ramey, S. L., Shure, M. B., & Long, B. (1993). The science of prevention: A conceptual framework and some directions for a national research program. *American Psychologist, 48*, 1013–1022.

Compas, B. E., Connor-Smith, J. K., Saltzman, H., Thomsen, A. H., & Wadsworth, M. (2001). Coping with stress during childhood and adolescence: Progress, problems, and potential. *Psychological Bulletin, 127*, 87–127.

Cowen, E. L. (2000). Psychological wellness: Some hopes for the future. In D. Cicchetti, J. Rappaport, I. Sandler, & R. P. Weissberg (Eds.), *The promotion of wellness in children and adolescents* (pp. 477–503). Washington, DC: CWLA.

Cowen, E. L., & Durlak, J. A. (2000). Social policy and prevention in mental health. *Development and Psychopathology, 12*, 815–834.

Crawford, E., Wright, M. O' D., & Masten, A. S. (2006). Resilience and spirituality in youth. In E. C. Roehlkepartain, P. E. King, L. Wagener, & P. L. Benson (Eds.), *The handbook of spiritual development in childhood and adolescence* (pp. 355–370). Thousand Oaks, CA: Sage.

Cummings, E. M., Davies, P. T., & Campbell, S. B. (2000). *Developmental psychopathology and family process*. New York, NY: Guilford.

Curtis, J., & Cicchetti, D. (2003). Moving resilience on resilience into the 21st century: Theoretical and methodological considerations in examining the biological contributors to resilience. *Development and Psychopathology, 15*, 773–810.

Del Giudice, M., Ellis, B. J., & Shirtcliff, E. A. (2011). The adaptation calibration model of stress responsivity. *Neuroscience and Behavioral Reviews., 35*(7), 1562–1592.

Diamond, A., Barnett, W. S., Thomas, J., & Munro, S. (2007). Preschool program improves cognitive control. *Science, 318*, 1387–1388.

DiLillo, D. (2001). Interpersonal functioning among women reporting a history of childhood sexual abuse: Empirical findings and methodological issues. *Clinical Psychology Review, 21*, 553–576.

DiLillo, D., & Damashek, A. (2003). Parenting characteristics of women reporting a history of childhood sexual abuse. *Child Maltreatment, 8*, 319–333.

Dong, M., Anda, R. F., Fellitti, V. J., Dube, S. R., Williamson, D. F., Thompson, T. J., Loo, C. M., & Giles, W. H. (2004). The interrelatedness of multiple forms of child abuse, neglect, and household dysfunction. *Child Abuse & Neglect, 28*, 771–784.

Dozier, M., Peloso, E., Lewis, E., Laurenceau, J.-P., & Levine, S. (2008). Effects of an attachment-based intervention on the cortisol production of infants and toddlers in foster care. *Development and Psychopathology, 20*, 845–859.

Egeland, B., Carlson, E., & Sroufe, L. A. (1993). Resilience as process. *Development and Psychopathology, 5*(4), 517–528.

Egeland, B., Weinfield, N. S., Bosquet, M., & Cheng, V. K. (2000). Remembering, repeating, and working through: Lessons from attachment-based interventions. In J. D. Osofsky & H. E. Fitzgerald (Eds.), *Infant mental health in groups at high risk* (WAIMH handbook of infant mental health, Vol. 4, pp. 35–89). New York, NY: Wiley.

Feder, A., Nestler, E. J., & Charney, D. S. (2009). Psychobiology and molecular genetics of resilience. *Nature Reviews Neuroscience, 10*, 446–457.

Finkelhor, D., Ormrod, R., Turner, H., & Holt, M. (2009). Pathways to poly-victimization. *Child Maltreatment, 14*, 316–329.

Fisher, P. A., Van Ryzin, M. J., & Gunnar, M. R. (2011). Mitigating HPA axis dysregulation associated with placement changes in foster care. *Psychoneuroendocrinology., 36*(4), 531–539.

Ford, D. H., & Lerner, R. M. (1992). *Developmental systems theory: An integrative approach.* Newbury Park, CA: Sage.

Furstenberg, F. F., Jr., Brooks-Gunn, J., & Morgan, S. P. (1987). *Adolescent mothers in later life.* Cambridge: Cambridge University Press.

Gaines, S. O., Marelich, W. D., Bledsoe, K. L., Steers, W. N., Henderson, M. C., Granrose, C. S., Barajas, L., Hicks, D., Lyde, M., Takahashi, Y., Yum, N., Ríos, D. I., García, B. F., Farris, K. R., & Page, M. S. (1997). Links between race/ethnicity and cultural values as mediated by racial/ethnic identity and moderated by gender. *Journal of Personality and Social Psychology, 72*, 1460–1476.

Galassi, J. P., & Akos, P. (2007). *Strength-based school counseling: Promoting student development and achievement.* London: Routledge.

Garmezy, N. (1985). Stress-resistant children: The search for protective factors. In J. E. Stevenson (Ed.), *Recent research in developmental psychopathology: Journal of Child Psychology and Psychiatry Book Supplement #4* (pp. 213–233). Oxford: Pergamon.

Garmezy, N., Masten, A. S., & Tellegen, A. (1984). The study of stress and competence in children: A building block for developmental psychopathology. *Child Development, 55*, 97–111.

Glantz, M. D., & Johnson, J. L. (1999). *Resilience and development: Positive life adaptations.* New York, NY: Kluwer Academic/Plenum Publishers.

Gone, J. P. (2009). A community-based treatment for Native American "historical trauma": Prospects for evidence-based practice. *Journal of Consulting and Clinical Psychology, 77*, 751–762.

Goodman, S. H. (2007). Depression in mothers. *Annual Review of Clinical Psychology, 3*, 107–135.

Gottlieb, G. (2007). Probabilistic epigenetics. *Developmental Science, 10*, 1–11.

Gunnar, M. R. (2001). Effects of early deprivation: Findings from orphanage-reared infants and children. In C. A. Nelson & M. Luciana (Eds.), *Handbook of developmental cognitive neuroscience* (pp. 617–629). Cambridge, MA: MIT.

Hawkins, J. D., Catalano, R. F., Kosterman, R., Abbott, R. D., & Hill, K. G. (1999). Preventing adolescent health-risk behavior by strengthening protection during childhood. *Archives of Pediatrics and Adolescent Medicine, 153*, 226–234.

Hawkins, J. D., Smith, B. H., Hill, K. G., Kosterman, R., Catalano, R. F., & Abbott, R. D. (2003). Understanding and preventing crime and violence. In T. P. Thornberry & M. D. Krohn (Eds.), *Taking stock of delinquency: An overview of findings from contemporary longitudinal studies* (pp. 255–312). New York, NY: Kluwer Academic.

Heckman, J. J. (2006). Skill formation and the economics of investing in disadvantaged children. *Science, 312*, 1900–1902.

Herbers, J. E., Cutuli, J. J., Lafavor, T. L., Vrieze, D., Leibel, C., Obradovi , J., & Masten, A. S. (2011). Direct and indirect effects of parenting on academic functioning of young homeless children. *Early Education and Development., 22*(1), p77–104.

Hill, R. (1999). *The strengths of African-American families: Twenty-five years later.* Lanham, MD: University Press of America.

Kim, U., Triandis, H. C., Kagitcibasi, S., Choi, S., & Yoon, G. (Eds.). (1994). *Individualism and collectivism: Theory, method and applications.* Thousand Oaks, CA: Sage.

Kim-Cohen, J., & Gold, A. L. (2009). Measured gene-environment interactions and mechanisms promoting resilient development. *Current Directions in Psychological Science, 18*, 138–142.

Kraemer, H. C., Kazdin, A. E., Offord, D. R., Kessler, R. C., Jensen, P. S., & Kupfer, D. J. (1997). Coming to terms with the terms of risk. *Archives of General Psychiatry, 54*, 337–343.

Kraemer, H. C., Stice, E., Kazdin, A. E., Offord, D. R., & Kupfer, D. J. (2001). How do risk factors work together? Mediators, moderators, and independent, overlapping, and proxy risk factors. *American Journal of Psychiatry, 158*, 848–856.

Kraemer, H. C., Wilson, G. T., Fairburn, C. G., & Agras, W. S. (2002). Mediators and moderators of treatment effects in randomized clinical trials. *Archives of General Psychiatry, 59*, 877–883.

LaFromboise, T. D., Oliver, L., & Hoyt, D. R. (2006a). Strengths and resilience of American Indian adolescents. In L. Whitbeck (Ed.), *This is not our way: Traditional culture and substance use prevention in American Indian adolescents and their families*. Tucson: University of Arizona Press.

LaFromboise, T. D., Oliver, L., Hoyt, D. R., & Whitbeck, L. B. (2006b). Family, community, and school influences on resilience among American Indian adolescents in the upper Midwest. *Journal of Community Psychology, 34,* 193–209.

Laub, J. H., Nagin, D. S., & Sampson, R. J. (1998). Trajectories of change in criminal offending: Good marriages and the desistence process. *American Sociological Review, 63,* 225–238.

Laub, J. H., & Sampson, R. J. (2002). Sheldon and Eleanor Glueck's Unraveling Juvenile Delinquency study: The lives of 1,000 Boston men in the twentieth century. In E. Phelps, F. F. Furstenberg Jr., & A. Colby (Eds.), *Looking at lives: American longitudinal studies of the twentieth century* (pp. 87–115). New York, NY: Russell Sage.

Longstaff, P. H. (2009). (Editorial) Managing surprises in complex systems: Multidisciplinary perspectives on resilience. *Ecology and Society* 14(1): 49. [online] URL: http://www.ecologyandsociety.org/vol14/iss1/art49/.

Luthar, S. S. (2006). Resilience in development: A synthesis of research across five decades. In D. Cicchetti & D. J. Cohen (Eds.), *Developmental psychopathology* (Risk, disorder, and adaptation 2nd ed., Vol. 3, pp. 739–795). Hoboken, NJ: Wiley.

Luthar, S. S., & Cicchetti, D. (2000). The construct of resilience: Implications for interventions and social policies. *Development and Psychopathology, 12,* 857–885.

Luthar, S. S., Cicchetti, D., & Becker, B. (2000). The construct of resilience: A critical evaluation and guidelines for future work. *Child Development, 71*(3), 543–562.

Masten, A. S. (1999). Resilience comes of age: Reflections on the past and outlook for the next generation of research. In M. D. Glantz, J. Johnson, & L. Huffman (Eds.), *Resilience and development: Positive life adaptations* (pp. 289–296). New York, NY: Plenum.

Masten, A. S. (2001). Ordinary magic: Resilience processes in development. *American Psychologist, 56*(3), 227–238.

Masten, A. S. (2006). Promoting resilience in development: A general framework for systems of care. In R. J. Flynn, P. Dudding, & J. G. Barber (Eds.), *Promoting resilience in child welfare* (pp. 3–17). Ottawa, ON: University of Ottawa Press.

Masten, A. S. (2007). Resilience in developing systems: Progress and promise as the fourth wave rises. *Development and Psychopathology, 19,* 921–930.

Masten, A. S. (2011). Resilience in children threatened by extreme adversity: Frameworks for research, practice, and translational synergy. *Development and Psychopathology., 23,* 493–506.

Masten, A. S. (2012). Risk and resilience in development. In P. D. Zelazo (Ed.), *Oxford handbook of developmental psychology*. New York, NY: Oxford University Press (in press).

Masten, A. S., Best, K. M., & Garmezy, N. (1990). Resilience and development: Contributions from the study of children who overcome adversity. *Development and Psychopathology, 2,* 425–444.

Masten, A. S., Burt, K. B., & Coatsworth, J. D. (2006). Competence and psychopathology in development. In D. Cicchetti & D. Cohen (Eds.), *Developmental psychopathology* (Risk, disorder and psychopathology 2nd ed., Vol. 3, pp. 696–738). New York, NY: Wiley.

Masten, A. S., Burt, K., Roisman, G. I., Obradović, J., Long, J. D., & Tellegen, A. (2004). Resources and resilience in the transition to adulthood: Continuity and change. *Development and Psychopathology, 16,* 1071–1094.

Masten, A. S., & Cicchetti, D. (2010). Editorial: Developmental cascades. Developmental cascades [Special Issue, Part 1]. *Development and Psychopathology, 22*(3), 491–495.

Masten, A. S., & Coatsworth, J. D. (1998). The development of competence in favorable and unfavorable environments: Lessons from successful children. *American Psychologist, 53,* 205–220.

Masten, A. S., & Curtis, W. J. (2000). Integrating competence and psychopathology: Pathways toward a comprehensive science of adaptation in development. *Development and Psychopathology, 12,* 529–550.

Masten, A. S., & Gewirtz, A. H. (2006). Vulnerability and resilience in early child development. In K. McCartney & D. Phillips (Eds.), *Handbook of early childhood development* (pp. 22–43). Malden, MA: Blackwell.

Masten, A. S., & Hubbard, J. J. (2003). *Global threats to child development: A resilience framework for humanitarian intervention*. University of Minnesota: Unpublished manuscript.

Masten, A. S., Hubbard, J. J., Gest, S. D., Tellegen, A., Garmezy, N., & Ramirez, M. L. (1999). Competence in the context of adversity: Pathways to resilience and maladaptation from childhood to late adolescence. *Developmental Psychopathology, 11,* 143–169.

Masten, A. S., Long, J. D., Kuo, S. I.-C., McCormick, C. M., & Desjardins, C. D. (2009). Developmental models of strategic intervention. *European Journal of Developmental Science, 3,* 282–291.

Masten, A. S., & Obradović, J. (2008). Disaster preparation and recovery: Lessons from research on resilience in human development. *Ecology and Society, 13*(1): 9 [online] URL: http://www.ecologyandsociety.org/vol13/iss1/art9/.

Masten, A. S., Obradović, J., & Burt, K. (2006). Resilience in emerging adulthood: Developmental perspectives on continuity and transformation. In J. J. Arnett & J. L. Tanner (Eds.), *Emerging adults in America: Coming of age in the 21st Century* (pp. 173–190). Washington, DC: American Psychological Association.

Masten, A. S., & Osofsky, J. (2010). Disasters and their impact on child development: Introduction to the special section. *Child Development, 81,* 1029–1039.

Masten, A. S., & Powell, J. L. (2003). A resilience framework for research, policy, and practice. In S. S. Luthar (Ed.), *Resilience and vulnerability: Adaptation in the context of childhood adversities* (pp. 1–25). New York, NY: Cambridge University Press.

Masten, A. S., & Reed, M.-G. (2002). Resilience in development. In C. R. Snyder & S. J. Lopez (Eds.), *The handbook of positive psychology* (pp. 74–88). New York, NY: Oxford University Press.

Masten, A. S., & Wright, M. O. (1998). Cumulative risk and protection models of child maltreatment. *Journal of Aggression, Maltreatment & Trauma, 2*(1), 7–30.

Masten, A. S., & Wright, M. O. (2010). Resilience over the lifespan: Developmental perspectives on resistance, recovery, and transformation. In J. W. Reich, A. J. Zautra, & J. S. Hall (Eds.), *Handbook of adult resilience* (pp. 213–237). New York, NY: Guilford.

McClain, D. B., Wolchik, S. A., Winslow, E., Tein, J.-Y., Sandler, I. N., & Millsap, R. E. (2010). Developmental cascade effects of the New Beginnings Program on adolescent adaptation outcomes. *Development and Psychopathology, 22*, 771–784.

McCormick, C. M., Kuo, S. I.-C., & Masten, A. S. (2011). Developmental tasks across the lifespan. In K. L. Fingerman, C. Berg, T. C. Antonucci, & J. Smith (Eds.), *The handbook of lifespan development.* New York, NY: Springer.

Meaney, M. J. (2010). Epigenetics and the biological definition of gene x environment interactions. *Child Development, 81*, 41–79.

Mulvey, E. P., Sternberg, L., Piquero, A. R., Besana, M., Fagan, J., Shubert, C., & Cauffman, E. (2010). Trajectories of desistance and continuity in antisocial behavior following court adjudication among serious adolescent offenders. *Development and Psychopathology, 22*, 453–475.

Nation, M., Crusto, C., Wandersman, A., Kumpfer, K. L., Seybolt, D., Morrissey-Kane, E., & Davino, K. (2003). What works in prevention: Principles of effective intervention programs. *American Psychologist, 58*, 449–456.

Norris, F. H., Steven, S. P., Pfefferbaum, B., Wyche, K. F., & Pfefferbaum, R. L. (2008). Community resilience as a metaphor, theory, set of capacities, and strategy for disaster readiness. *American Journal of Community Psychology, 41*, 127–150.

O'Dougherty, M., & Wright, F. S. (1990). Children born at medical risk: Factors affecting vulnerability and resilience. In J. Rolf, A. S. Masten, D. Cicchetti, K. H. Nuechterlein, & S. Weintraub (Eds.), *Risk and protective factors in the development of psychopathology* (pp. 120–140). New York, NY: Cambridge University Press.

Obradović, J. (2010). Effortful control and adaptive functioning of homeless children: Variable-focused and person-focused analyses. *Journal of Applied Developmental Psychology, 31*, 109–117.

Obradović, J., Shaffer, A., & Masten, A. S. (2012) Risk in developmental psychopathology: Progress and future directions. In L. C. Mayes & M. Lewis (Eds.), *The Cambridge handbook of environment of human development: A handbook of theory and measurement* (pp. 35–57). New York, NY: Cambridge University Press.

Park, C. L., & Folkman, S. (1997). Meaning in the context of stress and coping. *Review of General Psychology, 1*, 115–144.

Patterson, G. R., Forgatch, M. S., & DeGarmo, D. S. (2010). Cascading effects following intervention. *Development and Psychopathology, 22*, 941–970.

Pines, M. (1975, December). In praise of "invulnerables." *APA Monitor*, p. 7.

Plomin, R., Asbury, K., & Dunn, J. (2001). Why are children in the same family so different? Nonshared environment a decade later. *Canadian Journal of Psychiatry, 46*, 225–233.

Ramey, C. T., & Ramey, S. L. (1998). Early intervention and early experience. *American Psychologist, 53*, 109–120.

Reynolds, A. J., & Ou, S. R. (2003). Promoting resilience through early childhood intervention. In S. S. Luthar (Ed.), *Resilience and vulnerability: Adaptation in the context of childhood adversities* (pp. 436–459). New York, NY: Cambridge University Press.

Reynolds, A. J., & Temple, J. A. (2006). Economic benefits of investments in preschool education. In E. Zigler, W. Gilliam, & S. Jones (Eds.), *A vision for universal prekindergarten* (pp. 37–68). New York, NY: Cambridge University Press.

Riley, J. R., & Masten, A. S. (2005). Resilience in context. In R. DeV, B. L. Peters, & R. J. McMahon (Eds.), *Resilience in children, families, and communities: Linking context to practice and policy* (pp. 13–25). New York, NY: Kluwer Academic/Plenum.

Rutter, M. (1979). Protective factors in children's responses to stress and disadvantage. In M. W. Kent & J. E. Rolf (Eds.), *Primary prevention of psychopathology* (Social competence in children, Vol. 3, pp. 49–74). Hanover, NH: University Press of New England.

Rutter, M. (1987). Psychosocial resilience and protective mechanisms. *American Journal of Orthopsychiatry, 57*, 316–331.

Rutter, M. (2000). Resilience reconsidered: Conceptual considerations, empirical findings, and policy implications. In J. P. Shonkoff & S. J. Meisels (Eds.), *Handbook of early intervention* (2nd ed., pp. 651–681). New York, NY: Cambridge University Press.

Rutter, M., & The English and Romanian Adoptees (ERA) Study Team. (1998). Developmental catch-up and deficit, following adoption after severe global early privation. *Journal of Child Psychology and Psychiatry, 39*, 465–476.

Rutter, M., & Quinton, D. (1984). Long-term follow-up of women institutionalized in childhood: Factors promoting good functioning in adult life. *British Journal of Developmental Psychology, 18*, 225–234.

Sameroff, A. J. (1999). Ecological perspectives on developmental risk. In J. D. Osofsky & H. E. Fitzgerald (Eds.), *Infant mental health in groups at high risk* (WAIMH handbook of infant mental health, Vol. 4, pp. 233–248). New York, NY: Wiley.

Sameroff, A. J. (2000). Developmental systems and psychopathology. *Development and Psychopathology, 12,* 297–312.

Sameroff, A., Gutman, L. M., & Peck, S. C. (2003). Adaptation among youth facing multiple risks. In S. Luthar (Ed.), *Resilience and vulnerability: Adaptation in the context of childhood adversities* (pp. 364–391). New York, NY: Cambridge University Press.

Sampson, R. J., & Laub, J. H. (1993). *Crime in the making: Pathways and turning points through life.* Cambridge, MA: Harvard University Press.

Sandler, I., Wolchik, S., Davis, C., Haine, R., & Ayers, T. (2003). Correlational and experimental study of resilience in children of divorce and parentally bereaved children. In S. S. Luthar (Ed.), *Resilience and vulnerability: Adaptation in the context of childhood adversities* (pp. 213–240). New York, NY: Cambridge University Press.

Shonkoff, J. P., Boyce, W. T., & McEwen, B. S. (2009). Neuroscience, molecular biology, and the childhood roots of health disparities. *Journal of the American Medical Association, 301*(21), 2252–2259.

Sroufe, L. A., Carlson, E. A., Levy, A. K., & Egeland, B. (1999). Implications of attachment theory for developmental psychopathology. *Development and Psychopathology, 11,* 1–13.

Sroufe, L. A., & Rutter, M. (1984). The domain of developmental psychopathology. *Child Development, 55,* 17–29.

Steinberg, L., Dahl, R., Keating, D., Kupfer, D. J., Masten, A. S., & Pine, D. S. (2006). Psychopathology in adolescence: Integrating affective neuroscience with the study of context. In D. Cicchetti & D. Cohen (Eds.), *Developmental psychopathology* (Developmental neuroscience 2nd ed., Vol. 2, pp. 710–741). New York, NY: Wiley.

Szalacha, L. A., Erkut, S., García Coll, C., Fields, J. P., Alarcón, O., & Ceder, I. (2003). Perceived discrimination and resilience. In S. S. Luthar (Ed.), *Resilience and vulnerability: Adaptation in the context of childhood adversities* (pp. 414–435). New York, NY: Cambridge University Press.

Toth, S. L., Pianta, R. C., & Erickson, M. F. (2011). From research to practice: Developmental contributions to the field of prevention science. In D. Cicchetti & G. I. Roisman (Eds.), *The origins and organization of adaptation and maladaptation: Minnesota symposia on child psychology* (Vol. 36). New York, NY: Wiley.

Walsh, F. (1998). *Strengthening family resilience.* New York, NY: Guilford.

Weissberg, R. P., & Greenberg, M. T. (1998). School and community competence-enhancement and prevention programs. In I. E. Siegel & K. A. Renninger (Eds.), *Handbook of child psychology* (Child psychology in practice, Vol. 4, pp. 877–954). New York, NY: Wiley.

Weissberg, R. P., & Kumpfer, K. L. (2003). Special Issue: Prevention that works for children and youth. *American Psychologist, 58,* 425–490.

Weissberg, R. P., Kumpfer, K. L., & Seligman, M. E. P. (2003). Prevention that works for children and youth: An introduction. *American Psychologist, 58,* 425–432.

Werner, E. E., & Smith, R. S. (1982). *Vulnerable but invincible: A study of resilient children.* New York, NY: McGraw-Hill.

Werner, E. E., & Smith, R. S. (1992). *Overcoming the odds: High risk children from birth to adulthood.* Ithaca, NY: Cornell University Press.

Werner, E. E., & Smith, R. S. (2001). *Journeys from childhood to midlife: Risk, resilience and recovery.* Ithaca, NY: Cornell University Press.

Wright, M. O., Crawford, E., & Sebastian, K. (2007). Positive resolution of childhood sexual abuse experiences: The role of coping, benefit-finding and meaning-making. *Journal of Family Violence, 22,* 597–608.

Wright, M. O., & Littleford, L. N. (2002). Experiences and beliefs as predictors of ethnic identity and intergroup relations. *Journal of Multicultural Counseling and Development, 30,* 2–20.

Wright, M. O., & Masten, A. S. (1997). Vulnerability and resilience in young children. In J. D. Noshpitz, J. D. Osofsky, & S. Wieder (Eds.), *Handbook of child and adolescent psychiatry* (Infancy and preschoolers: Development and syndromes, Vol. 1). New York, NY: Wiley.

Wright, M. O., Masten, A. S., Northwood, A., & Hubbard, J. J. (1997). Long-term effects of massive trauma: Developmental and psychobiological perspectives. In D. Cicchetti & S. L. Toth (Eds.), *Rochester Symposium on Developmental Psychopathology* (The effects of trauma on the developmental process, Vol. 8, pp. 181–225). Rochester: University of Rochester Press.

Wyman, P. A. (2003). Emerging perspectives on context specificity of children's adaptation and resilience: Evidence from a decade of research with urban children in adversity. In S. S. Luthar (Ed.), *Resilience and vulnerability: Adaptation in the context of childhood adversities* (pp. 293–317). New York, NY: Cambridge University Press.

Wyman, P. A., Cowen, E. L., Work, W. C., & Kerley, J. H. (1993). The role of children's future expectations in self-system functioning and adjustment to life-stress. *Development and Psychopathology, 5,* 649–661.

Wyman, P. A., Sandler, I., Wolchik, S., & Nelson, K. (2000). Resilience as cumulative competence promotion and stress protection: Theory and intervention. In D. Cicchetti, J. Rapport, I. Sandler, & R. P. Weissberg (Eds.), *The promotion of wellness in children and adolescents* (pp. 133–184). Washington, DC: Child Welfare League of America.

Yates, T. M., Egeland, B., & Sroufe, L. A. (2003). Rethinking resilience: A developmental process perspective. In S. S. Luthar (Ed.), *Resilience and vulnerability: Adaptation in the context of childhood adversities* (pp. 234–256). New York, NY: Cambridge University Press.

Yehuda, R., Flory, J. D., Southwick, S., & Charney, D. S. (2006). Developing an agenda for translational studies of resilience and vulnerability following trauma exposure. *Annals of the New York Academy of Science, 1071*, 379–396.

Yoshikawa, H. (1994). Prevention as cumulative protection: Effects of early family support and education on chronic delinquency and its risks. *Psychological Bulletin, 115*, 28–54.

Zeanah, C. H., Smyke, A. T., & Settles, L. D. (2006). Orphanages as a developmental context for early childhood. In K. McCartney & D. Phillips (Eds.), *Blackwell handbook of early childhood development* (pp. 424–454). Malden, MA: Blackwell.

Reconceputalizing Resilience

Howard B. Kaplan[†]

The deceptively simple construct of resilience is in fact rife with hidden complexities, contradictions, and ambiguities. These have been recognized in earlier reviews of the relevant literature (Kaplan, 1999). More recent reviews have reaffirmed many of these difficulties and have offered suggestions in some cases for resolution of these problems (Luthar, Cicchetti, & Becker, 2000; Olsson, Bond, Burns, Vella-Brodrick, & Sawyer, 2003). By and large, however, problematic aspects of the concept of resilience persist.

Concepts by their nature are not true or false. However, they may be evaluated with regard to their usefulness. The utility of the construct of resilience in the study of adaptation to life stress depends upon resolving the confusion surrounding the concept that has led many scholars to question whether the idea of resilience helps to advance theory, research, or clinical practice (Bartelt, 1994; Kaplan, 1999; Liddle, 1994). In this chapter I outline what I perceive to be the sources of confusion surrounding the concept of resilience and offer suggestions regarding the conditions that must be fulfilled in defining resilience if that concept is to be useful in understanding human development and adaptations. These conditions implicate (1) equating resilience with a more narrowly focused set of phenomena than is currently associated with the concept and (2) the use of this more narrowly

conceived set of phenomena to compose an integrative explanatory theory of adaptation to life stress. The more focused set of concepts that is equated with resilience, and the theoretical framework that derives from concepts, relate to four sets of self-referent processes: self-cognition; self-evaluation; self-feelings; and self-enhancing and self-protective mechanisms.

(Mis)Understanding Resilience

Arguably, any consensus that exists regarding the nature of resilience rests upon the ideas of achievement of positively (or the avoidance of negatively) valued outcomes in circumstances where adverse outcomes would normally be expected. A close examination of this idea, however, reveals a number of unresolved questions that at best render the concept less than useful, and at worst, impede progress in understanding human adaptation. Among the more salient issues are the following:

1. *Does resilience refer to characteristics and outcomes of individuals* (children, adults, various categories of persons differentiate according to gender, race/ethnicity, or other psychosocial variables), or does it refer to characteristics and outcomes of more inclusive systems such as groups in general or particular kinds of groups, communities, or ecosystems? The literature finds the concept applied to a bewildering array of categories of individuals and systems. Regarding categories

[†]H.B. Kaplan (Deceased)

S. Goldstein and R.B. Brooks (eds.), *Handbook of Resilience in Children*,
DOI 10.1007/978-1-4614-3661-4_3, © Springer Science+Business Media New York 2013

of individuals, resilience has been studied with reference to women (Humphreys, 2003), children referred for learning problems (Sorenson et al., 2003), and adolescents (Olsson et al., 2003), to name but a few. Other discussions focus on higher-order interpersonal systems and refer to social and ecological resilience (Adger, 2000), cultural-community resilience (Clauss-Ehlers & Levi, 2002), or collective resilience, referring to look to reconstruct and maintain social relationships that have suffered trauma (Hernandez, 2002). More specifically, the term resilience has been applied frequently to couples (Conger, Rueter, & Elder, 1999) or families (Haan, Hawley, & Deal, 2002; Oswald, 2002; Patterson, 2002; Schwartz, 2002; Walsh, 2002) as units that are more or less resilient in the face of adversity.

Although it is conceivable that the term might usefully be applied to interpersonal as well as individual-level systems, the context for usage should be clarified in each instance. Certainly the nature of the outcomes in which resilience is manifested or the kinds of resilience mechanisms which influence benign outcomes would be expected to vary with the nature of the unit to which the term resilience is applied (Radke-Yarrow & Sherman, 1990).

> At a societal level, successful coping behaviors are those that contribute to the survival and well being of others. At a psychological level, we regard positive coping as the exercise of behaviors that contribute to the well being of the self. A child who becomes a survivor is one who is happy about one's self, who is physically healthy, whose behavior is masterful, and who is learning to be a positive contributor to one's immediate society. (p. 100)

2. *Is resilience isomorphic to, partially overlapping, or orthogonal to a variety of other terms that appear to be functionally equivalent to that term?* The functional equivalence of resilience and other terms has been recognized by numerous researchers, each selecting one of the terms and indicating the functional equivalence of the other terms. For example, Lösel, Bliesener, and Köferl (1989) observe: "There is a multitude of constructs that are related to invulnerability, such as resilience, hardiness,

adaptation, adjustment, mastery, plasticity, person-environment fit, or social buffering" (p. 187). Thus, resilience has been characterized as the positive counterpart of vulnerability (Rauh, 1989); and resilience has been likened to salutogenesis in that both address how people adapt in the face of adversity (Lindström, 2001).

3. *Is resilience the opposite of nonresilience or of vulnerability?* In the former case it is possible to lack resilience but still not be invulnerable as when the person has not experienced disvalued outcomes but is nevertheless vulnerable to unwelcome effects of adversity should they arise. In the latter case, the absence of resilience implies vulnerability to adversity. Thus, resilience and vulnerability are often viewed as opposite poles of a continuum reflecting susceptibility to adverse consequences or benign consequences upon exposure to high risk circumstances (Anthony, 1987). Ego-resilience is regarded as one pole of a dimension, the other end of which is ego-brittleness (Block & Block, 1980):

> Ego-resiliency, when dimensionalized, is first defined at one extreme by resourceful adaptation to changing circumstances and environmental contingencies, analysis of the "goodness of fit" between situational demands and environmental contingencies, and flexible invocation of the available repertoire of problem-solving strategies ("problem solving" being defined to include the social and personal domains as well as the cognitive). The opposite end of the ego-resilience continuum (ego-brittleness) implies little adaptive flexibility, an inability to respond to the dynamic requirements of the situation, a tendency to perseverate or to become disorganized when encountering changed circumstances or when under stress, and a difficulty in recouping after traumatic experiences. (p. 48)

Occasionally, however, the negative pole is defined in terms of nonresilience rather than vulnerability. Radke-Yarrow and Brown (1993) use these terms:

> Resilience was defined as having no diagnoses and not being on the borderline of reaching criteria for a diagnosis. Nonresilience was defined as the presence of one or more diagnoses of a serious nature, with problems persisting over time. (p. 583)

Whether or not positive and negative outcomes should represent polar opposites or the nature of the range between polar opposites remains problematic in the literature. Each desirable state does not necessarily have an undesirable state as a polar opposite. The presence of an undesirable state (illness) implies the absence of a desirable state (health). However, the absence of an undesirable state does not necessarily imply the presence of a desirable one. One may be asymptomatic without having fulfilled his or her potential for health. In studies of adaptation to life crisis, investigators typically equate a good outcome with the absence of physical symptoms and psychopathology. They usually fail to consider the possibility of a new and better level of adaptation that reflects personal growth rather than a return to the status quo (Schaefer & Moos, 1992, p. 149).

The way these issues are resolved has important implications for the definition of resilience and the other components of paradigms of resilience.

> Should positive factors associate with the reduction of risk and vulnerability be considered as leading to optimal development and thus be considered as benefits to the growing child, or should one assume that they contribute primarily to adequate development, and should thus be seen proactive? One view would hold that the possible influence of positive and negative factors could affect development on a full continuum running from poor to optimal functioning. The other possibility is that positive and negative factors affect the organisms on a continuum ranging from poor to adequate functioning only but do not affect optimal functioning. (Greenbaum & Auberbach, 1992, p. 12)

4. *Is resilience to be defined in terms of the nature of the outcomes in response to stress or in terms of factors which interact with stress to produce the outcomes?* Is resilience the valuation of good outcomes among individuals who are at risk for bad outcomes, or is resilience the qualities possessed by individuals who are at risk for bad outcomes, or is resilience the qualities possessed by individuals that enable them to have good outcomes? Is resilience a phenomenon that moderates the influence of risk factors on more or less benign outcomes? Or is resilience the fact of having achieved benign outcomes in the face of adversity? In the

latter case, resilience would be defined in terms of the presence of desirable outcomes and the absence of undesirable outcomes. In the former case, resilience would be defined in terms of the characteristics that moderate the effect of risk factors on benign outcomes and, less directly, the influence upon these factors.

Resilience is frequently defined in terms of the fact or process of approximating valued outcomes in the face of risk or adversity. Resilience refers to the fact of "maintaining adaptive functioning in spite of serious risk hazards" (Rutter, 1990, p. 209). Consistent with the definition, Lösel et al. (1989) state, "Our main interest is in resilient adolescents who are (still) psychologically healthy despite high multiple exposure to stressful life events and circumstances" (p. 194).

Individuals are considered as vulnerable to particular negative outcomes or to the absence of positive outcomes by virtue of being at risk. Vulnerable individuals are those who turn out poorly, while invulnerable individuals turn out well (Seifer & Sameroff, 1987). As one team operationalized the concepts, children who are being reared in chaotic and threatening conditions by emotionally ill parents are labeled "invulnerable" or "resilient" if they have no psychiatric diagnoses, relate well to peers and adult authorities in school and at home, have a positive self-concept, and are performing at grade level in school (Radke-Yarrow & Sherman, 1990). For Masten (1994), resilience relates to "how effectiveness in the environment is achieved, sustained or recovered despite adversity" (p. 4).

Resilience, in addition to, or instead of, being defined in terms of the fact of having benign or less malignant outcomes in the face of life stress may be thought of as a general construct that reflects specific characteristics and the mechanisms through which they operate that moderate the relationships between risk factors and outcome variables. One construct that is the functional equivalent of resilience used in this sense is hardiness.

The implication that resilience reflects characteristics of the person or environment that influences (other) desirable outcomes is apparent in Cohler's (1987) comments about the nature of resilience:

> In sum, the children of psychiatrically ill parents who are better able to cope with the adversity of unreliable and often emotionally inaccessible caretakers have innate ego strength, creative abilities, and increased personal and physical attractiveness; these traits enable children to continue to reach out to others for support...Finally, these children often have greater intelligence and come from families higher in social status; in turn, these qualities foster increased instrumental mastery and greater social skills. (p. 395)

In many instances it is difficult to determine which of the two definitions, resilience as outcomes vs. resilience as influential quality, is intended by the researcher. Indeed, outcomes in one context may be treated plausibly as influences upon outcomes in another context (Schuldberg, 1993):

> The same current indices can be viewed either as signs of positive adjustment or as protective or compensatory factors; in both cases the variables will predict future good outcomes. (pp. 139–140)

5. *What is the relationship between resilience and the experience of distressful life experiences?* Is a person said to be resilient because he or she bounces back from adversity? An affirmative response implies that a person cannot be resilient in the absence of preexisting experiences of adversity. One has to suffer before the consequences of suffering can be assuaged. However, it might be asserted that individuals are resilient because they are capable of recovering from adversity even if they have not yet experienced adversity. Should they experience disvalued life experiences they most likely would recover. Indeed, the very experience of risk might be forestalled by the characteristics that make a person or system resilient.

The issue of the applicability of the concept of resilience to "well-functioning/low-risk individuals" has been raised by many researchers or clinicians. Richters and Weintraub (1990), for example, assert that for:

> those who study the offspring of psychiatrically ill parents, the search for protective factors seems to stem from surprise at finding high-risk offspring who are doing well–so-called resilient children. The personal and environmental factors that characterize them are assumed to be protective factors. Presumably, children of nondiagnosed parents who are coping as well do not deserve the resilient label, nor are the personal and environmental factors that characterize them labeled protective. Why, then, are these concepts deemed so necessary to explain well-functioning children of psychiatrically ill parents? (p. 78)

Anthony (1987, pp. 27–28) highlights the issue of potential resilient or vulnerable individuals by referring to "pseudovulnerables who are vulnerable or extremely vulnerable individuals who have been 'blessed' with an overprotective environment (particularly the maternal portion of it), and are relatively unchallenged and thriving until the environment fails, and they fail along with it."

6. Where resilience is defined in relationship to the prior experience of distressful life experiences, the further question is raised as to *whether resilience is reflected in the ability to bounce back from adversity or is caused by adversity.* In the former case, a person's resilience is manifest in the person's ability to function adequately following adversity. The person's ability to function was first disrupted by the adversity but was subsequently restored. In the latter case, the adversity challenged the person (or system) to find strength that might not otherwise have been discovered. The person is better off because of the adversity than if the adversity had not been experienced:

> Life crises are viewed as constructive confrontations that spur development. Personal growth can be fostered by the disruption that crises generate and the subsequent reorganization that occurs in their wake. Stressors are a natural and potentially positive part of life; resilience develops from confronting stressful experiences and coping with them effectively...The process of confronting these experiences can promote a cognitive differentiation, self-confidence, and a more mature approach to life. A person who experiences pain and loss may develop a deeper understanding and empathy for others with similar problems. Exposure to novel crisis situations may broaden a person's perspective, promote new coping skills, and lead to new personal and social resources. (Schaefer & Moos, 1992 p. 150)

7. Where resilience is defined in terms of outcomes, *should resiliency be defined in terms of some overall criterion or in terms of particular context-specific favorable outcomes?* Resilience is often defined in general terms of the forestalling of adverse developmental outcomes in the face of characteristics of the individual or the individual's environment that would have led to the prediction of the adverse developmental outcome. However, except for this similarity, variation in the nature of the desirable or undesirable developmental outcomes had led to widely different definitions of resilience.

The subject may be manifesting resiliency according to one criterion, but not according to another. For example, Spencer, Cole, Dupree, Glymph, and Pierre (1993), conceptualizing resilience as adaptive coping, tested a model of risk and resilience to examine coping methods and competence outcomes as measured by academic performance and academic self-esteem. It is possible that those individuals may be judged to be resilient by these criteria but not according to the criteria representing competence in other spheres (per relations, family). The fact that individuals may vary in adjustment depending upon the domain under consideration has implications for the conceptualization of resilience. Luthar (1993) concludes:

> The current evidence indicates, then, that notions of overall resilience are questions of utility. In future research, it would be more useful if discussions were presented in terms of specific domains of successful coping (e.g. academic resilience, social resilience, or emotional resilience), along with those areas in which apparent survivors show high vulnerability. (p. 442)

Even within the same sphere of operation, judgments of resiliency can vary as outcome measures vary.

> While a child may appear to be adapting positively within the school arena if outcome measures focus solely on cognitive abilities, the same child may manifest impaired social relationships. Unless multiple domains of development are assessed, only a partial picture of adaptation can be formulated. (Cicchetti & Garmezy, 1993, pp. 499–500)

Further, outcomes are ordinarily defined in terms of arbitrary normative judgments regarding appropriate intrapsychic and behavioral responses, taking into account culture, environmental circumstances, and stage of development. This is a major limitation of utility of the construct since normative judgments are so variable. Bartelt (1994) offers the following example:

> Several representatives of Hispanic community organizations have put the following question to me: If family income is lower for Puerto Rican communities, the day-to-day needs of the household for additional economic resources are strongly present; and if there is a strong pro-family ideology within the community that is threatened by continued poverty; why should we not expect that our teenagers will seek to leave school and obtain full-time employment as soon as possible? In turn I must ask myself, isn't this is a form of resilience as we have come to define it? How do we distinguish academic success as resilience from dropping out as resilience? (p. 103)

8. Where resilience is defined in terms of protective factors, *which general or specific protective factors are equated with resilience?* Where vulnerability is defined in terms of the protective factors or related phenomena that permit the approximation of desirable outcomes, a good deal of definitional variability can be observed. Variability in definition is observed because the causes of resiliency vary according to the causes of diverse outcomes.

Since the same factors may not cause one outcome as opposed to another outcome, factors which mitigate the effects of stressors on one outcome may be expected to be different from those that mitigate the effect of stressors on another outcome. The implication of this is that "differences across spheres of adjustment must be carefully appraised and discussions on resilience should be presented in terms of the specific spheres of successful (and less successful) adaptation" (Luthar, 1993, p. 442).

9. Where resilience is defined in terms of benign outcomes or responses to adversity, stress or risk factors, *how does it determine the nature of the factors that place an individual or system at risk?* The definitions of resilience that have reference to risk factors have been widely

and justifiably criticized. There are not definite criteria by which a particular variable may be defined as a risk factor. Therefore, no clear criterion exists by which particular behaviors or outcomes may be defined as resilient. Judgment is always made after the fact and is based on the assignment of risk to particular conditions. Seifer and Sameroff (1987) also note:

There is currently no criterion by which a particular variable is determined to be a risk factor, a protective factor, or merely a measure that is related to the outcome in question. This issue of defining "risk" might be a trivial matter except for the fact that what determines vulnerability or invulnerability is dependent upon the initial determination of risk. To some extent, this is a logical dilemma. One could assume that any factor shown to affect child outcomes adversely should be considered a risk factor. But then there would be no possibility of finding a set of measures that consistently differentiate vulnerable from invulnerable, since anything that differentiates children with good outcomes from those with poor outcomes would be considered a risk factor. (pp. 64–65)

Cicchetti and Garmezy (1993) observe the difficulty of distinguishing between the factors that indeed place the individual at risk and factors that happen to distinguish between good and poor outcomes but have no causal significance. Frequently risk factors are stated in terms of marker variables rather than in terms of marker variables rather than in terms of underlying constructs. Therefore, the assumption of being exposed to risk may be faulty. The individual may have been exposed to the marker variable but not to the underlying construct that is said to be represented by the marker variable. Thus, people may be labeled resilient even though they have not in fact been exposed to the situation considered to be a stressor.

The idea of resilience has then a plethora of different meanings, many of which are vague and contradictory. The absence of specificity is traceable to several issues, many of which were categorized and described briefly above. So daunting is the number of such issues that have been raised with regard to the concept that one might despair of ever being able to resolve these various issues and offer a definition or, having offered a definition, to gain consensus on its usage.

However, a review of the literature on resilience offers some hope of focusing this concept on a more narrow set of phenomena namely, those relating to self-referent processes.

Resilience and Self-Referent Processes

Various conceptualizations of resilience, as we have noted above, focus on different appeals of a general process including, but not limited to: (absence of) subjective distress and more or less dysfunctional sequelae of such distress, risk (protective) factors that increase the likelihood of adverse (benign) outcomes; circumstances that mediate the influence of putative (protective) risk factors on (benign) adverse outcomes; and perhaps most importantly given to frequency with which they are discussed in the resilience literature, factors that moderate the degree to which hypothetical (protective) risk factors eventuate in more or less adverse outcomes. An examination of the theoretical and empirical literatures utilizing the notion of resilience and one or more of these components suggests that they have in common the manifest reflection of self-referent processes as operationalizations of these components, or are interpretable in these terms. It is unfortunate that the conceptualization of some of the self-referent processes suffer from many of the limitations that characterize the resilience construct. For example, frequently it is difficult to determine from the context if "self-esteem" refers to self-image, self-evaluation, or self-feeling. However, as we will develop in the next sections, these difficulties are more easily soluble for the self-referent construct than for resilience-related concepts. In any case, an overview of the resilience literature admits of the following generalizations regarding the relevance of self-referent responses for virtually all elements of what have been discussed frequently as part of the resilience phenomena.

1. In virtually all theoretical discussions or reports of empirical findings relating to resilience, the hypothetical protective and risk factors, and/or the more or less benign outcomes of these factors, either manifestly

reflect or are interpretable in terms of self-referent processes.

This conclusion holds for a wide variety of factors, outcomes, and subject populations. Considering those reports that deal with *protective factors and/or benign outcomes*, the following studies serve to illustrate this generalization.

If not invariably, self-esteem and/or related self-referent constructs often are presented as criterion outcome variables that are predicted by constructs said to reflect resilience for those outcomes (e.g., Filbert & Flynn, 2009). Thus, in an investigation of the resilience of foreign American college students in the face of perceived ethic discrimination self-esteem was observed to be an outcome of first order effects of ethnic identity pride and low perceived discrimination, the one precursor of high self-esteem, and the others the absence of a threat to self-esteem (Lee, 2005). Similarly, self-esteem, which along with optimism composed of a core construct of resilience, was inversely related to "mental distress" over a 1-year period (Mäkikangas, Kinnunen, & Feld, 2004); and among adolescents with sickle cell disease, higher levels of self-esteem were associated with lower levels of depression and anxiety (Simon, Barakat, Patterson, & Dampier, 2009).

A variety of self-referent processes have been implicated in the resilience process. For example, among subjects who have suffered abuse as children, in addition to self-esteem, such self-relevant processes include regulation of self-feelings and self-reliance as contributors to adaptive coping (Cicchetti & Rogosch, 2009).

Others have measured resilience exclusively in terms of such self-referent constructs such as self-esteem, self-confidence, and self-transcendence (Phillips-Salimi, Haase, Kintner, Monahan, & Azzouz, 2007). Thus, self-esteem, personal control, and optimism, conceived of as components of resilience, have been observed to influence outcomes that are less dysfunctional for organizations in which the person participates. Resilience, so defined, was related to willingness to accept change which, in turn, was inversely related to job dissatisfaction, intention to quit the job, and feeling of irritation in the workplace (Wanberg & Banas, 2000).

These observations regarding the relevance of a range of self-referent processes for resilience have important implications for social policy and planned interventions. Implicit in the observation that self-referent processes are implicated in the development of resilience is the expectation that resilience can be increased by, for example, facilitating participation in relationships that offer the promise of enhancing such processes, including a sense of empowerment, worth, and competence (Hartling, 2008).

Conversely, considering those reports that deal with *risk factors and/or undesirable* outcomes, the following studies serve to illustrate the near universal recognition that self-referent processes are manifestly or implicitly germane to the antecedents and/or outcomes of the resilience processes. Thus, the loss of personal control associated with aging-related loss of functions among those elderly individuals in a psychological autopsy study *whose self-esteem appeared to be contingent on being productive and in context* were said to develop an intolerable sense of vulnerability that leads to suicide (Kjølseth, Ekeberg, & Steihaug, 2009). It is the pervasive sense of vulnerability, caused by threats to salient self-evaluative standards and concomitant low self-esteem that defines the low resilience/at risk person.

In a three wave longitudinal study, the estimation of structural equation models revealed that, controlling for early levels of self-esteem, adolescents who reported peer victimization tended to have lower self-esteem across 1-year intervals (Overbeek, Zeevalkink, Vermulst, & Scholte, 2010). Presumably, the experience of peer victimization serves to communicate to the victims that (s)he is held in low regard by her(his) peers, which in turn adversely affect her(his) self-esteem. Moreover, it was observed that lower self-esteem tended to invite peer victimization, but only among a subgroup of overly self-controlled individuals. Among the explanations of this finding that present themselves is that which suggests that bullying peers are not inhibited from their victimizing behaviors since their over controlled intrapunitive victims are not likely to assert themselves and retaliate.

Among the outcomes of antecedent self-referent responses are dysphonic affective states. Thus, in a cross-sectional national sample of 16–19 year old adolescents in Iceland, low self-esteem was observed to be related to a higher probability of depressed mood and anger. Further, these effects were stronger for students who were sexually abused, a finding that is to be expected if the experience of sexual abuse reflects a self-devaluing experience that exacerbates the distressful self-feelings that follow upon the intensified need to attain or restore self-esteem (Asgeirsdottir, Gudjonsson, Sigurdsson, & Sigfusdttir, 2010).

Self-threatening experiences, in addition to having effects on intrinsically undesirable outcomes such as low self-esteem and other dysfunctional/deviant adaptations, often lead to the loss of resources, the acquisition or possession of which might forestall such outcomes. Such resources might include learned interpersonal skills and material resources and other social supports provided by one's interpersonal networks, the availability of which might be diminished by self-threatening circumstances. A case in point is the observed inverse relationship between earlier "protective self-cognitions" (self-efficacy and self-esteem) and later resource loss observed in a sample of women who experience childhood abuse and were at risk for contracting sexually transmitted diseases (Walter, Horsey, Palmieri, & Hobfoll, 2010).

Although to this point the citations reflect exclusively positive or exclusively negative outcomes, and exclusively risk or protective factors, it should be noted quite frequently self-referent processes may be reflected in both positive and negative outcomes, and/or as proactive and risk factors in the same study. In the former case, for example, high self-esteem is observed to have benign effects on outcomes of personal threats, that is, manifest resiliency, while frequently evoking extreme and antisocial defensive responses. What these counterveiling responses may have in common is "reactive approach-motivation processes" that are evoked by threat in high self-esteem individuals. In support of this hypothesis, are the results of a study in which experimentally induced uncertainty threat led individuals with high self-esteem to manifest increased "Relative Left Frontal (F7/F8) Electroencephalographic Activity" which is commonly understood to be a neural manifestation of resilient approach-motivation. The same normal pattern was observed in the effect of the interaction of self-esteem and threat on a variety of antisocial defenses (McGregor, Nash, & Inzlicht, 2009).

In the latter case, the simultaneous consideration of risk and protective factors in the same study is illustrated by the observed indirect effects of trait anxiety and trait resilience (via their influence on positive and negative affect) that are interpretable in terms of their implications for threats to self-esteem : trait anxiety reflecting sensitivity to the prevalence of such threats, and trait resilience reflecting the presence of self-protective mechanisms that forestall or reduce the distress associated with self-threatening circumstances (Benetti & Kambouropoulos, 2006).

2. Whether or not self-referent processes are reflected as risk/protective factors and/or as more or less benign outcomes in studies or theoretical discussions of resiliency, such self-referent processes have been widely reported to mediate and/or moderate these relationships.

With regard to their mediating functions, a number of studies previously cited as illustrative of relationships between risk/protective factors and more or less adverse outcomes that reflect self-relevant processes also illustrate the mediating role of such processes. Thus in a prospective study of women at risk for contracting sexually transmitted disease and who suffered childhood abuse, symptoms of posttraumatic stress disorder (PTSD) associated with experiences of childhood abuse were observed to be inversely related to a latent construct reflected in measures of self-efficacy and self-esteem. These "protective self-cognitions," in turn were inversely related to a latent construct, "resource loss" measured at a later point in time, reflected in measures of family resources, energy resources, material resources, and interpersonal resources (Walter et al., 2010).

Reports that positive and negative affect mediate the influence of self-threatening (anxiety) or self-protective (resilience) personal traits on self-esteem are interpretable in terms of the mediating influence of other self-referent processes (Benetti & Kambouropoulos, 2006). In this instance, scores on mediating positive and negative affect measures may reflect the ability to self- protectively regulate the negative/positive self-feelings that are the outcome of self-threatening or self-enhancing circumstances indicated by measures of trait anxiety and resilience, respectively, and that, in turn, influence self-esteem, that is, a measure of perceived self-worth. Also relevant is the cross-sectional study of a national sample of adolescents in Iceland, in which self-esteem was observed to indicate the influence of such variables as parental support and attitudes toward school on depressed mood and anger (Asgeirsdottir et al., 2010).

Consistent with the results of these studies, data collected by questionnaire from the municipal Police Office of Florence indicated that cumulative exposure to perceived personal threat that was a risk factor for posttraumatic stress is mediated by greater social support and by lower levels of perceived personal threat and peritraumatic distress (Pietrantoni, Prati, & Lori, 2009).

Even more prevalent than studies manifesting the mediating role of self-referent processes in relationships between risk/protective factors and adverse/benign outcomes are those investigations that describe how circumstances that manifestly reflect or are interpretable as reflecting self-referent processes moderate these relationships. In particular the moderating influence of self-esteem on resilience has been observed for a wide variety of putative risk factors, adverse consequences, and populations. For example Edwards and Romero (2008) observed that Mexican descent adolescents who were experiencing high levels of stress from discrimination and who reported particular coping patterns were able to protect their self-esteem from the adverse effects of prejudice and discrimination. In effect an interaction between level of discrimination and category of coping mechanisms influenced subsequent level of self-esteem. When the youth experiences higher levels of discrimination stress, and so is more motivated to restore or attain self-esteem, the adoption of primary continual engagement coping patterns (direct coping with the source of stress of one's emotions) influences higher levels of self-esteem.

Level of self-esteem moderates the effect of failure on responses to such failure. Individuals characterized by low self-esteem, by definition, have a stronger need to restore or attain self-esteem than characteristically high self-esteem people. Consequently, low self-esteem people who have their self-esteem on a particular domain (e.g., academic competence) would be more prone than high self-esteem individuals to respond to failure self-protectively by losing motivation to achieve academically while devaluing the evaluative significance of such achievement (Park, Crocker, & Kiefer, 2007). More specifically, low self-esteem people who experience failure in domains on which they base their self-esteem would be prone to respond to intimations of failure in those domains by reducing their motivation *to appear competent* in those areas.

In a study of homeless youth self-esteem has been observed to be a salient protective factor against loneliness, suicidal ideation, and feelings of being trapped (Kidd & Shahar, 2008). In addition, self-esteem is protective against the adverse effect of fearful (as opposed to secure) attachment on loneliness. Similarly, opportunities afforded to individuals to engage in activities that increased self-esteem among those residing in impoverished households apparently mitigated the expected adverse consequences of material deprivation (Canvin, Marttila, Burstrom, & Whitehead, 2009).

A variety of medical conditions are taken to reflect a concatenation of risk factors, the effects of which are somewhat mitigated by high self-esteem. Thus, for children with dyslexia (presumably a risk factor for adverse outcomes) the children who scored higher on a measure of global self-worth (as well as their parents) manifested more positive attitudes toward the difficulties in reading. Further, they were less likely to report a negative impact on relationships (Terras, Thompson, & Minnis, 2009).

In this regard, frequently self-esteem related constructs are viewed, not only as a component of resilience, but rather as the essential elements of this construct. Thus, Yi and associates (Yi, Vitaliano, Smith, Yi, & Weinger, 2008) defined resilience in terms of a factor score consisting of self-esteem, self-efficacy, self-mastery, and optimism. Resilience, thus defined, was observed to moderate the effect of diabetes-related distress on glycosylated hessoglobin among patients with diabetes. Patients with low or moderate resilience levels manifested a strong association between rising distress and worsening glycosylated hessoglobin. Those with high resilience did not demonstrate the same association. Nor did low resilience patience engage in self-care behaviors to the same degree as others in response to rising distress.

Finally, to further illustrate the moderating influence of self-esteem, according to the terror management theory (TNT) self-esteem buffers the anxiety—producing effects of increased awareness of one's mortality. Those with high self-esteem have successfully internalized and conformed to a system of self-values shared by an interpersonal network. Bolstered by these resources it is possible to manage what would otherwise be paralyzing terror evoked by mortality salience. However, low self-esteem individuals have failed to meet the culturally prescribed demands that allow full participation in their social system and the garnering of resources normally afforded to such participants. Consequently, for low self-esteem individuals increased awareness of one's mortality would evoke intensified feelings of death-related anxiety and the concomitant need to defend against such anxiety. Consistent with this reasoning, among individuals low in implicit (presumably true) self-esteem, but not those high in implicit self-esteem, increased mortality salience was associated with increased defensive responses. In addition to the foregoing an increase in implicit self-esteem reduced the effect of mortality salience on the defensive response. Finally, unique to a subset of individuals characterized by low implicit/high explicit self-esteem (suggesting highly vulnerable or defensive persons)

increased mortality salience was associated with increased endorsement of positive personality descriptions suggesting an increased need to defend against self-threatening circumstances by people who are particularly sensitive to self-criticism (Schmeichel et al., 2009).

Toward an Integrative Explanatory Framework

The importance of establishing a linkage between resilience-related constructs and a set of mutually influential self-referent constructs is twofold. On the one hand, it is possible to replace a diffuse and ambiguous resilience-related literature with a more narrowly focused group of concepts that appears to offer greater opportunities for conceptual clarity. At the same time, on the other hand, these self-referent concepts offer the promise of constituting the core of an explanatory theoretical framework that addresses the sources of life stress, the (in) direct and moderating influences of stressors on more or less adverse outcomes and the reciprocal influence of these outcomes on the aforementioned factors.

Over a period of more than 50 years I have formulated a general theory of behavior that focuses upon the antecedents and consequences of four classes of self-referent responses, the relations among the self-referent responses, and the mediators and moderators of these relations (Kaplan, 1972, 1975, 1980, 1984, 1986, 1996, 2001). Although initially formulated and tested as a general theory of deviant behavior (see Kaplan, 1980, 2003; Kaplan & Johnson, 2001 for an overview of several analyses), the theory has since been applied as an integrative framework for the literature in several other (partially overlapping) substantive areas, including psychosocial stress (Kaplan, 1996), the sociology of emotions (Kaplan, 2006), social psychology (Kaplan, 1986), and the several disciplines constituting the humanities (Kaplan & Kaplan, 2004/2005). Most recently the general theory was applied to the medical sociology literature (Kaplan, 2007).

Building upon the seminal observations of others regarding the reflexive nature of human behavior, social influence on self-conception and self-evaluation, and the motivational force of self-feelings (see in particular Cooley, 1902; James, 1915; Mead, 1934), the theoretical statement delineates: (1) structural and interactional effects on self-conceptions (cognitive responses directed toward one's own person, including self-perception, self-imagination, self-awareness, etc.); (2) the influence of self-cognition on self-evaluation (a subcategory of self-conception whereby persons judge themselves to be more or less proximate to or distant from self-relevant, situationally appropriate, hierarchically oriented evaluative standards); (3) the influence of self-evaluation on self-feelings (emotional responses to internalized needs stimulated by salient self-evaluations); (4) the influence of (negative) self-feelings on initiation of self-enhancing and self-protective responses (behavioral change to approximate self-evaluative standards, distortion of self-concept, reformulation of self-evaluative hierarchy, suppression of distressful self-feelings) evoked by the intensified need to diminish negative (and increase positive) self-feelings, occasioned by negative self-evaluations; and (5) the impacts of self-enhancing and self-protecting responses on behavior that is directed toward approximating salient self-evaluative standards, or directly diminishing the experience of distressful self-feelings (Kaplan, 1986). Although it is beyond the purpose of this paper to present a detailed description of an integrative explanatory theoretical framework, perhaps the following synopsis will serve to convey the utility of this approach in systematically encompassing the range of constructs that are normally considered in the resilience-related literature, including those that are regarded as risk or protective factors and a range of more or less (un)desirable outcomes, as well as the variables that mediate or moderate the relationships between them. Again, the constructs that compose the theoretical framework, in large measure, relate to the relevance of self-referent processes for explaining sociodevelopmental or contemporaneously socially structured phenomena.

To begin with the process of self-cognition, how an individual responds to himself along any of a number of cognitive dimensions is influenced by the person's attributes, behavior, and experiences in interaction with the situational context in which they appear, the system of concepts that the person has learned to use to structure stimuli, and the motivation to evaluate himself positively. The person's traits, behaviors, and experiences (including the individual and collective responses of others that purposely or otherwise have an impact on the person's outcomes) are social in nature, both in the sense that their meanings are provided by the current situation and in the sense that they have their origins in the course of past social interactions.

The most direct route by which personal traits, behaviors, or experiences may influence self-referent cognitive responses is by immediately becoming objects of self-awareness. The personal traits, behaviors, and experiences of which one becomes aware may be conceived of in terms of their objectively given forms or in terms of other, perhaps unobserved or unobservable, personal traits, behaviors, or experiences that are suggested by the immediate object of awareness.

The person's traits, behaviors, and experiences are mutually influential, whether over a relatively long or short period of time. Therefore, any particular trait, behavior, or experience may have an indirect effect on self-referent cognition by, first, influencing others' personal traits, behaviors, or experiences that, in turn, directly stimulate self-awareness and self-conceiving responses. Traits, behaviors, and experiences vary to the extent to which they may directly stimulate self-conceiving responses as opposed to indirectly influencing such responses through their mediating effects on other influential traits, behaviors, and experiences.

The nature of the influence of personal traits, behaviors, and experiences on self-referent cognitive responses is moderated by the situational context, the person's system of concepts that he habitually uses to structure the world and himself, and the person's motivation to acquire self-enhancing experiences. The situational context provides symbolic cues that (1) specify the relevance of particular traits, behaviors, and experiences for the person's current life situation from among the many traits, behaviors, and experiences in the person's repertoire and (2) provide a range and distribution of values along specific dimensions that allow and stimulate the person to discern the particular values that characterize himself along these dimensions. The person uses a relatively stable, more or less consensual system of concepts to guide the selective cognitive structuring of personal attributes—a system of concepts that is derived both from regularities in the person's responses and from the reinforcement value of (1) other' sanctions for the use of particular concepts and (2) the usefulness of the consensual concepts in anticipating other's responses to the person's behaviors. The person's need for positive self-evaluation motivates him to be sensitive to his own personal traits, behaviors, or experiences that are relevant to self-attitudes and to perceive and define them in ways that will enhance self-evaluation.

Self-referent cognitive responses have direct consequences, both for the person's own traits, behaviors, and experiences and for other modes of self-referent responses. The acts of responding to oneself cognitively in particular ways are themselves behaviors and may become personal attributes that, in turn, stimulate other self-referent cognitions. Self-cognitions, conjointly with the individual's need-value system, influence self-evaluative responses and self-enhancing responses.

Self-evaluative responses are personal judgments of the extent to which the person approximates desirable states. The initiation of a self-evaluative response is a function of the person's self-awareness and self-conceptualization and of the person's learned disposition to evaluate himself when becoming aware of himself. The nature (content) of the self-evaluative response is a function of the nature of the person's self-perceptions and of the personal system of evaluative standards (in particular, that aspect of the personal value system that encompasses self-values), according to which he judges that which he perceives about himself. The specific self-perception, in conjunction with social situational cues, stimulates self-judgments

with reference to the situationally applicable personal evaluative standards. The most inclusive self-value in the person's system of self-values is positive self-evaluation. The person's overall self-evaluation is a function of self-perceptions of approximating specific self-evaluative standards that are more or less salient (central, important) in the personal hierarchy of values.

Depending on the degree to which the person judges himself to be distant from positive self-evaluation, he will experience more or less negative self-feelings that motivate him to behave in ways that appear to reduce the likelihood of negative self-feelings and to maximize the probability of experiencing more positive self-feelings.

Self-feelings reflect the activation of need dispositions that are stimulated by the person's self-evaluative responses, that is, by self-judgments of being more or less distant from valued or disvalued states. Need dispositions are internalizations of self-values and reflect the readiness to behave in ways that will permit approximation of valued, and distancing from disvalued, states. Self-feelings as the experience of needs stimulated by self-evaluative responses are experienced as more or less intense and more or less durable affective or emotional responses to self-evaluative responses. The feelings are experienced as more or less distressful, depending on the self-evaluations of being more or less distant from the valued or disvalued states, and the certainty and immediacy of approaching these states. The most inclusive of the needs is the need for positive self-evaluation. The stimulation of this need is a function of the more or less salient self-evaluative responses of more specific personal traits, behaviors, or experiences and of the corresponding, more specific self-feelings that are evoked by self-referent evaluative responses to personal traits, behaviors, or experiences.

Affective or emotional responses to self-evaluation (i.e., self-feelings) become part of the repertoire of personal traits, behaviors, and experiences. As such, they stimulate self-awareness and self-conceptualization, and thereby stimulate self-evaluative responses relating to the propriety of the self-feelings.

Self-feelings, the experience of need, stimulate the person to behave in ways that will permit the person to satisfy his needs. These needs relate to the approximation of self-values, the most inclusive of which is overall positive self-evaluation. In view of this, the responses oriented to the satisfaction of needs, stimulated by self-values and expressed as self-feelings, are collectively considered to be self-protective and self-enhancing responses. These responses to self-feeling take the form of changes in: self-referent cognition; the person's need-value system; and other personal traits, behaviors, and experiences that have self-evaluative significance. Additionally, the responses may directly affect the experience of negative (positive) self-feelings.

Self-protective and self-enhancing responses are behaviors by the person that are more or less consciously oriented toward the goal of (1) forestalling the experience of self-devaluing judgments and consequent distressful self-feelings (self-protective patterns) and (2) increasing the occasions for positive self-evaluations and self-enhancing responses that may take any or all of four forms relating to the person's self-referent cognitive responses, the person's revision of the need-value system, the person's responses that are oriented to the approximation of salient self-value, and responses that directly impact the experiences of positive or negative self-feelings.

Self-referent cognitive responses serve self-protective functions by permitting the person (1) to perceive himself as having positively valued qualities; (2) to deny negative attributes; and (3) to be sensitive to those personal attributes, behaviors, and experiences that have self-evaluative relevance. This last function orients the person to responses that are likely to forestall self-devaluing and to facilitate self-enhancing experiences. Revisions in the need-value system permit individuals to selectively order self-values so that they are compatible with the person's present and anticipated traits, behaviors, and experiences. A third major form of self-protective and self-enhancing responses encompasses the person's purposive behaviors that are oriented to the approximation of self-evaluative standards. That is, the person behaves in ways that are instrumental

in the attainment of, or intrinsically reflect, salient self-values.

Responses that directly impact self-feelings may involve the use of pharmacologic substances that increase euphoric or decrease dysphoric self-feelings, or may implicate involuntary central and autonomic nervous system responses that preclude the experiences of unwelcome feelings. The responses in all of those categories may be expressed in ways that, in varying degrees, approximate conventional or deviant standards.

The occurrence and form of self-protective or self-enhancing responses are determined by the nature of the person's self-feelings, the person's beliefs about himself in relation to his environment, and the person's evaluation of the projected self-protective and self-enhancing responses as more or less closely approximating self-evaluative criteria. To the extent that the individual variously experiences chronic self-rejecting feelings or situational exacerbation of self-rejecting feelings, the person will be motivated to adopt self-protective or self-enhancing responses. The experience of positive self-feelings tends to reinforce those specific or general purposes that the person associates with the experience of positive self-feelings. Within these constraints, the specific forms of the self-protective and self-enhancing patterns are influenced by the person's beliefs about his own capabilities in relationship to the mutability of reality. The person will tend to adopt those response patterns that, based on earlier experiences, are believed to be within the person's capabilities and that are expected to serve self-protective or self-enhancing functions. The form of the self-protective or self-enhancing responses is influenced, further, by the personal evaluation of responses that are expected to serve these functions. Although a person may anticipate that certain responses will serve self-enhancing functions, he may not perform those behaviors if they are judged to reflect or to be instrumental in the approximation of disvalued states. Those behaviors will be acted out to the extent that such judgments are not made, whether because they were already compatible with the person's self-values or because the person reorders his self-values in such a way that the projected self-enhancing patterns are no longer incompatible with the person's self-evaluative criteria.

Conclusion

Although I have criticized the concept of resilience because it is so diffuse and ambiguous in its meanings it might be argued that the concept of resilience is useful precisely because it instigates so many conceptual or theoretical issues. The word evokes so many rich intellectual issues regarding intrapsychic and interpersonal resilience-related processes that increased understanding of human or higher-order systemic adaptive responses in all their ramifications must follow necessarily. Perhaps it is in serving this sensitizing function that "resilience" finds it raison d'etre. When it ceases to serve this function, if it has not already done so, because of the several contradictions and ambiguities inherent in the concept, it may be necessary to move beyond the definition of the concept.

"Moving beyond" involves both reconceptualization and theoretical integration. In the former case, resilience must be more precisely equated to constructs that reflect adversity and the psychosocial processes that mediate and moderate the reciprocal relations between them. Based on a review of the resilience-related theoretical and empirical literatures, I suggest that such precision and equivalency may be found in a concentration of self-referent constructs.

In addition, however, for resilience to serve a useful purpose it must be located in the context of a coherent theoretical framework. I argue that such a framework should be grounded in a matrix of interrelated propositions asserting (in) direct (non) recursive linear and moderative influences among four classes of self-referent processes: those relating to (1) self-cognition, (2) self-evaluation, (3) self-feeling, and (4) self-enhancing and self-protective mechanisms. This explanatory framework would address not only why individuals overcome adversity, but perhaps more importantly why and how they fail to do so.

In sensitizing us to the need to understand the mutual effects of antecedents of more or less positive outcomes, the conditional nature of these effects, and the fact that proximal and conditional variables have their own causes, the concept of resilience has served an important function. The concept has alerted us to the fact that people who according to conventional wisdom should have experienced adverse outcomes, do not in fact experience them. Having so alerted us to the phenomena, however, resilience may have served its purpose. In place of this concept, we must now redirect our attention to creating more general theoretical structures that take into account individual, environmental, and situational factors that influence each other and interact with each other to influence other variables in different ways at different stages of the developmental cycle and of the evolution of social structures to affect outcomes, the evaluative significance of which is only incidental to the purpose of explaining the phenomena in question.

Acknowledgments This work was supported by research grants (R01 DA 02497 and R01 DA 10016) and by a Research Scientist Award (K05 DA 00136) from the National Institute on Drug Abuse to the author.

References

Adger, W. N. (2000). Social and ecological resilience: Are they related? *Progress in Human Geography, 24*(3), 347–364.

Anthony, E. J. (1987). Risk, vulnerability and resilience: An overview. In E. J. Anthony & B. Cohler (Eds.), *The invulnerable child* (pp. 3–48). New York: Guilford.

Asgeirsdottir, B., Gudjonsson, G., Sigurdsson, J., & Sigfusdttir, I. (2010). Protective processes for depressed mood and anger among sexually abused adolescents: The importance of self-esteem. *Personality and Individual Differences, 49*, 402–407.

Bartelt, D. W. (1994). On resilience: Questions of validity. In M. C. Wang & E. W. Gordon (Eds.), *Educational resilience in inner-city America* (pp. 97–108). Hillsdale: Erlbaum.

Benetti, C., & Kambouropoulos, N. (2006). Affect-regulated indirect effects of trait anxiety and trait resilience on self-esteem. *Personality and Individual Differences, 41*, 341–352.

Block, J. H., & Block, J. (1980). The role of ego control and ego resiliency in the organization of behavior. In W. A. Collins (Ed.), *Development of cognition, affect, and social relations* (pp. 39–101). Hillsdale: Erlbaum.

Canvin, K., Marttila, A., Burstrom, B., & Whitehead, M. (2009). Tales of the unexpected? Hidden resilience in poor households in Britain. *Social Science & Medicine, 69*(2), 238–245.

Cicchetti, D., & Garmezy, N. (1993). Prospects and promises in the study of resilience. *Development and Psychopathology, 5,* 497–502.

Cicchetti, D., & Rogosch, F. A. (2009). Adaptive coping under conditions of extreme stress: Multilevel influences on the determinants of resilience in maltreated children. *New Directions for Child and Adolescent Development, 2009*(124), 47–59.

Clauss-Ehlers, C. S., & Levi, L. L. (2002). Violence and community, terms in conflict: An ecological approach to resilience. *Journal of Social Distress & the Homeless, 11*(4), 265–278.

Cohler, B. J. (1987). Adversity, resilience, and the study of lives. In E. J. Anthony & B. Cohler (Eds.), *The invulnerable child* (pp. 363–424). New York: Guilford.

Conger, R. D., Rueter, M. A., & Elder, G. H., Jr. (1999). Couple resilience to economic pressure. *Journal of Personality and Social Psychology, 76*(1), 54–71.

Cooley, C. H. (1902). *Human nature and the social order.* New York: Scribners.

Edwards, L., & Romero, A. (2008). Coping with discrimination among Mexican descent adolescents. *Hispanic Journal of Behavior Sciences, 30*(1), 24–39.

Filbert, K. M., & Flynn, R. J. (2009). Developmental and cultural assets and resilient outcomes in First Nations young people in care: An initial test of an explanatory model. *Children and Youth Services Review, 32*(4), 560–564.

Greenbaum, C. W., & Auberbach, J. G. (1992). The conceptualization of risk, vulnerability, and resilience in psychological development. In C. W. Greenbaum & J. G. Auerbach (Eds.), *Longitudinal studies of children at psychological risk: Cross-national perspectives* (pp. 9–28). Norwood: Ablex.

Haan, L. D., Hawley, D. R., & Deal, J. E. (2002). Operationalizing family resilience: A methodological stratedgy. *American Journal of Family Therapy, 30*(4), 275–291.

Hartling, L. M. (2008). Strengthening resilience in a risky world: It's all about relationships. *Women and Therapy, 31*(2–4), 51–70.

Hernandez, P. (2002). Resilience in families and communities: Latin American contributions from the psychology of liberation. *Family Journal—Counseling and Therapy for Couples and Families, 10*(3), 334–343.

Humphreys, J. (2003). Resilience in sheltered battered women. *Issues in Mental Health Nursing, 24*(2), 137–152.

James, W. (1915). *Psychology.* New York: Holt, Rinehart and Winston.

Kaplan, H. B. (1972). Toward a general theory of psychosocial deviance: The case of aggressive behavior. *Social Science & Medicine, 6,* 539–617.

Kaplan, H. B. (1975). *Self-attitudes and deviant behavior.* Pacific Palisades: Goodyear.

Kaplan, H. B. (1980). *Deviant behavior in defense of self.* New York: Academic.

Kaplan, H. B. (1984). *Patterns of juvenile delinquency.* Beverly Hills: Sage Publications.

Kaplan, H. B. (1986). *Social psychology of self-referent behavior.* New York: Plenum Press.

Kaplan, H. B. (1996). Psychosocial stress from the perspective of self theory. In H. B. Kaplan (Ed.), *Psychosocial stress: Perspectives on structure, theory, life course, and methods* (pp. 175–244). San Diego: Academic.

Kaplan, H. B. (1999). Toward an understanding of resilience: A critical review of definitions and models. In M. D. Glantz & J. L. Johnson (Eds.), *Resilience and development* (pp. 17–83). New York: Kluwer Academic/Plenum.

Kaplan, H. B. (2001). Self esteem and deviant behavior: A critical review and theoretical integration. In T. J. Owens, S. Stryker, & N. Goodman (Eds.), *Extending self-esteem theory and research: Sociological and psychological currents* (pp. 375–397). New York: Cambridge University Press.

Kaplan, H. B. (2003). Testing an integrative theory of deviant behavior: Theory syntonic findings from a long-term multigenerational study. In T. Thornberry & M. Krohn (Eds.), *Taking stock of delinquency* (pp. 185–204). New York: Springer.

Kaplan, H. B. (2006). Self-theory and emotions. In J. Turner & J. Stets (Eds.), *Handbook of the sociology of emotions* (pp. 224–253). New York: Springer.

Kaplan, H. B. (2007). Self-referent construct and medical sociology: In search of a integrative framework. *Journal of Health and Social Behavior, 48*(June), 99–114.

Kaplan, H., & Johnson, R. (2001). *Social deviance: Testing a general theory.* New York: Kluwer Academic/Plenum.

Kaplan, H. & Kaplan, D. (2004/2005). The structural integrity of the humanities: Self-related constructs as integrative mechanisms. *International Journal of the Humanities, 2,* 705–715.

Kidd, S., & Shahar, G. (2008). Resilience in homeless youth: The key role of self-esteem. *The American Journal of Orthopsychiatry, 78*(2), 163–172.

Kjølseth, I., Ekeberg, O., & Steihaug, S. (2009). "Why do they become vulnerable when faced with the challenges of old age?" Elderly people who committed suicide, described by those who knew them. *International Psychogeriatrics/IPA, 21*(50), 903–912.

Lee, R. M. (2005). Resilience against discrimination: Ethnic identity and other-group orientation as protective factors for Korean America. *Journal of Counseling Psychology, 52*(1), 36–44.

Liddle, H. A. (1994). Contextual resiliency. In M. C. Wang & E. W. Gordon (Eds.), *Educational resilience in inner-city America* (pp. 167–177). Hillsdale: Erlbaum.

Lindström, B. (2001). The meaning of resilience. International Journal of Adolescent Medicine and

Health. *Special Issue: Resilience and Adolescence: A Tribute to Emanuel Chigier, 13*(1), 7–12.

Lösel, F., Bliesener, T., & Köferl, P. (1989). On the concept of invulnerability: Evaluation and first results of the Bielefeld project. In M. Brambring, F. Lösel, & H. Skowronek (Eds.), *Children at risk: Assessment, longitudinal research, and intervention* (pp. 186–219). New York: Walter de Gruyter.

Luthar, S. S. (1993). Annotation: Methodological and conceptual issues in research on childhood resilience. *Journal of Child Psychology and Psychiatry, 34,* 441–453.

Luthar, S. S., Cicchetti, D., & Becker, B. (2000). The construct of resilience: A critical evaluation and guidelines for future work. *Child Development, 71*(3), 543–562.

Masten, A. S. (1994). Resilience in individual development: Successful adaptation despite risk and adversity. In M. C. Wang & E. W. Gordon (Eds.), *Educational resilience in inner-city America* (pp. 3–25). Hillsdale: Erlbaum.

McGregor, I., Nash, K., & Inzlicht, M. (2009). Threat, high self-esteem, and reactive approach-motivation: Electroencephalographic evidence. *Journal of Experimental Social Psychology, 45*(2009), 1003–1007.

Mead, G. H. (1934). *Mind, self, and society.* Chicago: University of Chicago Press.

Mäkikangas, A., Kinnunen, U., & Feld, T. (2004). Self-Esteem, dispositional optimism, and health: Evidence from cross-lagged data on employees. *Journal of Research in Personality, 38*(6), 556–575.

Olsson, C. A., Bond, L., Burns, J. M., Vella-Brodrick, D. A., & Sawyer, S. M. (2003). Adolescent resilience: A concept analysis. *Journal of Adolescence, 26*(1), 1–11.

Oswald, R. F. (2002). Resilience within the family networks of lesbians and gay men: Intentionality and redefinition. *Journal of Marriage and the Family, 64*(2), 374–383.

Overbeek, G., Zeevalkink, H., Vermulst, A., & Scholte, R. (2010). Peer victimization, self-esteem, and ego resilience types in adolescents: A prospective analysis of person-context interactions. *Social Development, 19*(2), 270–284.

Park, L., Crocker, J., & Kiefer, A. (2007). Contingencies of self-worth, academic failure, and goal pursuit. *Personality and Social Psychology Bulletin, 2007*(33), 1503.

Patterson, J. M. (2002). Understanding family resilience. *Journal of Clinical Psychology. Special Issue: A second Generation of Resilience Research, 58*(3), 233–246.

Phillips-Salimi, C. R., Haase, J. E., Kintner, E. K., Monahan, P., & Azzouz, F. (2007). Psychometric properties of the Herth Hope Index in adolescents and young adults with cancer. *Journal of Nursing Measures, 15*(1), 3–23.

Pietrantoni, L., Prati, G., & Lori, G. (2009). Risk and resilience factors in posttraumatic stress disorder when

working in the Municipal Police Force. *Psicoterapia Cognitiva e Comportamentale, 15*(1), 63–78.

Radke-Yarrow, M., & Brown, E. (1993). Resilience and vulnerability in children of multiple-risk families. *Development and Psychopathology, 5,* 581–592.

Radke-Yarrow, M., & Sherman, T. (1990). Hard growing: Children who survive. In J. Rolf, A. S. Masten, D. Cicchetti, K. H. Nuechterlein, & S. Weintraub (Eds.), *Risk and protective factors in the development of psychopathology* (pp. 97–119). New York: Cambridge University Press.

Rauh, H. (1989). The meaning of risk and protective factors in infancy. *European Journal of Psychology of Education, 4*(2), 161–173.

Richters, J., & Weintraub, S. (1990). Beyond diathesis: Towards an understanding of high-risk environments. In J. Rolf, A. S. Masten, D. Cicchetti, K. H. Nuechterlein, & S. Weintraub (Eds.), *Risk and protective factors in the development of psychopathology* (pp. 67–96). New York: Cambridge University Press.

Rutter, M. (1990). Psychosocial resilience and protective mechanisms. In J. Rolf, A. S. Masten, D. Cicchetti, K. H. Nuechterlein, & S. Weintraub (Eds.), *Risk and protective factors in the development of psychopathology* (pp. 181–214). New York: Cambridge University Press.

Schaefer, J. A., & Moos, R. A. (1992). Life crises and personal growth. In B. N. Carpenter (Ed.), *Personal coping: Theory, research, and application* (pp. 149–170). Westport: Praeger.

Schmeichel, B., Gailliot, M., Filardo, E., McGregor, I., Gitter, S., & Baumeister, R. (2009). Terror management theory and self-esteem revisited: The roles of implicit and explicit self-esteem in mortality salience effects. *Journal of Personality and Social Psychology, 96*(5), 1077–1087.

Schuldberg, D. (1993). Personal resourcefulness: Positive aspects of functioning in high research. *Psychiatry, 56,* 137–152.

Schwartz, J. P. (2002). Family resilience and pragmatic parent education. *Journal of Individual Psychology, 58*(3), 250–262.

Seifer, R., & Sameroff, A. I. (1987). Multiple determinants of risk and invulnerability. In E. J. Anthony & B. Cohler (Eds.), *The invulnerable child* (pp. 51–69). Guilford: New York.

Simon, K., Barakat, L. P., Patterson, C. A., & Dampier, C. (2009). Symptoms of depression and anxiety in adolescents with sickle cell disease: The role of intrapersonal characteristics and stress processing variables. *Child Psychiatry and Human Development, 40*(2), 317–330.

Sorenson, L. G., Forbes, P. W., Bernstein, J. H., Weiler, M. D., Mitchell, W. M., & Waber, D. P. (2003). Psychosocial adjustment over a two-year period in children referred for learning problems: Risk, resilience, and adaptation. *Learning Disabilities Research and Practice, 18*(1), 10–24.

Spencer, M. B., Cole, S. P., Dupree, D., Glymph, A., & Pierre, P. (1993). Self-efficacy among urban African American early adolescents: Exploring issues of risk, vulnerability, and resilience. *Development and Pschopathology., 5*, 719–739.

Terras, M., Thompson, L., & Minnis, H. (2009). Dyslexia and psycho-social functioning: An exploratory study of the role of self-esteem and understanding. *Dyslexia, 15*(4), 304–327.

Walsh, F. (2002). A family resilience framework: Innovative practice applications. *Family Relations: Interdisciplinary Journal of Applied Family Studies, 51*(2), 130–137.

Walter, K., Horsey, K., Palmieri, P., & Hobfoll, S. (2010). The role of protective self-cognitions in the relationship between childhood trauma and later resource loss. *Journal of Traumatic Stress, 23*(2), 264–273.

Wanberg, C., & Banas, J. (2000). Predictors and outcomes of openness to changes in a reorganizing workplace. *Journal of Applied Psychology, 85*(1), 132–142.

Yi, J., Vitaliano, P., Smith, R., Yi, J., & Weinger, K. (2008). The role of resilience on psychological adjustment and physical health in patients with diabetes. *British Journal of Health Psychology, 13*(2), 311–325.

Resilience in Gene–Environment Transactions*

4

Zhe Wang and Kirby Deater-Deckard

Resilient children are not simply "born that way," nor are they "made from scratch" by their experiences. Genetic and environmental factors operate conjointly as protectors against a variety of risks to healthy development, ranging from resistance to bacteria and viruses to resistance to maltreatment and rejection. The key question is how genes and environments work together to produce resilient children and adults.

Resilience in childhood is defined as typical development in the face of adverse circumstances that propel others to deleterious outcomes. The risks for minor or serious problems in mental and physical health are real and for a segment of the human population, are ever present. Nearly every child faces occasional adversity, and many experience chronic stressors such as abuse, poverty, or disease. However, even within populations of children who have or who experience powerful predictive risks for behavioral and emotional problems, there is wide variation in outcomes. Some will succumb to the vicissitudes of life, but many will thrive in spite of them. Our goal is to highlight several areas of research that demonstrate the integrative interplay between nature and nurture in the prediction of individual differences in resilience. We begin by considering several aspects of individuality that are critical to resilience in childhood, with an emphasis on temperament, cognitive skills, and social cognitions. We then turn to consideration of the resilience-building transactions that connect the individual and the environment, with emphasis on warm, supportive social relationships.

Nature and Nurture

Humans share a genome and live in environments that have many structural similarities. For numerous outcomes of interest to developmental scientists, the variation between people arises not from the presence or absence of genes or environments, but from functionally distinct *forms* of genes and environments. A variety of techniques are used to estimate the effects of these distinct forms on individual differences, based on quantitative and molecular biology models (Plomin, DeFries, McClearn, & McGuffin, 2008).

Molecular genetic techniques for the collection, storage, and analysis of DNA permit the examination of association and linkage between specific regions of chromosomes or specific genes, and human variation in measured attributes. Using these molecular approaches, scientists identify the genes that are involved in complex phenotypes (i.e., observed characteristics)—a level of

*This chapter is an updated and modified version of the chapter from the first edition (Deater-Deckard, Ivy, & Smith, 2004). The majority of the modifications involved inclusion of recent research on molecular genetic studies and findings. Some portions of the chapter were not modified from the prior edition.

Z. Wang • K. Deater-Deckard (✉)
Department of Psychology, Virginia Polytechnic Institute and State University, Blacksburg, VA 24061, USA
e-mail: wangzhe@vt.edu; kirbydd@vt.edu

specificity not afforded by traditional behavioral genetic techniques.

Quantitative behavioral genetic techniques do not require DNA analysis, but instead rely on mathematical models based on population genetics to estimate the relative strength of genetic and environmental contributions to individual differences. These are based on data from quasi-experimental designs involving identical and fraternal twins, adoptive and nonadoptive siblings, adoptive and biological parent–child pairs, and stepfamily members. If family member similarity on a variable of interest is predicted by genetic similarity, then genetic variance or *heritability* is present. If family member similarity remains after genetic similarity is controlled, then *shared environmental* variance is present. Shared environmental influences are the nongenetic effects that lead to family member similarity. *Nonshared environmental* variance is what remains—the nongenetic influences that do not account for family member similarities (Reiss, Neiderhiser, Hetherington, & Plomin, 2000).

Individual Differences and Resilience

There is ample quantitative behavioral genetic research (e.g., twin, adoption designs) that provides a basis for investigating the interplay between genes and environments. Some of the specific genes that may be involved in complex gene–environment transactions in development have also been identified. To exemplify this burgeoning literature, we describe findings from research on temperament and cognitive factors—both of which are strongly implicated as protective factors in development.

Temperament and Personality

Temperament includes individual attributes that are defined as being moderately stable across situations and over time, are biologically influenced, and are observable from infancy. Individual differences in temperament arise from transactions between genetic and environmental influences,

are mediated by brain mechanisms, are modified by experience and situational factors, and change with development (Prior, 1999; Rothbart & Bates, 1998). Temperament forms the foundation of personality dimensions (e.g., neuroticism, conscientiousness, agreeableness) that have patterns of heritable and environmental variance that are similar to temperament and are implicated in the development of resilience (Campbell-Sills, Cohan, & Stein, 2006; Carver & Connor-Smith, 2010; Costa, Somerfield, & McCrae, 1996; Matthews, Deary, & Whiteman, 2003; Rothbart, Ahadi, & Evans, 2000). Rothbart's theory of temperament is particularly helpful as an organizing framework for considering connections between individual differences, resilience, and gene–environment transactions (other prominent theories include Buss & Plomin, 1984; Thomas & Chess, 1977). According to this theory, there are multiple dimensions of temperament that represent reactivity to stimuli and the regulation of those reactions.

Extraversion/surgency. The first dimension is *Extraversion/surgency* and includes activity level, positive affect, low shyness, and positive anticipation/approach. *Activity level* represents amount and pacing of physical movement. A moderate activity level is optimal for resilience (e.g., Mendez, Fantuzzo, & Cicchetti, 2002). If too low, the child is sluggish and prone to weight gain, and if too high then the child is hyperactive and more difficult to manage. Between one-third and three-quarters of the variation in activity level is accounted for by genetic factors, with the remaining variance attributable to nonshared environment and error (Braungart, Plomin, DeFries, & Fulkner, 1992; Gagne, Vendlinski, & Goldsmith, 2009; Oniszczenko et al., 2003; Plomin, Pedersen, McClearn, Nesselroade, & Bergeman, 1988; Saudino, 2005; Wood, Rijsdijk, Saudino, Asherson, & Kuntsi, 2008). Surgency also includes positive emotionality, which shows genetic and nonshared enviornmental variance (Eid, Reimann, Angleitner, & Borkenau, 2003). Children who often experience and express positive moods (e.g., happiness, excitement, interest) are less likely to suffer the consequences of exposure to risk factors. Lengua (2002) found that positive emotionality predicted resilience in 8–10-year-olds, consistent with an earlier study by Masten et al. (1999)—although this effect was limited to females in the earlier study. *Shyness* represents slow or inhibited approach in novel or uncertain situations. Children who are less shy and more sociable may be protected against stressors (e.g., Lösel & Bliesener, 1994), although they also may be at greater risk for problems in coping with family conflict (Tschann, Kaiser, Chesney, Alkon, & Boyce, 1996). Genetic variance in twin studies, and a serotonin neurotransmitter gene in molecular genetic studies, has been implicated in the development of shyness (Arbelle et al., 2003). *Positive anticipation/approach* represents the extent to which the child seeks out and enjoys having new experiences. Children who are high in positive anticipation/approach may be protected from negative events through their exploration of new strategies, but may also be more easily frustrated when their anticipation is not fulfilled (Deater-Deckard et al., 2010). Heritability accounts for one-fourth to three quarters of the variance, with some studies showing modest shared environmental variance (Eid et al., 2003; Plomin & Rutter, 1998; Schmitz, 1994). Molecular genetic studies have indicated a functional role of the dopamine receptor 4 gene (DRD4) in individual differences in novelty-seeking behaviors (Ebstein, 2006).

Negative affectivity. This dimension includes sadness, anger, fear, discomfort, and problems in soothing when upset. Consistent with studies of trait neuroticism in adolescents and adults, children who are low in negative affectivity are less likely to show maladjustment in the face of difficult circumstances. For example, Kilmer, Cowen, and Wyman (2001) found that negative affectivity best discriminated resilient from maladjusted children in their study of highly stressed inner-city youth. Genetic factors account for one-third to two-thirds of the variance in negative affectivity (Goldsmith, Buss, & Lemery, 1997; Oniszczenko et al., 2003; Plomin et al., 1988). Molecular genetic studies have indicated that the serotonin transporter 5-HTTLPR gene and the catechol-*O*-methyltransferase gene

(COMT; one major enzyme that is involved degrading catecholamines) are associated with variation in anxiety and fear-related traits (Enoch, Xu, Ferro, Harris, & Goldman, 2003; Hariri et al., 2002; Melke et al., 2001; Sen, Burmeister, & Ghosh, 2004; Woo et al., 2004). The COMT gene also has been associated with anger and hostility (Rujescu, Giegling, Gietl, Hartmann, & Moller, 2003; Volavka et al., 2004).

Effortful control. This dimension includes enjoyment of low-intensity stimulation, greater perceptual sensitivity, and more control over impulses and attention. Effortful control is important to resilience. Children who are higher in effortful control show less negative affectivity, indicating an important connection between attentional control and the regulation of negative emotions (Rothbart et al., 2000). Thus, those who are better able to control cognitive and perceptual processing of information also may be better at regulating their emotions and behaviors so that they are less likely to develop psychopathologies that are associated with poor self-regulation (Buckner, Mezzacappa, & Beardslee, 2009; Gardner, Dishion, & Connell, 2008; Posner & Rothbart, 2006). In addition, the tendency to persist with challenging tasks is a protective factor among at-risk youth, for a variety of outcomes (Lösel & Bliesener, 1994; Wills, Sandy, Yaeger, & Shinar, 2001). Thus, children with more effortful control tend to have better academic achievement (Ponitz, McClelland, Matthews, & Morrison, 2009; Smith, Borkowski, & Whitman, 2008).

Effortful control and its underlying attributes are heritable, and some include shared environmental variance as well (Goldsmith et al., 1997). For task orientation and persistence, heritability estimates are moderate to substantial in early and middle childhood (Braungart et al., 1992; Deater-Deckard & Wang, 2012; Manke, Saudino, & Grant, 2001). Molecular genetic studies have identified the DRD4 and 5-HTTLPR genes as being involved in the regulation of sustained attentive behavior (Canli et al., 2005; Fan, Fossella, Sommer, Wu, & Posner, 2003; Krakowski, 2003). In addition to genetic influence, a portion of the variation in task persistence arises from shared environmental effects that are predicted by household socioeconomic status (SES) and maternal warmth (Petrill & Deater-Deckard, 2004).

In sum, there are various aspects of temperament that are indicative of good self-regulation and resilience. Persistence may help a child find appropriate coping strategies. Positive emotionality may increase proactive efforts to deal with stress and can promote the belief that the efforts will be successful. Furthermore, children who are easy to manage (i.e., adaptable, self-regulated, and happy) and who enjoy engaging in social interaction are more able to attract the care and attention of others who can assist them in coping with stressful situations. They may have "double protection," both in terms of their temperaments and the qualities of their social relationships with caregivers and others (Prior, 1999; Smith & Prior, 1995). In contrast, children who are irritable, easily distressed by changes in the environment, and more distractible may be less able to cope with adversity and more likely to attract or elicit harsh and rejecting parenting—particularly if the parent is distressed (Hetherington, 2006).

Cognitive Factors

Cognitive factors are also important in resilience processes. Research in this area of developmental science also exemplifies some of the ways genes and environments work together in promoting optimal development under nonoptimal conditions. Two broad domains of theory and research to consider include individual differences in children's cognitive abilities and their self-referent social cognitions.

Cognitive ability. Cognitive ability is a strong and consistent predictor of resilience in childhood and adolescence. Children who are more facile with information sources and strategies for solving problems not only are more likely to succeed academically, but have broader and more sophisticated repertoires of coping strategies at their disposal (Buckner et al., 2009; Kumpfer, 1999; Masten, 2001). In addition, children who have better cognitive executive function

are better at regulating their behaviors and emotions and therefore are protected against various externalizing and internalizing problems (Greenberg, 2006). Intelligence and its component skills include moderate to substantial genetic variance that increases in magnitude with development. Shared environmental variation is present in early childhood, but by adolescence this component of variance dissipates, so that all of the nongenetic variance becomes nonshared (McCartney, Harris, & Bernieri, 1990; Plomin et al., 2008).

Self-referent social cognitions. Although cognitive processing skills and abilities are important, the content of children's cognitions also are critical to resilience—in particular, social cognitions about the self, and control over things that threaten the integrity or safety of the self. Self-efficacy is the belief that goals can be accomplished, even when frustrations lie in the way. Self-worth or esteem stems from feeling valued by, and valuable to, other people. Anticipated outcomes also are important, with optimism defined as the anticipation of good outcomes, and pessimism defined as the anticipation of negative outcomes (Matthews, Schwean, Campbell, Saklofske, & Mohamed, 2000). These self-referent cognitions include moderate amounts of heritable and nonshared environmental variance, with some evidence of shared environmental influence in optimism and pessimism (Zuckerman, 2000). Twin and adoption studies of self-esteem yield heritability estimates in the 30–60% range, with the remaining variance accounted for by nonshared environmental variance (Kamakura, Ando, & Ono, 2007; Kendler, Gardner, & Prescott, 1998; McGuire et al., 1999; Neiderhiser & McGuire, 1994; Neiss, Sedikides, & Stevenson, 2002; Raevuori et al., 2007).

The development of self-concept and self-worth begins early in life. After gaining awareness of our own distinct qualities, we begin comparing ourselves to others. These cognitions become an integral part of how we perceive ourselves and how we think others perceive us. If we believe that we are valuable to others and that we can control our circumstances, we are more adept at planning coping strategies as well as evaluating and changing strategies that are not working (Zimmerman, 2000). Thus, high self-esteem and self-efficacy are effective protection against deleterious effects of a wide variety of risk factors (Buckner et al., 2009; Kumpfer, 1999; Neiderhiser & McGuire, 1994). In addition, those who believe that the worst will happen are less likely to adapt well when difficult circumstances arise. In contrast, those who are optimistic are more able to save and use their resources when they need them, and to be protected from subsequent stressors (Aspinwall, 2001).

In sum, there are a host of child attributes (including but not limited to temperament and personality, cognitive abilities, and self-referent social cognitions) that contribute to children's resilience. These attributes vary widely across children and emerge from the interplay between genetic and environmental influences.

Nongenetic Factors: Shared and Nonshared

Quasi-experimental behavioral genetic studies provide some of the clearest evidence of the role of nongenetic influences in the development of individual differences, particularly when compared to traditional family studies that lack quasi-experimental designs (Plomin, 1994). Of the ample nongenetic variance that typically is found in behavioral genetic studies, most is nonshared within families. This means that nongenetic factors contribute to attributes of each individual within the family in ways that do not make them more alike to one another. This nonshared nongenetic variance is pervasive, and its effects are often substantial. It is possible to identify potential nonshared factors using genetically informative designs (Reiss et al., 2000). Most of the prior work in this area has focused on sibling children's differential experiences with their parents. This is exemplified in a study of same-sex 3-year-old twins (for an overview see Deater-Deckard, 2009). Identical twin differences in mothers' expressed warmth accounted for 6–25% of the identical twin difference in behavior problems (e.g., aggression, noncompliance) and positive

mood. The identical twin who received more maternal warmth was more compliant, less aggressive, and happier. This differential process could not be attributed to sibling differences in genes because in this design the siblings were identical twins. A few other studies have used this and other methods for identifying nonshared mechanisms. The effort is worthwhile, although these mechanisms are difficult to find because nonshared nongenetic variance also includes effects arising from measurement error and non-systematic idiosyncratic factors (Reiss et al., 2000; Turkheimer & Waldron, 2000).

Shared environmental variance factors also can be identified using quantitative genetic methods. These reflect nongenetic factors that lead to family member similarity in attributes. For example, consider the link between child cognitive ability and maternal warmth—both of which are implicated in the development of resilience. Cognitive ability includes moderate levels of shared nongenetic variance in early childhood, and there is some evidence that a substantial portion of that effect in childhood is accounted for by maternal warmth and the family's SES (Petrill & Deater-Deckard, 2004).

Although a useful first step, testing mathematical models of potential genetic and nongenetic factors on individual differences in resilience lacks precision in specification of the mechanisms linking genes, environments, and children's resilience. On their own, these studies do not inform us about how it is that environmental protective factors such as warm supportive parenting operate in conjunction with specific genetic factors on risk and resilience. We turn now to a consideration of some of these gene–environment transactions.

Resilience as Process: Gene–Environment Transactions

There are a host of environmental factors that contribute to resilience in the home, the neighborhood, the school, and beyond. We focus here on warm, supportive parenting, because this is a consistent predictor of resilience in a wide range of populations and types of studies, and because parenting is the most frequently studied environmental domain in genetic studies of child development. Children who are at risk for developing behavioral and emotional problems are protected against those outcomes if their parents are sensitive and responsive, warm and accepting, and involved (Conger & Conger, 2002). These children are more likely to believe that others can be trusted, and that they are loved and accepted regardless of the difficulty of their circumstances. These are keys to children's developing self-efficacy and social competence, and to ameliorating the effects of risks to mental health (Rohner, Khaleque, & Cournoyer, 2005).

These environmental factors operate in transactions with genetic influences. There are two types of gene–environment transactions: gene–environment interaction and gene–environment correlation.

Gene–Environment Interaction

Through *gene–environment interaction*, the effect of a gene or genes on an outcome is conditioned on or moderated by an environmental factor or factors, or vice versa. This definition of gene–environment interaction fits well with most current definitions of resilience. Accordingly, children who have genetic risks for maladaptive outcomes will show fewer and less severe symptoms if certain environmental factors are present that functionally reduce or eliminate altogether the genetic effect. Furthermore, children who have more environmental risks for disturbances in development will have fewer adjustment problems if they also have forms of particular genes that reduce or eliminate the environmental risk effect.

Behavioral genetic studies have provided preliminary evidence suggesting the effect of gene–environment interaction on development of resilience. For example, studies have found that genetic influences in depression and anxiety are moderated by negative life events (Silberg, Rutter, Neale, & Eaves, 2001), whereby risk for anxiety is enhanced by more exposure to life stress (Eaves, Silberg, & Erkanli, 2003). Similarly,

genetic and environmental factors interactively influence aggression, conduct disorder, and adult antisocial behavior, such that adverse home environments increase the likelihood of these behavioral outcomes in the presence of genetic risk factors (Cadoret, Yates, Troughton, Woodworth, & Steward, 1995).

As molecular genetic techniques have become available to researchers, more studies are being conducted that examine the potential interactions between specific environmental factors and specific genes. Nonhuman primate studies provide preliminary models for human research. A series of studies have demonstrated an interactive effect between the serotonin transporter gene 5-HTTLPR and early attachment relationships on resilience and vulnerability on various negative behavioral outcomes in rhesus monkeys (Barr et al., 2003). A particular form of this gene is associated with reduced serotonin expression and function. This genotype along with poor early caregiving experiences has been associated with higher rates of conduct problems including aggression and alcohol consumption, whereas secure attachment relationships in early childhood appear to buffer against genetic risk for these outcomes (for reviews see Bennett, 2007, and Suomi, 2006).

Humans have the same functional serotonin transporter gene, and a similar interactive effect between this gene and adverse life experiences has been found in the prediction of depression (Caspi et al., 2003; Eley et al., 2004; Kaufman et al., 2004; Kendler, Kuhn, Vittum, Prescott, & Riley, 2005; but see Risch et al., 2009, regarding nonreplication of this effect). Individuals with the "risk" genotype have been found to exhibit higher amygdala activity in response to fear-related stimuli (Hariri et al., 2002; Heinz et al., 2005; for a review see Wurtman, 2005), with related weakened or strengthened connections to other neural systems involved in cognitive processing of emotion (Heinz et al., 2005; Pezawas et al., 2005). These neural characteristics are associated with increased sensitivity to adverse experiences through which they potentially exert their influences on development of depression and anxiety under conditions of life stress.

These gene–environment interaction processes clearly implicate malleability in the influences of environments and genes on development. Furthermore, their effects very likely depend in part on effects of still other genetic and environmental factors. For example, positive social support is a strong protective factor that guards children against depression and anxiety, even for those who may be genetically and environmentally at risk (Kaufam et al., 2006; Kaufman et al., 2004). Furthermore, the presence of a particular form of a gene for brain-derived neurotrophic factor or BDNF may minimize the interactive effect between the serotonin transporter gene and early life adversity (described above) on the development of depression (Kaufam et al., 2006).

Another interesting area of inquiry can be found in research on the gene for monoamine oxidase A (MAOA) and interaction with adverse life experiences. MAOA is an enzyme that metabolizes a neurotransmitter that contributes to the regulation of mood and behavior. For males with forms of the gene that are indicative of sufficient production of MAOA, family adversity (e.g., abuse or maltreatment) is only modestly associated with behavioral problems in childhood and adulthood (Caspi et al., 2002; Cohen et al., 2006; Foley et al., 2004), whereas the effect of early adversity on these outcomes is substantial among those with forms of the gene indicative of insufficient MAOA production. This finding has been replicated with females as well and with respect to a variety of behavioral maladjustment outcomes (Ducci et al., 2008; Widom & Brzustowicz, 2006).

Yet another area of interest lies in investigation of the COMT gene, which is involved in the metabolism of dopamine and other neurotransmitters. The "valine" (val) form is associated with lower levels of dopamine, while the "methionine" (met) form is associated with higher levels of dopamine. Studies have found that compared to individuals with two copies of the val allele, individuals with two copies of the met allele show higher level of fixation on negative affective stimuli (Drabant et al., 2006), higher sensory and affective response to pain (Zubieta et al., 2003), and higher harm avoid-

ance response (Enoch et al., 2003). These findings suggest that those individuals who have two copies of the met allele have an enhanced affective sensitivity to negative experiences and are at greater risk for developing behavioral and emotional problems such as anxiety and depression when faced with stress and adversity.

Several other genes involved in regulation of the neuroendocrine stress response (i.e., the hypothalamic-pituitary-adrenal or HPA axis) have been examined as well. These include the corticotrophin-releasing hormone receptor gene (CRHR1), the FKBP5 gene (involved in glucocorticoid signal transduction), and the glucocorticoid receptor gene. These have been implicated in the prediction of behavioral and emotional maladjustment in adulthood among those who also have histories of child abuse and maltreatment (Binder et al., 2008; Bradley et al., 2008). This gene–environment interaction may operate in part through impaired regulation of the HPA axis. When functioning in an adaptive way, the HPA axis is activated in response to stress but is also regulated by a feedback loop. Impaired function of HPA axis regulation has been associated with stress-related disorders, such as depression and posttraumatic stress disorder (Ising et al., 2008; Koenen et al., 2005; Kumsta et al., 2007; Van Rossum et al., 2006; Van West et al., 2006; for a review, see Gillespie, Phifer, Bradley, & Ressler, 2009).

Finally, genetic factors also interact with the prenatal environment to influence the development of various externalizing problems in childhood such as attention deficit hyperactivity disorder (ADHD). Studies have demonstrated that particular forms of the dopamine transporter DAT1 gene and the dopamine receptor DRD4 gene increase the risk of ADHD for children who have been exposed to alcohol and tobacco prenatally (Asherson, Kuntsi, & Taylor, 2005; Becker, EI-Faddagh, Schmidt, Esser, & Laucht, 2008; Kahn, Khoury, Nichols, & Lanphear, 2003; Neuman et al., 2007).

All the above examples demonstrate how genetic and environmental factors can interact in the prediction of individual differences in children's resilience or susceptibility to developing various forms of psychopathology. Identifying specific gene–environment interaction processes in resilience is important for the future of genetics research in psychology, because it informs us not only about bio-environmental processes but also informs us about ways to improve assessment and intervention.

Gene–Environment Correlation

Individual differences in resilience emerge from gene–environment interactions. However, these interactions do not arise as random transactions. Genetic and environmental factors can be correlated (*gene–environment correlation*, or r_{g-e}). Two general classes of gene–environment correlation (r_{g-e}) have been described and identified in quantitative genetic studies—passive and nonpassive forms (Plomin, 1994). Quantitative genetic models can be used to identify r_{g-e}, when variables representing the environmental factors of interest are incorporated into the statistical model that estimates genetic, shared environmental and nonshared environmental sources of variance in the outcomes of interest.

Passive r_{g-e} arises when a child is exposed to an environmental factor that a biological parent provides and that is correlated with their genotypes. Consider the example of the link between cognitive skills and achievement. Variation in these skills arises in part from genetic influences. At the same time, parents who value and enjoy experiences that challenge their minds are more likely to provide stimulating environments for their children that promote resilience (e.g., books, reading, challenging toys, and puzzles). These parents are more likely to have children who have better cognitive skills and who succeed in school. The mechanisms linking stimulation in the home and child cognitive skills typically are tested using correlations in family studies of biologically related parents and children. However, because parents also are providing genes to their children, the enriched environment and genetic influences are confounded. What may appear to be environmental causation based on family studies

may also arise from shared genes between parents and children (Petrill & Deater-Deckard, 2004).

Nonpassive r_{g-e} includes at least two mechanisms, including active and evocative (or reactive) effects (Deater-Deckard, 2009). Active r_{g-e} is environment selection, whereby an individual is more likely to experience certain things as a result of selecting into specific environments that are most consistent with her or his own attributes. For example, children who are highly sociable and gregarious—behaviors that are genetically influenced and implicated in resilience—are more likely to seek out and reinforce interaction with other people, in contrast to shy or socially anxious children. Evocative r_{g-e} occurs when a child's genetically influenced attribute or behavior elicits a particular response from other people—a response that can then serve to reinforce that attribute or behavior. For example, children's genetically influenced externalizing behavior problems (e.g., aggression, conduct problems) tend to evoke harsh, critical responses including rejection and hostile treatment from parents and peers (Burt, McGue, Krueger, & Iacono, 2005; Larsson, Viding, Rijsdijk, & Plomin, 2008; O'Connor, Deater-Deckard, Fulker, Rutter, & Plomin, 1998). Another source of evidence of evocative r_{g-e} comes from studies of differential parental treatment to his or her multiple children. When examining a parent's relationship with her or his two children (i.e., sibling differences), the warmth and acceptance in each parent–child dyad differs (Coldwell, Pike, & Dunn, 2008; Dunn, 1993; Kowal, Kramer, Krull, & Crick, 2002). The differential parental treatment of siblings emerges in part as a result of evocative r_{g-e}. In our research, we have found that mothers' self-reports of warmth toward each of her children, as well as observers' ratings of maternal warm and responsive behavior (based on ratings from brief mother–child dyadic interactions), yield data that implicate evocative r_{g-e}. Identical twins experience very similar levels of maternal warmth and responsiveness from their mothers, whereas fraternal twins and nontwin full siblings experience moderately similar levels of maternal warmth. In contrast, genetically unrelated adoptive siblings are only modestly correlated in the maternal warm supportive behavior that they experience. This evocative gene–environment correlation effect probably operates through genetic influences on children's responsiveness to and social engagement with their mothers (Deater-Deckard, 2009).

It is important to note that gene–environment transactions are not deterministic. For example, children with higher cognitive performance scores may seek and elicit more stimulation from caregivers and their physical environments, but experiments demonstrate that manipulating adults' perceptions of children's intellectual capacities causes improvements in children's achievement outcomes (Rosenthal & Jacobson, 1968). Similarly, children who are more difficult to care for because their behavior distresses and annoys their parents (e.g., irritable, aggressive, oppositional) are more likely to elicit harsh parenting. However, evaluation of parenting interventions show that parents can be taught strategies for responding differently to their children's aversive behaviors, which in turn promotes reductions in children's emotional and behavioral problems (Deater-Deckard, 2004). Gene–environment transactions linking protective influences and children's outcomes are flexible and can change when environments change.

Closing Comments

In closing, we address some implications of the research on gene–environment interplay and resilience.

Resilience Is a Developmental Process

Rutter (2006) has emphasized a focus on risk or protective *mechanisms and processes*, rather than identifying risk and protective factors. The goal should be to test for processes in development, because risk and protective influences are not static. This may be particularly important when genetic influences are being considered, given that there is a tendency to view genes as being somehow fixed in their effects. The actions of genes, and their transactions with environments, occur at many levels (within and outside of cells), and in real time. Although the form of a gene within an individual may not change, its function and effects on the individual can, and this may depend entirely on changes in the function of other genes and changes in environments.

There are numerous and complex transactions operating—between genes and genes, environments and environments, and genes and environments. Humans are not closed systems; the environment and the genome change, sometimes randomly. The "story" describing a gene–environment process in resilience may depend on the population being studied and the environmental context in which that population exists. The success of future research on gene–environment transactions in human development will depend on the extent to which these developmental transactions between genes and environments are taken seriously in research design, assessment, and data analysis.

Your Risk Factor Is My Protective Factor

What may be protective in some contexts may have no effect or further increment problematic outcomes in others (Rutter, 2006). For example, high levels of surgency can be adaptive in the face of adversity, because extraverted individuals are more likely to have access to and to seek out social support from other people. However, approach behavior predicts social withdrawal when there is a high degree of conflict in the family (Tschann et al., 1996). Another example comes from studies of peer relations and antisocial behavior. For most children and adolescents in most social groups, having one or several stable close friendships predicts social competence and scholastic achievement. However, when the youth in question are antisocial and violent, and their peer group consists of other antisocial children or teenagers (a common scenario in natural environments as well as treatment settings), those who are least embedded in their peer network and friendships show the most improvement in behavior over time (Berndt, 2007; Lösel &

Binder, 2003). For a child or adolescent with conduct problems, finding a close, supportive friend can greatly reduce or increase her or his antisocial symptoms, depending on whether or not the friendship is formed and maintained because of a shared interest in breaking the law and mistreating others (Gifford-Smith, Dodge, Dishion, & McCord, 2005).

That a genetic risk factor can also have protective effects, depending on the environment or context, is essentially required by evolutionary explanations for species change and adaptation. Genes that confer only deleterious effects are far more likely to drop in prevalence over time as affected individuals die before reproducing. However, genes that confer risks as well as protective influences are far more likely to remain over time, because individuals with those genes are able to produce offspring who themselves reproduce. Sickle cell anemia illustrates this point. This is a single gene recessive trait, in which its presence leads to malformation of red blood cells, rendering them ineffective and prone to clotting. Individuals who have both copies of the trait gene (one from each parent) have a wide variety of physical maladies due to problems in circulation, and the disease is life threatening. Those who have only one copy of the disease form of the gene are carriers and are mildly affected by comparison. Furthermore, they are protected against contracting malaria. This explains why the disease form of this gene is far more prevalent in areas of the world where malaria is a constant threat, such as West Africa. The very same disease-inducing form of this gene protects carriers from a common threat to health. If malaria were reduced or eradicated, carrier status would no longer confer a known protective effect in those regions of the world. The prevalence of the disease form of the gene would likely drop off, as has been happening in successive generations of African Americans (Connor & Ferguson-Smith, 1997). Thus, a genetic risk factor for a life-threatening and painful disease provides remarkable protection against a common external threat to health, but this protective effect becomes moot if the external biological threat is removed.

As specific gene–environment interactions are identified for psychological outcomes in childhood and beyond, we may see similar kinds of effects where the genes involved as protection against one outcome confer some risk for a different problematic outcome—but only under certain environmental conditions. This prediction does not sit well with definitions of resilience involving static deterministic protective factors. Rather, it is consistent with the idea that resilience is a dynamic developmental process (Belsky & Pluess, 2009).

The Environment of the Mind

The reality of resilience in development is thrust upon us when we find that within populations that apparently are homogeneous in terms of risk factors (e.g., poverty, family violence, low birth weight), children's outcomes are anything but uniform. Considering, assessing, and testing for protective mechanisms using objective measures of the environment is essential, but only tells half of the story. The other half requires venturing into the environment of the child's mind—her or his subjective reality. Although the research on resilience and self-concept and other self-relevant social cognitions (described earlier) is relevant to this end, what is needed are studies examining gene–environment transactions underlying children's interpretations of their environments and experiences, and how these subjective experiences influence developmental outcomes.

There has been interest in the past 2 decades in establishing robust empirical methods for assessing children's subjective experiences, at younger and younger ages. This emerging literature shows that children's social information processing biases—in particular, the attributions that they make regarding others' intentions, and their evaluations of alternative responses to provocations in social situations—help explain why some at-risk children become more aggressive over time, while others do not (Arsenio, 2010; Crick & Dodge, 1994). Results also point to comparable or better predictive validity for children's social cognitions compared to parents' reports of children's rearing environments (Kraemer et al., 2003).

There are several hints from theory and empirical data from genetic studies, suggesting that the environment of the mind should be studied more often. First, in theory, all experiences in the objective sense are filtered through the brain via perceptual and cognitive mechanisms. Although there are species typical brain pathways involved (e.g., visual systems feeding into memory systems), there also are individual differences in what it is that people attend to in their environments, what it is they store in memory and recall, and so forth. Theoretically, individual differences in information processing biases or preferences are just as likely as variations in behaviors (e.g., temperament) to arise from gene–environment transactions. The work to test this idea needs to be done and requires social cognition experiments using genetically informative designs.

A second finding implicating subjective experience is that the majority of environmental variance in quantitative genetic studies is nonshared; it is possible that much of the nongenetic influence on developmental outcomes is idiosyncratic. It follows logically that these idiosyncratic experiences need not arise solely from differences in "actual" experiences in the objective sense, but also can arise from idiosyncratic subjective experiences that differ between two people who have had the same "actual" experience. This type of research remains largely unexplored and requires experiments using genetically informative designs. However, one line of research suggests that studies like this will lead to some promising findings. Several studies examining sibling children's differential experiences with the same parent (a likely source of nonshared environmental influence) show that this differential treatment is associated with problem behaviors in the less favored child when he or she perceives the situation as being unfair (Coldwell et al., 2008; Kowal et al., 2002; McHale, Updegraff, Jackson-Newson, Tucker, & Crouter, 2000). Within families in which one child is treated more punitively than another, some children view this as being fair because the differential treatment reflects parents' fair and appropriate responses to sibling differences in misbehavior (i.e., the less favored child is getting what she or he deserves). In those families, the differential treatment does not appear to be associated with increases in problem behaviors in the less favored child. In contrast, some children view differential treatment as unjust, and it is these children who are most likely to show behavioral and emotional problems as a result of differential treatment. A complete picture requires consideration of both the objective (differential treatment of siblings) and the subjective (children's perceptions of whether the differential treatment is fair or not).

A third finding that points to subjective factors is that individual differences in concurrent and retrospective self-reports of rearing environments show clear evidence of genetic influence. Siblings who are more similar genetically also report more similar childrearing environments and experiences (Plomin, 1994). The most common interpretation of this finding is that active and evocative gene–environment correlations cause this effect, whereby siblings who are more similar genetically actually do have more similar experiences—and their self-reports reflect this reality. Another interpretation that has not been rigorously investigated is that there are genetically influenced information processing mechanisms that lead to similarity in interpretations of events even when the "actual" events are distinct. Again, testing this idea will require experiments using genetic research designs.

One empirical implication concerning the environment of mind is how data on environmental protective mechanisms in the home should be assessed and analyzed. More of the emphasis should be on child-specific factors within families, both in an objective and subjective terms, rather than on global measures of the home environment. For example, a researcher can focus on measuring a mother's control, warmth, and negativity with two or more of her children rather than with only one child. Often, the same mother's feelings about and behaviors toward her two (or more) children will differ, depending on the child in question. In addition, measures other than parent self-report should be utilized to assess various aspects of parenting. Specifically, child report is of great importance because it serves as an index of each child's subjective perception of parenting behavior. After all, it is not only what the parent actually does that matters; it is also what each child sees and feels that exerts an influence. The same can be said for a host of other environmental factors that typically are assessed at a level that does not capture the process for each individual child within each family. Examining each child individually permits tests of the most approximate candidate "environmental" mechanisms that protect him or her against various negative behavioral and emotional outcomes.

In conclusion, resilience is a developmental process that involves individual differences in children's attributes (e.g., temperament, cognitive abilities) and environments (e.g., supportive parenting, learning enriched classrooms). The genetic and environmental influences underlying these individual differences are correlated, and they interact with each other to produce the variation that we see between children, and over time within children. Elucidating these gene–environment transactions will allow better prediction. At the same time, it is imperative that scientists and practitioners recognize that these gene–environment transactions are probabilistic in their effects, and the transactions and their effects can change with shifts in genetic functions and environments.

References

Arbelle, S., Benjamin, J., Golin, M., Kremer, I., Belmaker, R. H., & Ebstein, R. P. (2003). Relation of shyness in grade school children to the genotype for the long form of the serotonin transporter promoter region polymorphism. *The American Journal of Psychiatry, 160*, 671–676.

Arsenio, W. F. (2010). Social information processing, emotions, and aggression: Conceptual and methodological contributions of the special section articles. *Journal of Abnormal Child Psychology, 38*(5), 627–632.

Asherson, P., Kuntsi, J., & Taylor, E. (2005). Unraveling the complexity of attention-deficit hyperactivity disorder: A behavioral genomic approach. *The British Journal of Psychiatry, 187*, 103–105.

Aspinwall, L. G. (2001). Dealing with adversity: Self-regulation, coping, adaptation, and health. In A. Tesser & N. Schwarz (Eds.), *Blackwell handbook of social psychology: Intraindividual processes* (pp. 591–614). Malden: Blackwell.

Barr, C. S., Newman, T. K., Becker, M. L., Parker, C. C., Chamoux, M., Lesch, K. P., et al. (2003). The utility of the non-human primate model for studying gene by environment interactions in behavioral research. *Genes, Brains, and Behavior, 2*(6), 336–340.

Becker, K., El-Faddagh, M., Schmidt, M. H., Esser, G., & Laucht, M. (2008). Interactions of dopamine transporter genotype with prenatal smoke exposure on ADHD symptoms. *The Journal of Pediatrics, 152*(2), 263–269.

Belsky, J., & Pluess, M. (2009). The nature (and nurture?) of plasticity in early human development. *Perspectives on Psychological Science, 4*, 345–351.

Bennett, A. J. (2007). Gene environment interplay: Nonhuman primate models in the study of resilience and vulnerability. *Developmental Psychology, 50*(1), 48–59.

Berndt, T. J. (2007). Children's friendships: Shifts over a half-century in perspectives on their development and their effects. In G. W. Ladd (Ed.), *Appraising the human developmental sciences: Essays in honor of Merrill-Palmer quarterly*. Detroit: Wayne State University Press.

Binder, E. B., Bradley, R. G., Liu, W., Epstein, M. P., Deveau, T. C., Mercer, K. B., et al. (2008). Association of FKBP5 polymorphisms and childhood abuse with risk of posttraumatic stress disorder symptoms in adults. *Journal of the American Medical Association, 299*(11), 1291–1305.

Bradley, R. G., Binder, E. B., Epstein, M. P., Tang, Y., Nair, H. P., Liu, W., et al. (2008). Influence of child abuse on adult depression: Moderation by the corticotrophin-releasing hormone receptor gene. *Archives of General Psychology, 65*(2), 190–200.

Braungart, J. M., Plomin, R., DeFries, J. C., & Fulkner, D. W. (1992). Genetic influence on tester-rated infant temperament as assessed by Bayley's infant behavior record: Nonadoptive and adoptive siblings and twins. *Developmental Psychology, 28*, 40–47.

Buckner, J. C., Mezzacappa, E., & Beardslee, W. R. (2009). Self-regulation and its relations to adaptive functioning in low income youths. *The American Journal of Orthopsychiatry, 79*, 19–30.

Burt, S. A., McGue, M., Krueger, R. F., & Iacono, W. G. (2005). How are parent-child conflict and childhood externalizing symptoms related over time? Results from a genetically informative cross-lagged study. *Development and Psychopathology, 17*, 145–165.

Buss, A. H., & Plomin, R. (1984). *Temperament: Early developing personality traits*. Hillsdale: Erlbaum.

Cadoret, R. J., Yates, W. R., Troughton, E., Woodworth, G., & Steward, M. A. (1995). Gene-environment interaction in the genesis of aggressivity and conduct disorder. *Archives of General Psychiatry, 52*, 916–924.

Campbell-Sills, L., Cohan, S. L., & Stein, M. B. (2006). Relationship of resilience to personality, coping, and psychiatric symptoms in young adults. *Behaviour Research and Therapy, 44*(4), 585–599.

Canli, T., Omura, K., Haas, B. W., Fallgatter, A., Constable, R. T., & Lesch, K. P. (2005). Beyond affect: A role for genetic variation of the serotonin transporter in neural activation during a cognitive attention task. *Proceeding of the National Academy of Sciences, 102*, 12224–12229.

Carver, C. S., & Connor-Smith, J. (2010). Personality and coping. *Annual Review of Psychology, 61*, 679–704.

Caspi, A., McClay, J., Moffitt, T. E., Mill, J., Martin, J., Craig, I. W., et al. (2002). Role of genotype in the cycle of violence in maltreated children. *Science, 297*, 851–854.

Caspi, A., Sugden, K., Moffitt, T. E., Taylor, A., Craig, I. W., Harrington, H., et al. (2003). Influence of life stress on depression: Moderation by a polymorphism in the 5-HTT gene. *Science, 301*, 386–389.

Cohen, J. K., Caspi, A., Taylor, A., Williams, B., Newcombe, R., Craig, I. W., et al. (2006). MAOA, maltreatment, and gene-environment interaction predicting children's mental health: New evidence and a meta-analysis. *Molecular Psychiatry, 11*, 903–913.

Coldwell, J., Pike, A., & Dunn, J. (2008). Maternal differential treatment and child adjustment: A multi-informant approach. *Social Development, 17*(3), 596–612.

Conger, R. D., & Conger, K. J. (2002). Resilience in Midwestern families: Selected findings from the first decade of a prospective, longitudinal study. *Journal of Marriage and the Family, 64*, 361–373.

Connor, J. M., & Ferguson-Smith, M. A. (1997). *Essential medical genetics* (5th ed.). London: Blackwell.

Costa, P. T., Somerfield, M. R., & McCrae, R. R. (1996). Personality and coping: A reconceptualization. In M. Zeidner & N. S. Endler (Eds.), *Handbook of coping: Theory, research, and applications* (pp. 44–61). New York: Wiley.

Crick, N., & Dodge, K. A. (1994). A review and reformulation of social information-processing mechanisms in children's social adjustment. *Psychological Bulletin, 115*, 74–101.

Deater-Deckard, K. (2004). *Parenting stress*. New Haven: Yale University Press.

Deater-Deckard, K. (2009). Parenting the genotype. In K. McCartney & R. Weinberg (Eds.), *Experience and development: A festschrift in honor of Sandra Wood Scarr* (pp. 141–161). New York: Taylor and Francis.

Deater-Deckard, K., Beekman, C., Wang, Z., Kim, J., Petrill, S., Thompson, L., et al. (2010). Approach/positive anticipation, frustration/anger and overt aggression in childhood. *Journal of Personality, 78*, 991–1010.

Deater-Deckard, K., Ivy, L., & Smith, J. (2004). Resilience as gene-environment transactions. In S. Goldstein & R. Brooks (Eds.), *Handbook of resilience in children* (pp. 49–63). New York: Plenum.

Deater-Deckard, K., & Wang, Z. (2012). Development of temperament and attention: Behavioral genetic approaches. In M. Posner (Ed.), *Cognitive neuroscience of attention* (2nd ed., pp. 331–342). New York: Guilford.

Drabant, E. M., Hariri, A. R., Meyer-Lindenberg, A., Munoz, K. E., Mattay, V. S., Kolachana, B. S., et al. (2006). Catechol-O-methyltransferase Val158Met genotype and neural mechanisms related to affective arousal and regulation. *Archives of General Psychiatry, 63*, 1396–1406.

Ducci, F., Enoch, M. A., Hodgkinson, C., Xu, K., Catena, M., Robin, R. W., et al. (2008). Interaction between a functional MAOA locus and childhood sexual abuse predicts alcoholism and antisocial personality disorder in adult women. *Molecular Psychiatry, 13*, 334–347.

Dunn, J. (1993). *Young children's close relationships: Beyond attachment*. Thousand Oaks: Sage.

Eaves, L., Silberg, J., & Erkanli, A. (2003). Resolving multiple epigenetic pathways to adolescent depression. *Journal of Child Psychology and Psychiatry, 44*, 1006–1014.

Ebstein, R. P. (2006). The molecular genetic architecture of human personality: Beyond self-report questionnaires. *Molecular Psychiatry, 11*, 427–445.

Eid, M., Riemann, R., Angleitner, A., & Bornenau, P. (2003). Sociability and positive emotionality: Genetic and environmental contributions to the covariation between different facets of extraversion. *Journal of Personality, 71*, 319–346.

Eley, T. C., Sugden, K., Corsico, A., Gregory, A. M., Sham, P., McGuffin, P., et al. (2004). Gene-environment interaction analysis of serotonin system markers with adolescent depression. *Molecular Psychiatry, 9*, 908–915.

Enoch, M. A., Xu, K., Ferro, E., Harris, C. R., & Goldman, D. (2003). Genetic origins of anxiety in women: A role for functional catechol-O-methyltransferase polymorphism. *Psychiatric Genetics, 13*, 33–41.

Fan, J., Fossella, J., Sommer, T., Wu, Y., & Posner, M. I. (2003). Mapping genetic variation of executive attention onto brain activity. *Proceedings of the National Academy of Sciences, 100*, 7406–7411.

Foley, D. L., Eaves, L. J., Wormley, B., Silberg, J. L., Maes, H. H., Kuhn, J., et al. (2004). Childhood adversity, monoamine oxidase A genotype, and risk for conduct disorder. *Archives of General Psychiatry, 61*(7), 738–744.

Gagne, J. R., Vendlinski, M. K., & Goldsmith, H. H. (2009). The genetics of childhood temperament. In Y.-K. Kim (Ed.), *Handbook of behavior genetics* (pp. 251–267). New York: Springer.

Gardner, T. W., Dishion, T. J., & Connell, A. M. (2008). Adolescent self-regulation as resilience: Resistance to antisocial behavior within the deviant peer context. *Journal of Abnormal Child Psychology, 36*, 273–284.

Gifford-Smith, M., Dodge, K. A., Dishion, T. J., & McCord, J. (2005). Peer influence in children and adolescents: Crossing the bridge from developmental to intervention science. *Journal of Abnormal Child Psychology, 33*(3), 255–265.

Gillespie, C. F., Phifer, J., Bradley, B., & Ressler, K. J. (2009). Risk and resilience: Genetic and environmental influences on development of the stress response. *Depression and Anxiety, 26*, 984–992.

Goldsmith, H. H., Buss, K. A., & Lemery, K. S. (1997). Toddler and childhood temperament: Expanded content, stronger genetic evidence, new evidence for the importance of environment. *Developmental Psychology, 33*, 891–905.

Greenberg, M. T. (2006). Promoting resilience in children and youth: Preventive interventions and their interface with neuroscience. *The New York Academy of Sciences, 1094*, 139–150.

Hariri, A. R., Mattay, V. S., Tessitorre, A., Kolachana, B., Fera, F., Goldman, D., et al. (2002). Serotonin transporter genetic variation and the response of the human amygdala. *Science, 297*, 400–403.

Heinz, A., Braus, D. F., Smolka, M. N., Wrase, J., Puls, I., Hermann, D., et al. (2005). Amygdala-prefrontal coupling depends on a genetic variation of the serotonin transporter. *Nature Neuroscience, 8*, 20–21.

Hetherington, E. M. (2006). The influence of conflict, marital problem solving, and parenting on children's adjustment in nondivorced, divorced, and remarried families. In A. Clarke-Stewart & J. Dunn (Eds.), *Families count: Effect on child and adolescent development* (pp. 203–236). Cambridge: Cambridge University Press.

Ising, M., Depping, A., Siebertz, A., Lucae, S., Unschuld, P. G., & Kloiber, S. (2008). Polymorphisms in the FKBP5 gene region modulate recovery from psychosocial stress in healthy controls. *European Journal of Neuroscience, 28*, 389–398.

Kahn, R. S., Khoury, J., Nichols, W. C., & Lanphear, B. P. (2003). Role of dopamine transporter genotype and maternal prenatal smoking in childhood hyperactive-impulsive, inattentive, and oppositional behaviors. *Journal of Pediatrics, 143*, 104–110.

Kamakura, T., Ando, J., & Ono, Y. (2007). Genetic and environmental effects of stability and change in self-esteem during adolescence. *Personality and Individual Differences, 42*(1), 181–190.

Kaufam, J., Yang, B. Z., Douglas-Palumberi, H., Grasso, D., Lipschitz, D., Krystal, J. H., et al. (2006). Brain-derived neurotrophic factor 5-HTTLPR gene interactions and environmental modifiers of depression in children. *Biological Psychiatry, 59*(8), 673–680.

Kaufman, J., Yang, B. Z., Douglas-Palumberi, H., Houshyar, S., Lipschitz, D., Krystal, J. H., et al. (2004). Social supports and serotonin transporter gene moderate depression in maltreated children. *Proceedings of the National Academy of Sciences of the United States of America, 101*(49), 17316–17321.

Kendler, K. S., Gardner, C. O., & Prescott, C. A. (1998). A population-based twin study of self-esteem and gender. *Psychological Medicine, 28*, 1403–1409.

Kendler, K. S., Kuhn, J. W., Vittum, J., Prescott, C. A., & Riley, B. (2005). The interaction of stressful life events and a serotonin transporter polymorphism in the prediction of episodes of major depression: A replication. *Archives of General Psychiatry, 62*, 529–535.

Kilmer, R. P., Cowen, E. L., & Wyman, P. A. (2001). A micro-level analysis of developmental, parenting, and family milieu variables that differentiate stress-resilient and stress-affected children. *Journal of Community Psychology, 29*, 391–416.

Koenen, K. C., Saxe, G., Prucell, S., Smoller, J. W., Bartholomew, D., Miller, A., et al. (2005). Polymorphisms in FKBP5 are associated with peritraumatic dissociation in medically injured children. *Molecular Psychiatry, 10*, 1058–1059.

Kowal, A., Kramer, L., Krull, J. L., & Crick, N. R. (2002). Children's perception of the fairness of parental preferential treatment and their socioemotional well-being. *Journal of Family Psychology, 16*, 297–306.

Kraemer, H. C., Measelle, J. R., Ablow, J. C., Essex, M. J., Boyce, W. T., & Kupfer, D. J. (2003). A new approach to integrating data from multiple informants in psychiatric assessment and research: Mixing and matching contexts and perspectives. *The American Journal of Psychiatry, 160*, 1566–1577.

Krakowski, M. (2003). Violence and serotonin: Influence of impulse control, affect regulation, and social functioning. *The Journal of Neuropsychiatry and Clinical Neurosciences, 15*(3), 294–305.

Kumpfer, K. L. (1999). Factors and processes contributing to resilience: The resilience framework. In M. D. Glantz & J. L. Johnson (Eds.), *Resilience and development: Positive life adaptations* (pp. 179–224). New York: Kluwer Academic/Plenum Publishers.

Kumsta, R., Entringer, S., Koper, J. W., van Rossum, E. F., Hellhammer, D. H., & Wust, S. (2007). Sex specific associations between common glucocorticoid receptor gene variants and hypothalamus-pituitary-adrenal axis responses to psychosocial stress. *Biological Psychiatry, 62*, 863–869.

Larsson, H., Viding, E., Rijsdijk, F. V., & Plomin, R. (2008). Relationships between parental negativity and childhood antisocial behavior over time: A bidirectional effects model in a longitudinal genetically informative design. *Journal of Abnormal Child Psychology, 36*(5), 633–645.

Lengua, L. J. (2002). The contribution of emotionality and self-regulation to the understanding of children's response to multiple risk. *Child Development, 73*, 144–161.

Lösel, F., & Binder, D. (2003). Protective factors and resilience. In D. P. Farrington & J. Coid (Eds.), *Early prevention of adult antisocial behavior* (pp. 130–204). Cambridge: Cambridge University Press.

Lösel, F., & Bliesener, T. (1994). Some high-risk adolescents do not develop conduct problems: A study of protective factors. *International Journal of Behavioral Development, 17*, 753–777.

Manke, B., Saudino, K. J., & Grant, J. D. (2001). Extremes analyses of observed temperament dimensions. In R. N. Emde & J. K. Hewitt (Eds.), *Infancy to early childhood: Genetic and environmental influences on developmental change* (pp. 52–72). New York: Oxford University Press.

Masten, A. S. (2001). Ordinary magic: Resilience process in development. *American Psychologist, 56*(3), 227–238.

Masten, A. S., Hubbard, J. J., Gest, S. D., Tellegen, A., Garmezy, N., & Ramirez, M. (1999). Competence in the context of adversity: Pathways to resilience and maladaptation from childhood to late adolescence. *Development and Psychopathology, 11*, 143–169.

Matthews, G., Deary, I. J., & Whiteman, M. C. (2003). *Personality traits* (2nd ed.). Cambridge: Cambridge University Press.

Matthews, G., Schwean, V. L., Campbell, S. E., Saklofske, D. H., & Mohamed, A. A. R. (2000). Personality, self-regulation, and adaptation: A cognitive-social framework. In M. Boekaerts, P. R. Pintrich, & M. Zeidner (Eds.), *Handbook of self-regulation* (pp. 171–207). New York: Academic.

McCartney, K., Harris, M. J., & Bernieri, F. (1990). Growing up and growing apart: A developmental meta-analysis of twin studies. *Psychological Bulletin, 107*, 226–237.

McGuire, S., Manke, B., Saudino, K. J., Reiss, D., Hetherington, E. M., & Plomin, R. (1999). Perceived competence and self-worth during adolescence: A longitudinal behavioral genetic study. *Child Development, 70*, 1283–1296.

McHale, S. M., Updegraff, K. A., Jackson-Newson, J., Tucker, C. J., & Crouter, A. C. (2000). When does parents' differential treatment have negative implications for siblings? *Social Development, 9*, 149–172.

Melke, J., Landen, M., Baghei, F., Rosmond, R., Holm, G., Bjorntorp, P., et al. (2001). Serotonin transporter gene polymorphisms are associated with anxiety-related personality traits in women. *American Journal of Medical Genetics, 105*, 458–463.

Mendez, J. L., Fantuzzo, J., & Cicchetti, D. (2002). Profiles of social competence among low-income African American preschool children. *Child Development, 73*, 1085–1100.

Neiderhiser, J. M., & McGuire, S. (1994). Competence during middle childhood. In J. C. DeFries, R. Plomin, & D. W. Fulkner (Eds.), *Nature and nurture during middle childhood* (pp. 141–151). Cambridge: Blackwell Publishers.

Neiss, M. B., Sedikides, C., & Stevenson, J. (2002). Self-esteem: A behavioural genetic perspective. *European Journal of Personality, 16*, 351–367.

Neuman, R. J., Lobos, E., Reich, W., Henderson, C. A., Sun, L., & Todd, R. D. (2007). Prenatal smoking exposure and dopaminergic genotypes interact to cause a sever ADHD subtype. *Biological Psychiatry, 61*, 1320–1328.

O'Connor, T. G., Deater-Deckard, K., Fulker, D. W., Rutter, M., & Plomin, R. (1998). Gene- environment correlations in late childhood and early adolescence. *Developmental Psychology, 34*, 970–981.

Oniszczenko, W., Zawadzki, B., Strelau, J., Riemann, R., Angleitner, A., & Spinath, F. M. (2003). Genetic and environmental determinants of temperament: A comparative study based on Polish and German samples. *European Journal of Personality, 17*, 207–220.

Petrill, S. A., & Deater-Deckard, K. (2004). Task orientation, parental warmth and SES account for a significant proportion of the shared environmental variance in general cognitive ability in early childhood: Evidence from a twin study. *Developmental Science, 7*(1), 25–32.

Pezawas, L., Meyer-Lindenberg, A., Drabant, E. M., Verchinski, B. A., Munoz, K. E., & Kolachana, B. S. (2005). 5-HTTLPR polymorphism impacts human cingulated-amygdala interactions: A genetic susceptibility mechanism for depression. *Nature Neuroscience, 8*(6), 828–834.

Plomin, R. (1994). *Genetics and experience: The interplay between nature and nurture*. Thousand Oaks: Sage.

Plomin, R., DeFries, J. C., McClearn, G. E., & McGuffin, P. (2008). *Behavioral genetics* (5th ed.). New York: Worth Publishers.

Plomin, R., Pedersen, N. L., McClearn, G. E., Nesselroade, J. R., & Bergeman, C. S. (1988). EAS temperaments during the last half of the life span: Twins reared apart and twins reared together. *Psychology and Aging, 3*, 43–50.

Plomin, R., & Rutter, M. (1998). Child development, molecular genetics, and what to do with genes once they are found. *Child Development, 69*, 1223–1242.

Ponitz, C. C., McCleliand, M. M., Matthews, S., & Morrison, F. K. (2009). A structured observation of behavioral self-regulation and its contribution to kindergarten outcomes. *Developmental Psychology, 45*, 605–619.

Posner, M. I., & Rothbart, M. K. (2006). *Educating the human brain*. Washington: American Psychological Association.

Prior, M. (1999). Resilience and coping: The role of individual temperament. In E. Frydenberg (Ed.), *Learning to cope: Developing as a person in complex societies* (pp. 33–52). Oxford: Oxford University Press.

Raevuori, A., Dick, D. M., Keski-Rahkonen, A., Pulkkinen, L., Rose, R. J., Rissanen, A., et al. (2007). Genetic and environmental factors affecting self-esteem from age 14 to 17: A longitudinal study of Finnish twins. *Psychological Medicine, 37*(11), 1625–1633.

Reiss, D., Neiderhiser, J., Hetherington, E. M., & Plomin, R. (2000). *The relationship code: Deciphering genetic and social influences on adolescent development*. Cambridge: Harvard University Press.

Risch, N., Herrell, R., Lehner, T., Liang, K.-Y., Eaves, L., Hoh, J., et al. (2009). Interaction between the serotonin transporter gene (5-HTTLPR), stressful life events, and risk of depression. *Journal of the American Medical Association, 301*, 2462–2471.

Rohner, R. P., Khaleque, A., & Cournoyer, D. E. (2005). Parental acceptance-rejection: Theory, methods, cross-cultural evidence, and implications. *Journal of the Society for Psychological Anthropology, 33*(3), 299–334.

Rosenthal, R., & Jacobson, L. (1968). *Pygmalion in the classroom*. New York: Holt, Rinehart & Winston.

Rothbart, M. K., Ahadi, S. A., & Evans, D. E. (2000). Temperament and personality: Origins and outcomes. *Journal of Personality and Social Psychology, 78*, 122–135.

Rothbart, M. K., & Bates, J. E. (1998). Temperament. In W. Damon (Series Ed.) and N. Eisenberg (Vol. Ed.), *Handbook of child psychology: Vol. 3, social, emotional and personality development* (5th ed, pp. 105–176). New York: Wiley.

Rujescu, D., Giegling, I., Gietl, A., Hartmann, A. M., & Moller, H. J. (2003). A functional single nucleotide polymorphism (V158M) in the COMT gene is associated with aggressive personality traits. *Biological Psychiatry, 54*, 34–39.

Rutter, M. (2006). Implications of resilience concepts of scientific understanding. *Annual New York Academy of Science, 1094*, 1–12.

Saudino, K. J. (2005). Behavioral genetics and child temperament. *Journal of Developmental and Behavioral Pediatrics, 26*(3), 214–223.

Schmitz, S. (1994). Personality and temperament. In J. C. DeFries, R. Plomin, & D. W. Fulkner (Eds.), *Nature and nurture during middle childhood* (pp. 120–140). Cambridge: Blackwell Publishers.

Sen, S., Burmeister, M., & Ghosh, D. (2004). Meta-analysis of the association between a serotonin transporter promoter polymorphism (5-HTTLPR) and anxiety-related personality traits. *American Journal of Medical Genetics, 127B*, 85–89.

Silberg, J., Rutter, M., Neale, M., & Eaves, L. (2001). Genetic moderation of environmental risk for depression and anxiety in adolescent girls. *The British Journal of Psychiatry, 179*, 116–121.

Smith, L. E., Borkowski, J. G., & Whitman, T. L. (2008). From reading readiness to reading competence: The role of self-regulation in at-risk children. *Scientific Studies of Reading, 12*, 131–152.

Smith, J., & Prior, M. (1995). Temperament and stress resilience in school-age children: A within-families study. *Journal of the American Academy of Child and Adolescent Psychiatry, 34*, 168–179.

Suomi, S. J. (2006). Risk, resilience, and gene x environment interactions in rhesus monkeys. *Annuals of the New York Academy of Science, 1094*, 52–62.

Thomas, A., & Chess, S. (1977). *Temperament and development*. New York: Brunner/Mazel.

Tschann, J. M., Kaiser, P., Chesney, M. A., Alkon, A., & Boyce, T. (1996). Resilience and vulnerability among preschool children: Family functioning, temperament, and behavior problems. *Journal of the American Academy of Child and Adolescent Psychiatry, 35*, 184–192.

Turkheimer, E., & Waldron, M. (2000). Nonshared environment: A theoretical, methodological, and quantitative review. *Psychological Bulletin, 126*, 78–108.

Van Rossum, E. F. C., Binder, E. B., Majer, M., Koper, J. W., Ising, M., Modell, S., et al. (2006). Polymorphisms of the glucocorticoid receptor gene and major depression. *Biological Psychiatry, 59*, 681–688.

Van West, D., Van Den, E. F., Del Favero, J., Souery, D., Norrback, K. F., van Duijin, C., et al. (2006). Glucocorticoid receptor gene-based SNP analysis in patients with recurrent major depression. *Neuropsychopharmacology, 31*, 620–627.

Volavka, J., Kennedy, J. L., Ni, X., Czobor, P., Nolan, K., Sheitman, B., et al. (2004). COMT158 polymorphism and hostility. *American Journal of Medical Genetics, 127B*, 28–29.

Widom, C. S., & Brzustowicz, L. M. (2006). MAOA and the "cycle of violence:" childhood abuse and neglect, MAOA genotype, and risk for violent and antisocial behavior. *Biological Psychiatry, 60*(7), 684–689.

Wills, T. A., Sandy, J. M., Yaeger, A., & Shinar, O. (2001). Family risk factors and adolescent substance use: Moderation effects for temperament dimensions. *Developmental Psychology, 37*, 283–297.

Woo, J. M., Yoon, K. S., Choi, Y. H., Oh, K. S., Lee, Y. S., & Yu, B. H. (2004). The association between panic disorder and the L/L genotype of catechol-O-methyltransferase. *Journal of Psychiatric Research, 38*, 365–370.

Wood, A. C., Rijsdijk, R., Saudino, K. J., Asherson, P., & Kuntsi, J. (2008). High heritability for a composite index of children's activity level measure. *Behavior Genetics, 38*(3), 266–276.

Wurtman, R. J. (2005). Genes, stress, and depression. *Metabolism, 54*, 16–19.

Zimmerman, B. J. (2000). Attaining self-regulation: A social cognitive perspective. In M. Boekaerts, P. R. Pintrich, & M. Zeidner (Eds.), *Handbook of self-regulation* (pp. 13–39). New York: Academic.

Zubieta, J. -K., Heitzeg, M. M., Smith, Y. R., Bueller, J. A., Xu, K., Xu, Y., et al. (2003). COMT val158met genotype affects μ-opioid neurotransmitter responses to a pain stressor. *Science, 299*, 1240–1243.

Zuckerman, M. (2000). Optimism and pessimism: Biological foundations. In E. C. Chang (Ed.), *Optimism & pessimism: Implications for theory, research, and practice* (pp. 169–188). Washington: American Psychological Association.

Relational Resilience in Girls

5

Judith V. Jordan

This chapter, mainly theoretical in orientation, also reviews recent research on resilience and gender. The theoretical orientation represented here is known as relational-cultural theory (RCT). At the core of this work is the belief that all psychological growth occurs in relationships and that movement out of relationship (chronic disconnection) into isolation constitutes the source of much psychological suffering. Moving away from a "separate self" model of development, RCT also suggests that resilience resides not in the individual but in the capacity for connection. A model of relational resilience is presented. Mutual empathy, empowerment, and the development of courage are the building blocks of this resilience. While this chapter seeks to explicate the importance of relational resilience for girls, it also suggests that growth-fostering connections are the source of resilience for both boys and girls.

Resilience is traditionally defined as the ability to "bounce back" from adversity, to manage stress effectively and to withstand physical or psychological pressures without showing major debilitation or dysfunction (Benard, 2004; Brooks & Goldstein, 2001; Hartling, 2003; Herrman et al., 2011; Jordan & Hartling, 2002). Often resilience is described as (1) good outcomes in high-risk children; (2) sustained competence in children under stress; and (3) recovery from trauma (Hartling, 2003; Masten, Best, & Garmezy, 1990). In these models resilience is most often seen as residing within the individual, in such traits as: temperament (Rutter, 1978, 1989, 1990), hardiness (Kobasa, 1979), or self-esteem (Schwalbe & Staples, 1991). Temperament and hardiness are usually depicted as involving innate physiological variables. It is noteworthy that the hardiness research which emphasized commitment and control, however, was conducted on White male middle-to-upper level business executives and then generalized to all people (Hartling, 2003). Contrary to these findings, Sparks (1999) described relational practices rather than internal traits as contributing to the resilience of African-American mothers on welfare. Internal locus of control is an individual characteristic, which has also been associated with resilience (Masten et al., 1990). "Children who take responsibility for their own successes and failures are said to have an internal locus of control" (Roediger, Capaldi, Paris, & Polivy, 1991, p. 352).

Recently, research in the field of neuroscience has opened new ways of understanding resilience, providing hopeful data about the lifelong malleability of the brain, and hence, of behavior. Davidson's research on resilient health indicates that a secure relationship history provides people with the resources to bounce back from emotional setbacks and losses (Goleman, 2006). When the left prefrontal cortex has time to recover from distress and thus remains robust, we continue to develop strategies for emotional regulation and recovery throughout life. Cozolino

J.V. Jordan (✉)
Jean Baker Miller Training Institute and Harvard Medical School, 114 Waltham St, Suite 17, Lexington, MA 02421, USA
e-mail: jvjordan@aol.com

S. Goldstein and R.B. Brooks (eds.), *Handbook of Resilience in Children*,
DOI 10.1007/978-1-4614-3661-4_5, © Springer Science+Business Media New York 2013

(2006) has written that the greatest contributor to neural plasticity is love; good relationships rework the circuitry of the prefrontal cortex. Siegel and Bryson (2011), in writing about interpersonal neurobiology, suggest that curiosity, openness, acceptance, and love support neural integration and openness to the present. Resilience is in part the ability to be present in the moment, responding rather than reacting, thus exhibiting emotional flexibility. The capacity for relational repair depends on flexibility, respect, safety, trust, and courage (Jordan, 2010). If the amygdala alert system has been overstimulated by abuse, neglect, or other signals of danger, however, a child's nervous system will be overstressed and excessive cortisol will be released. We know that cortisol has a negative impact on our bodies and our brains; it contributes to diabetes, depression, anxiety, and heart disease. If we seek comfort when stressed (Schore, 1994) and we participate in mutual empathy and regulation (Jordan, 2010), our systems will not be overwhelmed by adverse hormonal/chemical reactions and we will demonstrate some measure of resilience. What some have called "allostatic load" (Goldstein & Thau, 2011) represents a physiological response to social conflict that persists over time. This creates enormous wear and tear on the body and contributes to chronic stress. A reactive amygdala, overstimulated by unrelenting threats of danger, hijacks a person's response in a context that feels unsafe. In this case, more considered responsiveness is overridden by impulsive, disorganized responding. These patterns of reactivity often leave a person more cut off and therefore less able to find support and repair in safe, sustaining relationships. Isolation can become chronic, keeping people from participating in healing relationships. This is especially stressful for girls because girls and women experience connection as central to their well-being (Hossfeld, 2008).

Social pain overlap theory (Eisenberger & Lieberman, 2004) provides additional insights regarding resilience. Research shows that social pain travels the same neuronal pathways to the same place in the brain—the anterior cingulate cortex. This model confirms how core our need for connection is: being excluded is experienced as urgent at a biological level as hunger, thirst or pain avoidance. A cultural system that denies the importance of connection for growth and healing interferes with our ability to acknowledge our need for others and thus impedes our ability to turn to others when in distress. To the extent that dependency and need of others is devalued (Jordan, 2010), our capacity to form supportive and resilience building relationships is challenged. Girls and women are especially impacted by the negative cultural messages about our yearnings for connection. Despite the values and pressures in our culture that block the natural flow of disconnection–connection and healing in connection, our brains exhibit a robust ability to change.

Neuroscience studies using functional MRIs in particular have given us the data that establishes beyond a doubt that the brain is changed throughout the lifespan—neuroplasticity. People can move out of isolation and dysfunctionality throughout their lives (Cozolino, 2006; Goleman, 2006). Even when children have grown up in families where they have suffered terror or great instability, there is the opportunity to achieve more secure attachment by finding safe enough connection with therapists, teachers, professors, mentors, and friends (Cozolino, 2006; Farber & Siegel, 2011; Goleman, 2006). Love, connectedness, secure attachment, responsiveness from others, etc. actually resculpt the brain. Acute disconnections, reworked back into healthy connection, begin to shift underlying patterns of isolation and immobilization. The amygdala can be quieted; the prefrontal cortex can function more effectively. Some researchers have looked at the effect of early experience on glucocorticoid and catecholamine levels that influence neural activity in areas of the brain associated with executive function (Blair, 2010). Empathy can create change in the prefrontal cortex and blocks the production of certain hormones (glucocorticoids) that kill neurons in the hippocampus (Goldstein & Thau, 2011).

Toning the vagal nervous system also significantly impacts relational responsiveness. The vagal nerve plays a part in modulating emotional reactivity and particularly intervenes to move a person out of sympathetic (arousal) and parasympathetic (withdrawing, shutting down) patterns. What some have called the "smart vagus" allows us to stay in relationships even when we are angry or shamed (Banks, 2011), crucial skills for maintaining connection. We do not have to move into all or nothing, black or white reactivity. If we have poor vagal tone arising from a neglectful, abusive, or risk-filled childhood, we can achieve more resilient functioning by experiencing more modulated patterns of organization and disorganization, the ebb and flow of connection and disconnection (Goldstein & Thau, 2011). More recent resilience research has pointed to the dynamic nature of resilience throughout the lifespan (Herrman et al., 2011).

Gender

The effects of gender or context on resilience have not been well documented in traditional or neuropsychological approaches. In much of the resilience research, issues of control and power tend to be decontextualized; in particular there is a failure to recognize realities of racism, sexism, and heterosexism or other forces of discrimination and social bias which render certain people powerless and realistically lacking control. Brown, however, studies the impact of culture on girls' ability to speak up with their anger (2003). She suggests that "relational aggression" (Simmons, 2002; Wiseman, 2003) results not from girls' essential meanness (the mean girl phenomenon), but because girls are not provided with more direct ways to register their protests and anger. A contextual approach might reconsider the concept of internal sense of control, examining a person's engagement in mutually empathic and responsive relationships as the more likely source of resilience. While social support is often cited in studies of resilience, it is typically studied as a one-directional process in which one person is supported by another (Spiegel, 1991). The tradition in western psychology of studying individual traits and internal characteristics exists within a paradigm of "separate self." Separation is seen as primary and relatedness as secondary. What is inside the individual,

such as traits or intrapsychic structure, is seen as fundamentally determining an individual's well-being and psychological adjustment. There are now studies and models of development that question this separate self bias (Jordan, 2010; Jordan, Kaplan, Miller, Stiver, & Surrey, 1991; Spencer, 2000).

A study of 12,000 adolescents suggested that the single best predictor of resistance to high-risk behaviors (violence, substance abuse, and suicide) is "having a good relationship" with one adult, such as a teacher, parent, or mentor (Resnick et al., 1997; Resnick, Harris, & Blum, 1993). Connections "fortify" kids. I would suggest that growth-fostering connection is at the core of the notion of resilience; I would also like to address the additional factor of *resistance*, which points to the importance of contextual factors in resilience. By resistance, I refer to the capacity to resist the destructive and disempowering messages regarding gender, race, and sexual orientation coming from many sources such as immediate familial context and/or larger societal controlling images (Collins, 2000). While resistance is not always included in the concept of resilience, for a member of any marginalized group (i.e., nondominant, less powerful groups such as girls, people of color, homosexuals) the capacity to develop resistance to the distorting and hurtful influences impinging on them as a function of their marginality (and also contributing to their marginality) is essential (Brown, 2003; Ward, 2002). Gilligan, Lyons, & Hammer (1990) noted that there is a gender disparity with respect to times in development when children's resilience is at heightened risk: early in childhood in boys and in adolescence for girls. She suggests it is important for all children to be joined by adults in their resistance. In RCT the primary indicator of psychological development is an increasing capacity for significant and meaningful connection with others (Jordan, 2010; Miller & Stiver, 1997). Relationships are at the heart of growth, healthy resistance, and resilience. The societal or cultural context largely determines the kinds of relationships that are likely to occur for anybody and these determine one's capacity to respond to stress

Most models of child development are framed by the notion of growth toward autonomy and separation. The cultural mandate and myth is one of "standing alone," the lone ranger, the lone hero, the fully individuated person who is independent, separate, and autonomous. Resilience then is viewed as an internal trait or set of traits, the lone resilient individual recovering from the impingements of an adverse environment. The job of socialization in this model is to bring the dependent child into a place of separate, independent adulthood. These standards apply to all children but especially to boys.

As Bill Pollack (1998) notes, the "boy code" pushes boys towards extremes of self-containment, toughness, and separation. Men are encouraged to dread or deny feeling weak or helpless. Shame-based socialization for boys directs them towards being strong in dominant-defined ways: unyielding, not showing vulnerability, and displaying a narrow range of affect (i.e., anger). The standards for maturity involve being independent, self-reliant, autonomous. Yet these hallmarks of successful maturity and "strength" are generally unattainable since we are ultimately interdependent beings. These hyperindividualistic standards then create stress, shame, and enormous pain for all who are affected by them. Furthermore, the importance of connection with others is omitted in these models. Context and socially defined identity issues such as race and gender clearly impact resilience and yet they, too, are overlooked.

With regard to some unexamined gender issues, Seligman's concept of "learned helplessness" is seen as contributing to poor outcome (poor psychological health) and optimism is seen as leading to resilience and good outcome (Seligman, 1990). Yet gender may play a crucial role in the development of pessimistic or optimistic coping strategies (Dweck, 2006; Dweck & Goetz, 1978). Girls' expectations of future performance are affected more by past or present failures than by successes (Dweck & Reppucci, 1973). Girls attribute failure to internal factors and success to chance or external factors, while boys tend to attribute failure to external factors and success to internal factors.

Girls blame themselves far more than boys do and take less credit for success. Studies have shown that freedom from self-denigration is a powerful protector against stress-related debilitation (Peterson, Schwarz, & Seligman, 1981). Self-denigration is seen as contributing to poor self-esteem which in turn is thought to contribute negatively to resilience (Dumont & Provost, 1999). Self-esteem tends to be thought of as a core, internal trait. But self-esteem is a complicated concept. Self-esteem has been constructed in Western cultures based on a separate-self, hyperindividualistic model of development (Jordan, 1994). One "possesses" self-esteem and in a competitive culture often comparisons with others (better than or worse than) are at the core of self-esteem. As Harter (1993) notes "how one measure up to one's peers, to societal standards, becomes the filter through which judgments about the self pass" (p. 94). Groups that are "outside" the dominant definitions of merit, who may have differing standards of worth, are thus disadvantaged by these privileged standards (e.g., being emotionally responsive and expressive in a culture that overvalues the rational or being relational in a culture that celebrates autonomy). Yvonne Jenkins has suggested that we think of *social esteem* which implies a group-related identity that values interdependence, affiliation, and collaterality (1993). Social esteem, then, may be more relevant to psychological well-being than self-esteem, particularly in more communal cultures and subcultures. Feeling good about oneself depends a lot on how one is treated by others and whether one can be authentic and seen and heard in relationships with important others.

Data suggest that girls are more depressed and self-critical in adolescence than boys. Girls' rates of depression begin to climb in adolescence. Girls and women are twice as likely to develop depression throughout their lives (Gillham, Chaplin, Reivich, & Hamilton, 2008; Gladstone & Beardslee, 2009; Hankin & Abramson, 2001; Lewisohn & Essau, 2002) "For girls to remain responsive to themselves they must resist the convention of female goodness; to remain responsive to others, they must resist the values placed on self sufficiency and independence in North American culture" (Gilligan, 1990, p. 503). Girls lose connection with themselves and authentic connection with others during this period. Researchers have noticed that women's coping styles are more relational (i.e., talking about personal distress with friends, sharing sadness) (Lazarus & Folkman, 1984). Men's styles are more problem-focused or instrumental, taking action to solve the problem and seeking new strategies. Emotion-focused coping may be more adaptive in situations where one has little real control and problem-focused coping is useful where one can realistically expect to effect change. Those with less power and less real control (members of nondominant and marginalized groups) may develop more relational or "externalizing" ways of coping.

One of the core ideas of traditional Western Psychology is the notion of "fight or flight" in the face of stress. This knowledge has been passed along for generations and is quite relevant to the way we understand resilience. Prevailing studies have consistently suggested that when we are stressed we either mobilize aggressive, self-protective defenses (fight) or we flee (run away and avoid the possible confrontation with our own vulnerability). But a recent analysis by (Taylor et al. 2000; Taylor, 2002) points out that all the studies on "fight or flight" were completed with males (i.e., male albino rats and monkeys, men, etc.). In replicating some of these experiments with females, Taylor noted a very different response to stress, which she and her colleagues called the "tend-and-befriend" response. In times of stress they noted females engage in caretaking activities or in the creation of a network of associations to protect themselves and others from a threat. Women respond relationally to stress; they seek connection. Belle (1987) has also noted that women are more likely to mobilize social support in times of stress and turn to female friends more often than males. These data suggest it is imperative that we attend to social identity issues, particularly gender, when we seek to understand resilience.

Relational Resilience

Theorists at the Stone Center, Wellesley College, have created a relational model of development and resilience. The model was originally developed by listening to women's voices and studying women's lives, but it is increasingly seen as applicable to men as well. Most developmental and clinical models have been biased in the direction of overemphasizing separateness, particularly *the separate self*. This new model, called RCT, posits that we grow through and toward connection; that a desire to participate in growth-fostering relationship is the core motivation in life (Jordan, 1997, 2010; Jordan, et al., 1991; Miller & Stiver, 1997). Growth-fostering connections are characterized by mutual empathy and mutual empowerment and produce the following outcomes: zest, a sense of worth, productivity, clarity, and a desire for more connection (Miller & Stiver, 1997). All relationships arise within particular contexts and the socioeconomic/cultural context powerfully shapes the connections and disconnections that exist in people's lives. Isolation is viewed as the primary source of pain and suffering. In a stratified society, difference is always subject to distortions of power (Walker, 2002). When one group is dominant and possesses the power to define what is valuable, the less powerful group is left having to "fit in," to "make do" with rules of conduct and behavior that may not represent their experiences. Thus, Jean Baker Miller once said, "authenticity and subordination are totally incompatible" (1986, p. 98). In order to enjoy full authentic and growth-fostering interaction, one cannot be in a position of subordination. The role of power is to silence difference, limit authenticity, and to define merit.

RCT proposes we think of "relational resilience" as the capacity to move back into growth-fostering connections following an acute disconnection or in times of stress (Hartling, 2003; Jordan, 1992, 2010). RCT suggests that relationships that enhance resilience and encourage growth are characterized by a two-way experience of connection, involving mutual empathy, mutual empowerment, and movement toward mutuality. For instance, we would suggest that real courage, real growth, and real strength all occur in a relational context, not in a state of isolation or independent assertion. In short, resilience is not an internal trait. The dominant North American culture does not support the notion of interdependence among people. Yet there is an inevitable human need to turn to others for feedback, both appreciative and corrective, and to provide support to others as we make meaning of our lives. We all need to be responded to by others throughout our lives. This is different from one person needing support or approval from another person; we need to engage with others and to be engaged with, to participate in relationships that create growth for each person involved. It is about mutuality.

What is needed is a relational model of resilience which includes a notion of: (1) supported vulnerability; (2) mutual empathic involvement; (3) relational confidence or the ability to build relationships that one can count on; (4) empowerment which involves encouraging mutual growth; and (5) creating relational awareness alongside of personal awareness. Relational resilience emphasizes strengthening relationships rather than increasing an individuals' strength (Hartling, 2003). In this model the ability to ask for help is reframed as a strength. When we are stressed, personal vulnerability increases. Finding a way to tolerate vulnerability and turn toward others is a significant sign of resilience. When we turn away from others and move toward isolation, we are likely to become more inflexible, getting stuck in dysfunctional patterns. In order to reach out for support, we must have some reason to believe that a dependable, mutual relationship is possible in which putting oneself in a more vulnerable position does not pose a danger. A part of relational resilience, then, involves discerning the growth-fostering potential of a particular interaction or relationship.

Relational resilience involves movement toward mutually empowering, growth-fostering connections in the face of adverse conditions, traumatic experiences, and alienating social-cultural pressures. It is the ability to connect, reconnect, and/or resist disconnection. Characteristics such as temperament, intellectual development, self-esteem, locus of control, and mastery can be reframed from a relational perspective. The most important contribution of temperament to resilience may be the means by which a child is placed at risk or protected in terms of relational consequences. For instance, a hard to soothe child may contribute to a sense of helplessness and frustration in the parent which could lead to avoidance or neglect. Similarly "intellectual development" which is typically thought of as an internal trait largely deriving from genetic loading is now understood as formed to a great extent in relational contexts. Siegel (1999) notes that interpersonal relationships are the primary source of experience that shapes how the brain develops. "Human connections create neuronal connections" (Siegel, p. 85).

Self-esteem can also be thought of in a more contextual way by examining what Jordan (1999) has called *relational confidence*. Thus rather than emphasizing "the self" and its esteem, we suggest that one's capacity to develop growth-fostering relationships, which engender confidence in our connections with others, might be a more important variable for study than some supposed internal trait of self-esteem (Burnett & Denmar, 1996). Similarly, internal locus of control defined as a source of resilience may be understood better when we take context into account. In a culture that so values control and certainty one can understand why this might be seen as central. But studies have indicated that locus of control is influenced by cultural context and the realistic power that a group exercises in their culture. Locus of control may be seen as the ability to influence one's experience, environment, or relationship (Hartling, 2003).

Social support has also been viewed as vital to resilience (Masten & Coatsworth, 1998). Social support has been defined as emotional concern, instrumental aid, information, and appraisal. Most social support studies have emphasized one-way support, *getting* love, *getting* help. A relational perspective points to the importance of engaging in relationship that contributes to all people in the relationships. Data suggests that it is as rewarding to give to others as to be given to (Luks, 1992). The power of social support is more about *mutuality* than about *getting for the self*. But the mutuality is often obscured in the ways social support is construed; this appears to be true of the twelve step programs, misleadingly called *self-help groups* when they actually are about *mutual-help* and growth. In other words, we all have a need to be appreciated, valued, validated, and given to, but we also have a need to participate in the development of others.

Mutuality

At the core of relational resilience is the movement toward mutuality. The social support literature points to the importance of being given to and receiving support from others (Ganellen & Blaney, 1984; Spiegel, 1991). But recently research has uncovered the importance of "giving" to others (Luks, 1992). The research community has moved into the study of altruism as a way of understanding the benefits of giving to others. RCT would suggest that it is actually *mutually* growth-fostering relationships that create the beneficial effects for individuals not a trait such as altruism. That is, there is a need to give, to matter, to make a difference; we find meaning in contributing to the well-being of others (Jordan, 2010; Jordan, et al., 1991; Jordan, Walker & Hartling, 2004). But we also need to feel cared for, given to, and treated with respect. We need to feel that we matter, that we can have an impact on the other person and on the relationship. Imbalances in mutuality are the source of pain for many people. And when we feel "outside" mutual connection, we often experience isolation. To give to others in a situation where we are not being respected, responded to, and appreciated in the long run can lead to demoralization, a drop in resilience. It is not that we need to be "thanked" or valorized for our giving. We must feel that we are part of a respectful, mutual system. Mutual empathy holds the key to what we mean by mutuality. It is important that we see that we have had an impact on each other; we know, feel, see that we have made a difference.

Mutual empathy is not about reciprocal, back and forth empathizing although that happens in growth-fostering relationships as well. Mutual empathy is the process in which each person empathizes with the other in mutual growth; I see that I have moved you and you see that you have moved me. We matter to each other, we reach each other, we have an effect on one another. We can produce change in one another and in the relationship. This ultimately brings about a sense of relational competence. It brings us into the warmth of the human community where real resilience resides. And it contributes to the development of community, the ultimate source of resilience for all people.

The literature on competence motivation addresses the intrinsic need to produce an effect on our environment (White, 1959); the usual research looks at the way a child manipulates the physical world and how that enhances a child's sense of competence ("I made this happen"). While there is no doubt that physical ability and task competence serve to increase one's sense of efficacy and worth, it is clear that an equally, if not more, important source of competence is in the world of interpersonal effectiveness, being able to evoke a sought for response in another person.

Let us take the example of a child and parent where the child is not understood, heard, or responded to (Dunham et al., 2011). There may be an empathic failure and the child attempts to represent her hurt to the parent. If the parent responds and lets the child see that it matters to the parent that she has hurt the child, that she is affected by the impact (in this case hurtful) that she has on the child, and the parent communicates this to the child, the relationship is strengthened and the child's sense of relational competence is strengthened. The child feels seen, heard, and cared about; she feels she matters, her feelings matter. If on the other hand, the parent does not respond to the child's pain with empathy or caring, but denies the child's feelings or attacks the child in some way or simply does not respond at all (neglect), the child will experience a sense of not mattering, of having no impact on the other person or on the relationship. She will begin to keep these aspects of herself out of relationship and will move into isolation and inauthenticity. When this happens repeatedly, the child moves into chronic disconnection. She develops strategies of disconnection for survival. In the most egregious cases of chronic disconnection and violation such as physical or sexual abuse of a child, these strategies of disconnection lead to a massive sense of isolation, immobilization, self-blame, and shame, what Jean Baker Miller calls "condemned isolation" (Miller & Stiver, 1997). This state of condemned isolation is a state of minimal resilience. The person maintains rigid and overgeneralized relational images that maintain isolation and mistrust of others. The person is not free to move back into connection following current disappointments and disconnection. New learning and growth is blocked or limited. The biochemistry may also be altered in such a way so that dissociation, amygdala reactivity, and startle responses interfere with reestablishing connection (Banks, 2000).

Shame

Often these disconnections occur in a climate of shame. Shame moves people into isolation and thus disempowers and immobilizes people. Shame is the experience of feeling unworthy of love, of feeling outside the human community (Jordan, 1989). In shame one doubts that another person can be empathically present. One feels that one's very being is flawed in some essential way. While in guilt we can hope to make amends, in shame we anticipate only rejection and scorn. Our very "being" feels deficient. Shame is an intensely interpersonal effect, one of the original effects delineated by Tomkins (1987). Because it leads to silencing and isolation, shame is a major deterrent to resilience, particularly if one frames resilience as an interpersonal, relational phenomenon. To the extent that one moves away from relationship in the face of shame, the opportunity for restorative and corrective connection is lessened.

Shame arises spontaneously when one feels unworthy of love or connection, at the same time that one is aware of one's yearning for connection. Shaming is also done to people,

used to change an individual's or a group's behavior. Sometimes it is used to disempower and silence. Dominant societal groups often shame the subordinate groups into silence as a way of exercising social control. The implication often is that "your" reality (nondominant individual or group) is deficient or deviant. This applies to any marginalized group, whether it is girls, people of color, gays, and lesbians. To the extent that an individual or group feels shame, they will in fact be less resilient and less empowered, less able to give voice to difference.

Building Relational Resilience in Girls and Women

Resilience exists to the extent that empathic possibility is kept alive. To the extent that girls feel they are a part of mutually growth-fostering relationships in which they care about others and are cared about as well, they will experience a sense of flexibility, worth, clarity, creativity, zest, and desire for more connection, what Jean Baker Miller has called the "five good things" of good connection (Miller & Stiver, 1997). We grow and learn, expanding the quality of our relationships. In isolation we repeat old patterns, are caught in repetitive cognitions, and often are disempowered. Resilience implies energy, creativity, flexibility to meet new situations. Sometimes it involves courage, the capacity to move into situations when we feel fear or hesitation. Courage is not an internal trait; it is created in connection. As human beings, we *en-courage* one another, create courage in an ongoing way. Just as there is no such thing as an internal state of "self-esteem" that resides in a separate person, feelings of worth, strength, and creativity are also supported or destroyed in relationships. At a societal level, those at the margins, defined by the dominant "center" (Hooks, 1984), are often disempowered by the dominant group's definition of what defines them, their "defective differentness."

Resilience becomes especially salient for girls in adolescence, a time when according to Carol Gilligan (1982) girls begin to "lose their voices." Between the ages of 11 and 13, Caucasian girls show massive drops in self-esteem (Gilligan, Lyons, & Hanmer, 1990). Rates of depression increase. As Gilligan suggests, girls begin to be silenced and less authentic in relationships. They appear to lose their relational intelligence. They take themselves out of relationship (authentic relationship) in order to "stay in relationship" (appearance of relationship). They lose a sense of effectiveness and feel they must accommodate to other's needs (Jordan, 1987). Janie Ward has written with great insight about the importance for adolescent girls of color to find a way to resist the disempowering stereotypes that the dominant culture imposes on girls of color. This capacity to resist the controlling images (Collins, 2000) is a significant contributor to resilience.

Janie Ward (2002) has suggested in working with African-American girls that we help them build healthy resistance, originally called "resistance for liberation" (Robinson & Ward, 1991). She suggests four processes to help these girls remain strong and resilient. First she suggests we help these girls "*read it*." By this she means examine the message and the immediate context and larger sociopolitical context. Thus with disempowering messages, one does not get caught up in reacting, but examines and thinks carefully about the evidence for the message or stereotype. After reading it, it is important to *name it*: in this we acknowledge the presence of racism, sexism, or class bias. It involves "knowing what you know" and confronting the issue. It may involve keeping silent until safety is reached (e.g., bringing it to a trusted adult to get support and seek clarification). A failure to name can lead to internalization of the negative identity and shame. Naming gives one a sense of agency and strength. The third step is to *oppose the negative force*. As Janie Ward suggests, one engages in the action to defy or circumvent or avoid the negative force, such as racism. It involves opposing self-hatred, despair, contempt, hopelessness, anger, and complacency. And finally she suggests we support girls in *replacing it*. This means that one can hold fast to a belief or value a sense of reality that is different from the one that is being promoted and then put something new in the place of the feeling, attitude, or behavior that is being opposed.

For instance, a person resisting racism could take a stand for fairness and justice.

These steps can be applied to many situations that typically undermine the sense of strength and worth of an individual (Franz & Stewart, 1994). It is interesting that members of marginalized groups are encouraged to internalize blame. For instance there was a "psychiatric diagnosis" of drapetomania in the days of slavery which was applied to slaves who had "a need to run away from their masters." Their desire for freedom was pathologized and given a medical diagnosis. In a less extreme way, girls are taught to take responsibility for failure and are pathologized for their relational longings. And there is abundant data that indicate girls internalize failure and externalize success while boys do the opposite. If the default explanation for failure is self-blame, assuming that "I am the problem," depression, immobilization, and shame ensue. If, on the other hand, one assumes that failure results from chance factors or external forces and success is a result of one's ability or effort, one feels more empowered to act and more sense of worth. The context plays a large role in creating these styles of attribution.

Courage in Connection

In addition to resisting the forces of disempowerment (sexism, racism, classism, heterosexism), resilience involves the development of courage. While courage has also been constructed within a separate self-model, with images of lone heroes scaling mountains or jumping from airplanes in individual death defying acts, courage also might be considered to be an interpersonal experience. Courage develops in connection; we are *en-couraged* by others (Jordan, 1990). Courage, like resilience, is not a trait that exists within the individual. As human beings we are constantly in interactions that are either encouraging or discouraging. Growth-fostering relationships which promote zest, clarity, a sense of worth, productivity, and desire for more connection are intrinsically encouraging. They help us feel energetic, focused, strong, and seeking growth and connection. Much of parenting, teaching, and therapy is about en-couraging others, literally helping people develop a sense of courage, feeling the capacity to act on one's values and intentions.

For young adolescent girls, there is probably nothing more important than supporting the growth of courage. Girls in early adolescence begin to lose their voice, begin to lack confidence, and their self-esteem plummets. The early energy, confidence, and feistiness (Gilligan, 1990; Pipher, 1994) that researchers have written about in young girls evaporate for many. A part of this arises around heterosexual relationships where girls begin to feel objectified, lose touch with their own body experience, and feel that they must accommodate to others, often boys', desires and definitions of them. A preoccupation with body image (where one feels eternally deficient) and with control of sexuality and anger leaves girls feeling constricted and inauthentic. Girls feel they cannot represent their experience fully; they fear rejection from boys and exclusion from girls if they deviate from the group norms. The inclusion–exclusion factors (Eisenberger & Lieberman, 2004; Simmons, 2002) that have weighed heavily on girls in social relationships heat up even more during these years. And as they emulate boys' models of success, girls feel less and less able to show or share these feelings of fear and uncertainty. They're supposed to be cool and tough.

The prohibition on anger for girls (Brown, 2003; Miller, 1976, 1985) is a great obstacle to their developing resilience. If a person cannot represent her feelings as fully as possible, particularly feelings that inform relational health, she will move into silence and isolation. Anger is a necessary and important signal in any relationship; it often marks a place of hurt or injustice. People need to be able to move into conflict to avoid being silenced or subordinated (Jordan, 1990). By suggesting that anger is a necessary part of change and growth in relationship, I am not endorsing cathartic, expressive, impulsive anger. Nor am I supporting the use of aggression, force, or dominance against others. Authentic anger is not about being totally reactive,

expressive, or spontaneous. In all relationships we must act and speak with awareness of our possible impact on others. And if we value good relationships, we will use anticipatory empathy to avoid hurting others when possible. But anger is a signal that something is wrong, that something hurts, that there has to be a shift or change in the relationship. If girls are asked to suppress their anger, they are invited into accommodation, subordination, and inauthenticity. Helping an adolescent girl learn how to speak up, especially how to channel her anger, how to be strategic in her use of her anger, will support her courage and her sense of who she is. The messages from the culture, however, silence and distance girls from these interpersonal signals. Girls then become cut off from themselves and from authentic connection with others.

Promising interventions have been developed in response to the research indicating that adolescent girls are at particular risk for depression, anxiety, losing their sense of worth, and becoming less resilient. Girls define safety in terms of relationships (Schoenberg, Riggins, & Salmond, 2003). The "Girls Circle" model (Hossfeld, 2008; Irvine, 2005) integrates relational theory, resilience practices, and skills training in an effort to help girls increase their positive connections. It is meant to counteract social and interpersonal forces that impede girls' growth and development. Girls Circle is a gender-specific program. Benard has indicated that providing caring and meaningful participation in communities increases empathic responsiveness and helps girls navigate difficult peer relationships (Benard, 2004; Hossfeld, 2008; Johnston, O'Malley, & Bachman, 2002; LeCroy & Daley, 2001; LeCroy & Mann, 2008; Steese et al., 2006). Gender-specific programs become increasingly important as modern adolescents are exposed to risky behavior at a much earlier age. Another curriculum, "Go Grrrls" is a program aimed at strengthening girls' connections and friendships. Go Grrls was also found to improve girls' body images, assertiveness, efficacy, self-liking, and competence (LeCroy, 2004). The Penn Depression Prevention program and the Penn Resiliency Program (PRP) address personal relationships and cultural pressures in addition to cognitive change (Beck, 1976). The Penn program is a manualized program that can be delivered in schools, clubs, clinics, and other community setting (Gillham et al., 2003; 2008). Given the sex differences in depression in adolescence, the Penn project underscores the importance of addressing girls' depression and resilience separately from boys (Le, Munoz, Ippen, & Stoddard, 2003; Lewisohn & Essau, 2002). It focuses on cognitive risk factors and problem-solving strategies. Restriction of anger may also be linked to depression in girls (Chaplin & Cole, 2005). Girls respond to the physical changes of puberty more negatively than do boys. Further, the internalization of negative cultural messages increases girls' vulnerability to depression (Stice, Spangler, & Agras, 2001). A new initiative at the Penn Resilience project, "Girls in Transition" (GT), highlights issues important to girls in early adolescence. GT encourages girls to think critically about cultural messages that demean women or impose impossible body image standards (Chaplin et al., 2006). Successful mentoring programs are based on teaching skills, relational competence, fostering relationships between mentor and mentee, and fostering connection with community. They emphasize mutual support (Dubois et al., 2011).

As the research and many of the intervention programs point out, helping girls value connection and relationship is essential. Too often the larger culture invalidates or pathologizes a girl's desire for connection or her desire to participate in the growth of others (seen as a failure of "self-interest"). The courage to move into the necessary vulnerability of authentic connections is as important as the courage to move into conflict to protest personal and social injustice. Because there is little real support for the importance of relationships in people's lives, girls and women are viewed as "too needy" or "too dependent" when they express their strong desire for connection. By acknowledging and valuing the basic, lifelong human need for relationship (now strongly supported by neuroscience research), we support a girl's natural inclination toward connection and thereby help create a powerful pathway toward resilience.

In summary, all children experience a better outcome following adverse life conditions when they have a positive relationship with a competent adult, engage with other people, and have an area of competence valued by themselves or society (Masten, et al., 1990). Girls tend to seek more help from others in childhood and offer more help and support in the preadolescent years (Belle, 1987). For girls and women in particular, mutuality is a key factor in how much protection a relationship offers. Lower depressions scores are found in women who are in highly mutual relationships (Genero, 1995; Sperberg & Stabb, 1998). The importance of these relationships is not just that they offer support, but they also provide an opportunity to participate in a relationship, which is growth-fostering for the other person as well as for oneself (Jordan, 2010). Participation in growth-fostering connection and relational competence may well be the key to resilience in girls and women. It is likely that understanding resilience as a relational phenomenon rather than as a personality trait will lead us to deepen our understanding of the significance of connection for the well-being of all people.

References

Banks, A. (2000). *Post-traumatic stress disorder: Brain chemistry and relationships* (Project Rep. No 8). Wellesley MA: Stone Center working Paper Series.

Banks, A. (2011). *The smart vagus. Webinar.* Wellesley, MA: Jean Baker Miller Training Institute.

Beck, A. T. (1976). *Cognitive therapy and the emotional disorders.* New York: International Universities Press.

Belle, D. (1987). Gender differences in the social moderators of stress. In D. Belle (Ed.), *Gender differences in the social moderators of stress* (pp. 257–277). New York: Free Press.

Benard, B. (2004). *Resiliency, what we have learned.* San Francisco: WestEd.

Blair, C. (2010). Stress and the development of self regulation in context. *Child Development Perspectives, 4*(3), 181–188.

Brooks, R., & Goldstein, S. (2001). *Raising Resilient Children.* New York, NY: Contemporary.

Brown, L. M. (2003). *Girlfighting: Betrayal and rejection among girls.* New York: New York University Press.

Burnett, P. C., & Demnar, W. J. (1996). The relationships between closeness to significant others and self-esteem. *Journal of Family Studies, 1*(2), 121–129.

Chaplin, J. M., & Cole, P. M. (2005). The role of emotion regulation in the development of psychopathology. In B. Hankin & J. R. Abeal (Eds.), *Development of psychopathology: A vulnerability-stress perspective* (pp. 49–74). Thousand Oaks, CA: Sage.

Chaplin, T. M., Gillham, J. E., Reivich, K., Elkon, A. G. L., Samuels, B., Freres, D. R., et al. (2006). Depression prevention for early adolescent girls: A pilot study of all-girls versus co-ed groups. *Journal of Early Adolescence, 26*, 110–126.

Collins, P. H. (2000). *Black feminist thought: Knowledge, consciousness and the politics of empowerment.* New York: Routledge.

Cozolino, L. (2006). *The neuroscience of human relationships: Attachment and the developing social brain.* New York: W W Norton.

Dubois, D., Silverthorn, N., Pryce, J., Reeves, E., Sanchez, A., Ansu, A., et al. (2011). Mentorship: The GirlPOWER program. In C. LeCroy & J. Mann (Eds.), *Handbook of prevention and intervention programs for adolescent girls* (pp. 325–367). New York: Wiley.

Dumont, M., & Provost, M. A. (1999). Resilience in adolescents: Protective role of social support, coping strategies, and self-esteem and social activities on experience of stress and depression. *Journal of Youth and Adolescents, 28*(3), 343–363.

Dunham, S. M., Dermer, S. B., & Carlson, J. (2011). *Poisonous parenting: Toxic relationships between parents and their adult children.* New York: Routledge.

Dweck, C. (2006). *Mindset.* New York: Random House.

Dweck, C., & Goetz, T. (1978). Attributions and learned helplessness. In J. H. Harvery, W. Ickes, & R. F. Kidd (Eds.), *New directions in attribution research* (Vol. 2). Hilldale, NJ: Erlbaum.

Dweck, C., & Reppucci, N. (1973). Learned helplessness and reinforcement responsibility in children. *Journal of Personality and Social Psychology, 25*, 1090–1160.

Eisenberger, N., & Lieberman, M. (2004). Why rejection hurts: A common neural alarm system for physical and social pain. *Trends in Cognitive Sciences, 8*, 294–300.

Farber, H. R., & Siegel, D. J. (2011). Parental presence: An interpersonal neurobiology approach to healthy relationships between adults and their parents. In S. M. Dunham, S. B. Dermer, & J. Carlson (Eds.), *Poisonous parenting* (pp. 49–611). New York: Routledge.

Franz, C. E., & Stewart, A. J. (Eds.). (1994). *Women creating lives: Identities, resilience & resistance.* Boulder, CO: Westview Press.

Ganellen, R. J., & Blaney, R. H. (1984). Hardiness and social support as moderators of the effects of stress. *Journal of Personality and Social Psychology, 47*(1), 156–163.

Genero, N. (1995). Culture, resiliency and mutual psychological development. In H. I. McCubbin, E. A. Thompson, A. I. Thompson, & J. A. Gutrell (Eds.), *Resiliency in ethnic minority families: African American families* (pp. 1–18). Madison, WI: University of Wisconsin.

Gillham, J., Chaplin, T., Reivich, K., & Hamilton, J. (2008). Preventing depression in early adolescent girls: The Penn Resilience and Girls in Transition Programs. In C. W. LeCroy & J. E. Mann (Eds.), *Handbook of prevention and intervention programs for adolescent girls* (pp. 125–161). New York: Wiley.

Gillham, J., Jaycox, L., Reivich, K., Seligman, M., & Silver, T. (2003). *Penn Resiliency Project.* Unpublished manual, University of Pennsylvania and Adaptive Learning Systems.

Gilligan, C. (1982). *In a different voice.* Cambridge, MA: Harvard University Press.

Gilligan, C. (1990). Joining the resistance. Psychology, politics, girls and women. *Michigan Quarterly Review, 29*, 501–536.

Gilligan, C., Lyons, N., & Hanmer, T. (1990). *Making connections: The relational worlds of adolescent girls at Emma Willard School.* Cambridge, MA: Harvard University Press.

Gladstone, T. R., & Beardslee, W. R. (2009). The prevention of depression in children and adolescents; a review. *Canadian Journal of Psychiatry, 54*(4), 212–221.

Goldstein, S., & Thau, S. (2011). A brain-based understanding from the cradle to the grave. In S. M. Dunham, S. B. Dermer, & J. Carlson (Eds.), *Poisonous parenting: Toxic relationships between parents and their adult children* (pp. 63–79). New York: Routledge.

Goleman, D. (2006). *Social intelligence: The new science of human relationships.* New York: Bantam Books.

Hankin, B. L., & Abramson, L. Y. (2001). Development of gender differences in depression an elaborated cognitive vulnerability-transactional stress theory. *Psychological Bulletin, 127*, 773–796.

Harter, S. (1993). Causes and consequences of low self-esteem in children and adolescents. In R. Baumeister (Ed.), *Self-esteem: The puzzle of low self regard.* New York: Plenum Press.

Hartling, L. (2003). *Strengthening resilience in a risky world: it's all about relationships* (Work in Progress. # 101). Wellesley: Wellesley Centers for Women.

Herrman, H., Steward, D. E., Diaz-Grandos, B. E. L., Jackson, B., & Yuen, T. (2011). What is resilience? *Canadian Journal of Psychiatry, 56*(5), 258–265.

Hooks, B. (1984). *Feminist theory: From margin to center.* Boston, MA: South End Press.

Hossfeld, B. (2008). Developing friendships and peer relationships: Building social support with the Girls Circle Program. In C. W. LeCroy & J. E. Mann (Eds.), *Handbook of prevention and intervention programs for adolescent girls.* New York: Wiley.

Irvine, A. (2005). *Girls Circle summary of outcomes for girls in the juvenile justice system.* Report submitted by Cere Policy Research of the Girls Circle Association, Santa Cruz, CA.

Jenkins, Y. M. (1993). Diversity and social esteem. In J. L. Chin, V. DaLacamelas, & Y. M. Jenkins (Eds.), *Diversity in psychotherapy: The politics of race, ethnicity and gender* (pp. 45–63). Westport, CT: Praeger.

Johnston, L. D., O'Malley, P. M., & Bachman, J. (2002). *Monitoring the future: National results of adolescent drug use: overview of key findings* (HID Publications No. 02-5105). Bethesda, MD: National Institute on Drug Abuse.

Jordan, J. (1989). *Relational development: Therapeutic implications of empathy and shame*. (Work in Progress, No. 39). Wellesley, MA: Stone Center Working Paper Series.

Jordan, J. V. (1987). *Clarity in connection: Empathic knowing, desire and sexuality* (Work in Progress, No. 29). Wellesley, MA: Stone Center Working Paper Series.

Jordan, J. V. (1990). *Courage in connection: Conflict, compassion, creativity* (Work in Progress No. 45). Wellesley, MA: Stone Center Working Paper Series.

Jordan, J. V. (1992). *Relational resilience* (Work in Progress No 57). Wellesley, MA: Stone center Working Paper Series.

Jordan, J. V. (1994). *A relational perspective on self-esteem* (Work in Progress No. 70). Wellesley, MA: Stone center working paper series.

Jordan, J. V. (Ed.). (1997). *Women's growth in diversity: More writings form the Stone Center*. New York: Guilford.

Jordan, J. V. (1999). *Toward connection and competence* (Work in I progress No. 83). Wellesley, MA: Stone Center Working Paper Series.

Jordan, J. V. (2010). *Relational-cultural therapy*. Washington, DC: American Psychological Association Press.

Jordan, J. V., & Hartling, L. M. (2002). New developments in relational-cultural theory. In M. Ballou & L. Brown (Eds.), *Rethinking mental health and disorder*. New York: Guilford.

Jordan, J. V., Kaplan, A. G., Miller, J. B., Stiver, I. P., & Surrey, J. L. (1991). *Women's growth in connection: Writings form the stone center*. New York: Guilford Press.

Jordan, J., Walker, M., & Hartling, L. (Eds.) (2004). *The complexity of connection: Writings from the Stone Center's Jean Baker Miller Training Institute*. New York: Guilford.

Kobasa, S. C. (1979). Stressful life events, personality and health: An inquiry into hardiness. *Journal of Personality and Social Psychology, 37*, 1–11.

Lazarus, R. S., & Folkman, S. (1984). *Stress, appraisal and coping*. New York: Springer.

Le, H., Munoz, R. F., Ippen, C. G., & Stoddard, J. L. (2003). Treatment is not enough we must prevent major depression in women. *Prevention and Treatment, 6*, 2–21.

LeCroy, C. W. (2004). Experimental evaluation of "Go Girrrls" preventive intervention for early adolescent girls. *The Journal of Primary Prevention, 25*, 457–473.

LeCroy, C. W., & Daley, J. (2001). *Empowering adolescent girls: Examining the present and building skills for the future with the Go Grrrls program*. New York: Norton.

LeCroy, C. W., & Mann, J. E. (2008). *Handbook of prevention and intervention programs for adolescent girls*. New York: Wiley.

Lewisohn, P., & Essau, C. (2002). Depression in adolescents. In I. H. Gotlieb & C. Hammen (Eds.), *Handbook of depression* (pp. 541–559). New York: Guilford Press.

Luks, A. (1992). *The healing power of doing good*. New York: Faucett Columbine.

Masten, A. S., Best, K. M., & Garmezy, N. (1990). Resilience and development: Contributions from the study of children who overcome adversity. *Development and Psychopathology, 2*, 425–444.

Masten, A. S., & Coatsworth, J. D. (1998). The development of competence in favorable and unfavorable environments: Lessons from research on successful children. *The American Psychologist, 53*(2), 205–220.

Miller, J. (1986). *Toward a new psychology of woman*. (2nd ed.) Boston: Beacon Press.

Miller, J. B. (1976). *Toward a new psychology of women*. Boston: Beacon.

Miller, J. B. (1985). *The construction of anger in women and men* (Work in Progress, No. 4). Wellesley, MA: Stone Center Working Paper Series.

Miller, J., & Stiver, I. (1997). *The healing connection* Boston: Beacon Press.

Peterson, C., Schwarz, S., & Seligman, M. (1981). Self blame and depressive symptoms. *Journal of Personality and Social Psychology, 41*(2), 253–259.

Pipher, M. (1994). *Reviving Ophelia*. New York: Grosset/Putnam.

Pollack, W. S. (1998). *Real boys: Rescuing our sons from the myths of boyhood*. New York: Random House.

Resnick, M., Bearman, P., Blum, R., Bauman, H., Harris, K., Jones, J., et al. (1997). Protecting adolescents from harm: Findings from the National Longitudinal Study on Adolescent Health. *Journal of the American Medical Association, 278*(10), 823–832.

Resnick, M. D., Harris, L. J., & Blum, R. W. (1993). The impact of caring and connectedness on adolescent health and well-being. *Journal of Paediatrics and Child Health, 29*(1), S3–S9.

Robinson, T., & Ward, J. (1991). A belief in self far greater than anyone's disbelief: Cultivating resistance among African American female adolescents. In C. Gilligan, A. Rogers, & D. Tolman (Eds.), *Women, girls and psychotherapy: Reframing resistance* (pp. 87–103). New York: Harrington Press.

Roediger, H. L., Capaldi, E. D., Paris, S. G., & Polivy, J. (1991). *Psychology*. New York: Harper Collins.

Rutter, M. (1978). Early sources of security and competence. In J. Bruner & A. Garton (Eds.), *Human growth and development* (pp. 33–61). Oxford, UK: Clarendon.

Rutter, M. (1989). Temperament: Conceptual issues and clinical implications. In G. A. Kohnstarmm Jr., D. Bates, & M. K. Rothbart (Eds.), *Temperament in childhood* (pp. 463–479). New York: Wiley.

Rutter, M. (1990). Psychological resilience and protective mechanisms. In J. Rolf, A. Master, D. Cicchetti, K. H. Nuechterlein, & S. Weintraub (Eds.), *Risk and protective factors in development of psychopathology* (pp. 181–214). New York: Cambridge University Press.

Schoenberg, J., Riggins, T., & Salmond, K. (2003). *Feeling safe: What girls say* [Executive Summary]. New York: Girl Scouts of the United States of America, Girl Scouts Research Institute.

Schore, A. (1994). *Affect regulation and the origin of the self: The neurobiology of emotional development*. Hillsdale, NJ: Erlbaum.

Schwalbe, M., & Staples, C. (1991). Gender differences in sources of self esteem. *Social Psychology Quarterly, 54*(2), 158–168.

Seligman, M. (1990). *Learned optimism.* New York: Pocket Books.

Siegel, D. J. (1999). *The developing mind: Toward a neurobiology of interpersonal experience.* New York: Guilford Press.

Siegel, D. J., & Bryson, T. P. (2001). *The whole-brain child: 12 Revolutionary strategies to nurture your child's developing mind.* New York: Delacorte Press.

Simmons, R. (2002). *Odd girl out: The hidden culture of aggression in girls.* New York: Harcourt Press.

Sparks, E. (1999). *Against the odds. Resistance and resilience in African American welfare mothers* (Work in Progress, No 81). Wellesley, MA: Stone Center Working Paper Series.

Spencer, R. (2000). *A comparison of relational psychologies* (Work in Progress, No. 5). Wellesley, MA: Stone Center Working Paper Series.

Sperberg, E. D., & Stabb, S. D. (1998). Depression in women as related to anger and mutuality in relationships. *Psychology of Women Quarterly, 22,* 223–238.

Spiegel, D. (1991). A psychosocial intervention and survival time of patients with metastatic breast cancer. *Advances, 7*(3), 10–19.

Steese, D., Dollete, M., Phillips, W., Matthews, G., Hossfeld, E., & Taormina, G. (Spring 2006). Understanding Girls Circle as an intervention of perceived social support, body image, self efficacy, locus of control and self esteem. *Adolescence, 41,* 55–74.

Stice, E., Spangler, D., & Agras, W. S. (2001). Exposure to media-portrayed thin-ideal messages adversely affects vulnerable girls; a longitudinal experiment. *Journal of Social and Clinical Psychology, 20,* 270–288.

Taylor, S. (2002). *The tending instinct: How nurturing is essential to who we are and how we live.* New York: New York Times Books.

Taylor, S. E., Klein, L. C., Lewis, B. P., Greuenwarld, T. C., Gurney, R. A., & Upfdegraff, J. A. (2000). Biobehavioral responses to stress in females: Tend-and-befriend, not fight-or-flight. *Psychological Review, 102*(3), 411–429.

Tomkins, S. (1987). Shame. In D. Nathanson (Ed.), *The many faces of shame.* New York: Guilford Press.

Walker, M. (2002). *Power and effectiveness: Envisioning an alternative paradigm* (Work in Progress No 94). Wellesley, MA: Stone Center Working Paper Series.

Ward, J. (2002). *The skin we're in: Teaching our children to be emotionally strong, socially smart, spiritually connected.* New York: Free Press.

White, R. (1959). Motivation reconsidered: The concept of competence. *Psychological Review, 66,* 297–333.

Wiseman, R. (2003). *Queen bees and wannabees: Helping your daughter survive cliques, gossip, boyfriends and other realities of adolescence.* New York: Crown.

What Can We Learn about Resilience from Large-Scale Longitudinal Studies?

6

Emmy E. Werner

Since the mid-1980s, a number of investigators from different disciplines—child development, pediatrics, psychology, psychiatry, and sociology—have focused on the question why some children cope successfully with major adversities in their lives, while others develop severe and persistent psychopathology. The *resilience* these children display is conceived as an end-product of buffering processes that do not eliminate risks and stress in their lives, but that allow the individual to deal with them effectively (Rutter, 1987).

Lately, there has been a lively debate that centers on whether successful coping in the face of adversity is domain-specific, whether the protective factors that mitigate the effects of adversity tend to be universal or context-specific, and whether the factors that contribute to resilience among children exposed to high levels of childhood adversity are equally beneficial for those not exposed to these adversities.

These questions are not easily addressed in the existing literature. Much of the available evidence is based on cross-sectional studies, retrospective studies, short-term longitudinal studies of only a few years duration (mostly in middle childhood), and studies with relatively small samples without "low-risk" comparison groups.

Nonetheless, there are lessons to be learned from large-scale longitudinal studies that have focused on the process of resilience at different points in time—from infancy to adulthood—and that are much rarer than the numerous reviews and handbooks that have been devoted to this topic. A *caveat is in order*: resilience itself, as Luthar and Zelazo (2003) remind us, is never *directly* measured in these studies—instead it is *inferred*, based on the measurement of two component constructs: risk and positive adaptation.

There are currently about a dozen large-scale longitudinal studies of high-risk children in different geographical regions of the United States that have reported their findings from different time periods in the life cycle. They include African American, Asian American, Caucasian and Hispanic youngsters who managed to cope successfully, despite significant adversities in their lives, such as poverty, parental mental illness, child abuse, parental divorce, and/or an accumulation of multiple risk factors in their families.

These longitudinal studies have (a) maintained a core group of 100 to a 1,000 or more participants; (b) included both males and females in their samples; (c) used multiple and age-appropriate measures of adaptation; (d) followed the children at several points in time; (e) kept their attrition rates low, and (f) collected data on "low-risk" comparison groups.

This chapter will also draw on report from longitudinal studies from Great Britain, New Zealand, Australia, the Scandinavian countries, and Germany whose findings complement the results reported by American investigators.

E.E. Werner (✉)
University of California, Davis, CA, USA
e-mail: eewerner@ucdavis.edu

S. Goldstein and R.B. Brooks (eds.), *Handbook of Resilience in Children*,
DOI 10.1007/978-1-4614-3661-4_6, © Springer Science+Business Media New York 2013

Large-Scale Longitudinal Studies

U.S. Studies

The Kauai Longitudinal Study: Beginning in the prenatal period, the Kauai Longitudinal Study has monitored the impact of a variety of biological and psychosocial risk factors, stressful life events, and protective factors on the development of some 698 Asian, Caucasian, and Polynesian children, born in 1955, in the westernmost county of the United States. Some 30% of this cohort were exposed to four or more risk factors that included chronic poverty, perinatal complications, parental psychopathology, and family discord. Data on the children and their families were collected at birth, in the postpartum period, and at ages 1, 2, 10, 18, 32, and 40 years. The most comprehensive publication resulting from this study is the book *Journeys from childhood to midlife: risk, resilience, and recovery* (Werner & Smith, 2001). A follow-up in the mid-50s is planned.

The Minnesota Parent–child Project: Begun in 1975, this project followed some 190 of 267 low-income women and their first-born children in Minneapolis from the last trimester of pregnancy to ages 7 and 10 days, 3, 6, 9, 12, 18, 24, 30, 42, 48 months, and from grades 1, 2, 3, and 6 to age 25 years (Yates, Egeland, & Sroufe, 2003; Sroufe, Egeland, Carlson, & Collins, 2005).

Project Competence: Begun in 1977–1978, this study followed a normative school cohort of 205 third to sixth graders in the Minneapolis public schools (ages 8–12) after 7, 10, and 20 years, with high retention rates. Some 90% of the original cohort participated in the 20-year follow-up (Masten & Powell, 2003; Masten et al., 2004).

The Virginia Longitudinal Study of Divorce and Remarriage: Begun in 1971, the initial sample consisted of 144 white middle-class families, half divorced, half nondivorced, with a target child of 4 years. Children and families were studied at 2 months, and 1, 2, 6, 8, 11, and 20 years after divorce. Of the original 144 families, 122 are continuing to participate in the study. When the children were 10 years old, the sample was expanded to include 180 families. When the children were 15 years old, it was expanded to include 300 families, and when the young people were 24 years old, it was expanded to include 450 families (Hetherington, 1989).

The Hetherington and Clingempeel Study of Divorce and Remarriage: Begun in 1980, this study examined the adaptation in stepfamilies of adolescent children at 4, 17, and 26 months after their parents' remarriage. Participants in this study were 202 white middle-class families living in Philadelphia and its suburbs, with the nondivorced and stepfamilies studied at equal intervals (Hetherington & Kelley, 2002).

The Rochester Longitudinal Study: Begun in 1970, the study included a core sample of 180 out of 337 women showing a history of mental illness (and a normal control group) whose children were studied at birth, 4, 12, 30 months, 4 years, and through grades 1–12 (Sameroff, Gutman, & Peck, 2003).

A Study of Child Rearing and Child Development in Normal Families and Families with Affective Disorders: Begun in 1980, the study enrolled 80 (Maryland) families where parents had affective disorders, with two children each: a younger child in the age range from 15 to 36 months, and an older child between the ages of 5 and 8 years, and 50 control families. There were three follow-ups at ages 42–63 months; 7–9 years; and 11–13 years (Radke-Yarrow & Brown, 1993).

A Longitudinal Study of the Consequences of Child Abuse: Begun in 1975, the study included a core sample of 353 out of 439 children from Pennsylvania families served by abuse centers, and controls drawn from daycare and Head Start programs. The children were seen between 1 and 6 years, and followed at 6–12 years, and in late adolescence (Herrenkohl, Herrenkohl, & Egolf, 1994).

The Virginia Longitudinal Study of Child Maltreatment: Begun in 1986, the study focused on 107 maltreated children, identified from the statewide registry, and a normal control group of children attending public schools in Charlottesville. The children were assessed in grades 1–3, grades 4–5, and grades 6–7 (Bolger & Patterson, 2003).

The Notre Dame Adolescent Parenting Project (NDAPP) focused on the fate of more than a hundred teenage mothers and their children—born in the late 1980s and early 1990s across the first 14 years of their lives. The goal of the study was to understand the mechanisms and pathways through which risk and protective factors influenced the children's development at 6 months, 1, 3, 5, 8, 10, and 14 years of age (Borkowski et al., 2007).

The Chicago Longitudinal Study: Begun in 1983, this is a longitudinal quasi-experimental cohort design, including 989 low-income children who entered the Child–Parent Center programs (CPC) in preschool and 550 low-income children who participated in an all-day kindergarten program. The youngsters were followed at age 14 and age 20 years, when 1,281 sample participants were still active (Raynolds & Ou, 2003).

British Studies

The National Child Development Study (NCDS): This study has followed some 16,994 persons, born in Great Britain between March 3 and 9, 1958, until adulthood. Data were collected on the physical, psychosocial, and educational development of the cohort at ages 7, 11, 16, 23, and 33 years (Wadsworth, 1999).

The British Cohort Study (BCS70): This study has followed 14,229 children, born in the week between April 5 and 11, 1970, for 3 decades. Follow-up data were collected when the cohort members were age 5, 10, 16, and 26 years (Schoon, 2001, 2006).

The Avon Brothers and Sisters Study (ABSS): Is a longitudinal study of some 192 families, each with a child born between August 1991 and December 1992 and an older sibling over the age

of 7, but below age 17. The aim of the research was to explore sibling relationships in different family types (two-parent families, single-parent families, and stepfamilies) and the risk and protective factors that impact their development and adjustment (Gass, Jenkins, & Dunn, 2007).

New Zealand Studies

The Dunedin Multidisciplinary Health and Development Study: This is a longitudinal investigation of a cohort of infants, born between April 1, 1972, and March 31, 1973, in Dunedin, New Zealand. The base sample comprised 1,037 children, followed at ages 3, 5, 7, 9, 11, 13, 15, 18, and 21 years, with 992 participating at age 21. In the latest follow-up, at age 26, 847 of the cohort were assessed (Caspi et al., 2003).

The Christchurch Health and Development Study: Begun in the mid-1977s, this study consists of a birth cohort of 1,265 children, born in the Christchurch urban region, and followed at 4 months, 1 year, and annual intervals to age 16 years, and at ages 18 and 21 years. In the last follow-up, 991 participants were assessed (Fergusson & Horwood, 2003).

Australian Studies

The Mater-University of Queensland Study of Pregnancy (Brisbane): This is a prospective study of 8,556 pregnant women begun in 1981. The mothers and their offspring were assessed between the third and fifth day postpartum and at 6 months, 5 years, and 14–15 years when 5,262 children participated. A follow-up at age 21 is under way (Brennen, Le Brocque, & Hammen, 2002).

The Australian Temperament Project (ATP) is a longitudinal study of the psychosocial development of a representative sample of 2,443 children born in the Australian State of Victoria between September 1982 and January 1983. DNA data were available for 584 adolescents at age 15–16 years, and 544 at age 17–18 years (Chipman et al., 2007).

Danish Studies

The Copenhagen High-Risk Study: This study has traced 207 children of schizophrenic mothers and 104 matched controls from age 15 to ages 25 and 42 years. More than half had exhibited *no* psychopathology from mid-adolescence through mid-life (Parnas et al., 1993).

Swedish Studies

The Lundby Study: This is a prospective longitudinal study of the mental health of some 2,550 persons, including 590 children (mean age 8 years at first assessment) living in southern Sweden. Cederblad (1996) followed a subsample of 148 individuals who had been exposed to three or more psychiatric risk factors (such as parental mental illness, alcoholism, family discord, or abuse) in childhood. Three out of four were functioning well in midlife.

German Studies

There are two longitudinal studies of risk and protective factors in Germany: Losel and Bliesener (1990) have studied adolescents in residential institutions in Bielefeld; Laucht, Esser, & Schmidt (1999) have followed a birth cohort of 347 children in Mannheim from 3 months to 8 years. Reports on the findings of their studies are available in German in the book *Was Kinder starkt* (What Makes Children Strong?) (Laucht et al., 1999).

Individual Attributes and Sources of Support Associated with Successful Coping Among High-Risk Children

Tables 6.1 and 6.2 summarize the individual attributes and sources of support in the family and community associated with successful coping among high-risk children that have been replicated in a number of large-scale longitudinal studies in the United States of America and abroad. In most cases the factors that contributed to resilience among those exposed to high levels of childhood adversity also benefited "low-risk"

children, that is, they showed a main effect rather than an interaction effect in statistical analyses (Fergusson & Horwood, 2003).

Children who coped successfully with adversity tended to become less easily distressed than those who developed problems and had an active, sociable, "engaging" temperament that attracted adults and peers alike. They possessed good communication and problem-solving skills, including the ability to recruit substitute caregivers; they had a talent or special skill that was valued by their peers, and they had faith that their actions could make a positive difference in their lives.

They also drew on external resources in the family and community. Foremost were affectional ties that encouraged trust, autonomy, and initiative. These bonds were often provided by alternative caregivers who were members of the extended family, such as grandparents or older siblings. There were also informal support systems in the community that reinforced and rewarded the competencies of such youngsters and that provided them with positive role models, such as teachers, mentors, and peer friends.

The frequency with which the same predictors of resilience emerge from diverse studies with different ethnic groups, in different geographic and sociopolitical contexts, conveys a powerful message of universality (Masten & Powell, 2003). That does not preclude the possibility that some protective factors are more age-, gender-, and context-specific than others. For example, in the Kauai Longitudinal Study we found some variables that discriminated significantly between positive and negative developmental outcomes *only* when there was a series of stressful life events or when children were exposed to poverty. They did not discriminate between good and poor outcomes among middle-class children whose lives were relatively secure, stable, and stress-free (Werner & Smith, 1989).

Among such protective factors were autonomy and self-help skills in early childhood for the males and a positive self-concept in adolescence for the females. Among protective factors in the caregiving environment for *both* boys and girls were a positive parent–child relationship observed during the second year of life and the number of sources of emotional support they could draw on

Table 6.1 Individual attributes associated with successful coping in high-risk children-replicated in two or more large-scale longitudinal studies

Source notes	Characteristics of individual	Time period studied	Childhood adversities				
			Multiple (4+) risk factors	Poverty	Parental mental illness	Child abuse	Divorce
1	Low distress; low emotionality	Infancy–adulthood	+	+	+	+	+
2	Active; vigorous	Infancy–adulthood	+	+			
3	Sociable	Infancy–adulthood	+	+	+	+	
4	Affectionate "engaging" temperament	Infancy–childhood	+	+	+	+	+
5	Autonomy; social maturity	Early childhood	+	+			
6	Average-above average intelligence (incl. reading skills)	Childhood–adulthood	+	+	+	+	+
7	High achievement motivation	Childhood–adulthood	+	+	+		
8	Special talents	Childhood–adolescence	+	+	+		
9	Positive self-concept	Childhood–adolescence	+	+	+		+
10	Internal locus of control	Childhood–adulthood	+	+	+	+	+
11	Impulse control	Childhood–adulthood	+	+	+		
12	Planning; foresight	Adolescence–adulthood	+	+			
13	Faith; a sense of coherence	Adolescence–adulthood	+	+	+		
14	Required helpfulness	Childhood–adulthood	+	+	+		

Source notes:

1. Farber and Egeland (1987); Fergusson and Horwood (2003); Werner and Smith (1992, 2001)

2. Farber and Egeland (1987); Werner and Smith (1992, 2001)

3. Farber and Egeland (1987); Losel and Bliesener (1990); Werner and Smith (1992, 2001)

4. Farber and Egeland (1987); Hetherington (1989); Werner and Smith (1992, 2001)

5. Farber and Egeland (1987); Masten et al. (2004); Werner and Smith (1989, 1992, 2001)

6. Farber and Egeland (1987); Fergusson and Lynsky (1996); Hetherington and Elmore (2003); Losel and Bliesener (1990); Masten and Powell (2003); Masten et al. (2004); Seifer et al. (1992); Werner and Smith (1992, 2001)

7. Fergusson and Horwood (2003); Losel and Bliesener (1990); Masten and Powell (2003); Masten et al. (2004); Radke-Yarrow and Brown (1993); Schoon (2001); Werner and Smith (1992, 2001)

8. Anthony (1987); Werner and Smith (1992, 2001)

9. Cederblad (1996); Fergusson and Horwood (2003); Hetherington and Elmore (2003); Losel and Bliesener (1990); Radke-Yarrow and Brown (1993); Werner and Smith (1992, 2001)

10. Bolger and Patterson (2003); Cederblad (1996); Hetherington and Elmore (2003); Masten and Powell (2003); Seifer et al. (1992); Werner and Smith (1992, 2001)

11. Fergusson and Lynsky (1996); Fergusson and Horwood (2003); Masten and Powell (2003); Werner and Smith (1992, 2001)

12. Masten et al. (2004); Rutter (2000); Werner and Smith (1992, 2001)

13. Cederblad (1996); Hansson et al. (2008); Hetherington and Kelley (2001); Howard et al. (2007); Rumbaut (2000); Suarez-Oroczo (2001); Werner and Smith (1992, 2001)

14. Anthony (1987); Boyden (2009); Losel and Bliesener (1990); Werner and Smith (2001)

Table 6.2 Resources in the family and community associated with successful coping in high-risk children—replicated in two or more large-scale longitudinal studies

Source notes	Resources	Time period studies	Childhood adversities				
			Multiple (4+) risk factors	Poverty	Parental mental illness	Child abuse	Divorce
1	Small family (<4 children)	Infancy	+	+			
2	Maternal competence	Infancy–adolescence	+	+	+	+	
3	Close bond with primary caregiver	Infancy–adolescence	+	+	+	+	
4	Supportive grandparents	Infancy–adolescence	+	+	+	+	+
5	Supportive siblings	Childhood–adolescence	+	+	+	+	+
6	Competent peer friends	Childhood–adolescence	+	+		+	+
7	Supportive teachers	Preschool–adulthood	+	+	+		+
8	Successful school experiences	Childhood–adulthood	+	+	+		+
9	Mentors (elders)	Childhood–adulthood	+	+			
10	Prosocial organizations: (youth clubs, religious groups)	Childhood–adulthood	+	+			

Source:

1. Cederblad (1996); Werner and Smith (1992, 2001)
2. Egeland, Carlson, and Stroute (1993); Masten and Powell (2003); Seifer et al. (1992); Werner and Smith (1992, 2001)
3. Cederblad (1996); Fergusson and Horwood (2003); Losel and Bliesener (1990); Masten et al. (2004); Mednick et al. (1987); Rumbaut (2000); Seifer (2003); Werner and Smith (1992, 2001)
4. Farber and Egeland (1987); Herrenkohl et al. (1994); Hetherington (1989); Howard et al. (2007); Radke-Yarrow and Brown (1993); Werner and Smith (1992, 2001)
5. Gass et al. (2007); Hetherington (1989); Wallerstein and Blakeslee (1989); Werner and Smith (1992, 2001)
6. Bolger and Patterson (2003); Fergusson and Horwood (2003); Hetherington (1989); Losel and Bliesener (1990); Rumbaut (2000); Suarez-Oroczo (2001); Wallerstein and Kelley (1980); Werner and Smith (1992, 2001)
7. Hetherington (1989); Losel and Bliesener (1990); Radke-Yarrow and Brown (1993); Reynolds and Ou (2003); Rumbaut (2000); Werner and Smith (1992, 2001)
8. Fergusson and Lynskey (1996); Hetherington (1987); Masten et al. (2004); Schoon (2001, 2006); Wadsworth (1999); Werner and Smith (1992, 2001)
9. Howard et al. (2007); Yates et al. (2003); Werner and Smith (2001)
10. Howard et al. (2007); Masten and Powell (2003); McGee (2003); Rumbaut (2000); Suarez-Orozco (2001); Werner and Smith (1989, 1992, 2001); Wyman (2003)

in early and middle childhood. Further, in the Rochester Child Resilience Project, Wyman (2003) reported context-specific effects of involvement in structured after-school activities among high-risk teens. Participation in pro-social group activities lowered the risk for delinquent behavior for youngsters with many antisocial friends, but not for those with few antisocial friends.

The Importance of Early Developmental Competence and Support

Because the majority of research on resilience has focused on middle childhood and adolescence, an early history of developmental competence has received little attention in the literature on resilience. Yet, both the Kauai Longitudinal

Study and the Minnesota Parent–child Project have shown that an early history of positive adaptation, engendered by consistent and supportive care, is a powerful and enduring influence on children's adaptation, and it increases the likelihood that they will utilize both formal and informal sources of support in their environment at later stages in the life-cycle.

For example, Yates et al. (2003) found that children with early histories of secure attachment in infancy and generally supportive care in the first 2 years demonstrated a greater capacity to rebound from a period of poor adaptation when they entered elementary school compared to those with less-supportive histories. Likewise, children who exhibited positive transitions from maladaptation in middle childhood to competence in adolescence were able to draw on a positive foundation of early support and positive adaptation.

That the process of resilience is manifested at later stages in the developmental trajectory became apparent to us in our follow-up studies in early adulthood and midlife on Kauai (Werner & Smith, 1992, 2001). The majority of high-risk children who had become troubled teenagers (with delinquency records and mental health problems) recovered in the third and fourth decade of life and became responsible partners, parents, and citizens in their communities. The individuals who availed themselves of informal sources of support in the community, and whose lives subsequently took a positive turn, differed in significant ways from those who did not make use of such options. They had been exposed to more positive interactions with their primary caregivers in the first 2 years, that is, their early rearing conditions fostered a sense of trust.

events that heighten children's vulnerability and protective factors that enhance their resilience. The follow-up in adulthood in the Kauai Longitudinal Study, for example, found a few offspring of psychotic parents who had managed to cope successfully with a variety of stressful life events in childhood or adolescence, but whose mental health began to deteriorate in the third decade of life (Werner & Smith, 1992).

Other high-risk children had grown into competent, confident, and caring adults, but felt a persistent need to detach themselves from parents and siblings whose domestic and emotional problems threatened to engulf them. This was especially true for the adult offspring of alcoholic parents, some of whom had been physically and emotionally abused when they were young. The balancing act between forming new attachments to loved ones of their choice and the loosening of old family ties that evoked painful memories exacted a toll in their adult lives. The price they paid varied from stress-related health problems to a certain aloofness in their interpersonal relationships.

On the positive side, the Kauai study demonstrated that the opening of opportunities at major life transitions (high school graduation, entry into the world of work, marriage) enabled the majority of the high-risk individuals who had a troubled adolescence to rebound in their 20s and 30s. Among the most potent second chances for such youth were adult education, voluntary military service, active participation in a church community, and a supportive friend or marital partner. Likewise, *Project Competence* identified a number of young people who did poorly in adolescence but turned their lives around in the transition to adulthood (Masten & Wright, 2009).

The Shifting Balance Between Vulnerability and Resilience

Large-scale longitudinal studies that have followed boys and girls from birth to adulthood (whether children of poverty, divorce, or children coming from multirisk families) have repeatedly found a shifting balance between stressful life

Protective Mechanisms: Interconnections Over Time

Just as risk factors tend to co-occur in a particular population (i.e., children of poverty) or within a particular developmental period (i.e., adolescence), protective factors are also likely to occur together to some degree (Gore & Eckenrode,

1994). The presence of a cluster of (interrelated) variables that buffer adversity at one point in time also makes it more likely that other protective mechanisms come into play at a later period of time.

There are only a few large-scale longitudinal studies that have demonstrated such interconnections over time. The highlights of the results of the latent variable path analyses that were applied to the data from the Kauai Longitudinal Study at six points in the life cycle illustrate the complexity of the phenomenon of resilience. They show how individual dispositions and outside sources of support and stress are linked together from infancy and early childhood to middle childhood and adolescence, and how these variables in turn, predict the quality of adaptation in young adulthood and midlife (Werner & Smith, 1992, 2001).

When the links between individual dispositions and outside resources were examined, men and women who had made a successful adaptation at midlife—despite serious childhood adversity—had relied on sources of support within the family and community that *increased* their competence and efficacy, *decreased* the number of stressful life events they subsequently encountered, and *opened up* new opportunities for them.

The protective processes that fostered resilience manifested themselves early in life. Across a span of several decades, maternal competence in infancy was positively related to their offsprings' adaptation in adulthood (at 32 and 40 years). Girls whose mothers interacted in a consistently positive way with their infant daughters were more autonomous at age 2 and more competent at age 10. They also attracted more sources of emotional support in childhood and adolescence and encountered fewer stressful life events than did the daughters whose mothers were less competent caregivers. Males with more competent mothers were more successful at school at age 10, more resourceful and efficacious at age 18, and utilized more sources of emotional support in adulthood than did the sons of mothers who were less competent caregivers.

For both boys and girls there was a positive association between autonomy at age 2 and scholastic competence at age 10. Boys who were more autonomous at age 2 encountered fewer stressful life events in the first decade of life and had fewer health problems in childhood and adolescence. Girls who were more autonomous as toddlers had fewer health problems in each decade of life and fewer coping problems by age 40.

For both boys and girls, there was a positive association between the number of sources of emotional support they were attracted in childhood, their scholastic competence at age 10, and the quality of adaptation at age 40. Individuals who could count on more sources of emotional support in childhood reported fewer stressful life events at later stages of their lives than those who had little emotional support.

For both sexes, scholastic competence at age 10 was positively linked to self-efficacy and the ability to make realistic plans at age 18. Males with higher scholastic competence at age 10 had fewer health problems in adolescence and higher activity scores on the EAS Temperament Survey at age 32. They also availed themselves of more sources of emotional support in adulthood. Females with higher scholastic competence at age 10 attracted more sources of emotional support in adolescence. For both boys and girls, the number of sources of emotional support they could rely on in adolescence was positively linked to their self-efficacy and ability to make realistic plans at age 18.

Men and women who were more resourceful and more realistic in their educational and vocational plans at age 18 received higher scores on the Scales of Psychological Well-Being at age 40. Their temperament was related to the quality of their adult adaptation as well. Men who scored higher on the activity scale of the EAS Temperament Survey at age 32 coped better at age 40 than did males with lower activity scores. Women with higher distress scores at age 32 had more health problems and lower scores on the Scales of Psychological Well-Being at age 40.

Most of the variance in the quality of adaptation at age 40 was accounted for by earlier predictors of resilience (i.e., variables associated with successful coping at ages 2, 10, and 18). Most was attributed to four clusters of protective factors that had been independently assessed in the first decades of life: (1) *maternal competence* (a cluster of variables that included mother's age and education and the proportion of positive interactions with her child, observed independently at home at age 1, and during developmental examinations at age 2); (2) the number of *sources of emotional support available to the child between ages 2 and 10 years* (including members of the extended family); (3) *scholastic competence at age 10* (a cluster of variables that included IQ scores and scores on the PMA reasoning test and the STEP reading test); (4) the *health status* of the child (between birth and 2 years for females; between birth and 10 years for males).

Those findings point to the importance of the first decade of life in laying the foundations for later resilience—as has been also documented by Sroufe and his collaborators in the *Minnesota Parent–child Project* (Sroufe et al., 2005).

Gender Differences

All large-scale longitudinal studies of risk and resilience report gender differences that appear to vary with the stages of the life cycle and the demands made on each gender in the context of the prevailing sex role expectations.

At each developmental period, beginning in the prenatal period and infancy, more males than females perished. In childhood and adolescence, more boys than girls developed serious learning and behavior problems and displayed more externalizing symptoms. In contrast, in late adolescence and young adulthood, more girls than boys were subject to internalizing symptoms, especially depression (Caspi et al., 2003; Fergusson & Horwood, 2003; Werner & Smith, 1989).

But among the high-risk youths who had become "troubled teenagers," more women than men managed to make a successful transition into their 30s and 40s, at least on Kauai. Protective factors *within* the individual—an engaging temperament, scholastic competence, and self-efficacy—tended to make a greater contribution to the quality of adult adaptation for females than

for males who successfully coped with adversities in their lives. In contrast the sources of support available in the family and community tended to make a greater impact on the lives of the men who successfully overcame childhood adversities (Werner & Smith, 2001).

Biological Aspects of Resilience

Most of the longitudinal studies reviewed here were conducted by educators, psychologists, and sociologists, but there has been a growing interest in biological and genetic variables that may mitigate or modify the impact of stress and childhood adversities on the quality of adaptation at different stages of the life cycle (Curtis & Cicchetti, 2008).

Health

Surprisingly, the general health status of the individual tends to be overlooked in most studies concerned with resilience and vulnerability. Even in large-scale longitudinal studies, in which the original focus has been "health and development," the variables that are included in complex regression equations that look for "resiliency factors" tend to denote psychological or sociological constructs or are concerned with educational attainment rather than health (Fergusson & Horwood, 2003; Schoon, 2001).

Path analyses of the data of the Kauai Longitudinal Study suggest that it might be worthwhile to explore the effects of good health or debilitating illnesses or accidents on children's ability to cope with stressful life events and adversity. On Kauai, at each stage of the life cycle—from early childhood to adulthood—individuals who encountered more stressful life events also encountered more health problems. Health problems in *early childhood* (a count of serious illnesses or accidents reported by the parents between birth and age 2; the number of referrals to health care providers, and the pediatrician's low rating of the toddler's physical status at age 2) were significantly correlated with coping problems in adulthood, both at 32 and age 40 (Werner & Smith, 1992, 2001).

On the positive side, perinatal health (i.e., the absence of pregnancy and birth complications) was a significant protective factor in the lives of adolescents who were the offspring of mothers who suffered from mental illness. These finding have been replicated in the Copenhagen High-Risk Study (Parnas et al., 1993) and in a study of 15-year-old-children of depressed mothers who were participants in the Mater-University Study of Pregnancy and Outcomes in Brisbane, Australia (Brennen et al., 2002).

Biological Sensitivity to Context

An exciting new avenue of research has focused on the role of psychobiologic factors as moderators of children's vulnerability to stress. The concepts of "biological sensitivity to context" and "differential susceptibility to environmental influences" have been advanced to explore the possibility that some children are more sensitive to the influence of context than others, whether the context is adverse or beneficial (Belsky, Bakermans-Kranenburg, & van Ijzendorn, 2007; Ellis, Essex, & Boyce, 2005).

Biological reactivity to naturally occurring stressors appears to be a robust, replicable phenomenon that involves a set of complex responses within the neural circuitry of the brain, and within peripheral neuro-endocrine pathways regulating metabolic, immunologic, and cardiovascular functions. Boyce and his collaborators (2005) have demonstrated in several studies that a disproportionate number of preschool children in supportive home environments displayed high autonomic reactivity. Conversely, a relatively high proportion of children in very stressful family environments, followed from infancy to age 7, showed evidence of heightened adrenocortical and sympathetic reactivity. In both studies, children from moderately stressful home environments displayed the lowest reactivity levels.

These finding suggest that relations between levels of childhood support/adversity and the magnitude of stress reactivity are curvilinear, an observation supported by Belsky et al. (2007) who speculates that the anxiety displayed by fearful children reflects a highly sensitive nervous system on which experience registers powerfully—one that makes them especially susceptible to both negative and positive rearing effects.

Research on differential susceptibility has only just begun. Studies that include twins and other siblings from the same family (such as the Swedish Twin Registry) may prove especially powerful as they could distinguish genetically and environmentally induced variations in susceptibility (Hansson et al., 2007)

Gene-Environment Interactions

There is ample evidence of the important role genetic factors play in the susceptibility of individuals to psychopathology, such as alcoholism, antisocial behavior, and severe psychiatric illnesses (schizophrenia and bi-polar disorder). Several studies, including the Copenhagen High-Risk Study (Parnas et al., 1993) and the Kauai Longitudinal Study have reported findings that suggest that adverse environments, including serious pre- and perinatal stress, have the most negative impact on individuals who are genetically vulnerable, among them the offspring of alcoholic and schizophrenic mothers (Werner & Smith, 2001).

It stands to reason that gene–environment interactions also play a significant role in relation to the phenomenon of resilience. Evidence of gene–environment interactions in which an individual's response to the environmental insults appears to be moderated by his or her genetic makeup has been reported by Caspi et al. (2002, 2003) from the 26-year follow-up of the Dunedin (New Zealand) Multi-Disciplinary Health and Development Study, in which 847 Caucasian cohort members participated.

Individuals with one or two copies of the short allele of the 5-HTTLPR gene (a serotonin transporter) exhibited significantly more (self-reported) depressive symptoms in relation to four or more stressful life events between the ages of 21 and 26 than individuals homozygous for the long allele. Of special interest was the finding that childhood maltreatment in the first decade of life predicted adult depression *only* among individuals carrying a short allele, but not among individuals homozygous for the long allelle (Caspi et al., 2003).

In another analysis of data from the Dunedin Study, Caspi and his associates found that a functional polymorphism in the X-linked gene encoding the neurotransmitter-metabolizing enzyme monoamine oxidase A (MAOA) was found to moderate the effects of childhood maltreatment in males. Boys with a genotype conferring high levels of MAOA expression who had been maltreated in childhood were less likely to develop antisocial problems (conduct disorders between ages 10 and 18; convictions for violent crimes by age 26) than those with low levels of MAOA activity (Caspi et al., 2002). The authors wisely suggested that "until this study's findings are replicated, speculations about clinical implications are premature" (p. 853).

Kim-Cohen and her associates (2006) were able to replicate the original finding by showing that the MAOA genotype moderated the development of psychopathology after exposure to physical abuse in a cohort of 975 7-year-old British boys. Her meta-analysis of the results of five independent investigations (from Great Britain, New Zealand and the U.S.A.) demonstrated that across studies the association between childhood maltreatment and mental health problems was significantly stronger in the group of males with the genotype conferring low MAOA activity. These findings provide the strongest evidence to date suggesting that the MAOA gene influences vulnerability to environmental stress and that this biological process can be initiated early in life. But that evidence so far is based only on samples of Caucasian males.

Meta-analyses of studies of the interaction between the serotonin transporter gene (5-HTTLPR), stressful life events, and increased risk of major depression have yielded mostly negative results—though substantial resources have been devoted to replication efforts.

Risch et al. (2009) conducted a meta-analysis of 14 studies, using both published data and individual-level original data. Of a total of 14,250 participants, 1,769 were classified as having depression. In the meta-analysis of published data, the number of stressful life events was significantly associated with depression. No association was found between the 5-HTTLPR genotype and depression in any of the individual studies, and no interaction effect between genotype and stressful life events on depression was observed. This meta-analysis yielded no evidence that the serotonin transporter genotype alone or in interaction with stressful life events was associated with an elevated risk of depression in men alone, women alone, or in both sexes combined.

Munafo et al. (2009), at the University of Bristol, carried out an independent meta-analysis on 15 studies that focused on gene x environment interactions at the serotonin transporter locus and concluded that the main effects of the 5-HTTLPR genotype and the interaction effect between 5-HTTLPR and stressful life events on risk of depression are negligible. Only a minority of studies (Kaufman, 2008; Kendler, 2005) report a replication that is qualitative comparable to that in the original report. In general, the positive results for the 5-HTTLPR x stressful life events interactions were compatible with chance findings.

Diversity of methods and approaches used to measure environmental risk may explain the inconsistencies in results across G x E studies. Health practitioners, educators, and behavioral scientists need to recognize the importance of replication of findings from genetic analyses that seek to anchor in neurobiology individual differences in resilience (Reiss, 2010; Stein et al., 2009).

Resilience in a Cross-Cultural Context

Research on resilience needs to acquire a cross-cultural perspective that focuses on children in the developing world who have been exposed to many biological and psychosocial risk factors that increase their vulnerability far beyond that of their peers born in more stable and affluent conditions.

Immigrant and refugee children are the fastest growing segment of the U.S. child population. *The Children of Immigrants Longitudinal Study* (CILS) have examined the aspirations, educational performance, and psychological adaptation of more than 5,000 teenage youths in two key areas of immigrant settlements in the United States: southern California and south Florida (Rumbaut, 2000). The original survey (T1) conducted in spring 1992 interviewed 2,420 students enrolled in the eighth and ninth grade in the San Diego Unified School District and 2,842 students in public and private schools in the Miami area. Three years later, from 1995 to 1996, a second survey (T2) of the same youths was conducted, supplemented by interview with their parents. The students from San Diego were mostly of Mexican and Southeast Asian origin, the students from Florida came mostly from Latin America.

Regardless of their country of origin, immigrant children with higher school achievement, aspirations, and self-esteem relied on high levels of social support by their parents and the extended family, and on competent peers from the same ethnic group. Among protective factors that enhanced their psychological well-being was closeness with parents, religion, and social support from family, friends, and teachers.

A 5-year *Longitudinal Immigrant Student Adaptation* (LISA) *Study*, directed by Carola and Marcel Suarez-Oroczo (2001), reports similar findings. The LISA study followed some 400 immigrant children (ages 9–14) who came from five regions (China, Central America, the Dominican Republic, Haiti, and Mexico) to the Boston and San Francisco areas.

Qualitative interview data and quantitative survey data employed in the LISA study illustrated the importance of supportive friends, counselors, and members of the extended family in the social world of immigrant youths, and the protective role of religion and church-based relationships in the lives of immigrant teenagers.

Young Lives is a longitudinal study of childhood poverty in four developing countries: Ethiopia, India (Andhra Pradesh), Peru, and Vietnam (Hardgrove, Boyden, & Dornan, 2010). So far, data have been gathered on some 12,000 children and their families over a span of 15 years. The children are in two age groups: The older cohort was born in 1994–2010, the younger in 2001–2002. Some of the overall trends across the three rounds of available survey data (2002, 2006, 2009) are:

Maternal education is a significant correlate of an array of positive outcomes for poor children, especially their nutritional status. In turn, there is a strong relationship between nutrition and children's cognitive achievement and psychosocial well-being.

Intergenerational interdependency is crucial to children's well-being and resilience in poor families where children's efforts are combined with parents and elders to meet family needs. Norms concerning what constitues a "good child" tend to reinforce their work contributions.

Evidence on children's active contributions to the domestic economy suggests that it is not just essential to household maintenance in poor families, but can foster their sense of belonging and responsibility, and ease their transition to adulthood (Boyden, 2009). We found the same to be true in our longitudinal study of multiracial families on Kauai (Werner & Smith, 2001).

Evaluation Studies of the Effectiveness of Programs Designed to Foster Resilience

Scarr (1992) points out that it is not easy to intervene deliberately in children's lives. We know how to rescue children from extremely bad circumstances and to return them to normal developmental pathways, but only within the limits of their own heritable characteristics, such as intelligence, temperament (activity, excitability, sociability), and psycho-biologic reactivity (cardiac and immunologic responses under stress). Since the 1980s, many "competence enhancement" and "strength" or "asset" building programs for high-risk children have been introduced in North America, most of which have focused on preschool and school-age children. So far, there have been very few evaluation programs that have examined their long-term effectiveness.

Some of these programs are discussed in other chapters of this book.

A notable example is the Chicago Longitudinal Study, begun in 1983, an ongoing investigation of the effects of the CPC, the oldest extended childhood intervention program in the United States of America and the second-oldest federally funded preschool program (after Head Start). The program stresses center-based language learning and parent participation and provides educational and family support services to disadvantaged children from preschool to the early elementary grades (3–9 years). The data available on more than a thousand participants in the Chicago public schools cover nearly 2 decades of life.

Reynold and Ou (2003) reported the results of several path analyses that modeled the effect of preschool participation (from year 3 to 5), cognitive skills (at age 5), parent involvement at school (in the years 8–12), quality of school (at ages 10–14), on school achievement and grade retention (at ages 14–15), and on the diminished likelihood of special education placement and dropping out of high school by age 20.

Effect sizes on measures of social competence averaged 0.70 standard deviations, modest, but higher than those reported from several meta-analyses on the effectiveness of preventive mental health programs (average 0.34 SD) and of a wide range of psychological and behavioral treatments (0.47 SD). Children who attended programs in the poorest neighborhoods benefited most from the CPC programs.

Because the pathways that lead to positive adaptation despite childhood adversities are influenced by context, it is not likely we will discover a "magic bullet," a model intervention program that will succeed every time with every youngster who grows up under adverse circumstances. Knowing this does not mean we should despair. But it does mean, as Ruttrer (2002) admonishes us that "caution should be taken in jumping too readily onto the bandwagon of whatever happens to be the prevailing enthusiasm of the moment" (p. 15).

Conclusions

Large-scale longitudinal studies, extending from childhood to adulthood, have documented the shifting balance between stressful life events and risk factors that increase children's vulnerability, and internal dispositions and outside sources of support that enhance their resilience. This balance may change at different stages in life for each gender and is affected by the cultural context.

The frequency with which the same predictors of resilience emerge from longitudinal studies conducted with different ethnic groups and in different geographic settings is impressive. In most cases the factors that mitigated the negative effects of childhood adversity also benefited children who lived in stable and secure homes, but they appear to have particular importance when adversity levels are high.

Large-scale longitudinal studies have demonstrated that an early history of developmental competence, engendered by consistent and supportive care, is a powerful and enduring influence on children's adaptation at later stages of the life cycle and increases that likelihood that they will rebound from a "troubled" adolescence.

The pathways that lead to positive adaptation, despite childhood adversity, are complex, and there is great need to map the interconnections between individual dispositions and outside sources of support that increase competence and self-efficacy, decrease negative chain effects, and open up opportunities, whether in natural settings or in structured intervention programs.

Longitudinal research needs to focus more on the role of gene–environment interactions that moderate an individual's response to stressful life events. It also needs to acquire a cross-cultural perspective that focuses on children from the developing world. We need to know more about individual dispositions and sources of support in the family and community that enable these children to operate effectively in a variety of high-risk contexts.

References

Anthony, E. J. (1987). Children at high risk for psychosis growing up. In E. J. Anthony & B. J. Cohlcr (Eds.), *The invulnerable child* (pp. 147–184). New York: Guilford.

Barwick, C. L., Belser, M., & Edwards, G. (2002). Refugee children and their families: Exploring mental health risks and protective factors. In F. J. Cramer Asima & N. Grizenko (Eds.), *Immigrant and refugee children and their families* (pp. 37–63). Madison, CT: International Universal Press.

Belsky, J., Bakermans-Kranenburg, M. J., & Van Ijzcndoorn, M. H. (2007). For better and for worse: Differential susceptibility to environmental influences. *Current Directions in Psychological Science, 16*, 300–304.

Bolger, K. E., & Patterson, C. (2003). Sequelae of child maltreatment: Vulnerability and resilience. In S. S. Luthar (Ed.), *Resilience and vulnerability: Adaptation in the context of childhood adversities* (pp. 156–181). New York: Cambridge University Press.

Borkowski, J. G., Farris, J. R., Whitman, T. L., Carothers, S. S., Weed, K., & Keogh, D. A. (Eds.). (2007). *Risk and resilience: Adolescent mothers and their children grow up*. Mahwah, NJ: Lawrence Erlbaum.

Boyden, J. (2009). Risk and capability in the context of adversity: Children's contributions to household livelihoods in Ethiopia. *Children, Youth, and Environments, 19*, 2.

Boyden, J., & Mann, G. (2005). Children's risk, resilience, and coping in extreme situations. In M. Ungar (Ed.), *Handbook for working with children and youth: Pathways to resilience across cultures and contexts* (pp. 3–26). Thousand Oaks, CA: Sage.

Brennan, P., Le Broque, R., & Hammen, C. (2002, September). *Resilience in children of depressed mothers: A focus on psychological, behavioral and social outcomes at age 15 years*. Paper presented at the meeting of the Society for Life History Research in Psychopathology, New York.

Caspi, A., McClay, J., Moffitt, T. E., Mill, J., Martin, J., Craig, I. W., et al. (2002). Role of genotype in the cycle of violence in maltreated children. *Science, 297*, 851–853.

Caspi, A., Sugden, K., Moffitt, T. E., Taylor, A., Craig, I. W., et al. (2003). Influence of life stress on depression: Moderation by a polymorphism in the 5-HTT gene. *Science, 30*, 386–389.

Caspi, A., Hariri, A. R., Holmes, A., Uher, R., & Moffitt, T. E. (2010). Genetic sensitivity to the environment: The case of the serotonin transporter gene and its implications for studying complex diseases and traits. *The American Journal of Psychiatry, 167*, 509–527.

Cederblad, M. (1996). The children of the Lundby Study as adults: A salutogenic perspective. *European Child & Adolescent Psychiatry, 5*, 38–43.

Chipman, P., Jorm, A. F., Prior, M., Sanson, A., Smart, D., et al. (2007). No interaction between the serotonin transporter polymorphism (5-HTTLPR) and childhood adversity or recent stressful life events on symptoms of depression: Results from two community surveys. *American Journal of Medical Genetics, 144B*, 561–565.

Curtis, W. J., & Cicchetti, D. (2003). Moving research on resilience into the 21st century: Theoretical and methodological considerations in examining the biological contributors to resilience. *Development and Psychopathology, 15*, 773–810.

Egeland, B., Carlson, L., & Sroufe, L. A. (1993). Resilience as process. *Development and Psychopathology, 5*, 517–528.

Ellis, B. J., Essex, M. J., & Boyce, W. T. (2005). Biological sensitivity to context II: Empirical explorations of an evolutionary-developmental theory. *Development and Psychopathology, 17*, 303–328.

Farber, E. A., & Egeland, B. (1987). Invulnerability among abused and neglected children. In E. J. Anthony & B. J. Cohler (Eds.), *The invulnerable child* (pp. 253–288). New York: Guilford.

Fergusson, D. M., & Horwood, J. L. (2003). Resilience to childhood adversity: Results of a 21-year study. In S. S. Luthar (Ed.), *Resilience and vulnerability: Adaptation in the context of childhood adversities* (pp. 130–155). New York: Cambridge University Press.

Fergusson, D. M., & Lynskey, M. T. (1996). Adolescent resiliency to family adversity. *Journal of Child Psychology and Psychiatry, 37*, 281–292.

Gass, K., Jenkins, J., & Dunn, J. (2007). Are sibling relationships protective? A longitudinal study. *Journal of Child Psychology and Psychiatry, 48*, 167–175.

Gore, S., & Eckenrode, J. (1994). Context and process in research on risk and resilience. In R. J. Haggerty, L. R. Sherrod, N. Garmezy, & M. Rutter (Eds.), *Stress, risk, and resilience in children and adolescents* (pp. 19–63). New York: Cambridge University Press.

Grant, B. F. (2000). Estimates of U.S. children exposed to alcohol abuse and dependence in the family. *American Journal of Public Health, 90*, 112–115.

Hansson, K., Cederblad, M., Lichtenstein, P., Reiss, D., Pedersen, N., Belderhiser, J., et al. (2008). Individual resiliency factors from a genetic perspective: Results from a twin study. *Family Process, 47*, 537–551.

Hardgrove, A., Boyden, J., & Dornan, P. (2010). *Summary of findings on children's experiences of poverty from young lives: A focus on risk, resilience, and protection* (Working paper).

Herrenkohl, F. C., Herrenkohl, R. C., & Egolf, B. (1994). Resilient early school age children from maltreating homes: Outcomes in late adolescence. *The American Journal of Orthopsychiatry, 64*, 301–309.

Hetherington, E. M. (1989). Coping with family transitions: Winners, losers, and survivors. *Child Development, 60*, 1–14.

Hetherington, E. M., & Kelley, J. (2002). *For better or for worse: Divorce reconsidered*. New York: Norton.

Hetherington, E. M., & Elmore, A. M. (2003). Risk and resilience in children coping with their parents' divorce and remarriage. In S. S. Luthar (Ed.), *Resilience and vulnerability: Adaptation in the context of childhood adversities* (pp. 182–212). New York: Cambridge University Press.

Howard, S. K., Carothers, S. S., Smith, L. E., & Akri, C. E. (2007). Overcoming the odds: Protective factors in the lives of children. In J. G. Borkowski, J. R. Farris, T. L. Whitman, S. S. Carothers, K. Weed, & D. A. Keogh (Eds.), *Risk and resilience: Adolescent mothers and their children grow up* (pp. 205–231). Mahwah, NJ: Lawrence Erlbaum.

Kaufman, J. (2008). Genetic and environmental modifiers of risk and resiliency in maltreated children. In J. J. Hudziak (Ed.), *Developmental psychopathology and wellness: Genetic and environmental influences* (pp. 141–159). Washington, DC: American Psychiatric Publishing.

Kendler, K. S., Kuhn, J. W., Vittum, J., Prescott, C., & Riley, B. (2005). The interactions of stressful life events and serotonin transporter polymorphism in the prediction of episodes of major depression: A replication. *Archives of General Psychiatry, 62*, 529–535.

Kim-Cohen, J., & Gold, A. L. (2009). Measured gene-environment interactions and mechanisms promoting resilient development. *Current Directions in Psychological Science, 18*, 138–142.

Kim-Cohen, J., Caspi, A., Taylor, A., Williams, B., Newcombe, R., Craig, I. W., et al. (2006). MAOA, maltreatment, and gene-environment interaction predicting children's mental health: New evidence and a meta-analysis. *Molecular Psychiatry, 11*, 903–913.

Laucht, M., Esser, G., & Schmidt, M. H. (1998). Was wird aus Risikokindern? Ergebnisse der Mannheimer Längsschnittstudie im Überblick. In G. Opp, M. Fingerle, & A. Freytag (Eds.), *Was Kinder stärkt* [What makes children strong?] (pp. 71–93). München: Ernst Reinhardt.

Lösel, F., & Bliesener, T. (1990). Resilience in adolescence: A study on the generalizability of protective factors. In K. Hürrelmann & F. Lösel (Eds.), *Health hazards in adolescence* (pp. 299–320). Berlin: De Gruyter.

Luthar, S. S. (Ed.). (2003). *Resilience and vulnerability: Adaptation in the context of childhood adversities.* New York: Cambridge University Press.

Luthar, S. S., & Zelzao, L. B. (2003). Research on resilience: An integrative review. In S. S. Luthar (Ed.), *Resilience and vulnerability: Adaptation in the context of childhood adversities* (pp. 510–550). New York: Cambridge University Press.

Masten, A. S., & Coatsworth, J. D. (1998). Resilience in individual development. The development of competence in favorable and unfavorable environments: Lessons from research on successful children. *The American Psychologist, 53*(2), 205–220.

Masten, A. S., & Powell, J. L. (2003). A resilience framework for research, policy, and practice. In S. S. Luthar (Ed.), *Resilience and vulnerability: Adaptation in the context of childhood adversities* (pp. 1–28). New York: Cambridge University Press.

Masten, A. S., & Wright, M. O. (2009). Resilience over the lifespan: Developmental perspectives on resistance, recovery, and transformation. In J. W. Reich (Ed.), *Handbook of adult resilience* (pp. 213–237). New York: Guilford.

Masten, A. S., Burt, K. B., Roisman, G. I., Obradovic, J., Long, J. D., & Tellegen, A. (2004). Resources and resilience in the transition to adulthood: Continuity and change. *Development and Psychopathology, 16*, 1071–1094.

McGee, R. (2003, June). *Participation in clubs and groups from childhood to early adulthood: Effects on perceived competence and attachment.* Poster session presented at the 11th scientific meeting of the International Society for Child and Adolescent Psychopathology, Sydney, Australia.

Mednick, S. A., Parnas, J., & Schulsinger, F. (1987). The Copenhagen High Risk Project. *Schizophrenia Bulletin, 16*(3), 485–495.

Munafo, M. R., Durrant, C., Lewis, G., & Flint, J. (2008). Gene X environmental interactions at the serotonin transporter locus. *Biological Psychiatry, 65*, 211–219.

Parnas, J., Cannon, T. D., Jacobsen, B., Schulsinger, H., Schulsinger, F., & Mednick, S. A. (1993). Lifetime DSM-III-R diagnostic outcomes in the offspring of schizophrenic mothers: Results from the Copenhagen High Risk Study. *Archives of General Psychiatry, 56*, 707–714.

Plomin, R., & Haworth, M. A. (2010). Genetics and intervention research. *Perspectives on Psychological Science, 5*, 557–563.

Radke-Yarrow, M., & Brown, E. (1993). Resilience and vulnerability in children of multiple-risk families. *Development and Psychopathology, 5*, 581–592.

Reiss, D. (2010). Genetic thinking in the study of social relationships: Five points of entry. *Perspectives on Psychological Science, 5*, 502–515.

Reynolds, A. J., & Ou, S. R. (2003). Promoting resilience through early childhood intervention. In S. S. Luthar (Ed.), *Resilience and vulnerability: Adaptation in the context of childhood adversities* (pp. 436–462). New York: Cambridge University Press.

Risch, N., Herrell, R., Lehner, T., Liang, K. Y., Eaves, L., Holt, J., et al. (2009). Interaction between the serotonin transporter gene (5-HTTLPR), stressful life events and risk of depression: A meta-analysis. *Journal of the American Medical Association, 301*, 2462–2471.

Rumbaut, R. G. (2000). Profiles in resilience: Educational achievement and ambition. In R. D. Taylor & M. C. Wong (Eds.), *Resilience across contexts: Family, work, culture and community* (pp. 257–293). Mahwah, NJ: Lawrence Erlbaum.

Rutter, M. (1987). Psychosocial resilience and protective mechanisms. *The American Journal of Orthopsychiatry, 57*, 216–331.

Rutter, M. (2000). Resilience reconsidered: Conceptual considerations, empirical findings, and policy implications. In J. P. Shonkoff & S. J. Meisels (Eds.), *Handbook of early intervention* (2nd ed., pp. 651–681). New York: Cambridge University Press.

Rutter, M. (2002). Nature, nurture, and development: From evangelism through science toward policy and practice. *Child Development, 23*, 1–21.

Sameroff, A., Gutman, L. M., & Peck, S. C. (2003). Adaptation among youth facing multiple risks: Prospective research findings. In S. S. Luthar (Ed.), *Resilience and vulnerability: Adaptation in the context of childhood adversities* (pp. 364–391). New York: Cambridge University Press.

Scarr, S. (1992). Developmental theories for the 1990's: Development and individual differences. *Child Development, 63*, 1–19.

Schoon, I. (2001). Risk and resources: A developmental-contextual approach to the study of adaptation in the face of adversity. In R. K. Silbereisen & M. Reitzle (Eds.), *Psychologie 2000.* Berlin: Pabst Science Publishers.

Schoon, I. (2006). *Risk and resilience: Adaptations in changing times.* New York: Cambridge University Press.

Seifer, R. (2003). Young children with mentally ill parents: Resilient developmental systems. In S. S. Luthar (Ed.), *Resilience and vulnerability: Adaptation in the context of childhood adversities* (pp. 29–49). New York: Cambridge University Press.

Seifer, R., Sameroff, A. J., Baldwin, C. P., & Baldwin, A. (1992). Child and family factors that ameliorate risk between 4 and 13 years of age. *Journal of the American Academy of Child and Adolescent Psychiatry, 31*, 893–903.

Sroufe, L. A., Egeland, B., Carlson, E. A., & Collins, B. E. (2005). *The development of the person: The Minnesota study of risk and adaptation from birth to adulthood.* New York: Guilford.

Stein, M. B., Campbell-Sills, L., & Gelenter, F. (2009). Genetic variation in 5-HTTLPR is associated with emotional resilience. *American Journal of Medical Genetics, 150B*, 900–906.

Suarez-Orozco, C., & Suarez-Orozco, M. (2001). *Children of immigrants.* Cambridge, MA: Harvard University Press.

Taylor, S. E., & Stanton, A. (2007). Coping resources, coping processes and mental health. *Annual Review of Clinical Psychology, 3*, 377–401.

Ungar, M. (2005). Introduction: Resilience across cultures and contexts. In M. Ungar (Ed.), *Handbook for working with children and youth: Pathways to resilience across cultures and contexts* (pp. XV–XXXIX). Thousand Oaks, CA: Sage.

Wadsworth, M. (1999). Ergebnisse der Resilienzforschung in Grossbritannien. In G. Opp, M. Fingerle, & A. Freytag (Eds.), *Was Kinder starkt* [What makes children strong?] (pp. 59–70). Munchen: Ernst Reinhardt.

Wallerstein, J. S., & Blakeslee, S. (1989). *Second chances: Men, women, and children a decade after divorce.* New York: Ticknor and Fields.

Wallerstein, J. S., & Kelley, J. B. (1980). *Surviving the break-up: How children and parents cope with divorce.* New York: Basic Books.

Werner, E. E. (2000). Protective factors and individual resilience. In J. P. Shonkoff & S. J. Meisels (Eds.), *Handbook of early intervention* (2nd ed., pp. 115–132). New York: Cambridge University Press.

Werner, E. E., & Smith, R. S. (1989). *Vulnerable but invincible: A longitudinal study of resilient children and youth.* New York: Adams, Bannister, Cox. (Original work published by McGraw Hill, 1982)

Werner, E. E., & Smith, R. S. (1992). *Overcoming the odds: High risk children from birth to adulthood.* Ithaca, NY: Cornell University Press.

Werner, E. E., & Smith, R. S. (2001). *Journeys from childhood to midlife: Risk, resilience, and recovery.* Ithaca, NY: Cornell University Press.

Wyman, P. A. (2003). Emerging perspectives on context specificity of children's adaptation and resilience: Evidence from a decade of research with urban children in adversity. In S. S. Luthar (Ed.), *Resilience and vulnerability: Adaptation in the context of childhood adversities* (pp. 293–317). New York: Cambridge University Press.

Yates, T. M., Egeland, B., & Sroufe, L. A. (2003). Rethinking resilience: A developmental process perspective. In S. S. Luthar (Ed.), *Resilience and vulnerability: Adaptation in the context of childhood adversities* (pp. 243–266). New York: Cambridge University Press.

Part II

Environmental Issues

Poverty in Childhood and Adolescence: A Transactional–Ecological Approach to Understanding and Enhancing Resilience in Contexts of Disadvantage and Developmental Risk

Robert D. Felner and Melissa L. DeVries

The number of children in the United States who grow up in conditions of chronic poverty and social disadvantage remains a tragedy of epidemic proportions. Currently, approximately one out of every five children under age 18 lives in poverty (Proctor & Dalaker, 2003; DeNavas-Walt, Proctor, & Smith, 2008). Further, the overall numbers grew by approximately 400,000 from 2001 to 2002, to exceed 12 million children and youth who now live below the poverty line. When those who are considered "near poor"—calculated by the U.S. Census as those who have household incomes of less than 1.25 times the poverty income level—the percentage of all children below the age of 18 in the United States who experience serious economic hardship each day of rates edges close to one-quarter (22.3) of all children and youth. Poverty rates among minority children are even higher, with this level of severe economic disadvantage affecting approximately 30% of both Hispanic and African-American children (Proctor & Dalaker, 2003; DeNavas-Walt et al., 2008). Studies of the effects of poverty and other forms of socioeconomic disadvantage have underscored the potentially devastating impact that these conditions can have on the emotional, physical, and intellectual development of children and youth

(cf. Felner et al., 1995; Felner, Silverman, & Felner, 2000; Lipina & Colombo, 2009; Mrazek & Haggarty, 1994). Summarizing these findings, Schorr (1988) concluded "poverty is the greatest risk factor of all. Family poverty is relentlessly correlated with school-aged childbearing, school failure, and violent crime.... Virtually all other risk factors that make rotten outcomes more likely are also found disproportionately among poor children" (p. xxii). Little has changed since Schorr wrote those words to change the prognosis for children in poverty. Indeed, as we will discuss below, because of changes in society many of the conditions that have been associated with poverty, such as school failure, may be more likely to result in other compounding, comorbid difficulties than at any time in our nation's history.

Elsewhere in this volume there are extended discussions of approaches to building specific competencies, or specific supports (e.g., parental skills) to enable all children and youth, including those in poverty, to better withstand stressors and challenges, including ones from both nature and nurture (Deater-Deckard, Ivy & Smith, 2005), that they confront as they develop. It is neither the intent nor within the scope of the current chapter to cover that same ground in significant detail, except to refer to it as necessary. Rather, our intent is to offer a framework for more fully understanding the pathways by which poverty impacts and shapes the developmental course for children and youth, one that has shown promise for guiding both policy and other interventions that may be effective in reducing the ongoing toll

R.D. Felner
University of Louisville, Louisville, KY, USA

M.L. DeVries (✉)
Neurology, Learning and Behavior Center,
Salt Lake City, UT, USA
e-mail: Melissa@samgoldstein.com

S. Goldstein and R.B. Brooks (eds.), *Handbook of Resilience in Children*,
DOI 10.1007/978-1-4614-3661-4_7, © Springer Science+Business Media New York 2013

of poverty among our young. To be sure, what is offered here is but one element of what must be a far more extensive and comprehensive approach to enabling children and youth to be resilient in the face of the myriad of developmentally hazardous conditions that are associated with living in poverty. Further, the discussion offered here, although potentially making a useful contribution to considering the impact of poverty in non-western countries would be vastly different both in its focus and recommendations, although the transactional–ecological perspective is one that does generalize to the basic developmental processes of all living organisms, and in that way may have some utility.

As we considered where to focus the discussion in this chapter, of such a vast area (poverty), about which so much has been written, perhaps what was easiest to decide was what it did not need to do. Another chapter recounting all of the ills associated with poverty, or that had little utility for guiding action, was one thing that we clearly do not need. There are literally hundreds, if not thousands of government and public/private sector reports that recount the costs and impacts of poverty for children, adolescents, families, and others. This chapter does not do that. Similarly, it is not about the definitions of poverty, and we leave that to the economists. Instead, our focus is on the ways in which chronic disadvantage may act both directly, and through other social institutions, to negatively impact the developmental course of children and youth, as well as to offer some general understandings and specific examples of how we may reduce the population-level impacts of disadvantage.

A Mediated Effects Approach to Defining and Understanding the Experience of Poverty in Childhood and Adolescence

Transactional (Felner & Felner, 1989; Sameroff & Fiese, 1989) and ecological perspectives on human development (Bronfennbrenner, 1979), taken together as a transactional–ecological perspective (Felner, Felner, & Silverman, 2000),

provide an important organizing theoretical framework for understanding the ways in which conditions such as poverty and correlated forms of social and economic disadvantage (e.g., parental educational and occupational attainment) may impact adaptational outcomes. Here, it is important to distinguish poverty and related forms of socioeconomic disadvantage from other, conceptually distinct aspects of the ecology of child and adolescent development (Bronfennbrenner, 1979; McLoyd, 1990, 1998). In articulating this view, Felner et al. (2000) noted that social structural stress, major life events, and associated conditions from which they may derive, such as the forms of disadvantage noted earlier, are "distal" in that they do not directly describe the life circumstances and demands that result from them, nor the adaptive processes they require. That is, although there may be some conditions for which "poverty" may, for all children and youth, increase the marginal probability of experiencing, to talk about the experience of "poverty" can be very misleading.

Illustratively, given poverty's economic definition, where the level of income for a family is often the "yardstick," a family where the primary breadwinner is a well-educated, but new school teacher with several children can easily be seen as potentially meeting the standard for being either "in poverty" or at least "near poverty." Similarly, within the group of children/youth in poverty may be in families where the parent(s) is very young, has little education, few other resources, and yet have approximately the same income.

Families with the same income levels may also live in dramatically different communities where the developmental contexts experienced by their children may vary significantly. Kozol (1991) and others have talked about the "Savage inequalities" that may be present in the educational settings that are provided to students in neighborhoods and communities where pervasive poverty and social disadvantage are present. At the "next level" of the ecology of communities, Wilson (1987, 1996) and Xue, Leventhal, Brooks-Gunn, and Earls (2005) have shown the way that neighborhoods with high levels of unemployment, "dense" or "concentrated disadvantage" may be developmental contexts where the effects of family poverty are potentiated and magnified. Such neighborhoods often have substandard housing where high lead or other toxin levels may be present, significantly greater levels of crime, substance abuse and violence, fewer high quality after-school or childcare options, and they may also provide exposure to fewer positive models or opportunities that shape the dreams and aspirations of youth. It is also clear from both the works of Wilson (1987, 1996) and census reports that for some poverty or near poverty is a transitory experience, often persisting less than 1 year. For others, however, it may be ongoing, pervasive, and characterize much or all of the developmental period from prenatal to maturity. What is clear from the work of Sameroff and his colleagues (Masten & Sesma, 1999; Sameroff & Chandler, 1975; Sameroff & Fiese, 1989) is that exposure to additional conditions of risk is not simply additive in their impact but may, in fact, exponentially increase the probability of developmental difficulties. Hence, to discuss resilience in the face of poverty requires a framework that both reflects a full awareness of the "nested" and variable nature of poverty and that may guide action for affecting resilience in the vastly different contexts and conditions that may be associated with it.

According to this perspective, it is the more proximal person–environment transactions and developmental circumstances that define the particular experience of poverty by a child or adolescent. And, it is those immediate, day-to-day experiences that most directly shape the adaptation of youth and the developmental challenges that they confront (Abelev, 2009; Felner, Farber, & Primavera, 1980, 1983). Many of us know people who have said that they, "...were poor as a child, but did not know it. We didn't know it because there was always food, the same house (housing stability), a safe place to play, and clean clothes." But, for others who have grown up in poverty the developmental contexts were far more harsh.

There are several important implications of this view. First, conditions of social and economic disadvantage may, at least in part, exert their impact on adaptational outcomes via their effects on the relatively more proximal environmental conditions and experiences that characterize the lives of youth. The conceptual model implied by this view is one in which conditions of socioeconomic disadvantage influence proximal environmental experiences, and the same proximal experiences, in turn, have effects on child and adolescent adjustment. The model also allows for the possibility of direct effects of conditions of socioeconomic disadvantage on adjustment.

A second implication is that the more proximal developmental contexts (e.g., schools, neighborhoods, families) may provide and create powerful "compensatory effects" (Abelev, 2009; Costello, Swendsen, Rose, & Dierker, 2008; Felner et al., 1995) that are not only protective in their own right, but that provide developmental experiences that facilitate the development of individual level competencies in the children and youth in them, and that then magnifies the potential for positive outcomes. Here, we see the opportunity for the compliment to "rotten outcomes cluster." That is, where developmentally enhancing, compensatory settings are provided, "strengths may magnify in reciprocal ways between through transactions that enhance both protective features of the context and individual strengths of the inhabitants."

As noted, consistent with the hypothesized ecological–mediational linkages in the proposed model, numerous prior investigations have established both: (a) associations between indices of household socioeconomic disadvantage and the relatively more proximal experiences of children and youth in primary developmental contexts, including, but not limited to, heightened levels of parent–child conflict, family disorganization, negative experiences in school, and greater degrees of exposure to both acute and potentially chronic stressors (Garmezy, 1983; Mash & Dozois, 2003; McLoyd, 1998; Sameroff & Fiese, 1989; Sameroff, Seifer, Barocas, Zax, & Greenspan, 1987), and (b) associations between indices of proximal environmental experiences in many of these same domains and various aspects of child and adolescent adjustment including, but again not limited to, relative levels of self-esteem, symptoms relating to depression and anxiety, behavioral problems in home and school contexts, and academic achievement (Cicchetti, Rappaport, Sandler, & Wessberg, 2000; DuBois, Felner, Brand, Adan, & Evans, 1992; Felner, Aber, Primavera, & Cauce, 1985; Mash & Dozois, 2003; Nolen-Hoeksema, Girgus, & Seligman, 1992; Rowlison & Felner, 1988).

Findings from the relatively few studies which have examined patterns of association among all three types of variables provide some support for distal-proximal-adjustment mediated pathways (see McLoyd, 1990, for an excellent review of this literature). In her review, which focused on the effects of economic hardship among African-American families and children, she concluded that there was support for the hypothesis that the socioemotional functioning of children living in poor families is mediated by the effects of poverty on proximal contextual conditions in children's lives, such as the psychological functioning of parents and levels of distress in family interaction patterns. Of particular note for a mediated pathways perspective are those studies which have found that measures of relatively distal environmental factors no longer relate significantly to adjustment outcomes after their shared variance with key proximal conditions is removed. For example, in reviews of the literature concerning conduct disturbances several authors have, over the years (Hinshaw & Lee, 2003; Rutter, 1979) noted that in at least some studies the correlation between social class and conduct disturbance was either no longer evident, or far reduced, after controlling for measures of family discord and disorganization that were associated with social class differences.

In pursuing the line of inquiry outlined earlier, the manner in which relative levels of socioeconomic disadvantage have been assessed is critical to understanding and interpreting any findings. Although this would appear to be a straightforward issue, a consideration of prior work shows that it is anything but clear cut (Allen & Mitchell, 1998; Flouri, Tzavidis, & Kallis, 2010; McLoyd et al., 2009; Ruggles, 1992; Wilson, 1996). Instead, in studies of socioeconomic

disadvantage the defining parameters are often inconsistent, not well articulated, or embrace a broad spectrum of what even the most casual observer would agree are quite different conditions (cf. Featherman, Spenner, & Tsunematsu, 1988; Proctor & Dalaker, 2003). Of particular concern in the present work are distinctions between economic forms of disadvantage and those that cooccur and are frequently combined with economic circumstances to create a single index of socioeconomic status (e.g., educational disadvantage). When combined to create single indicators of socioeconomic status the differential relationships among various forms of disadvantage and child and adolescent adaptation may be obscured. Consistent with this view, Hollingshead (1975), in revising his classic scale for the assessment of socioeconomic status levels, argued strongly for the need to attend to distinctions between occupational and educational dimensions of socioeconomic disadvantage.

Relatedly, there is also a need to address the ways in which relative levels of advantage and disadvantage are defined. One area requiring greater attention in this regard is the extent to which, within each form of disadvantage, quantitative (i.e., continuous) vs. qualitative (i.e., discrete "level") assessments may differentially shape our understanding of the nature and magnitude of patterns of association between socioeconomic disadvantage and adjustment. In most prior work, indices of socioeconomic status typically have been represented through interval scales or continua. An implicit assumption of this approach is that there is an equivalent level of "distance" between each pair of adjacent scale points on the indices of socioeconomic status employed. As a result, qualitative and/or unequal differences in the adaptive implications among various status levels, which may be important for understanding linkages between socioeconomic disadvantage and adjustment, have largely been ignored in this work. Illustratively, on some indices of socioeconomic status the "distance" or number of scale points separating a "middle-class" background and an upper-class one is roughly equal to the distance between the former and a highly impoverished one (see, e.g., Hollingshead's (1975) nine-point scale Occupational Status Scale). Although in some ways this may be true, in others, such as their association with increased exposure to risk-related stressors, there may be a far greater "distance" between poverty and middle class than between the upper two points of the scale.

Felner et al. (1995) conducted one of the most extensive studies both sought to attend to the above issues and that investigated all three aspects of the proposed mediated pathway simultaneously, for example, household disadvantage, proximal environmental conditions, and child and adolescent adjustment. Among youth whose families were relatively economically or socially disadvantaged, those who were from homes in which adults were employed in low-income, unskilled occupations were found to have lower levels of school performance and achievement compared to those from homes in which adults were employed in semiskilled or skilled/professional occupations. Further, youth from families in which neither parent had graduated from high school exhibited significantly poorer socioemotional and academic adjustment than did those whose parents had higher educational levels, independent of family income levels. Youth who lived in relatively more disadvantaged homes also reported more negative experiences of proximal environmental conditions relating to family and school contexts and greater exposure to stressful life events. Most critically for a perspective that an ecological–mediational perspective is important for understanding patterns of linkage between socioeconomic disadvantage and levels of adjustment were the findings that proximal environmental experiences were significant predictors of adolescent adjustment, independent of their shared variance with conditions of household disadvantage, whereas conditions of disadvantage in several instances were no longer related significantly to indices of adjustment once their association with proximal environmental conditions was taken into account.

One of the more intriguing aspects of their findings was that economic and educational forms of disadvantage had somewhat differential patterns of association with indices of adjustment and proximal environmental experiences.

Youth from families where there was more serious economic hardship experienced more problematic parenting, felt less connected to school, and had greater exposure to other major stressful events—themselves repeatedly documented as relating to developmental negative outcomes (Mrazek & Haggarty, 1994; Vazsonyi, Pickering, & Bolland, 2006). But, a marker of family disadvantage that is combined with occupational status to create an aggregate indicator of socioeconomic status—parental education—had a notably different and more pervasive pattern of association with the proximal risk experiences of youth. Students from homes in which neither parent had graduated from high school experienced more "across the board" developmentally negative experiences, including higher levels of rejection from parents, less social support and emphasis on intellectual–cultural issues in their families, more negative feelings about school, and heightened levels of exposure to both major and relatively minor stressors.

These findings suggest that levels of parental education may be related to relatively greater or lesser levels of resilience among students, as well as to other developmental conditions that, even for children and youth who are not experiencing economic hardship, have been linked to resilience and/or disorder.

Collectively, the studies discussed earlier provide support for view that the effects of household disadvantage on socioemotional adaptation are mediated by the developing child's experiences at school, in the neighborhood, and in the other primary developmental contexts that define their life space. It seems clear that at least part of the impact that conditions of social and economic disadvantage have on developmental outcomes is accounted for by the ways in which these larger, more distal conditions, shape the more proximal environmental experiences of individuals. They suggest that, as we move toward attempting to build and enhance resilience among youth in poverty, the approach must address the multiple ecologically mediated pathways linking conditions of family occupational and educational disadvantage to poorer child and adolescent adjustment.

A Transactional–Ecological Frame for Understanding and Building Resilience About Children and Youth Experiencing Poverty and Disadvantage

Given the above understandings what is now required is a broader, systemic framework for understanding and predicting the differential emergence of resilience among children and youth from households and backgrounds characterized by poverty and disadvantage, as well as for guiding actions that may be useful for making significant gains in the face of conditions of risk that are so widespread.

A Transactional–Ecological perspective is best suited for explicating pathways to disorder that are congruent with tasks of understanding and building strengths and resilient outcomes for in children and adolescents in poverty (Felner & Felner, 1989; Felner et al., 2000; Lorion, Price, & Eaton, 1989; Sameroff & Fiese, 1989; Seidman, 1987). If the impact of poverty is mediated through the conditions that define the contexts and transactions that children and youth experience, and with which they must cope, then a framework that enables us to consider both the relationships between individuals and those environments, and the ways in which those environments and their experience may interact with each other, across contexts, is required. Research on developmental psychopathology and preventive interventions suggests that the principles of "healthy or normal" development central for understanding the emergence of disorder as well as resistance to disorder and dysfunction (Felner et al., 2000; Mash & Dozois, 2003; Sroufe & Rutter, 1984). Here, the focus is on understanding normal developmental trajectories as they are shaped by the interactions between the individual and the primary contexts in which they grow, as well as understanding the ways that contextual conditions may "bend" those pathways to build competencies or increase vulnerability.

Applying this developmental view to the issue of resilience among those in poverty we can identify a critical set of tasks that must be addressed if these understandings are to be useful for guiding action. These tasks are:

1. Assessment of the ways in which poverty is associated with disruption in normal developmental processes and contexts.
2. Identification of the ways that poverty and its correlates shape and impact the nature of disruptions and distortions in developmental processes.
3. Design and implementation of policies and interventions whose goals are to modify and "correct" these disrupted processes until they closely approximate those that lead to healthy, resilient, developmental outcomes.

Hence, this developmentally based approach starts by identifying those processes and contextual conditions that relate to "healthy" forms of the outcomes of concern (e.g., academic success instead of academic failure) even in the face of other challenges (e.g., economic hardship). They then consider the ways in which the proximal conditions experienced by those in poverty are different from those that would be desirable. Resilience building strategies are then aimed at closing this "gap" in the desired direction. Critically when thinking about what makes for "resilience," problematic outcomes are now seen as predictable and even "normal" results of the deviations in developmental conditions since the mechanisms and processes that lead to problematic developmental outcomes are the same as those that lead to positive ones. It is only the levels and forms of these processes that differ when problematic outcomes emerge. Thus, a guiding assumption of a developmentally based model is that any "healthy" child, youth, or adult, if exposed to the problematic developmental process of concern, is likely to show the similar problematic outcomes. Conversely, actions to attain resilient outcomes require that the disruptions in the proximal contexts of children and youth that have resulted from economic hardship be addressed.

Adopting this broad "developmental" approach is an important first step. But clearly such a broad developmental perspective does not possess sufficient specificity concerning the conditions and processes that shape "resilience" and the emergence of one specific set of outcomes over another. To attain such specificity we need greater precision and agreement in our definitions of the central concepts that mark potential points for intervention in developmental pathways to resilience or disorder. Of particular concern are the ways in which we define risk, vulnerability, resilience itself, protective conditions, and onset, as the failure to draw clear distinctions among these concepts may lead to ambiguity and confusions that hamper the systematic accumulation of a body of knowledge for guiding our understanding of "why some kids do well when they shouldn't" or, more scientifically, for reducing the marginal probability of the emergence of disorder in the fact of serious economic hardship and disadvantage.

Understanding Developmental Pathways to Resilience: Disentangling Vulnerability, Risk, Protective Factors, and Onset of Disorder or Maintaining Positive Developmental Trajectories

As is discussed elsewhere in this volume, most perspectives on disorder or health start with a fundamental "diathesis-stress" perspective. This model holds that individuals may have either genetically based or otherwise *acquired* vulnerabilities to the onset of disorder. These vulnerabilities are the diathesis side of the equation. They "set" the person's threshold of susceptibility to environmental conditions (e.g., stress; disadvantage) or hazards (e.g., high levels of contextual disorganization, restrictive opportunity structures, sharp changes in developmental demands; other forms of danger) that may precipitate the onset of disorder.

What is important to understand is that, although often misused and misapplied, the concept of *risk* is defined epidemiologically (Felner et al., 2000). It is "a conditional statement about the probability that any member of a given population or subpopulation will develop later disorder. Often overlooked in discussions of risk is that the designation of being a member of an 'at risk' group says little about any specific member of that group other than that they have been exposed to the condition(s) of risk under consideration. If the conditional probabilities of disorder in a population are 'X,' it is not that all members of that group posses 'X' levels of predisposition or 'riskness' for disorder." ...A risk designation is no more than an actuarial statement about the members of a selected group (Felner et al.). As discussed, there is perhaps no more widespread and pervasive set of conditions of risk to which children and youth are exposed than poverty and disadvantage. Efforts to build resilience have, as one implicit, if not explicit goal, a focus on addressing the probabilistic ways in which conditions of risk (poverty and its correlates) disrupt developmental processes in the lives of all children and youth in a cohort.

What is also important to understand in this discussion is that it now makes the widespread view that children or youth in poverty are "high risk" is completely inappropriate. They have clearly been potentially exposed to relatively greater levels of conditions of risk, and they may also be seen to be a *population* "at risk." But they are not "high-risk" individuals. Unfortunately, the term "risk" has been frequently applied to imply that all individuals in a "high-risk" group are somehow more fragile or *vulnerable* than all of those in lower risk groups. This is simply not the case. Indeed, from a resilience perspective, depending on other developmental attributes individuals may have acquired (see below) or proximal environmental conditions in their homes or schools, on an individual basis they may be far less likely—and therefore less at risk—than certain specific youth not in poverty.

This conceptual slippage stems, at least in part from the practice of individual-level variables, especially when aggregated for a population or group, being spoken about as risk markers (c.f. Catalano, Haggerty, Hawkins, & Elgin, 2011; Hawkins, Catalano, & Miller, 1992; Mrazek & Haggarty, 1994). For example, children who are shy, who show signs of behavioral problems in the classroom, or who have reading/learning problems are often designated "at risk." So, as a first step to differentiating among critical elements of pathways to resilience for children/youth in poverty it is important to avoid this terminology creep and be clear that actuarial statements cannot be made about particular individuals.

As we move to understanding risk for those exposed to poverty and disadvantage there are several corollaries of our definition of risk that are important. First, conditions of risk are primarily environmental in nature—disadvantage and poverty, as well as proximal disruptions in developmental contexts clearly fall into this category. This is not to say that being part of a population group that may have some genetic risk characteristics would also qualify, so long as we remember we are talking about a population-level attribute.

Second, and critically for understanding the nature and emergence of resilience for children and youth in poverty—such environmental conditions can have two quite distinct roles—as predisposing conditions and as precipitating/compensatory conditions. When environmental conditions act in a predisposing (or risk enhancing) fashion, vulnerabilities, which in our definition are always person-level variables, are acquired. This acquisition may result either from problematic interactions with environmental conditions that are present or the lack of exposure to important developmentally promoting conditions and resources. For example, poor early parent–child interactions may lead to the development of vulnerabilities and delays in a number of areas of child functioning.

Strengths and personal competencies may also be acquired from positive, more proximal and primary developmental contexts and are again person-level variables. In keeping with the mediational model discussed earlier, one way of enhancing resilience then is by supporting or enhancing the ability of proximal conditions (family patterns, opportunity-to-learn conditions in schools) to withstand the frequent negative impacts that may result from a lack of economic resources and the stresses or paucity of resources that may accompany such economic hardships. Failure to accurately understand that these person-level characteristics are, in fact, "first-order" developmental outcomes (i.e., acquired vulnerabilities and competencies/strengths) has, in the past, led to their being incorrectly labeled as individual-level *risk conditions or as early signs of "onset" of specific disorders.*

The levels of acquired competencies, strengths, and vulnerabilities all influence the probability that an individual will be resilient in the face of the experience of the more problematic contextual or conditions of risk that frequently defines the developmental conditions that surround children and youth whose families lack in economic resources. But, as we have seen, they are not markers of individual risk nor are they typically direct and inevitable markers of the onset of disorder. We must pause here to also note that to talk about building resiliencies in individuals also muddies these concepts. *Resilience, in a population level framework*, is an *outcome*, defined by a person or population's response to challenge and stress. Discussions of building "resiliencies" lose this essential defining element and obscure important differences between such outcomes and aspects of developmental pathways that produce them. What is "built" or acquired are strengths, vulnerabilities are acquired or avoided, and environmental resources and stressors interact with those in very specific ways so that even should a vulnerability be acquired, without exposure to triggering conditions, no difficulties may emerge. In this instance, resilience simply results from the child avoiding exposure to certain developmental demands, even though heightened vulnerability levels have been acquired. Indeed, put this way, primary development contexts that are resistant to being disrupted by poverty may themselves be resilient, that is, have or maintain positive developmental functioning in the face of serious risk and challenge.

Let us explore these issues a bit further. Environmental circumstances are now seen as potentially acting as precipitating or protective conditions, rather than simply predisposing ones. They can interact with *existing*, previously acquired, vulnerabilities and competencies to trigger the onset of more serious dysfunction. Similarly, protective conditions in proximal environments and developmental contexts may act in a compensatory fashion, reducing the likelihood that existing vulnerabilities will be "activated" when the child experiences conditions of risk.

Implicit in this view of unfolding pathways to disorder is that exposure to conditions of risk or the acquisition of vulnerabilities does not inevitably lead to the onset of disorder (see Fig. 7.1). Neither does exposure to protective factors nor the acquisition of competencies always result in health and resilience. Rather, these are the sequential, dynamically interactive elements of developmental trajectories to dysfunction and well-being (Felner et al., 2000). And it is these elements of the developmental trajectory that are the appropriate direct targets for change for efforts that seek to enhance resilience and prevent disorder. Framed this way, resilience enhancement efforts for children and youth whose lives are characterized by poverty and disadvantage should include focused strategies that (1) seek to reduce levels of conditions of risk or increase levels of protective factors; (2) directly, or indirectly through the previous step, reduce the incidence rates of person-level vulnerabilities or the enhancement of personal competencies and strengths; and (3) alter levels of conditions of risk and of protective factors that have been shown to interact with acquired vulnerabilities and strengths to trigger the onset of more serious disorder or to produce resilience in the face of serious challenge.

This conceptualization of developmental pathways has direct implications for the evaluation of resilience-focused initiatives. The initial assessments of the efficacy of such efforts may take place far sooner than is often thought to be possible. Illustratively, for some efforts that seek to enhance the resilience of children as the move through life it may be a number of years before the primary conditions and disorders we seek to impact are likely to develop. A perspective based on the above understandings of developmental pathways makes it far more possible to obtain relatively rapid assessments of the degree to which the program or policies, and their effects are "on course" and are likely to have the desired long-term effects. This can be done by assessing the degree to which the initiative has produced changes in the desired directions in key conditions that are earlier in the developmental pathway, even when they are far distant from the time when we might expect the onset of dysfunction. They also help us to better understand the levels of change and program required to obtain the desired effects.

For example, our first assessments of program impact would focus on the degree to which levels of risk have been reduced and levels of enhancing conditions increased. Next, we would assess the degree to which the incidence and prevalence of vulnerabilities and competencies in the population have been changed. Finally, as population members experience identifiable conditions that have been shown to have a high likelihood to act as precipitants (e.g., school transitions; being approached by gangs) and/or moves through developmental periods when maximum onsets are expected, we would examine differential rates of the occurrence of adaptive difficulties in order to assess the levels of resilience obtained. But, it is also the case that when we have clearly identified increased levels of strengths/reductions of vulnerabilities (e.g., marked increases in the reading skills and levels of children in poverty and reductions in "equity gaps") we would have clear evidence for the probability of having enhanced resilience in the population group (those in poverty) across the life span.

Mediating Conditions

Let us now revisit the issue of mediating conditions and mediated pathways as they fit within the current framework, so that we may link this perspective back to the initial studies we presented. Mediating conditions can now be seen to be a subset of the conditions of risk we have discussed earlier. They are those proximal

Risk/Protective Factors

Acquired Vulnerability/ Strengths and Competencies

Resilience/Disorder

Fig. 7.1 Felner risk/protective factors acquired vulnerability/strength and competencies resilience/disorder

circumstances in the child's developmental contexts that most directly shape daily experiences. For example, when children experience "poverty" it is, as we have seen, the associated changes in the conditions of the child's life that are actually responsible for the impacts that have been observed. For example, within families, poverty and economic scarcity are often associated with negative changes in parenting patterns, parental depression, and intra-parental conflict—conditions that have, themselves, been found to be frequently associated with multiple, comorbid, and complex patterns of developmental difficulties. From this perspective, poverty, disadvantage, and their correlates are seen as markers of the potentially higher levels of these more proximal changes and mediating conditions in the person's developmental context (Evans, Eckenrode, & Marcynszyn, 2010; Felner et al., 1983). In the model we have proposed in the current chapter, the direct focus of resilience building interventions would be on reducing the levels of these negative mediators (conditions of risk) as experienced by the entire population.

Implications for the Nature and Targeting of Resilience Enhancement-Focused Programming and Policies

Let us now consider the implications of the above framework to the targeting and appropriate shape of programmatic efforts that seek to enhance resilience among those children and youth who live in poverty. The first implications are that an approach that is based on individual screenings is neither advisable nor required to as we seek to identify appropriate target populations for resilience enhancing efforts. Instead, we can employ epidemiological data to focus accurately on entire populations whose members have a high probability of both experiencing the critical mediators and for identifying the specific vulnerabilities and strengths that may be the appropriate first-order outcomes on which the programmatic efforts should focus to enhance resilience in that population.

To this point we have built an argument that, as Lamb (1992) has noted, poverty is an economic and not a psychological variable. Its implication for developmental outcomes lies in its association with the ways these economic conditions relate to altered societal, community, material, and psychological conditions of risk that mediates or translate the economic conditions to direct daily experiences (Felner, 1992, 2000). Based on epidemiological data we can predict, with a high degree of certainty that children in economically distressed neighborhoods (here the neighborhood variable further defines the nature of the poverty and disadvantage with which the efforts will be concerned) will be exposed to substandard schooling, high levels of environmental stresses, a paucity of local conditions that lead to high expectations and aspirations, and literally dozens of other negative mediators (Mrug & Windle, 2009; Wilson, 1987).

Efforts that address these and other risk or developmentally promoting conditions, for all children living in such neighborhoods, will be far more cost effective and efficient in reaching our target group than would screening-based efforts that seek to target only some children and families (Felner, 1992, 2000; Felner et al., 2000). Illustratively, to screen all of the children in just one public housing community in a city like Chicago for the presence of conditions that may mediate the development of problem social and emotional outcomes would be incredibly costly. It would almost certainly require all of the funds that are available for conducting the intervention. Instead, interventions that target mediators that have a high probability of being of concern for the entire population would be far more cost effective and reduce the marginal probabilities of disorder across the population group while building important strengths that further facilitate the ability to deal with the range of challenges that stem from economic and neighborhood disadvantage. For example, the intervention might be provided to all children and families strong preschool programs, high quality educational environments, efforts to enhance the safety of the neighborhoods, and/or the modification removal of policies that create disincentives for family success, or that create barriers to access to quality employment opportunities. Put otherwise, more 2 decades ago, Zigler (1990) succinctly summarized the prospects and problems of early intervention programs and underscored the importance of efforts that target entire contexts by noting, "No amount of counseling, early childhood curricula, or home visits will ever take the place of jobs that provide decent incomes, affordable housing, appropriate health care, optimal family configurations, or integrated neighborhoods where children encounter positive role models" (p. xiii). For example, the New Hope intervention program which provided wage supplements, work supports, and child-care and health insurance subsidies to a low income working adults has been shown to affect children directly, boys in particular in this case, by increasing parents sense of control and confidence in their ability to protect their children, and by reducing their stress levels and use of discipline (Epps & Hutson, 2007).

Summary

In the model we have proposed thus far, the first-order, direct, or "immediate" targets of change in resilience enhancement efforts will typically be nonindividual level elements of developmental trajectories to adaptation and disorder. Strategies will focus on direct efforts to increase or decrease, as appropriate, the levels of conditions of risk, protective factors, and developmentally enhancing experiences to which a population is exposed. Changes in levels of these first-order elements of the developmental pathways of populations will, in turn, radiate to impact the degree to which second-order changes are accomplished. These second-order elements of developmental pathways should show changes, in desired directions, relatively soon after attainment of the first-order changes. These "early intermediate outcomes" provide preliminary evidence that the strategy is on course for being effective in achieving its long-term goals. Second-order targets of change in developmental pathways include levels of acquired vulnerabilities as well as strengths and competencies that may be required to attain

resilient outcomes. Interventions will thus involve systematic actions aimed at modifying the reciprocal and interactive influences of conditions of risk, strengths, vulnerabilities, and resources, in shaping trajectories to the developmental outcomes of concern (c.f. Fig. 7.1).

Given these understandings about those aspects of developmental pathways that are the direct and indirect, intermediate, targets of change, we turn to the question of "what are the appropriate long-term goals of resilience building interventions?" The answer we select for this question is critical as it defines those specific conditions earlier in developmental pathways with which we will be concerned. It is to these concerns that we now turn.

Targeting Resilience Enhancing Efforts for Children and Youth in Poverty: Issues of Outcome Specificity and Pathways to Disorder Outcome Specificity

Elsewhere in this volume several authors raise the questions and issues of the appropriate level of the specificity of the "targeting" of developmental difficulties. Some of the approaches in those chapters have focused on broad approaches to the enhancement of resilience, while others have discussed more focused concerns, such as issues of resilience as they relate to delinquency, depression, self-control, and learning disabilities. In considering the question of what are the appropriate goals of resilience efforts for children and youth in poverty, we now turn to the issue of whether programmatic efforts should have as their goal(s) the reduction of highly specific disorders or whether, at least when the issue of poverty serves as the focal condition of risk, our efforts should be focused on broad-based and multiple outcomes.

Historically, a major dimension on which most efforts to enhance resilience and resistance to risk, or prevent disorder, reflects two quite different assumptions about the specificity and uniqueness of developmental pathways. Single outcome focused programs, such as those targeted to substance abuse, delinquency, school failure, depression, teen suicide, and teen pregnancy reflect *a specific disease/disorder pathway* model that rests heavily on classic medical paradigms of disorder. These paradigms hold that dysfunction is caused by specifiable deficits, disease agents, or predispositions that interact with individual vulnerabilities that can also be specified.

A contrasting perspective to this position is one that holds that there is a need for a *comprehensive, multicausal and nonspecific developmental pathways/root causes* focused approach (c.f. Felner & Felner, 1989; Mrazek & Haggarty, 1994). This model recognizes that (1) most of the disorders we seek to prevent have a large number of common risk factors; (2) that conditions that protect against one disorder generally also protect against many others; and (3) that there are nonspecific personal vulnerabilities that increase a person's susceptibility to the onset of a wide array of dysfunction. The pathways to most of the social, emotional, and adaptive difficulties with which we are concerned are generally complex and shared by more than one disorder. Hence, for a wide range of developmental outcomes and sociopathologies it appears that efforts to identify specific and unique etiological "causal" agents are not appropriate.

For children and youth in poverty, given the wide array of different elements of the developmental pathway that poverty may impact, and that the condition of risk here is *entirely outside the control of individual*, comprehensive, broadly targeted approaches are clearly the most appropriate. Further, recent research from a number of converging research traditions shows the potential efficacy of such an approach to a population that has heightened probability of the onset of a broad array of disorder and dysfunction, that is so large, and that has such a broad set of potential disruptions in the proximal, mediating contexts that define the developmental experiences of the focal population. Studies of the adaptive impact of a wide array of developmental circumstances have shown that there are common developmental antecedents, such as family resources and interaction patterns, economic and social deprivation, other life stresses, powerlessness,

and an array of nonspecific protective resiliency factors (e.g., social support, sense of self-efficacy, hope) that all relate to the probability that persons in a population will develop an extraordinary assortment of mental and physical disorders (Allen & Mitchell, 1998; Mrazek & Haggarty, 1994; O'Connell, Boat, & Warner, 2009; Sameroff & Fiese, 1989; Silverman, 1989). Converging with this developmental evidence, the data on the epidemiology of serious disorders (Allen & Mitchell, 1998; Mrazek & Haggarty, 1994; O'Connell et al., 2009) have also pointed to the high levels of comorbidity among these more severe instances and further underscored the fact that they appear to share a common constellation of antecedent developmental experiences and root causes in their emergent pathways.

The nonlinear and overlapping nature of pathways to disorder, particularly among those who may be exposed to a wide array of developmental circumstances that are problematic such as those in poverty, is further underscored by a third set of studies on the stability of the developmental course of such difficulties (Cantwell & Baker, 1989). Summarizing the early findings pertaining to high levels of comorbidity of disorder, Rutter (1989) concluded, "Perhaps the most striking finding to emerge from all developmental epidemiological studies … has been the extremely high levels of comorbidity" (p.645). These findings have only been reinforced in subsequent years, including major studies by such groups as the Institute of Medicine (Mrazek & Haggarty, 1994; O'Connell et al., 2009). Similarly, in discussing commonalities across root causes and the need to consider broadly focused prevention approaches rather than that focus on specific outcomes, Sameroff and Fiese (1989) state that, "Whereas clear linkages have been found between some 'germs' and specific biological disorders, this has not been true for behavioral disorders…." (p.24). Less technically, but more succinctly, Lisbeth Schorr (1988) has, as noted, summarized the interconnectedness among social problems by noting that "Rotten outcomes cluster," and that children from high-risk environments [such as severe, pervasive, and/or dense poverty neighborhoods] encounter developmental experiences that are so severe as to increase the rates of morbidity they will develop across the full spectrum of human social, emotional, and health problems.

To this point we have emphasized in our discussions sets of interrelated but still discreet issues and understandings that need to be woven together for a more complete conceptual framework to guide the enhancement of resilience in the face of the multiple risks and challenge confronted by children and you in poverty. We now turn to a brief discussion of the application to this task of an integrative theoretical framework that we have proposed for this purpose (Felner et al., 2000) that allows us to accomplish this weaving. It is to a presentation of that framework we turn next.

Transactional–Ecological Models for Prevention

The *Transactional–Ecological* model is a framework that Felner and his colleagues (Felner et al., 2001; Felner & Felner, 1989; Felner, Silverman, & Adan, 1992; Felner, Silverman, & Adix, 1991) have both refined and demonstrated its utility for guiding interventions and policy, over the past several decades, particularly as it applies to prevention, promotion, and resilience enhancement. Other authors have also made important contributions to the model (c.f., Seidman, 1987, 1990). Felner (2000) has argued that the framework contains critical features for guiding strategies that have the necessary levels of comprehensiveness to address the range of issues raised earlier, while also providing for the degree of specificity required for interventions that meet the test of intentionality (Cowen, 2000).

This Transactional–Ecological (*T–E*) model obtains from a conceptual synthesis of two other highly complementary frameworks, the transactional (c.f. Sameroff & Fiese, 1989) and ecological (c.f. Bronfennbrenner, 1979) models of development. Full discussion of each of these approaches is beyond the parameters of this chapter. But let us attempt to capture the key features of each for the issues of concern here.

The Transactional Model has been articulated by Sameroff and Chandler (1975) and Sameroff and Fiese (1989) as a guide for efforts to enhance the developmental outcomes of children and youth preventive efforts. The model emphasizes the dynamic, reciprocal interactions between the individual and their context, with bidirectional influence being a fundamental element (Sarason & Doris, 1979). For example, the interactions between an infant and their parent, or between a youth and her peers, are thought to be a result of the child's influence on the parent or group, and the reciprocal effect of the environmental influence on the child.

A transactional perspective has, as its focal targets for change, key developmental processes that lead to strengths or disorder. But it is not sufficient for addressing the full range of conditions that must be considered by interventions when the concern is the developmental course of children and youth living in poverty. The transactional model is still, at best, dyadic. It can only deal with those proximal environments in which the person directly participates—and many of the contexts that impact the life of children in poverty, and others, extend well beyond their direct experience. Further, since the transactional model always views the sources of influence as bidirectional (Sarason & Doris, 1979), there are some proximal contexts on which individual behavior has little influence (e.g., schools) for which it is not well suited for providing directions for intervention. To address these limitations and provide for a comprehensive model of prevention, the author of this chapter and his colleagues as well as others (Felner et al., 1992, 2000, 2001; Felner & Felner, 1989; Seidman, 1987, 1990) have advocated for the joining of an ecological model of development (Barker, 1968; Bronfennbrenner, 1979; Lewin, 1951) to the transactional one.

Combining the ecological and transactional perspectives to create a *Transactional–Ecological* (*T–E*) model broadens the focus of each in important ways. Consistent with transactional perspectives, an ecological view holds that developmental trajectories are shaped by, "Progressive, mutual accommodation between an active, growing human being and the changing properties of the settings in which the developing person lives" (Bronfennbrenner, 1979, p.21). The ecological framework also provides for the consideration of additional elements of human contexts. It offers a comprehensive and integrative means of *viewing the interactions between the various parts of total ecological and psychological systems*, not just between individuals and their proximal environments. In particular, this perspective allows for the consideration of influences that shape the dynamic relationships between systems and the ways in which being part of these multiple systems influence human development. Given the breadth of the impact of poverty, typically both on all or most of the systems in which the child may participate directly and on those in which their parents/primary caregivers function, a perspective that considers the reciprocal influences of proximal systems across both the individuals who inhabit them and on each other is critical to fully appreciating the challenges and outcomes that are confronted by youth in poverty and in these systems.

There are at least three important ways in which the synthesis of ecological and transactional models enables us to address these concerns. First, it enables us to consider the etiological significance of conditions with which the child comes into direct contact, but on which their behavior does not have a significant bidirectional influence. Included in this category of conditions are such "social structural conditions" as the density and distribution of poverty and social disadvantage (Iceland, 2006; Jencks & Perterson, 1991; Schorr, 1988; Wilson, 1987), shifting economic conditions that influence both the prognosis of poverty and motivation (Halperin, 1998; Judy & D'Amico, 1997; W.T. Grant Foundation, 1988) and the regularities or structures of such primary developmental contexts as schools (Sarason, 1982, 1996).

Of particular interest for the current chapter is that this level allows us to consider those system-wide conditions that distort, in pathogenic ways, all of the dyadic transactions that take place within their reach. Clearly poverty, particularly when dense and persistent, is one of those systemwide conditions with such pervasive

impact. These conditions may occur at several different system levels. The smallest system level of this type is what have been termed *microsystems* (Bronfennbrenner, 1979) or immediate settings-level contexts. These systems are the primary developmental contexts in which people live. They include such contexts as schools, religious congregations, the family, the worksite, and peer groups. The regularities of these settings may be only influenced slowly, if at all, by the dyadic interactions that take place within them. For example, the overwhelming flux and disorganization that accompanies the transition to a high school "fed" by multiple middle schools is a condition that may seriously disrupt many of the dyadic patterns that are taking place within the school and peer groups (De Wit, Karioja, & Rye, 2010; Felner & Adan, 1988; Felner, Ginter, & Primavera, 1982). Similarly, the social regularities of a school or workplace, its resource patterns, and other formal system regularities may go far to shape the nature of the interpersonal interactions that take place within it (Sarason, 1982, 1996). But, in neither case will the dyadic interactions rapidly nor necessarily impact the system regularities that are shaping them.

At the level of *macrosystems* (*i.e., social structural conditions and regularities*)(Bronfennbrenner, 1979), the individual's behavior often has little effect. But, with more proximal settings (microsystems), these conditions have significant adaptive implications for individual behavior, both directly and through their impact on the other system relationships that a person experiences. For example, when considering the definition of a resilient outcome for those in poverty it is important to understand that shifts in macrosystemic conditions have both "raised the bar" both about what is expected, and shifted the value of what was, in the past, a motivating goal with clear rewards associated with it. Illustratively, due to societal changes the earning potential of a high school graduate has dropped more than 40% in the decades between 1970 and 1990 and has continued to decline (Halperin, 1998; Judy & D'Amico, 1997; National Academy of Science, 2010; W.T. Grant Foundation, 1988). This is a structural condition over which the individual has little control. But this shift may have profound effects both on the nature of those behaviors students view as adaptive. When this condition is coupled, for example, with others that indicate to youth that they have little hope for attending college—even if they complete high school—this fundamental shift in the economic meaning of graduation may make alternative, societally undesirable behaviors, such as early school leaving, early parenthood, and/or involvement in illicit activities to earn money, appear to be intelligent and attractive choices.

A second enhancement for efforts to understand and promote resilience in children and adolescents that derives from joining ecological views to transactional ones is that this synthesis allows for consideration of the ways in which interactions between individuals and any specific setting are influenced by differences and similarities between that setting and others that make up their life context (i.e., it allows for consideration of cross-contextual effects). Such relationships between microsystems have been labeled *mesosystems* (Bronfennbrenner, 1979). The need to consider transcontextual influences rests on the understanding that persons have a number of primary settings which comprise the *ecological map* of their life context. Each of these settings has unique demands that shape the nature of the transactions required by them. The solutions, skills, and abilities required by one context may, when applied in other settings, be complimentary, antagonistic, and/or irrelevant. Illustratively, for students in poverty, the skills and interaction styles required to be adaptive in an inner-city environment where safety may be an issue, when applied to a school setting, be maladaptive or irrelevant. Such conditions may result in children from inner-city environments being mislabeled as lacking in social competence or other abilities when, in fact, the actual problem is not that these children are deficient; rather, there is a poor match in the skills required among the different developmental contexts that make up their lives. For children and adolescents, who often have little ability to impact or select the primary settings that define their lives, understanding the dynamics among those settings as they act reciprocally to shape both adaptation of

individuals and each other is perhaps even more important than it is for adults, who may at least more easily "opt out" of settings that are poor matches for the other in their lives.

These mesosystemic relationships also add to our understanding of pathways to resilience and efforts to enhance it. They bring attention to conditions that surround resilience promoting efforts that may play a limiting role in the impact of such efforts and, if not adequately considered, may lead to false conclusions that a program effort, or the building of a particular set of skills that is relevant to resilience is ineffective when, in fact, it is a necessary but not a sufficient element of a more complete resilience development strategy.

There are a number of instances where this may occur. Illustratively, the impact of a resilience-focused emotional and social/behavioral problem-solving skill building curriculum will certainly be attenuated if the school context in which it takes place does not also provide adequate academic experiences to enable the students to develop necessary skills in these critical academic areas. Even with the best decision-making skills, and the motivation to make prosocial decisions, outcomes will be limited if the student is unable to read. Likewise, parent training programs for parents who have few economic resources may enable parents to gain important knowledge and skills, but, the degree to which they apply this new knowledge in their interactions with children may be influenced by conditions in other systems in their lives. If they are experiencing severe stress from economic hardship, or concerned over the adequacy and safety of the school, they may not be as likely to use those new skills at the requisite levels of quality and intensity. As the most highly trained developmental psychologists can tell you, when it has been a "bad day" outside the home, the quality of their parenting may be sharply diminished. Such "bad days" are, unfortunately, the stark day-to-day reality for parents with few economic resources, those in negative job surroundings, those in poverty, and other groups with chronic stressors. These conditions will all certainly reduce the degree to which newly acquired parenting skills are translated to action. Thus, an ecological analysis of the interrelated systems of the lives of those we seek to impact is critical for ensuring that change efforts are adequately comprehensive and that research on them does not lead to the incorrect conclusion that intervention elements which may be necessary, but not sufficient, do not have utility for the building of resilience.

Third, a comprehensive model for understanding the adaptation and resilience of children and youth must provide for consideration of the impact of settings on individuals with which they do not come into direct contact. Again, this is particularly important for children and youth who caregivers, throughout the day, are often parts of systems in which the child does not participate at all but which may shape the transactions of those caregivers with the child (e.g., parental workplaces; social welfare offices; teacher unions). Bronfenbrenner (1979) has referred to these as *exosystems*. Illustratively, a child may never have direct contact with the neighborhoods and conditions in which their parents or grandparents were raised, or with the workplaces of their parents. But traumas suffered in these earlier developmental contexts (Garbarino, 1990), values learned in them (Sarason, 1982), or conditions within the workplaces must all be part of a broader analysis of influences that contribute to the nature of the parent–child interactions that occur. And, of course, for those in children living in poverty, the likelihood that those caring for them are experiencing stressful or even problematic interactions elsewhere in the settings that define their lives is clearly elevated (e.g., high stress levels; high levels of job instability and underemployment; difficult, exhausting work). These setting level regularities would then be directly targeted by introducing systemwide conditions (e.g., on-site, child care centers that promote parent involvement; linking parents to appropriate employment opportunities) that reduce workers' stresses and enhance well-being and family support resources—thereby enhancing the resilience of children and youth in poverty without ever directly engaging them. These changes would also be expected to radiate to the family/microsystem level interactions of all workers in the setting for enhancing the probability or the acquisition of important strengths and reducing the acquisition of vulnerabilities that may have resulted in the case of more problematic family functioning.

To briefly summarize, joining an ecological perspective to a transactional one to create a T–E model expands our focus to include the ways in which person-setting interactions are impacted by relationships between settings, as well as the broader, macrosystemic contexts in which they may be nested. Equal weight is given to understanding dyadic transactions and to the analysis of the impact of and interactions among various settings, mesosystems, and macrosystems that may significantly influence developmental pathways.

There is an important corollary of the above features of the T–E model that makes it particularly useful for providing a more fully contextualized definition of resilience than might otherwise be developed. That is, the T–E model affords us the ability to view the definition of resilience as one that must be considered, and often can only be understood, in context. Some behaviors and outcomes that we would seek to reduce or promote do not require the assumption that there are deficits or defect in the persons/population targeted—a core factor in victim blaming and disorder-focused approaches to interventions. The T–E framework allows us to consider the ways in which the target "disorders" may, in fact, be *adaptive solutions to contextual conditions that are disordered or at least incongruent with broader societal expectations and demand*. Hence, an important understanding here is that acquired strengths that might enable a child to be resilient in a dysfunctional or problematic context—for example, where peer values and rewards may be at odds with those of the broader society requirements—may well be, in those other contexts (those same strengths are) vulnerabilities that lead to a lack of resilience. By utilizing the lens of a T–E perspective, many of the target conditions with which we are concerned can be seen to be the result of highly appropriate and adaptive efforts in disordered or alternative contexts. That is, "what might appear to be deviant outcomes may be those that any healthy child would exhibit in the environments and systems that define their lives … what might have been seen as disorder or disease may be better understood as a result of the child's appropriate, predictable, and highly adaptive attempts to adjust to contexts and conditions that require responses which are incompatible with those in other contexts in which they live." That is, … what might have been seen as a disorder or disease may be better understood as the child's appropriate, predictable, and highly adaptive attempts to adjust to contexts and conditions [that are developmentally inappropriate or disordered] (Felner & Felner, 1989, p. 21).

Applying this view to understanding and defining resilience and children's efforts to adapt in the contexts of poverty, the first, fundamental questions that must be asked are: "In what ways were the conditions and adaptive patterns (e.g., behavior, belief system, etc.) that we wish to modify adaptive at the time they developed?" and, "Are there factors that are associated with poverty or its correlates in the contexts of the child's life that make the interaction patterns, or the lack of them, continue to be adaptive?" *A basic assumption of this model is that any adaptive pattern—however problematic—originated as an attempt to positively adapt to conditions that existed at the time.* Given this assumption, efforts to understand or change any developmental pathway or outcome cannot take place independent of a consideration of the full set of historical, familial, economic, social, and political contexts that provide meaning to a person's life experiences. And, as is clear, for children and youth in poverty, particularly when coupled with racial or ethnic disadvantage, such consideration in the understanding of resilience and its enhancement are essential. Such an approach will allow us to see that many of the behaviors or interaction patterns we may have viewed as "not resilient" actually reflect high levels of resilience as they were simply intelligent, effective attempts at adaptive solutions to disordered contexts.

Illustratively, in the case of families in poverty, until recently social welfare policies often punished recipients for earning income, acquiring savings, and attempting to accumulate equity (Moynihan, 1986). These conditions may have led welfare recipients to behave in ways that society viewed as inappropriate (e.g., not saving; not seeking employment). Instead, the recipients were actually showing intelligent and adaptive problem solutions in the face of disordered contextual demands. To avoid the confusion that places the locus of such difficulties inside the person, particularly when dealing with individuals in communities where dense poverty and a lack of positive employment opportunities are pervasive, we might better refer to these and other positive adaptations to disordered contexts—that are dysfunctional in later or other developmental settings—as "*socio*"*pathology* rather than psychopathology, with the latter's inherent individual focus. This view further sharpens our focus on the characteristics of contexts that systematically distort normal developmental pathways to produce what appears to be a deviant outcome—but which are, in fact, better understood as positive, resilient, and often highly adaptive efforts to dysfunctional contexts when considered in their full ecological–developmental context.

Creating Resilience Enhancing Contexts

As should be clear from our discussion, broad-based, population-level programs are those that hold the most promise for being adequate to the challenge of addressing the levels of need and the forms of adaptive challenges confronted by children and youth in poverty. It is also the case that such resilience developing approaches may be well served by shifting their attention to, or at least making certain to include in their design, strategies and programmatic elements that impact the contexts in which children and youth in poverty grow, even if those contexts never directly engage the children. Indeed, a failure to attend to modifying these contexts, in ways that "naturally" build strengths and help youth avoid the acquisition of vulnerabilities, may limit the efficacy of any efforts that focus more directly on skill building or other individual-level enhancement approaches.

The most promising of these initiatives are those that seek to understand the ways in which elements of the school, community, peer, or home environment may be structured or reorganized to improve their match to the developmental needs and competencies of the populations that inhabit them, as well as to increase the degree of congruence in the developmental demands and expectations across the multiple settings inhabited by children in poverty. Such approaches promise to build resilience in a comprehensive and highly impactful way and to more full reflect the recommendations of the Institute of Medicine that state, "… The ultimate goal to achieve optimal prevention should be to build the principles of prevention into the ordinary activities of everyday life and into community structures to enhance development over the entire life span." Marazk & Haggarty, IOM, pp.298–299, p.323.

To correct this overly narrow view of resilience and its development, particularly if we are to deal with the enormity of the task of dealing with the epidemic levels of disorder and failure associated with poverty, what must be recognized is that legitimate efforts will include a focus on changes in social and educational policies and programming that increases the developmental appropriateness and resources, and reduce the conditions of risk, in all significant human contexts. School and welfare reform and transformation efforts; restructuring of work sites to increase worker participation, satisfaction, access, and productivity; community development efforts to change opportunity structures, safety, sense of community, and resource patterns for families; and family support programs, including and social and recreational "youth development programming" (Carnegie Council on Adolescent Development, 1989; Shinn & Yoshikawa, 2008) are but a few of the domains of initiatives that seek to change the ecology of the peoples' lives and that have, in the past, not been adequately recognized for their potential as core strategies in resilience development.

There are numerous other such efforts that may be targeted to children and families that are more ecologically congruent with the existing regularities and systems of their lives than those of the earlier generations of such efforts. For families in poverty and economically disadvantaged neighborhoods and communities, comprehensive efforts that target changes throughout the context are not only advisable but necessary for almost any more individually focused efforts to be viable. Parents who are concerned about their children cannot and will not go to work or to obtain additional education if it means leaving their children without adequate adult supervision and support in high-risk neighborhoods. Hence, although clearly not typically thought of as enhancing resilience, initiatives that provide child care may act to do so both directly, through their impact on the children who participate, but also indirectly, through the profound effects that such access may have on the lives of the parents of children in poverty. Indeed, it is important to understand that social programs and polices that require parents to go to work or pursue training without providing for high-quality child care are, in fact, asking parents to engage in what may well be chargeable neglect. These are precisely the kinds of problematic policies that may emerge without sufficient attention to the way in which what appear to be dysfunctional behaviors are, in fact, found to be adaptive ones when contextual regularities are considered. Indeed, given the changing nature of society quality child care and afterschool programming that provides both supervision as well as social and educational development aspects may be one of the most powerful setting-level interventions that may be mounted, for all families, under the "flag" of resilience enhancement and the promotion of positive outcomes. Additional family-support programs, such as those that provide homeless families and/or those who are socially and educationally disadvantaged with coordinated and necessary residential stabilization, medical, human service, and food resources also fall into this category.

Concluding Comments

We have presented what we see as a framework that can guide the development of the next generation of efforts to enhance the live outcomes of children and youth in poverty. As such efforts move toward their next generation of efforts, the contributions of those who provide the shoulders on which we stand in gaining our current vision should not be underestimated or underappreciated. Given this perspective and their "boost," we hope that the perspective provided in this chapter further changes our ways of "think about what we are thinking about" in the continued evolution of approaches that seek to ensure that all children have the developmental experiences and circumstances that allow them to grow to fully empowered adults, with all of the choices and opportunities that enable them to live satisfying and successful lives.

References

Abelev, M. S. (2009). Advancing out of poverty: Social class worldview and its relation to resilience. *Journal of Adolescent Research, 24*, 114–141.

Allen, L., & Mitchell, C. (1998). High-risk behaviors in patterns of problematic and adaptive development: An epidemiological perspective. In V. C. McLoyd & L. Steinberg (Eds.), *Studying minority adolescents: Conceptual, methodological, and theoretical issues* (pp. 29–54). Mahwah: Lawrence Erlbaum.

Barker, R. G. (1968). *Ecological psychology: Concepts and methods for studying the environment of human behavior.* Stanford: Stanford University Press.

Bronfennbrenner, U. (1979). *The ecology of human development: Experiments by nature and design.* Cambridge: Harvard University Press.

Cantwell, D. P., & Baker, L. (1989). Stability and natural history of DSM-III childhood diagnoses. *Journal of the American Academy of Child and Adolescent Psychiatry, 28*, 691–700.

Carnegie Council on Adolescent Development. (1989). *Turning points: Preparing America's Youth for the 21st Century.* New York: Carnegie Corporation of New York.

Catalano, R. F., Haggerty, K. P., Hawkins, J. D., & Elgin, J. (2011). Prevention of substance abuse and substance use disorders: Role of risk and protective factors. In Y. Kaminer & K. C. Winters (Eds.), *Clinical manual of adolescent substance abuse treatment* (pp. 25–63). Arlington: American Psychiatric Publishing.

Cicchetti, D., Rappaport, J., Sandler, I., & Wessberg, R. P. (2000). *The promotion of wellness in children and adolescents.* Washington: Child Welfare League of America.

Costello, D. M., Swendsen, J., Rose, J. S., & Dierker, L. C. (2008). Risk and protective factors associated with trajectories of depressed mood from adolescence to early adulthood. *Journal of Consulting and Clinical Psychology, 76*, 173–183.

Cowen, E. L. (2000). Psychological wellness: Some hopes for the future. In D. Cicchetti, J. Rappaport, I. Sandler, & R. P. Weissberg (Eds.), *The promotion of wellness in children and adolescents* (pp. 477–503). Thousand Oaks, CA: Sage.

Deater-Deckard, K., Ivy, L., & Smith, J. (2005). Resilience in gene-environment transactions. In S. Goldstein & R. B. Brooks (Eds.), *Handbook of resilience in children* (pp. 49–63). New York: Kluwer Academic/Plenum.

DeNavas-Walt, C., Proctor, B., & Smith, J. (2008). Income, poverty, and health insurance coverage in the United States: 2007. (Current Population Report. U.S. Census Bureau). Washington, DC Government Printing Office.

De Wit, D. J., Karioja, K., & Rye, B. J. (2010). Student perceptions of diminished teacher and classmate support following the transition to high school: Are they related to declining attendance. *School Effectiveness and School Improvement, 21*, 451–472.

DuBois, D. L., Felner, R. D., Brand, S., Adan, A. M., & Evans, E. G. (1992). A prospective study of life stress, social support, and adaptation in early adolescence. *Child Development, 63*, 542–547.

Epps, S. R., & Hutson, A. C. (2007). Effects of a poverty intervention policy demonstration on parenting and child behavior: A test of the direction of effects. *Social Science Quarterly, 88*, 344–365.

Evans, G. W., Eckenrode, J., & Marcynszyn, L. A. (2010). Chaos and the macrosetting: The role of poverty and socioeconomic status. In G. W. Evans & T. D. Wachs (Eds.), *Chaoes and its influence on children's development: An ecological perspective* (pp. 225–238). Washington: American Psychological Association.

Featherman, D. L., Spenner, K. L., & Tsunematsu, N. (1988). Class and the socialization of children: Constancy, change, or irrelevance? In E. M. Hetherington, R. M. Lemer, & M. Permutter (Eds.), *Child development in life-span perspective* (pp. 67–90). Hillsdale: Lawrence Erlbaum.

Felner, R. D. (2000). Educational reform as ecologically-based prevention and promotion: The project on high performance learning communities. In D. Cicchetti, J. Rappaport, I. Sandler, & R. P. Weissberg (Eds.), *The promotion of wellness in children and adolescents* (pp. 271–307). Washington: CWLA Press.

Felner, R. D., Aber, M. S., Primavera, J., & Cauce, A. M. (1985). Adaptation and vulnerability in high risk adolescents: An examination of environmental mediators. *American Journal of Community Psychology, 75*(4), 365–379.

Felner, R. D., & Adan, A. M. (1988). The school transitional environment project: An ecological intervention and evaluation. In R. H. Price, E. L. Cowen, R. P. Lorion, & J. Ramos-McKay (Eds.), *Fourteen ounces of prevention: A casebook for practitioners* (pp. 111–122). Washington: American Psychological Association.

Felner, R. D., Brand, S., DuBois, D. L., Adan, A. M., Mulhall, P. R., & Evans, E. G. (1995). Socioeconomic disadvantaged, proximal environmental experience, and socioemotional and academic adjustment in early adolescence: Investigation of a mediated effects model. *Child Development, 66,* 774–792.

Felner, R. D., Farber, S. S., & Primavera, J. (1980). Children of divorce, stressful life events and transitions: A framework for preventive efforts. In R. H. Price, R. F. Ketterer, B. C. Bader, & J. Monahan (Eds.), *Prevention in mental health: Research, policy and practice* (pp. 81–108). Beverly Hills: Sage.

Felner, R. D., Farber, S. S., & Primavera, J. (1983). Transitions and stressful life events: A model for primary prevention. In R. D. Felner, L. A. Jason, J. N. Moritsugu, & S. S. Farber (Eds.), *Preventive psychology: Theory, research, and prevention* (pp. 191–215). New York: Pergamon.

Felner, R. D., Favazza, A., Shim, M., Brand, S., Gu, K., & Noonan, N. (2001). Whole school improvement and restructuring as prevention and promotion: Lessons from project STEP to the project on high performance learning communities. *Journal of School Psychology, 39*(2), 177–202.

Felner, R. D., & Felner, T. Y. (1989). Prevention programs in the educational context: A transactional-ecological framework for program models. In L. Bond & B. Compas (Eds.), *Primary prevention in the schools* (pp. 13–49). Beverly Hills: Sage Publications.

Felner, R. D., Felner, T. Y., & Silverman, M. M. (2000). Prevention in mental health and social intervention: Conceptual and methodological issues in the evolution of the science and practice of prevention. In J. Rappaport & E. Seidman (Eds.), *Handbook of community psychology* (pp. 9–42). New York: Kluwer Academic/Plenum.

Felner, R. D., Ginter, M. A., & Primavera, J. (1982). Primary prevention during school transitions: Social support and environmental structure. *American Journal of Community Psychology, 10,* 277–290.

Felner, R. D. (Invited Address) (1992). *An ecological analysis for enhancing the developmental outcomes of children in poverty.* Fifth Annual Conference on Stress and Coping In Childhood and Adolescence, American Psychological Association (Committee on Children and Youth) and the University of Miami, Miami.

Felner, R. D., Silverman, M., & Adan, A. M. (1992). Risk assessment and prevention of youth suicide in educational contexts: A transactional-ecological perspective. In A. Maris, A. Berman, J. Maltsberger, & R. Yufit (Eds.), *Assessment and prediction of suicide* (pp. 420–447). New York: Guilford Press.

Felner, R. D., Silverman, M. M., & Adix, R. S. (1991). Prevention of substance abuse and related disorders in childhood and adolescence: A developmentally-based, comprehensive ecological approach. *Family and Community Health: The Journal of Health Promotion and Maintenance, 14*(3), 1–11.

Flouri, E., Tzavidis, N., & Kallis, C. (2010). Adverse life events, area socioeconomic disadvantage, and psychopathology and resilience in young children: The importance of risk factors' accumulation and protective factors' specificity. *European Child & Adolescent Psychiatry, 19,* 535–546.

Garbarino, J. (1990). The human ecology of early risk. In J. P. Shonkoff & S. J. Meisels (Eds.), *The handbook of early intervention.* New York: Cambridge University Press.

Garmezy, N. (1983). Stressors of childhood. In N. Garmezy & M. Rutter (Eds.), *Stress, coping and development in children* (pp. 43–84). New York: McGraw-Hill.

Halperin, S. (1998). *The forgotten half revisited: American youth and young families, 1988–2008.* Washington: American Youth Policy Forum.

Hawkins, J. D., Catalano, R. F., & Miller, J. Y. (1992). Risk and protective factors for alcohol and other drug problems in adolescence and early adulthood: Implications for substance abuse prevention. *Psychological Bulletin, 112*(1), 64–105.

Hinshaw, S. P., & Lee, S. S. (2003). Conduct and oppositional defiant disorders. In E. J. Mash & R. A. Barkley (Eds.), *Child psychopathology* (2nd ed., pp. 144–198). New York: Guilford Publishing.

Hollingshead, A. A. (1975). *Four-factor index of social status.* Unpublished manuscript. New Haven: Yale University.

Iceland, J. (2006). *Poverty in America: A handbook* (2nd ed.). Berkeley: University of California Press.

Jencks, C., & Perterson, P. E. (1991). *The urban underclass.* Washington: The Brookings Institution.

Judy, R. W., & D'Amico, C. (1997). *Workforce 2020: Work and workers in the 21st century.* Indianapolis: Hudson Institute.

Kozol, J. (1991). *Savage inequalities: Children in America's schools.* New York: Crown.

Lamb, M. (1992). *Developmental issues in addressing poverty.* Fifth Annual Conference on Stress and Coping In Childhood and Adolescence, American Psychological Association (Committee on Children and Youth) and the University of Miami, FL.

Lewin, K. (1951). *Field theory in social science: Selected theoretical papers.* New York: Harper.

Lipina, S. J., & Colombo, J. A. (2009). *Poverty and brain development during childhood: An approach from cognitive psychology and neuroscience.* Washington: American Psychological Association.

Lorion, R. P., Price, R. H., & Eaton, W. W. (1989). The prevention of child and adolescent disorders: From theory to research. In D. Schaffer, I. Phillips, N. B. Enzer, M. M. Silverman, & V. Anthony (Eds.), *Prevention of mental disorders, alcohol and other drug use in children and adolescents: OSAP Prevention Monograph-2* (pp. 55–96). Washington: DHHS Publications No. (ADM) 89-1646.

Mash, E. J., & Dozois, D. J. A. (2003). Child psychopathology: A developmental systems prespective. In E. J. Mash & R. A. Barkley (Eds.), *Child psychopathology* (2nd ed., pp. 3–71). New York: Guilford Publishing.

Masten, A. S., & Sesma, A., Jr. (1999). Risk and resilience among children homeless in Minneapolis. *CURA Reporter, 29,* 1–6.

McLoyd, V. C. (1990). The impact of economic hardship on black families and children: Psychological distress, parenting, and socioemotional development. *Child Development, 61*, 311–346.

McLoyd, V. C. (1998). Changing demographics in the American Population: Implications for research on minority children and adolescents. In V. C. McLoyd & L. Steinberg (Eds.), *Studying minority adolescents: Conceptual, methodological, and theoretical issues* (pp. 3–28). Mahwah: Lawrence Erlbaum.

McLoyd, V. C., Kaplan, R., Purtell, K. M., Bagley, E., Hardaway, C. R., & Smalls, C. (2009). Poverty and socioeconomic disadvantage in adolescence. In R. M. Lerner & L. Steinberg (Eds.), *Handbook of adolescent psychology, Vol 2: Contextual influences on adolescent development* (3rd ed.). Hoboken: Wiley.

Moynihan, D. P. (1986). *Family and nation.* Orlando: Harcourt Brace.

Mrazek, P. J., & Haggarty, R. J. (Eds.). (1994). *Reducing risk for mental disorders: Frontiers for preventive intervention research.* Washington: National Academy Press.

Mrug, S., & Windle, M. (2009). Mediators of neighborhood influences on externalizing behavior in preadolescent children. *Journal of Abnormal Child Psychology, 37*, 265–280.

National Academy of Science (NAS). (2010). *Rising above the gathering storm: Rapidly approaching category 5.* Washington: National Academies Press.

Nolen-Hoeksema, S., Girgus, J. S., & Seligman, M. E. P. (1992). Predictors and consequences of childhood depressive symptoms: A 5-year longitudinal study. *Journal of Abnormal Psychology, 101*, 405–427.

O'Connell, M. E., Boat, T., & Warner, K. E. (Eds.). (2009). *Preventing mental, emotional, and behavioral disorders among young people: Progress and possibilities.* Washington: National Academies Press.

Proctor, B. D., & Dalaker, J. (2003). *U.S. Census Bureau, Current Population Reports, P60-222, Poverty in the United States: 2002. Washington, DC.* Washington: U.S. Government Printing Office.

Rowlison, R. T., & Felner, R. D. (1988). Major life events, hassles and adaptation in adolescence: Confounding in the conceptualization and measurement of life stress and adjustment. *Journal of Personality and Social Psychology, 55*, 432–444.

Rutter, M. (1979). Protective factors in children's responses to stress and disadvantage. In M. Kent & J. Rolf (Eds.), *Primary prevention of psychopathology* (Vol. 3, pp. 49–74). Hanover: University Press of New England.

Rutter, M. (1989). Isle of wight revisited: Twenty-five years of child psychiatric epidemiology. *Journal of the American Academy of Child and Adolescent Psychiatry, 28*, 633–653.

Ruggles. P. (1992). Measuring Poverty. *Focus, 14*, 1–9.

Sameroff, A. J., & Chandler, M. J. (1975). Reproductive risk and the continuum of caretaking casualty. In F. D. Horowitz, M. Hetherington, S. Scarr-Salapatek, & G. Siegal (Eds.), *Review of child development research* (Vol. 4). Chicago: University of Chicago Press.

Sameroff, A. J., & Fiese, B. H. (1989). Conceptual issues in prevention. In D. Schaffer, I. Phillips, N. B. Enzer, M. M. Silverman, & V. Anthony (Eds.), *Prevention of mental disorders alcohol and drug use in children and adolescents: OSAP Prevention other Monograph-2* (pp. 23–54). DHHS Publication No. (ADM) 89-1646. Washington: U.S. Government Printing Office.

Sameroff, A. J., Seifer, R., Barocas, R., Zax, M., & Greenspan, S. (1987). I.Q. scores of 4-year-old children: Social-environmental risk factors. *Pediatrics, 79*(3), 343–350.

Sarason, S. B. (1982). *The culture of the school and the problem of change* (2nd ed.). Boston: Allyn & Bacon.

Sarason, S. B. (1996). *Revisiting the culture of the school and the problem of change.* New York: Teachers College Press.

Sarason, S. B., & Doris, J. (1979). *Educational handicap, public policy, and social history: A broadened perspective on mental retardation.* New York: Free Press.

Schorr, L. B. (1988). *Within our reach: Breaking the cycle of disadvantage.* New York: Doubleday.

Seidman, E. (1987). Toward a framework for primary prevention research. In J. A. Steinberg & M. M. Silverman (Eds.), *Preventing mental disorders: A research perspective* (pp. 2–19). DHHS Pub. No. (ADM) 87-1492. Washington: U.S. Government Printing Office.

Seidman, E. (1990). Pursuing the meaning and utility of social regularities for community psychology. In P. Tolan, C. Keys, F. Chertok, & L. Jason (Eds.), *Researching community psychology: Issues of theory and methods* (pp. 91–100). Washington: American Psychological Association.

Silverman, M. M. (1989). Commentary: The integration of problem and prevention perspectives: Mental disorders associated with alcohol and drug use. In D. Schaffer, I. Phillips, N. B. Enzer, M. M. Silverman, & V. Anthony (Eds.), *Prevention of mental disorders alcohol and other drug use in children and adolescents: OSAP Prevention Monograph-2* (pp. 7–22). (DHHS Publication No (ADW) 89-1646). Washington, DC: U.S. Government Printing Office.

Shinn, M., & Yoshikawa, H. (Eds.). (2008). *Toward positive youth development: Transforming schools and community programs.* New York: Oxford University Press.

Sroufe, L. A., & Rutter, M. (1984). The domain of developmental psychopathology. *Child Development, 55*, 17–29.

Vazsonyi, A. T., Pickering, L. E., & Bolland, J. M. (2006). Growing up in a dangerous developmental milieu: The effects of parenting processes on adjustment in inner-city African American adolescents. *Journal of Community Psychology, 34*, 47–73.

W.T. Grant Foundation. (1988). *The forgotten half: Non-college youth in America.* New York: W.T. Grant Foundation.

Wilson, W. J. (1987). *The truly disadvantaged: The inner-city, the underclass, and public policy.* Chicago: The University of Chicago Press.

Wilson, W. J. (1996). *When work disappears: The world of the new urban poor.* New York: Alfred A. Knopf.

Xue, Y., Leventhal, T., Brooks-Gunn, J., & Earls, F. J. (2005). Neighborhood residence and mental health problems of 5- to 11-year olds. *Archives of General Psychiatry, 62,* 554–563.

Zigler, E. F. (1990). Forward. In S. J. Meisels & J. P. Shonkoff (Eds.), *Handbook of early childhood intervention* (pp. ix–xiv). New York: Cambridge University Press.

Family Violence and Parent Psychopathology: Implications for Children's Socioemotional Development and Resilience

Sara R. Jaffee

Family violence, which refers to child maltreatment and intimate partner violence, is a widespread problem in the United States. In 2009, the most recent year for which figures are available, 702,000 children were found to be victims of maltreatment, including physical, sexual, and psychological abuse, and neglect (U.S. Department of Health and Human Services, 2010). A survey of 16,000 men and women in the United States found that the lifetime prevalence of intimate partner violence was 17% and approximately 1.3 million women and 834,732 men had been the victims of partner violence in the 12 months prior to the survey (Tjaden & Thoennes, 2000). Worldwide, the lifetime prevalence of intimate partner violence ranges from 15 to 71% (Garcia-Moreno, Jansen, Ellsberg, Heise, & Watts, 2006).

Many victims of partner violence live with children. A Bureau of Justice Statistics Special Report found that between 1993 and 1998, the average number of victims of intimate partner violence who lived with children under the age of 12 was 459,590 (Rennison & Welchans, 2000). Child maltreatment and intimate partner violence co-occur in families (Appel & Holden, 1998; Edleson, 1999; Hazen, Connelly, Kelleher, Landsverk, & Barth, 2004), with data from a nationally representative sample of American youth showing that 33.9% who had witnessed

intimate partner violence had also been victims of maltreatment in the past year and 56.8% who had ever witnessed intimate partner violence had been victims of maltreatment at some point in their lives (Hamby, Finkelhor, Turner, & Ormrod, 2010). Reviewing data from community and clinical samples, Edleson (1999) estimated that among those who were exposed to one form of family violence (i.e., child maltreatment or partner abuse), 30–60% were exposed to the other form of family violence as well.

Children who are exposed to intimate partner violence and children who are maltreated are at risk for a range of adverse outcomes in childhood and adolescence, including conduct problems, anxiety and depression, cognitive dysfunction, poor school performance, low self-esteem, and difficulties with peers (for reviews, see Holt, Buckley, & Whelan, 2008; Margolin & Gordis, 2000). Thus, child maltreatment and intimate partner violence constitute significant public health problems because of their high prevalence and co-occurrence rates and because of the adverse outcomes for parents and children involved in family violence.

In their efforts to understand the etiology of family violence, researchers in different fields have developed models that call on a subset of potential explanatory variables (Belsky & Vondra, 1989; Parke & Collmer, 1975). For example, psychiatric models of family violence emphasize the role that an individual's rearing history and psychological characteristics (e.g., low impulse control, alcohol and drug problems,

S.R. Jaffee (✉)
Institute of Psychiatry,
Kings College London, London, UK
e-mail: sara.jaffee@kcl.ac.uk

S. Goldstein and R.B. Brooks (eds.), *Handbook of Resilience in Children*,
DOI 10.1007/978-1-4614-3661-4_8, © Springer Science+Business Media New York 2013

depression or personality disorders) play in increasing risk for child (Kempe, Silverman, Steele, Droegemueller, & Silver, 1962; Spinetta & Rigler, 1972) or partner abuse (Dutton, 1995). Sociological models of family violence emphasize the degree to which social stressors (e.g., unemployment, poverty) and societal attitudes and values about violence undermine family functioning and are thus implicated in child or partner abuse (Gelles, 1973; Sugarman & Frankel, 1996; Tolan & Guerra, 1998). Finally, the "child effects" model highlights the degree to which the behavior of hard-to-manage children (e.g., premature infants, children with difficult temperaments) elicits harsh and abusive discipline from adults (Hurme, Alanko, Anttila, Juven, & Svedstrom, 2008; Kadushin & Martin, 1981; Wu et al., 2004) or causes disagreements about how to manage children that result in intimate partner violence (Straus, Gelles, & Steinmetz, 1980).

Working from a developmental–ecological framework, Belsky (1980, 1993) proposed that maltreatment occurs as a result of interactions between "contexts of maltreatment." Although Belsky's developmental–ecological model was formulated to explain child maltreatment, it can be generalized to other forms of family violence like intimate partner violence. According to the developmental–ecological model, factors that influence whether an individual will be abusive towards a child or an intimate partner operate at and across several levels of the ecology from the most proximal to the most distal. These include the level of the individual (e.g., individual personality or mental illness), the level of the microsystem (i.e., family-level factors including poverty, single parenthood, or unemployment), the level of the exosystem (e.g., community-level violence, unemployment rates, or social cohesion), and the level of the macrosystem (e.g., cultural attitudes to violence, regional policy on family violence).

The developmental–ecological model underscores the fact that family violence is determined by multiple factors and, as Belsky (1993) concluded, there appear to be no necessary or sufficient causes of family violence. Thus, although the focus of this chapter is on the asso-

ciation between mental illness in parents and family violence, I do not advocate the psychiatric model. Rather, as the following review of the literature will demonstrate, it is assumed that family violence has many causes and that the degree to which parents' psychopathology increases risk for family violence depends on the balance of other potentiating and compensatory factors that may change over time (Cicchetti & Rizley, 1981). Clearly, not all parents with a history of mental disorder are involved in family violence and not all of those involved in family violence have a history of mental disorder. However, a focus on parent psychopathology is worthwhile given the central role that parent personality plays in theories of the determinants of parenting (Belsky & Jaffee, 2005). Personality is what links a parent's developmental history (e.g., early experience of caregiving) with his or her current functioning as a parent. Personality also influences a range of contextual factors (marital quality, job satisfaction and stability) that increase or decrease risk for family violence (Belsky, 1984).

The goal of this chapter is to review the literature on the association between parent mental illness and two forms of family violence: violence against an intimate partner, referred to as partner violence, and violence against a child, referred to as child maltreatment. Although child maltreatment comprises physical, psychological, and sexual abuse as well as neglect, most of the studies reviewed in this chapter concern child physical abuse and neglect.

A review of the literature on family violence and parent mental illness is merited at this point in time because of the growing use of nationally representative datasets to estimate the co-occurrence of family violence and parent mental illness in the population vs. clinical samples where family violence and parent mental illness may be correlated with a host of other psychosocial risk factors that inflate co-occurrence estimates. Moreover, research based on nationally representative, *longitudinal* samples can address questions regarding the temporal association between mental illness and family violence. The temporal nature of these data has allowed researchers to explore whether parent mental illness is a predisposing risk factor for family violence or whether parent mental illness arises from the experience of violence victimization in the family, thus getting at the question of whether family violence occurs because parents are mentally ill or whether mental illness occurs because parents have been victims of violence.

In this chapter, I will review the evidence linking parent mental illness to family violence. I will then review evidence on what accounts for the link between parent mental illness and family violence. Finally, I will discuss the implications for children's well-being of growing up in a home where they are exposed to both family violence and parent mental illness. Despite the risk for poor adjustment associated with family violence and with parent psychopathology, many children who are exposed to such adversities show remarkable resilience over time and across a range of domains of functioning. I will consider the degree to which the *co-occurrence* of parent psychopathology and family violence may decrease the likelihood that children will manifest resilience.

The Prevalence of Psychopathology Among Perpetrators of Partner Violence

Personality disorders appear in up to 90% of males in domestic violence treatment programs (Craig, 2003) and clinical elevations in passive–aggressive and antisocial personality disorders best predict domestic violence (Dutton, 1994). However, batterers are a diverse group who differ in terms of the frequency and severity of their violence, the extent to which they are violent outside of the family, and the degree to which they are characterized by personality disorder and psychopathology (Dixon & Browne, 2003; Holtzworth-Monroe & Stuart, 1994). In an empirical test of their batterer typology, Holtzworth-Monroe, Meehan, Herron, Rehman, and Stuart (2000) reported that the generally violent antisocial group (16%) were characterized by high levels of psychopathy, substance use and abuse, and involvement in crime. The borderline-dysphoric group (15%) were characterized by

borderline personality organization and high scores on a number of Diagnostic and Statistical Manual (American Psychiatric Association, 2000) Axis I scales including major depression, anxiety, posttraumatic stress disorder, and symptoms of disordered thought. Over a third of the violent men in the sample (36%) corresponded to the family-only group and they were indistinguishable from the nonviolent control group in terms of psychopathology and criminal behavior.

Consistent with the notion that clinically significant psychopathology may characterize only a subset of batterers, Gleason (1997) conducted a review of psychological and social dysfunction among battering men and identified two types of batterers: one group characterized by frequent alcohol abuse, antisocial personality disorder, low intelligence, and criminal behavior and another group characterized by relatively low levels of psychological and social dysfunction.

Data from epidemiological studies of men and women who perpetrate partner violence are consistent with data from clinical samples, showing that perpetrators (men, in most studies) have elevated past-year rates of mood and anxiety disorders, substance use disorders, and antisocial personality disorder (Danielson, Moffitt, Caspi, & Silva, 1998; Eiden, Leonard, & Morrisey, 2001; Feingold, Kerr, & Capaldi, 2008; Magdol et al., 1997). A childhood history of antisocial behavior—and particularly early emerging antisocial behavior—has also been identified consistently as a risk factor for partner violence perpetration (Ehrensaft et al., 2003; Kerr & Capaldi, 2011; Lussier, Farrington, & Moffitt, 2009; Magdol, Moffitt, Caspi, & Silva, 1998; Woodward, Fergusson, & Horwood, 2002), with at least one study finding that male perpetrators were more likely than nonperpetrators to also have a childhood history of any mental health or substance use problem (Magdol et al., 1998). Finally, at least one study has shown that symptoms of depression, poly-drug use, and antisocial personality disorder differentiate male perpetrators from male nonperpetrators more strongly than they differentiate female perpetrators from female nonperpetrators (Magdol et al., 1997).

The Prevalence of Psychopathology Among Victims of Partner Violence

In a meta-analysis of the association between intimate partner violence and mental health problems, Golding (1999) reported that women's violence victimization significantly increased the odds of suicidality, posttraumatic stress disorder, and substance use/dependence in samples taken from psychiatric patient settings, battered women's shelters, and emergency rooms. Although Golding (1999) concluded that these results supported a model in which violence victimization was a cause of mental disorder in women, the analyses did not address the possibility that women who were victimized by their partners had a preexisting mental disorder that may have influenced their likelihood of entering abusive relationships.

Although the majority of research on victims of partner violence concerns women, there is a small literature on male victims. Similar to the findings for women, a review of this literature found that men who were victims of intimate partner violence were at increased risk of symptoms of posttraumatic stress, depression, and suicide (Randle & Graham, 2011).

Again, consistent with data from clinical samples, data from epidemiological studies show that male and female victims of partner violence are at increased risk for mood, anxiety, eating, substance use, antisocial personality, and psychotic disorders (Afifi et al., 2009; Bonomi et al., 2006; Carbone-Lopez, Kruttschnitt, & Macmillan, 2006; Coker et al., 2002a; Coker, Smith, & Fadden, 2005; Danielson et al., 1998; Magdol et al., 1997). The past-year prevalence of psychiatric disorders among men and women who have been victims of partner violence ranges from 25 to 66% depending on the severity of the abuse (Afifi et al., 2009; Danielson et al., 1998). As compared with male victims, female victims have been shown to have higher rates of anxiety (Afifi et al., 2009; Magdol et al., 1997) and to have lower rates of disruptive and substance use disorders (Afifi et al., 2009). Findings from community samples suggest that access to social

supports buffer women who experience intimate partner violence from risk of depression and posttraumatic stress symptoms (Beeble, Bybee, Sullivan, & Adams, 2009; Coker et al., 2002b; Escriba-Aguir et al., 2010; Mburia-Mwalili, Clements-Nolle, Lee, Shadley, & Yang, 2010).

Why Is Intimate Partner Violence Correlated with Psychopathology?

Research that establishes an association between intimate partner violence and mental illness can be interpreted in at least three ways: (a) mental disorder causes individuals to perpetrate or fall victim to intimate partner violence; (b) the experience of having been abused by an intimate partner increases risk for mental disorder; (c) the association between mental disorder and intimate partner violence is spurious and can be accounted for by a third set of variables (e.g., low socioeconomic status). As longitudinal data on partner violence and mental illness have become available, researchers have begun to exploit the temporal nature of these data to answer questions about whether the link between mental disorder and partner violence reflects social selection (individuals with a history of mental disorder are at increased risk of entering violent relationships), social causation (partner violence causes mental disorder), or a spurious association.

In one longitudinal study of a New Zealand birth cohort, individuals with a history of psychiatric disorder in adolescence were more likely than individuals without such a history to be victims of clinically abusive partner violence—resulting in injury or official intervention—in their mid-twenties (Ehrensaft, Moffitt, & Caspi, 2006). For male victims, a prior history of psychiatric disorder explained why they were subsequently at increased risk for psychiatric disorder. For female victims, however, the risk for psychiatric disorder associated with partner violence remained significant after controlling for psychiatric history (Ehrensaft et al. 2006). Thus, these data indicate that the experience of partner violence is not random—individuals with a history of mental disorder are more likely to enter abusive relationships than individuals without a history of mental disorder. However, for women at least, being victimized by a partner further increases risk for psychopathology.

Complicating this picture is the fact that most individuals who perpetrate violence against a partner have also been victims of violence (Anderson, 2002; Magdol et al., 1997). Thus, mental health problems may predict violence perpetration because perpetrators have themselves been victims of violence in the past and have developed mental health problems as a consequence. Using data from the National Survey of Families and Households, Anderson (2002) found that depressive symptomatology increased the odds of partner violence perpetration, even controlling for a range of sociodemographic variables and controlling for violence victimization. Thus, individuals who reported symptoms of depression were at increased risk of violence perpetration, even accounting for the fact that they might have been victims of violence in the past. In contrast, the authors detected a spurious association between drug and alcohol problems and violence perpetration. Drug and alcohol problems were associated with the perpetration of partner violence because both stemmed from the experience of having been the victim of violence in the past.

In summary, both clinical and nationally representative samples have established an association between partner violence perpetration, victimization, and mental disorder, although a substantial number of individuals involved in partner violence are not characterized by mental disorder (Holtzworth-Monroe et al., 2000). Longitudinal studies have shown that social selection and social causation are both at play for female victims of partner violence, but that processes of social selection primarily explain why male victims of partner violence have elevated symptoms of mental health problems (Ehrensaft et al., 2006). Moreover, some forms of disorder increase the risk of perpetration, regardless of an individual's history of victimization whereas other forms of disorder appear to be associated with violence perpetration because both stem from a history of victimization (Anderson, 2002).

More longitudinal research is needed to further explore the question of (a) whether psychopathology arises from the experience of partner violence, (b) whether partner violence exacerbates an underlying diathesis for psychopathology, or (c) whether partner violence is a manifestation of stable individual differences as indexed by an individual's history of psychopathology. Finally, relatively little research has explored whether "third variables" such as poverty, single parenthood, or unemployment account for the association between mental disorder and partner violence or whether these factors moderate the relationship such that mental disorders and partner violence are linked only under certain conditions.

Parental Psychopathology and Child Maltreatment

As is true for studies of mental disorder and intimate partner violence, researchers who study the association between parent mental disorder and child maltreatment have collected data from both clinic samples (e.g., studies of parents on protective service caseloads) as well as from parents in population samples.

Clinic samples. State child welfare records indicate that substance abuse is one of the top two problems exhibited by families in 81% of reported cases (Lung & Daro, 1996). Among confirmed cases of child maltreatment, 40% involve the use of alcohol or other drugs by a parent (Children of Alcoholics Foundation Inc, 1996). Crack cocaine has been held responsible by researchers and social workers for skyrocketing child protective service caseloads in the 1980s and early 1990s (Curtis & McCullough, 1993). Children of alcoholics may also be at increased risk of neglect as evidenced by research showing that such children suffer more injuries and poisonings than do children in the general population (Bijur, Kurzon, Overpeck, & Scheidt, 1992).

Substance abuse may influence the course and consequences of child maltreatment. In a comparison of drug and alcohol substance-abusing and non-substance-abusing parents involved in over 200 child protective cases brought to court in Massachusetts, Murphy et al. (1991) reported that parents with documented substance abuse histories were more likely than other maltreating parents to be repeat offenders with regard to child maltreatment and to have longer histories with child protective services. Parents with substance abuse histories were rated by court investigators as being at higher risk of continuing to maltreat their children, were more likely to reject court-ordered services (71% vs. 39%), and were more likely to eventually lose care and custody of their children (80% vs. 58%). These differences between substance-abusing and non-substance-abusing families remained significant even after controlling for socioeconomic status, as indexed by receipt of welfare benefits. Thus, in families where maltreatment co-occurs with a parent's substance abuse problem, maltreatment is more persistent, parents are more resistant to treatment, and children are more likely to be placed in care.

Although these studies show substantial rates of mental disorder among parents who maltreat their children, they do not clarify whether rates of disorder are significantly higher among these parents than among sociodemographically matched controls. In a study of 53 families who had been reported (and indicated) to child protective services, De Bellis et al. (2001) reported that prevalence rates of lifetime DSM-III and IV diagnoses for any anxiety disorder, any mood disorder, and alcohol and substance abuse/dependence disorders were significantly higher among maltreating mothers compared to sociodemographically similar control mothers. Compared to control mothers, mothers of maltreated children were also more likely to have had a history of violent behavior towards other adult family or community members, although the two groups did not differ with respect to criminal arrests.

Famularo and colleagues (Famularo, Kinscherff, & Fenton, 1992; Famularo, Stone, Barnum, & Wharton, 1986) matched 50 court-referred maltreating parents with 38 parents whose children were inpatients at a general pediatric hospital on age, income, race, and marital status. Maltreating parents were significantly more likely than control parents to meet Research and Diagnostic Criteria for a lifetime diagnosis of alcoholism (38% vs. 8%) and major depression (28% vs. 8%).

The clinic studies reported earlier have estimated rates of mental disorder among samples of parents on child protective service caseloads. Another approach to studying the link between parent mental disorder and child maltreatment is to estimate the prevalence of maltreatment among parents who are receiving mental health services or who have disclosed illicit drug use. At least four studies have detected elevated rates of physical abuse and neglect among drug users compared to sociodemographically matched controls (Kelley, 1992; McGlade, Ware, & Crawford, 2009; Street, Harrington, Chiang, Cairns, & Ellis, 2004; Wasserman & Leventhal, 1993). For example, Kelley (1992) reported that nearly 60% of the drug-exposed infants in her sample were the subject of subsequent substantiated reports of abuse or neglect compared to just over 8% of the control children. At 11 months of age, all of the control children were still living with their biological mothers in contrast to just over half of the drug-exposed children, 42% of whom had been placed by child protective services in foster care with relatives or others.

Finally, a recent study followed a sample of 999 youth released from juvenile justice facilities in New York. By the time they were 28 years old, 62% of the girls and 17% of the boys had been investigated by child welfare services for allegations of abuse or neglect (Colman, Mitchell-Herzfeld, Kim, & Shady, 2010). Although this study lacked a demographically matched control group of nondelinquents, it bears noting that rates of maltreatment perpetration were higher among female former delinquents than among individuals who themselves have a history of child maltreatment, roughly a third of whom are expected to maltreat their own children (Kaufman & Zigler, 1987).

In summary, when compared to sociodemographically matched controls, the association between child maltreatment and mental disorder (including major depressive, personality, and substance use disorders) is detected (a) in samples where prevalence rates of mental disorder are assessed in parents referred to child protective services and (b) in samples where the prevalence of child maltreatment is assessed prospectively among mothers who abuse drugs or who have been released from juvenile detention facilities. Several caveats bear note. First, several samples included parents who were judged potentially unfit to retain custody of their children (e.g., Famularo et al., 1992; Murphy et al., 1991). These families may represent a particularly severe group of maltreating parents and prevalence rates of disorder in this group may not represent prevalence rates of disorder among maltreating parents generally. Second, the over-representation of parents with substance abuse problems on child protective service caseloads may reflect detection bias, wherein such parents are perceived as being at greater risk to their children than other parents (Benjet, Azar, & Kuersten-Hogan, 2003).

Population samples. Several studies have reported on the association between child maltreatment and parents' mental disorder using data from the representative St. Louis Epidemiological Catchment Area (ECA) sample (Robins & Regier, 1991). Dinwiddie and Bucholz (1993) reported that the lifetime rate of self-reported child physical abuse among parents in the ECA sample was 4.1%. Compared to nonabusers, those who reported perpetrating child physical abuse were significantly more likely to have a lifetime history of alcohol abuse/dependence, drug abuse, antisocial personality disorder, major depressive disorder, and panic disorder.

Egami, Ford, Greenfield, and Crum (1996) explored the link between mental disorder and child maltreatment among all adults in the ECA sample and found that a lifetime history of any mental disorder increased the odds of child physical abuse by 2.72 times. A lifetime history of alcohol abuse or dependence and a lifetime history of affective disorders increased risk for physical child abuse even controlling for a range of sociodemographic variables as well as other psychiatric diagnoses.

Finally, Chaffin, Kelleher, and Hollenberg (1996) utilized the prospective, longitudinal design of the ECA survey to predict the onset of child physical abuse and neglect from sociode-mographic and psychiatric data measured at a previous wave. In models controlling for socio-demographic factors and psychiatric disorders, substance abuse remained a strong predictor of subsequent child physical abuse and mediated the association between a range of sociodemographic factors (e.g., parent's age, number in household, marital status, race) and the emergence of neglect.

This pattern of findings from the ECA study has been replicated in other large population samples. In a study of 1,200 unselected adults, the odds of engaging in violence against a spouse or partner, against a child, against someone outside the family or of engaging in child neglect were from 1.6 to 4.7 times higher among those who had a definite or possible diagnosis of antisocial personality disorder, alcohol abuse or dependence, or recurrent depression (Bland & Orn, 1986). Among individuals who were comorbid for two or more disorders, the odds of engaging in familial or extrafamilial violence were exponentially greater. Parent criminality and substance abuse were also implicated in child maltreatment in a study of 644 families who were part of a larger, unselected sample (Brown, Cohen, Johnson, & Salzinger, 1998). The odds of physical child abuse, neglect, and sexual abuse were four to six times higher among mothers who reported involvement with drugs, alcohol, and/or the police.

Similarly, retrospective data from the 8,548 participants in the Ontario Mental Health Supplement showed that adults who reported a history of childhood maltreatment were more likely to report that their own parents had psychiatric disorders and substance use problems compared with adults who did not report a history of childhood maltreatment; a parent's history of antisocial personality disorder increased the odds of child maltreatment by 7.5 (Walsh, MacMillan, & Jamieson, 2003; Walsh, McMillan, & Jamieson, 2002). Finally, although the sample was small, at least one prospective, longitudinal study of 224 low-income families followed for 10 years found that maternal drug use and maternal depressive symptoms predicted which families would become involved with child protective services (Dubowitz et al., 2011).

Summary. Clinic and population studies have detected an association between parent mental disorder and child maltreatment even controlling for a range of sociodemographic factors that might explain the association. Substance abuse, affective, and antisocial personality disorders have consistently been found to increase risk for child maltreatment.

Why Is Parent Psychopathology Correlated with Child Maltreatment?

Very few studies have explored why it is that parents who have a history of mental illness are at increased risk for family violence. Potential explanations may be common across mental disorders or may relate to specific disorders. Drawing from the literature on social cognition, it is possible that parent mental illness biases parents' cognitions about their children's behavior as well as their ability to recognize their children's emotions. Moreover, parents who are experiencing depression or substance use problems because they are also victims of partner violence may be at elevated risk of abusing or neglecting children because of difficulties in coping with social stressors. These hypotheses are reviewed below.

Social cognitive models of parenting posit that negative emotions bias parents' perceptions, interpretations, and evaluations of their children's behavior (Azar & Twentyman, 1986; Dix, 1991; Milner, 2003). Parents who are characteristically angry, depressed, or anxious are more likely to perceive children as acting in deliberately negative ways (Dix, 1991) and, consistent with those perceptions, to parent in a hostile, negative fashion (Rueger, Katz, Risser, & Lovejoy, 2011). Indeed, research shows that maltreating parents are more likely to attribute children's misbehavior to stable, global, and internal causes (for reviews see Azar, 2002; Milner, 2003; Seng & Prinz, 2008) and that parents who are at high risk for maltreating children have more readily accessible negative child-related schema (Crouch et al., 2010; Milner et al., 2011). Social cognitive models may also be applied in the context of partner violence, where negative emotionality may bias

an individual's perceptions of an intimate partner's behavior (Noller, Beach, & Osgarby, 1997).

A parent's depressogenic cognitive style (e.g., Abramson, Metalsky, & Alloy, 1989) may contribute to the perception that she or he is not competent in the parenting role and may cause the parent to withdraw from interaction with the child. In families where rates of parent–child interaction are low, children's misbehavior may be reinforced because it elicits a reaction from the withdrawn parent. These coercive exchanges may further undermine parents' perception of their competency (Azar, 2002). Low self-esteem and perceived control in parenting are characteristics of abusive parents (Trickett & Susman, 1988), suggesting the possibility that such parents have little faith in their ability to manage the child's behavior through less power-assertive means.

A third hypothesis proposes that parents who maltreat their children may have difficulties managing stress relative to other parents (Whipple & Webster-Stratton, 1991). Although exposure to social stressors may precipitate the onset or recurrence of mental disorder, a history of mental illness may also increase the risk of experiencing a range of social stressors including marital conflict, relationship and job instability, and the erosion of social supports. Thus, a parent's history of mental disorder may increase the probability of child maltreatment because of the greater number of stressors to which the parent is exposed and the parent's impaired capacity to manage stress (Abidin, 1992; McPherson, Lewis, Lynn, Haskett, & Behrend, 2009). Given the co-occurrence of partner violence and child maltreatment, partner violence itself may be a potent stressor that impairs the ability to parent effectively (Slep & O'Leary, 2001).

Implications for Children's Socioemotional Development and Resilience

The fact that family violence and parental psychopathology tend to co-occur poses interpretive difficulties for studies attempting to determine whether family violence is a causal risk factor for children's problem behaviors. This co-occurrence raises the possibility that gene variants common to parents and children explain the observed association between family violence and child psychopathology. That is, family violence may simply be a marker for genetic risk that parents transmit to children (DiLalla & Gottesman, 1991), a phenomenon known as passive gene–environment correlation (Plomin, DeFries, & Loehlin, 1977). Another possibility is that children inherit a genetic predisposition to engage in hard-to-manage behavior and that this behavior elicits abusive reactions from adults, a phenomenon known as evocative gene–environment correlation (Plomin et al., 1977).

Several studies using genetically informative research designs have ruled out these alternative hypotheses (Jaffee, Caspi, Moffitt, & Taylor, 2004; Jaffee, Strait, & Odgers, in press). Twin studies have shown that maltreatment is not significantly heritable (Jaffee, Caspi, Moffitt, Polo-Tomas et al., 2004; Schulz-Heik et al., 2009), suggesting that genetically influenced characteristics of the child do not explain why some children are more likely than others to experience maltreatment. Moreover, in models that estimate passive gene–environment correlations, adverse childhood events (including maltreatment and inter-parental conflict) have been shown to have direct effects on youth antisocial behavior (Eaves, Prom, & Silberg, 2010).

Although genotype is unlikely to account for the effect of maltreatment on children's risk for psychopathology, genotype is likely to moderate the effects of maltreatment (and other forms of victimization) on children's outcomes. The first evidence that a specific gene variant moderated the effect of maltreatment appeared in 2002 (Caspi et al., 2002). This study involved a cohort of 442 New Zealand men who had participated from birth in the Dunedin Longitudinal Study (Moffitt, Caspi, Rutter, & Silva, 2001). Among men who carried the low activity variant of the monoamine oxidase A gene (MAOA), those who experienced childhood adversities, including sexual and physical abuse, maternal rejecting behavior, harsh discipline, and frequent caretaker changes, had significantly higher levels of antisocial behavior in childhood and adulthood than those who had not experienced childhood adversity. Among men who carried the high activity variant, childhood adversity was not associated with later antisocial behavior. In a subsequent paper focused on a variant in the serotonin transporter gene-linked polymorphic region (5HTTLPR) (Caspi et al., 2003), they showed that among men and women who were homozygous for the short form of the serotonin transporter polymorphism, experiencing more adverse childhood events was associated with increased levels of depression in adulthood. This association was not observed among individuals who were homozygous for the long form of the serotonin transporter polymorphism.

There is plausible biological evidence from animals and humans that these genotype x environment interactions capture real biological processes (for a review, see Caspi, Hariri, Holmes, Uher, & Moffitt, 2010). MAOA is involved in metabolism of monoamines in the brain and other organs (Shih & Thompson, 1999) and 5HTTLPR is involved in the reuptake of serotonin at brain synapses (Heils et al., 1995). Results of studies that either knock out or functionally excise these genes support the involvement of MAOA in aggressive traits (Cases et al., 1995; Shih, 2004) and 5HTTLPR in anxious traits (Murphy & Lesch, 2008). Studies of nonhuman primates provide evidence of GxE that is consistent with the human findings (for review, see Caspi et al., 2010), and 5HTTLPR and MAOA have been associated with brain activity in regions implicated in depression and aggression in response to negative stimuli (Buckholtz & Meyer-Lindenberg, 2008; Munafo, Brown, & Hariri, 2008).

Subsequent efforts to replicate the original findings involving MAOA, 5HTTLPR, and family violence have been mixed, with meta-analyses identifying small, but significant interaction effects (Karg, Burmeister, Shedden, & Sen, 2011; Kim-Cohen et al., 2006; for negative findings, see Munafo, Durrant, Lewis, & Flint, 2009; Risch et al., 2009). If real, genotype x environment (GxE) interactions provide important clues to the biological basis of resilience. For example, the neuroimaging genetics literature has shown that individuals who are homozygous for the long form of the serotonin transporter polymorphism show lower levels of amygdala reactivity to negative vs. neutral stimuli, such as facial expressions of fear and sadness (Munafo et al., 2008). Amygdala reactivity may influence the cognitive processing of emotion expressions, with consequences for how individuals cope with their own or others' negative emotions. Other studies have shown that individuals who are homozygous for the long form of the serotonin transporter polymorphism produce lower levels of cortisol—a stress hormone—in response to a socially stressful task (Gotlib, Joormann, Minor, & Hallmayer, 2008). Because cortisol hyper-reactivity has been implicated in the pathophysiology of depression (Parker, Schatzberg, & Lyons, 2003) and cortisol hypo-reactivity has been implicated in antisocial behavior (van Goozen, Fairchild, Snoek, & Harold, 2007), genetic influences on stress response systems may provide a biological basis for resilience. However, because most studies of GxE focus on a single outcome (e.g., depression or antisocial behavior) more research is needed to determine whether risk for psychopathology in general is reduced if an individual has a particular genotype or if genotype x environment interactions involving specific gene variants reduce risk for specific forms of psychopathology, but not others.

Moreover, the fact that an individual is at genetic and environmental risk for maltreatment is no guarantee that the individual will suffer from mental health problems. At least one study found that children who had high levels of social support were at relatively low risk for depression even if they carried the short form of the serotonin transporter polymorphism and had been victims of maltreatment (Kaufman et al., 2004). There is a substantial literature on protective factors for child victims of family violence (many of whom will also be at genetic risk for psychopathology) implicating child-, family-, and community-level factors (for a review, see Afifi & MacMillan, 2011).

However, given that resilience is likely to arise from the balance of risk and protective factors available to a child (Masten & Coatsworth, 1998), the co-occurrence of parental mental illness and family violence is likely to decrease the probability of resilience. It is important to consider how the course of a parent's mental illness may alter this balance and, consequently, alter the child's ability to maintain positive psychological functioning. Depression, for example, tends to recur throughout adulthood (Post, 1992) and the timing of a parent's depressive episodes may influence not only the likelihood that family violence will occur (e.g., partner violence is more likely to occur when a parent is experiencing an episode of depression; Capaldi & Kim, 2003), but also the parent's interactions with the child (Goodman & Gotlib, 1999). For example, a parent may be better able to buffer a child against exposure to inter-parental violence when the parent is suffering relatively few symptoms of psychopathology than when a parent is experiencing a clinical episode of disorder. Parents may be better able to handle psychosocial stressors and, consequently, use nonabusive forms of discipline when they are psychologically well vs. when they are psychologically distressed.

In summary, although family violence is multiply determined, the association between family violence and parent mental illness is robust across studies, particularly for mood disorders, antisocial personality disorder, and substance abuse disorder. I argue that children's inherited vulnerability to disorder may be exacerbated by exposure to family violence, children's risk for a range of adverse outcomes increases with the number of psychosocial risk factors to which the child is exposed, and violence in families where a parent has a history of disorder is likely to be more severe, persistent, and pervasive than in families where violence and mental disorder do not co-occur. Clinicians working with victims or perpetrators of family violence should be especially aware of the degree to which mental illness may be a cause or consequence of violence because the co-occurrence of family violence and mental illness may jeopardize children's chances of positive adjustment.

References

Abidin, R. R. (1992). The determinants of parenting behavior. *Journal of Clinical Child Psychology, 21,* 407–412.

Abramson, L. Y., Metalsky, G. I., & Alloy, L. B. (1989). Hopelessness depression: A theory-based subtype of depression. *Psychological Review, 96,* 358–372.

Afifi, T. O., & MacMillan, H. L. (2011). Resilience following child maltreatment: A review of protective factors. *Canadian Journal of Psychiatry-Revue Canadienne de Psychiatrie, 56,* 266–272.

Afifi, T. O., MacMillan, H., Cox, B. J., Asmundson, G. J. G., Stein, M. B., & Sareen, J. (2009). Mental health correlates of intimate partner violence in marital relationships in a nationally representative sample of males and females. *Journal of Interpersonal Violence, 24,* 1398–1417.

Anderson, K. L. (2002). Perpetrator or victim? Relationships between intimate partner violence and well-being. *Journal of Marriage and the Family, 64,* 851–863.

Appel, A. E., & Holden, G. W. (1998). The co-occurrence of spouse and physical child abuse: A review and appraisal. *Journal of Family Psychology, 12,* 578–599.

Association, A. P. (2000). *Diagnostic and statistical manual of mental disorders: Text revision* (4th ed.). Washington: American Psychiatric Association.

Azar, S. T. (2002). Parenting and child maltreatment. In M. H. Bornstein (Ed.), *Handbook of parenting: Social conditions and applied parenting* (Vol. 4, pp. 361–388). Mahwah: Lawrence Erlbaum.

Azar, S. T., & Twentyman, C. T. (1986). Cognitive behavioral perspectives on the assessment and treatment of child abuse. In P. C. Kendall (Ed.), *Advances in cognitive behavioral research and therapy* (Vol. 5, pp. 237–267). New York: Academic Press.

Beeble, M. L., Bybee, D., Sullivan, C. M., & Adams, A. E. (2009). Main, mediating, and moderating effects of social support on the well-being of survivors of intimate partner violence across 2 years. *Journal of Consulting and Clinical Psychology, 77,* 718–729.

Belsky, J. (1980). Child maltreatment: An ecological integration. *American Psychologist, 35,* 320–335.

Belsky, J. (1984). The determinants of parenting: A process model. *Child Development, 55,* 83–96.

Belsky, J. (1993). Etiology of child maltreatment: A developmental-ecological analysis. *Psychological Bulletin, 114,* 413–434.

Belsky, J., & Jaffee, S. R. (2005). The multiple determinants of parenting. In D. Cicchetti & D. J. Cohen (Eds.), *Handbook of developmental psychopathology: Volume 3. Risk, disorder, and adaptation* (2nd ed., pp. 38–85). New York: Wiley.

Belsky, J., & Vondra, J. (1989). Lessons from child abuse: The determinants of parenting. In D. Cicchetti & V. Carlson (Eds.), *Child maltreatment: Theory and research on the causes and consequences of child abuse and neglect* (pp. 153–202). Cambridge: Cambridge University Press.

Benjet, C., Azar, S. T., & Kuersten-Hogan, R. (2003). Evaluating the parental fitness of psychiatrically diagnosed individuals: Advocating a functional-contextual analysis of parenting. *Journal of Family Psychology, 17,* 238–251.

Bijur, P. E., Kurzon, M., Overpeck, M. D., & Scheidt, P. C. (1992). Parental alcohol use, problem drinking and child injuries. *Journal of the American Medical Association, 23,* 3166–3171.

Bland, R., & Orn, H. (1986). Family violence and psychiatric disorder. *Canadian Journal of Psychiatry, 31,* 129–137.

Bonomi, A. E., Thompson, R. S., Anderson, M., Reid, R. J., Carrell, D., Dimer, J. A., et al. (2006). Intimate partner violence and women's physical, mental, and social functioning. *American Journal of Preventive Medicine, 30,* 458–466.

Brown, J., Cohen, P., Johnson, J. G., & Salzinger, S. (1998). A longitudinal analysis of risk factors for child maltreatment: Findings of a 17-year prospective study of officially recorded and self-reported child abuse and neglect. *Child Abuse & Neglect, 22,* 1065–1078.

Buckholtz, J. W., & Meyer-Lindenberg, A. (2008). MAOA and the neurogenetic architecture of human aggression. *Trends in Neurosciences, 31,* 120–129.

Carbone-Lopez, K., Kruttschnitt, C., & Macmillan, R. (2006). Patterns of intimate partner violence and their associations with physical health, psychological distress, and substance use. *Public Health Reports, 121,* 382–392.

Capaldi, D. M., & Kim, H. K. (2003). *Assortative partnering by antisocial behavior and depressive symptoms and risk for aggression to partner in young couples.* Poster presented at the Society for Research in Child Development meeting, Tampa, Florida.

Cases, O., Seif, I., Grimsby, J., Gaspar, P., Chen, K., Pournin, S., et al. (1995). Aggressive behavior and altered amounts of brain serotonin and norepinephrine in mice lacking MAOA. *Science, 268,* 1763–1766.

Caspi, A., Hariri, A. R., Holmes, A., Uher, R., & Moffitt, T. E. (2010). Genetic sensitivity to the environment: The case of the serotonin transporter gene and its implications for studying complex diseases and traits. *The American Journal of Psychiatry, 167,* 509–527.

Caspi, A., McClay, J., Moffitt, T. E., Mill, J., Martin, J., Craig, I. W., et al. (2002). Role of genotype in the cycle of violence in maltreated children. *Science, 297,* 851–854.

Caspi, A., Sugden, K., Moffitt, T. E., Taylor, A., Craig, I. W., Harrington, H., et al. (2003). Influence of life stress on depression: Moderation by a polymorphism in the 5-HTT gene. *Science, 31,* 386–389.

Chaffin, M., Kelleher, K., & Hollenberg, J. (1996). Onset of physical abuse and neglect: Psychiatric, substance abuse, and social risk factors from prospective community data. *Child Abuse & Neglect, 20,* 191–203.

Children of Alcoholics Foundation Inc. (1996). *Collaboration, coordination and cooperation: Helping children affected by parental addiction and family violence.* New York: Children of Alcoholics Foundation.

Cicchetti, D., & Rizley, R. (1981). Developmental perspectives on the etiology, intergenerational transmission, and sequelae of child maltreatment. *New Directions for Child Development, 11*, 31–55.

Coker, A. L., Davis, K. E., Arias, I., Desai, S., Sanderson, M., Brandt, H. M. et al. (2002a). Physical and mental health effects of intimate partner violence for men and women. *American Journal of Preventive Medicine, 23*, 260–268.

Coker, A. L., Smith, P. H., & Fadden, M. K. (2005). Intimate partner violence and disabilities among women attending family practice clinics. *Journal of Women's Health, 14*, 829–838.

Coker, A. L., Smith, P. H., Thompson, M. P., McKeown, R. E., Bethea, L., & Davis, K. E. (2002b). Social support protects against the negative effects of partner violence on mental health. *Journal of Women's Health, 11*, 465–476.

Colman, R. A., Mitchell-Herzfeld, S., Kim, D. H., & Shady, T. A. (2010). From delinquency to the perpetration of child maltreatment: Examining the early adult criminal justice and child welfare involvement of youth released from juvenile justice facilities. *Children and Youth Services Review, 32*, 1410–1417.

Craig, R. J. (2003). Use of the Millon Clinical Multiaxial Inventory in the psychological assessment of domestic violence: A review. *Aggression and Violent Behavior, 8*, 235–243.

Crouch, J. L., Risser, H. J., Skowronski, J. J., Milner, J. S., Farc, M. M., & Irwin, L. M. (2010). Does accessibility of positive and negative schema vary by child physical abuse risk? *Child Abuse & Neglect, 34*, 886–895.

Curtis, P., & McCullough, C. (1993). The impact of alcohol and other drugs on the child welfare system. *Child Welfare, 72*, 533–542.

Danielson, K. K., Moffitt, T. E., Caspi, A., & Silva, P. A. (1998). Comorbidity between abuse of an adult and DSM-III-R mental disorders: Evidence from an epidemiological study. *The American Journal of Psychiatry, 155*, 131–133.

De Bellis, M. D., Broussard, E. R., Herring, D. J., Wexler, S., Moritz, G., & Benitez, J. G. (2001). Psychiatric comorbidity in caregivers and children involved in maltreatment: A pilot research study with policy implications. *Child Abuse & Neglect, 25*, 923–944.

DiLalla, L. F., & Gottesman, I. I. (1991). Biological and genetic contributions to violence: Widom's untold tale. *Psychological Bulletin, 109*, 125–129.

Dinwiddie, S. H., & Bucholz, K. K. (1993). Psychiatric diagnoses of self-reported child abusers. *Child Abuse & Neglect, 17*, 465–476.

Dix, T. (1991). The affective organization of parenting: Adaptive and maladaptive processes. *Psychological Bulletin, 110*, 3–25.

Dixon, L., & Browne, K. (2003). The heterogeneity of spouse abuse: A review. *Aggression and Violent Behavior, 8*, 107–130.

Dubowitz, H., Kim, J., Black, M. M., Weisbart, C., Semiatin, J., & Magder, L. S. (2011). Identifying children at high risk for a child maltreatment report. *Child Abuse & Neglect, 35*, 96–104.

Dutton, D. G. (1994). The origin and structure of abusive personality. *Journal of Personality Disorders, 8*, 181–191.

Dutton, D. G. (1995). Intimate abusiveness. *Clinical Psychology: Science and Practice, 2*, 207–224.

Eaves, L. J., Prom, E. C., & Silberg, J. L. (2010). The mediating effect of parental neglect on adolescent and young adult anti-sociality: A longitudinal study of twins and their parents. *Behavior Genetics, 40*, 425–437.

Edleson, J. L. (1999). The overlap between child maltreatment and woman battering. *Violence Against Women, 5*, 134–154.

Egami, Y., Ford, D., Greenfield, S., & Crum, R. (1996). Psychiatric profile and sociodemographic characteristics of adults who report physically abusing or neglecting their children. *The American Journal of Psychiatry, 153*, 921–925.

Ehrensaft, M. K., Cohen, P., Brown, J., Smailes, E., Chen, H. N., & Johnson, J. G. (2003). Intergenerational transmission of partner violence: A 20-year prospective study. *Journal of Consulting and Clinical Psychology, 71*, 741–753.

Ehrensaft, M. K., Moffitt, T. E., & Caspi, A. (2006). Is domestic violence followed by an increased risk of psychiatric disorders among women but not among men? A longitudinal cohort study. *The American Journal of Psychiatry, 163*, 885–892.

Eiden, R. D., Leonard, K. E., & Morrisey, S. (2001). Paternal alcoholism and toddler noncompliance. *Alcoholism, Clinical and Experimental Research, 25*, 1621–1633.

Escriba-Aguir, V., Ruiz-Perez, I., Montero-Pinar, M. I., Vives-Cases, C., Plazaola-Castano, J., & Martin-Baena, D. (2010). Partner violence and psychological well-being: Buffer or indirect effect of social support. *Psychosomatic Medicine, 72*, 383–389.

Famularo, R., Kinscherff, R., & Fenton, T. (1992). Parental substance abuse and the nature of child maltreatment. *Child Abuse & Neglect, 16*, 475–483.

Famularo, R., Stone, K., Barnum, R., & Wharton, R. (1986). Alcoholism and severe child maltreatment. *The American Journal of Orthopsychiatry, 56*, 481–485.

Feingold, A., Kerr, D. C. R., & Capaldi, D. M. (2008). Associations of substance use problems with intimate partner violence for at-risk men in long-term relationships. *Journal of Family Psychology, 22*, 429–438.

Garcia-Moreno, C., Jansen, H. A. F. M., Ellsberg, M., Heise, L., & Watts, C. H. (2006). Prevalence of intimate partner violence: Findings from the WHO multi-country study on women's health and domestic violence. *Lancet, 368*, 1260–1269.

Gelles, R. (1973). Child abuse as psychopathology: A sociological critique and reformulation. *The American Journal of Orthopsychiatry, 43*, 611–621.

Gleason, W. G. (1997). Psychological and social dysfunctions in battering men: A review. *Aggression and Violent Behavior, 2*, 43–52.

Golding, J. M. (1999). Intimate partner violence as a risk factor for mental disorders: A meta-analysis. *Journal of Family Violence, 14*, 99–132.

Goodman, S. H., & Gotlib, I. H. (1999). Risk for psychopathology in the children of depressed mothers: A developmental model for understanding mechanisms of transmission. *Psychological Review, 106*, 458–490.

Gotlib, I. H., Joormann, J., Minor, K. L., & Hallmayer, J. (2008). HPA axis reactivity: A mechanism underlying the associations among 5-HTTLPR, stress, and depression. *Biological Psychiatry, 63*, 847–851.

Hamby, S., Finkelhor, D., Turner, H., & Ormrod, R. (2010). The overlap of witnessing partner violence with child maltreatment and other victimizations in a nationally representative survey of youth. *Child Abuse & Neglect, 34*, 734–741.

Hazen, A. L., Connelly, C. D., Kelleher, K., Landsverk, J., & Barth, R. (2004). Intimate partner violence among female caregivers of children reported for child maltreatment. *Child Abuse & Neglect, 28*, 301–319.

Heils, A., Teufel, A., Petri, S., Seemann, M., Bengel, D., Balling, U., et al. (1995). Functional promoter and polyadenylation site mapping of the human serotonin (5-HT) transporter gene. *Journal of Neural Transmission, 102*, 247–254.

Holt, S., Buckley, H., & Whelan, S. (2008). The impact of exposure to domestic violence on children and young people: A review of the literature. *Child Abuse & Neglect, 32*, 797–810.

Holtzworth-Monroe, A., Meehan, J. C., Herron, K., Rehman, U., & Stuart, G. L. (2000). Testing the Holtzworth-Monroe and Stuart (1994) batterer typology. *Journal of Consulting and Clinical Psychology, 68*, 1000–1019.

Holtzworth-Monroe, A., & Stuart, G. L. (1994). Typologies of male batterers: Three subtypes and differences among them. *Psychological Bulletin, 116*, 476–497.

Hurme, T., Alanko, S., Anttila, P., Juven, T., & Svedstrom, E. (2008). Risk factors for physical child abuse in infants and toddlers. *European Journal of Pediatric Surgery, 18*, 387–391.

Jaffee, S. R., Caspi, A., Moffitt, T. E., Polo-Tomas, M., Price, T. S., & Taylor, A. (2004). The limits of child effects: Evidence for genetically mediated child effects on corporal punishment but not on physical maltreatment. *Developmental Psychology, 40*, 1047–1058.

Jaffee, S. R., Caspi, A., Moffitt, T. E., & Taylor, A. (2004). Physical maltreatment victim to antisocial child: Evidence of an environmentally mediated process. *Journal of Abnormal Psychology, 113*, 44–55.

Jaffee, S. R., Strait, L. B., & Odgers, C. L. (2012). From correlates to causes: Can quasi-experimental studies and statistical innovations bring us closer to identifying the causes of antisocial behavior? *Psychological Bulletin, 138*(2), 272–295.

Kadushin, A., & Martin, J. (1981). *Child abuse: An interactional event*. New York: Columbia University Press.

Karg, K., Burmeister, M., Shedden, K., & Sen, S. (2011). The serotonin transporter promoter variant (5-HTTLPR), stress, and depression meta-analysis revisited: Evidence of genetic moderation. *Archives of General Psychiatry, 68*, 444–454.

Kaufman, J., Yang, B. Z., Douglas-Palumberi, H., Houshyar, S., Lipschitz, D., Krystal, J. H., et al. (2004). Social supports and serotonin transporter gene moderate depression in maltreated children. *Proceedings of the National Academy of Sciences of the United States of America, 101*, 17316–17321.

Kaufman, J., & Zigler, E. (1987). Do abused children become abusive parents? *The American Journal of Orthopsychiatry, 57*, 186–192.

Kelley, S. J. (1992). Parenting stress and child maltreatment in drug-exposed children. *Child Abuse & Neglect, 16*, 317–328.

Kempe, C. H., Silverman, F. N., Steele, B. B., Droegemueller, W., & Silver, H. K. (1962). The battered child syndrome. *Journal of the American Medical Association, 181*, 17–24.

Kerr, D. C. R., & Capaldi, D. M. (2011). Young men's intimate partner violence and relationship functioning: Long-term outcomes associated with suicide attempt and aggression in adolescence. *Psychological Medicine, 41*, 759–769.

Kim-Cohen, J., Caspi, A., Taylor, A., Williams, B., Newcombe, R., Craig, I. W., et al. (2006). MAOA, maltreatment, and gene-environment interaction predicting children's mental health: New evidence and a meta-analysis. *Molecular Psychiatry, 11*, 903–913.

Lung, C. T., & Daro, D. (1996). *Current trends in child abuse reporting and fatalities: The results of the 1995 annual fifity state survey*. Chicago: National Committee to Prevent Child Abuse.

Lussier, P., Farrington, D. P., & Moffitt, T. E. (2009). Is the antisocial child father of the abusive man? A 40-year prospective longitudinal study on the developmental antecedents of intimate partner violence. *Criminology, 47*, 741–780.

Magdol, L., Moffitt, T. E., Caspi, A., Newman, D. L., Fagan, J., & Silva, P. A. (1997). Gender differences in partner violence in a birth cohort of 21-year-olds: Bridging the gap between clinical and epidemiological approaches. *Journal of Consulting and Clinical Psychology, 65*, 68–78.

Magdol, L., Moffitt, T. E., Caspi, A., & Silva, P. A. (1998). Developmental antecedents of partner abuse: A prospective-longitudinal study. *Journal of Abnormal Psychology, 107*, 375–389.

Margolin, G., & Gordis, E. B. (2000). The effects of family and community violence on children. *Annual Review of Psychology, 51*, 445–479.

Masten, A. S., & Coatsworth, J. D. (1998). The development of competence in favorable and unfavorable environments. *American Psychologist, 53*, 205–220.

Mburia-Mwalili, A., Clements-Nolle, K., Lee, W., Shadley, M., & Yang, W. (2010). Intimate partner violence and depression in a population-based sample of women: Can social support help? *Journal of Interpersonal Violence, 25*, 2258–2278.

McGlade, A., Ware, R., & Crawford, M. (2009). Child protection outcomes for infants of substance-using mothers: A matched-cohort study. *Pediatrics, 124*, 285–293.

McPherson, A. V., Lewis, K. M., Lynn, A. E., Haskett, M. E., & Behrend, T. S. (2009). Predictors of parenting stress for abusive and nonabusive mothers. *Journal of Child and Family Studies, 18*, 61–69.

Milner, J. S. (2003). Social information processing in high-risk and physically abusive parents. *Child Abuse & Neglect, 27*, 7–20.

Milner, J. S., Rabenhorst, M. M., McCanne, T. R., Crouch, J. L., Skowronski, J. J., Fleming, M. T., et al. (2011). Event-related potentials: Search for positive and negative child-related schemata in individuals at low and high risk for child physical abuse. *Child Abuse & Neglect, 35*, 249–266.

Moffitt, T. E., Caspi, A., Rutter, M., & Silva, P. A. (2001). *Sex differences in antisocial behaviour: Conduct disorder, delinquency, and violence in the Dunedin Longitudinal Study*. Cambridge: Cambridge University Press.

Munafo, M. R., Brown, S. M., & Hariri, A. R. (2008). Serotonin transporter (5-HTTLPR) genotype and amygdala activation: A meta-analysis. *Biological Psychiatry, 63*, 852–857.

Munafo, M. R., Durrant, C., Lewis, G., & Flint, J. (2009). Gene x environment interactions at the serotonin transporter locus. *Biological Psychiatry, 65*, 211–219.

Murphy, J. M., Jellinek, M., Quinn, D., Smith, G., Poitrast, F. G., & Goshko, M. (1991). Substance abuse and serious child mistreatment: Prevalence, risk, and outcome in a court sample. *Child Abuse & Neglect, 15*, 197–211.

Murphy, D. L., & Lesch, K. P. (2008). Targeting the murine serotonin transporter: Insights into human neurobiology. *Nature Reviews Neuroscience, 9*, 85–96.

Noller, P., Beach, S., & Osgarby, S. (1997). Cognitive and affective processes in marriage. In W. K. Halford & H. J. Markman (Eds.), *Clinical handbook of marriage and couples interventions* (pp. 43–71). New York: Wiley.

Parke, R., & Collmer, C. (1975). Child abuse: An interdisciplinary review. In E. M. Hetherington (Ed.), *Review of child development research* (Vol. 5, pp. 509–590). Chicago: University of Chicago Press.

Parker, K. J., Schatzberg, A. F., & Lyons, D. M. (2003). Neuroendocrine aspects of hypercortisolism in major depression. *Hormones and Behavior, 43*, 60–66.

Plomin, R., DeFries, J. C., & Loehlin, J. C. (1977). Genotype-environment interaction and correlation in the analysis of human behavior. *Psychological Bulletin, 84*, 309–322.

Post, R. M. (1992). Transduction of psychosocial stress into the neurobiology of recurrent affective disorder. *The American Journal of Psychiatry, 149*, 999–1010.

Randle, A. A., & Graham, C. A. (2011). A review of the evidence on the effects of intimate partner violence on men. *Psychology of Men & Masculinity, 12*, 97–111.

Rennison, C. M., & Welchans, S. (2000). *Intimate partner violence*. (Rep. No. NCJ Publication No. 178247). Washington: U.S. Department of Justice.

Risch, N., Herrell, R., Lehner, T., Liang, K. Y., Eaves, L., Hoh, J., et al. (2009). Interaction between the serotonin transporter gene (5-HTTLPR), stressful life events, and risk of depression: A meta-analysis. *Journal of the American Medical Association, 301*, 2462–2471.

Robins, L. N., & Regier, D. A. (1991). *Psychiatric disorders in America: The Epidemiologic Catchment Area Study*. New York: The Free Press.

Rueger, S. Y., Katz, R. L., Risser, H. J., & Lovejoy, M. C. (2011). Relations between parental affect and parenting behaviors: A meta-analytic review. *Parenting-Science and Practice, 11*, 1–33.

Schulz-Heik, R. J., Rhee, S. H., Silvern, L., Lessem, J. M., Haberstick, B. C., Hopfer, C., et al. (2009). Investigation of genetically mediated child effects on maltreatment. *Behavior Genetics, 39*, 265–276.

Seng, A., & Prinz, R. (2008). Parents who abuse: What are they thinking? *Clinical Child and Family Psychology Review, 11*, 163–175.

Shih, J. C. (2004). Cloning, after cloning, knock-out mice, and physiological functions of MAO A and B. *Neurotoxicology, 25*, 21–30.

Shih, J., & Thompson, R. (1999). Monoamine oxidase in neuropsychiatry and behavior. *American Journal of Human Genetics, 65*, 593–598.

Slep, A. M. S., & O'Leary, S. G. (2001). Examining partner and child abuse: Are we ready for a more integrated approach to family violence? *Clinical Child and Family Psychology Review, 4*, 87–107.

Spinetta, J., & Rigler, D. (1972). The child abusing parent: A psychological review. *Psychological Bulletin, 77*, 296–304.

Straus, M. A., Gelles, R. J., & Steinmetz, S. K. (1980). *Behind closed doors*. New York: Anchor Press/Doubleday.

Street, K., Harrington, J., Chiang, W., Cairns, P., & Ellis, M. (2004). How great is the risk of abuse in infants born to drug-using mothers? *Child: Care, Health and Development, 30*, 325–330.

Sugarman, D. B., & Frankel, S. L. (1996). Patriarchal ideology and wife-assault: A meta-analytic review. *Journal of Family Violence, 11*, 13–40.

Tjaden, P., & Thoennes, N. (2000). *Extent, nature, and consequences of intimate partner violence: Findings from the National Violence Against Women Survey*. (Rep. No. Publication No. NCJ 181867). Washington: US Department of Justice.

Tolan, P. H., & Guerra, N. (1998). Societal causes of violence against children. In P. K. Trickett & C. J. Schellenbach (Eds.), *Violence against children in the family and the community* (pp. 195–209). Washington: American Psychological Association.

Trickett, P. K., & Susman, E. J. (1988). Parental perceptions of child-rearing practices in physically abusive and nonabusive families. *Developmental Psychology, 24*, 270–276.

U.S. Department of Health and Human Services. (2010). *Child maltreatment 2009*. Retrieved June 15, 2011 from http://www.acf.hhs.gov/programs/cb/stats_research/index.htm#can

van Goozen, S. H. M., Fairchild, G., Snoek, H., & Harold, G. T. (2007). The evidence for a neurobiological model of childhood antisocial behavior. *Psychological Bulletin, 133*, 149–182.

Walsh, C., MacMillan, H. L., & Jamieson, E. (2003). The relationship between parental substance abuse and child maltreatment: Findings from the Ontario Health Supplement. *Child Abuse & Neglect, 27,* 1409–1425.

Walsh, C., McMillan, H., & Jamieson, E. (2002). The relationship between parental psychiatric disorder and child physical and sexual abuse: Findings from the Ontario Health Supplement. *Child Abuse & Neglect, 26,* 11–22.

Wasserman, D. R., & Leventhal, J. M. (1993). Maltreatment of children born to cocaine-abusing mothers. *American Journal of Diseases of Children, 147,* 1324–1328.

Whipple, E. E., & Webster-Stratton, C. (1991). The role of parental stress in physically abuse families. *Child Abuse & Neglect, 15,* 279–291.

Woodward, L. J., Fergusson, D. M., & Horwood, L. J. (2002). Romantic relationships of young people with childhood and adolescent onset antisocial behavior problems. *Journal of Abnormal Child Psychology, 30,* 231–243.

Wu, S. S., Ma, C. X., Carter, R. L., Ariet, M., Feaver, E. A., Resnick, M. B., et al. (2004). Risk factors for infant maltreatment: A population-based study. *Child Abuse & Neglect, 28,* 1253–1264.

Understanding and Promoting the Development of Resilience in Families*

Susan M. Sheridan, Tara M. Sjuts, and Michael J. Coutts

Children spend the majority of their early lives within the context of the family. As the composition of the family system continues to change, the caregivers' role has become increasingly important in fostering healthy developmental trajectories for their children. Family relationships and interaction styles are central to developing competence and promoting adaptive educational, social, emotional, and behavioral functioning. Clearly, families serve a primary role in their children's development. Families give a child an informal education (Turnbull, Turnbull, Erwin, & Soodak, 2006), which is considered a prerequisite for successful experiences in the classroom (Adams & Christenson, 2000). Whereas the school environment sets up developmental tasks for students, the family serves as an important resource for the acquisition of these developmental tasks (Stevenson & Baker, 1987). Parents are considered to be providers of linguistic and social capital by presenting their child with learning experiences from early childhood through adult years. Such experiences consist of (a) exposing a child to ideas and activities that promote the acquisition of knowledge; (b) assisting in the socialization of gender, cultural, and peer roles; (c) establishing standards, expectations, and rules; and (d) delivering rewards and praise (Clark, 1988). Parents also play an important role in the development of children's behavioral, social, and emotional skills. Parents can teach their children appropriate behaviors through everyday interactions and strategies, such as providing positive attention, encouragement, and praise; setting clear and consistent limits; using natural and logical consequences for inappropriate behavior; and teaching problem-solving skills, social skills, and emotion regulation skills (Webster-Stratton, 2005).

Unfortunately, some families face various forms of stress and adversity, thereby challenging their abilities to optimally support their children's development. The purpose of this chapter is to articulate the concept of family resilience and its importance in helping families realize their fundamental responsibility of ensuring the healthy development and adaptation of children. Following a brief discussion of realities facing families in contemporary society, the notion of family resilience will be defined and couched in ecological theory. Characteristics of resilient families will be reviewed, and approaches for building family strength and resilience will be presented.

---

*Portions of this chapter were published originally in Sheridan, S. M., Eagle, J. W., & Dowd, S. E. (2005). Families as contexts for children's adaptation. In S. Goldstein & R. Brooks (Eds.), *Handbook of resiliency in children* (pp. 165–179). New York: Kluwer/Plenum Press.

S.M. Sheridan (✉) • T.M. Sjuts • M.J. Coutts
University of Nebraska, Lincoln, NE, USA
e-mail: ssheridan2@unl.edu; Tsjuts2@unl.edu; mcoutts@huskers.unl.edu

Definition of Family

The term "family" has been defined in a variety of ways and has evolved over time with recent trends within today's society. The U.S. Census Bureau defines a family household as consisting of at least two members related by birth, marriage, or adoption (Kreider & Elliott, 2009). Although this restricted definition is practical for collecting census data, it is neither inclusive nor functional for many contemporary households. Current conceptualizations of "family" no longer consider a direct relation through birth, marriage, or adoption to be a requisite condition for defining the term "family." In contemporary society and related research on the topic, families are viewed from a holistic lens to include individuals who fulfill important roles in one's life that are traditionally met by immediate family members, regardless of a direct relation (Turnbull et al., 2006). Thus, a family may best be viewed not as a direct kinship, but as a group of people that together fulfill the roles and functions historically bestowed upon family members. For the purposes of this chapter, we will use the following definition when discussing families:

> Families include two or more people who regard themselves as a family and who carry out the functions that families typically perform. These people may or may not be related by blood or marriage and may or may not usually live together (Turnbull et al., 2006, p. 7).

The Evolving Family Structure

Over recent decades, the landscape of the family structure has changed dramatically. The United States has seen a decrease in the "traditional" family, which is composed of two biological parents and consists of one parent in the workforce and the other in a caregiver role. The traditional family is now being replaced in many instances by an increasingly diverse family structure. The population of children living with two parents decreased from 77% in 1980 to 72% in 1990 and 69% in 2002 (Fields, 2003; U.S.

Census Bureau, 2003). This decline has leveled since 2002, with 69% of children living with two parents in 2010 (U.S. Census Bureau, 2010). Single-parent families and stepparent families have become more common, despite the fact that children from these families are at greater risk for low academic achievement and are more likely to drop out of school or bear children at an early age, as well as display psychological factors including depression, anxiety, stress, and aggression (Fields, Smith, Bass, & Lugaila, 2001). Currently, 23% of children are living in single-parent families headed by women compared to only 3% of children living in single-parent families headed by men (U.S. Census Bureau, 2010). Additionally, the average number of people per household has waned from 3.1 people per household in 1970 to 2.6 in 2007 (Kreider & Elliott, 2009).

The cultural and educational climate of the American family has also changed over the years. In 2010, 55% of all children in the United States were identified as White, non-Hispanic (U.S. Census Bureau, 2010). This is a sharp decline from the 64% reported in 2000 (U.S. Census Bureau, 2000). Currently, over 3% of children living in the United States are foreign born, with at least one foreign-born parent. Additionally, 33% of parents report the highest level of education of either parent in the home as a high school degree or less (U.S. Census Bureau, 2010). Other realities facing families in today's society include economic challenges and conflicts overseas, such as that being experienced in the Middle East.

The recent decline of the American economy has left many parents without jobs. In 2007, 91% of fathers and 68% of mothers were employed (Kreider & Elliott, 2009); however, in 2010, 67% of fathers and 63% of mothers were employed (U.S. Census Bureau, 2010). The dramatic drop in the number of working parents has led to poverty-related challenges. In 2010, 21% of children were living below the poverty line and 43% are considered low income (living below 199% of the poverty line); 19% of children were living in families that received food stamps; and 10% of children were not covered by health insurance (U.S. Census Bureau, 2010). The negative impact that poverty can have on children has been well documented. Children living in poverty or socioeconomic disadvantage experience lower rates of cognitive functioning, academic achievement, physical health status, and positive child adjustment, as well as increased rates of internalizing and externalizing symptoms (Conger et al., 2002; McLoyd, 1998; Petterson & Albers, 2001).

Poverty is one but not the only persistent social issue facing families in the United States. Due to the terroristic and military conflicts arising around the world, current generations of children are also impacted by the deployment of parents for military service. It is estimated that 700,000 children have had a parent deployed on military assignment since September 11, 2001 (Johnson et al., 2007). These deployments leave families and children devoid of one parent for extended periods of time, with the added stress of worrying about their parent's safety. Risk factors associated with a military family's lifestyle (e.g., deployment, frequent relocation, exposure to combat) have been theorized to have negative, indirect effects on child outcomes through increases in parental stress and psychopathology (Palmer, 2008). When a parent leaves for deployment, families are left with the responsibility of adapting to having one less member and are required to fulfill the missing member's roles within the family. This change can lead to ambiguity and role confusion within families and cause stress to the remaining family members (McFarlane, 2009).

The stress associated with issues such as poverty and deployment places a significant strain on parent–child relationships, which can have a detrimental impact on child development (Conger et al., 2002; Palmer, 2008). The presence of protective factors is related to families' abilities to successfully support their children's development even in the face of stress or adversity (e.g., poverty, military deployment). In times of family stress, protective factors take on an even greater importance. Therefore, promoting protective family characteristics is crucial in helping families create resiliency and perform their primary function: building competence in their children and enabling them to deal effectively with challenging

life circumstances (Seccombe, 2002). Given the large percentage of American families facing serious hardships, it is important to understand factors associated with resilience and methods for its promotion.

Definitions and Underpinnings of Family Resilience

Multiple definitions of resilience have been posited in the literature, and several have extended beyond a focus on individuals to encompass aspects important for family functioning (i.e., family resilience). Patterson (2002a) suggested that family resilience is "the processes by which families are able to adapt and function competently following exposure to significant adversity or crisis" (p. 352). Similarly, Simon, Murphy, and Smith (2005) defined family resilience as "the ability of a family to respond positively to an adverse situation and emerge from the situation feeling strengthened, more resourceful, and more confident than its prior state" (p. 427). Luthar, Cicchetti, and Becker (2000) proposed resilience as "a dynamic process encompassing positive adaptation within the context of significant adversity" (p. 543). Finally, Walsh (2003) offers a framework for family resilience as a process aimed at assisting families to "reduce stress and vulnerability in high-risk situations, foster healing and growth out of crisis, and empower families to overcome prolonged adversity" (p. 5).

Common definitions, such as those presented herein, have features that embrace context, process, and outcomes collectively characterizing the construct of family resilience. From a contextual perspective, it is commonly thought that resilience takes place within the context of an adverse situation or event within which the family finds itself. Adversity may take several forms and arise through issues internal to the family or its members (e.g., problems experienced by an individual, divorce) or within the broader society (e.g., economic strife, military activity). The manner and degree to which a family develops resiliency is typically considered a dynamic process requiring flexibility and adaptation.

The outcomes achieved as families develop resilience include greater levels of resourcefulness, confidence, and ability to avoid serious problems in the future (Conger & Conger, 2002). Thus, the notion of family resilience considers key processes that help families face challenges and that strengthen the family as a unit.

For purposes of this chapter, we define "resilience in families" as the ability of the family to respond to stress and challenge in a positive and adaptive manner, characterized by the demonstration of competence and confidence among its members, with the intentional goal of socializing children. It includes concomitant attention to the development of resilience in its individuals, while at the same time embracing the resilience of the entire family system. It is further conceptualized along a continuum. Families are not necessarily "resilient" or not; rather, they demonstrate varying degrees of resiliency in response to different stressors and may be more or less capable to adapt depending on unique situations and their consequences.

Several theories have shaped contemporary understandings of family resilience. An integration of ecological systems and developmental theories has contributed to our conceptualization of the construct. An ecological-systems approach (Bronfenbrenner, 1979) considers both the characteristics of the family and the reciprocal interactions among the family and the broader systems within which they function (e.g., workplace, community). Ecological theory posits that individual family members (and by extension, family units) exist in the context of multiple interacting systems, and the experiences and interactions within and among those systems both influence and are potentially influenced by each other. The multiple interacting systems in the life of a family exist at both the immediate and proximal level (i.e., microsystem, such as neighborhoods, church group affiliations) and at indirect or distal level (i.e., exosystem, such as governmental policies or cultural norms). The ability of a family and its members to develop resilience is thus influenced by relationships, patterns of interaction, and direct and indirect experiences within and across various systems. Further, all systems have

strengths that can be leveraged to help build family resilience. Therefore, by virtue of being embedded within interacting ecological systems, all families have the potential for resilience. The identification of family strengths and their ability to take advantage of social supports and resources from within their embedded systems provides mechanisms for the development of resilience.

A developmental perspective is also relevant in our notion of family resilience. In contrast to perspectives that view family resilience as a set of fixed traits or attributes, a developmental vantage point views resilience as a process in which interactions between risk and protective factors mediate a specified outcome (Walsh, 1996). Within a developmental framework, a family's ability to adapt and cope with adversity is a process determined by many co-existing and evolving factors that occur over time and are developed in response to complex and changing conditions within and outside of the family. Furthermore, what is "resilient" at one point in time may be considered ineffective or inappropriate at another, depending on the developmental progression of its members.

The concept of family resilience, embedded within ecological systems and developmental paradigms, is an ongoing and evolving process occurring at multiple levels (Patterson, 2002b). One level focuses on the interactions among individual family members within the family unit, and the second centers on interactions between the family unit and the broader ecology. This view of family resilience highlights the connection between the family system and larger community contexts, thereby emphasizing the importance of both family and community efforts in fostering resilience.

Finally, cultural awareness is significant when conceptualizing family resilience. Traits or characteristics may vary in their relevance and salience in relation to family resilience. For example, varying levels of family cohesion may be valued differently in Eastern and Western cultures. Additionally, the strategies families use to cope with adversity may be relevant in one culture but considered inappropriate in another culture. The resilient response of a family in the face of adversity is dependent upon the values present in a particular culture, how the members of that culture conceptualize the adverse event, and the cultural expectations regarding coping and adaptation.

Characteristics of Resiliency

An understanding of the characteristics that resilient families may exhibit is necessary when determining methods by which to promote family resilience. Key characteristics that are often present in resilient families include cohesion, positive parenting, affective involvement, parent engagement, communication, problem solving, and adaptability (see Table 9.1). Together, these characteristics support families in times of challenge and crisis, helping families respond in a positive and adaptive manner.

Cohesion

According to Turnbull and Turnbull (1997), family cohesion is defined as "family members' close emotional bonding with each other as well as the level of independence they feel within the

family system" (p. 108). The degree of emotional connectedness varies significantly between and within families and is influenced by the culture, age, and stage of life of the family members. Within connected relationships, family members display emotional closeness and loyalty while maintaining some friendships and leisure activities outside the family unit. There is mutual support and emphasis on shared time, collaboration, and a commitment to work through struggles together, but there is also a respect for individual needs and boundaries (Cohen, Slonim, Finzi, & Leichtentritt, 2002; Walsh, 2003). Behavioral outcomes highlight the importance of cohesion in a family. Behavioral problems are common in families with low levels of cohesion and high levels of internal conflict. Specifically, Lucia and Breslau (2006) reported that level of family cohesion was associated longitudinally with the extent of children's internalizing and attention problems, as well as with their externalizing behavior problems. Cohesion between a parent and child is enhanced by parent–child interactions; child outcomes are mediated by the affective nature of these interactions. Effective attachment, defined as the affective bond between a child and his or her caregiver, provides the child with a sense of security, assuring the child

Table 9.1 Characteristics of resilient families

Characteristic	Definition
Cohesion	Family cohesion is defined as "family members' close emotional bonding with each other as well as the level of independence they feel within the family system" (Turnbull & Turnbull, 1997, p. 108)
Adaptability	Family adaptability or flexibility refers to a family's ability to modify its rules, roles, and leadership; thus, restoring balance between (a) family members and the family unit and (b) the family unit and the community (Olson, 1993; Patterson, 2002b)
Communication	Communication is the exchange of information, ideas, or feelings from one person to another
Affective involvement	Affective involvement refers to the extent to which family members value and display interest in the activities of other family members (Epstein, Bishop, Ryan, Miller, & Keitner, 1993)
Engagement	Parent engagement is parents' psychological, affective, and active commitment to experiences supporting children's learning and development
Positive parenting	Five core components define positive parenting: ensuring a safe and engaging environment, creating a positive learning environment, using assertive discipline, having realistic expectations, and taking care of oneself as a parent (Sanders, 1999)
Problem solving	Problem solving can be defined as a systematic process that allows individuals to formulate solutions to identified problems and involves objectively identifying and defining a problem; generating potential alternatives; assessing, selecting, and implementing the best choice; and evaluating the outcomes in relation to its success at ameliorating the original problem

that the caregiver is available during times of adversity (Pianta & Walsh, 1996). Formation of an affective bond is related to the quality and quantity of caregiver responses (Epstein et al., 1993), and responses marked by warmth, nurturance, and sensitivity to the child's needs facilitate resiliency and adaptive development (Maccoby & Martin, 1983).

The link between caregiver responsiveness and child functioning permeates numerous areas of development. A highly connected response pattern is related to positive socioemotional outcomes in children (Clark & Ladd, 2000). Specifically, parent–child connectedness is associated with peer acceptance (Cohn, 1990), quality friendships (Kerns, Klepac, & Cole, 1996), and altruism and moral development (MacDonald, 1992). The nature of the affective bond also sets the stage for cognitive development and school achievement. Children with secure attachment bonds display problem-solving capabilities, emergent literacy skills, and overall school adjustment (Pianta & Walsh, 1996). In contrast, insecure attachments have been linked to low levels of mastery and peer competence in school settings (Sroufe, 1989).

Positive Parenting

Resilient families are also characterized by high levels of positive parenting. According to Sanders (1999), there are five core aspects of positive parenting: ensuring a safe and engaging environment, creating a positive learning environment, using assertive discipline, having realistic expectations, and taking care of oneself as a parent. First, in a safe and engaging environment, children are supervised while they explore, experiment, and play. Next a positive learning environment is established when parents respond positively and constructively to child-initiated interactions through incidental teaching opportunities. In environments that promote learning, children develop language, social, and problem-solving skills. The third aspect of positive parenting, assertive discipline, is accomplished when parents

set and discuss specific ground rules, give age-appropriate instructions in a clear and calm manner, and use behavioral consequences such as time out and planned ignoring. This manner of discipline serves as an alternative to harsh and ineffective practices, and it promotes a positive parent–child relationship. Fourth, creating realistic expectations involves choosing developmentally appropriate goals for the child's behavior. This reduces the risk of child abuse, which often stems from unrealistic expectations. The last core aspect of positive parenting focuses on promoting a parent's self-esteem and sense of well-being, so parents are able to develop and use coping strategies to address challenging emotions and stress.

Taken together, these five core principles of positive parenting promote family resilience and reduce the risk of negative child outcomes. Negative effects that are correlated with poor parenting practices include outcomes such as behavioral and emotional problems, substance abuse, antisocial behavior, and juvenile crime (Sanders, 1999). However, when parents provide age-appropriate rules and these rules are enforced in a predictable manner, family resilience is enhanced and child outcomes improve (Black & Lobo, 2008). Kwok et al. (2005) reported that positive parenting mediated the relationship between widowed parents' psychological distress and their children's mental health concerns. A longitudinal study (Conger & Conger, 2002) indicated that nurturing and involved parenting compensated for child distress related to economic hardship and interparental conflict. Additionally, positive outcomes of nurturing and involved parenting during adversity included positive school performance, effective social relationships, and high self-confidence. Low levels of antisocial behaviors and emotional distress, as well as few externalizing and internalizing problems for adolescents, were also correlated with positive parenting practices.

The parenting style and practices adopted by primary caregivers play a critical role in the growth and development of children. Parenting style is defined as "a constellation of attitudes toward the child that are communicated to the child and that, taken together, create an emotional climate in which the parents' behaviors are expressed" (Darling & Steinberg, 1993, p. 493). Authoritative parenting, which aligns with positive parenting (Kwok et al., 2005), has been demonstrated to be typically the most efficacious style of parenting, and it is marked by predictable discipline, mutual respect, warmth, affection, clear expectations, and a level of flexibility. Authoritative parenting has been positively linked to academic achievement, positive peer relationships, and independence in children (Keith & Christenson, 1997). Further, parenting practices characterized by positive, consistent discipline are correlated with resiliency to stress in children (Wyman, Cowen, Work, & Parker, 1991). Conversely, authoritarian styles are less positively related to child development and resilience. Authoritarian or harsh, inconsistent parenting has been associated with verbal aggressiveness and argumentativeness (Bayer & Cegala, 1992; Grusec & Goodnow, 1994), conduct problems (Frick, 1993), and conduct disorders (Short & Shapiro, 1993).

Affective Involvement and Family Engagement

Another correlate of resilience is active and affective family involvement. Affective involvement refers to the extent to which family members value and display interest in the activities of other family members (Epstein et al., 1993). An emphasis is placed on the amount of interest as well as the manner in which family members demonstrate their interest and investment in one another. Active family involvement fosters the development of resiliency and healthy adjustment in children, and a key area influenced by family involvement is educational outcomes. Parent involvement in school is correlated with children's positive attitudes toward school, school attendance, positive behaviors, and study and homework habits (Christenson & Sheridan, 2001). Further, family involvement is positively

linked to student performance; optimal levels of family involvement are positively related to children's scores on prereading (Hill, 2001), reading (Clark, 1988), and math tasks (Galloway & Sheridan, 1994). Whereas family involvement may be conceptualized as involvement with other family members, it can also be considered in the context of connections to broad support networks and community bases. Family resilience is fostered when there are ties between the family and the community, and when kin and social support are present (Cohen et al., 2002; Walsh, 2003). Black and Lobo (2008) describe family resiliency as an interaction between the family and community networks wherein the family receives information, companionship, services, and respite. This connection to the community is two way; the family not only receives support, but they invest in the community and give back. This connection to the community allows children to feel safe in their community and neighborhood, achieve higher grades, and exhibit fewer behavioral problems. Additionally, parents benefit in domains including perseverance, hope, and companionship.

An extension of family involvement, family engagement, is another characteristic of resilient families. Family involvement and family engagement are closely related, but a key distinction divides the two. Whereas family involvement can be defined in terms of activities, family engagement is concerned with the quality of interactions between parents and children, and parents and other caregivers as they participate or are involved in those activities. Specifically, we define family engagement as parents' psychological, affective, and active commitment to experiences supporting children's learning and development. Engagement is demonstrated through parents' consistent and responsive interactions with their children, and between themselves and other caregivers in their children's lives. Key features of this interaction might include attentiveness, warmth, sensitivity, enthusiasm, and positivity. This interaction between parents and children fosters family resilience.

Communication and Problem Solving

Another characteristic central to resilient families is communication. Communication is defined as the exchange of information, ideas, or feelings from one person to another. In families, clear communication fosters family resilience by allowing family members to develop a shared sense of meaning regarding stressors or crises, as well as coping strategies, informed decision making, and collaborative problem solving (Walsh, 2003). Clear communication also helps protect children because it discourages them from filling in gaps in their knowledge or understanding with inaccuracies. Communication allows families to achieve agreement and balance, as well as to be connected, flexible, and able to organize resources (Bayat, 2007).

Active problem solving is another characteristic of families that demonstrate resilience in the face of a crisis or consistent adverse conditions. Problem solving can be defined as a systematic process that allows individuals to formulate solutions to identified problems. When done effectively, it involves determining the basis of the problem through analysis, objectively identifying and defining a problem; generating potential alternatives; assessing, selecting, and implementing the best choice; and evaluating the outcomes in relation to its success at ameliorating the original problem. Problem solving contributes to resiliency when the problem is recognized by the family, lines of communication are open, and parents work together to coordinate each family member's ideas and opinions (Black & Lobo, 2008). Additionally, problem solving builds family resilience when it involves creative brainstorming among family members, joint decision making, productive conflict resolution, and a plan to prepare for future challenges (Cohen et al., 2002).

Parent communication during the problem-solving process has been linked to children's social functioning (O'Brien et al., 2009), interpersonal skills, and conflict resolution (Costigan, Floyd, Harter, & McClintock, 1997). Additionally, there are strong links between the approaches parents and adolescents take in problem solving and communication. Alternatively, deficits in family problem-solving skills are related to several types of childhood problems, including depression (Sanders, Dadds, Johnston, & Cash, 1992), delinquency in adolescence (Krinsley & Bry, 1991), and reduced psychosocial competence (Leaper, Hauser, Kremen, & Powers, 1989).

Adaptability, Flexibility, and Stability

Every family faces situations throughout their life course that present challenges to the manner in which family members relate to one another or how the family unit functions within the community (Patterson, 2002b). Family adaptability or flexibility refers to a family's ability to modify and reorganize its rules, roles, and leadership; thus restoring balance between family members and the family unit, and the family unit and the community (Black & Lobo, 2008; Olson, 1993; Patterson, 2002b). Walsh (2003) conceptualizes flexibility as providing families an opportunity to bounce forward, as opposed to bouncing back. This distinction is made because a family can recover from a crisis, but they will not revert to their previous state. Instead, with resilience, they will improve and move forward.

To function as a healthy system, families must be both adaptive and stable. Families that are able to determine the appropriate times to maintain stability or attempt change are more likely to be healthy, functional families (Black & Lobo, 2008; Cohen et al., 2002; Olson, 1993). Successful and adaptive families are proactive in the socialization and development of individual family members and understand the importance of maintaining the family unit (Patterson, 2002a). Accordingly, there are two central components of family adaptability: adoption of optimal parenting styles and problem-solving practices, and developing a shared set of beliefs or values within the family unit. This is consistent with an ecological framework that views both the interactions among family members and the relationship between the family unit and the community as essential pieces in developing family resilience.

An important component for the development of family adaptability is the establishment of shared beliefs within the members of the family. Shared values and beliefs are essential for family resilience and reinforce specific patterns in how a family reacts to new situations, life events, and crises (Antonovsky & Sourani, 1988; Walsh, 1996). When families have a strong set of shared beliefs, they may view their interaction with the world from a collective "we" vs. "I" orientation (McCubbin, McCubbin, & Thompson, 1993). Resilient families often have a shared set of values for critical aspects of family life, including financial issues and time management (McCubbin & McCubbin, 1988).

Promoting Resilience in Families

Our conceptualization of family resilience is one wherein family strengths and resources are leveraged to overcome obstacles and challenges. The ultimate function and purpose of families is to ensure the positive development and adaptation of children. Services or interventions intended to build resilience realize this fundamental responsibility. Thus, services that are family centered and strengths based (i.e., that support families as they strive to become effective and self-sufficient in promoting positive child development) are the cornerstone of programs for building resilience. In other words, the ultimate goal of services to promote family resilience is to build caregivers' competence and confidence in order to build competence and confidence in their children (Sheridan, Marvin, Knoche, & Edwards, 2008).

Family-centered services are intended to build family resilience based on the extensive and seminal work of Dunst and colleagues (Dunst & Trivette, 1987; Dunst, Trivette, & Deal, 1988; Dunst, Trivette, & Deal, 1994). Four operating principles define family-centered approaches: (1) intervention efforts are based on families' needs; (2) existing strengths and capabilities of families are used to mobilize resources and promote abilities; (3) social networks are used as a source of support; and (4) specific forms of helping behaviors on the part of professionals promote acquisition of family competencies. In addition, family-centered services promote resilience when they ensure positive and adaptive outcomes for families. These are described next, with emphasis on their relevance for bolstering family resilience.

Base intervention efforts on family-identified needs. From a family-centered perspective, families are in the best position to identify their most salient needs. Thus, services are developed that are responsive to the priorities identified by the family in collaboration with supportive professionals. Likewise, commitment to change may be greatest when families' needs are self-determined. To build resilience, professionals can assist families as they strive to identify issues interfering with optimal or desired levels of functioning, define them in manageable terms, establish shared and long-term goals, state clear objectives, determine objectives essential to attaining short- and long-term goals, and clarify foci for intervention.

Use existing family strengths and capabilities to mobilize family resources. An overarching principle of family-centered services is that all families have strengths and abilities. Circumstances causing a family stress or adversity may limit their abilities to recognize, access, or use their strengths. Services based on family-centered principles help family members to identify and mobilize their strengths and to use them to attain goals that they articulate for enhanced familial functioning (Garbarino, 1982).

Maximize social networks and supports. The development of collaborations and partnerships within and across systems is essential to facilitate families' development of resilience. Positive, proactive linkages and networks help family members mobilize resources and supports that are available to them but that may have been perceived as inaccessible. An essential system interacting with children and families is that of the school. Schools and classrooms represent significant contexts for development, and teachers are meaningful individuals in a child's life (Sheridan & Gutkin, 2000). The establishment of partnerships between families and schools can be critical for maximizing the growth potential for a child. Positive, constructive relationships with other primary systems (i.e., schools) can be instrumental in helping families develop competencies and utilize resources on behalf of their child's development (Dunst et al., 1988; Sheridan & Burt, 2009). The notion of "partnership" implies that family members are co-equal partners in the identification of needs and goals, creation of strategies and plans, and evaluation of outcomes as programs and resources are utilized (Christenson & Sheridan, 2001; Welch & Sheridan, 1995). Thus, services are not delivered "to" or "for" families, but "with" family members as active partners and decision makers.

Use helping behaviors that promote the acquisition of competencies. When building resilience through a family-centered framework, professional roles focus on developing competence and confidence among all family members. Capacity building begins with an understanding and appreciation for "where the family is." Rather than utilizing strategies to "treat" problems or remediate deficiencies, family-centered approaches strive to promote the acquisition of family and child competencies. Models focused on "correcting a problem" result in a limited, often short-term resolution of one presenting concern. To build family resilience, services must attend proactively to growth-producing behaviors. The development of strengths, assets, and skills is expected to lead to generalization and maintenance of resources to address a range of presenting challenges in the future.

Ultimately, for families to be competent, confident, and resilient, they must be empowered. Empowerment models support families in proactively identifying needs, mobilizing resources, and accomplishing goals through the development of personal capacities, strengths, and abilities. This is contrasted to expert models, which often lead to dependency on the professional, fail to produce personal resources (competence) and positive belief systems (confidence), and result in limited skills in assessing personal needs and mobilizing personal resources and support systems in the future.

Concern is with process as well as outcomes. The emphasis in family-centered services is not only on the final outcome experienced by the family system, but also the processes by which families work toward the desired outcomes. In fact, it is thought that the strengths-based empowering process is the mechanism through which adaptive outcomes are achieved. As a process that promotes resilience through involvement, communication, and adaptability, family-centered services assist family members to actively participate in enhancing their own lives. Families are engaged in identifying their own needs, mobilizing resources on their own behalf, and accomplishing self-determined goals through the development of personal capacities, strengths, and abilities. Through such processes, attainment of long-term, generalized positive outcomes is maximized.

The strengths-based process by which professionals help families achieve their own goals is the cornerstone of family-centered service delivery. By helping family members identify and prioritize needs, establish reasonable goals, and develop appropriate plans, opportunities for positive family outcomes are maximized. Furthermore, strategies that are relevant and feasible for families, that result in desired outcomes, and that provide new knowledge and skill will likely be used by family members in the future when similar needs are present.

Our work has focused on consultation models as means for providing services promoting families' acquisition of competencies and attainment of goals. Although many forms of consultation exist in the literature (Gutkin & Curtis, 2009), behavioral consultation has received the most empirical support (Martens & DiGennaro, 2008; Sheridan, Welch, & Orme, 1996). Conjoint behavioral consultation (CBC; Sheridan & Kratochwill, 2008; Sheridan, Kratochwill, & Bergan, 1996), an extension of traditional behavioral consultation, was developed with the specific goals of enhancing families' skills and developing cross-system partnerships. This model will be reviewed next, with attention to its alignment with the goals of family resilience.

Conjoint Behavioral Consultation

Based on an ecological-systems perspective, CBC is a strengths-based service delivery model acknowledging that families do not exist in a vacuum and that children function within and across various systems in their environment (Bronfenbrenner, 1977; Sheridan, Kratochwill, et al., 1996). The two primary systems in children's lives are the home and school systems. CBC recognizes that children, families, schools, and other systems have a bidirectional, reciprocal influence over each other, and that the connections among systems are essential for facilitating positive outcomes for children. CBC secures these connections by bringing together families, schools, and other support systems in a collaborative manner to build social support networks in efforts aimed at addressing the needs of children. The process of CBC acknowledges the vital role of families and empowers them to be equal participants in the problem-solving process.

CBC is defined as "a strength-based, cross-system problem-solving and decision-making model wherein parents, teachers, and other caregivers or service providers work as partners and share responsibility for promoting positive and consistent outcomes related to a child's academic, behavioral, and social-emotional development" (Sheridan & Kratochwill, 2008, p. 25). CBC can be instrumental in promoting family resilience when challenges associated with children's behavioral, academic, or social-emotional functioning create hardships for the family system. In CBC, parents and teachers engage in a structured problem-solving process with a consultant to collaboratively address the needs of children across home and school settings. Parents and teachers work as joint consultees to share in the identification of children's strengths and needs, and to develop, implement, and evaluate interventions to ameliorate those needs through proactive intervention aimed at strengthening children's skills and competencies.

CBC services are based on several principles that parallel family-centered constructs (see Table 9.2). The indirect nature of services allows professionals to work with families and other caregivers (e.g., teachers), who are ultimately responsible for implementing programs and plans. By definition, consultation models (and CBC) strive to enable individuals (including families) to

"…become better able to solve problems, meet needs, or achieve aspirations by promoting the acquisition of competencies that support and strengthen functioning in a way that permits a greater sense of individual or group control over its developmental course" (Dunst, Trivette, Davis, & Cornwell, 1994, p. 162). Like family-centered services, CBC is implemented in a manner that is responsive to families' needs, builds competencies and resilience within members, and promotes participation and collaboration among systems.

The CBC process consists of four stages, implemented in a collaborative manner with families and school personnel working with the guidance of a consultant. Three of the four stages are initiated in the context of a structured interview with parents and teachers. The stages are (a) conjoint needs identification, (b) needs analysis, (c) plan implementation, and (d) plan evaluation (Sheridan & Kratochwill, 2008). The objectives of each stage, including objectives necessary for both addressing concerns and enhancing relationships, are in Table 9.3. During the needs identification stage, consultants work together with parents and teachers to identify a child's needs across the home and school settings, and consultees decide upon target behaviors for intervention. Consultants also assist parents and teachers in identifying valid procedures for collecting baseline data on the target behaviors across settings. In the conjoint needs analysis stage of CBC, parents and teachers evaluate the baseline data, decide upon behavioral goals for the child, and discuss various factors that may influence the child's behavior (e.g., events functionally related to the target behaviors). Hypotheses are generated regarding the environmental or functional conditions that may contribute to the occurrence of the target behaviors, and a plan is developed collaboratively to address the needs of the child.

The third stage of CBC consists of plan implementation. During this stage, parents and teachers implement the intervention procedures in the home and school settings, supporting implementation across settings. The consultant remains in close contact with parents and teachers throughout implementation of the intervention to provide support, ensure understanding of the plan, offer

Table 9.2 Characteristics of family-centered services and conjoint behavioral consultation

Family-centered services (Dunst & Trivette, 1994)	Conjoint behavioral consultation (Sheridan & Kratochwill, 2008)
Help-giver	Consultant
Employs active and reflective listening	Uses open ended questions and frequent summarizations to ensure understanding
Helps clients clarify concerns and needs	Provides help that is congruent with parents' needs
Pro-offers help in response to help-seeker needs	Does not determine target behaviors and/or interventions independent of parents' priorities
Offers help that is congruent and matches the help-seeker's appraisal of needs	Develops data collection and intervention strategies based on what works in families' environments
Promotes acquisition of competencies to meet needs, solve problems, and achieve aspirations	Focuses on existing skills, strengths, and competencies
Allows locus of decision making to rest with the family member	Creates opportunities for families to acquire knowledge to manage concerns (e.g., problem-solving approach, data-based decision making strategies, specific interventions)
	Encourages skills learned in CBC to generalize for future problem solving
	Focuses on increased sense of self-efficacy and empowerment among parents
Promotes partnerships and parent-professional collaboration as the mechanism for meeting needs	Promotes collaborative problem solving
	Promotes joint responsibility among home and school systems for problem and problem solutions
	Assists parents in learning strategies for working across systems to meet needs of the child
	Approaches systems work in a positive and proactive manner
	Focuses on common goals across systems rather than on problems within systems

Adapted from: Sheridan, S. M., Erchul, W. P., Brown, M. S., Dowd, S. E., Warnes, E. D., Marti, D. C., et al., (2004). Perceptions of helpfulness in conjoint behavioral consultation: Congruity and agreement between teachers and parents. *School Psychology Quarterly, 19*, 121–140

assistance, reinforce parents' and teachers' intervention efforts, and determine the need for any immediate plan modifications. The final stage of CBC is the conjoint plan evaluation. During this stage, parents and teachers examine the behavioral data collected to evaluate the effects of the treatment and determine if the goals of consultation have been met across the home and school settings. The team discusses plans for continuation, modification, or termination of the intervention based on the child's progress towards his or her goal and the family's and/or teacher's ability to maintain that progress.

Goals of CBC

The CBC process described earlier provides a logical format for operationalizing the principles of family-centered services, as the goals of CBC directly address these important principles. Paralleling the goals of family-centered services outlined earlier, important goals of CBC include: (a) address the needs that family members have for children; (b) use family strengths to address concerns; (c) establish partnerships; and (d) develop and enhance the skills and competencies of family members (Sheridan & Kratochwill, 2008). These relevant CBC goals and family-centered principles are described below.

Address the needs that family members have for children. The primary goal of CBC is to effectively address the needs that parents, teachers, and other caregivers have for children. These needs comprise the focus of consultation and are the basis for the services provided across settings. CBC consultants do not make assumptions

Table 9.3 Behavioral and relational goals and objectives by CBC stage

Behavioral (child) goals/objectives	Relationship goals/objectives
Needs Identification Stage (Building on Strengths)	
Identify strengths of the child, family, teacher, systems	Establish joint responsibility in goal setting and decision making
Behaviorally define the concern or need as it is represented across home and school settings	Establish/improve working relationship between parents and teacher
Explore environmental conditions that may be contributing to or motivating problem behavior	Validate shared goals of supporting the child
Determine a shared goal for consultation	Identify strengths of the child, family, and school
Clarify specific settings within systems that will be the focus for intervention	Increase communication and knowledge regarding the child, goals, concerns, and culture of family and school
Explore within- and across-setting environmental factors that may contribute to or influence behaviors	
Establish and implement baseline data collection procedures to set the stage for careful, systematic, data-based decision making	
Needs Analysis/Intervention Planning Stage (Planning for Success)	
Explore baseline data collected across settings	Use inclusive language to strengthen partnerships between home and school
Identify setting events, ecological conditions, and cross-setting variables that may be impacting the target concerns	Encourage and validate sharing of parents' and teachers' perspectives of the priority behavior
Investigate trends across settings (e.g., home and school) and highlight when appropriate	Foster an environment that facilitates "give-and-take" communication across settings
Elicit and provide information about the function or motivating features of the behavior that are based on environmental (rather than internal) explanations	Promote collaborative decision making and shared responsibility for plan development
Collaboratively design an effective intervention plan across settings that is sensitive to setting-specific variables	
Link assessment to intervention through the interpretation of concerns in terms of environmental conditions and not internal causes	
Discuss general strategies and plans to be included in a treatment package across home and school settings	
Summarize the plan, being clear about what is to be done, when, how, and by whom	
Plan Implementation Stage (No formal meeting)	
Implement agreed-upon intervention across home and school settings	Increase continuity in addressing child's needs across settings
Address questions, provide feedback, make immediate modifications to plan as necessary	Communicate about strategies as they are being implemented across home and school
Assess changes in student's behavior	
Plan Evaluation Stage (Checking and Reconnecting)	
Analyze treatment data in relation to baseline data	Continue to promote open communication; home-school collaborative decision making
Determine if the shared goals of consultation have been attained	Reinforce joint efforts in addressing needs
Evaluate the effectiveness of the plan across settings	Discuss parents' and teachers' perceptions
Discuss strategies and tactics regarding the continuation, modification, or termination of the treatment plan across settings	Reinforce parents' and teachers' competencies for addressing future needs
Schedule additional interviews if necessary	Establish means for parents and teachers to continue to partner
Discuss ways to continue conjoint problem solving or shared decision making	

regarding the needs of families (i.e., what will become the focus of consultation services); rather, they provide opportunities for families to express their concerns and determine mutual goals with other caregivers. This is the central objective of the needs identification stage of CBC.

Families are engaged and empowered to participate in needs identification and goal development through intentional efforts by consultants as they build a partnership orientation. Consultants provide an opportunity for families to describe and prioritize their needs and co-select targets that are thought to create optimal family functioning. In this way, the needs addressed in CBC are those that are most central to families, thus increasing the probability that families will devote their resources of time and energy to follow through on plan development, implementation, and maintenance of positive change. Consultants also incorporate flexibility and responsiveness in the process of prioritizing concerns for intervention. For example, through data collection, parents may learn that the initial needs were misidentified and identify new priorities later in the CBC process. This flexibility helps to ensure that the family's most essential needs are met.

Similarly, the consultant incorporates flexibility in developing interventions and data collection methods used throughout the CBC process, helping families determine those that fit within their culture and environment. Successful data collection is more likely to occur if an effective, practical, and efficient method of information gathering is developed— one that fits within the family's routine. The same principle applies to selecting and implementing an intervention. The likelihood that families will feel both comfortable with and empowered by implementing a plan for their child increases as the plan matches the schedule and culture of the family.

Consultants encourage families to assess the various factors that may contribute to or influence the target behaviors and goals of consultation. This analysis allows the consultation team to examine various systemic factors that contribute to children's behavior (e.g., negative interactions with the child, ineffective routines, and/or lack of resources) and develop strategies aimed at strengthening or restructuring environmental contingencies that may support positive adaptation in the child.

Use family strengths to address concerns. Importantly, the CBC process allows for an examination of teacher and family strengths and competencies to address children's needs. In CBC, consultants acknowledge that teachers have expertise in educational interventions and families have expertise relevant to the home environment. Families have knowledge (e.g., information about supports in the home, interactions with children, children's developmental histories) that can be used to address children's needs in consultation. Throughout the consultation process, consultants affirm families' strengths and contributions, further promoting their involvement in identifying and developing intervention components. For example, the consultant may assess and highlight intervention procedures families are already using throughout their daily routines. Highlighting the family's existing strengths in the home setting provides a sense of self-efficacy for parents by acknowledging their abilities to affect positive change in their child's life (Dunst et al., 1988).

Rather than focusing on barriers or families' lack of resources to cope with problems or hardships, CBC consultants provide an atmosphere that supports families and allows their existing resources to set the foundation upon which resilience can be developed. Such a strength-based approach ensures that the focus of consultation is on families' capabilities rather than on what is lacking in parenting skills and resources. Building on existing family strengths is essentially a matter of "meeting the family where they are" (Dunst et al., 1988) and viewing family members as having strengths to be utilized to address the child's needs. In this way, consultants provide services that are congruent and consistent with consultees' needs.

Maximize partnerships and support networks. Strengthening social supports and promoting partnerships and collaboration among systems is an important principle outlined in family-centered services (Dunst & Trivette, 1987). CBC's focus on establishing home-school partnerships operationalizes this principle directly. In CBC, home and school systems work in collaboration with one another to address mutual goals for children. The CBC process allows schools and families to share in decision making and adopt equal responsibility for both the assessment of needs and development of solutions. Likewise, parents and teachers actively participate in data collection procedures and implementation of the interventions developed in CBC.

As a team, consultants, parents, and teachers examine and evaluate data to verify the nature and extent of children's needs. The consultant facilitates the process but ensures that the teacher and parent jointly determine goals and develop and implement plans. General agreement among the home and school systems regarding a shared goal for consultation helps ensure continued partnership between primary caregivers (i.e., parents and teachers) in the child's social support systems (i.e., the home and school), thereby promoting the immediate and future success of children and their families.

Develop and enhance the skills and competencies of parents and teachers. Consistent with a family-centered principle toward building competence among parents (Dunst, Trivette, Davis et al., 1994; Dunst, Trivette, & Deal, 1994), an important goal of CBC is to promote parents' acquisition of skills and knowledge (Sheridan & Kratochwill, 2008). The CBC process achieves this goal through supporting and guiding the families' engagement in identifying needs and formulating solutions. Given their active involvement, parents, teachers, and other caregivers gather essential knowledge about aspects of the process such as the importance of identifying and defining the child's or family's needs, assessing factors that may contribute to maintenance of a specific behavior, mobilizing the family's strengths and resources, and developing interventions to achieve positive outcomes.

Through the CBC process, families learn to prioritize their concerns for children. During needs identification, consultants help parents identify specific behaviors to target for intervention, allowing for a more focused approach to problem solving. Likewise, detailed strategies for monitoring primary concerns are discussed (i.e., methods of data collection and evaluation). Throughout the consultation process, parents and teachers collect data on specific targets and information regarding environmental conditions that may affect children's behaviors. Consultants assist parents in using this information to develop meaningful interventions that address children's needs. Similarly, data are used to develop socially valid goals and monitor progress. Continued assessment throughout the consultation process provides parents with an understanding of the data-based decision-making process. Parents learn strategies for determining if goals have been met based on existing data, rather than subjective perceptions. Additionally, team members learn procedures for modifying plans when behavioral goals are not met. Through this process, families learn the value of using data to guide decision making regarding the child's progress and the efficacy of the intervention. Each of the aforementioned skills developed through participation in the CBC process provides families with tools that can be used to address future family needs. Families are empowered by recognizing their existing competencies, strengthening their skills, and acquiring tools for independence, which lessens their dependence on professionals for assistance in the future.

Conclusion

Families in today's society face many challenges that can impede them from ensuring the healthy development and adaptation of children. Family resiliency is a concept by which families meet these challenges in a positive and adaptive manner, thus allowing them to fulfill their primary function of socializing children. Understanding how resiliency is developed and fostered within the family context can play a central role in the development of effective interventions as well as to help strengthen families when life stressors disrupt family functioning. Interventions that strengthen family resiliency can provide families with skills for enduring challenging situations as well as preparing families for handling similar situations in the future. CBC has been described in this chapter as an example of how current interventions can be used to promote family resiliency through an ecological, developmental, and multicultural framework.

References

Adams, K. S., & Christenson, S. L. (2000). Trust and the family-school relationship: Examination of parent-teacher differences in elementary and secondary grades. *Journal of School Psychology, 38,* 477–497.

Antonovsky, A., & Sourani, T. (1988). Family sense of coherence and family adaptation. *Journal of Marriage and the Family, 50,* 79–92. doi:10.2307/352429.

Bayat, M. M. (2007). Evidence of resilience in families of children with autism. *Journal of Intellectual Disability Research, 51,* 702–714. doi:10.1111/j.1365-2788.2007.00960.x.

Bayer, C. L., & Cegala, D. J. (1992). Trait verbal aggressiveness and argumentativeness: Relations with parenting style. *Western Journal of Communication, 56,* 301–310.

Black, K., & Lobo, M. (2008). A conceptual review of family resilience factors. *Journal of Family Nursing, 14,* 33–55.

Bronfenbrenner, U. (1977). Toward an experimental ecology of human development. *American Psychologist, 32,* 513–531.

Bronfenbrenner, U. (1979). *The ecology of human development: Experimental by nature and design.* Cambridge: Harvard University Press.

Christenson, S. L., & Sheridan, S. M. (2001). *Schools and families: Creating essential connections for learning.* New York: Guilford.

Clark, R. M. (1988). Parents as providers of linguistic and social capital. *Educational Horizons, 66,* 93–95.

Clark, K. E., & Ladd, G. W. (2000). Connectedness and autonomy support in parent–child relationships: Links to children's socioemotional orientation and peer relationships. *Developmental Psychology, 36,* 485–498. doi:10.1037/0012-1649.36.4.485.

Cohen, O., Slonim, I., Finzi, R., & Leichtentritt, R. D. (2002). Family resilience: Israeli mothers' perspectives. *American Journal of Family Therapy, 30,* 173–187. doi:10.1080/019261802753573876.

Cohn, D. A. (1990). Child-mother attachment of six-year-olds and social competence at school. *Child Development, 61,* 152–162. doi:10.2307/1131055.

Conger, R. D., & Conger, K. J. (2002). Resilience in Midwestern families: Selected findings from the first decade of a prospective, longitudinal study. *Journal of Marriage and Family, 64,* 361–373. doi:10.1111/j.1741-3737.2002.00361.

Conger, R. D., Wallace, L. E., Sun, Y., Simons, R. L., McLoyd, V. C., & Brody, G. H. (2002). Economic pressure in African American families: A replication and extension of the family stress model. *Developmental Psychology, 38,* 179–193.

Costigan, C. L., Floyd, F. J., Harter, K. M., & McClintock, J. C. (1997). Family process and adaptation to children with mental retardation: Disruption and resilience in family problem-solving interactions. *Journal of Family Psychology, 11,* 515–529. doi:10.1037/0893-3200.11.4.515.

Darling, N., & Steinberg, L. (1993). Parenting style as context: An integrative model. *Psychological Bulletin, 113,* 487–496. doi:10.1037/0033-2909.113.3.487.

Dunst, C. J., & Trivette, C. M. (1987). Enabling and empowering families: Conceptual and intervention issues. *School Psychology Review, 16,* 443–456.

Dunst, C. J., Trivette, C. M., Davis, M., & Cornwell, J. C. (1994). Characteristics of effective help-giving practices. In C. J. Dunst, C. M. Trivette, & A. G. Deal (Eds.), *Supporting and strengthening families. Vol. 1: Methods, strategies and practices* (pp. 171–186). Cambridge: Brookline.

Dunst, C. J., Trivette, C. M., & Deal, A. G. (1988). *Enabling and empowering families: Principles and guidelines for practice.* Cambridge: Brookline.

Dunst, C. J., Trivette, C. M., & Deal, A. G. (1994). *Supporting and strengthening families: Methods, strategies and practices.* Cambridge: Brookline.

Epstein, N. B., Bishop, D., Ryan, C., Miller, L., & Keitner, G. (1993). The McMaster Model view of healthy family functioning. In F. Walsh (Ed.), *Normal family processes* (pp. 138–160). New York: Guilford.

Fields, J. (2003). *Children's living arrangements and characteristics: March 2002 (Current Population Reports, P20-547).* Washington: U.S. Census Bureau.

Fields, J. M., Smith, K., Bass, L. E., & Lugaila, T. (2001). *A child's day: Home, school, and play (Selected indicators of child well-being) (Current Population Reports, P70-68).* Washington: U.S. Census Bureau.

Frick, P. J. (1993). Childhood conduct problems in a family context. *School Psychology Review, 22,* 376–385.

Galloway, J., & Sheridan, S. M. (1994). Implementing scientific practices through case studies: Examples using home-school interventions and consultation. *Journal of School Psychology, 32,* 385–413. doi:10.1016/0022-4405(94)90035-3.

Garbarino, J. (1982). *Children and families in the social environment.* New York: Aldine.

Grusec, J. E., & Goodnow, J. J. (1994). Impact of parental discipline methods on the child's internalization of values: A reconceptualization of current points of view. *Developmental Psychology, 30,* 4–19. doi:10.1037/0012-1649.30.1.4.

Gutkin, T. B., & Curtis, M. J. (2009). School–based consultation: The science and practice of indirect service delivery. In T. B. Gutkin & C. R. Reynolds (Eds.), *The handbook of school psychology* (4th ed., pp. 591–635). New York: Wiley.

Hill, N. E. (2001). Parenting and academic socialization as they relate to school readiness: The roles of ethnicity and family income. *Journal of Educational Psychology, 93,* 686–697. doi:10.1037/0022-0663.93. 4.686.

Johnson, S. J., Sherman, M. D., Hoffman, J. S., James, L. C., Johnson, P. L., Lochman, J. E., et al. (2007). *The psychological needs of U.S. military service members and their families: A preliminary report.* Washington: American Psychological Association.

Keith, P. B., & Christenson, S. L. (1997). Parenting styles. In G. G. Bear, K. M. Minke, & A. Thomas (Eds.), *Children's needs II: Development, problems and alternatives* (pp. 559–566). Bethesda: National Association of School Psychologists.

Kerns, K. A., Klepac, L., & Cole, A. (1996). Peer relationships and preadolescents' perception of security in the child-mother relationship. *Developmental Psychology, 32*, 457–466.

Kreider, R. M., & Elliott, D. B. (2009). *America's families and living arrangements: 2007 (Current Population Reports, P20-561)*. Washington: U.S. Census Bureau.

Krinsley, K. E., & Bry, B. H. (1991). Sequential analyses of adolescent, mother, and father behaviors in distressed and nondistressed families. *Child & Family Behavior Therapy, 13*, 45–62. doi:10.1300/J019v13n04_03.

Kwok, O., Haine, R. A., Sandler, I. N., Ayers, T. S., Wolchik, S. A., & Tein, J. (2005). Positive parenting as a mediator of the relations between parental psychological distress and mental health problems of parentally bereaved children. *Journal of Clinical Child and Adolescent Psychology, 34*, 260–271. doi:10.1207/s15374424jccp3402_5.

Leaper, C., Hauser, S. T., Kremen, A., & Powers, S. I. (1989). Adolescent–parent interactions in relation to adolescents' gender and ego development pathway: A longitudinal study. *The Journal of Early Adolescence, 9*, 335–361. doi:10.1177/0272431689093009.

Lucia, V. C., & Breslau, N. (2006). Family cohesion and children's behavior problems: A longitudinal investigation. *Psychiatry Research, 141*, 141–149. doi:10.1016/j.psychres.2005.06.009.

Luthar, S. S., Cicchetti, D., & Becker, B. (2000). The construct of resilience: A critical evaluation and guidelines for future work. *Child Development, 71*, 543–562.

Maccoby, E. E., & Martin, J. A. (1983). Socialization in the context of the family: Parent-child interaction. In E. M. Hetherington (Ed.), *Handbook of child psychology: Vol. 4, Socialization, personality, and social development* (pp. 469–546). New York: Wiley.

MacDonald, K. (1992). Warmth as a developmental construct: An evolutionary analysis. *Child Development, 63*, 753–773. doi:10.2307/1131231.

Martens, B. K., & DiGennaro, F. D. (2008). Behavioral consultation. In W. P. Erchul & S. M. Sheridan (Eds.), *Handbook of research in school consultation: Empirical foundations for the field*. New York: Taylor and Francis.

McCubbin, H. I., & McCubbin, M. A. (1988). Typologies of resilient families: Emerging roles of social class and ethnicity. *Family Relations, 37*, 247–254.

McCubbin, H. I., McCubbin, M. A., & Thompson, A. I. (1993). Resiliency in families: The role of family schema and appraisal in family adaptation to crises. In T. H. Brubaker (Ed.), *Family relations: Challenges for the future* (pp. 153–177). Newbury Park: Sage.

McFarlane, A. C. (2009). Military deployment: The impact on children and family adjustment and the need for care. *Current Opinion in Psychiatry, 22*, 369–373. doi:10.1097/YCO.0b013e32832c9064.

McLoyd, V. C. (1998). Socioeconomic disadvantage and child development. *American Psychologist, 53*, 185–204.

O'Brien, M. P., Zinberg, J. L., Ho, L., Rudd, A., Kopelowicz, A., Daley, M., et al. (2009). Family problem solving interactions and 6-month symptomatic and functional outcomes in youth at ultra-high risk for psychosis and with recent onset psychotic symptoms: A longitudinal study. *Schizophrenia Research, 107*, 198–205. doi:10.1016/j.schres.2008.10.008.

Olson, D. H. (1993). Circumplex model of marital and family systems: Assessing family functioning. In F. Walsh (Ed.), *Normal family processes* (2nd ed., pp. 104–137). New York: Guilford.

Palmer, C. (2008). A theory of risk and resilience factors in military families. *Military Psychology, 20*, 205–217.

Patterson, J. (2002a). Integrating family resilience and family stress theory. *Journal of Marriage and Family, 64*, 349–360. doi:10.1111/j.1741-3737.2002.00349.x.

Patterson, J. M. (2002b). Understanding family resilience. *Journal of Clinical Psychology, 58*, 233–246. doi:10.1002/jclp.10019.

Petterson, S. M., & Albers, A. B. (2001). Effects of poverty and maternal depression on early child development. *Child Development, 72*, 1794–1813.

Pianta, R. C., & Walsh, D. J. (1996). *High-risk children in schools: Constructing sustaining relationships*. New York: Routledge.

Sanders, M. R. (1999). The Triple P-Positive Parenting Program: Towards an empirically validated multilevel parenting and family support strategy for the prevention of behavior and emotional problems in children. *Clinical Child and Family Psychology Review, 2*, 71–90.

Sanders, M. R., Dadds, M. R., Johnston, B. M., & Cash, R. (1992). Childhood depression and conduct disorder: I. Behavioral, affective, and cognitive aspects of family problem-solving interactions. *Journal of Abnormal Psychology, 101*, 495–504. doi:10.1037/0021-843X.101.3.495.

Seccombe, K. (2002). "Beating the odds" versus "changing the odds": Poverty, resilience, and family policy. *Journal of Marriage and Family Therapy, 64*, 384–394.

Sheridan, S. M., & Burt, J. B. (2009). Family-centered positive psychology. In C. R. Synder & S. J. Lopez (Eds.), *Handbook of positive psychology* (2nd ed., pp. 551–559). New York: Oxford University Press.

Sheridan, S. M., & Gutkin, T. B. (2000). The ecology of school psychology: Examining and changing our paradigm for the 21st century. *School Psychology Review, 29*, 485–502.

Sheridan, S. M., & Kratochwill, T. R. (2008). *Conjoint behavioral consultation: Promoting family-school connections and interventions*. New York: Springer.

Sheridan, S. M., Kratochwill, T. R., & Bergan, J. R. (1996). *Conjoint behavioral consultation: A procedural manual*. New York: Plenum.

Sheridan, S. M., Marvin, C. A., Knoche, L. L., & Edwards, C. P. (2008). Getting ready: Promoting school readiness through a relationship-based partnership model. *Early Childhood Services, 3*, 149–172.

Sheridan, S. M., Welch, M., & Orme, S. (1996). Is consultation effective? A review of outcome research. *Remedial and Special Education, 17*, 341–354.

Short, R. J., & Shapiro, S. K. (1993). Conduct disorders: A framework for understanding and intervention in schools and communities. *School Psychology Review, 22*, 362–375.

Simon, J. B., Murphy, J. J., & Smith, S. M. (2005). Understanding and fostering family resilience. *The Family Journal, 13*, 427–436.

Sroufe, L. (1989). Pathways to adaptation and maladaptation: Psychopathology as developmental deviation. In D. Cicchetti (Ed.), *The emergence of a discipline: Rochester symposium on developmental psychopathology* (Vol. 1, pp. 13–40). Hillsdale: Erlbaum.

Stevenson, D. L., & Baker, D. P. (1987). The family-school relation and the child's school performance. *Child Development, 58*, 1348–1357.

Turnbull, A. P., & Turnbull, H. R. (1997). *Families, professionals, and exceptionality: A special partnership.* Upper Saddle River: Prentice-Hall.

Turnbull, A., Turnbull, R., Erwin, E. J., & Soodak, L. C. (2006). *Families, professionals, and exceptionality: Positive outcomes through partnerships and trust* (5th ed.). Upper Saddle River: Pearson Education.

U.S. Census Bureau. (2000). *U.S. census of population and housing.* Washington: U.S. Census Bureau.

U.S. Census Bureau. (2003). *March current population survey.* Washington: U.S. Census Bureau.

U.S. Census Bureau. (2010). *America's families and living arrangements: 2010.* Washington: U.S. Census Bureau.

Walsh, F. (1996). The concept of family resilience: Crisis and challenge. *Family Process, 35*, 261–281.

Walsh, F. (2003). Family resilience: A framework for clinical practice. *Family Process, 42*, 1–18. doi:10.1111/j.1545-5300.2003.00001.x.

Webster-Stratton, C. (2005). *The Incredible Years: A trouble-shooting guide for parents of children aged 2-8 years.* Seattle: Incredible Years.

Welch, M., & Sheridan, S. M. (1995). *Educational partnerships: Serving students at-risk.* San Antonio: Harcourt-Brace Jovanovich.

Wyman, P. A., Cowen, E. L., Work, W. C., & Parker, G. R. (1991). Developmental and family milieu correlates of resilience in urban children who have experienced major life stress. *American Journal of Community Psychology, 19*, 405–426.

Resiliency in Maltreated Children

10

Shadi Houshyar, Andrea Gold,
and Melissa DeVries

Child abuse is a pervasive societal problem, with nearly one million substantiated reports of child maltreatment each year (U.S. Department of Health and Human Services, 2001), many reported cases of actual abuse that are not verified (Kaufman & Zigler, 1996), and countless other cases that are never brought to the attention of authorities (Wolfner & Gelles, 1993). Extant research has identified a host of negative sequelae associated with child maltreatment, including deficits in interpersonal relationships, affect regulation, and self-development (Beeghly & Cicchetti, 1994; Crittenden, 1992; Egeland & Sroufe, 1981; Maughan & Cicchetti, 2002), as well as increased rates of multiple psychiatric diagnoses (Ammerman, Cassisi, Hersen, & Van Hasselt, 1986; Cicchetti & Carlson, 1989; Cicchetti & Toth, 1995; Egeland, Sroufe, & Erickson, 1983). Although not all abused children develop difficulties, many experience a chronic course of psychopathology, with

posttraumatic stress disorder (PTSD), depression, and behavioral disorders constituting the common psychiatric sequelae of maltreatment reported in children (Briere, Berliner, Bulkley, Jenny, & Reid, 1996; Chu & Dill, 1990; de la Vega, de la Osa, Ezpeleta, Granero, & Domènech, 2011; Famularo, Kinscherff, & Fenton, 1992; Kaufman, 1991; McLeer, Callaghan, Henry, & Wallen, 1994; Pynoos, Steinberg, & Wraith, 1995) and adults (Springer, Sheridan, Kuo, & Carnes, 2007; Windle, Windle, Scheidt, & Miller, 1995).

Given the deleterious and long-term effects of maltreatment, there is a continued need for research in this area. A resiliency framework can be especially productive in guiding maltreatment research given that resiliency research focuses on (a) delineating the pathways to *positive adaptation* in abused children and (b) examining *how* children who experience considerable risk factors and stressors, including physical trauma and neglect within the family context, come to "beat the odds." Resiliency research explores the processes, moderators, and mechanisms that facilitate positive adaptation and can provide a guide for the development of targeted intervention practices aimed at attenuating the deleterious effects of maltreatment.

To date, pioneering investigators have set a strong foundation for resiliency research in widely disseminated empirical and theoretical reports (Cowen & Work, 1988; Cowen, Work, & Wyman, 1992, 1997; Garmezy, 1992, 1993; Garmezy, Masten, & Tellegen, 1984; Luthar, Cicchetti, &

S. Houshyar
Yale University School of Medicine,
New Haven, CT, USA
e-mail: Shadi.houshyar@yale.edu

A. Gold
Department of Psychology, Yale University,
P.O. Box 208205, New Haven,
CT 06520-8205, USA
e-mail: andrea.gold@yale.edu

M. DeVries (✉)
Neurology, Learning and Behavior Center,
Salt Lake City, UT, USA
e-mail: melissa@samgoldstein.com

S. Goldstein and R.B. Brooks (eds.), *Handbook of Resilience in Children*,
DOI 10.1007/978-1-4614-3661-4_10, © Springer Science+Business Media New York 2013

Becker, 2000; Luthar, Doernberger, & Zigler, 1993; Luthar & Zigler, 1991; Masten, 2001; Masten & Coatsworth, 1998; Masten et al., 1999; Rutter, 1990, 1995, 1996; Werner, 1992, 1993, 1995). Seminal works by resiliency researchers have led to considerable advancements in the conceptualization, implementation, and dissemination of resiliency research. Owing to notable progress, researchers have identified a host of protective factors and mechanisms that contribute to resiliency in high-risk populations.

One protective or modifying factor that has been recurrently associated with positive outcomes in maltreated children is the presence of a supportive and stable caregiver. The availability of a caring and stable parent or alternate guardian has been identified as one of the most important factors that distinguish abused individuals with good developmental outcomes from those with more deleterious outcomes (Beeghly & Cicchetti, 1994; Cicchetti & Toth, 1995; Kaufman & Henrich, 2000; Pynoos et al., 1995). In children, it decreases the likelihood of the development of PTSD and depressive disorders (Kaufman, 1991; Pynoos et al., 1995), reduces the risk for the development of behavior problems (Newton, Litrownik, & Landsverk, 2000), and is associated with better school achievement (Cook, Fleishman, & Grimes, 1991). Adults who were maltreated in childhood who report the presence of a supportive parent or foster parent as a child have been found to have more years of education (Cook et al., 1991; Zimmerman, 1982), greater housing stability (Meier, 1965), higher rates of self-support (Zimmerman, 1982), decreased risk of persistent violent antisocial behavior (Widom, 1991), decreased likelihood of early parenthood (Cook et al., 1991), better parenting skills, and lower rates of problems in caring for the next generation (Kaufman & Zigler, 1989; Zimmerman, 1982).

Chapter Framework and Organization

This chapter is organized using a translational framework. Translational research in the behavioral and social sciences utilizes knowledge of basic behavioral and biological processes to inform clinical studies. This is becoming increasingly plausible with the growth and integration of brain and behavior research, the merging of the fields of developmental psychology and neuroscience, advancements in neuroimaging and genetics research methodology, and findings from preclinical (e.g., animal) studies that examine the impact of stress on behavior, physiological reactivity, neural circuitry, and gene expression (Cicchetti & Tucker, 1994; Maier & Watkins, 1998).

As an example of this approach, Field and her colleagues utilized findings from studies of rat pups separated from their mothers to design an intervention for preterm infants that required extended incubator stays and prolonged periods of mother–infant separation (Scafidi & Field, 1997; Schanberg & Field, 1987). Specifically, animal studies have long established that separation of a rat pup from its mother is associated with a host of negative behavioral and biological consequences, including decreased growth hormone secretion. Through a series of studies, investigators were able to determine that it was the absence of maternal tactile (e.g., licking) stimulation that was associated with decreased growth hormone secretion during periods of separation (Hofer, 1987), and they were able to prevent separation-induced decrements in growth hormone levels by simulating maternal tongue-licking behavior with a wet paintbrush during periods of mother–infant separation (Schanberg & Field, 1987). These findings were instrumental to the formulation of massage therapy for preterm infants that require maternal separation during incubator treatment. Massage treatment of preterm infants has been found to increase growth hormone secretion, improve weight gain, decrease the time required for intensive care, and increase performance on measures of social and motor skill development (Scafidi & Field, 1997; Wheeden, Scafidi, Field, & Ironson, 1993). Cocaine- and HIV-exposed preterm infants have also been found to benefit from massage therapy (Scafidi & Field, 1997; Wheeden et al., 1993). This example demonstrates how basic research can be utilized to delineate mechanisms involved in producing different deleterious outcomes (i.e., an absence of touch leading to a decrease in growth hormone secretion and blunted growth) and suggests novel intervention strategies for high-risk populations (i.e., massage therapy for premature infants). It also highlights that even though biological mechanisms may be responsible for producing certain deleterious outcomes (e.g., reduced growth hormone secretion leading to blunted growth), psychosocial interventions can still be effective.

This chapter on resiliency in maltreated children is comprised of seven sections. The first section reviews key structures and neurotransmitter systems involved in the stress response; the second section reviews preclinical studies of the neurobiological effects of early stress; and the third section discusses factors that modify the impact of these experiences. The fourth section highlights similarities in the neurobiological correlates of stress and PTSD in adults, the fifth section discusses developmental issues in the application of these research findings, and the sixth section briefly discusses factors that modify the impact of early maltreatment identified in clinical studies. The data reviewed in these sections preliminarily suggest that (a) *genetic* factors influence outcomes of maltreated children, (b) a positive supportive caregiver (i.e., attachment) is a protective factor that minimizes neurobiological changes and other negative sequelae associated with child maltreatment, and (c) more work is needed to understand gene–environment interactions in determining developmental outcomes of maltreated children.

In the final section of this chapter, the clinical implications of this research are discussed in the context of the Adoption and Safe Families Act (P.L. 105-89), legislation aimed at promoting secure and stable attachment relations for maltreated children. The objective of this chapter is to highlight the benefit of multidisciplinary research efforts in resiliency research with maltreated children with foci that span from neurobiology to social policy.

Key Structures and Neurotransmitter Systems Involved in the Stress Response: Overview

The brain responds to stress in a complex and orchestrated manner, with both general and stimuli-specific components to the stress response (Lopez, Akil, & Watson, 1999). However, knowledge about the structural and functional components of the stress system is still evolving. The review of the stress response included in this section is not exhaustive. It focuses on key components of the stress system and emphasizes the structures and neurotransmitter systems most extensively studied in preclinical studies examining the long-term effects of early stress. The reader is referred to additional reviews for a more detailed discussion of the central and peripheral components of the stress system (e.g., Chrousos, 1998; Gold & Chrousos, 2002; Heim & Nemeroff, 2001; Lopez et al., 1999; Manji et al., 2003; Vaidya & Duman, 2001).

Figure 10.1 depicts the functional connections among the different cortical and subcortical brain regions involved in the stress response (Kaufman, Plotsky, Nemeroff, & Charney, 2000). There is growing appreciation of the role of cortical inputs, with medial prefrontal cortex (PFC), anterior cingulate, and orbital PFC currently understood to play an important role in relaying information from primary sensory and association cortices to subcortical structures involved in the stress response (Lopez et al., 1999). The medial and orbital PFCs are reciprocally interconnected, and each has connections with the hypothalamus and amygdala (An, Handler, Ongur, & Price, 1998; Bernard & Bandler, 1998; Krout, Jansen, & Loewy, 1998; Ongur, An, & Price, 1998). These prefrontal regions appear to be critical in restraining the acute stress response (Herman & Cullinan, 1997). The mPFC is also reciprocally connected with the mediodorsal thalamic nucleus (Groenewegen, 1988) and has extensive connections with the ventral tegmental area, substantia nigra, nucleus accumbens, raphe, locus coeruleus (LC), and brainstem autonomic nuclei (Drevets, Ongur, & Price, 1998).

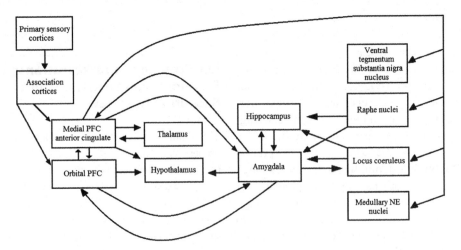

Fig. 10.1 Key cortical and subcortical structures involved in the stress response. Medial prefrontal cortex (PFC), anterior cingulate, and orbital PFC relay information from primary sensory and association cortices to subcortical structures involved in the stress response. Medial and orbital PFC are reciprocally interconnected. The medical and orbital cortices provide direct inputs to the hypothalamus, and are reciprocally connected with the amygdala. Not show in the diagram are indirect connections from these prefrontal structures to the hypothalamus and amygdala via inputs to the perdiaqueductal gray and parabrachial nucleus. The mPFC is also reciprocally connected with the mediodorsal thalamic nucleus and has extensive connections with the ventral tegmental area, substantia nigra, nucleus accumbens, raphe, locus coeruleus, and brainstem autonomic nuclei. These connections facilitate initiation and regulation of the endocrine response to stress that is mediated by the coeruleus. PFC = prefrontal cortex; straight line = stimulatory; dotted line = inhibitory. Source: Reprinted from Kaufman, Plotsky, Nemeroff, & Charmey, 2000

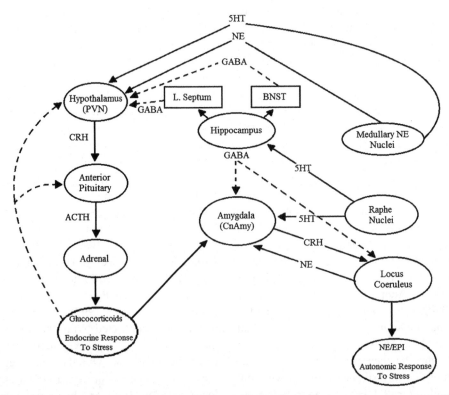

Fig. 10.2 Neurotransmitter systems utilized by subcortical structures involved in the stress response. The release of neurohormone CRH from the PVN of the hypothalamus initiates the endocrine response to stress. CRH then promotes the release of ACTH from the pituitary, which initiates the release of glucocorticoids from the adrenals.

Figure 10.2 depicts in more detail the relationship among subcortical structures involved in the stress response, and the neurotransmitter systems involved in the transmission of information between the different brain regions. Corticotropin releasing hormone (CRH) is the neurohormone that initiates the endocrine response to stress. It is secreted from the paraventricular nucleus (PVN) of the hypothalamus. Among the numerous inputs to the hypothalamus, noradrenergic inputs are primary in promoting the synthesis and release of CRH (Plotsky, Cunningham, & Widmaier, 1989). The main noradrenergic inputs into the hypothalamus appear to be derived from medullary sources, the nucleus of the solitary tract (NTS), and the ventrolateral medullary oblongata (Pacak, Palkovits, Kopin, & Goldstein, 1995). CRH then binds to receptors at the anterior pituitary gland and, through a cascade of intracellular events, promotes the release of adrenocorticotropin (ACTH). ACTH then promotes the synthesis and release of glucocorticoids (Cortisol in primates. corticosterone in rats) from the adrenal cortex (Arborelius, Owens, Plotsky, & Nemeroff, 1999). Glucocorticoids regulate energy availability and utilization and provide negative feedback to the stress system at the pituitary, hypothalamus, and other central sites involved in the stress response.

The LC appears to be the critical site in initiating the autonomic response to stress and promoting the release of norepinephrine (NE) and epinephrine (EPI) into the periphery. It receives endogenous CRH inputs from the central nucleus of the amgydala (Jezova, Ochedalski, Glickman, Kiss, & Aguilera, 1999; Page & Abercrombie,

1999; Valentino, Curtis, Page, Pavcovich, & Florin-Lechner, 1998). The amygdala is activated during stress by ascending catecholamine neurons originating in the brainstem and by cortical association neurons involved in processing stressful stimuli via direct and indirect medial and orbital prefrontal cortical connections (Lopez et al., 1999). CRH neurons in the amygdala respond positively to glucocorticoids and activate the LC/NE component of the stress system (Lopez et al.).

The hippocampus, in contrast, serves to inhibit the stress response via multiple direct and indirect links with several of the brain structures activated during stress (Lopez et al., 1999). For example, CRH synthesis in the amygdala is inhibited by gamma-aminobutyric acid (GABA) inputs from the hippocampus (Owens & Nemeroff, 1991). The hippocampus also inhibits the LC via direct connections and inhibits the hypothalamus via indirect inputs through the lateral septum and bed nucleus of the stria terminalis (BNST).

The stress response is further modified by serotonin (5HT) inputs from the raphe to the amygdala, hypothalamus, and the hippocampus (Lopez et al., 1999). The latter 5HT neurons terminate on inhibitory GABA neurons.

Neurobiological Effects of Early Stress: Preclinical Studies

Building on the seminal work of Levine and colleagues (Coe, Mendoza, Smotherman, & Levine, 1978; Levine, Wiener, & Coe, 1993; Wiener,

---

Fig. 10.2 (continued) Glucocorticoids provide negative feedback at the pituitary and PVN, among other sites. The release of CRH from the PVN is modified by mutliple neurotransmitters, but NE inputs from the medullary nuclei provide the primary stimulus for CRH synthesis and release. CRH also acts as a neurotransmitter to initiate the autonomic response to stress. The autonomic component of the stress response is initiated by CRH inputs from the CnAmy to the LC. Glucocorticoids provide positive stimulation to the CnAmy, which promotes the synthesis and release of CRH. The hippocampus serves to inhibit the stress response via multiple direct and indirect GABAergic inputs to the PVN, amygdala, and LC. The stress response is further modified by 5HT inputs from the

raphe nuclei to the PVN, hippocampus, and amygdala. GABAergic interneurons located at each of the structures likely further modify stress reactivity, as do connections from multiple other brain regions including the PFC, thalamus, association cortex, and mesocortical and mesolimbic structures. NE = norepinephrine; CRH = corticotropin releasing hormone; PVN = paraventricular nucleus; CnAmy = central nucleus of the amygdala; GABA = gamma-aminobutyric acid; 5-HT = serotonin; EPI = epinephrine; PFC = prefrontal cortex; L. Septum = lateral septum; BNST = bed nucleus stria terminalis; solid lines = stimulatory inputs; dotted lines = inhibitory inputs. Source: Reprinted from Kaufman, Plotsky, Nemeroff, & Charney, 2000

Johnson, & Levine, 1987), numerous investigators have documented long-term neurobiological changes in animals subjected to multiple prenatal and postnatal stress paradigms (Graham, Heim, Goodman, Miller, & Nemeroff, 1999; Takahashi & Kallin, 1991). This review focuses on long-term effects of early stress on hypothalamic pituitary adrenal (HPA) axis function and central CRH, NE, serotonin (5-HT), and gamma-aminobutyric acid/benzodiazepine (GABA/BZ) systems. Structural brain changes associated with early and/or severe stress will also be reviewed.

Extensive research has been conducted examining the neurobiological effects of early maternal separation, with these experiences associated with increased CRH and NE drive in adulthood (Francis, Diorio, Liu, & Meaney, 1999; Ladd, Owens, & Nemeroff, 1996; Liu, Caldji, Sharma, Plotsky, & Meaney, 2000). Rat pups separated from their mothers 6 h/day during the first 3 weeks of life have been found to have increased basal and stress induced ACTH concentrations and decreased CRH binding in the anterior pituitary (Ladd et al., 1996). Maternal deprivation has also been associated with increased CRH mRNA expression in the hypothalamus PVN and increased CRH concentration in the median eminence (Plotsky & Meaney, 1993). It has also been associated with increased CRH mRNA expression in the central nucleus of the amygdala; increased CRH content in the parabrachial nucleus, a region that adjoins the LC; increased CRH binding in the LC; and increased NE concentration in the hypothalamus (Menzaghi, Heinrichs, Pich, Weiss, & Koob, 1993). Nonhuman primates subjected to maternal separation early in life have also been found to have elevated cerebrospinal fluid NE in response to an acute stressor (Kraemer, Ebert, Schmidt, & McKinney, 1989) (for reviews see Francis, Diorio, et al., 1999; Ladd et al., 2000).

The increase in CRH and NE drive in maternally deprived rats is also associated with a decrease in tone of the inhibitory GABA/BZ system (Caldji, Francis, Sharma, Plotsky, & Meaney, 2000; Francis, Caldji, Champagne, Plotsky, & Meaney, 1999). Specifically, adult rats subjected to repeat separations from their mothers during

the first 3 weeks of life have been found in adulthood to have reduced $GABA_A$ receptor binding in the amygdala and the frontal cortex. They have also been found to have reduced central benzodiazepine binding in the amygdala, LC, and NTS. These effects are associated with decreased expression of mRNA for the 72 subunit that encodes for the benzodiazepine site of the $GABA_A$ receptor. In addition, adult rats separated from their mothers during the first 3 weeks of life also had increased mRNA expression for the a2 and a3 subunits and decreased expression of the a^ subunit mRNA (Caldji et al., 2000). This profile is associated with decreased GABA binding (Wilson, 1996). It is likely that the dampened GABAergic tone in rats exposed to maternal separation contributes to the enhanced CRH expression in the amygdala and the increased stress-induced activation of the noradrenergic systems (Francis, Caldji, et al., 1999).

In an attempt to more closely parallel the experience of neglectful parenting and exposure to stressful environments in young nonhuman primate infants, Coplan et al. (1996) subjected macaque infant–mother dyads to variable foraging demands. Primates in the low foraging demand condition had easy access to food, primates in the high foraging demand condition had to work hard to find food, but foraging demands and food supply were predictable, and primates in the variable foraging demand condition experienced changing and unpredictable access to food. In adulthood, consistent with the maternal deprivation rodent studies discussed above, monkeys reared in the variable foraging condition had higher cerebral spinal fluid CRH concentration than monkeys reared under the two other more predictable and less-stressful experimental conditions (Coplan et al., 1996). The variable foraging condition was also associated with overactivity of the NE system (Rosenblum et al., 1994).

In addition to the neurochemical alterations associated with early stress, severe stress also is associated with hippocampus volume loss. Neuronal atrophy in the CA3 region of the hippocampus can be caused by 3 weeks of exposure to stress and/or stress levels of glucocorticoids (Sapolsky, 1996; Woolley, Gould, & McEwen,

1990). At this level, glucocorticoids produce a reversible decrease in number of apical dendritic branch points and length of apical dendrites of sufficient magnitude to impair hippocampal-dependent cognitive processes, with the number of damaged cells in the CA3 region of the hippocampus found to correlate with the severity of deficits in learning escape behaviors in a T-maze (Watanabe, Gould, & McEwen, 1992). More sustained stress and/or glucocorticoid exposure can lead to neurotoxicity, which is actual permanent loss of hippocampal neurons. Adult rats exposed to high concentrations of glucocorticoids for approximately 12 h/day for 3 months experience a 20% loss of neurons specific to the CA3 region of the hippocampus (Sapolsky, Krey, & McEwen, 1985). Evidence of stress-induced neurotoxicity of cells in this region has been reported in mature nonhuman primates as well (Sapolsky, 1996; Uno et al., 1994). Reductions in hippocampal volume can also be affected by decreases in neurogenesis (Gould & Cameron, 1996). The granule cells in the dentate gyrus of the hippocampus continue to proliferate into adulthood, and neurogenesis in this region is markedly reduced by stress (Gould, Tanapat, Rydel, & Hastings, 2000; McEwen & Magarinos, 2001; Sapolsky, 2000).

In contrast to the negative effects of early stress, rats that were given positive stimulation via 15 min of handling per day during the first 3 weeks of life have been found to have reduced stress reactivity in adulthood when compared to nonhandled or maternally separated rats (Plotsky & Meaney, 1993). Specifically, in adulthood, rats handled in the first 3 weeks of life show decreased fearfulness in novel environments. The neurobiological alterations associated with early handling are essentially the opposite of those reported in maternally separated rats. Handled rats show reduced ACTH and corticosterone response to exogenous stressors, with quicker return of corticosterone to baseline levels. They also show enhanced negative feedback of circulating glucocorticoids, and increased glucocorticoid receptor mRNA expression and glucocorticoid receptor number in the hippocampus and the frontal cortex, sites involved in the inhibitory control of CRH synthesis in hypothalamic neurons.

Accordingly, handled rats have reduced CRH mRNA levels in the hypothalamus and reduced basal CRH concentration in the median eminence. Handled rats also have reduced CRH mRNA concentrations in the amygdala and lower CRH content in the LC (Francis, Caldji, et al., 1999; Ladd et al., 2000). They also have attenuated CRH-induced activation of the LC and smaller resulting increases in extracellular NE levels in the hypothalamus after acute restraint stress (Liu et al., 2000). Handled rats have increased GABAA receptor levels in noradrenergic cell body regions of the LC and NTS, as well as increased central benzodiazepine receptor levels in the amygdala, LC, and NTS (Francis, Caldji, et al., 1999). In addition, as adults, handled rats have attenuated age-related cell loss in the hippocampus and improved performance on hippocampal-mediated cognitive tasks (Meaney, Aitken, Bhatnagar, & Sapolsky, 1991; Meaney et al., 1993) (for additional reviews see Francis, Diorio, et al., 1999; Ladd et al., 2000).

Factors That Modify the Impact of Early Stress: Preclinical Studies

The studies reviewed in the prior section demonstrate that early life experiences can have profound effects on brain structure and function. There are emerging data to suggest, however, that the subsequent caregiving environment can moderate the adverse effects of early stress. In conducting the handling experiments, Meaney et al. noted that there were marked differences in the maternal behavior of the mothers of handled and nonhandled pups, with the former group spending significantly more time licking and grooming their offspring than the latter group (Woodside, Meaney, & Jans, unpublished observation).

To determine if the differences in maternal behavior were related to differences in stress reactivity of handled and nonhandled rats, Meaney and colleagues examined multiple indices of stress reactivity in adult rats reared by mothers with similar natural occurring differences in maternal behaviors (Caldji et al., 1998, Liu et al., 1997, 2000). They found that the adult offspring of high-licking and grooming mothers reared without any experimental manipulations showed greater exploration in novel environments and had reduced plasma ACTH and corticosterone response to acute stress. The animals also showed increased hippocampal glucocorticoid receptor mRNA expression, enhanced glucocorticoid negative feedback sensitivity, and decreased hypothalamic CRH mRNA levels. They also had decreased CRH mRNA expression in the amygdala, increased central benzodiazepine receptor number in the amygdala and LC, decreased CRH receptor density in the LC, and decreased stress-induced NE secretion from the hypothalamus. These results parallel the findings observed in handled rats and suggest that maternal licking and grooming behaviors may "program" the development of the neural systems that mediate reactivity to stress (Caldji et al., 1998). These studies raised questions as to whether the neurobiological changes associated with maternal separation and handling were due to the early experimental manipulation or to subsequent differences in maternal behavior.

To determine if the neurobiological changes associated with early experimental manipulations could be altered by subsequent caregiving experiences, rat pups exposed to early handling or maternal separation experiences were cross-fostered with dams whose pups were assigned the same or opposite condition (Gonzalez, Ladd, Huot, Owens, & Plotsky, 1999). In the initial set of experiments, handled pups were either cross-fostered to other dams assigned to the handled condition or to dams assigned to the maternal separation condition. Similar cross-fostering was performed on pups exposed to the maternal separation condition. When tested as adults, the handled pups cross-fostered to dams assigned to the maternal separation condition reacted to novel stressors like rats subjected to maternal separation during the neonatal period. Conversely, maternally separated pups reared by dams assigned to the handling condition looked more like handled animals.

In a second set of experiments (Gonzalez et al., 1999), dams assigned the maternal separation conditions were provided with an age-matched foster litter during the period when their own pups were away. This simple manipulation seemed to normalize maternal behavior by the dams and the adult offspring that had been assigned to the maternal separation condition appeared like handled animals rather than like maternally separated animals. These findings are consistent with the results of studies examining the effects of prenatal stress. In these studies "adoption" with "optimal parenting" has also been found to reverse the HPA axis alterations typically observed in these experiments (Barbazanges et al., 1996; Maccari et al., 1995). These results are consistent with emerging data demonstrating the powerful role of different components of mother–infant interaction (e.g., tactile stimulation) in regulating physiological systems involved in the stress response (Caldji et al., 1998; Feldman, Singer, & Zagoory, 2010; Kuhn & Schanberg, 1998).

These preclinical studies suggest that the effects of early experiences can be modified by subsequent rearing experiences. As the influence of genetic factors or strain effects has been well established in preclinical studies of stress reactivity (Dhabhar, McEwen, & Spencer, 1997), the cross-fostering studies raise questions as to whether manipulations in parenting can overcome genetic and/or breed differences in stress reactivity. To address this question, Anisman and colleagues subjected BALB/cByJ and C57BL/6ByJ mice to early handling experiences and randomly assigned them to BALB/cByJ or C57BL/6ByJ mothers for subsequent rearing (Anisman, Zaharia, Meaney, & Merali, 1998; Zaharia, Kulczycki, Shanks, Meaney, & Anisman, 1996). BALB/cByJ mice are inherently high reactors and have elevated corticosterone and brain catecholamine (NE) responses to acute stressors. In addition, mice of this strain exhibit impaired performance on a Morris water-maze, a hippocampal mediated memory task that is exacerbated by foot-shock (e.g., stress) application. Early handling of BALB/cByJ mice reduced the learning impairments seen when mice were tested in the Morris water-maze as adults and prevented stress-induced elevations of corticosterone and disturbances with task performance. Likewise, cross-fostering BALB/cByJ mice with C57BL/6ByJ dams prevented corticosterone hyperactivity and performance deficits. However, cross-fostering and handling did not alter stress-induced changes in NE concentration in the hypothalamus, LC, hippocampus, or PFC. Early handling and cross-fostering of the more resilient C57BL/6ByJ mice had no impact on maze performance, corticosterone stress reactivity, or brain NE. A similar set of findings was reported by investigators studying two different high- and low-reactive rat species (Steimer, Escorihuela, Femandez-Teruel, & Driscoll, 1998). Effects of handling and cross-fostering were only observed in the high-reactive rats, and these experimental manipulations only affected stress-induced corticosterone levels, not central NE measures.

These studies highlight the need for a better understanding of gene and environmental interactions in determining an individual's stress reactivity. They suggest that species with more intrinsic reactivity are more responsive to the effects of environmental manipulations than species that are less intrinsically reactive, and that environmental manipulations have greater impact on some (e.g., HPA axis), more than other (e.g., central NE), neurobiological systems. Most importantly they suggest the adverse effects associated with early stress are not inevitable and can be modified by intrinsic and extrinsic factors, with the quality of the subsequent caregiving environment especially important in determining the long-term impact of early stress.

Similarities in the Neurobiological Correlates of Stress and Posttraumatic Stress Disorder in Adults

PTSD is one of the most common sequelae of early child maltreatment. As highlighted earlier, PTSD is but one of the many negative sequelae associated with a history of abuse. This section focuses on the neurobiological correlates of PTSD in adults to illustrate the utility of a translational research approach in understanding the sequelae of stress, as preclinical studies of the effects of stress provide a valuable heuristic for thinking about the pathophysiology of PTSD and organizing findings of the neurobiological correlates of PTSD, in adults.

Specifically, many of the biological alterations associated with early stress in preclinical studies have been reported in *adults* with PTSD. For example, adults with PTSD have been reported to have multiple alterations of the HPA axis, including: abnormal basal Cortisol secretion; altered negative feedback at the level of the pituitary; and blunted ACTH secretion in response to administration of endogenous CRH (Arborelius et al., 1999). They have also been found to have increased central CRH drive, as evidenced by reports of elevated concentrations of cerebrospinal fluid CRH (Baker et al., 1999; Bremner, Licinio, et al., 1997), increased central NE function, as evidenced by higher cerebrospinal fluid NE concentration (Geracioti et al., 2001), and altered activity in the orbitofrontal, prefrontal, and temporal cortices after yohimbine administration, an NE antagonist (Bremner, Innis, et al., 1997). Adults with PTSD also appear to have decreased GABA/BZ drive, as assessment with single photon emission computed tomography (SPECT) imaging of [^{123}I] iomazenil binding found adults with PTSD to have a reduced GABA/BZ receptor number and/or binding in the PFC (Bremner et al., 2000).

Structural changes have also been reported in adults with PTSD, with reduced hippocampal volume in PTSD patients as compared to normal controls the most highly replicated finding (Bremner et al., 1995; Bremner, Randall, et al., 1997; Driessen et al., 2000; Gurvits et al., 1996; Stein, Koverola, Hanna, Torchia, & McClarty, 1997; Villarreal et al., 2002; Vythilingam et al., 2002), and magnitude of volume loss correlated with functional deficits in verbal memory ability (Bremner et al., 1995; Bremner, Randall, et al., 1997). In addition, in studies using magnetic resonance spectroscopy (MRS) to assess neurochemical changes in the brain, individuals with PTSD were found to have reduced A^-acetyl-L-aspartic acid (NAA) and creatine in the hippocampus region when compared to controls (Freeman, Cardwell, Karson, & Komoroski, 1998; Schuff et al., 2001; Villarreal et al., 2002). NAA reduction is typically interpreted as an indication of neuronal loss or damage (De Stefano, Matthews, & Arnold, 1995), with associated loss in neuron number, density, or neuronal metabolism (Birken & Oldendorf, 1989). Creatine reductions are suggestive of decreases in high energy phosphate metabolism (Urenjak, Williams, Giadian, & Noble, 1993).

The neurobiological correlates reported in adults with PTSD are very similar to the neurobiological changes associated with experiences of early stress, with changes in key cortical and subcortical structures involved in the stress response consistently reported in adults with PTSD.

Developmental Factors

One very important caveat to add, however, is that there are important developmental issues that need to be better understood before preclinical research findings in this area can be optimally informative in understanding the effects of stress on children. Although the preclinical studies examining the neurobiological effects of early stress provide a powerful heuristic for thinking about the pathophysiology of PTSD in adults, the application of this literature for understanding the neurobiology of PTSD in children is more limited.

Specifically there have been 13 structural neuroimaging studies to date in children with PTSD (Carrion et al., 2001; Carrion, Weems, & Reiss, 2007; De Bellis, Hall, et al., 2001; De Bellis & Keshevan, 2003; De Bellis et al., 1999, 2002; De Bellis & Kuchibhatla, 2006; Jackowski et al., 2008; Karl et al., 2006; Teicher et al., 2004; Tupler & De Bellis, 2006) with only two of the studies reporting evidence of changes in hippocampal volume in children and adolescents with PTSD (Carrion et al., 2007; Tupler & De Bellis, 2006). Interestingly, Tupler and De Bellis observed increases in hippocampal volume in children with PTSD that was positively correlated with age at trauma and severity of psychopathology. While Carrion et al. noted reductions in hippocampal volume in children with PTSD, their study did not include use of a comparison group.

Instead of hippocampal atrophy, children and adolescents with PTSD were found to have a decreased area in the medial and posterior portions of the corpus callosum (De Bellis & Keshevan, 2003; De Bellis et al., 1999, 2002; Karl et al., 2006; Teicher et al., 2004). Consistent with these reports, in a recent study using diffusion tensor imaging (DTI), children with PTSD were noted to have reductions in integrity of the medial and posterior areas of the corpus callosum (Jackowski et al., 2008).

Other areas of the brain that have been examined for changes in children and adolescents with PTSD (De Bellis et al., 2002; De Bellis & Kuchibhatla, 2006) revealed that children and adolescents with PTSD had smaller overall cerebellar volume as compared to children with generalized anxiety disorder and a group of nonabused healthy controls. De Bellis and Keshevan (2003) observed that adolescents with a history of maltreatment and subsequent PTSD, and youth with PTSD and a history of suicidal ideation had larger pituitary volume when compared a control group. De Bellis et al. (2002) utilized magnetic resonance imaging to demonstrate that maltreated children and adolescents with PTSD had increased volume of the superior temporal gyrus as compared with controls, possibly due to increased sensitivity to conditioned auditory stimuli during development.

To the best of our knowledge, there is only one published structural MRI study in prepubescent nonhuman primates that had been subjected to early stress (Sanchez, Hearn, Do, Rilling, & Herndon, 1998). Most preclinical studies of early stress have examined the long-term impact of these experiences on brain development in adult animals. Interestingly, the study with the young primates also failed to find evidence of hippocampal atrophy. Instead, consistent with the child and adolescent studies described above, the investigators reported reductions in the medial and caudal portions of the corpus callosum in the juvenile, nonhuman primates subjected to early stress (Sanchez et al., 1998).

The medial and caudal portions of the corpus callosum contain interhemispheric projections from the cingulate, posterior temporal–parietal sensory association cortices, superior temporal sulcus, retrosplenial cortex, insula, and parahippocampal structures (Pandya & Seltzer, 1986). Several of the regions with interhemispheric projections through the medial and caudal portions of the corpus callosum have direct connections with prefrontal cortical areas and are involved in circuits that mediate the processing of emotion and various memory functions—core types of disturbances observed in individuals with PTSD.

Given the prominence of corpus callosum alterations in children and adolescents with PTSD, our group has conducted a preliminary study using DTI in 14 maltreated children with PTSD and 16 normal controls (Jackowski, Douglas-Palumberi, Jackowski, Win, Schultz, Staib, Krystal, & Kaufman, 2008). DTI can be used to assess the integrity of white matter tracts in the brain. Children with PTSD had significantly greater mean diffusivity in the medial and posterior regions of the corpus callosum, a finding that is consistent with the possibility of reduced axonal pruning early in development and decreased fractional anisotropy, a finding that is consistent with the possibility of reduced myelination in children with PTSD compared to aged-matched controls. (Jackowski et al., 2008).

The utilization of a developmental framework in future preclinical and clinical studies will help to enhance our understanding of the neurobiological mechanisms that link child maltreatment with PTSD and other negative sequelae across the life cycle. As noted above, most preclinical studies of early stress have examined the long-term impact of these experiences on brain development in adult animals. There is a need for more developmental work in this area.

Factors That Modify the Impact of Early Stress: Clinical Studies

As in the preclinical studies, emerging research in clinical populations highlights the importance of examining gene and environmental interactions in understanding the long-term impact of early child maltreatment. Work in this area is still preliminary, and to date researchers have primarily only documented the impact of familial and genetic factors and the quality of the subsequent caregiving environment on behavioral and clinical outcomes (Caspi et al., 2002; Kaufman & Henrich, 2000). The modifying effect of these factors on neurobiological sequelae has been little explored (Kaufman et al., 1997). However, as with the preclinical studies,

the emerging clinical findings suggest the adverse effects associated with early child maltreatment are not inevitable and can be modified by intrinsic and extrinsic factors, with the quality of the subsequent caregiving environment especially important in determining the long-term impact of early abuse.

Clinical Implications

As discussed previously, the neurobiological correlates reported in adults with PTSD are very similar to the neurobiological changes associated with experiences of early stress. Translational research approaches have been very productive in delineating the pathophysiology of PTSD in adults and suggesting novel treatments for adults with this disorder.

For example, the finding that administration of NE blocking agents immediately following an acute stressor reduced the long-term neurobiological effects of the stressor in rodents led to the trial of propranolol, a beta-adrenergic NE blocker, to prevent the onset of PTSD in adults who suffered an acute trauma (Pittman et al., 2002). Preliminary positive findings in the prevention of PTSD in adults administered propranolol following an acute trauma are very encouraging. The convergence of findings in preclinical and clinical studies has also lead to the development of CRH receptor type 1 antagonist drugs that are currently being tested for their efficacy in treating PTSD (Arborelius et al., 1999). In addition, as chronic antidepressant treatment with selective serotonin reuptake inhibitors (SSRIs) has been found to reverse hippocampal atrophy and promote neurogenesis in adult rodents (Duman, Nakagawa, & Malberg, 2001; Malberg, Eisch, Nestler, & Duman, 2000). SSRI medications have been found to be effective treatments for PTSD in adults, with chronic treatment associated with improvement of verbal declarative memory deficits and an increase in hippocampal volume (Vermetten, Vythilingam, Southwick, Chamey, & Bremner, 2003).

This section, however, focuses primarily on the clinical implications of the stress research for children and adolescents with a history of child maltreatment. We currently know very little about the pharmacological treatment of PTSD in children. For example, a small pilot study examining the effectiveness of propanolol in reducing PTSD symptoms in pediatric injury patients failed to reveal significant main effects for pharmacological intervention. Findings suggested that gender may influence outcomes, with boys showing nonsignificant decreases in PTSD symptoms when treated with propanolol. Girls, however, showed a significant increase in PTSD symptoms when treated with the same medication (Nugent et al., 2010). More work is needed in this area, and, as discussed previously, more developmentally focused preclinical work is needed to guide research efforts with children and adolescents.

The extant preclinical and clinical literature reviewed, however, strongly suggests that facilitating the formation of stable, secure, and positive relationships is essential to promoting good outcomes for children with a history of maltreatment (Kaufman & Henrich, 2000; Zielinski & Bradshaw, 2006). The Adoption and Safe Families Act (P.L. 105-89), passed in November 1997, was designed to facilitate permanency-planning efforts on behalf of maltreated children. Permanency planning involves the systematic implementation of interventions to secure a caring, legally recognized, and continuous family for traumatized children (CWLA, 1994). These efforts aim to maximize the likelihood of children having at least one adult that they identify as a psychological parent (Goldstein, Solnit, Goldstein, & Freud, 1996). Permanency efforts can result in family reunification, placement with kin, or child adoption.

Although the quality of child protection services departments varies from state to state, nationwide it is estimated that investigation is the only "service" provided in response to reports of child maltreatment in 40% of substantiated cases of child abuse and neglect (McCurdy & Daro, 1992). In these cases, no interventions are provided to reduce the risk of future maltreatment or alleviate the effects of past abuse. Research is beginning to

emerge, however, that provides preliminary support for abuse prevention programs, and those that aim to prevent the recurrence of abuse/neglect and the deleterious effects of those maltreated youth (as reviewed by MacMillan et al., 2009).

It has also been estimated that at least 50% of all child welfare cases involve substance abuse, with rates as high as 90% reported in some parts of the country (National Center on Addiction and Substance Abuse, 1999). Birth parents cannot be a viable attachment choice for children unless they are given intervention to address their substance abuse problems.

Several states have developed innovative approaches to increase services to address substance abuse problems, including having adult addiction services liaisons work in child welfare offices to facilitate client referral for treatment (McAlpine, Marshall, & Doran, 2001); hiring substance abuse counselors to work in child welfare offices to perform onsite evaluations and identify appropriate resources for clients (Semidei, Radel, & Nolan, 2001); and establishing family drug courts that provide a highly structured venue within which treatment services are offered, sanctions are applied for noncompliance, and program progress is meticulously monitored allowing case planning decisions to be made more quickly on the basis of better information (Semidei et al.). Dialectical behavior therapy (DBT) programs for substance abusing parents can be an additional alternative promising approach worthy of evaluation with protective service cases, as DBT programs have been found to be more effective than treatment-as-usual for substance abusing patients with borderline personality disorder (Linehan et al., 1999)—patients who exhibit many of the core difficulties observed among protective service clients (e.g., history of early childhood trauma, dissociative symptoms, intense unstable relationships, difficulty tolerating distress, labile affect, impulsiveness).

There are several promising model programs aimed at promoting permanency for maltreated children that warrant further systematic evaluation (Lieberman, 2003; Zeanah et al., 2001).

Without permanency, the likelihood of positive outcomes is significantly diminished.

Future Directions and Closing Remarks

Resiliency researchers have made considerable advancements in recent years. Use of a translational framework to guide the design of future studies will enrich resiliency research and provide improved insights into psychological, physiological, and biological mechanisms and processes involved in resiliency. As the examples depicted in the chapter framework and preclinical sections illustrate, even when biological mechanisms are responsible for producing certain deleterious outcomes (e.g., reduced growth hormone secretion leading to blunted growth; brain changes that alter stress reactivity), psychosocial interventions can be effective.

Resiliency is an important area of research that serves to inform social policymakers and interventionists of factors that make a difference in the lives of at-risk children. It has direct and practical implications for programs aimed at promoting the healthy development of children. In future research, it is important to continue to work toward building methodological consensus, greater research integration, and the development of consistent and accurate assessments of resiliency that ultimately serve to make resiliency research more effective.

The problem of child maltreatment is enormous, both in terms of its costs to the individual and its cost to society. The growing body of research suggests that not all maltreated children will experience problems. Understanding resilience in maltreated children requires examination of genetic factors, the modifying role of attachment relationships, and gene and environmental interactions. As system failures and repeat out-of-home placements often compromise the development of maltreated children, multidisciplinary research and treatment efforts are required to address this problem, with foci that span from neurobiology to social policy.

References

Ammerman, R. T., Cassisi, J. E., Hersen, M., & Van Hasselt, V. B. (1986). Consequences of physical abuse and neglect in children. *Clinical Psychology Review, 6*(4), 291–310.

An, X., Handler, R., Ongur, D., & Price, J. L. (1998). Prefrontal cortical projections to longitudinal columns in the midbrain periaqueductal gray in macaque monkeys. *The Journal of Comparative Neurology, 401*(4), 455–479.

Anisman, H., Zaharia, M. D., Meaney, M. J., & Merali, Z. (1998). Do early-life events permanently alter behavioral and hormonal responses to stressors? *International Journal of Developmental Neuroscience, 16*(3–4), 149–164.

Arborelius, L., Owens, M. J., Plotsky, P. M., & Nemeroff, C. B. (1999). The role of corticotropin-releasing factor in depression and anxiety disorders. *Journal of Endocrinology, 160*(1), 1–12.

Baker, D. G., West, S. A., Nicholson, W. E., Ekhator, N. N., Kasckow, J. W., Hill, K. K., et al. (1999). Serial CSF corticotropin-releasing hormone levels and adrenocortical activity in combat veterans with posttraumatic stress disorder. *The American Journal of Psychiatry, 156*(4), 585–588.

Barbazanges, A., Vallee, M., Mayo, W., Day, J., Simon, H., Le Moal, M., et al. (1996). Early and later adoptions have different long-term effects on male rat offspring. *Journal of Neuroscience, 16*(23), 7783–7790.

Beeghly, M., & Cicchetti, D. (1994). Child maltreatment, attachment, and the self-system: Emergence of an internal state lexicon in toddlers at high social risk. *Development and Psychopathology, 6*(1), 5–30.

Bernard, J. R., & Bandler, R. (1998). Parallel circuits for emotional coping behaviour: New pieces in the puzzle. *The Journal of Comparative Neurology, 401*(A), 429–436.

Birken, D. L., & Oldendorf, W. H. (1989). N-acetyl-L-aspartic acid: A literature review of a compound prominent in IH-NMR spectroscopic studies of the brain. *Neuroscience Biobehavioral Review, 13*, 23–31.

Bremner, J. D., Innis, R. B., Ng, C. K., Staib, L. H., Salomon, R. M., Bronen, R. A., et al. (1997). Positron emission tomography measurement of cerebral metabolic correlates of yohimbine administration in combat-related posttraumatic stress disorder. *Archives of General Psychiatry, 54*(3), 246–254.

Bremner, J. D., Innis, R. B., Southwick, S. M., Staib, L., Zoghbi, S., & Charney, D. S. (2000). Decreased benzodiazepine receptor binding in prefrontal cortex in combat-related posttraumatic stress disorder. *The American Journal of Psychiatry, 157*(1), 1120–1126.

Bremner, J. D., Licinio, J., Darnell, A., Krystal, J. H., Owens, M. J., Southwick, S. M., et al. (1997). Elevated CSF corticotropin-releasing factor concentrations in posttraumatic stress disorder. *The American Journal of Psychiatry, 154*(5), 624–629.

Bremner, J. D., Randall, P., Vermetten, E., Staib, L., Bronen, R. A., & Mazure, C. (1997). Magnetic resonance imaging-based measurement of hippocampal volume in posttraumatic stress disorder related to childhood physical and sexual abuse—a preliminary report. *Biological Psychiatry, 41*(1), 23–32.

Brenmer, J. D., Randall, P., Scott, T. M., Bronen, R. A., Seibyl, J. P., Southwick, S. M., et al. (1995). MRI-based measurement of hippocampal volume in patients with combat-related posttraumatic stress disorder. *The American Journal of Psychiatry, 152*(1), 973–981.

Briere, J., Berliner, L., Bulkley, J. A., Jenny, C., & Reid, T. (1996). *The APS AC handbook on child maltreatment.* Thousand Oaks, CA: Sage.

Caldji, C., Francis, D., Sharma, S., Plotsky, P. M., & Meaney, M. J. (2000). The effects of early rearing environment on the development of GABAA and central benzodiazepine receptor levels and novelty-induced fearfulness in the rat. *Neuropsychopharmacology, 22*(3), 219–229.

Caldji, C., Tannenbaum, B., Sharma, S., Francis, D., Plotsky, P. M., & Meaney, M. J. (1998). Maternal care during infancy regulates the development of neural systems mediating the expression of fearfulness in the rat. *Proceedings of the National Academy of Sciences, 95*(9), 5335–5340.

Carrion, V. G., Weems, C. F., & Reiss, A. L. (2007). Stress predicts brain changes in children: A pilot longitudinal study on youth stress, posttraumatic stress disorder, and the hippocampus. *Pediatrics, 119*, 509–516.

Carrion, V. G., Weems, C. F., Eliez, S., Patwardhan, A., Brown, W., Ray, R. D., et al. (2001). Attenuation of frontal asymmetry in pediatric posttraumatic stress disorder. *Biological Psychiatry, 50*, 943–951.

Caspi, A., McClay, J., Moffitt, T. E., Mill, J., Martin, J., Craig, I. W., et al. (2002). Role of genotype in the cycle of violence in maltreated children. *Science, 297*(5582), 851–854.

Child Welfare League of America (CWLA). (1994). *Kinship care: A natural bridge.* Washington, DC: Child Welfare League of America.

Chrousos, G. P. (1998). Stressors, stress, and neuroendocrine integration of the adaptive response. The 1997 Hans Selye Memorial Lecture. *Annals of the New York Academy of Sciences, 851*, 311–335.

Chu, J. A., & Dill, D. L. (1990). Dissociative symptoms in relation to childhood physical and sexual abuse. *The American Journal of Psychiatry, 147*(1), 887–892.

Cicchetti, D., & Carlson, V. (1989). *Child maltreatment: Theory and research on the causes and consequences of child abuse and neglect.* New York: Cambridge University Press.

Cicchetti, D., & Toth, S. (1995). A developmental psychopathology perspective on child abuse and neglect. *Journal of the American Academy of Child and Adolescent Psychiatry, 34*(5), 541–565.

Cicchetti, D., & Tucker, D. (1994). Development and self-regulatory structures of the mind. *Development and Psychopathology, 6*(4), 533–549.

Coe, C. L., Mendoza, S. P., Smotherman, W. P., & Levine, S. (1978). Mother-infant attachment in the squirrel monkey: Adrenal response to separation. *Behavioral Biology, 22*(2), 256–263.

Cook, R., Fleishman, E., & Grimes, V. (1991). *A national evaluation of Title IV-E foster care independent living programs for youth: Phase 2, final report* (Vol. 1). Unpublished report. Rockville, MD: Westat, Inc.

Coplan, J. D., Andrews, M. W., Rosenblum, L. A., Owens, M. J., Friedman, S., Gorman, J. M., et al. (1996). Persistent elevations of cerebrospinal fluid concentrations of corticotropin-releasing factor in adult nonhuman primates exposed to early-life stressors: Implications for the pathophysiology of mood and anxiety disorders. *Proceedings of the National Academy of Sciences, 93*(4), 1619–1623.

Cowen, E. L., & Work, W. C. (1988). Resilient children, psychological wellness, and primary prevention. *American Journal of Community Psychology, 16*(4), 591–607.

Cowen, E. L., Work, W. C., & Wyman, P. A. (1992). Resilience among profoundly stressed urban schoolchildren. In M. Kessler & S. E. Goldston (Eds.), *The present and future of prevention: In honor of George W. Albee. Primary prevention of psychopathology* (Vol. 15, pp. 155–168). Thousand Oaks, CA: Sage.

Cowen, E. L., Work, W. C., & Wyman, R. A. (1997). The Rochester Child Resilience Project (RCRP): Facts found, lessons learned, future directions divined. In S. S. Luthar & J. A. Burack (Eds.), *Developmental psychopathology: Perspectives on adjustment, risk, and disorder* (pp. 527–547). New York: Oxford University Press.

Crittenden, P. M. (1992). Children's strategies for coping with adverse home environments: An interpretation using attachment theory. *Child Abuse & Neglect, 76*(3), 329–343.

De Bellis, M. D., Hall, J., Boring, A. M., Frustaci, K., & Moritz, G. (2001). A pilot longitudinal study of hippocampal volumes in pediatriac maltreatment-related posttraumatic stress disorder. *Biological Psychiatry, 50*, 305–309.

De Bellis, M. D., & Keshevan, M. S. (2003). Sex differences in brain maturation in maltreatment-related pediatric posttraumatic stress disorder. *Neuroscience & Biobehavioral Reviews, 27*, 103–117.

De Bellis, M. D., Keshavan, M. S., Clark, D. B., Casey, B. J., Giedd, J. N., Boring, A. M., et al. (1999). Developmental traumatology. Part II: Brain development. *Biological Psychiatry, 45*(10), 1271–1284.

De Bellis, M. D., Keshevan, M. S., Frustaci, K., Shifflett, H., Iyengar, S., Beers, S. R., et al. (2002). Superior temporal gyrus volumes in maltreated children and adolescents with PTSD. *Biological Psychiatry, 51*, 544–552.

De Bellis, M. D., & Kuchibhatla, M. (2006). Cerebellar volumes in pediatric maltreatment-related posttraumatic stress disorder. *Biological Psychiatry, 60*, 697–703.

de la Vega, A., de la Osa, N., Ezpeleta, L., Granero, R., & Domènech, J. M. (2011). Differential effects of psychological maltreatment on children of mothers exposed to intimate partner violence. *Child Abuse & Neglect, 35*, 524–531.

De Stefano, N., Matthews, P. M., & Arnold, D. L. (1995). Reversible decreases in N-acetylaspartate after acute brain injury. *Magnetic Resonance in Medicine, 34*, 721–727.

Dhabhar, F. S., McEwen, B. S., & Spencer, R. L. (1997). Adaptation to prolonged or repeated stress—comparison between rat strains showing intrinsic differences in reactivity to acute stress. *Neuroendocrinology, 65*(5), 360–368.

Drevets, W. C., Ongur, D., & Price, J. L. (1998). Neuroimaging abnormalities in the subgenual prefrontal cortex: Implications for the pathophysiology of familial mood disorders. *Molecular Psychiatry, 3*(3), 220–226, 190–221.

Driessen, M., Hermann, J., Stahl, K., Zwann, M., Meier, S., Hill, A., et al. (2000). Magnetic resonance imaging volumes of the hippocampus and the amygdala in women with borderline personality disorder and early traumatization. *Archives of General Psychiatry, 57*, 1115–1122.

Duman, R. S., Nakagawa, S., & Malberg, J. (2001). Regulation of adult neurogenesis by antidepressant treatment. *Neuropsychopharmacology, 25*, 836–844.

Egeland, B., Sroufe, A., & Erickson, M. (1983). The developmental consequence of different patterns of maltreatment. *Child Abuse & Neglect, 7*(4), 459–469.

Egeland, B., & Sroufe, L. A. (1981). Developmental sequelae of maltreatment in infancy. *New Directions for Child Development, 11*, 77–92.

Famularo, R., Kinscherff, R., & Fenton, T. (1992). Psychiatric diagnoses of maltreated children: Preliminary findings. *Journal of the American Academy of Child and Adolescent Psychiatry, 31*(5), 863–867.

Feldman, R., Singer, M., & Zagoory, O. (2010). Touch attenuates infants physiological reactivity to stress. *Developmental Science, 13*, 271–278.

Francis, D., Caldji, C., Champagne, F., Plotsky, P. M., & Meaney, M. J. (1999). The role of corticotropin-releasing factor—Norepinephrine systems in mediating the effects of early experience on the development of behavioral and endocrine responses to stress. *Biological Psychiatry, 46*(9), 1153–1166.

Francis, D., Diorio, J., Liu, D., & Meaney, M. J. (1999). Nongenomic transmission across generations of maternal behavior and stress responses in the rat. *Science, 286*(5442), 1155–1158.

Freeman, T. W., Cardwell, D., Karson, C. N., & Komoroski, R. A. (1998). In vivo proton magnetic resonance spectroscopy of the medial temporal lobes of subjects with combat-related posttraumatic stress disorder. *Magnetic Resonance in Medicine, 40*(1), 66–71.

Garmezy, N. (1992). Resiliency and vulnerability to adverse developmental outcomes associated with poverty. In T. Thompson & S. C. Hupp (Eds.), *Saving children at risk: Poverty and disabilities* (Vol. 131, pp. 45–60). Thousand Oaks, CA: Sage Focus Editions.

Garmezy, N. (1993). Vulnerability and resilience. In D. C. Funder, R. D. Parke, et al. (Eds.), *Studying lives through time: Personality and development* (pp. 377–398). Washington, DC: American Psychological Association.

Garmezy, N., Masten, A. S., & Tellegen, A. (1984). The study of stress and competence in children: A building block for developmental psychopathology. *Child Development, 55*(1), 97–111.

Geracioti, T. D., Jr., Baker, D. G., Ekhator, N. N., West, S. A., Hill, K. K., Bruce, A. B., et al. (2001). CSF norepinephrine concentrations in posttraumatic stress disorder. *The American Journal of Psychiatry, 755*(8), 1227–1230.

Gold, P. W., & Chrousos, G. P. (2002). Organization of the stress system and its dysregulation in melancholic and atypical depression: High vs. low CRH/NE states. *Molecular Psychiatry, 7*(3), 254–275.

Goldstein, J., Solnit, A., Goldstein, S., & Freud, A. (1996). *The best interest of the child: The least detrimental alternative*. New York: Free Press.

Gonzalez, M. E., Ladd, C. O., Huot, R., Owens, M. J., & Plotsky, P M. (1999). *Prevention of HPA axis changes in response to neonatal maternal separation by providing dams with foster pups during the absence of her litter* (Abstract #583.6). In Paper presented at the Society for Neuroscience, Miami, FL, October 22–28, 1999.

Gould, E., & Cameron, H. A. (1996). Regulation of neuronal birth, migration and death in the rat dentate gyrus. *Developmental Neuroscience, 18*(1–2), 22–35.

Gould, E., Tanapat, P., Rydel, T., & Hastings, N. (2000). Regulation of hippocampal neurogenesis in adulthood. *Biological Psychiatry, 48*(S), 715–720.

Graham, Y. R., Heim, C., Goodman, S. H., Miller, A. H., & Nemeroff, C. B. (1999). The effects of neonatal stress on brain development: Implications for psychopathology. *Developmental Psychopathology, 77*(3), 545–565.

Groenewegen, H. J. (1988). Organization of the afferent connections of the mediodorsal thalamic nucleus in the rat, related to the mediodorsal-prefrontal topography. *Neuroscience, 24*(2), 379–431.

Gurvits, T. V., Shenton, M. E., Hokama, H., Ohta, H., Lasko, N. B., Gilbertson, M. W., et al. (1996). Magnetic resonance imaging study of hippocampal volume in chronic, combat-related posttraumatic stress disorder. *Biological Psychiatry, 40*(11), 1091–1099.

Heim, C., & Nemeroff, C. B. (2001). The role of childhood trauma in the neurobiology of mood and anxiety disorders: Preclinical and clinical studies. *Biological Psychiatry, 49*(12), 1023–1039.

Herman, J. P., & Cullinan, W. E. (1997). Neurocircuitry of stress: Central control of the hypothalamo-pituitaryadrenocortical axis. *Trends in Neuroscience, 20*(2), 78–84.

Hofer, M. A. (1987). Early social relationships: A psychobiologist's view. *Child Development, 58*(3), 633–647.

Jackowski, A. P., Douglas-Palumberi, H., Jackowski, M., Win, L., Schultz, R. Staib, L. W., et al. (2008). Corpus callosum in maltreated children with posttraumatic stress disorder: A diffusion tensor imaging study. *Psychiatry Research, 162*(3), 256–261.

Jezova, D., Ochedalski, T., Glickman, M., Kiss, A., & Aguilera, G. (1999). Central corticotropin-releasing hormone receptors modulate hypothalamic-pituitary-adrenocortical and sympathoadrenal activity during stress. *Neuroscience, 94*(3), 797–802.

Karl, A., Schaefer, M., Malta, L. S., Dorfel, D., Rohleder, N., & Werner, A. (2006). A meta-analysis of structural brain abnormalities in PTSD. *Neuroscience Biobehavioral Review, 30*, 1004–1031.

Kaufman, J. (1991). Depressive disorders in maltreated children. *Journal of the American Academy of Child and Adolescent Psychiatry, 30*(2), 257–265.

Kaufman, J., Birmaher, B., Perel, J., Dahl, R. E., Moreci, P., & Nelson, B. (1997). The corticotropin-releasing hormone challenge in depressed abused, depressed nonabused, and normal control children. *Biological Psychiatry, 42*(8), 669–679.

Kaufman, J., & Henrich, C. (2000). Exposure to violence and early childhood trauma. In C. Zeanah Jr. (Ed.), *Handbook of infant mental health* (pp. 195–207). New York: Guilford.

Kaufman, J., Plotsky, P., Nemeroff, C., & Charney, D. (2000). Effects of early adverse experience on brain structure and function: Clinical implications. *Biological Psychiatry, 48*(S), 778–790.

Kaufman, J., & Zigler, E. (1989). The intergenerational transmission of child abuse. In D. Cicchetti & V. Carlson (Eds.), *Child maltreatment: Theory and research on the causes and consequences of child abuse and neglect.* Cambridge: Cambridge University Press.

Kaufman, J., & Zigler, E. (1996). Child abuse and social policy. In E. Zigler, S. Kagan, & N. Hall (Eds.), *Children, families and government: Preparing for the twenty-first century* (pp. 233–255). New York: Cambridge University Press.

Kraemer, G. W., Ebert, M. H., Schmidt, D. E., & McKinney, W. T. (1989). A longitudinal study of the effect of different social rearing conditions on cerebrospinal fluid norepinephrine and biogenic amine metabolites in rhesus monkeys. *Neuropsychopharmacology, 2*(3), 175–189.

Krout, K. E., Jansen, A. S., & Loewy, A. D. (1998). Periaqueductal gray matter projection to the parabrachial nucleus in rat. *The Journal of Comparative Neurology, 401*(4), 437–454.

Kuhn, C. M., & Schanberg, S. M. (1998). Responses to maternal separation: Mechanisms and mediators. *International Journal of Developmental Neuroscience, 16*(3–4), 261–270.

Ladd, C. O., Huot, R. L., Thrivikraman, K. V., Nemeroff, C. B., Meaney, M. J., & Plotsky, P. M. (2000). Longterm behavioral and neuroendocrine adaptations to adverse early experience. In E. Mayer & C. Sape (Eds.), *Progress in brain research: The biological basis for mind body interactions* (Vol. 122, pp. 79–101). Amsterdam: Elsevier.

Ladd, C. O., Owens, M. J., & Nemeroff, C. B. (1996). Persistent changes in corticotropin-releasing factor neuronal systems induced by maternal deprivation. *Endocrinology, 137*(4), 1212–1218.

Levine, S., Wiener, S. G., & Coe, C. L. (1993). Temporal and social factors influencing behavioral and hormonal responses to separation in mother and infant squirrel monkeys. *Psychoneuroendocrinology, 18*(4), 297–306.

Lieberman, A. F. (2003). The treatment of attachment disorder in infancy and early childhood: Reflections from clinical intervention with later-adopted foster care children. *Attachment & Human Development, 5*(3), 279–282.

Linehan, M. M., Schmidt, H., III, Dimeff, L. A., Craft, J. C., Kanter, J., & Comtois, K. A. (1999). Dialectical behavior therapy for patients with borderline personality disorder and drug-dependence. *American Journal of Addiction, 8*, 279–292.

Liu, D., Caldji, C., Sharma, S., Plotsky, P. M., & Meaney, M. J. (2000). Influence of neonatal rearing conditions on stress-induced adrenocorticotropin responses and norepineherine release in the hypothalamic paraventricular nucleus. *Journal of Neuroendocrinology, 72*(1), 5–12.

Liu, D., Diorio, J., Tannenbaum, B., Caldji, C., Francis, D., Freedman, A., et al. (1997). Maternal care, hippocampal glucocorticoid receptors, and hypothalamic-pituitary-adrenal responses to stress. *Science, 277*(5332), 1659–1662.

Lopez, J. R., Akil, H., & Watson, S. J. (1999). Neural circuits mediating stress. *Biological Psychiatry, 46*(11), 1461–1471.

Luthar, S. S., Cicchetti, D., & Becker, B. (2000). The construct of resilience: A critical evaluation and guidelines for future work. *Child Development, 77*(3), 543–562.

Luthar, S. S., Doemberger, C. H., & Zigler, E. (1993). Resilience is not a unidimensional construct: Insights from a prospective study of inner-city adolescents. *Development and Psychopathology, 5*(4), 703–717.

Luthar, S. S., & Zigler, E. (1991). Vulnerability and competence: A review of research on resilience in childhood. *The American Journal of Orthopsychiatry, 67*(1), 6–22.

Maccari, S., Piazza, P. V., Kabbaj, M., Barbazanges, A., Simon, H., & Le Moal, M. (1995). Adoption reverses the long-term impairment in glucocorticoid feedback induced by prenatal stress. *Journal of Neuroscience, 75*(1 Pt 1), 110–116.

MacMillan, H. L., Wathen, C. N., Barlow, J., Fergusson, D. M., Leventhal, J. M., & Taussig, H. N. (2009). Interventions to prevent child maltreatment and associated impairment. *The Lancet, 373*, 250–266.

Maier, S. F., & Watkins, L. R. (1998). Cytokines for psychologists: Implications of bidirectional immune-to-brain communication for understanding behavior, mood, and cognition. *Psychological Review, 105*(1), 83–107.

Malberg, J. E., Eisch, A. E., Nestler, E. J., & Duman, R. S. (2000). Chronic antidepressant treatment increases neurogenesis in adult rat hippocampus. *Journal of Neuroscience, 20*, 9104–9110.

Manji, H. K., Quiroz, J. A., Spom, J., Payne, J. L., Denicoff, K., Zarate, C. A., Jr., et al. (2003). Enhancing neuronal plasticity and cellular resilience to develop novel, improved therapeutics for difficult-to treat depression. *Biological Psychiatry, 53*(8), 707–742.

Masten, A. S. (2001). Ordinary magic: Resilience processes in development. *American Psychologist, 56*(3), 227–238.

Masten, A. S., & Coatsworth, J. D. (1998). The development of competence in favorable and unfavorable environments: Lessons from research on successful children. *American Psychologist, 53*(2), 205–220.

Masten, A. S., Hubbard, J. J., Gest, S. D., Tellegen, A., Garmezy, N., & Ramirez, M. (1999). Competence in the context of adversity: Pathways to resilience and maladaptation from childhood to late adolescence. *Development and Psychopathology, 77*(1), 143–169.

Maughan, A., & Cicchetti, D. (2002). Impact of child maltreatment and interadult violence on children's emotion regulation abilities and socioemotional adjustment. *Child Development, 73*(5), 1525–1542.

McAlpine, C., Marshall, C. C., & Doran, N. H. (2001). Combining child welfare and substance abuse services: A blended model of intervention. *Child Welfare, 80*, 129–149.

McCurdy, K., & Daro, D. (1992). *Current trends in child abuse reporting and fatalities: The results of the 1992 annual fifth state survey*. Report of the National Center on Child Abuse Prevention Research, Chicago.

McEwen, B. S., & Magarinos, A. M. (2001). Stress and hippocampal plasticity: Implications for the pathophysiology of affective disorders. *Human Psychopharmacology, 76*(S1), S7–S19.

McLeer, S. V., Callaghan, M., Henry, D., & Wallen, J. (1994). Psychiatric disorders in sexually abused children. *Journal of the American Academy of Child and Adolescent Psychiatry, 33*(3), 313–319.

Meaney, M. J., Aitken, D. H., Bhatnagar, S., & Sapolsky, R. M. (1991). Postnatal handling attenuates certain neuroendocrine, anatomical, and cognitive dysfunctions associated with aging in female rats. *Neurobiology of Aging, 72*(1), 31–38.

Meaney, M. J., Bhatnagar, S., Diorio, J., Larocque, S., Francis, D., O'Donnell, D., et al. (1993). Molecular basis for the development of individual differences in the hypothalamic-pituitary-adrenal stress response. *Cell and Molecular Neurobiology, 13*(4), 321–347.

Meier, E. G. (1965). Current circumstances of former foster children. *Child Welfare, 44*, 196–206.

Menzaghi, R., Heinrichs, S. C., Pich, E. M., Weiss, F., & Koob, G. F. (1993). The role of limbic and hypothalamic corticotropin-releasing factor in behavioral responses to stress. *Annals of the New York Academy of Sciences, 697*, 142–154.

National Center on Addiction and Substance Abuse (1999). *No safe haven: Children of substance-abusing parents*. New York: Author.

Newton, R. R., Litrownik, A. J., & Landsverk, J. A. (2000). Children and youth in foster care: Distangling the relationship between problem behaviors and number of placements. *Child Abuse & Neglect, 24*, 1363–1374.

Nugent, N. R., Christopher, N. C., Crow, J. P., Browne, L., Ostrowski, S., & Delahanty, D. L. (2010). The efficacy of early propanolol administration at reducing PTSD symptoms in pediatric injury patients: A pilot study. *Journal of Traumatic Stress, 23*, 282–287.

Ongur, D., An, X., & Price, J. L. (1998). Prefrontal cortical projections to the hypothalamus in macaque monkeys. *The Journal of Comparative Neurology, 401*(4), 480–505.

Owens, M. J., & Nemeroff, C. B. (1991). Physiology and pharmacology of corticotropin-releasing factor. *Pharmacological Review, 43*(4), 425–473.

Pacak, K., Palkovits, M., Kopin, I. J., & Goldstein, D. S. (1995). Stress-induced norepinephrine release in the hypothalamic paraventricular nucleus and pituitary-adrenocortical and sympathoadrenal activity: In vivo microdialysis studies. *Front Neuroendocrinology, 76*(2), 89–150.

Page, M. E., & Abercrombie, E. D. (1999). Discrete local application of corticotropin-releasing factor increases locus coeruleus discharge and extracellular norepinephrine in rat hippocampus. *Synapse, 55*(4), 304–313.

Pandya, D. N., & Seltzer, B. (1986). The topography of commissural fibers. In F. Lepore, M. Ptito, & H. H. Jasper (Eds.), *Two hemispheres—One brain: Functions of the corpus callosum* (pp. 47–73). New York: Liss.

Pittman, R. K., Sanders, K. M., Zusman, R. M., Healy, A. R., Cheema, F., Lasko, N. B., et al. (2002). Pilot study of secondary prevention of posttraumatic stress disorder with propranolol. *Biological Psychiatry, 57*(2), 189–192.

Plotsky, P. M., Cunningham, E. T., Jr., & Widmaier, E. P. (1989). Catecholaminergic modulation of corticotropin-releasing factor and adrenocorticotropin secretion. *Endocrinology Review, 10*(4), 437–458.

Plotsky, P. M., & Meaney, M. J. (1993). Early, postnatal experience alters hypothalamic corticotropin-releasing factor (CRF) mRNA, median eminence CRF content and stress-induced release in adult rats. *Brain Research and Molecular Brain Research, 18*(3), 195–200.

Pynoos, R., Steinberg, A., & Wraith, R. (1995). A developmental model of childhood traumatic stress. In D. Cicchetti & D. Cohen (Eds.), *Developmental psychopathology: Risk, disorder, and adaptation* (Vol. 2, pp. 72–95). New York: Wiley.

Rosenblum, L. A., Coplan, J. D., Friedman, S., Bassoff, T., Gorman, J. M., & Andrews, M. W. (1994). Adverse early experiences affect noradrenergic and serotonergic functioning in adult primates. *Biological Psychiatry, 35*(4), 221–227.

Rutter, M. (1990). Psychosocial resilience and protective mechanisms. In J. E. Rolf & A. S. Masten (Eds.), *Risk and protective factors in the development of psychopathology* (pp. 181–214). New York: Cambridge University Press.

Rutter, M. (1995). Psychosocial adversity: Risk, resilience and recovery. *Southern African Journal of Child & Adolescent Psychiatry, 7*(2), 75–88.

Rutter, M. (1996). Stress research: Accomplishments and tasks ahead. In R. J. Haggerty & L. R. Sherrod (Eds.), *Stress, risk, and resilience in children and adolescents: Processes, mechanisms, and interventions* (pp. 354–385). New York: Cambridge University Press.

Sanchez, M. M., Hearn, E. F., Do, D., Rilling, J. K., & Herndon, J. G. (1998). Differential rearing affects corpus callosum size and cognitive function of rhesus monkeys. *Brain Research, 812*, 38–49.

Sapolsky, R. M. (1996). Stress, glucocorticoids, and damage to the nervous system: The current state of confusion. *Stress, 1*(1), 1–19.

Sapolsky, R. M. (2000). The possibility of neurotoxicity in the hippocampus in major depression: A primer on neuron death. *Biological Psychiatry, 48*(8), 755–765.

Sapolsky, R. M., Krey, L. C., & McEwen, B. S. (1985). Prolonged glucocorticoid exposure reduces hippocampal neuron number: Implications for aging. *Journal of Neuroscience, 5*(5), 1222–1227.

Scafidi, R., & Field, T. (1997). HIV-exposed newborns show inferior orienting and abnormal reflexes on the Brazelton scale. *Journal of Pediatric Psychology, 22*(1), 105–112.

Schanberg, S. M., & Field, T. M. (1987). Sensory deprivation stress and supplemental stimulation in the rat pup and preterm human neonate. *Child Development, 58*(6), 1431–1447.

Schuff, N., Neylan, T. C., Lenoci, M. A., Du, A. T., Weiss, D. S., Marmar, C. R., et al. (2001). Decreased hippocampal N-acetylaspartate in the absence of atrophy in posttraumatic stress disorder. *Biological Psychiatry, 50*(12), 952–959.

Semidei, J., Radel, L. F., & Nolan, C. (2001). Substance abuse and child welfare: Clear linkages and promising responses. *Child Welfare, 80*, 109–128.

Springer, K. W., Sheridan, J., Kuo, D., & Carnes, M. (2007). Long-term physical and mental health consequences of childhood physical abuse: Results from a large population-based sample of men and women. *Child Abuse & Neglect, 31*, 517–530.

Steimer, T., Escorihuela, R. M., Femandez-Teruel, A., & Driscoll, P. (1998). Long-term behavioural and neuroendocrine changes in Roman high-(RHA/Verh) and low-(RLA-Verh) avoidance rats following neonatal handling. *International Journal of Developmental Neuroscience, 76*(3–4), 165–174.

Stein, M. B., Koverola, C., Hanna, C., Torchia, M. G., & McClarty, B. (1997). Hippocampal volume in women victimized by childhood sexual abuse. *Psychological Medicine, 27*(4), 951–959.

Takahashi, L. K., & Kallin, N. H. (1991). Early developmental and temporal characteristics of stress-induced secretion of pituitary-adrenal hormones in prenatally stressed rat pups. *Brain Research, 555*(1), 75–78.

Teicher, M. H., Dumont, N. L., Ito, Y., Vaituzis, C., Giedd, J. N., & Andersen, S. L. (2004). Childhood neglect is associated with reduced corpus callosum area. *Biological Psychiatry, 56*, 80–85.

Tupler, L. A., & De Bellis, M. D. (2006). Segmented hippocampal volume in children and adolescents with posttraumatic stress disorder. *Biological Psychiatry, 59*, 523–529.

U.S. Department of Health and Human Services. (2001). National Center on Child Abuse and Neglect. *Child maltreatment 2001: Reports from the states to the National Center on Child Abuse and Neglect Data System.* Washington, DC: U.S. Government Printing Office.

Uno, H., Eisele, S., Sakai, A., Shelton, S., Baker, E., DeJesus, O., et al. (1994). Neurotoxicity of glucocorticoids in the primate brain. *Hormones and Behaviour, 28*(4), 336–348.

Urenjak, J., Williams, S. R., Giadian, D. G., & Noble, M. (1993). Proton nuclear magnetic resonance spectroscopy unambiguously identifies different neuronal cell types. *Journal of Neuroscience, 13*, 981–989.

Vaidya, V. A., & Duman, R. S. (2001). Depression—emerging insights from neurobiology. *British Medical Bulletin, 57*, 61–79.

Valentino, R. J., Curtis, A. L., Page, M. E., Pavcovich, L. A., & Florin-Lechner, S. M. (1998). Activation of the locus ceruleus brain noradrenergic system during stress: Circuitry, consequences, and regulation. *Advances in Pharmacology, 42*, 781–784.

Vermetten, E., Vythilingam, M., Southwick, S. M., Chamey, D. S., & Bremner, J. D. (2003). Long-term treatment with paroxetine increases verbal declarative memory and hippocampal volume in posttraumatic stress disorder. *Biological Psychiatry, 54*(1), 693–702.

Villarreal, G., Hamilton, D. A., Petropoulos, H., Driscoll, I., Rowland, L. M., Griego, J. A., et al. (2002). Reduced hippocampal volume and total white matter volume in posttraumatic stress disorder. *Biological Psychiatry, 52*(2), 119–125.

Vythilingam, M., Heim, C., Newport, J., Miller, A. H., Anderson, E., Bronen, R., et al. (2002). Childhood trauma associated with smaller hippocampal volume in women with major depression. *The American Journal of Psychiatry, 759*(12), 2072–2080.

Watanabe, Y., Gould, E., & McEwen, B. S. (1992). Stress induces atrophy of apical dendrites of hippocampal CA3 pyramidal neurons. *Brain Research, 588*(2), 341–345.

Werner, E. E. (1992). The children of Kauai: Resiliency and recovery in adolescence and adulthood. *Journal of Adolescent Health, 13*(4), 262–268.

Werner, E. E. (1993). Risk, resilience, and recovery: Perspectives from the Kauai longitudinal study. *Development and Psychopathology, 5*(4), 503–515.

Werner, E. E. (1995). Resilience in development. *Current Directions in Psychological Science, 4*(3), 81–85.

Wheeden, A., Scafidi, F. A., Field, T., & Ironson, G. (1993). Massage effects on cocaine-exposed preterm neonates. *Journal of Developmental and Behavioral Pediatrics, 14*(5), 318–322.

Widom, C. S. (1991). The role of placement experiences in mediating the criminal: Consequences of early childhood victimization. *The American Journal of Orthopsychiatry, 61*, 195–209.

Wiener, S. G., Johnson, D. F., & Levine, S. (1987). Influence of postnatal rearing conditions on the response of squirrel monkey infants to brief perturbations in mother-infant relationships. *Physiology and Behavior, 39*(1), 21–26.

Wilson, M. A. (1996). GABA physiology: Modulation by benzodiazepines and hormones. *Critical Reviews in Neurobiology, 70*(1), 1–37.

Windle, M., Windle, R. C., Scheidt, D. M., & Miller, G. B. (1995). Physical and sexual abuse and associated mental disorders among alcoholic inpatients. *The American Journal of Psychiatry, 752*(9), 1322–1328.

Wolfner, G. D., & Gelles, R. J. (1993). A profile of violence toward children: A national study. *Child Abuse & Neglect, 17*(2), 197–212.

Woolley, C. S., Gould, E., & McEwen, B. S. (1990). Exposure to excess glucocorticoids alters dendritic morphology of adult hippocampal pyramidal neurons. *Brain Research, 531*(1–2), 225–231.

Zaharia, M. D., Kulczycki, J., Shanks, N., Meaney, M. J., & Anisman, H. (1996). The effects of early postnatal stimulation on Morris water-maze acquisition in adult mice: Genetic and maternal factors. *Psychopharmacology, 128*(3), 227–239.

Zeanah, C. H., Larrieu, J. A., Heller, S. S., Valliere, J., Hinshaw-Fuselier, S., Aoki, Y., et al. (2001). Evaluation of a preventive intervention for maltreated infants and toddlers in foster care. *Journal of the American Academy of Child and Adolescent Psychiatry, 40,* 214–221.

Zielinski, D. S., & Bradshaw, C. P. (2006). Ecological influences on the sequelae of child maltreatment: A review of the literature. *Child Maltreatment, 11,* 49–62.

Zimmerman, R. B. (1982). Foster care in retrospect. *Tulane Studies in Social Welfare, 14,* 7–13.

Part III

Resilience as a Phenomenon in Childhood Disorders

Resilience and the Disruptive Disorders of Childhood

11

Sam Goldstein and Richard Rider

Introduction

The Disruptive Behavior Disorders of childhood (DBD) are comprised of Attention Deficit Hyperactivity Disorder (ADHD), Oppositional Defiant Disorder (ODD), and Conduct Disorder (CD) (APA, 2001). These conditions are among the most commonly treated in mental health settings with epidemiological studies suggesting that between 3 and 16% of all youth meet the diagnostic criteria for at least one, if not two or more, of these conditions (Eiraldi, Power, & Nezu, 1997; Loeber, Burke, Lahey, Winters, & Zera, 2000; for review see Barkley, 1998 and Goldstein & Goldstein, 1998). These conditions have traditionally been referred to as "externalizing disorders" as opposed to the "internalizing disorders" such as anxiety, depression, or learning disability. The former disrupt and disturb the immediate environment and are easily visible to the observer. Symptoms and impairments of the latter are not as often observed nor are environments as disrupted by affected children and adolescents.

S. Goldstein (✉)
Neurology, Learning and Behavior Center,
Salt Lake City, UT 84102, USA
e-mail: info@samgoldstein.com

R. Rider
Bellin Psychiatric Center, Green Bay, WI, USA
e-mail: Rfrider47@gmail.com

Given that the behavior of children with DBD's are rarely viewed as benign by parents, teachers, and community professionals, it is not surprising that these conditions are comprised of patterns of impulsive, hyperactive, aggressive, and defiant behaviors. These pose a significant adverse risk factor for a host of outcome variables into the late adolescent and young adult years. In fact, even a single DBD compromises the probability of positive life adjustment into young adulthood. A combination of DBD's (e.g., ADHD and CD, ODD and CD) speak to significant adverse outcome in major life domains, including school, family, health, vocation, and even activities such as driving (Barkley & Gordon, 2002; Goldstein, 2002). The DBD's may also act catalytically reducing a child's opportunity for normal life adjustment by precipitating a cascade of adverse outcomes into adulthood.

A small percentage of children with ADHD and CD and an even greater percentage of children with ODD alone manage to transition and adjust reasonably well into young adulthood (Teeter Ellison, 2002). Thus, if a specific risk such as chronically demonstrating a DBD significantly contributes to adverse outcome, and current treatment efforts for DBD demonstrate that symptoms can be managed but symptom relief in the long-term doesn't appear to significantly alter the adult outcome of these conditions, then researchers and clinicians must identify and understand those variables within the child, immediate family, and community that predict better outcome. Thus, there has been an interest in studying resilience processes in children with DBD's. If a group of children suffering from one or more DBD's can be identified who demonstrate the ability to transition successfully into the late adolescent and young adulthood years, then perhaps the lessons learned from studying these youth can generate a treatment protocol of those thoughts, feelings, behaviors, experiences, attitudes, and opportunities enhance resilience in a group of children whose adult outcome have been demonstrated to be significantly more risk-filled than those of others. Particularly for youth with DBD's, an increasing body of literature operating from a developmental pathways model has demonstrated that a number of childhood variables can be used to predict risk of adult problems as well as to identifying insulating or protective factors that reduce risk and increase the chances of a satisfactory transition into adult life (for review see Katz, 1997). As a field, researchers in the DBD's are slowly beginning to examine these protective factors. Though much is known about the risk factors, for the time being, there is only limited data available about protective factors; however, it is quite likely that those factors that insulate and protect children from other psychiatric conditions affect those with DBD's as well. Thus, living in an intact household, above the poverty level, with parents free of serious psychiatric problems, consistent in their parenting style, and available to their children whenever needed, appear to be among the most powerful factors predicting resilience in all children as well as those with DBD's (for review see Goldstein & Goldstein, 1998).

In a long-term follow-up studies, at least 70–80% of adolescents with a childhood diagnosis of ADHD or another DBD continue to meet the diagnostic criteria for at least one DBD with at least 60% reporting impairing symptoms but fewer meeting the diagnostic criteria during the adult years (for review Ingram, Hechtman, & Morgenstern, 1999). These authors suggest that the decrease in prevalence is in part due to the developmental nature of the diagnostic protocols for DBD's. Prognosis for individuals with ADHD in adulthood for example appears to be influenced by the severity of their symptoms, comorbid conditions, level of intellectual functioning, family situations, such as, parental pathology, family adversity, socio-economic status, and treatment history (Goldstein, 2002). These variables are likely predictive for the other DBD's as well.

There is a broader literature available concerning the absence of certain negative phenomena in predicting the outcome. For example, Herrero, Hechtman, and Weiss (1994) demonstrated that females may experience less risk of adverse outcome with DBD simply due to their gender. Subtype differences in ADHD, specifically children with the inattentive type, may also reduce risk. The absence of impulsive behavior appears to predict to better outcome. In fact, it has been hypothesized that problems with self-control characteristic of all three of the DBD's may be the best predictors of future adult outcome into young adulthood when evaluating young children (for review see Barkley, 1997).

Not surprisingly, aggressive behavior in general, is a diagnostic characteristic of ODD and CD, as well as a common consequence of ADHD, has been found to predict outcome into adulthood (Loney, Whaley-Klahn, & Kosier, 1983). Emotional lability has also been highly correlated with aggression (Hechtman, Weiss, & Perlman, 1984). It is also likely that within the symptom listing for the DBD's, some may hold stronger positive or negative predictive power. Algorithmic research with these conditions has slowly begun to identify the presence or absence of certain symptoms as not only predictive of condition presence but also speaking to outcome (Mota & Schachar, 2000).

This chapter will provide an overview of the DBD's, diagnostic symptoms, definition, and prevalence. We will provide an overview of risk and resilience factors that may contribute to acquisition and exacerbation of these conditions over time. The chapter will conclude with a proposed set of guidelines for the clinicians.

Overview

Over the past quarter century, multiple longitudinal and retrospective studies have demonstrated that youth exhibit two broad dimensions of disruptive behaviors. The first dimension present for many children at a young age is characterized by a trinity of inattentive, hyperactive, and impulsive behaviors. Over the last 100 years this trinity first described by George Still (1902) as a disorder of defective moral control, has been described by various labels attesting to hypothesized cause (minimal brain dysfunction), or key symptom (hyperactivity or inattention), but is increasingly recognized as not so much a behavioral disorder but one of faulty cognitive functioning (Barkley, 1997). The second dimension of disruptive behavior falls in two distinct groups. The first, a group of oppositional and aggressive behaviors, has consistently been found to be distinct from a second group of covert behaviors (Fergusson, Horwood, & Lynskey, 1994; Frick, Lahey, & Loeber, 1993). Overt behaviors include, but are not limited to, fighting, disobedience, tantrums, destruction, bullying, and attention seeking. The second set of covert behaviors include, but are not limited to, theft without confrontation of the victim, choice of bad companions, school truancy, running away, lying, and loyalty to delinquent friends (Achenbach, Conners, Quay, Verlhulst, & Howell, 1989; Loeber & Schmaling, 1985). Two aspects of this dimension have traditionally been thought to be strongly influenced by experience but likely also find their roots in genetic vulnerability. Further, overt behaviors can be divided into those that are nondestructive such as simply resisting adult authority and those that are aggressive towards others and destructive of property. The covert behaviors can be further divided into those again that do not confront victims, such as vandalism and those that are nondestructive such as truancy or running away from home (Lahey, Frick, et al., 1990).

Within the DBD's, ADHD has consistently been found as distinct from ODD and CD (for review see Barkley, 1998; Goldstein & Goldstein, 1998; Hinshaw, 1987). The DBD's can also be clearly distinguished from the internalizing disorders of depression and anxiety (Taylor, Schachar, Thorley, & Wieselberg, 1986). ODD and CD appear to be distinct, although the two disorders may well overlap in a number of behaviors such as mild aggression and lying. The onset of ODD in comparison to CD appears to be earlier. Children manifesting CD before age 10 appear to have a much worse prognosis than those demonstrating symptoms after that time (Moffitt, 1990; Patterson, Debarshye, & Ramsey, 1989). Although some children demonstrate the onset of CD and ODD simultaneously, the most serious symptoms of CD, including vandalism, repeatedly running away, truancy, shoplifting, breaking, and entering, rape, assault and homicide, generally emerge at a later age than the symptoms of ODD.

It can be easily argued that the DBD's fall on a continuum from mild to severe beginning with ADHD then progressing through ODD and CD. Though not all children with ADHD develop ODD and CD, a significant percentage of youth with CD have histories of ADHD. The younger a child progresses to CD, the more adverse is his or her outcome (Biederman, Faraone, Milberger, Guite, et al., 1996; Campbell, 1991). Further, boys experiencing CD in comparison to those with only ODD, scored lower on tests of intelligence, came from families of lower socio-economic status and had a history of greater conflict with school and judicial systems (Robins, 1991). Boys with CD demonstrated the strongest family history of antisocial personality, a problem that could reflect a combination of family, environment, and shared family genetics.

Diagnostic Overview

ADHD

ADHD is described as a "persistent pattern of inattention and/or hyperactivity" more frequent in severity than is typical of children in a similar level of development (APA, 2001). Some symptoms must have been apparent before the age of 7 years, although many children are diagnosed at later ages after symptoms have been observed for several years. Impairment must be present in at least two settings and interfere with developmentally appropriate functioning in social, academic, or work setting. Assessment of impairment has been an increasing focus in making the diagnosis of ADHD. ADHD appears more common in males than females, a problem that may or may not be a function of the DSM field studies and/or differences in prevalence and presentation (Goldstein & Gordon, 2003). ADHD is characterized by developmentally inappropriate, often limited attention span and/or hyperactivity and impulsivity. Six of nine inattentive symptoms must be present to confirm the inattentive aspect of the disorder. DSM-IV-TR (2001) did not delineate these symptoms by importance. As noted, algorithmic research finds some symptoms that may in fact demonstrate better negative or positive predictive power than others (Mota & Schachar, 2000). The inattentive symptoms include failing to give close attention to details, problems with sustained attention, not listening when spoken to directly, failing to complete tasks, difficulty with organization, avoiding or reluctant to engage in tasks requiring sustained mental effort, losing things, being easily distracted, and forgetful in daily activities.

Six of nine hyperactive-impulsive symptoms must be met to confirm the hyperactive-impulsive aspect of the disorder. The hyperactive symptoms include fidgeting, having trouble remaining seated, demonstrating inappropriate activity, difficulty in engaging in leisure activities quietly, acting as if driven by a motor, and talking excessively. The impulsive symptoms include blurting out answers before questions have been completed, difficulty waiting turn, and interrupting others. If in fact ADHD represents failure to develop effective self-discipline as evidenced by impulsive behavior, then 3 of 18 symptoms reflecting this phenomenon may well be a problem (Barkley, 1997). Diagnosis is made by confirming six or more symptoms in the inattention domain, hyperactivity-impulsive domain or both. An individual may qualify for ADHD Inattentive Type, Hyperactive-Impulsive Type or Combined Type. It is important to note that the diagnosis (Part D) requires that there must be "clear evidence of clinically significant impairment in social, academic, or occupational functioning."

ODD/CD

ODD is described in the DSM-IV-TR as a recurrent pattern of negativistic, defiant, disobedient, and hostile behavior towards authority figures. This pattern of behavior must have lasted for at least 6 months and be characterized by frequent occurrence of at least four of the following: loss of temper, arguments with adults, defiance or refusal to comply with adults' request or rules, deliberately doing things that annoy people, blaming others for personal failings, touchiness, anger, resentment, spite, or vindictiveness. CD is described in the DSM-IV-TR as a "repetitive and persistent pattern of behavior in which the basic rights of others or major age appropriate societal norms or rules are violated." ODD reflects an enduring pattern of negativistic, hostile, and defiant behaviors in the absence of serious violation of societal norms and the rights of others. Thus, children with ODD argue with adults, lose their temper, and are quick to anger. They frequently defy reasonable requests or rules and deliberately annoy others. They tend to blame others for their mistakes.

CD appears to reflect an enduring set of behaviors that evolve over time. CD is characterized most often by significant aggression and violation of the rights of others. The average age of CD is younger in boys than in girls. Boys may meet the diagnostic criteria for CD if it is going to develop by 12 years of age, whereas girls often reach 14–16 before the diagnosis is made. Three or more of the following behaviors must occur within a 12 month period with at least one present in the past 6 months for youth to qualify for a diagnosis of CD: bullying, threatening or intimidating others, initiating physical fights, using a weapon that causes serious harm, stealing with confrontation of the victim, physically cruel to others, physically cruel to animals, forcible sexual activity with others, lying to avoid obligation, staying out overnight without permission, stealing items of nontrivial value, deliberately engaging in fire setting with the intention of causing harm, deliberately destroying others' property, running away from home overnight, at least twice, truant from school, and burglary. The diagnostic protocol for CD includes two different types, Child—Onset and Adolescent—Onset. These are largely based on the classification system identified by Moffitt (1993). Moffitt utilized a developmental approach to distinguish between individuals who engage in temporary vs. persistent antisocial behavior. Life-course-persistent individuals were thought to demonstrate risk factors such as neuropsychological abnormalities and poor home environments contributing to their difficulty. Individuals classified as adolescent-limited did not demonstrate these risk factors and had no prior engagement in antisocial behavior.

The life-course-persistent pattern might well equate with the juvenile court characterization of delinquency. To test her dual trajectory theory, Moffitt examined a birth cohort of over 1,000 children in New Zealand for trends in parent, teacher, and self-reported antisocial behavior biennially from ages 3 to 15 years. Five percent of the sample accounted for nearly 70% of the stability of crime across time. Despite these efforts at delineation there continues to be little consensus as to the distinction between CD as a clinical diagnosis and delinquency as a legal/societal description.

The DBD's and Delinquency

There is little consensus in defining delinquency as a condition distinct from CD. In fact, most professionals and lay persons use the terms CD, delinquency, and even antisocial behavior interchangeably. However, in a legal sense a delinquent is defined as someone who breaks the law, those that apply to youth as well as adults. Tremblay (2003) suggests that the term "delinquent" should be used to describe youth in studies that specifically focus upon legal issues. He suggests three classes of delinquent behavior from a legal perspective. These are: (1) vandalism and theft with or without confrontation of a victim; (2) physical, verbal or indirect aggression, predatory or defensive; and (3) status offenses of underage youth (e.g., consuming alcohol prior to age 21). Aggression alone has not always been found to predict delinquency (Anderson, Bergman, & Magnusson, 1989). These authors suggest that delinquency is best predicted when aggression is accompanied by peer rejection and other problems, many of which are present in most youth with ADHD. In young children, a combination of aggression and social problems appear to be predictive of later drug abuse and duress (Kellam, Simon, & Ensminger, 1983). Rose, Rose, and Feldman (1989) suggested that early antisocial behavior predicts more than the single well-established developmental path that ends in delinquency. Early signs of DBD among a preschool population, including tantrums, defiance and overactivity predicted the diagnosis of a DBD by mid-childhood in 67% and later delinquency (Campbell & Ewing, 1990).

In 2001, Moffitt and Caspi attempted to identify the childhood risk factors of life-course-persistent delinquence. Their results with the same 1,000 individuals found that males and females classified as life-course-persistent delinquents were highly similar on most risk factors and had significantly higher levels of risk factors in their adolescence-limited peers. With regard to childhood risk factors, life-course-persistent individuals demonstrated significantly greater risk on 21 of the 26 factors measured. In contrast, the risk factors reported by adolescence-limited individuals were similar to their comparison peers with no history of juvenile court involvement on all but one of the factors measured. Thus, youth who exhibit rule violations that are limited to their adolescent years tended to have fewer pathological histories, personality problems, reading problems, inadequate parenting, and broken attachments and relationships than life-course persistent delinquents. Although Moffitt and others (Moffitt, Caspi, Harrington, & Milne, 2002; White, Bates, & Buyske, 2001) refer to both adolescence-limited and life-course-persistent youth problems as delinquency, it would appear that the latter group certainly provide a better working definition of the community's perception of the chronic, recurrent antisocial behaviors exhibited by delinquents. White et al. (2001)'s extension of Moffitt's work demonstrated that delinquents manifested higher disinhibition, impulsivity and parental hostility and lower harm avoidance, and less intact family structure than non-delinquents.

Perhaps a distinction between CD and delinquency should also focus upon persistence. CD, based upon DSM-IV field studies tends to have an average length of duration of 3 years. That is, most youth meeting the CD criteria recover within that period of time. CD may thus equate with Moffitt's conceptualization of adolescence-limited delinquency. It should be noted, however, that receiving a diagnosis of CD is not a benign phenomena over time. Associations between parent and teacher reports of conduct problems at age 8 and psychosocial outcomes at 18 report elevated rates of educational underachievement, juvenile offending, substance abuse/dependence, and mental health problems at 18 even after adjusting for social disadvantage, attention problems, and I.Q. (Fergusson & Lynskey, 1998). Further, maternal communication/problem solving skills and family variables (e.g., marital status, maternal depressed mood, and interparental conflict) during early adolescence, both independently and interactively, predicts severe delinquent behaviors during early adulthood (Klein & Forehand, 1997).

Developmental Course

The greatest comorbidity for the DBD's may be with each other rather than other psychiatric conditions. Comorbidity may in fact reflect the differentiation in what begins as unitary pattern of disruptive symptoms. For example, Bauermeister (1992) generated factor analytic data suggesting that at 4–5 years of age disruptive symptoms appear to fall on a single dimension.

ADHD

ADHD appears to develop relatively early in childhood before the other DBD's present. The majority of children with ADHD are identified within their first year of school. Early signs of inattention, hyperactivity, and impulsivity in children quickly cause impairment in multiple settings leading to problems with social relations, self-esteem and underachievement (Barkley, Fischer, Edelbrock, & Smallish, 1990). Interpersonal difficulties with peers, adults, and family members often result in rejection and subsequent social neglect due to the inappropriate

pattern of behavior resulting from an impulsive manner of dealing with thoughts, feelings, and others (Milich & Landau, 1981; Milich, Landau, Kilby, & Whitten, 1982). Problems with language impairment may further contribute to poor interpersonal relations, school achievement, and developing self-regulatory patterns of behavior (Cantwell & Baker, 1977; Cantwell & Baker, 1989; Cantwell, Baker, & Mattison, 1981). In a vicious cycle, isolation from peers due to the combined effect of ADHD and its impact on the normal course of development as well as other adversities leads to reduced opportunity to develop appropriate social interaction, self-esteem, coping skills, academic progress, and likely resilience processes (Brooks, 1998). The academic performance and achievement problems in youth with ADHD have been reported to be well over 50% (Fischer, Barkley, Fletcher, & Smallish, 1990; Semrud-Clikeman et al., 1992). Poor persistence and limited motivation (Milich, 1994), organizational deficits (Zentall, Harper, & Stormont-Spurgin, 1993), careless mistakes (Teeter, 1998), and noncompliant behavior (Weiss & Hechtman, 1993) have all been implicated as contributing to the pervasive scholastic problems experienced by youth with ADHD. Problems with independent seat work, school performance, deficient study skills, poor test taking, disorganized notebooks, desks, and reports, as well as lack of attention to lectures and group discussions, are consistent themes for youth with ADHD (DuPaul & Stoner, 2003). This pattern of impairment results in a variety of negative consequences in the social arena (Coie, Dodge, & Coppotelli, 1982), poor test performance (Nelson & Ellenberg, 1979), impaired working memory (Douglas & Benezra, 1990), and poor overall success in school (DuPaul & Stoner, 2003). As Teeter Ellison (2002) notes, an inability to persist and be vigilant interferes with classroom behavior, especially when tasks are repetitive or boring. These difficulties, unfortunately, present early and in particular when classroom expectations require sustained attention, effort, and goal directedness. Many children with ADHD, as Teeter Ellison notes, are "exquisitely attuned to the fact that they are not performing up to their peer group, that they are not meeting the expectations of important adults in their lives and that they are not well liked by their peers" (pg. 10). This cycle, described by others (Goldstein & Goldstein, 1990) creates increased vulnerability limiting opportunities for youth with ADHD to develop resilient qualities. Self-doubt and lack of confidence, combined with academic, social and avocational (e.g., sporting activities) failure, impedes self-esteem, increasing vulnerability for conditions such as depression and anxiety. By late elementary, many youth with ADHD may disengage from the learning environment as a means of avoiding failure, choosing instead patterns of inappropriate behavior, preferring to be labeled misbehaving rather than "dumb" (Brooks, 1991). Because elementary experience provides the basis foundational skills necessary to learn, including basic achievement, study, test taking, and organizational skills, many youth with ADHD enters the middle school years ill-prepared for the increasing demands of autonomy required by the upper grades. This then fuels their problems leading to a cycle of increased risk for drop out, school failure, academic underachievement, and significant risk in transitioning successfully into adulthood (Barkley et al., 1990; Barkley & Gordon, 2002).

The preponderance of these data argue strongly that symptoms of ADHD, in particular failure to develop what can be referred to as self-discipline, dramatically reduces positive outcome and thus opportunities to demonstrate resilience in the face of these adversities. Unfortunately, this pattern continues and intensifies in the adolescent years. What is most disturbing about the increasing body of research about ADHD in the adolescent years is the growing evidence of the widespread effects of ADHD on all aspects of academic, interpersonal, behavioral, emotional, and daily living activities. Up to 80% of youth carrying a diagnosis of ADHD continued to demonstrate clinically significant symptoms into their adolescent years (Barkley et al., 1990; Biederman, Faraone, Milberger, Guite et al., 1996; Biederman, Faraone, Milberger, Jetton et al., 1996; Weiss & Hechtman, 1993). Even early studies examining outcome found only a significant minority (between 20 and 30%) of children with ADHD followed into their adolescent years demonstrating limited differences

from controls. Seventy percent of a cohort followed over 20 years demonstrated significant academic, social, and emotional difficulties relative to their ADHD (Hechtman, 1999). The emerging literature suggests that adolescents with ADHD demonstrate significantly greater than expected presentation of comorbid disorders that during the adolescent years also appear to influence the development of adverse personality styles (e.g., antisocial or borderline personality disorder). Further, adolescents with ADHD demonstrate signs of social disability and appear at significantly greater risk for mood, anxiety, disruptive, and substance abuse disorders than comparison boys without social disability (Greene, Biederman, Faraone, Sienna, & Garcia-Jones, 1997). In this 4-year longitudinal study of boys with ADHD, the presence of social disability predicted poor social and psychiatric outcome including substance abuse and conduct disorder. The authors concluded that assessing social function in adolescents with ADHD is critical to their treatment. Once again, ADHD is demonstrated to strip away or limit the potential to develop critical, resilient phenomena. These include the ability to connect and maintain satisfying reciprocal relationships with others, achieve in school, and maintain mental health facilitate resilience (Brooks & Goldstein, 2001).

ODD and CD

Not surprisingly, with ODD and CD, less serious symptoms tend to precede moderate symptoms which precede the presentation of more serious symptoms. Preschoolers demonstrate a single disruptive pattern of behavior often composed of oppositionality and mild aggression (Achenbach, Edelbrock, & Howell, 1987). These findings are consistent with the developmental view that ODD usually precedes the onset of CD. The risk of onset of CD was found to be four times higher in children with ODD than in those without (Cohen & Flory, 1998). Multiple authors have investigated developmental pathways of these patterns of behavior, identifying three often parallel pathways as (1) overt, (2) covert, and (3) authority conflict (Kelly, Loeber, Keenan, & DeLamatre, 1997; Loeber et al., 1988; Loeber, Keenan, & Zhang, 1997). On the overt pathway, minor aggression leads to physical fighting and finally violence. On the covert pathway, minor covert behaviors such as stealing from home often lead to property damage (e.g., fire setting) and then to moderate to serious forms of recurrent status and criminal behavior. On the authority conflict pathway, problems progress from stubborn behavior to defiance and authority avoidance (e.g., truancy and running away). Youth often start down this pathway well before age 12, though it is not well understood whether aggression in preschoolers in and of itself significantly increases risk to precede down one of these pathways (Nagin & Tremblay, 1999).

Prevalence

When DSM symptoms are used epidemiologically, an incidence rate of up to 15% is found for ADHD. In a study of nearly 500 children evaluated on an outpatient basis at a children's hospital, 15% received a diagnosis of ADHD based on a comprehensive assessment (McDowell & Rappaport, 1992). Field studies for the DSM-IV identified nearly 9% of the population as meeting at least one of the diagnostic subtypes for ADHD (Applegate et al., 1997). When a careful analysis is conducted, the rate of ADHD most likely falls between 3 and 6% (for review see Goldstein & Goldstein, 1998; Jensen & Cooper, 2002; Boyle et al., 2011). A higher incidence of ADHD as well as other DBD's occurs in lower socio-economic families. A variety of additional life variables appear to affect the prevalence of ADHD as well as the other DBD's. For example, among adopted or foster families the incidence of ADHD has been found to be twice as high as among other children (Molina, 1990).

Few studies have generated consistent prevalence data for ODD or CD as a function of age. Epidemiological studies estimating the occurrence of CD in the general population vary from just over 3% of 10-year-olds (Rutter, Tizard, & Whitmore, 1970) to almost 7% of 7-year-olds (McGee, Silva, & Williams, 1984). Based on a review of the existing literature, Kazdin in 1987 suggested a range of 4–10% for CD. The rate of ODD in the general population has been reported as equally high (Anderson, Williams, McGee, and Silva, 1987). Oppositional, negativistic, behavior may be developmentally normal in early childhood. However, epidemiological studies of negativistic traits in nonclinical populations found such behavior in between 16 and 22% of school age children (Loeber, Lahey, & Thomas, 1991). Although ODD may begin as early as 3 years of age, it typically does not begin until 8 years of age and usually not later than adolescence. In boys, aged 5–8 years, fighting, temper tantrums, disobedience, negativism, irritability, and quickness to anger appear to decrease with increasing age (Werry and Quay, 1971). MacFarlane, Allen, and Honziak (1962) found similar decreases with age for both sexes in the prevalence of lying, destructiveness, negative behavior, and temper tantrums. The greatest decline in these problems appeared to take place during the elementary years. Tremblay (2003) reported a decline in oppositional behavior in boys, particularly between the first and second grades. Anderson, Williams, McGee, and Silva (1987) report that mothers ratings of aggressive behavior decreased for their children between the ages of 5 and 11 years in children without a reported history of psychiatric problems. In contrast, teacher rated aggression scores for this same group increased for children with histories of psychiatric problems. Certain covert disruptive behaviors such as alcohol and drug use, as well as various forms of theft appear to increase from late childhood to adolescence (Loeber & Schmaling, 1985). Lying, interestingly enough appears to present at all age levels (Achenbach & Edelbrock, 1981). Further, there is little doubt that prevalence varies as diagnostic criteria changes. For example, when comparing the revised third edition of the DSM with the original third edition ADHD criteria, the revised criteria were found to identify 14% more children than the original criteria identified (Lahey,

Loeber et al., 1990). Lahey, Loeber, et al. (1990) concluded that boys are more likely to meet criteria for DSM definitions of CD than their female counterparts.

Table 11.1, though a number of years old, provide an overview of risk factors that increase the probability of youth receiving a psychiatric diagnosis, including the DBD's. Although none of these studies assess variability of problems across situations, a consistent set of diagnostic criteria were utilized. Further, educational risk factors including lower cognitive skills, weaker academic self-esteem, lower academic achievement, and school repetition appear to consistently present in youth at increased risk for emotional and behavioral problems in these studies. Readers will note that many of these risk factors have been identified as those which increase vulnerability and adverse outcome in studies of resilience in childhood.

Comorbidity

ADHD co-occurs with other DBD's as well as multiple other developmental and psychiatric disorders in children to such an extent that authors have suggested subtypes of ADHD to include combinations of ADHD with other DBD (e.g., ADHD and CD) as well as with internalizing disorders (e.g., ADHD and Anxiety) (Jensen, Martin, & Cantwell, 1997). ADHD coexists with other disorders at a rate well beyond chance (Seidman, Benedict, Biederman, & Bernstein, 1995). As described, impulsiveness likely acts as a catalyst, increasing risk for development of other problems, especially in the face of additional risk factors (e.g., family, developmental, educational).

Goldstein and Goldstein (1998) posit that certain events instigate or increase the probability that ADHD will be diagnosed. These include

Table 11.1 Other factors associated with increased risk for psychiatric disorder

Factor	Risk increased for	
Anderson et al. (1989) (age 11)	Lower cognitive abilities	ADD, multiple
	Lower academic self-esteem	Emotional, ADD[a], multiple
	Lower general self-esteem	Emotional, ADD, multiple
	Poor health	Any
	Poor peer socialization	Multiple
	Family disadvantage	Emotional, ADD
Bird et al. (1988) (ages 4–16)	Lower academic achievement	Behavioral, depressed
	Poor family functioning	Depressed
	High life stress	Behavioral, depressed
Velez et al. (1989) (ages 9–19)	Family problems	Behavioral
	Repeated school grade	Any
	High life stress	Behavioral, overanxious
Costello (1989) (ages 7–11)	Urban (vs. suburban)	Behavioral
	Repeated school grade	Behavioral
	High life stress	Any
	No father in home	Oppositional
Offord et al. (1987) (ages 4–16)	Family dysfunction	Any
	Repeated school grade	Behavioral
	Parental psychiatric problems	Somatization (boys only)
	Parent arrested	Conduct and oppositional
	Chronic mental illness	Any (4–11) only for hyperactivity

Source: Costello (1989). Copyright, 1989. Used with permission of the author and publisher
[a]ADD attention deficit disorder

individual characteristics such as intellectual functioning, biological pre-disposition, and the physical and psychosocial environment. Events in the school or home then either strengthen or decrease the behavioral symptoms of ADHD. Once ADHD is diagnosed, the risk of depression is increased as the result of social problems, school failure, and possibly the side effects of medication. The risk for CD is increased by school and social problems as well as the presentation of antisocial role models which has been demonstrated as a critical risk factor.

In a review of empirical studies, Biederman, Newcorn, and Sprich (1991) attempted to define the comorbidity of ADHD with other disorders. The authors suggest that the literature supports considerable comorbidity of ADHD with CD, ODD, mood disorders, anxiety disorders, learning disabilities, and other disorders such as mental retardation, Tourette's disorder, and borderline personality disorder. The qualities of ADHD may act as a catalyst: Leave them alone and they may not be terribly aversive; mix them with negative life events or risk factors and they appear to catalytically worsen those events and the impact they have on children's current and future functioning (Goldstein & Goldstein, 1998).

In a community sample of over 15,000 14–18-year-old adolescents, Lewinsohn, Rhode, and Seeley (1994) compared six clinical outcome measures with four major psychiatric disorders (depression, anxiety, substance abuse, and disruptive behaviors). The impact of comorbidity was strongest for academic problems, mental health treatment utilization, and past suicide attempts; intermediate on measures of role, function, and conflict with parents and non-significant and physical symptoms. The greatest incremental impact of comorbidity was on anxiety disorders; the least was on substance abuse. Substance use and disruptive behavior were more common in males, depression, and anxiety in females. The effect of comorbidity was not due to psychopathology. The authors conclude as others have that there is a high rate of comorbidity in adolescence referred in clinical practice.

In clinic referred populations, the comorbidity between ADHD and CD has been reported as high as 50% with an incidence of 30–50% reported in epidemiological or comorbidity samples (Szatmari, Boyle, & Offord, 1989). Children with ADHD and comorbid ODD and CD exhibit greater frequencies of antisocial behavior such as lying, stealing, and fighting than those with ADHD who do not develop the second disruptive comorbid disorder (Barkley, 1998). It has also been suggested that this combined group is at greater risk for peer rejection. These children may be neglected due to their lack of social skills and rejected due to their aggressive behavior. Common sense dictates that the comorbid group is going to require more intensive and continuous service delivery. The comorbid group also holds the greatest risk for later life problems. In fact, it is likely the co-occurrence of CD with ADHD that speaks to the significant adult problems a subgroup of those with ADHD appear to develop. As Edelbrock (1989) noted more predictive of outcome than severity of ADHD symptoms is the development in children with ADHD of oppositional and aggressive behaviors. Environmental consequences, including parent psychopathology, marital discord, ineffective parenting, parent aggressiveness, and antisocial parent behavior are better predictors of life outcome for children with ADHD than the ADHD diagnosis per se. In fact these factors become highly stable over time and are resistant to change. Data also suggests that the comorbid conditions presenting before age 10 have a much worse prognosis than the second behavior disorder develops after age 10 (McGee & Share, 1988).

After careful review of the literature, Loeber et al. (1991) suggest that CD and ODD are strongly and developmentally related but clearly different. Factor analyses indicate that distinct covarying groups of ODD and CD can be identified but that certain symptoms relate to both disorders particularly, mild aggression and lying. As noted, age of onset for ODD is earlier than most CD symptoms. Nearly all youth with CD have a history of ODD but not all ODD cases progress to CD. Interestingly, in some studies children with ODD demonstrate the same forms of parental psychopathology and family adversity but to a lesser degree than for CD. Clearly the age of onset of some CD symptoms, specifically fighting, bullying, lying, and vandalism suggest that some youth with CD show nearly simultaneous onset of ODD and CD. However, the more serious symptoms of CD such as vandalism, running away, truancy, shoplifting, breaking and entering, rape, and assault appear to emerge at a much later age than ODD symptoms. Biederman, Faraone, Milberger, Jetton, et al. (1996) generated data suggesting two types of ODD which appear to have different correlates, course, and outcome. One type appeared prodromal for CD the other sub-syndromal to CD and not likely to progress into CD in later years. Not surprisingly, the higher risk form of ODD was characterized by a stronger profile of negative, provocative, spiteful, and behavior.

There is a growing body of literature suggesting that DBD's and anxiety disorders are often comorbid. Loeber and Keenan (1994) found that CD and anxiety disorders are comorbid substantially higher than chance during childhood and adolescence.

Epidemiologically the overlap between ADHD and depression occurs at a beyond chance level with some studies suggesting nearly 30% (McClelland, Rubert, Reichler, & Sylvester, 1989). While Capaldi (1992) found that CD is likely a precursor to depression in some children, Biederman, Faraone, Mick, and Lelon (1995) questioned the psychiatric comorbidity among referred juveniles with major depression. In a sample of 424 children and adolescents consecutively referred to a psychiatric facility, nearly 40% were identified with a depressive disorder. They had a history of chronic course and severe psychosocial dysfunction. They also demonstrated a high rate of CD, anxiety disorder, and ADHD. Seventy-four percent with severe major depression and 77% with mild major depression received a diagnosis of ADHD compared to 74% of the psychiatric controls and none of the normal controls. The authors hypothesized that major depression was more likely the outcome rather than the cause of co-occurring disorders based on an analysis of age of symptom onset.

Risk for Acquisition and Exacerbation

Biological, psychological, and psychosocial factors are all posited to be risk factors for the development of a DBD. Burke, Loeber, and Birmaher (2002)

considered genetics, intergenerational transmission, neuroanatomy, neurotransmitters, pre-autonomic nervous system, pre- and perinatal problems and neurotoxins as biological risk factors for the development of a DBD. While the evidence is not conclusive, several studies suggest a moderate genetic influence on DBD's. Eaves et al. (2000) concluded that there is a high genetic correlation across gender in the liability for ODD and CD.

Several researchers, for example, Lahey et al. (1998) have found that a history of parental antisocial behavior disorders is associated with pre-adolescent onset of CD. Loeber, Green, Keenan, and Lahey (1995) concluded that parental substance abuse, low socio-economic status, and oppositional behavior are key factors in boys' progression to CD.

Biological

Frontal lobe dysfunction has been associated with the increased risk of violent behavior (Pliszka, 1999). Impairments in the functioning of the amygdala are associated with deficits in the reading of social cues and the connection between the amygdala and prefrontal cortical regions serves to aid in the suppression of negative emotion (Davidson, Putnam, & Larson, 2000).

Low levels of serotonin in cerebral spinal fluid have been linked to aggression (Clark, Murphy, & Constantino, 1999; Kruesi et al., 1990). Moffitt, Brammer, and Caspi (1998) found that in men metabolites of serotonin in the general population sample of 21-year-olds was related to past year self-reported and life time court recorded violence. Burke et al. (2002) concluded that the link between serotonin and aggression reflects a complex relationship between neuroanatomical and neurochemical interconnectivity, executive brain function, and behavioral dysregulation.

Pliszka (1999) reported that individuals with DBD experienced general physiological under-arousal. Lower heart rates have been reported to be associated with adolescent antisocial behavior (Mezzacappa, Tremblay, & Kindlon, 1997) and predictive of later criminality (Raine, Venables, & Williams, 1990).

Evidence exists of the contributions of genetic factors to DBD as well as the contributions of pre-natal and early developmental exposure to toxins, other perinatal problems and physical damage to brain structures (Burke et al., 2002). Maternal smoking during pregnancy has been found to predict CD in boys (Wakschlag et al., 1997). Pregnancy and birth complications have also been shown to be associated with the development of behavior problems in offspring (Raine et al., 1990). Environmental toxins such as lead have also been implicated in the development of DBD's. Elevated levels of lead in bones of children at age 11 are associated with greater parent and teacher ratings of aggressiveness, higher delinquency scores, and greater somatic complaints (Needleman, Riess, Tobin, Biesecker, & Greenhouse, 1996). The psy-chological substrates of temperament, attachment, neuropsychological functioning, intelligence, aca-demic performance, and social cognition have all been found to influence an individual's propensity to develop a DBD. Sanson and Prior (1999) con-cluded that early temperament (specifically nega-tive emotionality, intense, and reactive responding and inflexibility), is predictive of externalizing behavior problems by late childhood.

Low intelligence is often considered a precur-sor to DBD. However, as Loeber et al. (1991) point out, the issue of the association between CD, ADHD, and IQ is not well understood. Additionally, IQ appears to be related to low achievement and school failure which are also related to later antisocial behavior (Farrington, 1995). Moreover, high intelligence does not pre-clude conduct problems. Boys with psychopathic characteristics, parental antisocial personality dis-order, and conduct problems were found to have IQ's equivalent to those of controls and higher than those with boys with conduct problems but without psychopathology and parental APD (Christian, Frick, Hill, Tyler, & Frazer, 1997).

Psychological and Psychosocial Factors

Several aspects of child rearing practices such as degree of involvement, parent–child conflict man-agement, monitoring, and harsh and inconsistent discipline have been correlated with children's disruptive or delinquent behavior (Frick, 1994; Wasserman, Miller, Pinner, & Jaramilo, 1996). Coercive parenting behaviors appear to lead to aggressive behaviors in younger girls as well as boys (Eddy, Leve, & Fagot, 2001).

Fergusson, Lynskey, and Horwood (1996) reported that harsh or abusive parenting style such as sexual or physical abuse significantly increased the risk of CD. Childhood victimization of boys and girls, including abuse and neglect is predictive of later antisocial personality disorder (Luntz & Widom, 1994). Peer effects also appear to be importantly related to potential development and maintenance of DBD symptoms. The stability of peer rejection in children identified as having con-duct problems is significant (Coie & Dodge, 1998; Coie & Lenox, 1994) and related to aggressive responding (Dodge, Price, Bachorowski, & Newman, 1990). Association with deviant peers appears to lead to the initiation of delinquent behav-ior in boys (Elliott & Menard, 1996). Exposure to delinquent peers may enhance preexisting delin-quency (Coie & Miller-Johnson, 2001).

Disruptive behaviors among children are par-ticularly associated with poor and disadvantage neighborhoods (Loeber et al., 1995). Wickström and Loeber (2000) found that the effects of living in public housing countered the impact of any indi-vidual protective factors that were present. Specific social and economic risk factors such as unemploy-ment (Fergusson, Lynskey, & Horwood, 1997), neighborhood violence (Guerra, Huesmann, Tolan, Van Acker, & Eron, 1995), family poverty, and children's aggression (Guerra et al., 1995), low SES and duration and poverty (McLoyd, 1998) are associated with antisocial behavior. Finally, expo-sure to daily stressors may add to the risk for DBD in children and as noted can be exacerbated by life circumstances caused having a DBD.

Are Some Youth with DBD More Resilient Than Others?

The biological bases of resilience have yet to be studied, but likely will be found to play a role in predicting outcome. Traditionally, within the

DBD's the study of positive outcome has focused on reduction of symptom severity over time and the reduction of exposure to significant adverse family, educational and environmental phenomena. Yet, there is an increasing interest in studying individuals who suffered from DBD's, in particular CD and manage to transition successfully into adult life despite struggling through adolescence and at times young adulthood. Stories collected by the Office of Juvenile Justice and Delinquency Prevention (Office of Juvenile Justice and Delinquency Prevention, 2000) exemplify that efforts focusing upon rehabilitation, providing mentors and individual attention and most importantly, providing youth with a second chance, can and have been demonstrated to be a part of the formula that leads to resilience.

Enhancing Resilience in Youth with DBD: Guidelines for Clinical Practice

What are the factors that help some youth and adults bounce back while others become overwhelmed with feelings of helplessness and hopelessness. Some attain success that could have never been predicted by early life circumstances, finding the inner strength to overcome obstacles in their paths. Those who find success are viewed as resilient. Their positive outcome in the face of adversity precisely reflects the scientific studies that have demonstrated positive outcome in the face of variety of youthful problems, including those related to DBD's. A number of later chapters in this volume are devoted to developing and applying a clinical psychology of resilience. The remainder of this chapter provides a very brief overview of nine proposed guidelines for clinical practice.

1. Develop strategies with these youth to help them learn to rewrite negative scripts. Negative scripts are those words or behaviors that are followed day after day with predictable negative results.
2. Provide youth with a DBD opportunities to develop stress management skills.
3. Take the time to nurture and develop the capacity for empathy in youth with DBD's.

4. Teach effective communication through modeling and instruction. Effective communication includes an appreciation for both understanding as well as seeking to be understood.
5. Help youth with a DBD accept themselves without feeling inadequate or like second class citizens.
6. Facilitate connections to others, including providing opportunities for youth with DBD to help and serve as teachers for others.
7. Youth with DBD's view mistakes as challenges to appreciate and overcome rather than signs of inadequacy.
8. Help every youth with a DBD experience success and develop an island of competence, an area of strength in which success is experienced and appreciated by others.
9. Patiently help youth with a DBD develop self-discipline and self-control.

Summary

The DBD's encompass the most common and disruptive childhood symptom composites. They affect wide percentage of children, often present in combination and are catalytic in fueling a variety of adverse outcomes. The DBD's act to reduce protective influences, decreasing the opportunity to develop a resilient mindset and a resilient outcome into adulthood. An increasing body of research is providing an understanding of those protective factors that may mitigate and insulate youth with DBD's. Efforts at clinically applying the qualities of resilience and strategies to enhance a resilience mindset offer the promise of helping youth with DBD's overcome the adverse odds as they transit into adulthood.

References

Achenbach, T. M., Conners, C. K., Quay, H. C., Verlhulst, F. C., & Howell, C. T. (1989). Replication of empirically derived syndromes as a basis for taxonomy of child/adolescent psychopathology. *Journal of Abnormal Child Psychology, 17*, 299–320.
Achenbach, T. M., & Edelbrock, C. S. (1981). Behavioral problems and competencies reported by parents of

normal and disturbed children aged 4 through 16. *Monographs of the Society for Research and Child Development, 46* (Serial No. 188).

Achenbach, T. M., Edelbrock, C. S., & Howell, C. T. (1987). Empirically based assessment of the behavioral/emotional problems of 2- and 3-year-old children. *Journal of Abnormal Child Psychology, 15*, 629–650.

American Psychiatric Association. (2001). *Diagnostic and statistical manual—text revision* (4th ed.). Washington: American Psychiatric Association.

Anderson, T., Bergman, L. R., & Magnusson, D. (1989). Patterns of adjustment problems and alcohol abuse in early childhood: A prospective longitudinal study. *Development and Psychopathology, 1*, 119–131.

Anderson, D. J., Williams, S., McGee, R., & Silva, P. A. (1987). DSM-111 disorders in preadolescent children: Prevalence in a large sample from the general population. *Archives of General Psychiatry, 44*, 69–76.

Applegate, B., Lahey, B. B., Hart, E. L., Biederman, J., Hynd, G. W., Barkley, R. A., et al. (1997). Validity of the age of onset criterion for ADHD. A report from the DSM-IV field trials. *Journal of the American Academy of Child and Adolescent Psychiatry, 36*, 1211–1221.

Barkley, R. A. (1997). *The nature of self-control*. New York: Guilford.

Barkley, R. A. (1998). *Attention deficit hyperactivity disorder* (3rd ed.). New York: Guilford.

Barkley, R. A., Fischer, M., Edelbrock, C. S., & Smallish, L. (1990). The adolescent outcome of hyperactive children diagnosed by research criteria: I. An eight-year prospective follow-up study. *Journal of the American Academy of Child and Adolescent Psychiatry, 29*, 546–557.

Barkley, R. A., & Gordon, M. (2002). Research on comorbidity, adaptive functioning, and cognitive impairments in adults with ADHD: Implications for a clinical practice. In S. Goldstein & S. Teeter Ellison (Eds.), *Clinician's guide to adult ADHD: Assessment and intervention*. New York: Academic.

Bauermeister, J. J. (1992). Factor analyses of teacher ratings of attention deficit hyperactivity disorder and oppositional defiant symptoms in children aged four through thirteen years. *Journal of Clinical Child Psychology, 21*, 27–34.

Biederman, J., Faraone, S., Mick, E., & Lelon, E. (1995). Psychiatric comorbidity among referred juveniles with major depression: Fact or artifact? *Journal of the American Academy of Child and Adolescent Psychiatry, 34*, 579–590.

Biederman, J., Faraone, S., Milberger, S., Guite, J., Mick, E., Chen, L., et al. (1996). A prospective 4-year follow-up study of attention-deficit hyperactivity and related disorders. *Archives of General Psychiatry, 53*, 437–446.

Biederman, J., Faraone, S., Milberger, S., Jetton, J. G., Chen, L., Mick, E., et al. (1996). Is childhood oppositional defiant disorder a precursor to adolescent conduct disorder? Findings from a four-year follow-up study of children with ADHD. *Journal of the American Academy of Child and Adolescent Psychiatry, 35*, 1193–1204.

Biederman, J., Newcorn, J., & Sprich, S. (1991). Comorbidity of attention-deficit hyperactivity disorder with conduct, depressive, anxiety and other disorders. *The American Journal of Psychiatry, 148*, 564–577.

Bird, H. R., Canino, G., Rubio-Stipec, M., Gould, M. S., Ribera, J., Sesman, M., et al. (1988). Estimates of the prevalence of childhood maladjustment in a community survey in Puerto Rico. *Archives of General Psychiatry, 45*, 1120–1126.

Boyle, C. A., Boulet, S., Schieve, L. A., Cohen, R. A., Blumberg, S. J., et al. (2011). Trends in the prevalence of developmental disabilities in US children, 1997–2008. *Pediatrics, 127*, 1034–1042.

Brooks, R. (1991). *The self-esteem teacher*. Circle Pines: AGS.

Brooks, R. (1998). Self-esteem: Helping your child become a confident, resilient and persistent learner. In S. Goldstein & N. Mather (Eds.), *Overcoming underachieving: An action guide to helping your child succeed in school*. New York: Wiley.

Brooks, R., & Goldstein, S. (2001). *Raising resilient children*. New York: Contemporary Books.

Burke, J. D., Loeber, R., & Birmaher, B. (2002). Oppositional defiant disorder and conduct disorder: A review of the past 10 years, Part II. *Journal of the American Academy of Child and Adolescent Psychiatry, 41*, 1275–1293.

Campbell, S. B. (1991). Longitudinal studies of active and aggressive pre-schoolers: Individual differences in early behavior and outcome. In D. Cicchetti & S. L. Toth (Eds.), *Rochester symposium on developmental psychopathology*. New Jersey: Erlbaum.

Campbell, S. B., & Ewing, L. J. (1990). Follow-up of hard-to-manage preschoolers: Adjustment at age 9 and predictors of continuing symptoms. *Journal of Child Psychology and Psychiatry, 31*, 871–890.

Cantwell, D. P., & Baker, L. (1977). Psychiatric disorder in children with speech and language retardation. *Archives of General Psychiatry, 34*, 583–591.

Cantwell, D. P., & Baker, L. (1989). Stability and natural history of DSM-III childhood diagnoses. *Journal of the American Academy of Child and Adolescent Psychiatry, 28*, 691–700.

Cantwell, D. P., Baker, L., & Mattison, R. (1981). Prevalence, type and correlates of psychiatric disorder in 200 children with communication disorder. *Journal of Developmental and Behavioral Pediatrics, 2*, 131–136.

Capaldi, D. M. (1992). The co-occurrence of conduct problems and depressive symptoms in early adolescent boys, II: a 2-year follow-up at grade 8. *Developmental Psychology, 4*, 125–144.

Christian, R. E., Frick, P. J., Hill, N. L., Tyler, L., & Frazer, D. R. (1997). Psychopathy and conduct problems in children. II: implications for subtyping children with conduct problems. *Journal of the American Academy of Child and Adolescent Psychiatry, 36*, 233–241.

Clark, R. A., Murphy, D. L., & Constantino, T. N. (1999). Serotonin and externalization behavior in young children. *Psychiatry Research, 86*, 29–40.

Cohen, P., & Flory, M. (1998). Issues in the disruptive behavior disorders: Attention Deficit disorder without hyperactivity and the differential validity of oppositional defiant and conduct disorders. In T. A. Widiger, A. J. Frances, & H. J. Pincus (Eds.), *DSM-IV sourcebook* (Vol. 4, pp. 455–463). Washington: American Psychiatric Press.

Coie, J. D., & Dodge, K. A. (1998). Aggression and antisocial behavior. In W. Damon (Series Ed.) & N. Eisenberg (Vol. Ed.), *Handbook of child psychology. Social, emotional and personality development* (5th ed., Vol. 3, pp. 779–862). New York: Wiley.

Coie, J. D., Dodge, K. A., & Coppotelli, H. (1982). Dimensions and types of social status: A cross-age perspective. *Developmental Psychology, 18*, 557–570.

Coie, J. D., & Lenox, K. F. (1994). The development of antisocial individuals. In D. C. Fowles, P. Sutker, & S. H. Goodman (Eds.), *Progress in experimental personality and psychopathology research* (pp. 45–72). New York: Springer.

Coie, J. D., & Miller-Johnson, S. (2001). Peer factors and interventions. In R. Loeber & D. P. Farrington (Eds.), *Child delinquents* (pp. 191–209). Thousand Oaks: Sage.

Costello, E. J. (1989). Developments in child psychiatric epidemiology. *Journal of the American Academy of Child and Adolescent Psychiatry, 28*, 836–841.

Davidson, R. J., Putnam, K. M., & Larson, C. L. (2000). Dysfunction in the neuro circuitry of emotion regulation as a possible preclude to violence. *Science, 289*, 591–594.

Dodge, K. A., Price, J. M., Bachorowski, J. A., & Newman, J. P. (1990). Hostile attributional biases in severely aggressive adolescents. *Journal of Abnormal Psychology, 99*, 385–392.

Douglas, V. I., & Benezra, E. (1990). Supraspan verbal memory in attention deficit disorder with hyperactivity normal and reading disabled boys. *Journal of Abnormal Child Psychology, 18*, 617–638.

DuPaul, G. J., & Stoner, G. (2003). *ADHD in the schools* (2nd ed.). New York: Guilford.

Eaves, L., Rutter, M., Silberg, J. L., Shillady, L., Maes, H., & Pickles, A. (2000). Genetic and environmental causes of covariation in interview assessments of disruptive behavior in child and adolescent twins. *Behavioral Genetics, 30*, 321–334.

Eddy, J. M., Leve, L. D., & Fagot, B. I. (2001). Coercive family processes: A replication and extension of Patterson's coercion model. *Aggressive Behavior, 27*, 14–25.

Edelbrock, C. (1989). *Childhood conduct problems: Developmental consideration and a proposed taxonomy.* Unpublished manuscript. Worcester: University of Massachusetts Medical Center.

Eiraldi, R. B., Power, T. J., & Nezu, C. M. (1997). Patterns of comorbidity associated with subtypes of attention deficit/hyperactivity disorder among six-to-twelve year-old children. *Journal of the American Academy of Child and Adolescent Psychiatry, 36*, 503–514.

Elliott, D. S., & Menard, S. (1996). Delinquent friends and delinquent behavior: Temporal and developmental patterns. In J. D. Hawkins (Ed.), *Delinquency and crime: Current theories.* New York: Cambridge University Press.

Farrington, D. P. (1995). The development of offending and antisocial behavior from childhood: Key findings from the Cambridge study in delinquentprogram. *Journal of Child Psychology and Psychiatry, 36*, 929–964.

Fergusson, D. M., Horwood, L. J., & Lynskey, M. T. (1994). Structure of DSM-III-R criteria for disruptive childhood behaviors: Confirmatory factor models. *Journal of the American Academy of Child and Adolescent Psychiatry, 33*, 1145–1155.

Fergusson, D. M., & Lynskey, M. T. (1998). Conduct problems in childhood and psychosocial outcomes in young adulthood: A prospective study. *Journal of Emotional and Behavioral Disorders, 6*, 2–18.

Fergusson, D. M., Lynskey, M. T., & Horwood, L. J. (1996). Factors associated with continuity and change in disruptive behavior patterns between childhood and adolescence. *Journal of Abnormal Child Psychology, 24*, 533–553.

Fergusson, D. M., Lynskey, M. T., & Horwood, L. J. (1997). Attentional difficulties in middle childhood and psychosocial outcomes in young adulthood. *Journal of Child Psychology and Psychiatry, 38*, 633–644.

Fischer, M., Barkley, R. A., Fletcher, C. S., & Smallish, L. (1990). The adolescent outcome of hyperactive children diagnosed by research criteria: II. Academic, attentional and neuropsychological status. *Journal of Consulting and Clinical Psychology, 58*, 580–588.

Frick, P. J. (1994). Family dysfunction and hte disruptive behavior disorders: A review of recent empirical findings. *Advances in Clinical Child Psychology, 16*, 203–226.

Frick, P. J., Lahey, B. B., & Loeber, R. (1993). Oppositional defiant disorder and conduct disorder: A meta-analytic review of factor analyses and cross-validation in a clinical sample. *Clinical Psychology Review, 13*, 319–340.

Goldstein, S. (2002). Continuity of ADHD in adulthood: Hypothesis and theory meet reality. In S. Goldstein & S. Teeter Ellison (Eds.), *Clinician's guide to adult ADHD: Assessment and intervention.* New York: Academic.

Goldstein, S., & Goldstein, M. (1990). *Understanding and managing attention deficit disorder in children.* New York: Wiley.

Goldstein, S., & Goldstein, M. (1998). *Understanding and managing attention deficit hyperactivity disorder in children* (2nd ed.). New York: Wiley.

Goldstein, S., & Gordon, M. (2003). Gender issues and ADHD: Sorting fact from fiction. *The ADHD Report, 11*(4), 7–11.

Greene, R. W., Biederman, J., Faraone, S. V., Sienna, M., & Garcia-Jones, J. (1997). Adolescent outcome of boys with attention-deficit/hyperactivity disorder and social disability: Results from a four-year longitudinal follow-up study. *Journal of Consulting and Clinical Psychology, 65*, 758–767.

Guerra, N. G., Huesmann, L. R., Tolan, P. H., Van Acker, R., & Eron, L. D. (1995). Stressful events and individual beliefs as correlates of economic disadvantage and aggression among urban children. *Journal of Consulting and Clinical Psychology, 63*, 518–528.

Hechtman, L. (1999). Attention-deficit/hyperactivity disorder. In M. Weiss, L. T. Hechtman, & G. Weiss (Eds.), *ADHD in adulthood: A guide to current theory, diagnosis and treatment* (pp. 17–38). Baltimore: John Hopkins University Press.

Hechtman, L., Weiss, G., & Perlman, T. (1984). Hyperactives as young adults: Initial predictors of adult outcome. *Journal of the American Academy of Child and Adolescent Psychiatry, 25*, 250–260.

Herrero, M. E., Hechtman, L., & Weiss, G. (1994). Children with deficits in attention, motor control and perception almost grown up: The contribution of various background factors to outcome at age sixteen years. *European Child & Adolescent Psychiatry, 3*, 1–15.

Hinshaw, S. P. (1987). On the distinction between attention deficits/hyperactivity and conduct problems/aggression in child psychopathology. *Psychological Bulletin, 101*, 443–463.

Ingram, S., Hechtman, L., & Morgenstern, G. (1999). Outcome issues and ADHD: Adolescent and adult long-term outcome. *Mental Retardation and Developmental Disabilities Research Reviews, 5*, 243–250.

Jensen, P. S., & Cooper, J. R. (2002). *Attention deficit hyperactivity disorder: State of the science.* Kingston: Civic Research Institute.

Jensen, P. S., Martin, D. P., & Cantwell, D. P. (1997). Comorbidity in ADHD: Implications for research practice and DSM-V. *Journal of the American Academy of Child and Adolescent Psychiatry, 36*, 1065–1079.

Katz, M. (1997). *On playing a poor hand well.* New York: Norton.

Kellam, S. G., Simon, M. B., & Ensminger, M. E. (1983). Antecedents in first grade of teenage substance use and psychological well-being: A ten-year community-wide perspective study. In D. F. Ricks & B. S. Dohrenwend (Eds.), *Origins of psychopathology.* Cambridge: Cambridge University Press.

Kelly, B. T., Loeber, R., Keenan, K., & DeLamatre, M. (1997). *Developmental pathways in boys' disruptive and delinquent behavior.* Washington: Office of Juvenile Justice and Delinquency Prevention, U.S. Department of Justice.

Klein, K., & Forehand, R. (1997). Delinquency during the transition to early adulthood: Family and parenting predictors from early adolescence. *Adolescence, 32*, 61–78.

Kruesi, M. J. P., Rapoport, J. L., Hamburger, S., Hibbs, E., Potter, W. Z., Lenane, M., et al. (1990). Cerebrospinal fluid monoamine metabolites, aggression, and impulsivity in disruptive behavioral disorders of children and adolescents. *Archives of General Psychiatry, 47*, 419–426.

Lahey, B. B., Frick, P. J., Loeber, R., Tannenbaum, B. A., Van Horn, Y., & Christ, M. A. G. (1990). *Oppositional and conduct disorder: I. A meta-analytic review.* Unpublished manuscript. Athens: University of Georgia.

Lahey, B. B., Loeber, R., Quay, H. C., Applegate, B., Shaffer, D., Waldman, I., et al. (1998). Validity of DSM-IV subtypes of conduct disorder based on age of onset. *Journal of the American Academy of Child and Adolescent Psychiatry, 37*, 435–442.

Lahey, B. B., Loeber, R., Stouthamer-Loeber, M., Christ, M. A. G., Green, S., Russo, M. F., et al. (1990). Comparison of DSM-III and DSM-III-R diagnoses for prepubertal children: Changes in prevalence and validity. *Journal of the American Academy of Child and Adolescent Psychiatry, 29*, 620–626.

Lewinsohn, P. M., Rhode, P., & Seeley, J. R. (1994). Adolescent psychopathology: III. The clinical consequences of comorbidity. *Journal of the American Academy of Child and Adolescent Psychiatry, 34*, 510–519.

Loeber, R., Burke, J., Lahey, B. B., Winters, A., & Zera, M. (2000). Oppositional defiant and conduct disorder: A review of the past 10 years, Part I. *Journal of the American Academy of Child and Adolescent Psychiatry, 39*, 1468–1484.

Loeber, R., Green, S. M., Keenan, K., & Lahey, B. B. (1995). Which boys will fare worse? Early predictors of the onset of conduct disorder in a six-year longitudinal study. *Journal of the American Academy of Child and Adolescent Psychiatry, 34*, 499–509.

Loeber, R., & Keenan, K. (1994). Interaction between conduct disorder and its comorbid conditions: Effects of age and gender. *Clinical Psychology Review, 14*, 497–523.

Loeber, R., Keenan, K., Russo, M. F., Green, S. M., Lahey, B. B., & Thomas. (1988). Secondary data analyses for DSM-IV on the symptoms of oppositional defiant disorder and conduct disorder. In T. A. Widiger, A. J. Frances, H. J. Pincus (Eds.), *DSM-IV sourcebook* (Vol. 4, pp. 465–490). Washington: American Psychiatric Press.

Loeber, R., Keenan, K., & Zhang, Q. (1997). Boys' experimentation and persistence in developmental pathways toward serious delinquency. *Journal of Child and Family Studies, 6*, 321–357.

Loeber, R., Lahey, B. B., & Thomas, C. (1991). Diagnostic conundrum of oppositional defiant disorder and conduct disorder. *Journal of Abnormal Psychology, 100*, 379–390.

Loeber, R., & Schmaling, K. B. (1985). Empirical evidence for overt and covert patterns of antisocial conduct problems. *Journal of Abnormal Child Psychology, 100*, 379–390.

Loney, J., Whaley-Klahn, M. A., & Kosier, T. (1983). Hyperactive boys and their brothers at 21: Predictors of aggressive and antisocial outcomes. In K. T. Van Dusen & S. A. Mednick (Eds.), *Prospective studies of crime and delinquency* (pp. 181–206). Boston: Kluwer-Nijhoff.

Luntz, B. K., & Widom, C. S. (1994). Antisocial personality disorder in abused and neglected children grown up. *The American Journal of Psychiatry, 151*, 670–674.

MacFarlane, J. W., Allen, L., & Honziak, M. P. (1962). *A developmental study of the behavior problems of normal children between twenty-one months and fourteen years.* Berkeley: University of California Press.

McClelland, J. M., Rubert, M. P., Reichler, R. J., & Sylvester, C. E. (1989). Attention deficit disorder in children at risk for anxiety and depression. *Journal of the American Academy of Child and Adolescent Psychiatry, 29*, 534–539.

McDowell, M. J., & Rappaport, L. R. (1992). *Neurodevelopmental comorbidity with attention deficit hyperactivity disorder: A clinical review.* Paper presented at the 10th annual meeting of the Society for Behavioral Pedicatrics, St. Louis.

McGee, R., & Share, D. L. (1988). Attention deficit disorder hyperactivity and academic failure: Which comes first and what should be treated. *Journal of the American Academy of Child and Adolescent Psychiatry, 27*, 318–325.

McGee, R., Silva, P. A., & Williams, S. (1984). Behavior problems in a population of seven-year-old children: Prevalence, stability and types of disorder—a research report. *Journal of Child Psychology and Psychiatry, 25*, 251–259.

McLoyd, V. C. (1998). Socioeconomic disadvantage and child development. *American Psychology, 53*, 185–204.

Mezzacappa, E., Tremblay, R. E., & Kindlon, D. (1997). Anxiety, antisocial behavior, and heart rate regulation in adolescent males. *Journal of Child Psychology and Psychiatry, 38*, 457–469.

Milich, R. (1994). The response of children with ADHD to failure: If at first you don't succeed, do try, try again? *School Psychology Review, 23*, 11–28.

Milich, R., & Landau, S. (1981). Socialization and peer relations in the hyperactive child. In K. D. Gadow & I. Bailer (Eds.), *Advances in learning and behavior disabilities* (Vol. 1). Greenwich: JAI Press.

Milich, R., Landau, S., Kilby, G., & Whitten, P. (1982). Preschool peer perceptions of the behavior of hyperactive and aggressive children. *Journal of Abnormal Child Psychology, 10*, 497–510.

Moffitt, T. E. (1990). Juvenile delinquency and attention deficit disorder: Developmental self-reported delinquents. *Developmental Psychopathology, 1*, 105–118.

Moffitt, T. E. (1993). Adolescence limited and life-course-persistent to anti-social behavior: A developmental taxonomy. *Psychological Review, 100*, 674–701.

Moffitt, T. E., Brammer, G. L., & Caspi, A. (1998). Whole blood serotonin relates to violence in epidemiological study. *Biological Psychiatry, 43*, 446–457.

Moffitt, T. E., & Caspi, A. (2001). Childhood predictors differentiate life-course-persistent in adolescence-limited anti-social pathways among males and females. *Development and Psychopathology, 13*, 355–375.

Moffitt, T. E., Caspi, A., Harrington, H., & Milne, B. J. (2002). Males on the life-course-persistent and adolescence-limited anti-social pathways: Follow-up at age twenty-six years. *Development and Psychopathology, 14*, 179–207.

Molina, L. R. (1990). Adoptees may be at risk for hyperactivity but no one knows why. *Adopted Child, 9*, 1–2.

Mota, V. L., & Schachar, R. J. (2000). Reformulating ADHD according to signal detection theory. *Journal*

of the American Academy of Child and Adolescent Psychiatry, 39, 1144–1151.

Nagin, D. S., & Tremblay, R. E. (1999). Trajectories of boys' physical aggression, opposition, and hyperactivity on the path to physically violent and nonviolent juvenile delinquency. *Child Development, 70*(5), 1181–1196.

Needleman, H. L., Riess, J. A., Tobin, M. J., Biesecker, G. E., & Greenhouse, J. B. (1996). Bone lead levels and delinquent behavior. *Journal of the American Medical Association, 275*, 363–369.

Nelson, K. B., & Ellenberg, J. H. (1979). Apgar scores and long-term neurological handicap (Abstract). *Annals of Neurology, 39*, 6.

Offord, D. R., Boyle, M. H., Szatmari, P., Rae-Grant, N., Links, P. S., Cadman, D. T., et al. (1987). Ontario child health study: II. Six month prevalence of disorder and rates of service utilization. *Archives of General Psychiatry, 44*, 832–836.

Office of Juvenile Justice and Delinquency Prevention. (2000). Second chances: Giving kids a chance to make a better choice. *U.S. Department of Justice, Publication #NCJ181680 (May, 2000).* Washington, DC.

Patterson, G. R., DeBaryshe, B. D., & Ramsey, E. (1989). A developmental perspective on antisocial behavior. *American Psychologist, 44*, 329–335.

Pliszka, S. R. (1999). The psychobiology of oppositional defiant disorder and conduct disorder. In H. C. Quay & A. E. Hogan (Eds.), *Handbook of disruptive behavior disorders* (pp. 371–395). New York: Kluwer Academic/Plenum.

Raine, A., Venables, P. H., & Williams, M. (1990). Relationships between central and autonomic measures of arousal at age 15 years and criminality at age 24 years. *Archives of General Psychiatry, 47*, 1060–1064.

Robins, L. N. (1991). Conduct disorder. *Journal of Child Psychology and Psychiatry, 32*, 193–212.

Rose, S. L., Rose, S. A., & Feldman, J. F. (1989). Stability of behavior problems in very young children. *Development and Psychopathology, 1*, 5–19.

Rutter, M., Tizard, J., & Whitmore, K. (1970). *Education health and behaviour.* London: Longmass.

Sanson, A., & Prior, M. (1999). Temperament and behavioral precursors to oppositional defiant disorder and conduct disorder. In H. C. Quay & A. E. Hogan (Eds.), *Handbook of disruptive behavior disorder* (pp. 397–417). New York: Kluwer Academic/Plenum.

Seidman, L. J., Benedict, K. B., Biederman, J., & Bernstein, J. H. (1995). Performance of children with ADHD on the Rey-Osterrieth Complex Figure: A pilot neuropsychology study. *Journal of Child Psychology and Psychiatry, and Allied Disciplines, 36*, 1459–1473.

Semrud-Clikeman, M., Biederman, J., Sprich-Buckminister, S., Krifcher, L., Lehman, B., Faraone, S. V., et al. (1992). The incidence of ADHD and concurrent learning disabilities. *Journal of the American Academy of Child and Adolescent Psychiatry, 31*, 439–448.

Still, G. F. (1902). The Coulstonian lectures on some abnormal physical conditions in children. *Lancet, 1*, 1008–1012.

Szatmari, P., Boyle, M., & Offord, D. R. (1989). ADHD and conduct disorder: Degree of diagnostic overlap and differences among correlates. *Journal of the American Academy of Child and Adolescent Psychiatry, 28*, 865–872.

Taylor, E., Schachar, R., Thorley, G., & Wieselberg, M. (1986). Conduct disorder and hyperactivity: I. Separation of hyperactivity and antisocial conduct in British child psychiatric patients. *The British Journal of Psychiatry, 149*, 760–767.

Teeter, P. A. (1998). *Interventions for ADHD: Treatment in developmental context*. New York: Guilford.

Teeter Ellison, A. (2002). An overview of childhood and adolescent ADHD: Understanding the complexities of development into the adult years. In S. Goldstein & S. Teeter Ellison (Eds.), *Clinician's guide to adult ADHD: Assessment and intervention*. New York: Academic.

Tremblay, R. E. (2003). Why socialization fails: The case of the chronic physical aggression. In B. B. Lahey, T. E. Moffitt, & A. Caspi (Eds.), *Causes of conduct disorder and juvenile delinquency* (pp. 185–206). New York: Guilford.

Velez, C. N., Johnson, J., & Cohen, P. (1989). A longitudinal analysis of selected risk factors of childhood psychopathology. *Journal of the American Academy of Child and Adolescent Psychiatry, 29*, 782–784.

Wakschlag, L. S., Lahey, B. B., Loeber, R., Green, S. M., Gordon, R., & Leventhal, B. L. (1997). Maternal smoking during pregnancy and the risk of conduct disorder in boys. *Archives of General Psychiatry, 54*, 670–676.

Wasserman, G. A., Miller, L. S., Pinner, E., & Jaramilo, B. (1996). Parenting predictors of early conduct problems in urban, high-risk boys. *Journal of the American Academy of Child and Adolescent Psychiatry, 35*, 1227–1236.

Weiss, G., & Hechtman, L. (1993). *Hyperactive children grown up: ADHD in children, adolescents and adults* (2nd ed.). New York: Guilford.

Werry, J. S., & Quay, H. C. (1971). The prevalence of behavior symptoms in younger elementary school children. *The American Journal of Orthopsychiatry, 41*(1), 136–143.

White, H. R., Bates, M. E., & Buyske, S. (2001). Adolescence-limited versus persistent delinquency: Extending Moffitt's hypothesis into adulthood. *Journal of Abnormal Psychology, 110*, 600–609.

Wickström, P. O., & Loeber, R. (2000). Do disadvantaged neighborhoods cause well-adjusted children to become adolescent delinquents? A study of male juvenile serious offending, risk and protective factors, and neighborhood context. *Criminology, 38*, 1109–1141.

Zentall, S. S., Harper, G., & Stormont-Spurgin, M. (1993). Children with hyperactivity and their organization abilities. *The Journal of Educational Research, 87*, 112–117.

From Helplessness to Optimism: The Role of Resilience in Treating and Preventing Depression in Youth

12

Karen Reivich, Jane E. Gillham, Tara M. Chaplin, and Martin E.P. Seligman

Some of the most common psychological disorders in children and adolescents are internalizing disorders such as depression and anxiety. Research on the development of depression and anxiety suggests that internalizing disorders can be reduced, even prevented, by promoting more accurate cognitive styles, problem-solving skills, and supportive family relationships. Several cognitive–behavioral interventions have shown promise in treating and preventing depression and anxiety. We review the Penn Resiliency Program (PRP) as an example of such an intervention. We suggest that most of the skills covered in the PRP and similar preventive interventions are not specific to depression or anxiety and can be useful for increasing young people's resiliency more generally. Interventions that teach and reinforce these skills can help children to navigate a variety of difficult situations they are likely to encounter during adolescence and adulthood.

K. Reivich (✉) • T.M. Chaplin • M.E.P. Seligman
University of Pennsylvania, Pennsylvania, PA, USA
e-mail: revich@psych.upenn.edu;
tchaplin@psych.upenn.edu; seligman@psych.upenn.edu

J.E. Gillham
Department of Psychology, Swarthmore College,
Swarthmore, PA, USA
e-mail: jgillha1@swarthmore.edu

Depression in Children and Adolescents

At any point in time, approximately 2–3% of children and 6–9% of adolescents have a major depressive disorder (Cohen et al., 1993; Lewinsohn, Hops, Roberts, & Seeley, 1993). Approximately one in five adolescents will have had a major depressive episode by the end of high school (Lewinsohn et al.). Anxiety disorders, which often precede and co-occur with depression, are found in 10–21% of children and adolescents (Kashani & Orvaschel, 1990; Romano, Tremblay, Vitaro, Zoccolillo, & Pagani, 2001). It is notable that rates of depression increase as children enter adolescence (Hankin, Abramson, Moffitt, Silva, & McGee, 1998), indicating that the transition to adolescence is a particularly vulnerable developmental period for depression. In addition, several studies indicate that rates of depression and anxiety have increased dramatically over the past 50 years (Klerman et al., 1985; Twenge, 2000), so that young people today are much more likely to suffer from depression and anxiety than their parents or grandparents were.

This chapter focuses on unipolar depression,[1] one of the most common types of internalizing disorders, because our research program focuses

[1] We will not focus on bipolar disorder, or manic-depression, which is relatively rare in children and which appears to be more heavily biologically based (Hammen & Rudolph, 2003).

S. Goldstein and R.B. Brooks (eds.), *Handbook of Resilience in Children*,
DOI 10.1007/978-1-4614-3661-4_12, © Springer Science+Business Media New York 2013

primarily on the prevention of this disorder and its symptoms. We will also discuss anxiety symptoms since there is considerable co-occurrence of depression and anxiety among children and most of the cognitive–behavioral risk and resilience factors and interventions discussed here in the context of depression also apply to anxiety disorders and symptoms (Kendall, 1994).

Unipolar depression, also known as major depression, is characterized by intense sadness or irritability, disrupted concentration, sleep, eating, and energy levels, and feelings of hopelessness and suicidal thoughts. Major depression in youth is not simply a phase of development; rather, it is a serious psychological problem that shows stability over time and can significantly interfere with children's ability to function. Depressed youth have a lowered ability to function in daily life, with 85–87% of adolescents with depressive disorders rated as having "major" impairments in functioning (Whitaker et al., 1990). Moreover, a significant portion of children with major depression continue to show depression in adulthood. For example, Harrington et al. found that 60% of children treated for major depression had at least one bout of major depression in adulthood (Harrington, Fudge, Rutter, Pickles, & Hill, 1990). Depression is not only burdensome to the individual but it is also very costly for society. In the United States, the yearly expenditure for major depressive disorder is about $43 billion, including loss of productivity, premature death, and cost of treatment (Hirschfeld et al., 1997).

The problems associated with depression extend beyond those meeting diagnostic criteria for a depressive disorder. Many children and adolescents have elevated, but subclinical, levels of internalizing symptoms. For example, 10–15% of middle school children may report moderate to severe levels of depressive symptoms (Nolen-Hoeksema, Girgus, & Seligman, 1986). Research suggests that children with high levels of depressive symptoms experience the same kinds of difficulties as do children with depressive disorders (Gotlib, Lewinsohn, & Seeley, 1995). Children and adolescents who suffer from high levels of depressive symptoms or depressive disorders are more likely to have academic and interpersonal difficulties.

They are more likely to smoke cigarettes, use other substances, and attempt suicide (Covey, Glassman, & Stetner, 1998; Garrison, Addy, Jackson, McKeown, & Waller, 1991). Despite the often severe concomitants of depression, it is underdetected and undertreated in adolescence—only about 20–25% of adolescents who are clinically depressed receive adequate treatment (Hirschfeld et al., 1997). Given the seriousness of depression and the number of children and adolescents who experience it, the identification, treatment, and prevention of depression in youth have become important areas for research.

Cognitive–Behavioral Models of the Development of Depression

Developmental psychopathologists theorize that depression is caused by a complex interaction of biological, cognitive, emotional, and interpersonal risk factors (Sroufe & Rutter, 1984). The focus of this chapter is mainly on cognitive and behavioral factors involved in the development of depression, although we acknowledge the importance of other systems and the interactions of those systems with cognitive and behavioral systems. For example, the interpersonal risk of fighting with a parent can interact with a child's negative cognitive style ("It was all my fault. I am a bad kid.") and the presence of a biological risk factor such as shyness or an anxious temperament to produce depression.

The Learned Helplessness Model was one of the first cognitive–behavioral models of depression (Seligman, 1975). Seligman observed that individuals who were exposed to uncontrollable negative events often overgeneralized from this experience and became passive in other situations that were in fact controllable. These individuals exhibited apathy, decreased appetite, despair, and other symptoms of clinical depression. The experience of uncontrollable negative events seemed to produce expectations of helplessness. That is, the individuals believed they could not control future negative events in their lives. Seligman also observed that some individuals seemed resistant to helplessness. These individuals remained persistent and hopeful even when exposed to uncontrollable negative events. Further cognitive–behavioral theories were developed to explain these individual differences.

More recent cognitive–behavioral theories generally posit that a tendency to view one's self, the world, and the future in overly negative ways, combined with a lack of behavioral coping skills, puts one at risk for depression and anxiety (Beck, 1976). Conversely, a realistic thinking style and positive coping skills promote resilience and may buffer children from internalizing problems. The Reformulated Learned Helplessness (RLH) model was introduced to explain why some people exhibit helplessness and depression in the face of adversity while others are more resilient. According to this theory, over time, people develop cognitive styles for explaining the events in their lives. Individuals who develop a pessimistic explanatory style attribute negative events to internal, stable, and global factors and positive events to external, unstable, and specific factors (Abramson, Seligman, & Teasdale, 1978). More recently, the hopelessness theory of depression posits that pessimistic explanatory style is one of three cognitive styles that can lead to depression. The others are the tendency to view the self as flawed and deficient following negative events and the tendency to catastrophize the consequences of negative events (Abela, 2001; Abramson, Metalsky, & Alloy, 1989). Taking the Reformulated Learned Helplessness and Hopelessness theories together, an adolescent with a hopeless cognitive style who fails a math test might think to him- or herself 'Math is impossible,' 'I'm stupid,' or 'I'm never going to do well.' Following a success, this adolescent might think 'that was lucky' or 'the test was easy.' This pattern of thoughts leads to helplessness (the student expects failure to continue and believes that there is nothing he or she can do to improve performance). When this kind of interpretive style is used to explain multiple events over time, it can lead to a more generalized sense of helplessness, which, in turn, leads to passivity, hopelessness, and despair. Numerous studies have linked a pessimistic or hopeless interpretive style to depression in adults and children (for reviews, see Abela

& Hankin, 2008; Gladstone & Kaslow, 1995; Robins & Hayes, 1995; Sweeny, Anderson, & Bailey, 1986)."

Other interpretive styles and problem-solving deficits have also been implicated in the development of depression. For example, Quiggle, Garber, Panak, and Dodge (1992) found that depressed children show a hostile attributional bias; that is, they tend to see actions of others as hostile, even when the action is actually ambiguous. This may help to explain the overlap between depression and conduct disorder that is often seen during adolescence (Rhode, Lewisohn, & Seeley, 1991). In addition to difficulties with interpreting social cues, depressed children may also lack behavioral skills for coping with social situations and regulating emotions (for review, see Kaslow, Brown, & Mee, 1994). For example, Altmann and Gotlib (1988) found that depressed fourth- and fifth-grade children spent more time alone and had higher numbers of negative interactions with peers in their school playground than their nondepressed classmates. Longitudinal research indicates that reliance on maladaptive coping strategies increases risk for depression. For example, children and adolescents with ruminative response styles (who dwell on negative emotions and negative experiences) are at increased risk for depression (Abela, Aydin, & Auerbach, 2007; Abela & Hankin, 2011). In contrast, children and adolescents who engage in problem-solving or adaptive coping are at lower risk for depression (Abela et al., 2007; Auerbach, Abela, Zhu, & Yao, 2010).

Developmentally, cognitive–behavioral factors associated with depression appear to become more important as children mature and become more cognitively sophisticated. In early childhood, occurrences of depression are relatively rare and tend to be reactions to overwhelming life events, such as the loss of a caregiver or a prolonged period with inadequate caregiving (e.g., Bemporad, 1994; Spitz, 1946). As children mature, depression occurs at higher rates and increasingly involves cognitive interpretations of events (Garber & Flynn, 1998; Garber, Quiggle, & Shanley, 1990). By middle childhood, pessimistic explanatory styles can be reliably measured and are related to symptoms of depression (e.g., Blumberg & Izard, 1985; Nolen-Hoeksema, Girgus, & Seligman, 1992). The increases in abstract thinking, self-consciousness, and thinking about future possibilities that occur in adolescence can intensify pessimistic explanatory styles, helpless expectations, and, in turn, depressive symptoms. Socially and biologically, adolescents face a number of transitions, including physical changes associated with puberty, changes in peer and family relationships, and changes in school structure from elementary school to middle school (Eccles & Midgley, 1990; Petersen & Hamburg, 1986). These events are often quite stressful and require adolescents to utilize resilient coping and problem-solving strategies. Children who enter adolescence without solid problem-solving skills can be at increased risk for depression.

Cognitive–Behavioral Therapies for Depression in Children and Adolescents

Cognitive–behavioral therapies for depression and anxiety target cognitive styles and problem-solving skills. Clients are taught to identify their negative interpretations, to consider the evidence for and against these interpretations, and to generate alternative interpretations that are more realistic. Additionally, clients are often taught specific coping and problem-solving skills, including relaxation and assertiveness techniques (e.g., Beck, Rush, Shaw, & Emery, 1979).

Several studies have demonstrated the efficacy of cognitive–behavioral therapies in treating depression in adults (e.g., Elkin et al., 1989). More recent research indicates that cognitive–behavioral therapies can be effective for treating depression in children and adolescents (for reviews, see Weisz, McCarty, & Valeri, 2006). For example, Lewisohn and colleagues developed a cognitive–behavioral group treatment for depressed adolescents, which focuses on decreasing automatic negative thoughts, increasing engagement in positive activities, and enhancing behavioral coping skills and interpersonal skills (Lewinsohn, Clarke, Hops, & Andrews, 1990;

Lewinsohn, Clarke, Rohde, Hops, & Seeley, 1996). Lewinsohn et al. tested this program both with and without a complementary parent training program and found that both forms of the program decreased depression significantly more than a wait-list control. Similar cognitive–behavioral therapies have also been successful in treating anxiety disorders in children (e.g., Flannery-Schroeder & Kendall, 2000; Kendall, 1994; Muris, Meesters, & van Melick, 2002).

Cognitive–Behavioral Prevention of Depression

There is growing evidence that cognitive–behavioral techniques can be effective in preventing depression as well as treating it. For example, adults treated with cognitive–behavioral therapy are less likely to experience a recurrence of depression than adults treated with medication (Shea et al., 1990). Additionally, several cognitive–behavioral interventions have shown promise in preventing depressive symptoms or depressive disorder in adults and children (see Cjuipers, van Straten, Smit, Mihalopoulos, & Beekman, 2008; Horowitz & Garber, 2006; Stice, Shaw, Bohon, Marti, & Rohde, 2009). The intervention with the best results to date was developed by Clarke et al. (1995). Clarke et al. evaluated their prevention program with 13–18-year-olds with high but subclinical levels of depressive symptoms. Adolescents who participated in this intervention were significantly less likely to develop depressive disorders than controls (Clarke et al., 1995, 2001; Garber et al., 2009).

The Penn Resiliency Program

Our research group has developed a cognitive–behavioral intervention, the PRP, for younger adolescents. PRP has 12 90-min intervention sessions designed to be delivered by school counselors and teachers who are trained and supervised in intervention delivery. The techniques we used have been adapted from adult cognitive–behavioral therapy (Beck, 1976; Beck et al., 1979; Ellis, 1962) and are incorporated in many other intervention programs. Our emphasis is on helping the students to use the skill set to improve their problem solving and to enhance their ability to navigate the daily stressors of life, as well as to bounce back from major setbacks such as parental loss or divorce. In this section, we describe several techniques included in PRP that may be especially important for building and promoting resilience and preventing anxiety and depression.

Based on our work, and the resilience literature more broadly, we have identified seven key intrapersonal factors or abilities that appear to increase overall resilience (see Reivich & Shatte, 2002 for full description of these factors). We will show how the skills of PRP impact each of these abilities (see Table 12.1). Briefly, the seven abilities are: (1) emotion regulation—being able to identify, label, and express emotions and control emotions when it is appropriate to do so; (2) impulse control—the ability to identify impulses and resist impulses that are counterproductive for the situation at hand or for long-term goal attainment; (3) causal analysis—being able to identify multiple and accurate causes of problems; (4) realistic optimism—thinking as optimistically as possible within the bounds of reality; (5) self-efficacy—being confident in one's ability to identify and implement coping and problem-solving skills that are well suited to the situation; (6) empathy—being able to accurately identify and connect with the emotional states in others; (7) reaching out—being comfortable and willing to connect with others in order to deepen

one's relationships and gain support through difficult times.

PRP builds on the ABC model developed by Ellis (1962), which suggests that different people feel and respond differently to the same event because of idiosyncratic beliefs about those events. In Ellis's model, A stands for activating event. The As are not the direct cause of the consequences (Cs, emotions and behaviors) that we experience. Rather, according to Ellis, it is our thoughts and beliefs about the event (our Bs) that mediate the effects of events on our behavior and feelings. We teach adolescents in our program how to identify the link between their thoughts and feelings/behaviors, and in this process they come to understand that their belief systems may not be wholly accurate. Practicing ABC is particularly important for children and adolescents who are struggling with anxiety and depression issues because it serves as the first step toward changing the beliefs that are fueling their maladaptive emotional reactions. More generally, the ABC model helps to build emotion awareness, a central component of emotion regulation, because through the use of this skill, adolescents practice identifying their emotional reactions, differentiating among emotions, and assessing the intensity of the emotion they feel. In addition, we believe this skill helps promote empathy by helping adolescents learn how to anticipate, identify, and label the emotions that others experience in a variety of common stressors and adversities.

We first teach students the ABC model with three-panel cartoons. In some instances, they are presented with an adversity and the emotional consequences, and they must fill in a thought bubble with a belief that fits the logic of ABC. In others, they are provided the adversity and the character's beliefs and they must identify the emotional reaction that the belief would likely generate. For example, in one cartoon, the first frame depicts a student being yelled at by a coach. The third frame has an illustration of the student feeling extremely sad. The adolescents are asked to identify what the boy is feeling and then to suggest what the boy might be saying to himself that is causing him to feel that emotion (e.g., "I'm never going to be good enough" or "I stink at sports," etc.).

Table 12.1 Summary of PRP skills and the resilience abilities targeted

PRP skill	Resilience ability targeted
ABC	Emotion regulation and empathy
Explanatory style	Realistic optimism and casual analysis
Self-disputing	Self-efficacy
Putting it in perspective	Realistic optimism and self-efficacy
Goal setting	Impulse control
Assertiveness and negotiation	Reaching out
Decision making	Self-efficacy, impulse control, empathy

Once the students are able to accurately link Bs and Cs in the cartoon worksheets, the students practice identifying their own self-talk in current problem situations and the emotions and behaviors generated by that self-talk. We have found that it is helpful to the adolescents to liken their Bs to an internal radio station (one that plays nothing but you, you, you 24/7) and we help them to turn the volume of this radio station up so that it is loud enough for them to hear what it is they are saying to themselves, particularly during times of adversity or stress. In so doing, the adolescents become more aware of their beliefs as well as the effect their beliefs have on their mood and behavior. We emphasize that negative emotions are not "bad"—that instead, they are a healthy part of life and serve an important function from an evolutionary perspective. We also make clear that the goal is not to eradicate all negative emotion from one's life. Rather, we guide the students in thinking about whether they tend to overexperience certain emotions and to identify the patterns in their thinking that might be leading them to experience one emotion much more frequently than others.

The ABC skill represents a glimpse into one's thoughts or beliefs during a particular activating event. Although this is useful, it is also important for the adolescents to begin to notice patterns in how they think about the events in their lives. It has been well documented that our automatic thoughts are influenced by our styles (or schemas) of processing information, which, to some degree, predetermine our responses to any given event. Our goal is to help the adolescents detect patterns in their thinking and emotions that may be counterproductive for them. As one seventh-grade boy put it, "I never really thought about how much of the time I feel embarrassed. I guess I kind of thought all kids feel embarrassed all the time. Now I'm starting to see that maybe I don't have to feel this way so much; that maybe I'm worrying too much about what other kids are thinking of me—when they probably aren't even thinking about me!"

One example of a style or schema is explanatory style, our habitual and reflexive way of explaining the events in our lives (Abramson et al., 1978).

We teach adolescents to identify their explanatory style (using the terms "me versus not me," "always versus not always," "everything versus not everything") and, most important, to question the accuracy of their beliefs. Although pessimistic explanations tend to lead to helplessness, depression, and anxiety, our goal is to teach the students how to think accurately about the causes and implications of the problems they face, not to swap a pessimistic style for an optimistic one. This reattribution training specifically targets realistic optimism and causal analysis. Our aim is to help students to think more flexibly about the multiple and varied causes of problems, instead of merely replacing negative thoughts with "happy thoughts." In fact, some of the adolescents we have worked with have had explanatory styles that were too optimistic. These adolescents believed that others were always to blame for their problems, and that they had complete control to change any aspect of a situation they did not like. We helped these students to understand how this very optimistic view might actually be hindering their resilience and problem solving rather than bolstering it.

We call this skill of generating more accurate beliefs "self-disputing." Adolescents are guided in using the three dimensions of explanatory style for generating other ways of understanding the causes of the event. In essence, we help them to "think outside the box" that their explanatory style puts them in. For example, if they tend to be overly internal, they are encouraged to generate plausible explanations about how other people or circumstances contributed to the problem. Similarly, if their explanations indicate that they believe the causes of the problem are wholly unchangeable, they are encouraged to think about other explanations that focus on more changeable, controllable, and temporary causal factors. We have found that using the knowledge of one's explanatory style in the process of generating alternatives is quite important. When students are not aware of their tendency to explain the causes of events in a set pattern, the alternatives they generate tend to fall within their pattern rather than become more inclusive. So, an adolescent who tends to be highly external can generate four alternatives to the belief "I fought with my parents because they are too strict," but the alternatives are each as external as that initial belief (for example, "They're old-fashioned," "They don't understand me," "They're control-freaks," etc.). There are several problems with this, none the least of which is that this process serves to reinforce the adolescent's style rather than broaden it.

After the students have generated alternative beliefs, they are taught how to use evidence to determine which beliefs are most accurate and to identify potential solutions that their new, richer understanding of the situation affords them. We have found self-disputing is a powerful tool for overcoming the negative beliefs that often fuel hopelessness and depression, and we believe that the process of self-disputing increases adolescents' self-efficacy because they have learned a skill that enables them to more effectively solve problems. As we often tell the participants in our program, you cannot solve a problem until you know what caused it.

PRP also teaches a skill called "putting it in perspective," which can be used when beliefs are about the implications of an activating event, or what we call "what next" beliefs. At this point in the program, we begin to focus on beliefs about the future rather than beliefs about the causes of problems. Like self-disputing, putting it in perspective helps students to view the future with greater realistic optimism, and it also increases their self-efficacy for dealing with anticipated negative events. We have found this skill to be particularly helpful for children and adolescents who are at risk for depression and anxiety because, as ABC predicts, catastrophizing is often the consequence of unrealistic beliefs about the likelihood of horrible things happening in the future. For adolescents prone to anxiety, small problems are seen as insurmountable and dreaded outcomes are feared.

Putting it in perspective encourages adolescents to identify and list their worst-case thoughts about the implications of adversity. By getting these thoughts out of their heads and onto a piece of paper, the adolescents begin to have distance from their beliefs and are better able to start to consider the likelihood of the feared events. These thoughts tend to come in chains of ever increasing severity; for example, imagine a student who does not get asked to a school dance. "If I don't get asked to the dance then everyone will talk behind my back. If they're all talking about me, then I'll become the joke of the school and everyone will make fun of me. If that happens I'll have to switch schools because I'll never be able to put it behind me. But if I switch schools, then I'll be the new kid and the outcast at that school too!" The causal link between not getting asked to a dance and becoming a social outcast across schools is extremely weak, but the connection from link to link seems more plausible, particularly for the anxious adolescent.

To stop the process of catastrophizing, we guide children out of their dreaded fantasy by teaching them to estimate the probability of each link given that only the initial adversity (not being asked to the dance) has occurred. Participants are then taught to generate equally improbable best-case scenarios (for example, "Everyone will realize that the mailman made a mistake and failed to deliver an engraved invitation to the dance from the most popular boy"). This step is important because the very silliness of the best-case scenario helps to jolt the adolescent out of his or her catastrophic thinking and tends to lower anxiety and increase positive affect. The next step is to use worst-case and best-case scenarios as anchors to arrive at most-likely outcomes. Once the most-likely outcomes have been identified, the adolescents are taught to develop a plan for dealing with them. The skill of putting it in perspective not only reduces adolescents' anxiety, but it also helps them to develop strategies for dealing with the real-world outcomes of the problems they face—and thus, increases optimism and self-efficacy. In PRP we also teach goal setting, a skill that is important for all adolescents and particularly valuable for those who feel pessimistic or hopeless about their futures. Adolescents who learn to set obtainable goals and to develop plans for reaching their goals have developed a valuable system for combating the impulsiveness that can undercut resilience. In PRP, we teach realistic goal setting and the "one step at a time" technique for making large projects more manageable by breaking the project into doable steps. We also help adolescents to identify beliefs that can fuel procrastination or impulsiveness and derail them from their plan, and we apply the skill of self-disputing to test the accuracy and usefulness of these beliefs.

PRP also includes assertiveness and negotiation training. We have found that these skills, particularly assertiveness, help adolescents to feel more hopeful about approaching others with their concerns, needs, or requests. From a resilience perspective, assertiveness helps to foster reaching out by helping adolescents to connect with others in ways that will maximize the likelihood that their needs will be heard by others. Because depression-prone adolescents often underestimate the likelihood that a situation can be improved, they tend to respond to interpersonal problems with passivity. In PRP, we first apply the skills of self-disputing and putting it in perspective to beliefs that fuel passivity such as: "She won't listen to me anyway," or "If I ask her to stop she'll think I'm a nag." Other adolescents often have beliefs that fuel aggressiveness, such as: "The only way to get respect is to come on strong," or "If I don't fight for what I want, no one will listen to me." Regardless of whether the adolescent is relying on passive or aggressive interaction styles, our goal is to help the adolescent evaluate how well the strategy is working and to challenge the beliefs that may be fueling counterproductive behaviors. In addition, we make explicit that speaking up and asking for help is a valuable coping strategy that is helpful when dealing with adversities and trauma.

After the adolescents have challenged the beliefs that fuel nonassertive behaviors, we teach them a four-step approach to assertiveness. This skill is particularly challenging for adolescents—especially those feeling hopeless—so we include assertiveness practice in many of the sessions. We have found that many adolescents are initially reluctant to practice assertiveness, but that with practice, they find assertiveness to be one of the most useful and potent skills they have learned in

the program. Given their initial reluctance, it is important to continue to identify their beliefs about trying the skill and to help them to use the basic cognitive skills of the program to challenge any pessimistic beliefs.

We also teach decision making and creative problem solving as part of the PRP skill. Both skills work to increase students' self-efficacy, optimism, impulse control, and empathy. As with assertiveness and "one step at a time," our goal is first to identify beliefs that might be pushing the adolescent toward counterproductive and nonresilient decisions or solutions. Once students are able to evaluate the accuracy and usefulness of these beliefs, we then provide them with decision-making and problem-solving models. In both decision making and creative problem solving, we emphasize the importance of slowing the process to make sure they are not responding impulsively. We guide them in identifying their goals, gathering thorough information about the situation, and then work with them to generate a series of possible routes to achieve the goal. We also help them to consider the plusses and minuses associated with each potential decision, both from a time perspective (short term versus long term) and a self–other perspective (How will this affect me? How will this affect the other people in the situation?). By focusing on how their decisions and solution strategies can affect others, we help them to build empathy for the other people involved in the situation. As the students start to see real-world differences in their ability to handle difficult, complex situations we hear them share stories about increased confidence, greater hope for the future, and a sense of feeling more in control of their actions.

Penn Resiliency Program Findings

In our initial studies of PRP, we evaluated PRP as a depression prevention program among students who reported higher than average symptoms of depression, family conflict, or both. Students who participated in the intervention were compared with a matched control group. Our findings indicated that the intervention improved explanatory styles and that this effect lasted 3 years following the intervention. The intervention group also reported lower levels of depressive symptoms through 2 years of follow-up, and the group members were less likely than controls to report moderate to severe levels of depressive symptoms (Gillham & Reivich, 1999; Gillham, Reivich, Jaycox, & Sehgman, 1995). Yu and Seligman (2002) replicated these findings through 6 months of follow-up with a sample of Chinese school children. Roberts, Kane, Thompson, Bishop, and Hart (2003) attempted to replicate these findings with 11–13-year-olds in rural Australia who reported elevated depressive symptoms. In this study, PRP significantly reduced anxiety symptoms but not depressive symptoms relative to a standard health curriculum. We are continuing to evaluate PRP as an intervention for high-risk participants. However, we have also begun to evaluate PRP as a universal intervention, an intervention that is offered to all students regardless of risk level. We believe that the cognitive and problem-solving skills covered in PRP are important for increasing resilience more generally and are beneficial to most children. In support of this, a recent meta-analytic review of PRP studies found significant benefits of PRP when tested with both high risk and universal samples (Brunwasser, Gillham, & Kim, 2009). In addition, in some studies, we have found that PRP prevents depressive symptoms in children with low levels of symptoms (as well as in children with high levels of symptoms) (Gillham et al., 1995), although findings have not always been consistent. For example, Cardemil, Reivich, and Seligman (2002) evaluated the PRP as a universal program for inner-city students. In an inner-city Latino sample, PRP participants reported significantly fewer symptoms than controls following the intervention. However, in an inner-city African American sample, depressive symptoms fell dramatically in both the intervention and control group, and the difference between the groups was not significant. Pattison and Lynd-Stevenson (2001) evaluated PRP as a universal intervention with children in rural Australia. They found that PRP did not significantly reduce depression or anxiety relative to a control group.

However, this study followed a very small sample, which may have limited the researchers' ability to find effects. Our research group is currently conducting further evaluations of PRP that focus on ways to boost the intervention's effectiveness.

Including Parents in Resilience Training

One of the ways we are enhancing the PRP is by including parents in the intervention. Depression in youth can be best prevented by interventions that include parents. Children of depressed parents are at greatly increased risk for depression themselves (Downey & Coyne, 1990). The link between parental and child depression appears to be due to several factors that tend to co-occur or result from parental depression, but also can occur in parents who are not depressed. Parents who are depressed have been found to have fewer positive interactions with their children (Field, 1984). Depressed parents are also more likely to display and model negative interpretive styles and passive or maladaptive coping skills. When parents give pessimistic explanations for events in their own lives, children can adopt these same types of interpretive patterns when confronting problems of their own. They might expect that negative events will be long lasting and difficult or impossible to overcome. When parents give pessimistic explanations for child-related events (for example, "You failed the test because you're lazy"), children can internalize these explanations and interpret future adversity through a similar lens. Garber and Flynn (2001) found that children's explanatory styles are correlated with parents' explanatory styles, particularly parents' explanatory styles for child-related events.

The Penn Resiliency Program for Parents (PRP-P) was designed with two major goals in mind: (1) to increase the parents' overall resilience by teaching them the core skills of PRP (adapted for adults), and (2) to teach parents how to model the skills effectively for their children and to coach their children in the skills taught in PRP. PRP-P meets for six 90-min sessions, facilitated at the schools by school guidance counselors, social workers, and psychologists who have been certified through a 30-h training with senior members of our research team.

The sessions are comprised of two components. The first, and central, component focuses on teaching the parents how to use the skills in their own lives. Parents discuss adversities ranging from professional issues to marital issues to specific challenges confronted by parents with children at risk for depression. The second component addresses how to model/coach the skills with their own children. Our emphasis here is on helping parents to notice "teachable moments" and to help them become comfortable sharing their own practicing of the skills in ways that are both appropriate and nonintrusive for their adolescents.

The first five sessions of PRP-P are devoted to the core cognitive resilience skills: ABC (the link between thoughts and feelings/behaviors); self-disputing (challenging inaccurate beliefs), putting it in perspective (challenging catastrophic beliefs), real-time resilience (disputing counterproductive beliefs in real time), and assertiveness. The final session is devoted to reviewing the skill set, reinforcing ways to effectively promote the skills in the context of the family, and identifying upcoming stressors and the skills that could be used to deal with these stressors.

We conducted a small pilot study of the combined parent and adolescent PRP intervention. Forty-four middle school students and their parents were randomly assigned to the combined intervention or a control condition. Students who were assigned to the intervention condition participated in the PRP for adolescents; their parents participated in the PRP for parents. Results indicated that the combined intervention prevented depression and anxiety symptoms through the 1-year follow-up. Findings were particularly strong for anxiety; controls were almost five times more likely than intervention participants to report moderate to severe levels of anxiety (Gillham et al., 2006). Although promising, these findings should be interpreted with caution since this was a pilot study with a very small sample. We are currently conducting a large-scale evaluation of the PRP for parents as an added component to PRP.

Surprisingly, only a few other programs have attempted to prevent depression or anxiety by including parenting components. Results of other programs have also been positive. Beardslee et al. (1997) developed an intervention for families in which one or both parents suffered from unipolar or bipolar depression. The major goal of the intervention was to educate parents about the effects of depression, to improve family communication, and to increase children's understanding of parental depression so they would be less likely to blame themselves for parental symptoms and behavior. Beardslee et al. found that participants in the family intervention reported improved communication relative to participants in a lecture intervention condition. Children in the family intervention reported greater understanding of parental depression and greater global functioning. Children in the family intervention were less likely than those in the lecture intervention to develop depressive disorders, although this difference was not statistically significant. Dadds et al. (1997) found that a cognitive–behavioral school-based intervention that included a parent component was effective in preventing anxiety in children and adolescents. Recently, Compas et al. found that their cognitive–behavioral family-based prevention program significantly reduced depression and anxiety symptoms in children and adolescents (Compas et al., 2009).

Discussion, Limits, and Future Directions

Making Interventions More Powerful

Research on the psychological interventions that treat and prevent depression and anxiety has identified several promising interventions. However, intervention success rates are often far from ideal. Although effective for many participants, a sizable minority of participants in cognitive–behavioral therapy do not improve significantly. For example, in a large study on therapy for depression, 65% of depressed adults who were treated with cognitive–behavioral therapy showed a full improvement in symptoms, but 35% continued to show fairly high levels of depression even after completing the intervention (Elkin et al., 1989). Similarly, some participants in prevention programs develop clinical depression or anxiety, despite efforts in the program to promote resilience. Future research should focus on strengthening interventions and making them effective for more people.

One way to strengthen the effects of interventions is to incorporate other parts of the adolescent's world as targets of interventions. Historically, psychological treatments have focused on the individual child or adolescent. However, children's lives are imbedded within family, school, peer, and neighborhood systems (Bronfenbrenner, 1986). Thus, it is important to understand how resiliency is built within family systems and larger communities. In the PRP intervention, initial findings suggest that providing an intervention for parents in addition to the adolescent groups can be an effective way to increase effectiveness of the intervention. In addition, efforts could be made to incorporate interventions into the larger community through neighborhood programs or schoolwide programs that work to create more positive relationships and more hopefulness for communities as a whole.

Universal Versus Targeted Interventions

One of the debates within the prevention literature concerns the feasibility and effectiveness of targeted versus universal interventions. Targeted interventions, like Clarke et al.'s (1995) prevention program and our initial evaluations of PRP discussed earlier, are provided to at-risk participants, such as participants with elevated levels of symptoms. In contrast, universal interventions are administered broadly to the entire population regardless of risk. In general, effects for the average participant are larger in targeted interventions than universal interventions. This is because targeted intervention participants are more likely to develop the disorder or problem and there is thus greater room for change in each individual. However, universal interventions that have small effects for the average participant can have large effects for society (Offord, 1996).

Over the past decade, we have come to believe that cognitive–behavioral interventions, like the PRP, can have important applications as universal interventions. The shift in our thinking is reflected in the change to the name of the program, from the Penn Prevention Program to the PRP. All children and adolescents encounter challenges and stressful events in their lives. Most of the skills covered in PRP and other programs are useful for responding to these day-to-day challenges, as well as more serious events that children encounter. These cognitive–behavioral skills (e.g., thinking realistically about problems, perspective taking, considering a variety of solutions to a problem, considering consequences when making decisions) overlap with competences that are discussed in the resilience literature (e.g., Brooks & Goldstein, 2002). Some of these skills are also taught in problem-solving programs and interventions designed to reduce or prevent aggression, substance abuse, and other maladaptive behaviors (Caplan et al., 1992). Interventions that incorporate these skills should be relevant to most students and could have effects on a variety of positive and negative outcomes. We believe that the development and evaluation of such broad-based interventions will equip children to respond resiliently to the challenges they will no doubt encounter in their future.

Acknowledgment Research on the effectiveness of the Penn Resiliency Project is funded by a grant from the National Institute of Mental Health (MH52270). The Penn Resiliency Program is owned by the University of Pennsylvania. The University of Pennsylvania has licensed this program to Adaptive Learning Systems. Drs. Reivich and Seligman own Adaptive stock and could profit from the sale of this program.

References

Abela, J. R. Z. (2001). The hopelessness theory of depression: A test of the diathesis-stress and causal mediation components in third and seventh grade children. *Journal of Abnormal Child Psychology, 29,* 241–254.

Abela, J. R. Z., Aydin, C. M., & Auerbach, R. P. (2007). Responses to depression in children: Reconceptualizing the relation among response styles. *Journal of Abnormal Child Psychology, 35,* 913–927.

Abela, J. R. Z., & Hankin, B. L. (2008). Cognitive vulnerability to depression in children and adolescents: A psychopathology perspective. In J. R. Z. Abela & B. L. Hankin (Eds.), *Handbook of depression in children and adolescents* (pp. 35–78). New York, NY: Guilford Press.

Abela, J. R. Z., & Hankin, B. L. (2011). Rumination as a vulnerability factor to depression during the transition from early to middle adolescence: A multiwave longitudinal study. *Journal of Abnormal Psychology, 120,* 259–271.

Abramson, L. Y., Metalsky, G. I., & Alloy, L. B. (1989). Hopelessness depression: A theory-based subtype of depression. *Psychological Review, 96,* 358–372.

Abramson, L. Y., Seligman, M. E. P., & Teasdale, J. D. (1978). Learned helplessness in humans: Critique and reformulation. *Journal of Abnormal Psychology, 87,* 49–74.

Altmann, E. O., & Gotlib, I. H. (1988). The social behavior of depressed children: An observational study. *Journal of Abnormal Child Psychology, 16,* 29–44.

Auerbach, R. P., Abela, J. R., Zhu, X., & Yao, S. (2010). Understanding the role of coping in the development of depressive symptoms: Symptom specificity, gender differences, and cross- cultural applicability. *British Journal of Clinical Psychology, 49,* 547–561.

Beardslee, W. R., Wright, E. J., Salt, P., Drezner, K., Gladstone, T. R. G., Versage, E. M., et al. (1997). Examination of children's responses to two preventive intervention strategies over time. *Journal of the American Academy of Child and Adolescent Psychiatry, 36,* 196–204.

Beck, A. T. (1976). *Cognitive therapy and the emotional disorders.* New York: International Universities Press.

Beck, A. T., Rush, J. A., Shaw, B. F., & Emery, G. (1979). *Cognitive therapy of depression.* New York: Guilford.

Bemporad, J. (1994). Dynamic and interpersonal theories of depression. In W. M. Reynolds & H. F. Johnston (Eds.), *Handbook of depression in children and adolescents. Issues in clinical child psychology* (pp. 81–95). New York: Plenum.

Blumberg, S., & Izard, C. E. (1985). Affective and cognitive characteristics of depression in 10- and 11-year-old children. *Journal of Personality and Social Psychology, 49,* 194–202.

Bronfenbrenner, U. (1986). Ecology of the family as a context for human development: Research perspectives. *Developmental Psychology, 22,* 723–742.

Brooks, R., & Goldstein, S. (2002). *Raising resilient children: Fostering strength, hope, and optimism in your child.* New York: McGraw-Hill.

Brunwasser, S. M., Gillham, J. E., & Kim, E. (2009). A meta-analytic review of the Penn Resiliency Program's effects on depressive symptoms. *Journal of Consulting and Clinical Psychology, 77,* 1042–1054.

Caplan, M., Weissberg, R. P., Grober, J. S., Sivo, P. J., Grady, K., & Jacoby, C. (1992). Social competence promotion with inner-city and suburban young adolescents: Effects on social adjustment and alcohol use.

Journal of Consulting and Clinical Psychology, 60, 56–63.

Cardemil, E. V., Reivich, K. J., & Seligman, M. E. P. (2002). The prevention of depressive symptoms in inner-city middle school students. *Prevention and Treatment, 5,* n.p.

Cjuipers, P., van Straten, A., Smit, F., Mihalopoulos, C., & Beekman, A. (2008). Preventing the onset of depressive disorders: A meta-analytic review of psychological interventions. *American Journal of Psychiatry, 165,* 1272–1280.

Clarke, G. N., Hawkins, W., Murphy, M., Sheeber, L. B., Lewinsohn, R. M., & Seeley, J. R. (1995). Targeted prevention of unipolar depressive disorder in an at-risk sample of high school adolescents: A randomized trial of a group cognitive intervention. *Journal of the American Academy of Child and Adolescent Psychiatry, 34,* 312–321.

Clarke, G. N., Hombrook, M., Lynch, R., Polen, M., Gale, J., Beardslee, W., et al. (2001). A randomized trial of a group cognitive intervention for preventing depression in adolescent offspring of depressed parents. *Archives of General Psychiatry, 58,* 1127–1134.

Cohen, P., Cohen, J., Kasen, S., Velez, C. N., Hartmark, C., Johnson, J., et al. (1993). An epidemiological study of disorders in late childhood and adolescence: I. Age and gender-specific prevalence. *Journal of Child Psychology and Psychiatry, 34,* 851–867.

Compas, B. E., Forehand, R., Keller, G., Champion, J. E., Rakow, A., Reeslund, K. L., et al. (2009). Randomized controlled trial of a family cognitive-behavioral preventive intervention for children of depressed parents. *Journal of Consulting and Clinical Psychology, 77,* 1007–1020.

Covey, L. S., Glassman, A. H., & Stetner, F. (1998). Cigarette smoking and major depression. *Journal of Addictive Diseases, 17,* 35–46.

Dadds, M. R., Spence, S. H., Holland, D. E., Barrett, R. M., & Laurens, K. R. (1997). Prevention and early intervention for anxiety disorders: A controlled trial. *Journal of Consulting & Clinical Psychology, 65,* 627–635.

Downey, G., & Coyne, J. C. (1990). Children of depressed parents: An integrative review. *Psychological Bulletin, 108*(1), 50–76.

Eccles, J. S., & Midgley, C. (1990). Changes in academic motivation and self-perception during early adolescence. In R. Montemayor, G. R. Adams, & T. P. Gullotta (Eds.), *From childhood to adolescence: A transitional period? Advances in adolescent development: An annual book series* (Vol. 2, pp. 134–155). Thousand Oaks, CA: Sage.

Elkin, I., Shea, M. T., Watkins, J. T., Imber, S. D., Sotsky, S. M., Collins, J. R., et al. (1989). National Institute of Mental Health treatment of depression collaborative research program: General effectiveness of treatments. *Archives of General Psychiatry, 46,* 971–982.

Ellis, A. (1962). *Reason and emotion in psychotherapy.* New York: Lyle Stuart.

Field, T. M. (1984). Early interactions between infants and their postpartum depressed mothers. *Infant Behavior and Development, 7,* 517–522.

Flannery-Schroeder, E., & Kendall, P. C. (2000). Group and individual cognitive-behavioral treatment for youth with anxiety disorders: A randomized clinical trial. *Cognitive Therapy and Research, 24,* 251–278.

Garber, J., Clarke, G. N., Weersing, V. R., Beardslee, W. R., Brent, D. A., Gladstone, T. R. G., et al. (2009). Prevention of depression in at-risk adolescents: A randomized controlled trial. *Journal of the American Medical Association, 301,* 2215–2224.

Garber, J., & Flynn, C. (1998). Origins of depressive cognitive style. In D. K. Routh & R. J. DeRubeis (Eds.), *The science of clinical psychology: Accomplishments and future directions* (pp. 53–93). Washington, DC: American Psychological Association.

Garber, J., & Flynn, C. (2001). Predictors of depressive cognitions in young adolescents. *Cognitive Theory and Research, 25,* 353–376.

Garber, J., Quiggle, N., & Shanley, N. (1990). Cognition and depression in children and adolescents. In R. E. Ingram (Ed.), *Contemporary psychological approaches to depression: Theory, research, and treatment* (pp. 87–116). New York: Plenum.

Garrison, C. Z., Addy, C. L., Jackson, K. L., McKeown, R. E., & Waller, J. L. (1991). A longitudinal study of suicidal ideation in young adolescents. *Journal of the American Academy of Child and Adolescent Psychiatry, 30,* 597–603.

Gillham, J. E., & Reivich, K. J. (1999). Prevention of depressive symptoms in school children: A research update. *Psychological Science, 10,* 461–462.

Gillham, J. E., Reivich, K. J., Freres, D. R., Lascher, M., Litzinger, S., Shatté, A., et al. (2006). School-based prevention of depression and anxiety symptoms in early adolescence: A pilot of a parent intervention component. *School Psychology Quarterly, 21,* 323–348.

Gillham, J. E., Reivich, K. J., Freres, D. R., Shatté, A. J., & Seligman, M. E. P. (2003). [School-based prevention of depression and anxiety symptoms: Pilot of a parent component to the Penn Resiliency Program.] Unpublished raw data.

Gillham, J. E., Reivich, K. J., Jaycox, L. H., & Seligman, M. E. P. (1995). Preventing depressive symptoms in schoolchildren: Two year follow-up. *Psychological Science, 6,* 343–351.

Gillham, J. E., Shatte, A. J., & Freres, D. R. (2000). Preventing depression: A review of cognitive-behavioral and family interventions. *Applied and Preventive Psychology, 7,* 63–88.

Gladstone, T. R. G., & Kaslow, N. J. (1995). Depression and attributions in children and adolescents: A meta-analytic review. *Journal of Abnormal Child Psychology, 23,* 597–606.

Gotlib, I. H., Lewinsohn, P. M., & Seeley, J. R. (1995). Symptoms versus a diagnosis of depression: Differences in psychosocial functioning. *Journal of Consulting and Clinical Psychology, 63,* 90–100.

Hammen, C., & Rudolph, K. D. (2003). Childhood mood disorders. In E. J. Mash & R. A. Barkley (Eds.), *Child psychopathology* (2nd ed., pp. 233–278). New York: Guilford.

Hankin, B. L., Abramson, L. Y., Moffitt, T. E., Silva, P. A., & McGee, R. (1998). Development of depression from preadolescence to young adulthood: Emerging gender differences in a 10-year longitudinal study. *Journal of Abnormal Psychology, 107,* 128–140.

Harrington, R., Fudge, H., Rutter, M., Pickles, A., & Hill, J. (1990). Adult outcomes of childhood and adolescent depression: Psychiatric status. *Archives of General Psychiatry, 47,* 465–473.

Hirschfeld, R., Keller, M., Panico, S., Arons, B., Barlow, D., Davidoff, F., et al. (1997). The National Depressive and Manic-Depressive Association consensus statement on the undertreatment of depression. *Journal of the American Medical Association, 277,* 333–340.

Horowitz, J. L., & Garber, J. (2006). The prevention of depressive symptoms in children and adolescents: A meta-analytic review. *Journal of Consulting and Clinical Psychology, 74,* 401–415.

Kashani, J. H., & Orvaschel, H. (1990). A community study of anxiety in children and adolescents: Current progress and future research directions. *American Journal of Psychiatry, 147,* 313–318.

Kaslow, N. J., Brown, R. T., & Mee, L. L. (1994). Cognitive and behavioral correlates of childhood depression: A developmental perspective. In W. M. Reynolds & H. F. Johnston (Eds.), *Handbook of depression in children and adolescents* (pp. 97–121). New York: Plenum.

Kendall, P. C. (1994). Treating anxiety disorders in children: Results of a randomized clinical trial. *Journal of Consulting and Clinical Psychology, 65,* 366–380.

Klerman, G. L., Lavori, P. W., Rice, J., Reich, T., Endicott, J., Andreasen, N. C., et al. (1985). Birth cohort trends in rates of major depressive disorder: A study of relatives of patients with affective disorder. *Archives of General Psychiatry, 42,* 689–693.

Lewinsohn, P. M., Clarke, G. N., Hops, H., & Andrews, J. (1990). Cognitive-behavioral group treatment of depression in adolescents. *Behavior Therapy, 21,* 385–401.

Lewinsohn, P. M., Clarke, G. N., Rohde, P., Hops, H., & Seeley, J. (1996). A course in coping: A cognitive-behavioral approach to the treatment of adolescent depression. In E. D. Hibbs & P. S. Jensen (Eds.), *Psychosocial treatments for child and adolescent disorders: Empirically based strategies for clinical practice* (pp. 109–135). Washington, DC: American Psychological Association.

Lewinsohn, P. M., Hops, H., Roberts, R., & Seeley, J. (1993). Adolescent psychopathology: I. Prevalence and incidence of depression and other DSM-III-R disorders in high school students. *Journal of Abnormal Psychology, 102,* 110–120.

Muris, P., Meesters, C., & van Melick, M. (2002). Treatment of childhood anxiety disorders: A preliminary comparison between cognitive-behavioral group therapy and a psychological placebo intervention. *Journal of Behavior Therapy and Experimental Psychiatry, 33,* 143–158.

Nolen-Hoeksema, S., Girgus, J. S., & Seligman, M. E. P. (1986). *Depression in children of families in turmoil.* Unpublished manuscript, University of Pennsylvania.

Nolen-Hoeksema, S., Girgus, J. S., & Seligman, M. E. P. (1992). Predictors and consequences of childhood depressive symptoms: A five-year longitudinal study. *Journal of Abnormal Psychology, 101,* 405–422.

Offord, D. R. (1996). The state of prevention and early intervention. In R. D. Peters & R. J. McMahon (Eds.), *Preventing childhood disorders, substance abuse, and delinquency* (pp. 329–344). Thousand Oaks, CA: Sage.

Pattison, C., & Lynd-Stevenson, R. M. (2001). The prevention of depressive symptoms in children: The immediate and long-term outcomes of a school based program. *Behaviour Change, 18*(2), 92–102.

Petersen, A. C., & Hamburg, B. A. (1986). Adolescence: A developmental approach to problems and psychopathology. *Behavior Therapy, 17,* 480–499.

Quiggle, N. L., Garber, J., Panak, W. F., & Dodge, K. A. (1992). Social information processing in aggressive and depressed children. *Child Development, 63,* 1305–1320.

Reivich, K. J., & Shatte, A. (2002). *The resilience factor.* New York: Random House-Doubleday.

Rhode, P., Lewisohn, P., & Seeley, J. (1991). Comorbidity of unipolar depression: II. Comorbidity with other mental disorders in adolescents and adults. *Journal of Abnormal Psychology, 100,* 214–222.

Roberts, C., Kane, R., Thompson, H., Bishop, B., & Hart, B. (2003). The prevention of depressive symptoms in rural school children: A randomized controlled trial. *Journal of Consulting and Clinical Psychology, 71,* 622–628.

Robins, C. J., & Hayes, A. M. (1995). The role of causal attributions in the prediction of depression. In G. M. Buchanan & M. E. P. Segliman (Eds.), *Explanatory style* (pp. 71–97). Hillsdale, NJ: Erlbaum.

Romano, E., Tremblay, R. E., Vitaro, P., Zoccolillo, M., & Pagani, L. (2001). Prevalence of psychiatric diagnoses and the role of perceived impairment: Findings from an adolescent community sample. *Journal of Child Psychology and Psychiatry and Allied Disciplines, 42,* 451–461.

Seligman, M. E. P. (1975). *Helplessness: On depression, development, and death.* San Francisco: Freeman.

Shea, M. R., Elkin, I., Imber, S. D., Sotsky, S. M., Watkins, J., Collins, J. F., et al. (1990). Course of depressive symptoms over follow-up: Findings from the National Institute of Mental Health treatment of depression collaborative research program. *Archives of General Psychiatry, 49,* 782–787.

Spitz, R. (1946). Anaclitic depression. *Psychoanalytic Study of the Child, 5,* 113–117.

Sroufe, L. A., & Rutter, M. (1984). The domain of developmental psychopathology. *Child Development, 55,* 17–29.

Stice, E., Shaw, H., Bohon, C., Marti, C. N., & Rohde, P. (2009). A meta-analytic review of depression prevention programs for children and adolescents: Factors that predict magnitude of intervention effects. *Journal of Consulting and Clinical Psychology, 77,* 486–503.

Sweeny, P. D., Anderson, K., & Bailey, S. (1986). Attributional style in depression: A meta-analytic review. *Journal of Personality and Social Psychology, 50,* 974–991.

Twenge, J. M. (2000). The age of anxiety? Birth cohort change in anxiety and neuroticism, 1952–1993. *Journal of Personality and Social Psychology, 79,* 1007–1021.

Weisz, J. R., McCarty, C. A., & Valeri, S. M. (2006). Effects of psychotherapy for depression in children and adolescents: A meta-analysis. *Psychological Bulletin, 132,* 132–149.

Whitaker, A., Johnson, J., Shaffer, D., Rapoport, J. L., Kalikow, K., Walsh, B. T., et al. (1990). Uncommon troubles in young people: Prevalence estimates of selected psychiatric disorders in a nonreferred adolescent population. *Archives of General Psychiatry, 47,* 487–496.

Yu, D. L., & Seligman, M. E. P. (2002). Preventing depressive symptoms in Chinese children. *Prevention and Treatment, 5,* n.p.

Resilience and Self-Control Impairment

13

Wai Chen and Eric Taylor

Introduction

The Concept of Self-Control and ADHD

Self-control has been a pervasive idea in developmental psychology. At a neurocognitive level, the organism's control (or lack of it) over its own responsiveness to stimuli has been regarded as a central topic in attention/executive function research and attention deficit (e.g., Taylor, 1995). Behavioral control is a more complex idea: clearly, a planned and rule-governed organization of activity can have many advantages and has arguably been a crucial acquisition in the evolution of man. Emotional control relates to the idea that it is adaptive to moderate the immediate affective reaction and to respond in a willed rather than a passionate fashion.

Self-control and its absence are appealing concepts for explaining a wide variety of psychopathological presentations. Impaired self-control can be seen as a risk for nearly all the disorders presenting with unruly or undesirable behavior—hyperactivity, attention deficit, impulse disorders

such as gambling, bulimia, or kleptomania, substance abuse, oppositional and conduct disorders, and the complex tics of Tourette disorder (Strayhom, 2002a); or it can be seen as a part of those disorders or the result of them. The ability to control oneself can be seen as a protective factor in an even wider range of disorders—either because one can use self-control to avoid acquiring even greater developmental risks, such as substance abuse, or because the ability to control oneself is a necessary condition for the success of some forms of treatment, such as cognitive therapy (Strayhom, 2002b).

This widespread use of the idea already points to a difficulty. If the idea is applicable to so many sorts of problem, perhaps it should not be seen as an explanatory concept, but rather as a somewhat nonspecific description. There is a certain circularity in it: if the only evidence needed for poor behavioral self-control is the presence of undesirable behavior, then it cannot also be used to explain that behavior. It constitutes, in effect, a theory about the cause of behavior disorders. In this case, independent evidence for its presence is essential. Operational definitions have been hard to achieve. The difficulty is akin to that inherent in the closely related idea of the will: if an act is caused by a volition, what causes the volition?

When considered as a theory of cause, then impaired self-control must compete with others. Consider a group of children in a classroom who are behaving riotously. Some may be doing this in a planned and willful fashion; for instance, they may prefer to impress their peers rather than

W. Chen (✉)
Ashurst Hospital, Lyndhurst Road, Southampton,
MRC SGDP, Institute of Psychiatry,
King's College London, UK
e-mail: wai.2.chen@kcl.ac.uk

E. Taylor
MRC SGDP, Institute of Psychiatry,
King's College London, UK
e-mail: E.taylor@iop.kcl.ac.uk

please their teacher. This may be regrettable, but it is not uncontrolled; it is a different organization rather than a lack of organization. Others may have no idea that they are infringing serious expectations; their egotism is so great that they are following their own inclinations without regard to the reactions of others. Another child would, in reflecting on it, realize that his or her interests would better be served by being less unruly; but the child either will not or cannot take the time to reflect and translate the understanding into action. It is this latter child who could be described as "lacking in self-control" or "impulsive" or "lacking in inhibition"; but it is not an operational definition of behavior—rather, it is based on inferences about the current and other possible states of mind.

In this chapter, we will focus on the most clearly operationalized behaviors that can be seen as evidence for impaired self-regulation: overactivity and impulsiveness. Within this narrow operationalized definition, attention deficit hyperactivity disorder (ADHD) represents a classic paradigm. ADHD is characterized by age-inappropriate levels of inattentiveness, hyperactivity, and impulsivity, with an onset in early to middle childhood. We describe the behaviors as they have emerged from observational studies and briefly summarize a large literature on their neurocognitive basis, which has suggested an altered function of brain structures involved in self-organization. The outcome studies will then be reviewed, to the effect that the resulting behavioral changes are indeed a risk factor for later psychological adjustment. This leads to a consideration of the factors that can promote resilience in the face of this risk, including what can be achieved by treatment.

Core Problems in ADHD

In ADHD, symptoms and impairments should be persistent over time and pervasive across settings. *Inattentiveness* denotes a reduced length of time spent on a task or toy; an increase in the number of orientations away from a centrally presented task; and more rapid changes between activities (Dienske, de Jonge, & Sanders-Woudstra, 1985;

Milich, Loney, & Landau, 1982). *Overactivity* implies an excess of movements, and this cannot be simply reduced to impulsiveness or inattentiveness (Porrino et al., 1983). *Impulsivity* means acting without reflecting, and it can be conceptualized as overrapid responsiveness, sensation seeking, excessive attraction to immediate reward, aversion to waiting, and a failure to plan ahead. DSM-IV classification of ADHD contains three subtypes: (1) predominantly inattentive; (2) predominantly hyperactive–impulsive; and (3) combined. The third variant is comparable to the European diagnosis of hyperkinetic disorder and the syndrome of pervasive hyperactivity. The validity of this separation, however, has not been empirically established. At the time of writing, the draft for DSM-V has retained the subtypes (though admitting their dubious nosological status) but has added a fourth: "restrictive inattentive." The notion behind this is the clinical suspicion that children with inattention but no trace of hyperactivity are different from the "predominantly inattentive" subjects who enter studies—and who are often just sub-threshold for hyperactive–impulsive symptoms. ADHD is a disabling condition, associated with increased risk for learning disabilities, educational failure, impaired social functioning, relationship problems, employment difficulties, delinquencies, and multiple psychiatric disorders, including conduct disorder, and in later life, substance abuse, personality disorders, and mood disorders.

Neuropsychological Correlates of ADHD

In the field of ADHD research, the hypotheses of deficits in response inhibition and self-control as the core psychopathology have been gaining attention. Though the apparent inattentiveness and distractibility are prominent observed features of ADHD, research of neuropsychological correlates has consistently failed to detect deficits in selective attention or attention filter. That is, the deficit appears not to lie in sensory inputs or screening out unwanted information, but rather in response outputs. In other words, ADHD is more a disorder of inhibition and of maladaptive response patterns than a disorder of attention.

There are several theoretical accounts of this change in response organization, and they compete to give the closest representation of the problems: (1) response inhibition theory (Barkley, 1997); (2) delay aversion theory (Sonuga-Barke, Taylor, & Heptinstall, 1992; Sonuga-Barke, Taylor, Sembi, & Smith, 1992); (3) state regulation theory (Van der Meere, 2002); (4) working memory deficit theory (Castellanos & Tannock, 2002); (5) cognitive-energetic theory (Sergeant, 2000); and (6) temporality (perception of time) deficits theory. More recently, a dual pathway model has been proposed, combining response inhibition theory with delay aversion theory (Sonuga-Barke, 2003).

The contention of response inhibition theory is that the core deficit of ADHD resides in impaired inhibition of unwanted outputs, for instance, in inhibition of a prepotent response; withholding an established ongoing response pattern (thus permitting a delay for a decision); and protecting this period of delay from interference or disruptions from extraneous events. These give rise to other secondary impairments in executive functions involved in self-control.

State regulation theory gives more emphasis to the contextual factors; the poor performance of children with ADHD on certain tasks is believed to reflect a nonoptimal state of energetic pools, arousal, activation, and effort. By introducing, for example, reward or a faster event rate, the states of these ADHD children can be optimized so their performance can be potentially brought to the level of control children. This theory offers an explanation for the observed variability or inconsistency in response in ADHD subjects; and also, that the degree of their variability is altered under different experimental situations of stimuli presentation, such as improvements under reward conditions and under a fast rate of stimuli presentation.

Delay aversion theory proposes that impulsive, and therefore uncontrolled, behavior does not stem from an inability to withhold response, but from a motivational change: a deep-rooted dislike for waiting and therefore a reluctance to delay. The influence of context is even stronger in this formulation because if the delay characteristics are controlled—if the child has to wait no matter which choice he or she makes—then it is possible to set up experimental arrangements in which children with ADHD do not demonstrate impulsiveness.

In short, it cannot be assumed from the cognitive studies so far that we are dealing with a deficit of inhibitory control rather than an alteration in the ways that decisions about inhibition are made. Either notion could apply. They are not mutually exclusive; in fact, they could give rise to each other. A deficit of inhibition can cause children to be averse to delay because they have suffered many experiences of failure in delay situations. Delay aversion will discourage children from experiencing situations in which delay is involved, and can therefore hold them back from learning the skills of inhibition. Indeed, we do not see the theories of inhibition and delay aversion as competing for the sole explanation of impulsive behavior. Rather, they describe two possible pathways into impulsiveness, resulting either in two subgroups of children with ADHD or in the problems for the same individual. In the model of volitional control presented by Taylor (1999), the two theories represent changes at different stages of the formulation of a planned and intended response—the executive planning and decision of what to do, the elaboration of the intent into a plan, the choice of one plan over others, and the suppression of competing plans.

All these abnormalities of inhibitory control could follow directly from genetically determined changes in the microstructure and metabolism of the brain. The brain structures that are involved in the suppression of inappropriate responses (e.g., right frontal and striatal areas) are rich in dopamine and dopamine receptors. Their activity could well be impaired by genetically determined reductions in the efficiency of synaptic transmission. It would, however, be too simple to assume that this direct route must be the key one; interactions with the psychological environment also need to be considered. There are strong genetic influences on hyperactive behavior, but much less is known about the inheritance of the putative cognitive abnormalities. Experience may influence both simple and complex processes, but it is perhaps easier to see how complex processes can be modified by learning and motivation. The decision to inhibit—to withhold a prepotent response or one known to lead to immediate gratification—must be determined in part by the organism's previous history. A child, for example, whose experience favors the idea that delayed reinforcers will never in fact arrive (as might be the case in the children of some impulsive parents) may well not evolve a style of preferring to wait. Similarly, the decision to allocate protracted consideration and analysis to a problem is likely to be conditioned by the extent to which doing just that in the past has been rewarded by success or by the reactions of caregiving adults. In theory, this opens the way to cognitive and self-instructional methods of intervening; in practice, they have not yet proven their clinical value.

Kuntsi et al. (2010) conducted a multivariate familial factor analysis to examine whether the apparent multiple neuropsychological impairments share common or separate etiological pathways. The goal was to examine and identify common latent familial factors which underlie the slow and variable reaction times, impaired response inhibition, and choice impulsivity associated with ADHD. The study used an ADHD and control sibling-pair design. The results of the final model consisted of two familial factors. The first larger factor captured the familial influences on mean reaction time and reaction time variability. This factor explained 98–100% of the familial influences of these measures. The second, smaller factor, captured 62–82% of the familial influences on commission and omission errors. Choice impulsivity was excluded in the final model because of poor fit. The findings suggest the existence of two familial pathways to cognitive impairments in ADHD.

The idea that there are several different neurocognitive routes into dysregulation implies that it could be useful—both for research and clinical practice—to distinguish subtypes on this basis and offer separate approaches to remediation. Indeed, studies which discriminate those with ADHD from controls on the basis of combining tests of different processes look very promising. Solanto et al. (2001) achieved a much stronger discrimination with a combination of inhibitory control and delay aversion tests than with either type of test alone; Gupta, Kar, and Srinivasan (2010) have achieved better than 90% correct classification using a set of four tests. More research is needed

to establish the reliability and stability of test results, but it looks as though we may be moving towards more objective assessment and more prescriptive education.

Resilience, Outcome Studies, and Methodological Issues

Taylor, Chadwick, Heptinstall, and Danckaerts (1996) described a follow-up study of children with pervasive hyperactivity who were identified by parent and teacher ratings in a large community survey of 7- and 8-year-olds. Nine years later, at the age of 17, they were reassessed with parental ratings, as well as a detailed interview using Parent Account of Childhood Symptoms (PACS) rating system. Hyperactivity was a risk factor for later maladjustments, even after allowing for the coexistence of conduct disorder problems and excluding children who showed the problems of emotional disorder. Nearly half of the affected children had developed a psychiatric diagnosis, and more showed problems such as persisting hyperactivity, violence and other conduct problems, and social and peer problems. Although hyperactivity presents as a chronic and debilitating disorder, a minority of the children interestingly seemed to escape complications and grew out of the disorder, so that their young adult outcome was not severely compromised. In other words, resilience in the presence of pervasive hyperactivity does indeed exist. Yet resilience among children with ADHD has not been a major focus of research.

In the field of resilience, a number of studies have been conducted on children exposed to early adversities and deprivations. The researchers examined predictors of good adjustments in later life as indicators of resilience. Though one could infer similar predictors are applicable to ADHD children, nevertheless, direct and robust empirical evidence is still lacking. Furthermore, empirical studies sometimes can yield counterintuitive findings, that is, results opposite to what one may logically predict. This subject is discussed in a review article by Hechtman (1991) and Chap. 6. It is important to emphasize here that the large-scale resilience studies were not conducted on children with ADHD or hyperactivity. In order to avoid confusion, we will not review their findings here. However, we have included studies that have touched on these issues that had been conducted on hyperactive or ADHD subjects.

In ADHD psychological treatment, in relation to resilience, a new trend has emerged, challenging the conventional conceptualization of resilience based on the *deficit or weakness-based model* (Brooks & Goldstein, 2001). In the deficit or weakness-based model, a disorder is conceived to embody symptoms, abnormalities, deficits, and weaknesses; resilience is conceptualized as factors that reduce symptoms and thereby improve outcome. As an alternative, a *strength-based model* has been proposed. This model places emphasis on the development of skills, strengths, and "islands of competence," in spite of the disorder (Brooks & Goldstein). In essence, the new approach demarcates "abilities" from "disabilities"; and it advocates the development of "abilities" and the "talents" associated with the condition. In contrast to the traditional paradigm, the new paradigm also postulates that "strengths" can minimize the negative impacts of "symptoms" in promoting resilience.

There is no substantive intervention trial that evaluates the efficacy of this novel paradigm, that is, to test whether promoting development of abilities or ADHD-associated strengths or islands of strengths, in the absence of reducing symptoms, improves outcomes in ADHD. In this review, we shall therefore examine the available published evidence on (1) the natural history of the condition and its implication on resilience; (2) predictors of resilience and predictors of adverse outcomes in ADHD; (3) predictors of treatment response; and (4) whether an emphasis on strengths in the absence of symptom reduction is likely to promote resilience in children with ADHD.

Before this main review, we would like to draw attention to some methodological issues in evaluating published evidence in this field. Research evidence on ADHD broadly derives from two groups: those conducted on subjects with hyperactivity (on a dimensional scale) and those with ADHD or a comparable diagnosis (by

a categorical definition). The latter category comprises children who have been diagnosed to have a clinical disorder (i.e., ADHD) by clinicians or by researchers using validated diagnostic instruments. These subjects are usually ascertained through specialist clinics. On the other hand, study subjects with hyperactivity are often derived from community samples and classified according to the level of activity (plus or minus inattentiveness). These perceived hyperactive subjects represent the extreme end of a continuous dimension but may not necessarily have the clinical disorder of ADHD.

Research on ADHD children is often subject to referral bias, that is, children who are referred to doctors may have more severe symptoms or comorbid conditions that are troublesome to adults, such as aggression and conduct problems, which are more common among boys. Furthermore, results from these studies are heavily influenced by whether the control or comparison groups have been well chosen and representatively selected. A comparison group can be overmatched, leading to underdetection of differences, and undermatching can lead to detection of false differences.

On the other hand, research on hyperactivity, the extreme end of the dimensional spectrum, is usually conducted on community samples. They are less subject to selection bias. But the qualities of the data gathered often lack details and precision. Often they are confined to rating scale measures, recording behaviors over a short time frame, and completed by parents or teachers who are not trained to distinguish normality from disorder. The information gathered is therefore vulnerable to measurement errors, rater bias, and information bias, leading to misclassification of subjects. Furthermore in the analysis, the cut-off between "normality" and "abnormality" can be arbitrarily defined, for example, with a cut-off threshold made at the top 5, 10, 20, or 25%. Thus a child can be designated as a "case" for a range of reasons: he or she has been overrated by an overstrict parent, going through a bad phase at the time of data collection, or having an activity at the upper end of normality but below the lower boundary of a disorder. Birth cohorts are sometimes too small to contain adequate numbers of children who meet the criteria for the presence of disorder and thus lack statistical power to identify the true effects of a disorder. The inferred relevance of the findings of these studies to ADHD needs to be taken with caution.

Natural Outcomes of Hyperactivity and ADHD

Evidence from Community Samples of Subjects with Hyperactivity

The natural course of the undiagnosed and untreated disorder can be inferred from longitudinal studies of epidemiologically ascertained community samples, that is, subjects drawn from large-scale surveys of unreferred individuals such as birth cohorts. These longitudinal epidemiological studies are difficult and expensive to carry out, and have generally been reported from cohort studies that were designed for other purposes. The classification of hyperactivity may be derived from proxy measures, which often lack precision and specificity for ADHD. The key studies are derived from five major cohorts: Dunedin, Christchurch, Isle of Wight, East London (Taylor et al., 1996), and Cambridge.

Fergusson, Lynskey, and Horwood (1997) have analyzed the Christchurch birth cohort with parent and teacher rating scales ascertained at different time points of development. They found no significant association between hyperactive/inattentive behavior and later offending, once coexisting conduct problems were adjusted in the analysis. The former only appeared as a risk because of its prior association with conduct disorder, which, they suggested, was the true risk. However, the negative consequence of hyperactivity was not trivial, for it did predict educational underachievement. Furthermore, a very strong correlation exists between the two conditions. Moffitt (1990) analyzed the Dunedin birth cohort and came to different conclusions. Even when early aggressive behavior (at age 5) was statistically controlled, hyperactive behavior predicted antisocial behaviors in adolescence.

This finding was confirmed by the Cambridge cohort, which Farrington reanalyzed to evaluate the effect of childhood inattention/hyperactivity on later criminal outcome (Farrington, Loeger, & van Kammen, 1990). Four hundred and eleven males were derived from a working-class area in London and followed-up at age 8, 10, 14, 16, 18, 21, and 25. He found that inattention/hyperactivity predicted later criminality, and this was partly independent of conduct problems, especially for early conviction and multiple offending before age 25. His analysis indicated that hyperactivity and conduct problems were discrete, but overlapping, predictors for delinquency.

Only a few studies have been able to base their conclusions about natural history on cases of disorder. Schachar, Rutter, and Smith (1981) reanalyzed the Isle of Wight longitudinal epidemiological study and concluded that hyperactivity, if it was pervasive across situations and informants, strongly predicted the persistence of psychological deviance between the ages of 9 and 14. However, the initial stratification of cases had been studied for other types of disorders, so their cases of hyperactivity were particularly likely to show comorbid disorder. It is therefore possible that their prediction resulted, not from hyperactivity being a specific risk, but from its being a marker to increased severity of psychological disturbance.

The East London cohort delineated a diagnostic syndrome in an urban community sample by a two-stage process of screening followed by detailed assessment of high-risk and a proportion of low-risk subjects. This brings the advantages of having precise clinical details on subjects derived from a sample unaffected by clinic referral bias. Taylor et al. (1996) found that initial hyperactivity predicted later conduct problems, violence, and also covert antisocial behaviors, even after allowing for baseline coexisting conduct symptoms.

On balance, the evidence from community samples indicates that hyperactivity is associated with later maladjustments, ranging from poor academic achievement to antisocial behaviors, violence, and overt and covert conduct problems. We can now turn to the findings from individuals with syndromic diagnosis of ADHD or its equivalents and examine their outcomes and implications.

Evidence from Diagnosed ADHD Samples

On syndromal persistence, a meta-analysis (Faraone, Biederman, & Mick, 2006) combined the findings of published longitudinal studies and estimated an approximate persistent rate of 15%. When the adult phenotype included "ADHD in partial remissions" (that is, symptomatic cases below the threshold for childhood syndrome), the persistence rate increased to 65%, indicating that about two-thirds of childhood cases continue to show significant symptoms and impairment in adulthood, despite a smaller proportion fulfilling the strict diagnostic definition.

A consistent finding across follow-up studies of children with ADHD is that they continue to have persistent problems with restlessness, over-activity, impulsive behavior, and inattention. Much of the published data on natural history of the disorder was derived from six major cohort samples (with representative authors in parentheses): New York (Gittelman & Mannuzza), Montreal (Weiss, Hechtman, & Milroy), Wisconsin (Barkley, 1997; Fischer, Barkley, Smallish, & Fletcher, 2002), California (Lambert), East London (Taylor et al., 1996), and Sweden (Rasmussen & Gillberg, 2000). Other clinic cohorts with a shorter follow-up period included Harvard (Biederman, Mick, & Faraone, 2000), Pittsburgh (Molina & Pelham, 2003), Portland (Satterfield, Swanson, Schell, & Lee, 1994), and Iowa (Loney, Kramer, & Milich, 1981). The East London and Swedish cohorts are unique in that the diagnosed cohorts were ascertained through epidemiological samples by screening. The other cohorts were clinic patients and thus subjected to selection bias.

In the New York cohort, Gittelman et al. prospectively followed 101 hyperactive males in adolescence and adulthood and compared them with matched normal controls. They found that the majority (68 out of 101) of the subjects still

suffered from ADHD in early adolescence; 27% had conduct problems, and 20% had multiple convictions (Gittelman, Mannuzza, Shenker, & Bonagura, 1985; Mannuzza, Klein, Konig, & Gismpino, 1989). Gittelman et al. identified the continuing presence of hyperactivity, *not* the baseline hyperactivity at early childhood, as the best prediction for later risk of conduct problems and delinquency in adolescence, suggesting that chronic persistence of hyperactive symptoms is the key risk factor for adverse outcomes (Gittelman et al., 1985). In adulthood, only 4% still fulfilled the criteria for ADHD diagnosis, but more of the hyperactive subjects had antisocial personality disorders and nonalcohol drug use (Mannuzza, Klein, Bessler, Malloy, & Lapadula, 1998). Their low rate of persistence of diagnosis may be due to the artifacts of diagnostic threshold for adult condition or high attrition rate. It is well known that those who refused or were lost at follow-up tend to have more problems. A follow-up study was carried out when the subjects reached 18 years of age (Mannuzza, Klein, Abikoff, & Moulton, 2004); the authors found that low levels of CD-type problems are not innocuous, because they predict later CD among children with ADHD but without a comorbid CD diagnosis at baseline. When the subjects reached 39 years of age, Mannuzza, Klein, and Moulton (2008) found that even in the absence of comorbid conduct disorder in childhood, ADHD increased the risk of developing antisocial and substance use disorders (SUDs) in adolescence, which, in turn, increases the risk for criminal behavior in adulthood.

In the Montreal cohort, Weiss, Minde, Werry, Douglas, and Neneth (1971) compared 91 clinic-referred hyperactive subjects with a control group matched for age, sex, IQ, and social class. At the 5-year follow-up, they found that the hyperactive adolescents had lower self-esteem and more academic problems. Most continued to be distractible, impulsive, and emotionally immature, although less hyperactive. In addition, 25% of the hyperactive subjects had delinquent behaviors. Similar results were found by Akeman, Dykman, and Peters (1977); the hyperactive subjects had more oppositional or delinquent behavior and lower self-esteem when compared with a group of normal controls and other comparison group with learning difficulties. Satterfield et al. (1994) found a five times higher rate of arrest among the hyperactive subjects compared with matched controls in committing a felony (burglary, theft, or assault with a weapon). At a 10- to 12-year follow-up of the Montreal cohort, at approximately age 19, Weiss, Hechtman, Perlman, Hopkins, and Werner (1979) found them to have less education, have had more car accidents, and to have made more geographical moves when compared with normal matched controls. Hyperactive subjects had less friends, completed fewer years of education, failed more grades, and received lower marks. They also had more court referrals, had tried nonmedical drugs more often, and had more personality trait problems, most frequently of "impulsive" and "immature-dependent" types. They were more impulsive on cognitive style tests. During face-to-face research interviews, they reported more feelings of restlessness and exhibited more signs of restlessness. At the 15-year follow-up when the same cohort was in their early 20s (Weiss et al., 1985), they found 66% of hyperactive subjects still had at least one disabling symptom of ADHD and 23% suffered from an antisocial personality disorder. There had also been more suicide attempts in the hyperactive group. According to Hechtman, Weiss, Perlman, and Tuck (1981), there are three categories of outcome. The first group had a fairly normal outcome. The second group consist of those with persistent attentional, social, emotional, and impulse problems; and as adults, they continued to have difficulties with work, interpersonal relationships, low self-esteem, impulsive behavior, irritability, anxiety, and emotional lability. The majority of young adults fell into this group. The third group included those with more serious psychiatric compUcations, including heavy dependence on drugs or alcohol, severe depression with suicidal problems, and anfisocial personality pathologies. Their last finding published some 20 years ago has recently been replicated in other studies. One recent follow-up study extended the analysis further to identify predictors of antisocial personality disorder. Fischer et al.

(2002) conducted a self-report survey on psychiatric and personality disorders in a follow-up study on the Wisconsin ADHD cohort (then in their early 20s) and examined a number of predictors for psychiatric morbidity. About 21% of hyperactive probands qualified for antisocial personality disorder (ASPD), a fivefold increase compared with the control group. Their findings were in keeping with previous studies at New York (27% vs 8% of controls), Montreal (23% vs 2.3%), and Sweden (18% vs 2.1%). They all suggest hyperactivity in childhood predisposes a person to ASPD in adulthood. Fischer's study, however, has extended the finding further by demonstrating that this elevated risk for ASPD is substantially influenced by severity of childhood conduct problems (odds ratio [OR]; OR = 4.54 with 95% confidence interval of 1.44–14.31), as well as teenage conduct problems (OR = 1.56 with 95% confidence interval of 1.20–2.02), even after controlling for the severity of childhood symptoms as covariants. Their findings provided support to Lynam's (1996) view that coexisting hyperactivity and conduct problems in the same child constitute a greater risk for antisocial outcomes in adulthood than when either problem occurs alone. Another interesting finding was that histrionic and passive-aggressive personality disorders were also significantly overrepresented among their subjects (12% and 18% respectively); and these disorders were not a function of childhood conduct problems. However, elevated borderline personality disorder (14%) was associated with teenage conduct disorder (OR = 1.32 with 95% confidence interval of 1.05–1.66). Major depression was significantly greater in the hyperactive than control group, especially in the presence of ASPD (OR = 3.59) and borderline PD (OR = 5.56). In this study, they found no evidence of increase in substance abuse.

Research has been inconsistent with regards to increased risk for substance abuse. Some found a greater prevalence of alcohol or drug use in New York (16% vs. 3% by age 18) (Gittelmanet al., 1985), 12% vs. 4% at age 24 (Mannuzza et al., 1998), and 16% vs. 4% at age 26 (Mannuzza, Klein, Bessler, Malloy, & LaPadula, 1993). In the Swedish sample, only alcohol misuse disorders occurred more often (24% vs. 4%) (Rasmussen & Gillberg, 2000). In the Montreal sample, significant differences were found for "use of narcotics in last 5 years" (14% vs. 4%), "use of nonmedical drug" (74% vs. 55%), and "sold non-medical drug" (18% vs. 5%); while no significant difference was found for "use of hash, speed, and barbiturates" (Weiss, Hechtman, Perlman, Hopkins, & Werner, 1979). In Fischer et al.'s (2002) study, the rate of "any drug disorder" among hyperactive subjects was 43%, which is high compared with controls of other studies. But in their study, this rate was not significantly different from their normal control (31%). The authors believed that this was due to an elevated rate of substance use in their control group, perhaps reflecting a secular trend in more prevalent substance misuse in the U.S. population, leading to no increase in relative risk (Fischer et al., 2002). It is likely that the risks in development of substance abuse among hyperactive subjects is influenced by both exposure to and availability of illegal drugs, which in turn are related to the time, country, and urban or nonurban settings in which they live. Hence, prevalence of substance abuse as an outcome is more variable across studies.

Molina and Pelham (2003) evaluated the correlates and predictors of substance use in a follow-up study of 142 children with ADHD into adolescence (13–18 years old) comparing with 100 same-aged non-ADHD controls. They found associations between hyperactive subjects with higher levels of alcohol, tobacco, and illegal drug use. They identified three correlates: first, severity of childhood inattention symptoms predicted later multiple substance use; second, childhood oppositional defiant disorder/conduct disorder symptoms predicted later illegal drug use; and third, persistence of ADHD and adolescent conduct problems correlated with elevated substance use behaviors. Their findings suggested that elevated risks of subsequent drug use were mediated via both oppositional/conduct problems and severity of inattentive symptoms.

Lynskey and Hall (2001) suggested that the key mediator for substance abuse in ADHD is the presence of conduct problems. In other words, in the absence of conduct disorder, ADHD is not

associated with an increased risk of substance use problems in males. Biederman, Wilens, Mick, Faraone, and Spencer (1998), however, found ADHD to be associated with substance abuse independent of comorbid conditions. In their study of a clinic-referred ADHD adult sample, they found twofold increased risk for psychoactive substance use disorder (PSUD) and an increased likelihood of progressing from alcohol use disorder to a drug use disorder (hazard ratio = 3.8) for ADHD subjects. The authors suggested that individuals who used drugs for psychopathological reason (i.e., ADHD symptoms and pathologies) were more likely to progress to dependence and abuse after exposure and were less likely to abstain than those who used drugs for social or recreational reasons. In another study on adults with ADHD, the researchers found a slower remission rate, longer duration of PSUD, and slower recovery in their hyperactive subjects compared with nonhyperactive users (Wilens, Biederman, & Mick, 1998). Recently, Flory, Milich, Lynam, Leukefeld, and Clayton (2003) reported that ADHD and conduct disorder (CD) symptoms interacted to predict marijuana dependence symptoms as well as hard drug use and dependence symptoms. They concluded that individuals with comorbid ADHD and CD are at a greater risk for substance abuse than either condition occurring alone.

Overall, studies suggested three different paths leading to substance abuse: conduct problems, core pathology of ADHD, and unique interaction between comorbid ADHD and conduct problems. As persistent ADHD is highly correlated with CD, family history of ADHD, and psychosocial adversity, these findings suggest that the subgroup exposed to both a high dose of ADHD genetic loading and a high dose of environment insults are most likely to be at risk and thus least resilient.

Summary

Several themes emerge from the reviewed longitudinal studies. First, ADHD is not a benign condition, it is a chronic illness with significant psychological, social, and emotional morbidity.

Second, for the majority of cases, significant or residual ADHD symptoms will persist and result in serious academic, social, and emotional problems in adolescence and in adulthood, even in the absence of more severe complications. Third, certain patterns are more indicative of a malignant course: persistence of symptoms over time, the presence of conduct problems and aggression, and the emergence of substance abuse and personality difficulties in adolescence and early adult life. The coexistence of conduct problems with ADHD appears to represent the strongest risk factor for severe maladjustments in later life. The implications of these findings are that (1) adequate control of ADHD symptoms (i.e., reducing persistence of symptoms) and (2) controlling aggression and factors leading to conduct problems can improve resilience.

Predictors of Resilience and Adverse Outcome in ADHD

In a review paper, Hechtman (1991) examined a range of factors associated with resilience among at-risk children (though not ADHD subjects), and related these factors to ADHD in a single case report. Factors reviewed included child characteristics (health, temperament, IQ, autonomy, psychological parameters) and family characteristics (socioeconomic status, emotional warmth and support, family size, and characteristics of the wider community). Research on at-risk children (though not ADHD subjects) shows that resilient children are healthier. They have fewer health problems in utero, perinatally, and in infancy. Their temperaments are more likely to be active, adaptable, and socially responsive, eliciting a more positive response from their caretakers and environment. They are more able to find solace and satisfaction. They also have more reflective vs. impulsive cognitive styles and more able to control their feelings appropriately. Children with higher IQs fare better in difficult circumstances, much as those with more advanced self-help abilities and more problem solving capacities and language development and communication skills. Resilient children had a greater sense of autonomy,

internal locus of control, and more positive self-esteem. They have better ego strengths and coping skills. They can ask help of others and are generally more optimistic about themselves and their futures, along with showing better capacities for empathy, good peer relationship, and sense of humor. Protective family characteristics include closer supervision, higher social status, and a warm, cohesive, and supportive family atmosphere, where emotional expression, open communication, and independence are encouraged. Parental mental health and physical health are associated with the presence or absence of such a positive environment. Positive factors in the network of extended family, friends, school, and church can provide support that is lacking at home and can also confer protection. In this case study of an ADHD subject, Hechtman reported the subject to have a high IQ, a good sense of humor, and charm. His family was middle class, stable, loving, and supportive. There were significant figures in his life who believed in him. He thrived and coped well in his early adulthood, despite significant impairments and setbacks experienced at higher education and at work related to persistent symptoms of hyperactivity, restlessness, impulsivities, and inappropriate talkativeness. This was a single case report with evident methodological limitations. It nevertheless suggests that similar resilient predictors for at-risk children can be applied to ADHD subjects. There is no ADHD research that systematically examines whether this wide range of predictors for resilience for at-risk children also applies to ADHD subjects. Nevertheless, our review of published evidence suggests that child, family, and environmental factors can influence resilience in ADHD. Favorable child-predictive factors include: (a) lack of perinatal complications, (b) higher baseline IQ, academic, emotional, and social functioning, (c) childhood temperament, frustration tolerance and emotional stability, (d) desisting symptom trajectory or symptom reduction as response to treatment, (e) lower baseline symptoms, and (f) lack of baseline aggressive and conduct disorder symptoms, all predicting better subsequent adjustments. Favorable family and environmental factors include: (a) lower family conflict, (b) lower parental negative expressed emotions, (c) higher socioeconomic status, (d) emotional health of family members and emotional climate of the home and child-rearing practices, (e) parental supervision and control, and (f) nonurban dwelling, which appear to modify the risk of exposure to drugs, deviant peers, and criminal activities. Weiss et al. (1971) found that children with initial high IQs and lower initial scores of hyperactivity and distractibility fared better academically in adolescence. Furthermore, a quarter of hyperactive adolescents with significant antisocial behavior had higher initial ratings of aggressive behaviors. This finding was also replicated by Loney et al. (1981) who demonstrated that initial aggression predicted aggression and antisocial behavior in adolescence.

Loney's sample was derived from 124 children (ages 2–12) with the diagnosis of hyperkinetic/minimal brain dysfunction syndrome who had been referred to an Iowa child psychiatry clinic. In their follow-up at age 12–18, they measured three broad domains of outcomes: (1) symptoms at outcome, (2) delinquent behaviors, and (3) academic achievement. They carried out multiple regressions, expressing effect size of the predictors as "squared multiple correlation," which can be transformed to represent a percentage that accounts for the total variation of the outcome measure.

For the symptoms outcome domain, they examined three separate variables: (1) adolescent hyperactivity and inattention, (2) aggression, and (3) negative effects at follow-up. For adolescent hyperactivity scores (rated by the mother), they found three predictors to account for about 20% of the outcome measure: (1) parental socioeconomic status, (2) baseline aggression, and (3) a history of perinatal complications. Interestingly, baseline hyperactivity scores did not predict later hyperactive symptoms. Inattention was predicted by age of onset (effect size—5%). Adolescent negative effects were weakly predicted by response to medication and parental control (combined effect size—9%). For delinquency outcome domain, they examined aggression/offenses and illegal drug use. "Offenses against property" were predicted by urban dwelling, size of family, and baseline aggression (combined

effect size—37%). "Offenses against person" was predicted by parental control, the presence of neurological signs, and aggression at baseline (combined effect size—36%). "Involvement with illegal drugs" was predicted by baseline aggression, age of referral, urban dwelling, and response to drug treatment (negative) (combined effect size—40%). For academic achievement domain, they examined reading, arithmetic, and spelling abilities. Reading scores were predicted by past reading and response to drug treatment (combined effect size—63%). Arithmetic skills were predicted by past academic ability, response to treatment, family size (negative direction), maternal hostility, reading abilities, and perinatal compactions (combined effect size—69%). Spelling was predicted by past academic ability, maternal control, hyperactivity, and family size (combined effect size—79%).

To put the results another way, their findings suggest that response to treatment (symptom reduction) promotes resilience in lowering the risk of later drug use and improving later academic achievement. Parent control confers resilience by increasing academic skills and reducing negative effect. However, perinatal complications predicted aggression, persistence of hyperactivity, and lower arithmetic skills. Urban dwelling increases the risk of drug use and offenses against property. Large family size increases the risk of offenses against property and lowered later academic achievement. Thus, lack of the latter factors would increase resilience, in a similar way that the absence of conduct and aggressive problems at baseline would improve outcome.

A prospective study of 123 hyperactive children also examined similar predictive factors (Fischer, Barkley, Fletcher, & Smallish, 1993). For positive predictors they found that childhood cognitive and academic competence predicted adolescent academic skills; and parental personal competence predicted social competence in adolescence. For negative predictors they found that family stress at baseline predicted conduct problems; and the combined effects of paternal antisocial tendencies and the severity of childhood impulsivity–hyperactivity predicted later oppositional defiant behaviors. Child defiance, but not hyperactivity, predicted later arrests. Overall, the study suggested that no single predictor cut across all domains.

In the Montreal cohort at 10- to 12-year follow-up (Weiss et al., 1979), hyperactive subjects (around age 20) were asked what had helped them most during their childhood. The most common response was a positive relationship with a significant adult; for instance, one parent (nearly always the mother) who believed in their final success or a teacher who seemed to turn the tide of failure. Another response was discovering that they had some special talents. When asked what made things worse, the most common responses were family fights (usually concerning the hyperactive subject), feeling different (inferior, "dumb"), and being criticized. Significantly more hyperactives than controls rated their childhood as unhappy. However, the authors did not report whether these factors were correlated with outcomes in their study.

In a later publication by the same group, Hechtman, Weiss, Perlman, and Amsel (1984) examined a range of childhood predictors of outcome in early adulthood. The outcome measures studied include: (1) emotional adjustment, (2) academic performance, (3) police involvement, (4) car accidents, and (5) substance and alcohol misuse. The authors identified baseline personal characteristics such as IQ, aggressiveness, emotional stability, and low frustration tolerance, and family characteristics, such as socioeconomic class, child-rearing practices, home emotional atmosphere, and parental mental health, to be significant predictors of successful adult outcome.

Within family measures, the specific effect of parental negative expressed emotions influencing the development of antisocial behaviors in hyperactive children has been studied by Rutter et al. (1997). Negative expressed emotions denote criticism, disapproval, negative attributions, as well as rejecting and hostile attitudes toward the child. They are coded independently of emotional warmth. Emotional over involvement (EOI) was originally conceptualized as a component of "expressed emotion" in the Camberwell Family Interview for adults. As dependency is age-appropriate for children, the validity of this construct in childhood-related measurement is questionable. EOI has thus not been included in most childhood studies of expressed emotions.

Rutter et al. (1997) conducted a longitudinal follow-up study on pervasively hyperactive subjects ascertained in a community epidemiological sample and examined the effect of expressed emotions on disruptive behaviors. Hyperactive children who were exposed to a high level of negative expressed emotions from parents exhibited more antisocial and disruptive behaviors at follow-up compared with the hyperactive counterparts exposed to a low level. The pathogenic effect of negative child–parent relationship applied also to nonhyperactive subjects in the same study, though the effect was less marked, that is, the rates of antisocial and disruptive behaviors were also raised in the nonhyperactive children exposed to a high level of negative expressed emotion; but the overall rates were lower than in the hyperactive counterparts. The findings suggest a possible causal relationship between expressed emotions and antisocial/disruptive behaviors.

The impact of emotional dysregulation on adjustments has recently received attention. Barkley and Fischer (2010) published a study, which followed-up 135 hyperactive children into adulthood and measured their Emotional Impulsiveness (EI) symptoms. Of the hyperactive children now adults, 55 were classified as having persistent ADHD (ADHD-P); and 80 as having nonpersistent ADHD (ADHD-NP). They were also compared with a community sample of 75 subjects followed-up concurrently. They found significantly more EI symptoms in ADHD-P subjects, than their nonpersistent and community control counterparts. EI was measured with seven items: (1) find it difficult to tolerate waiting— impatient; (2) quick to get angry or become upset; (3) easily frustrated; (4) overreact emotionally; (5) easily excited by activities going on around me; (6) lose my temper; (7) am touchy or easily annoyed by others. EI was found to contribute uniquely to major impairments in multiple domains—occupational, educational, criminal, driving, financial and social relationship—after adjusting for the confounding effects of inattention and hyperactivity/ impulsivity symptoms. The authors concluded that

"EI is as much a component of ADHD as are its two traditional dimensions and is associated with impairments beyond those contributed by the two traditional dimensions."

Wilmshurst, Peele, and Wilmshurst (2011) found that subjects with a diagnosis of ADHD who nevertheless became college students represented an especially resilient group. This group reported significantly higher paternal support and greater support from friends than non-ADHD college students. The authors suggested that college students with ADHD should form a focus of research, as they had achieved success against the odds.

Mikami and Hinshaw (2003) found a complex relationship between protective factors and adaptive behaviors in girls with and without ADHD. Peer rejection was related to higher levels of aggressive behavior and depressed/anxious behavior, confirming peer problems as a risk factor. For all girls, popularity with adults predicted lower levels of aggression while goal-directed solitary play predicted lower levels of anxiety/depression. Popularity with adults was most protective among the peer-accepted subgroup, whereas solitary play was most protective among the peer-rejected subgroup. For ADHD girls (not controls), engaging in meaningful solitary play was a stronger predictor of lower levels of anxious/depressed behavior. In the follow-up study, Mikami and Hinshaw (2006) hypothesized protective factors to be childhood measures of self-perceived scholastic competence, engagement in goal-directed play when alone and popularity with adults. In adolescents the authors examined a range of outcomes, including externalizing and internalizing symptoms, academic achievement, eating pathology, and substance use as outcomes. ADHD and peer rejection predicted an increased risk for all these outcome measures except for substance use, which was predicted by ADHD only. ADHD and peer rejection predicted lower adolescent academic achievement but not adolescent externalizing and internalizing behavior. As a buffer, self-perceived scholastic competence in childhood (with control of academic achievement) predicted resilient adolescent functioning. However, the protective effect of meaningful solitary play was not detected in adolescents.

To investigate biological factors that promote resilience, Nigg, Nikolas, Friderici, Park, and Zucker (2007) examined two independent samples: children were classified as resilient if they avoided developing ADHD, oppositional defiant disorder (ODD) or conduct disorder (CD) in the face of family adversity. The first sample consisted of ADHD-combined subtype, ADHD-inattentive subtype and controls. The second replication sample was a prospective cohort of children from high-risk families with high levels of alcohol and drug misuse. Adversity was indexed by low socioeconomic status, parental psychopathology, marital conflict, and exposure to stressful events. Resilience was defined as being below the diagnostic threshold for attention, oppositional, and conduct problems despite adversity. Two specific biological protective factors were examined, given their potential relevance to prefrontal brain development. These were (1) neuropsychological response inhibition, as assessed by the Stop task, and (2) a composite catecholamine genotype risk score. Resilient children were characterized in both samples as displaying more effective response inhibition. A composite high-risk genotype index was developed by summing the presence of high-risk allele markers on three genes expressed in prefrontal cortex: dopamine transporter (SLC6A3), dopamine D4 receptor (DRD4), and noradrenergic alpha-2 receptor (ADRA2A). Homozygous insertion genotype was classified as high risk for DRD4. High-risk SNP (single nucleotide polymorphism) alleles were "G" (A/G or G/G) for SLC6A3, and "T" (C/T or T/T) for ADRA2A. The authors found that a low score in risk genotype was a reliable resilience indicator against development of ADHD and CD—but not ODD—in the face of psychosocial adversity. Amidst moderate or moderate-to-high adversity, biological characteristics of the child provided broad protection, if the child had protective genotypes or had strong response inhibition or both. Notably, genotype and response inhibition were uncorrelated and did not interact; the authors suggested these to be two distinct neurobiologically based protective mechanisms. The catecholamine genes analyzed are expressed primarily in prefrontal cortex and involved in executive functions; whereas response inhibition is associated with the integrity of basal ganglia and striatum as well as prefrontal–subcortical network, influenced by other putative factors. The authors suggest that moderate to high levels of family adversity, which disrupt socialization experiences and prefrontal cortical functions necessary for adjustment and regulation, could be one route in a multipathway causal model of ADHD. Furthermore, stress events alter neural development in regions involving hippocampus, amygdala and frontal cortex, important in inhibitory control. The results provided preliminary evidence for key biological factors linked to prefrontal cortex function, which may enable children to avoid developing ADHD and CD in the presence of psychosocial adversity.

In summary, studies on predictors of outcomes in hyperactive subjects suggest that factors in the child, family, and environment can all influence later resilience and maladjustments. We now turn to examine the issues of resilience and developmental trajectories.

Developmental Trajectories and Resilience: The Effects and Predictors of Remitting and Persistent Life Course and Normalization of Function for Persisters

In a prospective study on a clinic sample of ADHD subjects, Biederman et al. (1996) examined the rate of desistence and persistence over time, and identified the predictors for desistent and persistent life course of ADHD. Their sample consisted of Caucasian boys aged 6–17 with IQs over 80 and who had an intact nuclear family. At 4-year follow-up, they identified a high rate of persistence of 85%, with only 15% remitted. The high rate of persistence found was likely due to the broad definition of persistence they used (see later). Of the 15% whose ADHD was a transient disorder, half of the remission occurred in childhood and the other half in adolescence. Predictors of persistence included family history, severity of ADHD, psychosocial adversity, and comorbidity with conduct, mood, and anxiety disorders. ADHD in the family history influenced persistence:

45% for persisters vs. 33% for late desisters vs. 10% for early desisters. The persistent form of ADHD also differed in the family history (34% vs. 11% vs. 10%). This suggested a stronger effect of familiality and perhaps a heavier genetic loading in the persisters. As an indicator of psychosocial adversity, persisters were exposed to a higher level of family conflict. Subjects' own characteristics also differed. Among the persisters, there were more severe inattentive and hyperactive symptoms and a greater level of functional impairments at both baseline and follow-up. Persisters also had more symptoms of oppositional/defiance disorder and depression and anxiety problems. Furthermore, the persisters showed a trend of having a lower IQ at baseline, but the differences did not reach statistical significance (109.2 vs. 110.8 vs. 111.7; $p = 0.063$). The GAF (global assessment functioning) scores were significantly lower for the persisters at baseline (47 vs. 53 vs. 53; $p = 0.0001$) and at follow-up (52 vs. 60 vs. 64; $p = 0.0001$). Overall, the persisters had higher exposure to family conflicts, a stronger family history of ADHD, and were more severely affected and impaired by ADHD at both baseline and follow-up. In other words, resilience (better functioning and escaping impairments at outcome) was associated with a desisting life course, which in turn was predicted by lower symptom levels, better adjustment, lack of family history, and lack of family conflict at the baseline.

Chen and Simonoff (unpublished) studied a U.K. birth cohort with parental and teacher rating scales and found that hyperactivity (HA) exerted a relatively weak and nonenduring antecedent effect on conduct problems, a moderate dose–response effect (length of exposure as dosage), and a very strong proximity effect of HA on the development of conduct problems. This finding offers support to the idea that it is the maintenance and chronic course of HA, rather than its simple presence in earlier childhood, that leads to conduct problems with their ensuing complications. In the same study, it was also suggested that declining HA life trajectories were protective against conduct problems at age 16. Furthermore, a shorter exposure to HA was associated with a lower risk of conduct problems at age 16 in the longitudinal follow-up study. This would mean that a short course and discontinuity of HA symptoms was associated with a low level of conduct problems and their ensnaring consequences. It was not clear whether treatment and therapeutic reduction in symptoms would confer the same benefit.

With regards to the definition of persistence, Biederman et al. (2000) identified a shift in the patterns of symptoms and impairments with age. The symptoms of inattention remitted for fewer subjects than did symptoms of hyperactivity or impulsivity. To some extent, it seemed the proportion of subjects experiencing remission varied considerably with the definition used (highest for syndromatic remission, lowest for functional remission). This finding was also supported by an earlier longitudinal follow-up study of 106 boys with DSM-III-R ADHD (Hart, Lahey, Loeber, Applegate, & Frick, 1995). Hyperactivity/impulsivity symptoms declined with increasing age, but inattention symptoms did not. Inattention declined only from the first to the second assessment and remained stable thereafter in boys of all ages. The rate of decline in hyperactivity–impulsivity symptoms was independent of the amount and type of treatment received. Furthermore, they found that boys who still met the criteria for ADHD at follow-up were significantly more hyperactive/impulsive and more likely to exhibit conduct disorder at baseline than boys who no longer met the criteria at follow-up. The findings suggest possible heterogeneity in the childhood form of ADHD, with one subtype traversing a symptom-declining trajectory and another a more symptom-persistent trajectory.

So far we have examined maladjustment in relation to persistent ADHD trajectory and resilience in relation to desisting trajectory. We now turn to the interesting question on predictors of resilience despite persistence of symptoms. That is, can resilience exist in spite of persistent ADHD, and if it does, what are they? In a follow-up study of a clinic sample comprised of 85 boys with persistent ADHD diagnosed by DSM-III-R criteria, Biederman, Mick, and Faraone (1998) attempted to disentangle syndromic persistence from functional outcome in ADHD youths. The subjects were followed prospectively into mid-adolescence and compared with 68 non-ADHD boys. Three domains of functioning were recorded

at baseline and follow-up: school, social, and emotional. At follow-up, the persistent ADHD sample fell into three groups: 20% functioning poorly in all domains, 30% functioning well, and 60% with intermediate outcomes. They found that impulsivity reduced the likelihood for normalization of functioning (odds ratio [OR] for normalization of functioning=0.7 with 95% CI of 0.5–0.9). That is, among those persistent ADHD subjects, those with a high level of impulsivity had more impaired function. Likewise, psychiatric comorbidity (OR=0.3 with 95% CI of 0.1–0.7), exposure to maternal psychopathology (OR=0.3 with 95% CI of 0.1–0.8), and larger number of siblings (OR=0.5 with 95% CI of 0.3–0.9) all predicted lower adjustments. Learning difficulties impeded normalization of school functioning (OR=0.15 with 95% CI of 0.05–0.53). The converse was also true, that is, the absence of these risk factors was associated with improved functioning despite persistence of ADHD. Furthermore, improvement in one area of functioning had a snowball effect, increasing the chance of improvement in other areas. Good baseline functioning also predicted normalized functioning at follow-up. Good emotional functioning at baseline predicted normalized function of both emotional functioning (OR=5.6 with 95% CI of 2.2–14.6) and school functioning (OR=2.4 with 95% CI of 1.01–5.8). Good social functioning at baseline predicted normalized emotional functioning at follow-up (OR=3.1 with 95% CI of 1.05–9.3). Good school functioning at baseline predicted normalized school functioning at follow-up (OR=3.6 with 95% CI of 1.4–9.1). In short, good baseline functioning and lack of adverse predictors confer relative resilience despite persistence of ADHD. This suggests that normalization of functioning and syndromic persistence of ADHD may be partially independent.

Genetic Influence: The Role of Gene and Environment Interaction

There is only scanty published evidence in the field of ADHD demonstrating the effect of gene and environment interaction in moderating resilience. As already mentioned, a study examined the effect of psychosocial adversity and genetic risks in developing ADHD, ODD and CD. A composite catecholamine genotype risk score was used by summing presence of risk across markers on three genes expressed in prefrontal cortex: dopamine transporter, dopamine D4 receptor, and noradrenergic alpha-2 receptor. A low score in risk genotype was reported to be a reliable resilience indicator against development of ADHD and CD, but not ODD, in the face of psychosocial adversity (Nigg et al. 2007). We anticipate this topic to be an area of interest for ADHD research. For non-ADHD subjects, two highly cited publications have demonstrated that genetic factors can influence resilience following exposure to childhood abuse and life stress.

Caspi et al. (2003) investigated the role of genetic contribution to account for why some children who are maltreated grow up to develop antisocial behavior, whereas others do not. A functional polymorphism in the gene encoding the neurotransmitter-metabolizing enzyme mono-amine oxidase A (MAOA) was found to moderate the effect of maltreatment. Subjects with a genotype conferring high levels of MAOA expression (associated with an increased level of this enzyme in the brain) were less likely to develop antisocial problems following exposure to childhood maltreatment. Those with a genotype conferring low levels of MAOA expression had an increased risk of developing antisocial behaviors. Their findings suggested that the genotype associated with a high level of MAOA expression can also confer resilience following exposure to childhood abuse. They also provided early evidence that genotypes can moderate children's sensitivity to environmental insults.

In the second study by the same group, Caspi et al. (2003) investigated why stressful experiences led to depression in some people but not in others. They used a prospective longitudinal study of a representative birth cohort and investigated the moderating effects of a functional polymorphism in the promoter region of the serotonin transporter (5-HTT) gene. There are two common variants of this gene: a short and a long form (or allele). They found that subjects who are homozygous or heterozygous (with one or two copies respectively) of the short allele of the

5-HTT promoter polymorphism exhibited more depressive symptoms, diagnosable depression, and suicidality following exposure to stressful life events than individuals homozygous for the long allele. This study again provides another piece of early evidence that an individual's response and resilience to environmental insults can be moderated by his or her genetic makeup.

In the field of ADHD, there is early evidence that comorbid ADHD and CD may be an etiologically distinct disorder entity as suggested by analysis of familial history and aggregates (Faraone, Biederman, Jetton, & Tsuang, 1997; Thaper, Harrington, & McGuffin, 2001); and also that adult ADHD may be a more homogenous condition with stronger familial etiological risk factors than the childhood form (Biederman et al., 1995). Within the childhood form, there are likely to be subtypes of persistent and nonpersistent variants, possibly mediated by different genetic and environmental influences. A transient course of ADHD is associated with better prognosis; in contrast, both persistent ADHD and the comorbid form of ADHD/CD are associated with greater maladjustment. If genetic factors are proven to be associated with these varying subtypes of clinical phenotypes, genetic makeup will also influence resilience and vulnerability in the presence of ADHD. We anticipate that genetic research and gene–environment interaction research in the near future may provide interesting insights into the biological and environmental substrates that confer resilience.

Resilience, Treatments, and Lessons from the MTA

Here, we examine the effects of treatment and medication in terms of symptom reduction and "normalization" of behaviors. In particular, we summarize some of the key relevant findings from the recent publications from the Multimodal Treatment of Attention-Deficit Hyperactivity Disorder (MTA, 1999) study. A reader may refer to an overview summary paper on the MTA (Jensen, Hinshaw, Swanson, et al., 2001) and one on the effect of comorbidities in the MTA (Jensen, Hinshaw, Kraemer, et al., 2001).

There are in excess of 200 published studies reporting the efficacy and effectiveness by stimulant treatment on inattentive and hyperactive symptoms. More interestingly, there are other studies examining the effects of stimulants on symptomatic impulsivity, aggression, and conduct problems, as well as on executive function and the impacts on parental negative expressed emotions.

In both laboratory and naturalistic settings, stimulants have been found to be effective in reducing aggression and impulsivity. Improvements in social and interpersonal functioning as a result of reduction in aggression and impulsivity have been confirmed in naturalistic studies. In other words, the effects of stimulants are not only confined to attention, they also affect emotional and social processing and can correct disruptive, intrusive, and aggressive behaviors, which often render hyperactive children unpopular among their peers. In nonhyperactive children with CD, a study (Klein et al., 1997) reported improvements in conduct symptoms with stimulant treatment, confirming the effect of stimulants on nonhyperactive symptoms.

The positive effects of stimulant medication on social functioning within the family have been demonstrated. In a double-blinded crossover treatment study, Schachar, Taylor, Wieselberg, Thorley, and Rutter (1987) found that the family function and relationships improved in children who responded to methylphenidate treatment: there was a reduction in negative sibling encounters and a reduction of parental negative expressed emotions. Treatment response was defined as 50% or greater reduction in hyperactive symptoms while on stimulant treatment. Measures of maternal warmth, criticism, contacts with parents, parental coping, and positive/negative encounters with siblings were gathered by raters blinded to the treatment and response status. Among responders, methylphenidate was significantly associated with more expressed maternal warmth, less criticism, increased contact between mother and child, and fewer negative encounters between the child and his siblings.

If symptom control by treatment can improve social, interpersonal, and cognitive functioning, then it is important to identify the most effective form of treatment. The MTA study compared the effects of different modes of treatment.

ADHD Symptoms

In the MTA, subjects were randomized to four arms: community care (CC), intensive behavioral treatment (Beh), state-of-the-art medication management (Med), and a combination of Beh and Med (Comb). The key initial finding was that for core ADHD symptoms, the Comb and Med treatments were more effective than Beh and CC (i.e., Comb ~ Med > Beh – CC, with an effect size [ES] of 0.50–0.60). Ninety percent of children on Comb and 88% on Med no longer met the full criteria for ADHD at the study end point. Two more recent secondary analyses (one using a composite outcome measure and another using a categorical outcome measure) identified a significant but marginal superiority of Comb over Med in additional to the initial findings (i.e., Comb > Beh ~ CC, with ES = 0.70; and Comb > Med with ES = 0.28).

The difference between Med and CC was striking. Interestingly, two-thirds of CC subjects also took medication. But there were important differences between the community practice and study protocol in medication management. Subjects in the Med arm were given a detailed initial dose titration over 28 days. This was followed by monthly review, with adjustment of dosage, or change of medication if indicated. The prescribing clinicians also contacted the teachers before each monthly review. Adjustments of medication after initial dose titration were common, and only about 30% of the children remained on the initial dose established by initial titration by the end of the 14-month trial period. This means that about 70% of the children needed continuing monitoring and dose adjustment to obtain the optimal treatment response. Interestingly, most of the dose adjustment was toward a higher dosing, especially for those starting on a low and intermediate posttitration dose. Med subjects were on three times daily dosing, with a higher average daily dose (average total daily dose = 32.8 mg) and 12 visits per year; in contrast, CC subjects were on twice daily dosing, with a lower average daily dose (average total daily dose = 18.7 mg) and an average of 2.3 visits per year. It appears that initial dose titration followed by close monitoring and effective dosing with careful adjustment to maintain response over time and to avoid side effects will markedly improve the immediate efficacy of stimulants.

Non-ADHD Symptoms

The study also examined non-ADHD outcome measures. These measures included parent–child relationship, teacher-rated social skills, anxiety/depression symptoms, and oppositional/defiance symptoms as well as academic achievement and functioning. Comb had a small but statistical significant superiority to Beh for (1) academic functioning, (2) WIAT reading scores, (3) controlling internalizing, and (4) oppositional/defiance symptom (with ES range 0.26–0.28). Comb was also superior to CC in improving parent–child relationship, additional to the above four measures. Med was located in between Comb and CC, not statistically different from either. The nonsignificant differences should not be regarded as "no difference" as MTA was designed to have 80% power to detect ES of 0.4 or greater; so any real difference of a magnitude smaller than this ES is less likely to be detected.

Moderators

Factors whose presence alters the likelihood of treatment response are known as moderators. Moderators identified by the MTA were: (1) comorbid anxiety disorder and patterns of comorbidities, (2) socioeconomic status and educational background of the parents, and (3) comorbidity status. These factors were already present prior to the randomization, so the influences of moderators on the outcome of the study are protected by the randomization process. They should be distinguished from "mediators," which are factors that occur after the randomization process, such as clinic attendance, compliance, adherence to treatment, and therapeutic alliance with the therapists; and the latter are thus not protected by the randomization process.

Children with comorbid anxiety are more likely to respond to Beh. That is, Beh appeared more effective than indicated in the primary analyses. First, it diverged from CC, and converged with Med. Second, Comb treatment was also more effective, diverging from Med. Differences in treatment effects were most evident in outcome

measures on (1) parent-reported hyperactivity and inattention, (2) parent–child relationship, and (3) teacher-rated social skills. Perhaps children with anxiety symptoms are biologically more sensitive and hence responsive to conditioning. About 33% of subjects met DSM-III-R criteria for an anxiety disorder excluding simple phobias. Moderating effect of anxiety favors the inclusion of psychosocial treatment for them. This positive effect was also identifiable in parent-reported outcome measures on disruptive behavior, internalizing symptoms, and inattention (March et al., 2000).

Family socioeconomic status (SES) can be fractionated into two independent measures: parental education and parental occupation. The key departures from the primary finding (Comb ~ Med > Beh ~ CC) due to moderating effect of SES were for disruptive behavioral, inattentive, and hyperactive symptoms. For families with a low SES, Comb was more effective than all three other treatments (Comb > Med ~ Beh ~ CC) for oppositional/defiance symptoms only. There is no additional advantage of Comb for ODD symptoms among children from families with higher occupational status. For the high educational status group, Comb is more effective than Med (Comb > Med > Beh ~ CC) for hyperactive and inattentive symptoms. One explanation for these findings is that perhaps ODD symptoms in children from advantageous background were more biologically determined, whereas in children from disadvantageous backgrounds the same symptoms were more attributable to poor parenting. Correcting parenting skills in low SES families thus had a more marked effect than the other group. Second, core ADHD symptoms could be more recalcitrant to behavioral treatment, requiring parents with higher educational backgrounds to implement the program more effectively. In recommending treatment, clinicians should identify target symptoms and familial characteristics and offer the optimal intervention plan accordingly (Rieppi et al., 2002).

Finally, the presence of comorbid conditions also moderates treatment response. Jensen, Hinshaw, Kraemer, et al. (2001) found that the presence of anxiety symptoms (ANX) with ADHD regardless of CD status increased the likelihood of response to behavioral treatment.

ANX status confers benefits on ADHD children regardless of the presence of oppositional defiance/conduct disorder symptoms (ODD/CD). Its presence exerted ameliorating effects on concurrent ODD/CD (i.e., ADHD + ANX + ODD/CD vs. ADHD + ODD/CD). As a simple rule for predicting treatment response, ADHD plus ANX subjects were likely to respond to any of the three treatments: behavioral alone, medication alone, and combination of medication and behavioral intervention. In other words, all interventions are likely to be effective for them. In contrast, ADHD only and ADHD plus ODD/CD subjects usually responded only to interventions that included medication. That is, for these two groups, medication appeared especially indicated, and behavioral intervention alone seemed contraindicated. However, for the doubly comorbid group with ADHD plus ANX plus ODD/CD, combination interventions appeared to offer substantial advantages over other treatments.

In summary, the MTA study identified that management with state-of-the-art medication alone is—at least over 14 months—more effective than conventional medication management and behavioral management combined. The additional benefit of combination treatment should be reserved for special cases, such as children with double comorbidities (ADHD + ANX + CD/ODD) and children from low SES background with severe ODD/CD symptoms. Children with comorbid anxiety disorder can be given behavioral management as the first line of treatment, especially if they are from high SES background and targeted for inattentive and hyperactive symptoms. Behavioral treatment alone is not as effective for children with ADHD only and ADHD plus CD (but of course some families will prefer the option, knowing that adverse effects are probably less likely in behavioral treatment). Treatment should be tailored according to the psychosocial and clinical profiles of a child. There is no single treatment strategy that would confer universal benefits for all subtypes of ADHD.

The 3- and 8-year follow-ups of the MTA subjects have, however, found no superiority of the intensively medicated group to that receiving only behavioral approaches or, indeed, to the routinely treated community control group. The practical conclusions of this equifinality can be argued over. Some will say that this calls for extending intensity of treatment delivery over a longer time span. Others will consider that equifinality is only to be expected, given that randomization stopped at the 14-month point. The self-selection that followed would mean that families chose whichever therapy was best for them, and would imply that they mostly chose wisely. The main implication for this chapter is that a period, even as long as 14 months, in which symptoms are intensively controlled is not sufficient to promote resilience.

Resilience, Stimulant Treatment, and Subsequent Substance Abuse

Data from more than 200 randomized clinical trials have consistently found stimulants an effective treatment for children and adults with ADHD. One study reported that childhood treatment with stimulants for ADHD increased the risk for subsequent cigarette smoking and nicotine and cocaine dependence in adulthood (Lambert & Hartsough, 1998). This study received much media attention, and public concerns have been raised whether early exposure to stimulant medication predisposes to subsequent substance abuse and dependency.

This study, however, represents the only study so far reporting such an association. Twelve other studies have not found evidence that childhood-stimulant treatment for ADHD leads to an increased risk for substance experimentation, use, dependence, or abuse by adulthood. Wilens, Faraone, Biederman, and Gunawardene (2003) conducted a meta-analysis on six of the larger published studies, two studies with follow-up in adolescence and four in young adulthood. The analysis comprised 674 medicated and 360 unmedicated subjects. The combined estimate of the odds ratio using random-effect meta-analysis indicated a 1.9-fold reduction in risk (95% CI 1.1–3.6) for SUD for those exposed to childhood-stimulant treatment compared with those not exposed. The age effect showed that studies with follow-up into adolescence showed a greater protective effect (OR 5.8) than studies with follow-up to adulthood (OR 1.4). It was possible that the extended follow-up period to adulthood increased the likelihood of exposure to drug experimentation and hence misuse. Alternatively, this might be due to higher dropout in stimulant treatment in early adulthood, leading to loss of risk protection. However, data on duration of exposure to pharmacotherapy were not available and did not allow further analysis to test the hypothesis. Another explanation was that enhanced parental supervision for youths receiving medication might have confounded the analysis.

Furthermore, there were major methodological problems with the study by Lambert et al. They found that stimulant treatment increased the risk of subsequent drug use in young adults. In particular, they found that exposure to earlier stimulant treatment was linearly related to nicotine and cocaine abuse, with similar trends to alcohol abuse. There were, however, significant differences on baseline characteristics between the medicated and unmedicated subjects, conduct disorder was overrepresented in the medicated group. Prospective studies have consistently identified conduct disorder as a major risk factor for the development of SUD among ADHD subjects. Conduct disorder, therefore, represents an important confounder in their analysis, which was likely to give rise to a false association. Overall, the evidence indicates no harmful association between childhood exposure to stimulant treatment to ADHD and subsequent substance abuse in adolescence and adulthood. There is evidence from the pooled estimates derived from meta-analysis to suggest that effective treatment reduces the risk of subsequent substance abuse, and thus confers resilience.

Conclusion

This review of available published literature suggests that resilience is related to characteristics of the child, family, and environment. Aggression, low frustration tolerance, severity, and persistence of ADHD symptoms appear to increase risks of later maladjustment in the child. Urban dwelling, poor parental control, a high level of expressed

emotions, and the presence of parental psychopathologies also increase risks. The presence of conduct problems in conjunction with ADHD represents a particularly strong predictor of adverse outcome, in terms of subsequent antisocial behaviors, social and occupational impairments, substance abuse, antisocial personality disorders, and associated mood problems. Positive endowments such as high IQ, emotional stability, minimal impairments of functioning, and favorable family background with the presence of supportive adults all confer resilience. Symptom reduction, associated with either a desisting hyperactive symptom trajectory or response to treatment, predicts better outcomes. Behavioral modifications can sometimes be enough in themselves, in milder cases, without recourse to medication: given without medication they can be helpful particularly for preschool children, children with anxiety symptoms, and children with very resourceful parents. They are nearly always desirable *in conjunction with* medication, and especially for comorbid children and those in disadvantaged families. Strengths and skills development by cognitive methods alone have not been shown to confer protection against social impairment. Social skills training however (together with parent training and the use of behaviorally oriented recreational camps) has received support in controlled trials (reviewed by Fabiano et al., 2009). The use of "neurofeedback" in training components of the EEG has also obtained recent trial evidence (Arns, De Ridder, Strehl, Breteler, & Coenen, 2009). The role of genetic and environmental contributions to resilience is likely to represent an area of expanding research interest, and may well generate new ideas about what the targets of intervention should be.

References

Akeman, P., Dykman, R., & Peters, J. (1977). Teenage status of hyperactive and non hyperactive learning disabled boys. *The American Journal of Orthopsychiatry, 47,* 577–596.
Arns, M., De Ridder, S., Strehl, U., Breteler, M., & Coenen, A. (2009). Efficacy of neurofeedback treatment in ADHD: The effects on inattention, impulsivity

and hyperactivity: A meta-analysis. *Clinical EEG and Neuroscience, 40*(3), 180–189.

Barkley, R. (1997). *ADHD and the nature of self-control.* New York: Guilford.

Barkley, R. A., & Fischer, M. (2010). The unique contribution of emotional impulsiveness to impairment in major life activities in hyperactive children as adults. *Journal of the American Academy of Child and Adolescent Psychiatry, 49*(5), 503–513.

Biederman, J., Faraone, S., Milberger, S., Curtis, S., Chen, I., Marrs, A., et al. (1996). Predictors of persistence and remission of ADHD into adolescence: Results from a four-year prospective follow-up study. *Journal of the American Academy of Child and Adolescent Psychiatry, 35*(3), 343–351.

Biederman, J., Faraone, S. V., Mick, E., Spencer, T., Wilens, T., Kiely, K., et al. (1995). High risk for attention deficit hyperactivity disorder among children of parents with childhood onset of the disorder: A pilot study. *The American Journal of Psychiatry, 152*(3), 431–435.

Biederman, J., Mick, E., & Faraone, S. V. (1998). Normalized functioning in youths with persistent attention deficit/hyperactivity disorder. *Journal of Pediatrics, 133*(4), 544–551.

Biederman, J., Mick, E., & Faraone, S. V. (2000). Age-dependent decline of symptoms of attention deficit hyperactivity disorder: Impact of remission definition and symptom type. *The American Journal of Psychiatry, 757*(5), 816–818.

Biederman, J., Wilens, T. E., Mick, E., Faraone, S. V., & Spencer, T. (1998). Does attention-deficit hyperactivity disorder impact the developmental course of drug and alcohol abuse and dependence? *Biological Psychiatry, 44*(4), 269–273.

Brooks, R., & Goldstein, S. (2001). *Raising resilient children.* New York: Contemporary Books.

Caspi, A., Sugden, K., Moffitt, T. E., Taylor, A., Craig, I. W., Harrington, H., et al. (2003). Influence of life stress on depression: Moderation by a polymorphism in the 5-HTT gene. *Science, 301*(5631), 386–389.

Castellanos, F. X., & Tannock, R. (2002). Neuroscience of attention-deficit/hyperactivity disorder: The search for endophenotypes. *Nature Reviews Neuroscience, 3*(8), 617–628.

Dienske, H., de Jonge, G., & Sanders-Woudstra, J. A. R. (1985). Quantitative criteria for attention and activity in child psychiatric patients. *Journal of Child Psychology and Psychiatry, 26*, 895–916.

Fabiano, G. A., Pelham, W. E., Jr., Coles, E. K., Gnagy, E. M., Chronis-Tuscano, A., & O'Connor, B. C. (2009). A meta-analysis of behavioural treatments for attention-deficit/hyperactivity disorder. *Clinical Psychology Review, 29*, 129–140.

Faraone, S. V., Biederman, J., Jetton, J. G., & Tsuang, M. T. (1997). Attention deficit disorder and conduct disorder: Longitudinal evidence for a familial subtype. *Psychological Medicine, 27*(2), 291–300.

Faraone, S. V., Biederman, J., & Mick, E. (2006). The age-dependent decline of attention deficit hyperactivity disorder: A meta-analysis of follow-up studies. *Psychological Medicine, 36*(2), 159–165.

Farrington, D., Loeger, R., & van Kammen, W. B. (1990). Long-term criminal outcomes of hyperactivity-impulsivity-attention deficit and conduct problems in childhood. In L. Robins & M. Rutter (Eds.), *straight and devious pathways from childhood and adulthood* (pp. 72–73). Cambridge: Cambridge University Press.

Fergusson, D. M., Lynskey, M. T., & Horwood, L. J. (1997). Attentional difficulties in middle childhood and psychosocial outcomes in young adulthood. *Journal of Child Psychology and Psychiatry, 38*(6), 633–644.

Fischer, M., Barkley, R. A., Fletcher, K. E., & Smallish, L. (1993). The adolescent outcome of hyperactive children: Predictors of psychiatric, academic, social, and emotional adjustment. *Journal of the American Academy of Child and Adolescent Psychiatry, 52*(2), 324–332.

Fischer, M., Barkley, R. A., Smallish, L., & Fletcher, K. E. (2002). Young adult follow-up of hyperactive children: Self-reported psychiatric disorders, comorbidity, and the role of childhood conduct problems and teen CD. *Journal of Abnormal Child Psychology, 30*(5), 464–475.

Flory, K., Milich, R., Lynam, D. R., Leukefeld, C., & Clayton, R. (2003). Relation between childhood disruptive behavior disorders and substance use and dependence symptoms in young adulthood: Individuals with symptoms of attention-deficit/hyperactivity disorder and conduct disorder are uniquely at risk. *Psychology of Addictive Behaviors, 17*(2), 151–158.

Gittelman, R., Mannuzza, S., Shenker, R., & Bonagura, N. (1985). Hyperactive boys almost grown up: I. Psychiatric status. *Archives of General Psychiatry, 42*(10), 937–947.

Gupta, R., Kar, B. R., & Srinivasan, N. (2010). Cognitive-motivational deficits in ADHD: Development of a classification system. *Child Neuropsychology, 17*(1), 67–81.

Hart, E. L., Lahey, B. B., Loeber, R., Applegate, B., & Frick, P. J. (1995). Developmental change in attention-deficit hyperactivity disorder in boys: A four-year longitudinal study. *Journal of Abnormal Child Psychology, 23*(6), 729–749.

Hechtman, L. (1991). Resilience and vulnerability in long term outcome of attention deficit hyperactive disorder. *Canadian Journal of Psychiatry, 36*(6), 415–421.

Hechtman, L., Weiss, G., Perlman, T., & Amsel, R. (1984). Hyperactives as young adults: Initial predictors of adult outcome. *Journal of the American Academy of Child Psychiatry, 23*(3), 250–260.

Jensen, R. S., Hinshaw, S. P., Kraemer, H. C., Lenora, N., Newcom, J. H., Abikoff, H. B., et al. (2001). ADHD comorbidity findings from the MTA study: Comparing comorbid subgroups. *Journal of the American Academy of Child and Adolescent Psychiatry, 40*(2), 147–158.

Jensen, P. S., Hinshaw, S. P., Swanson, J. M., Greenhill, L. L., Conners, C. K., Arnold, L. E., et al. (2001). Findings from the NIMH multimodal treatment study of ADHD (MTA): Implications and applications for primary care providers. *Journal of Developmental and Behavioral Pediatrics, 22*(1), 60–73.

Klein, R. G., Abikoff, H., Klass, E., Ganeles, D., Seese, L. M., & Pollack, S. (1997). Clinical efficacy of methylphenidate in conduct disorder with and without attention deficit hyperactivity disorder. *Archives of General Psychiatry, 54*(12), 1073–1080.

Kuntsi, J., Wood, A. C., Rijsdijk, F., Johnson, K. A., Andreou, P., Albrecht, B., et al. (2010). Separation of cognitive impairments in attention-deficit/hyperactivity disorder into 2 familial factors. *Archives of General Psychiatry, 67*(11), 1159–1167.

Lambert, N. M., & Hartsough, C. S. (1998). Prospective study of tobacco smoking and substance dependencies among samples of ADHD and non-ADHD participants. *Journal of Learning Disabilities, 31*(6), 533–544.

Loney, J., Kramer, J., & Milich, R. (1981). The hyperkinetic child grows up: Predictors of symptoms, delinquency and achievement at follow-up. In K. Gadow, J. Loney (Eds.), *Psychosocial aspects of drug treatment for hyperactivity.* AAAS selected symposium.

Lynam, D. R. (1996). Early identification of chronic offenders: Who is the fledgling psychopath? *Psychological Bulletin, 120*(2), 209–234.

Lynskey, M. T., & Hall, W. (2001). Attention deficit hyperactivity disorder and substance use disorders: Is there a causal link. *Addiction, 96*(6), 815–822.

Mannuzza, S., Klein, R. G., Abikoff, H., & Moulton, J. L., III. (2004). Significance of childhood conduct problems to later development of conduct disorder among children with ADHD: A prospective follow-up study. *Journal of Abnormal Child Psychology, 32*(5), 565–573.

Mannuzza, S., Klein, R. G., Bessler, A., Malloy, P., & LaPadula, M. (1993). Adult outcome of hyperactive boys. Educational achievement, occupational rank, and psychiatric status. *Archives of General Psychiatry, 50*(1), 565–576.

Mannuzza, S., Klein, R. G., Konig, P. H., & Gismpino, T. L. (1989). Hyperactive boys almost grown up: IV. Criminality and its relationship to psychiatric status. *Archives of General Psychiatry. 46*(12), 1073–1079.

Mannuzza, S., Klein, R. G., Bessler, A., Malloy, P., & LaPadula, M. (1998). Adult psychiatric status of hyperactive boys grown up. *The American Journal of Psychiatry, 155*(4), 493–498.

Mannuzza, S., Klein, R. G., & Moulton, J. L., III. (2008). Lifetime criminality among boys with attention deficit hyperactivity disorder: A prospective follow-up study into adulthood using official arrest records. *Psychiatry Research, 160*(3), 237–246.

March, J. S., Swanson, J. M., Arnold, L. E., Hoza, B., Conners, C. K., Hinshaw, S. P., et al. (2000). Anxiety as a predictor and outcome variable in the multimodal treatment study of children with ADHD (MTA). *Journal of Abnormal Child Psychology, 28*(6), 527–541.

Mikami, A. Y., & Hinshaw, S. P. (2003). Buffers of peer rejection among girls with and without ADHD: The role of popularity with adults and goal-directed solitary play. *Journal of Abnormal Child Psychology, 31*(4), 381–397.

Mikami, A. Y., & Hinshaw, S. P. (2006). Resilient adolescent adjustment among girls: Buffers of childhood peer rejection and attention-deficit/hyperactivity disorder. *Journal of Abnormal Child Psychology, 34*(6), 825–839.

Milich, R., Loney, J., & Landau, S. (1982). The independent dimensions of hyperactivity and aggression: Evaluation with playroom observation data. *Journal of Abnormal Psychology, 91*, 183–198.

Moffitt, T. E. (1990). Juvenile delinquency and attention deficit disorder: Boys' developmental trajectories from age 3 to 15. *Child Development, 61*, 893–910.

Molina, B. S., & Pelham, W. E., Jr. (2003). Childhood predictors of adolescent substance use in a longitudinal study of children with ADHD. *Journal of Abnormal Psychology, 112*(3), 497–507.

MTA Cooperative Group. (1999). A 14-month randomized clinical trial of treatment strategies for attention deficit/hyperactivity disorder. Multimodal Treatment Study of Children with ADHD. *Archives of General Psychiatry, 56*, 1073–1086.

Nigg, J., Nikolas, M., Friderici, K., Park, L., & Zucker, R. A. (2007). Genotype and neuropsychological response inhibition as resilience promoters for attention-deficit/hyperactivity disorder, oppositional defiant disorder and conduct disorder under conditions of psychosocial adversity. *Development and Psychopathology, 19*(3), 767–786.

Porrino, L. J., Rapoport, J. L., Behar, D., Sceery, W., Ismond, D., & Bunney, W. E. (1983). A naturalistic assessment of the motor activity of hyperactive boys: I. Comparison with normal controls. *Archives of General Psychiatry, 40*, 681–687.

Rasmussen, P., & Gillberg, C. (2000). Natural outcome of ADHD with developmental coordination disorder at age 22 years: A controlled, longitudinal, community-based study. *Journal of the American Academy of Child and Adolescent Psychiatry, 39*(11), 1424–1431.

Rieppi, R., Greenhill, L. L., Ford, R. E., Chuang, S., Wes, M., Davies, M., et al. (2002). Socioeconomic status as a moderator of ADHD treatment outcomes. *Journal of the American Academy of Child and Adolescent Psychiatry, 41*(3), 269–277.

Rutter, M., Maughan, B., Meyer, J., Pickles, A., Silberg, J., Simonoff, E., et al. (1997). Heterogeneity of antisocial behavior: Causes, continuities, and consequences. *Nebraska Symposium on Motivation, 44*, 45–118.

Satterfield, J., Swanson, J., Schell, A., & Lee, F. (1994). Prediction of antisocial behavior in attention-deficit hyperactivity disorder boys from aggression/defiance scores. *Journal of the American Academy of Child and Adolescent Psychiatry, 33*(2), 185–190.

Schachar, R., Rutter, M., & Smith, A. (1981). The characteristics of situationally and pervasively hyperactive children: Implications for syndrome definition. *Journal of Child Psychology and Psychiatry, 22*(4), 375–392.

Schachar, R., Taylor, E., Wieselberg, M., Thorley, G., & Rutter, M. (1987). Changes in family function and relationships in children who respond to methylphenidate. *Journal of the American Academy of Child and Adolescent Psychiatry, 2*(5), 728–732.

Sergeant, J. (2000). The cognitive-energetic model: An empirical approach to attention-deficit hyperactivity disorder. *Neuroscience and Biobehavioral Reviews, 24*, 7–12.

Solanto, M. V., Abikoff, H., Sonuga-Barke, E., Schachar, R., Logan, G. D., Wigal, T., et al. (2001). The ecological validity of delay aversion and response inhibition as measures of impulsivity in AD/HD. *Journal of Abnormal Child Psychology, 29*, 215–228.

Sonuga-Barke, E. J. (2003). The dual pathway model of AD/HD: An elaboration of neuro-developmental characteristics. *Neuroscience and Biobehavioral Reviews, 27*(1), 593–604.

Sonuga-Barke, E. J., Taylor, E., & Heptinstall, E. (1992). Hyperactivity and delay aversion—II. The effect of self versus externally imposed stimulus presentation periods on memory. *Journal of Child Psychology and Psychiatry, 33*(2), 399–409.

Sonuga-Barke, E. J., Taylor, E., Sembi, S., & Smith, J. (1992). Hyperactivity and delay aversion—I. The effect of delay on choice. *Journal of Child Psychology and Psychiatry, 33*(2), 387–398.

Strayhom, J. M., Jr. (2002a). Self-control: Theory and research. *Journal of the American Academy of Child and Adolescent Psychiatry, 41*(1), 7–16.

Strayhom, J. M., Jr. (2002b). Self-control: Toward systematic training programs. *American Academy of Child and Adolescent Psychiatry, 41*(1), 17–27.

Taylor, E. (1995). Dysfunctions of attention. In D. Cicchetti & D. J. Cohen (Eds.), *Developmental psychopathology* (Risk, disorder, and adaptation, Vol. 2, pp. 243–273). New York: Wiley.

Taylor, E. (1999). Disorders of volition in childhood. In C. Williams & A. Sims (Eds.), *Disorders of volition and action in psychiatry* (pp. 229–247). London: Gaskell.

Taylor, E., Chadwick, O., Heptinstall, E., & Danckaerts, M. (1996). Hyperactivity and conduct problems as risk factors for adolescent development. *Journal of the American Academy of Child and Adolescent Psychiatry, 35*, 1213–1226.

Thaper, A., Harrington, R., & McGuffin, P. (2001). Examining the comorbidity of ADHD-related behaviours and conduct problems using a twin study design. *The British Journal of Psychiatry, 179*, 224–229.

Van der Meere, J. J. (2002). The role of attention in hyperactivity disorders. In S. Sandberg (Ed.), *Hyperactivity and attention disorders of childhood* (pp. 162–171). Cambridge: Cambridge University Press.

Weiss, G., Hechtman, L., Milroy, T., & Perlman, T. (1985). Psychiatric status of hyperactives as adults: A controlled prospective 15 year follow-up of 63 hyperactive children. *Journal of the American Academy of Child Psychiatry, 23*, 211–220.

Weiss, G., Hechtman, L., Perlman, T., Hopkins, J., & Werner, A. (1979). Hyperactives as young adults: A controlled prospective ten-year follow-up of 75 children. *Archives of General Psychiatry, 36*, 675–681.

Weiss, G., Minde, K., Werry, S. J., Douglas, V., & Neneth, E. (1971). The hyperactive child. VII: Five-year followup. *Archives of General Psychiatry, 24*, 409–414.

Wilens, T. E., Biederman, J., & Mick, E. (1998). Does ADHD affect the course of substance abuse? Findings from a sample of adults with and without ADHD. *The American Journal on Addictions, 7*(2), 156–163.

Wilens, T. E., Faraone, S. V., Biederman, J., & Gunawardene, S. (2003). Does stimulant therapy of attention deficit/hyperactivity disorder beget later substance abuse? A meta-analytic review of the literature. *Pediatrics, 111*(1), 179–185.

Wilmshurst, L., Peele, M., & Wilmshurst, L. (2011). Resilience and well-being in college students with and without a diagnosis of ADHD. *Journal of Attention Disorders, 15*(1), 11–17.

Part IV

Assessment

Measuring Resilience in Children: From Theory to Practice*

Jack A. Naglieri, Paul A. LeBuffe, and Katherine M. Ross

Introduction

The concept of resilience, like all psychological constructs, must have certain characteristics in order to be subjected to experimental testing so as to be effectively applied to benefit our constituency. A primary characteristic is that resilience must be operationally defined in a way that is reliable across time, subjects, and researchers. Once a concept is operationalized in a reliable manner, then its validity can be examined. When we have sufficiently operationalized the concept of resilience, and there is evidence that it can be measured in

_____

*We write this chapter in order to provide essential information about measurement of resilience and the tools that are currently available for that purpose. It is important for the reader to recognize that the first two authors of this chapter are authors of several of the scales included here. In order to provide as complete a view as possible of all the scales currently available for measuring protective factors, we also included scales developed by other authors. We have, therefore, limited any evaluative comments about these scales but do provide a factual presentation of their characteristics. It is our expectation that this information will provide readers sufficient information to arrive at their own conclusions regarding the relative advantages and disadvantages of these tools.

J.A. Naglieri (✉)
University of Virginia,
Charlottesville, VA, USA
e-mail: jnaglieri@gmail.com

P.A. LeBuffe • K.M. Ross
Devereux Center for Resilient Children, Villanova, PA, USA
e-mail: plebuffe@Devereux.org; kross@devereux.org

a reliable and valid way, then application in clinical and educational settings becomes possible. This is an ideal sequence for the development tools for testing new concepts, but it is not how many concepts and tests used in education and psychology have been promulgated.

In practice, there is great emphasis on helping clients and pressure to implement new approaches even if they have only been minimally tested. If an idea appears logical and appears to help clients then it seems reasonable to believe that the construct possesses validity, however ill-defined that may be. Unfortunately, what seems logical and consistent with clinical experience may not be true. As noted by Garb (2003, p. 32), "Results from empirical studies reveal that it can be surprisingly difficult for mental health professionals to learn from clinical experience." This sobering point suggests that we should weigh empirical findings more heavily than clinical experience not vice versa. Science should temper enthusiasm. This is especially true when a new approach to treatment or a new concept is introduced.

There is a natural and desirable interplay between scientific research and applied practice in psychology because of the very nature of the field. We can assume that ultimately the field will advance because of the mutual respect and collaboration of those that emphasize science more than practice, and practice more than research. The need for the balanced contribution of science and practice is well illustrated by the study of factors related to resilience. Clearly, this area of study has benefited from the outstanding contributions made by those professionals whose goal has been to help children and adults survive and thrive in the face of adversity and by those researchers who have studied the complex interrelationships of variables that may be predictive of good outcome. All of these individuals, however, must be able to clearly define their constructs and measure them reliably before the validity of the concept can be assessed. That is the focus of this chapter— the challenge of reliable and valid measurement of factors related to resilience.

Resilience: Measurement Issues

Defining the Concept: What Is Resilience?

Although resilience has been studied and described since the 1950s, it has been only in about the past 2 decades that some consistency has emerged in the definition of this construct. Most contemporary researchers now agree that resilience refers to positive outcomes, adaptation or the attainment of developmental milestones or competencies in the face of significant risk, adversity, or stress. As Masten (2001) points out, the claim of resilience in an individual requires two judgments. First, that the individual has been exposed to significant risk or adversity and, second, that the individual has attained at least typical or normal developmental outcomes.

The paradigm for resilience research therefore consists first of enumerating or measuring the risks and sources of adversity in individuals' lives. Two general approaches have been used to ascertain and measure risk. The *major life events* approach focuses on episodic, highly traumatic events such as the death or divorce of a parent. Typically, major life events are measured using checklists that assess a wide range of traumatic events that have occurred in the individual's lifetime. Examples include the *Sources of Stress Inventory* (Chandler, 1981) or the *Life Events Checklist* (Work, Cowen, Parker, & Wyman, 1990).

Although major life events are clearly important sources of risk and adversity, a reliance on this approach in isolation has been criticized as incomplete. To gain a more complete picture of risk and adversity, a measure of daily hassles is recommended. Daily hassles denotes sources of risk that have lower acuity, but greater chronicity when compared to major life events. Examples for young children might include frequent changes in caregivers, poor quality childcare, and inconsistent or overly harsh discipline. The *Daily Hassles Scale* (Kanner, Coyne, Schaefer, & Lazarus, 1981) is a good example of this approach.

After having ascertained the risk in an individual's life, developmental outcomes can be assessed. This may consist of the attainment of developmental milestones or the accomplishment of major developmental tasks within normal limits. Positive outcome has also been characterized as the absence of psychopathology in an at-risk population. If the individual has attained typical or superior outcomes in the presence of risk or adversity, then resilience is inferred.

Challenges in Measuring Resilience

Measurement of those variables that allow some children to cope successfully with adversities in their lives is not simple. This is especially so because resilience is assessed on an inferential basis by an examination of risk and positive adaptation factors (Luthar & Zelazo, 2003). Resilience is an outcome, rather than a psychological construct in and of itself that can be defined and, perhaps, measured. This has led to efforts to identify variables that lead to, and therefore, can be used to predict, resilience rather than measuring it directly. These factors that lead to resilient outcomes are referred to as protective factors and are defined as characteristics or processes that moderate or buffer the negative effects of stress resulting in more positive behavioral and psychological outcomes than would have been expected in their absence (Masten & Garmezy, 1985). Rather than measuring resilience per se, assessments have instead focused on measuring these protective factors that predict resilience.

Further complicating the situation is the fact that researchers in this field (e.g., Werner, 2005; Wright & Masten, 2005) have found that risk and protective factors occur at multiple levels including the community (e.g., dangerous neighborhoods/ quality after school programs), the family (e.g., domestic violence/effective parenting), and characteristics of the child (e.g., difficult temperament/good coping skills). Although resilience is a function of the complex interaction of these multiple level protective and risk factors, and therefore, most likely is a multivariate construct, most assessments have focused only on the personal characteristics, often referred to as "within-child" protective factors. Moreover, this complex interaction may differ from person to person; that is, the impact of risk factors and the protection afforded by specific protective factors may be very person-specific. As an example, being part of a faith community is widely regarded as an important protective factor, yet the impact of a faith life in moderating risk and adversity differs from person to person. Given this complexity, how can these variables be reliably measured? How can these variables be aggregated to yield a reliable predictor of resilience?

Measurement of the wide variety of variables used to study resilience in children has been accomplished using a variety of experimental methods as well as formal and informal tests, including both standardized and unstandardized methods. The list ranges from published behavior rating and self-concept scales to informal ratings based on clinical criteria; sociometric ratings to social skills rating scales; tests of achievement to yearly grades and IQ test results; parent interviews to parenting quality questionnaires; and positive and negative emotionality, to name just a few. The field is awash in variables that have been studied. It appears that measures of most of the major psychological and educational constructs have been included in one study or another as putative protective factors. It leads one to ask the question: "What has *not* been included in the study of protective and risk factors?" Is there any variable or variables that are *unique* to this line of research?

The inclusion of such a wide variety of variables used to assess the potential for resilience suggests that researches have taken a case study approach to the research question. The typical list of measures of protective factors reads like a psychological report that includes major areas such as the child's history (physical attributes); status of the home environment (socioeconomic status, parents, siblings, etc.); current academic performance (class grades, standardized achievement test scores); intelligence test scores, behavioral and emotional status (parent and teacher rating scales, interviews, measures of self-concept, clinical classifications). The goal of casting such a broad net has been to determine which of these many variables are most important. This assessment, however, is complicated by the fact that not all of these variables share equal psychometric qualities.

The use of both formal and informal measures of protective factors offers a means of studying the field but the disadvantage of leading to inconsistencies within and across research investigations. For example, social status can be assessed using interviews, unstandardized questionnaires, and peer nominations but the extent to which such methods can be reliably reproduced by other researchers should also be studied. Moreover, the transition from research setting to practical application will require more refined instrumentation than is currently available to practitioners. While these methods may assist in the development of the research base for the study of resilience, well developed, reliable and valid measures are required if the important theoretical contributions made thus far can be utilized in applied settings so that children and other consumers may benefit.

In order to advance instrumentation and measurement in the field of resilience, we will present some suggestions to researchers and practitioners. In the sections that follow, we will discuss some basic measurement issues and illustrate their relevance to clinical practice. Our emphasis is on the application of concepts of resilience by child-serving professionals including both teachers and mental health professionals.

How a Test of Resilience Could Be Developed

Development of a system for measuring variables related to resilience is a task that requires important and well-established test development procedures be followed. The many methods and issues are amply described, for example, by Crocker and Algina (1986), Nunnally and Bernstein (1994), and Thorndike (1982). Essentially, the typical test development process involves a series of steps designed to yield a defensible and usable measure of a construct or constructs. The process begins with a clear operational definition of the construct or constructs to be measured. This means that all variables of interest must be defined with such clarity that they can be evaluated via some method, be that a rating scale, observational method, or performance test. In the area of resilience, concepts such as sociability, negative affectivity, adaptability, self-referent social cognitions, which have been invoked to explain or understand resilience, would have to be defined with clarity because without a clear definition, hopes for reliable and valid measurement would be difficult at best. Definitional clarity is the sine-qua-non for the development of psychometrically sound assessment measures and approaches. This requirement is made considerably more difficult because of the evolving nature of the field of resilience.

After clearly defining the construct or constructs to be measured, the next step is the development of an initial pool of items to measure those constructs, followed by pilot testing of the items. A key consideration at this stage is adequate sampling of the various behaviors related to the construct under consideration to ensure adequate breadth of coverage, that is, content validity. The items also need to be clear, one-dimensional (that is, describe only one behavior) and, to the extent possible, free of cultural bias. The subsequent pilot tests are designed to evaluate the clarity of the items as well as the general approach to obtaining scores. At this initial stage the ways the items are presented on the page, size of the fonts, clarity of the directions, colors used on the form, position of the items on the sheet of paper, and so on, are considered. Questions like reliability and validity are not usually examined at this point because sample size typically precludes adequate examination of such questions. The goal of pilot testing is very simple—to quickly and efficiently determine if the form seems to work, if the users understand what they need to do, are we on the right track?

The next step is to conduct experiments with larger samples that allow for an examination of the psychometric qualities of the items and their correspondence to the constructs of interest. This phase is repeated until the author has sufficient confidence that the items and the scales have been adequately operationalized and the constructs adequately sampled. In each of the many iterations, experimental evidence is used to answer questions such as:

- What is the mean and standard deviation (SD) of each item?
- Do items designed to measure the same construct correlate with each other?
- Do items designed to measure the same construct correlate with other items designed to measure that same construct at higher levels than they correlate with items designed to measure different constructs?
- What is the internal reliability of those items organized to measure each construct?
- What effect does elimination of each item have on the reliability of the scale on which it is temporarily included?
- What is the factor structure of the set of items and how can item elimination be used to clarify the factor structure?
- Does the scale seem to have validity (defined in a number of different ways)?

This phase, sometimes referred to as a "tryout" stage is repeated until the scale has demonstrated at least minimally acceptable reliability and validity to warrant proceeding with standardization. The number of actual data collection efforts depends on the quality of the original concepts, the quality of the initial pool of items, the quality of the sampling used to obtain the data used to examine these questions, and the results that are found. The goal is to produce a version that is ready to be subjected to large-scale national standardization. The idea is that the cost of standardization is so great that the current status of the instrument must be of high enough quality that the risk of the final assessment failing to meet demonstrates adequate reliability and validity is greatly reduced.

The next to the last step in development of a measure for use in clinical settings is standardization and data collection to establish the reliability and validity of the final measure. This process first requires that a sample of persons who represent the population with whom the measure will be used is administered the measure so that (a) a final group of items and scales is determined and (b) normative values can be computed. Typically, this is a nationally representative sample. Development of norms is an art as much as a science and there are several ways in which this task can be accomplished (see Crocker & Algina, 1986; Nunnally & Bernstein, 1994; Thorndike, 1982). The second task at this stage is collection of data for the purpose of establishing reliability (internal, test–retest, inter-rater, intra-rater) and validity (construct, criterion, and content, for example). Of these two, validity is clearly the more difficulty psychometric quality to assess.

There are many types of validity and, therefore, validity is not established by any single study. According to the Standards for Educational and Psychologist Testing (AERA, APA, & NCME, 1999) evidence for validity "integrates various strands of evidence into a coherent account of the degree to which existing evidence and theory support the intended interpretation of test scores for specific uses" (p. 17). It is important to note that it is not the test that is valid (as is commonly thought) but rather the interpretations and uses of test scores. In other words, the authors of the assessment have to demonstrate that the inferences about the construct (e.g., the strength of the individual's protective factors) and the decisions that are made (e.g., the individual is at risk) based on the interpretive guidelines presented in the manual are supported by evidence. That book provides 24 standards that relate to validity issues that should be addressed by test developers. This includes, for example, the need to provide evidence:

- That evidence exists to support interpretations based on the scores the instrument yields
- About the internal structure of the test
- About the organization of scales and composites within a test
- Of the relationship between the scores the instrument yields and one or more criterion variables
- For the utility of the measure across a wide variety of demographic groups or its limitations thereof
- That the measure differentiates between groups as intended

This list represents some of the issues that need to be addressed and is not intended to describe all the issues that should be examined. In the field of resilience, we believe that there are some particularly salient validity issues. For example, can variables related to resilience be operationalized into some measurable system? How effective is the measure for differentiating between children who are at risk and those who are not? How many variables need to be measured to maximally predict resilience? Is a combination of variables related to protective factors in the environment, the family, and the child, the best way to predict resilience? Do protective factors enhance outcomes only for children who are at significant risk, or all children? Can the extensive lists of child protective factors be reduced to a few key characteristics that predict which children may be resilient? The answers to these questions will help define the future of this field.

Once development of an instrument is completed then the important task of documentation begins. There is wide variation in the extent to which test authors document the development, standardization, reliability, and validity, of their measure. Some test manuals provide little if any information of the types we have described above, others provide ample descriptions. We refer the reader to examples such as the Kaufman Assessment Battery for Children—Second Edition (Kaufman & Kaufman, 2004), the Devereux Student Strength Assessment (LeBuffe, Shapiro, & Naglieri, 1999), and the Cognitive Assessment System (Naglieri & Das, 1997). We use these examples because not only do these authors provide detailed discussion of the various phases of development, but they provide extensive discussion of how the tests should be used and the scores the tests yield interpreted.

Development of a measure does not end with the writing of the sections in the manual that describe the development, standardization, and reliability/validity of the instrument. The authors have the added responsibility to inform the users about how the scores can be used to enhance practice and improve outcomes for the individual being assessed (AERA, APA, & NCME, 1999). This may include how the scores on various scales should be compared with one another and with scores from other tests (if appropriate) to gain a better understanding of the relative strengths and needs of the individual. Increasingly important in this era of evidence-based practice is guidance on the use of scale scores from pretests and posttests to document growth, change, or response to treatment in the individual. It is essential that the authors provide the users with the values needed for determining significance when the various scores a measure provides are compared. The test manuals should provide a thorough discussion of interpretive methods to guide the practitioner. This will enable the user to interpret the scores from an instrument in a manner that is consistent with the intent of the authors and the reliability and validity evidence that was accumulated.

The Importance of Psychometric Characteristics

Why Reliability Matters

Good reliability is essential for all measurements used for research as well as in applied settings to ensure accuracy. Reliability is important to the practitioner because it reflects the amount of error in the measurement. Recall that any obtained score is comprised of the true score plus error (Crocker & Algina, 1986). Because we can never directly determine the true score, we describe it on the basis of a range of values within which the person's score likely falls with a particular level of probability. The size of the range is determined by the reliability of the measurement with higher reliability resulting in smaller ranges. This is why in practice we say, for example, that a child earned an IQ of 105 (±5); meaning that there is a 90% likelihood that the child's true IQ score falls within the range of 100–110 (105 ± 5). The range of scores (called the confidence interval) is computed by first obtaining the standard error of measurement (SEM) from the reliability coefficient and the standard deviation (SD) of the score in the following formula (Crocker & Algina, 1986):

$$SEM = SD \times \sqrt{1 - \text{reliability}}$$

The SEM is considered the average standard deviation (68% of the normal curve is in this range) of the theoretical distribution of a person's scores around the true score. Thus, if we add and subtract 1 SEM from an obtained score, we can say that there is a 68% chance (the percentage of scores contained within ± 1 SD) that the person's true score is contained within that range. Recall that 68% of cases in a normal distribution fall within +1 and −1 standard deviation. Second, the SEM is multiplied by a z value of, for example 1.64 or 1.96, to obtain a confidence interval at the 90 or 95% levels, respectively. The resulting value is added to and subtracted from the obtained score to yield the confidence interval. For example, the 95% confidence range for a test score with a reliability of 0.95 and an obtained score of 100 is 93 (100−7) to 107 (100+7). It is important to note that the higher the reliability the smaller the interval of scores that can be expected to include the child's true score. The smaller the range, the more precise practitioners can be in their interpretation of the results, resulting in more accurate decisions regarding the child. The relationships between reliability and confidence intervals are provided in Fig. 14.1 for T-scores ($M=50$; SD=10) and IQ scores ($M=100$; SD=15).

The SEM is, of course, most important when individual decisions are made because the larger the SEM the more likely scores will differ as a function of low reliability. The lower the reliability, the more likely there will be disparity among scores, for example on a variety of measures of protective factors. These inconsistent results can complicate the interpretation of findings and make a clear understanding of a child's strengths and needs more difficult. Without reliable measures of strengths and needs, planning effective support strategies or interventions becomes problematic and ultimately child outcomes may be adversely impacted.

Reliability of specific scores also influences the comparisons among scores. For example, if a researcher or practitioner is concerned with determining if a particular protective factor score received by a child is significantly higher than the scores received on other protective factor scales and therefore represents a significant strength for

Fig. 14.1 Relationship between reliability and confidence intervals

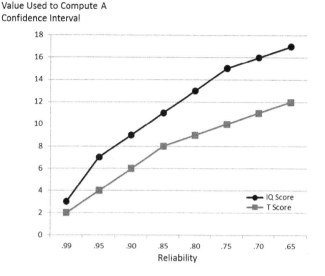

Value Used to Compute A Confidence Interval

Fig. 14.2 Differences required for significance when comparing IQ or *T*-scores based on scale reliability

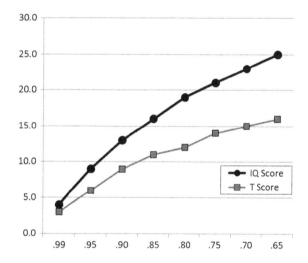

the child, the ability to make that determination is directly related to each factor's reliability coefficient because the calculation of the SEM is based on the reliability. In fact, the formula for the difference between two scores earned by an individual is calculated using the SEM of each score.

$$\text{Difference} = Z \times \sqrt{\text{SEM } 1^2 + \text{SEM } 2^2}$$

Applying this formula to IQ test scores and *T*-scores as shown in Fig. 14.2, we see that as the reliability goes down, the differences needed when comparing two scores increase dramatically. This means that scores from measures with

reliability of 0.70 from two different teachers would have to differ by 15 points to be significant at the 95% level. This means that test scores with higher reliability reduce the influence of *measurement error* on the different scores. Clearly, in both research and clinical settings, variables with high reliability are needed.

How Much Reliability Is Needed?

Bracken (1987) provided suggested thresholds for acceptable levels of test reliability. He suggested that individual variables should have at least an internal reliability estimate of 0.80 or greater and total scales an internal consistency of 0.90 or greater. These guidelines should be further considered in light of the decisions being made. For example, if a score is used for screening purposes where over identification is preferred to under identification, a 0.80 reliability standard for a total score may be acceptable. If, however, important decisions are made, for example, dealing with special educational placement, then a higher (e.g., 0.95) standard should be deemed more appropriate (Nunnally & Bernstein, 1994).

In summary, it is advisable that researchers and clinicians who examine scores from measures of protective factors look for scores that have internal reliability estimates of 0.80 or higher and composite scores comprised of several variables that have an internal reliability estimates of 0.90 or greater. If a rating scale's score has not been constructed to meet these requirements, then its inclusion in research and applied practice should be questioned. This is particularly important because the extent to which two variables can reliably correlate is influenced by the reliability of each variable. Clinicians are advised not to use measures that do not meet these standards because there will be too much error in the measurement to allow for confidence in the result. This is especially important because the decisions clinicians make can have significant impact on the life of a child. We therefore urge the reader to carefully examine the reliability findings of any tool they choose to use.

Why Validity Matters

Validity refers to the extent to which empirical evidence and theory supports the recommended uses and interpretations of scores derived from an assessment. Researchers who study resilience are faced with the first responsibility of carefully and clearly defining the construct they intend to evaluate. Given the inferential nature of the study of resilience, one of the greatest validity questions concerns which variables are associated with or predictive of resilience and how is the relevance

of each variable demonstrated. Much of the research conducted in this area has attempted to examine these issues to varying degrees. The field has increasingly focused on identifying those variables that predict resilience in the face of adversity.

Validity of a measure of resilience is, therefore, more complicated than demonstrating the validity of an achievement test or measure of depression, for example. The number of variables that has been examined is substantial, there is considerable inconsistency in the psychometric quality of the variables studied, and the research on the relative importance of the many variables is still evolving. This makes for an exciting area of research but one that clinicians should approach with appropriate cautions.

Our view is that practitioners have a responsibility to use measures that have been developed in the manner we have briefly outlined above and that nonstandardized approaches should be avoided. We believe that the quality of the decisions made based on any assessment tool is directly related to the quality of the assessments themselves. Responsible practitioners should be aware of the psychometric attributes of any tools that are used. We will, therefore, discuss the psychometric characteristics of a number of measures available to practitioners so that the relative advantages and limitations of the tools can be understood.

Tools to Measure Variables Related to Resilience

The assessment of factors related to resilience in clinical practice is in its early stages. Although informal, nonstandardized tests and procedures are valuable as initial approaches to assessment, they lack the needed research and development base as well as norms calibrated on a representative national standardization sample to make them useful in research and defensible in practice. To assist educational and clinical professionals who would like to incorporate the assessment of resilience in their professional practice, we provide a review of the tools currently available for this purpose that meet certain criteria. To be included in this listing, the evaluation tools must: (1) be published so as to be readily available to practitioners, (2) be a standardized, norm-referenced tool, (3) have a technical manual or other accessible source of psychometric information including standardization sample, reliability and validity, (4) be intended for use with children, defined as birth to 18 years. The tools that met these criteria are presented in alphabetical order.

Ages and Stages Questionnaire: Social Emotional

Purpose: The Ages and Stages Questionnaire: Social Emotional (ASQ-SE; Squires, Bricker, & Twombly, 2002) was developed for early identification and remediation of social and emotional deficits in young children. The ASQ-SE was designed for cost-effective large-scale screening of children aged 6–60 months. There are separate questionnaires for each 6-month age interval. The main purpose of the ASQ-SE is to act as a screening test, but, according to the authors, it can also be used to monitor progress, plan for intervention, and conduct research within a comprehensive community-based program.

Scale description: Each of the eight ASQ-SE questionnaires is designed for a specific age range. The number of questions ranges from 22 to 36 depending on the age. The ASQ-SE items cover seven concepts: self-regulation, compliance, communication, adaptive functioning, autonomy, affect, and interaction with people. There is also a section to identify general concerns and comments. Responses are calibrated using a multiple point format (*most of the time*, *sometimes*, or *never or rarely*). The rater can also indicate if a particular item is of particular concern. The ASQ-SE yields a total raw score, by adding the item scores; a high score is problematic. Children who receive a total score above a recommended cut-off should be referred for further evaluation. The ASQ-SE can only be completed by a parent rater. The reading level is that of a fifth to sixth grader (Squires, Bricker, & Twombly, 2003).

Psychometric characteristics: The ASQ-SE was standardized on a sample of 2,633 children with approximately 175 cases in each age group. Cronbach's alpha coefficient was reported to range from 0.67 to 0.91. The level of agreement between the total scores over two time intervals (1–3 weeks) was reported as 94%. The overall sensitivity (the ability to accurately identify children with social–emotional disabilities) was reported as 78%. The authors also measured the utility of the ASQ-SE by surveying parents. The results indicated that 97% of parents thought the assessment was "easy to understand and appropriate" (Squires et al., 2003).

Behavioral and Emotional Rating Scale

Purpose: The Behavioral and Emotional Rating Scale, Second Edition (BERS-2; Epstein, 2004) measures behavioral and emotional strengths in children aged 5–19 years using parent, teacher, and a youth self-report rating scales. The BERS-2 is intended to identify protective factors related to the child and the child's family, relying on resilience theory (King, Swerrdlik, & Schneider, 2005). Other purposes outlined in the manual are to identify children who lack strengths and who may be in need of further intervention. The BERS-2 scores can also be used to guide intervention, monitor progress, and evaluate the effectiveness of instructional programs (Epstein, 2004).

Scale description: The BERS-2 has 52–57 items, depending on the rating form. The items are divided into five scales: Interpersonal Strength, Family Involvement, Intrapersonal Strength, School Function, and Affective Strength. There is a Career Strength scale on the youth and parent form as well. The BERS-2 uses a Likert-type format where the rater is asked to reflect on the child's behavior from the last 3 months and answer "not at all like the youth" to "very much like." In addition, there are eight open-ended questions to capture additional information that may aid follow-up assessments or interventions (King et al., 2005). The results of the BERS-2 yield percentile ranks and standard scores for each scale, with a mean of 10 and standard deviation of 3. The summation of the five scales yields the Strength Index. The rater also receives a summary form that can be used to compare results with other raters (Epstein, 2004).

Psychometric characteristics: The BERS-2 utilized the same standardization sample from the original BERS to create the norms for the teacher form. These norms were based on a sample of 2,176 normally developing children and adolescents, and 861 children and adolescents with emotional/behavioral disorders (King et al., 2005). The parent and youth forms were created and normed with the new standardization samples of 927 and 1,301 youth, respectively. The standardization sample closely matched the 2002 U.S. census data, although slightly under- or over-representing: females, Hispanics, and certain family income levels. The authors reported alpha internal consistency with coefficients ranging from 0.79 to 0.96. Test–retest reliability studies yielded correlations of 0.87–0.99 for the Strength Index. Inter-rater reliability studies indicated correlations of 0.98 for teacher–teacher and 0.54 for parent–child for the Strength Index. The subscales were slightly less reliable with correlations of 0.85–0.96 for teacher–teacher, 0.50–0.63 for parent–child, and 0.20–0.67 for parent–teacher. Validity was examined by comparing the BERS-2 to the Walker-McConnell Scale of Social Competence and School Adjustment—Adolescent Version (Walker & McConnell, 1995), the Systematic Screening for Behavior Disorders (SSBD; Walker & Severeson, 1992), the Scale for Assessing Emotional Disturbance (SAED; Epstein & Cullinan, 1998), the Social Skills Rating System (SSRS; Gresham & Elliot, 1990), and the Achenbach Teacher Report Form (TRF; Achenbach, 1991). Correlations are reported in the form of a table contained in the Examiner's manual (Epstein, 2004).

Devereux Early Childhood Assessment

Purpose: The Devereux Early Childhood Assessment (DECA: LeBuffe & Naglieri, 1999) is a nationally standardized rating scale designed to be used by preschool program directors, teachers, preschool mental health, and early childhood special educators to evaluate protective factors related to resilience in children aged 2–5 years. One of the main goals of the DECA is to help determine if children have developed adequate skills in three areas (Initiative, Self-control, and Attachment) that are related to resilience. Children who receive comparatively low scores in these three strength-based, within-child protective factors may be at risk for developing social and emotional challenges or disorders. By identifying these at-risk children early, strategies can be implemented at school and at home to help develop these protective factors, increasing the odds that the child will be able to successfully adapt to current and future risk and adversity. The rating scale also includes a brief rating of behavioral concerns.

Scale description: The DECA uses a behavior rating scale format which evaluates the frequency with which a child aged 2–5 years demonstrates specific behaviors over the past 4-week interval. A family member or early care and educational professional completes the 37 items which are scored using a 0 (Never) to 4 (Very Frequently) scale. The DECA items are organized into two dimensions: protective factors and behavioral concerns. The Protective Factors included are Initiative (11 items), Self-Control (8 items), and Attachment (8 items). A screener for behavioral concerns (10 items) is included to help identify children with emerging problem behaviors. Items on the Initiative scale assess the child's use of independent thought and action to meet his or her needs. The Self-Control scale includes items about the child's ability to experience a range of feelings and express them appropriately using words and actions. Attachment items determine if the child has developed mutual, strong, and long-lasting relationships with other children and adults. In addition, a Total Protective Factors Scale is provided. The Behavioral Concerns items measure a wide variety of problem behaviors seen in some young children. Separate norms are provided for parent and teacher raters and yield both percentile ranks and *T*-scores. Recommended descriptive terms are provided to aid in communication with parents, teachers, and other professionals. The term "Strength" is used for protective factor T-scores of 60 or above. "Typical" is used to describe T-scores of 41–59 inclusive. "Concern" is used to describe low protective factor scores of 40 or below.

Psychometric characteristics: The DECA was standardized on a national sample of 2,017 children aged 2–5 years. The Total Protective Factors Scale reliabilities for Parents and Teachers is 0.93. The average reliabilities across raters for the separate scales are as follows: Initiative (0.87), Self-Control (0.88), Attachment (0.81), and Behavioral Concerns (0.76). The validity of the DECA was studied by comparing children who varied in their social and emotional health. Two samples of children were compared: one group with known emotional/behavioral problems ($N=95$) and another that were considered typical ($N=86$). The results showed that the children with emotional/behavioral problems earned lower scores (less desirable) on the measures of Initiative (effect size (ES) of 0.78), Self-Control (ES$=1.01$), Attachment (ES$=0.47$), Total Protective Factors (ES$=0.89$), and higher scores (also less desirable) on the measure of Behavioral Concerns (ES$=1.08$). These results and others presented in the DECA Technical Manual (LeBuffe & Naglieri, 1999) indicated that the children with demonstrated emotional and behavioral problems earned scores that reflect the behavioral difficulties they have and their need for stronger factors that are associated with resilience. See Chap. 10 for more information.

It is important to note that at the time of this writing, the second edition of the DECA is in the final stages of development. The second edition has a larger standardization sample and new norms. More information about this edition can be found in the manual that will be published along with the rating scale.

Devereux Early Childhood Assessment for Infants and Toddlers

Purpose: The Devereux Early Childhood Assessment for Infants and Toddlers (DECA-I/T; Mackrain, LeBuffe, & Powell, 2007) was created to evaluate social–emotional skills in infants and toddlers. The DECA-I/T assesses three protective factors related to resilience: Attachment/Relationships, Initiative, and Self-Regulation. The results of this assessment can be used to identify young children's social–emotional skills and to help identify children who may be at risk or need additional assistance. The DECA-I/T can also be used as an outcome measure for early childhood programs and be used as a research tool.

Scale description: The DECA-I/T is a behavior rating scale for children aged 1 month up to 36 months. The Infant form has 33 items comprised from two protective factor scales: Initiative (18 items) and Attachment/Relationships (15 items). The Toddler form has 36 items comprised from three protective factors scales: Attachment/Relationships (18 items), Initiative (11 items), and Self-Regulation (7 items). The DECA-I/T asks family members and early care and education providers to rate the child's behavior from the past 4-week interval using a 0 (Never) to 4 (Very Frequently) scale. The Attachment/Relationship scale assesses if a mutual, strong, long-lasting relationship has developed between the infant or toddler and a significant adult. The Initiative scale determines the infant or toddler's ability to use independent thought or actions to meet his or her needs. The Self-Regulation scale assesses the toddler's ability to gain control of and manage emotions, and sustain focus and attention. A Total Protective Factors scale is provided, in addition to T-scores and percentile ranks for each scale.

Psychometric characteristics: The DECA-I/T was standardized on a national sample of 2,183 infants and toddlers between 4 weeks and 3 years of age. The internal reliability coefficients for the Infant form on the Total Protective Factors scale ranged from 0.90 to 0.94 for parents, and 0.93 to 0.94 for teachers. The reliabilities for the Attachment/Relationships scale ranged from 0.80 to 0.92 for parents and 0.89 to 0.93 for teachers. The reliabilities for the Initiative scale ranged from 0.86 to 0.90 for parents and 0.87 to 0.91 for teachers. The internal reliability coefficients for the Toddler form on the Total Protective Factors scale was 0.94 for parents and 0.95 for teachers. The reliabilities for the separate scares are as follows: Attachment/Relationships (0.87 for parents and 0.90 for teachers), Initiative (0.92 for parents and 0.94 for teachers), Self-Regulation (0.79 for parents and 0.83 for teachers). The validity of the DECA-I/T was investigated by a contrasted groups approach, examining the scale scores for an identified vs. community samples. Results from both the infant and toddler forms indicate significant and meaningful differences between the identified and community samples on all scales (d-ratios range from 0.75 to 1.52). These results are presented in the Technical Manual (Powell, Mackrain, & LeBuffe, 2007).

Devereux Early Childhood Assessment—Clinical Form

Purpose: The Devereux Early Childhood Assessment—Clinical Form (DECA-C; LeBuffe & Naglieri, 2003) is designed to assess factors related to both resilience and emotional/behavioral problems. DECA-C is intended to be used as part of a larger assessment of emotional health and to develop intervention plans that may be needed. For this reason, the DECA-C is intended to be used by those professionals (e.g., psychologists, counselors, and those with clinical training) who have the necessary qualifications to interpret and use this clinical tool as part of child assessment. The information about both protective factors and behavior concerns provides at least three important advantages to the clinician. First, a balanced examination of the child from both positive and concern perspectives is achieved. Second, the examination of the relationships between these dimensions leads to a more complete understanding of how they individually and jointly influence the child's behavior. Third, the inclusion of both dimensions provides important information for intervention planning. See Chap. 10 for more information.

Scale description: The DECA-C uses a behavior rating scale format to evaluates the frequency with which a child aged 2–5 years demonstrated specific behaviors over the past 4-week interval.

A family member or early care and educational professional completes the items which are scored using a 0 (Never) to 4 (Very Frequently) scale. The DECA-C is organized into three scales related to resilience (Initiative, Self-control, and Attachment) and four scales about behavioral concerns. These are: Attention Problems (7 items which assess difficulties with focus, distractibility, impulsivity, and hyperactivity); Aggression (7 items used to measure hostile and destructive acts); Emotional Control Problems (8 items which measure the child's difficulties in modifying the overt expression of negative emotions); and Withdrawal/Depression (9 items which address behaviors related to social isolation and lack of reciprocal interactions as well as depressed affect). Like the Total Protective Factors scale, these four Behavioral Concerns scales are combined into a Total score.

The DECA-C was standardized on a national sample of 2,017 children aged 2–5 years and normed to yield T-scores set at a mean of 50 and SD of 10. The Total Protective Factors Scale reliabilities for Parents and Teachers is 0.93 and the average reliabilities across raters for the separate scales are: Initiative (0.87), Self-Control (0.88), Attachment (0.81), and Behavioral Concerns (0.76). The average Behavioral Concerns scale internal reliabilities across parent and teacher raters are as follows: Withdrawal/Depression (0.73), Emotional Control Problems (0.83), Attention Problems (0.83), and Aggression (0.82) and the Total Behavioral Concerns Scale (0.91).

Psychometric characteristics: The validity of the DECA-C was examined in a series of research studies summarized in the Manual. In summary, the DECA-C effectively differentiated the groups of children who had known emotion and behavior problems with a matched comparison group of typical preschool children (see LeBuffe & Naglieri, 2003); children with known emotional and behavioral problem showed more signs of behavioral concerns and fewer signs of strong protective factor scores than the DECA-C normative sample; and that the children with documented emotional and behavioral problems in this study had needs in the Protective Factors and Behavioral Concerns Scales of the DECA-C.

The validity of the DECA-C was assessed using several other studies which are reported in the Manual by LeBuffe and Naglieri (2003) and in Chapter 15 in this volume.

Devereux Student Strengths Assessment

Purpose: The Devereux Student Strengths Assessment (DESSA; LeBuffe, Shapiro, & Naglieri, 2009) is a rating scale designed to assess social–emotional competencies that serve as protective factors for children in kindergarten through the eighth grade. The DESSA is completed by parents, teachers, or staff at schools and child-serving agencies, including after-school, social service, and mental health programs. The assessment is comprised entirely of 72 items that are described as strength-based (e.g., how well does the child get along with others). The DESSA is intended to provide a psychometrically sound, strength-based, measure of social–emotional competence in children and youth that can be used to identify individuals at risk of developing social–emotional problems before those problems emerge and identify the strengths and needs of individuals already been identified as having social, emotional, and behavioral concerns.

Scale description: The DESSA is organized into eight conceptually-derived scales that provide information about social–emotional competencies. They are: Self-Awareness (7 items), Social-Awareness (9 items), Self-Management (11 items), Goal-Directed Behavior (10 items), Relationship Skills (10 items), Personal Responsibility (10 items), Decision Making (8 items), and Optimistic Thinking (7 items). The combination of these scales is used to obtain a Social–Emotional Composite score. This composite score provides an overall indication of the strength of the child's social–emotional competence and the eight DESSA scales are used to create profiles for individuals as well as the entire classroom that describe the strengths and needs of the student and/or groups of students as compared to national norms. This information can also be used to compare ratings across raters, environments, and time to monitor progress and evaluate outcomes.

Psychometric characteristics: The DESSA was standardized on a national sample of 2,494 children in grades K through 8 by teachers and parents using both paper and pencil and online versions of the scale. The DESSA standardization sample closely approximated the K–8 population of the United States with respect to age, gender, geographic region of residence, race, ethnicity, and socioeconomic status based on the 2008 U.S. census bureau. The DESSA reliability coefficients for the Social–Emotional Composite for parent raters (0.98) and teacher raters (0.99) both exceed the 0.90 value for a total score suggested by Bracken (1987). The internal reliability coefficients for the eight social–emotional competence scales vary from 0.82 (Optimistic Thinking and Self-Awareness—Parent Raters) to 0.94 (Relationship Skills—Teacher Raters). The median reliability coefficient across these eight scales was 0.86 for parent raters and 0.92 for teacher raters. These values well exceed the 0.80 minimum suggested by Bracken (1987). The validity evidence provided in the scale's Manual suggested that DESSA scores *d* differentiate between groups of children with and without the special education designation of serious emotional disturbance, that the scales do show strong convergent validity with similar measures, and that the Social–Emotional Composite can be considered a measure of within-child protective factors. See LeBuffe, Shapiro, and Naglieri (2009) for more details or Chapter 15 in this volume.

Devereux Student Strengths Assessment—Second Step Edition

Purpose: Devereux Student Strengths Assessment—Second Step Edition (DESSA-SSE; LeBuffe, Naglieri, & Shapiro, 2011) is a 36-item, standardized, norm-referenced behavior rating scale that assesses the social–emotional competencies that serve as protective factors for children in kindergarten through the fifth grade. Developed on the basis of the social–emotional content covered in the Second Step curriculum (Committee for Children, 1997), the DESSA-SSE can be completed by parents, teachers, or staff at schools and child-serving agencies, including after-school, social service, and mental health programs. Like all the other scales in this line from the Devereux Center for Resilient Children, the assessment uses only strength-based items. The DESSA-SSE was developed to provide a way to evaluate those specific social–emotional competencies taught in the Second Step curriculum. Specifically, the DESSA-SSE has been designed to describe the social–emotional competence of groups of children so that children's progress through the Second Step social–emotional learning program can be evaluated using a psychometrically sound, nationally normed tool.

Scale description: The DESSA-SSE is organized into five scales: Skills for Learning (9 items), Empathy (9 items), Emotional Management (9 items), Problem Solving (9 items), and a Social–Emotional Composite based on all 36 items. Raw scores on each scale are converted to *T*-scores and corresponding percentile ranks and categorical descriptions. The DESSA-Second Step Edition was standardization and normed on a sample of a total of 1,250 children in kindergarten through fifth grades who closely approximated the U.S. population with respect to age, gender, geographic region of residence, race, ethnicity, and socioeconomic status according to the 2008 U.S. census.

Devereux Student Strengths Assessment—Mini

Purpose: The Devereux Student Strengths Assessment—Mini (DESSA-mini) (Naglieri, LeBuffe, & Shapiro, 2010) is a universal screening tool developed to measure social–emotional skills that are related to mental, emotional, and behavioral disorders in order to make early intervention more possible. The DESSA-mini can be used by professionals with or without clinical training to offer a brief summary of a child's current overall social–emotional competence to determine if additional skill development should be provided. The scale can also be used for ongoing progress monitoring during the course of social–emotional interventions. The DESSA-mini

is comprised entirely of strength-based items (e.g., get along with others) which are scored on a 5-point scale about how often the student engaged in each behavior over the past 4 weeks.

Scale description: The DESSA-mini is comprised of four 8-item forms which were developed to be highly correlated with the full DESSA and equal in reliability and very similar in overall mean scores. The standardization and normative sample was comprised of a total of 1,250 children and youth in kindergarten through eighth grade who closely approximated the K–8 population of the United States with respect to age, gender, geographic region of residence, race, ethnicity, and socioeconomic status according to the 2008 U.S. census. Each DESSA-mini form yields a *T*-score from the sum of the 8-item ratings.

Psychometric characteristics: The internal reliability of the four 8-item DESSA-mini forms range from 0.91 (mini 4) to 0.92 (mini 3). Each of the DESSA-mini reliability coefficients exceed the 0.90 value for a total score suggested by Bracken (1987). Validity evidence presented in the manual indicates that the DESSA-mini can be used with confidence as a screener for social–emotional competence because (a) DESSA-mini Social–Emotional Total scores are strongly correlated with the Social–Emotional Composite scores on the full DESSA; (b) there is considerable agreement between identification rates based on the DESSA and each DESSA-mini form; (c) the DESSA-mini *T*-scores differentiate groups of children with and without known social–emotional problems; and (d) the DESSA-mini and the DESSA identify children similarly regardless of race or ethnicity.

Hierarchical

Penn Interactive Peer Play Scale

Purpose: The Penn Interactive Peer Play Scale (PIPPS; Fantuzzo, Coolahan, et al., 1998; Fantuzzo et al., 1995) was developed on the idea that children's play interactions are highly indicative of their social and emotional health and predictive of future social and academic success.

This behavioral rating scale was developed with Head Start teachers and parents, assessing peer play interactions with high-risk urban youth. There is a teacher form, which is utilized in the classroom and on the playground, and there is a parent form, which is utilized in the home and neighborhood (Fantuzzo et al., 1995). The PIPPS aims to measure children's play strengths in kindergarten and is intended to be used for screening, assessment, informing curriculum, and promoting communication between parents and teachers (Fantuzzo & Hampton, 2000). The PIPPS is also only intended to be used with urban, low-income, minority children. The PIPPS was developed to identify resilient children in high-risk situations, differentiate children with positive peer interactions from those who were less successful, and to inform interventions (Fantuzzo et al., 1995).

Scale description: The PIPPS was originally standardized on a group of 312 African American high-risk children aged 38–63 months. The participants included 38 teachers from five different Head Start programs. Fantuzzo et al. utilized an exploratory factor analysis of the original items to uncover three constructs: Play Interaction, Play Disruption, and Play Disconnection. Both the teacher and the parent versions consist of 32 items. This behavior rating scale is in a Likert-type format (*never*, *seldom*, *often*, or *always*) revealing how often the teacher or parent witnessed the child displaying a certain behavior. The Play Interaction scale measures the child's play strengths, the Play Disruption scale measures antisocial behaviors that can interrupt play interactions, and the Play Disconnection scale measures withdrawal from play. The PIPPS is not intended to categorize students. If the results indicate that a child has poor play interactions, further evaluation is recommended in addition to efforts to bolster the child's skills in that area (Fantuzzo et al., 1995).

Psychometric characteristics: The PIPPS demonstrates reliability and validity in urban, low-income, African American, Kindergarten youth. Cronbach's alpha for the three scales ranges from 0.87 to 0.91. The construct validity of the PIPPS was determined using exploratory factor analysis. The PIPPS was reported to be significantly correlated with the SSRS. The PIPPS also demonstrates reliability and validity in low-income preschool children, utilizing the same comparisons as articulated above (Hampton & Fantuzzo, 2003).

Preschool Behavioral and Emotional Rating Scale

Purpose: The Preschool Behavioral and Emotional Rating Scale (PreBERS; Epstein & Synhorst, 2009) is an assessment that measures the emotional and behavioral strengths in preschool children aged 3–5 years. The preBERS can be used to identify children with low levels of emotional and behavior strengths, inform IEPs or IFSPs, guide intervention, and monitor progress. This rating scale can be completed by any adult with adequate exposure to the child and can be scored and interpreted by any professional adult who had appropriate training in tests and measurement. The preBERS is entirely strength-based and grounded in resilience research. The overarching goal of this assessment is early identification of children who may need additional support or interventions (Epstein & Synhorst, 2009).

Scale description: The preBERS has 42 items that are divided into four dimensions: Emotional Regulation (13), School Readiness (13), Social Confidence (9), and Family Involvement (7). There are seven open-ended questions that aim to capture any additional social, family, or community strengths. The assessment is written at a fifth-grade reading level and was created to be completed in 10 min. Each item is rated on a Likert-type scale (0 = not at all like the child, 1 = not much like the child, 2 = like the child, and 3 = very much like that child) (Drevon, 2011). The subscales each yield a raw score, a percentile rank, and scaled standard scores. The summation of the subscales yields the total scaled score or Strength Index, which is also reported in a percentile rank and a descriptive term (*Very Superior, Superior, Above Average, Average, Below Average, Poor,* or *Very Poor*) (Epstein & Synhorst, 2009).

Psychometric characteristics: The preBERS has a set of norms for three different standardization samples: typical preschool children, Head Start preschool children, and Special Education preschool children. The sample size for these groups was 1,471, 962, and 1,103, respectively. Each sample was compared to the U.S. census by region, race, ethnicity, gender, parental education, family income, and disability status. The samples were mostly representative, but with some regional discrepancies in both the Head Start and Special Education groups (Drevon, 2011). The preBERS reported good internal consistency for the Strength Index, with correlations ranging from 0.96 to 0.98. Correlations were good for each subscale, as well, ranging from 0.84 to 0.97. Short-term test–retest data for the Strength Index indicated high corrected correlations, equaling 0.80 in teachers and 0.95 in parents. The subscale correlations ranged from 0.81 to 0.89 in teachers and 0.88 to 0.97 in parents. Long-term test–retest data revealed a corrected correlation of 0.79 in teachers and 0.85 in parents for the Strength Index and subscale correlations ranging from 0.72 to 0.89 in teachers and 0.83 to 0.92 in parents. The preBERS reported teacher and paraprofessional inter-rater corrected correlations between 0.71 and 0.85 for the subscales, with a 0.72 corrected correlation in the Strength Index (Epstein & Synhorst, 2009).

Resiliency Scales for Children and Adolescents

Purpose: The Resiliency Scales for Children and Adolescents (RSCA; Prince-Embury, 2008) aims to identify and measure personal qualities and vulnerabilities related to resiliency in youth aged 9–18 years. The RSCA is a screener, but can also be utilized to plan and monitor progress and outcomes. The scales are available only in a self-report format and can be administered by qualified supervisors who are professionals, knowledgeable of psychological tests and assessments (Prince-Embury & Steer, 2010). The RSCA can be used to evaluate children and adolescents' personal resiliency.

Scale description: The RSCA items are written on a third-grade reading level and use a 5-point

Likert-type scale 0 (*never*) to 4 (*almost always*) to measure three global scales: Sense of Mastery (20 items), Sense of Relatedness (24 items), and Emotional Reactivity (20 items), for a total of 64 items. Each global scale consists of a group of subscales—sense of mastery: optimism, self-efficacy, and adaptability; sense of relatedness: trust, perceived social support, comfort, and tolerance; emotional reactivity: sensitivity, recovery, and impairment. The raw scores of the RSCA are converted to *T*-scores (Prince-Embury & Steer, 2010).

Psychometric characteristics: The RSCA was standardized on a group of 200 children aged 15–18 years. The sample was compared to the U.S. census on both parent education and ethnicity within each year of age and also by gender (Prince-Embury, 2008). All three global scales displayed good internal consistency scores, with alpha coefficients ranging from 0.83 to 0.95. The RSCA indicated test–retest reliability through a 12-day interval (on average), yielding correlations of 0.70–0.92. To establish validity, the RSCA was correlated with the Reynolds Bully Victimization Scale (Reynolds, 2004), the Brown ADD Scales for Children (Brown, 2001), and then Beck Youth Inventories (BYI-II; Beck, Beck, Jolly, & Steer, 2005; Sink & Mvududu, 2010). Psychometric properties for the RSCA were further explored in clinical samples of children ($n=110$) and adolescents ($n=178$) revealing good internal consistency among the three global scales with alpha coefficients ranging from 0.82 to 0.90 in the child population and from 0.92 to 0.94 in the adolescent population (Prince-Embury, 2010).

Conclusions

Initial conceptualizations of psychological concepts have a history of being retained across generations of psychologists. Once an idea is proposed, and especially if it is operationalized in a practical method, it can become widely used before researchers have adequately determined the ultimate value and utility of the concept. Perhaps one of the best examples is the Stanford-Binet and Wechsler IQ tests which have changed

Table 14.1 Psychometric characteristics of scales used to measure variables related to resilience

Rating scale	No. of items	Age range	Informants	Scores for scales	Comparison sample size	Sample description	Match to US population
Ages and Stages Questionnaire: Social–Emotional (ASQ-SE)	Varies	3–66 months	Parents	Raw score	2,633	National sample	No
Behavioral and Emotional Rating Scale (BERS)	52	6–9 years	Teachers, parents, self	Raw scores, percentiles, scales scores	2,176	National sample	Yes
Devereux Early Childhood Assessment (DECA)	37	2–5 years	Parents and teachers	T-score	2,000	National sample	Yes
Devereux Early Childhood Assessment—Clinical (DECA-C)	62	2–5 years	Parents and teachers	T-score	2,000	National sample	Yes
Devereux Early Childhood Assessment—Infant Toddler (DECA-IT)	33 (infant form) and 36 (toddler form)	1–36 months	Parents and teachers	T-score	2,183	National sample	Yes
Devereux Student Strengths Assessment (DESSA)	72	5–14 years	Parents and teachers	T-score	2,500	National sample	Yes
Devereux Student Strengths Assessment—Mini (DESSA-mini)	Four 8 item forms	5–14 years	Teachers	T-score	1,250	National sample	Yes
Devereux Student Strengths Assessment—Second Step Edition (DESSA-SSE)	36 items	5–14 years	Teachers	T-score	1,250	National sample	Yes
Penn Interactive Play Scale	32	preK & K	Parents and teachers	T-score	312	African American Head Start populations living in high-risk, low income urban populations	No
Preschool Behavioral and Emotional Rating Scale (preBERS)	42	3–6 years	Parents and teachers	Scaled scores	1,471	Typical preschool, head start, and early childhood special education	Yes
Resiliency Scales for Children and Adolescents (RSCA)	64	9–18 years	Self report	T-score	650	National sample	No

little since they were first published in the early 1900s. Similarly, because initial conceptualizations have such an important influence on the field, advocates of a concept such as resilience and the variables that lead to it should be mindful of the power of initial conceptualizations.

Researchers and practitioners need to be mindful that the various tools summarized in Table 14.1 of this chapter have both definitional and operational influence. Although there is a growing number of new methods for assessing the likelihood of resilience there is, as yet, much more work has to be accomplished just to adequately define the concept and the methods used in the assessment process. The use of any one of the tools described in this chapter may provide useful information about a child, but such information needs to be integrated into a larger picture. Each of the tools summarized in this chapter provides a limited examination of the child and they should be used accordingly. This is particularly important because the list of variables that influence resilience is very large and diverse, including the child's characteristics (psychological and physical), the family, both immediate and extended, as well as the community and larger societal factors. Additionally, the determination of which combination of variables best predicts resilience and the complex interactions of these variables is still evolving.

Transformation of research findings into clinical practice is always tricky, and it is especially so for the concept of resilience. Application of this concept in the educational and clinical environments would benefit from greater consensus regarding the definition of resilience, the identification and measurement of protective factors, and agreement on which protective factors should be measured. Most importantly, which protective factors, especially in the within-child domain, can be strengthened, and how, and to what effect?

Clinicians should be cautious when applying the concept of resilience and they should be particularly mindful of the psychometric issues that limit application. We suggest that when given the option, measures that have documented psychometric characteristics and have norms based on a national standardization should be preferred and used within the boundaries specified by the authors. The use of well-developed, psychometrically sound assessments will greatly enhance the likelihood that we will be able to (a) obtain good information about the variables related to resilience and (b) develop and evaluate ways to improve social and emotional outcomes for children.

References

Achenbach, T. M. (1991). *Teacher Report Form.* Burlington: Department of Psychiatry, University of Vermont.

American Educational Research Association, American Psychological Association, & National Council on Measurement in Education. (1999). *Standards for educational and psychological testing.* Washington, DC: American Educational Research Association, American Psychological Association, National Council on Measurement in Education.

Beck, J. S., Beck, A. T., Jolly, J. B., & Steer, R. A. (2005). *Beck Youth Inventories* (2nd ed.). San Antonio, TX: Pearson.

Bracken, B. A. (1987). Limitations of preschool instruments and standards for minimal levels of technical adequacy. *Journal of Psychoeducational Assessment, 5,* 313–326.

Brown, T. E. (2001). *Brown Attention-Deficit Disorder Scales for Children and Adolescents.* San Antonio, TX: Pearson.

Chandler, L. A. (1981). The source of stress inventory. *Psychology in the Schools, 18*(2), 164–168.

Committee for Children. (1997). *Second step: A violence prevention curriculum* (2nd ed.). Seattle, WA: Committee for Children.

Crocker, L., & Algina, J. (1986). *Introduction to classical and modern test theory.* New York: Hold, Rinehart and Winston.

Drevon, D. D. (2011). Test review [Review of the preschool behavioral and emotional rating scale, by M. H. Epstien & L. Synhorst]. *Journal of Psychoeducational Assessment, 29*(1), 84–88.

Epstein, M. H. (2004). *Behavioral and emotional rating scale, second edition: Examiner's manual.* Austin, TX: PRO-ED, Inc.

Epstein, M. H., & Cullinan, D. (1998). *Scale for Assessing Emotional Disturbance.* Austin, TX: PRO-ED.

Epstein, M. H., & Synhorst, L. (2009). *Preschool behavioral and emotional rating scale: Examiner's manual.* Austin, TX: PRO-ED, Inc.

Fantuzzo, J., Coolahan, K., Mendez, J., McDermott, P., & Sutton-Smith, B. (1998). Contextually-relevant validation of peer play constructs with African American head start children: Penn interactive peer play scale. *Early Childhood Research Quarterly, 13,* 411–431.

Fantuzzo, J., Sutton-Smith, B., Coolahan, K. C., Manz, P. H., Canning, S., & Debnam, D. (1995). Assessment of preschool play interaction behaviors in young low-income children: Penn Interactive Play Scale. *Early Childhood Research Quarterly, 10*, 105–120.

Fantuzzo, J. W., & Hampton, V. R. (2000). Penn Interactive Peer Play Scale: A parent and teacher rating system for young children. In K. Gitlin-Weiner, A. Sandgrund, & C. Schaefer (Eds.), *Play diagnosis and assessment* (2nd ed., pp. 599–620). Hoboken, NJ: Wiley.

Garb, J. N. (2003). Clinical judgement and mechanical prediction. In J. R. Graham & J. A. Naglieri (Eds.), *Handbook of psychology, (Assessment psychology, Vol. 10*, pp. 27–43). New Your: Wiley.

Gresham, F. M., & Elliot, S. N. (1990). *Social Skills Rating System test manual.* Circle Pines, MN: American Guidance Service.

Hampton, V. R., & Fantuzzo, J. W. (2003). The validity of the Penn Interactive Play Scale with urban, low-income kindergarten children. *School Psychology Review, 10*(1), 77–91.

Kanner, A. D., Coyne, J. C., Schaefer, C., & Lazarus, R. S. (1981). Comparison of two modes of stress management: Daily hassles and uplifts versus major life events. *Journal of Behavioral Medicine, 4*(1), 1–37.

Kaufman, A. S., & Kaufman, N. L. (2004). *Kaufman assessment battery for children* (2nd ed.). San Antonio, TX: Pearson.

King, J., Swerrdlik, M. E., & Schneider, J. W. (2005). Review of behavioral and emotional rating scale. In R. A. Spies & B. S. Plake (Eds.), *The sixteenth mental measurements yearbook* (2nd ed.). Lincoln, NE: Buros Institute of Mental Measurements.

LeBuffe, P. A., & Naglieri, J. A. (1999). *Devereux Early Childhood Assessment (DECA) assessment, technical manual, and user's guide.* Lewisville, NC: Kaplan.

LeBuffe, P. A., & Naglieri, J. A. (2003). *Devereux early childhood assessment—clinical form.* Lewisville, NC: Kaplan.

LeBuffe, P. A., Naglieri, J. A., & Shapiro, V. B. (2011) *The Devereux Student Strengths Assessment–Second step edition (DESSA-SSE).* Lewisville, NC: Kaplan.

LeBuffe, P. A., Shapiro, V. B., & Naglieri, J. A. (2009). *The Devereux Student Strengths Assessment (DESSA) assessment.* Lewisville, NC: Kaplan.

Luthar, S. S., & Zelazo, L. B. (2003). Research on resilience: An integrative review. In S. S. Luthar (Ed.), *Resilience and vulnerability: Adaptation in the context of childhood adversities* (pp. 510–549). Cambridge: Cambridge University Press.

Mackrain, M., LeBuffe, P. A., & Powell, G. (2007). *The Devereux Early Childhood Assessment for Infants and Toddlers (DECA-I/T) assessment,* Lewisville, NC: Kaplan.

Masten, A., & Garmezy, N. (1985). Risk, vulnerability, and protective factors in developmental psychopathology. In B. Lahey & A. Kazdin (Eds.), *Advances in clinical child psychology.* New York: Plenum Press.

Masten, A. S. (2001). Ordinary magic: Resilience processes in development. *American Psychologist, 56*, 227–238.

Naglieri, J. A., & Das, J. P. (1997). *Cognitive assessment system interpretive handbook.* Itasca: Riverside Publishing Company.

Naglieri, J. A., LeBuffe, P. A., & Shapiro, V. B. (2010). *The Devereux Student Strengths Assessment–Mini (DESSA-Mini) assessment,* Lewisville, NC: Kaplan.

Nunnally, J. C., & Bernstein, I. H. (1994). *Psychometric theory.* New York: McGraw-Hill.

Powell, G., Mackrain, M., & LeBuffe, P. (2007). *The Devereux Early Childhood Assessment for Infants and Toddlers (DECA-I/T), technical manual,* Lewisville, NC: Kaplan.

Prince-Embury, S. (2008). *Resiliency Scales for Children & Adolescents (RSCA).* San Antonio, Pearson.

Prince-Embury, S. (2010). Psychometric properties of the resiliency scales for children and adolescents and use for youth with psychiatric disorders. *Journal of Psychoeducational Assessment, 28*(4), 291–302.

Prince-Embury, S., & Steer, R. A. (2010). Profiles of personal resiliency for normative and clinical samples of youth assessed by the resiliency scales for children and adolescents. *Journal of Psychoeducational Assessment, 28*(4), 303–314.

Reynolds, W. (2004). *Reynolds Bully Victimization Scale.* San Antonio, TX: Pearson.

Sink, C., & Mvududu, N. R. (2010). Review of the resiliency scales for children and adolescents. In R. A. Spies, K. F. Geisinger, & J. F. Carlson (Eds.), *The eighteenth mental measurements yearbook.* Lincoln, NE: Buros Institute of Mental Measurements.

Squires, J., Bricker, D., & Twombly, E. (2002). *The ASQ:SE user's guide.* Baltimore: Paul H. Brookes Publishing.

Squires, J., Bricker, D., & Twombly, E. (2003). *The ASQ:SE User's Guide for the Ages & Stages Questionnaires, social-emotional: A parent completed, child-monitoring system for social-emotional behaviors.* Baltimore, MD: Paul H. Brookes Publishing.

Thorndike, R. L. (1982). *Applied psychometrics.* Boston: Houghton-Mifflin.

Walker, H. M., & McConnell, S. R. (1995). *The Walker-McConnell Scale of Social Competence and School Adjustment–Adolescent Version.* San Diego: Singular.

Walker, H. M. & Severeson, H. H. (1992). *Systematic screening for behavior disorders.* Longmont, CO: Sopris West.

Werner, E. E. (2005). What can we learn about resilience from large-scale longitudinal studies? In S. Goldstein & R. Brooks (Eds.), *Handbook of resilience in children.* New York, NY: Kluwer.

Work, W. C., Cowen, E. L., Parker, G. R., & Wyman, P. A. (1990). Stress resilient children in an urban setting. *Journal of Primary Prevention, 11*(1), 3–17.

Wright, M. O., & Masten, A. S. (2005). Resilience processes in development: Fostering positive adaptation in the context of adversity. In S. Goldstein & R. Brooks (Eds.), *Handbook of resilience in children.* New York, NY: Kluwer.

Assessment of Social-Emotional Competencies Related to Resilience

15

Jack A. Naglieri, Paul A. LeBuffe,
and Valerie B. Shapiro

Introduction

In the past 50 years there has been a growing interest in promoting, sustaining, and restoring the well-being of young people by nurturing their positive attributes and assets. This strength-based approach is predicated on the belief that "everybody has knowledge, talents, capacities, skills, and resources that can be used as building blocks toward their aspirations, the solution of their problems, the meeting of their needs, and the boosting of the quality of their lives" (Saleebey, 2008). A strength-based orientation suggests that, even in the face of adversity, individuals can overcome the odds and achieve better-than-expected outcomes (Masten, 2001). Studies of children that have beaten the odds suggest that these children share common characteristics—many of which can be nurtured in their natural environments (Werner & Smith, 1992). The Devereux Center for Resilient Children (DCRC) has transformed the findings from this body of research into resources that parents and professionals can use to promote these characteristics in children and youth. This chapter first describes

some of the fields of research and practice that have guided the incorporation of a strength-based approach to children's mental health into the DCRC resources. Next, this chapter focuses on the specific resources within the DCRC collection that were designed to help practitioners collect relevant, empirical information about a child's strengths. It concludes by providing examples of how these assessment tools can be used to plan and monitor interventions that promote resilience in children.

Positive Youth Development

The DCRC resources can be used as part of a comprehensive program to promote positive youth development (PYD). PYD, as defined by the United States Department of Health and Human Services, is an orientation toward providing services and opportunities that support all young people development a sense of competence, usefulness, belonging, and empowerment (National Clearinghouse on Families & Youth, 2007). The concept of PYD is not a single intervention, but a policy perspective that uses both prevention and intervention strategies in an integrated fashion to provide opportunities, develop skills, and reinforce prosocial behavior. The United States government has embraced PYD since the 1960s as a means to deal with crime and poverty. When such programs are aligned with the science of human development and behavior change, PYD has been shown to improve mental health

J.A. Naglieri (✉)
University of Virginia, Charlottesville, VA, USA
e-mail: jnaglieri@gmail.com

P.A. LeBuffe
Devereux Center for Resilient Children, Villanova, PA, USA

V.B. Shapiro
University of California, Berkeley, CA, USA

S. Goldstein and R.B. Brooks (eds.), *Handbook of Resilience in Children*,
DOI 10.1007/978-1-4614-3661-4_15, © Springer Science+Business Media New York 2013

outcomes, prevent violence and delinquency, and reduce the onset of early sexual activity (Catalano, Hawkins, & Toumbourou, 2008).

There are several explanations for the positive effect of PYD. Although many theories have been proposed, the Social Development Model (Catalano & Hawkins, 1996) is an example that has influenced preventative interventions for over 30 years. This approach posits that youth first need opportunities for involvement in prosocial activities. Once provided with opportunities for involvement, they need the skills to realize the potential of these opportunities. When skills are used, the behavior needs to be reinforced. Youth form emotional attachments to the source of the reinforcement, and then internalize the values of the person or institution to which they are bonded. This explanation can explain why some youth feel bonded to their families and their schools, while other youth develop a sense of attachment to neighborhood gangs. Gangs can also provide leadership opportunities, skill training, and tangible rewards, but result in quite different, and often antisocial, behaviors.

In PYD initiatives, the Devereux Center for Resilience Children assessment tools help practitioners identify which skills (referred to as competencies) a youth already has and which ones need development. The assessments then serve as goal-setting tools to direct attention and resources toward promoting skills that the child needs in order to cope with set-backs and make the most of opportunities. When the development of social-emotional competencies occurs within an environment that is abundant with engaging opportunities and is plentiful in recognition, bonding and the internalization of prosocial values occurs.

When a PYD model is put into place within a school building, it is often called *School-wide Positive Behavior Support (PBS)* (Sawka-Miller & Miller, 2007). PBS involves the "careful assessment and reengineering of whole school environments to effect positive and lasting behavior change in the student population" (McCurdy, Mannella, & Eldridge, 2003, p. 160). This is done through the implementation of school-wide proactive behavior management strategies (e.g., rule and procedure clarification), prosocial skill instruction, and behavior-modification techniques to reinforce prosocial behavior. The aspect of PYD in which children and adolescents receive direct skill instruction to promote social and emotional competencies is often referred to as *Social-Emotional Learning (SEL)*, the topic of a later section in this chapter. While many DCRC resources can be used to create opportunities, support engagement, and identify reinforcers, the assessment tools in particular have been primarily designed as a tool to support the implementation and progress monitoring of competence-building interventions. The PYD movement influenced the DCRC assessments to be strength-based, or more specifically, measures of the frequency of desirable or positive behaviors in children. This reflects a recent clarification of the goal of PYD, to not only be the reduction of problem behavior, mental illness, and delinquency, but also to promote mental health and engagement in a way that expands upon our vision for health and quality of life. This has been reflected in the movement of many human service disciplines towards positive psychology (Keyes, 2007; Seligman et al., 2005), strength-based practice (Clark & Whitaker, 2002; Nickerson, 2007), asset building (Benson, Scales, Hamilton, & Sesma, 2006), and whole-child education (ASCD Commission on the Whole Child, 2007).

Risk Factors, Protective Factors, and Resilience

The Devereux Center for Resilience Children resources utilizes a risk and protective factor framework. This emphasis reflects the field's improved understanding of the etiology of health and behavior problems, which give PYD coalitions a refined ability to identify and target the predictors and precursors of problem behavior and, therefore, enhance the effectiveness of their prevention and early intervention work (Catalano et al., 2008). The identified predictors of developmental outcomes are commonly called risk and protective factors.

Risk Factors are those environmental or individual attributes that are associated with negative developmental outcome (e.g., truancy, mental illness, delinquency). Risk factors in contemporary American society may include a history of abuse and neglect, a developmental disability, experiences of poverty, discrimination, academic failure, neighborhood crime, and substance abuse. Children that have numerous risk factors, in the absence of protective factors, are described as *vulnerable* (Masten et al., 1999).

Protective Factors are those environmental and/or individual attributes that counter the impact of risk and decrease the likelihood of negative outcomes. Protective factors for children include consistent caregivers, a positive school climate, good social-emotional skills, and a bond with a prosocial adult. Children who have strong protective factors that help them to overcome risk and adversity are known as *resilient* (Werner, 1984).

The implementation of programs that promote protective factors within a resilience framework require the ability to reliably assess protective factors in children. The DCRC resources provide users with a practical and psychometrically sound means of assessing protective factors as part of their efforts to gather information, plan interventions, and evaluate efforts. Risk and protective factors exist on societal, community, familial, and individual (also known as within-person) levels. Although the DCRC assessments target malleable within-child protective factors, child-serving agencies will best serve their target populations by reducing risk and promoting protection simultaneously on as many levels as pragmatically possible, within the scope of their organization's mission. By building protective factors, we may be able to prevent or minimize the negative outcomes caused by unmediated stressors and achieve a more positive developmental trajectory for our children.

Social-Emotional Learning

SEL programs and practices are curricula and instructional techniques that promote the development of social-emotional competencies, such as those measured by the DCRC Assessments. The National Registry of Evidence-Based Programs and Practices (http://nrepp.samhsa.gov)

assists the public in identifying such efficacious approaches to promote social-emotional well-being and positive functioning. The site currently lists 18 programs (e.g., Promoting Alternative Thinking Strategies, Second Step, Guiding Good Choices) that have demonstrated the achievement of these goals in populations of children aged 6–12, through a randomized control trial with at least one replication. In the context of Positive Youth Development and a Risk and Protective Factor Framework, SEL is an effort to give students the individual capacities to moderate the impact of stress and make the most of opportunities. SEL has been demonstrated to impact a broad array of important outcomes (Greenberg et al., 2003).

The Collaborative for Academic, Social and Emotional Learning (CASEL) has grouped these capacities into five categories: self-awareness, social-awareness, self-management, relationship skills, and responsible decision making (Devaney, O'Brien, Tavegia, & Resnik, 2005). A review of after-school programs teaching these skills reported that SEL programs have the potential to (1) improve feelings of self-confidence and self-esteem, (2) promote school bonding (positive feelings and attitudes toward school), (3) improve school grades, (4) reduce aggression, noncompliance, and conduct problems, and (5) reduce recreational drug use (Durlak & Weissberg, 2007). A second meta-analysis reported that when SEL programs were implemented in schools, they were found to (1) increase social and emotional skills, (2) improve student attitudes about themselves, others, and the school, (3) enhance social and classroom behavior, (4) reduce emotional distress related to stress and depression, and (5) promote academic achievement. Durlak and colleagues further connected SEL to academic achievement by reporting that, when SEL programs were well implemented, students experienced meaningful increases on standardized achievement tests as compared to students uninvolved in the SEL programming (Durlak, Weissberg, Dymnicki, Taylor, & Schellinger, 2011; Zins, Bloodworth, Weissberg, & Walberg, 2004). Noting the impact of SEL programs on student's capacities for learning (Abbott et al., 1998; Domitrovich, Cortes, & Greenberg, 2007), policy-makers have begun to recognize SEL as an important part of the school curriculum. In 2004, Illinois adopted SEL learning standards at the state level, requiring each school district to develop an instructional plan, and other states (e.g., New York) and local educational agencies (e.g., Anchorage, Alaska) have followed suit. The need for user-friendly, scientifically sound, child-centered measurement tools to assess the individual and aggregate social-emotional capacities of students has hindered the implementation of SEL programs in the years since these policies have been adopted. The DCRC resources have been designed for this purpose and thus support the widespread adoption of social-emotional learning programs and practices.

From Theory to Practice

The Devereux Center for Resilience Children (DCRC) assessment tools were designed to help practitioners collect relevant, empirical information about a child's strengths, and then plan for—and monitor the results of—interventions designed to promote resilience in children. A variety of assessment tools have been created to meet the needs of children at various developmental stages that fit into the organizational contexts and practice routines of the systems that serve them. In the sections that follow, we will briefly discuss each of these rating scales as designed for infants and toddlers, preschool children aged 2 through 5 years, and school-aged students in kindergarten through the eighth grade. Readers should refer to Chap. 14 for a more thorough description of the six scales from the DCRC.

Infants and Toddlers

The Devereux Early Childhood Assessment for Infants and Toddlers (DECA-I/T; Mackrain, LeBuffe, & Powell, 2007) evaluates social-emotional skills in infants and toddlers up to 36 months of age. The DECA-I/T was standardized on a national sample of 2,183 infants and toddlers

between 4 weeks and 3 years of age. The DECA-I/T Infant form has 33 items and yields two protective factor scales; Initiative (18 items) and Attachment/Relationships (15 items). The Toddler form has 36 items comprising three protective factors scales; Attachment/Relationships (18 items), Initiative (11 items), and Self-Regulation (7 items). The DECA-I/T items are rated by family members and early care and education providers based on behaviors observed over the past 4 weeks using a 0 (Never) to 4 (Very Frequently) scale. The Attachment/Relationship scale assesses if a mutual, strong, long-lasting relationship has developed between the infant or toddler and a significant adult. The Initiative scale determines the infant or toddler's ability to use independent thought or actions to meet his or her needs. The Self-Regulation scale assesses the toddler's ability to manage emotions and sustain focus and attention. A Total Protective Factors scale provides a summary score across these scales. Each scale and total score is reported in T-score units as well as percentile ranks to facilitate interpretation and give meaning to the score.

Preschoolers

The Devereux Early Childhood Assessment (DECA: LeBuffe & Naglieri, 1999) measures protective factors related to resilience and was standardized on a national sample of 2,017 children aged 2 through 5 years of age. Like the DECA-I/T, the DECA uses a behavior rating scale format which evaluates the frequency with which a child demonstrates specific behaviors over the past 4 weeks. A family member or early care and educational professional completes the 37 items which are scored using a 0 (Never) to 4 (Very Frequently) scale. The DECA items are organized into Protective Factor (Initiative, Self-Control, and Attachment) Scales and also include a brief screener for Behavioral Concerns. Similar to the DECA-I/T, the items on the Initiative scale assess the child's use of independent thought and action to meet his or her needs, and the Self-Control scale includes items about the child's ability to experience a range of feelings and express them appropriately using words and actions. The Attachment Scale items determine if the child has developed mutual, strong, and long-lasting relationships not only with adults, but also with other children. In addition, a Total Protective Factors Scale is provided. The brief Behavioral Concerns Screener provides an initial look at a wide variety of problem behaviors seen in some young children. Separate norms are provided for parent and teacher raters and yield both percentile ranks and T-scores. At the time that this chapter is being written, the DECA is being revised. The revised version will be known as the Devereux Early Childhood Assessment for Preschoolers—Revised (DECA-P2) and is scheduled to be published in 2012.

The Devereux Early Childhood Assessment—Clinical Form (DECA-C; LeBuffe & Naglieri, 2003) is a modified version of the DECA. This rating scale is designed to fully assess factors related to both resilience and emotional/behavioral problems. Therefore, the DECA-C is appropriate for use with children with significant known social and emotional needs as part of a larger assessment of emotional health and to guide the development of intervention plans. The DECA-C uses a behavior rating scale format to evaluate the frequency with which a child aged 2 through 5 years demonstrated specific behaviors over the past 4-week interval according to a family member or early care and educational professional. The protective factor scales of the DECA-C were standardized on a nationally representative sample of 2,000 children aged 2 through 5 years of age. The Behavioral Concerns Scale was standardized on a nationally representative sample of 1,108 children aged 3 through 5 years. The DECA-C is organized into three scales related to resilience (initiative, self-control, and attachment) and four scales about behavioral concerns (attention problems, aggression, emotional control problems, and withdrawal/depression). The three scales related to resilience and the four scales related to behavioral concerns are respectively combined into two total scores, Total Protective Factors and Total Behavioral Concerns.

School Age Children

There are three rating scales that are appropriate for students aged 5–14 years. The first is the Devereux Student Strengths Assessment (DESSA; LeBuffe, Shapiro, & Naglieri, 2009), which is designed to assess social-emotional competencies that serve as protective factors for children in kindergarten through the eighth grade. The DESSA was standardized on a national sample of 2,494 children in grades K through 8 by teachers and parents using both paper and pencil and online versions of the scale. The DESSA is completed by parents, teachers, or staff at child-serving agencies, including after-school, social service, and mental health programs. The assessment is comprised of 72-items that are entirely strength-based. The DESSA is organized into eight conceptually derived scales that provide information about social-emotional competencies. They are self-awareness, social-awareness, self-management, goal-directed behavior, relationship skills, personal responsibility, decision making, and optimistic thinking. The total of these scales is used to obtain a Social-Emotional Composite score.

The second scale for this age group is the Devereux Student Strengths Assessment—Mini (DESSA-mini; Naglieri, LeBuffe, & Shapiro, 2011). The scale was standardization on a sample of 1,250 children and youth in kindergarten through the eighth grade rated by teachers or program staff. The DESSA-mini is a series of four brief (8 item), parallel forms comprised of entirely strength-based items which are scored on a five-point scale about how often the student engaged in each behavior over the past 4 weeks. The DESSA-mini can be used to obtain a snapshot of a child's overall social-emotional competence to determine if additional assessment or skill development should be a provided. The four different forms are designed for ongoing progress monitoring (OPM) during the course of social-emotional interventions. Each DESSA-mini form yields a single T-score, the Social-Emotional Total (SET), from the standardized sum of the 8-items. Because the four forms are equivalent, the SET scores from each form can be directly compared.

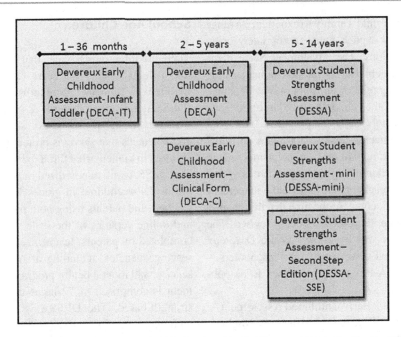

Fig. 15.1 Scales for assessing social-emotional skills developed by the Devereux Center for Resilient Children

This enables the use of the various DESSA-mini forms to monitor progress in acquiring social-emotional competence across time.

The third scale for this age group is the Devereux Student Strengths Assessment—Second Step Edition (DESSA-SSE; LeBuffe, Naglieri, & Shapiro, 2011). This scale of strength-based items was developed on the basis of the social-emotional skill areas covered in the Second Step program (Committee for Children, 2011) in order to facilitate assessment and evaluation as part of the use of that SEL program. The scale was standardized and normed on the same sample as the DESSA. The DESSA-SSE is organized into four scales: Skills for Learning, Empathy, Emotion Management, and Problem Solving, and includes a composite score based on all 36 items. The DESSA-SSE is especially useful for the assessment of those specific social-emotional skill areas taught in the Second Step program. In addition, the DESSA-SSE can be used for evaluating the gains in social-emotional skills as a result of the Second Step program at both the individual child and group (e.g., classroom, school) levels (Fig. 15.1).

The DESSA Comprehensive System for Ages 5–14 Years

The DCRC assessments have each been designed to help practitioners collect relevant, empirical information about a child's social-emotional competencies, giving careful consideration to how these assessment tools can be used to plan for and monitor interventions that promote resilience in children. This implies developing resources that reflect and enhance the organizational practices that occur in child-serving settings. For example, there is increasing interest in schools in the use of brief universal screening procedures for academic subjects such as reading and math in order to prevent academic failure and promote the attainment of educational standards for school-aged children. The use of screening tools for all students in a class enables educators to effectively and efficiently identify those children who are currently showing poor progress and therefore are at risk of continued and future academic failure. Once identified as at-risk, these students are given a more thorough assessment to determine their specific areas of need as well as academic strengths. This information is then used to identify targeted strategies to address any academic needs. We have designed the school-aged DCRC assessments in a way that helps schools to extend this approach to promoting the social-emotional competence of children, which is also essential for academic success.

The *DESSA Comprehensive System* is a practice model that integrates the use of the DESSA-Mini and the DESSA to encourage universal social-emotional skill instruction, school-wide screening and monitoring of the entire student body, and comprehensive assessment and planning for students who need more targeted instruction than what is available in the standard curriculum. In this way, the social-emotional competence of all children is being promoted, and the social-emotional competence of no child slips through the cracks. By adopting a primary prevention, strength-based approach, we can intervene before the emergence of emotional and behavioral problems occurs and individualize the school environment and instructional supports and programs to increase the likelihood of success in school and life for all children.

Three resources are required to implement the DESSA Comprehensive System. These are (a) the four alternate forms of the DESSA-mini; (b) the full 72-item DESSA and DESSA Classroom Profile; and (c) the DESSA-mini OPM form. Utilization of these resources is summarized in the text that follows.

Time 1: Universal Screening and Selective Assessment

The implementation of the DESSA Comprehensive System begins with universal screening of all children using Form 1 of the DESSA-mini. This will most likely occur near the beginning of a school year, after the required 4-week observation period has occurred. It can be expected that most children will obtain a DESSA-mini SET *T*-score of 41 or higher, placing them in the Typical (*T*-scores of 41–59 inclusive) or Strength range (*T*-scores of 60 or higher). These children will benefit from universal (i.e., Tier 1) social and emotional learning programs and a safe and supportive school climate.

Those students who obtain a DESSA-mini *T*-score that is in the Need for Instruction range (*T*-scores of less than or equal to 40) should be provided targeted social-emotional instruction. In order to better understand the students' specific areas of need, these children should be assessed with the full 72-item DESSA to help determine the nature of the targeted interventions that should be provided. These interventions should be based on specific social-emotional scores on the eight DESSA scales and an examination of individual item scores as specified in the DESSA Manual.

As noted above, children who were not identified at Time 1 will continue to benefit from the universal social-emotional instruction and a healthy school climate. If at any time a teacher or parent should become concerned about a child's social-emotional status, however, a full DESSA should be completed. If warranted, based on DESSA results, the child could move from Tier 1 (standard, universal, school-wide practice) to a higher Tier (individualized support) at any point during the year.

Tier 2: Ongoing Progress Monitoring

The services at Tier 2 apply only to those children who were identified as needing targeted social-emotional instruction and related supports. The goal of OPM at Tier 2 is to use alternative DESSA-mini Forms 2, 3, and 4 to provide feedback to the teacher, student support personnel, student, and caregivers on the progress that the child is making on acquiring social-emotional competencies. Typically, the alternate forms of the DESSA-mini are administered at 30–90 day intervals, depending on the needs of the student. If necessary, the DESSA-mini forms can be used repeatedly throughout the year. The results of each administration are recorded and graphically displayed using the DESSA-mini OPM form. This form allows the user to record changes in

T-scores from one DESSA-mini administration to the next. Guidelines are presented in the DESSA-mini manual on how to interpret changes and modify targeted interventions and supports based on the student's progress.

Time 4: Documenting Outcomes and Preparing for the Next School Year

At the end of the year, we recommend a second DESSA be completed for all those children that have been receiving Tier 2 supports. Using the pretest–posttest comparison procedure described in the DESSA manual, the child's growth or decline on each of the eight DESSA scales can be determined. This information can be useful for both documenting outcomes, planning for sustaining growth over the summer break, and preparing for the next school year. If the analysis indicates that a child failed to respond to targeted interventions, a referral for more intensive services (Tier 3) in the next school year should be considered.

In addition to evaluating the outcomes for individual students, the results of the pretest–posttest comparison technique can be aggregated across students who have been receiving Tier 2 supports. These data can indicate areas where staff have, on the whole, been more or less successful at promoting specific competencies. For instance, this analysis might reveal that 75% of children receiving targeted supports to address social skills showed improvement, whereas only 25% of children receiving supports for self-awareness showed improvement. This information can readily inform professional development strategies for staff, resource acquisition and mobilization in the school or community, and summer safety planning for youth.

A Time 4, all children who have not been reassessed with the DESSA as described above should be rescreened with the DESSA-mini. This is in recognition that risk and protective factors can wax and wane over the course of the school year. A child who had a Typical score in the fall may have experienced additional risk and adversity and now scores in the Need for Instruction range.

The Use of the DESSA at Tier 3

The DESSA also provides valuable information for children who are being evaluated for, or have already been deemed eligible for special education services. In particular, the individual item analysis technique described in the DESSA manual can identify empirically grounded and instructionally relevant strengths to be incorporated into the child's Individualized Education Plan (IEP). A review of the scale scores on the DESSA can also provide insights on how the disability is affecting the child's social and emotional competence.

Contemporary Debates

Some professionals (e.g., Shinn, Tindal, & Stein, 1988) have suggested that determining which students in a class should be considered "at-risk" and qualified for targeted services should be based on local rather than national norms. This presumes that local norms can more accurately identify students who may be at risk based upon the comparison of a student directly to other children in his or her immediate environment. A counter ideology suggests that high hopes and expectations should be maintained for all students, even those in local environments where low achievement is prevalent. In other words, this viewpoint suggests that "at risk" status should be determined by comparing a student to a well-defined reference point rather than to an artificial (and changing) standard determined in part by the availability of local resources rather than authentic student need. This interesting debate places two ideological approaches in contrast to each other, but the impact of such a decision is not often examined empirically.

In order to shed light on the differences between the way in which local and national norming practices could impact the assessment of resilience in children, we analyzed data from the DESSA standardization sample. The data used for this illustration (see Table 15.1) reflect three levels of DESSA scores. One group with an average *T* score around 40 (a student body with significant needs), another with an average around 50 (a typical student body), and one with an average around 60 (a student body with significant competence). The tabled values for these three

Table 15.1 Comparison of national and local norms

Student	T-scores based on national norms			T-scores based on local norms		
	Classroom 1	Classroom 2	Classroom 3	Classroom 1	Classroom 2	Classroom 3
1	44	48	60	53	48	51
2	26	31	39	37	34	32
3	26	38	46	37	40	38
4	34	41	52	44	42	44
5	48	58	66	57	56	56
6	21	27	38	32	30	31
7	26	35	45	37	37	37
8	49	58	69	58	56	59
9	28	41	50	38	42	42
10	38	50	58	48	50	49
11	48	57	66	57	55	56
12	42	50	60	51	50	51
13	42	53	58	51	52	49
14	53	66	74	62	63	64
15	40	53	60	50	52	51
16	38	50	58	48	50	49
17	24	33	45	35	35	37
18	40	53	60	50	52	51
19	58	68	76	66	65	65
20	37	50	54	47	50	46
21	49	64	67	58	61	57
22	53	68	74	62	65	64
23	42	48	60	51	48	51
24	53	68	76	62	65	65
25	44	50	56	53	50	47
26	40	50	62	50	50	53
27	56	68	76	65	65	65
28	28	38	46	38	40	38
29	56	64	69	65	61	59
30	29	37	48	39	39	40
Mean	40.4	50.5	58.9	50.0	50.0	50.0
SD	10.7	12.0	11.1	10.0	10.0	10.0
N<41	15	7	2	8	7	7

Note: *Shaded cells* include values less than 41, the recommended cutoff for being at risk and in need of social-emotional instruction

groups, based on the DESSA national norms, appear in the left portion of the table. The scores for each of the 30 cases across the three groups are provided. Using our rule that a score of 40 or less (−1 standard deviation; 16th percentile) would indicate that the child is in need of social-emotional instruction we would conclude that 15 students in Group A, 7 in Group B, and 2 in Group C are in need of targeted services.

The scores in the right side of the table are those that were calibrated based on local norms that were constructed by transforming the original scores to z scores based upon the means and standard deviations for each group. For example, the score for student #1 based on the DESSA normative sample is 44. In order to compute a local normative value for that student, the following formula was used: $((44-40.4)/10.7) \times 50 + 10.$

When converted to a local normative value, student #1's score of 44 now becomes a score of 53 (*T* score based on Group A mean and standard deviation). The values in this table show the national and local norm values for three groups of 30 cases. The findings illustrate the differences between these methods.

As seen in Table 15.1, the mean scores for the three Groups differed considerably. The average for Group A is very low (40.4) and for Group C quite high (58.9). As an artifact of the local norming process, each of the group *T*-score means on the right side will be 50. Because the student body in Group B is typical, meaning that their average is close to the national average, there is little difference between the local and national norm values. This is not the case for those groups that have an average score that deviates from 50. The scores in Group 1 go up (from 40.4 to 50.0) and the scores in Group 3 go down (from 58.9 to 50.0). Importantly, the number of students who are identified as at risk goes down for Group 1 and up for Group 3. That is, 7 (47%) of the 15 cases in Group 1 that were at risk on a national basis are no longer identified. For example, case #16 has a *T* score of 38 when compared to the national mean, but a score of 48 when compared to the rest of the cases in Group 1. That means that a child who is about one standard deviation below the national mean could be treated as a typically developing child and disqualified from receiving services if the scores of the other children in his local community are very low.

The cases which comprise Group 3 are generally high, and as a group, the students are almost one standard deviation above the national mean. Using the cut score of 40, the national norm would lead to the conclusion that two students are at risk. When the local norm is calculated, five additional students are identified as being at risk. Those students in schools where the mean is high will earn comparatively low scores based on the local mean, and may be treated differently and allocated resources, despite actually being quite typical on a national basis. Beyond misleading, it is concerning that these students will likely receive supports that they may not need while other students who are in considerable need for social-emotional skills in Group A will be overlooked through the use of local norms. This analysis raises concerns about the capacity of local norms to accurately access students and allocate resources in the most equitable way possible.

Conclusions

All of the assessments developed by the DCRC share certain key features. First, they are strength-based. In order to support primary prevention and mental health promotion, it is essential that a strengths orientation is utilized. More traditional deficit or problem-oriented scales can only identify children in need of services after the challenging behaviors have exceeded some threshold. The goal of the DCRC assessments are to promote healthy social and emotional development and to identify children who are at risk of developing emotional and behavioral problems due to low protective factors *before the problem behaviors emerge.* Second, all of the assessments meet or exceed professional standards for well-developed assessments. Because teachers, staff, and parents have many demands upon their time, we should only expect individuals to complete, score, and use assessments if those tools provide valid, reliable, and useful information. Third, quality assessment should precede and guide intervention. All of the DCRC assessments have been developed to help guide effective interventions to support the social and emotional competence of children. For this reason, many of the assessments (DECA, DECA-I/T) are accompanied by strategy guides for parents and teachers and the DESSA-SSE was developed to support the Second Step social and emotional learning program. We have developed these tools to give professionals who work in infant and toddler programs, preschools, schools, after-school programs, and child welfare and mental health facilities a way to make data-based decisions to promote the social-emotional competencies of children in order to facilitate their success in school and life.

References

Abbott, R. D., O'Donnell, J., Hawkins, J. D., Hill, K. G., Kosterman, R., & Catalano, R. F. (1998). Changing teaching practices to promote achievement and bonding to school. *The American Journal of Orthopsychiatry, 68*, 542–552.

Association for Supervision and Curriculum Development. (2007). *The learning compact redefined: A call to action. A report of the commission on the whole child.* Alexandria, VA: Association for Supervision and Curriculum Development.

Benson, P. L., Scales, P. C., Hamilton, S. F., & Sesma, A. (2006). Positive youth development: Theory, research, and applications. In W. Damon & R. M. Lerner (Eds.), *Handbook of child psychology* (Theoretical models of human development 6th ed., Vol. 1, pp. 894–941). Hoboken, NJ: Wiley.

Catalano, R. F., & Hawkins, J. D. (1996). The social development model: A theory of antisocial behavior. In J. D. Hawkins (Ed.), *Delinquency and crime: Current theories* (pp. 149–197). New York: Cambridge University Press.

Catalano, R. F., Hawkins, J. D., & Toumbourou, J. W. (2008). Positive youth development in the United States: History, efficacy, and links to moral and character education. In L. Nucci & D. Narvaez (Eds.), *Handbook of moral and character education* (pp. 459–483). New York: Routledge.

Clark, S., & Whitaker, T. (2002). *Pippah pack: Promoting positive youth environments.* Washington, DC: National Association of Social Workers.

Committee for Children. (2011). *Second step: Skills for social and academic success.* Seattle, WA: Committee for Children.

Devaney, E., O'Brien, M. U., Tavegia, M., & Resnik, H. (2005). Promoting children's ethical development through social and emotional learning. *New Directions for Youth Development, 108*, 107–116.

Domitrovich, C. E., Cortes, R., & Greenberg, M. T. (2007). Improving young children's social and emotional competence: A randomized trial of the preschool PATHS curriculum. *The Journal of Primary Prevention, 28*, 67–91.

Durlak, J. A., & Weissberg, R. P. (2007). *The impact of after-school programs that promote personal and social skills.* Chicago, IL: Collaborative for Academic, Social, and Emotional learning.

Durlak, J. A., Weissberg, R. P., Dymnicki, A. B., Taylor, R. D., & Schellinger, K. B. (2011). The impact of enhancing students' social and emotional learning: A meta-analysis of school-based universal interventions. *Child Development, 82*, 405–432.

Greenberg, M. T., Weissberg, R. P., O'Brien, M. U., Zins, J. E., Fredericks, L., Resnik, H., et al. (2003). Enhancing school-based prevention and youth development through coordinated social, emotional, and academic learning. *The American Psychologist, 58*, 466–474.

Keyes, C. L. M. (2007). Promoting and protecting mental health as flourishing: A complementary strategy for improving national mental health. *The American Psychologist, 62*, 95–108.

LeBuffe, P. A., & Naglieri, J. A. (1999). *Devereux Early Childhood Assessment (DECA) assessment, technical manual, and user's guide.* Lewisville, NC: Kaplan.

LeBuffe, P. A., & Naglieri, J. A. (2003). *Devereux Early Childhood Assessment—Clinical form.* Lewisville, NC: Kaplan.

LeBuffe, P. A., Naglieri, J. A., & Shapiro, V. B. (2011). *The Devereux Student Strengths Assessment (DESSA) assessment—Second step edition.* Lewisville, NC: Kaplan.

LeBuffe, P. A., Shapiro, V. B., & Naglieri, J. A. (2009). *The Devereux Student Strengths Assessment (DESSA) assessment, technical manual, and user's guide.* Lewisville, NC: Kaplan.

Mackrain, M., LeBuffe, P. A., & Powell, G. (2007). *The Devereux Early Childhood Assessment for Infants and Toddlers (DECA-I/T) assessment, technical manual, and user's guide.* Lewisville, NC: Kaplan.

Masten, A. (2001). Ordinary magic. *The American Psychologist, 56*, 227–238.

Masten, A. S., Hubbard, J. J., Gest, S. D., Tellegen, A., Garmezy, N., & Ramirez, M. (1999). Competence in the context of adversity: Pathways to resilience and maladaptation from childhood to late adolescence. *Development and Psychopathology, 11*, 143–169.

McCurdy, B. L., Mannella, M., & Eldridge, N. (2003). Positive behavior support in urban schools: Can we prevent the escalation of antisocial behavior? *Journal of Positive Behavior Interventions, 5*, 158–170.

Naglieri, J. A., LeBuffe, P. A., & Shapiro, V. B. (2011). *The Devereux Student Strengths Assessment—Mini (DESSA-Mini) assessment, technical manual, and user's guide.* Lewisville, NC: Kaplan.

National Clearinghouse on Families & Youth. (2007). *Putting positive youth development into practice: A resource guide.* Silver Spring, MD: U.S. Department of Health and Human Services Administration for Children and Families, Administration on Children, Youth, and Families, & Family and Youth Services Bureau.

Nickerson, A. B. (2007). The use and importance of strength-based assessment. *School Psychology Forum: Research in Practice, 2*, 15–25.

Saleebey, D. (2008). The strengths perspective: Putting possibility and hope to work in our practice. In K. M. Sowers & C. N. Dulmus (Series Ed.) & B. W. White (Vol. Ed.), *Comprehensive handbook of social work and social welfare: Vol. 1. The profession of social work* (pp. 123–142). Hoboken, NJ: Wiley.

Sawka-Miller, K. D., & Miller, D. N. (2007). The third pillar: Linking positive psychology and school-wide positive behavior support. *School Psychology Forum: Research in Practice, 2*, 26–38.

Seligman, M. E. P., Berkowitz, M. W., Catalano, R. F., Damon, W., Eccles, J. S., Gilham, J. E., et al. (2005).

The positive perspective on youth development. In D. L. Evans, E. B. Foa, R. E. Gur, H. Hendin, C. P. O'Brien, M. E. P. Seligman, & B. T. Walsh (Eds.), *Treating and preventing adolescent mental health disorders: What we know and what we don't know* (pp. 498–527). New York: Oxford University Press, The Annenberg Foundation Trust at Sunnylands, & The Annenberg Public Policy Center of the University of Pennsylvania.

Shinn, M. R., Tindal, G. A., & Stein, S. (1988). Curriculum-based measurement and the identification of mildly handicapped students: A research review. *Professional School Psychology, 3*, 69–85.

Werner, E. E. (1984). Resilient children. *Young Children, 40*, 68–72.

Werner, E. E., & Smith, R. S. (1992). *Overcoming the odds: High risk children from birth to adulthood.* Ithaca, NY: Cornell University Press.

Zins, J. E., Bloodworth, M. R., Weissberg, R. P., & Walberg, H. (2004). The scientific base linking social and emotional learning to school success. In J. Zins, R. P. Weissberg, M. Wang, & H. J. Walberg (Eds.), *Building academic success on social and emotional learning: What the research says.* New York: Teachers College Press.

The Resiliency Scales for Children and Adolescents: Constructs, Research and Clinical Application

16

Sandra Prince-Embury

What qualities buffer youth who are faced with more than the average burden of hardship? Do these qualities strengthen children generally in times of greater uncertainty and exposure? Are they the same qualities that characterize children and adolescents who can weather the transitions and upheavals that frequently accompany normal development? Accumulating research and theory suggest that it is possible to objectively measure qualities of resiliency although many forces may shape them. The *Resiliency Scales for Children and Adolescents*™ (Prince-Embury, 2007) is based on the findings of previous research of personal resiliency in children and adolescents and are grounded in developmental theory. The Resiliency Scales were designed to systematically identify and quantify core personal qualities of resiliency in youth, as expressed in their own words about their own experience. The function of the scales is to theoretically and empirically provide sound assessment of core characteristics underlying personal resiliency in children and adolescents (ages 9–18). The purpose of the scales is to allow for easy communication of this information to youth and their caregivers for the purpose of education, screening, prevention, and counseling. The scales are based on the assumption that personal resiliency reflects adequate personal resources that match or exceed emotional reactivity

to internal or external stress. It is also assumed that this relationship may be expressed as a Personal Resiliency Profile unique to each child or adolescent.

Although resilience has been the focus of much discussion and research over the past decades, the operational definition has varied considerably over time as hardiness, optimism, competence, self-esteem, social skill, achievement, or the absence of pathology in the face of adversity. Resilience in the face of adversity has been studied extensively by developmental psychopathologists for the past 50 years. This body of work has generally defined resilience as the ability to weather adversity or to bounce back from a negative experience and has focused on success defined as having observable assets, achievement, developmental milestones, or absence of symptoms. Much of resilience research has examined the interaction of protective factors and risk in high-risk populations. The focus of this work has been the identification of factors that were present in the lives of those who thrived in the face of adversity as compared to those who did not (Garmezy, Masten, & Tellegen, 1984; Luthar, 1991, 2003; Masten, 2001; Rutter, Harrington, Quinton, & Pickles, 1994; Werner & Smith, 1982, 1992, 2001).

Protective factors identified in previous research include personal qualities of children that may have allowed them to cope with various types of adversities. The personal qualities identified include intellectual ability (Baldwin et al., 1993; Brooks, 1994; Jacelon, 1997; Luthar & Zigler,

S. Prince-Embury (✉)
The Resiliency Institute of Allenhurst, LLC,
West Allenhurst, NJ, USA
e-mail: sandraprince-embury@earthlink.net

S. Goldstein and R.B. Brooks (eds.), *Handbook of Resilience in Children*,
DOI 10.1007/978-1-4614-3661-4_16, © Springer Science+Business Media New York 2013

1991, 1992; Masten & Coatsworth, 1998; Rutter, 1987; Wolff, 1995; Wright & Masten, 1997), easy temperament (Jacelon, 1997; Luthar & Zigler, 1991; Rende & Plomin, 1993; Werner & Smith, 1982; Wright & Masten, 1997; Wyman, Cowen, Work, & Parker, 1991), autonomy (Jacelon, 1997; Werner & Smith, 1982), self-reliance (Polk, 1997), sociability (Brooks, 1994; Luthar & Zigler, 1991), effective coping strategies (Brooks, 1994; Luthar & Zigler, 1991), and communication skills (Werner & Smith, 1982).

Another group of protective factors identified in previous research pertains to the child's social environment, including family. Included in this group of factors are family warmth, cohesion, structure, emotional support, positive styles of attachment, and a close bond with *at least one* caregiver (Baldwin et al., 1993; Brooks, 1994; Cowen & Work, 1988; Garmezy, 1991; Gribble et al., 1993; Luthar & Zelazo, 2003; Luthar & Zigler, 1991; Masten & Coatsworth, 1998; Rutter, 1987; Werner & Smith, 1982; Wolff, 1995; Wright & Masten, 1997; Wyman et al., 1991, 1992).

Environmental protective factors outside the immediate family have been identified and include positive school experiences (Brooks, 1994; Rutter, 1987; Werner & Smith, 1982; Wright & Masten, 1997), good peer relations (Cowen & Work, 1988; Jacelon, 1997; Werner & Smith, 1982; Wright & Masten, 1997), and positive relationships with other adults (Brooks, 1994; Conrad & Hammen, 1993; Garmezy, 1991; Werner, 1997; Wright & Masten, 1997). For an extensive review of research and findings pertaining to resilience, see Luthar (2006a, 2006b).

Conceptually, the findings of earlier research in developmental psychopathology seemed to imply that resilient youth were extraordinary and that this quality was not accessible to every child. More recently, resiliency has been identified as a characteristic of normal development and not applicable in adverse circumstances only (Masten, 2001; Masten & Powell, 2003). Masten (2001) suggested that fundamental systems, already identified as a characteristic of human functioning, have great adaptive significance across diverse stressors and threatening situations. She recommends that these systems would include

individual attributes, such as attachment, defined as systems underlying close relationships in development; mastery motivation, defined as pleasure from mastering developmental tasks; self-regulation, defined as emotional and behavioral regulation and impulse control; and cognitive development and learning. Masten also suggested that the dominance of a medical model that emphasizes deficits has impeded the development of good measures of positive aspects of behavior (Masten & Curtis, 2000).

Other researchers and clinicians have expressed a need for a further shift toward clinical application. If resiliency, as suggested by Masten (2001), is part of normal development, why should not psychology focus on developing these qualities in all children? Goldstein and Brooks (2005) and Brooks and Goldstein (2001) have called for a clinical psychology of resiliency. These authors focus on the interaction between the child and the child's social environment. Brooks and Goldstein have written on the importance of the mindset of a resilient parent in raising a child with a resiliency mindset and the importance of teaching parents how to identify and foster these qualities. These authors focus on changing the family environment to be more supportive of the child's resiliency.

Seligman (1995, 1998, 2000) has written on the need for developing a systematic science of positive psychology to offset the prevailing focus on pathology. He points out that the major strides in prevention have come from a perspective of systematically building competency, not on correcting weakness. Seligman's approach, based on cognitive theory, is to provide structured interventions designed to build resilient attitudes that will then buffer against symptoms of depression.

The creation of the Resiliency Scales began with the identification and operationalizing of personal qualities that are critical for resiliency adaptation of youth (Prince-Embury, 2006b). While acknowledging the critical importance of environmental forces, the scales are predicated on the knowledge that what youth bring to their environments is also highly influential for their overall well-being. The focus here, therefore, is on the types of personal attributes that generally allow some youth to do better than others in the face of adversities. The dimensions of personal strength captured in the Resiliency Scales overlap conceptually with the notion of ego resiliency as a personal integrative characteristic in adults presented by Block and Block (1980). The Blocks' notion of ego resiliency encompasses a set of traits reflecting general resourcefulness and sturdiness of character and flexibility in functioning in response to varying environmental circumstances. Personal resiliency as presented in the RSCA is described in terms of three developmental systems that are recognized as beginning early in development and maintaining saliency across the lifespan.

Resiliency and Sense of Mastery

A child's sense of mastery and self-efficacy is recognized by most experts as a core characteristic of resiliency in children and adults. White (1959) introduced the construct as a sense of mastery/efficacy in children and adolescents that provides the opportunity for them to interact with and enjoy cause and effect relationships in the environment. According to White, a sense of competence, mastery, or efficacy is driven by an innate curiosity, which is intrinsically rewarding and the source of problem-solving skills. Other theories have emphasized learning rather than intrinsic motivation. Bandura and others (1981, 1977, 1993, 1997) spent many years studying the mechanisms by which self-efficacy is learned and developed. Bandura's theory focuses on the internal mediating mechanism of learned expectation through direct and indirect interaction with the social environment. The critical implication of Bandura's work is that self-efficacy experiences can be systematically structured for students to maximize the likelihood of their learning to have greater belief in their own self-efficacy. Several studies conducted as part of the Rochester Child Resiliency Project supported the hypothesis that positive expectation is related to resiliency. Positive efficacy expectations in 10–12-year-olds predicted better behavioral adaptation and classification of the child as stress resilient (Cowen, Pryor-Brown, Hightower, & Lotyczewski, 1991). Positive expecta-

tions about their future predicted lower anxiety, higher school achievement, and better classroom behavior control in these children (Wyman, Cowen, Work, & Kerley, 1993).

Resiliency and Sense of Relatedness

A second body of literature links a youth's relational experience and ability with personal resiliency. Bowlby (1969) and Ainsworth and Wittig (1969) systematically studied and established the importance of the interaction between a mother and her infant in the development of attachment. Masten and Coatsworth (1998) identified the significance of an attachment system to the resiliency of an organism. Luthar and Zelazo (2003) argued that strong, supportive relationships lie at the core of resilient adaptation. The implication from this body of literature is that social relatedness allows external buffering in several ways. First, the youth may view relationships as generally available as needed. In addition, the youth may view relationships as available for specific supports in specific situations. On another level, internal mechanisms reflecting the cumulative experience of previous support may in some way shield the child from negative psychological impact. Research and theory regarding internalized mechanisms of relatedness suggest more than one pathway for this influence.

Relationships as Buffers

Relationships and relational ability as mediators of resiliency have been supported in research by developmental psychopathologists such as Emmy Werner. Throughout her writing, Werner has stressed the importance of children having relationships with caring adults other than, or in addition to, their parents. In *Vulnerable but Invincible*, Werner and Smith (1982) noted that resilient youth sought support from non-parental adults more often, especially teachers, ministers, and neighbors, and that these supports were seen as influential in fostering resiliency. Werner's research suggests that it is not only the presence of supportive individuals at the time of adversity that protects the child, but also the internal mechanism of being able to relate to others in a meaningful and long-lasting way that constitutes resiliency.

Previous research has indicated that perceived support, as distinguished from actual support, is the dimension of social support that is most strongly related to psychological well-being in adults and children (Barrera, 1986; Cohen & Wills, 1985; Jackson & Warren, 2000; Sarason, Shearon, Pierce, & Sarason, 1987). According to Thompson, Flood, and Goodvin (2006) "confidence in the availability and helpfulness of social partners is crucial to maintaining a sense that assistance is available and the hope that can ensue even in difficulty (this is what is meant by a secure attachment relationship early in life)" (p. 13).

Internal Mechanisms of Relatedness

Psychosocial theories of development, such as that of Erikson (1963), identified the first developmental psychosocial process that occurred in infancy through interaction between the child and the primary caregiver as the development of trust vs. distrust. The significance of trust was identified by Erikson (1963) as the first stage of social–emotional development, upon which all other social development is built. Erikson defined basic trust as the ability to receive and accept what is given. A number of theorists observing the interaction between the infant and primary caregiver conceptualized this early social interactive process as the development of attachment, which they claimed has implications for the individual's ability to relate to others throughout their lifetime. Neurophysiologists claim that the presence of an adequate attachment experience in infancy and childhood impacts more basic functioning of the individual, such as the ability to self-regulate. Fonagy, Steele, Steele, Higgitt, and Target (1994) cited other researchers who have found that children identified as securely attached at age 2 later score higher on measures of social behavior, affect regulation, endurance in challenging task

situations, orientation to social resources, and cognitive resourcefulness than insecurely attached children. Success in relationships has been defined as a source of modifying stress (self-comforting ability) and effecting positive outcome, such as social competence, social skill, and positive self-esteem (Cicchetti & Toth, 1997). Allen, Hauser, and Borman-Spurrell (1996) examined the long-term sequalae of severe adolescent psychopathology from the perspective of adult attachment theory. These authors reported findings that supported a substantial and enduring connection between attachment organization and severe adolescent psychopathology. A molecular genetics study by Kaufman et al. (2004) indicated that social support may moderate the effects of biological vulnerability and a history of maltreatment on children's proneness to depressive symptomatology. Social support is likely not only to have a direct relationship to the development of psychopathology, but it also mediates the effects of other risk factors in complex ways. Research suggests a complex interaction between early attachment and the development of the capacity for self-regulation. The presence of a secure relationship in infancy mediates the regulation of affect and models that regulation for the child. Self-regulation then impacts the child's development in many ways, including the ability to relate to others.

Resiliency and Emotional Reactivity

Much research in the field of developmental psychopathology has found that whether a child develops pathology in the presence of adversity is related in some way to the child's emotional reactivity and his/her ability to modulate and regulate this reactivity. Strong emotional reactivity and associated difficulty with self-regulation has been strongly linked with behavioral difficulty and vulnerability to pathology. Conversely, the ability to modulate or otherwise manage emotional reactivity has been found to be a significant factor in fostering resiliency. Reactivity has been labeled alternately as vulnerability, arousability, or threshold of tolerance prior to the occurrence of adverse events or circumstances. Rothbart and Derryberry (1981) indicated that reactivity is the speed and intensity of a child's negative emotional response, and that regulation is the child's capacity to modulate that negative emotional response. Relative reactivity may have physiological basis, such as temperament (Thomas & Chess, 1977), genetic predisposition, learning disability, physical impairment, or congenital anomaly, but it may also be modified by adverse experience. Developmental psychology has focused on self-regulation as the organism's way of maintaining the delicate balance or homeostasis required for functioning. Within this context, self-regulation has been defined in several ways: a set of abilities that allow children to regulate their own attention, emotions, and behavior (Cicchetti & Tucker, 1994; Pennington & Welsh, 1995; Rothbart & Bates, 1998); and the intra- and extra organismic factors by which emotional arousal is redirected, controlled, modulated, and modified so that an individual can function adaptively in emotionally challenging situations (Cicchetti, Ganiban, & Barnett, 1991; Thompson, 1990). Emotion regulation may be defined as a part of self-regulation, which in turn refers to a set of tools that allow children to regulate their own attention, emotions, and behavior (Cicchetti & Tucker, 1994; Pennington & Welsh, 1995; Rothbart & Bates, 1998).

Resiliency Scales for Children and Adolescents (RSCA)

Conceptually, the RSCA draw from the three core theoretical areas described above. Each scale is designed to reflect one of these core areas and the implied system of underlying mechanisms that mediate between the environment and the child's internal experience of sense of mastery, sense of relatedness, or emotional reactivity. The three self-report scales are written at a third-grade reading level and consist of 20–23 items each with a total of 64 items. Response options for each item are rated on a 5-point Likert scale: 0 (Never), 1 (Rarely), 2 (Sometimes), 3 (Often), and 4 (Almost Always).

Sense of Mastery Scale and Subscale

A sense of mastery in children and youth provides the opportunity for them to interact with and enjoy cause and effect relationships in the environment. As described previously, the construct of mastery has been discussed by different theorists in slightly different ways. The Sense of Mastery scale consists of 20 items and distinguishes three personal characteristics that combine to form the underpinnings of a youth's sense of mastery—Optimism, Self-Efficacy, and Adaptability. The purpose of this distinction is to include these aspects and to potentially assess the relative contribution of each to a youth's sense of mastery or lack thereof. Sense of Optimism is defined as a positive attitude(s) about the world/life in general and about an individual's life specifically, currently, and in the future. Self-efficacy is defined as the sense that one can master his or her environment and is manifested by the presence of problem-solving strategies and a sense of accomplishment. Adaptability is conceptualized as the ability to learn from one's mistakes and to accept feedback from others.

Sense of Relatedness Scale and Subscales

The Sense of Relatedness scale consists of 24 items and includes four component aspects that contribute to a sense of relatedness: sense of trust, perceived access to support, comfort with others and tolerance. These aspects are conceptually and developmentally interrelated but are at the same time conceptually distinct. Sense of Trust is conceptualized as the extent to which others are perceived as reliable and the extent to which one can be authentic in relationship with others. Access to support is conceptualized as the extent to which a youth believes that there are others who care and to whom he/she can go for help in the face of adversity. Comfort with others is conceptualized as being at ease with others, having friends, spending time with friends and generally being liked by others. Tolerance of differences is conceptualized as being able to express and experience differences in relationship with others. This would manifest itself in assertiveness and forgiveness in relationships.

Emotional Reactivity Scale and Subscales

Emotional reactivity may be viewed as pre-existing vulnerability, arousal, or threshold of tolerance to stimulation prior to the occurrence of adverse events or circumstances. Relative reactivity may have physiological bases, such as temperament, genetic predisposition, learning disability, physical impairment, or congenital anomaly. Siegel (1999) proposed a conceptual framework of self-regulation in which he identified some basic components: regulation of intensity, sensitivity, specificity, windows of tolerance, recovery, access to consciousness, and external expression. The Sensitivity subscale assesses how easily upset or triggered the child is and the intensity of the reaction. The Recovery subscale is designed to assess the perceived time it takes for emotionality to dissipate. The Impairment subscale measures the degree to which a child's emotional reactivity overwhelms his or her capacity to function effectively. In this way, the Emotional Reactivity Scale reflects the extent to which the youth experiences him or herself as maintaining an even keel when emotionally aroused.

Personal Resiliency Profiles

Scholars now underscore the need to consider the unique profiles and associated intervention needs of youth (Luthar, 2006a, 2006b; Luthar & Zelazo, 2003; Zucker, Wong, Puttler, & Fitzgerald, 2003). The second phase of the development of the RSCA included an examination of the relationship between the three core constructs of the model underlying the RSCA. The three global resiliency scales, converted to a common metric, may be plotted together to form a unique Resiliency Profile for each child or adolescent. This Resiliency Profile allows the user to see the youth's relative strengths and vulnerability at a given point in time. The Resiliency Profile also

allows strengths and vulnerabilities to be considered in relation to each other for each youth. In addition, the profile may be compared to what is normative for children of a specific age and gender and/or be compared with profiles that have been observed for specific population. Kumar, Steer, and Gulab (2010) and Mowder, Cummings, and McKinney (2010) provide examples of Personal Resiliency Profiles in clinical and juvenile detention populations.

Resource and Vulnerability Indexes

The need to condense information for the purpose of initial screening led to the development of the Resource and Vulnerability Indexes. The Indexes are not intended to replace the information provided by the Resiliency Scales and/or the Resiliency Profile, as these provide rich information with which to develop intervention strategies for children and adolescents. The indexes are meant to identify students in universal preventive screening for additional monitoring or for proactive intervention (see Prince-Embury, 2010a, 2010b for more information).

The Resource Index

The Resource Index takes into consideration both the individual's Sense of Mastery and Sense of Relatedness Scale scores. Although these core dimensions of resiliency have distinct developmental pathways, these are highly inter-related. Therefore, for screening purposes, combining assessment of these qualities is an expedient way of summarizing the positive strengths available to the individual. The Resource Index score is the standardized mean of the sum of the Sense of Mastery and Sense of Relatedness Scale scores.

The Vulnerability Index

Personal vulnerability is quantified and estimated by the discrepancy between the youth's Emotional Reactivity Scale score and his or her Resource Index score described above. The Vulnerability

Index is consistent with a notion of resiliency as having personal resources which match or exceed one's emotional reactivity, and vulnerability as having personal resources which are significantly below one's level of emotional reactivity.

Reliability Evidence

Cicchetti (1994) suggests that coefficient alphas at or above 0.70 are adequate, at or above 0.80 are good, and at or above 0.90 are excellent. Alphas of 0.90 are thought of as adequate for tracking individual scores over time. Alphas of 0.80 or more are considered adequate for tracking group scores over time. Using these criteria, reliability evidence was excellent for the RSCA Index Scores, good for the three global scale scores, and adequate for most subscales (see RSCA technical manual for details, Prince-Embury, 2007). The RSCA index and global scale scores show good or excellent internal consistency across age and gender groups and, as expected, greater internal consistency was evidenced with increased age (Prince-Embury). For children aged 9–11, the *RSCA Index* scores and the *Emotional Reactivity Scale* score meet the criterion of alpha >0.90 for individual-level tracking. The *Sense of Mastery* and *Sense of Relatedness Scale* scores meet the criterion of alpha >0.80 for group level tracking. For children aged 12–14, the *RSCA Index* scores and all three global scores meet the criterion for individual-level tracking. Six of the *RSCA* subscales met the criterion for group-level tracking. For youth aged 15–18, both Index scores, three global scale scores, and three subscale scores meet the criterion for individual-level tracking. All scores meet the criterion for group-level tracking. Hence, the RSCA demonstrates good to excellent internal consistency, supporting the empirical derivation of the scale, subscales, and indices.

Test–Retest Reliability

Most RSCA scales have at least adequate test–retest consistency across 2 weeks for both the child and adolescent sample. Test–retest reliability is good for the Index and global scale scores. As expected, adolescents evidenced more consistency over time than children (for more detailed information on RSCA reliability, see Prince-Embury, 2007).

Developmental Consistency of Constructs

Although the Resiliency Scales were originally developed and normed for use with adolescents (Prince-Embury, 2006b), they were designed at a third-grade reading level so that the same instrument could be used across a wide age range extending from childhood through adolescence. Before extending the scales downward, the question of whether the core constructs salient for adolescents would be the same for younger children was considered. At different ages and developmental levels, optimism, self-efficacy, mastery, and personal competencies may be exhibited differently. Preschoolers may reveal these strengths in their play, whereas elementary-school-age children may do so verbally, and adolescents may do so cognitively, leaving parents to witness only the outcome. Preliminary analysis examined the developmental consistency of the core constructs underlying the Resiliency Scales on two levels. The more global level of analysis confirmed that the three-factor structure was a better fit than a one or two factor structure across the entire normative sample 9–18 (Prince-Embury, 2007; Prince-Embury & Courville, 2008a). The second level of analysis examined measurement invariance of the three-factor structure across age band. Prince-Embury and Courville (2008b) found support for measurement invariance of this three-factor structure across three age bands.

Validity Evidence

Protective Factors: Self-Concept

Construct validity evidence for the RSCA as a measure of resiliency may be explored in the relationship between RSCA scores and measures of related protective factors. Previous theorists have suggested that resiliency is associated with positive self-concept or self-esteem (see Rutter, Luthar, & Brooks). Research by Dumont and Provost (1999) and others have previously provided support for this assumption. Prince-Embury (2007) described the relationship between the positive Self-Concept score of the Beck Youth Inventory—Second Edition (BYI-II) (Beck, Beck, Jolly, & Steer, 2005) and the RSCA protective factor scores for children and adolescents. Significant positive correlations were found between a positive BYI-II Self-Concept score (Beck et al.) and the RSCA Resource Index (0.78, 0.79), Sense of Mastery (0.74, 0.80), and Sense of Relatedness (0.70, 0.70) Scale scores for child and adolescent groups, suggesting convergent validity for these scores as reflective of protective factors. The RSCA Self-Efficacy subscale was most significantly related to positive self-concept for both children (0.75) and adolescents (0.77) supporting the idea that self-efficacy is an important aspect of resiliency as well as positive self-concept.

The relationship between personal resiliency and positive self-concept was explored in a separate study using the Pier-Harris Children's Self-Concept Scale, Second Edition (Piers-Harris 2; Piers, 2002) (Prince-Embury, 2007). The RSCA Sense of Mastery, Sense of Relatedness Scale, and Resource Index scores were positively correlated with the Pier Harris 2 Total Score (0.60, 0.55, 0.59). The Behavior Adjustment Domain subscale of the Piers Harris 2 was most strongly related to the RSCA scores (0.70, 0.61, 0.69). The RSCA subscale most strongly correlated with Piers Harris 2 Total and Domain scores was the Optimism subscale of the Sense of Mastery Scale. In summary, these findings suggest that positive self-concept is strongly related to but not identical to the Sense of Mastery Scale of the RSCA.

Protective Factor: Parent Attachment

Developmental theory has identified positive parental attachment as a far-reaching protective factor. Construct validity of the RSCA and the Sense of Relatedness Scale in particular may be explored in relation to parental attachment as

examined by the Inventory of Parent and Peer Attachment (IPPA; Armsten & Greenberg, 1987). The IPPA was developed in order to assess the adolescents' perceptions of the positive and negative affective/cognitive dimensions of relationships with the parents. Three broad dimensions are assessed: degree of mutual trust, quality of communication, and extent of anger and alienation. The overall attachment score combines these three. One study of 157 adolescents attending high school in a low socio-economic area of Connecticut correlated overall attachment scores for mother and father with RSCA Index and global scale scores (Luthar, 2006b). The overall attachment score with mother was significantly and positively correlated with the RSCA Resource Index Score (0.52), Sense of Mastery Scale score (0.48), and Sense of Relatedness Scale score (0.50). The overall attachment with father was related to a lesser extent to the three RSCA protective scores (0.36, 0.29, and 0.33). Moderate convergent construct validity was provided by the positive and significant relationships between RSCA protective scores and mother and father attachment scores. Correlations between the Sense of Relatedness Scale scores and attachment scores are slightly but not significantly higher than those between Sense of Mastery scores and attachment. The Resource Index Score correlates most strongly with parental attachment suggesting that combined resources are most related to strength of parent attachment.

Vulnerability, Emotional Reactivity and Measures of Negative Affect, and Behavior

Prince-Embury (2007, 2008) reported strong positive correlations between the Vulnerability Index Score and the Emotional Reactivity score and all BYI-II (Beck et al., 2005) scores of negative affect and behavior for the standardization sample of 200 adolescents. This sample was the normative sample for both the RSCA and the BYI-II and consisted of 100 males and 100 females, each group stratified to represent the US

Census by parent education level and race/ethnicity. The Vulnerability Index score had significant positive correlations with the BYI-II scores; 0.65 with Anxiety, 0.66 with Disruptive Behavior, 0.75 with Depression, and 0.77 with Anger. Similarly, high positive correlations were found between the Emotional Reactivity Scale score and scores on all BYI-II scores; 0.65 with Anxiety, 0.67 with Disruptive Behavior, 0.74 with Depression, and 0.76 with Anger. These findings support the hypothesis that a high degree of emotional reactivity is associated with negative affect and behavior. It might be noted that the Vulnerability Index score and the Emotional Reactivity Scale scores correlate with BYI-II scores across affective domains in adolescents and are not limited to any one affective domain although depression and anger showed the strongest correlations. There are also high negative correlations between the Resource Index score and the BYI-II scores: −0.51 with Disruptive Behavior, −0.53 with Anxiety, −0.61 with Depression, and −0.62 with Anger. Similarly, high negative correlations were found between the Sense of Mastery (−0.51 to −0.61) and the Sense of Relatedness (−0.45 to −0.57) Scales and all BYI-II scores of negative affect and behavior.

Similar results were found in correlational studies of the RSCA with other assessments of problem behaviors such as the Connors Adolescent Symptom Scale (CASS; Conners, 1997) (see Prince-Embury, 2007). In a sample of 89 children aged 9–14, conduct problems as assessed by the CASS were positively correlated with the RSCA Vulnerability Index score (0.62) and the Emotional Reactivity Scale score (0.59). Conversely, the CASS conduct problems score was negatively correlated with the RSCA Resource Index (−0.56), the Sense of Mastery Scale score (−0.51), and the Sense of Relatedness Scale score (−0.57).

Personal Resiliency, Bullying, and Victimization

A study correlating RSCA scores with bullying and victimization scores of the *Reynolds Bully*

Victimization Scales (Reynolds, 2004) for 47 children aged 9–14 suggested some gender differences between the relationship of these behaviors with vulnerability and resources in children (see Prince-Embury, 2007). For boys, the Vulnerability Index and Emotional Reactivity Scale score were significantly positively related to self-reported bullying (0.60, 60) and victimization (0.54, 0.45). Resource Index scores were less significantly related to bullying (−0.21 to −0.38) and victimization (0.02 to −0.21) for boys. For girls, on the other hand, a lower Resource Index score was most significantly related to both bullying and victimization. For girls, the Resource Index, Sense of Mastery, and Sense of Relatedness Scale scores were negatively correlated with self-reported bullying and victimization in the following manner: (Resource Index, −0.75, −0.57), (Sense of Mastery, −0.77, −0.44), and (Sense of Relatedness, −0.63, −0.61). Emotional Reactivity was less related to bullying and victimization for girls (0.26, 0.08). It must be noted that these results are preliminary and should be replicated and expanded upon in larger studies of bullying and victimization. However, if replicated these results would suggest that bullying is related to aspects of personal resiliency and that prevention programs might differ for males and females. Interventions might focus more on managing emotional reactivity for males and on enhancing sense of mastery and relatedness for females.

Personal Resiliency and Risk Behavior

A normative adolescent sample of 100 males and 100 females, aged 15–18, responded to the *Adolescent Risk Behavior Inventory* (ARBS; Prince-Embury, 2006b) which consists of item clusters tapping frequency of alcohol and drug abuse, sexual behavior, self-harm ideation, and sensation seeking, as well as completing the RSCA (Prince-Embury, 2006a, unpublished study). The sample which comprised the normative adolescent sample for the RSCA was stratified by race/ethnicity and parent education level within gender and age (see Prince-Embury,

2007, for details of the sample). The results for females and male adolescents were the following: Emotional Reactivity was positively correlated with self-reported frequency of substance use (0.51), sexual behavior (0.42), self-harm ideation (0.67), and sensation seeking (0.33). Sense of Relatedness was negatively correlated with frequency of substance use (−0.40), sexual behavior (−0.29), self-harm ideation (−0.53), and sensation seeking (−0.24). Sense of Mastery was negatively correlated with frequency of substance use (−0.40), sexual behavior (−0.22), self-harm ideation (−0.53), and sensation seeking (−0.19). Correlations above 0.30 were significant at the $p < 0.001$ level and correlations above 0.20 were significant at the $p < 0.05$ level. These findings suggest that higher Emotional Reactivity is related to higher frequency of risk behavior and ideation in non-clinical adolescents. This was particularly true for ideation of self-harm and use of drugs or alcohol. The protective factors of Sense of Relatedness and Sense of Mastery have modest relationships with lower frequency of risk behavior, particularly use of drugs or alcohol. These findings support the relevance of aspects of personal resiliency to behaviors of concern among adolescents and the relevance of screening for resiliency and vulnerability among non-clinical samples.

Evidence of Criterion Group Differences

Prince-Embury (2007) reported significant differences between mean scores of clinical groups and matched control groups for children and adolescents across several diagnostic groupings. The non-clinical groups scored consistently higher on the Resource Index score, Sense of Mastery, Sense of Relatedness Scales, and subscales. The clinical samples scored consistently higher on the Vulnerability Index, Emotional Reactivity Scale, and subscale scores. Effect sizes were large for all differences (see Prince-Embury, 2007 for details).

Personal Resiliency Profiles

The RSCA Personal Resiliency Profile employs scores on the three global scales, Sense of Mastery, Sense of Relatedness, and Emotional Reactivity, to be charted with respect to each other for the purpose of graphically displaying the relative strengths and vulnerabilities of individuals or groups of individuals. Personal Resiliency Profiles have been described for normative samples (Prince-Embury & Steer, 2010), clinical samples (Kumar et al., 2010; Prince-Embury, 2007), and youth in juvenile detention (Mowder et al., 2010).

Characteristic Personal Resiliency Profiles in the RSCA standardization sample were identified using cluster analysis, a statistical technique for summarizing the variability of profiles into profiles that most characterize the sample (Prince-Embury & Steer, 2010). This method produced three Personal Resiliency Profiles that most characterize the normative sample of children and adolescents. These profiles are displayed in Fig. 16.1. Profile A suggesting High Resiliency represents 31% of the normative samples and is characterized by high Sense of Mastery and Sense of Relatedness along with a low Emotional Reactivity Scale score. Profile B suggesting Adequate Resiliency represents 44% of the normative samples and is characterized by all three global scale scores in the average range. Profile C suggesting High Vulnerability represented 25% of the normative samples and is characterized by low mean Sense of Mastery and Sense of Relatedness Scale scores along with a high mean Emotional Reactivity Scale Score. These three Personal Resiliency Profiles lend support to Masten's concept of resiliency as "ordinary magic." In that 75% of the normative samples would have at least adequate resources to handle most of life's ordinary adversities. The extent to which a high resiliency profile is an advantage remains a question to be examined in future research. The 25% of the normative samples characterized by Low Resiliency have Personal Resiliency Profiles similar to those of clinical

Fig. 16.1 Profiles of personal resiliency in a normative sample, $n = 641$ (Prince-Embury & Steer, 2010)

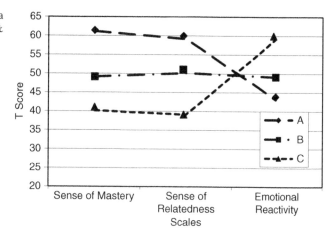

samples studies although these individuals were undiagnosed at the time of testing. We may speculate that these youth with Low Resiliency Profiles are symptom free because they have not encountered sufficient adversity to precipitate the emergence of symptoms. On the other hand, it may be that this 25% of the normative samples are symptomatic but undiagnosed. Preventive screening using the RSCA would potentially identify those youth with Low Resiliency for preventive psychosocial intervention.

Resiliency Profiles of Adolescent Clinical Disorder Groups

Figure 16.2 displays Resiliency Profiles for five adolescent clinical groups and the nonclinical adolescent sample based on the mean T scores for the Sense of Mastery, Sense of Relatedness, and Emotional Reactivity scales for each diagnostic group (see technical manual for description of samples, Prince-Embury, 2007). As anticipated, the profile for the nonclinical group is relatively flat with mean T scores close to 50 on all three scales. This profile is similar to Profile B in Fig. 16.1 characterizing 44% of the normative samples. In contrast, the profiles for the clinical groups slope up to the right on the chart. This profile is due to characteristically low scores on the Sense of Mastery and Sense of Relatedness Scales and characteristically high scores on

Emotional Reactivity Scale for adolescents diagnosed with clinical disorders. The Depressive Disorder, Anxiety Disorder, Conduct Disorder, and Bipolar Disorder groups scored below average or low on the Sense of Mastery and Sense of Relatedness Scales. These groups scored in the above average or high range for the Emotional Reactivity Scale. The Nonspecific group, which had been in treatment and/or on medication for over a month, indicated a profile that was within the average range unlike the other clinical groups but still distinct from the nonclinical sample. This group manifested Sense of Mastery and Sense of Relatedness Scale scores in the low average range and Emotional Reactivity in the high average range. In summary, the adolescent clinical disorder groups have a tendency to report low Sense of Mastery and Sense of Relatedness, on one hand, and high Emotional Reactivity, on the other, relative to the nonclinical samples. Differences in the shape of the profiles are also notable. The shape of the Resiliency Profile of the nonclinical samples is flat and in the average range. In contrast, the profiles of the clinical groups have reverse slopes or elbow shapes with similar reports of Sense of Mastery and Sense of Relatedness, and a large discrepancy between these strength scores and an elevated Emotional Reactivity Scale score. The shape of the clinical Resiliency Profiles is consistent with the construction of the Vulnerability Index as the discrepancy between personal resources and emotional reactivity.

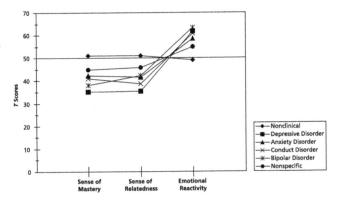

Fig. 16.2 Profiles of personal resiliency in adolescent clinical and non-clinical samples (reprinted Table 3.2 on page 29 of the RSCA Manual, Prince-Embury, 2007)

Preventive Screening Using the RSCA Index Scores

The relationships between the three global RSCA scores illustrated in the profiles in Figs. 16.1 and 16.2 above may be quantified and expressed in the two Index scores described earlier in this chapter. The Resource Index combines the Sense of Mastery and Sense of Relatedness Scale scores. The Vulnerability Index score quantifies the difference between the Emotional Reactivity scale score and the Resource Index score. As illustrated in Fig. 16.2, the graphic presentation of the resiliency profile allows us to view this discrepancy across clinical groups. Validity evidence discussed earlier in this chapter suggests that the Vulnerability Index is correlated with negative affect and discriminates significantly between clinical and non-clinical samples (Prince-Embury, 2007, 2008). Therefore, preventive screening may use the Vulnerability Index to identify students who may be at risk for developing clinical symptoms and other difficulties before the emergence of disabling symptoms. Students who have Vulnerability Index T-scores in the high ranges (T60 or above) may be screened for further examination. See Prince-Embury (2010a, 2010b) for additional information on use of the RSCA in preventive screening.

A Clinical Case Study

Below is an example of how the RSCA may be used to assess a youth's relative strengths and vulnerabilities as a guide for treatment in an outpatient setting. Also illustrated is use of the RSCA to assess treatment outcome with respect to changes in general and specific strengths and vulnerabilities.

Figure 16.3 displays the RSCA Personal Resiliency Profile and Index Scores for Ellen, a 17-year-old girl, at her initial therapy session. On the right-hand side of the chart, we see that Ellen's Vulnerability Index score is extremely high (T80) and her Resource Index score is extremely low (T26). On the left-hand side of the chart, Ellen's Emotional Reactivity Scale score is extremely high (T80) and her Sense of Mastery (T30) and Sense of Relatedness Scale score (T25) are both extremely low. This profile expresses severe vulnerability and was in fact accompanied by subjectively reported distress and extremely elevated scores on various symptom measures. This protocol called for referral for psychiatric and medication consultation and ruling out the possible need for hospitalization. From a treatment planning perspective, this protocol indicated a need to reduce Emotional Reactivity followed by interventions to increase Sense of Relatedness and Sense of Mastery. Examination of subscale scores discussed below elaborates on the issues indicated above in Ellen's profile.

Ellen's subscale scores on the Emotional Reactivity Scale were the following: Sensitivity (17), Recovery (14), and Impairment (20) based on a scale of 1–19 with a mean of 10 and standard deviation of 3. These subscale scores are consistent with parent reports that Ellen had shown Impairment as poor judgment in her behavior by skipping school, driving without a license, and other risk-taking behaviors. She manifested high

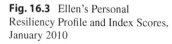

Fig. 16.3 Ellen's Personal Resiliency Profile and Index Scores, January 2010

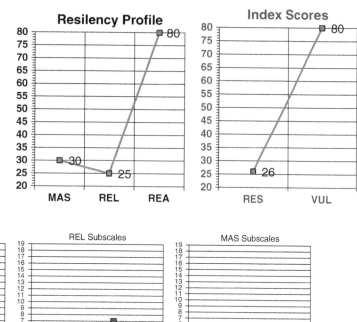

Fig. 16.4 Ellen's subscale scores at first session in January 2010

Sensitivity in reaction to her parents and any attempts to restrict her behavior. This extreme Emotional Reactivity was dealt with by explaining emotional reactivity to Ellen and her parents and discussing ways to control it using time outs and avoiding trigger events. Specific attention was paid to illustrating the role of emotional reactivity in impairing Ellen's functioning. This was important in helping the family understand that not all of Ellen's behaviors were informed by rational choice. Referral for medication evaluation was also initiated (Fig. 16.4).

Ellen's subscale scores on the Sense of Relatedness Scale were the following: Trust (6), Support (0), Comfort (7), and Tolerance (3). These subscale scores underlined the conflict and lack of support experience by Ellen in relation to her parents. Discussion of these scores led to discussion of ways that Ellen's parents could communicate more support to her. It was noted that Ellen's comfort with others was a strength which was manifested in the fact that she had several friends.

Ellen's subscale scores on the Sense of Mastery Scale were the following: Optimism (4), Self-efficacy (5), and Adaptability (5). These subscale scores were consistent with the fact that Ellen who was customarily a good student had begun doing poorly recently. Discussion with Ellen's family who emphasized good grades focused on the need to help Ellen lower her emotional reactivity and experience more support as necessary in order to help her improve her functioning. Item level examination of Ellen's Adaptability score indicated that she did not ask others for help or accept help when offered. Exploration of these themes revealed that there was a perceived culture of self-reliance within the family within which asking for help was viewed as weakness. Family sessions focused on disputing and changing this family culture. Subsequent therapy sessions and maintained medication regime for depression and mood stabilization were aimed at controlling emotional reactivity. Therapy and increasing support led to improvement over a 3-month period. Ellen's RSCA Profiles 3 months later are shown below.

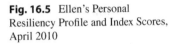

Fig. 16.5 Ellen's Personal
Resiliency Profile and Index Scores,
April 2010

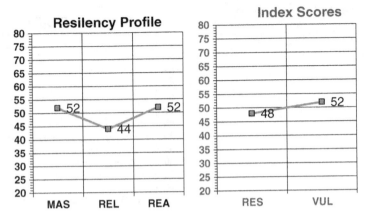

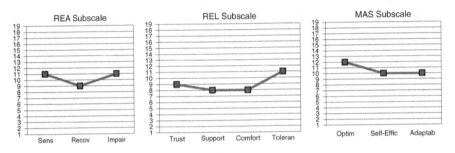

Fig. 16.6 Ellen's subscale scores at first session in April 2010

Ellen's Personal Resiliency Profile and Index scores in April after 3 months of therapy indicate positive change with decreased overall Vulnerability (*T*52) and Emotional Reactivity (*T*52) to within the average range. Also shown are increases in Sense of Mastery (*T*52) to the average range and increase in Sense of Relatedness (*T*44) to slightly below average. Subscale scores indicate more detail about these more global changes (Fig. 16.5).

Ellen's subscale scores when tested in April after 3 months of therapy were all in the average range (Fig. 16.6). The lowering of Ellen's Emotional Reactivity Scale score with the aid of medication helped relieve her distress and helped her to regain academic functioning. Therapy sessions helped to improve communication within the family which in turn increased Ellen's Sense of Support. It should be noted that Ellen's functioning in the average range was supported by continued medication to help her in controlling her Emotional Reactivity. Ellen's increased

understanding of the Emotional Reactivity concept helped her to understand the potentially impairing effect of uncontrolled reactivity, and the importance of compliance to her medication regime. In addition, repeated emphasis on the importance of communication in the family sessions was needed as the family tended to return to more familiar patterns of non-communication. In this case, achieving adequate personal resiliency in order to support adequate functioning was the goal of therapy.

Conclusion

In summary, this chapter has presented the *Resiliency Scales for Children and Adolescents* as an assessment tool designed to tap core developmental processes underlying personal resiliency as experienced by children and adolescents and expressed in their own words. Reference has been made to three major bodies of theory and literature related to the three global scales of the RSCA although a thorough review of this literature would be beyond the scope of this chapter. Reliability and validity evidence for the RSCA have been referenced although a more extensive understanding of this work may be found in the RSCA technical manual (Prince-Embury, 2007) and related publications (Prince-Embury & Courville, 2008a, 2008b; Prince-Embury & Steer, 2010).

The Personal Resiliency Profile has been presented as a tool for graphically comparing relative strengths and vulnerabilities within individuals and across normative and clinical groups of children and adolescents. Reference has been made to the use of the Vulnerability Index for preventive screening to identify youth who may have insufficient personal resources and may be vulnerable to the emergence of disabling psychological symptoms. The advantage of screening that is not pathology based and stigmatizing is discussed further in Prince-Embury (2010a, 2010b). Finally, a clinical case has been presented to illustrate the use of the RSCA for treatment planning and progress monitoring.

References

Ainsworth, M. D. S., & Wittig, B. A. (1969). Attachment and exploratory behavior of one-year-olds in a strange situation. In B. M. Foss (Ed.), *Determinants of infant behaviour* (Vol. 4, pp. 111–136). London: Methuen & Company.

Allen, J. P., Hauser, S. T., & Borman-Spurrell, E. (1996). Attachment theory as a framework for understanding sequelae of severe adolescent psychopathology: An 11-year follow-up study. *Journal of Consulting and Clinical Psychology, 64*(2), 254–263.

Armsten, G. C., & Greenberg, M. T. (1987). Inventory of Parent and Peer Attachment: Individual differences and their relationship to psychological well-being in adolescents. *Journal of Youth and Adolescents, 16*(5), 427–454.

Baldwin, A. L., Baldwin, C. P., Kasser, T., Zax, M., Sameroff, A., & Seifer, R. (1993). Contextual risk and resiliency during late adolescence [Special issue]. *Development and Psychopathology, 5*(4), 741–761.

Bandura, A. (1977). Self-efficacy: Toward a unifying theory of behavioral change. *Psychological Review, 84*(2), 191–215.

Bandura, A. (1993). Perceived self-efficacy in cognitive development and functioning. *Educational Psychologist, 28*(2), 117–148.

Bandura, A. (1997). *Self-efficacy: The exercise of control.* New York: Freeman.

Bandura, A., & Schunk, D. H. (1981). Cultivating competence, self-efficacy, and intrinsic interest through proximal self-motivation. *Journal of Personality and Social Psychology, 41*(3), 586–598.

Barrera, M. (1986). Distinction between social support concepts, measures and models. *American Journal of Community Psychology, 14*, 413–445.

Beck, J. S., Beck, A. T., Jolly, J. B., & Steer, R. A. (2005). *Beck youth inventories—Second edition.* San Antonio, TX: Harcourt Assessment, Inc.

Block, J. H., & Block, J. (1980). The role of ego-control and ego-resiliency in the organization of behavior. In W. A. Collins (Ed.), *Development of cognition, affect, and social relations. The Minnesota symposia on child psychology* (Vol. 13, pp. 39–101). Hillsdale, NJ: Lawrence Erlbaum.

Bowlby, J. (1969). *Attachment and loss: Vol. 1. Attachment.* New York: Basic Books.

Brooks, R., & Goldstein, S. (2001). *Raising resilient children: Fostering strength, hope, and optimism in your child.* San Antonio, TX: The Psychological Corporation.

Brooks, R. B. (1994). Children at risk: Fostering resilience and hope. *The American Journal of Orthopsychiatry, 64*(4), 545–553.

Cicchetti, D. V. (1994). Guidelines, criteria, and rules of thumb for evaluating normed and standardized assessment instruments in psychology. *Psychological Assessment, 6*(4), 284–290.

Cicchetti, D., Ganiban, J., & Barnett, D. (1991). Contributions from the study of high-risk populations to understanding the development of emotion regulation. In J. Garber & K. A. Dodge (Eds.), *The development of emotion regulation and dysregulation* (pp. 15–48). Cambridge, UK: Cambridge University Press.

Cicchetti, D., & Toth, S. L. (1997). Transactional ecological systems in developmental psychopathology. In S. S. Luthar, J. A. Burack, D. Cicchetti, & J. R. Weisz (Eds.), *Developmental psychopathology: Perspectives on adjustment, risk, and disorder* (pp. 317–349). Cambridge, UK: Cambridge University Press.

Cicchetti, D., & Tucker, D. (1994). Development and self-regulatory structures of the mind [Special issue]. *Development and Psychopathology, 6*(4), 533–549.

Cohen, S., & Wills, T. A. (1985). Stress, social support and the buffering hypothesis. *Psychological Bulletin, 98*, 310–357.

Conners, C. K. (1997). *Conners' rating scales—revised technical manual.* Toronto: Multi-Health Systems, Inc.

Conrad, M., & Hammen, C. (1993). Protective and resource factors in high- and low-risk children: A comparison of children with unipolar, bipolar, medically ill, and normal mothers [Special issue]. *Development and Psychopathology, 5*(4), 593–607.

Cowen, E. L., Pryor-Brown, L., Hightower, A. D., & Lotyczewski, B. S. (1991). Age perspectives on the stressfulness of life-events for 10–12 year old children. *School Psychology Quarterly, 6*(4), 240–250.

Cowen, E. L., & Work, W. C. (1988). Resilient children, psychological wellness, and primary prevention. *American Journal of Community Psychology, 16*(4), 591–607.

Dumont, M., & Provost, M. A. (1999). Resilience in adolescents: Protective role of social support, coping strategies, self-esteem, and social activities on experience of stress and depression. *Journal of Youth and Adolescence, 28*(3), 343–363.

Erikson, E. H. (1963). *Childhood and society* (2nd ed.). New York: W. W. Norton & Company.

Fonagy, P., Steele, M., Steele, H., Higgitt, A., & Target, M. (1994). The Emanuel Miller Memorial Lecture 1992: The theory and practice of resilience. *Journal of Child Psychology and Psychiatry, 35*(2), 231–257.

Garmezy, N. (1991). Resiliency and vulnerability to adverse developmental outcomes associated with poverty. *American Behavioral Scientist, 34*(4), 416–430.

Garmezy, N., Masten, A. S., & Tellegen, A. (1984). The study of stress and competence in children: A building block for developmental psychopathology. *Child Development, 55*, 97–111.

Goldstein, S., & Brooks, R. B. (Eds.). (2005). *Handbook of resilience in children*. New York: Kluwer Academic.

Gribble, P. A., Cowen, E. L., Wyman, P. A., Work, W. C., Wannon, M., & Raoof, A. (1993). Parent and child views of parent-child relationship qualities and resilient outcomes among urban children. *Journal of Child Psychology and Psychiatry, 34*(4), 507–519.

Jacelon, C. S. (1997). The trait and process of resilience. *Journal of Advanced Nursing, 25*, 123–129.

Jackson, Y., & Warren, J. S. (2000). Appraisal of social support and life events: Predicting outcome behavior in school age children. *Child Development, 71*, 1441–1457.

Kaufman, J., Yang, B., Douglas-Palumberi, H., Houshyar, S., Lipschitz, D., Krystal, J. H., et al. (2004). Social supports and serotonin transporter gene moderate depression in maltreated children. *Proceedings of the National Academy of Sciences, 101*, 17316–17321.

Kumar, G., Steer, R., & Gulab, N. (2010). Profiles of personal resiliency in child and adolescent inpatients. *Journal of Psychoeducational Assessment, 28*(4), 315–325.

Luthar, S. S. (1991). Vulnerability and resilience: A study of high-risk adolescents. *Child Development, 62*, 600–616.

Luthar, S. S. (2003). *Resilience and vulnerability: Adaptation in the context of childhood adversities*. Cambridge, UK: Cambridge University Press.

Luthar, S. S. (2006a). Resilience in development: A synthesis of research across five decades. In D. Cicchetti & D. J. Cohen (Eds.), *Developmental psychopathology: Risk, disorder, and adaptation* (2nd ed., Vol. 3, pp. 739–795). Hoboken, NJ: Wiley.

Luthar, S. S. (2006b). Unpublished study.

Luthar, S. S., & Zelazo, L. B. (2003). Research on resilience: An integrative review. In S. S. Luthar (Ed.), *Resilience and vulnerability: Adaptation in the context*

of childhood adversities (pp. 510–549). Cambridge: Cambridge University Press.

Luthar, S. S., & Zigler, E. (1991). Vulnerability and competence: A review of research on resilience in childhood. *The American Journal of Orthopsychiatry, 61*(1), 6–22.

Luthar, S. S., & Zigler, E. (1992). Intelligence and social competence among high-risk adolescents. *Development and Psychopathology, 4*, 287–299.

Masten, A. S. (2001). Ordinary magic: Resilience processes in development. *American Psychologist, 56*(3), 227–238.

Masten, A. S., & Coatsworth, J. D. (1998). The development of competence in favorable and unfavorable environments: Lessons from research on successful children. *American Psychologist, 53*(2), 205–220.

Masten, A. S., & Curtis, W. J. (2000). Integrating competence and psychopathology: Pathways toward a comprehensive science of adaptation in development [Special issue]. *Development and Psychopathology, 12*, 529–550.

Masten, A. S., & Powell, J. L. (2003). A resilience framework for research, policy, and practice. In S. S. Luthar (Ed.), *Resilience and vulnerability: Adaptation in the context of childhood adversities* (pp. 1–25). Cambridge, UK: Cambridge University Press.

Mowder, M., Cummings, J., & McKinney, R. (2010). Resiliency Scales for Children and Adolescents: Profiles of juvenile offenders. *Journal of Psychoeducational Assessment, 28*(4), 326–337.

Pennington, B. F., & Welsh, M. (1995). Neuropsychology and developmental psychopathology. In D. Cicchetti & D. J. Cohen (Eds.), *Developmental psychopathology: Vol. 1. Theory and methods* (pp. 254–290). Oxford, England: Wiley.

Piers, E. (2002). *Piers-Harris children's self-concept scale* (2nd ed.). Los Angeles: Western Psychological Services.

Polk, L. V. (1997). Toward a middle-range theory of resilience. *Advances in Nursing Science, 19*(3), 1–13.

Prince-Embury, S. (2006b). *Adolescent Risk Behavior Inventory*. Unpublished study.

Prince-Embury, S. (2006b). *Resiliency scales for adolescents: A profile of personal strengths*. San Antonio, TX: Harcourt Assessment, Inc.

Prince-Embury, S. (2007). *Resiliency Scales for Children and Adolescents: A profile of personal strengths*. San Antonio, TX: Harcourt Assessment, Inc.

Prince-Embury, S. (2008). The Resiliency Scales for Children and Adolescents, psychological symptoms and clinical status in adolescents. *Canadian Journal of School Psychology, 23*(1), 41–56.

Prince-Embury, S. (2010a). Psychometric properties of the Resiliency Scales for Children and Adolescents and use for youth with psychiatric disorders. *Journal of Psychoeducational Assessment, 28*(4), 291–303.

Prince-Embury, S. (2010b). Assessment for integrated screening and prevention using the Resiliency Scales for Children and Adolescents. In B. Doll, W. Pfohl, &

J. Yoon (Eds.), *Handbook of youth prevention science.* New York: Routledge.

Prince-Embury, S., & Courville, T. (2008a). Comparison of a one, two and three factor models of the Resiliency Scales for Children and Adolescents. *Canadian Journal of School Psychology, 23*(1), 11–25.

Prince-Embury, S., & Courville, T. (2008b). Measurement invariance of the Resiliency Scales for Children and Adolescents across gender and age cohorts. *Canadian Journal of School Psychology, 23*(1), 26–40.

Prince-Embury, S., & Steer, R. (2010). Profiles of personal resiliency for normative and clinical samples of children and adolescents using the Resiliency Scales for Children and Adolescents. *Journal of Psychological Assessment, 28*(4), 303–315.

Rende, R., & Plomin, R. (1993). Families at risk for psychopathology: Who becomes affected and why? [Special issue]. *Development and Psychopathology, 5*(4), 529–540.

Reynolds, W. (2004). *Reynolds bully victimization scale.* San Antonio, TX: Harcourt Assessment.

Rothbart, M. K., & Bates, J. E. (1998). Temperament. In W. Damon (Series Ed.) & N. Eisenberg (Vol. Ed.), *Handbook of child psychology: Vol. 3. Social, emotional, and personality development* (5th ed., pp. 105–176). New York: Wiley.

Rothbart, M. K., & Derryberry, D. (1981). Development of individual differences in temperament. In M. E. Lamb & A. L. Brown (Eds.), *Advances in developmental psychology* (Vol. 1, pp. 37–86). Hillsdale, NJ: Lawrence Erlbaum Associates.

Rutter, M. (1987). Psychosocial resilience and protective mechanisms [Special report]. *The American Journal of Orthopsychiatry, 57*(3), 316–331.

Rutter, M., Harrington, R., Quinton, D., & Pickles, A. (1994). Adult outcome of conduct disorder in childhood: Implications for concepts and definitions of patterns of psychopathology. In R. D. Ketterlinus & M. E. Lamb (Eds.), *Adolescent problem behaviors: Issues and research* (pp. 57–80). Hillsdale, NJ: Lawrence Erlbaum Associates.

Sarason, B. R., Shearon, E. N., Pierce, G. R., & Sarason, I. (1987). Interrelations of social support measures: Theoretical and practical implications. *Journal of Personality and Social Psychology, 50,* 845–855.

Seligman, M. E. P. (1998). The prediction and prevention of depression. In D. K. Routh & R. J. DeRubeis (Eds.), *The science of clinical psychology: Accomplishments and future directions* (pp. 201–214). Washington, DC: American Psychological Association.

Seligman, M. E. P. (2000). Positive psychology. In J. E. Gillham (Ed.), *Science of optimism and hope: Research essays in honor of Martin E. P. Seligman* (pp. 415–429). Philadelphia, PA: Templeton Foundation Press.

Seligman, M. E. P. (with Reivich, K., Jaycox, L., & Gillham, J.). (1995). *The optimistic child.* New York: Houghton Mifflin.

Siegel, D. J. (1999). *The developing mind: How relationships and the brain interact to shape who we are.* New York: Guilford Press.

Thomas, A., & Chess, S. (1977). *Temperament and development.* New York: Brunner/Mazel.

Thompson, R. A. (1990). Emotion and self-regulation. In R. Dienstbier (Series Ed.) & R. Thompson (Vol. Ed.), *Nebraska symposium on motivation 1988: Socioemotional development* (pp. 367–467). Lincoln, NE: University of Nebraska Press.

Thompson, R. A., Flood, M. F., & Goodvin, R. (2006). Social support and developmental psychopathology. In D. Cicchetti & D. J. Cohen (Eds.), *Developmental psychopathology: Risk, disorder, and adaptation* (2nd ed., Vol. 3, pp. 1–37). Hoboken, NJ: Wiley.

Werner, E. E. (1997). Vulnerable but invincible: High-risk children from birth to adulthood. *Acta Paediatrica, 422*(Suppl.), 103–105.

Werner, E. E., & Smith, R. S. (1982). *Vulnerable but invincible: A longitudinal study of resilient children and youth.* New York: McGraw-Hill.

Werner, E. E., & Smith, R. S. (1992). *Overcoming the odds: High risk children from birth to adulthood.* Ithaca: Cornell University Press.

Werner, E. E., & Smith, R. S. (2001). *Journeys from childhood to midlife: Risk, resilience, and recovery.* Ithaca: Cornell University Press.

White, R. W. (1959). Motivation reconsidered: The concept of competence. *Psychological Review, 66*(5), 297–333.

Wolff, S. (1995). The concept of resilience. *The Australian and New Zealand Journal of Psychiatry, 29*(4), 565–574.

Wright, M. O., & Masten, A. S. (1997). Vulnerability and resilience in young children. In J. D. Noshpitz (Series Ed.) & S. Greenspan, S. Weider, & J. Osofsky (Vol. Eds.), *Handbook of child and adolescent psychiatry: Vol. 1. Infants and preschoolers: Development and syndromes* (pp. 202–224). New York: Wiley.

Wyman, P. A., Cowen, E. L., Work, W. C., & Kerley, J. H. (1993). The role of children's future expectations in self-system functioning and adjustment to life stress: A prospective study of urban at-risk children [Special issue]. *Development and Psychopathology, 5*(4), 649–661.

Wyman, P. A., Cowen, E. L., Work, W. C., & Parker, G. R. (1991). Developmental and family milieu correlates of resilience in urban children who have experienced major life stress. *American Journal of Community Psychology, 19*(3), 405–426.

Wyman, P. A., Cowen, E. L., Work, W. C., Raoof, A., Gribble, P. A., Parker, G. R., et al. (1992). Interviews with children who experienced major life stress: Family and child attributes that predict resilient outcomes. *Journal of the American Academy of Child and Adolescent Psychiatry, 31*(5), 904–910.

Zucker, R. A., Wong, M. M., Puttler, L. I., & Fitzgerald, H. E. (2003). Resilience and vulnerability among sons of alcoholics: Relationship to developmental outcomes between early childhood and adolescence. In S. S. Luthar (Ed.), *Resilience and vulnerability: Adaptation in the context of childhood adversities* (pp. 76–103). Cambridge, UK: Cambridge University Press.

Part V

Resilience in the Clinical and School Settings

Resilience and Positive Youth Development: A Relational Developmental Systems Model

17

Richard M. Lerner, Jennifer P. Agans, Miriam R. Arbeit, Paul A. Chase, Michelle B. Weiner, Kristina L. Schmid, and Amy Eva Alberts Warren

Adolescents are not resilient. Resilience is also not a functional feature of the ecology of adolescent development (e.g., as may be represented by the concept of "protective factors"). Rather, resilience is a concept denoting that the *relationship* between an adolescent and his or her ecology has adaptive significance. That is, the relationship involves a fit between characteristics of an individual youth and features of his or her ecology that reflects either adjustment (change) in the face of altered or new environmental threats, challenges, or "processes," or constancy or maintenance of appropriate or healthy functioning in the face of environmental variations in the resources needed for appropriate or healthy functioning. As such, the individual–context relationship summarized by the term "resilience" reflects individual well-being at a given point in time, and thriving across the adolescent period, in the face of features within the ecological context that challenge adaptation. In turn, this relationship also implies that, for the ecology or context, there are actions that could maintain or further the quality of its structure (e.g., the family, schools, or community programs for youth development) or its function in the service of supporting healthy adolescent behavior and development (e.g., parenting that reflects warmth and appropriate monitoring; low student–teacher ratios involving engaged students and high quality institutions; and access to competent, caring, and committed mentors in out-of-school-time [OST] youth development programs, respectively).

Resilience is, then, a dynamic attribute of a relationship between an individual adolescent and his or her multilevel and integrated (relational) developmental system. We represent this mutually influential relation between a youth and the context as individual $\longleftrightarrow$ context relations. In our view, the process of individual $\longleftrightarrow$ context relations involved in resilience is *not* distinct from the relations involved in human functioning in general. What is distinct, however, is that exchanges involving resilience are located at a portion of a theoretical probability distribution of these relations that may be described as involving nonnormative levels of risk or high levels of adversity (see Fig. 17.1). In short, the process we study in seeking to understand resilience differs from the other instances of individual $\longleftrightarrow$ context relations only in regard to location in this distribution.[1]

Accordingly, since resilience is not a characteristic of either component of the individual

---

[1] Clearly, the translation of this theoretical probability distribution into empirical reality will vary in relation to individuals across the course of adolescence, as well as in relation to group differences and diverse contexts. In short, there is intraindividual variability, and between-group differences in intraindividual changes in the empirical probability distribution pertinent to resilience.

R.M. Lerner (✉) • J.P. Agans • M.R. Arbeit • P.A. Chase • M.B. Weiner • K.L. Schmid • A.E.A. Warren
Tufts University, Medford, MA, USA
e-mail: richard.lerner@tufts.edu

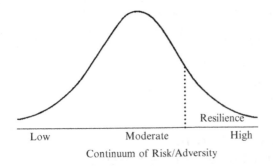

Fig. 17.1 Theoretical probability distribution of instances of adaptive individual ←→ context relations in the face of differing levels of risk and adversity

←→context relationship (i.e., resilience is not an attribute of the adolescent or of the context), it should be studied within a nonreductionist theoretical frame and through the use of change-sensitive and multilevel (and hence multivariate) developmental methods, including longitudinal designs that involve measurement models that are sensitive to change and diversity (e.g., Collins, 2006; Lerner, Schwartz, & Phelps, 2009a; Little, Card, Preacher, & McConnell, 2009). To approach the conceptualization, study, and measurement of resilience in this manner entails the use of contemporary relational developmental systems theoretical models of human development, which—today—are at the cutting-edge of developmental science (e.g., Lerner, 2012; Overton, 2006, 2010; Overton & Mueller, in press).

Indeed, the scientific study of resilience within the developmental system is an excellent sample case of the utility of such theoretical models as frames with which to elucidate the basic, relational processes of adolescent development and, as well, for the application of developmental science to promote positive youth development (PYD; Lerner, 2006; Masten, 2009; Masten & Obradović, 2006; Wachs, 2006; see, too, Lerner, Weiner, Arbeit, Chase, Agans, Schmid, Warren, 2012). Accordingly, to understand the nature and significance of basic and applied facets of the developmental science of adolescence to the study of resilience, it is useful to specify the features of current developmental systems models.

This discussion will afford specification of the dynamic, relational character of resilience.

The Developing Context of the Concept of Development

Developmental psychology has been transformed into developmental science. As richly illustrated by the chapters across the four volumes of the *Handbook of Child Psychology*, 6th edition (Damon & Lerner, 2006), as well as in other major publications in the field (e.g., Bornstein & Lamb, 2010; Lamb & Freund, 2010; Lerner, Easterbrooks, & Mistry, in preparation; Overton, 2010), the study of human development has evolved from being either a psycogenic or a biogenic approach to conceptualizing and studying the life span, to a multidisciplinary approach that seeks to integrate variables from biological through cultural and historical levels of organization into a synthetic, coactional system (Elder, 1998; Gottlieb, 1997, 1998; Hood, Halpern, Greenberg, & Lerner, 2010). As such, reductionist accounts of development that adhere to a Cartesian dualism, and that pull apart facets of the integrated developmental system, are rejected by proponents of relational, developmental systems theories (Mistry, 2011; Mistry & Wu, 2010; Overton, 2010). These reductionist views typically raise as key developmental issues such split formulations as nature vs. nurture, continuity vs. discontinuity, stability vs. instability, or basic vs. applied.

We eschew such thinking. In turn, we favor post-postmodern, relational models stressing the integration of different levels of organization as a means to understand and to study life-span human development (Overton, 2010; Overton & Mueller, in press). Thus, as exemplified by the focus of inquiry in the contemporary study of resilience, the conceptual emphasis of relational developmental systems theory is placed on the nature of mutually influential individual ←→ context relations, that is, the focus is on the "rules," the processes that govern exchanges between individuals and their contexts. Brandtstädter (1998) terms these relations "developmental regulations" and notes that where developmental regulations involve mutually beneficial individual ←—→ context relations, they constitute *adaptive* developmental regulations. As suggested earlier, we believe that adaptive developmental regulations are the essence of resilience. Table 17.1 summarizes the set of defining features of relational developmental systems models.

The combined ideas presented in the table suggest that the possibility of adaptive developmental relations between adolescents and their contexts, and the potential plasticity of human development that is a defining feature of ontogenetic change within the relational developmental system, are distinctive features of this approach to youth development. As well, the core features of relational developmental systems models—including integration and mutual influence of levels of organization, plasticity, and diversity—provide a rationale for making a set of methodological choices that differ in design, measurement, sampling, and data analytic techniques from selections made by researchers using split or reductionist approaches to developmental science (Overton, 2010). For example, the emphasis on how the individual acts on the context to contribute to the plastic relations within it fosters an interest in person-centered (as compared to variable-centered) approaches to the study of human development.

Adding to the complexity of the study of human development is the fact that the array of individual and contextual variables involved in person–context relations constitutes a virtually open set. Estimates are that the odds of two genetically identical genotypes arising in the human population is about 1 in 6.3 billion, and each of these potential human genotypes may be coupled across life with an even larger number of life course trajectories of social experiences (Hirsch, 2004). Thus, the number of human phenotypes that can exist is fundamentally equivalent to infinity, and the diversity of development becomes a prime, substantive focus for developmental science. This diversity may be approached with the expectation that positive changes can be promoted across all instances of variation, as a consequence of health-supportive alignments

between youth and settings. With this stance, diversity becomes the necessary subject of inquiry in developmental science, and in the study of resilience.

We define resilience here as relations reflecting the maintenance or enhancement of links that are mutually beneficial to individual youth and contexts.[2] In order to understand the bases of and, in turn, to promote individual ←—→ context relations that may be characterized as resilient among diverse youth, scholars must ask a complex, multipart question. They must ascertain: *what fundamental attributes of individual youth* (e.g., what features of cognition, motivation, emotion, ability, physiology, or temperament); among *adolescents of what status attributes* (e.g., youth at what portions of the adolescent period, and of what sex, race, ethnic, religious, geographic location, etc. characteristics); in relation to *what characteristics of the context* (e.g., under what conditions of the family, the neighborhood, social policy, the economy, or history); are likely to be associated with *what facets of adaptive functioning, or PYD* (e.g., maintenance of health and of active, positive contributions to family, community, and civil society)?

Addressing such a set of interrelated questions requires, at the least, a systematic program of research. Nevertheless, the linkage between the ideas of plasticity and diversity that gave rise to this set of questions provides a rationale for extending relational developmental systems thinking to an optimistic view of the potential to apply developmental science to promote individual ←—→ context exchanges that may reflect and/or promote health and positive, successful youth development; in other words, that may reflect resilience. Accordingly, employing a relational developmental systems frame for the application of developmental science affords a basis for forging a new, strength-based vision of and vocabulary for the nature of youth development and for specifying the set of individual and ecological

---

[2]Individual actions that are not supportive of the institutions and agents of the ecology (that are acting to support the individual) are ultimately not reflective of resilience and, as well, are not sustainable (Lerner, 2004).

Table 17.1 Defining features of relational developmental systems theories

A relational metamodel

Predicated on a post-modern philosophical perspective that transcends Cartesian dualism, developmental systems theories are framed by a relational metamodel for human development. There is, then, a rejection of all splits between components of the ecology of human development, e.g., between nature- and nurture-based variables, between continuity and discontinuity, or between stability and instability. Systemic syntheses or integrations replace dichotomizations or other reductionist partitions of the developmental system

The integration of levels of organization

Relational thinking and the rejection of Cartesian splits is associated with the idea that all levels of organization within the ecology of human development are integrated, or fused. These levels range from the biological and physiological through the cultural and historical

Developmental regulation across ontogeny involves mutually influential individual $\longleftrightarrow$ context relations

As a consequence of the integration of levels, the regulation of development occurs through mutually influential connections among all levels of the developmental system, ranging from genes and cell physiology through individual mental and behavioral functioning to society, culture, the designed and natural ecology and, ultimately, history. These mutually influential relations may be represented generically as Level 1 $\longleftrightarrow$ Level 2 (e.g., Family $\longleftrightarrow$ Community) and, in the case of ontogeny may be represented as individual $\longleftrightarrow$ context

Integrated actions, individual $\longleftrightarrow$ context relations, are the basic unit of analysis within human development

The character of developmental regulation means that the integration of actions—of the individual on the context and of the multiple levels of the context on the individual (individual $\longleftrightarrow$ context)—constitute the fundamental unit of analysis in the study of the basic process of human development

Temporality and plasticity in human development

As a consequence of the fusion of the historical level of analysis—and therefore temporality—within the levels of organization comprising the ecology of human development, the developmental system is characterized by the potential for systematic change, by plasticity. Observed trajectories of intraindividual change may vary across time and place as a consequence of such plasticity

Plasticity is relative

Developmental regulation may both facilitate and constrain opportunities for change. Thus, change in individual $\longleftrightarrow$ context relations is not limitless, and the magnitude of plasticity (the probability of change in a developmental trajectory occurring in relation to variation in contextual conditions) may vary across the life span and history. Nevertheless, the potential for plasticity at both individual and contextual levels constitutes a fundamental strength of all human development

Intraindividual change, interindividual differences in intraindividual change, and the fundamental substantive significance of diversity

The combinations of variables across the integrated levels of organization within the developmental system that provide the basis of the developmental process will vary at least in part across individuals and groups. This diversity is systematic and lawfully produced by idiographic, group differential, and generic (nomothetic) phenomena. The range of interindividual differences in intraindividual change observed at any point in time is evidence of the plasticity of the developmental system, and makes the study of diversity of fundamental substantive significance for the description, explanation, and optimization of human development

Optimism, the application of developmental science, and the promotion of positive human development

The potential for and instantiations of plasticity legitimate an optimistic and proactive search for characteristics of individuals and of their ecologies that, together, can be arrayed to promote positive human development across life. Through the application of developmental science in planned attempts (i.e., interventions) to enhance (e.g., through social policies or community-based programs) the character of humans' developmental trajectories, the promotion of positive human development may be achieved by aligning the strengths (operationalized as the potentials for positive change) of individuals and contexts

Multidisciplinarity and the need for change-sensitive methodologies

The integrated levels of organization comprising the developmental system require collaborative analyses by scholars from multiple disciplines. Multidisciplinary knowledge and, ideally, interdisciplinary knowledge is sought. The temporal embeddedness and resulting plasticity of the developmental system requires that research designs, methods of observation and measurement, and procedures for data analysis be change-sensitive and able to integrate trajectories of change at multiple levels of analysis

Source: Adapted from Lerner (2006)

conditions that, together, may reflect resilience. The plasticity-diversity linkage within relational developmental systems theory and method provides the basis for the formulation of a PYD perspective, one where the potential for adolescent resilience is ubiquitous across this period of life (and indeed across the life span).

Key Facets of a PYD Perspective

The key feature of a PYD perspective predicated on relational developmental systems theory is an emphasis on individual strengths (e.g., the possession of relative plasticity) and the presence of resources within the adolescent's ecology (termed "developmental assets"; Benson, Scales, Hamilton, & Sesma, 2006; Benson, Scales, & Syvertsen, 2011) that, when coupled across adolescence with the strengths of an individual, foster thriving (positive and healthy functioning). Given the ubiquity of relative plasticity across the life span (Lerner, 1984), the PYD perspective posits that all youth have the potential to develop more positively by enhancing adaptive (mutually beneficial) developmental regulations. We emphasize here that resilience is, in fact, adaptive developmental regulation. From a relational developmental systems perspective, all adolescents have the potential to be in relations with their context that reflect resilience. The goal of the developmental science of adolescence is, then, to identify the individual and ecological conditions that reflect resilience and to then apply this information in ways that optimize the chances that diverse youth will manifest these adaptive developmental regulations.

As implied in an earlier discussion of our definition of resilience, of relational developmental systems theory, and of adaptive developmental regulations, such mutually beneficial individual ←→ context relations occur when the strengths of youth are aligned with those resources (the developmental assets) present in the ecology of adolescent development that maximize the probability that the individual's strengths are linked to instances of positive functioning or healthy developmental outcomes. A key idea within the PYD perspective is that youth are embedded in contexts (e.g., families, schools, and communities) that possess such assets, and there is abundant research supporting this idea (e.g., see Benson et al., 2006, 2011; for reviews).

For instance, Theokas and Lerner (2006) have identified four types of ecological developmental assets. Other individuals constitute the ecological asset most likely to be linked to PYD (Theokas & Lerner, 2006). While the peers of adolescents represent important instances of the individuals that may serve as resources for PYD (Brown & Larson, 2009), across adolescence the social support provided by adults constitute a major source of such developmental assets (Rhodes & Lowe, 2009). For example, authoritative parents, who provide high quantities of high quality time with their adolescent children (e.g., involving high monitoring and warmth; Bebiroğlu, 2009), may foster thriving among them (Laursen & Collins, 2009). In addition, adults may serve as effective mentors of adolescents, particularly when they are competent, committed, and continuously present (for at least 1 year; Rhodes, 2002). Teachers or coaches can also enhance, of course, the academic and extracurricular behavior and development of students (Elmore, 2009), and spiritual leaders or guides can promote senses of mattering and meaning in the lives of youth (King, Carr, & Boitor, 2011; Oman, Flinders, & Thoresen, 2008).

Three additional developmental asset categories were identified by Theokas and Lerner (2006). They pointed to institutions (e.g., libraries, parks, or community-based OST programs); to opportunities for interpersonal interaction and collaboration (e.g., as in community programs involving adults and youth working together on food drives or in soup kitchens); and to accessibility (e.g., local OST programs for youth, or the availability of transportation to reach recreational activities or facilities).

Accordingly, within the PYD perspective, as well as within relational developmental systems models that give rise to this view of human development, the ubiquity of both human strengths and contextual developmental assets means that both adolescents and their ecologies are active contributors to the developmental process and to the possible promotion of healthy youth development. Resilience is likely to occur when individual youth possess the capacities, or skills, to align themselves with developmental assets in the face of individual ←→ context relations that vary from normative or expected exchanges between the adolescent and his or her ecology and that may be marked by atypical levels of risk or high levels of adversity. Considerable research has identified the individual contributors to adaptive individual ←→ context relations that enhance the likelihood of resilience. This research pertains to the topic of self-regulation (e.g., Geldhof, Little, & Colombo, 2010; Lerner et al., in press; McClelland, Ponitz, Messersmith, & Tominey, 2010).

The Role of Self-Regulation in Resilience

Across the life span, individuals live in complex physical, social, cultural, and historical contexts. To be resilient—indeed to thrive (acting in manners that optimize one's chances for a life marked by health and positive exchanges with one's world)—individuals make decisions about how to act in ways that meet personal needs and environmental demands (Brandtstädter, 2006; Lewontin, 2000). In other words, youth must act in ways that support their own healthy functioning and, as well, are of benefit to their context. Accordingly, across the adolescent period, youth need to accomplish several adaptive tasks involving self and context. First, they must establish and then build knowledge about the evolving requirements for personal adjustment, given their particular characteristics of physiological, physical, psychological, and behavioral individuality; they must learn also the demands for adaptation present in their specific ecological niche. Second, a foundation must be established and then enhanced for attaining the cognitive and behavioral skill sets needed for setting goals necessary for survival and, even more, for thriving.

To accomplish these ends, strategic thinking and executive functioning need to be coupled with the actions required for turning life goals into reality, that is, into successful personal adjustment and ecological adaptation (Baltes, 1997; Baltes, Lindenberger, & Staudinger, 2006). These adaptive tasks—developing links between thinking and action in the service of adaptation—must occur in the face of a changing body (associated with pubertal maturation; Susman & Dorn, 2009) and a changing world. During adolescence, these individual and ecological changes may necessitate a rapidly evolving developmental trajectory. Such trajectories involve changing neurological, cognitive, emotional, somatic, and behavioral characteristics that evolve in relation to normative and often nonnormative changes in key contexts of life, including families, peer groups, schools, and communities (Bronfenbrenner, 1979, 2005). The foundational and developmental knowledge acquisition and skill attainment required for thriving across adolescence, and the embeddedness of these requirements in multiple and complex trajectories across the developmental system, are enormous (and arguably ontogenetically distinct) across the adolescent period.

Organismic and Intentional Self-Regulation

Developmental science has recognized the theoretical importance across life of establishing and maintaining adaptive developmental regulations for individual thriving and, as well, for understanding the contribution of individuals to the quality of their contexts. For instance, Posner and Rothbart (2000) have stated that "understanding self-regulation is the single most crucial goal for advancing an understanding of development" (p. 427). Not surprisingly, then, in the last decade, there has been a focus in theory and research on self-regulation, that is, on the ways in which the developing physiological, psychological, and behavioral attributes of individuals coalesce to provide the means for them to actively contribute to mutually beneficial individual ←→ context relations. Within this literature, self-regulation is a term that encompasses multiple forms of functioning, ranging from physiological functions to complicated, intentional thought processes. Self-regulation also involves actions designed to either enact strategies for attaining the goals for selected transactions with the context or for compensating effectively when goals are blocked or initial actions fail (Baltes, 1997; Geldhof et al., 2010; Gestsdóttir & Lerner, 2008; McClelland et al., 2010).

As such, self-regulation pertains to all aspects of adaptive developmental regulation, as individuals alter their behaviors—as well as thoughts, attention, and emotions—to react to different contexts and modulate their reactions to and actions aimed at influencing their contexts (Shonkoff & Phillips, 2000). Thus, self-regulation may be defined as "the ability to flexibly activate, monitor, inhibit, persevere and/or adapt one's behavior, attention, emotions and cognitive strategies in response to direction from internal cues, environmental stimuli and feedback from others, in an attempt to attain personally-relevant goals" (Moilanen, 2007, p. 835).

Clearly, these conceptions of self-regulation encompass two integrated but nevertheless distinguishable processes: ones involving either primarily physiological, or organismic, processes, and ones involving primarily intentional processes. Gestsdóttir and Lerner (2008) have explained that intentional self-regulations are contextualized actions that are actively aimed towards harmonizing demands and resources in the context with personal goals in order to attain better functioning and to enhance self-development. Intentional self-regulation is characterized by goal-directed behaviors. Processes of intentional self-regulation are more readily available to consciousness than processes and structures of organismic regulation, which are broad, ontogenetically consistent (i.e., relatively continuous) attributes of a person that involve biologically based, physiological structures and functions that contribute to the relationship an individual has with the environment. Such organismic characteristics, including hypothalamic control of body temperature, circadian rhythms, pubertal timing, and temperamental attributes such as threshold of response or quality of mood, are under no or limited control of the person, and do not involve

intentional efforts of the person to regulate his or her individual ←→ context exchanges.

Both organismic and intentional self-regulation processes must be integrated across life for adaptive developmental regulations to exist and for the developing person to thrive, not only within particular developmental periods but, as well, across the transitions into and out of successive portions of ontogeny. The development of and interindividual differences in organismic self-regulation influence the individual's contributions to adaptive individual ←→ context relations, both directly and in connection to intentional self-regulation (a point to which we will return later in this chapter). Moreover, across the life span, changes in the nature of intentional self-regulation are arguably the major means through which the active individual contributes to the adaptive developmental regulations that mark resilience.

Baltes, Freund, and colleagues agree (e.g., Baltes, 1997; Baltes & Baltes, 1990; Freund & Baltes, 2002; Freund, Li, & Baltes, 1999). These scholars have found that individuals' capacities for intentional self-regulation are important, indeed key, strengths enabling individuals to access the resources needed to optimize the chances that the positive goals they select are attained *or* to compensate effectively when optimization skills (such as resource recruitment, executive functioning, or strategic tracking) fail or when goal-oriented behaviors are blocked. Scholars whose work is focused on adolescence also place a prominent emphasis on the importance of processes of intentional self-regulation for adaptive developmental regulations.

Geldhof and Little (2011) underscored the idea that self-regulation represents a core aspect of human functioning that influences positive development in adolescence. Consistent with the ideas of Baltes (1997), Freund and Baltes (2002), Brandtstädter (1998, 2006), and Heckhausen (1999), Geldhof and Little discuss self-regulation within the context of what they term an action-control model. They regard such a model as a fundamental facet of self-regulation during the first 2 decades of life, in that it links cognitions (beliefs) about the sources of control over behavior with the actions of individuals. In particular, they discuss the development of action-control beliefs. They note that there are at least several action-control beliefs involved in the relationships among agents (self or others), means, and outcomes/ends, and that research has primarily focused on means-ends, agency, and control-expectancy beliefs. As such, they focus on action-control beliefs and their links to positive development. They explain that action-control beliefs are related to physiological well-being, and thus point to the interrelation between organismic and intentional facets of self-regulation. They provide ideas about how the integration of the action-control model with other theories of self-regulation can inform understanding of self-regulation processes across the life span.

Data derived from the 4-H Study of Positive Youth Development (e.g., Lerner, Almerigi, Theokas, & Lerner, 2005; Lerner, von Eye, Lerner, & Lewin-Bizan, 2009b; Lerner, von Eye, Lerner, Lewin-Bizan, & Bowers, 2010) provide information about development during the second decade of life that are consistent with the views of Geldhof and Little (2011). For instance, Gestsdóttir, Urban, Bowers, Lerner, and Lerner (2011) discuss the development of intentional self-regulation in adolescence and the implications of such development for thriving. Indexing intentional self-regulation through the Freund and Baltes (2002) Selection (S), Optimization (O), and Compensation (C; SOC) measure, they summarize the results of several studies that have examined the development of the SOC processes among youth in Grades 5 through 10. They point to positive links among intentional self-regulation, ecological developmental assets, and thriving in adolescence but note, as well, the need for more systematic examination of the longitudinal, bidirectional relationships among individual strengths and contextual assets in relation to outcomes in adolescence and adulthood. To illustrate, Urban, Lewin-Bizan, and Lerner (2010) found that positive development in adolescence is more likely when these SOC skills are aligned with ecological developmental resources associated with community-based, youth development programs.

However, Napolitano, Bowers, Gestsdóttir, and Chase (2011), note that other findings from the 4-H Study data set suggest that an adolescent's SOC skills undergo significant change throughout adolescence while nevertheless playing an important, positive role in promoting his or her thriving. For instance, research indicated that in fifth and sixth graders, SOC existed as a global construct, rather than as the tripartite construct found in adult and aged samples and as described above (Gestsdóttir & Lerner, 2007). This globality of the SOC structure suggested that younger adolescents, while still possessing intentional self-regulation strategies in some sense, had not yet fully developed the distinct and independent components that comprise the SOC model. Younger adolescents had simply "strong SOC" or "weak SOC," rather than a complex combination of these skills. Results indicated that higher SOC scores were positively related to PYD and negatively related to risk or problem behaviors in fifth, sixth, and seventh graders, and as well, predicted placement in the most-optimal developmental trajectories across the same age range (Gestsdóttir et al., 2011; Zimmerman, Phelps, & Lerner, 2007).

Subsequent research involving the 4-H Study indicated that SOC did exist as a tripartite, differentiated, adult-like construct in adolescents in Grades 8 through 10 (Gestsdóttir, Lewin-Bizan, von Eye, Lerner, & Lerner, 2009). Consistent with Werner's orthogenetic principle (1957), which holds in part that development progresses, across life to states of greater differentiation, older adolescents now presented complex combinations of S, O, and C, and, in other research with Grade 10 youth, also of loss-based selection (LBS) behaviors, i.e., behaviors involving the selection of a new goal when an initial one is not attainable (Gestsdóttir, Bowers, von Eye, Napolitano, & Lerner, 2010). While overall SOC scores of adolescents from Grades 8 to 10 were positively correlated with PYD, there were differences in relations with PYD when examining the individual components of SOC. That is, high levels of O, C, and LBS—but not S—were strongly associated with PYD (Gestsdóttir et al., 2009, 2010). Studying the influences and outcomes related to these complex patterns of S, O, C, and LBS development among older adolescents will be an important focus in future research.

In summary, the data from the 4-H Study indicate that a key component for the development of PYD in adolescence may be developmentally and contextually appropriate manifestations of the intentional self-regulation characteristics of selection, optimization, and compensation. As such, we agree with Baltes et al. (2006) that:

> When orchestrating the optimization of development by processes such as selection and compensation, the appraisal of resources is of central importance. Questions such as how to evolve a goal structure and the associated goal-relevant means and motivational investment strategies, how to deal with selection-related disengagements from other possible goals, when to accept a loss and re-orient one's life, and when to still strive harder because current behavior is not yet employed to its fullest capability become crucial in composing life development (p. 643).

Clearly, there is a growing body of scholarship that reflects the theoretical and empirical use of a relational individual ←→ context approach to resilience during the adolescent period, especially one wherein the contribution of youth to this relational process involves the enactment of the cognitive, emotional, and behavioral facets of intentional self-regulation. However, to more fully instantiate this approach to the study of resilience in adolescence, especially as it is manifested within and across the transitions that mark this period of ontogeny and in relation to the key contexts of human development, several important conceptual and methodological issues will need to be addressed.

Problematics in the Study of Resilience Across the Life Span

From a relational developmental systems perspective (Overton, 2010), adaptive individual ←→ context relations constitute the fundamental reflection of resilience. As we have emphasized, resilience exists when developmental regulations involve mutually beneficial actions of the individual youth on the context, and actions of the context on individual adolescents, in relation to nonnormative levels of risk or high levels of adversity. We have argued that the cognitive, emotional, and behavioral attributes, or skill sets, that are involved in intentional self-regulation reflect the fundamental features of the actions of youth that are pertinent to resilience. In turn, when the provision of developmental assets by the ecology of youth development (i.e., resources provided by people or societal institutions or social structures) are secured by youth using intentional self-regulation skills to attain these assets, then adolescents thrive. As such, they are apt to act to maintain the healthy or positive structure, function, and integrity of these developmental assets. Figure 17.2 presents an illustration of this relational developmental systems conception of resilience in adolescence.

However, such integration of actions between youth and their ecologies, while ubiquitous across the adolescent period in signifying resilience, may nevertheless undergo developmental transitions and transformations. That is, we may ask what facets of the system of relations depicted in Fig. 17.2 show quantitative and/or qualitative *continuity* and what facets show quantitative and/or qualitative *discontinuity* across the adolescent decade. We would expect, for instance, that both organismic and intentional self-regulation show developmental variation (intraindividual change) across this period of ontogeny. Thus, the nature of the interrelation between these two fundamental facets of self-regulation should change as well. Moreover, completing this link between organismic and individual self-regulation is the likelihood that the content of intentional self-regulation needs to change as the individual undergoes normative development from the end of childhood through the beginning of adulthood. For instance, such developmental change will occur as different facets of development emerge, and as the resources needed from the context to promote PYD vary in relation to the different developmental tasks of successive portions of adolescence. Indeed, we noted earlier in this chapter that both the structure of intentional self-regulation, as indexed by SOC scores, and

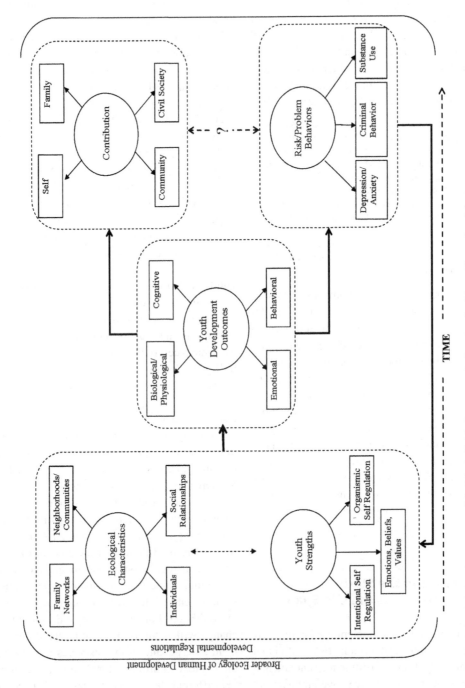

Fig. 17.2 A relational developmental systems model of the individual-context relations involved in resilience in adolescence

of ecological developmental assets may vary across development (e.g., Gestsdóttir & Lerner, 2007; Gestsdóttir et al., 2009, 2010; Zimmerman et al., 2007).

Given these developmental trends, we may ask if there are different structures of ecological developmental assets that covary along with developmental changes in the structure of intentional self-regulation. No research exists in regard to this question of developmental transformation. Similarly, would answers to this question vary if research were focused on adolescents in different cultural contexts? Would answers vary if the focus was on the transitions across this developmental period? Would the fundamental sequence of the linkages across adolescence between intentional self-regulation and developmental assets vary in relation to interindividual differences in intraindividual changes in organismic self-regulation? Again, no research exists to answer these questions.

In addition, how do nonnormative developmental changes or nonnormative historical events interrelate with normative individual and ecological transformations and transitions? Do such individual and ecological variations alter the content or structure of intentional self-regulation and/or ecological assets and, in so doing, constitute a different array of adaptive challenges that, in essence, make the nature of resilience qualitatively or quantitatively different within or across portions of adolescence? Moreover, do answers to these questions vary in regard to the ecological niches within which individual adolescents are interacting? We would expect so. Successful individual ←→ context relations within one's family of origin may involve different facets of intentional self-regulation and of organismic self-regulation (e.g., involving "difficult" temperament styles; Chess & Thomas, 1999). In addition, different facets of intentional self-regulation may be most salient when individual youth engage with different types of ecological resources in middle school vs. in high school, preparing to leave the family of origin to live independently, or in the playground vs. in the place of part-time employment. Once again, research remains to be conducted to address such nuanced questions.

As such research is undertaken, we believe that issues of measurement are paramount. Several interrelated problems exist here. First, there is a tripartite measurement issue involved in the present formulation of resilience. That is, research must develop psychometrically sound indices of the person, of the context and, in particular, of the individual ←→ context relation. Measuring any one of these three foci of inquiry is difficult enough; measurement of all three of these targets of assessment in an integrated way seems particularly challenging, especially given the complicated and evolving methodological issues involved in relational, fit, or difference scores (e.g., Baltes, Reese, & Nesselroade, 1977; Chiou & Spreng, 1996; Cronbach & Furby, 1970; Singer & Willett, 2003; von Eye, 1982).

In addition, there exist issues of measurement equivalence, both across conventional demographic categories (age, race, sex, religion, and culture) and, as well, across these diverse ecological niches to which we have just pointed (e.g., Little et al., 2009). Moreover, measurement in normative settings may not be the same as measurement in the face of nonnormative situations such as wars or natural disasters. Nonnormative settings may transform qualitatively or structurally the requirements that exist for the adaptive individual ←→ context relations reflecting resilience to be identified.

Furthermore, as the sort of research to which we are pointing is pursued, these issues of measurement may be expected to be complicated further by the fact that, as is the case in all facets of adolescent behavior and development, some of the variance in resilience will involve nomothetic, group differential, or idiographic features of human functioning (Kluckhohn & Murray, 1948). For instance, nomothetic characteristics that may play a role in resilience may involve brain structures (such as the amygdala); the sympathetic and the parasympathetic systems, and the endocrine system. Group differential components of human functioning may be marked by the demographic variables we noted above or may be reflected by variation in the social capital available to some social groups, such as religious denominations, but not to others (King & Furrow, 2004; Putnam, 1995), or by the institutions of civil society present in some nations, but not others (Zaff, Kawashima-Ginsberg, & Lin, 2011). Idiographic features may be illustrated by the specific sets of organismic and intentional self-regulatory processes possessed by a person, for instance, particular temperamental attributes (e.g., easy, difficult, or slow-to-warm-up characteristics of temperament; Chess & Thomas, 1999) or the attributes of intentional self-regulation (e.g., elective selection, loss-based selection, optimization, compensation; Freund & Baltes, 2002; tenacious goal pursuit or flexible goal adjustment; Brandtstädter, 1998; or primary or secondary control processes; Heckhausen, 1999) used by an adolescent in a given instance of individual ←→ context relations.

The combination of nomothetic, differential, and idiographic attributes that are present in every adolescent not only makes the study of resilience difficult from a measurement perspective but, along with the other measurement issues we have noted, also requires that a new generation of resilience research be framed by an expression of the complex, interrelated set of questions we noted earlier: For youth with diverse ideographic, group differential, and nomothetic features of functioning, what characteristics of intentional self-regulation (with what structure and content); within or across what portions of adolescence; in what normative or nonnormative proximal (e.g., family, school, or OST activity) and distal (e.g., community, society, culture, or historical epoch) facets of the ecology, and in interrelation with what array of developmental assets, are adaptive individual ←→ context relations instantiated?

Obviously, addressing this complex question involves engaging in a long-term program of research. Perhaps equally as obvious, however, is that answers to these questions have important implications for applications to youth development programs and policies. This observation leads to some final comments about the study of resilience in adolescence.

Conclusions and Recommendations for Application

The promotion of PYD is of fundamental concern to the developmental science of adolescence in that it affords insight into how to test theoretically predicated explanations of fundamental ontogenetic processes by actualizing the optimization goals of the field (Baltes, 1997; Baltes et al., 2006; Lerner, 2004). As such, a focus on resilience in adolescence will elucidate the ways in which relations between active youth and active facets of their ecologies can be constituted to be mutually beneficial to the young person and his or her world.

The relational developmental systems approach to the study of resilience across adolescence provides a largely nascent program of research to account for the facets of contexts and of individual youth, groups of youth, and adolescents in general that must be aligned to optimize the life chances of our diverse humanity. While this research is ongoing, and we still have much to learn about the adaptive developmental regulations that reflect resilient functioning across adolescence, we already have enough knowledge to suggest to practitioners and policy makers that their actions should focus on both individual youth and context and, in particular, on mutually beneficial exchanges between the two, for any adolescent and for adolescents in general to thrive.

In addition, the theoretically framed knowledge base we have presented affords other recommendations for application. For instance, practitioners may take a strength-based approach to promoting successful interactions between youth and their context. If resilience reflects successful functioning when the adolescent's individual ←→ context relations involve high levels of risk and adversity (see Fig. 17.1), then practitioners may explore the developmental history or current circumstances of youth in order to identify such successful relations and seek to replicate them when the adolescent is not showing resilience. In addition, since resilience is not just a person-level characteristic, practitioners should seek to identify the resources in the environment that can enhance the probability that past successes will be reenacted or that will create new, innovative, and healthier individual $\longleftrightarrow$ context interactions in adolescence.

Simply, our message for application is to build on strengths, try to use the resources that keep individual $\longleftrightarrow$ context relations below the tipping point requiring resilience, enhance previous successes, and look for new contextual resources to enhance the probability of resilience among youth in those situations where it is requisite. The evaluation of programs and policies predicated on such a relational developmental systems approach to PYD may, then, feed back to researchers by clarifying steps that may work in enhancing the presence of resilience and the ensuing quality of the condition of young people across the second decade of life.

Acknowledgments The preparation of this chapter was supported in part by grants from the National 4-H Council, the Thrive Foundation for Youth, and the John Templeton Foundation.

References

Baltes, P. B. (1997). On the incomplete architecture of human ontology: Selection, optimization, and compensation as foundation of developmental theory. *The American Psychologist, 23*, 366–380.

Baltes, P. B., & Baltes, M. M. (1990). Psychological perspectives on successful aging: The model of selective optimization with compensation. In P. B. Baltes & M. M. Baltes (Eds.), *Successful aging: Perspectives from the behavioral sciences* (pp. 1–34). New York, NY: Cambridge University Press.

Baltes, P. B., Lindenberger, U., & Staudinger, U. M. (2006). Life span theory in developmental psychology. In W. Damon & R. M. Lerner (Eds.), *Handbook of child psychology* (Theoretical models of human development 6th ed., Vol. 1, pp. 569–664). New York, NY: Wiley.

Baltes, P. B., Reese, H. W., & Nesselroade, J. R. (1977). *Life-span developmental psychology: Introduction to research methods*. Monterey, CA: Brooks/Cole.

Bebiroğlu, N. (2009). *From family to society: The role of parenting behaviors in promoting youth civic engagement*. Doctoral dissertation, Available from ProQuest Dissertations and Theses database (UMI No. 1742035841).

Benson, P. L., Scales, P. C., Hamilton, S. F., & Sesma, A. (2006). Positive youth development: Theory, research and application. In W. Damon & R. M. Lerner (Eds.), *Handbook of child psychology* (Theoretical models of human development 6th ed., Vol. 1, pp. 894–941). New York, NY: Wiley.

Benson, P. L., Scales, P. C., & Syvertsen, A. K. (2011). The contribution of the developmental assets framework to positive youth development theory and practice. In R. M. Lerner, J. V. Lerner, & J. B. Benson (Eds.), *Advances in child development and behavior: Positive youth development* (Vol. 41, pp. 198–227). London, England: Academic.

Bornstein, M. H., & Lamb, M. E. (Eds.). (2010). *Developmental science: An advanced textbook* (6th ed.). New York, NY: Taylor and Francis.

Brandtstädter, J. (1998). Action perspectives on human development. In R. M. Lerner (Ed.), *Handbook of child psychology: Vol. 1. Theoretical models of human development* (5th ed., pp. 807–863) (Editor-in-Chief: W. Damon). New York, NY: Wiley.

Brandtstädter, J. (2006). Action perspectives on human development. In R. M. Lerner (Vol. Ed.) & W. Damon & R. M. Lerner (Eds.), *Handbook of child psychology: Vol. 1. Theoretical models of human development* (6th ed., pp. 516–568). Hoboken, NJ: Wiley.

Bronfenbrenner, U. (1979). *The ecology of human development: Experiments by nature and design*. Cambridge, MA: Harvard University Press.

Bronfenbrenner, U. (2005). *Making human beings human: Bioecological perspectives on human development*. Thousand Oaks, CA: Sage.

Brown, B. B., & Larson, J. (2009). Peer relationships in adolescence. In R. M. Lerner & L. Steinberg (Eds.), *Handbook of adolescent psychology* (Contextual influences on adolescent development 3rd ed., Vol. 2, pp. 74–104). Hoboken, NJ: Wiley.

Chess, S., & Thomas, A. (1999). *Goodness of fit: Clinical applications from infancy through adult life*. Ann Arbor, MI: Edwards Brothers.

Chiou, J., & Spreng, R. A. (1996). The reliability of difference scores: A re-examination. *Journal of Consumer Satisfaction, Dissatisfaction, and Complaining Behavior, 9*, 158–167.

Collins, L. M. (2006). Analysis of longitudinal data: The integration of theoretical model, temporal design, and statistical model. *Annual Review of Psychology, 57*, 505–528.

Cronbach, L. J., & Furby, L. (1970). How we should measure "change"—Or should we? *Psychological Bulletin, 74*, 68–80.

Damon, W., & Lerner, R. M. (Eds.). (2006). *Handbook of child psychology* (6th ed.). Hoboken, NJ: Wiley.

Elder, G. H., Jr. (1998). The life course and human development. In R. M. Lerner (Vol. Ed.) & W. Damon (Ed.), *Handbook of child psychology: Vol. 1. Theoretical models of human development* (5th ed., pp. 939–991). New York, NY: Wiley.

Elmore, R. F. (2009). Schooling adolescents. In R. M. Lerner & L. Steinberg (Eds.), *Handbook of ado-

lescent psychology (Contextual influences on adolescent development 3rd ed., Vol. 2, pp. 193–227). Hoboken, NJ: Wiley.

Freund, A. M., & Baltes, P. B. (2002). Life-management strategies of selection, optimization and compensation: Measurement by self-report and construct validity. *Journal of Personality and Social Psychology, 82,* 642–662.

Freund, A. M., Li, K. Z. H., & Baltes, P. B. (1999). Successful development and aging: The role of selection, optimization, and compensation. In J. Brandtstädter & R. M. Lerner (Eds.), *Action and self-development: Theory and research through the life span* (pp. 401–434). Thousand Oaks, CA: Sage.

Geldhof, G. J., & Little, T. D. (2011). Influences of children's and adolescents' action-control processes in school achievement, peer relationships, and coping with challenging life events. *New Directions for Child and Adolescent Development, 2011,* 45–59.

Geldhof, G. J., Little, T. D., & Colombo, J. (2010). Self-regulation across the life span. In M. E. Lamb & A. M. Freund (Eds.), *Handbook of life-span development* (Social and emotional development, Vol. 2, pp. 116–157). Hoboken, NJ: Wiley.

Gestsdóttir, S., Bowers, E. P., von Eye, A., Napolitano, C. M., & Lerner, R. M. (2010). Intentional self regulation in middle adolescence: The emerging role of loss-based selection in Positive Youth Development. *Journal of Youth and Adolescence, 39*(7), 764–782.

Gestsdóttir, S., & Lerner, R. M. (2007). Intentional self-regulation and positive youth development in early adolescence: Findings from the 4-H Study of Positive Youth Development. *Developmental Psychology, 43*(2), 508–521.

Gestsdóttir, G., & Lerner, R. M. (2008). Positive development in adolescence: The development and role of intentional self regulation. *Human Development, 51,* 202–224.

Gestsdóttir, S., Lewin-Bizan, S., von Eye, A., Lerner, J. V., & Lerner, R. M. (2009). The structure and function of selection, optimization, and compensation in middle adolescence: Theoretical and applied implications. *Journal of Applied Developmental Psychology, 30*(5), 585–600.

Gestsdóttir, S., Urban, J. B., Bowers, E. P., Lewin-Bizan, S., Lerner, J. V., & Lerner, R. M. (2011). Intentional self regulation, ecological assets, and thriving in adolescence: A developmental systems model. In R. M. Lerner, J. V. Lerner, E. P. Bowers, S. Lewin-Bizan, S. Gestsdottir, & J. B. Urban (Eds.), *New Directions for Child and Adolescent Development, 133,* 61–76.

Gottlieb, G. (1997). *Synthesizing nature-nurture: Prenatal roots of instinctive behavior.* Mahwah, NJ: Lawrence Erlbaum Associates.

Gottlieb, G. (1998). Normally occurring environmental and behavioral influences on gene activity: From central dogma to probabilistic epigenesis. *Psychological Review, 105,* 792–802.

Heckhausen, J. (1999). *Developmental regulation in adulthood: Age-normative and sociocultural constraints as*

adaptive challenges. New York, NY: Cambridge University Press.

Hirsch, J. (2004). Uniqueness, diversity, similarity, repeatability, and heritability. In C. Garcia Coll, E. Bearer, & R. M. Lerner (Eds.), *Nature and nurture: The complex interplay of genetic and environmental influences on human behavior and development* (pp. 127–138). Mahwah, NJ: Erlbaum.

Hood, K. E., Halpern, C. T., Greenberg, G., & Lerner, R. M. (Eds.). (2010). *The handbook of developmental science, behavior and genetics.* Malden, MA: Wiley Blackwell.

King, P. E., Carr, D., & Boitor, C. (2011). Religion, spirituality, positive youth development, and thriving. In R. M. Lerner, J. V. Lerner, & J. B. Benson (Eds.), *Advances in child development and behavior* (Vol. 41, pp. 164–197). London, England: Academic.

King, P. E., & Furrow, J. L. (2004). Religion as a resource for positive youth development: Religion, social capital, and moral outcomes. *Developmental Psychology, 40*(5), 703–713.

Kluckhohn, C., & Murray, H. (1948). Personality formation: The determinants. In C. Kluckhohn & H. Murray (Eds.), *Personality in nature, society, and culture.* New York, NY: Knopf.

Lamb, M. E., & Freund, A. M. (Eds.). (2010). *Handbook of life-span development: Vol. 2. Social and emotional development* (Editor-in-Chief: Richard M. Lerner). Hoboken, NJ: Wiley.

Laursen, B., & Collins, W. A. (2009). Parent-child relationships during adolescence. In R. M. Lerner & L. Steinberg (Eds.), *Handbook of adolescent psychology* (Contextual influences on adolescent development 3rd ed., Vol. 2, pp. 3–42). Hoboken, NJ: Wiley.

Lerner, R. M. (1984). *On the nature of human plasticity.* New York: Cambridge University Press.

Lerner, R. M. (2004). *Liberty: Thriving and civic engagement among America's youth.* Thousand Oaks, CA: Sage.

Lerner, R. M. (2006). Developmental science, developmental systems, and contemporary theories of human development. In W. Damon & R. M. Lerner (Eds.), *Handbook of child psychology* (Theoretical models of human development 6th ed., Vol. 1, pp. 1–17). Hoboken, NJ: Wiley.

Lerner, R. M. (2012). Developmental science and the role of genes in development. *GeneWatch, 25*(1–2), 34–35.

Lerner, R. M., Almerigi, J., Theokas, C., & Lerner, J. V. (2005). Positive youth development: A view of the issues. *The Journal of Early Adolescence, 25*(1), 10–16.

Lerner, R. M., Easterbrooks, M. A., & Mistry, J. (in press). Foundations of development across the life span. In I. B. Weiner (Editor-in-Chief) & R. M. Lerner, M. A. Easterbrooks, & J. Mistry (Eds.), *Handbook of psychology: Vol. 6. Developmental psychology* (2nd ed.). Hoboken, NJ: Wiley.

Lerner, R. M., Lerner, J. V., Bowers, E. P., Lewin-Bizan, S., Gestsdottir, S., & Urban, J. B. (2011). Self-regulation processes and thriving in childhood and adolescence:

A view of the issues. In R. M. Lerner, J. V. Lerner, E. P. Bowers, S. Lewin-Bizan, S. Gestsdottir, & J. B. Urban (Eds.), Thriving in childhood and adolescence: The role of self regulation processes. *New Directions for Child and Adolescent Development 133*, 1–9.

Lerner, R. M., Schwartz, S. J., & Phelps, E. (2009a). Problematics of time and timing in the longitudinal study of human development: Theoretical and methodological issues. *Human Development, 52*, 44–68.

Lerner, R. M., von Eye, A., Lerner, J. V., & Lewin-Bizan, S. (2009b). Exploring the foundations and functions of adolescent thriving within the 4-H Study of Positive Youth Development: A view of the issues. *Journal of Applied Developmental Psychology, 30*(5), 567–570.

Lerner, R. M., Weiner, M. B., Arbeit, M. R., Chase, P. A., Agans, J. P., & Schmid, K. L., et al. (2012). Resilience across the life span. In G. C. Smith & B. Hayslip, Jr. (Eds.), *Annual review of gerontology and geriatrics* (Vol. 32, Number 1, pp. 275–299). New York: Springer.

Lewontin, R. C. (2000). *The triple helix: Gene, organism and environment*. Cambridge, MA: Harvard University Press.

Little, T. D., Card, N. A., Preacher, K. J., & McConnell, E. (2009). Modeling longitudinal data from research in adolescence. In R. M. Lerner & L. Steinberg (Eds.), *Handbook of adolescent psychology, individual bases of adolescent development* (pp. 15–54). Hoboken, NJ: Wiley.

Masten, A. S. (2009). Ordinary magic: Lessons from research on resilience in human development. *Education Canada, 49*(3), 28–32.

Masten, A. S., & Obradović, J. (2006). Competence and resilience in development. *Annals of the New York Academy of Sciences, 1094*, 13–27.

McClelland, M. M., Ponitz, C. C., Messersmith, E., & Tominey, S. (2010). Self-Regulation: Integration of cognition and emotion. In W. Overton (Vol. Ed.) & R. M. Lerner (Editor-in-Chief), *Handbook of life-span development: Vol. 1: Cognition, biology, and methods* (pp. 509–553). Hoboken, NJ: Wiley.

Mistry, J. (2011). Integrative theoretical perspectives: Nature and processes of development: Commentary on Raeff. *Human Development, 54*, 44–48.

Mistry, J., & Wu, J. (2010). Navigating cultural worlds and negotiating identities: A conceptual model. *Human Development, 53*, 5–25.

Moilanen, K. L. (2007). The adolescent self-regulatory inventory: The development and validation of a questionnaire of short-term and long-term self-regulation. *Journal of Youth and Adolescence, 36*, 835–848.

Napolitano, C. M., Bowers, E. P., Gestsdóttir, S., & Chase, P. (2011). The development of intentional self-regulation in adolescence: Describing, explaining, and optimizing its link to positive youth development. In R. M. Lerner, J. V. Lerner, & J. B. Benson (Eds.), *Advances in child development and behavior* (Vol. 41, pp. 19–38). London, England: Academic.

Oman, D., Flinders, T., & Thoresen, C. E. (2008). Integrating spiritual modeling into education: A college course for stress management and spiritual growth. *The International Journal for the Psychology of Religion, 18*(2), 79–107.

Overton, W. F. (2006). Developmental psychology: Philosophy, concepts, methodology. In W. Damon & R. M. Lerner (Eds.), *Handbook of child psychology* (Theoretical models of human development 6th ed., Vol. 1, pp. 18–88). Hoboken, NJ: Wiley.

Overton, W. F. (2010). Life-span development: Concepts and issues. In R. M. Lerner (Editor-in-Chief) & W. F. Overton (Vol. Ed.), *The handbook of life-span development: Vol. 1. Cognition, biology, and methods* (pp. 1–29). Hoboken, NJ: Wiley

Overton, W. F., & Mueller, U. (in press). Development across the life span. In I. B. Weiner (Editor-in-Chief) & R. M. Lerner, A. M. Easterbrooks, & J. Mistry (Eds.), *Handbook of psychology: Vol. 6. Developmental psychology* (2nd ed.). Hoboken, NJ: Wiley.

Posner, M. I., & Rothbart, M. K. (2000). Developing mechanisms of self-regulation. *Development and Psychopathology, 12*, 427–441.

Putnam, R. D. (1995). Bowling alone: America's declining social capital. *Journal of Democracy, 6*, 65–78.

Rhodes, J. E. (2002). *Stand by me: The risks and rewards of mentoring today's youth*. Cambridge, MA: Harvard University Press.

Rhodes, J. E., & Lowe, S. R. (2009). Mentoring in adolescence. In R. M. Lerner & L. Steinberg (Eds.), *Handbook of adolescent psychology* (Contextual influences on adolescent development 3rd ed., Vol. 2, pp. 152–190). Hoboken, NJ: Wiley.

Shonkoff, J. P., & Phillips, D. A. (Eds.). (2000). *From neurons to neighborhoods: The science of early childhood development*. Washington, DC: National Academies Press.

Singer, J. D., & Willett, J. B. (2003). *Applied longitudinal data analysis. Modeling change and event occurrence*. New York, NY: Oxford University Press.

Susman, E. J., & Dorn, L. D. (2009). Puberty: Its role in development. In R. M. Lerner & L. Steinberg (Eds.), *Handbook of adolescent psychology* (Individual bases of adolescent development 3rd ed., Vol. 1, pp. 116–151). Hoboken, NJ: Wiley.

Theokas, C., & Lerner, R. M. (2006). Observed ecological assets in families, schools, and neighborhoods: Conceptualization, measurement and relations with positive and negative developmental outcomes. *Applied Developmental Science, 10*(2), 61–74.

Urban, J. B., Lewin-Bizan, S., & Lerner, R. M. (2010). The role of intentional self regulation, lower neighborhood ecological assets, and activity involvement in youth developmental outcomes. *Journal of Youth and Adolescence, 39*(7), 783–800.

von Eye, A. (1982). Statistische und methodologische Problemstellungen psychologischer Präventionsforschung. In J. Brandtstädter & A. von Eye (Eds.), *Psychologische Prävention: Grundlagen, Programme, Methoden* (pp. 305–439). Bern, Switzerland: Huber.

Wachs, T. D. (2006). Contributions of temperament to buffering and sensitization processes in children's development. *Annals of the New York Academy of Sciences, 1094*, 28–39.

Werner, H. (1957). The concept of development from a comparative and ogranismic point of view. In D. B. Harris (Ed.), *The concept of development* (pp. 125–148). Minneapolis, MN: University of Minnesota Press.

Zaff, J. F., Kawashima-Ginsberg, K., & Lin, E. S. (2011). Advances in civic engagement research: Issues of civic measures and civic context. In R. M. Lerner, J. V. Lerner, & J. B. Benson (Eds.), *Advances in child behavior and development* (Positive youth development: Research and applications for promoting thriving in adolescence, Vol. 41, pp. 275–308). Amsterdam: Elsevier.

Zimmerman, S., Phelps, E., & Lerner, R. M. (2007). Intentional self-regulation in early adolescence: Assessing the structure of selection, optimization, and compensations processes. *European Journal of Developmental Science, 1*(3), 272–299.

A Resilience Framework for Treating Severe Child Trauma

David A. Crenshaw

After more than 42 years of direct clinical work with severe trauma in children what amazes the author most is the courage, awesome spirit, and the resilience of these children. These are children who in their brief lives have suffered more than most human beings experience in a life time. They are children who have seen things that no child's eyes should ever see; children who have heard things that no child should ever hear. These are children who've been hurt in ways that no child should ever be hurt. But there is something else that is quite striking about these children. From the pile of rubble heaped high by the atrocities that some adults in their worst moments commit towards children emerges a child who often in spite of all justification refuses to give up. These children reveal a vital spark that is not easily extinguished—what James Garbarino (1999) called the "divine spark." Resilient children are determined to surmount even the most formidable odds—they display courage and strength in the face of obstacles that would demolish the spirit of many less hardy individuals.

Resilience in the Face of Severe Child Trauma

The American Psychiatric Association (2000) defined a stressor as traumatic when an individual is exposed to a life-threatening experience or a threat to physical integrity that is accompanied by a subjective response of fear and helplessness. Terr (1991) distinguished between Type I trauma that results from exposure to a single event as contrasted with Type II trauma that is a result of repeated or prolonged exposure to trauma. Resilience in the face of severe trauma in childhood, that is, the focus of this chapter, is best thought of as Type II trauma as described by Terr. Type II traumas have also been termed *complex trauma* (Herman, 1992) and *developmental trauma disorder* (van der Kolk, 2005, 2007). The terms complex trauma and developmental trauma disorder call attention to the fact that the PTSD diagnosis does not capture the disruptive developmental effects of trauma in childhood when development is still in process.

Trauma in childhood can disrupt affect regulation, attachment patterns, and interfere with the achievement of core competencies. Thus the impact of Type II traumas in childhood can have a pervasive disruptive effect on development. These Type II traumas often take the form of sexual and/or physical abuse or torture and thus are deliberately inflicted on children by other human beings, often by adults whom they would

D.A. Crenshaw (✉)
Children's Home of Poughkeepsie,
Poughkeepsie, NY, USA
e-mail: dcrenshaw@childrenshome.us

S. Goldstein and R.B. Brooks (eds.), *Handbook of Resilience in Children*,
DOI 10.1007/978-1-4614-3661-4_18, © Springer Science+Business Media New York 2013

ordinarily turn to for protection and safety, namely their parents or caregivers.

While it is important not to overreach with the concept of resilience and thereby expect youth to rise above their circumstances regardless of the conditions they face, this needs to be balanced by a healthy appreciation of the amazing capacity of the human spirit to adapt and overcome formidable odds. Stories of amazing endurance and survival in the face of overwhelming hardship or obstacles are recorded in Biblical times, most notably the story of Moses surviving a harsh beginning in life and the story of David overcoming unimaginable odds to triumph in his battle against Goliath. Other Biblical stories of resilient children include among many others: Isaac (who was bound to an altar and was about to be stabbed by a knife wielded by his father Abraham but saved by the last moment intervention of an angel but according to the story, Isaac lived until the age of 180, the longest-lived of the patriarchs); and Joseph (who was sold into slavery by his jealous brothers, yet rose to become the most powerful man in Egypt next to the Pharaoh; saving many lives from the 7-year famine).

Resilience of Children in the Wake of Recent Disasters and Severe Trauma

In more recent times remarkable stories of survival, courage, resilience, and heroism regarding children of military families affected by the wars in Iraq and Afghanistan; children impacted by 9/11 and Hurricane Katrina also underline the capacity of children to sometimes overcome unfathomable circumstances (Solt, 2010). In addition more clinical case reports of healing in contrast to simply documenting the damage in the aftermath of deliberate as compared to accidental trauma, namely witnessing domestic violence, exposure to neglect, physical, and sexual abuse have appeared in the recent literature (Crenshaw & Garbarino, 2008; Crenshaw & Hardy, 2005; Crenshaw & Hill, 2008; Crenshaw & Lee, 2008; Cristantiello, Crenshaw, & Tsoubris, 2008; Fillette, 2010; Green, Crenshaw, & Kolos, 2010; Hardy & Crenshaw, 2008; Noziska-Kenny,

2010; Seymour, 2010; Solt, 2010: Soracco, 2010; Wingo et al., 2010).

Recent research reports of large scale disasters have also expanded our knowledge base of severe trauma. Among the seminal research recently reported include postwar adjustment in adolescents in Bosnia (Layne et al., 2010); Sierra Leone's former child soldiers (Betancourt et al., 2010); political violence in Kenya (Kithakye, Morris, Terranova, & Myers, 2010); survivors of Katrina (Kilmer & Gil-Rivas, 2010; Kronenberg, Hansel, Brennan, Lawrason, & Osofsky, 2010; Vigil, Geary, Granger, & Flinn, 2010); tsunami survivors of Sri Lanka (Catani et al., 2010; Fernando, Miller, & Berger, 2010); and the 9/11 World Trade Center terrorist disaster (Gershoff, Aber, Ware, & Kotler, 2010).

Child Soldiers in Uganda

A good contemporary example of such awe-inspiring resilience in children is described in a study of posttraumatic resilience in former Ugandan child soldiers (Klasen et al., 2010). The children abducted and coerced into becoming child soldiers for the rebels were typically cruelly abused and often forced to inflict atrocities on others.

In the study by Klasen and colleagues, 330 former Ugandian child soldiers from war torn districts of Uganda were evaluated for posttraumatic resilience defined as the absence of clinically significant psychopathology in the aftermath of exposure to severe trauma. The children were assessed after returning from the armed rebel group for a minimum of 6 months and at the time of follow-up were between 11 and 17 years of age. Of the 330 former child soldiers in the study, 48.5% were girls. Since the late 1980s, Klasen et al. report that an estimated 25,000 children and adolescents were recruited by force into the rebel forces of the Lord's Resistance Army (LRA). The study delineated the exposure to severe trauma as follows:

90.6% of the children were beaten by armed forces

87.9% witnessed murder

86.4% were threatened with death

25.8% were raped by members of the armed group (22.4% for boys; 29.4% for girls)

65.2% looted houses

52.6% abducted other children

52.6% killed another person

38.6% of the children had been abducted more than once

43.1% of the children had lost both parents

36.7% of the children had lost one parent

88.8% reported frequent experiences of domestic and community violence after leaving forced military service

In spite of this picture of severe trauma, it is extraordinary that more than one fourth (27.6%) showed a resilient mental health outcome. Given the brutal circumstances forced on these children who spent an average of 19.81 months in abduction and were abducted at the average age of 10.75 years, it is not surprising that 72.4% showed significant symptoms of psychopathology at outcome (33% met criteria for major depression, 33% met criteria for PTSD, and 18.5% warranted the diagnosis of both disorders).

Klasen's et al. (2010) important study yielded some important clues as to what enables some children to survive psychologically intact after exposure to horrific, almost unimaginable circumstances. These researchers found that perceived spiritual support was a significant contributor to resilience in these children and adolescents. Revenge motivation, on the other hand, contributed to a negative outcome for the former child soldiers. The preoccupation with revenge and also guilt were risk factors for these youth. Children in this study had frequently been forced to torture or kill others, sometimes even their relatives in order to survive.

A major drawback of this study is that it was cross-sectional rather than longitudinal and it is not clear what changes in psychological functioning of these youth would occur over a longer span of time. Even with this caveat, the results are still quite stunning and a compelling testament to the will to survive and the resilience of children. The authors observed, "One of the most impressive phenomena of child development is the ability of many children to develop into healthy, well-adapted adults despite adversity

and trauma" (Klasen et al., 2010, p. 1097). Compared to the voluminous research on psychopathology, positive adaptation in the face of harsh conditions is understudied.

Richard Akena: Transformation and Resilience of a Former Child Soldier

A compelling example of a former child soldier in Uganda, Richard Akena who was not a part of the sample in the Klasen et al. (2010) study, granted the author permission to share his story. Richard Akena as a child was not abducted just once by the LRA but four times. He was rescued the first three times but not the fourth. Prior to the third abduction his parents were killed by the LRA in a raid on his village. Richard was wounded in this battle but his physical wounds could not match the devastating pain to his heart caused by the murder of his parents.

Richard's experience is not unique. Some of the children in order to survive were required to kill their own parents (Eichstaedt, 2009). In his book *First Kill Your Family: Child Soldiers of Uganda and the Lord's Resistance Army*, Eichstaedt, a journalist, summarized what he encountered when going there to become a senior editor for Uganda Radio Network in 2005: "Northern Uganda is a world out of control, where right is wrong, and wrong is right, where carnage and chaos are the normal state of affairs. An army of brutal killers has been committing atrocities day after day, month after month, year after year, with no end in sight" (Eichstaedt, 2009, p. 5).

Devastating Trauma of War

A shaky peace has come to Northern Uganda. Since June of 2006 peace has returned to the areas ravaged by an internal war waged by the LRA. But this peace is barely trusted by those whose lives have been ravaged for more than 20 years by rapes, murders, abductions, and pillaging of their homes and villages. Raids by the LRA are less frequent but still occur and are no less devastating than ever. Slowly the rebuilding of the North is taking place, but the infrastructure is being rebuilt at a snail's pace.

Richard Akena's mission in life is rebuilding the lives of children who have suffered so deeply during the war years, whose hearts still tremble with fear as night comes, whose faces show the emotional scars within; some of the children show the visible scars of war such as lips, ears, noses chopped off by machetes which were wielded for the most part by child soldiers. Children who in cold blood killed members of their own family, their own clans, and their own tribe—the abducted children turned into killers, like zombies running amok due to the terror tactics of the LRA.

Richard Akena was one of those abducted children turned into killers by their captors. Richard was born when the LRA was already on a rampage. He grew up in fear of them. The children and their families never knew when the LRA would strike. Richard Akena and thousands like him were robbed of their childhood, of their innocence, of their ability to laugh and dream of a hope filled future.

Richard Akena was on his way to school when he was captured by the LRA for the fourth time and this time there was no rescue; a 14-year-old boy's life changed forever. Beaten, brainwashed, and coerced, Richard was turned from a 14-year-old into a killer, a child soldier, where he only thought of self-preservation and did what he was told to do. He saw and did things he never thought were possible; his mind became numb; his heart cold and yet there was a longing within to escape, to leave the insanity and cruelty of the LRA behind.

Richard Akena as a teenager saw death, participated in killings, saw and participated in lootings, abductions, beatings, the cutting off of lips, noses, ears, and limbs, all leaving his heart and soul imprinted with images that would flash by him, day and night, for years to come. Richard was made a corporal since he distinguished himself in battles and raids. He was nicknamed *Apiiremo* meaning "Blood" since he was a tough fighter who did not show fear, and yet within him was the hope of going home, or to what was left of it.

When the LRA was attacked by the Ugandan Army, Richard saw his chance and he began to run away, 12 km in all. Richard came across some hunters who were out and killed them fearing to be captured. Finally he reached safety in Acholibur and a government official placed him in a Displaced People's Camp, but there was no food for him. The World Food Program would only hand out food once a month and Richard went without food for 3 days.

Turning Points

A kind lady took Richard in and fed him and gave him shelter. He went to Kampala, hoping for a better life, only to find more despair. It was hard to adjust from being a child soldier to living as a civilian; normality eluded him and that is when he converted to Christianity, purpose and meaning entered his life.

Richard pursued an education, finishing High School and then onward to higher education even pursuing a Degree in Public Administration from Makerere University. As he returned to the North of Uganda, he began to see the ugly consequences of what the LRA had caused. Children who lived in fear, scarred within, orphans whose parents had been killed by the LRA, children who had been physically maimed by lips, ears, noses being cut off, hands amputated by a machete, but most of all he saw orphans. The LRA war produced countless numbers of parentless children in Northern Uganda.

Richard established Pader Orphans Caring Project which is a registered nonprofit organization in Uganda taking in the "throw away" children of the area giving them a place to call home. Richard did not and still today has little funding—the need is so great—but the generosity of his heart is greater than the need and he prays each day for the daily bread of the children and he believes that somehow little miracles will happen.

Richard Akena, former child soldier with the LRA explained in a personal communication that he is now fighting only for food for the 300 orphans that he feeds and cares for every day.

Richard is a voice for the voiceless—a person who has found his true purpose in life; to care for those who were child soldiers like him, who like himself were made orphans by the LRA, and those scarred physically and emotionally by the LRA.

Richard is a man with a dream to help the helpless of Northern Uganda—each day that dream becomes more of a reality—the ghosts of his past still haunt some nights—but his faith in God has enabled him to foster hope for a brighter future for the orphans and former child soldiers of Northern Uganda. (Adapted with minor editing with permission from Richard Akena from the Pader Orphans Caring Project website: http://www.paderorphanscareproject.webs.com/).

Richard Akena's story is one of such severe exposure to trauma that it inspires hope for so many children in all parts of the world who have been forcefully confronted with conditions that many people can hardly imagine. It is interesting in the light of the research by Klasen et al. (2010) that a key turning point for Akena was his conversion to Christianity. In fact in the study by Klasen and colleagues the children's perceived spiritual support was not only a protective factor but almost doubled the odds of resilience in their subjects. The triumph of the spirit of children in the face of these horrific conditions is a testament to a side of the story that has not received the attention it deserves. The damage done to children by such horror is well documented, the resilience, courage, and determination to prevail over such conditions has unfortunately received much less attention.

A Resilience Framework for Treatment of Severe Trauma in Children: Basic Tenets

In this section, some of the key tenets of the conceptual approach to a resilience framework in treating severe trauma are delineated followed by a detailed case example of the treatment of a family that suffered unusually severe and prolonged trauma. The case example will illustrate how recent research in severe child trauma and disasters can guide and inform the treatment process.

The Crucial Role of Mind-Sets

Mind-sets influence what we see and hear when meeting with a child as described eloquently by Brooks (2010). Minuchin and Colapinto (1994) explained that even the way the clinician gathers information, the questions that are asked, reflect the mind-set of the therapist and communicate to the child and family what is of greater interest: pathology or resilience. Mental health professionals are well trained, if not overtrained to identify pathology but recognizing and honoring resilience in children offers far more leverage for change. Minuchin and Colapinto (1994) stated that if you wish to be a diagnostic center then you focus on pathology. But if you wish to become a change center, then you focus on strengths. Goldstein and Brooks (2005) pointed out, "Symptom relief has simply not been found to be robustly synonymous with changing long-term outcome" (p. xiv). Resilience research widens the lens to include a view of the intrapersonal and interpersonal dimensions of children adapting to challenges, and more importantly can provide a new lens of understanding for therapists from many theoretical backgrounds to incorporate a strengths-based approach to child and family therapy (Seymour & Erdman, 1996).

The Remarkable Self-Reparative Forces in Children

While Robert White (1959) wrote about competence and striving for mastery from infancy onward more than 50 years ago, the integration of these concepts into child treatment has been neglected relative to the focus on pathology and trauma. A refreshing exception is the recent book edited by Gil (2010a) containing chapters focused on the powerful innate healing forces in children exposed to severe trauma (Crenshaw, 2010a; Drewes, 2010; Gil, 2010b, 2010c, 2010d; Goldin, 2010; Green, 2010; Jalazo, 2010; Ludy-Dobson & Perry, 2010, Shaw, 2010; Sobol, 2010). In the face of trauma, the deleterious impact can't be ignored or minimized but reverence and profound respect for the innate and powerful drive to adapt, to grow, and to heal should likewise never be ignored or minimized. The case studies in Gil's edited book provide ample testament to this self-reparative drive to be honored and appreciated in children.

One of the ways that the self-healing drive becomes evident in work with children of severe trauma is the desire to unburden, to tell their stories, and to have someone they've learned gradually to trust to witness their pain. The pathology side of this equation is well known. One of the cardinal features of posttraumatic stress disorder is avoidance of reminders of the trauma. It is true that children don't usually want to think about or talk about trauma events and they do their best to avoid any reminder of these devastating events but that is only part of the story. The other part of the story is that these children long to unburden and when sufficient trust is developed their innate drive to heal will often overtake the natural inclination to avoid and to distract from the pain.

The Resilience and Healing Powers of Families

Waters and Lawrence (1993) significantly contributed to this shift from the "pathology mindset" in work with families by emphasizing competence, courage, love, hope, and vision in families. Waters and Lawrence didn't ignore pathology but rather found the seeds of strength within the family often embedded in their pathology. This refreshing approach to work with families brought into the therapy room a focus not just on dysfunction and illness, but health and competence, strength, and important qualities rarely talked about before in family therapy including the family's vision, hope, their love, and compassion. The work of Waters and Lawrence was inspired by White's (1959) work on the concept of competence. White emphasized the innate desire of human beings to master their surroundings and environment which he referred to as an underlying *competence motivation*. If one closely observes young children, it is fascinating to watch their persistent attempts to master their world.

Salvador Minuchin, considered one of the pioneers of family therapy in a presentation at the Psychotherapy Networker Symposium in 2009 reflected on nearly 50 years of doing family therapy. Minuchin (2009) shared with the audience that his thinking has changed considerably since he started working with families. Minuchin explained that in the beginning of his career, he considered that families were simply wrong in the way they viewed their problems. Now, he still believes that families are wrong, but they are wrong because they "are richer than they think." Minuchin elaborated by saying that families possess rich resources for resolving problems of which they are often unaware. Basically Minuchin has shifted his mind-set from one that was originally problem-focused to his current mind-set that emphasizes strengths and resilience in the family.

In the case of severe trauma, healing is facilitated by enlisting the support and resources of the available family so the child does not undertake the journey isolated and alone. In the cases of deliberate trauma, including domestic violence, physical, or sexual abuse the family may not be available or it may not be feasible to enlist whatever healthy resources exist in the family to assist in the child's healing but this clinical decision should not be made without careful evaluation. It is easy to dismiss such families as not being helpful resources in the healing process, but the opposite may be true.

Pipher (2005) observed, "Families for all their flaws are one of our remaining ancient and true shelters. Families, not therapists, will be there for our clients if they lose their jobs, go to the hospital, or need someone to show up at their bowling tournaments" (p. 31).

In the heartbreaking stories of the Uganda child soldiers when they were rescued or able to escape the LRA many were confronted with the harsh reality that their parents had been killed. In that case they would seek out an uncle or a brother or sister, or anyone left in their family. Sadly the returning soldiers were often rejected by their surviving family members because of the atrocities the child soldiers were forced to commit (Eichstaedt, 2009). In addition to the theft of their childhoods, many also had to face either the disappearance of their families or rejection by their surviving family upon their return.

The Strengths that Reside in Communities

The community is an extension of the family and helps to support, guide, and reinforce the values of the dominant culture. Silverstein (1995) suggested that contemporary culture has deprived many of what makes life endurable, a sense of community, a connection to a larger context that gives life meaning and purpose. Beginning with the Industrial Revolution and the migration of agricultural families to the cities to work in factories there has been a splintering of family ties. The more frequent relocations in modern society often due to work transfers, weakens ties to home communities. If it takes a whole village to raise a child, children exposed to severe trauma need the acceptance, backing, and support of whole communities in order to heal. In a study of child soldiers in the Sierra Leone war, Betancourt et al. (2010) found that community acceptance was a key protective factor for the recovery of the children after they returned from the conflict.

Another important feature of the community that plays an important role in recovery is the return to schools. Prompt reestablishment of schooling was one of the best practices endorsed by a wide range of studies (Ager, Stark, Akesson, & Boothby, 2010; Betancourt et al., 2010; Kronenberg et al., 2010; Masten & Osofsky, 2010). In the family case study in this chapter, the children were able to return within a week to their same schools following the last in a series of horrific trauma events.

Hope as a Healing Ingredient

Hope is a cornerstone of successful therapy but especially occupies a central role in the treatment of a child or family confronted with severe trauma. Hopelessness due to the devastating impact particularly of deliberate trauma, and Type II multiple traumas that gradually erode the spirit of even the most courageous children, can represent a formidable obstacle to the treatment process.

Jerome Frank (1968) in a classic paper highlighted the critical role of hope in psychotherapy

in combating demoralization. One of the features of children and families in treatment of Type II traumas is what Garbarino (1999) has called "terminal thinking" and Hardy refers to as a "survival orientation" (Crenshaw & Hardy, 2005). In other words the repeated assaults on one's dignities and threats to one's very survival lead to an adaption that entails keeping hopes at low levels. Survival depends on keeping expectations low because when your dreams are crushed over and over again you can't afford to risk further disappointment. It might be more than the psychic can bear.

As understandable and as functional as this coping mechanism may be, it makes it hard for such children and families to envision new possibilities and to be receptive to risking themselves in new relationships or in the wider world because their assumptions of safety and trust in the world have long ago been shattered, sometimes in cruel ways. Hope is the fuel people draw on to keep going when the going gets tough, when the road is treacherous or lonely. It was hope that allowed Richard Akena to get through the horrific experiences of being brutalized and coerced into brutality towards others. He kept alive in his heart his secret hope that he would someday escape and return to his home and community. Yet hope can also be dangerous for people who are chronically exposed to trauma. The loss of hope, the loss of vision, and the loss of dreams are harrowing losses and can decimate the spirit. Children may be extremely reluctant to be put in that vulnerable position of embracing hope and risk exposure to still another crushing blow because it might be the "tipping point" for their psychic survival.

From the beginning of the work with the Taliaferro family (fictitious name) that will be described in the next section, the mother of this family with the support and encouragement of the treatment team gave the children the firm and clear message: "We will get through this together as a family!" Sometimes hope is a conscious decision. It is a decision even though your world has been blown apart, to get up the next morning, put your best clothes on and go out the door to meet the world even if it means quite deliberately simply putting one foot in front of the other, just one step at a time. I frequently challenge hopelessness in children and families by stating with conviction, "It is only hopeless, if you decide it is hopeless."

Facilitating hope in therapy, particularly in families that have been battered by a series of tragedies, requires sensitivity to a delicate balance that I (2010b) described in the title of an edited book: *Reverence in Healing: Honoring Strengths without Trivializing Suffering.* If a family is stuck in a survival orientation no matter how warranted, they may feel that the clinician is trying to move them to a more hopeful place to meet the validation needs of the therapist rather than their own needs. The family may also feel that the therapist is insensitive to the depth of their suffering and hasn't taken adequate time to truly hear their story and honor their suffering.

Survival for these families may have been partly the result of pride in being able to cope with their struggles and bear their suffering. Families may believe in keeping with their spiritual faith that they are being tested as to how much they can bear and that their tragedies in life are according to God's will. Unless therapists take time to hear the stories of suffering and the meaning the families attach to their adversities, the families may feel their suffering is being trivialized and that the therapist simply doesn't understand or respect how difficult their journey has been or they may feel their religious beliefs or faith are disrespected. Creating hope requires the healers to be sensitive to the delicate balance and the necessity of pacing the therapy according to what the family can handle at any one point in time.

A Clinical Case Example of the Taliaferro Family: A Resilience Framework

The research literature was carefully reviewed and informed the treatment of the Taliaferro family. The goal of undertaking the literature review was to find current research findings that could translate into clear guiding principles for the treatment of severe trauma in children. Since the magnitude and duration of the trauma experienced by this family was beyond the parameters typical of even severe trauma conditions, the research review of larger scale disasters proved especially helpful in guiding the work with the eight children of this family and their surviving parent.

Among the seminal research recently reported and particularly instructive for guiding the work with this family are the following studies: postwar adjustment in adolescents in Bosnia (Layne et al., 2010); Sierra Leone's former child soldiers (Betancourt et al., 2010); political violence in Kenya (Kithakye et al., 2010); survivors of Katrina (Kilmer & Gil-Rivas, 2010; Kronenberg et al., 2010; Vigil et al., 2010); tsunamic survivors of Sri Lanka (Catani et al., 2010; Fernando et al., 2010); and the 9/11 World Trade Center disaster (Gershoff et al., 2010). The following key components of intervention were derived from the above studies and the summary of the findings of this research (Masten & Osofsky, 2010).

Establish a Therapeutic Relationship that Creates Safety for the Gradual Unburdening of the Trauma Stories

More than 2,000 studies (Kazdin, 2005) point to the crucial role of the therapeutic alliance in psychotherapy outcome research. Kazdin has shown that the quality or strength of the therapeutic relationship early in treatment statistically predicts treatment outcome among adults. In addition research has shown the better the therapeutic alliance the greater the change in treatment (Hovarth & Bedi, 2002). Since the stories of traumatic exposure are particularly difficult to share, the trust developed within the therapeutic relationship is especially cogent in trauma treatment with children as well as adults.

The relationship forged with the Taliaferro family whose amazing story of courage and determination unfolded dramatically in the crucible of trauma when I met the mother and her 19-year-old son for the first time just minutes before she told her other eight children the horrible news that their father had killed himself. I provided support to the mother and children on an intensive basis beginning with that Friday night and continuing through the weekend as I spent considerable time on the campus of the Children's Home of Poughkeepsie (CHP) where the children had been placed on an emergency basis. I talked frequently with the children and their mother on the days that followed. I attended at the children's request the funeral service for the father and I was present when their mother and her extended family and the children gathered for dinner on the night prior to the funeral service. I met members of the extended family including the maternal grandmother, an uncle, an older sister, and her family. I was present when the children made their first return visit to their own home after being in placement for 6 months. I observed the joy of the children as they played with their dogs, and with each other. I watched them sing and dance and they showed me their rooms.

The Taliaferro's allowed me into the inner circle of their family and into their hearts even though they had been betrayed and mistreated for years, somehow they found the generosity of heart to trust me and I will always consider that a great honor and privilege.

The extensive degree of trust needed to tell the trauma stories of children who've experienced the cruel blows of deliberately inflicted trauma is often the result of two complicating factors. The first complication is the shame and stigma associated with the trauma exposure. Children who've experienced sexual abuse frequently feel tainted and damaged as a result of the exploitation by adults, often adults that they had once trusted and loved. The shame tends to silence them. Revealing shame in therapy is a shaming experience itself and requires an uncommon degree of trust in the therapist for the child to risk exposure to possible further humiliation and rejection.

The second complicating factor is that many of these children who have been abused or terrorized by adults were threatened by the perpetrator that they or someone they love will suffer great harm if they ever tell (Crenshaw, Rudy, Triemer, & Zingaro, 1986). To break the "silent bond" requires not only enormous courage on the part of the child, but a degree of trust not easily achieved in therapy when the child has suffered repeated abuse, and betrayals. The strength of the bond that was formed between the Taliaferro family and me enabled us to have many difficult and sensitive conversations and to persevere in spite of many disappointments and setbacks that occurred along the way in the treatment journey. In the end the mission to heal the wounds of this family and see them reunited successfully again was viewed by all treatment providers and team members as more than worthy of the struggle.

The healing relationship with this family consisted of many therapeutic relationships not just the relationship formed with the family by the author. A key relationship that was vitally supportive and helpful to the mother and the children throughout the children's placement at CHP was with the child care supervisor in their group, Miss Nora. When the sibling group was subsequently moved to a new house established just for them, Miss Nora went with them and became the supervisor in the new home. Miss Nora formed a close and trusting relationship with the mother, the children truly respected her and she was with them throughout their time at CHP.

In addition the children benefitted from important therapeutic relationships with their individual therapists and workers from other community agencies who came regularly to CHP to work with them on various skills and to take them into the community for recreation and excursions. The family was virtually surrounded by opportunities for healing relationships. The children formed positive relationships with a number of the treatment team staff, administrators in the program, other child care staff and with their teachers in school. The story is a familiar one: it is relationships not techniques that heal the psychic wounds of children.

Not all relationships went smoothly and some did not go well at all as would be expected with a family that had suffered such extensive betrayal. But it is a compelling testament to the strengths and courage of these eight children and their mother that such conflictual relationships were the exception rather than the norm.

Honor and Strengthen Family Bonds

One of the most consistent of all protective or ameliorative factors in the resilience research is the presence of a stable and supportive caregiver

(Houshyar & Kaufman, 2005). Even with children with a history of deliberate trauma the availability of a supportive and stable caregiver or an alternative mentor or guardian is one of the critical factors that distinguish between a good vs. a poor outcome (Beeghly & Cicchetti, 1994; Cicchetti & Toth, 1995; Houshyar & Kaufman, 2005; Kaufman & Henrich, 2000; Pynoos, Steinberg, & Wraith, 1995).

In view of the robust influence of a stable and consistent caretaker and the support of the surviving family, one of the overriding principles in the treatment of the Taliaferro family after the children were removed from their home and separated from their surviving parent, their mother, was to keep the siblings together while in placement and involve their mother extensively in the treatment process; supporting her vital role with the children by frequent visits. In summarizing the implications of research following disasters, Masten and Osofsky (2010) emphasized the importance of reuniting children and adults with attachment bonds if they have to be separated.

Watching the Taliaferro family on a snowy Sunday in December, 2010 playing with great zest and joy, making a snowman, sledding, and throwing snowballs you would never guess that the eight children in this family has been removed from their home just 9 months before by Dutchess County Child Protective Services (CPS). Nor would it be apparent to any casual observer that the day after their placement in the CHP's Group Emergency Foster Care (GEFC) program that their father committed suicide. Hearing the gales of laughter accompanying the playfulness of the children and their mother in the snow, it would never be assumed that the children and their mother were terrorized by the violence of the father and controlled to such a degree that it took on many of the earmarks of a family cult.

Family members ranging in age from 8 to 19 were subjected to long hours of listening to country western music of the father's choosing sometimes late into the night while the father drank heavily and no one dared move, not even to go to the bathroom. The children knew better than to cross their father when he was in a rage, always exacerbated when he was drinking. Stories of

witnessing numerous beatings of their mother, times when the father held a loaded gun to the head of their mother and threatened to pull the trigger, extensive sexual abuse of two of the adolescent girls, and beatings of the kids gradually emerged in the months following their placement. A prisoner in their own home; accounts of the mother and at times the children being locked in their rooms for long periods of time added to the horrific nature of the abuse and terror that the family experienced. In addition, the father favored some of the children and gave them power and authority over the others while telling them not to listen to their mother because "she did not love them."

As the story of their nightmare that lasted at least 10 years for the older kids and their mother unfolded, tales of his actively pitting the children against each other and all the children against their mother emerged. On some occasions the other children would be ordered by the father to physically attack a child at whom the father was angry. Because of concern that the mother of the children may have been complicit with the abuse by the father, CPS didn't let the children return home even after the tragic death of their father. The mother LaNora (fictitious name), however, visited everyday and the children attended the memorial service for their father. Since I was present when LaNora told her children of the father's death and witnessed the way she comforted, consoled, and hugged them, I viewed the mother as a huge asset in the healing process and someone who had been severely traumatized as well due to the terrorizing conditions including threats to her life, reinforced by beatings and forced confinement on multiple occasions. Nine months later, two of the eight children returned home as a result of turning 18 and signing themselves out of care. The other six remained at CHP.

While this case was complex due to the size of the family and the severity of the abuse and terror suffered and the prolonged out-of-home placement after the father's suicide, evidence-based principles were applied to the treatment of this family. Since maintaining connections with their surviving parent was deemed essential, even if visits and phone calls were required to be supervised during the first 8 months of placement, the mother visited the children nearly every day. The children gained meaningful comfort and consolation from the mother's visits and the treatment team consulted LaNora frequently on issues related to the children and how best to handle situations that arose. The sibling group was kept together in one cottage. The unwavering dedication of LaNora and her whole-hearted commitment to reuniting her family was a major contribution to the positive outcome with this family.

Forge Alliances and Collaborations to Facilitate the Healing Power of Community

Research regarding healing and restoration following severe trauma emphasizes the importance of a supportive community and the function of cultural and community practices that include support for families and their children (Masten & Osofsky, 2010). Included are restoration of participation in schools, support of family spiritual practices (Garbarino, 2010) and involvement of community agencies that serve children and their families (Betancourt et al., 2010; Klasen et al., 2010; Masten & Osofsky, 2010). The children were transported to the same schools they had previously attended, and their spiritual practices were honored and supported. On the night the children were told that their father committed suicide, LaNora, her children, and the staff ended that unforgettable gathering of the family in the living room at CHP by joining hands with all the family members and the staff present including the author in a circle and saying together the "Lord's Prayer." On the night of the wake for the father when the family and members of the extended family gathered at the Children's Home for a dinner; following the dinner they once again joined hands in a circle in the living room and asked me to join them in the circle for prayer.

Due to pervasive trauma of long duration and severity impacting every family member from youngest to oldest, CHP enlisted a wide variety of treatment services within the community. The agency enjoyed the support and backing of the Dutchess County Department of Social Services (DSS) and CPS in securing these services. Behavioral Crisis services were provided by the Dutchess County Department of Mental Hygiene on the night of the father's suicide. Each child received individual therapy and psychiatric evaluation and treatment from a community mental health clinic operated by a nonprofit agency Astor Services for Children & Families (ASCF). In addition, various community intervention programs were enlisted including Family Preservation and Bridges to Health (both programs offered by ASCF) that provided a wide array of services to individual family members including psychoeducational, crisis, and vocational services, and will also provide follow-up services to the children once they return to their family home. The CHP itself has enjoyed the wide support of the surrounding community since it was founded in 1847.

A wide range of services were also offered to LaNora including individual therapy (with the author), crime victims' assistance services through Family Services, Inc., another nonprofit agency within the community, battered women's counseling and parenting classes from Family Services as well. Family therapy during the children's placement was provided by the author and during the later stages of the work I was joined by a co-therapist, Amanda Dixon, a clinical staff member at CHP. The insidious pitting by the father of the children against each other and the children as a group against their mother was a primary focus of the family therapy sessions with the goal of repairing and restoring the relational bonds between siblings and between the children and their mother. Thus the collaborative effort of numerous community agencies with the support and encouragement of DSS provided a positive, supportive environment to promote healing of a severely battered and traumatized mother and eight children who had been terrorized for years.

Five months into the placement, CHP leased a house off-campus for the family to be together, separate from the other children on the main campus. The collaborative decision with DSS to establish a separate house for this family is believed to be the first of its kind in New York State—an innovative partnership between a public agency (DSS) with the approval of the New York Office of Children and Family Services (OCFS—a state agency), and a private nonprofit agency (CHP).

LaNora was invited to participate to the fullest degree possible including getting the children up in the morning and off to school and greeting them upon their return from school in the afternoon. This dedicated mother would set her alarm for 5:30 in the morning in order to travel to the group boarding home where she helped wake the children, serve breakfast, and get them out to the buses for school on time. She would also accompany the children to their numerous therapy appointments at Astor's Community Clinic and to medical appointments. She attended school open house, teachers' conferences, and any Committee for Special Education (CSE) meetings for her children. The Hyde Park Central School District (HPCSD) and its teachers were also part of the community network of support and vital services for this family. Close coordination and communication with the school district was maintained by LaNora as well as the educational coordinator at CHP. Several of the children had learning problems and individual educational plans (IEPs) that required close monitoring.

LaNora was also deemed a full-fledged member of the treatment team and participated with the staff in weekly treatment team meetings where the progress of each child was reviewed. The input and recommendations of the mother was highly valued by all team members. Since she knew her children far better than we, the team often deferred to her judgment when deciding on changes to be made in the house or in the treatment plan.

Support Normalizing Routines and Activities

In their review of the research on disasters and their impact on child development, Masten and Osofsky (2010) stated the importance of supporting normalizing routines and activities after disasters. This was especially important for a family that had not been allowed normalized activities.

The children had not been permitted by the father to engage in school sports or school-related activities. Nor could they have friends over or even go into the community without being accompanied by the father except to go to school. The children eagerly participated at CHP in a wide range of sports, recreational, creative, and artistic activities including participation by two of the girls in an annual talent show that showcases the performing arts' talents of CHP's residents. The enthusiasm and delight that the children took in these activities was quite moving to observe and was an important step to reintegration within a more normalized sense of community.

Provide a Sanctuary for Healing

The *Sanctuary Model*, a trauma-informed treatment program developed by Sandra Bloom (2005) for the residential treatment of children was adapted from a program she developed for the inpatient treatment of adults (Bloom, 1997). Bloom developed a model for creating or changing an organizational culture in order to more effectively provide a cohesive context within which healing from psychological and social traumagenic experiences can be facilitated. CHP adopted this model in 2008 and since then has conducted extensive Sanctuary training for all staff. Key features of the model include empowerment of children in placement through community meetings and red flag meetings that can be called by any child or any staff member to address issues that are not going well in treatment. The latter meeting is a collaborative problem solving and strategizing meeting with the child and staff together generating creative solutions. The community meetings are designed to ensure that children and adolescents have a voice in small as well as large matters that arise within their living group.

The children also submit letters to the treatment team to request certain privileges or considerations and they are reviewed and responded to by the treatment team at a weekly meeting. When appropriate, children are included in the team meetings to discuss certain requests or issues.

A unique feature of Bloom's model is the emphasis on the parallel process nature of chronic stress as seen in the behavior of children and of staff, as well as the organization as a whole. The Sanctuary model creates a sense of community within the treatment environment that enriches the experience of community outside of the program. The Sanctuary Model creates an environment of dignity and respect that should be the foundation of any trauma-informed treatment program.

The Taliaferro children actively participated in Sanctuary through community meetings, team letters, and participation in red flag meetings, and LaNora became the first parent to go through the complete Sanctuary training that we offer our staff. CHP introduced a new variation to the Sanctuary model consistent with a strengths-based model called a "green flag" meeting to recognize significant progress and success by a child in the program.

Honor Strengths of Children and Families

CHP is so committed to the strengths-based approach that honors competence both in children and adults and the power of mind-sets (Brooks, 2010) that it printed on the forms to be filled out at every quarterly treatment plan review for each child a section entitled: "Islands of Competence" (Brooks, 1994). As Brooks emphasized every child has strengths, talents, assets, interests, as well as their deficits or pathology but the change process is greatly facilitated by punctuating the strengths and highlighting the "islands of competence." By requiring all treatment plan reviews to reflect on the child's strengths and competencies the program ensures that the vital resources for growth and healing are not overlooked. Resilience theory and research finding are highly congruent with strengths-based treatment (Masten, Herbers, Cutuli, & Lafavor, 2008).

In the Taliaferro family it would have been easy to just focus on the pathology, to document the damage. But each family member, the children as well as their mother, possessed unique strengths, talents, and positive personal qualities that became the foundation of their healing. Each of these children as well as their mother touched the hearts of our staff in unforgettable ways by their courage, love, loyalty, and determination to heal.

Titrate Treatment According to a Dose–Response Gradient

A key finding of research studies in severe child trauma is that the response to disaster is often determined by the severity of exposure sometimes referred to as a "dose–response gradient" but is also influenced by previous exposures to trauma and to the conditions either facilitating or hindering recovery (Masten & Osofsky, 2010). Research has also shown a differential effect of severe trauma and disaster based on gender and age. Studies reveal that females report more symptoms in response to trauma and disaster than males (Masten & Osofsky, 2010; Tolin & Foa, 2006). Younger children are typically more vulnerable to trauma if it disrupts the quality of caregiving on which they are so dependent (Osofsky, 2004). Older children and adolescents, however, are at higher risk for severe trauma because they are typically less protected from higher dose exposures to trauma (such as rape or military duty) and they also are more aware than younger children of what is happening and its consequences (Masten & Osofsky, 2010). Thus the treatment of severe trauma in children can't be a "one size fits all" approach.

It should be noted that only three of the children in the Taliaferro family were the biological offspring of these two parents. The rest were adopted and without exception there were differential trauma issues suffered by the children prior to the adoptions. One of the children was identified as experiencing a pervasive developmental disorder. Each of the adopted children came into the family already suffering a combination of biological vulnerabilities and exposure to psychosocial trauma. In spite of these challenges and the subsequent severe and prolonged exposure to trauma within the family, LaNora and each of the children in individual ways manifested clear and unmistakable posttraumatic growth and healing.

Izabella: Transformation and Healing

Beginning Stage

Space does not allow me to detail the posttraumatic growth and healing of each member of the family but I will give an example. I should note that I did not pick Izabella (fictitious name) because she has grown the most, and it would be hard to pick one on that basis because they each made significant developmental strides in their own ways. Izabella, the second oldest, age 17 at the time of placement, and a biological child of the two parents had dropped out of school prior to removal from the family. Izabella said that the reason she dropped out at the beginning of her senior year was that she was taunted by other students at the new school she entered because of the clothes she wore. Although this was likely a factor, a bigger reason, in my judgment, was that Izabella was the protector of her mother and her siblings and she didn't want to be away from home and then worry about her mother.

The courage that Izabella showed in standing up to her father, when he was threatening or beating her mother or siblings, was amazing and a remarkable sign of resilience in itself. In spite of numerous beatings she received as a result of taking these stands, she remains to this day protective of both her mom and siblings. Another feature stood out about Izabella when I first met her on the night that LaNora told the children that their father had killed himself and in the days and months following, was the clothes she wore. Although a tall and strikingly pretty girl, she wore no makeup even on special occasions; she always wore baggy clothes, and her trademark heavily worn flannel shirts.

Return to School

While in placement, Izabella returned to school and completed high school. A graduation party was planned by the program and Izabella's mother that entailed the entire family along with some of the treatment staff going on a train to NYC, eating out, and then taking a boat trip to visit the Statue of Liberty and Ellis Island. Six months into the placement Izabella had enrolled and was taking classes at Dutchess Community College. Izabella made a serious heartfelt investment in her individual therapy and actively participated in family therapy. She also made good use of the community services provided by Astor's Bridges to Health program.

In her individual therapy, Izabella worked hard to confront the trauma issues that for a long time the children were forced to remain silent about for fear of devastating retaliation. She had witnessed her father hold a gun to her mother's head on more than one occasion and had endured many a severe beating herself. The children, even the older ones, were seldom allowed outside of the home except in the company of the father. If they bore bruises or marks from beatings they were kept home from school. It took several weeks after the children were placed before any of them could acknowledge what they had been through.

The Healing Process Begins

Once again, the mother took a leading role in the healing process. We gathered the children together in the living room at CHP after we had planned this intervention with the mother's full approval and support. LaNora said to the children in a firm and courageous voice, "We are no longer going to keep secrets." She explained to the children that she herself had suffered repeated abuse by their father, had been locked in her room numerous times as punishment and she will not remain silent any longer. Furthermore, she told the kids that she wanted them to be truthful and to be able to talk about what they had experienced and they too no longer had to live in fear and remain silent. During that meeting and later that day in a separate meeting I had with the three older girls including Izabella, the disclosures began of the physical and sexual abuse that two of the older girls experienced and Izabella disclosed the physical abuse that she had suffered.

The Healing Deepens

After working hard in individual therapy for 8 months, Izabella with her individual therapist at Astor Clinic decided she had reached a point of maximum benefit from processing and working through the trauma experiences. Prior to finishing her course of individual therapy as part of an agreed upon therapeutic ritual, Izabella smashed to pieces in the yard at their home the stereo that her father used to play at loud volumes his country and western music and that they had been forced to listen to for hours at a time.

At one stage of the work when the children were preparing to move to the new home that CHP secured for the family to live together, we had a meeting with the family including their mother to go over the ground rules. In this meeting, Izabella stormed out and slammed the door extremely hard. It was the beginning of her expressing overtly the anger that she had always internalized but was not safe to express thus leading to an anxious and depressed way of functioning. We realized as a treatment team not only was this a healthy step in Izabella becoming comfortable with her anger and finally feeling safe enough to express it but that also we had been insensitive to the experience of these children. This family had been controlled in an extreme and sadistic way, therefore it was a mistake to sit them down and go over a list of rules and restrictions without considering the impact on them.

An Amazing Transformation

Gradually an amazing transformation in Izabella's self-presentation took place. No longer dressing in oversized clothes and raggedy flannel shirts, she started to dress and look like the pretty 17-year-old girl that she had never been allowed to be including wearing makeup on special occasions. After another dramatic display of anger when she stormed out of one of our family therapy sessions, and some angry clashes with her siblings, which I

viewed as an overcorrection of the suppressed anger that she had contained for at least the past 10 years, her anger was expressed in less exaggerated form. The face she showed to the world and to us dramatically changed. It should be noted that this same dramatic change in self-presentation was seen in her mother and her siblings as well over the course of their placement. Izabella was frequently seen smiling and laughing and her mother and siblings as well as our entire staff saw a new, much happier Izabella.

Izabella's posttraumatic growth and healing was dramatically evident when she sent me a copy of a paper that she wrote for her college English class about the day the children were removed from the home. The paper was a moving and gripping account of the terror that she and her siblings experienced on that last day they spent with their father, the day they were removed from the home by CPS. The story she wrote included the father leaving the house before the police arrived with a gun hidden in a cereal box.

Remarkable Courage

A few weeks later after she shared her paper with me, I told Izabella that I was preparing a training presentation on "Resilience and Hope" for the clinical and child care staff at CHP and asked if she would like to read her paper to the group of 60 or more staff. I asked her if she thought this would be helpful to her in her healing process. Izabella immediately agreed to do it and her mom said she would also say a few words to our staff about what had been helpful and anything that we've done that was not helpful.

I told Izabella that it is a courageous thing to stand up in front of a large group of people, mostly staff members she knew, but some far better than others, and that she could change her mind even up to the very last moment. But she was there when that day arrived. When I gave a brief introduction, Izabella stood up tall and proud, and started reading her story. She broke down in a few places; her mother was standing right next to her with her arm around her, and for a brief period when Izabella was sobbing her mother took over the reading. But Izabella quickly took the paper back and finished it. When she stopped I gave her a big hug and among the entire room full of people, there was hardly a dry eye. The staff stood up and gave Izabella and her mother a standing ovation. It is not something that anyone who was there will ever forget.

I was so inspired by the courage, resilience, irrepressible spirit of this family, the love of the children for their mother and her love for them that I wrote a tribute to the family in a poetry book written to honor the healing mission of the CHP called *A Place of Healing and Hope* (Crenshaw, 2010c). The tribute was called "A Place of Beauty."

> I want to write about a place of beauty.
> Although there is much beauty in the world around us,
> This place of beauty in not in nature,
> But exists deeply in the hearts of a family
> I've been privileged to know.
>
> I want to write about courage.
> Courage abounds among heroic soldiers and firefighters.
> But I am talking about courage in a mother.
> Courage and heroism in her sons and daughters,
> In a family I've been privileged to know.
>
> I want to write about strength.
> Superheroes symbolize strength and power.
> But the strengths important to me are not about biceps or jumping off tall buildings.
> Rather these strengths show in a determination to move past the pain
> In a family I've been privileged to know.
>
> I want to write about goodness.
> There is plenty of evil but also much goodness in the world.
> Goodness abounds in people, in families as well.
> I've seen it as clear as a shiny star on a crystal clear night
> In the family I've been privileged to know (p. 28).

In February of 2011, a heartwarming and joyous party celebrating the remarkable courage and resilience of this family was held at the Children's Home on the occasion of the discharge of the six children and the reuniting of the family after 11 months in placement. The community of providers were not only invited to come and join in this honoring of this family but also to recognize the unique healing partnership created by the numerous community agencies.

As the children were preparing for their discharge, they decided to make me the "honorary grandfather" of the family. Izabella explained that along with their mother that "I had been there for the family throughout." This was a very meaningful and generous act because the family had previously identified that a pivotal point in the life of the family was the death of the maternal grandfather. The maternal grandfather was much loved in the family and was very protective of the children, and the father's abuse and reign of terror did not begin until after his death. The family could not recall a single happy Christmas after the grandfather died 12 years ago until this past Christmas after the father's death. I've never been so honored and I couldn't be more proud of "my grandchildren."

Summary

Stories of children triumphing over seemly impossible odds date back to Biblical times. It is not reasonable to expect that any child regardless of circumstances will simply be able to arise above their circumstances because there are conditions that can overwhelm the best of resilience and some children by virtue of their biological, genetic endowment and exposure to cumulative severe trauma will simply be more vulnerable than others. Repeated severe trauma can undermine the resilience that is part of the normal adaptation processes of children. But neither should we underestimate the resilient, innate healing forces in children nor their awe-inspiring spirit. Recent research has shown that some children can emerge from even the most severe trauma exposure and resume their developmental stride when intervention is comprehensive and multidimensional, recognizes and enlists the strengths and resources of the child, family, and community, and the treatment program addresses in depth the wounds to the soul of the child and family inflicted by the blunt instrument of deliberate trauma. There is no more challenging, nor rewarding work that a clinician could ever undertake, inspired by the courage of the children, their families and the commitment of a community of healers.

References

Ager, A., Stark, L., Akesson, B., & Boothby, N. (2010). Defining best practice in care and protection of children in crisis-affected settings: A Delphi study. *Child Development, 81*, 1271–1286.

American Psychiatric Association. (2000). *Diagnostic and statistical manual of mental disorders: DSM-IV-TR* (4th ed.). Washington, DC: APA.

Beeghly, M., & Cicchetti, D. (1994). Child maltreatment, attachment, and the self-system: Emergence of an internal state lexicon in toddlers at high social risk. *Development and Psychopathology, 6*(1), 5–30.

Betancourt, T. S., Borisova, I. I., Williams, T. P., Brennan, R. T., Whitfield, T. H., de las Soudiere, M., et al. (2010). Sierra Leone's former child soldiers: A follow-up study of psychosocial adjustment and community reintegration. *Child Development, 81*(4), 1077–1095.

Bloom, S. L. (1997). *Creating sanctuary: Toward the evolution of sane societies.* New York: Routledge.

Bloom, S. L. (2005). The Sanctuary model of organizational change for children's residential treatment. *Therapeutic Community: The International Journal for Therapeutic and Supportive Organizations, 26*(1), 65–81.

Brooks, R. (1994). Children at risk: Fostering resilience and hope. *The American Journal of Orthopsychiatry, 64*, 545–553.

Brooks, R. (2010). Power of mind-sets: A personal journey to nurture dignity, hope, and resilience in children. In D. A. Crenshaw (Ed.), *Reverence in healing: Honoring strengths without trivializing suffering* (pp. 19–40). Lanham, MD: Jason Aronson/Rowman & Littlefield.

Catani, C., Gewirtz, A. H., Wieling, E., Schauer, E., Elbert, T., & Neuner, F. (2010). Tsunami, war, and cumulative risk in the lives of Sri Lankan school children. *Child Development, 81*(4), 1176–1191.

Cicchetti, D., & Toth, S. (1995). A developmental psychopathological perspective on child abuse and neglect. *Journal of the American Academy of Child and Adolescent Psychiatry, 34*(5), 541–565.

Crenshaw, D. A. (2010a). "Stitches are stronger than glue": A child directs the healing of her shattered heart. In E. Gil (Ed.), *Working with children to heal interpersonal trauma: The power of play* (pp. 200–219). New York: Guilford.

Crenshaw, D. A. (Ed.). (2010b). *Reverence in healing: Honoring strengths without trivializing suffering.* Lanham, MD: Jason Aronson/Rowman & Littlefield.

Crenshaw, D. A. (2010c). *A place of healing and hope: A tribute in poetry and prose to the heartfelt mission of the Children's Home of Poughkeepsie.* Poughkeepsie, NY: Children's Home of Poughkeepsie Publication.

Crenshaw, D. A., & Garbarino, J. (2008). Hidden dimensions: Unspeakable sorrow and buried human potential in violent youth. In D. A. Crenshaw (Ed.), *Child and adolescent psychotherapy* (pp. 79–92). Lanham, MD: Jason Aronson/Rowman & Littlefield.

Crenshaw, D., & Hardy, K. V. (2005). Fawns in gorilla suits: Understanding and treating the aggression of children in the foster care system. In N. Boyd-Webb (Ed.), *Working with traumatized youth in child welfare* (pp. 171–195). New York: Guilford.

Crenshaw, D. A., & Hill, L. (2008). When grief is a luxury children can't afford. In D. A. Crenshaw (Ed.), *Child and adolescent psychotherapy* (pp. 93–106). Lanham, MD: Jason Aronson/Rowman & Littlefield.

Crenshaw, D. A., & Lee, J. (2008). A spectrum of dynamic forces that silence children. In D. A. Crenshaw (Ed.), *Child and adolescent psychotherapy* (pp. 107–121). Lanham, MD: Jason Aronson/Rowman & Littlefield.

Crenshaw, D. A., Rudy, C., Triemer, D., & Zingaro, J. (1986). Psychotherapy with abused children: Breaking the silent bond. *Residential group care and treatment, 3*, 25–38.

Cristantiello, S., Crenshaw, D. A., & Tsoubris, K. (2008). "Diamonds in the Rough": A strengths-based approach to healing children and families. In D. A. Crenshaw (Ed.), *Child and adolescent psychotherapy* (pp. 63–78). Lanham, MD: Jason Aronson/Rowman & Littlefield.

Drewes, A. A. (2010). The gift of time: Helping to heal through long-term treatment involving complex trauma and cultural issues. In E. Gil (Ed.), *Working with children to heal interpersonal trauma: The power of play* (pp. 263–287). New York: Guilford.

Eichstaedt, P. (2009). *First kill your family: Child soldiers of Uganda and the Lord's Resistance Army.* New York: Lawrence Hill Books.

Fernando, G. A., Miller, K. E., & Berger, D. E. (2010). Growing paints: The impact of disaster-related and daily stressors on the psychological and psychosocial functioning of youth in Sri Lanka. *Child Development, 81*(4), 1192–1210.

Fillette, R. (2010). A home of healing and reverence. In D. A. Crenshaw (Ed.), *Reverence in healing: Honoring strengths without trivializing suffering* (pp. 239–254). Lanham, MD: Jason Aronson/Rowman & Littlefield.

Frank, J. D. (1968). The role of hope in psychotherapy. *International Journal of Psychiatry, 5*, 383–395.

Garbarino, J. (1999). *Lost boys: Why our sons turn violent and how we can save them.* New York: Anchor Books.

Garbarino, J. (2010). Reverence for spirituality in the healing process. In D. A. Crenshaw (Ed.), *Reverence in healing: Honoring strengths without trivializing suffering* (pp. 41–50). Lanham, MD: Jason Aronson, Rowman & Littlefield.

Gershoff, E., Aber, J. L., Ware, A., & Kotler, J. (2010). Exposure to 9/11 among youth and their mothers in

New York City: Enduring associations with mental health and sociopolitical attitudes. *Child Development, 81*(4), 1142–1160.

Gil, E. (Ed.). (2010a). *Working with children to heal interpersonal trauma: The power of play.* New York: Guilford.

Gil, E. (2010b). Children's self-initiated gradual exposure: The wonders of posttraumatic play and behavioral enactments. In E. Gil (Ed.), *Working with children to heal interpersonal trauma: The power of play* (pp. 44–67). New York: Guilford.

Gil, E. (2010c). Silent grieving in a world without words: A child witnesses his brother's murder. In E. Gil (Ed.), *Working with children to heal interpersonal trauma: The power of play* (pp. 67–91). New York: Guilford.

Gil, E. (2010d). "This mommy has no milk!" A neglected child's adaptation to loss and hunger. In E. Gil (Ed.), *Working with children to heal interpersonal trauma: The power of play* (pp. 288–310). New York: Guilford.

Goldin, M. L. (2010). A tornado disrupts the wedding, to the relief of the unwilling bride: A girl's quest for healing after sexual abuse. In E. Gil (Ed.), *Working with children to heal interpersonal trauma: The power of play* (pp. 149–170). New York: Guilford.

Goldstein, S., & Brooks, R. (Eds.). (2005). *Handbook of resilience in children.* New York: Kluwer Academic/Plenum.

Green, E. J. (2010). Manny's story: A soul ascending. In E. Gil (Ed.), *Working with children to heal interpersonal trauma: The power of play* (pp. 220–239). New York: Guilford.

Green, E. J., Crenshaw, D. A., & Kolos, A. (2010). Counseling children with preverbal trauma. *International Journal of Play Therapy, 19*(2), 95–105.

Hardy, K. V., & Crenshaw, D. (2008). Healing the wounds to the soul camouflaged by rage. In D. A. Crenshaw (Ed.), *Child and adolescent psychotherapy* (pp. 15–30). Lanham, MD: Jason Aronson/Rowman & Littlefield.

Herman, J. L. (1992). Complex PTSD: A syndrome in survivors of prolonged and repeated trauma. *Journal of Traumatic Stress, 5*, 377–391.

Houshyar, S., & Kaufman, J. (2005). Resiliency in maltreated children. In S. Goldstein & R. B. Brooks (Eds.), *Handbook of resilience in children* (pp. 181–200). New York: Kluwer Academic/Plenum Publishers.

Hovarth, A. O., & Bedi, R. (2002). The alliance. In J. C. Norcross (Ed.), *Psychotherapy relationships that work: Therapist contributions and responsiveness to patients* (pp. 37–69). New York: Oxford University Press.

Jalazo, N. E. (2010). The owner of a broken heart: The cumulative trauma of surgery and sexual abuse. In E. Gil (Ed.), *Working with children to heal interpersonal trauma: The power of play* (pp. 92–116). New York: Guilford.

Kaufman, J., & Henrich, C. (2000). Exposure to violence and early childhood trauma. In C. Zeanah Jr. (Ed.), *Handbook of infant mental health* (pp. 195–207). New York: Guilford.

Kazdin, A. E. (2005). Treatment outcomes, common factors, and continued neglect of mechanisms of change. *Clinical Psychology: Science and Practice, 12*, 184–188.

Kilmer, R., & Gil-Rivas, V. (2010). Exploring posttraumatic growth in children impacted by Hurricane Katrina: Correlates of the phenomenon and developmental considerations. *Child Development, 81*(4), 1211–1227.

Kithakye, M., Morris, A. S., Terranova, A. M., & Myers, S. S. (2010). The Kenyan political conflict and children's adjustment. *Child Development, 81*(4), 1114–1128.

Klasen, F., Oettingen, G., Daniels, J., Post, M., Hoyer, C., & Adam, H. (2010). Posttraumatic resilience in former Ugandian Child Soldiers. *Child Development, 81*(4), 1096–1113.

Kronenberg, M. E., Hansel, T. C., Brennan, A. M., Lawrason, B., & Osofsky, J. D. (2010). Children of Katrina: Lessons learned about post-disaster symptoms and recovery patterns. *Child Development, 81*(4), 1241–1259.

Layne, C. M., Olsen, J. A., Baker, A., Legerski, J.-P., Isakson, B., Pasalic, A., et al. (2010). Unpacking trauma exposure risk factors and differential pathways of influence: Predicting post-war mental distress in Bosnian adolescents. *Child Development, 81*(4), 1053–1076.

Ludy-Dobson, C. R., & Perry, B. D. (2010). The role of healthy relational interactions in buffering the impact of childhood trauma. In E. Gil (Ed.), *Working with children to heal interpersonal trauma: The power of play* (pp. 26–43). New York: Guilford.

Masten, A. S., Herbers, J. E., Cutuli, J. J., & Lafavor, T. L. (2008). Promoting competence and resilience in the school context. *Professional School Counseling, 12*(2), 76–84.

Masten, A. S., & Osofsky, J. D. (2010). Disasters and their impact on child development: Introduction to the special section. *Child Development, 81*(4), 1029–1039.

Minuchin, S. (2009). Interview with Salvador Minuchin on 50 years of doing family therapy conducted by Rich Simon. 2009 Psychotherapy Networker Symposium. Washington, DC.

Minuchin, S. & Colapinto, J. (1994, October). *Consultations to the Astor Home for Children.* Rhinebeck, NY.

Noziska-Kenny, S. (2010). A strengths-based approach to working with abused and traumatized children. In D. A. Crenshaw (Ed.), *Reverence in healing: Honoring strengths without trivializing suffering* (pp. 123–136). Lanham, MD: Jason Aronson/Rowman & Littlefield.

Osofsky, J. (2004). *Young children and trauma: Interventions and treatment.* New York: Guilford.

Pipher, M. (2005). *Letters to a young therapist.* New York: Basic Books.

Pynoos, R., Steinberg, A., & Wraith, R. (1995). A developmental model of childhood traumatic stress. In D. Cicchetti & D. Cohen (Eds.), *Developmental psychopathology: Risk, disorder, and adaptation* (Vol. 2, pp. 72–95). New York: Wiley.

Seymour, J. W. (2010). Resiliency-based approaches an and the healing process in play therapy. In D. A. Crenshaw (Ed.), *Reverence in healing: Honoring strengths without trivializing suffering* (pp. 71–84). Lanham MD: Jason Aronson/Rowman & Littlefield.

Seymour, J. W., & Erdman, P. (1996). Family play therapy using a resilience model. *International Journal of Play Therapy, 5,* 19–30.

Shaw, J. A. (2010). A review of current research on the incidence and prevalence of interpersonal childhood trauma. In E. Gil (Ed.), *Working with children to heal interpersonal trauma: The power of play* (pp. 12–25). New York: Guilford.

Silverstein, O. (1995). *Inclusion/exclusion. A presentation at the Ackerman Institute for the Family.* New York: Ackerman Institute.

Sobol, B. (2010). "I am an artist": A sexually traumatized girl's self-portraits in paint and clay. In E. Gil (Ed.), *Working with children to heal interpersonal trauma: The power of play* (pp. 240–262). New York: Guilford.

Solt, M. (2010). What survivors of military families, 9/11, and Hurricane Katrina teach us about resilience in the wake of trauma. In D. A. Crenshaw (Ed.), *Reverence in healing: Honoring strengths without trivializing suffering* (pp. 165–184). Lanham, MD: Jason Aronson/Rowman & Littlefield.

Soracco, J. (2010). Strengths-based healing with youth in juvenile detention. In D. A. Crenshaw (Ed.), *Reverence in healing: Honoring strengths without trivializing suffering* (pp. 227–238). Lanham, MD: Jason Aronson/Rowman & Littlefield.

Terr, L. C. (1991). Childhood traumas: An outline and overview. *The American Journal of Psychiatry, 148,* 10–20.

Tolin, D. F., & Foa, E. B. (2006). Sex differences in trauma and posttraumatic stress disorder: A quantitative review of 25 years of research. *Psychological Bulletin, 132,* 959–992.

van der Kolk, B. A. (2005). Developmental trauma disorder. Towards a rational diagnosis for chronically traumatized children. *Psychiatric Annals, 35,* 401–408.

van der Kolk, B. A. (2007). The developmental impact of childhood trauma. In L. J. Kirmayer, R. Lemelson, & M. Barad (Eds.), *Understanding trauma: Integrating biological, clinical, and cultural perspectives* (pp. 224–241). New York: Cambridge University Press.

Vigil, J. M., Geary, D. C., Granger, D. A., & Flinn, M. V. (2010). Sex differences in salivary cortisol, alpha-amylase, and psychological functioning following Hurricane Katrina. *Child Development, 81*(4), 1228–1240.

Waters, D., & Lawrence, E. (1993). *Competence, courage, and change: An approach to family therapy.* New York: Norton.

White, R. (1959). Motivation reconsidered: The concept of competence. *Psychological Review, 66,* 297–333.

Wingo, A. P., Wrenn, G., Pelletier, T., Gutman, A. R., Bradley, B., & Ressler, K. J. (2010). Moderating effects of resilience on depression in individuals with a history of childhood abuse or trauma exposure. *Journal of Affective Disorders, 126,* 411–414.

Resilience and the Child with Learning Disabilities

19

Nicole Ofiesh and Nancy Mather

In this chapter we address how the factors of risk and resilience affect children with learning disabilities. Because learning disabilities encompass varied disorders associated primarily with difficulty learning, and due to the fact that time spent in school is a substantial part of the day, our central focus is upon children attending school. Both positive and negative school experiences shape children's self-perceptions and contribute to their academic self-concepts. Unfortunately, for many children with learning disabilities, their lowered academic self-perceptions are influenced by difficulties in both the academic and social aspects of school (Vaughn & Elbaum, 1999). In the first part of this chapter, we discuss how self-perception and, subsequently, resilience are shaped by school experiences. In the second part, we review various ways to help children with learning disabilities increase their resiliency and preserve their self-esteem and feelings of self-worth.

Learning Disabilities and Risk Factors

For the child with learning disabilities, the school environment is riddled with conditions that place the child at risk for negative experiences. Risk can be defined as the negative or potentially negative conditions that impede or threaten normal development (Keogh & Weisner, 1993). These conditions can stem from both internal characteristics associated with the child's disability and external characteristics associated with people and events in the child's world. Risk factors then are the hazards or adverse events that increase the likelihood of negative outcomes (Spekman, Herman, & Vogel, 1993). Because of difficulties at school, children with learning disabilities are particularly vulnerable and experience ongoing challenges in their emotional, behavioral, and social development (Maag & Reid, 2006; Montague, Enders, Dietz, Dixon, & Cavendish, 2008). These students feel less competent than their peers in these areas as well as academically (Smith & Nagle, 1995). Essentially, they become members of what Steele (1995) has described as an ability-stigmatized group. Fortunately since the writing of the first edition of this chapter, a number of researchers have continued to identify both the factors that place children with learning disabilities at risk as a result of their disabilities and several "success attributes" and factors that contribute to resilience (Goldberg, Higgins, Raskind, & Herman, 2003; Lackaye & Margalit, 2006; McNamara & Willoughby, 2010).

N. Ofiesh (✉)
Stanford University,
Stanford, CA, USA
e-mail: nofiesh@stanford.edu

N. Mather
University of Arizona, Tucson, AZ, USA
e-mail: nmather@u.arizona.edu

S. Goldstein and R.B. Brooks (eds.), *Handbook of Resilience in Children*,
DOI 10.1007/978-1-4614-3661-4_19, © Springer Science+Business Media New York 2013

Resilience is viewed less and less as a fixed trait that is innate or as one that grows in response to a deficit. Instead, it is more often conceptualized as a dynamic quality that can be nurtured internally and externally, by the multiple places and ways individuals interact with children (Margalit, 2004). As a child's resilience increases, so do his or her abilities to cope with or overcome risk and adversity (Doll & Lyon, 1998).

Difficulty Learning and School Failure

Although a learning disability in and of itself does not predict positive or negative outcomes (Morrison & Cosden, 1997), many students with learning disabilities have a multitude of school experiences that erode their feelings of confidence and damage their academic self-concepts (Gans, Kenny, & Ghany, 2003; Nalavany, Carawan, & Rennick, 2011). The finding that many students with learning disabilities maintain a positive global self-concept despite poor feelings about how well they perform in school is encouraging (Meltzer, 1995; Meltzer, Roditi, Houser, & Perlman, 1998). This suggests that fundamentally children with learning disabilities seem to know that their difficulties are primarily academically related and do not reflect a summation of their self-worth.

Nevertheless, unlike an adult who has the option of choosing a career path that capitalizes on personal strengths, children with learning disabilities are often required to read, write, and perform math 5 days a week. Failed attempts at completing or mastering tasks result in feelings of frustration rather than accomplishment (Lerner, 2000). Moreover, elementary age children are oriented to the present moment; they encounter the struggles of each school day with the perception that these school experiences will take place for the rest of their lives, with struggles that will last an eternity!

In describing a student with writing difficulties, Mather and Gregg (2003) provided the following illustration: On one afternoon, Ms. Jaffe, a third-grade teacher, asked her students to write a description of their favorite animal. Edward wanted to write about the giraffe, but because he

Fig. 19.1 Sorry I ripped it

could not think of how to spell the word, he decided to write about his pet rat. He thought for several minutes and then attempted to write the first sentence. Feeling unhappy with both the content and the appearance of his writing, he ripped the paper into several pieces. After recess, Edward asked Ms. Jaffe for some tape. Ready to try again, he taped the pieces back together, and wrote the following note, presented in Fig. 19.1, on the top of his paper: "Sorry I ripped it." Ms. Jaffe sat down with Edward and began to teach him a strategy for writing. She taught him to brainstorm his thoughts without paying attention to spelling at that moment. She explained they would edit the paper together for spelling later. Edward was then able to complete his description.

Edward's attempt to try again is an example of resilient behavior; he is able to keep his academic self-concept intact and persist on the task with effort. Indeed a child who can maintain a positive academic self-concept is more likely to persist in areas that are difficult, as well as be perceived by their teachers as working hard (Meltzer et al. 2004). When Ms. Jaffe taught Edward a new strategy, she contributed to his future success. As Meltzer et al. write,

> When students with LD are successful academically as a result of hard work and strategy use, they value these strategies and feel empowered to work hard and to recognize that their persistence will lead to academic success. (p. 42)

Ms. Jaffe is a powerful role model for teachers. She was able to recognize Edward's frustration as well as intervene which is not always commonplace. Lerner (2000) observed, "School is often a place that makes no allowances for the shortcomings of these students, a place where teachers are unable to comprehend their difficulties" (p. 538).

Shawn is an example of a young woman who was not well understood during her school years. During an evaluation to document her learning disabilities and provide justifications for accommodations, Shawn, a college freshman, shared her school experiences (B. J. Wendling, pers. comm., Feb 1, 2003). Shawn described school as being fun until first grade when it all changed. She was placed in the bottom reading group but that was not low enough so the teacher made a new, lower group just for her. She then repeated first grade and remained the sole member of the lowest reading group. Shawn was first tested for learning disabilities in second grade in the public school. Although she had significant discrepancies between her intelligence and basic reading and writing skills, the school determined that because her full-scale intelligence score was in the superior range, she did not require services at that time.

In third grade, the teacher wrote on her report card that Shawn was painfully aware of her reading difficulties. She was evaluated again that year at a hospital clinic and the diagnoses were (a) developmental dyslexia, (b) fine motor weaknesses, (c) attentional difficulties, and (d) anxiety and depression. The public school agreed to provide services and Shawn received resource help through eighth grade. In high school, the counselor encouraged her parents to discontinue special education, stating that she would have a better chance of being admitted to the college of her choice if she were not enrolled in special education. She started college, but dropped out after a couple of weeks because of anxiety over the academic load. Throughout school Shawn felt she was struggling just to keep up and working incredibly hard, but having few successes. Even now she does not understand how she can be so smart about some things (e.g., oral language and math), but then struggle so much with reading and spelling. She described that recently, while reading a book to a child, she forgot how to sound out a simple word. When spelling, she will sometimes forget how to spell even the most common words. As with the case of Shawn, 50% of children later identified as having learning disabilities are retained in the first grade (McKinney, Osborne, & Schulte, 1993). Thus, a negative cycle is set in motion where the child believes that things will not improve, and this sense of hopelessness becomes a barrier to future successes (Brooks, 2001). Moreover, students with learning disabilities who have negative self-perceptions are likely to work less hard (but may perceive themselves as working hard), be strategy deficient, and be judged by their teachers as exerting less effort (Lackaye & Margalit, 2006; Meltzer et al., 2004). Some may have difficulty forming an accurate perception of how hard they try (Klassen & Lynch, 2007).

Shawn did not receive help until third grade. By that time depression and anxiety had set in. Recent research underscores what Shawn and many other children like her have experienced. Students with learning disabilities demonstrate increased levels of anxiety and depression during the public school period compared to students without disabilities (Montague et al. 2008; Mugnaini, Lassi, La Malfa, & Albertini, 2009; Sideridis, 2007). Most recently, results from a meta-analysis have indicated that students with learning disabilities had statistically significant increased scores on measures of anxiety (Nelson & Harwood, 2011a). While research continues in this area, these students seem to be at higher risk for developing, experiencing, and displaying characteristics of both depression and anxiety, but for many not to clinically significant levels (Maag & Reid, 2006; Nelson & Harwood, 2011a, 2011b). Thus many children do not receive the help they need to reduce their anxiety which in turn can cause additional processing problems especially with attention, working memory, and executive functioning (Eysenck, Derakshan, Santos, & Calvo, 2007). Nelson and Harwood (2011b) found that parents and teachers rate students with learning disabilities as experiencing significantly greater depression than students rate themselves. They speculate that one reason for this may be the difficulties some students with learning disabilities have with the metacognitive skills necessary to sense and understand their emotions. As we discuss later in the chapter, teachers can play a critical role in providing children with social emotional support.

In a PBS video on learning disabilities, *Last One Picked, First One Picked On,* Richard Lavoie provides an explanation using poker chips to illustrate how students with learning disabilities gradually lose their resilience and are no longer willing to take risks. The high-achieving student has many daily gratifying experiences that help develop feelings of confidence and self-worth. This student has thousands of poker chips from accomplishments, as well as peer, teacher, and parental praise of acknowledgment and approval. When it is time to play, this student can afford to make numerous bets and take risks with little to lose and plenty of chips to spare. In contrast, a student with learning disabilities often has daily negative experiences and rejections that undermine the development of self-worth and strip away poker chips. This student clutches the small pile of poker chips firmly in one hand. Participation in a game only creates a fear of failure and the risk of losing the few remaining chips.

Even when they receive additional support and assistance, students with learning disabilities may not feel more competent scholastically over time (Smith & Nagle, 1995). Figure 19.2 displays several journal comments written by Maria, an eighth-grade student with reading and spelling difficulties. She has been receiving resource services since third grade. Maria admits that school is stressful and her self-esteem is very low. Even as adults, stress, anxiety, and a negative self-concept continue to be ever-present issues (Crawford, 2002; Shessel & Reiff, 1999). Maria's last comment, however, indicates that she is proud because she was able to accomplish something independently.

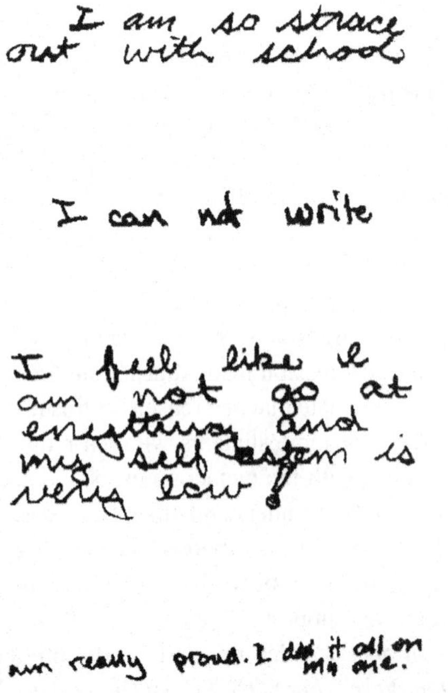

In discussing how poor reading skill affects an individual's development, Fernald (1943) indicated that the greatest liability is not poor reading per se, but rather the emotional complex that accompanies the reading failure. Stanovich (1986) aptly described the broad impact of reading failure:

> Slow reading acquisition has cognitive, behavioral, and motivational consequences that slow the development of other cognitive skills and inhibit performance on many academic tasks. In short, as reading develops, other cognitive processes linked to it track the level of reading skill. Knowledge bases that are in reciprocal relationships with reading are also inhibited from further development. The longer this developmental sequence is allowed to continue, the more generalized the deficits will become, seeping into more and more areas of cognition and behavior. Or to put it more simply and sadly—in the words of a tearful 9-year-old, already failing frustratingly behind his peers in reading progress, "Reading affects everything you do." (p. 390)

In exploring the relationship between behavior problems and early reading performance, the results of one study indicated that first graders with reading problems were more likely to display poor task engagement, poor self-control, and behavior problems in third grade. Unfortunately, they were also likely to still exhibit poor reading (Morgan, Farkas, Tufis, & Sperling, 2008). Morgan et al. reiterate the need to provide systematic early reading and behavioral interventions to children in need. To put it simply, as skills increase, so do resilient behaviors (Sorensen et al., 2003).

Fig. 19.2 Maria's journal comments

Negative Teacher and Peer Feedback

Clearly, negative teacher and peer feedback contribute to feelings of low self-worth. At times, students' completed products are greeted with comments that suggest that the assignment is not their best work and reflects limited effort. Jason, a second grader with severe fine motor weaknesses, was assigned a worksheet for handwriting practice. After evaluating the worksheet, the teacher placed a comment on the top of the paper that stated: "Work carefully, please." This feedback suggests that Jason is not putting forth his best effort and lacks motivation. Similarly, a comment on Jason's paper from third grade, "Can't read" conveys the teacher's frustration over his poor handwriting, rather than providing instructive, positive feedback. One is tempted to respond to the comment with a succinct reply: "Can't write." Although the teacher's feedback is most likely well intentioned, children frequently perceive these types of comments in a negative and accusatory way (Brooks, 2001); they can cause disappointment, increase vulnerability, and contribute to feelings of incompetence and inadequacy. Students with learning disabilities want teachers who acknowledge and praise them for their efforts and provide verbal encouragement. Many teachers are reluctant to praise children if they do not see "successful performance" (Klassen & Lynch, 2007). While academic achievement is one of the best ways to increase social emotional well-being, simple encouragement and praise can help students increase their academic competence. Without positive teacher feedback, the child may attempt to hide his or her lower levels of academic competence. In her autobiography, Crawford (2002) described how she would try to avoid humiliation in third grade by sitting in a beanbag chair pretending to be reading. She noted:

> I couldn't even understand what I was reading; I couldn't remember any of what the teachers had taught us. I wanted it to end. I would run away in my mind to a place that was safe, my own world in which I was the winner, in which I was recognized for what I could do. NO MORE BOOKS! With the tears streaming down my face, I would still pretend to read, but I knew the truth; I knew it was useless. (p. 71)

Some individuals will even refuse to do a task or participate in an activity, rather than risk humiliation by revealing incompetence. When called upon in class, the child's apprehension and fear of failure are often readily apparent. Instead of being supportive, the school environment often exposes what children do not know (Brooks & Goldstein, 2001).

We are reminded of the *Peanuts* character Peppermint Patty who has trouble staying awake in class. When she is not sleeping, she spends time analyzing the probability patterns of true/false tests, rather than attempting to read and actually answer the questions. In one cartoon, the teacher asks Peppermint Patty to come to the front of the room to work out an arithmetic problem on the blackboard. Patty ponders this request and inquires "in front of the whole class…at the blackboard?" As she walks up to the board, she comments: "Black, isn't it?" For children with learning difficulties, the fear of making mistakes is a hidden presence that casts a dark shadow over what happens in the classroom (Brooks & Goldstein, 2001).

Even when teachers are supportive and understanding, students with learning disabilities are often humiliated by their classmates' performance in comparison to their low levels of academic skills, as well as their difficulties mastering specific tasks. The child feels like an impostor worried about exposure, and the wounds caused by early experiences never heal (Salza, 2003; Shessel & Reiff, 1999). Spence, a fifth grader, recalls the parting words of a classmate retreating from a playground argument: "Well, guess who goes to the resource room. Guess who has a learning disability. You're a retard, man." Although Spence shared the experience with his teacher and the young man was rebuked, the damage to Spence's self-esteem had already been done. Similarly during an evaluation, Ben, an adolescent in seventh grade, stated, "I want you to help me get out of RSP (resource specialist program) 'cause everyone at school knows it stands for Really Stupid People." Ben's comments are not surprising given that children with learning disabilities tend to want the same activities, books, homework, grading criteria, and grouping practices as their classmates (Klassen & Lynch, 2007; Klingner & Vaughn, 1999). Especially during adolescence and secondary school, students are at risk for a depression in relation to self-concept

(Montague et al., 2008) and have a strong desire to simply fit in and not be seen as different (Bender, 2008). Yet for many children with learning disabilities, the social and emotional problems they experience are not predicted by where they receive special education support (e.g., resource room, self-contained class, or general education setting) (Wiener & Tardif, 2004). Spekman, Goldberg, and Herman (1993) observed, "They may enter school eager to learn and with expectations for success, but then run head-on into academic difficulties, extreme frustration, feelings of being different or retarded, peer rejection, and resultant low self-esteem and confidence" (p. 12).

It is not uncommon to hear adults with learning disabilities share painful experiences of being teased, bullied, and ridiculed during their school years (Higgins, Raskind, Goldberg, & Herman, 2002). Their perceptions of being different resulted in feelings of fear, confusion, and anger. These adults described these school-age misunderstandings as being traumatic and as resulting in humiliation, emotional insecurity, and self-doubt (McNulty, 2003). During interviews, 14 postsecondary students with learning disabilities described their repeated struggles and adversity, as well as the lasting emotional scarring of learning differently (Orr & Goodman, 2010). The combination of the disability and people's responses to it can create personal disruption and devastation (Crawford, 2002). Crawford recalls her feelings about failure: "There's nothing worse than failing every day: My body would shake, my stomach would ache, my head would pound with pain, and I would cast my eyes down in an attempt to hide the tears" (p. 71). In addition to repeated failure experiences, several other factors also affect the development of resiliency.

Type and Severity of Learning Disability

The type and severity of the learning disability appear to influence the level of resilience and long-term outcomes (Spekman, Goldberg, et al., 1993; Spekman, Herman, et al., 1993; Wong, 2003), and thus, it is necessary to determine the specific nature and characteristics of the condition. In reality, the term "learning disabilities" is vague, nondescript, and only causes confusion. Instead, it is more accurate to refer to domain-specific disabilities, such as reading disabilities, writing disabilities, math disabilities, or nonverbal learning disabilities (Stanovich, 1999), and to label and treat them separately. In addition to making the descriptor more accurate, specific labels also help to convey that the problem is circumscribed and not global in nature. Moreover, some types of learning disabilities exacerbate specific risk factors. For example, despite good verbal skills, students with nonverbal learning disabilities demonstrate markedly deficient social skills (Galway & Metsala, 2011), placing them substantially at risk for alienating teachers and peers who could provide needed support. In addition, some evidence suggests that students who are less academically adept and those who have nonverbal learning disabilities are less resilient and manifest higher rates of both depression and suicide (Bender, Rosenkrans, & Crane, 1999).

Social Support and Competence

Social support is considered an index of resiliency in that it serves as a stress-buffering condition (Robertson, Harding, & Morrison, 1998). Subsequently, students who lack the ability to create and maintain relationships tend to lose the support network needed to resolve life's challenges and crises. In addition to academic difficulties, many students with learning disabilities experience problems with peer acceptance and are more neglected and rejected than peers (Kuhne & Wiener, 2000). This lack of peer acceptance may be partially because children with learning disabilities appear to have limited interpersonal understanding, resulting in social difficulties in the classroom (Kravetz, Faust, Lipshitz, & Shalhav, 1999), on the playground, and with problem-solving (Elliot & McKinnie, 1994; Vaughn & Haager, 1994). Regardless, the individual's social life also impacts academic learning (Bryan, 2003).

Lindsey, a fourth-grade student with a nonverbal learning disability, described the experience of being unaccepted by and then losing her friends: "When I see other friends teasing each other about food on their clothes or toilet paper on their shoes, everyone laughs and they're still all friends…but whenever I try to make a joke about one of my friends, they're not my friend anymore and nobody laughs…they just don't like me anymore." For some students, difficulty with social competence can stem from their difficulty in understanding and using language, as well as reading social cues (Robertson et al., 1998). As with students with nonverbal learning disabilities, students with language-based learning disabilities are atypically at risk for school and peer alienation and school dropout (Morrison & D'Incau, 1997; Voeller, 1991). In the earliest grades teachers often suspect the child has a hearing problem because they present with such peculiar responses to directions.

For example, Ms. Martin commented that during the first few weeks of school, one of her first-grade students, Ralph, who had yet to be diagnosed as having a language-based learning disability, wrote his name anywhere on the front of a sheet of paper when told to "write your name at the "top" of the paper." Puzzled by his behavior and the observation that he did not model the behavior of his peers, Ms. Martin asked Ralph to show her where the *bottom* of the paper was. He turned it over and pointed to the backside. Ralph was an avid swimmer who conceptualized the terms top and bottom as he would in the swimming pool. It made perfect sense to him—and to Ms. Martin once she figured it out. Fortunately, as an extremely supportive teacher, she quickly demonstrated to Ralph where to place his name on the paper and how top and bottom could mean slightly different places on a paper and within a pool. Over the years, Ralph's problems with language comprehension caused him to get in trouble with teachers and peers on the playground although he rarely understood why. Through much role playing with the school's speech and language specialist, he was able to successfully navigate the social dynamics of school. As an adult he became a cabinet maker and happily worked for himself. He recently said his biggest challenge was making sure he understood what his customers wanted, but he had developed strategies for double checking his understanding. Sorensen et al. (2003) observed: "From a mental health perspective, special education services may need to focus not only on helping children acquire skills, but also on helping them develop strategies for coping with their learning impairment in the very setting where this impairment can be expected to be most stressful for them" (pp. 20–21).

In one study some individuals who spoke about growing up with a learning disability shared social difficulties across several contexts beyond school such as work, recreation, or family settings. These individuals did not know where or how to meet new people, how to make or sustain friendships, and they developed romantic relationships later than their peers (Goldberg et al., 2003). Interestingly, several studies have indicated that despite their lower level of social functioning, students with learning disabilities tend to feel positive about how their teachers and peers view them (Morrison, 1985; Robertson et al., 1998) though the quality of relating and friendships may differ (Wiener & Tardif, 2004). This discrepancy between the real and perceived events can in fact be a result of the disability itself (Palombo, 2001) or simply a coping mechanism (Robertson et al., 1998). It may also be evidence of the resilience that parents, teachers, and professionals seek to foster when they help students with learning disabilities understand the nature of their disability (Kloomok & Cosden, 1994; Palombo, 2001; Sorensen et al., 2003).

Gender

Although both boys and girls with learning disabilities can encounter social difficulties, some believe that gender may also play a role in the response of children to social failure (Settle & Milich, 1999; Wong, 2003), as well as the protective factors that they develop. Recent research shows no differences between boys and girls, across grade levels with the risk factors of anxiety, depression, and academic self-concept (Montague et al., 2008; Nelson & Harwood, 2011a). While more research has been conducted on the risk and protective factors that affect males (Morrison & Cosden, 1997), several studies have described differences between factors affecting risk and resiliency in boys and girls. For example, in one study, in order to make a successful transition into adulthood, intrinsic characteristics such as temperament and self-concept were more important for females, whereas outside sources of support from the family and community made a greater difference in the lives of males (Werner, 1993, 1999).

Strategies for Building Resilience

Fortunately, many individuals with learning disabilities do succeed and regain confidence in later years once they enter adulthood and the workforce. In a longitudinal study, Werner (1999) found that between the ages of 10–18, only one out of four children with learning disabilities had improved their academic and social status, but by the age of 32, three out of the four individuals had improved and had adapted successfully to the demands of work, marriage, and family life. Another longitudinal study found clear predictors of success for individuals with learning disabilities and underscored the importance of working on social emotional factors as much as academic skills (Goldberg et al., 2003; Raskind, Goldberg, Higgins, & Herman, 1999). These findings suggest that many individuals with learning disabilities are able to succeed in life. The fact that so many of these individuals have positive adult outcomes points to the powerful role of environmental factors (Dyson, 2003; Wong, 2003). Many adults with learning disabilities find innovative ways to teach themselves and thus prove that the ability to learn was always present, but perhaps, the knowledge of how to teach these individuals was absent (Reiff, Gerber, & Ginsberg, 1993). The successful experiences of many adults with learning disabilities indicate that children raised with multiple risk factors can still achieve

positive adult outcomes once they leave school (Goldberg et al., 2003).

How then can we increase children's successes in school? A variety of protective factors appear to help children with learning disabilities overcome risk and cultivate resiliency, the ability to spring back from the negative outcomes associated with stress factors and risks (Bender et al., 1999). Protective factors are those life situations or events that enhance the chances of positive outcomes (Keogh & Weisner, 1993). Several protective factors that appear to mitigate positive outcomes for children with learning disabilities are discussed.

Promote Self-Understanding and Acceptance

One critical factor for overcoming risk appears to be self-understanding, acceptance, and a feeling of control over one's life. In studying successful adults with learning disabilities, Gerber, Ginsberg, and Reiff (1992) found that having a sense of control over their lives was the most critical factor. One way that individuals are able to take control of their lives is by setting realistic goals that are possible to achieve. The capacity to accomplish goals is influenced by the accuracy of one's self-knowledge and self-perceptions (Nalavany, Carawan, & Rennick, 2011). In fact, the central problem is not the disability, but the capacity to confront the various challenges that one faces in living with and overcoming it (Gerber & Ginsberg, 1990). Individuals who have a greater understanding of their disability are more likely to adjust successfully to adult life because they seek help when needed and find educational and vocational opportunities that incorporate their strengths (Cosden, 2001; Nalavany et al., 2011). Goldberg et al. (2003) found that successful individuals with learning disabilities set goals that were specific but flexible; included a strategy; and appeared to be concrete, realistic, and attainable. Moreover, many of the successful adults in their longitudinal study indicated that their goals had been with them since their youth, and had provided both meaning and direction to their lives.

Without an understanding of their disability, students with learning disabilities have been described as having an external locus of control, or attributing their academic performance to reasons outside of their own thoughts and behaviors (Borkowski, Carr, Rellinger, & Pressley, 1990). They often attribute their academic successes to external factors such as luck or that the task was too easy. After several trials of reteaching, Andy, a fourth-grade boy with a mathematics disability, correctly solved a double-digit multiplication problem. In an effort to reinforce the correct procedure, his teacher enthusiastically asked Andy how he figured it out. His response was, "Well Ms. Hill, I guess it's just my lucky day." Andy simply could not see how his effort could influence the events in his life.

Since research has shown that an internal locus of control contributes to resilience (Blocker & Copeland, 1994; Wyman, Cowen, Work, & Keriey, 1993), teachers and parents need to explicitly convey and support the relationships between a child's efforts and the positive outcomes of those efforts. Instead of just saying, "Wow, you did a great job," students need to hear comments like: "Do you see how that strategy worked for you?" "You are listening carefully and looking at me." "You remembered to bring your homework back," "Do you see that you can understand these problems when you ask for help?" With specific praise, children can know exactly which behaviors have worked and what is expected (Smith, 2003a).

In one study, college students with and without learning disabilities differed significantly on resilience, stress, and need for achievement, but not on locus of control (Hall, Spruill, & Webster, 2002). We can learn from these students with learning disabilities who have successfully entered postsecondary education about the importance of teaching students how to understand the nature of their difficulties and how their efforts can pay off. In a 20-year longitudinal project tracing the lives of individuals with learning disabilities, Higgins et al. (2002) found

that the most successful participants accepted their learning disability and could talk about their strengths, as well as their weaknesses. Understanding of the disability and self-awareness then form protective factors that facilitate lowered levels of anxiety and provide the foundation for acceptance (Morrison & Cosden, 1997; Vogel, Hruby, & Adelman, 1993). Moreover, Dyson (2003) found that as time passed after a clinical evaluation, parents felt they understood their child better and reported a decline in their child's depression and adjustment problems and improvement in conduct. Seth's disability service provider helped him to learn about his disability in college. He wrote,

> "She looked at my files and we sat and talked about my disability. She wanted all the students with disabilities to really know what their disability was so that when they asked for help, they could explain their own strengths and weaknesses. She always was a person that would encourage you." (Orr & Goodman, 2010, p. 221)

Counselors and therapists can also help children with learning disabilities increase their self-understanding. Palombo (2001) advised that to treat children with learning disorders successfully, the therapist must both understand the effects of the learning disorder on the child, as well as be able to distinguish between thoughts and behaviors caused by the disorder from those resulting from a reaction to the disorder. For example, a therapist must be able to distinguish if a child did not comply with a parent's or teacher's request due to difficulty understanding or following directions, or if the noncompliance was a result of depression resulting from an external event. Parents and teachers often misunderstand these children because they do not recognize that the child's thoughts are neurologically driven, rather than motivated by psychological factors. To illustrate this point, Palombo provided the following example: "Simply put there is a failure to distinguish between 'she won't' and 'she can't.' A child with dyslexia does not fail to learn to read because she *does not want* to learn but because she *cannot* learn" (p. 7).

In discussing and explaining the learning disability to the student, parents and teachers need to be open, honest, and supportive (Miller & Fritz, 1998). As with the college students in the Hall et al. (2002) study, Gerber et al. (1992) found that successful adults understood and accepted their learning disabilities. They wanted to succeed, set achievable goals, and confronted their learning disabilities (Gerber & Ginsberg, 1990). In addition to understanding one's strengths and weaknesses, the person must also be able to see himself or herself as being more than "learning disabled" (Bender et al., 1999). Some successful adults are able to reframe their learning disabilities in a positive light so that the disability itself functions as a protective factor, making them stronger, more resilient, and more self-actualized (Gerber, Reiff, & Ginsberg, 1996; Shessel & Reiff, 1999).

Smith (1989) described the different types of masks that students with learning disabilities wear to hide their poor skills. Often they first put on these masks in first or second grade when they realize that they cannot read like the other students. She encouraged teachers to recognize the common masks that students wear to hide their inabilities: helplessness, invisibility, the clown, and the victim. When students realize why they are having difficulties learning and that they are not stupid, the masks can be removed and the problems treated.

The Role of Supportive Adults

Supportive adults or mentors are able to foster trust and bolster the self-esteem of children with learning disabilities (Bender et al., 1999; Brooks, 2001; Werner, 1993, 1999; Wong, 2003). Oftentimes teachers in the school environment can serve as protective factors for children. In describing the characteristics of resilient children, Segal (1988) wrote:

> From studies conducted around the world, researchers have distilled a number of factors that enable such children of misfortune to beat the heavy odds against them. One factor turns out to be the presence in their lives of a charismatic adult, a person with whom they can identify and from whom they gather strength. And in a surprising number of cases that person turns out to be a teacher. (p. 2)

Successful individuals with learning disabilities have at least one person in their lives who accepts them unconditionally and serves as a mentor who acts as the "gatekeeper for the future" (Werner, 1993; Wong, 2003). Hallowell (2003) recalled how he struggled to learn to read in first grade. As he tried to pronounce the words, his teacher, Mrs. Eldredge, put her arm around him protectively and took away his fear of learning to read. Now as a psychiatrist, he still recalls the power of her arm and the effect it had on his development:

> "None of this would have happened had it not been for Mrs. Eldredge's arm. That arm has stayed around me ever since first grade. Even though Mrs. Eldredge resides now in heaven, perhaps reclining on an actual cloud as I write these words, she continues to help me, her arm to protect me, and I continue to thank her for it, almost every day." (p. 7)

Teachers play a significant role in fostering resilience because through daily encounters, they are able to address the child's emotional, as well as academic, needs (Segal, 1988; Werner, 1993). Children with LD who have the mentoring relationship of an adult during adolescence have a greater likelihood of high school completion and improved self-esteem. Moreover, this same research indicates that teachers and guidance counselors who have cultivated meaningful relationships with their students have a greater impact on high school completion than other types of adult mentors (Ahrens, DuBois, Lozano, & Richardson, 2010). Thus, educators have the power to offset certain risk factors as they touch the mind, heart, and spirit of children by creating school climates where all students will succeed (Brooks, 2001). They provide children with positive experiences that enhance their self-esteem and competence, thereby reinforcing their resilience (Brooks, 1991; Rutter, 1985). They teach children not to be afraid of making mistakes and help students appreciate that mistakes are part of the learning process (Brooks & Goldstein, 2001). The long-term educational benefits from positive school experiences stem more from children's attitudes toward learning and their self-esteem than from what they are specifically taught (Rutter, 1985). Orr and Goodman (2010) collected statements from postsecondary students with learning disabilities regarding those individuals who had supported them along through school. One student commented on a person who inspired her in high school. She explained that this teacher consultant was, "… the one person that told me I need to go to college, and that I was smart" (p. 221). Another participant commented about a counselor who had particularly inspired her. She wrote, "He pulled me to the side and asked if I needed help. He helped me put things into perspective, think about what I was doing with my life" (p. 221).

Parental support is another key factor that helps children develop a healthy perspective of self (Cosden, Brown, & Elliott, 2002). Parents or guardians can advocate for their children in school and provide emotional support (Wiener, 2003). Individuals with learning disabilities who have positive adult outcomes grow up in home environments that foster emotional stability (Hechtman, 1991). In addition, parental acceptance of academic limitations, as well as acknowledgment of strengths, may reduce the stress caused by the learning disability (Morrison & Cosden, 1997). Individuals with learning disabilities who became successful adults reflected on their relationships with their families and how their families had shaped their lives. In their descriptions they stressed that their families had been extraordinarily supportive, had provided them with financial support and a healthy dependence, and an understanding that the learning disabilities had caused at times stresses on particular family members (Goldberg et al., 2003). After reading a long email from a teacher, describing her daughter's most recent failure to meet the requirements of a middle school assignment, Annie's mother wrote, "I hate to see her so defeated. I will be her cheerleader today. It is hard because I get down too and I know I have to stay up…recognize her struggle but keep her going." Parents and teachers, sometimes together, sometimes alone, often end up not only being a cheerleader, but the entire cheerleading squad. Thus, an interdisciplinary effort among parents, teachers, pediatricians, therapists, and psychologists is needed to forge a chain of protective fac-

tors that will reduce the negative impact of a learning disability (Werner, 1999). Caring parents and teachers can help preserve the self-esteem of children.

Provide School-Based Intensive Interventions

Within the school setting, teachers and administrators have to recognize that a child's psychological, academic, and social well-being should be addressed. In a meta-analytic review of 64 intervention studies, Elbaum and Vaughn (2001) found that the types of interventions that were effective varied based upon grade level. The interventions that were most effective in elementary schools were those that directly focused on improving academic performance, requiring considerable time and intensity. In middle school and high school, counseling interventions were more effective. In general, interventions were more effective with middle school students than they were with elementary or high school students. The extent of positive impact depends upon the type and quality of service, as well as the depth and breadth of intervention (Spekman, Goldberg, et al., 1993; Spekman, Herman, et al., 1993). A large and growing body of literature emphasizes two important points. First, academic achievement is a protective factor; when we find ways to teach children with learning disabilities strategies to succeed, they are more likely to thrive. Second, providing instruction in social emotional skills, including self-awareness, is just as important as teaching academic skills.

Vogel et al. (1993) found that the availability of long-term tutoring and one-to-one instruction characterized the education of successful adults with learning disabilities. Unfortunately, many students with learning disabilities do not receive differentiated instruction and, with continued failures, their perceptions of their academic competence are diminished. Schumm, Moody, and Vaughn (2000) interviewed third-grade teachers and students with learning disabilities. Overall, the teachers reported using whole-class instruction that included the same materials for all students in the class regardless of levels of performance. All students were expected to read grade-level materials even if they could not read the words in the material. Furthermore, students with learning disabilities did not receive instruction directed at improving their word analysis skills. One teacher voiced strong opposition to providing instruction in word analysis: "By the time they come to third grade they really should have those skills" (p. 483). With undifferentiated instruction and minimal direct instruction in reading, the students with learning disabilities made little academic improvement and their attitudes about reading declined. In contrast to general education placements, the identification process resulting in placement in special education programs does not appear to negatively affect the self-concept of students with learning disabilities, at least within the early grades (Vaughn, Haager, Hogan, & Kouzekanani, 1992).

To address students' learning disparities, teachers must help students make as much academic progress as possible. This cannot be accomplished by having the student use the same educational materials as their classmates. The academic difficulties of children with learning problems are chronic, even when they have individualized educational plans (Sorensen et al., 2003). A student with learning disabilities requires differentiated, carefully engineered educational programming. Although the student must be treated as equitably as others, the type of instruction that is provided will differ substantially from that provided to students without learning disabilities. In the short run, students who are behind in reading may feel better about their reading abilities if they have the same books as their peers; but in the long run, if their skills do not improve, they will have little basis for positive self-perceptions of their academic competence (Vaughn & Elbaum, 1999). Even the same students who reported wanting to have the same materials as their peers explained that they "… value teachers who slow down instruction when needed, explain concepts and assignments clearly, teach learning strategies, and teach the same material differently so that everyone can learn" (Klingner & Vaughn, 1999, p. 23). Students with learning disabilities require intensive and explicit instruction that focuses on their specific needs (Schumm et al., 2000). Additionally, participants in one study were seen to lack metacognitive skills, but be very aware of what they wanted from teachers. These adolescents wished for help that was *discreetly* provided by teachers sensitive to the fact they are self-conscious adolescents, and that these teachers offered help to the whole class rather than only to the students with learning disabilities (Klassen & Lynch, 2007).

Select the Most Appropriate Placement

Students with learning disabilities need a social environment that supports their academic efforts and sustains their achievement (Elbaum & Vaughn, 2001). Although the field continues to debate the most appropriate service delivery system for children with learning disabilities, findings from studies addressing self-concept and educational placements (general education, resource room, or self-contained) are equivocal, and no one placement is clearly preferable to another (Wiener & Tardif, 2004). The continuum of placements must be preserved in order to increase the likelihood that children will be able to get the individualized instruction they need.

Elbaum found that some studies showed higher self-concepts for students in more restrictive settings; others showed higher self-concept for students in less restrictive settings; and still others showed no difference. The age of the student can also affect his or her response to the type of classroom placement. Howard and Tryon (2002) investigated the relationship of depressive symptomology in a sample of adolescents with learning disabilities placed in general education or self-contained classrooms. Although their self-ratings did not differ based upon the type of placement, the guidance counselors rated the students with learning disabilities in general education classes as being more depressed than those in self-contained classes. This finding suggests that negative teacher and peer feedback can be more prevalent in inclusive settings and that sensitivity to disability may be less than that experienced in self-contained settings.

In another study, children with learning disabilities in four types of special education settings were compared in terms of social acceptance, number of friends, quality of friendships, quality of relationship with best friends, self-concept, loneliness, depression, social skills, and problem behaviors. The results suggested a preference toward the inclusive classroom for social and emotional adjustment; however, the researchers suggested that given the size of the differences it would be inappropriate to conclude that the major variable influencing social and emotional adjustment is the special education placement (Wiener & Tardif, 2004). The National Longitudinal Transition Study 2 (NLTS2) is a comprehensive report that provides an analysis of a large number of factors that influence the education of children with disabilities (Wagner et al., 2003). The authors underscore that school programs, support services, and other experiences have a significant influence on children with disabilities, particularly in the domains of academic engagement and performance (Wagner et al., 2003). The NLTS2 research team identified many factors that relate to better school outcomes for students with disabilities. Based on these findings parents are encouraged to:

- Maintain high expectations for future education and independence
- Stay actively involved in the child's school experiences
- Support extracurricular activities

Teachers and parents are encouraged to:

- Teach persistence at home and at school. The importance of persistence is tremendous (Wagner et al., 2003)
- Teach social skills
- Carefully consider placement in general education classrooms.
- Results are mixed in terms of advantages and disadvantages of placement: while the general education setting fostered both learning and social skills, grades earned by students with disabilities in the general education classroom tended to be lower than their peers without

disabilities. However, even though their grades were lower, they performed closer to grade level in both reading and mathematics than peers who did not take as many general education classes (Blackorby, Chorost, Garza, & Guzman, 2003). As Wagner et al. (2003) wrote, "Poor grades can send a message of failure to youth that could militate against the benefits of inclusion and erode the commitment to school over time" (p. 12).

One fact is clear: students with learning disabilities need a strong support system throughout their school careers. This system can help preserve self-concept and self-worth by: (a) keeping failure at a minimum, (b) increasing acknowledgment of nonacademic talents and other competencies, and (c) emphasizing learning goals over performance goals (Lerner, 2000). A learning goal rewards effort, even though the final product (the performance goal) can be partially complete or incorrect. Because social life and status impact school learning (Bryan, 2003), to ensure that children with learning disabilities succeed, their feelings of low self-worth and self-esteem must also be addressed. Whether a child receives services in a resource room or in a general education class, the child needs to be in an academic environment that is safe and secure so that learning will flourish (Brooks, 2001). When school teams are making decisions about educational placement, they should consider the student's own preferences, as well as his or her academic, social, and emotional needs (Elbaum, 2002). Some evidence suggests students with learning disabilities prefer resource services or pull-out programs to in-class service delivery (Jenkins & Heinen, 1989; Le Mare & de la Ronde, 2000). Regardless of the placement, school environments must be benevolent, supportive, and developmentally appropriate for all children (Bryan, 2003).

Acknowledge Accomplishments in Nonacademic Domains

Another way to foster resilience is to support positive development in other areas of performance besides traditional school subjects

(Werner, 1999). Unfortunately, many parents and teachers often feel that if they take away the activity the child enjoys the most and use it as a reward, it can motivate the child to perform academically. These adults need to be reminded that all children need to experience success, and caution should be used when taking away the one thing that makes a child smile, relax, or feel that he or she is indeed good at something. Harter's (1985) multidimensional model of self-concept includes the following six domains of self-perception: academic, social, athletic, physical, behavioral, and global self-worth. Although students with learning disabilities often have lower academic self-concepts than their peers, successful accomplishments in other domains can help offset low academic self-perceptions and help students maintain self-esteem (Smith & Nagle, 1995; Vaughn & Elbaum, 1999). Success in any arena of life leads to enhanced self-esteem and a feeling of self-efficacy (Rutter, 1985). Students with learning disabilities often find success in a nonacademic arena, such as sports, the arts, or technology.

In a posting to a listserv, Mary Perfitt-Nelson (2002) noted how different schools would be if the curriculum, rules, materials, and tests were developed by artists, musicians, athletes, or mathematicians. She wrote:

> "We meet and discuss kids and how they are doing in *our* environment. If they are not excelling, few of us even consider that the environment is not supporting the student's strengths. Changing the environment is rarely considered, nor is it even thought necessary. Districts have done away with technical courses. We are left with some variation of the college track, where the failure rate is astounding. And yet each child could be an expert in some area. It is important that we help the mathematicians and musicians find their way during the 12 years they must spend in a place designed for someone else."

Salza (2003) expressed similar sentiments and provided the following analogy to illustrate how the success of adults with dyslexia is often unexpected because we incorrectly assume that the skills needed for school success are the same as those needed for life success:

> "Consider the giant green sea turtle lumbering across the sand to lay her eggs. She heaves herself across the sand and struggles mightily for every inch of ground she covers. She looks awkward, vulnerable, disabled, and poorly adapted. Consider the same green sea turtle swimming in the ocean. She swims with power and grace, dives deep, stays down for long periods of time, and comes up practically dry! Schools can and must give children, at the least, a glimpse and perhaps a taste of the sea to which they are headed as they struggle across this patch of ground we call school." (p. 27)

Thus, it is important to recognize and acknowledge the unique talents of individuals with learning disabilities and to remind them that successful school performance does not guarantee or negate successful life outcomes. Young children do not have the ability to shift their perspective on their own. Parents and teachers need to help them realize that a report card does not reflect how successful they will be as an adult; furthermore they need to be reminded that school is not a life sentence! At some point, they will be able to choose where and how they learn, as well as what they do. This is big news to an elementary school child who has already started to compare her grades with that of her classmates and wonder if life will always be like it is on report card day.

The late Sally Smith, founder of the Lab School in Washington, DC, wrote, "The most important help that parents and teachers can give is to dig deep into the secret, unseen pockets of their children and students and search for the treasures. All of us have talent in something" (Smith, 2003b, p. 44). Many individuals have successful lives despite having a learning disability. They develop positive attitudes toward themselves and life. Werner (1993) found that a positive temperament did not reduce negative outcomes in late adolescence, but did predict positive adjustment by the age of 32.

Acknowledge Accomplishments in Academic Domains

For many students with learning disabilities, the problems are circumscribed or domain-specific. For example, the student can struggle with reading, but excel in math or science. Or the student can be an avid reader, but experience great difficulty with spelling. Because specific cognitive and linguistic mechanisms affect functioning differentially, a student with learning disabilities will struggle with certain academic tasks, but not others. For example, a student with a circumscribed weakness in phonological awareness will exhibit difficulties in word analysis and spelling tasks, but not typically in math activities (unless reading is involved). One important consideration is to identify specific academic areas in which students with learning disabilities can be educated with peers using the same materials and procedures (Klingner & Vaughn, 1999; Miller & Fritz, 1998). Simply having the same book is not the same as using and profiting from the same book. Students must be able to read and learn from the books they are provided. Thus, for students with learning disabilities, it is important to identify domain-specific academic strengths and match curricular materials accordingly. Children and adults who view their disabilities as circumscribed and not as affecting global functioning are more likely to have positive self-esteem (Cosden, 2001; Rothman & Cosden, 1995). For example, Miguel a high school sophomore received intensive reading support, but then served as a math tutor for classmates struggling in algebra class. Acknowledgment of his math competence helped Miguel maintain a positive self-image, despite his difficulties with reading and spelling.

Regardless of the level of performance, students with learning disabilities must experience realistic accomplishments (Brooks, 2001). Vail (2003) noted that self-esteem grows from the inside out, not from the outside in, and that competence leads to confidence, which then increases motivation and results in genuine self-regard.

Teachers and parents are to be reminded of the power of positive praise on behavior. In a recent workshop on resilience, a parent commented, "When I look at my son's writing, I just can't think of anything to praise." At the end of the workshop she had a list of ten items! Often we understandably take for granted many of the little steps it takes to get our children to even the place where they are struggling. Comments like, "I'm glad you have your school supplies with

you" or "That's great that you read the directions so clearly; what part do you need help with?" or "Wow! You capitalized the beginning of every sentence" can go a long way in helping children to persevere. Why does this work? Children crave attention even for those behaviors that they value as challenging to them, rather than easy tasks. Every time an adult recognizes the genuine efforts that a child has made with sincere praise, it makes the child feel anchored. Moreover, this works because struggling learners do not intuitively know what they do right in the academic realm because in their minds they have already tried hard and very often "were wrong." These children who are keenly aware that they are struggling need to know what has been done correctly so that they can do more of it. Table 19.1 reviews important ideas for both parents and teachers for enhancing a child's resilience.

Conclusion

Both general and special education teachers need to work together to provide effective instruction to students who are often confused and searching for personal survival and accomplishments (Masters, Mori, & Mori, 1993). When teachers give students powerful reasons to attend their classes and minimize their failure experiences, many students with learning disabilities will not only survive, but they will thrive (Sabornie & deBettencourt, 2008). Miller and Fritz (1998) encourage teachers to be the one a student will recall favorably when asked, "Tell me about a teacher you remember." Well-functioning schools can serve as a protective factor for children's development and accomplishments (Keogh & Weisner, 1993; Rutter, 1978). Schools must be effective, benevolent, supportive, and developmentally appropriate for all children (Bryan, 2003). This requires all educators to share a vision and create a plan. We are reminded of the advice that the Cheshire cat gave to Alice while she visited Wonderland, when she asked which way to go upon reaching an intersection. The cat inquired: "Where are you going?" Alice responded: "I have no idea." The cat then replied: "When you don't know where you are going, any road will do." We need to be clear and rigorous in our

Table 19.1 Twenty ways to foster resiliency in children with learning disabilities

1. Support and promote interest in nonacademic and academic areas. Do not use these activities as rewards or punishment. Every child needs to feel good at something. As Smith said, "Dig deep to find the treasures in your child" (Smith, 2003b)

2. Provide opportunities to cultivate relationships with other adults who can offer inspiration and hope

3. Offer a shift of perspective on school achievement. Help children to understand that report cards reflect only one aspect of life. They are not an indication of how successful a person will be as an adult. This conversation should take place repeatedly over time because children hear this message differently across the age span

4. Help the child develop an understanding of the nature of his or her learning disability. This may take the assistance of a teacher, school psychologist, or other professional. A child needs to k now how a disability impacts school, home, social life, and how to reduce the impact of the disability

5. Nurture strengths. Children need to know what strengths they possess and how those strengths can offset factors related to the disability

6. When learning takes place, provide specific praise so that the child is aware that it was his or her actions that made the learning successful, rather than it just being "a lucky day" or chance event

7. When learning strategies are taught, be specific about how the strategy worked. Children need to understand what behaviors make them a successful learner. This encourages future efforts

8. Provide basic reading instruction in secondary school for children who need it. Do not give up even though reading is no longer a "subject" in school

9. Teach social awareness and social skills for children who need them

10. Pay attention to the personal learning strategies students may develop on their own; if they are successful, praise them for coming up with a strategy that works for them and reinforce it

11. Help children set and achieve attainable goals. Promote ongoing hope by planning for the future

12. Foster collaboration between general and special education teachers. All teachers and tutors need to be working together. The IEP meeting is a good time to foster this collaboration

13. Before placement in or removal from the general education classroom, weigh carefully the academic vs. social implications

14. Reward effort when it is apparent. Help students gauge and reflect upon their level of effort, persistence, and perseverance. Rework tasks to build success and encourage persistence

15. Address anxiety and/or depression when indicated through clinical therapy, and/or consultation with a medical provider. These emotional factors can be as detrimental to learning as the disability itself

16. Watch your child perform schoolwork and every month identify five new behaviors that were done well and praise him or her. Praise should be sincere and the behaviors should be meaningful to the child

17. Respect a student's sensitivity when providing feedback in class. Be discreet

18. Praise a child's efforts during homework time. Provide breaks, humor, and try to be a good cheerleader even when it hurts to see your child struggle. Be a model of resilience

19. Not all learning disabilities are the same. Make an effort to understand the nature of a particular disability

20. Pay attention to all struggling learners in your class. Teacher support is critical

thinking (Donahue & Pearl, 2003). We must know where our roads are going and be ever vigilant as we plan curriculum and select activities for children with learning disabilities. Brooks (2001) so aptly described the common mind-set of effective educators: "We can accomplish this by being empathetic; by treating students in the same ways that we would like to be treated, by finding a few moments to smile and make them feel comfortable, by teaching them in ways they can learn successfully, by taking care to avoid any words or actions that might be accusatory, by minimizing their fears of failure and humiliation, by encouraging them, and by recognizing their strengths" (p. 20).

This is the road we must follow, a road paved with effective instruction, support, and empathy.

References

Ahrens, K., DuBois, D. L., Lozano, P., & Richardson, L. P. (2010). Naturally acquired mentoring relationships and young adult outcomes among adolescents with learning disabilities. *Learning Disabilities Research & Practice, 25*, 207–216.

Bender, W. N. (2008). *Learning disabilities: Characteristics, identification, and teaching strategies*. Toronto, ON: Pearson.

Bender, W. N., Rosenkrans, C. B., & Crane, M. K. (1999). Stress, depression, and suicide among students with learning disabilities: Assessing the risk. *Learning Disability Quarterly, 22*, 143–156.

Blackorby, J. Chorost, M., Garza, N., & Guzman, A., (2003). The academic performance of secondary school students with disabilities (pp. 1–15). In Wagner, M., Marder, C., Blackorby, J., Cameto, R., Newman, L., Levine, P., & Davies-Mercier, E. (with Chorost, M., Garza, N., Guzman, A., & Sumi, C.). *The achievements of youth with disabilities during secondary school. A report from the National Longitudinal Transition Study-2 (NLTS2).* Menlo Park, CA: SRI International. Retrieved from National Longitudinal Transition Study-2. Retrieved on 02 Jan, 2011 from website: www.nlts2.org/reports/2003_11/nlts2_report_2003_11_complete.pdf.

Blocker, L. S., & Copeland, E. P. (1994). Determinants of resilience in high-stressed youth. *The High School Journal, 77*, 286–293.

Borkowski, J. G., Carr, M., Rellinger, L., & Pressley, M. (1990). Self-regulated cognition: Interdependence of metacognition, attributions, and self-esteem. In B. Jones & L. Idol (Eds.), *Dimensions of thinking and cognitive instruction* (pp. 53–92). Hillsdale, NJ: Erlbaum.

Brooks, R. B. (1991). *The self-esteem teacher.* Loveland, OH: Treehaus Communications.

Brooks, R. B. (2001). Fostering motivation, hope, and resilience in children with learning disorders. *Annals of Dyslexia, 51*, 9–20.

Brooks, R., & Goldstein, S. (2001). *Raising resilient children: Fostering strength, hope, and optimism in your child.* Lincolnwood, IL: Contemporary Books.

Bryan, T. (2003). The applicability of the risk and resilience model to social problems of students with learning disabilities: Response to Bernice Wong. *Learning Disabilities Research & Practice, 18*, 94–98.

Cosden, M. (2001). Risk and resilience for substance abuse among adolescents and adults with LD. *Journal of Learning Disabilities, 34*, 352–358.

Cosden, M., Brown, C., & Elliott, K. (2002). Development of self-understanding and self-esteem in children and adults with learning disabilities. In B. Y. L. Wong & M. Donahue (Eds.), *Social dimensions of learning disabilities* (pp. 33–51). Mahwah, NJ: Erlbaum.

Crawford, V. (2002). *Embracing the monster: Overcoming the challenges of hidden disabilities.* Baltimore, MD: Paul Brookes.

Doll, B., & Lyon, M. (1998). Risk and resilience: Implications for the delivery of educational and mental health services in school. *School Psychology Review, 27*, 348–363.

Donahue, M. L., & Pearl, R. (2003). Studying social development and learning disabilities is not for the fainthearted: Comments on the risk/resilience framework. *Learning Disabilities Research & Practice, 18*, 90–93.

Dyson, L. L. (2003). Children with learning disabilities within the family context: A comparison with siblings in global self-concept, academic self-perception, and social competence. *Learning Disabilities Research & Practice, 18*, 1–9.

Elbaum, B. (2002). The self-concept of students with learning disabilities: A meta-analysis of comparisons across different placements. *Learning Disabilities Research & Practice, 17*, 216–226.

Elbaum, B., & Vaughn, S. (2001). School-based interventions to enhance the self-concept of students with learning disabilities: A meta-analysis. *The Elementary School Journal, 101*, 303–329.

Elliot, S., & McKinnie, D. (1994). Relationships and differences among social skills, problem behaviors, and academic competence for mainstreamed learning-disabled and nonhandicapped students. *Canadian Journal of School Psychology, 10*, 1–14.

Eysenck, M. W., Derakshan, N., Santos, R., & Calvo, M. G. (2007). Anxiety and cognitive performance: Attentional control theory. *Emotion, 7*, 336–353.

Fernald, G. (1943). *Remedial techniques in basic school subjects.* New York, NY: McGraw-Hill.

Galway, T. M., & Metsala, J. L. (2011). Social cognition and its relations to psychosocial adjustment in children with nonverbal learning disabilities. *Journal of Learning Disabilities, 44*, 33–49.

Gans, A. M., Kenny, M. C., & Ghany, D. L. (2003). Comparing the self-concept of students with and without learning disabilities. *Journal of Learning Disabilities, 36*, 287–295.

Gerber, P. J., & Ginsberg, R. J. (1990). *Identifying alterable patterns of success in highly successful adults with learning disabilities.* Washington, DC: OSERS: National Institute for Disability and Rehabilitation Research.

Gerber, P. J., Ginsberg, R. J., & Reiff, H. B. (1992). Identifying alterable patterns in employment success in highly successful adults with learning disabilities. *Journal of Learning Disabilities, 25*, 475–487.

Gerber, P. J., Reiff, H. B., & Ginsberg, R. (1996). Reframing the learning disabilities experience. *Journal of Learning Disabilities, 29*, 98–101.

Goldberg, R. J., Higgins, E. L., Raskind, M. H., & Herman, K. L. (2003). Predictors of success in individuals with learning disabilities: A qualitative analysis of a 20-year longitudinal study. *Learning Disabilities Research & Practice, 18*, 222–236.

Hall, C. W., Spruill, K. L., & Webster, R. E. (2002). Motivational and attitudinal factors of college students with and without learning disabilities. *Learning Disabilities Quarterly, 25*, 79–86.

Hallowell, E. M. (2003). Life and death and reading words. *Perspectives, 29*(3), 6–7.

Harter, S. (1985). *Manual for the self-perception profile for children.* Denver, CO: University of Denver.

Hechtman, L. (1991). Resilience and vulnerability in long-term outcomes of attention deficit hyperactivity disorders. *Canadian Journal of Psychiatry, 36*, 415–421.

Higgins, E. L., Raskind, M. H., Goldberg, R. J., & Herman, K. L. (2002). *Learning Disability Quarterly, 25*, 3–18.

Howard, K. A., & Tryon, G. S. (2002). Depressive symptoms in and type of classroom placement for adolescents with LD. *Journal of Learning Disabilities, 35*, 186–190.

Jenkins, J. R., & Heinen, A. (1989). Students' preferences for service delivery: Pull-out, in-class, or integrated models. *Exceptional Children, 55*, 516–523.

Keogh, B. K., & Weisner, T. (1993). An ecocultural perspective on risk and protective factors in children's development: Implications for learning disabilities. *Learning Disabilities Research & Practice, 8*, 3–10.

Klassen, R. M., & Lynch, S. L. (2007). Self-efficacy from the perspective of adolescents with LD and their specialist teachers. *Journal of Learning Disabilities, 40*, 494–507.

Klingner, J. K., & Vaughn, S. (1999). *Exceptional Children, 66*, 23–37.

Kloomok, S., & Cosden, M. (1994). Self-concept in children with learning disabilities: The relationship between global self-concept, academic "discounting," nonacademic self-concept, and perceived social support. *Learning Disability Quarterly, 17*, 140–153.

Kravetz, S., Faust, M., Lipshitz, S., & Shalhav, S. (1999). LD, interpersonal understanding, and social behavior in the classroom. *Journal of Learning Disabilities, 32*, 248–255.

Kuhne, M., & Wiener, J. (2000). Stability of social status of children without and without learning disabilities. *Learning Disability Quarterly, 23*, 64–75.

Lackaye, T. D., & Margalit, M. (2006). Comparisons of achievement, efforts, and self perceptions among students with learning disabilities and their peers from different achievement groups. *Journal of Learning Disabilities, 39*, 432–446.

Le Mare, L., & de la Ronde, M. (2000). Links among social status, service delivery mode, and service delivery preference in LD, low-achieving, and normally achieving elementary-aged children. *Learning Disability Quarterly, 23*, 52–62.

Lerner, J. W. (2000). *Learning disabilities: Theories, diagnosis, and teaching strategies*. Boston, MA: Houghton Mifflin.

Maag, J. W., & Reid, R. (2006). Depression among students with learning disabilities: Assessing the risk. *Journal of Learning Disabilities, 39*, 3–10.

Margalit, M. (2004). Second-generation research on resilience: Social-emotional aspects of children with learning disabilities. *Learning Disabilities Research & Practice, 19*, 45–48.

Masters, L. R., Mori, B. A., & Mori, A. A. (1993). *Teaching students with mild learning and behavior problems: Methods, materials, strategies*. Austin, TX: PRO-ED.

Mather, N., & Gregg, N. (2003). "I can rite": Informal assessment of written language. In S. Vaughn & K. L. Briggs (Eds.), *Reading in the classroom: Systems for observing teaching and learning* (pp. 179–219). Baltimore, MD: Paul H. Brookes.

McKinney, J. D., Osborne, S. S., & Schulte, A. C. (1993). Academic consequences of learning disability: Longitudinal prediction of outcomes at 11 years of age. *Learning Disabilities Research & Practice, 8*, 19–27.

McNamara, J. K., & Willoughby, T. (2010). A longitudinal study of risk-taking behavior in adolescents with learning disabilities. *Learning Disabilities Research & Practice, 25*, 11–24.

McNulty, M. A. (2003). Dyslexia and the life course. *Journal of Learning Disabilities, 36*, 363–381.

Meltzer, L. J. (1995). Strategic learning in students with learning disabilities: The role of students' self-awareness and self-perceptions. In T. E. Scruggs & M. Mastropieri (Eds.), *Advances in learning and behaviorial disabilities* (Vol. 10, pp. 181–199). Greenwich, CT: JAI.

Meltzer, L. J., Ranjini, R., Ollica, L. S., Roditi, B., Sayer, J., & Theokas, C. (2004). Positive and negative self-perceptions: Is there a cyclical relationship between teachers' and students' perceptions of effort, strategy use, and academic performance? *Learning Disabilities Research & Practice, 19*, 33–44.

Meltzer, L. J., Roditi, B., Houser, R. F., & Perlman, M. (1998). Perceptions of academic strategies and competence in students with learning disabilities. *Journal of Learning Disabilities, 31*, 437–451.

Miller, M., & Fritz, M. F. (1998). A demonstration of resilience. *Intervention in School and Clinic, 33*, 265–271.

Montague, M., Enders, C., Dietz, S., Dixon, J., & Cavendish, W. (2008). A longitudinal study of depressive symptomology and self-concept in adolescents. *The Journal of Special Education, 42*(2), 67–78.

Morgan, P. L., Farkas, G., Tufis, P. A., & Sperling, R. A. (2008). Are reading and behavior problems risk factors for each other? *Journal of Learning Disabilities, 41*, 417–436.

Morrison, G. M. (1985). Differences in teacher perceptions and student self-perceptions for learning disabled and nonhandicapped learners in regular and special education settings. *Learning Disabilities Quarterly, 1*, 32–41.

Morrison, G. M., & Cosden, M. A. (1997). Risk, resilience, and adjustment of individuals with learning disabilities. *Learning Disability Quarterly, 20*, 43–60.

Morrison, G. M., & D'Incau, B. (1997). The web of zero tolerance: Characteristics of students who are recommended for expulsion from school. *Education and Treatment of Children, 20*, 316–335.

Mugnaini, D., Lassi, S., La Malfa, G., & Albertini, G. (2009). Internalizing correlates of dyslexia. *World Journal of Pediatrics, 5*, 255–264.

Nalavany, B. A., Carawan, L. W., & Rennick, R. A. (2011). Psychosocial experiences associated with confirmed and self-identified dyslexia: A participant-driven concept map of adult perspectives. *Journal of Learning Disabilities, 44*, 63–79.

Nelson, J. M., & Harwood, H. (2011a). Learning disabilities and anxiety: A meta-analysis. *Journal of Learning Disabilities, 44*, 3–17.

Nelson, J. M. & Harwood, H. (2011b). A meta-analysis of parent and teacher reports of depression among students with learning disabilities: Evidence for the importance of multi-informant assessment. *Psychology in the Schools, 48*, 371–384. Retrieved on 02 Jan, 2011 from (www.wileyonline.com).

Orr, A. C., & Goodman, N. (2010). "People like me don't go to college": The legacy of a learning disability.

Journal of Ethnographic & Qualitative Research, 4, 213–225.

Palombo, J. (2001). *Learning disorders and disorders of the self.* New York, NY: Norton.

Perfitt-Nelson, M. (2002, Dec 16). "G," Sam makes sense. Message posted to Retrieved on 02 Jan, 2011 from http://IAPCHC@yahoogroups.com.

Raskind, M. H., Goldberg, R. J., Higgins, E. L., & Herman, K. L. (1999). Patterns of change and predictors of success in individuals with learning disabilities: Results from a twenty-year longitudinal study. *Learning Disabilities Research & Practice, 14,* 35–49.

Reiff, H. B., Gerber, P. J., & Ginsberg, R. (1993). Definitions of learning disabilities from adults with learning disabilities: The insiders' perspectives. *Learning Disability Quarterly, 16,* 114–125.

Robertson, L. M., Harding, M., & Morrison, G. (1998). A comparison of risk and resilience indicators among Latino/a students: Differences between students identified as at-risk, learning disabled, speech impaired, and not at-risk. *Education and Treatment of Children, 21,* 333–354.

Rothman, H. R., & Cosden, M. (1995). The relationship between self-perception of a learning disability and achievement, self-concept and social support. *Learning Disability Quarterly, 18,* 203–212.

Rutter, M. (1978). Early sources of security and competence. In J. S. Bruner & A. Garten (Eds.), *Human journal of development* (pp. 49–74). London: Clarendon.

Rutter, M. (1985). Resilience in the face of adversity: Protective factors and resistance to psychiatric disorder. *The British Journal of Psychiatry, 147,* 598–611.

Sabornie, E. J., & deBettencourt, L. U. (2008). *Teaching students with mild disabilities at the secondary level.* Upper Saddle River, NJ: Prentice-Hall.

Salza, L. (2003). Struggling to learn in school: Confessions of a lunch-pail school head. *Perspectives: The International Dyslexia Association, 29*(2), 26–27.

Schumm, J. S., Moody, S. W., & Vaughn, S. (2000). Grouping for reading instruction: Does one size fit all? *Journal of Learning Disabilities, 33,* 47–78.

Segal, J. (1988). Teachers have enormous power in affecting a child's self-esteem. *Brown University Child Behavior and Development Newsletter, 4,* 1–3.

Settle, S. A., & Milich, R. (1999). Social persistence following failure in boys and girls with LD. *Journal of Learning Disabilities, 32,* 201–212.

Shessel, I., & Reiff, H. B. (1999). Experiences of adults with learning disabilities: Positive and negative impacts and outcomes. *Learning Disability Quarterly, 22,* 305–316.

Sideridis, G. D. (2007). Why are students with LD depressed? A goal orientation model of depression vulnerability. *Journal of Learning Disabilities, 40,* 526–539.

Smith, D. S., & Nagle, R. J. (1995). Self-perceptions and social comparisons among children with LD. *Journal of Learning Disabilities, 28,* 364–371.

Smith, S. L. (1989). The masks students wear. *Instructor,* 27–28, 31–32.

Smith, S. L. (2003a). What do parents of children with learning disabilities, ADHD, and related disorders deal with? *LDA Newsbriefs, 38*(4), 3–8, 16.

Smith, S. L. (2003b). *The power of the arts: Creative strategies for teaching exceptional learners.* Baltimore, MD: Brookes.

Sorensen, L. G., Forbes, R. W., Bernstein, J. H., Weiler, M. D., Mitchell, W. M., & Waber, D. R. (2003). Psychosocial adjustment over a two-year period in children referred for learning problems: Risk, resilience, and adaptation. *Learning Disabilities Research & Practice, 18,* 10–24.

Spekman, N. J., Goldberg, R. J., & Herman, K. L. (1993). An exploration of risk and resilience in the lives of individuals with learning disabilities. *Learning Disabilities Research & Practice, 8,* 11–18.

Spekman, N. J., Herman, K. L., & Vogel, S. A. (1993). Risk and resilience in individuals with learning disabilities: A challenge to the field. *Learning Disabilities Research & Practice, 8,* 59–65.

Stanovich, K. E. (1986). Matthew effects in reading: Some consequences of individual differences in the acquisition of literacy. *Reading Research Quarterly, 21,* 360–407.

Stanovich, K. E. (1999). The sociopsychometrics of learning disabilities. *Journal of Learning Disabilities, 32,* 350–361.

Steele, C. M. (1995). Stereotype threat and intellectual test performance of African Americans. *Journal of Personality and Social Psychology, 69,* 797–811.

Vail, R. L. (2003). Tenets for parents. *Perspectives, 29*(3), 22.

Vaughn, S., & Elbaum, B. (1999). The self-concept and friendships of students with learning disabilities: A developmental perspective. In R. Gallimore, L. P. Bernheimer, D. L. MacMillan, D. L. Speece, & S. Vaughn (Eds.), *Developmental perspectives on children with high-incidence disabilities* (pp. 15–31). Mahwah, NJ: Erlbaum.

Vaughn, S., & Haager, D. (1994). Social competence as a multifaceted construct: How do students with learning disabilities fare? *Learning Disability Quarterly, 12,* 253–266.

Vaughn, S., Haager, D., Hogan, A., & Kouzekanani, K. (1992). Self-concept and peer acceptance in students with learning disabilities: A four- to five-year prospective study. *Journal of Educational Psychology, 84,* 43–50.

Voeller, K. K. S. (1991). Social-emotional learning disabilities. *Psychiatric Annals, 21,* 735–741.

Vogel, S. A., Hruby, P. J., & Adelman, P. B. (1993). Educational and psychological factors in successful and unsuccessful college students with learning disabilities. *Learning Disabilities Research & Practice, 8,* 35–43.

Wagner, M., Marder, C., Blackorby, J., Cameto, R., Newman, L., Levine, P.,...Sumi, C. (2003). *The achievements of youth with disabilities during secondary school. A report from the National Longitudinal Transition Study-2 (NLTS2).* Menlo Park, CA: SRI International. Retrieved from National Longitudinal Transition Study-2. Retrieved on 02

Jan, 2011 from website: www.nlts2.org/reports/2003_11/nlts2_report_2003_11_complete.pdf.

Werner, E. E. (1993). Risk and resilience in individuals with learning disabilities: Lessons learned from the Kauai longitudinal study. *Learning Disabilities Research & Practice, 8*, 28–34.

Werner, E. E. (1999). Risk and protective factors in the lives of children with high-incidence disabilities. In R. Gallimore, L. P. Beerheimer, D. L. MacMillan, D. L. Speece, & S. Vaughn (Eds.), *Developmental perspectives on children with high-incidence disabilities* (pp. 15–31). Mahwah, NJ: Erlbaum.

Wiener, J. (2003). Resilience and multiple risks: A response to Bernice Wong. *Learning Disabilities Research & Practice, 18*, 77–81.

Wiener, J., & Tardif, C. Y. (2004). Social and emotional functioning of children with learning disabilities: Does special education placement make a difference? *Learning Disabilities Research & Practice, 19*, 20–32.

Wong, B. Y. L. (2003). General and specific issues for researchers' consideration in applying the risk and resilience framework to the social domain of learning disabilities. *Learning Disabilities Research & Practice, 18*, 68–76.

Wyman, R. A., Cowen, E. L., Work, W. C., & Keriey, J. H. (1993). The role of children's future expectations in self-esteem functioning and adjustment to life stress: A prospective study of urban at-risk children. *Development and Psychopathology, 5*, 649–661.

Promoting Educational Equity in Disadvantaged Youth: The Role of Resilience and Social-Emotional Learning

Jazmin A. Reyes, Maurice J. Elias, Sarah J. Parker, and Jennifer L. Rosenblatt

We are all concerned about the future of American education. But as I tell my students, you do not enter the future—you create the future. The future is created through hard work.
Jaime Escalante, Latino Educator

As we enter the second decade of the twenty-first century, education in America is at a critical turning point. Call for reform is widespread and exemplified by the documentary film *Waiting for Superman*, which highlights the fact that for many American children, access to a quality education is often literally a lottery. Equal access to educational opportunity is the philosophical cornerstone of the American public education system. Although significant advances towards realizing this goal have been made over recent decades, educational quality still varies widely, with Latino and African-American children being more likely to attend disadvantaged schools (Cauce, Cruz, Corona, & Conger, 2011). The agents of this inequity are familiar to most in disadvantaged educational environments: educator stress, low academic expectations, and impaired relations with students; ecological instability; and a culture that discourages academic achievement and healthy behavior—as well as a host of other circumstances that demand the attention of students and educators at the expense of learning. While years of policy initiatives have worked to eliminate these problems, the future of American public education and its ability to produce a skilled workforce capable of competing in an increasingly challenging and technical global market remains uncertain (Education in America, 2010).

One certainty regarding the future American workforce, however, will be its multiracial and multiethnic composition. By the year 2050, roughly 47% of working Americans will be members of a racial/ethnic minority group. Of these, approximately 24% will be Latino (Toosi, 2006). Latinos (or Hispanics) are individuals of "Cuban, Mexican, Puerto Rican, South or Central American, or other Spanish culture or origin, regardless of race" (Office of Management and Budget (OMB), 1997). Currently, Latinos are the largest ethnic minority group in the U.S., accounting for 15% of the U.S. population. In addition to being the largest minority group, Latinos are the

J.A. Reyes (✉) • M.J. Elias
Department of Psychology, Rutgers, The State University of New Jersey, Tillett Hall, Room 101, 53 Avenue E, Piscataway, NJ 08904, USA
e-mail: reyesja@eden.rutgers.edu

S.J. Parker
Department of Psychiatry, Columbia University, New York, NY, USA

J.L. Rosenblatt
New York University Child Study Center, New York, NY, USA

S. Goldstein and R.B. Brooks (eds.), *Handbook of Resilience in Children*,
DOI 10.1007/978-1-4614-3661-4_20, © Springer Science+Business Media New York 2013

youngest group, with one-in-five U.S. school children being of Latino descent and one-in-four newborns being born to Latina mothers (Pew Hispanic Center, 2009).

The Latino youth of today will undoubtedly shape American society in the twenty-first century. Yet, research indicates that Latino youth face significant challenges and engage in many risky behaviors that can hinder positive development and well-being. For example, national statistics reveals that Latino youth engage in higher rates of attempted suicide, lifetime cocaine use, and unprotected sex than African-American and Caucasian youth (Centers for Disease Control and Prevention, 2007), with Latinas having the highest teen pregnancy rate among major ethnic groups in the U.S. (Umaña-Taylor, 2009). Latino youth also have the highest school dropout rate. Approximately 21.4% of Latino youth drop out of high school, which is four times the rate among Caucasian youth (5.3%) and nearly triple the rate among African-American youth (8.4%) (U.S. Department of Education, 2009). Latino children and adolescents are also more likely to live in poverty. The poverty rate among Latino children is three times that of Caucasian children (28% Latino vs. 9% Caucasian) (Prelow & Loukas, 2003).

It should be noted that considerable variability exists among Latinos in terms of national origin, immigration and migration histories, as well as different levels of education, socioeconomic status, acculturation, and immigration status. Differences among Latinos likely impact the extent and nature of risk exposure and the availability of resources and protective factors Latino children and adolescents experience in their daily lives, as well as differences in rates of engagement in delinquent behaviors and opportunities for positive developmental outcomes (Kuperminc, Wilkins, Roche, & Alvarez-Jimenez, 2009). Considering the diversity that exists among and within the various Latino groups is essential for understanding the experiences of Latino youth in the U.S. (Umaña-Taylor, 2009).

Despite the risk statistics highlighted above, Latinos have high aspirations for themselves. A recent poll revealed that 89% of Latino youth reported that career success is important in their lives (Pew Hispanic Center, 2009). However, Latinos face a disproportionate number of barriers to their academic achievement including poverty, lack of participation in preschool, attendance at poor quality elementary and secondary schools, and limited neighborhood resources. Poor academic achievement, in turn, results in low labor force participation, higher unemployment rates, and greater poverty (Zambrana & Zoppi, 2002). What can be done to help Latino youth create better futures that match their career and life aspirations while recognizing that social conditions are not likely to change quickly? A promising means to foster attainments among Latino youth is the application of school-based interventions consistent with resilience theoretical models and research.

Conceptualizing Resilience

It is impossible to enter into any discussion of resilience without first addressing the complex, and largely unresolved, conceptual issues surrounding the construct. Since Norman Garmezy's introduction of the concept of resilience over 50 years ago (Rolf, 1999), many empiricists have adopted the term and applied it towards their own work. The term, "resilience," though, is often subjected to a variety of disparate usages (Glantz & Johnson, 1999; Greene & Conrad, 2002). A now substantial body of theoretical literature has developed in response to this problem, propelling an ongoing debate over the ultimate utility of the concept (see Glantz & Johnson, 1999). While challenges to the construct's parsimony and integrity are numerous and valid (e.g., Kaplan, 1999), many researchers are reluctant to abandon a concept that has such powerful heuristic value (Luthar, Cicchetti, & Becker, 2000).

It is beyond the scope of this chapter to enter fully into this highly nuanced debate. The present focus is on formulating a practical, working definition of resilience that maximizes its utility in the development of educational interventions for economically disadvantaged ethnic minority youth, particularly Latinos. For the resilience construct to have potential influence on improving the life trajectory of Latino youth, two key criteria must be met: (1) the resiliency construct must add value to existing (and perhaps more parsimonious) constructs and (2) the concept of resilience must be able to inform the design of interventions.

Resilience as Protective Processes

At a preliminary level, several competing definitions of "resilience" seem good candidates for meeting these criteria. The simplest of these holds the term to be conceptually equivalent to "protective processes" in models of risk and protection. The latter concept is of undoubted importance in the formulation of educational interventions in under-resourced communities. The identification of these processes resulted in an important shift in how researchers viewed the life courses of individuals within challenging environments (Garmezy, 1985). Rather than solely focusing on preventing negative outcomes, researchers expanded their focus and intervention efforts to bolstering processes that were associated with adaptive outcomes—outcomes frequently termed "resilient." Different types of protective forces were identified and studied; Luthar (1991), for example, identified two different types: The first, "protective processes," counteract the harmful effect of stressors (such as educators providing normative coping strategies for students during school transitions, or providing parents with explicit approaches they can use to manage the dramatic influx of homework their children receive as they move through primary and secondary school); the second, called "protective-enhancing processes," strengthen children's competence so that they are better able to manage stressors (these include social-emotional skills, which are described later in the chapter, or training children in how to handle sexual harassment by a caretaking adult). The former mediate the effect of stressors on the child through changing environmental characteristics; the latter mediate harm by changing the child's ability to handle challenges.

The basic premise underlying these ideas—that avenues for intervention exist even when the removal of negative forces seems unfeasible—is key for educational interventions in areas where many of the negative forces a child faces (e.g., racism, poverty) exist on a macro level beyond the direct influence of most community-based efforts. In this way, the "protective processes" definition of resilience satisfies the criterion of being able to inform interventions. Where this definition falters, however, is in the first criterion: offering value-added to other existing constructs. Though the importance of risk and protective models is well established, there seems to be little advantage accrued by attaching the label "resilience" to these models.

Resilience as the Interaction of Protection and Risk

Some theorists have argued that equating the term "resilience" with protective processes, reduces the potentially unique and powerfully predictive concept of resilience to a description of competing probabilities among risk and protective processes (Kaplan, 1999). Such a description does not identify the mechanisms that intervention strategies can use to target specific risks. Although researchers and educators may have good descriptions of processes that may be helpful to most individuals, they still do not have a clear understanding of how to best help those individuals who have the highest likelihood of poor outcomes.

This gap in models of risk and protection offers a window in which some have argued resilience may offer the greatest value. One compelling view defines resilience as a transactional and three-dimensional (person, environment, and time) theoretical framework that outlines how a subset of protective processes specific to "at-risk" populations interacts with agents of environmental risk and with individual characteristics and developmental processes to influence outcome.

In this way "resilience" refers to a process in which specific protective influences moderate the effect of risk processes within both individual and environment in order to foster adaptive outcomes. This framing of resilience would neither include protective processes that affect outcome by lessening the magnitude of risk processes by acting on them directly, nor those protective processes that impact on outcomes uniformly, regardless of the presence of risk. Instead, "resilience" would comprise interactions between risk and protective processes, and in this way might offer the substantial informative value of being able to prescribe particular protective processes as ameliorative to specific areas of risk.

Such transactional models of resilience, however, have been plagued by two significant challenges. The first, outlined by Luthar and Cushing (1999), is of a statistical nature: in relying on an interaction term to identify "resilient" individuals, researchers not only are unable to specify the actual number of individuals represented by the interaction but also are frequently unable to replicate their findings because of the typically small effect sizes associated with interaction terms. Models of resilience based on interactions between risk and protective processes face an additional challenge: No matter how detailed the model may be, it can nevertheless be refined further. Kaplan (1999) argues convincingly how individuals identified as "resilient" were likely never at risk in the same manner as their "vulnerable" peers; instead, they were included in models of resilience only because the field had an inadequate predictive model of how risk operates in combination with other factors.

An example can illustrate this situation. "Resilient" outcomes have been found within troubled schools (risk factor) by those with strong internal locus of control and social problem-solving skills (protective factors). However, one could argue that those individuals are not in fact "resilient" because they were never at risk. The model fails to distinguish the presence of protective processes from the lack of risk. Therefore, in this example, the phenomenon is not so much "resilience" as it is possession of appropriate locus of control and problem-solving skills.

Resilience as a Conceptual Placeholder

In the 1999 chapter that detailed the preceding argument, Kaplan concludes convincingly that resilience is a once-useful construct whose time has since passed. Indeed, conceptualizations of resilience as a character trait or a consistent process cannot stand close scrutiny; there is no tangible, observable, defining feature common across all individual instances of "resilience." Resilience is an aberration—a failure in the predictive model—and the potential causes for this aberration are infinite (Kaplan, 1999). They range from a child's broad social context to minute features of a child's environment at the precise moment outcome was measured, or any combination of the factors in between. We may be able to identify variables that account for this aberration in a significant number of people, but it is of greater theoretical and practical utility to include these variables in a refined predictive model that applies to all "at-risk" individuals than to partition them off into a separate category of "resilience." In this way, "resilience" is not seen as a specific phenomenon per se, but rather as a conceptual tool in the development of increasingly refined predictive models. This conceptual tool would function as a "placeholder"—highlighting a group for whom the predictive model has failed, and reserving a space in the model for an as-yet undiscovered set of variables that may explain this failure.

In essence, Kaplan and those who hold "the placeholder" view do not differ in their conceptualizations of the bounds of utility for the resilience construct. The difference lies in their beliefs about the expiration of that utility. While Kaplan sees resilience as a concept that has historically served to highlight some predictive failures and models in need of refinement, he argues that this function has acted on a broad conceptual level, and, having done so, resilience has served out its utility. In contrast, we see resilience as having continued applicability in the process of refining each individual predictive model—prescribing an examination of unexpected outcomes and holding a place in the model for variables that will explain them. The concept of resilience, then, takes on a sustained utility—not only in the development of new models, but also the continued refinement of old ones. This process cannot be expected to end in a model yielding perfect predictions, but models can (and should) be refined in a series of successive approximations towards that goal. Each stage of this process can be aided by examining instances of "resilient" outcome and analyzing these instances for systematic differences that may inform the identification of new predictors. The "placeholder" conceptualization of resilience, as depicted in Fig. 20.1, offers practical utility in formulating educational interventions for youth considered to be at risk, thereby satisfying the first criterion for defining the term. The refinement of predictive models is clearly central to this task, both in helping to identify intervention targets accurately, and to discover the specific risk and protective processes the intervention should be formulated to address. The specific directives the resilience construct adds to the refinement process meet the second, value-added criterion.

Culture and Resilience

While culture plays an important role in children's development, it is typically afforded a distal or indirect role in models of resilience. Culture refers to the common language, history, symbols, beliefs, unquestioned assumptions, and institutions that are part of the heritage of members of an ethnic group (Roosa, Morgan-Lopez, Cree, & Specter, 2002). Culture and cultural practices exert significant influence on children's development and there is much to be learned about the many possible ways that cultural practices enhance or interfere with resilience (Masten & Motti-Stefanidi, 2009). Forces within a child's ethnic culture may serve as a buffer against adverse social circumstances. For example, the Latino cultural value of *familism*, which emphasizes the importance of the family unit and stresses the obligations and support that family members owe to both nuclear and extended kin is believed to protect Latino youth against externalizing problems (German, Gonzales, & Dumka, 2008). At the same time, sociocultural factors may hinder resilience. Research indicates that certain cultural beliefs and practices, such as focusing more on spiritual than medical cures, can greatly influence the utilization of medical and mental health services and treatment adherence. This, in turn, will affect a child's recovery from an illness or disease (Antshel, 2002).

Researchers have begun to pay increasing attention to the role of culture in models of risk and resilience. Kuperminc et al. (2009) have proposed a cultural-ecological-transactional model for studying resilience among Latinos and other ethnic minority groups in the U.S. In this model, the interaction between a child's culture of origin and the mainstream culture plays a central role in development. Thus, cultural factors, including values, behaviors, and norms interact and transact with every level of a child's ecology and help shape outcomes. The placeholder conceptualization of resilience calls for special attention to cultural risk and protective factors, as these variables are often not taken into account and may help explain unexpected outcomes.

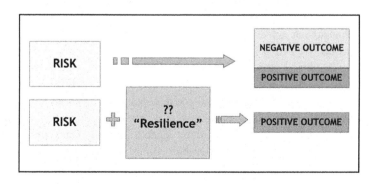

Fig. 20.1 The placeholder conceptualization of resilience

Remaining Conceptual Challenges

One remaining challenge is determining what constitutes a positive outcome, even within an educational environment. Such decisions necessarily rely on the culturally and temporally biased perspective of the researcher, a perspective that may overlook key factors at work in the population of interest. However, in the specific context of urban, low-SES educational institutions serving predominantly minority groups, outcomes are easier to grasp. Although school achievement and completion are indeed "positive" outcomes only because they are valued by the dominant culture, they are nonetheless agreed-upon by the educational system and its participants. Arguably, families who participate in the public education system enter into an unwritten social contract with their schools that is fulfilled when schools engender an exchange of adequate levels of skill accumulation and degree attainment for a certain amount of schooling. Using this "contract" helps to delineate more objectively what comprise positive outcomes in a model of educational resilience, as well as making clear that generating sufficient skill accumulation to overcome contextual disadvantage for poor Latino students will require an above-average educational effort by schools if the contract is to be honored.

Focusing on resilience within educational settings also allows researchers to avoid another common critique that the resilience field has faced: in order to accommodate the statistical and logistical demands of research, those who study resilience often define positive outcomes narrowly, failing to acknowledge the numerous aspects of life in which a person can succeed. This has resulted in models of resilience that seemingly ignore important areas in which those who did not achieve "resilient" outcomes have succeeded. An educational resilience model avoids this by restricting its focus to the K–12 educational experience; by doing so, it can employ a widely accepted, context-specific definition of "positive adaptation" (i.e., graduation, grades, and achievement on standardized tests) while acknowledging that individuals who

do not reach optimal functioning within this context can still do so in other aspects of their lives.

Overall, working within the educational resilience framework retains many of the benefits of "resilience" while excising some of its hazards. Within the bounds of this restricted focus, we will use academic achievement (including grade point average, standardized test scores, educator ratings of academic performance, and level of schooling completed) during the typical urban, low-SES K–12 educational experience as the measure of positive adaptation in the process of educational resilience.

Formulating Interventions to Improve Academic Achievement Outcomes

The "placeholder" conceptualization of resilience is rooted largely in this construction's ability to dictate a clear structure within which predictive models may be refined and interventions may be designed. Our interpretation of resilience leads us to a four-step approach:

1. *Identify distal agents of risk.* Given our overarching goal of working towards equalizing educational opportunity, our starting point is the identification of a single-risk process—attending a low-SES school—and a single-associated outcome—high school dropout.

2. *Identify instances of resilience.* The next step requires us to identify those students who have defied our initial predictive relationship. For instance, Latino students who graduate despite their disadvantaged school setting.

3. *Look for systematic differences that differentiate instances of resilience.* These differences are perhaps best conceptualized as the absence of risk processes, the presence of protective processes, or a set of such processes interacting. While the operational distinction between the absence of risk and the presence of protection is often difficult to delineate, such distinctions are rarely of practical import. As outlined in the following section, we propose that social and emotional skills constitute a set of protective processes that systematically differentiate

academically successful students in high-risk settings.

4. *Identify best options for intervention.* Once a theoretical understanding of those processes associated with instances of resilience is established, interventionists must adopt a practical stance in assessing the implications of these findings. Decisions must be made as to the relative feasibility of lessening specific risk processes or bolstering specific protective processes. Particularly in under-resourced communities, it is essential to design interventions such that they provide the optimal balance of efficacy and efficiency, with sustainability over time.

Social and Emotional Learning

The remainder of this chapter applies the preceding framework to our specific concern: equalizing educational opportunity. Given this point of entry, the identified distal agent of risk is low-SES educational settings. Students in such environments are clearly at heightened risk for poor academic outcome (Elias et al., 1997). However, while these associations between risk and outcome offer a prediction, they do not offer a prognosis. Some students are exceptions to the rule; they find pathways to academic success despite challenging school environments. The educational resilience paradigm directs us to look to these exceptions to find ways to change the rule. The next step, then, involves examining ways in which these students differ from their peers. An increasing body of research points to social and emotional skills as a key factor distinguishing students who attain academic success in challenging environments. Resilience holds a place

for variables in a predictive model that can accommodate these instances of academic success; social and emotional learning (SEL) may be one such variable (Fig. 20.2).

Social and Emotional Learning Defined

Just as students arrive at school with unique bodies of knowledge and cognitive strategies, they come equipped with their own social and emotional skills. They have often developed these techniques through interactions in their homes and communities; as such, they can learn new strategies in the school environment through SEL programs. These initiatives broadly aim to develop "social competence," defined as "the capacity to integrate cognition, affect, and behaviors, to achieve specified social tasks and positive developmental outcomes… [It is] a set of core skills, attitudes, abilities, and feelings given functional meaning by the contexts of culture, neighborhood, and situation" (Elias, Kress, & Neft, 2003, p. 1023). In short, SEL interventions help students accumulate knowledge and skills that facilitate the optimal emotional processing of their social contexts. Targeted competencies include self-awareness, self-management, social awareness, relationship skills, and decision making (Collaborative for Academic, Social, and Emotional Learning (CASEL), 2003a).

SEL as a Predictor of "Resilience"

The claim that SEL skills constitute important variables explaining instances of resilience requires empirical support on two levels. The first level is the demonstration that SEL skills

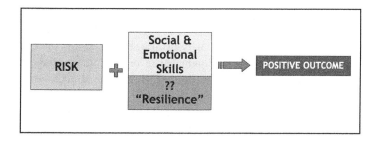

Fig. 20.2 Theoretical model of social and emotional learning (SEL) as a variable in explaining resilience

can reliably differentiate instances of resilience from more typical academic outcome. Such research is necessarily correlational in nature and, as such, is restricted in its ability to infer causation. Causation may be better examined at the second level of research: intervention evaluation. Intervention evaluations allow approximate experimental control of targeted skills, thereby affording stronger support for model formulation.

At the first level, a number of studies have found SEL skills (or closely related constructs) to be associated with instances of academic resilience. For example, studies have identified associations between school achievement and positive social and emotional skills (Caprara, Barbaranelli, Pastorelli, Bandura, & Zimbardo, 2000; Haynes, Ben-Avie, & Ensign, 2003). Research has also linked social and emotional skills with higher achievement on standardized tests (Welsh, Parke, Widaman, & O'Neil, 2001; Wentzel, 1993). Conversely, antisocial conduct often co-occurs with poor academic performance (Hawkins, Farrington, & Catalano, 1998).

SEL intervention research. These associations are encouraging, but far from conclusive as to the specific role SEL skills play in instances of resilience. Research at the second, intervention evaluation level helps to elucidate the patterns of causality in these relationships. While a true experimental manipulation of SEL is logistically impossible, intervention research approximates such manipulations by providing experimental groups with opportunities for the development of SEL. Well-designed studies also provide SEL measures to check for the success of skill acquisition. While the exact mechanisms responsible for any differences in the experimental group cannot be concluded with certainty, this method arguably offers the most scientific method available for maximizing this certainty.

To that end, a number of analyses of school-based prevention programs conducted in recent years provide general agreement that some of these programs are effective in reducing maladaptive behaviors, including those related to school success (e.g., Durlak, 1995; Elias, Gara, &

Ubriaco, 1985; Gottfredson, 2001). Recently, Durlak, Weissberg, Dymnicki, Taylor, and Schellinger (2011) conducted a meta-analysis of 213 universal, school-based SEL intervention outcome studies to examine the impact of SEL programming on social and emotional skills, attitudes towards self and others, positive social behavior, conduct problems, emotional distress, and academic performance. The analyses included 270,034 kindergarten through high school students. Results revealed that compared to controls, students' SEL skills, attitudes, positive social behaviors, and academic performance improved following intervention. Students also demonstrated fewer conduct problems and had lower levels of emotional distress (Durlak et al., 2011). While these findings offer empirical justification for the implementation of SEL programs, they offer little theoretical explanation for their demonstrated efficacy. The remainder of the chapter will focus on propositions as to *why* SEL interventions are effective—their mechanisms of action and their key implementational advantages. It should be emphasized that this discussion is theoretical and heuristic, rather than empirical, in nature. One of the goals of future research in this area will be to design studies such that the specific processes underlying the success of SEL interventions may be delineated.

A guiding assumption in the current discussion is that any variable that might explain educational resilience will ultimately be dependent on a dynamic interaction of three dimensions: person, environment, and time. By nature, these three dimensions are mutually determined, so there is little meaning in the examination of one in the absence of the other two. Thus, this discussion of the probable agents of educational resilience presumes them to be of a three-dimensional nature. School-based SEL programs counteract common mechanisms of risk and foster the protective resources in all of three dimensions of educational resilience: the students themselves, their educational and social environments, and the interaction of these dimensions over time.

In order to come to a clearer understanding of the mechanisms through which ethnic minority students demonstrating educational resilience may be buffered from negative influences on academic outcomes, it is necessary to parse the broad-risk processes associated with "poverty" into their more proximal agents of risk in an educational context. The following sections identify such mechanisms that are hypothesized to mediate the relationship between poverty and suboptimal academic achievement. The discussion covers categories of risk that were culled from a review of literature from the education-reform, resilience, and educational-resilience fields. Processes selected were those that theoretically and/or empirically were found to a greater degree among low-SES schools with high proportions of minority students than among their wealthier counterparts. The processes were also linked with poor academic outcomes in such communities and were theoretically and/or empirically demonstrated as mediators of the relationship between SES and academic outcomes. Risk categories described in the following sections were then created by grouping together those mechanisms that theoretically and/or empirically were elements of the same larger process. This method yielded the following broad mechanisms for intervention: factors that influence the student–educator dynamic (i.e., educator stress/frustration, low academic expectations, and impaired educator–student relationships) and factors that influence the student–community dynamic (i.e., ecological instability and disconnect between school and community cultures). The processes through which SEL interventions interact and ameliorate each of these risk factors will be outlined theoretically and supported with relevant research in the following discussion.

Student–Educator Interactions

The manner in which students and their educators and/or school administrators interact has enormous influence on student learning (Wang, Hertel, & Walberg, 1997). Often, the emotional climate in low-SES, underperforming schools can affect educators in ways that ultimately harm the academic outcomes of their students. Specifically, the emotional climate can function proximally to students through high levels of educator stress and low academic expectations, both of which have been identified as more common within low-SES educational environments (Peng & Lee, 1994). These factors hamper student achievement by discouraging educators from spending time and energy supporting and motivating their students in positive ways. As depicted in Fig. 20.3, the result of this interaction is poor educator–student relationships and lowered academic performance, both of which continue cycles of educator stress and low academic expectations.

This is an especially worrying cycle within low-SES schools because positive educator–student relationships have been found to protect at-risk students from negative academic outcome (Esposito, 1999; Haberman, 2004). Some research has suggested that these relationships may hold particular protective value for minority students (Meehan, Hughes, & Cavell, 2003; Wang et al., 1997). Unfortunately, data also suggest that minority students are less likely to enjoy strong relationships with their educators in comparison to their more advantaged peers. Contributing factors within disadvantaged school districts have been identified above and in Fig. 20.3, and they include widespread disengagement of faculty and

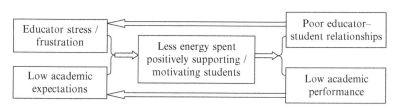

Fig. 20.3 Reciprocal influences in high-risk school settings

staff; a lack of interpersonal and self-regulatory skills among students to form strong relationships with adults; and everyday challenges that absorb student and teacher energy at the expense of educator–student relationships (Haberman, 2004; Kozol, 2005).

SEL interventions can ameliorate the cycle of educator stress, low expectations, poor student–teacher relationships, and low academic performance in two ways: (1) through professional development that helps educators to manage their stress and to understand the role that low expectations might play in student behavior and (2) by encouraging students to change their behavior in such a way that they are able to persist on difficult academic tasks and elicit more support from educators. These mechanisms of action are discussed in further detail below.

SEL and Poor Educator–Student Interactions

Educator effects. When school environments are chaotic, the effort that educators might otherwise apply to educating and motivating students in a positive way must be diverted to managing problematic student behavior and their own worries about personal safety. The stress and frustration brought about by this and other aspects of the school environment decrease educators' levels of commitment to their students and their careers, and may ultimately lead to "burnout." Positive correlations between number of years of educator experience and student achievement (Glass, 2002) suggest that the cycle of educator stress/burnout and low student academic achievement may be self-propagating.

SEL programs address educator stress through professional development. The orientation and training received through most empirically supported SEL programs help educators gain the same emotion-regulation and social problem-solving skills as they are expected to foster in their students. These skills help them better manage the stress and demands that often arise in their role, and can increase educators' career efficacy and satisfaction (CASEL, 2003b). The best SEL

programs provide professional development before program implementation, tools for internal and external personnel to observe program implementation, and feedback and coaching for educators (CASEL, 2003b). In this way, educators are empowered to use new and frequently more effective ways to maintain a positive and productive atmosphere in their classrooms.

Many SEL programs offer support for educators; one such program offering extensive professional development is The Responsive Classroom (http://www.responsiveclassroom.org). The program places less emphasis on social and emotional skill instruction and more emphasis on changing teaching strategies, employing six practices that help accomplish the program's goal: classroom organization, morning meetings, rules and consequences, academic choice, guided discovery, and family communication. These strategies help educators manage their classrooms in positive ways, which helps reduce their frustration and anxiety. The strategies also foster more open and effective educator–student relationships, which also can reduce educator stress. Responsive Classroom's professional development includes workshops, summer intensive programs, individual, on-site consultation, and comprehensive guidelines that help the educator implement and integrate the program into existing curricula (CASEL, 2003b). This approach has demonstrated a positive impact on student behavior and academic performance (Rimm-Kaufman, Fan, Chiu, & You, 2007).

Student effects. In addition to improving relations between educators and their students by reducing educators' levels of stress and frustration, SEL interventions explicitly teach social problem-solving skills that can generalize from students' peer relationships to their interactions with adults. These skills increase the likelihood that students will elicit positive, supportive behavior from their teachers. Primary social and emotional skills that help students become aware of their own and others' emotions, regulate their behavior, and make good behavioral decisions all help students communicate more effectively and openly with their teachers. The Caring School Community program, for example, employs a number of strategies specifically aimed at strengthening educator–student relationships. The vehicle for these strategies is a schedule of regular class meetings in which communication and relationship-management skills are taught and practiced by both students and educators. Meetings are used to discuss problems, plan classroom activities, make class decisions, and reflect on classroom events. Emphasis is placed on creating an environment in which students are comfortable expressing their opinions and feel valued as contributing members of the classroom community.

SEL programs can dramatically improve classroom climate by providing educators with positive and effective classroom-management techniques; these techniques reduce educator stress and remove many distractions that detract from learning and teaching (Elias & Schwab, 2006). SEL programs also help educators and students learn open and effective ways of communicating about conflict and emotional distress; when these skills are applied in the classroom, educator–student relations improve, and educators are better able to motivate students and convey course information.

Low Academic Expectations

A large body of research has demonstrated that educator expectations can have a powerful impact on students' academic outcomes, regardless of the degree of congruity between these expectations and students' actual prior achievement (Rosenthal & Jacobson, 1968; Rosenthal & Rubin, 1978; Wang & Haertel, 1987). These findings also have been replicated in urban samples (Gill & Reynolds, 1999; Haberman, 2004; Kuklinski & Weinstein, 2001). Some data suggest that educators tend to have lower expectations for Latino and African-American youth. Recently, McKown and Weinstein (2008) conducted a study examining teacher expectations of year-end math and reading achievement in a diverse sample of 640 first-, third-, and fifth-grade children from 30 urban elementary school classrooms. Results revealed that teachers were more likely to expect Asian and Caucasian children to

achieve higher math and reading grades than Latino and African-American children regardless of prior student achievement. There are several potential explanations for this inequity. First, lowered expectations may be an artifact of educators' stereotypical beliefs about members of minority and low-SES groups. A number of theorists have offered a second explanation, positing that educators' perceptions may be influenced by observing students within an educational structure based on the value system of a dominant culture (e.g., Kozol, 2005). Finally, given that race and economic status are significant risk factors for academic difficulty, educators may simply be forming expectations based on their own experience.

Educator effects. SEL programs target negative teacher expectations directly and indirectly. The more immediate approach consists of professional development that explicates the goals of SEL, the processes through which those goals are achieved, and the research supporting their effectiveness. This process makes explicit the potential of all students to learn, a phenomenon that contradicts low academic expectations. Such training also offers specific strategies to help educators become aware of and alter how they convey expectations to students. The Skills, Opportunities, and Recognition (SOAR) program, for example, helps educators develop and communicate clear standards for their students. In addition, educators are encouraged to actively seek out individual areas of strength for each student and provide recognition for students based on these strengths. SOAR techniques are directly contrary to having low academic expectations, thereby reducing the likelihood that low expectations will be conveyed to students (http://www.preventionscience.com).

A second, less direct SEL program approach to modifying low academic expectations consists of bolstering student performance, the mechanisms of which are discussed in the following section. Many empirically supported SEL programs have been linked to improved academic performance (Elias & Arnold, 2006; Zins, Weissberg, Wang, & Walberg, 2004). Educators who witness this change are provided with evidence that does not support their low expectations;

as depicted in Fig. 20.3, if educators respond to this by conveying higher academic expectations to their students, they often elicit better academic performance. The cycle of raised expectations and performance then can be maintained by students meeting increasingly higher academic expectations from their educators.

Student effects. SEL programs bolster students' meta-cognition and self-efficacy with regard to academic and other tasks. These skills help students—especially those from historically disadvantaged groups—recognize and persevere in the face of low academic expectations. The High/Scope educational program, for example, aims to foster self-confidence, social competence, and a "can-do" attitude in each of its program participants (High/Scope Educational Research Foundation, 2003). Kindergarten through third-grade students who participated in High/Scope had significant improvement in 18 of 25 academic indicators, as compared to two control groups; strongest results were found for low-SES students (High/Scope Educational Research Foundation).

Community–Student Interactions

Characteristics of the environment outside of the school can play significant roles in student achievement within the school (Leventhal & Brooks-Gunn, 2000). This is true of both advantaged and disadvantaged communities; in the former, external characteristics tend to exert positive influences on student achievement. Wealth, for example, plays a stabilizing role in the life of a family, which facilitates student focus on academic material when in the classroom. Communities that share their schools' values—such as the importance of succeeding in and completing high school and higher education while young—reinforce academic achievement. Access to health information and resources, which often characterize wealthier communities, results in better student health choices and reduced consequences when they make poor choices. These outcomes reduce the negative impact of health behavior on student achievement. However, many characteristics of disadvantaged communities play different roles in

the academic achievement of their students. These roles, and how SEL programs can change them, are detailed in the sections that follow.

Ecological Instability

A number of factors related to ecological instability and transition have been found to increase students' risk for academic difficulty. Familial instability and divorce (Masten, Best, & Garmezy, 1990; Wang & Gordon, 1994), frequent relocation (Lash & Kirkpatrick, 1994; Scanlon & Devine, 2001; Temple & Reynolds, 1999), and middle school transition (Elias et al., 1985) have all been linked with lower academic performance and increased rates of school behavior problems.

Not surprisingly, children in low-SES communities tend to experience a greater degree of ecological instability than do their peers from more advantaged environments. Disadvantaged families are more likely to be headed by a single mother, and disadvantaged single mothers are more likely to experience instability in relationship partners, creating frequent changes in household composition and location. Poor families are also subject to more frequent residence changes in general (Kerbow, 1996), often resulting in multiple school changes. Relative to other ethnic groups in the U.S., Latinos are more likely to raise their children in two parent families (Grau, Azmitia, & Quattlebaum, 2009). However, there is considerable diversity within Latinos concerning marriage, single parenthood rates, and other demographic variables. For example, some of the highest rates of nonmarital fertility and cohabitation can be found among those of Puerto Rican origin. Those of Cuban decent, on the other hand, have a higher average age at marriage and lower nonmarital fertility rates (Glick & Van Hook, 2008). Nevertheless, single parenthood among Latinos is on the rise. Roughly 33% of the children born to Latinos were born to unmarried mothers in 2002 (Grau et al., 2009).

The risk posed by ecological instability seems to be additive; that is, the more simultaneous changes experienced by a student, the greater that student's academic decline (Simmons, Burgeson,

Carlton-Ford, & Blyth, 1987). The logical inference from these data is that schools in low-SES, highly unstable environments may help increase academic performance by fostering a stable school environment (Cohen & Elias, 2011). Research supports this inference: In a study examining the long-term impacts of family transitions on children, researchers found that structured, safe, and predictable school environments helped buffer children of divorced families from adverse environments (Hetherington, 1989).

Intervention strategies should therefore aim to increase the stability and predictability of the school environment. SEL programs achieve this end by offering a consistent and coherent framework that can encompass many of the disparate disciplinary policies and psychoeducational activities that often coexist in the school environment. Professional development in SEL strategies help educators foster a collaborative and mutually reinforcing learning environment in which students experience a consistent set of behavior expectations, classroom-management strategies, and extracurricular support (such as mentoring and emotional health groups) across schools, grades, and classrooms (Elias & Arnold, 2006; Elias et al., 1997). Such consistency eases transitions between grades and schools.

Not only do SEL programs target ecological instability directly by creating consistent educational environments, but they also ameliorate the risks students face by helping them develop skills that buffer against the negative impact of an unstable environment. A direct evaluation of a school-based intervention designed to bolster social problem-solving skills found that program participation mitigated the normative decline in academic performance associated with middle school transitions (Elias et al., 1985). This research implies that social and emotional competence can protect children against the deleterious academic effects of an unstable environment.

Two SEL programs include specific materials to help districts promote high academic achievement while supporting environmental consistency through school-wide implementation: the Lions-Quest "Skills" curricula (Lions Clubs International Foundation, 2003) and the Community of Caring

program (Community of Caring: See Appendix). The Lions-Quest program, which targets social and emotional skills, positive health behaviors, and service learning, for example, helps schools create committees of faculty members, students, and parents to monitor the educational environment (CASEL, 2003b). The program also is designed to be continuous across grades, facilitated by school-wide programs and disciplinary strategies and professional development for staff to increase program consistency (Lions Clubs International Foundation, 2003). Unpublished studies of Lions-Quest programs that have been implemented with Caucasian, Asian, and African-American students showed not only that students in the program had better social skills and fewer educator-reported behavior problems, but also had higher overall GPAs and math and English grades than did a control group (CASEL, 2003b).

The Community of Caring Program addresses health behaviors and academic achievement through a whole-community approach that "works to implement and encourage five values—caring, responsibility, respect, trust, and family" (Community of Caring: See Appendix). The curriculum provides extra materials to aid implementation throughout the school (CASEL, 2003b) and involves on-site professional development for faculty and staff. Unpublished data from 1,000 Caucasian, Asian, and African-American ninth-grade students indicated improved academic and behavioral outcomes for those who participated in the program.

The consistent school environment created by SEL programs seem able to counteract some of the negative effects of ecological instability that are experienced by many disadvantaged youth. The structured setting and consistent management and disciplinary techniques encouraged by SEL curricula can smooth transitions between grades and schools and can help students maintain a sense of security and predictability when other parts of their lives may be in flux. They also learn skills to better allow them to manage strong emotions and new situations. This helps students devote the energy they would have spent on managing stress and learning new rules towards learning. That programs implemented throughout entire schools and districts have been linked with improved academic outcomes supports these claims.

Disconnect Between School and Community

One risk process identified in poor academic performance is incongruity between cultures inside and outside the school (Roosa, Dumka, Gonzales, & Knight, 2002; Roosa, Morgan-Lopez, et al., 2002; Tharp, 1989; Wang et al., 1997). When the values espoused inside of school are not in accord with those lauded outside of school by students' communities, families, and peers, they have difficulty identifying with and accomplishing academic goals (Roosa, Dumka, et al., 2002; Roosa, Morgan-Lopez, et al., 2002; Tharp, 1989). School personnel should pay particular attention to differences between the mainstream cultural values of schools and the values of Latino families. For example, in a study of immigrant Mexican families, Valdes (1996 as cited by Woolley, Kol, & Bowen, 2009) found there were major differences in parent and teacher definitions of education. Latino parents were deeply concerned with their children's educación (focusing more on behavior, respect for adults, and interpersonal skills). Teachers, on the other hand, were concerned with the children's education (focusing on academics). These cultural differences lead each to incorrectly conclude that the other was neglecting the children's learning. Such misinterpretations can often lead to parents avoid contact with teachers and teachers feeling frustrated and giving up on making connections with parents (Woolley et al.). Lack of communication between parents and school personnel puts Latino students at a disadvantage, as parents do not receive informational resources regarding their children's education (i.e., enrollment in Advanced Placement courses, taking the SAT, the process of entering college and mechanisms for financial assistance) (Zambrana & Zoppi, 2002).

Like parents, Latino students may become disconnected from school if their cultural and family values and assets are not valued in school. Latino culture is rich with protective factors related to resilience, including "having religious faith, emphasizing a collective orientation, valuing children and engaging in multiple affective gestures from early on, teaching children values which include responsibility to others, collective responsibility, respecting elders and authority figures, and sibling responsibility, and valuing civility such as the expression of politeness and helpful behaviors" (Zambrana & Zoppi, 2002, p. 45). Latino students often attend schools where few personnel are of Latino background. Despite the fact that Latino youth account for about 20% of the U.S. student population, only 4% of public school teachers and 4.1% of school principals are Latino (Zambrana & Zoppi). This demographic imbalance makes Latino issues less likely to be addressed within school systems. Additionally, the conflict between family values and mainstream American cultural values, such as independence, assertiveness, and competitiveness can decrease Latino students learning and achievement (Zambrana & Zoppi).

SEL programs strive to align school cultures with those outside of the educational environment in a way that fosters positive development among youth. In support of this claim, two of the three key strategies identified by Greenberg et al. (2003) in a review of research on SEL programs involved aligning the school environment with the community and family environments. In addition, studies have found that interventions that connect families with their children's schools and the larger community with its schools promote educational resilience (Wang & Haertel, 1987) and have larger- and longer-term effects (Epstein, Coates, Salinas, Sanders, & Simon 1997, Haynes & Comer, 1996; Walberg, 1984).

School–Community Partnerships. SEL programs bridge the gap between schools and their families and communities in a variety of ways. One strategy is to improve the alliance directly through school–community or school–family partnerships (Greenberg, Domitrovich, & Bumbarger, 2001). Service learning and family outreach initiatives are especially effective at bridging the gaps between communities and families and their schools. For example, Lions-Quest programs (Lions Clubs International Foundation, 2003) provide evidence-based, developmentally appropriate interventions for grades K–12 through school–community partnerships. In an effort to align the values of families with those of their children's schools, the program includes homework assignments that students complete with their guardians and skills-building workshops for parents. The Lions-Quest program targets community culture through its high school curriculum, Skills for Action; this segment involves service learning in the surrounding community and has resulted in "gains in positive community values" and increased empathy and ability to work with and relate to diverse groups (Lions Clubs International Foundation). More importantly in a discussion of educational resilience, the program also reduced dropout risk (Lions Clubs International Foundation).

Caring School Community (The Child Development Project: See Appendix) also has specific strategies for fostering a sense of cohesive culture within all ecological levels in which the child functions: in the classroom through class meetings, within the school through buddy programs, within the family through conversation prompts, and throughout the community through school–community programs. Grade-school students who went through the program had a stronger sense of the school as a community and more liking for their school (The Child Development Project). Even after the students transitioned to middle school, they maintained a stronger feeling of community and still reported more liking for their schools and greater trust in their educators than if they had not received the program (The Child Development Project).

Confronting a Culture of Violence, Sex, and Substance Use. Many urban, disadvantaged communities struggle with a subculture that promotes violent solutions to interpersonal problems and glamorizes sex and substance use. This subculture frequently carries over into the community's educational institutions, undermining academic achievement, healthy development, and prosocial behavior (U.S. Department of Health and Human Services, 2001). Various health behaviors have been identified as risk factors for low academic achievement and/or school dropout, including

drug abuse (McCluskey, Krohn, Lizotte, & Rodriquez, 2002), alcohol use (McCluskey et al.), smoking (Newcomb et al., 2002), and unprotected sexual activity (resulting in STDs or unwanted or early pregnancy) (McGee & Newcomb, 1992). As noted above, Latino youth suffer from higher than average rates of substance abuse, have an earlier age of onset of sexual activity than Caucasian youth, and are less likely to use condoms, which results in higher rates of teen pregnancy and risk of contracting STDs (Lescano, Brown, Raffaelli, & Lima, 2009). Currently, 20% of all people living with and newly diagnosed with AIDS between the ages of 13 and 24 are Latino (Lescano et al.).

These circumstances are widely associated with lower academic achievement in terms of grades, test scores, and school completion and tend to occur at significantly higher rates in low-SES communities. Poor health choices also have strong connections to greater likelihoods of violence. It is estimated that 9% of Latino males between the ages of 12 and 17 are victims of violence (National Center for Mental Health Promotion and Youth Violence Prevention, 2004). Moreover, after unintentional injury, homicide is the leading cause of death for Latino youth (Shetgiri et al., 2009) and Latino gangs make up 46% of all gangs in the U.S. (Kuperminc et al., 2009). Furthermore, the culture that values violence poses risks not only for the aggressors but also for those around them, such that small groups of physically or emotionally destructive individuals can have disproportionately large negative effects on entire schools.

Research indicates that urban school children experience growth in aggression over the course of each school year; empirically supported SEL programs, such as the Resolving Conflict Creatively Program (RCCP), slow and virtually halt this process. SEL programs directly target violent and poor health behaviors through comprehensive, multimodal violence-prevention and health-promotion modules that have been shown to foster healthy decision making and reduce high-profile aggressive acts (such as bullying and gang involvement) and lower profile and more commonplace antisocial behavior (such as interpersonal aggression and theft). They accomplish this through promoting five commonly identified social and emotional competencies, which constitute the focus for many SEL programs (CASEL, 2003a; Zins et al., 2004). Bolstering students' skills in self-awareness (recognizing one's own emotions), social awareness (recognizing emotions in other people), self-management (acting on one's emotions in a controlled, productive, prosocial manner), relationship management (responding calmly and constructively to others' behavior), and decision making (focusing on long-term rather than short-term goals) all work to de-escalate stressful interpersonal situations that frequently lead to poor health choices and violence at school and in the community. Decreased drug and alcohol use, pregnancy rates, health problems, and violent interactions result in less energy and time being devoted to managing these problems and their emotional effects (such as anxiety, anger, and grief) in students and educators. The time that administrators, educators, and students would have diverted toward those ends can then be applied to the task of teaching and learning, thereby fostering positive educational outcomes among students.

Many SEL programs identify violence prevention as a primary aim, and they use different techniques to achieve that aim. The I Can Problem Solve (ICPS; formerly, Interpersonal Cognitive Problem Solving) curriculum (Shure, 1992a, 1992b, 1992c), for example, focuses on five main problem-solving skills to reduce violence: means-end thinking, weighing pros and cons, alternative solution thinking, consequential thinking, and empathy. These skills have been shown to increase problem-solving skills and foster positive relationships and prosocial behavior both inside and outside the classroom, with effects lasting up to 4 years. ICPS has been shown to both intervene and prevent problem behavior such as bullying and violence. Another program, Peace Works, was based on resiliency theory and research, and prevents violence through multimodal intervention in three dimensions: the learning environment, the student's social competence, and problem behavior reduction. Studies of the program have found reduction in fights (Peace Works: See Appendix). The Second Step curriculum (Committee for Children: See Appendix) has similarly been found

to increase frequency of neutral and positive student behavior and their understanding of social skills; educators reported that the program helped with classroom management, and that it decreased disruptive and aggressive behavior in the classroom (Grossman et al., 1997).

The same social, emotional, and decision-making skills that decrease violent behaviors also support better health choices among youth. Know Your Body (American Health Foundation) targets general health behaviors through frequent lessons that target five areas: self-esteem, decision making, communication, goal setting, and stress management. Several evaluation studies have shown that Know Your Body results in improved health behaviors, including reduced rates of smoking. Teenage Health Teaching Modules (Education Development Center) is notable in its comprehensive programming that goes beyond drug prevention, healthy sexual development, and general health promotion and targets academic skills, citizenship, and violence prevention (CASEL, 2003b). A study of this program in high school found that it reduced tobacco, illicit drug, and alcohol use, along with consumption of fried foods (CASEL). However, another, unpublished study's findings of the program's effects in middle school were less conclusive (CASEL).

In general, SEL programs reduce or mediate the effects of negative forces in the community outside of the school, thereby supporting positive academic outcomes among youth. By providing students with safe, predictable educational environments that are responsive to the values of the context in which they function, schools can help students devote more energy to academic topics, and do so in a more efficient manner. SEL programs provide holistic frameworks that help educators achieve these aims through systematic change (Elias & Arnold, 2006).

Implementation of the Educational Resilience Model

Research to date indicates that effectively implemented SEL programs are particularly far-reaching interventions that are associated with overcoming the clustering risks endemic to urban, low-SES school environments. To the extent that SEL programs are implemented across grade and schools within a district—as they are designed to be—they can be particularly effective at ameliorating the chronic nature of risk factors that interfere with the achievement of developmental milestones (Gore & Eckenrode, 1994). However, the ability of the programs described in this chapter to build educational opportunity and contribute to resilient outcomes varies with, and in most cases, depends upon their level of implementation (Elias, 2007; Greenberg et al., 2003). This fact presents the most pressing issue for SEL researchers and supporters to resolve: barriers to implementation. Enacting the scope and degree of system change that are necessary to realize the positive effects of these programs is challenging for nearly all school districts, and can be especially so for ones whose financial, personnel, and physical assets are limited. Gathering the organizational and motivational resources to implement and subsequently evaluate an SEL program across a district's educators, grades, schools, and academic subjects can be overwhelming; fortunately there are numerous resources that outline best practices for accomplishing such an initiative. Recommended resources are listed in "SEL Implementation Resources."

One foundation of successful implementation is selecting an SEL program with strong empirical validation. A number of programs exist with well-documented efficacy. The Collaborative for Academic, Social, and Emotional Learning (CASEL) has created a guide (CASEL, 2003a; *Safe and Sound*, available for download from http://www.casel.org) evaluating the efficacy of and evidence supporting widely available SEL programs. All of the curricula mentioned in this chapter are among the 22 programs given CASEL's "select" designation, based on program quality and evidence of effectiveness. A list of these programs is provided in Appendix.

However, selecting such programs may be viewed as necessary but still insufficient conditions for effective implementation. Research shows clearly that even empirically validated programs are neither "implementation proof," nor can they be rendered such (Gager & Elias,

1997). Still, the challenges involved in establishing a comprehensive SEL program need not deter educators from the task. Their status confers them a unique capability to build opportunity for their students. As institutions that are mandated to educate all children within a certain geographical area, schools are able to have unparalleled, far-reaching influence on their constituents. As institutions that are often respected and prominent in their communities, schools are able to set standards for and exert positive influence on numerous ecological levels: students, parents and families, neighborhoods, and the wider public. In addition, their ability to influence students over the course of time, across developmental stages and milestones, grants schools vast promise as a source of systematic, comprehensive change (Elias & Arnold, 2006). The potential for such efficient and powerful enactment of social transformation provides the impetus for school administrators to choose an empirically validated SEL program and allocate the resources necessary for its full implementation.

Limitations and Directions for Future Research

All research on the risk and protective forces in academic success carries with it the limitations of the educational field's current correlational methodologies. Although all of the risk factors discussed in this chapter have been focused on low-SES, Latino status, and academic difficulty, educational resilience research has yet to build a robust, empirically based understanding of mechanisms that link poverty, culture, and poor academic outcomes. However, SEL programs have been shown repeatedly to increase academic achievement, and such programs ameliorate many of the risk factors that have been proposed to hinder youth's academic achievement.

Furthermore, research designs and statistical analyses are often not focused on examining those who do not follow the paths of central tendency defined by the data. Optimal application of a transactional approach to resilience would include greater use of idiographic, person-based methodologies, to supplement the more usual nomothetic, variable-based methods. The resiliency paradigm offers a framework for continuing research in which exceptions to the predictive model inform us as to the ongoing refinement of our models, in a series of successive approximations towards greater explanatory power.

Despite years of research, progress toward social and educational equity has been disappointingly slow. This is particularly the case for Latino youth whose presence in the American population is growing but who are not receiving proportionate attention with regard to their academic and social-emotional needs. Youth growing up now in low-SES communities face challenges too numerous and pervasive to be effectively eradicated during their formative years. Without a particular focus on Latino youth, schools will find themselves unable to move ahead to their potential because they will have left behind a sizable subgroup, one, paradoxically, that is deeply supportive of educational values and characterized by many protective processes that are supportive of educational success. The educational resiliency paradigm posits that this reality need not be deterministic of negative outcomes. Efforts to reduce these structural agents of risk should be pursued broadly and continuously at the level of policy; meanwhile, SEL offers an additional, and perhaps more immediately feasible, approach by ameliorating the negative effects of many of these structural agents of risk within disadvantaged educational environments. In essence, the application of the resiliency paradigm as articulated herein offers a means of reducing educational inequity, or at least its most negative effects, on those most at risk by targeting both the educational environment itself and by fostering students' internal resources.

Appendix: CASEL's Select SEL Programs (Adapted from CASEL, 2003a)

Caring School Community (Child Development Project), http://www.devstu.org

Community of Caring (Growing Up Caring), http://www.communityofcaring.org

High/Scope Educational Approach for Preschool and Primary Grades, http://www.highscope.org

I Can Problem Solve (ICPS), http://www.researchpress.com

Know Your Body, http://www.kendallhunt.com

Learning for Life, http://www.learningforlife.org/

Lions-Quest ("Skills series"), http://www.lions-quest.org

Michigan Model for Comprehensive Health Education, http://www.emc.cmich.edu

PATHS (Promoting Alternative Thinking Strategies), http://www.preventionscience.com

Peace Works (Peace Education Foundation), http://www.peaceeducation.com

Productive Conflict Resolution Program: A Whole School Approach, http://www.school-mediationcenter.org

Reach Out to Schools: Social Competency Program (Open Circle Curriculum), http://www.open-circle.org

Resolving Conflict Creatively Program (RCCP), http://www.esrnational.org

Responsive Classroom, http://www.responsiveclassroom.org

Second Step, http://www.cfchildren.org

Skills, Opportunities, and Recognition (SOAR), http://www.preventionscience.com

Social Decision Making and Problem-Solving Program, http://www.umdnj.edu/spsweb

References

Antshel, K. M. (2002). Integrating culture as a means of improving treatment adherence in the Latino population. *Psychology, Health & Medicine, 7*, 435–449.

Caprara, G. V., Barbaranelli, C., Pastorelli, C., Bandura, A., & Zimbardo, P. G. (2000). Prosocial foundations of children's academic achievement. *Psychological Science, 11*, 302–306.

Cauce, A. M., Cruz, R., Corona, M., & Conger, R. (2011). The face of the future: Risk and resilience in minority youth. In G. Carlo, L. J. Crockett, & M. Carranza (Eds.), *Health disparities in youth and families: Research and applications* (pp. 13–32). New York, NY: Springer.

Centers for Disease Control and Prevention. (2007). *National Youth Risk Behavior Survey: Health risk behaviors by race/ethnicity*. Retrieved June 10, 2010, from http://

www.cdc.gov/HealthyYouth/yrbs/pdf/yrbs07_us_dis-parity_race.pdf.

Collaborative for Academic, Social, and Emotional Learning (CASEL). (2003a). *Safe and sound: An educational leader's guide to evidence-based social and emotional learning (SEL) programs*. Chicago, IL: Author.

Collaborative for Academic, Social, and Emotional Learning (CASEL). (2003b). *Program descriptions: A companion to safe and sound: An educational leader's guide to evidence-based social and emotional learning (SEL) programs*. Chicago, IL: Author.

Durlak, J. A. (1995). *School-based prevention programs for children and adolescents*. Thousand Oaks, CA: Sage.

Durlak, J. A., Weissberg, R. P., Dymnicki, A. B., Taylor, R. D., & Schellinger, K. B. (2011). The impact of enhancing students' social and emotional learning: A meta-analysis of school based universal interventions. *Child Development, 82*(1), 405–432.

Education in America. (2010, September). It's a bird? It's a plane? *The Economist*. Retrieved March 6, 2011, from http://www.economist.com/node/17148968.

Elias, M. J., Gara, M., & Ubriaco, M. (1985). Sources of stress and support in children's transition to middle school: An empirical analysis. *Journal of Clinical Child Psychology, 14,* 112–118.

Elias, M. J., Kress, J. S., & Neft, D. (2003). Social and emotional learning, adolescence. In T. P. Gullotta & M. Bloom (Eds.), *Encyclopedia of primary prevention and health promotion* (pp. 1023–1028). New York, NY: Kluwer Academic/Plenum.

Elias, M. J., & Schwab, A. Y. (2006). From compliance to responsibility: The impact of social and emotional learning on classroom management. In C. M. Evertson & C. S. Weinstein (Eds.), *Handbook for classroom management: Research, practice, and contemporary issues*. New York, NY: Wiley.

Elias, M. J., Zins, J. E., Weissberg, R. P., Frey, K. S., Greenberg, M. T., Haynes, N. M., et al. (1997). *Promoting social and emotional learning: Guidelines for educators*. Alexandria, VA: Association for Supervision and Curriculum Development.

Epstein, J. L., Coates, L., Salinas, K. C., Sanders, M. G., & Simon, B. (1997). *School, family, community partnerships: Your handbook for action*. Thousand Oaks, CA: Corwin Press.

Esposito, C. (1999). Learning in urban blight: School climate and its effect on the school performance of urban, minority, low-income children. *School Psychology Review, 28,* 365–377.

Gager, P. J., & Elias, M. J. (1997). Implementing prevention programs in high-risk environments: Application of the resiliency paradigm. *The American Journal of Orthopsychiatry, 67,* 363–373.

Garmezy, N. (1985). Stress-resistant children: The search for protective factors. In J. E. Stevenson (Ed.), *Recent research in developmental psychopathology. Journal of Child Psychology and Psychiatry book supplement no. 4* (pp. 213–233). Oxford, England: Pergamon Press.

German, M., Gonzales, N. A., & Dumka, L. (2008). Familism values as a protective factor for Mexican-origin adolescents exposed to deviant peers. *The Journal of Early Adolescence, 29,* 16–42.

Gill, S., & Reynolds, A. J. (1999). Educational expectations and school achievement of urban African American children. *Journal of School Psychology, 37,* 403–424.

Glantz, M. D., & Johnson, J. L. (Eds.). (1999). *Resilience and development: Positive life adaptations*. New York, NY: Kluwer Academic/Plenum.

Glass, G. V. (2002). Teacher characteristics. In A. Molnar (Ed.), *School reform proposals: The research evidence*. Retrieved Jan 2, 2011, http://www.asu.Edu/educ/epsl/EPRU/documents/EPRU%202002-101/Chapter%2008-Glass-Final.pdf.

Glick, J. E., & Van Hook, J. (2008). Through children's eyes: Families and households of Latino children in the United States. In H. Rodríguez, R. Sáenz, & C. Menjívar (Eds.), *Latinas/os in the United States* (pp. 72–86). New York, NY: Springer.

Gore, S., & Eckenrode, J. (1994). Context and process in research on risk and resilience. In R. J. Haggerty, L. R. Sherrod, N. Garmezy, & M. Rutter (Eds.), *Stress, risk, and resilience in children and adolescents: Processes, mechanisms, and interventions*. New York, NY: Cambridge University Press.

Gottfredson, D. C. (2001). *Schools and delinquency*. New York: Cambridge University Press.

Grau, J. M., Azmitia, M., & Quattlebaum, J. (2009). Latino families: Parenting, relational, and developmental processes. In F. A. Villarruel, G. Carlo, J. M. Grau, M. Azmitia, N. J. Cabrera, & T. J. Chahin (Eds.), *Handbook of U.S. Latino psychology: Developmental and community-based perspectives* (pp. 153–170). Thousand Oaks, CA: Sage.

Greenberg, M. T., Domitrovich, C. E., & Bumbarger, B. (2001). The prevention of mental disorders in school-aged children: Current state of the field. *Prevention & Treatment, 4,* Article 1.

Greenberg, M. T., Weissberg, R. P., Utne O'Brien, M., Zins, J. E., Fredericks, L., Resnik, H., et al. (2003). Enhancing school-based prevention and youth development through coordinated social, emotional, and academic learning. *The American Psychologist, 58*(6/7), 466–474.

Greene, R. R., & Conrad, A. P. (2002). Basic assumptions and terms. In R. R. Greene (Ed.), *Resiliency: An integrated approach to practice, policy, and research* (pp. 29–62). Washington, DC: National Association of Social Workers Press.

Grossman, D. C., Neckerman, H. J., Koepsell, T. D., Liu, P. Y., Asher, K. N., Beland, K., et al. (1997). Effectiveness of a violence prevention curriculum among children in elementary school. A randomized controlled trial. *Journal of the American Medical Association, 277*(20), 1605–1611.

Haberman, M. (2004). *Urban education the state of urban schooling at the start of the 21st century*. Retrieved Jan 2, 2011, http://www.habermanfoundation.org/Articles/Default.aspx?id=10.

Hawkins, J. D., Farrington, D. P., & Catalano, R. F. (1998). Reducing violence through the schools. In D. S. Elliott, B. A. Hamburg, & K. R. Williams (Eds.), *Violence in American schools: A new perspective* (pp. 188–216). New York: Cambridge University Press.

Haynes, N. M., & Comer, J. P. (1996). Integrating schools families and communities through successful school reform. *School Psychology Review, 25*(4), 501–506.

Hetherington, E. M. (1989). Coping with family transitions: Winners, losers, and survivors. *Child Development, 60*, 1–14.

High/Scope Educational Research Foundation. (2003). *Elementary approach: Fundamental goals and purposes.* Retrieved August 23, 2003, from http://www.highscope.org/EducationalPrograms/Elementary/fundamentalgoals.htm.

Kaplan, H. B. (1999). Toward an understanding of resilience: A critical review of definitions and models. In M. D. Glantz & J. L. Johnson (Eds.), *Resilience and development: Positive life adaptations* (pp. 17–83). New York, NY: Kluwer Academic/Plenum.

Kerbow, D. (1996). Patterns of urban student mobility and local school reform. *Journal of Education for Students Placed at Risk, 1*, 147–169.

Kozol, J. (2005). Apartheid in America? *Phi Delta Kappan, 87*(4), 264–275.

Kuklinski, M. R., & Weinstein, R. S. (2001). Classroom and developmental differences in a path model of educator expectancy effects. *Child Development, 72*, 1554–1578.

Kuperminc, G. P., Wilkins, N. J., Roche, C., & Alvarez-Jimenez, A. (2009). Risk, resilience, and positive development among Latino youth. In F. A. Villarruel, G. Carlo, J. M. Grau, M. Azmitia, N. J. Cabrera, & T. J. Chahin (Eds.), *Handbook of U.S. Latino psychology: Developmental and community-based perspectives* (pp. 213–234). Thousand Oaks, CA: Sage.

Lash, A., & Kirkpatrick, S. (1994). Interrupted lessons: Teacher views of transfer student education. *American Educational Research Journal, 31*(4), 813–843.

Lescano, C. M., Brown, L. K., Raffaelli, M., & Lima, L. (2009). Cultural factors and family-based HIV prevention intervention for Latino youth. *Journal of Pediatric Psychology, 34*, 1041–1052.

Leventhal, T., & Brooks-Gunn, J. (2000). The neighborhoods they live in: The effects of neighborhood residence on child and adolescent outcomes. *Psychological Bulletin, 126*, 309–337.

Lions Clubs International Foundation. (2003). *Lions Quest evaluation report.* Retrieved August 23, 2003, from http://www.lions-quest.org/content/OurPrograms/EvaluationReport/evalreport.html.

Luthar, S. S. (1991). Vulnerability and resilience: A study of high-risk adolescents. *Child Development, 62*, 600–616.

Luthar, S. S., Cicchetti, D., & Becker, B. (2000). The construct of resilience: A critical evaluation and guidelines for future work. *Child Development, 71*, 543–562.

Luthar, S. S., & Cushing, G. (1999). Measurement issues in the empirical study of resilience. In M. D. Glantz & J. L. Johnson (Eds.), *Resilience and development: Positive life adaptations* (pp. 129–160). New York, NY: Kluwer Academic/Plenum.

Masten, A., Best, K., & Garmezy, N. (1990). Resilience and development: Contributions from the study of children who overcome adversity. *Development and Psychopathology, 2*, 425–444.

Masten, A. S., & Motti-Stefanidi, F. (2009). Understanding and promoting resilience in children: Promotive and protective processes in schools. In C. R. Reynolds & T. B. Gutkin (Eds.), *The handbook of school psychology* (4th ed., pp. 721–738). Danvers, MA: Wiley.

McCluskey, C. P., Krohn, M. D., Lizotte, A. J., & Rodriquez, M. L. (2002). Early substance use and school achievement: An examination of Latino, Caucasian, and African American youth. *Journal of Drug Issues, 32*, 921–943.

McGee, L., & Newcomb, M. D. (1992). General deviance syndrome: Expanded hierarchical evaluations at four ages from early adolescence to adulthood. *Journal of Consulting and Clinical Psychology, 60*, 766–776.

McKown, C., & Weinstein, R. S. (2008). Teacher expectations, classroom content, and the achievement gap. *Journal of School Psychology, 46*, 235–261.

Meehan, B. T., Hughes, J. N., & Cavell, T. A. (2003). Educator-student relationships as compensatory resources for aggressive children. *Child Development, 74*, 1145–1157.

National Center for Mental Health Promotion and Youth Violence Prevention. (2004, April). *Meeting the needs of Latino youth.* Retrieved March 30, 2010, from http://promoteprevent.org/documents/prevetion_belief_latino_youth.pdf.

Newcomb, M. D., Abbott, R. D., Catalano, R. F., Hawkins, J. D., Battin-Pearson, S., & Hill, K. (2002). Mediational and deviance theories of late high school failure: Process roles of structural strains, academic competence, and general versus specific problem behaviors. *Journal of Counseling Psychology, 49*, 172–186.

Office of Management and Budget (OMB). (1997, October). *Federal register notice: Revisions to the standards for the classification of federal data on race and ethnicity.* Retrieved April 1, 2010, from http://www.whitehouse.gov/omb/rewrite/fedreg/ombdir15.html.

Peng, S. S., & Lee, R. M. (1994). Educational experiences and needs of middle school students in poverty. In K. K. Wong & M. C. Wang (Eds.), *Rethinking policy for at-risk students* (pp. 49–64). Berkeley, CA: McCutchan Publishing.

Pew Hispanic Center. (2009, December). *Between two worlds: How young Latinos come of age in America.* Retrieved December 11, 2009, from http://pewhispanic.org/files/reports/117.pdf.

Prelow, H. M., & Loukas, A. (2003). The role of resource, protective, and risk factors on academic achievement-related outcomes of economically disadvantaged Latino youth. *Journal of Community Psychology, 31*, 513–529.

Rimm-Kaufman, S., Fan, X., Chiu, Y., & You, W. (2007). The contribution of the Responsive Classroom Approach on children's academic achievement: Results from a three year longitudinal study. *Journal of School Psychology, 45*(4), 401–421.

Rolf, J. E. (1999). Resilience: An interview with Norman Garmezy. In M. D. Glantz & J. L. Johnson (Eds.), *Resilience and development: Positive life adaptations* (pp. 5–14). New York, NY: Kluwer Academic/Plenum.

Roosa, M. W., Dumka, L. E., Gonzales, N. A., & Knight, G. P. (2002). Cultural/ethnic issues and the prevention scientist in the 21st century. *Prevention & Treatment, 5,* Article 5. Retrieved Jan 2, 2011, from http://journals.apa.org/prevention/volume5/pre0050005a.html.

Roosa, M. W., Morgan-Lopez, A. A., Cree, W. K., & Specter, M. M. (2002). Ethnic culture, poverty, and context: Sources of influence on Latino families and children. In J. M. Contreras, K. A. Kerns, & A. M. Neal-Barnett (Eds.), *Latino children and families in the United States: Current research and future directions* (pp. 27–44). Westport, CT: Praeger.

Rosenthal, R., & Jacobson, L. (1968). Pygmalion in the classroom. *The Urban Review, 3*(1), 16–20.

Rosenthal, R., & Rubin, D. B. (1978). Interpersonal expectancy effects: The first 345 studies. *The Behavioral and Brain Sciences, 1,* 377–416.

Scanlon, E., & Devine, K. (2001). Residential mobility and youth well-being: Research, policy, and practice issues. *Journal of Sociology and Social Welfare, 28,* 119–138.

Shetgiri, R., Kataoka, S. H., Ryan, G. W., Askew, L. M., Chung, P. J., & Schuster, M. A. (2009). Risk and resilience in Latinos: A community-based participatory research study. *American Journal of Preventive Medicine, 37,* S217–S224.

Shure, M. B. (1992a). *I Can Problem Solve (ICPS): An interpersonal cognitive problem solving program (preschool).* Champaign, IL: Research Press.

Shure, M. B. (1992b). *I Can Problem Solve (ICPS): An interpersonal cognitive problem solving program (kindergarten/primary grades).* Champaign, IL: Research Press.

Shure, M. B. (1992c). *I Can Problem Solve (ICPS): An interpersonal cognitive problem solving program (intermediate elementary grades).* Champaign, IL: Research Press.

Simmons, R. G., Burgeson, R., Carlton-Ford, S., & Blyth, D. A. (1987). The impact of cumulative change in early adolescence. *Child Development, 58,* 1220–1234.

Temple, J. A., & Reynolds, A. J. (1999). School mobility and achievement: Longitudinal findings from an urban cohort. *Journal of School Psychology, 37,* 355–377.

Tharp, R. G. (1989). Psychocultural variables and constants: Effects on teaching and learning in schools. *The American Psychologist, 44,* 349–359.

Toosi, M. (2006). *A new look at long-term labor force projections to 2050.* Retrieved March 8, 2011, from http://www.bls.gov/opub/mlr/2006/11/art3full.pdf.

U.S. Department of Education, National Center for Education Statistics. (2009). *The Condition of Education 2009* (NCES 2009-081), Table A-20-2. Retrieved June 10, 2010, from http://nces.ed.gov/fastfacts/display.asp?id=16.

U.S. Department of Health and Human Services. (2001). *Youth violence: A report of the Surgeon General.* Rockville, MD: U.S. Department of Health and Human Services.

Umaña-Taylor, A. J. (2009). Research with Latino early adolescents. *The Journal of Early Adolescence, 29,* 5–15.

Walberg, H. J. (1984). Improving the productivity of America's schools. *Educational Leadership, 41*(8), 19–27.

Wang, M. C., & Gordon, E. W. (1994). *Educational resilience in inner-city America: Challenges and prospects.* Hillsdale, NJ: Lawrence Erlbaum.

Wang, M. C., & Haertel, G. D. (1987). Educational resilience. In M. C. Wang, M. C. Reynolds, & H. J. Walberg (Eds.), *Handbook of special education: Research and practice.* New York, NY: Pergamon Press.

Wang, M. C., Haertel, G. D., & Walberg, H. J. (1997). Toward a knowledge base for school learning. *Review of Educational Research, 63,* 249–294.

Welsh, M., Parke, R. D., Widaman, K., & O'Neil, R. (2001). Linkages between children's social and academic competence: A longitudinal analysis. *Journal of School Psychology, 39,* 463–481.

Wentzel, K. R. (1993). Does being good make the grade? Social behavior and academic competence in middle school. *Journal of Educational Psychology, 85,* 357–364.

Woolley, M. E., Kol, K. L., & Bowen, G. L. (2009). The social context of school success for Latino middle school students: Direct and indirect influences of teachers, family, and friends. *The Journal of Early Adolescence, 29,* 43–70.

Zambrana, R. E., & Zoppi, I. M. (2002). Latina students: Translating cultural wealth into social capital to improve academic success. *Journal of Ethnic & Cultural Diversity in Social Work: Innovation in Theory, Research & Practice, 11,* 33–53.

Zins, J. E., Weissberg, R. P., Wang, M., & Walberg, H. J. (Eds.). (2004a). *Building school success through social and emotional learning: Implications for practice and research.* New York, NY: Teachers College Press.

SEL Implementation Resources

Cohen, J., & Elias, M. J. (2011). *School climate: Building safe, supportive and engaging classrooms & schools.* Port Chester, NY: National Professional Resources (http://www.nprinc.com).

Dunkelblau, E. (2009). *Social-emotional and character development: A laminated resource card for teachers, for students, for parents.* Port Chester, NY: National Professional Resources (http://www.nprinc.com).

Elias, M. J. (2007). From model implementation to sustainability: A multisite study of pathways to excellence in social-emotional learning and related school programs.

In A. M. Blankstein, P. D. Houston, & R. W. Cole (Eds.), *Sustaining professional learning communities: The soul of educational leadership series* (pp. 59–95). Thousand Oaks, CA: Paul Chapman Publishing.

Elias, M. J., & Arnold, H. (Eds.). (2006). *The educators' guide to emotional intelligence and academic achievement: Social and emotional learning in the classroom.* Thousand Oaks, CA: Corwin Press.

Elias, M. J., Zins, J. E., Graczyk, P. A., & Weissberg, R. P. (2003). Implementation, sustainability, and scaling up of social-emotional and academic innovations in public schools. *School Psychology Review, 32*, 303–319.

Haynes, N., Ben-Avie, M., & Ensign, J. (Eds.). (2003). *How social and emotional development add up: Getting results in math and science education.* New York, NY: Teachers College Press.

Ji, P., Axelrod, J., Foster, C., Keister, S., O'Brien, M. U., Orgen, K., et al. (2008). A model for implementing and sustaining schoolwide social and emotional learning. *The Community Psychologist, 42*, 39–42.

Kam, C., Greenberg, M. T., & Walls, C. T. (2003). Examining the role of implementation quality in school-based prevention using the PATHS curriculum. *Prevention Science, 4*, 55–63.

Novick, B., Kress, J. S., & Elias, M. J. (2002). *Building learning communities with character: How to integrate academic, social, and emotional learning.* Alexandria, VA: Association for Supervision and Curriculum Development.

Pasi, R. J. (2001). *Higher expectations: Promoting social emotional learning and academic achievement in your school.* New York, NY: Educators College Press.

Shelton, C. M., & Stern, R. (2004). *Understanding emotions in the classroom: Differentiating teaching strategies for optimal learning.* New York, NY: Dude Publishing.

Zins, J. E., Weissberg, R. P., Wang, M. C., & Walberg, H. J. (Eds.). (2004b). *Building academic success on social and emotional learning: What does the research say?* New York, NY: Teachers College Press.

Resilience Through Violence and Bullying Prevention in Schools

Jennifer Taub and Melissa Pearrow

When asked to write a chapter focusing on school for this book, we thought of the many fine books, chapters, and articles written about the multitude of school-based programs targeted at the prevention of social and emotional problems in children and adolescents. The majority of these programs target specific issues, such as drug and alcohol prevention, weapons-reduction, school-community partnerships, school-based mental health clinics, and school-based family support services (to name, but a few). All of them target the social and emotional well-being of our nation's students, and could be said to broadly foster resilience. In this chapter, however, we will not be discussing programs that target youth who have been identified as having problems, programs with a clinical or mental health focus, or other programs that have a secondary or tertiary prevention focus. Programs that target students with identified problems are more likely to have a clinically focused symptom-reduction emphasis rather than a wellness-promotion resiliency model (Cowen, 1994; Cowen, Hightower, Pedro-Carroll, Work, Wyman, & Haffey, 1996). They typically target a small proportion of the overall student population; for example, the U.S.

Department of Education (2007) estimates that 0.67% of students between 6 and 21 years of age are identified as having an emotional disturbance and qualifying them for services under IDEA. We strongly support such programs and believe they have a vital role in our nation's schools. We also believe that such programs contribute, directly or indirectly, to the reduction of factors related to violence in schools, as well as the promotion of factors related to resilience in our nation's student population.

In our focus on "school-wide" interventions, we are taking a primary prevention perspective, defined by Durlak and Wells (1997) as "an intervention intentionally designed to reduce the future incidence of adjustment problems in currently normal populations as well as efforts directed at the promotion of mental health functioning" (p. 117), where interventions target students with or without problem behaviors and are delivered to all students. We believe that schools play a critical and unique role in the development of resilience in young people as "current models of resilience assume that a systemic perspective is important for building protective factors that support children in an integrative manner" (Esquivel, Doll, & Oades-Sese, 2011; p. 650). This chapter will broadly focus on school- and classroom-based programs that are implemented within the school environment, are specifically designed to promote social and emotional competence and prevent the development of bullying and/or violent behaviors. As such, treatments and strategies that target only

J. Taub (✉)
Boston Chinatown Neighborhood Center, Inc.,
Boston, MA, USA
e-mail: Jennifer.taub@bcnc.net

M. Pearrow
University of Massachusetts Boston,
Boston, MA, USA

S. Goldstein and R.B. Brooks (eds.), *Handbook of Resilience in Children*,
DOI 10.1007/978-1-4614-3661-4_21, © Springer Science+Business Media New York 2013

individuals already identified as displaying problem behaviors (secondary prevention) will not be addressed, and our focus will be on universal (school-wide) and primary prevention programs that target the entire school population. There are many such programs which have found to be effective in increasing prosocial behaviors and reducing negative, bullying, aggressive, and violent behaviors by addressing individuals and the whole school climate (Hahn et al., 2007). We believe a resilience focus necessitates enhancing social and emotional learning (SEL) and competence, and promoting stress hardiness in all children to reduce the overall incidence of violence and bullying. The importance of such universal programs in school settings will be explored, as well as how they can enhance resilience through their implementation in the day-to-day activities of children and adolescents. Prevention programs that have been empirically validated will be reviewed, as well as strategies for implementation and examination and the needs and future directions of violence prevention programming and research.

Resilience and Primary Prevention

Resilience has been defined as an individual's capacity for adapting to change and stressful events in healthy and flexible ways. Or, as Henderson and Milstein (1996) state simply, it is how adults and children bounce back from stress, trauma, and risk in their lives. In research studies, resilience has been identified as a characteristic of youth who, when exposed to multiple risk factors, show successful responses to challenge and use this learning to achieve successful outcomes (e.g., Hawkins, Catalano, & Miller, 1992; Masten, Best, & Garmezy, 1990; Rutter, 1985; Werner, 1989). The National Academy of Sciences (Reiss & Roth, 1993) defined resilience as patterns that protect children from adopting problem behaviors in the face of risk. Resilience involves adaptive responses to such environmental stressors as changes in family or community circumstances, or exposure to trauma (Huizinga, Loeber, & Thornberry, 1995; Overstreet & Mathews, 2011).

In order for schools to foster resiliency, it is necessary to characterize the resilient child. As reviewed extensively in earlier chapters, there are two general groupings of protective factors associated with resiliency in children - internal and external. Internal protective factors are those that are located within the individual, such as impulse control, good decision-making, social problem solving, and the ability to form positive relationships with others (Henderson & Milstein, 1996). External factors include having families, schools, and communities with characteristics such as setting and enforcing clear boundaries, limits, norms, and rules, encouraging supportive and caring relationships with others, and possessing values of altruism and cooperation (Henderson & Milstein). A school-wide program designed to foster resiliency can use as its mechanism the bolstering of internal factors by working at the student (individual) level. Such a program can teach skills such as conflict resolution or social problem solving to students. External (school) factors can be enhanced through implementing environmental changes such as introducing a peer mediation program or making changes in a school's disciplinary policies.

The focus on primary prevention is grounded in a public health orientation (Doll & Cummings, 2008). Primary prevention has been defined as "actions taken *prior* to the onset of disease to intercept its causation or to modify its course before pathology is involved" (Goldston, 1985, p. 454). As such, these programs are educational rather than clinical in nature, since they do not necessarily target disease or the amelioration of symptoms. For prevention programs to be effective, interventions must begin early in life, target developmental levels, and include aspects of the individual and the environment, since many of the undesirable behaviors related to later aggression and the attitudes that accompany such behaviors are evident long before adolescence (Reiss & Price, 1996). Some programs target identified students; for example, aggressive children demonstrate deficits in social skills knowledge and are more likely to respond impulsively when confronted with social problems (Dodge, Pettit, McClaskey, & Brown, 1986). Thus, intervention programs are effective in increasing social skills knowledge, improving social behavior, and in preventing declines in social behavior (e.g., Catalano, Berglund, Ryan, Lonczak, & Hawkins, 2002; Durlak & Wells, 1997; Leff, Power, Manz, Costigan, & Nabors, 2001; Olweus & Limber, 2010). As such, interventions should start early as they are more cost-effective, and since the resources spent on an adolescent are enormous compared to the cost of interventions spent early in a child's life (Doll, Jones, Osborn, Dooley, & Turner, 2011; Flannery & Williams, 1999). By the time children get to middle school, large numbers have engaged in aggressive, risky, or bullying behaviors (Bosworth, Espelage, DuBay, Dahlberg, & Daytner, 1996; Englander, 2011; Johnson & Johnson, 1995; Petersen, Pietrzak, & Speaker, 1998). For instance, one large-scale survey found that children in grades three through five reported that during the past week, 15% had been sent to the office for disciplinary problems, 13% tried to start a fight, 27% hit someone, and 12% reported being threatened with a gun or knife (Embry, Flannery, Vazsonyi, Powell, & Atha, 1996).

Universal, primary prevention programs target all students in a school, not just particular students. There is a strong need to target the majority of school-aged children, even if they do not meet criteria for mental health diagnoses, as over 50% of elementary school children, over 60% of middle school children, and two-thirds of high school students report having been bullied in the past year. Most common is name calling, reported by about 50% of elementary students, and over 60% of older students. Elementary school boys report experiencing more physical bullying (41%), while about 25% of elementary school girls and the same number of older students report being victims of physical bullying. Social exclusion and rumors as a form of bullying starts in elementary school (14% of boys, 27% of girls), and increases in middle (36%) and high school (45%) (Englander, 2011). Social exclusion and rumors as a form of bullying starts in elementary school (14% of boys, 27% of girls), and increases in middle (36%) and high school (45%) (Englander, 2011). While approximately 80% of bullying incidents are witnessed by a bystander, less than 20% of bystanders report or intervene in some way (Nickerson, Mele, & Princiotta, 2008). Given the prevalence of such incidents, most students will at some point be in the role of bystander. Being a bystander can have negative consequences including feelings of guilt and distress (Twemlow, Fonagy, & Sacco, 2004). Some researchers have categorized types of bystanders, including those who egg on and encourage the bullies ("active accomplice"), those who laugh ("encouraging accomplice"), those who do nothing ("passive accomplice") and those who intervene on behalf of the victim ("defender") (Olweus & Limber, 2010). Defenders are more likely to be agreeable, prosocial, cooperative, and trustworthy (Tani, Greenman, & Schneider, 2003). It is therefore highly beneficial for programs to engage, together, the range of bystanders so that the skills of the defenders can be modeled for the passive bystanders and accomplices.

The profound need to address issues of bullying and violence prevention has resulted in legislative mandates with resources to support implementation of prevention programs (Naglieri, LeBuffe and Shapiro, 2011). At present, 48 states have legislation on the books aimed at the prevention of bullying in schools; two-thirds of those laws also address cyberbullying. Laws such as the one in our state (Massachusetts) have significantly expanded the domains in which schools are able and compelled to respond to situations that occur between students whether they occur at school or in the community. This creates a new and challenging level of responsibility for schools, as they are impelled to address situations which may occur outside of school, and which may be unseen (e.g., texting or cyberbullying).

Importance of Prevention Programming in Schools

Schools are the largest system capable of impacting the majority of children and their families. The President's New Freedom Commission (2003) called for a transformation in the delivery of mental health services, and the role of school mental health services was highlighted since schools are uniquely positioned to play a central role in enhancing the mental health promotion and prevention programming. Schools provide the opportunity to observe and intervene directly in the setting where the child spends a significant amount of time while also reducing issues of stigma related to mental health treatment. It is estimated that approximately 70% of children and adolescents in need of treatment do not receive mental health services, and for children who do receive mental health services, schools are the primary providers (Hoagwood & Erwin, 1997). Schools are particularly well suited to promote children's development in the area of social adjustment and can be a refuge where children who have many environmental risks can find structure and effective methods of success (Comer, 1980; Doll & Lyon, 1998). Moreover, over 180 studies have demonstrated that when schools implement universal programs that target social-emotional learning (SEL), the students demonstrate significant increases in self-control, decision-making, attitudes towards self and others, social behaviors, and decreases in conduct problems and aggression and emotional distress (Payton et al., 2008).

Schools afford the opportunity to promote social competence within this naturalistic setting - in classrooms, on the playground - where the skills can be developed, generalized, and moreover, are more effective than efforts utilized in traditional person-centered interventions or through other community organizations (Weissberg, Caplan, & Sivo, 1989). School effectiveness research demonstrates that schools do have major effects on children's development and offer "the most efficient and systematic means available to promote the psychological, social, and physical health of school-age children" (Weissberg, Caplan, & Harwood, 1991, p. 833). Factors like strong leadership, high and consistent academic and behavioral expectations, and creating a sense of belonging have been identified as strongly contributing to effective schools (Johnson, Schwartz, Livingston, & Slate, 2000). Moreover, the largest expenditure of state budgets is on education, totaling $567 billion in 2009 (U.S. Census Bureau, 2011). No other state supported agency that provides services primarily to children and youth receives comparable financial support to address these issues.

There are several factors which impact the ways in which violence and aggressive behavior is managed within a school including the overall climate, policies and procedures, and implicit and explicit rules. There is increasing recognition of the range of behaviors which can and should be addressed to make schools safe places, which promote resiliency for all students (Bostic & Brunt, 2011; Greenberg et al., 2003). However, individual factors, such as whether or not a teacher was bullied as a child, also impact how such incidents are dealt with in school settings (Ransford, Greenberg, Domitrovich, Small, & Jackson, 2009; Yoon, 2004). Teachers are more likely to see physical and verbal aggression as more damaging than social exclusion, which is not necessarily true (Yoon & Kerber, 2003). In some schools, teachers and school staff can be perceived as bullying towards students (Twemlow, Fonagy, & Sacco, 2006). Teachers who feel self-efficacy in dealing with bullying and aggression are more able to manage the situations effectively. Involving the entire school community, including parents, teachers, bus drivers, cafeteria staff, etc. is associated with less violence and aggression. Other factors associated with decreases in bullying and school violence include: Staff discussions about bullying, clear rules for the school that are posted and enforced, student involvement, community partnerships with local organizations, strong school leadership, professional development for teachers and staff, increased adult supervision, non-punitive consequences for aggressors/bullies, and access to mental health services for all students in need (Pepler, 2006).

Recently, there has been attention focused on the behaviors that broadly fall under the category of "bullying," including most acts thought of as "violent" and directed at another individual. In addition to physical acts such as pushing or hitting, there are other behaviors, often more frequent and just as negative to both school climate and individual student welfare, that fall under the bullying category. Such behaviors include acts that cause emotional harm such as cyberbullying, damage to one's property, threats or intimidation, social exclusion, and relational aggression (e.g., spreading rumors). Victims of such acts have outcomes just as negative as those who are victims of physical aggression, including being more likely to develop anxiety, somatic complaints, eating disorders, depression, and suicidality (Fekkes, Pijpers, & Verloove-Vanhorick, 2004). Recent research has shown that as many as half of middle school students surveyed said they have been victims of cyberbullying, and a third said they had been perpetrators of cyberbullying (Smith, Mahdavi, & Carvalho, 2008). While boys cyberbully both those they know and those they don't, girls are more likely to cyberbully their friends, and research suggests girls are more likely to be both victims and perpetrators of cyberbullying than boys (Snell & Englander, 2010).

These surveys document the high incidence of problem behaviors in school-age children, with a high level of unmet need for these problems. Violence prevention research has demonstrated that engaging in violence prevention activities increases standardized academic achievement scores (Payton et al., 2008; Twemlow et al., 2001) and reduces various problems that impact academic development, ranging from suspensions to time out of class visiting the school nurse (e.g., Farrington, 2002; Hausman, Pierce, & Briggs, 1996; Krug, Dahlberg, Brener, Ryan, & Powell, 1997). And critically, tragic events such as mass school shootings perpetrated by youth, or children who have attempted or completed suicide where bullying was a primary factor, have underscored the profound need for violence-prevention programs in schools.

Mechanisms for Prevention Programs

School-wide prevention and intervention programs, which fit within a public health orientation, that involve teachers, family, community members, and peers have shown to produce positive outcomes even for the most vulnerable youth (Power, Mautone, & Ginsburg-Block, 2010). Universal programs are delivered to all children, whether or not they have identified needs, are proactive and reduce the risk of stigma while also maximizing resources by providing services to large groups of children (Macklem, 2011; Power et al., 2010). Positive behavior intervention and supports (PBIS) is an overarching term in the field of education to describe strategies that support the development of social emotional competencies, prevent disruptive behaviors, enhance the school's organizational health, and foster the resilience of students and teachers (Bradshaw, Zmuda, Kellam, & Ialongo, 2009; Stoiber & Gettinger, 2011). School-wide PBIS is a noncurricular universal prevention strategy that aims to alter the school environment by creating improved systems (e.g., reinforcement, data management), and procedures (e.g., office referral, training) that promote positive change in staff and student behaviors (Bradshaw, Koth, Bevans, Ialongo, & Leaf, 2008). PBIS is organized by the three-tiered prevention model where universal school-wide components of the model are complemented by the secondary (classroom), and tertiary (individual) systems of support (for a review, see Carr et al., 2002; Sugai & Horner, 2006). The focus on organizational structures is critical and there is strong research support for the aforementioned strategies; readers are referred to these sources for additional information.

There are two primary mechanisms for the prevention of violence in schools. The first is to promote resiliency through the enhancement of protective factors, such as the promotion of prosocial behaviors, social competency, and other resilience-related factors. The second mechanism is through risk reduction, decreasing violence-related behaviors, and antecedents of those behaviors. Within each mechanism, there are both internal and external levels. At the internal level are student-centered programs, which include individually based interventions such as teaching the expression of feelings, assertiveness training, conflict resolution, perspective taking, and anger management. At the external level is environment or school-centered programs, which include interventions such as changes in school policies for students' disruptive behavior, implementation of peer mediation programs, programs that address teachers' classroom organization, changes in scheduling and staffing to provide more adult supervision, or parent components.

A comprehensive meta-analysis of primary prevention programs conducted by Durlak and Wells (1997) indicated that, overall, school-centered programs show small yet meaningful effect sizes (mean ES = 0.35), while student-centered programs show small to large effect sizes (mean ES = 0.25–0.93), depending on the age of student and the mode of intervention. These authors found that programs targeting younger children (ages 2–7) tend to show the greatest effect sizes, whether the approach is primarily affective education (mean ES = 0.70) or interpersonal problem solving (mean ES = 0.93). Student-centered programs targeting children over the age of 7 tend to show small effect sizes (mean ES = 0.24–0.36), similar to those seen in school-centered programs. Programs that focus on self-control or social competency, utilizing cognitive-behavioral or behavioral instructional methods, also show small yet significant positive results in a meta-analytic study (Wilson, Gottfredson, & Najaka, 2001).

Many school-wide violence prevention programs strive to enhance protective factors, as well as reduce risk, although some programs focus on just one or the other. Most programs are geared toward the internal level, using as their primary mechanism the direct teaching of both cognitive and affective skills to students. It is easier to enhance social competencies than decrease violence-related behaviors (e.g., Hudley & Graham, 1993; Taub, 2002), and research on single-approach programs reducing violence are more likely to demonstrate results than those involving family, peers, and community given the issues of complexity (Park-Higgerson, Perumean-Chaney, Bartolucci, Grimley, & Singh, 2008). This makes sense, as a new prosocial skill will need to be learned before it can be used in place of an anti-social, violent, or aggressive behavior.

Review of Universal Prevention Programs

Given our focus on prevention and resilience, in this section we describe primary prevention programs, designed for school-wide implementation.

A great number of secondary prevention programs, targeting those children who have displayed problem behaviors, have been implemented in schools targeting the reduction of aggressive student behaviors, and related problems. Many of these programs are effective in their goals, and would likely work well as companions to a universal prevention program such as the ones described below. Reviewing these programs is, however, outside the scope of this chapter.

Here we list some of the programs with the strongest current research base, utilizing the Standards of Evidence Criteria for Efficacy, Effectiveness, and Dissemination outlined by the Society for Prevention Research (2004). In order to assist those working in school settings, we also provide the most current information available regarding the materials, costs, and training needed to implement these programs. As such information can change, we recommend that you use the information provided about costs as a guideline, and consult the programs' websites for the most up-to-date information. Programs are presented in alphabetical order.

Good Behavior Game http://www.jhsph.edu/bin/i/h/gbg.pdf.

Classroom Prevention Program (Good Behavior Game + Academic Enhancement): http://toptierevidence.org/wordpress/wp-content/uploads/Classroom-Prevention-Program-Manual-Werthamer-1993.pdf.

The Good Behavior Game (GBG) is an approach to the management of classroom behavior that rewards positive group behavior for displaying appropriate on-task behaviors during instructional times. It has been designed for use in first grade classrooms. The class is divided into two or three teams and a point is given to a team for any inappropriate behavior displayed by one of its members. Any team with four or fewer check marks at the end of a specified time - ranging from 10 min at the start of the year to a full day later on - is rewarded. If both teams keep their points below a preset level, then both teams share in the reward (Barrish, Saunders, & Wold, 1969). Tangible rewards (e.g., stickers) are used early in the school year and less tangible rewards (e.g., working on a project) are added.

The GBG is supplemented by weekly teacher-led class meetings designed to build children's skills in social problem solving. The most effective components of the game are division of the class into teams, consequences for a team winning of the game, and criteria set for winning the game (Harris & Sherman, 1973). Approximately 20 independent replications of the GBG across different grade levels (e.g., elementary school, high school), different types of students (e.g., regular education, special education), different settings (e.g., classroom, lunchroom, urban, suburban), and some with long-term follow-up show strong, consistent impact on impulsive, disruptive behaviors of children and teens as well as reductions in substance use or serious antisocial behaviors (Embry, 2002; Kleinman & Saigh, 2011; Lannie & McCurdy, 2007; McCurdy, Lannie, & Barnabas, 2009).

The GBG has also been combined with an enhanced academic curriculum to create the Classroom Prevention Program (CPP) (Werthamer, Cooper, & Lombardi, 1993). This combined program has been extensively researched and has shown positive outcomes in across a number of domains. A 17-year longitudinal follow-up study of 18 randomized inner city school first grade classrooms found those in the CPP intervention had: lower likelihood of smoking at age 13 (Storr, Ialongo, Kellam, & Anthony, 2002); by grade 12 had higher educational attainment (21% more likely to receive a GED or HS diploma; 62% more likely to attend college); were 36% less likely to have received special education services; and scored approximately one grade level higher in reading and math (Bradshaw et al., 2009).

The Coalition for Evidence Based Policy's Top Tier Initiative's Expert Panel (2011) considers the stand alone GBG to be "promising but not yet Top Tier or Near Top Tier" and the combined CPP to be "Near Top Tier."

Materials

GBG: There is no cost, and no specific materials are needed to implement the GBG. Teachers can implement this program in their classroom with little to no outside support or assistance. A manual on the GBG developed by the Baltimore Prevention Program is available at http://www.jhsph.edu/bin/i/h/gbg.pdf.

CPP: Teachers receive approximately 60 h of training in the program prior to implementation, as well as supervision and feedback from program experts on a monthly basis during the year. The program's training and content is standardized; its cost is approximately $500 per student per year in 2010 dollars.

The manual for the combined program is available here: http://toptierevidence.org/wordpress/wp-content/uploads/Classroom-Prevention-Program-Manual-Werthamer-1993.pdf.

Olweus Bullying Prevention: http://www.olweus.org/public/bullying_prevention_program.page

Recommended in the *Blueprints for Violence Prevention* series (Olweus, Limber, & Mihalic, 1999) as a model program, the Olweus Bullying Prevention program has been shown to lead to a substantial reduction in reports of bullying and victimization in Norway, and has had mixed findings in the US. Evaluation in Norway in 42 schools over a 2-year period found that the frequency of bully/victim problems decreased by 50–70% (Olweus, 1997), and have shown a significant reduction in students' reports of general antisocial behavior such as vandalism, fighting, theft, and truancy, and significant improvements in the "social climate" of the class, as reflected in students' reports of improved order and discipline, more positive social relationships, and a more positive attitude toward schoolwork and school (Olweus et al., 1999).

In the US, there have been no randomized controlled trials. One recent longitudinal evaluation study in an urban school district over 4 years found the number of bullying incidents per 100 student hours decreased by 65% following implementation of the program. Components associated with decreased incidents were: posting of rules, consistent enforcement of positive and negative consequences, and training adult monitors to engage students in activities (Black & Jackson,

2007). A nonrandomized controlled trial with ten public middle schools indicated no reductions in bullying in the intervention schools overall, but found positive effects (reductions in bullying) for white students (Bauer, Lozano, & Rivara, 2007). A research report (non-peer reviewed) in Pennsylvania reported that Olweus school have "seen large reductions in bullying, increased staff response to bullying, and promoted a better understanding of the impact of bullying throughout the community" (Chilenski, Bumbarger, Kyler, & Greenberg, 2007, p. 4).

This program utilizes both student-level and school-level approaches, which include environmental changes in school climate and in the opportunity and reward structures for bullying behavior and sanctions for rule violations in school.

Materials

Costs for this program include a coordinator for the program, plus approximately $200 per school to purchase the questionnaires, materials, and DVD needed, and approximately $55 *per teacher* to cover costs of classroom materials. The establishment of a Bullying Prevention Coordinating Committee is a prerequisite for implementation, as is completion of 2 day training for one or two committee representatives, at a cost of $3000. These individuals are then responsible for training school staff. Additional phone consultation (at $125/hour) is recommended throughout the first year of program implementation.

Promoting Alternative Thinking Strategies

Information: http://www.prevention.psu.edu/projects/PATHS.html.

Materials (for purchase): http://www.channing-bete.com/prevention-programs/paths/paths.html.

The Promoting Alternative Thinking Strategies (PATHS) curriculum is a student-level program focusing on promoting emotional and social competencies and reducing aggression and behavior problems through a classroom-based intervention. The approach is a combination of cognitive-behavioral and affective education (Greenberg, Kusché, & Mihalic, 1998). This program has been held up as a model program by SAMHSA, a "best practices" program by the Centers for Disease Control and Prevention, and is listed as a "promising program" by the US Department of Education and the surgeon general's report on youth violence, and included in the *Blueprints for Violence Prevention* services (Greenberg et al., 1998). Evaluations of the PATHS curriculum found the program positively impacted students' emotional understanding and interpersonal problem-solving skills (Curtis & Norgate, 2007; Greenberg & Kusché, 1996). A review by Leff, Power, Manz, Costigan, and Nabors (2001) found the PATHS program to be a "possibly efficacious" program, based in part upon findings of evaluations of the PATHS program used in conjunction with another program (Families and Schools Together - FAST). A recent controlled trial found significant improvement in all dimensions for the intervention group but not the control. Teacher interviews also indicated that they perceived the program to help children acquire better understanding of emotions, and to improve empathy and self-control skills (Curtis & Norgate, 2007). A self-published report of the evaluation of the PATHS program in Pennsylvania reported that the program has increased elementary students' ability to prevent and resolve conflicts and resulted in significant decreases in classroom behavior problems (Chilenski et al., 2007).

Materials

A kit for kindergarten through sixth grade costs between $400–800, depending on the age level. Each grade requires a separate kit, so the total for PreK-4th grade would be $1,950; a counselor kit is $1900 (grades 1-4) or $2,700 (Preschool - 4th grade). Materials are estimated at between $15-45 per student per year. The lower figure would apply to a school that chooses to deliver the program through current staff who are trained in

PATHS, and the higher cost would apply to a school that hires a PATHS coordinator to deliver the program.

PeaceBuilders: http://www. peacebuilders.com/

This is a universal, elementary-school-based violence prevention program that attempts to alter the climate of a school by teaching students and staff simple rules and activities aimed at improving a child's social competence and reducing aggressive behavior. PeaceBuilders activities are built into the school environment and the daily interactions among students, teachers, and administrative staff, all of whom are taught a common language and provided models of positive behavior, environmental cues to signal such behavior, opportunities to rehearse positive behavior, and rewards for practicing it (Embry et al., 1996). A study in eight schools with comparison sites found significant gains in teacher-reported social competence for students in kindergarten through second grades, in child self-reported "peace building" behavior in kindergarten through fifth grades, and reductions in aggressive behavior in grades three through five (Flannery et al., 2003). Another study found the program to be more effective with the highest risk children, who experienced the greatest gains in social skills and the greatest reductions in aggressive behavior following program implementation (Vazsonyi, Belliston, & Flannery, 2004).

Materials

Costs of materials are $8 per elementary student, and include student and teacher materials. There are also training expenses of $1,500 and up, depending on the type of training. This fee includes "train the trainer" training for up to four staff people. Training and materials packages can be tailored to the needs of a school or district. Materials are available through www. PeaceBuilders.com.

Peacemakers Project

This program, geared toward students in grades four through eight, has both primary prevention and secondary prevention components. The primary prevention component is delivered by teachers in classrooms and consists of a psychoeducational curriculum and procedures for infusing program content into the school environment. The secondary prevention component targets students who have preexisting disciplinary problems and is delivered by school counselors. A large-scale study with a comparison group in an urban public school system was conducted on this curriculum and was found to have significant, positive program effects on six of the seven variables assessed (Shapiro, Burgoon, Welker, & Clough, 2002). These positive effects included increased knowledge of psychosocial skills, decreased self-reported aggression, and teacher-reported aggression. In comparison to controls, a 41% decrease in aggression-related disciplinary incidents and a 67% reduction in suspensions for violent behavior were found in the intervention schools (Shapiro et al., 2002).

Materials

A variety of program materials are available through their PeaceBuilders website. Training for each site is required; PeaceBuilders send a trainer directly to the site and will train up to 40 staff at once. The 4 h "Essentials" training is required ($2,500) and a variety of other training modules are available, such as PeaceBuilders for parents ($1,250).

Resolving Conflict Creatively Program: http://esrnational.org/professional-services/elementary-school/prevention/resolving-conflict-creatively-program-rccp/

The Resolving Conflict Creatively Program (RCCP) includes a K-12 classroom curriculum and a student-led mediation program. As such, the program has both student-level and environment-level components. The RCCP focuses on teaching conflict resolution and intergroup relations through constructive problem solving, perspective taking, cost–benefit analysis, decision-making, and negotiation (DeJong, 1994). There are also training components for teachers, administrators, and parents (Lantieri, DeJong, & Dutrey, 1996). An evaluation of the RCCP in 11 elementary schools found preservation of competence-related processes and slower growth in aggression-related processes when compared with students taught few or no RCCP lessons (Aber, Jones, Brown, Chaudry, & Samples, 1998). A more recent study of over 11,000 students found RCCP has a positive impact on aggressive behaviors and related beliefs, and children with more RCCP lessons also did better in math (Aber, Brown, & Jones, 2003).

Materials

Trainings for implementation of RCCP are individualized and personalized, and costs are not listed online currently. With the training come all relevant materials and on-site classroom visits and coaching. Training includes a planning meeting, data collection, school needs assessment, 3-4 day introductory workshop, peer mediation training, administrator and school staff training, and parent training.

Responding in Peaceful and Positive Ways: http://www.preventionopportunities.com/

The Responding in Peaceful and Positive Ways (RIPP) program is a middle school (6th–86th grades) universal violence prevention program that combines the use of a student-level, social-cognitive, problem-solving model where specific skills for violence prevention are taught throughout the school year in the classroom. RIPP also employs a school-wide peer mediation program.

The program is grounded in social/cognitive learning theory and targets the influence of intrapersonal attributes, behaviors, and environmental factors, following Perry and Jessor's (1985) health promotion model to reduce risk factors associated with violence by promoting nonviolent alternatives. An evaluation of the curriculum in randomized classrooms found that RIPP participants had fewer disciplinary violations for violent offenses and in-school suspensions, more frequent use of peer mediation, and reductions in fight-related injuries than students in the control group. The reduction in suspensions was maintained at 12-month follow-up for boys but not for girls. The program's impact on violent behavior was more evident among those with high pretest levels of problem behavior (Farrell, Meyer, & White, 2001). An extension of the RIPP curriculum into seventh-grade classrooms found students who participated in RIPP-7 had fewer disciplinary code violations for violent offenses during the following school year (Farrell, Meyer, Sullivan, & Kung, 2003). RIPP is recommended on the SAMHSA National Registry of Evidence Based Programs.

Materials

The 3-day, on-site training (includes instructor manual) is $850 per person plus travel expenses. Instructor manuals are $350 per grade level, and student workbooks are $5 each.

Second Step: http://www.cfchildren.org/programs/ssp/overview/

The Second Step program, based on the work of Shure and Spivack (1978), attempts to improve children's social competence by developing student skills in the areas of perspective taking, social problem solving, impulse control, and anger management (Beland, 1992; Committee for Children, 1992). This is a school-wide program for kindergarten through eighth grade with several controlled research studies to show effectiveness in the elementary grades. The Second

Step curriculum was selected as a Model Program by the US Substance Abuse and Mental Health Services Administration (SAMHSA) for inclusion in their National Registry of Effective Prevention Programs. Preliminary research in urban and suburban areas indicated that after participation in Second Step, children's perspective taking and social problem-solving abilities improved significantly when compared with controls (Sylvester & Frey, 1997). This research, however, did not assess changes in children's behavior after the intervention. In another study, a large-scale, randomized controlled trial of the Second Step was conducted in six urban schools. The researchers found modest reductions in levels of observed aggressive behavior and increases in neutral and prosocial behavior, especially in the playground and cafeteria settings, among second and third graders (Grossman et al., 1997). Another evaluation of this program with rural third through sixth graders found significant improvements in independent behavioral observations of engaging appropriately with peers, and on teacher ratings of social competencies and antisocial behaviors at the intervention school when compared with students at a comparison site (Taub, 2002). Second Step was discussed as a promising "universal" school-based violence prevention program in a 2001 review of programs (Leff et al., 2001). Since that time, a variety of peer reviewed studies have shown Second Step to have positive effects in a variety of areas, such as decreasing aggressive behavior and improving impulse control (Edwards, Hunt, Meyers, Grogg, & Jarrett, 2005), increasing prosocial skills and empathy (Cooke, Ford, Levine, Bourke, Newell, & Lapidus, 2007; Edwards, et al., 2005; Frey, Nolen, Edstrom, & Hirschstein, 2005) and with a range of populations, including with low SES Middle school students (Holsen, Iversen, & Smith, 2009),

Second Step has good teacher buy in (Cooke, et al., 2007; Edwards et al., 2005), and is shown to be most effective when implemented schoolwide, with administrative support and endorsement (Larsen & Samdal, 2008).

Materials

Program kits, which can be obtained from the Committee for Children, cost roughly $1,500 for a kit for all of the elementary grades. Individual grade level kits can also be purchased. Training is needed to implement the program, which is available online. Currently the training is being offered for free, although there have been fees in the past.

Conclusions

There are many good programs available for universal implementation in schools to help children develop social and emotional competences, thereby increasing resiliency and reducing violent and socially inappropriate behavior in children. We suspect that one of the factors associated with the positive findings of the reviewed programs is the teaching of a shared language and skills for positive and healthy interpersonal interactions within entire school communities. A shared language allows all parties - students, teachers, and staff - to communicate positively and effectively, enhance social interactions, reduce interpersonal conflict, and foster resilience, and implementation effectiveness will also be determined by the support of school leadership.

As the review of programs exemplifies, schools also have a number of choices of programs that are affordable once the commitment to implementation and training is made. Many of these programs can very well be time-efficient and cost-effective in the long run as well, especially if they result in a reduction of teacher and staff time for responding to students' behavior and more time for classroom instruction, and if they lead to increased student time spent in the classroom instead of in the principal's office, in detention, or on suspension.

It is important to note that primary prevention programs are more effective when targeting younger children (Doll et al., 2011; Durlak & Wells, 1997; Hahn et al., 2007). Children in preschool through the early elementary grades are likely to benefit most from interventions that increase students' awareness and expression of feelings, as well as interventions that enhance cognitively based social problem-solving skills. Such interventions will most likely enhance resilience and decrease aggression and violence. Although there is not a great deal of longitudinal data available, we would also hope that comprehensive interventions in the early school years would help to establish a repertoire of healthy interpersonal interactions that will serve as a strong base for years to come.

Although there is a general need for more research in this area, there is also an incumbent need for further research of these prevention programs with children of various ethnically and linguistically diverse backgrounds. One of the authors has had the anecdotal experience of using the Second Step program (Committee for Children, 1992) in an elementary classroom where nearly half of the children were of Asian descent. The cultural norm of restricting the expression of affect (Sue & Sue, 1999) impacted the role play and modeling activities that are central to the program. These sorts of experiences highlight the need to identify the context and ecological variables in which prevention and intervention strategies are effective.

We also look forward to long-term longitudinal studies to help elucidate some of the lasting effects of universal, primary violence prevention programs delivered to school-age children. In order for these studies to be adequately conducted, federal and state agencies will need to support research and program evaluations with a commitment to examining long-term, rather than short-term, outcomes. This support will also require effective collaboration between the education, mental health, and public health domains to address the multiple aspects of development. It is hoped that these studies will include, but not be limited to, some of the following issues: Does participation in earlier grades impact disciplinary infractions in later grades? Does participation in such programs reduce later involvement in juvenile justice or mental health? Does delivery to younger children (preschool) have differential effects? Do teacher variables contribute to the implementation of these programs? We trust that our colleagues are and will investigate these and other questions related to the effects of school-wide violence prevention programs.

References

Aber, J. L., Brown, J. L., & Jones, S. M. (2003). Developmental trajectories toward violence in middle childhood: Course, demographic differences, and response to school-based intervention. *Developmental Psychology, 39*, 324–348.

Aber, L. J., Jones, S. M., Brown, J. L., Chaudry, N., & Samples, F. (1998). Resolving conflict creatively: Evaluating the developmental effects of a school-based violence prevention program in neighborhood and classroom context. *Development and Psychopathology, 10*, 187–213.

Barrish, H. H., Saunders, M., & Wold, M. M. (1969). Good behavior game: Effects of individual contingencies for group consequences on disruptive behavior in a classroom. *Journal of Applied Behavior Analysis, 2*, 119–124.

Bauer, N. S., Lozano, P., & Rivara, F. P. (2007). The effectiveness of the Olweus Bullying Prevention Program in public middle schools: A controlled trial. *Journal of Adolescent Health, 40*, 266–274.

Bostic, J. Q., & Brunt, C. (2011). Cornered: An approach to school bullying and cyberbullying, and forensic implications. *Child and Adolescent Psychiatric Clinics of N. America., 20*(3), 447–465.

Beland, K. (1992). *Second Step: A violence prevention curriculum for grades 1–5, Revised*. Seattle, WA: Committee for Children.

Black, S. A., & Jackson, E. (2007). Using bullying incident density to evaluate the Olweus Bullying Prevention Programme. *School Psychology International, 28*, 623–638.

Bosworth, K., Espelage, D., DuBay, T., Dahlberg, L. L., & Daytner, G. (1996). Using multimedia to teach conflict-resolution skills to young adolescents. *American Journal of Preventive Medicine, 12*(5), 65–74.

Bradshaw, C. P., Koth, C. W., Bevans, K. B., Ialongo, N. S., & Leaf, P. J. (2008). The impact of school-wide positive behavior interventions and supports (PBIS) on the organizational health of elementary schools. *School Psychology Quarterly, 23*, 462–473.

Bradshaw, C. P., Zmuda, J. H., Kellam, S. G., & Ialongo, N. S. (2009). Longitudinal impact of two universal preventive interventions in first grade on educational outcomes in high school. *Journal of Educational Psychology, 101*, 926–937.

Carr, E. G., Dunlap, G., Horner, R. H., Koegel, R. L., Turnbull, A. P., Sailor, W., et al. (2002). Positive behavior support: Evolution of an applied science. *Journal of Positive Behavior Interventions, 4*, 4–16.

Catalano, R. F., Berglund, M. L., Ryan, J. A. M., Lonczak, H. S., & Hawkins, J. D. (2002). Positive youth development in the United States: Research findings on evaluations of positive youth development programs. *Prevention and Treatment, 5*, Retrieved from Nov, 2011, http://journals.apa.org/prevention/volume5/pre0050015a.html.

Chilenski, S. M., Bumbarger, B. K., Kyler, S. & Greenberg, M. T. (2007). *Reducing youth violence and delinquency in Pennsylvania*: PCCDs Research-based Programs Initiative. Prevention Research Center for the Promotion of Human Development at the Pennsylvania State University. Retrieved from Nov, 2011 http://prevention.psu.edu/pubs/docs/PCCD_ReducingYouthViolence.pdf.

Coalition for Evidence Based Policy. (2011). *Social programs that work*. Top Tier Initiative Expert Panel. Retrieved from Nov, 2011 http://evidencebasedprograms.org/wordpress/?page_id=81.

Comer, J. P. (1980). *School power: Implications of an intervention project* (Understanding and preventing violence, Vol. 1). New York: Free Press.

Committee for Children. (1992). *Second step: A violence prevention curriculum*. Seattle, WA: Committee for Children.

Cooke, M. B., Ford, J., Levine, J., Bourke, C., Newell, L., & Lapidus, G. (2007). The effects of city-wide implementation of "Second Step" on elementary school students' prosocial and aggressive behaviors. *The Journal of Primary Prevention, 28*(2), 93–115.

Cowen, E. L. (1994). The enhancement of psychological wellness: Challenges and opportunities. *American Journal of Community Psychology, 22*, 149–179.

Cowen, E. L., Hightower, A. D., Pedro-Carroll, J. L., Work, W. C., Wyman, P. A., & Haffey, W. G. (1996). *School-based prevention for children at risk: The primary mental health project*. Washington, DC: American Psychological Association.

Curtis, C., & Norgate, R. (2007). An evaluation of the promoting alternative thinking strategies curriculum at key stage 1. *Educational Psychology in Practice, 23*, 33–44.

DeJong, W. (1994). *Building the peace: The resolving conflict creatively program*. Washington, DC: U.S. Department of Justice, National Institute of Justice.

Dodge, K. A., Pettit, G. S., McClaskey, C. L., & Brown, M. M. (1986). Social competence in children. *Monographs of the Society for Research in Child Development, 51*(Serial No. 213).

Doll, B., & Cummings, J. (2008). Why population-based services are essential for school mental health and how to make them happen in your school. In B. Doll & J. Cummings (Eds.), *Transforming school mental health services: Population-based approaches to promoting the competency and wellness of children* (pp. 1–20). Thousand Oaks, CA: Corwin Press in cooperation with the National Association of School Psychologists.

Doll, B., Jones, K., Osborn, A., Dooley, K., & Turner, A. (2011). The promise and caution of resilience models for schools. *Psychology in the Schools, 48*, 652–659.

Doll, B., & Lyon, M. (1998). Risk and resilience: Implications for the practice of school psychology. *School Psychology Review, 27*, 348–363.

Durlak, J. A., & Wells, A. M. (1997). Primary prevention mental health programs for children and adolescents: A meta-analytic review. *American Journal of Community Psychology, 25*, 115–152.

Edwards, D., Hunt, M. H., Meyers, J., Grogg, K. R., & Jarrett, O. (2005). Acceptability and student outcomes of a violence prevention curriculum. *The Journal of Primary Prevention, 26*, 401–418.

Embry, D. (2002). The Good Behavior Game: A best practice candidate as a universal behavioral vaccine. *Clinical Child and Family Psychology Review, 5*, 273–297.

Embry, D., Flannery, D. J., Vazsonyi, A. T., Powell, K. E., & Atha, H. (1996). PeaceBuilders: A theoretically driven, school-based model for early violence prevention. *American Journal of Preventive Medicine, 12*(5 Suppl.), 91–100.

Englander, E. (2011). *MARC report: Bullying in grades 3-12 in Massachusetts*. The Massachusetts Aggression Reduction Center at Bridgewater State University. Retrieved from Nov, 2011 http://webhost.bridgew.edu/marc/MARC%20REPORT-Bullying%20In%20Grades%203-12%20in%20MA.pdf.

Esquivel, G. B., Doll, B., & Oades-Sese, G. V. (2011). Introduction to the special issue: Resilience in schools. *Psychology in the Schools, 48*, 649–651.

Farrell, A. D., Meyer, A. L., Sullivan, T. N., & Kung, E. M. (2003). Evaluation of the responding in peaceful and positive ways (RIPP) seventh grade violence prevention curriculum. *Journal of Child and Family Studies, 12*, 101–120.

Farrell, A. D., Meyer, A. L., & White, K. (2001). Evaluation of responding in peaceful and positive ways (RIPP): A school-based prevention program for reducing violence among urban adolescents. *Journal of Clinical Child Psychology, 30*, 451–463.

Farrington, D. P. (2002). The effectiveness of school-based violence prevention programs. *Archives of Pediatric and Adolescent Medicine, 156*, 748–749.

Fekkes, M., Pijpers, F. I., & Verloove-Vanhorick, S. P. (2004). Bullying behavior and associations with psychosomatic complaints and depression in victims. *Journal of Pediatrics, 144*(1), 17–22.

Flannery, D. J., Vazsonyi, A. T., Liau, A. K., Guo, S., Powell, K. E., Atha, H., et al. (2003). Initial behavior outcomes for the PeaceBuilders universal school-based violence prevention program. *Developmental Psychology, 39*, 292–308.

Flannery, D. J., & Williams, L. (1999). Effective youth violence prevention. In T. P. Gullotta & S. J. McElhaney (Eds.), *Violence in homes and communities: Prevention, intervention, and treatment* (pp. 207–244). Thousand Oaks, CA: Sage.

Frey, K. S., Nolen, S. B., Edstrom, L. V., & Hirschstein, M. K. (2005). Effects of a school-based social-emotional competence program: Linking children's goals, attributions, and behavior. *Journal of Applied Developmental Psychology, 26*, 171–200.

Goldston, S. E. (1985). Primary prevention: Historical perspectives and a blueprint for action. *American Psychologist, 41*, 453–460.

Greenberg, M. T., & Kusché, C. (1996). *A*. The PATHS Project: A preventive intervention for children. Final report to the National Institute for Health.

Greenberg, M. T., Kusché, C., & Mihalic, S. F. (1998). *Blueprints for violence prevention, Book Ten: Promoting Alternative Thinking Strategies (PATHS).* Boulder, CO: Center for the Study and Prevention of Violence.

Greenberg, M. T., Weissberg, R. P., O'Brien, M. U., Zins, J. E., Fredericks, L., Resnik, H., et al. (2003). Enhancing school-based prevention and youth development through coordinated social, emotional and academic learning. *American Psychologist, 58*, 466–474.

Grossman, D. C., Neckerman, H. J., Koepsell, T. D., Liu, P. Y., Asher, K. N., Beland, K., et al. (1997). Effectiveness of a violence prevention program among children in elementary school: A randomized controlled trial. *Journal of the American Medical Association, 277*, 1605–1611.

Hahn, R., Fuqua-Whitley, D., Wethington, H., Lowy, J., Crosby, A., Fullilove, M., et al. (2007). Effectiveness of universal school-based programs to prevent violent and aggressive behavior: A systematic review. *American Journal of Preventive Medicine, 33*(2 Suppl.), S114–S129.

Harris, V. W., & Sherman, J. A. (1973). Use and analysis of the "good behavior game" to reduce disruptive class-room behavior. *Journal of Applied Behavior Analysis, 6*, 405–417.

Hausman, A., Pierce, G., & Briggs, L. (1996). Evaluation of comprehensive violence prevention education: Effects on student behavior. *Journal of Adolescent Health, 19*, 104–110.

Hawkins, J. D., Catalano, R. F., & Miller, J. Y. (1992). Risk and protective factors for alcohol and other drug problems. *Psychological Bulletin, 112*, 64–105.

Henderson, N., & Milstein, M. M. (1996). *Resiliency in school: Making it happen for students and educators.* Thousand Oaks, CA: Corwin.

Hoagwood, K., & Erwin, H. D. (1997). Effectiveness of school-based mental health services for children: A 10-year research review. *Journal of Child and Family Studies, 6*, 435–451.

Holsen, I., Iversen, A. C., & Smith, B. (2009). Universal social competence programme in school: Does it work for children with low socio-economic background? *Advances in School Mental Health Promotion, 2*(2), 51–60.

Hudley, C., & Graham, S. (1993). An attributional intervention to reduce peer-directed aggression among African-American boys. *Child Development, 64*, 124–138.

Huizinga, D., Loeber, R., & Thornberry, T. P. (1995). *Urban delinquency and substance abuse. Research Summary.* Rockville, MD: Juvenile Justice Clearinghouse.

Johnson, D., & Johnson, T. (1995). Why violence prevention programs don't work—and what does. *Educational Leadership, 52*, 63–68.

Johnson, J. P., Schwartz, R. A., Livingston, M., & Slate, J. R. (2000). What makes a good elementary school? A critical examination. *The Journal of Educational Research, 93*, 339–348.

Kleinman, K. E., & Saigh, P. A. (2011). The effects of the Good Behavior Game on the conduct of regular education New York City high school students. *Behavior Modification, 35*, 95–105.

Krug, E. G., Dahlberg, L. L., Brener, N. D., Ryan, G. W., & Powell, K. E. (1997). The impact of an elementary school-based violence prevention program on visits to the school nurse. *American Journal of Preventive Medicine, 13*, 459–463.

Lannie, A. L., & McCurdy, B. L. (2007). Preventing disruptive behavior in the urban classroom: Effects of the Good Behavior Game on student and teacher behavior. *Education and Treatment of Children, 1*, 85–98.

Lantieri, L., DeJong, W., & Dutrey, J. (1996). Waging peace in our schools: The resolving conflict creatively program. In A. M. Hoffman (Ed.), *Schools, violence, and society* (pp. 241–251). Westport, CT: Praeger.

Larsen, T., & Samdal, O. (2008). Facilitating the implementation and sustainability of Second Step. *Scandinavian Journal of Educational Research, 52*, 187–204.

Leff, S. S., Power, T. J., Manz, P. H., Costigan, T. E., & Nabors, L. A. (2001). School-based aggression prevention programs for young children: Current status and implications for violence prevention. *School Psychology Review, 30*, 344–362.

Macklem, G. (2011). *Evidence-based school mental health services: Affect education, emotion regulation training, and cognitive behavioral therapy.* New York: Springer.

Masten, A. S., Best, K., & Garmezy, N. (1990). Resilience and development: Contribution from the study of children who overcome adversity. *Development and Psychopathology, 2*, 425–444.

McCurdy, B. L., Lannie, A. L., & Barnabas, E. (2009). Reducing disruptive behavior in an urban school cafeteria: An extension of the Good Behavior Game. *Journal of School Psychology, 47*, 39–54.

Naglieri, J. A., LeBuffe, P., & Shapiro, V. B. (2011). Universal screening for social-emotional competencies: A study of the reliability and validity of the Dessa-Mini. *Psychology in the Schools, 48*, 660–671.

Nickerson, A. B., Mele, D., & Princiotta, D. (2008). Attachment and empathy as predictors of roles as defenders or outsiders in bullying interactions. *Journal of School Psychology, 46*(6), 687–703.

Olweus, D. (1997). Bully/victim problems in school: Knowledge base and an effective intervention program. *Irish Journal of Psychology, 18*, 170–190.

Olweus, D., & Limber, S. (2010). Bullying in school: Evaluation and dissemination of the Olweus Bullying Prevention Program. *The American Journal of Orthopsychiatry, 80*(1), 124–134.

Olweus, D., Limber, S., & Mihalic, S. F. (1999). *Blueprints for violence prevention, Book Nine: Bullying Prevention Program*. Boulder, CO: Center for the Study and Prevention of Violence.

Overstreet, S., & Mathews, T. (2011). Challenges associated with exposure to chronic trauma: Using a public health framework to foster resilient outcomes among youth. *Psychology in the Schools, 48*, 738–754.

Park-Higgerson, H., Perumean-Chaney, S. E., Bartolucci, A. A., Grimley, D. M., & Singh, K. P. (2008). An evaluation of school-based violence prevention programs: A meta-analysis. *Journal of School Health, 78*, 465–479.

Payton, J., Weissberg, R. P., Durlak, J. A., Dymnicki, A. B., Taylor, R. D., Schellinger, K. B., & Pachan, M. (2008). *The positive impact of social and emotional learning for kindergarten to eighth-grade students: Findings from three scientific reviews*. Chicago: Collaborative for Academic, Social, and Emotional Learning.

Pepler, C. L. (2006). Bullying interventions: A binocular perspective. *Journal of the Canadian Academy of Child and Adolescent Psychiatry, 15*, 16–20.

Perry, C. L., & Jessor, R. (1985). The concept of health promotion and the prevention of adolescent drug abuse. *Health Education Quarterly, 12*, 169–184.

Petersen, G. J., Pietrzak, D., & Speaker, K. M. (1998). The enemy within: A national study on school violence and prevention. *Urban Education, 33*, 331–359.

Power, T. J., Mautone, J. A., & Ginsburg-Block, M. (2010). Training school psychologists for prevention and intervention in a three-tiered model. In M. R. Shinn & H. M. Walker (Eds.), *Interventions for achievement and behavior problems in a three-tiered model including RTI* (pp. 151–173). Bethesda, MD: NASP.

President's New Freedom Commission on Mental Health. (2003). Remarks by President Bush in announcing the New Freedom Commission on Mental Health. Retrieved on June 1, 2008 Retrieved from Nov, 2011 http://govinfo.library.unt.edu/mentalhealthcommission/address.html.

Ransford, C. R., Greenberg, M. T., Domitrovich, C. E., Small, M., & Jackson, L. (2009). The role of teachers' psychological experiences and perceptions of curriculum supports on the implementation of a social and emotional learning curriculum. *School Psychology Review, 38*, 510–532.

Reiss, D., & Price, R. H. (1996). National research agenda for prevention research: The National Institute of Mental Health Report. *American Psychologist, 51*, 1109–1115.

Reiss, A. J., & Roth, J. A. (Eds.). (1993). *Understanding and preventing violence* (Vol. 1). Washington, DC: National Academy of Science.

Rutter, M. (1985). Resilience in the face of adversity: Protective factors and resistance to psychiatric disorders. *The British Journal of Psychiatry, 147*, 598–611.

Shapiro, J. P., Burgoon, J. D., Welker, C. J., & Clough, J. B. (2002). Evaluation of the Peacemakers program: School-based violence prevention for students in grades four through eight. *Psychology in the Schools, 39*, 87–100.

Shure, M. B., & Spivack, G. (1978). *Problem-solving techniques in child rearing*. San Francisco: Jossey-Bass.

Smith, P. K., Mahdavi, J., & Carvalho, M. (2008). Cyberbullying: Its nature and impact in secondary school pupils. *Journal of Child and Adolescent Psychiatry, 49*(4), 376–385.

Snell, P. A., & Englander, E. (2010). Cyberbullying victimization and behaviors among girls: Applying research findings in the field. *Journal of Social Sciences, 6*(4), 510–514.

Society for Prevention Research. (2004). *Standards of evidence: Criteria for efficacy, effectiveness and dissemination*. Retrieved from Nov, 2011 http://www.preventionscience.org/StandardsofEvidencebook.pdf.

Stoiber, K. C., & Gettinger, M. (2011). Functional assessment and positive support strategies for promoting resilience: Effects on teachers and high-risk children. *Psychology in the Schools, 48*, 686–706.

Storr, C. L., Ialongo, N. S., Kellam, S. G., & Anthony, J. C. (2002). A randomized controlled trial of two primary school intervention strategies to prevent early onset tobacco smoking. *Drug and Alcohol Dependence, 66*, 51–60.

Sue, D. W., & Sue, D. (1999). *Counseling the culturally different: Theory and practice* (2nd ed.). New York: Wiley.

Sugai, G., & Horner, R. (2006). A promising approach for expanding and sustaining school-wide positive behavior support. *School Psychology Review, 35*, 245–259.

Sylvester, L., & Frey, K. (1997). *Summary of "Second Step" program evaluations (all grade levels)*. Seattle, WA: Committee for Children.

Tani, F., Greenman, P. S., & Schneider, B. H. (2003). Bullying and the big five. *School Psychology International, 24*, 131–146.

Taub, J. (2002). Evaluation of the "Second Step" violence prevention program in a rural elementary school. *School Psychology Review, 31*, 186–200.

Twemlow, S. W., Fonagy, P., & Sacco, F. C. (2006). Teachers who bully students: A hidden trauma. *International Journal of Social Psychiatry, 52*, 187–198.

Twemlow, S. W., Fonagy, P., & Sacco, F. C. (2004). The role of the bystander in the social architecture of bullying and violence in schools and communities. *Annals of NY Academy of Sciences, 1036*, 215–232.

Twemlow, S. W., Fonagy, P., Sacco, F. C., Gies, M. L., Evans, R., & Ewbank, R. (2001). Creating a peaceful school learning environment: A controlled study of an elementary school intervention to reduce violence. *The American Journal of Psychiatry, 158*, 808–810.

U.S. Census Bureau, Department of Commerce. (2011). *State government finances summary: 2009*. Retrieved from Nov, 2011 http://www2.census.gov/govs/state/09statesummaryreport.pdf.

U.S. Department of Education, Institute of Education Sciences. (2007). *Number and percentage of children ages 3 to 5 and ages 6 to 21 served under the Individuals with Disabilities Education Act (IDEA), by race/ethnicity and type of disability.* Retrieved from Nov, 2011 http:// nces.ed.gov/pubs2010/2010015/tables/table_8_1b.asp.

Vazsonyi, A. T., Belliston, B. M., & Flannery, D. J. (2004). Evaluation of a school-based, universal violence prevention program: Low-, Medium-, and High-Risk Children. *Youth Violence and Juvenile Justice, 2*(2), 185–206.

Weissberg, R. P., Caplan, M., & Harwood, R. L. (1991). Promoting competent young people in competence-enhancing environments: A systems-based perspective on primary prevention. *Journal of Consulting and Clinical Psychology, 59,* 830–841.

Weissberg, R. P., Caplan, M. Z., & Sivo, P. J. (1989). A new conceptual framework for establishing school-based social competence promotion programs. In L. A. Bond & B. E. Compas (Eds.), *Primary prevention and promotion in the schools* (Primary prevention of psychopathology, Vol. 12, pp. 255–296). Beverly Hills, CA: Sage.

Werner, E. E. (1989). High-risk children in young adulthood: A longitudinal study from birth to 32 years. *The American Journal of Orthopsychiatry, 59,* 72–81.

Werthamer, L., Cooper, J. E. & Lombardi, J. (1993). *Classroom prevention program manual.* The Baltimore City Public Schools and The Johns Hopkins Prevention Center. Retrieved from Nov, 2011 http://toptierevidence.org/wordpress/wp-content/uploads/Classroom-Prevention-Program-Manual-Werthamer-1993.pdf.

Wilson, D. B., Gottfredson, D. C., & Najaka, S. S. (2001). School-based prevention of problem behaviors: A meta-analysis. *Journal of Quantitative Criminology, 17,* 247–272.

Yoon, J. (2004). Predicting teacher interventions in bullying situations. *Education and Treatment of Children, 27,* 37–45.

Yoon, J., & Kerber, K. (2003). Bullying: Elementary teachers' attitudes and intervention strategies. *Research in Education, 69,* 27–35.

Caring for the Caregiver: Promoting the Resilience of Teachers

22

Jennifer L. Fleming, Mary Mackrain,
and Paul A. LeBuffe

Social and emotional competence is a critical factor in children's development and school readiness. According to the New Freedom Commission on Mental Health (2003), one in every five children has social and emotional or mental health concerns. An estimated two-thirds of all young people with concerns are not getting the help they need (Mental Health America, 2011). These concerns, if left unaddressed, predict school failure and more serious mental health problems such as depression, anxiety, and conduct disorders which are expensive and difficult to treat (Raver & Knitzer, 2002). Social and emotional competence has been defined as "the ability of children to successfully interact with other children and adults in a way that demonstrates an awareness of, and ability to manage, emotions in an age- and context-appropriate manner" (LeBuffe, Shapiro, & Naglieri, 2009, p. 5).

These social and emotional competencies are critical skills that often serve as protective factors, buffering children from the negative effects of risk and adversity and thereby supporting their resilience (Masten & Garmezy, 1985). Children who experience chronic adversity fare better or recover more successfully when they have a positive relationship with competent adults or prosocial peers, they are good learners and problem-solvers, they are engaging to other people,

and they have areas of competence and perceived efficacy valued by self or society (Masten, Best, & Garmezy, 1990). For example, LeBuffe et al. (2009) reported that children with higher social and emotional competence as measured by the Devereux Student Strengths Assessment (DESSA) had fewer and less severe behavioral problems than children with lower social and emotional competence. This result was found for both high-risk and low-risk children suggesting that social and emotional competence had a main effect in decreasing the negative impact of risk and thereby promoting resilience. The importance of promoting social and emotional competence in children is being increasingly recognized in research, practice, and policy (Durlak, Weissberg, Dymnicki, Taylor, & Shellinger, 2011; Payton et al., 2008). Durlak et al. (2011) conducted a meta-analysis of 213 school-based studies involving more than 270,000 students that investigated the outcomes of universal social and emotional learning (SEL) programs. They found that students in well-implemented SEL programs showed positive outcomes compared to students in control groups in a wide range of domains. The SEL programs resulted in increased social and emotional skills; improved attitudes toward self, school, and others; decreased behavioral concerns; and, importantly, an average 11 percentile point gain in tests of academic achievement.

In regards to practice, the promotion of social and emotional well-being and resilience is becoming a required area of competence for some child-serving professions. For example, the

J.L. Fleming (✉) • M. Mackrain • P.A. LeBuffe
Devereux Center for Resilient Children,
Villanova, PA, USA
e-mail: jflemin2@Devereux.org

S. Goldstein and R.B. Brooks (eds.), *Handbook of Resilience in Children*,
DOI 10.1007/978-1-4614-3661-4_22, © Springer Science+Business Media New York 2013

Model for Comprehensive and Integrated School Psychological Services of the National Association of School Psychologists (NASP, 2010) defines the core competencies of contemporary school psychologists to include the provision of "effective services to help children and youth succeed academically, socially, behaviorally and emotionally" (p. 1). School psychologists are expected to "have knowledge of … evidence-based strategies to promote social-emotional functioning and mental health" (p. 2) as well as "promote the development and maintenance of learning environments that support resilience…" (p. 6). Similarly, in the early care and education field, the National Association for the Education of Young Children (NAEYC) recommends the use of *developmentally appropriate practice*, which includes a strong emphasis on a teacher nurturing a child's social and emotional development by basing all practices and decisions on (1) theories of child development, (2) individually identified strengths and needs of each child uncovered through authentic assessment, and (3) the child's cultural background as defined by his community, family history, and family structure (Bredekamp & Copple, 1997). These practice standards reflect the recognition of the importance of SEL by leading professional organizations concerned with the well-being of children.

With respect to policy, as of the summer of 2011, eight states had adopted or were drafting explicit K-12 educational standards in the social and emotional domain. The remaining 42 states as well as 6 United States Territories had included some SEL goals or benchmarks in their educational standards (Collaborative for Academic, Social, and Emotional Learning (CASEL), 2011). Similarly, all states had preschool educational standards related to SEL, with 48 of these states having comprehensive, free standing standards for SEL. In addition, the Academic, Social and Emotional Learning Act of 2011 was introduced to the 112th Congress. This proposed legislation is still under consideration as this chapter is being written, but if passed, will support the implementation of SEL programs in the schools, particularly through providing funds through the Elementary and Secondary Education Act (ESEA) to support training in SEL programs for principals and teachers.

As the evidence for the critical importance of social and emotional competence in promoting resilience and success in school and life continues to accrue, and as more state and local educational agencies adopt SEL standards, teachers are increasingly expected to teach and promote these skills in the classroom. For many teachers, this is yet one more mandate to add to their growing list of responsibilities. Paradoxically then, the expectation that teachers promote the resilience of their students may be a source of stress for the teachers themselves and jeopardize their own resilience. It is our contention that the effectiveness of the teacher in promoting the social and emotional competence and resilience of students is directly influenced by the social and emotional well-being and resilience of the teacher him or herself. Therefore, if we desire to promote the resilience of the students, we should also commit to supporting the resilience of the teachers. This chapter will explore three facets of this issue. First, we will present some of the common stressors affecting teachers. Second, we will discuss how these stressors, mediated through the teachers, negatively influence children. Last, we will present some promising approaches for promoting the resilience of all adults, with an emphasis on teachers.

Common and Unique Stressors Experienced by Teachers

According to the American Psychological Association, the United States is an "overstressed nation" (American Psychological Association (APA), 2010, p. 5). In this survey of over 1,000 adults, one-third (32%) of parents report that their stress levels are extreme and parents overall say that they are living with stress levels that exceed their definition of healthy. Adults experience multiple sources of stress including money (76%), work (70%), family responsibilities (58%), and relationships (55%). Some sources of stress, especially the economy and work stability have been exacerbated by the current recession.

Teachers experience these and many other sources of stress as well. Since the passage of the No Child Left Behind (NCLB) Act in 2002, teachers have been under considerable pressure to ensure that all children demonstrate proficiency in reading and mathematics by 2014. In addition to the demands of NCLB, many teachers are also adversely affected by administrative demands such as excessive paperwork and severe time constraints (Kyriacou, 2001; Lambert, McCarthy, O'Donnell, & Wang, 2009). As noted by McCarthy and Lambert (2006), working conditions have also deteriorated for many teachers with more children displaying problem behaviors, lacking motivation, or coming to school sleep-deprived. Furthermore, teachers are coping with an increasing number of demanding or unsupportive parents. The pressure due to school reform efforts, inadequate administrative support, poor working conditions, lack of participation in school decision making, the burden of paperwork, and lack of resources have all been identified as common factors that can cause stress among school staff (Hammond & Onikama, 1997).

Effects of Stressors on Teachers

Given the multiple stressors present for teachers it is no surprise that their health and well-being is often compromised. Although stress that is infrequent can impact the physical and emotional health of teachers, it is the influence of chronic stress that is more alarming. Across occupations, chronic exposure to a variety of stressors such as high job demands and workload, lack of personal control, insufficient rewards, quality of interactions in the workplace, perceived fairness in work decisions, and values related to the job can lead to the development of burnout over time when coping resources are inadequate (Maslach & Leiter, 2005, 2008; Maslach, Schaufeli, & Leiter, 2011). The phenomenon of burnout has been well-documented in the education field and has

been linked with experiencing job stressors such as high work demands and low personal control (Betoret, 2009; Santavirta, Solovieva, & Theorell, 2007). In fact, Lambert et al. (2009) asserted that there are more studies of burnout in teachers than any other professional group.

Burnout is defined as a psychological response comprised of emotional exhaustion, depersonalization, and reduced personal accomplishment (Maslach & Jackson, 1981). The most central aspect of burnout, emotional exhaustion, is characterized by a feeling of being emotionally overextended and drained of mental resources. It includes feelings of fatigue, loss of energy, and being worn out. Depersonalization is defined as a negative or cynical attitude towards aspects of the job, including the people one works with, such as students, parents, or colleagues. The third component of burnout involves reduced personal accomplishment at work, such as feelings of incompetence, low morale, or reduced meaning or fulfillment with the job. Within the education field, teachers report considerable burnout (Bauer et al., 2006; Kyriacou, 2001; Schonfeld, 1990), which has been characterized by indicators such as job dissatisfaction, changes in attitudes about teaching, and impaired job performance (Guglielmi & Tatrow, 1998; Montgomery & Rupp, 2005; Santavirta et al., 2007; Tennant, 2001).

Furthermore, research suggests that chronic stress and burnout are linked to poor physical health in teachers, such as an increased risk of headaches, gastrointestinal problems, cold and flu episodes, sleep disturbances, muscle tension, and hypertension (Melamed, Shirom, Toker, Berliner, & Shapira, 2006; for a review; see Leiter & Maslach, 2000) in addition to mental health problems such as depressed mood, reductions in self-esteem and self-efficacy, decreased motivation, and job dissatisfaction (Burke, Greenglass, & Schwarzer, 1996; Jurado, Gurpegui, Moreno, & de Dios, 1998; Montgomery & Rupp, 2005; Santavirta et al., 2007; Schonfeld, 2001; Tennant, 2001). These physical and mental health problems can impact teachers' personal and professional lives and result in increased teacher absences and turnover.

The problem of teacher turnover has received increasing attention in recent years. Although reports have varied on the incidence of turnover in public schools, it appears that teachers are leaving the profession at an increasing rate (Provasnik & Dorfman, 2005). Current estimates by the National Center for Education Statistics (Keigher, 2010) suggest that about 15.6% of public school teachers were in transition during the school years of 2007–2008 to 2008–2009. Of these teachers, approximately 8.0% left teaching employment (attrition) and 7.6% moved to a different school (migration). Even more troubling are the rates for early childhood teachers. Estimates suggest that the annual job turnover rate for child care providers is estimated to be between 25% and 40% (Center for the Child Care Workforce, 2004). This combined turnover is associated with substantial financial costs. One estimate by the Alliance for Excellent Education (2005) used public teacher turnover cost estimates from the U.S. Department of Labor to compute an annual cost of about $4.9 billion to schools.

How Stress Impacts Adult Ability to Care for and Teach Children

Of equal concern to the effects of stressors on the teachers' well-being are the effects of teacher stress on students. The negative impacts of teacher stress on students are many; in this chapter we will focus on only three: (1) reduced teacher availability and the impact on attachment and relationships with children, (2) impairments in ability of teachers to model social and emotional competence, and (3) direct negative effects on children.

Reduced Teacher Availability. Teachers experiencing high levels of stress are less available to students both physically and emotionally. In addition to the higher rates of transition described above, highly stressed teachers also have impaired job performance, lower productivity, and increased absenteeism (Leithwood, Menzies, Jantzi, & Leithwood, 1999; Tennant, 2001). As a result of the physical sequelae of stress noted above and the decreased morale associated with burnout,

teachers experiencing high levels of stress are not physically present in the classroom as much as teachers with lower levels of stress. High rates of teacher turnover and absenteeism can disrupt the formation of relationships between teacher and students and can negatively impact on the quality of care provided to children (Helburn, 1995; Howes & Hamilton, 1993).

Even when physically present in the classroom, highly stressed teachers who are experiencing burnout may be less emotionally available to their students; believe they no longer contribute to student learning and growth; and show lower quality interactions with students (Belsky et al., 2007; Hamre & Pianta, 2004; Helburn, 1995). In their study of over 500 teachers, Lambert et al. (2009) reported that high-stress teachers had a tendency to both depersonalize and distance themselves from their students, seeing "the children as objects rather than developing individuals" (p. 986). The impact of these outcomes influences both the teacher's ability to form healthy relationships with children and the ability to effectively manage the classroom, both of which contribute to the overall classroom climate and may negatively influence children's social, emotional, behavioral, and academic outcomes (Jennings & Greenberg, 2009). In addition, distressed teachers are less able to handle misbehavior or provide guidance to their students (Biglan, 2008).

For young children especially, the ability to form close relationships and attachment to teachers or caregivers is critical for healthy development. Early developing attachment may be distorted by parental or caregiver unresolved losses, traumatic events, or chronic stressors (Shirilla & Weatherston, 2002). When adults are stressed and unsupported it can negatively impact their ability to provide the level of quality caregiving that infants and children need to prepare them for school and life success. Research is clear that an adult's neglect of a child's physical or emotional needs, use of harsh or inconsistent punishment, little expressive speech, and frequent changes in routines, which are all behaviors related to experiencing high levels of stress, lead to developmental risk. When adults provide clear, consistent expectations, positive emotional expression, stability, and responsive caregiving it promotes a child's potential (Rintoul et al., 1998) and lays the emotional foundation that enables readiness for learning (Norman-Murch, 1996). Children grow and thrive in the context of close and dependable relationships that provide love and nurturance, security, responsive interaction, and encouragement for exploration. According to Werner and Smith (1992), common factors among resilient children include having a close bond with at least one person that provided stable care, mothers' modeling of competence, and positive relationships with extended family members and caregivers when parental ties were not available. When the teacher or caregiver is unavailable to the young child as a result of chronic stress, these relationships can be disrupted and the consequences can be severe and long-lasting (Shonkoff & Phillips, 2000).

Impairments in the Ability of Teachers to Model Social and Emotional Competence. According to Bandura (1977), individuals, including children, are able to learn through the observation and imitation of others, a phenomenon described as social learning. Within this theory, children perceive adults' behavior and may later imitate that behavior. This theory has been applied to help explain the development of prosocial behavior in children. For example, parental modeling of empathy and concern for others influences children's prosocial behaviors (Eisenberg, Fabes, Schaller, Carlo, & Miller, 1991; Fabes, Eisenberg, & Miller, 1990) and parents' ability to manage emotions influences the way children experience and express their own emotions (Eisenberg, Fabes, Carlo, & Karbon, 1992; Roberts & Strayer, 1987).

Teachers too, influence the social and emotional development of children. A multitude of social-emotional learning curricula exist to promote these skills in children.[1] These programs typically emphasize both direct instruction and continual modeling of the skills by teachers in the classroom. This modeling provides children with the opportunities to apply concepts to their daily lives, for example by observing a teacher appropriately manage a frustrating event or problem-solving through a peer conflict. Numerous studies have demonstrated the effectiveness of social-emotional learning programs for students (Durlak et al., 2011; Greenberg et al., 2003) and suggest that teacher willingness and ability to generalize social-emotional skills by modeling during interactions with students throughout the day impacts student behavior (Conduct Problems Prevention Research Group, 1999).

However, teachers who are already overwhelmed by the demands of teaching may find it difficult to model appropriate social-emotional behaviors for children. Teachers are constantly exposed to emotionally challenging situations, and if they are already experiencing high levels of stress, they may not have the capacity to effectively manage those emotions in the presence of children. Similarly, it may be difficult to model an appropriate conflict-resolution approach for students if teacher emotions, such as frustration, are already at a high level. When this occurs, students miss out on critical opportunities to apply learned skills to their everyday lives, and may instead imitate inappropriate or ineffective behaviors. This may ultimately impact their ability to internalize these skills and may contribute to later emotional or behavioral concerns.

Direct Negative Effects on Children. In addition to social learning outcomes, stress-related negative behaviors evidenced by teachers most likely engenders negative emotions and behaviors in students. For example, research has suggested that teachers low on self-efficacy (which is associated with high stress and burnout) demonstrate less effective teaching practices, impacting student achievement, motivation, and self-efficacy (Skaalvik & Skaalvik, 2007; Tschannen-Moran & Woolfolk Hoy, 2001). Additionally, teacher reports of stress have been linked to student apathy (Jenkins & Calhoun, 1991) and student misbehavior in the classroom (Yoon, 2002).

---

[1] For a list of evidence-based K-12 social and emotional learning programs, see the Collaborative for Academic, Social, and Emotional Learning (CASEL; http://casel.org/publications/safe-and-sound-an-educational-leaders-guide-to-evidence-based-sel-programs/). For a list of evidence-based early childhood social and emotional programs, see the Technical Assistance Center on Social Emotional Intervention (http://www.challengingbehavior.org/do/resources/documents/roadmap_2.pdf).

The negative effects of parental stress on children are well documented. According to the 2010 Stress in America Study (APA, 2010) 69% of parents believe that their stress has little or no impact on their children, although this apparently is not the case. The overwhelming majority of children (91%) reported that they were aware of their parents' stress. Perceived parental stress resulted in youth ages 8–17 reporting feeling sad (39%), worried (39%), frustrated (31%), and helpless (21%). Children who reported that their parents experienced high levels of stress were eight times more likely to report being stressed themselves as compared to children of low stress parents (17% vs. 2%). Although these data pertain to parents and children, it is reasonable to suggest that a similar effect would be found with students reacting to perceived teacher stress.

Programs Promoting Adult Resilience

A multitude of adult resilience programs specific to workplace employees exist throughout the US and internationally, many of which are designed and offered at the company level and provide limited evidence of effectiveness. There are, however, programs applicable to a variety of workplace sites that offer promising results, including, but not limited to, the Promoting Adult Resilience (PAR) Program (Liossis, Shochet, Millear, & Biggs, 2009; Millear, Liossis, Shochet, & Biggs, 2008); the READY program (Resilience and Activity for Every Day; Burton, Pakenham, & Brown, 2010); and the Personal Resilience and Resilient Relationships (PRRR) worksite training program (Waite & Richardson, 2004).

Given the negative impact of stress on teachers' health, job satisfaction, and career longevity, as well as on student attachment and relationships, social and emotional competence, and self-perceived stress, it is understandable that attention is being given to fostering the well-being and resilience of teachers. Several recent studies have examined characteristics of teachers who have managed to thrive in the education profession despite facing a variety of stressors, such as working in disadvantaged or high-need

areas. The protective factors which emerged include a strong personal satisfaction from their work (Brunetti, 2006; Castro, Kelly, & Shih, 2010; Howard & Johnson, 2004; Stanford, 2001; Williams, 2003); strong social support from family, friends, colleagues, and school leadership (Brunetti, 2006; Howard & Johnson, 2004; Stanford, 2001); and a strong belief in the ability to control what happens to them, such as the ability to depersonalize unpleasant events, learning from the events and then moving on, and seeking to understand others' motivation and circumstances (Howard & Johnson, 2004).

In addition, recent studies have highlighted some of the skills resilient teachers working in high-need areas possess. These include asking for help, advice, or resources when needed; utilizing effective problem-solving approaches; the ability to manage relationships with colleagues and parents effectively; and seeking ways to rejuvenate and finding ways to balance life and work (Castro et al., 2010; Patterson, Collins, & Abbott, 2004).

A number of programs exist that target and promote many of these attributes in teachers. One such program is the Inner Resilience Program (IRP; Simon, Harnett, Nagler, & Thomas, 2009), designed following September 11, 2001 to enhance the well-being and resilience of teachers living in lower Manhattan. Following a pilot study, the program was expanded to include educators from public schools across New York City. Teachers participated in a variety of activities designed to reduce stress and burnout; increase attention, concentration, and job satisfaction; and improve relationships with colleagues. Activities included yoga classes, a series of monthly group classes, a weekend retreat, and curriculum training for a classroom component. Following the program, teachers reported reduced stress levels, increased mindfulness and attention levels, and improved relationships with colleagues.

The Emotional Intelligent Teacher (EIT; Brackett & Caruso, 2006) program, one component of a larger school-based SEL initiative, provides explicit training to teachers on fundamental skills drawn from emotional intelligence theory (Mayer & Salovey, 1997), a theory complementary to resilience. In this one-day workshop, teachers learn information about emotion-related skills (i.e., identifying, understanding, and managing of emotions) and how these emotion-related skills can be applied to classroom situations experienced by teachers (Brackett & Katulak, 2006).

The programs described in this section address a critical need and have demonstrated positive outcomes, but have some limitations as well. These are organized group interventions that require an organizational sponsor such as an employer. If one does not work at an organization that is committed to supporting the resilience of staff through programs such as these, access is very limited. Furthermore, many schools are facing difficult funding situations that may make these programs difficult to implement at this time. Additionally, employees in a group session with their coworkers may feel some reluctance to self-disclose the sources of stress in their lives or the success of prior attempts at coping.

The Devereux Approach to Fostering Adult Resilience

The Devereux Center for Resilient Children, recognizing the critical need for supporting the resilience of the adult as a requisite for enhancing the social and emotional competence and resilience of children, developed *The Devereux Adult Resilience Survey* (DARS; Mackrain, 2007). This self-reflective instrument is designed to help adults, including teachers, reflect on the presence of important protective factors in their lives. The DARS items are based on information gleaned from a thorough literature review of adult resilience, national focus groups with adults who care for and work on behalf of young children (e.g., parents, home visitors, infant mental health specialists, and early care and education providers) and conversations with national experts. The focus groups and conversations with national experts focused on gathering information related to (1) what behaviors adults felt were important to help them "bounce back" or cope successfully with risk and adversity as well as, (2) what behavior adults need to provide nurturing, quality care

and instruction to young children. The DARS was developed to accompany the Devereux Early Childhood Assessment Program for Infants and Toddlers (Mackrain, LeBuffe, & Powell, 2007), therefore the focus groups and literature reviews focused on parents, teachers, and other caregivers of young children. However, the protective factors identified and the items on the DARS are applicable to all adults.

The result of this process was the creation of a set of 23 items that relate to four adult protective factor domains. The *Relationships* grouping (5 items) addresses behaviors that reflect *the mutual, long-lasting, back-and-forth bond we have with another person in our lives*. Sample Relationship items include "I have good friends who support me," and "I have a mentor or someone who shows me the way." The *Initiative* grouping (8 items) inquires about *the ability to make positive choices and decisions and act upon them.* Sample Initiative items include "I try many ways to solve a problem," and "I can ask for help." *Internal Beliefs* (6 items) asks the adult to reflect on *the feelings and thoughts we have about ourselves and our lives, and how effective we think we are at taking action in life.* Sample Internal Beliefs items include, "My role as a caregiver is important," and "I am hopeful about the future." The *Self-Control* grouping (4 items) probes behaviors related to *the ability to experience a range of feelings, and express them using the words and actions that society considers appropriate.* Sample Self-Control items include, "I set limits for myself," and "I can calm myself down." Adults completing the DARS are asked to reflect on the presence of these protective factors in their lives and then check 1 of 3 boxes for each of the 23 items indicating that, "Yes" that protective factor is present in their lives, "Sometimes" it is present, or it is "Not Yet" present.

Staff at the Devereux Center for Resilient Children investigated the reliability and validity of the DARS by correlating participants' scores on the DARS with their respective scores on the Connor–Davidson Resilience Scale (CD-RISC; Connor & Davidson, 2003), a 25-item scale comprising four factors related to resilience: personal competence, intuition/coping with stress, secure relationships, and spiritual influences. A total of 721 teachers completed both measures in counterbalanced order. This sample population had a distribution similar to the U.S. Census Bureau (2007) population data in regards to race, ethnicity, and age, however in regards to gender, more females participated in the study than males. Findings revealed that the DARS had high internal consistency ($\alpha = 0.76$), and correlated highly with CD-RISC scores (Spearman rho $= 0.58$, $p = 0.01$), supporting the psychometric properties of the DARS.

A guiding principle of the Devereux Center for Resilient Children is that assessments should provide information that guides the development and implementation of strategies to enhance the resilience of the person who is the subject of the assessment. That is, the purpose of assessments developed by the Center is to promote, not just measure, resilience. In keeping with this principle, the DARS is accompanied by a self-reflective journal, *Building Your Bounce: Simple Strategies for a Resilient You* (Mackrain & Bruce, 2009). In addition to including the DARS, this resource provides strategies, derived from both research and practice, which are linked to the 23 items and designed to promote adult resilience. For example, in relation to the Internal Beliefs item, "My role as a caregiver is important" one of the strategies is to first list all of the routine, sometimes tedious, things that one does as a teacher. Next the adult is asked to reflect and write down the positive effects of these routines on him or herself. A teacher might list as a routine task writing weekly progress notes on each child, but then reflects and realizes that those notes enable her to see progress in her students' abilities and communicate that news to parents and the student. After completing the DARS, the adult selects one or more of the items that receive a rating of "Sometimes" or "Not Yet" and then selects a related strategy from Building Your Bounce to promote the development of that protective factor.

As a self-directed and self-reflective approach, the DARS and Building Your Bounce can be utilized by any adult interested in enhancing his or her resilience. Although it can be used in group settings, it can also be utilized by a single adult. Furthermore as a self-reflective approach, the results do not have to be shared or discussed with others enabling participants to be more honest and forthright. In addition, as Kyriacou (2001) noted, it is important for teachers to discover which strategies work best for them. Although training is available from the Devereux Center for Resilient Children in the use of the DARS and Building Your Bounce, it is not required. As such, these resources are easily used by a variety of adults and complement the group interventions described above.

Conclusions

Nearly all adults in the United States experience stressors of too many demands and too little time. Apparently, most adults feel that their level of stress has increased over the past 5 years (APA, 2010). The current "Great Recession" is exacerbating concerns over employment and financial stability for many adults and their families. For teachers the stressors are many and multiplying. Demands to meet annual yearly progress on high stakes testing, children who come to school not ready to learn, increasing behavior problems in the classroom, to name but a few common stressors are in some cases overwhelming the coping resources of teachers. It is critical that schools promote the well-being of teachers so they can in turn support students in acquiring the social and emotional skills that are essential for school and life success. Supporting teachers' resilience is a promising practice that is critical to educational planning efforts at the national, state, and local levels.

References

Academic, Social, and Emotional Learning Act of 2011, H.R. 2437, 112th Cong. (2011). Retrieved September 6, 2011, from http://www.govtrack.us/congress/billtext.xpd?bill=h112-2437.

Alliance for Excellent Education. (2005, August). *Teacher attrition: A costly loss to the nation and to the states* (Issue brief). Washington, DC: Author. Retrieved

February 25, 2011, from http://www.all4ed.org/files/archive/publications/TeacherAttrition.pdf.

American Psychological Association. (2010). *Stress in America report*. Retrieved September 6, 2011, from http://www.apa.org/news/press/releases/stress/index.aspx.

Bandura, A. (1977). *Social learning theory*. Englewood Cliffs, NJ: Prentice-Hall.

Bauer, J., Stamm, A., Virnich, K., Wissing, K., Mueller, U., Wirsching, M., et al. (2006). Correlation between burnout syndrome and psychological and psychosomatic symptoms among teachers. *International Archives of Occupational and Environmental Health, 79*, 199–204.

Belsky, J., Vandell, D. L., Burchinal, M., Clarke-Stewart, K. A., McCartney, K., & Owen, M. T. (2007). Are there long-term effects of early child care? *Child Development, 78*, 681–701.

Betoret, F. D. (2009). Self-efficacy, school resources, job stressors and burnout among Spanish primary and secondary school teachers: A structural equation approach. *Educational Psychology, 29*, 45–68.

Biglan, A. (2008, Fall). Teacher stress and collegiality: Overlooked factors in the effort to promote evidence-based practices. *Association for Behavior Analysis International Newsletter, 31*(3). Retrieved February 25, 2011, from http://www.abainternational.org/ABA/newsletter/vol313/Biglan.asp.

Brackett, M. A., & Caruso, D. R. (2006). *The emotionally intelligent teacher*. Ann Arbor, MI: Quest Education.

Brackett, M. A., & Katulak, N. A. (2006). Emotional intelligence in the classroom: Skill-based training for teachers and students. In J. Ciarrochi & J. D. Mayer (Eds.), *Applying emotional intelligence: A practitioner's guide* (pp. 1–27). New York, NY: Psychology Press.

Bredekamp, V. S., & Copple, C. (Eds.). (1997). *Developmentally appropriate practice in early childhood programs*. Washington, DC: NAEYC.

Brunetti, G. J. (2006). Resilience under fire: Perspectives on the work of experienced, inner city high school teachers in the United States. *Teaching and Teacher Education, 22*, 812–825.

Burke, R., Greenglass, E., & Schwarzer, R. (1996). Predicting teacher burnout over time: Effects of work stress, social support, and self-doubts on burnout and its consequences. *Anxiety, Stress, and Coping, 9*, 261–275.

Burton, N. W., Pakenham, K. I., & Brown, W. J. (2010). Feasibility and effectiveness of psychosocial resilience training: A pilot study of the READY program. *Psychology, Health & Medicine, 15*, 266–277.

Castro, A. J., Kelly, J., & Shih, M. (2010). Resilience strategies for new teachers in high-needs areas. *Teaching and Teacher Education, 26*, 622–629.

Center for the Child Care Workforce. (2004, June). *Current data on the salaries and benefits of the U.S. early childhood education workforce*. Retrieved February 25, 2011, from http://www.aft.org/yourwork/teachers/reports/ece.cfm.

Collaborative for Academic, Social, and Emotional Learning. (2011). *SEL in your state*. Retrieved September 6, from 2011, http://casel.org/research/sel-in-your-state/.

Conduct Problems Prevention Research Group. (1999). Initial impact of the FAST Track prevention trial for conduct problems: II. Classroom effects. *Journal of Counseling and Clinical Psychology, 67*, 648–657.

Connor, K. M., & Davidson, J. R. (2003). Development of a new resilience scale: The Connor-Davidson Resilience Scale (CD-RISC). *Depression and Anxiety, 18*, 76–82.

Durlak, J. A., Weissberg, R. P., Dymnicki, A. B., Taylor, R. D., & Shellinger, K. B. (2011). The impact of enhancing students' social and emotional learning: A meta-analysis of school-based universal interventions. *Child Development, 82*, 405–432.

Eisenberg, N., Fabes, R. A., Carlo, G., & Karbon, M. (1992). Emotional responsivity to others: Behavioral correlates and socialization antecedents. *New Directions for Child and Adolescent Development, 55*, 57–73.

Eisenberg, N., Fabes, R. A., Schaller, M., Carlo, G., & Miller, P. A. (1991). The relations of parental characteristics and practices to children's vicarious emotional responding. *Child Development, 62*, 1393–1408.

Fabes, R. A., Eisenberg, N., & Miller, P. A. (1990). Maternal correlates of children's vicarious emotional responsiveness. *Developmental Psychology, 26*, 639–648.

Greenberg, M. T., Weissberg, R. P., O'Brien, M. U., Zins, J. E., Fredericks, L., Resnik, H., et al. (2003). Enhancing school-based prevention and youth development through coordinated social, emotional, and academic learning. *The American Psychologist, 58*, 466–474.

Guglielmi, R. S., & Tatrow, K. (1998). Occupational stress, burnout and health in teachers: A methodological and theoretical analysis. *Review of Educational Research, 68*, 61–69.

Hammond, O. W., & Onikama, D. L. (1997). *At risk teachers*. Honolulu, HI: Pacific Resources for Education and Learning.

Hamre, B. K., & Pianta, R. C. (2004). Self-reported depression in nonfamilial caregivers: Prevalence and associations with caregiver behavior in child-care settings. *Early Childhood Research Quarterly, 19*, 297–318.

Helburn, S. W. (1995). *Cost, quality and child outcomes in child care centers (Technical report)*. Denver, CO: Department of Economics, Center for Research in Economic and Social Policy, University of Colorado at Denver.

Howard, S., & Johnson, B. (2004). Resilient teachers: Resisting stress and burnout. *Social Psychology of Education, 7*, 399–420.

Howes, C., & Hamilton, C. (1993). The changing experience of child care: Changes in teachers and in teacher-child relationships and children's social competence with peers. *Early Childhood Research Quarterly, 8*, 15–32.

Jenkins, S., & Calhoun, J. F. (1991). Teacher stress: Issues and intervention. *Psychology in the Schools, 28,* 60–70.

Jennings, P. A., & Greenberg, M. T. (2009). The prosocial classroom: Teacher social and emotional competence in relation to students and classroom outcomes. *Review of Educational Research, 79,* 491–525.

Jurado, D., Gurpegui, M., Moreno, O., & de Dios, L. J. (1998). School setting and teaching experience as risk factors for depressive symptoms in teachers. *European Psychiatry, 13,* 78–82.

Keigher, A. (2010). *Teacher attrition and mobility: Results from the 2008–09 teacher follow-up survey* (NCES 2010-353). U.S. Department of Education. Washington, DC: National Center for Education Statistics. Retrieved February 25, 2011, from http://nces.ed.gov/pubsearch.

Kyriacou, C. (2001). Teacher stress: Directions for future research. *Educational Review, 53,* 27–35.

Lambert, R. G., McCarthy, C., O'Donnell, M., & Wang, C. (2009). Measuring elementary teacher stress and coping in the classroom: Validity evidence for the classroom appraisal of resources and demands. *Psychology in the Schools, 46,* 973–988.

LeBuffe, P. A., Shapiro, V. B., & Naglieri, J. A. (2009). *The Devereux Student Strengths Assessment (DESSA), technical manual, and user's guide.* Lewisville, NC: Kaplan.

Leiter, M. P., & Maslach, C. (2000). Burnout and health. In A. Baum, T. Revenson, & J. Singer (Eds.), *Handbook of health psychology* (pp. 415–426). Hillsdale, NJ: Erlbaum.

Leithwood, K. A., Menzies, T., Jantzi, D., & Leithwood, J. (1999). Teacher burnout: A critical challenge for leaders of restructuring schools. In R. Vandenberghe & M. Huberman (Eds.), *Understanding and preventing teacher burnout: A sourcebook of international research and practice* (pp. 1–13). New York, NY: Cambridge University Press.

Liossis, P. L., Shochet, I. M., Millear, P. M., & Biggs, H. (2009). The Promoting Adult Resilience (PAR) Program: The effectiveness of the second, shorter pilot of a workplace prevention program. *Behaviour Change, 26,* 97–112.

Mackrain, M. (2007). *Devereux Adult Resilience Survey.* Villanova, PA: The Devereux Foundation.

Mackrain, M., & Bruce, N. (2009). *Building your bounce: Simple strategies for a resilient you.* Lewisville, NC: Kaplan.

Mackrain, M., LeBuffe, P. A., & Powell, G. (2007). *The Devereux Early Childhood Assessment for Infants and Toddlers (DECA-I/T) assessment, technical manual, and user's guide.* Lewisville, NC: Kaplan.

Maslach, C., & Jackson, S. E. (1981). The measurement of experienced burnout. *Journal of Occupational Behavior, 2,* 99–113.

Maslach, C., & Leiter, M. P. (2005). Stress and burnout: The critical research. In C. L. Cooper (Ed.), *Handbook of stress medicine and health* (2nd ed., pp. 153–170). London, UK: CRC Press.

Maslach, C., & Leiter, M. P. (2008). Early predictors of job burnout and engagement. *Journal of Applied Psychology, 93,* 498–512.

Maslach, C., Schaufeli, W. B., Leiter, M. P. (2011). Job burnout. *Annual Review of Psychology, 52*(1), 397–422.

Masten, A. S., Best, K. M., & Garmezy, N. (1990). Resilience and development: Contributions from the study of children who overcome adversity. *Development and Psychopathology, 2,* 425–444.

Masten, A. S., & Garmezy, N. (1985). Risk, vulnerability and protective factors in developmental psychopathology. In B. B. Lahey & A. E. Kazdin (Eds.), *Advances in clinical child psychology* (Vol. 8, pp. 1–512). New York, NY: Plenum.

Mayer, J. D., & Salovey, P. (1997). What is emotional intelligence? In P. Salovey & D. Sluyter (Eds.), *Emotional development and emotional intelligence: Educational implications* (pp. 3–34). New York, NY: Basic Books.

McCarthy, C. J., & Lambert, R. G. (2006). Helping teachers balance demands and resources in an era of accountability. In R. Lambert & C. McCarthy (Eds.), *Understanding teacher stress in an age of accountability* (pp. 215–226). Greenwich, CT: Information Age Publishing.

Melamed, S., Shirom, A., Toker, S., Berliner, S., & Shapira, I. (2006). Burnout and risk of cardiovascular disease: Evidence, possible causal paths, and promising research directions. *Psychological Bulletin, 132,* 327–353.

Mental Health America. (2011). *Children's mental health statistics.* Retrieved September 6, 2011, from http://www.nmha.org/go/information/get-info/children-s-mental-health/children-s-mental-health-statistics.

Millear, P., Liossis, P., Shochet, I. M., & Biggs, H. (2008). Being on PAR: Outcomes of a pilot trial to improve mental health and wellbeing in the workplace with the Promoting Adult Resilience (PAR) Program. *Behaviour Change, 25,* 215–228.

Montgomery, C., & Rupp, A. A. (2005). A meta-analysis for exploring the diverse causes and effects of stress in teachers. *Canadian Journal of Education, 28,* 458–486.

National Association of School Psychologists. (2010). *Model for comprehensive and integrated school psychological services.* Retrieved September 6, 2011, from http://www.nasponline.org/standards/2010standards/2_PracticeModel.pdf.

New Freedom Commission on Mental Health. (2003). *Achieving the promise: Transforming mental health care in America* (DHHS Pub. No. SMA-03-3832). Rockville, MD: U.S. Department of Health and Human Services, Substance Abuse and Mental Health Services Administration.

Norman-Murch, T. (1996). Reflective supervision as a vehicle for individual and organizational development. *Zero to Three, 17*(2), 16–20.

Patterson, J. H., Collins, L., & Abbott, G. (2004). A study of teacher resilience in urban schools. *Journal of Instructional Psychology, 31*, 3–11.

Payton, J., Weissberg, R. P., Durlak, J. A., Dymnicki, A. B., Taylor, R. D., Schellinger, K. B., et al. (2008). *The positive impact of social and emotional learning for kindergarten to eighth-grade students: Findings from three scientific reviews*. Chicago, IL: Collaborative for Academic, Social, and Emotional Learning.

Provasnik, S., & Dorfman, S. (2005). *Mobility in the teacher workforce: Findings from the condition of education 2005*. Washington, DC: National Center for Education Statistics.

Raver, C. C., & Knitzer, J. (2002). *Ready to enter: What research tells policymakers about strategies to promote social and emotional school readiness among three- and four-year-old children (Promoting the emotional well-being of children and families policy paper no. 3)*. New York, NY: National Center for Children in Poverty, Columbia University Mailman School of Public Health.

Rintoul, B., Thorne, J., Wallace, I., Mobley, M., Goldman-Fraser, J., & Luckey, H. (1998). *Factors in child development. Part 1: Personal characteristics and parental behavior*. Prepared for Centers for Disease Control and Prevention Public Health Service, U.S. Department of Health and Human Services by the Research Triangle Institute. Retrieved September 6, 2011, from http://www.rti.org/pubs/child-development.pdf.

Roberts, W. L., & Strayer, J. (1987). Parents' responses to the emotional distress of their children: Relations with children's competence. *Developmental Psychology, 23*, 415–422.

Santavirta, N., Solovieva, S., & Theorell, T. (2007). The association between job strain and emotional exhaustion in a cohort of 1,028 Finnish teachers. *The British Journal of Educational Psychology, 77*, 213–228.

Schonfeld, I. S. (1990). Psychological distress in a sample of teachers. *The Journal of Psychology, 124*, 321–338.

Schonfeld, I. S. (2001). Stress in first-year women teachers: The context of social support and coping. *Genetic, Social, and General Psychology Monographs, 127*, 133–168.

Shirilla, J., & Weatherston, D. (2002). *Case studies in infant mental health: Risk, resiliency and relationships*. Washington, DC: Zero to Three.

Shonkoff, J. P., & Phillips, D. A. (Eds.). (2000). *From neurons to neighborhoods: The science of early childhood development*. Washington, DC: National Academy Press.

Simon, A., Harnett, S., Nagler, E., & Thomas, L. (2009). *Research on the effect of the Inner Resilience Program on teacher and student wellness and classroom climate*. Metis Associates. Retrieved September 6, 2011, from http://www.metisassoc.com/publications.html.

Skaalvik, E. M., & Skaalvik, S. (2007). Dimensions of teacher self-efficacy and relations with strain factors, perceived collective teacher efficacy, and teacher burnout. *Journal of Educational Psychology, 99*, 611–625.

Stanford, B. H. (2001). Reflections of resilient, persevering urban teachers. *Teacher Education Quarterly, 28*, 75–87.

Tennant, C. (2001). Work-related stress and depressive disorders. *Journal of Psychosomatic Research, 51*, 697–704.

Tschannen-Moran, M., & Woolfolk Hoy, A. (2001). Teacher efficacy: Capturing an elusive construct. *Teaching and Teacher Education, 17*, 783–805.

Waite, P., & Richardson, G. (2004). Determining the efficacy of resilience training in the worksite. *Journal of Allied Health, 33*, 178–183.

Werner, E. E., & Smith, R. S. (1992). *Overcoming the odds: High risk children from birth to adulthood*. Ithica, NY: Cornell University Press.

Williams, J. S. (2003). Why great teachers stay [commentary]. *Educational Leadership, 60*, 71–75.

Yoon, J. S. (2002). Teacher characteristics as predictors of teacher-student relationships: Stress, negative affect, and self-efficacy. *Social Behavior and Personality, 30*, 485–493.

Beth Doll

Schools have historically been the great equalizer in the American landscape—the "ticket out" for youth struggling to overcome conditions of adversity and poverty (Pianta & Walsh, 1998). For immigrants to the eastern seaboard, schools were safe havens where children learned English, received public health services, and became literate and employable (Pulliam & Van Patten, 2007). As each wave of homesteaders moved west across the country, schools popped up alongside the newly broken sod. Universal access to public education has been a defining feature of the North American culture, and schools are fertile settings for promoting the intellectual, psychological, and personal competence of youth (Masten & Coatsworth, 1998).

Poignant tales of schooling and learning have passed down through my own family. My grandmother told vivid stories of being 12 years old and traveling alone by train from her parents' land in Montana to central Kansas. In 1912, schools had not yet been built near their new homestead but, in Kansas, she could live with relatives and attend school. My father remembered riding a pony to a one-room Montana schoolhouse, and then going out at lunchtime to break the ice on the water bucket so that the

horses could drink. At 18, he worked with his father for a mountain lumber company and, 65 years later, he was still grateful to the owner for telling him that he would be fired each fall and rehired each summer because he ought to be in college. My father would shake his head gently and remember, "He said I was too smart to be lumbering for the rest of my life."

Then, and now, schools are vested with the responsibility of ensuring the success of each generation's youth (Pianta & Walsh, 1998). Indeed, a central tenet of the No Child Left Behind Act (NCLB, Public Law No. 107-110, 115 Stat. 1425, 2002) was that schools are responsible for successfully teaching all children, regardless of their socioeconomic status, ethnicity, language, or parents' education. Threaded through contentious and passionate debates about the adequacy of schools and correctness of their practices, political will in the United States reiterates and reinforces the central importance of public education. To quote the prominent journalist, Dan Rather, children's dream for success "begins with a teacher who believes in you, who tugs and pushes and leads you to the next plateau, sometimes poking you with a sharp stick called truth." In response, schools do "deliberately intervene in children's lives" (Werner, 2006, p. 102), and they are entrusted by the public to do so.

The purpose of this chapter is to reframe this American dream around current research and conceptual frameworks of resilience, and to show how these frameworks can become a foundation for local micro-studies to identify classroom strategies

B. Doll (✉)
Educational Psychology, College of Education
and Human Sciences, University of Nebraska,
Lincoln, 238 Mabel, Lee Hall Lincoln, NE, USA
e-mail: Bdoll2@unl.edu

S. Goldstein and R.B. Brooks (eds.), *Handbook of Resilience in Children*, 399
DOI 10.1007/978-1-4614-3661-4_23, © Springer Science+Business Media New York 2013

that contribute to students' psychological wellness and strengthen their competence. This chapter uses Masten and Coatsworth's (1998) very simple definition of resilience: "Resilience is how children overcome adversity to achieve good developmental outcomes" (p. 205). This narrows the definition of resilience beyond its usage in the popular press. Within this definition, my own son and daughter would not be considered "resilient" although they are highly successful, because they have not struggled with any significant adversity in their first 3 decades of life. Alternatively, in many schools where I have worked, substantial numbers of children came to school hungry, frightened, with inadequate clothing, or with shocking memories of family or community violence or abuse. Resilience describes the conditions that allow these children to triumph nevertheless.

This chapter's translation from resilience research into classroom practices relies heavily on an essential assumption articulated by Egeland, Carlson, and Sroufe (1993) and reiterated by Pianta and Walsh (1998): Resilience emerges out of a constellation of child, family, and community factors. Consequently, practices to strengthen children's resilience are best integrated into the natural contexts where children live their daily lives (Masten, 2001). Moreover, it makes no sense to speak about resilience as a characteristic of children because children do not achieve resilience by "pulling themselves up by their own bootstraps" (Doll, Zucker, & Brehm, 2004). Instead, resilience is a characteristic that emerges out of the systemic interdependence of children with their families, communities, and schools.

This chapter examines resilience as a characteristic of school settings because schools dominate children's lives for at least 15,000 hours (Rutter, Maughan, Mortimore, Ouston, & Smith, 1979), and represent a secondary and highly important source of childhood caretaking. Even more narrowly, this chapter focuses very deliberately on resilience of classrooms. Other scholars have described the resilience of schools, school climates that promote wellness, and school–community partnerships that promote student success (Comer, Haynes, Joyner, & Ben-Avie, 1996; National Research Council/Institute of Medicine

[NRC/IOM], 2004; Slavin & Madden, 2001). These are worthy endeavors. However, at its core, resilience often emerges out of very personal interactions that occur between children and adults, and between children and other children (Masten & Coatsworth, 1998; Pianta & Walsh, 1998). This gives special relevance to the daily classroom interactions that occur between and among adults and children.

The remainder of this chapter will first describe the characteristics of classrooms that make it possible for children to overcome adversity and experience success and competence. Next, we will describe the data-based decision-making strategy that we use to translate this definition into classroom practices, including how we conduct needs assessments of classrooms, the ways in which plans are crafted and put into place to strengthen classroom resilience, and the ways in which evaluations of the classroom changes are embedded into the strategy. Sprinkled throughout this description will be the lessons that we have learned in carrying out these classroom change strategies with teachers and students. We will close with a candid discussion of the research that we have not yet done—the next steps. Throughout the chapter, the singular focus of our work is to develop and refine a practical strategy that teachers can use (alone or in partnership with colleagues) to create classroom environments that predispose their students to success.

Classroom Conditions That Foster Resilience

A useful description of the classroom conditions that make it possible for children to succeed despite the odds can be culled from the past 50 years' developmental research on risk and resilience (Coie et al., 1993; Doll & Lyon, 1998; Werner, 2006). This tradition began with a large number of longitudinal studies, many initiated in the 1950s and 1960s that followed participants from their birth through adolescence or even adulthood. Werner (2006) describes ten of these large-scale studies that continue to follow their participants into the present. The essential question examined in the studies was: what are the characteristics of children, their families, or their communities that predicted which children would be identified with disabilities or disturbances in adolescence or adulthood? Researchers gathered comprehensive data on the children, their family, their community at the time of birth, and then meticulously followed the children through decades. Results of these studies have been very competently summarized in Werner (2006). A brief and over-simplified synopsis is this: there was a remarkable concordance across the various studies conducted on different continents and with different predicted outcomes. Across the studies, the same 8–10 factors were potent predictors of childhood risk. Many of these factors were characteristics of families and communities rather than characteristics of individual children. Moreover, the number of factors rather than the precise combination of factors was a powerful indicator that the children were likely to succumb to risk. Thus, the results suggest that children could weather some adversity but were far more vulnerable when struggling with multiple adversities piled one on top of the other.

While the examination of risk was worthwhile in its own right, our operational framework for understanding classroom conditions that promote resilience grew out of a subsequent question began to be raised in the 1980s (Doll & Lyon, 1998; Werner, 2006). Each study had participants who were quite successful even though, by all rights and because they were growing up with multiple risk factors, they would have been predicted to fail. These were the resilient children. An important question was: What were the characteristics of children, their families, and their communities that predicted which children would overcome adversity and succeed? These characteristics have come to be called "protective factors" because, when present in sufficient numbers, they appear to insulate children from the deleterious effects of risk and make it more likely that they will grow into successful adults with ample education, rewarding vocations, satisfying family lives, and making important contributions to their communities.

Between eight and ten essential protective factors were identified in developmental resil-

ience research (Werner, 2006). Several of these same factors were also identified in rigorous educational research as predictors of the academic success of students who experienced significant psychosocial disadvantages outside of school (NRC/IOM, 2004). Prominent among these are rewarding and caring relationships between and among the adults and children who populate a classroom. Within our operational definition of resilient classrooms, my colleagues and I have emphasized three of these relational characteristics as essential to resilient classrooms: (1) the quality of the relationships that exist between the teacher and students in the classroom; (2) the nature of the peer relationships that exist among classmates; and (3) the degree of collaboration and connectedness that exists between the classroom and students' families (Doll et al., 2004). Another important set of protective classroom practices are those that promote students' autonomy and self-regulation. Again, we have emphasized two of these autonomy characteristics as essential to resilient classrooms, (4) the degree to which the students are empowered to set goals and make decisions on their own behalf (academic self-determination); and (5) the degree to which the students' are supported in managing their own behavior (academic self-control). Finally, but equally importantly, resilient classrooms foster children's optimism and hope. Within our operational definition, we emphasize (6) the degree to which classrooms support students' confident expectations that they will succeed in class (academic efficacy). More extensive descriptions of these six characteristics of classroom resilience, and the research that underlies their selection, can be found in Doll, LeClair, and Kurien (2009) and Doll, Kurien, et al. (2009).

Translating Resilience Research into Classroom Practices

The central thesis of our work is that it is possible to deliberately embed these protective factors into the fabric of everyday practices in classrooms; and that doing so increases the likelihood that children will learn and be successful in these classrooms even when they are struggling with many and very significant social and economic disadvantages (Doll et al., 2004). To implement these contextual changes within classrooms, we have adapted a familiar data-based problem-solving strategy that begins with a needs assessment to identify essential protective factors that are present or missing within a classroom, the data which are thoughtfully examined and interpreted by teachers in collaboration with their students and colleagues to become the basis for planned modifications in classroom practices that address the needs, the effects of which are carefully monitored by re-collecting some of the needs assessment data. We think of this as a classroom micro-study in which members of the class conduct local research to verify that they are fostering a classroom environment that maximizes the competence and success of all students who are its members. All that is needed to put this micro-study framework into place are clear operational definitions of the classroom characteristics that act as protective factors; measures of these characteristics that are technically sound, meaningful, and practical to collect in classrooms; and a "toolbox" of classroom strategies and modifications that can strengthen those characteristics that are found to be wanting.

When described in these terms, our classroom change strategy is deceptive in its simplicity. The challenge is that all of these occur within the existing system of schools, in which classrooms exist within grade level teams which, in turn, exist within schools, then school districts, and then communities. Moreover, even though classrooms operate under the legitimate authority of teachers and administrators, classroom changes emerge transactionally out of the interactions of adults and children within and among each other. Thus, it is a very complex endeavor to implement classroom change strategies while simultaneously respecting the existing classroom system.

Classroom needs assessment: There is an essential, common sense reason for beginning classroom resilience interventions with a needs assessment: precious resources should never be squandered on strengthening protective factors that are already amply represented within a classroom. As an example, the majority of needs assessments that we have conducted in elementary schools have often shown that teachers' relationships with their students were exceptionally strong and caring (Doll, Spies, Champion, et al., 2010; Doll, Spies, LeClair, Kurien, & Foley, 2010). Similarly, in most classrooms, students had satisfying peer friendships within which they felt supported and appreciated. Simultaneously, students frequently reported that their classmates argued a lot with each other, picked on each other, and were often disruptive in the classroom. In these modal classrooms, the logical focus of classroom changes will be on these aspects of peer conflict and student disruption. This planful decision about where to intervene and what to strengthen is not necessarily the norm in classroom change programs. In too many cases, manualized preventive interventions are implemented in a standard format without regard to the strengths that already exist within a classroom. With the wisdom of a child, a fourth-grader told me why this is a problem, explaining "We really like you and we don't mind doing this stuff. But we think you ought to know—we already know this."

Within a data-based problem-solving cycle, the measures underlying the needs assessment must be simultaneously sound technically and practical to use. As a result, we have spent an inordinate amount of energy developing class-wide measures of the six characteristics that are reliable, valid, brief, simple to collect, easily collated, and analyzed, with results that can be readily organized into a diagram or graph. A needs assessment that was highly time consuming would intrude into the instructional mission of classrooms, and that would prevent its use. If results of needs assessments were highly complicated, they would not "speak" to the teachers and children who populated the classroom, and so would not catalyze the suggestions for change. Given these constraints, we were impressed with the usefulness of anonymous student surveys that were aggregated across all students in a classroom.

The resulting ClassMaps Survey (Doll, Spies, Champion, et al., 2010; Doll, Spies, LeClair, et al.,

2010) is a 55-item anonymous student survey with eight subscales: three peer relationships subscales examining peer friendships in the classroom (My Classmates), peer conflict (Kids In This Class), and worries about being victimized (I Worry That); two other relationships subscales that examine teacher–student relationships (My Teacher) and parents' participation in students' learning (Talking With Parents); and three self-regulation subscales describing students' discipline (Following Class Rules), expectations for success (Believing in Me), and self-determination (Taking Charge). Students complete the survey by selecting "never," "sometimes," "often," or "almost always" for each item, and the results are aggregated across all students in a class. To ensure higher scores uniformly represent more supportive classroom environments, negative items are reverse coded. Early research has established that the resulting survey factors consistently into the six classroom characteristics have strong internal consistency (α ranges from 0.79 to 0.93 in elementary classrooms and from 0.82 to 0.91 in middle school classrooms), and correlates in predicted ways with other indices of the six characteristics.

The advantages of these aggregated classroom surveys are that they provide information that teachers are not always privy to—students' private perceptions of the support they experience from classmates and teachers, their personal sense of belonging and expectations of success, and their felt responsibility for charting their own course into academic success. Any single student's sense of their classroom emerges out of the interactions between their personal characteristics and temperament, and the social and behavioral contexts provided by the classroom. However, the collective experience of all students in a class is an invaluable barometer of the "felt experience" of the class as a whole and a stable reflection of classroom-level characteristics. Combined with teachers' own experience of the classroom, and focused very specifically on aspects of classrooms that have been linked to the success of students-at-risk, these intersecting perspectives begin to articulate the ecological system of the classroom in a way that is highly relevant to student resilience.

Ideally, using simple classroom data to reframe daily routines and practices can contribute to a classroom's efficiency as well as its effectiveness. Nevertheless, carving out time to collect data is very challenging in today's rushed classrooms and can become a significant barrier to a micro-study. Consequently, we are experimenting with a computer administration of an online ClassMaps Survey. We administer our beta version in one of a school's computer labs. Each student's computer station is logged onto the online ClassMaps Survey using a password and file name that is unique to the classroom teacher. Students wear headphones so that the survey is individually read to each of them as they proceed through the items. They click on their grade and gender, and then each item is displayed and read aloud, one at a time. As soon as students click on their answer, the program takes them to the next item. Once they answer the last item, a colorful "thank you" picture flashes up on the screen, signaling to the teacher that they have finished. The students then pull up one of the other instructional programs that the class is working on, while waiting for the classmates to finish the survey. When all the students are finished with the survey, the teacher can log onto the teacher screen, and immediately access and print graphs describing the class's responses to the surveys. Use of the online ClassMaps Survey cuts administration times to approximately 15 min for an elementary or middle school classroom, and the teachers can use their confidential password to access the summary data moments after the last student finishes.

Other measures could be used instead of the ClassMaps Survey within this micro-studies framework. Examples include school records of discipline reports, students possessive "votes" on the occurrence of teasing or arguments during recess, homework completion records, or playground maps on which the students have marked the places where students do or do not get along. Where these measures of one or more of the six classroom resilience characteristics were already available to the class, they were useful in addition to or instead of the ClassMaps Survey results. In other cases, teachers or students became emboldened by their experiences with micro-studies, and began to write their own survey questions, specific to the unique needs of their class.

Planning for classroom modifications: The essential purpose of any micro-study is to enhance the protective factors in classrooms that contribute to students' academic, behavioral, and social success. There are three immediately obvious ways in which this might occur (Masten & Coatsworth, 1998): (a) by providing scaffolded assistance that allows students to act in more competent ways than they could achieve alone; (b) by removing the barriers to students' competence that might be embedded within the context; and (c) by refining the classroom definition of competence so that it matches developmentally appropriate expectations. Our original plans had been to simply show ClassMaps Survey results from the classroom to teachers, and to support them in crafting plans that might accomplish one or all of these three purposes in response to weaknesses identified in the data.

The simple act of showing teachers data about their classroom can be highly reactive. In our very early investigations of school playgrounds (Doll, Murphy, & Song, 2003), we had to carefully guard data describing recess problems from teachers' eyes or they would step in and "fix" the problems before the study's conclusion. Eventually, realizing that this was actually what we wanted, we began to deliberately share classroom data with teachers. In turn, they were quick to share the data with the students in simple classroom meetings. When this occurred, students' interpretations of the data's veracity and meaning, and their suggestions for effective solutions, were often quite different from those of the teachers. For example, teachers thought that a class needed more playground supervisors and stricter playground rule enforcement, and students thought that there needed to be more games so that students kept busy playing instead of fighting at recess. Teachers thought that there needed to be more serious consequences when students were inattentive and disruptive during mathematics period, but students thought that they were wiggly because the work was much too difficult

and they were afraid of failing the weekly test. Classroom changes that took student perceptions into account alongside teacher perceptions were often simple and quickly effective.

Some teachers have been immediately comfortable with collecting and thinking about classroom data and quickly took leadership over their classroom micro-studies; other teachers have thought of "collecting data" as a very complex and time-consuming task, and were slow to look at and be responsive to their classrooms' results. Over time, we have learned to overtly market classroom data to be highly attractive and acceptable to reluctant classroom teachers. Classroom data are most attractive and more readily interpreted when displayed in graphs or figures than in long lists of tables. Data that are collapsed onto a single sheet of paper (one or two-sided) are most usable. Teachers' interest has been heightened when we have packaged their data into regularly scheduled newsletters printed in full color, annotated with graphics, with embedded comments describing other resources or material that we can make available upon request, and timed to coincide with teachers' existing school-improvement meetings.

Several master teachers showed us the critical importance of classroom meetings to classroom micro-studies. By including students in interpreting and planning from classroom data, the meetings broadened teachers' ecological perspectives on classroom practices and diversified the solutions that they used to strengthen classroom routines. We plan these classroom meetings around four simple questions to the students: is the classroom data accurate? What do students believe causes the strengths and weaknesses in the classroom? What could teachers do to make the classroom a better place for kids to learn? And, what could students do that would strengthen the classroom? Brief chart notes focused the students' attention on the questions, and the listed answers became permanent records that teachers could consult when planning classroom modifications. Students appreciated being included in the planning, and had a clearer sense of the purpose and potential of the classroom micro-study. As one seventh grader noted, "I get it now. This is all about trying to fix our school."

In this frame of mind, students were more receptive to the classroom changes that they owned and had helped to plan. Still while some student perspectives were refreshingly frank, others were more guarded, particularly as students became older and more self-conscious about their reputations with their classmates. In response, one inventive teacher supplemented the open class discussion with computer-aided "chats" in which students could type in additional private observations simultaneous with the open discussion. These private notes were particularly revealing in describing the cross-gender tensions that were heightened by a co-ed soccer game that dominated their recess.

Sometimes, simple but very necessary changes in classroom routines and practices were quickly apparent to teachers as soon as they leafed through their classroom data and discussed it with their students. Many of these could be implemented immediately—providing students with direct instruction in test-taking strategies; incorporating stress-reducing strategies into the preparations for an exam; arranging students in small groups or tables and vesting them with the responsibility for reminding each other of pending assignments or appointments; or adding more games to the recess playground. For example, in many schools where we have worked, playground soccer games were a common source of frequent and disturbing peer conflict. Students disagreed about what the "right" rules were for soccer; they struggled to find fair ways to choose balanced teams, they played soccer on fields that were too small (and the ball flew off into the middle of nearby ball courts or games) or that were too large (and students could not easily tell where the sidelines and goals were located). Students often spent so much time figuring out how to play soccer that they never had very much time left to play it. Often, these disagreements followed the students back into classroom instructional time. Teachers' solutions have included such common sense strategies as: researching the rules for soccer during the classroom social studies lesson; choosing teams every Monday and keeping the same teams for the full week; relocating the soccer field or marking it more clearly; dividing recess soccer into two separate games so that each field is less crowded.

In other classrooms, the needed changes were neither simple nor readily apparent to the teachers and they were quickly overwhelmed when confronted with classroom data describing weaknesses that they did not know how to address. One natural, systemic way to extend the number and quality of teachers' solutions was to pair them with two or three other teachers at similar grades, or to pair inexperienced teachers with an experienced master teacher. Within these peer-support groupings, teachers shared strategies that had previously proven successful in changing classroom relationships or autonomy. In other cases, a master teacher or a school mental health professional (school psychologist, school counselor, or school social worker) acted as a consultant to teacher teams who were conducting micro-studies in their classrooms. When we served this consultant role, we learned to bring one-page strategy sheets for classroom problems that were evident in a classroom's data. The top halves of the strategy sheets list 8–10 classroom modifications that teachers have used with good success to address similar problems; the bottom halves list routines and practices that have been described in the published literature. Rather than "teach" the solution lists, we simply laid them out on the table when teachers were planning and allowed teachers to scan them for strategies that seemed most relevant and about which they wanted more information. Then we described these strategies in more detail. In still other cases, teachers have asked us to go back into the literature and search for additional information or sources that meet a particular need in their classroom.

By far, the most common barrier to classroom change has been time—time for teachers to stop and reflect on their classroom environments, time to search out new information or gather together simple data, and time to implement changed routines. When classrooms lack the resources to implement a routine or practice that is too time consuming, we drew upon the untapped resource that is plentiful in almost every classroom—the time and energy of the students.

Indeed, our use of students has sometimes pushed the limits of reason and, to our surprise, they rarely disappointed us. As examples, students in both elementary and middle school grades have collected and collated simple data such as weekly "teasing thermometers" in which students rate the level of teasing in the classroom, or goal-achievement data in which students record their mastery of classroom academic standards. Students have created the graphs for the data, been "coaches" who remind classmates to carry out a new routine, served on advisory boards that conduct mini-studies of their own, searched out rule manuals for playground games, and written newsletters home for parents.

Implementing modified routines and practices and monitoring their impact: The best-made plans for classroom modifications have little impact unless they are actually acted upon. Planned classroom changes were more likely to be carried out if they were carefully written down, described as discrete steps, and clearly assigned to one or more person in the classroom. This written plan could also be used as a checklist that the teacher or a student used to check off steps as each was completed. Ultimately, the checklist recorded the degree to which the plan was followed with fidelity, and this record made it possible to interpret data describing the changes' impact within the context of what actually happened in the classroom. Still, fidelity is a bi-directional phenomenon. When planned changes were not carefully implemented, the fault sometimes lay with the plan itself. Plans were abandoned if they overreached the resources of a classroom. In one case, a school leadership team had planned to hold bi-weekly coordinating meetings with all of the paraprofessionals who supervised the recess playground at lunchtime. In fact, the supervisors' time was already scheduled into other student support activities and the school did not have the funds to pay for additional paraprofessional time to attend a meeting. Sometimes plans conflicted with the needs or interests of the teachers or students. For example, a fourth-grade classroom had created a teasing worksheet that walked students through a problem-solving conversation when they had become involved in a hurtful teasing incident. Half of the worksheet would be completed by the student who was teased and the other half would be completed by the student who did the teasing. However, none of the teasing worksheets was ever used. The students found a written worksheet to be a bit aversive, and so they simply talked through the recess problems to avoid completing the worksheet. Certain elements of plans were overlooked or deliberately omitted if these were over-ambitious, did not fit seamlessly into a classroom day, or competed with other demands on the classroom. The fact that this had occurred became obvious once the plan checklists were reviewed, and teachers could then focus their attention on what could be done to fix the plan or fix the implementation.

Once planned changes had been in place for between 4 and 6 weeks, simple evaluations were conducted to describe changes in the classrooms' targeted protective factors. At a minimum, the micro-studies collected pre–post data to verify whether classroom environments had improved during the time when the changed routine or practice was put into place. Thus, we deliberately designed the ClassMaps Survey so that any one of the subscales could be administered separate from the full survey, and most micro-studies re-collected only those subscales that were relevant to their planned changes. Comparisons of pre–post data were not sufficient to determine whether classroom modifications caused any improvements that were seen. However, on a very pragmatic level, the degree to which the changes are to blame for the improvements may not be an urgent question for teachers to answer. If the classroom modifications were convenient and fit seamlessly into the classroom's day, and the classroom relationships and autonomy were stronger, teachers' decisions to simply continue the modifications were reasonable ones. Alternatively, when the classroom modifications required significant resources, needed administrative consent, or represented a change in policy, teachers required a more ambitious evaluation. For example, by collecting classroom data repeatedly across brief intervals (e.g., daily or two or three times a week), it was possible for teachers to examine trends in the data and determine whether improvements in the data co-occurred with the changed routine. Thus, classrooms sometimes created small mini-surveys of 1–3 questions and students were assigned to collect these daily. Alternatively, more sophisticated small-n research designs might be important to verify the need for an intervention, show size of the intervention's effect, examine the effect's persistence over time, show that the results could be replicated in other classrooms, or establish that the intervention is worth the cost for stakeholders like administrators, school-board members, or community representatives. Such results could justify the continuation of a less convenient but highly effective classroom modification.

In some cases, the micro-study results showed that nothing had changed or that the classroom's protective factors had deteriorated. In this event, a logical next step was to implement evidence-based intervention that rigorous, peer-reviewed studies have demonstrated to hold promise for strengthening classrooms' relationships, student autonomy, or expectations of success (Kratochwill & Stoiber, 2002). Several resources are available for identifying evidence-based educational interventions, including interventions listed on the website of the What Works Clearinghouse (www. whatworks.ed.gov), several Response-to-Intervention resources (e.g., www.intervention-central.org); the Collaborative for Academic, Social and Emotional Learning (http://www.casel.org); and the UCLA Center for Mental Health in the Schools (http://smhp.psych.ucla.edu).

Next Steps

The rich tradition of research in developmental resilience holds special relevance to schooling because it establishes the characteristics of social and psychological environments that are optimal for children's capacity to overcome adversity. Our efforts to translate resilience research into classroom practices began by operationalizing its most robust and universal findings into a set of class-wide characteristics that could define a "resilient classroom." To date, our work has been dedicated to establishing that these characteristics of classrooms matter for children's learning, that they can be reliably and validly assessed, and that the results of these assessments can support practical plans to strengthen the classroom learning environment. In brief, we have worked to create a micro-study template that allows teachers and their students to empirically examine the resilience-promoting features of their own classroom.

Now, we are directing much of our attention towards carefully specifying the intervention strategies that teachers can use to strengthen the six classroom characteristics. Originally, we had assumed that this would require that we carefully "manualize" the micro-study consultation procedures; create sourcebooks of classroom routines, practices, and manualized interventions; and then implement these in large sample, random assignment, treatment-control studies. We anticipated that our most ambitious challenge would be specifying the consultative process in meticulous ways so that it could be replicated with good fidelity, all the while refining the procedures to be highly acceptable to classroom teachers. Instead, it has become increasingly apparent that our most difficult task has been to frame the micro-study procedures so that these accommodate the many diverse systems that exist within the classrooms. Clearly, one size does not fill all classrooms, and our micro-study procedures need to be innovative and flexible enough to fit the pragmatic realities of daily classroom practices. Ultimately, the success of the micro-studies will be sustained over time if teachers find the micro-study strategy to be viable, interesting, authentically relevant to their teaching, a strategy that saves them time and maximizes their impact with students—in short, a strategy that is worth their time.

Eighteen years ago, Coie et al. (1993) argued that practice ought to inform developmental research in the same way that developmental research ought to inform practice. Our most compelling lesson has been to listen carefully to teachers and their students, and thoughtfully attend to the wisdom in their observations about their classrooms, the change strategies that they use, and the accommodations they have made to the micro-study procedures. Then, we have infused the best of these teacher-generated ideas into our framework so that its potential is enhanced. The micro-study strategy has become more effective when we have crafted balanced partnerships with teachers and, in some cases, with students, and they work alongside us as we translate developmental resilience research into classroom practices. In essence, it has been important that classroom practices inform our promotion of resilience as much as our research is informing classroom practices.

One particularly compelling question that we are addressing with teacher partners is this: Which of the six resilience-promoting characteristics ought be emphasized in plans to strengthen classroom resilience? Are each of these equally important for the classrooms' support for student success and competence? In addition, it is not yet clear whether or how the relative importance of these factors might shift from one school to another, one cultural community to another, across generations, for high vs. low risk youth, or given different outcomes indicators of success. Most of the current research on classroom effectiveness has only examined one of these characteristics, independent of the others. In real classrooms, though, these merge into a psychosocial climate and interventions to strengthen this climate must work with the complexity of the system.

The central purpose of our classroom change efforts is not merely to change school procedures, but to enhance youth success. We remain convinced that it is absolutely essential to draw broadly from developmental resilience research, and work carefully to apply educational and developmental research on classroom relationships and student autonomy. Much of the research on these domains has been academic and theoretical rather than practice oriented. Still, the act of translating this research into practice is shifting our frame of reference and inherently reshapes our understanding of resilience. In the final analysis, we expect that this will make our understanding of classroom resilience stronger.

Finally, an important feature of the micro-study strategy is that it is not a remedial strategy for struggling teachers. Instead, micro-studies provide committed teachers with one more tools that they can use to stretch their capacities as teachers, maximize the match between their students' needs and their classroom practices, and nudge their students towards rewarding and successful adulthood. Deliberately intervening to strengthen children's lives is an essential goal of most dedicated teachers.

References

Coie, J. D., Watt, N. F., West, S. G., Hawkins, J. D., Asarnow, J. R., Markan, H. J., et al. (1993). The science of prevention: A conceptual framework and some directions for a national research program. *American Psychologist, 48*, 1013–1022.

Comer, J. P., Haynes, N. M., Joyner, E. T., & Ben-Avie, M. (Eds.). (1996). *Rallying the whole village: The Comer process for reforming education*. New York: Teachers College Press.

Doll, B., Kurien, S., LeClair, C., Spies, R., Champion, A., & Osborn, A. (2009). The ClassMaps survey: A framework for promoting positive classroom environments. In R. Gilman, S. Huebner, & M. Furlong (Eds.), *Handbook of positive psychology in the schools* (pp. 213–227). New York: Routledge.

Doll, B., LeClair, C., & Kurien, S. (2009). Effective classrooms: Classroom learning environments that foster school success. In T. Gutkin & C. Reynolds (Eds.), *The handbook of school psychology* (pp. 791–807). Hoboken, NJ: Wiley.

Doll, B., & Lyon, M. (1998). Risk and resilience: Implications for the practice of school psychology. *School Psychology Review, 27*, 348–363.

Doll, B., Murphy, P., & Song, S. (2003). The relationship between children's self-reported recess problems, and peer acceptance and friendships. *Journal of School Psychology, 41*, 113–130.

Doll, B., Spies, R. A., Champion, A., Guerrero, C., Dooley, K., & Turner, A. (2010). The ClassMaps survey: A measure of students' perceptions of classroom resilience. *Journal of Psychoeducational Assessment, 28*, 338–348.

Doll, B., Spies, R. A., LeClair, C., Kurien, S., & Foley, B. P. (2010). Student perceptions of classroom learning environments: Development of the ClassMaps survey. *School Psychology Review, 39*, 203–218.

Doll, B., Zucker, S., & Brehm, K. (2004). *Resilient classrooms: Creating healthy environments for learning*. New York: Guilford Publications.

Egeland, B., Carlson, E., & Sroufe, L. A. (1993). Resilience as process. *Development and Psychopathology, 5*, 517–528.

Kratochwill, T. R., & Stoiber, K. C. (2002). Special issue: Evidence-based interventions in school psychology: The state of the art and future directions. *School Psychology Quarterly, 17*, 341–389.

Masten, A. S. (2001). Ordinary magic: Resilience processes in development. *American Psychologist, 56*, 227–238.

Masten, A. S., & Coatsworth, J. D. (1998). The development of competence in favorable and unfavorable environments: Lessons from research on successful children. *American Psychologist, 53*, 205–220.

National Research Council and the Institute of Medicine. (2004). *Engaging schools: Fostering high school students' motivation to learn*. Committee on Increasing High School Students' Engagement and Motivation to Learn; Board on Children, Youth, and Families; Division of Behavioral and Social Sciences and Education. Washington, DC: The National Academies Press.

Pianta, R. C., & Walsh, D. J. (1998). Applying the construct of resilience in schools: Cautions from a developmental systems perspective. *School Psychology Review, 27*, 407–417.

Pulliam, J. D., & Van Patten, J. J. (2007). *History of education in America* (9th ed.). Upper Saddle River, NJ: Merrill Prentice Hall.

Rutter, M., Maughan, B., Mortimore, P., Ouston, J., & Smith, A. (1979). *Fifteen thousand hours: Secondary schools and their effects on children*. Cambridge, MA: Harvard University Press.

Slavin, R. E., & Madden, N. A. (2001). *Success for all: Research and reform in elementary education*. Mahwah, NJ: Lawrence Erlbaum Associates.

Werner, E. E. (2006). What can we learn about resilience from large-scale longitudinal studies. In S. Goldstein & R. B. Brooks (Eds.), *Handbook of resilience in children*. New York: Springer.

Jonathan Cohen

Life is full of ups and downs. What allows some people to be able to "bounce back" and some not? Virtually all scholars appreciate that this capacity to "bounce back" or be resilient is a biopsychosocially informed interactive process that refers to the findings that some individuals have relatively good psychosocial outcomes despite suffering risk experience that would be expected to bring about complicating effects (Rutter, 2006a, b). There has been an important debate about the nature of resiliency that is reflected in many of the chapters in this book and elsewhere (e.g., Greenberg, 2006). This chapter will not address the history and controversies that have shaped our unfolding understanding of this fundamentally important capacity. Here we will use the term resiliency to refer to the person's capacity to overcome stress or adversity. Resilience is not a trait that people either have or do not have. It involves behaviors, thoughts, and actions that can—at least to some extent—be learned and developed in anyone.

This chapter will describe how measuring K-12 school climate and using this data to engage students, parents, and school personnel is a practical, helpful, and data-driven school improvement strategy that provides the foundation for resilience, student learning, and positive youth development.

Social, Emotional and Civic Competence, School Climate Reform and Resiliency

This chapter honors and builds on other chapters in this volume that have underscored how healthy, consistent, engaged, and "connected" student–adult relationships (Jordon, Chap. 7; Werner, Chap. 8), instructional and school-wide efforts designed to promote children's (and adults) social, emotional, and civic competencies (Elisa, Parker & Rosenblatt, Chap. 22; Scales, Chap. 26; Winslow, Sandler & Wolchik, Chap. 28; Shure & Aberson, Chap. 29), empathic socially and emotionally "smart" parenting and healthy families (Sheridan, Dowd & Eagle, Chap. 12; Brooks, Chap. 27) promotes social and emotional competencies and healthy relationships that provide a foundation for resiliency.

The ideas presented in this chapter rest on the assumption that developing social, emotional, and civic competencies as well as growing up in safe, supportive, engaged schools and homes will promote what Brooks and Goldstein (2001) have described as a resilient mindset that are associated with specific skills (Goldstein & Brooks, 2005).[1] These include feeling appreciated and

---

[1] There is correlational support for this assumption. There is not experimental or quasi-experimental data yet to confirm or disconfirm that notion that enhanced social, emotional and civic abilities as well as safe, supportive, engaging and helpfully challenging learning environments promote resiliency.

J. Cohen (✉)
National School Climate Center, New York, NY, USA
e-mail: jonathancohen@schoolclimate.org

S. Goldstein and R.B. Brooks (eds.), *Handbook of Resilience in Children*,
DOI 10.1007/978-1-4614-3661-4_24, © Springer Science+Business Media New York 2013

competent; learning to become more (intrinsically) motivated; having learned realistic goals and expectations for self; they have developed social and emotional skills (e.g., reflective and empathic capacities); flexible problem solving/ decision making; perspective taking, clear communication and dispositions (e.g., viewing mistakes and obstacles as challenges rather than "bad things" to avoid) that provide the foundation for learning and healthy social relations.

Social, emotional, and civic skills, knowledge and dispositions can be learned (Cohen, 2006; Zins et al., 2004). This overlaps with findings from Positive Psychology suggesting that many aspects of resilience are teachable (Reivich & Shatte, 2002; Seligman, 1990). And, Seligman, Ernst, Gillham, Reivich, and Linkins (2009) suggests that when children develop the skills of "emotional fitness" it promotes resiliency. Again in an overlapping manner, there seem to be a number of evidence-based protective factors that contribute to resilience, some of which overlap with social, emotional and civic abilities, and dispositions (e.g., optimism, effective problem solving, impulse control, empathy) that contribute to resilience (Masten & Reed, 2002).

Brooks, Brooks, and Goldstein (2012) have recently summarized an important and growing body of empirical research that supports the notion that when we teach children to become more (intrinsically) motivated and promote engagement, we are also promoting resilience.

These ideas overlap with and compliment the American Psychological Associations' (2010) recent summary of factors that support the development of resiliency:

- *Making connections.* Good relationships with close family members, friends, or others strengthen resilience. Some people find that being active in civic groups, faith-based organizations, or other local groups provides social support and can help with reclaiming hope. Assisting others in their time of need also can benefit the helper.
- *Avoid seeing crises as insurmountable problems.* You can't change the fact that highly stressful events happen, but you can change how you interpret and respond to these events. How we interpret "the moment" is profoundly

shaped by how reflective we are (Cohen & Pickeral, 2009).
- *Accept that change is a part of living.* Certain goals may no longer be attainable as a result of adverse situations. Accepting circumstances that cannot be changed can help you focus on circumstances that you can alter. Again, this capacity is fundamentally related to how reflective the person is or how able they are to be in the moment and be a flexible and creative problem solver/decision maker.
- *Move toward your goals.* Develop some realistic goals. Do something regularly—even if it seems like a small accomplishment—that enables you to move toward your goals. Instead of focusing on tasks that seem unachievable, ask yourself, "What's one thing I know I can accomplish today that helps me move in the direction I want to go?"
- *Take decisive actions.* Act on adverse situations as much as you can. Take decisive actions, rather than detaching completely from problems and stresses and wishing they would just go away.
- *Look for opportunities for self-discovery.* People often learn something about themselves and may find that they have grown in some respect as a result of their struggle with loss. Many people who have experienced tragedies and hardship have reported better relationships, greater sense of strength even while feeling vulnerable, increased sense of self-worth, a more developed spirituality, and heightened appreciation for life.
- *Nurture a positive view of yourself.* Developing confidence in your ability to solve problems and trusting your instincts helps build resilience.
- *Keep things in perspective.* Even when facing very painful events, try to consider the stressful situation in a broader context and keep a long-term perspective. Avoid blowing the event out of proportion.
- *Maintain a hopeful outlook.* An optimistic outlook enables you to expect that good things will happen in your life. Try visualizing what you want, rather than worrying about what you fear.
- *Take care of yourself.* Pay attention to your own needs and feelings. Engage in activities

that you enjoy and find relaxing. Exercise regularly. Taking care of yourself helps to keep your mind and body primed to deal with situations that require resilience.

We will now turn to school climate reform as a data-driven strategy that mobilizes the "whole school community" to support the development of social, emotional and civic competencies, and a resilient mindset.

School Climate: Research, Policy, and Practice Trends

Educators have studied school climate for over 100 years (Cohen, McCabe, Michelli, & Pickeral, 2009). Over the last 3 decades there has been a growing body of empirical research that has studied which factors color and shape the learning environment at school (for reviews, see: Cohen et al., 2009; Freiberg, 1999; National School Climate Council, 2007). In 2007 the Education Commission of the States and the National School Climate Center (formerly the Center for Social and Emotional Education) formed the National School Climate Council (www.schoolclimate.org/about/council.php): a group of practice and policy leaders committed to narrowing the gap between school climate research on the one hand, and school climate policy, practice and teacher education on the other hand (National School Climate Council, 2007). The National School Climate Council (2009) worked to synthesize research on the subject and developed the following consensually created definition of school climate and a sustainable, positive school climate:

> School climate refers to the quality and character of school life. School climate is based on patterns of people's experience of school life and reflects norms, goals, values, interpersonal relationships, teaching, learning, leadership practices, and organizational structures.

> A sustainable, positive school climate fosters youth development and learning necessary for a productive, contributing, and satisfying life in a democratic society. This climate includes norms, values, and expectations that support people feeling socially, emotionally, intellectually, and physically safe. People are engaged and respected. Students, families, and educators work together to develop, live, and contribute to a shared school vision.

Educators model and nurture an attitude that emphasizes the benefits and satisfaction from learning. Each person contributes to the operations of the school and the care of the physical environment.

Some scholars and researchers have argued that it is useful to distinguish "climate" and "culture" and "supportive learning environments" or "conditions for learning" (e.g., Deal & Peterson, 2009; Schoen & Teddlie, 2008). The National School Climate Council (2007) considers these as overlapping terms. We suggest that what is most important is that we are clear about what we are operationally referring to when we use any or all of these terms.

Over the last 3 decades, educators and researchers have worked to identify specific elements that make up school climate. Although there is not "one list" that summarizes these elements, virtually all researchers suggest that there are four major areas that are essential to pay attention to: *Safety* (e.g., rules and norms; physical safety; social–emotional safety); *Relationships* (e.g., respect for diversity; social support: adults; social support: students; leadership); *Teaching and learning* (e.g., social, emotional, ethical, and civic learning; support for learning; professional relationships); and, the *Institutional Environment* (e.g., school connectedness/engagement; physical surrounding).[2] Over time, empirical research will help to refine, redefine and further develop our understanding of what aspects of school climate can and need to be assessed.

As summarized below, there is a compelling and robust body of empirical research that underscores how various aspects of safety, relationships, teaching and learning, and the environment affect and/or predict learning and positive youth

---

[2] The US Departments of Education's Division of Safe and Drug Free Schools has recently suggested that States consider including an assessment of "wellness" as well as rates of substance use/abuse. This stems from mandates to "track" these public health-related concerns. Although school climate surveys do assess aspects of health (e.g., supportiveness; connectedness to school) "wellness" is a somewhat neglected element that most school climate scholars have not explicitly focused on. Another limitation of all current school climate measures is that they do not yet recognize the "voice" of community leaders and/or members.

development. As summarized below there are predictive as well as a larger body of correlational findings that support the notion that when school community members learn and work together to create positive and sustained school climate, academic achievement, and school connectedness and graduate rates all increase. This contributes to the development of what Brooks and Goldstein have referred to as a resilient mind set.

Research: Over the last 40-some years, there has been a growing body of empirical research confirming that school climate matters. Positive and sustained school climate predicts and/or is associated with increased academic achievement, positive youth development, effective risk prevention, health promotion efforts, and teacher satisfaction and retention (for detailed summaries of this research, see Cohen, McCabe, Michelli, & Pickeral, 2009; Cohen & Geier, 2010). As a result of this research several government institutions, including the US Department of Justice (2004), the Centers for Disease Control and Prevention (2009) the US Department of Education's, as well as a growing number of state departments of education emphasize the importance of safe, civil and caring schools, school connectedness (or the belief by students that adults in the school care about their learning and about them as individuals) and/or positive school climates.

Policy: In theory, research shapes policy, which in turn dictates and encourages quality practice. But, there are a variety of factors that commonly undermine this logical framework (Hess, 2008). For whatever sets of reasons, the federal government and state departments of education have not yet responded adequately to school climate research findings. Recent State Department of Education school policy scans revealed significant shortcomings in how climate is defined, measured, and incorporated into policies (see Cohen et al., 2009 for details about the five major problems that currently define these policy shortcomings).

This troubling gap is curious given that most classroom, building, district, state and federal educational leaders appreciate the importance of school climate (e.g., Jennings, 2009; National Middle School Association, 2003; National School Board Association, 2009).

At the invitation of a State Department of Education, The National School Climate Council has developed *National School Climate Standards*: *Benchmarks to promote effective teaching, learning and comprehensive school improvement* (www.schoolclimate.org/climate/standards.php). The following five standards (that are linked to a set of indicators and subindicators) are designed to support local school communities addressing three essential questions: (1) what is our vision for the kind of school we want for our children and/or students? (2) Given this vision, what kinds of policies and rules do we need? And, (3) Given this vision and set of policies and/or rules, what kinds of instructional and systemic practices do we need to actualize this vision? The five standards are:

1. The school community has a shared vision and plan for promoting, enhancing, and sustaining a positive school climate.
2. The school community sets policies specifically promoting (a) the development and sustainability of social, emotional, ethical, civic, and intellectual skills, knowledge, dispositions and engagement and (b) a comprehensive system to address barriers to learning and teaching and reengage students who have become disengaged.
3. The school community's practices are identified, prioritized and supported to (a) promote the learning and positive social, emotional, ethical, and civic development of students; (b) enhance engagement in teaching, learning, and school-wide activities; (c) address barriers to learning and teaching and reengage those who have become disengaged; and (d) develop and sustain an appropriate operational infrastructure and capacity building mechanisms for meeting this standard.
4. The school community creates an environment where all members are welcomed, supported, and feel safe in school: socially, emotionally, intellectually, and physically.
5. The school community develops meaningful and engaging practices, activities, and norms that promote social and civic responsibilities and a commitment to social justice.

A number of States are now in the process as well as considering adopting or adapting these standards.

Practice trends: School leaders have been invested in measuring and working to improve school climate for some time. However, until recently most building leaders used "home grown" school climate assessments tools that were neither reliable nor valid (Cohen et al. 2009). And, the federal *No Child Left Behind* educational act has powerfully focused funding and school improvement efforts on the four current measures that driven American public education: reading, math, and science scores as well as rates of physical violence.

This is changing. In late 2009, the *Safe and Drug Free Schools Division* of the US Department of Education began to examine ways to use school climate as an organizing data-driven concept and process, one that recognizes the range of prosocial, risk prevention and health-mental health promotion efforts that protect children and encourages social, emotional, ethical, and civic learning (Jennings, 2009). The *Safe and Drug Free Schools Division* has recently allocated over 155 million dollars to support 11 states to develop statewide school climate assessment and improvement systems to support low achieving schools and create and sustain quality school climate. And, in the last few years, several large districts (e.g., Anchorage, Chicago, New York, Denver) have begun to measure school climate or many important aspects of climate.

Current School Climate Measurement Tools and Improvement Systems: Supporting the Development of a Resilient Mindset

An underlying premise for this chapter is that what is measured is what counts. And, that measuring and hence recognizing the social, emotional, and civic as well as intellectual dimensions of learning and using this data to mobilize school community members to create even safer, more supportive, engaging, and helpfully challenging learning environments supports the development of a resilient mindset. Today, there are hundreds of school climate measures. However, very few are reliable, valid, and comprehensive in two ways: (1) recognizing student, parent/guardian, and school personal "voice" as well as (2) measuring all of the dimensions that the National School Climate Council suggests need to be evaluated in a comprehensive school climate assessment.

A recent study of 102 school climate measures revealed that only three met American Psychological Association criteria for being reliable and valid: the Comprehensive School Climate Inventory (CSCI); the School Climate Inventory-Revised (SCI-R), and the Western Alliance for the Study of School Climate's School Climate Assessment Inventory (Gangi, 2009). And, a recent independent evaluation by Social Development Research Group (University of Washington) of 72 (1) social emotional learning (SEL) measures and (2) school climate surveys for middle schools reported that ten met their criteria for being reliable and valid and aligned with SEL related criteria. The CSCI was one of these ten measures and the only school climate measure that was recommended (Haggerty, Elgin, & Woolley, 2011).

Table 24.1 presents examples of major indicators and sample questions linked to each of the major school climate factors.

The US Departments of Education funding in this area (noted above) will support at least 11 states developing reliable and valid measurement tools and systems over the next 4 years. Pending congressional approval, the US Department of Education plans to significantly increase funding in this area so that a growing number of States will develop school climate assessment and improvement systems.

In public education today, measurement systems or data is too often used as a "hammer" or a way of simplistically giving schools, districts, or States a literal or figurative "grade" which can have immediate funding implications. This is why it is not uncommon that educators lie about test scores. Measurement systems and educational data should be a "flashlight" rather than a "hammer"—information that guides learning and improvement efforts. And, it to this topic that we

Table 24.1 Four essential dimensions of school climate (and some of the elements included within each)

Dimension	Major indicators and sample questions
Safety	
Rules and norms	Clearly communicated rules about physical violence and verbal abuse and clear and consistent enforcement
	In my school, there are clearly stated rules against insults, teasing, harassment, and other verbal abuse
	Adults in the school will stop students if they see them physically hurting each other (e.g., pushing, slapping, or punching)
Physical safety	Sense that students and adults feel safe from physical harm in the school
	I feel physically safe in all areas of the school building
	I have seen other students being physically hurt at school more than once (e.g., pushed, slapped, punched, or beaten up)
Social and emotional security	Sense that students feel safe from verbal abuse, teasing, and exclusion
	I have been insulted, teased, harassed, or otherwise verbally abused more than once in this school
	There are groups of students in the school who exclude others and make them feel bad for not being a part of the group
Teaching and learning	
Support for learning	Supportive teaching practices, such as constructive feedback and encouragement for positive risk taking, academic challenge, individual attention, and opportunities to demonstrate knowledge and skills in a variety of ways
	My teachers show me how to learn from my mistakes
	My teachers encourage me to try out new ideas (think independently)
	My teachers help me figure out how I learn best
Social and civic learning	Support for the development of social and civic knowledge and skills, including effective listening, conflict resolution, reflection and responsibility, and ethical decision making
	In my school, we have learned ways to resolve disagreements so that everyone can be satisfied with the outcome
	In my school, we talk about the way our actions will affect others
Interpersonal relationships	
Respect for diversity	Mutual respect for individual differences at all levels of the school–student–student; adult–student; adult–adult
	Students in this school respect each other's differences (e.g., gender, race, culture, etc.)
	Adults in this school respect each other's differences (e.g., gender, race, culture, etc.)
Social support: adults	Collaborative and trusting relationships among adults and adult support for students in terms of high expectations for success, willingness to listen, and personal concern
	Adults in my school seem to work well with one another
	If students need to talk to an adult in school about a problem, there is someone they trust who they could talk to
Social support: students	Network of peer relationships for academic and personal support
	Students have friends at school they can turn to if they have questions about homework
	Students have friends at school they can trust and talk to if they have problems
Institutional environment	
School connectedness/ engagement	Positive identification with school, sense of belonging, and norms for broad participation in school life for students and families
	I feel good about what I accomplish in school
	I think my parents/guardians feel welcome at my school
	My school encourages students to get involved in other things than schoolwork (e.g., sports, music/drama clubs, etc.)

(continued)

Table 24.1 (continued)

Dimension	Major indicators and sample questions
Physical surroundings	Cleanliness, order, and appeal of facilities and adequate resources and materials
	My school is physically attractive (pleasing architecture, nicely decorated, etc.)
	My school building is kept in good condition
	My school has up-to-date computers and other electronic equipment available to students

Source: National School Climate Center *Comprehensive School Climate Inventory* (www.schoolclimate.org/programs/csci.php). Used with permission

now turn: how can we use school climate data to "lead the way" in supporting positive youth development, learning (student and adult!) and the promotion of a resilient mindset.

The School Climate Improvement Road Map

Growing out of the work of the National School Climate Council (2007) as well as our Center's work with thousands of schools and districts across America, we have developed a five-stage school climate model that integrates the "problem solving" process that shapes all school reform efforts, with research and best practices that grow out of character education, social emotional learning, community schools and risk prevention/health promotion research and best practices (Cohen, 2006; Cohen & Pickeral, 2009; Devine & Cohen, 2007). Each of these five stages is characterized by a series of tasks and challenges that we have listed below in Table 24.2 below.

What follows is a brief discussion of some of the tasks and challenges that define each of the first three stages of the school climate improvement process and how they support the development of safe, supportive, engaging and helpfully challenging schools for students and adults to learn, teach and "grow up" in. But, before I describe some of these tasks/challenges and how they related to the development of resilient mind sets, I want summarize three, overlapping and organizing ideas related to (i) recognizing the essential social, emotional, and civic aspects of learning; (ii) engagement; and the (iii) coordina-

tion of risk prevention, health promotion, and educational efforts.

School climate recognizes essential social, emotional, ethical, civic and intellectual aspects of learning and our school improvement efforts: Einstein wisely suggested "not everything that can be counted counts, and not everything that counts can be counted." But, in K-12 education, as in business and medicine, it is commonly accepted that "what is measured is what counts." In fact, we are always—to a greater or lesser extent—measuring or taking stock: consciously, systemically, in valid and reliable ways or not![3]

When we measure school climate in valid and reliable ways, we are, by definition, recognizing the essential social, emotional, ethical, and civic as well as intellectual aspects of the learning process (Cohen, 2006; Durlak, Weissberg, Dymnicki, Taylor, & Schellinger, 2011; Hawkins, Kosterman, Catalano, Hill, & Abbott, 2008). We are also assessing important ethical and civic dispositions such as the fairness of school norms or the role of people as bystander (who collude with bullies actively or passively) or upstanders (who says

---

[3] It is interesting and often surprising to reflect on how powerfully measurement shapes all of our day-to-day lives. Consider how you identify people (e.g., health care providers or accountants) organizations (the school we send our children to; clubs; work places) to work with and/or join. Consider how we make judgments about "how did today go?" and/or how healthy or "rich" (in however we define "rich") we are. And, when it is discovered that 1% of a community is spending 30% of its health care costs, these (shocking) measurements can actually set in motion meaningful health care reform (Gawande, 2011). We are continually making judgments based on formal and/or informal data and assessment systems.

Table 24.2 The school climate improvement process: stages, tasks, and challenges

Stage one: preparation and planning
Forming a representative SC improvement leadership team and establishing ground rules collaboratively
Building support and fostering "Buy In" for the school climate improvement process
Establishing a "no fault" framework and promoting a culture of trust
Ensuring your team has adequate resources to support the process
Celebrating successes and building on past efforts
Reflecting on Stage One work
Stage Two: Evaluation
Systematically evaluating the school's strengths, needs, and weaknesses with any number of school climate as well as other potential measurement tools
Developing plans to share evaluation findings with the school community
Reflecting on our Stage Two work
Stage Three: Understanding the findings, engagement, and developing an action plan
Understanding the evaluation findings
Digging into the findings to understand areas of consensus and discrepancy in order to promote learning and engagement
Prioritizing goals
Researching best practices and evidence-based instructional and systemic programs and efforts
Developing an action plan
Reflecting on Stage Three work
Stage Four: Implementing the action plan
Coordinating evidence-based pedagogic and systemic efforts designed to (a) promote students' social, emotional, and civic as well as intellectual competencies; and (b) improve the school climate by working toward a safe, caring, participatory, and responsive school community
The instructional and/or school-wide efforts are instituted with fidelity, monitored and there is an ongoing attempt to learn from successes and challenges
The adults who teach and learn with students work to further their own social, emotional, and civic learning
Reflecting on Stage Four work
Stage Five: Reevaluation and development of the next phase
Reevaluating the school's strengths and challenges
Discovering what has changed and how
Discovering what has most helped and hindered further the school climate improvement process
Revising plans to improve the school climate
Reflecting on Stage Five work

"no" directly or indirectly) to bully-victim behavior (Devine & Cohen, 2007).

An assumption that underlies this chapter is that we can and need to recognize the social, emotional, ethical, and civic as well as intellectual aspects of learning and development to support the development of a resilient mindset.

Supporting meaningful engagement: students, parent/guardian and school personnel learning and working together: Comprehensive school climate improvement practices include, by definition, "the whole village."[4] There is a long-standing and growing body of research that supports the notion that when students are meaningfully engaged in the process of learning, positive youth development and academic achievement increases and student drop out rates decreases (Akey, 2006; Hardre & Reeve, 2003; Newman, 1992). Today, only one in two students feel engaged in schools (Quaglia Institute for Student Aspirations, 2010)! In an overlapping manner, research underscores the importance of parents and guardians being engaged in the life of the school and as active partners with teachers and how these essential educator–parent/guardian partnerships promote positive youth development and student learning (Epstein et al., 2009; Henderson, Mapp, Johnson, & Davies, 2007; Patrikakou, Weissberg, Redding, & Walberg, 2005). There is significant support for the notion that family strengthening approaches have the greatest impact on increasing resilience (Kumpfer & Summerhays, 2006). But the challenge is how to do so? The school climate improvement process provides a series of practical and meaningful opportunities to engage students and parents/guardians as well as school personnel in ways that support student learning and their healthy development.

During the first stage of the school climate improvement process, *Planning and Preparation*, school leaders have an opportunity to introduce the school climate assessment as an engagement strategy. When a principal is able to say to students, parents/guardians and school personnel, "We need to understand what you think are our strengths and needs. We need to learn together about how to prioritize our goals. And we need to work together to actualize the instructional and/or systemic goals that have grown out of our school climate evaluation." Naturally, this will contribute to people feeling recognized and honored. It powerfully supports collaborative learning and working together: the foundation for authentic learning communities.

One of the first tasks in the *Planning and Preparation* phase is to create a truly representative leadership team. This is challenging. There is no simple way to insure true and complete representation of the whole school community. But we can take meaningful steps in this direction. Rather than selecting students from honors classes and/or the range of existing student leadership positions, school leaders can go to the cafeteria and pick a student from each table. Students who are part of various cliques tend to sit together. In this way, the team of student's chosen speaks for the whole school. Students are initially incredulous. But, as they come to know that the adults really want to understand their perceptions and goals, a truly representative student leadership team grows (Preble & Taylor, 2009).

Students can and need to become co-leaders in any school climate improvement process. They can, for example, become involved with the process of understanding comprehensive school climate findings and can be active in developing "change projects" that grow out of this data. Then we are not only promoting school connectedness (Centers for Disease Control and Prevention, 2009); we are promoting the skills and dispositions that support student participation, student engagement and an engaged citizenry (Cohen, Pickeral & Levine, 2010; Northwest Regional Educational

---

[4] As noted above the major limitation of all current school climate surveys is that they do not recognize the 'voice" of community leaders. The Public Education Network has developed a Civic Index (http://civicindex4education.org/main/home.cfm?Category=What_is&Section=Main) and the federally funded *Communities that Care* program (http://ncadi.samhsa.gov/features/ctc/resources.aspx) are two important examples of data driven efforts that seek to recognize the essential voice of community leaders. In partnership with the Public Education Network, our Center is now developing a new forth scale for the Comprehensive School Climate Inventory (CSCI) (www.schoolclimate.org/climate/practice.php) that will recognize the voice of community leaders and members.

Regional Educational Laboratory, 2008). Middle and high school students are sometime cynical about whether the adults at school really care about what they think and need (Quaglia, 2008, 2010). But in scores of schools we've seen, the ability of students to identify problems and goals are meaningful to them in important and far reaching ways (e.g., Devine & Cohen, 2007; Preble & Taylor, 2009; Wessler & Preble, 2003)!

School climate improvement provides a model that recognizes and supports the coordination of effective risk prevention, health/mental health promotion and prosocial efforts: One of the most serious challenges that educators face is the number of children who enter school and come each day with a host of factors that interfere with school readiness. These range from neighborhood, family, school, peer, and individual factors. These factors become major barriers to learning. There are a number of reasons why K-12 education fails to apply recent research findings about effective child and adolescent health and mental health, interventions and treatments to school improvement efforts (Adelman & Taylor, 2006, 2007). This failure is one of the most important factors contributing to inequities in American public education (Rothstein, Jacobsen & Wilder, 2005). Poverty, for example, powerfully undermines and complicates the ability of a parent or guardian to adequately address children's basic needs.

Neither are educators educated to understand and appreciate the nutritional and social, emotional, and civic dimensions of development and learning.[5] This may contribute to a common phenomenon: many K-12 educators are disinclined or even frightened by "mental health and illness" related matters that provide an essential foundation for the development of a resilient mindset. Even terms of educational movements like "social emotional learning" and "character

education" are often dismissed by middle and high school educators as the latest "flavor of the month" or "not my area or focus." Unless the child's symptoms significantly disrupt functioning, many parents and too many educators are, understandably, unsure when to confer with a mental health professional.

It is critical that schools recognize children's needs and support effective risk prevention and health/mental health as well as their prosocial educational needs. School climate improvement, like all school improvement efforts, need to be a continuous process that is grounded in a flexible and creative problem solving cycle. Research on school climate and best practice from prosocial education, risk prevention, and health/mental health promotion has resulted in a five-stage school climate improvement model (Cohen & Pickeral, 2009; Devine & Cohen, 2007). In this model, schools begin by preparing for the next phase of the school climate/improvement efforts, and then assessing school climate; understanding the findings and developing an action plan. After they have developed an action plan, the next phase focuses on implementation the instructional and/or systemic efforts; and the next phase begins the cycle anew. As outlined in Table 24.1, each of these stages involves a series of tasks and challenges that can be embedded into any and all comprehensive models for systemic change and school transformation.

Too often, school improvement efforts are fragmented and uncoordinated. For example, schools often focus on improving reading instruction *or* promoting safety *or* engaging parents/guardians. These goals in fact, overlap. How safe students feel, for example, will color and shape language (and other aspects of) learning. And, how engaged parents/guardians are in the life of the school powerfully colors our ability to protect students and promote their learning. School climate evaluations provide a snapshot of safety, relationships, teaching, and learning within the school, as well as other environmentally related strengths and needs. Depending on how the findings are used (see below), the school community then has the opportunity to learn, plan, and implement improvement efforts that built on current strengths and needs.

---

[5]Over the last 2 decades there certainly has been extraordinary educational efforts to support pre-K educators about these issues. Organizations like *Zero to Three* (www.zerotothree.org) have had a profound and just impact on federal and state pre-K policy and practice. However, this has not become a facet of K-12 policy and practice.

Conclusion

In conclusion, measuring and improving school climate is an important, research-based strategy that supports the whole child and the whole school community working and learning together. Current educational policy does not recognize the array of children's needs and as a result, tragically, guarantees that American public education will leave children behind.

Clearly, school climate assessment and improvement efforts are useful if we are to support children developing the skills, knowledge, and dispositions they need as the foundation to love, work, and effective participation in a democratic society. When we measure and work to improve school climate we are: recognizing the essential social, emotional, ethical, and civic as well as intellectual aspects of learning; furthering our school improvement efforts; supporting shared leadership and learning; promoting School–Family–Community Partnerships: and, spurring student engagement. And, in doing so we are promoting the development of resilient mindsets.

We now have sets of policy and practice tools and guidelines that will narrow the socially unjust gap between school climate research, policy, practice guidelines, and teacher education. For too many years, American public education has focused all its energies on reading and math scores. As important as linguistic and mathematical competences are, it is unfair and in ways socially unjust that we do not recognize the whole child and the whole school community. In fact, I suggest that this is violation of children's rights (Cohen, Shapiro, & Fisher, 2006; Greene, 2006). Measuring and improving school climate is a practical, prosocial strategy that supports all children and their ability to become healthy, life long learners.

References

Adelman, H. S., & Taylor, L. (2006). *The school leader's guide to student learning supports: New directions for addressing barriers to learning*. Thousand Oaks, CA: Corwin Press.

Adelman, H. S., & Taylor, L. (2007). *Fostering school, family, and community involvement*. Portland, OR: North-West Regional Educational Laboratory & Hamilton Fish Institute. Retrieved September 20, 2010, from http://smhp.psych.ucla.edu/publications/44%_0guide%_0_%_0fostering%_0school%_0family%_0and%_0community%_0involvement.pdf

Akey, T. M. (2006, January). *School context, student attitudes and behavior, and academic achievement: An exploratory analysis*. New York: MDRC. Retrieved April 23, 2007, from http://www.mdrc.org/publications/419/full.pdf

American Psychological Association. (2010). *The road to resilience*. Retrieved January 7, 2011, from http://www.apa.org/helpcenter/road-resilience.aspx.

Brooks, R., & Goldstein, S. (2001). *Raising resilient children: Fostering strength, hope, and optimism in your child*. New York, NY: Contemporary Books.

Brooks, R., Brooks, S. & Goldstein, S. (2012). The power of mindsets: Nurturing engagement, motivation, and resilience in students. In S. L. Christenson, A. L. Reschly, & C. Wylie (Eds.) *Handbook of research in student engagement*. Springer.

Cohen, J. (2006). Social, emotional, ethical and academic education: Creating a climate for learning, participation in democracy and well-being. *Harvard Educational Review*, 76(2), Summer, 201–237. www.hepg.org/her/abstract/8.

Cohen, J., Shapiro, L., & Fisher, M. (2006). Finding the heart of your school: Using school climate data to create a climate for learning. *Principal Leadership (The Journal of the National Association of Secondary School Principals)*, 7(4), 26–32.

Cohen, J., Pickeral, T., & McCloskey, M. (2008). The challenge of assessing school climate. [Online article]. *Educational Leadership*, 66(4). Retrieved December 2, 2008, from www.ascd.org/publications/educational_leadership/dec08/vol66/num04/toc.aspx.

Cohen, J., McCabe, E. M, Michelli, N. M, & Pickeral, T. (2009). School climate: research, policy, teacher education and practice. *Teachers College Record*, 111(1), 180–213. http://www.tcrecord.org/Content.asp?ContentId=15220.

Cohen, J. & Pickeral, T. (2009). *The school climate implementation road map: Promoting democratically informed school communities and the continuous process of school climate improvement*. New York, NY: National School Climate Center www.schoolclimate.org/climate/roadmap.php.

Cohen, J., Pickeral, T., & Levine, P. (2010). The foundation for democracy: Social, emotional, ethical, cognitive skills and dispositions in K-12 schools. *Inter-American Journal of Education for Democracy*, 3(1), 73–94. http://scholarworks.iu.edu/journals/index.php/ried/index.

Cohen, J., & Geier, V. (2010). *School climate research summary—2009. A school climate brief*. New York: National School Climate Center.

Comer, J. P. (2005). *Leave no child behind: Preparing today's youth for tomorrow's world*. New Haven: Yale University Press.

Centers for Disease Control and Prevention. (2009). *School connectedness: Strategies for increasing protective factors among youth.* Atlanta, GA: Author. Retrieved December 3, 2009, from http://www.cdc.gov/healthyyouth/adolescenthealth/pdf/connectedness.pdf

Deal, T. E., & Peterson, K. D. (2009). *Shaping school culture: Pitfalls, paradoxes, & promises* (2nd ed.). San Francisco: Jossey-Bass.

Devine, J., & Cohen, J. (2007). *Making our school safe: Strategies to protect children and promote learning.* New York, NY: Teachers College Press.

Durlak, J. A., Weissberg, R. P., Dymnicki, A. B., Taylor, R. D., & Schellinger, K. R. (2011). The impact of enhancing students' social and emotional learning: A meta-analysis of school-based universal interventions. *Child Development, 82*(1), 405–432.

Epstein, J. L., Sanders, M. G., Sheldon, S. B., Simon, B. S., Clark Salinas, K., Rodriguez Jansorn, N., Van Voorhis, F. L., Martin, C. S., Thomas, B. G., Greenfeld, D. G., Hutchins, D. J., & Williams, K. J. (2009). *School, family, and community partnerships: Your handbook for action* (3rd ed.). Thousand Oaks, CA: Corwin Press.

Eyman, W., & Cohen, J. (2009). *Breaking the bully-victim-passive bystander tool kit: Creating a climate for learning and responsibility.* New York: National School Climate Center. Retrieved April 20, 2009, from http://www.schoolclimate.org/climate/toolkit.php

Freiberg, H. J. (Ed.). (1999). *School climate: Measuring, improving and sustaining healthy learning environments.* Philadelphia: Falmer Press.

Gangi, T. A. (2009). *School climate and faculty relationships: Choosing an effective assessment measure.* St. John's University New York. Retrieved November 1, 2009, from http://gradworks.umi.com/33/88/3388261.html.

Goldstein, S., & Brooks, R. (2005). *Handbook of resilience in children.* New York, NY: Kluwer Academic/Plenum.

Greenberg, M. T. (2006). Promoting resilience in children and youth. *Annuals of the New York Academy of Science, 1094,* 116–124.

Greene, M. (2006). Bullying in schools: A plea for a measure of human rights. *Journal of Social Issues, 62*(1), 63–79.

Gawande, A. (2011, January 24). The hot spotters: Can we lower medical costs by giving the neediest patients better care? *The New Yorker,* pp. 41–51.

Haggerty, K., Elgin, J. & Woolley, A. (2011). *Social-emotional learning and school climate assessment measures for middle school youth.* A Social Development Research Group University of Washington report. Funded by the Raikes Foundation.

Hardre, P. L., & Reeve, J. (2003). A motivational model of rural students' intentions to persist in, versus drop out of, high school. *Journal of Educational Psychology, 95*(2), 347.

Hawkins, J. D., Kosterman, R., Catalano, R. F., Hill, K. B., & Abbott, R. D. (2008). Effects of social development interventions in childhood: Fifteen years later. *Archives of Pediatrics & Adolescent Medicine, 162,* 1133–1141.

Henderson, A. T., Mapp, K. L., Johnson, V. R., & Davies, D. (2007). *Beyond the bake sale: The essential guide to family-school partnerships.* New York, NY: New Press.

Hess, F. H. (2008). *When research matter.* Cambridge, MA: Harvard Education Press.

Jennings, K. (2009, November 12). *Federal education priorities and creating safe schools.* US Department of Education, Washington, DC.

Kumpfer, K. L., & Summerhays, J. F. (2006). Prevention approaches to enhance reliance among high-risk youths. *Annuals of the New York Academy of Science, 1094,* 151–163.

Masten, A. S., & Reed, M. G. J. (2002). Resilience in development. In C. R. Snyder & S. J. Lopez (Eds.), *Handbook of positive psychology* (pp. 74–88). New York, NY: Oxford University Press.

National Middle School Association. (2003). *This we believe: Successful schools for young adolescents.* Westerville, OH: NMSA.

National School Climate Council. (2007). *The school climate challenge: Narrowing the gap between school climate research and school climate policy, practice guidelines and teacher education policy.* New York, NY: National School Climate Center. Retrieved September 15, 2007, from www.schoolclimate.org/climate/policy.php/.

National School Climate Council. (2009). National School Climate Standards: Benchmarks to promote effective teaching, learning and comprehensive school improvementt. National School Climate Center. http://www.schoolclimate.org/climate/standards.php.

National School Board Association. (2009). *Becoming a better board member: A guide to effective board service* (3rd ed.). Alexandria, VA: National School Boards Association.

Newman, F. (1992). *Student engagement and achievement in American secondary schools.* New York: Teachers College Press.

Northwest Regional Educational Regional Educational Laboratory. (2008). *Student engagement gains ground: A research brief.* Retrieved August 14, 2009, from http://www.nwrel.org/nwedu/13-03/dept/research.php

Patrikakou, E. N., Weissberg, R. P., Redding, S., & Walberg, H. J. (Eds.). (2005). *School-family partnerships for children's success.* New York, NY: Teachers College Press.

Preble, W., & Taylor, L. (2009). School climate through students' eyes. *Educational Leadership, 66*(4), 35–40.

Quaglia Institute for Student Aspirations. (2010). *My Voice national student report (grades 6–12).* Portland, ME: Author. Retrieved January 29, 2012, from http://www.qisa.org/publications/docs/MyVoiceNationalStudentReport%286-12%292010.pdf

Reivich, K., & Shatte, A. (2002). *The resilience factor: Seven essential skills for overcoming life's inevitable obstacles.* New York, NY: Broadway Books.

Rothstein, R., Jacobsen, R., & Wilder, T. (2005). *Grading education: Getting accountability right*. New York: Teachers College Press.

Rutter, M. (2006a). The promotion of resilience in the face of adversity. In A. Clarke-Stewart & J. Dunn (Eds.), *Families count: Effects on child and adolescent development* (pp. 26–52). New York, NY: Cambridge University Press.

Rutter, M. (2006b). Implications of resilience concepts for scientific understanding. *Annuals of the New York Academy of Science, 1094*, 1–12.

Schoen, L. T., & Teddlie, C. (2008). A new model of school culture: A response to a call for conceptual clarity. *School Effectiveness and School Improvement, 19*(2), 129–153.

Seligman, M. E. P. (1990). *Learned optimism*. New York, NY: Knopf.

Seligman, M. E. P., Ernst, R. M., Gillham, J., Reivich, K., & Linkins, M. (2009). Positive education and classroom interventions. *Oxford Review of Education, 35*, 293–311.

U.S. Department of Justice. (2004). *Toward safe and orderly schools—The national study of delinquency prevention in schools*. Office of Justice Programs, National Institute of Justice, Report # 205005. Retrieved July 20, 2006, from http://www.ojp.usdoj.gov/nij

Wessler, S. L., & Preble, W. (2003). *The Respectful school: How educators and students can conquer hate and harassment*. Alexandria, VA: Association for Supervision and Curriculum Development (ASCD).

Zins, J., Weissberg, R. W., Wang, M. C., & Walberg, H. (Eds.). (2004). *Building school success on social emotional learning: What does the research say?* New York: Teachers College Press.

Part VI

Shaping the Future of Children and Adults

Positive Adaptation, Resilience and the Developmental Assets Framework

25

Arturo Sesma Jr., Marc Mannes, and Peter C. Scales

Advances in our understanding of adaptation are rooted in the seminal work of Garmezy, Rutter, Werner, and others who "discovered" a not inconsiderable proportion of children who, thought to be at risk for current and future maladaptation, showed few or no signs of pathology and often exhibited high levels of competence (Garmezy, 1974; Rutter, 1979; Werner & Smith, 1982). Investigating what made a difference in this group of children's lives led at first to descriptions of correlates of positive development among children living in high-risk contexts and has progressed to complex process models allowing for multiple causal effects across multiple ecologies (Masten, 1999a). Two of the great contributions from this line of work have focused on elucidating the mechanisms thought to underlie both adaptive and maladaptive developmental trajectories under conditions of adversity, as well as advancing the position that studies of positive adaptation and competence should be studied alongside the more dominant models of risk, pathology, and treatment (Garmezy, 1974; Rutter, 1979; Masten, 2001). These advancements in turn have been instrumental in current

intervention and prevention practices (Rolf & Johnson, 1999).

This attention to the broad array of factors that facilitate healthy youth development has fueled a relatively new set of models focusing on the strengths, resources, and positive experiences of youths and of their communities (Benson & Pittman, 2001). Under the broader rubric of positive youth development, and with the knowledge gained from decades of research on resilience and risk and protective factors, these models seek new ways of conceptualizing, measuring, and promoting optimal outcomes for youth (Benson, Scales, Hamilton, & Sesma, 2006; Connell, Gambone, & Smith, 2001; Eccles & Gootman, 2002; Pittman, Irby, & Ferber, 2001).

One of these models is Search Institute's developmental assets framework. Over the past 20 years, Search Institute has been a leading force in theoretical and empirical work examining the relations among developmental resources, optimal development, and community mobilization (Benson, 2003; Brown, 2008; Eccles & Gootman, 2002; Lerner, 2003), with the primary goal of establishing an interdisciplinary and applied line of inquiry exploring the viability and developmental significance of the "informal, natural, and nonprogrammatic capacity of community" (Benson & Saito, 2001, p. 146).

In this chapter we describe the developmental assets framework and its relation to resilience models by addressing three dimensions salient to both approaches: (1) the taxonomy of factors thought to promote positive development and

A. Sesma Jr. (✉)
St. Catherine University, St. Paul, MN, USA
e-mail: agsesma@stkate.edu

M. Mannes
Booz Allen Hamilton, Minneapolis, MN, USA

P.C. Scales
Search Institute, Minneapolis, MN, USA

S. Goldstein and R.B. Brooks (eds.), *Handbook of Resilience in Children*,
DOI 10.1007/978-1-4614-3661-4_25, © Springer Science+Business Media New York 2013

adaptation; (2) the criteria used to determine or define positive developmental outcomes; and (3) strategies and mechanisms for enhancing the development of youth. In the process, we highlight points of convergence and distinction from resilience models along these three dimensions. Given that resilience is not a homogeneous arena of research, with differences in models, terminology, and assumptions, we will draw on broad themes to provide the context for the description of the developmental assets model.

Facilitators of Positive Development: The Developmental Assets Framework

The developmental assets framework is part of the rapidly developing field of positive youth development (PYD). PYD is the umbrella term for a number of approaches that, by and large, share the following characteristics (see also Benson et al., 2006; Hamilton, Hamilton, & Pittman, 2003):

- *A strength-based approach to development.* An emphasis on elements that facilitates optimal (thriving) development rather than factors associated with problematic behavior. The converse of strength-based models is the *risk or deficit-model*, where the emphasis is on problem behaviors and how to reduce or prevent them.
- *Multiple agents across multiple sectors.* Children develop in families, schools, neighborhoods, and in the context of multiple relationships. Any model that purports to describe development must reflect the various settings in which development proceeds.
- *Focus on relationships.* Positive development as a function of intentional and meaningful relationships with youth—getting to know them, asking their opinions, acknowledging that youth have a voice and something to contribute.
- *Facilitating positive development is an everyday, commonplace occurrence.* Promoting youth development is not solely the province of professionals or practitioners; everyone in a

community has a role and a responsibility in the lives of youth.

Search Institute's attempt at capturing these four elements lies in our work on how young people experience various "developmental assets." Developmental assets are defined as a set of interrelated experiences, relationships, skills, and values that are known to enhance a broad range of youth outcomes and are assumed to operate similarly for all youth (Benson, Leffert, Scales, & Blyth, 1998; Scales & Leffert, 2004). We have identified 40 of these assets, which reflect broad conceptualizations about strength-based, positive child and youth development that are rooted in explications of key developmental socialization processes of connection, support, regulation, autonomy, and competencies (Barber & Olsen, 1997; Benson, Scales, & Mannes, 2003; Scales & Leffert, 2004).

These developmental processes, however, need to be understood in light of the multiple and interactive influences on child well-being. The asset framework borrows heavily from Bronfenbrenner's (1979) notion that successful development is a function of the individual in constant transaction with multiple supportive ecologies. Additionally, the work of Jessor (1993) and Sameroff, Seifer, and Bartko (1997) on the "shared causation" and cumulative nature of risk and protective factors have informed the development and interpretation of developmental assets. Thus, one of the main purposes of the asset framework is to identify correlates and predictors of short- and long-term positive outcomes in order to guide theory and research on developmental strengths. Central to these efforts is an examination of interactive and richly layered community effects on youth development. Like various lists of protective factors (Eccles & Gootman, 2002; Hawkins, Catalano, & Miller, 1992; Masten, 2001; Masten & Reed, 2002; Werner & Smith, 1993), the assets framework identifies both external and internal qualities (see Table 25.1). The external assets (i.e., health-promoting features of the environment) are grouped into four categories: (1) support; (2) empowerment; (3) boundaries and expectations; and (4) constructive use of time. The internal

Table 25.1 Search Institute's developmental assets framework

External assets	Support	1. Family support—Family life provides high levels of love and support
		2. Positive family communication—Young person and her or his parent(s) communicate positively, and young person is willing to seek advice and counsel from parents
		3. Other adult relationships—Young person receives support from three or more nonparent adults
		4. Caring neighborhood—Young person experiences caring neighbors
		5. Caring school climate—School provides a caring, encouraging environment
		6. Parent involvement in schooling—Parent(s) are actively involved in helping young person succeed in school
	Empowerment	7. Community values youth—Young person perceives that adults in the community value youth
		8. Youth as resources—Young people are given useful roles in the community
		9. Service to others—Young person serves in the community 1 h or more per week
		10. Safety—Young person feels safe at home, at school, and in the neighborhood
	Boundaries and expectations	11. Family boundaries—Family has clear rules and consequences and monitors the young person's whereabouts
		12. School boundaries—School provides clear rules and consequences
		13. Neighborhood boundaries—Neighbors take responsibility for monitoring young people's behavior
		14. Adult role models—Parent(s) and other adults model positive, responsible behavior
		15. Positive peer influence—Young person's best friends model responsible behavior
		16. High expectations—Both parent(s) and teachers encourage the young person to do well
	Constructive use of time	17. Creative activities—Young person spends 3 or more hours per week in lessons or practice in music, theater, or other arts
		18. Youth programs—Young person spends 3 or more hours per week in sports, clubs, or organizations at school and/or in the community
		19. Religious community—Young person spends 1 or more hours per week in activities in a religious institution
		20. Time at home—Young person is out with friends "with nothing special to do" two or fewer nights per week
Internal assets	Commitment to learning	21. Achievement motivation—Young person is motivated to do well in school
		22. School engagement—Young person is actively engaged in learning
		23. Homework—Young person reports doing at least one hour of homework every school day
		24. Bonding to school—Young person cares about her or his school
		25. Reading for pleasure—Young person reads for pleasure 3 or more hours per week
	Positive values	26. Caring—Young person places high value on helping other people
		27. Equality and social justice—Young person places high value on promoting equality and reducing hunger and poverty
		28. Integrity—Young person acts on convictions and stands up for her or his beliefs
		29. Honesty—Young person "tells the truth even when it is not easy"
		30. Responsibility—Young person accepts and takes personal responsibility
		31. Restraint—Young person believes it is important not to be sexually active or to use alcohol or other drugs

(continued)

Table 25.1 (continued)

Internal assets	Social competencies	32. Planning and decision-making—Young person knows how to plan ahead and make choices
		33. Interpersonal competence—Young person has empathy, sensitivity, and friendship skills
		34. Cultural competence—Young person has knowledge of and comfort with people of different cultural/racial/ethnic backgrounds
		35. Resistance skills—Young person can resist negative peer pressure and dangerous situations
		36. Peaceful conflict resolution—Young person seeks to resolve conflict nonviolently
	Positive identity	37. Personal power—Young person feels he or she has control over "things that happen to me"
		38. Self-esteem—Young person reports having a high self-esteem
		39. Sense of purpose—Young person reports that "my life has a purpose"
		40. Positive view of personal future—Young person is optimistic about her or his personal future

assets (i.e., competencies and skills that young people use to guide their behavior) are placed in four categories as well: (1) commitment to learning; (2) positive values; (3) social competencies; and (4) positive identity. Search Institute's studies collectively involving more than three million 6th–12th graders (Benson, 2006; Benson, Scales, Leffert, & Roehlkepartain, 1999; Leffert et al., 1998; Scales, Benson, Leffert, & Blyth, 2000), as well as our extensive synthesis of empirical studies on development in adolescence (Scales & Leffert, 2004), middle childhood (Scales, Sesma, & Bolstrom, 2004), and early childhood (VanderVen, 2008) have yielded numerous positive conclusions about the contribution of developmental assets to students' avoidance of high-risk behaviors and measures of thriving, including helping others, overcoming adversity, and school success, as well as hopeful purpose and positive emotionality (Benson & Scales 2009a, 2009b).

Though important to our conceptual and empirical work on positive development, this framework was also designed with highly applied objectives as well. Thus, a second purpose of the asset model is to create an easily accessible language around positive development that can act as a catalyst for community mobilization and action on behalf of its youth. The significance of this facet cannot be overstated. Developmental assets were specifically chosen to reflect the kinds of relationships, environments, norms, and competencies over which people in a community have some degree of control (Benson, Scales, & Mannes, 2003). As Scales and Leffert (1999) put it: although not everyone can offer youth a well-designed experience that builds their planning and decision-making skills, everyone can talk with adolescents, keep an eye on them when their parents are not around, protect them, and give them help when they need it. Everyone can help make youth feel valued and supported (p. 13).

Much of the research and applied fieldwork conducted at Search Institute addresses the significance of these kinds of experiences for youth, including how to mobilize individuals within communities to begin engaging in these kinds of intentional relationships with youth.

The Relation of Developmental Assets to Outcomes

The fundamental assumption of the asset model is that the more positive experiences youth possess, the greater the likelihood they will succeed developmentally. Studies from Search Institute and others consistently show that youth who report relatively more assets are less likely to engage in problematic risk behavior patterns and more likely to endorse engaging in positive, socially constructive behaviors (Benson & Scales, 2009b; Scales et al., 2000; Taylor et al., 2002). For example, 50% of youth with 0–10 assets report engaging in a pattern of problematic alcohol use, compared to only 3% of youth with 31–40 assets, a 17-fold risk ratio. Conversely, 89% of youth with 31^4-0 assets report that they value and affirm cultural diversity, while only 34% of youth with 0–10 assets report this. Similarly, 32% of asset-depleted youth report engaging in early sexual intercourse, vs. only 3% for asset-rich youth, and only 8% of asset-depleted youth report getting mostly. As in school, compared with 49% of asset-rich youth (Search Institute, 2001). Multivariate analyses investigating the cumulative effect of assets indicate that the total number of assets explains 57% of the variance in a composite index of risk behaviors (Leffert et al., 1998), and between 47 and 54% of the variance in a composite index of positive behaviors (Scales et al., 2000), all over and above demographic variables such as maternal education, grade, and gender. Similar cumulative effects are found when the sample is broken down by race/ethnicity and SES levels (Sesma & Roehlkepartain, 2003).

Another way of showing this effect is to create a cumulative asset gradient. Figure 25.1 depicts the mean number of high-risk behavior patterns (e.g., problematic alcohol use, antisocial behavior) and thriving outcomes (e.g., values diversity, succeeds in school, exhibits leadership; see next section below) plotted as a function of the number of assets experienced by youth. These linear functions mirror the more oft-cited cumulative risk graph, wherein *risk* factors are plotted along the jc-axis. The concept of cumulative risk grew

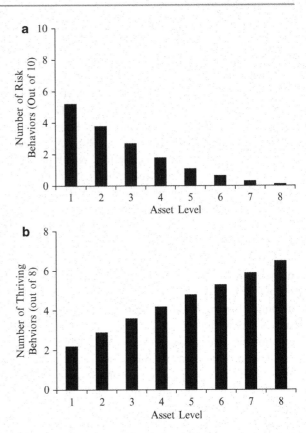

Fig 25.1 Cumulative asset gradient—number of risk behaviors (**a**) and thriving behaviors (**b**) reported by youth as a function of cumulative assets (each asset point is in increments of 5 assets; 1 = 0–5 assets, 2 = 6–10 assets, etc.). Unpublished Search Institute data

out of two consistent findings: risk factors often co-occur, and that it is the accumulation of many risk factors, not just one, that thwarts developmental progress (Belsky & Fearon, 2002; Sameroff & Fiese, 2000). Few factors moderate this linear function, as it has been documented across age, gender, race/ethnicity, socioeconomic status (SES) level, and cross-culturally (Keating & Hertzman, 1999). What these findings from cumulative risk effects suggest is that the power of assets lies in the cumulative pile-up of effects across multiple contexts. A corollary to this echoes the admonition from resilience researchers when discussing risk factors: there is unlikely to be one asset or set of assets that is the "most important" for enhancing development. Attempts at identifying the "magic bullet" of assets violates the assumption of the multifinality of positive development and are unlikely to yield fruitful results (Masten, 1999b; Scales & Leffert, 2004).

Although the majority of studies show point-in-time connections between assets and positive youth outcomes, some also demonstrate the link between assets at one point in time and outcomes one or more years later. Both the amount of an asset (or the number of assets if multiple assets are studied) and specific clusters of assets are related to outcomes over time. For example, Scales and Roehlkepartain (2003; Scales, Benson, Roehlkepartain, Sesma, & van Dulmen, 2006) found that each increase in the level of assets young people reported (from 0–10, to 11–20, 21–30, and 31–40 assets) in 1998, when the sample was in seventh through ninth grades, was associated with a significantly higher grade point average (GPA) 3 years later, when the sample was in the 10th–12th grades; this finding also held when Time 1 GPA was controlled. This is significant because GPA tends to be very stable over time, such that one's previous grades are by far, in all studies, the single best predictor of one's future grades. Moreover, assets in one year are strongly related to grades that same year. These results support the hypothesis that early asset levels provide significant independent contribution to later academic performance. Benson & Scales (2009b) also found that higher asset levels in middle school predicted lower levels of violent and antisocial behavior 3 years later in high school. In a study of whether changes in assets are related to changes in outcome, Taylor and his colleagues (2002) measured assets and positive functioning a year apart for youth involved in gang activity and a control group of youth involved in a community-based organization (CBO). Among the results reported was that for both gang- and CBO-involved youth, changes in positive functioning covaried positively with increases in assets over the year interval.

Developmental Assets and Resilience Constructs

Even though the fundamental distinction between developmental assets and protective factors would seem to be that protective factors are, by definition, operative only under the context of risk (Rutter, 2000), while assets are presumed to be operative regardless of any presumed moderator (e.g., risk/adversity, gender, SES, etc.), attempts at greater terminological clarity of resilience constructs have blurred this distinction (Luthar, Cicchetti, & Becker, 2000). Thus, terms like "protective-stabilizing" and "vulnerability" are added to the resilience lexicon in order to lend greater precision to the putative interactions among risk, moderating attributes, and competence outcomes (Luthar et al., 2000). Using these more differentiated constructs, developmental assets seem to be most closely related to *protective factors* (Luthar et al., 2000), *promotive factors* (Sameroff, 1999), or *assets* (Masten & Reed, 2002). The core element of all of these constructs is a direct positive influence on development regardless of risk status. Though it is likely that some of the developmental assets interact with or moderate risk effects (i.e., should really be characterized as protective-enhancement or protective-stabilizing factors), we do not posit the kinds of complex interactions across assets and risk as outlined by some resilience researchers, for at least two reasons.

First, the preponderance of research on each of these assets shows, in general, similar predictive utility across different groups of youth (Benson et al., 2003; Scales & Leffert, 2004).

Second, our work with communities indicates that individual adults are more likely to be engaged and active in intentional activities if the focus is shifted from vulnerable youth and adolescents to all children and adolescents. Focusing on at-risk and vulnerable youth seems to have the unfortunate effect of strengthening the belief that youth development is the responsibility of the professional sector (clinicians, program implementers, social workers), which has the concomitant effect of fostering civic disengagement (Benson et al., 1998). Of course, this does not preclude examinations of how assets interact with risk-only factors, such as ADHD or poverty (Stouthamer-Loeber et al., 1993). Studies investigating the moderating effects of developmental assets, both with other assets as well as with risk factors, are currently under way. Furthermore, it seems that most of the developmental assets fall into what Sameroff (1999) and Rutter (2000) call dimensional factors, and what Stouthamer-Loeber and her colleagues (1993) call protective plus risk effects. These are factors that, depending on the spectrum one chooses to emphasize, can either be a risk or a protective factor. For example, one of our assets is *family support*, which is defined in a way that emphasizes the positive end of the construct. However, other researchers can use the same global construct (a facet of family functioning) and focus on the negative pole (lack of family support; high degree of family conflict) and call this a risk factor. This does not appear to be all that problematic, given that one's theoretical model should dictate how one chooses to define relevant constructs (so long as the dimensionality of the construct is not forgotten), but also since the effect seems to be the same whether one is increasing protective factors or reducing risk factors (Sameroff, Bartko, Baldwin, Baldwin, & Seifer, 1999).

Beyond Competence to Thriving

The second dimension relevant to both assets and resilience models refers to how each model operationalizes competence or positive development. Masten and Curtis (2000), using the concept of stage-salient tasks, define competence as a track record of "adapta-tional success in the developmental tasks expected of individuals of a given age in a particular cultural and historical context" (p. 533). Other resilience researchers define competence as the absence of psychopathology or problems, while still others incorporate both stage-salient tasks and absence of symptoms to determine their outcome criteria (Masten, 2001). Luthar et al. (2000) attempt to refine the criteria and standards used to determine competence by positing that the selection of outcomes should be dictated by the type and severity of stress, and by a conceptual link between the presenting risk factors and the outcome. They suggest that perhaps the outcome criterion be excellent or superior functioning in a theoretically related domain when risk levels are low or moderate. This criterion for determining an outcome—excellent or optimal functioning—comes closer to Search Institute's work on defining what it means to *thrive* developmentally (Benson & Scales 2009a, 2009b; Scales & Benson, 2005), but Benson and Scales and other scholars (see Lerner, Brentano, Dowling, & Anderson, 2002) go farther, suggesting that thriving must reflect not just on optimal development of the person but mutually enhancing growth of the person and their *contexts*.

Scholars and practitioners are beginning to focus more on what defines not just normal or adequate development, but optimally successful development, or thriving. A new science of "positive psychology" is emerging that focuses on human happiness, optimism, and fulfillment rather than on the pathology and deficits that have driven psychology for the past 50 years (Seligman & Csikszentmihalyi, 2000). The integration of the positive aspects of Erikson's life cycle framework and the core principles of positive psychology, resilience, positive youth development, and the developmental assets framework together may provide an even more comprehensive canvas on which the strength-based child and adolescent research and practice of the coming decades unfolds.

A developmental systems focus on such constructs of human thriving echoes the notions of maximum personal fulfillment reflected in Maslow's theory of self-actualization. However, conceptualizations of thriving must give greater emphasis to this construct not only as an element of personal actualization, but also as inextricably bound with the moral ethos of the larger community in which persons live and to which, even as young people, they are essential contributors. In other words, when young people thrive, they are not simply doing well as individuals; they also are connected and contributing in meaningful ways to the common good that is realized through the groups, neighborhoods, communities, and societies to which they belong (Lerner, Brentano, Dowling, & Anderson, 2002).[1]

Differences Between Developmental Assets and Thriving Indicators

The concept of thriving encompasses not only the relative absence of pathology, but also more explicit indicators of healthy and even optimal development. There is some conceptual similarity between the notion of developmental assets and that of thriving indicators, in that both concepts focus on the presence of strengths in young people's lives. However, there are some important differences between these concepts.

Most important, thriving signifies an optimal developmental process (and outcomes), not just adequate, competent functioning. As such, thriving indicators are unipolar constructs. That is, the absence of thriving in the sense defined here is not necessarily negative. The individual may still be experiencing adequate development and achieving basic competency across various outcomes. In contrast, the relative absence or lower levels of developmental assets, as reflected in the research findings to date, seems associated with poorer developmental outcomes among the adolescents (Benson et al., 1999).

---

[1]Specifically, thriving may be understood as a developmental process of recursive cause and effect engagement with one's ecology *over* time that repeatedly results in optimal outcomes as viewed at any *one* point in time. Thriving in this sense reflects processes that are unique to or more pronounced in particular stages of development, such as the successful navigation of rapidly expanding peer relationships in middle childhood, or the significant cognitive maturation in early adolescence that can radically affect, for better or worse, young people's construction of supportive social environments.

Second, assets are conceptualized as *building blocks* of success, whereas thriving indicators are seen as *signs or markers* of success. In explanatory terms, developmental assets experienced cumulatively over time are considered predictors of or contributors to developmentally optimal outcomes that are represented by thriving indicators. If the assets are conceptualized as the "building blocks" of success, the question can then be raised, building toward what? The thriving indicators represent the "what" that the assets are helping young people build toward. Experiencing the assets defines conditions under which the attainment of those thriving outcomes is made more likely. To some extent, "thriving" can only be judged subjectively, by the individual him- or herself. For example, who can say that people are not thriving who are happy, emotionally open, and socially generous, but not as rich or powerful as they could have been, because they exercised their autonomy to make a choice not to pursue such paths? Perhaps they did so precisely because the pursuit of riches and power would have conflicted with other "well-being outcomes" they valued even more, such as a wonderful marriage, lots of time with their own kids, and other people's kids, or the in-depth pursuits of hobbies or volunteering.

Nevertheless, thriving suggests not only internal satisfaction, but also demonstrable excellence *or* substantive positive growth in a dimension of life. This may be measured either by comparison to others or by comparison to where one was before on that "outcome." Without this criterion as a form of one's "personal best," the concept of thriving becomes elitist. Instead, with the dual notion of thriving signifying demonstrable excellence *or* substantive positive growth, everyone is capable of thriving. In addition, some people are more capable of thriving by being "better" than others in given areas.

Thriving Indicators for Adolescents

Compared to the voluminous literature on adolescent risk-taking and negative behaviors, or the substantial literature on adequate development or competence, there is a relative paucity of research around what constitutes thriving in adolescence. The orientation of both the public and researchers toward young people is predominantly toward naming and reducing negative behavior, or, at best, how to promote adequate or competent functioning among young people (Benson, 2006; Scales, 2001; Scales et al., 2003). The territory of thriving is beginning to be discussed, but until recently, has been largely uncharted. Thus, public and scientific consensus has been more difficult to achieve on what constitutes adolescent "thriving" than it has been to agree about the constellation of risk behaviors that is desirable to reduce in adolescence.[2]

Undoubtedly, that relative difficulty also is partly due to notions of "thriving" being more rooted in moral worldviews and more culturally contextualized than are ideas about risk (Scales & Benson, 2005). For example, youth involvement in violence or cigarette smoking is plainly harmful to them and can kill them. These effects are appreciable regardless of one's cultural background or moral orientation. But showing leadership ability or being individually successful in other ways may not be so highly valued within a culture or moral orientation that values self-effacement and group harmony more highly. Thus, any taxonomy of thriving indicators necessarily reflects a particular moral and cultural framework that is likely to have less universality than competing taxonomies of risk or basic competence.

---

[2]Two early exceptions were two special issues of the *Journal of Adolescent Research*, one that was devoted to "positive aspects of adolescence" (Adams, 2001) and the other that called for youth social policy to focus on positive outcomes as much as it does on negative ones (Pittman, Diversi, & Ferber, 2002). Toward that end, for example, Child Trends, Inc., and the Chapin Hall Center for Children at the University of Chicago, in collaboration with the US Department of Health and Human Services, also played an early leadership role by hosting a conference of state leaders in 2002 to suggest positive indicators of youth development (later released as a book (Moore & Lippman, 2005)). If added to state-level data collection, such indicators would better inform policymakers' decisions about child, youth, and family policies and programs. But there are relatively few examples of studies or policy initiatives that go beyond measuring only negative or just adequate behavior among youth.

In addition, definitions of thriving clearly need to vary by age. Although the main focus of our work has been on adolescence, a useful framework of thriving also must include constructs that are continuous from earlier stages, as well as constructs that are unique to particular developmental stages. For example, there likely are some potential thriving indicators that are developmentally relevant to adolescence but not to middle childhood, such as having a significant girlfriend or boyfriend relationship. At the same time, valid thriving indicators for adolescence likely include some that are essentially the same as developmentally valid indicators for middle childhood. Young people's active helping of others might be an example. The items used to measure the "helping others" indicator might differ between those two developmental stages, but the essence of the prosocial behavior as an indicator of thriving would not. For example, perhaps we would expect adolescents to formally volunteer more as an indicator of thriving, whereas we would expect younger children's helping to be demonstrated more by informal helping of their friends and neighbors.

Originally, Search Institute studied seven indicators of thriving among adolescents: school success, helping others, valuing diversity, exhibiting leadership, overcoming adversity, maintaining physical health, and delaying gratification (Scales et al., 2000). These original seven indicators of well-being status were selected for study for two main reasons. First, a wealth of research suggests that these indicators are related to numerous positive physical, socioemotional, psychological, and cognitive outcomes, both proximally and distally, and that these positive associations occur among diverse young people by gender, race/ethnicity, and socioeconomic background (see review in Scales & Leffert, 2004). Second, these thriving indicators collectively reflect that adolescents have accomplished at least adequately and perhaps excellently a number of developmental tasks conceived as important for all young people, regardless of cultural background. These would include developing their intellectual capacities and a sense of belonging, being able to explore and enlarge their worlds while minimizing risks, and being able to persist and succeed despite challenge

(detailed in Scales et al., 2000). Such thriving indicators seem to satisfy what Takanishi, Mortimer, and McGourthy (1997) defined as their "primary" criterion for indicators of positive adolescent development: the attainment of social competency for adult roles and responsibilities. That broad criterion includes being an educated and productive worker, a person who can maintain a healthy lifestyle, a caring family member, and an involved citizen in a diverse society.

Our more recent definition of 'thriving' encompasses similar "status" descriptions of optimal functioning, but goes beyond them to reflect a more dynamic, process-oriented approach, characterized by three key, interconnected parts[3]. As we describe in Benson and Scales (2009a, 2009b, p. 90), thriving:

1. Represents a dynamic and bi-directional interplay over time of a young person intrinsically animated and energized by discovering his/her specialness, and the developmental contexts (people, places) that know, affirm, celebrate, encourage, and guide its expression.

2. Involves 'stability of movement' or the 'balance' of movement toward something (Bill Damon, personal conversation, May 11, 2006), that is, thriving is a process of experiencing a balance between continuity and discontinuity of development over time that is optimal for a given individual's fused relations with her or his contexts (per discussion of developmental continuity and discontinuity in Lerner, 2003).

3. Reflects both where a young person is currently in their journey to idealized personhood, and whether they are on the kind of path to get there that could rightly be called one of exemplary adaptive development regulations.

Given the complex balance and plasticity that these parts of the thriving definition reflect between person and context, continuity and discontinuity, and status and process, we also prefer to describe a young person at any point in time as more or less thriving oriented, rather than as thriving or not.

---

[3] A thorough description of the evolution of the theory of thriving is found in Benson and Scales (2010).

Fostering Positive Development: Developmentally Attentive Communities

The final dimension relates to the way in which positive development or adaptation is achieved. From a resilience perspective, the dominant delivery system for fostering resilience is via science-based intervention and prevention programs that, ideally, reduce risk factors and enhance protective factors (Rolf & Johnson, 1999). Masten and Reed's (2002) tripartite typology for promoting resilience highlights this goal by suggesting strategies that prevent or reduce risks and stressors, strategies that improve the number and/or quality of resources or assets, and strategies that bolster and strengthen basic human adaptive systems (e.g., cognitive functioning, attachment relationships). Prevention and intervention programs are increasingly targeting multiple risk and protective factors across multiple contexts in fostering resilience and positive development, at times with impressive results (Catalano, Berglund, Ryan, Lonczak, & Hawkins, 2002; Eccles & Gootman, 2002; Weissberg & Greenberg, 1998).

From a developmental asset perspective, programs are important, but cannot be the sole strategy in facilitating healthy outcomes for youth. Programs alone cannot offer the kinds of supports, opportunities, and relationships young people need. This work requires a broader strategy in which multiple contexts in young people's lives are strengthened to promote the kinds of factors that sustain and support positive development for all youth (Benson & Saito, 2001; Connell et al., 2001; Scales, Roehlkepartain, & Benson, 2009; Villaruel, Perkins, Borden, & Keith, 2003).

One way to conceive of this broader approach is through the notion of a "developmentally attentive community." This conception of community is rooted in strategies that identify mutually reinforcing lines of action, all intended to make communities places that promote youth development. Through our study of community change models and observations of hundreds of community initiatives that are using the framework, we have identified five components (as depicted in Table 25.2) that can transform communities into more developmentally attentive places; that is, places that are more intentional in their efforts to foster the healthy development of their children and adolescents. Central to this multifaceted approach is to mobilize young people, such that youth themselves are engaged in a community's activities. This echoes others' assertions that from a positive youth perspective, young people are seen as resources and contributors to their environments (Eccles & Gootman, 2002; Lerner et al., 2002; Whitlock & Hamilton, 2003). Importantly, our studies also have shown that when young people experience higher levels of such "voice" and empowerment, they enjoy far better outcomes, across academic, psychological, social, and behavioral domains (Scales, Roehlkepartain, & Benson, 2009). Another strategy is to activate the various sectors of a community; that is, the organizations, institutions, and settings that are able to promote youth development, including schools, families, faith-based organizations, neighborhoods, and youth organizations. Rallying the multiple settings of a community around positive youth development provides an important redundancy of messages and experiences to youth regarding their value in the community. A third strategy, engaging adults, refers to adults both in their formal roles as citizens, leaders, members, and decision makers who can influence the sectors, but also to adults as individuals who by their actions and statements in their ongoing daily relationships with young people can build youths' assets (Scales et al., 2003).

Becoming a mentor is a formal illustration of such engagement, but informal interactions can also be important (Lopez & McKnight, 2002). When many adults demonstrate their respect and appreciation of youth and when they actively seek to get to know them, the community becomes more welcoming and more growth-enhancing. Fourth, influencing civic decisions is necessary to both promote and sustain a community's activities.

Finally, the last component of a developmentally attentive community is the presence of

Table 25.2 Search Institute's five action strategies for a developmentally attentive community

Engage adults. Engage adults from all walks of life to develop sustained, strength-building relationships with children and adolescents, both within families and in neighborhoods

> Young people need the adults in their lives to acknowledge them, affirm them, and connect with them. They need these things from the adults who are not paid to work with them, as well as the professionals who are

> Engaging parents as asset builders—and affirming the many ways they already build assets—is particularly important, given their central role in children's lives

Mobilize young people. Mobilize young people to use their power as asset builders and change agents

> Many youth feel devalued by adults. And most report their community does not provide useful roles for young people. It should become normative in all settings where children and youth are involved to seek their input and advice, to make decisions with them, and to treat them as responsible, competent allies in all asset-building efforts

> It is also important to help young people tap their own power to build assets for themselves, their peers, and younger children

Activate sectors. Activate all sectors of the community—such as schools, congregations, children and youth, businesses, human services, and health care organizations—to create an asset-building culture and contribute fully to young people's healthy development

> Young people are customers, employees, patients, participants—members of their community in many of the same ways adults are. All sectors have opportunities to examine the ways they come in contact with young people and identify ways they can support their healthy development

Invigorate programs. Invigorate, expand, and enhance programs to become more asset rich and to be available to and accessed by all children and youth

> Though much asset-building occurs in daily, informal interactions, programs young people take part in throughout their community must also become more intentional about asset building. Opportunities for training, technical assistance, and networking should be made available in these settings

Influence civic decisions. Influence decision makers and opinion leaders to leverage financial, media, and policy resources in support of this positive transformation of communities and society

> Community-wide policies, messages, and priorities not only shape people's perceptions of youth, but they also can motivate and support individuals, organizations, and sectors to make asset building an ongoing priority

effective programs. As noted above, programs have the potential to significantly alter maladaptive developmental trajectories, indeed, evidence suggests that, however, without significantly changing the environments in which youth live may lead to the kinds of modest short- and long-term effects often reported in reviews of prevention programs (Eccles & Gootman, 2002). Indeed, this raises an interesting moderating hypothesis: Are the effects of a proven program enhanced when implemented in a community characterized by these other four components? Questions such as this one are possible when we begin to think beyond program models as the only planned or intentional efforts at influencing development and start to acknowledge the powerful role that a community can play when united around its youth.

What should be clear from this model is our assumption that not only are programs not sufficient to promote positive development across many groups of youth, but also that youth cannot

be the only target of change—adults are implicated as much if not more so in this work. Unless adults believe that they have the potential to play a significant role in the lives of youth, much of the work described in this chapter cannot take place. Thus, the strategies and assumptions that stem from our work do not focus on fixing or changing young people's behavior as much as they focus on influencing the attitudes, perceptions, and behaviors of adults toward youths (Benson, 2006).

There is no single model for how a community-wide, asset-building initiative is launched and sustained. We believe that each community brings a unique mix of strengths, history, and existing efforts into the planning and implementation of its initiative. However, certain dynamics appear essential.

• *Cultivate a shared vision.* Invite community members to articulate and keep alive a shared vision for an asset-rich community. Develop a shared community-wide vision centered on increasing the asset base for all children and adolescents. Know that reaching this target cannot be rushed or done with a single new idea or program.

Positive Adaptation, Resilience, and the Developmental Assets Framework

Rather, it will take long-term commitment, multiple and coordinated changes, and a passion for the vision that will sustain your efforts.

• *Recruit and network champions*. Nurture relationships with people who have the passion to spread the word and help make the vision a reality. Create opportunities for these champions to learn from, support, and inspire each other.
• *Communicate*. Distribute information, make presentations, and tap the media to raise awareness about asset building and local efforts. Share with your community what young people experience. Emphasize the ability of *all* community members—including young people—to build assets.
• *Strengthen capacity*. Provide or facilitate training, technical assistance, coaching, tools, or other resources that help individuals and organizations in their asset-building efforts.
• *Reflect, learn, and celebrate*. Reflect on and learn from current progress and challenges. Many people, places, and programs already build assets. Highlight and honor existing and new asset-building efforts in the community.
• *Manage and coordinate*. Manage and coordinate schedules, budgets, and other administrative tasks, as needed.

Asset-building communities mobilize people, organizations, institutions, and systems to take action around a shared understanding of positive development. Ultimately, rebuilding and strengthening the developmental infrastructure in a community is not a program run by professionals. It is a movement that creates a community-wide sense of common purpose. It places residents and their leaders on the same team moving in the same direction, and creates a culture in which all residents are expected, by virtue of their membership

in the community, to promote the positive development of children and youth.

Conclusion

As this review suggests, there is a great deal of consonance between the developmental assets framework and models of resilience. Both approaches identify multiple sources of developmental nutrients across numerous ecologies likely to foster adaptive functioning and optimal development. Likewise, both approaches provide complementary notions regarding the configurations of positive developmental outcomes for youth. And both affirm the significance of programs as a mechanism for promoting healthy behaviors and attitudes.

Because the developmental assets framework is different from a programmatic approach, the scope and implications of our work are broader. This work represents a shift away from relying solely on prevention and intervention efforts to the intentional mobilization and engagement of individuals and systems within communities in the service of healthy youth development. This is no simple task, not the least of which because "community" as the unit of analysis is far less wieldy than a controlled program design, but also because of the paucity of research examining the role of deliberate community-wide effects on the health and well-being of youth. Note though that this discussion of community mobilization in no way is meant to replace or supplant targeted programmatic efforts; one of the implications of the asset model is that strong and effective programs are a necessary component of a developmentally attentive community and that programs are eminently complementary to positive youth development approaches (Catalano, Hawkins, Berglund, Pollard, & Arthur, 2002; Resnick, 2000; Whitlock & Hamilton, 2003).

Nevertheless, if, as Bronfenbrenner and Morris (1998) note, the "growing chaos in … everyday environments in which human beings live their lives…interrupts and undermines the formation and stability of relationships and activities that are necessary for psychological growth" (p. 1022), then working toward bringing structure and intentionality to these environments under the banner of positive youth development provides a promising approach to increasing the developmental outcomes for young people.

References

Adams, G. R. (2001). Positive aspects of adolescence—Part II. *Journal of Adolescent Research, 16*, 427–428.

Barber, B. K., & Olsen, J. A. (1997). Socialization in context: Connection, regulation, and autonomy in the family, school, and neighborhood, and with peers. *Journal of Adolescent Research, 72*, 287–315.

Belsky, J., & Fearon, R. M. P. (2002). Infant-mother attachment security, contextual risk, and early development: A moderational analysis. *Development and Psychopathology, 14*, 293–310.

Benson, P. L. (2006). *All kids are our kids: What communities must do to raise caring and responsible children and adolescents* (2nd ed.). San Francisco, CA: Jossey-Bass.

Benson, P. L. (2003). Developmental assets and asset-building community: Conceptual and empirical foundations. In R. M. Lerner & P. L. Benson (Eds.), *Developmental assets and asset-building communities* (pp. 19–43). New York, NY: Kluwer Academic/Plenum.

Benson, P. L., Leffert, N., Scales, P. C., & Blyth, D. A. (1998). Beyond the "village" rhetoric: Creating healthy communities for children and adolescents. *Applied Developmental Science, 2*, 138–159.

Benson, P. L., & Pittman, K. J. (2001). *Trends in youth development: Visions, realities and challenges*. Boston, MA: Kluwer.

Benson, P. L., & Saito, R. N. (2001). The scientific foundations of youth development. In P. L. Benson & K. J. Pittman (Eds.), *Trends in youth development: Visions, realities, and challenges* (pp. 135–154). Norwell, MA: Kluwer.

Benson, P. L., & Scales, P. C. (2010). Thriving and sparks: Development and emergence of new core concepts in youth development. In R. J. R. Levesque (Ed.), *Encyclopedia of adolescence*. New York, NY: Springer.

Benson, P. L., & Scales, P. C. (2009a). The definition and preliminary measurement of thriving in adolescence. *The Journal of Positive Psychology, 4*, 85–104.

Benson, P. L., & Scales, P. C. (2009b). Positive youth development and the prevention of youth aggression and violence. *European Journal of Developmental Science, 3*, 218–234.

Benson, P. L., Scales, P. C., Hamilton, S. F., & Sesma, A., Jr. (2006). Positive youth development: Theory, research, and applications. In W. Damon & R. M. Lerner (Eds.), *Handbook of child psychology* (Theoretical models of human development 6th ed., Vol. 1, pp. 894–941). New York, NY: Wiley.

Benson, P. L., Scales, P. C., Leffert, N., & Roehlkepartain, E. R. (1999). *A fragile foundation: The state of developmental assets among American youth*. Minneapolis, MN: Search Institute.

Benson, P. L., Scales, P. C., & Mannes, M. (2003). Developmental strengths and their sources: Implications for the study and practice of community building. In R. M. Lerner, F. Jacobs, & D. Wertlieb (Eds.), *Handbook of applied developmental science* (Applying developmental science for youth and families: Historical and theoretical foundations, Vol. 1, pp. 369–406). Newbury Park, CA: Sage.

Bronfenbrenner, U. (1979). *The ecology of human development: Experiments by nature and design*. Cambridge, MA: Harvard University Press.

Bronfenbrenner, U., & Morris, P. A. (1998). The ecology of developmental processes. In W. Damon (Series Ed.) & R. M. Lerner (Vol. Ed.), *Handbook of child psychology: Vol. L. Theoretical models of human development* (5th ed., pp. 993–1028). New York, NY: Wiley.

Brown, B. V. (Ed.). (2008). *Key indicators of child and youth well-being*. New York, NY: Erlbaum.

Catalano, R. F, Berglund, M. L., Ryan, J. A. M., Lonczak, H. S., & Hawkins, J. D. (2002). Positive youth development in the United States: Research findings on evaluations of positive youth development programs. *Prevention and Treatment, 5*(15).

Catalano, R. F., Hawkins, J. D., Berglund, M. L., Pollard, J. A., & Arthur, M. W. (2002). Prevention science and positive youth development: Competitive or cooperative frameworks? *Journal of Adolescent Health, 31*, 230–239.

Connell, J. P., Gambone, M. A., & Smith, T. J. (2001). Youth development in community settings: Challenges to our field and our approach. In P. L. Benson & K. J. Pittman (Eds.), *Trends in youth development: Visions, realities, and challenges* (pp. 291–307). Boston: Kluwer Academic.

Eccles, J. S., & Gootman, J. A. (Eds.). (2002). *Community programs to promote youth development*. Washington, DC: National Academy Press.

Garmezy, N. (1974). The study of competence in children at risk for severe psychopathology. In E. J. Anthony & C. Koupernik (Eds.), *The child in his family* (Children as psychiatric risk, Vol. 3, pp. 77–97). New York, NY: Wiley.

Hamilton, S. F., Hamilton, M. A., & Pittman, K. J. (2003). Principles for youth development. In S. F. Hamilton & M. A. Hamilton (Eds.), *The youth development handbook: Coming of age in American Communities* (pp. 3–22). Thousand Oaks, CA: Sage.

Hawkins, J. D., Catalano, R. F., & Miller, J. Y. (1992). Risk and protective factors for alcohol and other drug problems in adolescence and early adulthood: Implications for substance abuse prevention. *Psychological Bulletin, 772*, 64–105.

Jessor, R. (1993). Successful adolescent development among youth in high-risk settings. *American Psychological Bulletin, 48*, 117–126.

Keating, D., & Hertzman, C. (Eds.). (1999). *Developmental health and the wealth of nations: Social, bio-*

logical, and educational dynamics. New York, NY: Guilford.

Leffert, N., Benson, P. L., Scales, P. C., Sharma, A. R., Drake, D. R., & Blyth, D. A. (1998). Developmental assets: Measurement and prediction of risk behaviors among adolescents. *Applied Developmental Science, 2,* 209–230.

Lerner, R. M. (2003). Developmental assets and asset-building communities: A view of the issues. In R. M. Lerner & P. L. Benson (Eds.), *Developmental assets and asset-building communities* (pp. 3–18). New York, NY: Kluwer/Academic.

Lerner, R. M., Brentano, C., Dowling, E. M., & Anderson, P. M. (2002). Positive youth development: Thriving as the basis of personhood and civil society. In R. M. Lerner, C. S. Taylor, & A. von Eye (Eds.), *New directions for youth development* (Pathways to positive development among diverse youth, Vol. 95, pp. 5–33). San Francisco, CA: Jossey-Bass.

Lopez, S. J., & McKnight, C. G. (2002). Moving in a positive direction: Toward increasing the utility of positive youth development efforts. *Prevention & Treatment, 5.*

Luthar, S. S., Cicchetti, D., & Becker, B. (2000). The construct of resilience: A critical evaluation and guidelines for future work. *Child Development, 77,* 543–562.

Masten, A. S. (1999a). The promise and perils of resilience research as a guide to preventive interventions. In M. D. Glantz & J. L. Johnson (Eds.), *Resilience and development: Positive life adaptations* (pp. 251–257). New York, NY: Plenum.

Masten, A. S. (1999b). Resilience comes of age: Reflections on the past and outlook for the next generation of research. In M. D. Glantz & J. L. Johnson (Eds.), *Resilience and development: Positive life adaptations* (pp. 282–296). New York, NY: Plenum.

Masten, A. S. (2001). Ordinary magic: Resilience processes in development. *American Psychologist, 56,* 227–238.

Masten, A. S., & Curtis, W. J. (2000). Integrating competence and psychopathology: Pathways toward a comprehensive science of adaptation in development. *Development and Psychopathology, 12,* 529–550.

Masten, A. S., & Reed, M. G. J. (2002). Resilience in development. In C. R. Snyder & S. J. Lopez (Eds.), *Handbook of positive psychology* (pp. 74–88). New York, NY: Oxford University Press.

Moore, K. A., & Lippman, L. H. (Eds.). (2005). *What do children need to flourish? Conceptualizing and measuring indicators of positive development. New York.* New York, NY: Springer.

Pittman, K., Diversi, M., & Ferber, T. (2002). Social policy supports for adolescence in the twenty-first century: Framing questions. *Journal of Research on Adolescence, 12,* 149–158.

Pittman, K. J., Irby, M., & Ferber, T. (2001). Unfinished business: Further reflections on a decade of promoting youth development. In P. L. Benson & K. J. Pittman (Eds.), *Trends in youth development: Visions, realities, and challenges* (pp. 3–50). Boston, MA: Kluwer.

Resnick, M. D. (2000). Protective factors, resiliency, and healthy youth development. *Adolescent Medicine: State of the Art Reviews, 77*(1), 157–164.

Rolf, J. E., & Johnson, J. L. (1999). Opening doors to resilience intervention for prevention research. In M. D. Glantz & J. L. Johnson (Eds.), *Resilience and development: Positive life adaptations* (pp. 229–249). New York, NY: Plenum.

Rutter, M. (1979). Protective factors in children's responses to stress and disadvantage. In M. W. Kent & J. E. Rolf (Eds.), *Primary prevention of psychopathology* (Social competence in children, Vol. 3, pp. 49–74). Hanover, NH: University Press of New England.

Rutter, M. (2000). Resilience reconsidered: Conceptual considerations, empirical findings, and policy implications. In J. P. Shonkoff & S. J. Meisels (Eds.), *Handbook of early childhood intervention* (2nd ed., pp. 651–682). New York, NY: Cambridge University Press.

Sameroff, A. J. (1999). Ecological perspectives on developmental risk. In J. D. Osofsky & H. E. Fitzgerald (Eds.), *WAIMH handbook of infant mental health* (Infant mental health groups at risk, Vol. 4, pp. 223–248). New York, NY: Wiley.

Sameroff, A. J., Bartko, W. T., Baldwin, A., Baldwin, C., & Seifer, R. (1999). Family and social influences on the development of child competence. In M. Lewis & C. Feiring (Eds.), *Families, risk, and competence* (pp. 161–186). Mahwah, NJ: Erlbaum.

Sameroff, A. J., & Fiese, B. H. (2000). Transactional regulation: The developmental ecology of early intervention. In J. P. Shonkoff & S. J. Meisels (Eds.), *Handbook of early childhood intervention* (2nd ed., pp. 135–159). New York, NY: Cambridge University Press.

Sameroff, A. J., Seifer, R., & Bartko, W. T. (1997). Environmental perspectives on adaptation during childhood and adolescence. In S. S. Luthar, J. A. Burack, D. Ciccetti, & J. R. Weisz (Eds.), *Developmental psychopathology: Perspectives on adjustment, risk, and disorder* (pp. 507–526). New York, NY: Cambridge University Press.

Scales, P. C. (2001). The public image of adolescents. *Society, 38,* 64–70.

Scales, P. C., & Benson, P. L. (2005). Adolescence and thriving. In C. B. Fisher & R. M. Lerner (Eds.), *Encyclopedia of applied developmental science* (pp. 15–19). Thousand Oaks, CA: Sage.

Scales, P. C., Benson, P. L., Leffert, N., & Blyth, D. A. (2000). Contribution of developmental assets to the prediction of thriving among adolescents. *Applied Developmental Science, 4,* 27–46.

Scales, P. C., Benson, P. L., Mannes, M., Roehlkepartain, E. C., Hintz, N. R., & Sullivan, T. K. (2003). *Other people's kids: Social expectations and American adults' involvement with children and adolescents.* New York, NY: Kluwer/Plenum (Search Institute Series on Developmentally Attentive Community and Society).

Scales, P. C., Benson, P. L., Roehlkepartain, E. C., Sesma, A., & van Dulmen, M. (2006). The role of developmental assets in predicting academic achievement: A longitudinal study. *Journal of Adolescence, 29*, 691–708.

Scales, P. C., & Leffert, N. (2004). *Developmental assets: A synthesis of the scientific research on adolescent development* (2nd ed.). Minneapolis, MN: Search Institute.

Scales, P. C., & Leffert, N. (1999). *Developmental assets: A synthesis of the scientific research on adolescent development*. Minneapolis, MN: Search Institute.

Scales, P. C., & Roehlkepartain, E. C. (2003). Boosting student achievement: New research on the power of developmental assets. *Search Institute Insights & Evidence, 7*(1), 1–10. www.search-institute.org/research/Insights.

Scales, P. C., Roehlkepartain, E. C., & Benson, P. L. (2009). *Teen voice 2009: Tapping the hidden strengths of 15-year-olds*. Minneapolis, MN: Search Institute and Best Buy Children's Foundation.

Scales, P. C., Sesma, A., Jr., & Bolstrom, B. (2004). *Coming into their own: How developmental assets promote positive growth in middle childhood*. Minneapolis, MN: Search Institute.

Search Institute. (2001). *Developmental assets: A profile of your youth*. Minneapolis, MN: Search Institute.

Seligman, M. E. P., & Csikszentmihalyi, M. (2000). Positive psychology: An introduction. *American Psychologist, 55*, 5–14 (special issue on Happiness, Excellence, and Optimal Human Functioning).

Sesma, A., Jr., & Roehlkepartain, E. C. (2003). Unique strengths, shared strengths: Developmental assets among youth of color. *Search Institute Insights & Evidence, 1*(2), 1–13. www.search-institute.org/research/Insights.

Stouthamer-Loeber, M., Loeber, R., Farrington, D. P., Zhang, Q., van Kammen, W., & Maguin, E. (1993). The double edge of protective and risk factors for delinquency: Interrelations and developmental patterns. *Development and Psychopathology, 5*, 683–701.

Takanishi, R., Mortimer, A. M., & McGourthy, T. J. (1997). Positive indicators of adolescent development: Redressing the negative image of American adolescents. In R. M. Hauser, B. V. Brown, & W. R. Prosser (Eds.), *Indicators of children's well-being* (pp. 428–441). New York, NY: Russell Sage.

Taylor, C. S., Lerner, R. M., von Eye, A., Balsano, A. B., Dowling, E. M., Anderson, P. M., et al. (2002). Individual and ecological assets and positive developmental trajectories among gang and community-based organization youth. In R. M. Lerner, C. S. Taylor, & A. von Eye (Eds.), *New directions for youth development* (Pathways to positive development among diverse youth, Vol. 95, pp. 57–72). San Francisco, CA: Jossey-Bass.

VanderVen, K. (2008). *Promoting positive development in early childhood: Building blocks for a successful start*. New York, NY.: Springer.

Villaruel, F. A., Perkins, D. E., Borden, L. M., & Keith, J. G. (2003). *Community youth development: Programs, policies, and practices*. Thousand Oaks, CA: Sage.

Werner, E. E., & Smith, R. S. (1982). *Vulnerable but invincible: A study of resilient children*. New York, NY: McGraw-Hill.

Werner, E. E., & Smith, R. S. (1993). *Overcoming the odds: High risk children from birth to adulthood*. New York, NY: Cornell University Press.

Weissberg, R. P., & Greenberg, M. T. (1998). School and community competence enhancement and prevention programs. In W. Damon (Series Ed.) & I. E. Siegel & K. A. Renninger (Vol. Eds.), *Handbook of child psychology* (5th ed., Vol. 5, pp. 877–954). New York, NY: Wiley.

Whitlock, J. L., & Hamilton, S. F. (2003). The role of youth surveys in community youth. *Applied Developmental Science, 7*, 39–51.

The Power of Parenting

26

Robert B. Brooks

I have focused for almost 30 years on examining the impact that parents have in nurturing hope, self-esteem, and an optimistic outlook in their children (Brooks, 1998; Brooks & Goldstein, 2001, 2003, 2011). My intention in this chapter is to examine specific steps that parents can take on a daily basis to reinforce a resilient mindset and lifestyle in their children. Before describing both the characteristics of this mindset and strategies to strengthen it in youngsters, I believe it is necessary to address the following two questions:

1. What is meant by the concept of resilience?
2. Do parents *really* have a major influence on the development of resilience in their children?

What Is Resilience?

Resilience may be understood as the capacity of a child to deal effectively with stress and pressure, to cope with everyday challenges, to rebound from disappointments, mistakes, trauma, and adversity, to develop clear and realistic goals, to solve problems, to interact comfortably with others, and to treat oneself and others with respect and dignity (Brooks & Goldstein, 2001).

R.B. Brooks(✉)
Department of Psychology,
McLean Hospital and Harvard Medical School,
60 Oak Knoll Terrace, Needham, MA 02478, USA
e-mail: contact@drrobertbrooks.com

In scientific circles, research related to resilience has primarily studied youngsters who have overcome trauma and hardship (Beardslee & Podorefsky, 1988; Brooks, 1994; Crenshaw, 2010; Hechtman, 1991; Herrenkohl, Herrenkohl, & Egolf, 1994; Masten, Best, & Garmezy, 1990; Rutter, 1985; Werner & Smith, 1992). However, several researchers and clinicians have raised important issues, such as: "Does a child have to face adversity in order to be considered resilient?" or "Is resilience reflected in the ability to bounce back from adversity or is it caused by adversity?" (Kaplan, 2005).

My colleague Sam Goldstein and I believe that the concept of resilience should be broadened to apply to every child and not restricted to those who have experienced adversity (Brooks & Goldstein, 2001, 2003). All children face challenge and stress in the course of their development and even those who at one point would not be classified as "at-risk" may suddenly find themselves placed in such a category. This abrupt shift to an at-risk classification was evident on a dramatic scale for the hundreds of children who lost a parent or loved one as a consequence of the terrorist attacks on 9/11. Nurturing resilience should be understood as a vital ingredient in the process of parenting every child whether that child has been burdened by adversity or not.

Other mental health specialists have also expanded the definition or scope of resilience to go beyond bouncing back from adversity. Reivich

S. Goldstein and R.B. Brooks (eds.), *Handbook of Resilience in Children*,
DOI 10.1007/978-1-4614-3661-4_26, © Springer Science+Business Media New York 2013

and Shatte (2002) contend that "everyone needs resilience" and they write:

> … resilience is the capacity to respond in healthy and productive ways when faced with adversity and trauma; it is essential for managing the daily stress of life. But we have come to realize that the same skills of resilience are important to broadening and enriching one's life as they are to recovering from setbacks (p. 20).

A more inclusive definition of resilience that embraces all youngsters encourages us to consider and adopt parenting practices that are essential for preparing children for success and satisfaction in their future lives. A guiding principle in each interaction parents have with children should be to strengthen their ability to meet life's challenges with thoughtfulness, confidence, purpose, responsibility, empathy, and hope. These qualities may be subsumed under the concept of resilience. The development of a resilient mindset, which will be described in detail later in this chapter, is not rooted in the number of adversities experienced by a child, but rather in particular skills and a positive attitude that caregivers reinforce in a child.

Do Parents Have a Major Influence on the Development of Resilience in Their Children?

Many people convinced of the profound influence that parents exert on a child's development and resilience, might wonder why it is necessary to pose this question. However, the answer is not as clearcut as many may believe (Goldstein & Brooks, 2003). Recently developed, sophisticated scientific instruments have highlighted the significant impact of genetics on adult personality, adaptation, and cognitive and behavioral patterns. As a consequence, the degree to which parents influence their child's development has been questioned by several researchers (Harris, 1998; Pinker, 2002).

In her book *The Nurture Assumption*, Harris (1998) presented evidence to suggest that the extended environment outside of the home, particularly the impact of peers, explained much of the non-genetic differences in human behavioral traits. Though some have lauded Harris for her contribution to the field of child development, she has also been widely criticized by professionals who have interpreted her conclusions as suggesting that parents are inconsequential players in their children's lives (Pinker, 2002).

However, Harris' position may be interpreted not as a dismissal of the influence of parents, but rather as a call to be more precise in understanding the impact of parents on the present and ultimately, future lives of their children. Pinker (2002), citing a number of studies of fraternal and identical twins reared together or apart, contends that it is not that parents don't matter; they in fact matter a great deal. It's that over the long term, parent behavior does not appear to significantly influence a child's intelligence or personality. In contrast, Siegel (1999) has posited that a child's attachment and relationship with caregivers is a major determinant of mental health and adaptation.

The position taken in this chapter is that even if those personality qualities in a child attributed to parental influence are in a statistical equation much smaller than previously assumed, they may in the daily lives of children be the difference in determining whether or not a child succeeds in school, develops satisfying peer relationships, or overcomes a developmental or behavioral impairment. Parents possess enormous influence in the lives of their children. Data suggesting that a particular parenting style may play a minimal role in intelligence or personality development does not absolve parents of their responsibility to raise their children in moral, ethical, and humane ways. The quality of daily parent-child relationships makes a vital difference in the behavior and adjustment of children. As Sheridan, Eagle, and Dowd (2005) note, "The development of resiliency and healthy adjustment among children is enhanced through empathetic family involvement practices" (p. 168).

Not surprisingly, the impact of parental behavior on children is less debatable when the behavior in question is inappropriate, humiliating, or abusive compared with that which is positive or benign. For example, Jaffee (2005) has highlighted the devastating effects on a child's emotional well-being and resilience when confronted with parents who have a history of mental disorder and also engage in violent and abusive behavior. Kumpfer and Alavarado (2003), emphasizing the significance of parental behavior write:

> The probability of a youth acquiring developmental problems increases rapidly as risk factors such as family conflict, lack of parent-child bonding, disorganization, ineffective parenting, stressors, parental depression, and others increase in comparison with protective or resilience factors. Hence, family protective mechanisms and individual resiliency processes should be addressed in addition to reducing risk factors… . Resiliency research suggests that parental support in helping children develop dreams, goals, and purpose in life is a major protective factor (p. 458).

Pinker (2002) notes, "Childrearing is above all an ethical responsibility. It is not okay for parents to beat, humiliate, deprive, or neglect their children because those are awful things for a big strong person to do to a small helpless one" (p. 398). Similarly, Harris writes, "If you don't think the moral imperative is a good enough reason to be nice to your kid, try this one: Be nice to your kid when he's young so that he will be nice to your when you're old" (p. 342).

Pinker (2002) poignantly captures the moral dimension of parenting practices in the following statement:

> There are well-functioning adults who still shake with rage when recounting the cruelties their parents inflicted on them as children. There are others who moisten up in private moments when recalling a kindness or sacrifice made for their happiness, perhaps one that the mother or father has long forgotten. If for no other reason, parents should treat their children well to allow them to grow up with such memories (p. 399).

Given the complexity of a child's development, it is unlikely that a specific number will ever be assigned as a "parent's share" or percentage of that development. As Deater-Deckard, Ivy, and Smith (2005) wisely observe, "The question is no longer whether and to what degree genes or environments matter, but how genes and environments work together to produce resilient children and adults" (p. 49).

They conclude:

> … resilience is a developmental process that involves individual differences in children's attributes (e.g., temperament, cognitive abilities) and environments (e.g., supportive parenting, learning enriched classrooms). The genetic and environmental influences underlying these individual differences are correlated, and they interact with each other to produce the variation that we see between children, and over time within children… . It is imperative that scientists and practitioners recognize that these gene-environment transactions are probabilistic in their effects, and the transactions and their effects can change with shifts in genes or environments (p. 60).

Although researchers and clinicians debate the extent to which particular parenting practices impact on children in specified areas, it seems that all agree that parents make a significant difference either in the day-to-day and/or future lives of their children. We concur with this position and believe that it is essential that we identify both those parental practices that nurture the skills, positive outlook, and stress hardiness necessary for children to manage an increasingly complex and demanding world as well as those that do harm to children. We must search for consistent ways of raising children that will increase the likelihood of their experiencing happiness, success in school, contentment in their lives, and satisfying relationships. If children are to realize these goals they must develop the inner strength to deal competently and successfully, day after day, with the challenges and pressures they encounter (Brooks & Goldstein, 2001).

The Characteristics of a Resilient Mindset

Resilient children possess certain qualities and/or ways of viewing themselves and the world that are not apparent in youngsters who have not been successful in meeting challenges. The assumptions that children have about themselves influence the behaviors and skills they develop. In turn, these behaviors and skills influence this set of assumptions so that a dynamic process is constantly operating. This set of assumptions may be classified as a mindset (Brooks & Goldstein, 2001).

An understanding of the features of a resilient mindset can provide parents with guideposts for nurturing inner strength and optimism in their children. Parents adhering to these guideposts can use each interaction with their children to reinforce a resilient mindset. While the outcome of a specific situation may be important, even more essential are the lessons learned from the process of dealing with each issue or problem. The knowledge gained therefore supplies the nutrients from which the seeds of resiliency will flourish.

The mindset of resilient children contains a number of noteworthy characteristics that are associated with specific skills. These include:
They feel special and appreciated.
They have learned to set realistic goals and expectations for themselves.
They believe that they have the ability to solve problems and make sound decisions and thus are more likely to view mistakes, setbacks, and obstacles as challenges to confront rather than as stressors to avoid.
They rely on effective coping strategies that promote growth and are not self-defeating.
They are aware of and do not deny their weaknesses and vulnerabilities but view them as areas for improvement rather than as unchangeable flaws.
They recognize and enjoy their strong points and talents.
Their self-concept is filled with images of strength and competence.
They feel comfortable with others and have developed effective interpersonal skills with peers and adults alike. This enables them to seek out assistance and nurturance in a comfortable, appropriate manner from adults who can provide the support they need.
They are able to define the aspects of their lives over which they have control and to focus their energy and attention on those rather than on factors over which they have little, or any, influence.

The process of nurturing this mindset and associated skills in children requires parents to examine their own mindset, beliefs, and actions. We will now examine guideposts that can facilitate this process together with case examples.

Parenting Practices That Nurture Resilience in Children

Following is a list of ten guideposts proposed by Brooks and Goldstein (2001, 2003) that form the scaffolding for reinforcing a resilient mindset and lifestyle in children. These guideposts are relevant for all the interactions parents and other caregivers have with children whether coaching them in a sport, helping them with homework, engaging them in an art project, asking them to assume certain responsibilities, assisting them when they make mistakes, teaching them to share, or disciplining them. While the specific avenues through which these guideposts can be applied will differ from one child and one situation to the next, the guideposts themselves remain constant.

1. Being empathic

A basic foundation of any relationship is empathy. Simply defined, in the parenting relationship empathy is the capacity of parents to place themselves inside the shoes of their children and to see the world through their eyes. Empathy does not imply that you agree with what your children do, but rather you attempt to appreciate and validate their point of view. Also, it is easier for children to develop empathy when they interact with adults who model empathy on a daily basis.

It is not unusual for parents to believe they are empathic, but the reality is that empathy is more fragile or elusive than many realize. Experience shows that it is easier to be empathic when our children do what we ask them to do, meet our expectations, and are warm and loving. Being empathic is tested when we are upset, angry, or disappointed with our children. When parents feel this way, many will say or do things that actually work against a child developing resilience.

To strengthen empathy, parents must keep in mind several key questions, questions that I frequently pose in my clinical practice and workshops. They include:

"How would I feel if someone said or did to me what I just said or did to my child?"

"When I say or do things with my children, am I behaving in a way that will make them most responsive to listening to me?"

"How would I hope my child described me?"

"Do I behave in ways that would prompt my child to describe me in the way I hope?"

"How would my child actually describe me and how close is that to how I hope my child would describe me?"

While thinking about these questions as the essential features of effective parenting, they are often neglected when parents are confronted with frustration and anger. This is evident in the following two case examples.

Mr. and Mrs. Kahn were perplexed why their son John, a seventh grader, experienced so much difficulty in completing his homework. John was an excellent athlete but had a long history of struggling to learn to read. His parents, noticing John's lack of interest in school activities, believed he was "lazy" and he could do the work if he "put his mind to it." They often exhorted him to "try harder" and they angrily reminded him on a regular basis how awful he would feel as a senior in high school when he was not accepted into the college of his choice.

Although perhaps well-intentioned, when Mr. and Mrs. Kahn told John to "try harder" they failed to consider how these words were experienced by their son. Many youngsters who are repeatedly told to "try harder" interpret this statement not as helpful or encouraging but rather as judgmental and accusatory, intensifying their frustration rather than their motivation to improve. Thus, the words the Kahns used worked against their goal to motivate John. If they had reflected upon how they would feel if they were having difficulty at work and their boss yelled, "Try harder," they may have refrained from using these words.

Mr. and Mrs. Kahn learned that by placing themselves inside John's shoes, they could communicate with him in ways that would lessen defensiveness and increase cooperation. They told him that they realized they came across as "nagging" but did not wish to do so. They said

that they knew he possessed much strength, but there were areas that were more challenging for him such as reading. By being empathic they transformed an accusatory attitude into a problem-solving framework by asking John what he thought would help. This more positive approach made it easier for John to acknowledge his difficulties in school and prompted his willingness to receive tutoring.

Sally, a shy 8-year-old, was frequently reminded by her parents, Mr. and Mrs. Carter, to say hello when encountering family or friends. Yet, from a young age Sally's temperament left her feeling anxious, fearful, and easily overwhelmed in new situations. It was not unusual for Sally to seek refuge behind her mother when people she did not know visited the Carter home. Both of the Carters were outgoing and were perplexed by Sally's cautiousness and fearfulness, especially since they viewed themselves as supportive and loving parents. They felt that Sally could be less shy "if she just put her mind to it."

The Carters became increasingly frustrated and embarrassed by Sally's behavior, prompting them to warn her that if she failed to say hello to others she would be lonely and have no friends. They frequently asked her after school if she had taken the initiative to speak with any of the children in her class. These kinds of comments backfired, prompting Sally to become more anxious.

Mr. and Mrs. Carter, desiring their daughter to be more outgoing, failed to appreciate that Sally's cautious demeanor was an inborn temperamental trait and could not be overcome by simply telling her to "say hello" to others. They were to discover that each reminder on their part not only intensified Sally's discomfort and worry but also compromised a warm, supportive relationship with their daughter.

In parent counseling sessions the Carters learned that they could assist Sally to be less shy, but they first had to reflect upon how their current actions and words impacted on their daughter. They had to ask, "If I were shy would I want anyone to say to me what I say to Sally?" or "Am I saying things to Sally that are helping or hindering the process of her becoming more comfortable with others?" In essence, these kinds of questions helped them to assume a more empathic stance. Both parents learned that telling a shy person to try to become less shy is often experienced as accusatory and not as a source of encouragement.

Mr. and Mrs. Carter informed Sally that they knew that it was not easy for her to say hello to people she did not know and added that it was not easy for many other children as well. They said that maybe working together with Sally they could figure out steps she could take to make it less difficult to greet others. These comments served to empathize and validate what Sally was experiencing and also to convey a feeling of "we're here to help, not criticize." Finally, they communicated to Sally, "Many kids, who have trouble saying hello when they're young, find it easier as they get older." This last statement conveyed realistic hope. And hope is a basic characteristic of a resilient mindset.

Being empathic permitted the Carters to communicate with Sally in a nonjudgmental way and in the process they nurtured their daughter's resilience.

2. Communicating effectively and listening actively

Empathy is closely associated with the ways in which parents communicate with their children. Communication is not simply how we speak with another person. Effective communication involves actively listening to our children, understanding, and validating what they are attempting to say, and responding in ways that avoid power struggles by not interrupting them, by not telling them how they should be feeling, by not derogating them, and by not using absolute words such as *always* and *never* in an overly critical, demeaning fashion (e.g., "You never help out"; "You always act disrespectful").

Resilient children demonstrate a capacity to communicate their feelings and thoughts effectively and their parents serve as important models in the process. When 10-year-old Michael insisted on completing a radio kit by himself and then was not able to do so, his father, Mr. Burton, angrily retorted, "I told you it wouldn't work. You don't have enough patience to read the directions carefully." Mr. Burton's message worked

against the development of a resilient mindset in his son since it contained an accusatory tone, a tone focusing on Michael's shortcomings rather than on his strengths. It did not offer assistance or hope.

Covey (1989), describing the characteristics of effective people, advocates that we first attempt to understand before being understood. What he is suggesting is that prior to expressing our views, we would be well-advised to practice empathy by listening actively and considering what messages the other person is delivering. Effective communication is implicated in many behaviors associated with resilience, including interpersonal skills, empathy, and problem-solving and decision-making abilities.

Given the significance of effective communication skills in our lives, during my therapeutic activities and my workshops I frequently pose the following questions for parents to consider when they interact with their children:

"Do my messages convey and teach respect?"

"Am I fostering realistic expectations in my children?"

"Am I helping my children learn how to solve problems?"

"Am I nurturing empathy and compassion?"

"Am I promoting self-discipline and self-control?"

"Am I setting limits and consequences in ways that permit my children to learn from me rather than resent me?"

"Am I truly listening to and validating what my children are saying?"

"Do my children know that I value their opinion and input?"

"Do my children know how special they are to me?"

"Am I assisting my children to appreciate that mistakes and obstacles are part of the process of learning and growing?"

"Am I comfortable in acknowledging my own mistakes and apologizing to my children when indicated?"

If parents keep these questions in mind, they can communicate in ways that reinforce a resilient mindset. However, this task is not always easy to accomplish as was evident at a family session with Mr. and Mrs. Berlin and their 13-year-old daughter Jennifer. The Berlins sought a consultation given for Jennifer's sadness and what they called "her pessimistic attitude towards everything."

At the first session, Jennifer said, "I feel very sad and unhappy."

Mrs. Berlin instantly countered, "But there's no reason for you to feel this way. We are a loving family and have always given you what you need."

Jennifer's expression suggested both sadness and anger at her mother's remark. While Mrs. Berlin may have intended to reassure her daughter, her comment served to rupture communication. People do not want to be told how they should or should not feel. If someone says she feels depressed, she does not want to hear that there is no reason to feel this way.

What might Mrs. Berlin have said? A good place to start is validation. Parents must first validate what their child is saying. Validation does not mean you agree with the other person's statement, but that you convey to that person you "hear" what is being said. Consider the following response that Mrs. Berlin might have offered:

> I know you've been feeling depressed. I'm not certain why, but I'm glad you could tell us. That's why we're seeing Dr. Brooks to try and figure out what will help you to feel better and also, how dad and I can help.

If the messages of parents are filled with empathy, validation, and support, a climate is established for nurturing resilience.

3. Changing negative scripts

Well-meaning parents have been known to apply the same approach with their children for weeks, months, or years even when the approach has proven ineffective. For instance, a set of parents reminded (nagged) their children for years to clean their rooms, but the children failed to comply. When I asked why they used the same unsuccessful message for years, they responded, "We thought they would finally learn if we told them often enough."

Similar to the reasoning offered by these parents, many parents believe that children should be the ones to change, not them. Others believe if they change their approach, it is like "giving in to a child" and they are concerned that their children will take advantage of them. One mother said, "My son forgets to do his chores and I keep reminding him and we keep getting into battles. But I can't back off. If I do my son will never learn to be responsible. He will become a spoiled brat like too many other kids are these days." Without realizing it, the mother's constant reminders backfired. They not only contributed to tension in the household, but in addition, they reinforced a lack of responsibility in her son by always being there to remind him of what he was expected to do rather than having him learn to remember his responsibilities on his own.

Parents with a resilient mindset of their own recognize that if something they have said or done for a reasonable amount of time does not work, then they must change their "script" if their children are to change theirs. This position does not mean giving in to the child or failing to hold the child accountable. It suggests that we must have the insight and courage to consider what we can do differently, lest we become entangled in useless, counterproductive power struggles. It also serves to teach children that there are alternatives ways of solving problems. If anything, it helps children learn to be more flexible and accountable in handling difficult situations.

Mr. Lowell was imprisoned by a negative script, especially towards his 12-year-old son Jimmy. The moment Mr. Lowell arrived home, the first question he asked Jimmy each and every day was, "Did you do your homework? Did you do your chores?" Even if Jimmy had not done his homework or chores, he quickly responded "yes" just to "get my father off my back." Over several years their relationship deteriorated. Jimmy felt all his father cared about were grades and chores. Mr. Lowell felt his son was "lazy" and needed daily "prodding" to become more responsible.

In counseling sessions, Mr. Lowell became aware of how his words echoed those of his father when Mr. Lowell was Jimmy's age. With impressive insight he said, "Jimmy must see me just like I saw my father, an overbearing man who rarely complimented me but was quick to tell me what I did wrong."

Mr. Lowell ruefully asked, "Why do we do the same things toward our kids that we didn't like our parents doing to us?"

It is a question frequently raised. While the answer may differ to some extent from one person to the next, the basic issue is how easily we become creatures of habit, incorporating the script of our own parents even if we were not happy with that script. We practice what we have learned.

Yet, parents are not destined to follow these ineffective, counterproductive scripts. Once they are aware of their existence they can consider other scripts to follow. Mr. Lowell, equipped with new insight, no longer greeted Jimmy with questions about his homework or chores, but instead showed interest in his son's various activities, including drawing and basketball. He and Jimmy signed up for an art class together offered by a local museum and they "practiced hoops" on a regular basis. Similar to the Kahn's approach with John and the Carter's with Sally, Mr. Lowell recognized that if Jimmy were to change, he, as the adult, would have to make the initial changes.

4. Loving our children in ways that help them to feel special and appreciated

It is well established that a basic foundation of resilience is the presence of at least one adult (hopefully several) who believes in the worth and goodness of the child. The late psychologist Julius Segal referred to that person as a "charismatic adult," an adult from whom a child "gathers strength" (Segal, 1988). One must never underestimate the power of one person to redirect a child toward a more productive, successful, satisfying life.

Parents, keeping in mind the notion of a charismatic adult, might ask each evening, "Are my children stronger people because of the things I said or did today or are they less strong?" Certainly, Mr. Burton yelling at his son Michael when the latter had difficulty in completing a radio kit or Mr. and Mrs. Carter questioning Sally each day if she had initiated conversations with classmates were actions that diminished their children's emotional well-being. Neither Michael nor Sally was likely to gather strength when confronted with their parents' statements and questions.

Unconditional love, which we will discuss in greater detail in the next guidepost, is an essential feature that charismatic adults bestow on children. If children are to develop a sense of security, self-worth, and self-dignity, they must have people in their lives who demonstrate love not because of something they accomplish but because of their very existence. When such love is absent, it is difficult to develop and fortify a resilient mindset.

When I have asked adults to recall a favorite occasion from their childhood when their parents served as a charismatic adult for them, one of the most common memories involved doing something pleasant and alone with the parent. One man described having his father's "undivided attention." He said, "My father really listened to me when no one else was around and we could talk about anything. It was tougher to do when my older sister and younger brother were also there."

Similarly, a woman said, "I loved bedtime when my mother or father read me a story. If my mother was reading to me, my father was reading to my brother. If my father was reading to me, my mother was reading to my brother." With a smile, this woman added, "Don't get me wrong, I loved my brother and I enjoyed when we did things as a family, but I think I felt closest to my parents when I did something alone with each. My husband and I do the same things with our kids today."

The power of "special times," poignantly captured in the words of this man and woman, are recalled by many adults. It is recommended that parents create these times in the lives of their children. Parents of young children might say, "When I read to you or play with you, it is so special that even if the phone rings I won't answer it." One young child said, "I know my parents love me. They let the answering machine answer calls when they are playing with me."

When children know that they will have a time alone with each parent, it helps to lessen sibling rivalry and vying for the parent's undivided attention. A parent of six children asked at a workshop,

"Is it possible to create special moments with each child when you have six." The answer is that it is more difficult with six than with two children in the household, but it is still possible. It requires more juggling, but if these times result in children feeling special in the eyes of their parents, the struggle to juggle one's schedule is worth the effort. As Pinker (2002) advised, "If for no other reason, parents should treat their children well to allow them to grow up with such memories" (p. 399).

Children are very sensitive if a parent is not present at their birthday, at a holiday, at their first Little League game, or at a talent show. In today's fast-paced world many parents work long hours and travel and thus, it is likely they may miss some of their children's special moments, but these absences should be kept to a minimum. One adult patient recalled that his father missed all but a couple of his birthdays between the ages of 5 and 12. "I know he had to travel for his business, but he knew when my birthday was. I think he could have scheduled his business trips to be there for my birthday." Tears came to his eyes as he added, "You certainly don't feel loved when your father misses your birthday. And to make matters worse, most of the time he forgot to call."

Time alone with each child does not preclude family activities that also create a sense of belonging and love. Sharing evening meals and holidays, playing games, attending a community event as a family, or taking a walk together are all opportunities to convey love and help children feel special in the eyes and hearts of their parents.

5. Accepting our children for who they are and helping them to establish realistic expectations and goals

One of the most difficult but challenging parenting tasks is to accept our children for who they are and not what we want them to be. Before children are born, parents have expectations for them that may be unrealistic given the unique temperament of each child. Chess and Thomas (1987), two of the pioneers in measuring temperamental differences in newborns, observed that some youngsters enter the world with so-called easy temperaments, others with cautious or shy temperaments, while still others with "difficult" temperaments.

When parents lack knowledge about these inborn temperaments, a powerful determinant of personality and behavior according to Harris (1998), they may say or do things that compromise satisfying relationships and interfere with the emergence of a resilient mindset. This dynamic certainly occurred in Mr. and Mrs. Carter's initial approach to their daughter Sally's shy demeanor. Basically, they exhorted her to make friends, feeling that her cautious, reserved nature could easily be overcome. They did not appreciate how desperately Sally wished to be more outgoing and have more friends, but it was difficult to do so, given her temperament. It was only when her parents demonstrated empathy and communicated their wish to help, that Sally felt accepted.

Another example concerned 10-year-old Carl. He dawdled in the morning, often missing the school bus. His parents, Mr. and Mrs. Thomas, found themselves obligated to drive him to school. A neighbor suggested them not to drive Carl to school, that by doing so they were just "reinforcing his lateness." They took this neighbor's advice and told Carl if he was not ready when the school bus arrived, they would not drive him and he would miss school. Carl missed school, which upset him. However, much to the dismay of his parents, his upset did not prepare him to be ready for school the next day. They were confused about what to do next and became increasingly angry with their son for his irresponsibility. As a further motivation to be ready on time, they decided to restrict many of his pleasurable activities if he were late. Unfortunately, that failed to bring about the desired results.

Carl's parents were unaware that his difficulty with lateness was not because he was irresponsible, but rather because he moved at a slow pace and was distractible, frequently becoming drawn into other activities. Instead of yelling and punishing, it would have been more effective to accept that this is their son's style and to engage him in a discussion of what he thinks would help to get ready on time. As we shall see under the guidepost for developing responsibility discussed below, when given the opportunity even young children are capable of offering sound solutions to problems they encounter.

In addition, collaborating with Carl's school to have a motivating "job" or responsibility waiting for him might have provided a positive incentive to assist him to consider ways to be ready on time even with his slower temperament. I frequently use such a strategy. A child with whom I worked who was tardy on a regular basis was given the job of "tardy monitor" at his school, a position that entailed arriving early and keeping track of which students were late. The child loved the responsibility and arrived on time with renewed purpose.

Accepting children for who they are and appreciating their different temperaments does not imply that we excuse inappropriate, unacceptable behavior but rather that we understand this behavior and help to modify it in a manner that does not assault a child's self-esteem and sense of dignity. It means developing realistic goals and expectations for our children. Fortunately, in the past 10–15 years there have been an increasing number of publications to help parents and teachers appreciate, accept, and respond effectively to a child's temperament and learning style (Carey, 1997; Keogh, 2003; Kurcinka, 1991; Levine, 2002, 2003; Sachs, 2001).

6. Helping our children experience success by identifying and nurturing their "islands of competence"

Resilient children do not deny problems that they may face. Such denial runs counter to mastering challenges. However, in addition to acknowledging and confronting problems, youngsters who are resilient are able to identify and utilize their strengths. Unfortunately, many children who feel poorly about themselves and their abilities experience a diminished sense of hope. Parents sometimes report that the positive comments they offer their children fall on "deaf ears," resulting in parents' becoming frustrated and reducing positive feedback.

It is important for parents to be aware that when children lack self-worth they are less receptive to accepting positive feedback. Parents should continue to offer this feedback, but must recognize that genuine self-esteem, hope, and resilience are based on children experiencing success in areas of their lives that they and significant others deem to be important. This requires parents to identify and reinforce a child's "islands of competence." Every child possesses these islands of competence or areas of strength and we must nurture these rather than overemphasize the child's weakness.

During an evaluation of a child, I regularly ask the parents to describe their child's islands of competence. I ask the child to do the same, often via the question, "What do you think you do well?" or "What do you see as your strengths?" For children who respond, "I don't know," I answer, "That's okay, it can take time to figure out what we're good at, but it's important to figure out." If we are to reinforce a more optimistic attitude in children, it is imperative that we place the spotlight on strengths and assist children to articulate the strengths that they possess.

One problem related to the issue of acceptance discussed in the previous guidepost, is when parents minimize the importance of their child's island of competence. For example, 13-year-old George struggled with learning problems. Unlike his parents, Mr. and Mrs. White, or his 16-year-old sister, Linda, he was not gifted academically or athletically. When his parents were asked during an evaluation to identify George's islands of competence, they responded with an intriguing, "We're somewhat embarrassed to tell you. We just don't think it's the kind of activity that a 13-year-old boy should be spending much of his time doing."

Eventually, Mr. White revealed, "George likes to garden and take care of plants. That would be okay if he did well in school and was involved in other activities. How can a 13-year-old boy be so interested in plants?"

Rather than my finding fault with the Whites' reactions to George's interests, it was vital to help them understand the importance of identifying and building on his strengths even if those strengths were not initially valued by them. To be resilient, children need to feel that they are skilled in at least one or two areas that are esteemed by others.

Clinicians and educators should insure that treatment and educational plans begin with a list of the child's strengths and include strategies that can be used to reinforce and display these strengths for others to see and praise. Of what use are a child's strengths if they are not observed and supported by others?

Laurie, a teenager, had difficulty in getting along with her peers, but young children gravitated towards her. Her parents described her as the "pied piper" of the neighborhood. Given this strength, she began to baby-sit. As the responsibilities involved with baby-sitting helped her to develop confidence, she was more willing to examine and change her approach with her peers, which led to greater acceptance. Similarly, 10-year-old Brian, a boy with reading difficulties, had a knack for artwork, especially drawing cartoons. His parents and teachers displayed his cartoons at home and school, an action that boosted his self-esteem and in a concrete way communicated that his reading problems did not define him as a person, that he also possessed strengths.

When children discover their islands of competence, they are more willing to confront those areas that have been problematic for them. Adults must be sensitive to recognizing and bolstering these islands.

7. Helping children realize that mistakes are experiences from which to learn

There is a significant difference in the way in which resilient children view mistakes compared with nonresilient children. Resilient children tend to perceive mistakes as opportunities for learning. In contrast, children who are not very hopeful often experience mistakes as an indication that they are failures. In response to this pessimistic view, they are likely to flee from challenges, feeling inadequate, and often blaming others for their problems. If parents are to raise resilient children, they must help them develop a healthy attitude about mistakes from an early age.

The manner in which children respond to mistakes provides a significant window through which to assess their self-esteem and resilience.

For example, in a Little League game two children struck out every time they came to bat. One child approached the coach after the game and said, "Coach, I keep striking out. Can you help me figure out what I'm doing wrong?" This response suggests a child with a resilient mindset, a child who entertains the belief that there are adults who can help him to lessen mistakes (strikeouts).

The second child, who unfortunately was not resilient, reacted to striking out by flinging his bat to the ground and screaming at the umpire, "You are blind, blind, blind! I wouldn't strike out if you weren't blind!" Much to the embarrassment of his parents he then ran off the field in tears, continuing to blame the umpire for striking out. Since this child did not believe he could improve, he coped with his sense of hopelessness by casting fault on others.

Parents can assist their children to develop a more constructive attitude about mistakes and setbacks. Two questions that can facilitate this task are to ask parents to consider what their children's answers would be to the following questions:

"When your parents make a mistake, when something doesn't go right, what do they do?"

"When you make a mistake, what do your parents say or do to you?"

In terms of the first question, parents serve as significant models for handling mistakes. It is easier for children to learn to deal more effectively with mistakes if they see their parents doing so. However, if they observe their parents blaming others or becoming very angry and frustrated when mistakes occur or offering excuses in order to avoid a task, they are more likely to develop a self-defeating attitude towards mistakes. In contrast, if they witness their parents use mistakes as opportunities for learning, they are more likely to do the same.

The second question also deserves serious consideration by parents. Many well-meaning parents become anxious and frustrated with their children's mistakes. Given these feelings they may say or do things that contribute to their children fearing rather than learning from setbacks. For instance, parental frustration may lead to such comments as: "Were you using your brains?" or "You never think before you act!" or "I told you it wouldn't work!" These and similar remarks serve to corrode a child's sense of dignity and self-esteem.

No one likes to make mistakes or fail, but parents can use their children's mistakes as teachable moments. They can engage their children in a discussion of what they can do differently next time to maximize chances for success. Using empathy, they can refrain from saying things that they would not want said to them (e.g., how many parents would find it helpful if their spouse said to them, "Were you using your brains?").

Parents must also have realistic expectations for their children and not set the bar too high or too low. If the bar is set too high, children will continually experience failure and are likely to feel they are a disappointment to their parents. Setting the bar too low may rob children of experiences that test their abilities and their capacity to learn to manage setbacks. Very low expectations also convey the message, "We don't think you are capable."

If parents are to reinforce a resilient mindset in their children, their words and actions must convey a belief that we can learn from mistakes. The fear of making mistakes and being humiliated is one of the most potent obstacles to learning, one that is incompatible with a resilient lifestyle.

8. Developing responsibility, compassion, and a social conscience by providing children with opportunities to contribute

Parents often ask what they can do to foster an attitude of responsibility, caring, and compassion in their children. One of the most effective ways of nurturing responsibility is offering children opportunities to help others. When children are enlisted in helping others and engaging in responsible behaviors, parents communicate trust in them and faith in their ability to handle a variety of tasks. In turn, involvement in these tasks reinforces several key characteristics of a resilient mindset including empathy, a sense of satisfaction in the positive impact of one's behaviors, a more confident outlook as islands of competence

are displayed, and the use of problem-solving skills.

Too often parents label the first responsibilities they give children "chores." Most children and adults are not thrilled about doing chores, whereas almost every child from an early age appears motivated to help others. The presence of this "helping drive" is supported by research in which adults were asked to reflect on their school experiences and to write about one of their most positive moments in school that boosted their self-esteem and motivation (Brooks, 1991). The most frequently cited memory was being asked to assist others (e.g., tutoring a younger child, painting murals in the school, running the film projector, passing out the milk, and straws).

To highlight the importance of teaching responsibility and compassion, I typically ask parents how their children would answer the following questions:

"What are the ways in which your parents show responsibility?"

"What behaviors have you observed in your parents that were not responsible?"

"What charitable activities have your parents been involved with in the past few months?"

"What charitable activities have they and you have been involved with together in the past few months?"

Parents would be well-advised to say as often as possible to their children, "We need your help" rather than "Remember to do your chores." In addition, parents who involve their children in charitable endeavors, such as walks for hunger or AIDS or food drives, appreciate the value of such activities in fostering self-esteem and resilience. Responsibility and compassion are not promoted by parental "lectures" but rather by opportunities for children to assume a helping role and to become part of a "charitable family," a family that is engaged in acts of compassion and giving.

9. Teaching our children to solve problems and make decisions

Children with high self-esteem and resilience believe that they are masters of their own fate and that they can define what they have control over and what is beyond their control. A vital ingredient of this feeling of control is the belief that when problems arise, they have the ability to solve problems and make decisions. Resilient children are able to articulate problems, consider different solutions, attempt what they judge to be the most appropriate solution, and learn from the outcome (Shure, 1996; Shure & Aberson, 2005).

If parents are to reinforce this problem-solving attitude in their children, they must refrain from constantly telling their children what to do. Instead it is more beneficial to encourage children to consider different possible solutions. To facilitate this process, parents might wish to establish a "family meeting time" every week or every other week during which the problems facing family members can be discussed and solutions considered.

Jane, a 9-year-old girl, came home from school in tears and sobbed to her mother, Mrs. Jones, that some of her friends refused to sit with her at lunch, telling her they did not want her around. Jane felt confused and distressed and asked her mother what to do. Mrs. Jones immediately replied that Jane should tell the other girls that if they did not want to play with her, she did not want to play with them. While this motherly advice may have been appropriate, quickly telling Jane what to do and not involving her in a discussion of possible solutions took away an opportunity to strengthen her own problem-solving skills.

As another example, Barry and his older brother, Len, constantly bickered. According to their parents, Mr. and Mrs. Stern, they fought about everything, including who would sit in the front seat of the car and who would use the computer. Len was frequently reminded by his parents to be more tolerant since he was the older of the two. They warned him that his failure to comply with their request would result in punishment. Len's response was to become angry and distant, feeling he was being treated unfairly. Eventually, the parents sat down with Barry and Len, shared with them the negative impact that their arguing was having on the family, and asked them to come up with possible solutions to particular problems and to select what they considered to be the best solution.

Much to the surprise of Mr. and Mrs. Stern, their sons came forth with solutions that were noteworthy for being grounded in simple rules. The boys decided that they would take turns sitting in the front seat as well as alternating every half hour in the use of the computer.

As Shure (1996) has found in her research, even preschool children can be assisted to develop effective and realistic ways of making choices and solving problems. When children initiate their own plans of action with the guidance of parents, their sense of ownership and control is reinforced, as is their resilience.

10. Disciplining in ways that promote self-discipline and self-worth

To be a disciplinarian is one of their most important roles that parents assume in nurturing resilience in their children (Brooks & Goldstein, 2007). In this role parents must remember that the word *discipline* relates to the word *disciple* and thus is a teaching process. The ways in which children are disciplined can either reinforce or erode self-esteem, self-control, and resilience.

Two of the major goals of effective discipline are: (a) to ensure a safe and secure environment in which children understand and can define rules, limits, and consequences, and (b) to reinforce self-discipline and self-control so that children incorporate these rules and apply them even when parents are not present. A lack of consistent, clear rules and consequences often contributes to chaos and to children feeling that their parents do not care about them. On the other hand, if parents are harsh and arbitrary, if they resort to yelling and spanking, children are likely to learn resentment rather than self-discipline.

There are several key principles that parents can follow to employ discipline techniques that are positive and effective. Given the significant role that discipline plays in parenting practices and in nurturing resilience, they are described in detail.

Practice prevention: It is vital for parents to become proactive rather than reactive in their interactions with their children, especially in regard to discipline. For example, discipline problems were minimized in one household when a young, hyperactive boy was permitted to get up from the dinner table when he could no longer remain seated. This approach proved far more effective than the previous one used by the parents, namely, to yell and punish him; when a punitive atmosphere was removed, this boy also learned greater self-control. In another home, a boy's tantrums at bedtime ended when he was allowed to have a nightlight in his room and keep a photo of his parents by his bedside (both were his ideas to deal with nightmares he was experiencing).

Work as a parental team: In homes with two parents, it is important that parents set aside time for themselves to examine the expectations they have for their children as well as the discipline they use. This dialog can also occur between divorced parents. While parents cannot and should not be clones of each other, they should strive to arrive at common goals and disciplinary practices, which most likely will involve negotiation and compromise. This negotiation should take place in private and not in front of their children.

Be consistent, not rigid: The behavior of children sometimes renders consistency a Herculean task. Some children, based on past experience, believe that they can outlast their parents and that eventually their parents will succumb to their whining, crying, or tantrums. If guidelines and consequences have been established for acceptable behavior, it is important that parents adhere to them. However, parents must remember that consistency is not synonymous with rigidity or inflexibility. A consistent approach to discipline invites thoughtful modification of rules and consequences such as when a child reaches adolescence and is permitted to stay out later on the weekend. When modifications are necessary, they should be discussed with children so that they understand the reasons for the changes and can offer input.

Select one's battlegrounds carefully: Parents can find themselves reminding and disciplining their children all day long. It is important for parents to ask what behaviors merit discipline and which are not really relevant in terms of nurturing

responsibility and resilience. Obviously, behaviors concerning safety deserve immediate attention. Other behaviors will be based on the particular values and expectations in the house. If children are punished for countless behaviors, if parents are constantly telling them what to do in an arbitrary manner, then the positive effects of discipline will be lost.

Rely when possible on natural and logical consequences: Children must learn that there are consequences for their behavior. It is best if these consequences are not harsh or arbitrary and are based on discussions that parents have had with their children. Discipline rooted in natural and logical consequences can be very effective. *Natural* consequences are those that result from a child's actions without parents having to enforce them such as a child having a bicycle stolen because it was not placed in the garage. While *logical* consequences sometimes overlap with natural consequences, logical consequences involve some action taken on the part of parents in response to their child's behavior. Thus, if the child whose bicycle was stolen asked parents for money to purchase a new bicycle, a logical consequence would be for the parents to help the child figure out how to earn the money needed to pay for the new bicycle.

Positive feedback and encouragement are often the most powerful forms of discipline: Although most of the questions I am asked about discipline focus on negative consequences or punishment, it is important to appreciate the impact of positive feedback and encouragement as disciplinary approaches. Parents should "catch their children doing things right" and let them know when they do. Children crave the attention of their parents. It makes more sense to provide this attention for positive rather than negative behaviors. Well-timed positive feedback and expressions of encouragement and love are more valuable to children's self-esteem and resilience than stars or stickers. When children feel loved and appreciated, when they receive encouragement and support, they are less likely to engage in negative behaviors.

Concluding Remark

Research may never be able to assign a precise percentage to capture the impact of a parent on a child's development. However, as noted earlier, whatever the percentage, we know that the day-to-day interactions parents have with their children are influential in determining the quality of lives that their children will lead. Parents can serve as charismatic adults to their children. They can assume this role by understanding and fortifying in their children the different characteristics of a resilient mindset, by believing in them, by conveying unconditional love, and by providing them with opportunities that reinforce their islands of competence and feelings of self-worth and dignity. Nurturing resilience is an immeasurable, lifelong gift parents can offer their children. It is part of a parent's legacy to the next generation.

References

Beardslee, W. R., & Podorefsky, D. (1988). Resilient adolescents whose parents have serious affective and other psychiatric disorders: Importance of self-understanding and relationships. *The American Journal of Psychiatry, 145*, 63–69.

Brooks, R. (1991). *The self-esteem teacher*. Loveland, OH: Treehaus Communications.

Brooks, R. (1994). Children at risk: Fostering hope and resilience. *The American Journal of Orthopsychiatry, 64*, 545–553.

Brooks, R. (1998). Parenting a child with learning disabilities: Strategies for fostering self-esteem, motivation, and resilience. In T. Citro (Ed.), *The experts speak: Parenting a child with learning disabilities* (pp. 25–45). Waltham, MA: Learning Disabilities Association of Massachusetts.

Brooks, R., & Goldstein, S. (2001). *Raising resilient children: Fostering strength, hope, and optimism in your child*. New York: McGraw-Hill.

Brooks, R., & Goldstein, S. (2003). *Nurturing resilience in our children. Answers to the most important parenting questions*. New York: McGraw-Hill.

Brooks, R., & Goldstein, S. (2007). *Raising a self-disciplined child: Help your child become more responsible, confident, and resilient*. New York: McGraw-Hill.

Brooks, R., & Goldstein, S. (2011). Raising resilient children. In G. P. Koocher & A. M. La Greca (Eds.), *The parents guide to psychological first aid: Helping children and adolescents cope with predictable life crises* (pp. 142–150). New York, NY: Oxford University Press.

Carey, W. B. (1997). *Understanding your child's temperament*. New York: Macmillan.

Chess, S., & Thomas, A. (1987). *Know your child*. New York: Basic Books.

Covey, S. (1989). *The seven habits of highly effective people*. New York: Simon & Schuster.

Crenshaw, D. A. (Ed.). (2010). *Reverence in healing: Honoring strengths without trivializing suffering*. New York: Jason Aronson.

Deater-Deckard, K., Ivy, L., & Smith, J. (2005). Resilience in gene-environment transactions. In S. Goldstein & R. Brooks (Eds.), *Handbook of resilience in children* (pp. 49–63). New York: Kluwer.

Goldstein, S., & Brooks, R. (2003). *Does it matter how we raise our children?* June article on websites www.samgoldstein.com and www.drrobertbrooks.com

Harris, J. R. (1998). *The nurture assumption: Why children turn out the way that they do*. New York: Free Press.

Hechtman, L. (1991). Resilience and vulnerability in long term outcome of attention deficit disorder. *Canadian Journal of Psychiatry, 36*, 415–421.

Herrenkohl, E. C., Herrenkohl, R. C., & Egolf, B. (1994). Resilient early school-age children from maltreating homes: Outcomes in late adolescence. *The American Journal of Orthopsychiatry, 64*, 301–309.

Jaffee, S. (2005). Family violence and parental psychopathology: Implications for children's socioemotional development and resilience. In S. Goldstein & R. Brooks (Eds.), *Handbook of resilience in children* (pp. 149–163). New York: Kluwer.

Kaplan, H. (2005). Understanding the concept of resilience. In S. Goldstein & R. Brooks (Eds.), *Handbook of resilience in children* (pp. 39–47). New York: Kluwer.

Keogh, B. K. (2003). *Temperament in the classroom: Understanding individual differences*. Baltimore, MD: Brookes Publishing.

Kumpfer, K. L., & Alavarado, R. (2003). Family-strengthening approaches for the prevention of youth problem behaviors. *American Psychologist, 58*, 457–465.

Kurcinka, M. S. (1991). *Raising your spirited child*. New York: HarperCollins.

Levine, M. D. (2002). *A mind at a time*. New York: Simon & Schuster.

Levine, M. D. (2003). *The myth of laziness*. New York: Simon & Schuster.

Masten, A. S., Best, K. M., & Garmezy, N. (1990). Resilience and development: Contributions from the study of children who overcome adversity. *Development and Psychopathology, 2*, 425–444.

Pinker, S. (2002). *The blank slate: The modern denial of human nature*. New York: Viking.

Reivich, K., & Shatte, A. (2002). *The resilience factor*. New York: Broadway Books.

Rutter, M. (1985). Resilience in the face of adversity: Protective factors and resistance to psychiatric disorders. *The British Journal of Psychiatry, 147*, 598–611.

Sachs, B. E. (2001). *The good enough child: How to have an imperfect family and be perfectly satisfied*. New York: HarperCollins.

Segal, J. (1988). Teachers have enormous power in affecting a child's self-esteem. *The Brown University Child Behavior and Development Newsletter, 4,* 1–3.

Sheridan, S. M., Eagle, J. W., & Dowd, S. E. (2005). Families as contexts for children's adaptation. In S. Goldstein & R. Brooks (Eds.), *Handbook of resilience in children* (pp. 165–179). New York: Kluwer.

Shure, M. B. (1996). *Raising a thinking child.* New York: Pocket Books.

Shure, M. B., & Aberson, B. (2005). Enhancing the process of resilience through effective thinking. In S. Goldstein & R. Brooks (Eds.), *Handbook of resilience in children* (pp. 373–394). New York: Kluwer.

Siegel, D. S. (1999). *The developing mind: How relationships and the brain interact to share who we are.* New York: Guilford Press.

Werner, E. E., & Smith, R. S. (1992). *Overcoming the odds: High risk children from birth to adulthood.* New York: Cornell University Press.

Building Resilience in All Children: A Public Health Approach

Emily B. Winslow, Irwin N. Sandler,
Sharlene A. Wolchik, and Colleen Carr

In this chapter, we present a conceptual framework for the promotion of resilience in children that integrates concepts from the study of resilience with a public health approach to improving mental health at the population level. The chapter begins with a review of resilience and public health concepts and describes how these perspectives can be integrated within a broad framework for the promotion of health and prevention of dysfunction. We then present examples of evidence-based preventive interventions and policies that have successfully implemented components of this framework. Given our focus on promoting resilience, we limit discussion and examples of interventions to those designed to create resources for children not diagnosed with mental health disorder, although the framework could readily be extended to interventions for children with clinical levels of dysfunction. Finally, we provide an overview of how the framework might be used by planners to create resources in their communities that will promote resilience, as well as examples of tools currently available to assist planners in this process.

E.B. Winslow (✉) • I.N. Sandler • S.A. Wolchik
• C. Carr
Department of Psychology, Arizona State University,
Tempe, AZ, USA
e-mail: emily.winslow@asu.edu; Irwin.sandler@asu.edu;
Wolchik@asu.edu; Colleen.carr@asu.edu

Resilience Concepts

We define resilience as "a child's achievement of positive developmental outcomes and avoidance of maladaptive outcomes under significantly adverse conditions" (Wyman, Sandler, Wolchik, & Nelson, 2000). Three concepts are central to this definition: adversity, positive outcomes, and the resources that are responsible for achieving positive outcomes under conditions of adversity.

Adversity

Adversity is conceptualized as a relationship between children and their environment in which satisfaction of basic needs and goals is threatened or in which accomplishment of age-appropriate developmental tasks is impeded (Sandler, 2001). Adversities can be conceptualized as occurring in individual, family, or community-organizational domains. Adversities in the individual domain include experiences such as illnesses, injuries, or abuse, which compromise children's relations with their environments. Adversities in the family domain include changes in family structure (e.g., divorce, death) or functioning (e.g., conflict) that threaten children's well-being. Adversities in the community-organizational domain include characteristics of communities (e.g., poverty, disorganization)

S. Goldstein and R.B. Brooks (eds.), *Handbook of Resilience in Children*,
DOI 10.1007/978-1-4614-3661-4_27, © Springer Science+Business Media New York 2013

or social institutions (e.g., school violence) that diminish children's satisfaction of basic needs and accomplishment of developmental tasks.

Relations between exposure to adversities in childhood and the development of a wide range of mental health and social adaptation difficulties in childhood and adulthood are well established (Grant et al., 2003; Sandler, Ayers, Suter, Schultz, & Twohey, 2003). Illustratively, based on a study of 9,508 members of a large HMO, Felitti et al. (1998) observed that exposure to four or more adversities in childhood was associated with a 4–12-fold increase in risk for alcoholism, drug abuse, depression, and suicide attempts in adulthood. Similarly, Furstenberg and colleagues found that the odds of negative mental health outcomes for children exposed to eight or more adversities was 5.7 times greater than for children exposed to three or fewer adversities (Furstenberg, Cook, Eccles, Elder, & Sameroff, 1999). Studies have also demonstrated consistent relations between mental health and social adaptation problems and exposure to specific adversities in childhood such as parental divorce (Lansford, 2009), family and neighborhood poverty (Edin & Kissane, 2010; Winslow & Shaw, 2007), parental mental illness (Goodman & Brand, 2008), child maltreatment (Cicchetti & Toth, 2005), exposure to domestic or community violence (Evans, Davies, & DiLillo, 2008; Fowler, Tompsett, Braciszewski, Jacques-Tiura, & Baltes, 2009), and bereavement (Melham, Walker, Moritz, & Brent, 2008).

Resources

Studies of resilience focus on identifying resources that facilitate the occurrence of positive outcomes and the avoidance of negative outcomes for children in the face of adversity (Luthar, 2006). Positive and negative outcomes are conceptualized as interrelated and include successful accomplishment of developmental tasks and avoidance of emotional and behavioral problems and mental disorders. Resources in the individual, family, and community-organizational domains facilitate positive outcomes by either promoting effective adaptation processes or by reducing the child's exposure to adversities (Sandler, 2001). Individual resources include cognitive, emotional, and behavioral skills, such as high cognitive ability, effective emotion regulation, and adaptive coping efforts. An important protective resource in the family domain involves positive parenting, which is characterized by warmth, responsivity, effective discipline, and support for effective coping. Community-organizational resources include access to high-quality schools, prosocial neighborhoods, and opportunities for involvement in other formal or informal systems that provide support or protect against the occurrence of adversities, such as religious or secular youth groups, organized sports, community volunteer groups, groups that develop specific talents (e.g., music, art, drama), and relationships with extended family members.

Public Health Approach

In contrast to the resilience perspective, which focuses on delineating resources and protective processes that promote healthy outcomes among individuals or families facing adversity, the public health approach to prevention focuses on how to change population-level behaviors, environmental factors, or processes to reduce incidence rates of disorders (i.e., number of new cases) and to increase healthy outcomes in a population (Rose, 1992). To effectively impact population-level outcomes while addressing individual differences (i.e., varying levels of adversities, resources, and problems), the public health model incorporates multiple intervention levels: mental health *promotion* interventions to enhance well-being of the general public or a whole population, *universal* prevention programs to prevent disorders in the general population or in a whole population that has not been identified based on individual risk, *selective* interventions for those at-risk due to exposure to specific adversities, and *indicated* programs for individuals experiencing sub-diagnostic symptomatology (National Research Council and Institute of Medicine [NRC/IOM], 2009).

Promotion Programs

Mental health promotion programs are typically offered to the general public or a whole population to enhance individuals' life skills (e.g., social competence) and promote well-being, as well as to strengthen individuals' ability to cope with adversity (NRC/IOM, 2009). Although such programs typically help prevent disorders as well, their primary purpose is to promote healthy outcomes (e.g., self-esteem, morality, friendships). Promotion programs may be less stigmatizing than prevention programs, particularly compared to prevention programs that target specific subgroups; because the emphasis is placed on maximizing individuals' potential rather than avoiding the development of disorder (NRC/IOM, 2009).

Universal Prevention Programs

Universal prevention programs are given to the general public or a whole population group not identified on the basis of individual risk and aim to reduce the incidence of mental health disorders (NRC/IOM, 2009). Although conceptually distinct, universal prevention and promotion interventions typically overlap considerably in practice, because effective mental health promotion programs also prevent maladjustment, and universal preventive interventions often promote well-being in addition to preventing disorders (Catalano, Berglund, Ryan, Lonczak, & Hawkins, 2002; Payton et al., 2008). Given the substantial overlap, we discuss universal prevention and promotion programs interchangeably in the rest of the chapter.

To justify inclusion of all individuals in a population and to maximize the benefit-cost ratio, universal programs must be able to be delivered to everyone, should be low in costs per individual, should be effective for and acceptable to the population, and have little potential for harm (NRC/IOM, 2009). Universal promotion and prevention programs can provide several benefits, particularly when incorporated within a multilevel system of strategies,

such as increasing population awareness, providing support and recruitment for more intensive prevention efforts, reducing stigmatization for those participating in targeted programs, and reinforcing common messages provided via different outlets (Offord, 2000; Stormshak, Kaminski, & Goodman, 2002). For example, parents who participate in an intensive parenting skills intervention may feel supported by their community, rather than stigmatized, if universal efforts have been successful at promoting the importance of positive parenting and value of actively improving one's parenting skills (Sanders, Turner, & Markie-Dadds, 2002). Universal programs may also be integrated into community structures or organizations that serve the full population (e.g., schools, health systems), and thus may promote policies or cultural practices (e.g., parental involvement in schools) that can benefit the entire population. Further, because a great number of people are involved, universal programs have the potential for producing large effects at the population level, although the benefits received by each individual may be relatively small (Rose, 1992; Shamblen & Derzon, 2009).

Selective Programs

Selective preventive interventions target specific individuals or subgroups of the population whose risk for mental disorder significantly exceeds that of the general population due to exposure to one or more adversities (e.g., parental mental illness), and who can be identified based on some marker variable rather than individual assessment of problematic functioning (NRC/IOM, 2009). Although selective programs are not delivered to all members of the general population, these interventions could involve a large number of individuals, particularly if selected adversities are highly prevalent (e.g., parental divorce). Therefore, selective programs should not exceed moderate costs per individual and should be characterized by low risk for potential iatrogenic intervention effects (NRC/IOM, 2009).

Selective prevention programs can provide important services that supplement universal efforts. Selective programming provides a potentially efficient way to direct additional resources to individuals with higher than average need for services (Offord, 2000). In addition, targeting specific subgroups allows provision of services tailored to the unique needs of these subgroups (i.e., needs not shared by other subgroups of the population). For example, children who experience traumatic events, such as parental divorce, death, or abuse, may benefit from specialized preventive services provided to caregivers and/or children that are designed to facilitate positive adjustment to the specific adversity.

Indicated Programs

In addition to programs for subgroups identified on the basis of exposure to adversities, indicated preventive interventions target children manifesting sub-diagnostic levels of mental health symptoms or families experiencing problems adapting to adversity (e.g., high conflict divorces) based on individual assessment of child or family functioning (NRC/IOM, 2009). For example, children may be selected to participate in a behavioral management program on the basis of parent or teacher report of high levels of disruptive behavior. The primary goal of indicated programs is to reduce the occurrence of new cases of mental disorder or other serious outcomes (i.e., incidence) by decreasing symptomatology and reversing the progression of severity. Indicated prevention programs are often moderately to highly intensive interventions that may include multiple components (e.g., parent education plus school-based behavior management) and/or may involve individualized approaches, such as one-on-one sessions with a mental health counselor. Similar to selective prevention programs, indicated interventions provide additional resources (i.e., beyond universal level) to prevent the development of serious problems in families and children who are most at risk.

Framework for Building Resilience in All Children

As illustrated in the previous sections, the public health approach incorporates multiple intervention levels that fulfill distinct and mutually reinforcing roles when implemented simultaneously in a community. In such cases, all children or families in a population would have access to universal promotion and prevention programs. Subgroups identified on the basis of exposure to adversity would receive these services as well as more specialized selective program(s). Those experiencing sub-diagnostic levels of symptomatology would have access to universal promotion and prevention programs as well as indicated programs, which may include multiple intervention components designed to reduce symptoms and reverse the progression of severity. A minority of families would qualify for both selective and indicated services and would have access to all levels of intervention.

From a resilience perspective, this multilevel framework takes into account the varying levels of exposure to adversity and availability of protective resources among members of a population. Table 27.1 shows how multiple domains of interventions to promote resilience processes can be subsumed within the classification of universal promotion/prevention, selective, and indicated interventions. Interventions at each level build individual, family, and/or community-organizational resources associated with resilient outcomes among children facing adversity. We refer to these as "constructed resilience resources" given they are promoted by interventions designed for that purpose. By looking across columns within each row of the matrix, one can see the range of interventions that might be used to construct resources in a given domain. For example, mutually reinforcing programs to improve parenting might be developed for the general population, as well as for those experiencing specific adversities or early levels of problems. By looking across the rows within each column, one can see how resources could be constructed in multiple domains to promote resilience in a defined

Table 27.1 Strategies to construct resilience resources across multiple domains and levels

Resource domain	Intervention level		
	Universal Promotion/Prevention	Selective	Indicated
Child	Promote child strengths to cope with stressors, problem solve, regulate affect, and deal with potential problem situations (e.g., peer conflict)	Teach coping skills and provide information to children experiencing a specific stressor (e.g., parental divorce)	Teach skills (e.g., cognitive appraisals of stress) to children with elevated problems or skill deficits
Family	Promote parenting practices that enhance child adaptive outcomes and help avoid future adversities or strengthen the child's ability to cope effectively	Promote effective parenting for children exposed to a specific adversity (e.g., poverty)	Teach parenting skills to counteract ongoing problems (e.g., child externalizing behavior)
Community-organizational	Promote community or organizational changes that reduce the occurrence of adversities or provide support for all children to adapt effectively to normative events (e.g., transition to junior high school)	Change ecologies of existing organizations (e.g., courts) to promote healthy adjustment for at-risk subgroups (e.g., divorced families). Develop new organizations to provide services for children exposed to a specific adversity (e.g., parental death)	Develop community structures to deal more effectively with youth experiencing sub-diagnostic levels of problems to strengthen their ability to cope effectively or prevent exposure to future adversities

population. For example, complementary child, family, and organizational programs might be developed for the entire community to build resources that promote well-being and developmental competencies and prevent disorder.

Universal promotion and prevention programs construct resources that promote resilience by reducing the occurrence of adversities for the full population or facilitating skills that promote healthy adaptation when adversities occur. These interventions may be designed to enhance *child* capacities (e.g., coping skills, academic competence), *family* competencies (e.g., parental warmth, effective discipline, communication), or *organizational* resources (e.g., learning structures, curricula, peer structures, school policies, neighborhood empowerment). Selective programs build resources to promote effective adaptation to specific adversities, such as *child* coping skills for parental divorce, parenting skills for *families* living in poverty, or *community-school* partnerships to facilitate successful transitions to high school for inner-city youths. Indicated interventions construct resources to improve adaptation processes for those exhibiting mental health problems, such as positive thinking skills for *adolescents* experiencing sub-diagnostic depressive symptoms, parent behavior management skills for *families* with oppositional children, or court *organizational* procedures for diverting delinquents to interventions rather than detention. In the following sections, we provide examples of programs with demonstrated efficacy in promoting child well-being through universal promotion/prevention, selective, or indicated intervention strategies that construct resources in child, family, or community-organizational domains.

Resources Constructed in the Child Domain

Universal Promotion and Prevention Programs

Promotion programs in the child domain focus on enhancing children's development in one or more areas, such as building skill competencies, fostering self-efficacy, and promoting prosocial relationships (Catalano et al., 2002; Payton et al., 2008). Similarly, universal preventive interventions are designed to build child resources based on the theory that promoting skills and strengths will help children effectively adapt to conditions of adversity (current and future) and decrease the likelihood of future adversities, thereby preventing the development of disorders and facilitating successful attainment of developmental tasks (Sandler, 2001). A variety of universal promotion and prevention programs designed for general populations have impacted child well-being outcomes by constructing resources in the child domain, including programs that teach skills such as problem-solving, social skills, conflict resolution, affect regulation, cognitive restructuring, empathy, impulse control, and leadership qualities (see Durlak, Weissberg, & Pachan, 2010; Hahn et al., 2007; Neil & Christensen, 2009; Payton et al., 2008; Soole, Mazerolle, & Rombouts, 2008 for reviews).

For example, the Promoting Alternative Thinking Strategies (PATHS) elementary school, multiyear curriculum is designed to build children's social and emotional competence through more than 50 lessons on knowledge about emotional states, skills for regulating affect, problem-solving, and social skills (Conduct Problems Prevention Research Group [CPPRG], 1999; Greenberg, Kusche, Cook, & Quamma, 1995). Several randomized controlled trials have indicated that when PATHS is supported by schools and well implemented by teachers, the curriculum is successful in promoting academic engagement and social, emotional, and behavioral competence in a variety of populations (CPPRG, 1999, 2010a; Curtis & Norgate, 2007; Domitrovich, Cortes, & Greenberg, 2007; Kam, Greenberg, & Walls, 2003). Researchers have also found that PATHS helps prevent problem outcomes, including socially withdrawn behavior, conduct problems, and peer difficulties (CPPRG, 2010a; Curtis & Norgate, 2007; Domitrovich et al., 2007).

Selective Programs

In contrast to universal interventions, which are designed for all individuals in a population, selective prevention programs build resources for subgroups confronting specific adversities. Selective interventions in the child domain typically focus on bolstering coping skills needed to effectively handle the challenges posed by adversities such as parental divorce (Pedro-Carroll, 1997; Stolberg & Mahler, 1994), parental death (Sandler, Ayers, et al., 2010) or trauma (Enright & Carr, 2002); or enhancing cognitive skills to counteract the deleterious effects of adversities such as social disadvantage (Lange & Carr, 2002).

For example, the Children of Divorce Intervention Project (CODIP) is a 12-session, group intervention for school-age children whose parents have divorced and is designed to help children identify and appropriately express emotions, cope effectively, restructure divorce-related misconceptions, and create positive perceptions of themselves and their families (Pedro-Carroll, 1997; Pedro-Carroll & Cowen, 1985). Pedro-Carroll and colleagues found that participation in CODIP improved children's coping, problem-solving skills, and classroom competence (e.g., social skills, task orientation) and resulted in decreases in anxiety and classroom adjustment problems (e.g., acting out, learning problems) compared to a no-intervention control group at posttest and 2 years following the intervention (Pedro-Carroll, Sutton, & Wyman, 1999).

Indicated Programs

Indicated prevention programs are designed to meet the needs of individuals within a population who are experiencing mental health problems but do not meet criteria for a mental health diagnosis. Indicated prevention programs in the child domain typically teach youths skills such as how to identify feelings, manage anger, or challenge distorted cognitions. This approach has been beneficial in reducing dysfunction among youths experiencing internalizing and/or externalizing

symptoms (Bienvenu & Ginsburg, 2007; Payton et al., 2008; Stice, Shaw, Bohon, Marti, & Rohde, 2009; Wilson & Lipsey, 2007).

For example, the Coping with Depression (CWD) course is a cognitive-behavioral intervention that has been adapted for many different target populations, including as an indicated prevention program for adolescents with sub-diagnostic levels of depressive symptomatology (Cuijpers, Muñoz, Clarke, & Lewinsohn, 2009). This intervention teaches adolescents how to identify and challenge negative thoughts using cartoons, role-plays, and group discussions. A meta-analysis of 25 randomized controlled trials of CWD found that for the 6 trials that used CWD as an indicated prevention program, adolescents who participated in the intervention had a 38% lower chance of developing a depressive disorder than adolescents in the control group (Cuijpers et al.). Garber et al. (2009) conducted a multicenter, randomized control trial of this preventive intervention with adolescents who had current or past depressive symptomatology and at least one parent with a current or past depressive disorder. They found significant preventive effects on both diagnosis of depression and self-reported depressive symptoms through a 9-month follow-up period but only for adolescents whose parents were not currently depressed.

Resources Constructed in the Family Domain

Universal Promotion and Prevention Programs

Promotion programs in the family domain target aspects of the home environment that could be optimized to enhance child development. For example, Whitehurst et al. (1988) developed and evaluated a shared reading program, called *dialogic reading*, to promote language development in toddlers and preschoolers. The 6-week program, which has been tested in both group- and video-based formats (Arnold, Lonigan, Whitehurst, & Epstein, 1994), encourages parents to make book reading interactive by asking the child open-ended questions about the story, praising and elaborating on children's verbalizations, and prompting the child to relate aspects of the story to his/her own life. A meta-analysis of 16 experimental studies found significant positive effects of the dialogic reading program on language development compared to reading-as-usual control groups, with stronger effects on expressive than receptive language skills, for younger (i.e., toddler and preschool age) than older (i.e., kindergarten age) children, and for higher SES than lower SES families (Mol, Bus, de Jong, & Smeets, 2008), although several studies have demonstrated positive effects of dialogic reading for children experiencing socioeconomic adversity (see Zevenbergen & Whitehurst, 2003 for a review).

Universal prevention programs in the family domain typically focus on improving parenting practices and communication patterns to help children learn skills such as effective coping and self-regulation skills to foster competence and prevent dysfunction. Several universal family-based programs have been shown to build family resources, increase child competence, and reduce the likelihood of substance abuse and other mental health problems (Lochman & van den Steenhoven, 2002; NRC/IOM, 2009; Sandler, Schoenfelder, Wolchik, & MacKinnon, 2011).

For example, Spoth and colleagues have evaluated the effects of two universal family-based prevention programs: the 5-session Preparing for the Drug Free Years (PDFY) (now called Guiding Good Choices) and the 7-session Iowa Strengthening Families Program (ISFP) (now called the Strengthening Family Program for Parents and Youth: 10–14) (Spoth, Redmond, & Shin, 1998, 2001; Spoth, Trudeau, Guyll, Shin, & Redmond, 2009). Both programs were designed to construct family resources, such as positive parent–child involvement and communication and effective parent management; however, PDFY intervenes primarily with parents, whereas ISFP includes parents and youths together in most sessions. Results of randomized controlled evaluations with rural families of sixth grade children have shown that both ISFP and PDFY improved parent–child warmth and effective

discipline at posttest, compared to a minimal-contact control group (Spoth et al., 1998). Long-term follow-up 10-years post-intervention demonstrated that youths whose families participated in the programs had lower rates of alcohol and polydrug use in young adulthood compared to the comparison group. The program indirectly impacted substance use in young adulthood by reducing substance use initiation in adolescence (Spoth et al., 2009). Although both programs have empirical support, findings have been more robust for the ISFP (Spoth et al.), and initial benefit-cost analyses suggest that ISFP may be more cost-effective than PDFY: the benefit-cost ratio for ISFP was $9.60 per $1 invested vs. $5.85 per $1 for PDFY (Spoth, Guyll, & Day, 2002).

Selective Programs

Family-based selective interventions build resources to counteract conditions of adversity, such as premature birth, parental divorce, death, abuse, or poverty, by providing parent or family skills training. Several family-based selective prevention programs have been shown to positively impact child and adolescent well-being (Lochman & van den Steenhoven, 2002; NRC/IOM, 2009; Sandler et al., 2011; Webster-Stratton & Taylor, 2001).

For example, the Family Bereavement Program was found to reduce mental health problems of both bereaved children and their spousally bereaved parents 6 years following their participation in the program, thus showing a "double prevention effect" (Sandler, Ayers, et al., 2010). This program was designed to change multiple risk and protective factors that had previously been found to be related to problem outcomes among bereaved children. The intervention focuses on changing the family environment (e.g., positive parenting, surviving parent's mental health, stressful events following the death) as well as promoting youth's adaptive coping (Sandler et al., 2008). At the 6-year follow-up, the program was found to strengthen family protective factors (e.g., positive parenting), to reduce externalizing problems and grief in youths

(Sandler, Ayers, et al., 2010; Sandler, Ma, et al., 2010), and to reduce depression in spousally bereaved parents (Sandler, Ayers, et al., 2010).

Wolchik and colleagues found that families facing multiple adversities benefited most from a parenting program for divorced mothers, the New Beginnings Program (NBP) (Dawson-McClure, Sandler, Wolchik, & Millsap, 2004; Wolchik et al., 2002; Wolchik, Sandler, Weiss, & Winslow, 2007). NBP was designed for divorced families of school-age children to improve mother–child relationships, increase effective discipline, promote father–child contact, and decrease children's exposure to interparental conflict and negative divorce events (Wolchik et al., 2000; Wolchik, West, Westover, & Sandler, 1993). Two randomized controlled trials conducted on NBP have shown that the program successfully decreased exposure to negative events and bolstered several family resources, including mother–child relationship quality, effective discipline, and willingness to change visitation (Wolchik et al., 1993, 2000).

Long-term follow-up of the second experimental trial demonstrated a wide array of program benefits lasting 6 years post-intervention, when youths were ages 15–18, including main effects of the program to reduce rates of diagnosed mental disorder and number of sexual partners, as well as to increase grade point averages, for the NBP group compared to the control group (Wolchik et al., 2007). Results from structural equation modeling showed that the NBP initiated a positive cascade of outcomes across development (Bonds et al., 2010). For example, the program increased mothers' effective discipline at posttest, which led to decreases in externalizing behavior several months later, which subsequently led to higher academic achievement in adolescence (Bonds et al.).

For several outcomes (i.e., externalizing, internalizing, and mental health symptomatology; alcohol and drug use; and self-esteem), youths who showed the greatest long-term benefit from the NBP were those who entered the program with higher risk for subsequent mental health problems (based on a risk index of externalizing behaviors and family adversities) (Wolchik et al.,

2007). These findings are consistent with research demonstrating that children exposed to multiple adversities, rather than single stressors, are most at risk for mental health problems and therefore most in need of selective prevention programs that build resources to reduce the negative effects of these adversities (Sandler et al., 2003).

Indicated Programs

Indicated programs for externalizing problems often include an individual- or group-based parent behavior management training approach (see Lochman & van den Steenhoven, 2002; NRC/IOM, 2009; Sandler et al., 2011; Webster-Stratton & Taylor, 2001 for reviews). For example, the Incredible Years BASIC program (Webster-Stratton, 2001) is a 14-session, group, parent training intervention that employs videotaped parent–child interactions and group discussion to teach effective parenting practices, such as child-directed play time, effective commands, praise for prosocial behavior, and nonviolent consequences for misbehavior (i.e., time out; natural and logical consequences). The program's ability to reduce externalizing problems has been demonstrated in several randomized controlled trials as an indicated prevention program for children exhibiting sub-diagnostic conduct problems (e.g., Jones, Daley, Hutchings, Bywater, & Eames, 2007; Reid, Webster-Stratton, & Hammond, 2007).

Resources Constructed in the Community-Organizational Domain

Universal Promotion and Prevention Programs

Promotion programs in the community-organizational domain focus on creating system-level changes to enhance children's social, emotional, and cognitive competencies. In a meta-analysis of positive youth development programs that targeted system-level changes, Durlak et al. (2007) found promotion programs in the school domain successfully changed school-wide and classroom-level processes, with overall effect sizes in the moderate to large range.

For example, the School Development Program (SDP; Comer & Emmons, 2006) is a whole-school intervention that focuses on changing school culture to support positive youth development. The SDP is a process model of school reform that involves three teams—the School Planning and Management Team, the Student and Staff Support Team, and the Parent Team. The teams develop, implement, and monitor a comprehensive school reform plan to improve school climate and student achievement. Periodic assessments are conducted and modifications are made as needed. The SDP specifies three guidelines for facilitating positive working relationships among team members: (1) a focus on problem-solving, not blaming; (2) the use of consensus decision-making rather than majority rule; and (3) members working collaboratively rather than alone. Multiple studies, including randomized controlled trials (e.g., Cook, Murphy, & Hunt, 2000), have shown that the SDP has short-term effects on improving school climate and long-term effects on student achievement. In a meta-analysis of 29 school reform programs, the SDP emerged as one of three programs with the strongest evidence of program effects based on the quantity and quality of research conducted to date (Borman, Hewes, Overman, & Brown, 2003).

Universal prevention programs that focus on building resources in the community or organizational domain are based on the theory that changing aspects of children's macro-level environments will reduce the likelihood of future adversities and provide support to help all children effectively manage stressors that occur in these settings (Sandler, 2001). Organizationally based universal programs have been developed to change school ecologies to prevent behavioral and academic problems (Felner et al., 2001; Flannery et al., 2003) and improve classroom management strategies to decrease undesirable student behaviors (Embry, 2002).

For example, the Good Behavior Game (GBG) is a classroom-based, behavior management intervention, which is based on the theory that

disruptive behaviors by students in the classroom occur because peers reinforce misbehavior through reactions such as smiles, giggles, laughs, and pointing; therefore, reinforcement for negative behaviors can be diminished by providing group-based rewards for inhibiting them (Embry, 2002). The GBG intervention is presented as a game in which teachers positively reinforce student *teams* who do not exceed negative behavior standards set by the teacher. GBG is played periodically over the school year, beginning with highly predictable procedures and immediate rewards and evolving into less predictable times and locations with deferred rewards (Kellam, Ling, Merisca, Brown, & Ialongo, 1998). In a large, randomized controlled trial of first grade students from 19 Baltimore public schools, Dolan et al. (1993) found significant reductions in aggression at posttest for both boys and girls in the intervention group as compared to the control group. At 5-year follow-up, intervention effects on teacher-rated aggression remained for boys who were elevated in aggression at baseline (Kellam, Rebok, Ialongo, & Mayer, 1994). Long-term follow-up with young adults aged 19–21 who had participated in GBG in their first and second grade classrooms found intervention effects on reduced drug and alcohol disorders, regular smoking, and antisocial personality disorder for participants who had been more aggressive and disruptive at baseline (Kellam et al., 2008). The GBG intervention appears to improve behaviors of the more aggressive males by changing the ecology of the classroom to be less aggressive overall (Kellam et al., 1998) and to be more conducive to developing prosocial affiliations with nondeviant peers (van Lier, Vuijk, & Crijnen, 2005).

School restructuring is another example of universal prevention in the organizational domain. Restructuring programs have been developed to reduce the adjustment problems of youths making the transition to junior high or high school. These school transitions are associated with increased risk for multiple negative outcomes including decreased grades, lower self-esteem, and higher distress, which place youths at increased risk for later problems such as depression and further academic difficulties (Seidman, Aber, & French, 2003). Developmental theorists have proposed that these negative effects are due to a mismatch between the school environment and adolescent needs for autonomy, identity formation, and close affiliation with peers and adults (Eccles et al., 1993). The School Transitional Environment Project (STEP) was designed to restructure the school context to better meet the needs of students during these high-risk transitions by creating a small group of students who move through all primary classes together and by assigning a single adult to serve as counselor, advisor, and liaison for their families (Felner et al., 1993). Thus, the program restructures the high school experience to increase social support from peers and adults.

Evaluations have demonstrated that students who experienced the STEP program had better emotional adjustment, grades, and attendance levels, and were less likely to drop out of school by 12th grade, as compared to a random sample of students who experienced the usual high school transition (Felner et al., 1993, 2001).

Selective Programs

Society develops institutions, policies, and practices to deal with children and families experiencing stressful life situations such as poverty, parental divorce, bereavement, or physical illness. For example, the domestic relations court provides an institutional structure within which families obtain a divorce and resolve legal issues (e.g., parental rights and responsibilities), as well as decide how financial assets will be divided. Alternative policies and practices may have significant impact on children's exposure to postdivorce stressors, such as interparental conflict, loss of contact with a parent or economic hardship, as well as on the quality of children's adjustment following divorce. Consequently, the courts have been proactive in developing alternative practices to reduce conflict (e.g., mediation of disputes), increase children's involvement with both parents (e.g., joint custody), and strengthen parental functioning following divorce (e.g.,

mandatory parenting programs) (Braver, Hipke, Ellman, & Sandler, 2003).

Postdivorce child custody is an example of policy in the organizational domain that has been shown through empirical research to be related to children's adjustment. Specifically, Bauserman (2002) conducted a meta-analysis of 33 studies comparing children's adjustment in joint- vs. sole-custody arrangements. Although the magnitude of effects tended to be small, Bauserman (2002) found that when families were awarded joint custody rather than sole custody, family relationships were better and children showed better adjustment across a variety of outcomes, including higher self-esteem and better emotional, behavioral, and divorce-specific adjustment. Although parents awarded joint custody were less conflictual before and after divorce than those awarded sole custody, interparental conflict did not account for differences in adjustment of children in sole- vs. joint-custody families.

In one prospective, longitudinal study, custody arrangement predicted children's later adjustment, even after controlling for a large number of pre-divorce selection factors, including interparental relationships, maternal and paternal parenting, parental adjustment, child adjustment, and demographic variables (Gunnoe & Braver, 2001). Causality cannot be inferred from these static-group investigations because families are not randomly assigned to different custody arrangements. However, the findings suggest that a judicial presumption in favor of joint custody for most families (i.e., those without parental fitness concerns) may help promote resilience among children who have experienced parental divorce (Gunnoe & Braver).

Indicated Programs

Organizational interventions to improve adaptation for youths already manifesting problem behaviors target policies or social structures designed to deal with these problems. The theory underlying these interventions is that policies or organizational structures can decrease or prevent the worsening of problems either by reducing future occurrence of adversities or by marshaling resources to promote resilience. Examples of such interventions include school policies for dealing with pregnant adolescents (Schellenbach, Leadbeater, & Moore, 2003), court approaches to dealing with juvenile delinquents (Sturza & Davidson, 2006), and a service system for children in foster care (Leve, Fisher, & Chamberlain, 2009).

Although policies and organizational structures to deal with problem behaviors are ubiquitous, their effects on adversities, resilience resources, and problem outcomes have rarely been examined empirically. One well-evaluated program in the organizational domain to promote resilience in children experiencing behavior problems is the Adolescent Diversion Project (Sturza & Davidson, 2006). This program is based on theoretical propositions concerning the harmful effects of social labeling on the future course of delinquency and on the value of mobilizing community resources to support the competencies of juvenile offenders in adapting to prosocial roles in the community. The program targeted youths identified by law enforcement as involved in delinquent behaviors but not yet officially adjudicated in the juvenile justice system. As an alternative to involvement in the justice system, delinquents participated in advocacy, family, or behavioral interventions to improve their community adaptation.

Multiple randomized controlled trials have demonstrated the efficacy of the diversion program model. Illustratively, in one study, youths were randomly assigned to one of three conditions: diversion with services (the Adolescent Diversion Project), diversion without services, and treatment-as-usual (e.g., court-processed). Each individual in the diversion with services condition was assigned a family worker from a local service agency who assisted the youth and family in developing behavioral goals and a reward system for the youth and in assessing community resources available to support the youth's educational advancement and civic involvement. Results indicated that participants assigned to the diversion with services condition showed decreased recidivism rates compared to the diversion without services and control conditions at 1-year follow-up (Smith, Wolf, Cantillon, Thomas, & Davidson, 2004).

Constructing Resources Across Domains and Levels

As the previous sections illustrate, a variety of interventions have been empirically shown to promote resilience and prevent dysfunction by constructing resources in child, family, or organizational domains using universal promotion/prevention programs, selective prevention approaches, and indicated interventions. Efficacious interventions have been identified for all nine cells in the matrix presented in Table 27.1. While single efforts to build resilience can be described within each of the matrix cells, building resilience in all children requires coordinated efforts that combine interventions across domains (rows) and levels (columns) to address individual differences in adversities, resources, and needs among children in a community. Several evidence-based prevention programs have combined interventions across domains and/or levels to promote resilience and prevent dysfunction (CPPRG, 2002, 2007, 2010b; Hawkins, Guo, Hill, Battin-Pearson, & Abbott, 2001; Metropolitan Area Child Study Research Group, 2002; Reid et al., 2007; Sanders et al., 2002; Vitaro, Brendgen, & Tremblay, 2001).

For example, the Seattle Social Development Project (SSDP) is an evaluation of a universal intervention provided to students exposed to community-school adversity (i.e., children attending public elementary schools in high-crime areas of Seattle) (Hawkins, Catalano, Kosterman, Abbott, & Hill, 1999). In this non-randomized controlled trial, three conditions were compared: full intervention, late intervention, and no intervention. In the full intervention condition, services were provided in grades 1 through 6 and included interventions in child, family, and organizational domains: social competence training for children, parenting classes, and annual teacher training. The late intervention included the same services provided only in grades 5 and 6.

Long-term follow-up studies of the SSDP into adolescence and young adulthood have indicated that those who received the full intervention (but not the late intervention) had higher levels of educational and occupational attainment; engaged in significantly less violent behavior, criminal activity, and risky sexual behavior; had fewer anxiety symptoms; and females were less likely to become pregnant, as compared to those in the control group (Hawkins, Smith, Hill, Kosterman, & Catalano, 2007).

In contrast to interventions such as SSDP that build resources across multiple domains, the Triple P—Positive Parenting Program (Sanders et al., 2002) is an example of a program that promotes a specific resource (i.e., effective parenting) across multiple intervention levels. The Triple P model is based on the principle that individual families within a community differ with respect to the amount of support and assistance needed to promote positive parenting. Rather than being a single program, Triple P is a system of five intervention levels that vary in intensity from a media-based, universal parenting program to a brief, video-based selective program to more intensive, group-based indicated interventions. Multiple randomized controlled trials have been conducted on most of Triple P's intervention levels and have provided evidence for their efficacy in promoting effective parenting and children's prosocial behavior (de Graaf, Speetjens, Smit, de Wolff, & Tavecchio, 2008a, 2008b; Nowak & Heinrichs, 2008). Recently, Prinz, Sanders, Shapiro, Whitaker, and Lutzker (2009) conducted a population-level dissemination trial on the full Triple P system. In this experimental trial, 18 counties were randomly assigned to either a services-as-usual control condition or a county-wide Triple P dissemination condition, in which the existing child service provider workforce was trained to implement the Triple P system. The researchers found that dissemination of the multilevel, Triple P system led to a significant reduction in child maltreatment cases at the population level (Prinz et al., 2009).

Putting Science into Practice

A growing number of efficacious prevention programs have been identified that promote resilience for children who experience adversities. These programs share two key characteristics. First, they build individual, family, and/or community-organizational resources associated with resilient outcomes for children facing adversities. Second, these programs have been shown to be efficacious in bolstering resources, preventing problem outcomes, and promoting resilience through well-controlled evaluation studies. Without evidence from well-controlled evaluations, programs can offer only promissory notes, not proven benefits. Unfortunately, many communities have not adopted evidence-based programming, relying instead on interventions that have been well packaged but not adequately evaluated (Backer, 2000; Ennett et al., 2003; Redmond et al., 2009). In the following sections, we examine some of the main issues and challenges communities must tackle to make effective use of evidence-based, resource-building interventions, as well as tools and systems that have been developed to help communities successfully navigate the process of putting science into practice.

Needs Assessment

An important challenge a community initially faces involves conducting a needs and resources assessment of the population (Hawkins, Catalano, & Arthur, 2002; Wandersman, Imm, Chinman, & Kaftarian, 2000). This process is critical for defining the problems and generating specific goals the community hopes to achieve. The process involves collecting epidemiologic data on adversities, resources, and problems prevalent in the community, which are used to guide goal setting and the selection of intervention strategies. Identification of adversities, resources, and problems is facilitated by the use of multiple sources of data, including community member perceptions (i.e., youth and adult reports) and archival data (e.g., census, court, school records) (Wandersman et al.).

Given that community leaders are likely to be unfamiliar with needs assessment methodology, a variety of tools and systems have been devised to guide leaders through this process (Chinman, Tremain, Imm, & Wandersman, 2009; Glaser, Van Horn, Arthur, Hawkins, & Catalano, 2005). For example, the Search Institute[1] has developed surveys to assist community leaders in identifying whether "developmental assets" (i.e., research-based protective resources) are present or absent in their communities (Scales & Leffert, 2004). The "Profiles of Student Life: Attitudes and Behaviors" survey is a 158-item questionnaire administered in one 50-min classroom period to students in grades 6 through 12. This survey assesses the availability of 20 external assets in students' families and communities (e.g., nurturing relationships with adults, supportive institutions, enrichment opportunities, collective youth monitoring) and 20 internal assets (e.g., student commitment to learning, prosocial values, social skills, positive self-identity). This survey also obtains information on student demographics, high-risk behaviors (e.g., substance use), resilience indicators (e.g., school success), and developmental deficits (e.g., abuse history). Research supports the reliability and validity of this assessment tool (Leffert et al., 1998; Reininger et al., 2003; Zullig, Ward, King, Patton, & Murray, 2009). The institute's fee-based service includes telephone consultation on administration issues, an administration manual, student survey forms, computerized scanning of forms and analysis by the institute, a summary report of survey results, and resources to aid community mobilization efforts to develop asset-building strategies for promoting positive youth outcomes.

Communities That Care (CTC)[2] is a similar service developed to help communities formulate strategies for promoting healthy behaviors and preventing negative mental health outcomes

among youths (Hawkins et al., 2002). CTC is a comprehensive, manualized system for guiding community leaders through the entire process of planning and implementing science-based prevention strategies including: (a) assessing community readiness to use CTC; (b) introducing prevention science and CTC principles to key stakeholders and community members; (c) establishing a community prevention board to carry out CTC activities; (d) collecting community-specific data on risk and protective factors, adolescent substance use, and other mental health and behavior problems; (e) using assessment data to develop an action plan; (f) selecting science-based prevention strategies shown to be effective in reducing community-specific risk factors and enhancing protective processes; (g) implementing the selected prevention strategies; and (h) monitoring and evaluating implementation.

During the needs assessment phase, the CTC community board develops a profile of community strengths and challenges based on results of student surveys and archival data (e.g., census) that measure risk behaviors (i.e., substance use, delinquency), adversities, and resources across four domains: community, school, family, and peer-individual (Glaser et al., 2005; Hawkins et al., 2002, 2009). A community map is created detailing the distribution of adversities and resources across different neighborhoods in the community, allowing the board to focus efforts on high-risk neighborhoods.

Whitlock and Hamilton (2003) conducted an informal study based on interviews with representatives of New York communities that used one or more youth survey approaches including those described here. They concluded that successful implementation of these approaches depended on widespread community buy-in and participation, combined with flexibility regarding the roles and actions of community coalition boards.

Intervention Strategy Selection

After the needs assessment and goal-setting phase, communities face the challenge of selecting

---

[1] Search Institute surveys: http://www.search-institute.org/survey-services

[2] CTC website: http://www.sdrg.org/ctcresource

intervention strategies to meet the community's goals (Chinman et al., 2009; Hawkins et al., 2002). A multilevel approach that includes a mix of evidence-based universal promotion/prevention, selective, and indicated programs that counteract adversities and construct resources across multiple domains has the potential to provide an efficient way of meeting the diverse needs of individuals within the community, while building resilience at the population level (Hawkins et al., 2002; Sanders et al., 2002; Sheeber, Biglan, Metzler, & Taylor, 2002). The conceptual framework presented in this chapter could help guide the process of selecting appropriate intervention strategies. Community leaders could use data collected on adversities, problems, and resources prevalent in their area to choose selective interventions to counteract specific adversities that are highly prevalent in their community, universal promotion and prevention strategies within a domain to bolster resources lacking, and indicated programs to address substance use and mental health problems.

However, to effectively choose programs that meet a community's needs, community leaders need to have access to concise information regarding programs that have been shown to promote specific resources, counteract specific adversities, and reduce specific adjustment problems. Recognizing the necessity of providing this type of information to communities and practitioners, a variety of federal and nonprofit organizations have developed principles of effectiveness to guide the identification of promotion and prevention programs that work, as well as registries listing effective programs and details regarding the conditions under which these programs have been shown to be effective: Substance Abuse and Mental Health Service (SAMHSA)'s National Registry of Evidence-Based Programs and Practices (NREPP)[3]; Office of Juvenile Justice and Delinquency Prevention (OJJDP)[4]; U.S. Department of Education's What Works Clearinghouse[5]; the

Collaborative for Academic, Social, and Emotional Learning (CASEL)'s Safe and Sound Program Guide[6]; and Child Trends Lifecourse Interventions to Nurture Kids Successfully (LINKS) database.[7] For example, SAMHSA's NREPP website offers a searchable database of more than 170 mental health promotion, prevention, and treatment interventions, as well as substance abuse prevention and treatment programs, that have been shown to be effective through methodologically rigorous evaluations. Users can search for programs based on type (e.g., prevention, treatment); outcomes impacted (e.g., alcohol use, delinquency); age, gender, and ethnicity of children with whom the program has been implemented; as well as intervention settings (e.g., school, home) and locations (e.g., urban, suburban). Programs are described with respect to intervention level (i.e., universal, selective, indicated), intervention strategies employed, target populations served, key outcomes impacted, any iatrogenic effects that have been reported, quality of the research, readiness for dissemination, cost estimates, and program developer contacts.

Implementation and Evaluation

Selecting evidence-based programs does not guarantee that programs will be successfully implemented in a community. Even when evidence-based programs are selected, often they are not well implemented in natural service delivery systems (Gottfredson et al., 2006; Greenberg et al., 2003). Fidelity of implementation has been identified as an important factor determining whether or not evidence-based programs delivered in community settings produce the same effects as the original intervention models (Berkel, Mauricio, Schoenfelder, & Sandler, 2011; Durlak & DuPre, 2008). Therefore, program packages need to include training programs, ongoing technical assistance, and procedures for monitoring implementation as ways to promote

---

[3] SAMSHA NREPP: http://nrepp.samhsa.gov

[4] OJJDP website: http://www.strengtheningfamilies.org

[5] Department of Education What Works Clearinghouse: http://ies.ed.gov/ncee/wwc

[6] CASEL Safe & Sound Program Guide: http://www.casel.org/programs/selecting.php

[7] Child Trends LINKS database: http://childtrends.org/links

adherence to interventions (Durlak & DuPre; Redmond et al., 2009).

In addition to intervention packaging features, client characteristics, provider preferences, and organizational issues have been identified as factors that influence the quality of implementation and the sustainability of interventions (Backer, 2000; Durlak & DuPre, 2008; Mayer & Davidson, 2000). It is important to ensure that organizations implementing prevention programming possess or develop characteristics associated with successful implementation, such as a shared vision about the value and purpose of the program, staff with appropriate skills and cultural competence, adequate resources to support the program, strong organizational leadership, and a shared decision-making process (Durlak & DuPre, 2008; Wandersman, 2009; Wandersman et al., 2000). Further, to improve the effectiveness of evidence-based prevention programming delivered in community settings, implementation steps must be clearly defined and planned out (e.g., timeline, responsibility assignments), and continuous quality improvement strategies need to be used to systematically assess and feed back information about intervention planning, implementation, and program outcomes (Wandersman, 2009; Wandersman et al., 2000).

Experimental trials evaluating the effectiveness of systems that guide community leaders through the process of putting science into practice have produced promising results (Chinman et al., 2009; Hawkins et al., 2009; Redmond et al., 2009). For example, Hawkins et al. (2009) conducted a population-level evaluation of the CTC system in which 24 towns were randomly assigned to CTC or a control condition. Risk and protective factors and youth outcomes were assessed using annual student surveys conducted longitudinally for 4 years with 4,407 middle-school students. The investigators found that the CTC system was implemented with fidelity (Fagan, Hanson, Hawkins, & Arthur, 2009). Significant effects of the CTC system were found for reducing the incidence and prevalence of substance use (i.e., tobacco and alcohol) and delinquency compared to control communities, controlling for baseline prevalence (for substance

use outcomes) and demographic variables (Hawkins et al., 2009). For the most part, findings held equally for both boys and girls and by risk status, although stronger effects were found for reducing substance use among boys in eighth grade and for reducing delinquency among students who were nondelinquent at baseline (Oesterle, Hawkins, Fagan, Abbott, & Catalano, 2010).

Although these results are encouraging, the potential public health impact of CTC and systems like it could be improved by integrating more effective methods of engaging parents into family-based prevention programs. For example, in the CTC trial, communities rarely met their goal of providing parenting services to at least 20% of families (Fagan et al., 2009). In fact, initiation rates ranged from 4 to 7% across 4 years. In a large-scale trial of the multilevel Triple P Positive Parenting Program, family engagement rates were also low (1% engaged in the 8-session parenting program; <10% engaged in any Triple P level) (Prinz et al., 2009). Even in a study that obtained a relatively higher participation rate, Redmond and colleagues' (2009) trial of PROSPER (PROmoting School-university-community Partnerships to Enhance Resilience), only a small minority of families participated in the family-focused intervention (17%).

Given the well-established effectiveness of evidence-based, preventive parenting interventions (Lochman & van den Steenhoven, 2002; Sandler et al., 2011; Webster-Stratton & Taylor, 2001), it is critical to develop more effective strategies for engaging parents into these programs to maximize their public health impact (Spoth, Clair, Greenberg, Redmond, & Shin, 2007). Several factors have been shown to predict participation, such as high parent education and income, perceived need for and benefits of participating in the intervention, and lower perceived barriers to participation (e.g., Dumas, Nissley-Tsiopinis, & Moreland, 2007; Spoth, Redmond, & Shin, 2000; Winslow, Bonds, Wolchik, Sandler, & Braver, 2009). Targeting potentially modifiable predictors of participation, such as perceived benefits and barriers, and adapting strategies that have worked in other fields such as child treatment (McKay,

Stowe, McCadam, & Gonzales, 1998; Nock & Kazdin, 2005), may help researchers develop more effective engagement strategies, which would increase the population-level impact of effective family-based prevention programs.

Conclusions

In this chapter, we have presented a conceptual framework that integrates concepts from resilience with a public health approach to building resilience and preventing mental health problems for all children. Individuals within a population are characterized by varying levels of adversities, resources, mental health problems, and developmental competencies. A multidomain, multilevel approach that includes a combination of universal promotion/prevention, selective, and indicated programs holds promise as an efficient, effective way to address the diversity of needs and simultaneously impact population-level mental health problems and developmental competencies. A variety of universal promotion/prevention, selective, and indicated interventions have been rigorously tested and shown to construct resources across multiple domains to promote resilience and prevent mental health problems. Unfortunately, most communities have not implemented evidence-based programming, highlighting the importance of refining, evaluating, and disseminating methods for assisting community leaders to conduct needs assessments, select effective programs, engage families, implement programs with fidelity, and evaluate the impact of programs on youth outcomes. Building resilience in all children will require communities to identify specific goals regarding child competencies to promote and problems to prevent, assess the adversities that threaten those goals and the resources that promote them, and implement a coordinated combination of evidence-based interventions that construct resources across multiple domains and levels.

Acknowledgments Work on this edition of the chapter was supported by grants from the National Institute of Mental Health (NIMH) to support Winslow (5 K01 MH074045) and Sandler and Wolchik (P30 MH068685).

References

Arnold, D. H., Lonigan, C. J., Whitehurst, G. J., & Epstein, J. N. (1994). Accelerating language development through picture book reading: Replication and extension to a videotape training format. *Journal of Educational Psychology, 86*(2), 235–243.

Backer, T. (2000). The failure of success: Challenges of disseminating effective substance abuse prevention programs. *Journal of Community Psychology, 28*(3), 363–373.

Bauserman, R. (2002). Child adjustment in joint-custody versus sole-custody arrangements: A meta-analytic review. *Journal of Family Psychology, 16*(1), 91–102.

Berkel, C., Mauricio, A. M., Schoenfelder, E., & Sandler, I. N. (2011). Putting the pieces together: An integrated model of program implementation. *Prevention Science, 12*, 23–33.

Bienvenu, O. J., & Ginsburg, G. S. (2007). Prevention of anxiety disorders. *International Review of Psychiatry, 19*(6), 647–654.

Bonds, D., Wolchik, S., Winslow, E., Tein, J., Sandler, I., & Millsap, R. (2010). Developmental cascade effects of the New Beginnings Program on adolescent adaptation outcomes. *Development and Psychopathology, 22*(4), 771–784.

Borman, G. D., Hewes, G. M., Overman, L. T., & Brown, S. (2003). Comprehensive school reform and achievement: A meta-analysis. *Review of Educational Research, 73*(2), 125–230.

Braver, S. L., Hipke, K. N., Ellman, I. M., & Sandler, I. N. (2003). Strengths-building public policy for children of divorce. In K. Maton, C. J. Schellenbach, B. J. Leadbeater, & A. L. Solarz (Eds.), *Investing in children, youth, families and communities: Strengths-based research and policy* (pp. 53–73). Washington, DC: American Psychological Association.

Catalano, R. F., Berglund, M. L., Ryan, J. A. M., Lonczak, H. S., & Hawkins, J. D. (2002). Positive youth development in the United States: Research findings on evaluations of positive youth development programs. *Prevention and Treatment, 5*, Article 15.

Chinman, M., Tremain, B., Imm, P., & Wandersman, A. (2009). Strengthening prevention performance using technology: A formative evaluation of interactive getting to outcomes. *The American Journal of Orthopsychiatry, 79*(4), 469–481.

Cicchetti, D., & Toth, S. (2005). Child maltreatment. *Annual Review of Clinical Psychology, 1*, 409–438.

Comer, J. P., & Emmons, C. (2006). The research program of the Yale Child Study Center School Development Program. *Journal of Negro Education, 75*(3), 353–372.

Conduct Problems Prevention Research Group. (1999). Initial impact of the Fast Track prevention trial for conduct problems: II. Classroom effects. *Journal of Consulting and Clinical Psychology, 67*(5), 648–657.

Conduct Problems Prevention Research Group. (2002). Evaluation of the first 3 years of the Fast Track prevention trial with children at high risk for adolescent conduct problems. *Journal of Abnormal Child Psychology, 30*(1), 19–35.

Conduct Problems Prevention Research Group. (2007). Fast track randomized controlled trial to prevent externalizing psychiatric disorders: Findings from grades 3 to 9. *Journal of the American Academy of Child and Adolescent Psychiatry, 46*(10), 1250–1262.

Conduct Problems Prevention Research Group. (2010a). The effects of a multiyear universal social-emotional learning program: The role of student and school characteristics. *Journal of Consulting and Clinical Psychology, 78*(2), 156–168.

Conduct Problems Prevention Research Group. (2010b). Fast track intervention effects on youth arrests and delinquency. *Journal of Experimental Criminology, 6*, 131–157.

Cook, T. D., Murphy, R. F., & Hunt, H. D. (2000). Comer's School Development Program in Chicago: A theory-based evaluation. *American Educational Research Journal, 37*(2), 535–597.

Cuijpers, P., Muñoz, R. F., Clarke, G. N., & Lewinsohn, P. M. (2009). Psychoeducational treatment and prevention of depression: The "coping with depression" course thirty years later. *Clinical Psychology Review, 29*, 449–458.

Curtis, C., & Norgate, R. (2007). An evaluation of the promoting alternative thinking strategies curriculum at key stage 1. *Educational Psychology in Practice, 23*(1), 33–44.

Dawson-McClure, S., Sandler, I., Wolchik, S., & Millsap, R. (2004). Risk as a moderator of the effects of prevention programs for children from divorced families: A six-year longitudinal study. *Journal of Abnormal Child Psychology, 32*, 175–190.

de Graaf, I., Speetjens, P., Smit, F., de Wolff, M., & Tavecchio, L. (2008a). Effectiveness of the Triple P Positive Parenting Program on behavioral problems in children: A meta-analysis. *Behavior Modification, 32*(5), 714–735.

de Graaf, I., Speetjens, P., Smit, F., de Wolff, M., & Tavecchio, L. (2008b). Effectiveness of the Triple P Positive Parenting Program on parenting: A meta-analysis. *Family Relations, 57*, 553–566.

Dolan, L., Kellam, S., Brown, C., Werthamer-Larsson, L., Rebok, G., Mayer, L., et al. (1993). The short-term impact of two classroom-based preventive interventions on aggressive and shy behaviors and poor achievement. *Journal of Applied Developmental Psychology, 14*, 317–345.

Domitrovich, C. E., Cortes, R. C., & Greenberg, M. T. (2007). Improving young children's social and emotional competence: A randomized trial of the preschool "PATHS" curriculum. *The Journal of Primary Prevention, 28*(2), 67–91.

Dumas, J., Nissley-Tsiopinis, J., & Moreland, A. (2007). From intent to enrollment, attendance, and participation in preventive parenting groups. *Journal of Child and Family Studies, 16*, 1–26.

Durlak, J. A., & DuPre, E. P. (2008). Implementation matters: A review of research on the influence of implementation on program outcomes and the factors affecting implementation. *American Journal of Community Psychology, 41*, 327–350.

Durlak, J. A., Taylor, R., Kawashima, K., Pachan, M., DuPre, E., Celio, C., et al. (2007). Effects of positive youth development programs on school, family, and community systems. *American Journal of Community Psychology, 39*, 269–286.

Durlak, J. A., Weissberg, R. P., & Pachan, M. (2010). A meta-analysis of after-school programs that seek to promote personal and social skills in children and adolescents. *American Journal of Community Psychology, 45*, 294–309.

Eccles, J. S., Midgley, C., Wigfield, A., Buchanan, C. M., Reuman, D., Flanagan, C., et al. (1993). The impact of stage-environment fit on young adolescents' experiences in schools and families. *The American Psychologist, 48*, 90–101.

Edin, K., & Kissane, R. J. (2010). Poverty and the American family: A decade in review. *Journal of Marriage and Family, 72*, 460–479.

Embry, D. (2002). The Good Behavior Game: A best practice candidate as a universal behavioral vaccine. *Clinical Child and Family Psychology Review, 5*(4), 273–297.

Ennett, S., Ringwalt, C., Thorne, J., Rohrbach, L., Vincus, A., Simons-Rudolph, A., et al. (2003). A comparison of current practice in school-based substance use prevention programs with meta-analysis findings. *Prevention Science, 4*(1), 1–14.

Enright, S., & Carr, A. (2002). Prevention of post-traumatic adjustment problems in children and adolescents. In A. Carr (Ed.), *Prevention: What works with children and adolescents?* (pp. 314–335). New York: Brunner-Routledge.

Evans, S., Davies, C., & DiLillo, D. (2008). Exposure to domestic violence: A meta-analysis of child and adolescent outcomes. *Aggression and Violent Behavior, 13*, 131–140.

Fagan, A. A., Hanson, K., Hawkins, J. D., & Arthur, M. W. (2009). Translational research in action: Implementation of the Communities That Care prevention system in 12 communities. *Journal of Community Psychology, 37*(7), 809–829.

Felitti, V., Anda, R., Nordenberg, D., Williamson, D., Spitz, A., Edwards, V., et al. (1998). Relationship of childhood abuse and household dysfunction to many of the leading causes of death in adults: The Adverse Childhood Experiences (ACE) Study. *American Journal of Preventive Medicine, 14*(4), 245–258.

Felner, R., Favazza, A., Shim, M., Brand, S., Gu, K., & Noonan, N. (2001). Whole school improvement and restructuring as prevention and promotion: Lessons from STEP and the Project on High Performance Learning Communities. *Journal of School Psychology, 39*(2), 177–202.

Felner, R. D., Brand, S., Mulhall, P., Standiford, S., Adan, A., & Brenner, J. (1993). Restructuring the ecology of the school as an approach to prevention during school transitions: Longitudinal follow-ups and extensions of the School Transitional Environment Project (STEP). *Prevention in Human Services, 10*(2), 103–136.

Flannery, D., Vazsonyi, A., Liau, A., Guo, S., Powell, K., Atha, H., et al. (2003). Initial behavior outcomes for the PeaceBuilders universal school-based violence prevention program. *Developmental Psychology, 39*(2), 292–308.

Fowler, P., Tompsett, C., Braciszewski, J., Jacques-Tiura, A., & Baltes, B. (2009). Community violence: A meta-analysis on the effect of exposure and mental health outcomes of children and adolescents. *Development and Psychopathology, 21*, 227–259.

Furstenberg, F., Cook, T., Eccles, J., Elder, G., & Sameroff, A. (1999). *Managing to make it: Urban families and adolescent success.* Chicago: University of Chicago Press.

Garber, J., Clarke, G. N., Weersing, V. R., Beardslee, W. R., Brent, D. A., Gladstone, T. R. G., et al. (2009). Prevention of depression in at-risk adolescents: A randomized controlled trial. *Journal of the American Medical Association, 301*(21), 2215–2224.

Glaser, R. R., Van Horn, M. L., Arthur, M. W., Hawkins, J. D., & Catalano, R. F. (2005). Measurement properties of the Communities That Care Youth Survey across demographic groups. *Journal of Quantitative Criminology, 21*(1), 73–102.

Goodman, S. H., & Brand, S. R. (2008). Parental psychopathology and its relation to child psychopathology. In M. Hersen & A. Gross (Eds.), *Handbook of clinical psychology* (Children and adolescents, Vol. 2, pp. 937–965). Hoboken, NJ: Wiley.

Gottfredson, D., Kumpfer, K., Polizzi-Fox, D., Wilson, D., Puryear, V., Beatty, P., et al. (2006). The strengthening Washington D.C. Families Project: A randomized effectiveness trial of family-based prevention. *Prevention Science, 7*(1), 57–74.

Grant, K., Compas, B., Stuhlmacher, A., Thurm, A., McMahon, S., & Halpert, J. (2003). Stressors and child and adolescent psychopathology: Moving from markers to mechanisms of risk. *Psychological Bulletin, 129*(3), 447–466.

Greenberg, M., Kusche, C., Cook, E., & Quamma, J. (1995). Promoting emotional competence in school-aged children: The effects of the PATHS curriculum. *Development and Psychopathology, 7*(1), 117–136.

Greenberg, M., Weissberg, R., O'Brien, M., Zins, J., Fredericks, L., Resnik, H., et al. (2003). Enhancing school-based prevention and youth development through coordinated social, emotional and academic learning. *The American Psychologist, 58*(6/7), 466–474.

Gunnoe, M. L., & Braver, S. (2001). The effects of joint legal custody on mothers, fathers, and children controlling for factors that predispose a sole maternal versus joint legal award. *Law and Human Behavior, 25*(1), 25–43.

Hahn, R., Fuqua-Whitley, D., Wethington, H., Lowy, J., Crosby, A., Fullilove, M., et al. (2007). Effectiveness of universal school-based programs to prevent violent and aggressive behavior: A systematic review. *American Journal of Preventive Medicine, 33*(2S), S114–S129.

Hawkins, J. D., Catalano, R., & Arthur, M. (2002). Promoting science-based prevention in communities. *Addictive Behaviors, 27*, 951–976.

Hawkins, J. D., Catalano, R., Kosterman, R., Abbott, R., & Hill, K. (1999). Preventing adolescent health-risk behaviors by strengthening protection during childhood. *Archives of Pediatrics & Adolescent Medicine, 153*, 226–234.

Hawkins, J. D., Guo, J., Hill, K., Battin-Pearson, S., & Abbott, R. (2001). Long-term effects of the Seattle Social Development Intervention on school bonding trajectories. *Applied Developmental Science, 5*(4), 225–236.

Hawkins, J. D., Oesterle, S., Brown, E. C., Arthur, M. W., Abbott, R. D., Fagan, A. A., et al. (2009). Results of a type 2 translational research trial to prevent adolescent drug use and delinquency: A test of Communities That Care. *Archives of Pediatrics & Adolescent Medicine, 163*(9), 789–798.

Hawkins, J. D., Smith, B. H., Hill, K. G., Kosterman, R., & Catalano, R. F. (2007). Promoting social development and preventing health and behavior problems during the elementary grades: Results from the Seattle Social Development Project. *Victims and Offenders, 2*, 161–181.

Jones, K., Daley, D., Hutchings, J., Bywater, T., & Eames, C. (2007). Efficacy of the incredible years basic parent training programme as an early intervention for children with conduct problems and ADHD. *Child: Care, Health and Development, 33*(6), 749–756.

Kam, C., Greenberg, M., & Walls, C. (2003). Examining the role of implementation quality in school-based prevention using the PATHS curriculum. *Prevention Science, 4*(1), 55–63.

Kellam, S., Ling, X., Merisca, R., Brown, C. H., & Ialongo, N. (1998). The effect of the level of aggression in the first grade classroom on the course and malleability of aggressive behavior into middle school. *Development and Psychopathology, 10*, 165–185.

Kellam, S., Rebok, G., Ialongo, N., & Mayer, L. (1994). The course and malleability of aggressive behavior from early first grade into middle school: Results of a developmental epidemiologically-based preventive trial. *Journal of Child Psychology and Psychiatry, 35*, 359–382.

Kellam, S. G., Brown, C. H., Poduska, J. M., Ialongo, N. S., Wang, W., Toyinbo, P., et al. (2008). Effects of a universal classroom behavior management program in first and second grades on young adult behavioral, psychiatric, and social outcomes. *Drug and Alcohol Dependence, 95*(Suppl 1), S5–S28.

Lange, G., & Carr, A. (2002). Prevention of cognitive delay in socially disadvantaged children. In A. Carr (Ed.), *Prevention: What works with children and adolescents?* (pp. 41–63). New York: Brunner-Routledge.

Lansford, J. (2009). Parental divorce and children's adjustment. *Perspectives on Psychological Science, 4*(2), 140–152.

Leffert, N., Benson, P., Scales, P., Sharma, A., Drake, D., & Blyth, D. (1998). Developmental assets:

Measurement and prediction of risk behaviors among adolescents. *Applied Developmental Science, 2*(4), 209–230.

Leve, L. D., Fisher, P. A., & Chamberlain, P. (2009). Multidimensional treatment foster care as a preventive intervention to promote resiliency among youth in the child welfare system. *Journal of Personality, 77*(6), 1869–1902.

Lochman, J., & van den Steenhoven, A. (2002). Family-based approaches to substance abuse prevention. *The Journal of Primary Prevention, 23*(1), 49–114.

Luthar, S. (2006). Resilience in development: A synthesis of research across five decades. In D. Cicchetti & D. J. Cohen (Eds.), *Developmental psychopathology* (2nd ed., Vol. 3, pp. 739–795). Hoboken, NJ: Wiley.

Mayer, J., & Davidson, W. (2000). Dissemination of innovation as social change. In J. Rappaport & E. Seidman (Eds.), *Handbook of community psychology* (pp. 421–443). Dordrecht, Netherlands: Kluwer Academic Publishers.

McKay, M., Stoewe, J., McCadam, K., & Gonzales, J. (1998). Increasing access to child mental health services for urban children and their caregivers. *Health & Social Work, 23*(1), 9–15.

Melham, N. M., Walker, M., Moritz, G., & Brent, D. A. (2008). Antecedents and sequelae of sudden parental death in offspring and surviving caregivers. *Archives of Pediatrics & Adolescent Medicine, 162*(5), 403–410.

Metropolitan Area Child Study Research Group. (2002). A cognitive-ecological approach to preventing aggression in urban settings: Initial outcomes for high-risk children. *Journal of Consulting and Clinical Psychology, 70*(1), 179–194.

Mol, S. E., Bus, A. G., de Jong, M. T., & Smeets, D. J. H. (2008). Added value of dialogic parent-child book readings: A meta-analysis. *Early Education and Development, 19*(1), 7–26.

National Research Council and Institute of Medicine. (2009). Preventing mental, emotional, and behavioral disorders among young people: Progress and possibilities. Committee on the Prevention of Mental Disorders and Substance Abuse Among Children, Youth, and Young Adults: Research Advances and Promising Interventions. In: M. E. O'Connell, T. Boat, & K. E. Warner (Eds.), *Board on children, youth, families, division of behavioral and social sciences and education*. Washington, DC: National Academies Press.

Neil, A. L., & Christensen, H. (2009). Efficacy and effectiveness of school-based prevention and early intervention programs for anxiety. *Clinical Psychology Review, 29*, 208–215.

Nock, M., & Kazdin, A. (2005). Randomized controlled trial of a brief intervention for increasing participation in parent management training. *Journal of Consulting and Clinical Psychology, 73*(5), 872–879.

Nowak, C., & Heinrichs, N. (2008). A comprehensive meta-analysis of Triple P- Positive Parenting Program using hierarchical linear modeling: Effectiveness and moderating variables. *Clinical Child and Family Psychology Review, 11*, 114–144.

Oesterle, S., Hawkins, J. D., Fagan, A. A., Abbott, R. D., & Catalano, R. F. (2010). Testing the universality of the effects of the Communities That Care prevention system for preventing adolescent drug use and delinquency. *Prevention Science, 11*, 411–423.

Offord, D. (2000). Selection of levels of prevention. *Addictive Behaviors, 25*(6), 833–842.

Payton, J., Weissberg, R., Durlak, J., Dymnicki, A., Taylor, R., Schellinger, K., et al. (2008). *The positive impact of social and emotional learning for kindergarten to eighth-grade students: Findings from three scientific reviews*. Chicago, IL: Collaborative for Academic, Social, and Emotional Learning.

Pedro-Carroll, J. (1997). The Children of Divorce Intervention Program: Fostering resilient outcomes for school-aged children. In G. Albee & T. Gullotta (Eds.), *Primary prevention works. Issues in children's and families' lives* (Vol. 6, pp. 213–238). Thousand Oaks, CA: Sage Publications.

Pedro-Carroll, J., & Cowen, E. (1985). The Children of Divorce Intervention Program: An investigation of the efficacy of a school-based prevention program. *Journal of Consulting and Clinical Psychology, 53*(5), 603–611.

Pedro-Carroll, J., Sutton, S. E., & Wyman, P. A. (1999). A two-year follow-up evaluation of a preventive intervention for young children of divorce. *School Psychology Review, 28*(3), 467–476.

Prinz, R. J., Sanders, M. R., Shapiro, C. J., Whitaker, D. J., & Lutzker, J. R. (2009). Population-based prevention of child maltreatment: The U.S. Triple P system population trial. *Prevention Science, 10*, 1–12.

Redmond, C., Spoth, R. L., Shin, C., Schainker, L. M., Greenberg, M. T., & Feinberg, M. (2009). Long-term protective factor outcomes of evidence-based interventions implemented by community teams through a community-university partnership. *The Journal of Primary Prevention, 30*, 513–530.

Reid, M. J., Webster-Stratton, C., & Hammond, M. (2007). Enhancing a classroom social competence and problem-solving curriculum by offering parent training to families of moderate-to high-risk elementary school children. *Journal of Clinical Child and Adolescent Psychology, 36*(4), 605–620.

Reininger, B., Evans, A. E., Griffin, S. F., Valois, R. F., Vincent, M. L., Parra-Medina, D., et al. (2003). Development of a youth survey to measure risk behaviors, attitudes and assets: Examining multiple influences. *Health Education Research, 18*(4), 461–476.

Rose, G. (1992). Strategies of prevention: The individual and the population. In M. Marmot & P. Elliott (Eds.), *Coronary heart disease epidemiology: From aetiology to public health* (pp. 311–324). Oxford: Oxford University Press.

Sanders, M., Turner, K., & Markie-Dadds, C. (2002). The development and dissemination of the Triple P—Positive Parenting Program: A multilevel, evidence-based system of parenting and family support. *Prevention Science, 3*(3), 173–189.

Sandler, I. (2001). Quality and ecology of adversity as common mechanisms of risk and resilience. *American Journal of Community Psychology, 29*(1), 19–61.

Sandler, I., Ayers, T., Suter, J., Schultz, A., & Twohey, J. (2003). Adversities, strengths and public policy. In K. Maton, C. Schellenbach, B. Leadbeater, & A. Solarz (Eds.), *Investing in children, youth, families, and communities: Strengths-based research and policy.* Washington, DC: American Psychological Association.

Sandler, I., Ayers, T., Tein, J., Wolchik, S., Millsap, R., Khoo, S. T., et al. (2010). Six-year follow-up of a preventive intervention for parentally-bereaved youth: A randomized controlled trial. *Archives of Pediatrics & Adolescent Medicine, 164*(10), 907–914.

Sandler, I. N., Ma, Y., Tein, J. Y., Ayers, T. S., Wolchik, S., Kennedy, C., et al. (2010). Long-term effects of the Family Bereavement Program on multiple indicators of grief in parentally bereaved children and adolescents. *Journal of Consulting and Clinical Psychology, 78*, 131–144.

Sandler, I. N., Schoenfelder, E. N., Wolchik, S. A., & MacKinnon, D. P. (2011). Long-term impact of prevention programs to promote effective parenting: Lasting effects but uncertain processes. *Annual Review of Psychology, 62*(18), 18.1–18.31.

Sandler, I. N., Wolchik, S. A., Ayers, T. S., Tein, J. Y., Coxe, S., & Chow, W. (2008). Linking theory and intervention to promote resilience of children following parental bereavement. In M. Stroebe, M. Hansson, W. Stroebe, & H. Schut (Eds.), *Handbook of bereavement research: Consequences, coping and care* (pp. 531–550). Washington, DC: American Psychological Association.

Scales, P., & Leffert, N. (2004). *Developmental assets: A synthesis of the scientific research on adolescent development* (2nd ed.). Minneapolis: Search Institute.

Schellenbach, C., Leadbeater, B., & Moore, K. (2003). Enhancing the developmental outcomes of adolescent parents and their children. In K. Maton, C. Schellenbach, B. Leadbeater, & A. Solarz (Eds.), *Investing in children, youth, families, and communities: Strengths-based research and policy.* Washington, DC: American Psychological Association.

Seidman, E., Aber, J. L., & French, S. E. (2003). The organization of schooling and adolescent development. In K. Maton, C. J. Schellenbach, B. J. Leadbeater, & A. L. Solarz (Eds.), *Investing in children, youth, families and communities: Strengths-based research and policy* (pp. 233–251). Washington, DC: American Psychological Association.

Shamblen, S. R., & Derzon, J. H. (2009). A preliminary study of the population-adjusted effectiveness of substance abuse prevention programming: Towards making IOM program types comparable. *The Journal of Primary Prevention, 30*, 89–107.

Sheeber, L., Biglan, A., Metzler, C., & Taylor, T. (2002). Promoting effective parenting practices. In L. Jason & D.

Glenwick (Eds.), *Innovative strategies for promoting health and mental health across the life span* (pp. 63–84). New York: Springer.

Smith, E. P., Wolf, A. M., Cantillon, D. M., Thomas, O., & Davidson, W. S. (2004). The Adolescent Diversion Project: 25 years of research on an ecological model of intervention. *Journal of Prevention & Intervention in the Community, 27*(2), 29–47.

Soole, D. W., Mazerolle, L., & Rombouts, S. (2008). School-based drug prevention programs: A review of what works. *Australian and New Zealand Journal of Criminology, 41*(2), 259–286.

Spoth, R., Clair, S., Greenberg, M., Redmond, C., & Shin, C. (2007). Toward dissemination of evidence-based family interventions: Maintenance of community-based partnership recruitment results and associated factors. *Journal of Family Psychology, 21*(2), 137–146.

Spoth, R., Guyll, M., & Day, S. (2002). Universal family-focused interventions in alcohol-use disorder prevention: Cost-effectiveness and cost-benefit analyses of two interventions. *Journal of Studies on Alcohol, 63*, 219–228.

Spoth, R., Redmond, C., & Shin, C. (1998). Direct and indirect latent-variable parenting outcomes of two universal family-focused preventive interventions: Extending a public health-oriented research base. *Journal of Consulting and Clinical Psychology, 66*, 385–399.

Spoth, R., Redmond, C., & Shin, C. (2000). Modeling factors influencing enrollment in family-focused preventive intervention research. *Prevention Science, 1*, 213–225.

Spoth, R., Redmond, C., & Shin, C. (2001). Randomized trial of brief family interventions for general populations: Adolescent substance use outcomes 4 years following baseline. *Journal of Consulting and Clinical Psychology, 69*(4), 627–642.

Spoth, R., Trudeau, L., Guyll, M., Shin, C., & Redmond, C. (2009). Universal intervention effects on substance use among young adults mediated by delayed adolescent substance initiation. *Journal of Consulting and Clinical Psychology, 77*(4), 620–632.

Stice, E., Shaw, H., Bohon, C., Marti, C. N., & Rohde, P. (2009). A meta-analytic review of depression prevention programs for children and adolescents: Factors that predict magnitude of intervention effects. *Journal of Consulting and Clinical Psychology, 77*(3), 486–503.

Stolberg, A., & Mahler, J. (1994). Enhancing treatment gains in a school-based intervention for children of divorce through skill training, parental involvement, and transfer procedures. *Journal of Consulting and Clinical Psychology, 62*(1), 147–156.

Stormshak, E., Kaminski, R., & Goodman, M. (2002). Enhancing the parenting skills of Head Start families during the transition to kindergarten. *Prevention Science, 3*(3), 223–234.

Sturza, M. L., & Davidson, W. S. (2006). Issues facing the dissemination of prevention programs: Three decades of research on the Adolescent Diversion Project. *Journal of Prevention & Intervention in the Community, 32*(1/2), 5–24.

van Lier, P. A. C., Vuijk, P., & Crijnen, A. A. M. (2005). Understanding mechanisms of change in the development of antisocial behavior: The impact of a universal intervention. *Journal of Abnormal Child Psychology, 33*(5), 521–535.

Vitaro, F., Brendgen, M., & Tremblay, R. (2001). Preventive intervention: Assessing its effects on the trajectories of delinquency and testing for mediational processes. *Applied Developmental Science, 5*(4), 201–213.

Wandersman, A. (2009). Four keys to success (theory, implementation, evaluation, and resource/system support): High hopes and challenges in participation. *American Journal of Community Psychology, 43*, 3–21.

Wandersman, A., Imm, P., Chinman, M., & Kaftarian, S. (2000). Getting to outcomes: A results-based approach to accountability. *Evaluation and Program Planning, 23*, 389–395.

Webster-Stratton, C. (2001). The incredible years: Parents, teachers, and children training series. *Residential Treatment for Children and Youth, 18*(3), 31–45.

Webster-Stratton, C., & Taylor, T. (2001). Nipping early risk factors in the bud: Preventing substance abuse, delinquency, and violence in adolescence through interventions targeted at young children (0–8 years). *Prevention Science, 2*(3), 165–192.

Whitehurst, G., Falco, F., Lonigan, C., Fischel, J., DeBaryshe, B., Valdez-Menchaca, M., et al. (1988). Accelerating language development through picture-book reading. *Developmental Psychology, 24*, 552–558.

Whitlock, J., & Hamilton, S. (2003). The role of youth surveys in community youth development initiatives. *Applied Developmental Science, 7*(1), 39–51.

Wilson, S. J., & Lipsey, M. W. (2007). School-based interventions for aggressive and disruptive behavior: Update of a meta-analysis. *American Journal of Preventive Medicine, 33*(2S), S130–S143.

Winslow, E. B., Bonds, D., Wolchik, S., Sandler, I., & Braver, S. (2009). Predictors of enrollment and retention in a preventive parenting intervention for divorced families. *The Journal of Primary Prevention, 30*(2), 151–172. doi:10.1007/s10935-009-0170-3.

Winslow, E. B., & Shaw, D. S. (2007). Impact of neighborhood disadvantage on overt behavior problems during early childhood. *Aggressive Behavior, 33*, 207–219.

Wolchik, S., Sandler, I., Millsap, R., Plummer, B., Greene, S., Anderson, E., et al. (2002). Six-year follow-up of preventive interventions for children of divorce: A randomized controlled trial. *Journal of the American Medical Association, 288*(15), 1874–1881.

Wolchik, S., Sandler, I., Weiss, L., & Winslow, E. (2007). New beginnings: An empirically-based program to help divorced mothers promote resilience in their children. In J. M. Briesmeister & C. E. Schaefer (Eds.), *Handbook of parent training: Helping parents prevent and solve problem behaviors* (3rd ed., pp. 25–62). New York: Wiley.

Wolchik, S., West, S., Sandler, I., Tein, J., Coatsworth, D., Lengua, L., et al. (2000). An experimental evaluation of theory-based mother and mother-child programs for children of divorce. *Journal of Consulting and Clinical Psychology, 68*(5), 843–856.

Wolchik, S., West, S., Westover, S., & Sandler, I. (1993). The children of divorce parenting intervention: Outcome evaluation of an empirically based program. *American Journal of Community Psychology, 21*(3), 293–331.

Wyman, P., Sandler, I., Wolchik, S., & Nelson, K. (2000). Resilience as cumulative competence promotion and stress protection: Theory and intervention. In D. Cicchetti et al. (Eds.), *The promotion of wellness in children and adolescents* (pp. 133–184). Washington, DC: Child Welfare League of America.

Zevenbergen, A., & Whitehurst, G. (2003). Dialogic reading: A shared picture book reading intervention for preschoolers. In A. van Kleeck, S. Stahl, & E. Bauer (Eds.), *On reading books to children* (pp. 177–200). Mahwah, NJ: Lawrence Erlbaum.

Zullig, K. J., Ward, R. M., King, K. A., Patton, J. M., & Murray, K. A. (2009). Testing the feasibility of developmental asset measures on college students to guide health promotion efforts. *Assessment, 16*, 31–42.

Enhancing the Process of Resilience Through Effective Thinking

28

Myrna B. Shure and Bonnie Aberson

In the first edition of this book, a problem-solving approach to resiliency was illustrated to show how early high-risk behaviors as physical and verbal aggression could be reduced and prevented, and how clinical applications of the problem-solving approach could enhance the resiliency of children exhibiting emotional disturbance and ADHD. We have now learned that a different form of aggression, called relational aggression, popularized by the "mean girls syndrome" (e.g., Simmons, 2002; Wiseman, 2002) can stifle resilience, and how the problem-solving approach can help both the perpetrator and the victim of such behaviors. We have also learned how a feeling of bonding to school can increase resilience, and how the problem-solving approach can promote that feeling. Finally, we have discovered that in addition to emotional disturbance and ADHD, children with other diagnoses can be helped with the problem-solving approach, and how this can transpire with Asperger's syndrome will be illustrated.

No one doubts that clinicians, parents, teachers, and other caregivers are in a unique position to affect social adjustment and interpersonal competence in children. There is, however, a reason to wonder whether we have a thorough grasp

of the subtleties of this process. We know that some families, for instance, can adjust in reasonably adaptive ways to what appear to be circumstances very similar to those in families who cannot. Even among the very poor, many of whom experience insurmountable pressures of daily living, some can cope better than others and can have children who emerge as stellar examples of healthy human functioning.

This chapter will describe an interpersonal cognitive problem-solving (ICPS) approach that George Spivack developed with the first author (Shure), an approach that can provide a protection against stress—protection that can provide a significant mediator of resilience that helps people cope with insurmountable pressures, frustration, and even failures in life. First, socially adjusted and interpersonally competent children and those in regular classrooms displaying varying degrees of high-risk behaviors such as impulsivity and inhibition will be discussed. Examples of how the problem-solving approach has helped both adjusted and high-risk children develop resilience in typical, everyday conflict situations will be illustrated. How school bonding can promote resilience, and how interpersonal problem-solving can help children bond to their school environment will also be discussed. Examples of how clinicians can put into practice the efforts of controlled, empirical research of the first author and others will then be described through vignettes reported by the second author (Aberson) in her work with children diagnosed with clinical and neurological disorders.

M.B. Shure (✉)
Drexel University, Philadelphia, PA, USA
e-mail: mshure@drexel.edu

B. Aberson
Joe Dimaggio Children's Hospital, Hollywood, FL, USA

S. Goldstein and R.B. Brooks (eds.), *Handbook of Resilience in Children*,
DOI 10.1007/978-1-4614-3661-4_28, © Springer Science+Business Media New York 2013

Traditionally, educators and clinicians believed that if emotional tension could be relieved, it would be easier for children to think "straight." It seemed to George Spivack and Shure just as reasonable to believe that if one could think "straight," it would be easier to relieve emotional tension. Let's look at Zachary (all names are pseudonyms), a 4-year-old who wanted a wagon that Richard was playing with. When Richard refused his request, Zachary did not create a new problem by becoming disorganized in the face of stress. His ability to think of other options created the opportunity for him to demonstrate flexibility, and this led him to another tactic "If you let me have the wagon, I'll give it right back." Richard did not answer. Zachary then asked him, "Why can't I have it?" Richard replied, "Because I *need* it. I'm pulling the rocks." Zachary paused, then quietly offered, "I'll pull them with you." "Okay," said Richard. And the two children played with the wagon together.

Zachary's teacher may not have agreed with the way this problem was solved.

She might have thought Richard should have let Zachary have the wagon when he first asked for it because Richard already had his turn. But Zachary was satisfied with pulling together. Instead of ending up in dissatisfaction and frustration, both children responded warmly toward each other and felt good about their own decision. Zachary was able to think about his original desire, the wagon, and when faced with resistance could then think of alternative ways to solve the problem (ask for it; promise a quick return; suggest playing together). He was able to understand the other child's feelings and incorporate them into a solution that ended up successful. Like other good problem solvers, Zachary may have *thought* about hitting or pushing Richard or just pulling the wagon away, and he may also have been able to anticipate the consequences of such acts. But most importantly, his ability to think of other options prevented Zachary from experiencing frustration and failure. He could bounce back. He didn't have to give up too soon. Perhaps this was possible because Zachary had available to him more than one way to solve his problem.

Let's look at Sara, who asked her sister to let her play with her doll, and like Zachary, was told she couldn't have it. Could she think of other ways to get her sister to let her play with her doll? If not, she might become frustrated with her sister and react aggressively, or perhaps avoid the problem entirely by withdrawing. Sara might have hit her sister, not as an impulsive reaction to frustration, but after *deciding* that hitting is one way to get it. If this were the case, the new question is whether she also thought about the potential consequences of her hitting and whether that might have influenced her decision to hit. She might have foreseen that her sister could hit her back and not let it concern her. She might go ahead and hit her anyway. Perhaps she could not think of anything else to do. When Sara's sister told her she could play with her doll after she was finished with it, Sara thought of something different to do while she waited, an important coping strategy in itself. Sara was able to wait without getting impatient, flying off the handle, hitting her sister, or giving up.

What do Zachary and Sara have that children who are not so successful in negotiating for what they want but do not have? These two children have the ability to think of more than one way to solve a typical interpersonal problem, to mesh their needs with the needs of the other child, and to consider what might happen next if they were able to carry out a particular solution.

Problem-Solving and Resilience

Arend, Gove, and Sroufe (1979) found that 5-year-olds who can think of more options to interpersonal problems are more likely to display ego resiliency, defined as "the ability to respond flexibly, persistently, and resourcefully, especially in problem situations" (p. 951). The authors continue: "Individuals presumably have a typical or preferred level or threshold of control. Being ego-resilient implies the ability to modulate this preferred level of control in situational appropriate ways." The ego-brittle individual, on the other hand, "implies inflexibility—an inability to respond to changing requirements of the situation—and a tendency to become disorganized in the face of novelty or stress." This individual will be "impulsive (or constrained) even in situations when such behavior is clearly inappropriate." Perhaps having more than one way to solve problems that involve other people available in one's repertoire of thought provides the very flexibility and resourcefulness that creates an ego-resilient individual. In addition to being flexible and able to bounce back in the face of failure, Brooks and Goldstein (2001) observe that resilient children "have learned to set realistic goals and expectations for themselves. They have developed the ability to solve problems and make decisions and thus are more likely to view mistakes, hardships, and obstacles as challenges to confront rather than as stressors to avoid. They have developed effective interpersonal skills with peers and adults alike" (p. 5).

Children who are empathic and good problem solvers have developed effective interpersonal skills, as they have more friends and are less frustrated when things don't go their way. And, as Brooks and Goldstein note, parents can help by being empathic, communicating effectively, teaching our children to solve problems and make decisions, and disciplining in a way that promotes self-discipline and self-worth. Children who can plan their own actions that have positive, not negative, consequences are better able to take control of their lives, instead of letting life take control of them.

Problem-Solving Skills that Foster Resiliency

In youngsters as young as 4 and 5 years of age, Spivack and Shure measured the ability to think of *alternative solutions* to two types of problems: (a) wanting a toy another child has and (b) how to keep mother from being angry after having broken something of value to her. Using the Preschool Interpersonal Problem Solving (PIPS) test (Shure & Spivack, 1972), it was possible to distinguish good from poor problem solvers as early as preschool. To obtain a chance to play with a toy another child has, poor problem solvers thought of "Ask," "Grab it," "Hit him," or "Tell the

teacher." Good problem solvers could think of those solutions too, but added solutions as, "Take turns," "Say, 'I'll give it right back,'" "Tell him he'll be his friend," and more creative ones as, "Put her name on it and she'll think it's hers," and "Say, 'you'll have more fun if you play with me than if just play by yourself.'" Although good problem solvers could, like poor ones, think of "Take it," they were also more likely to offer, "Wait 'till he's finished," and surprisingly, "Wait 'til he's not looking and then take it." Poor problem solvers might have thought of "Say 'I'm sorry'" for breaking the flower pot, "I won't do it again," and perhaps some form of "fix it," while good problem solvers could add, "Paint it her favorite color," "Put her favorite flower in it," "Pretend he's asleep and mommy can't spank him," and "Bring her mommy a drink and she'll feel better."

Shure, Spivack, and Jaeger (1971) found that good problem solvers were, compared to poor ones, less physically and emotionally aggressive, less likely to fly off the handle when things don't go their way, better able to wait their turn and share things, more aware of, if not genuinely concerned for, peers in distress, and more sought after by their classmates. They were also less likely to display inhibited behaviors in the classroom, such as timidity, fear of jumping into play with others, and ability to stand up for their rights. The efficacy of ICPS for adjustment in youngsters from preschool through adolescence has been confirmed by others who have found poor ICPS skills to be associated naturally with high-risk impulsive and inhibited behaviors as well as display of fewer positive prosocial behaviors in both lower- and middle-income groups (for a thorough review of these studies, see Spivack and Shure 1982). Importantly, the very behaviors with which poor ICPS skills are associated are also, as longitudinal research has found, early predictors of later, more serious outcomes as violence, substance abuse, unsafe sex, and some forms of psychopathology, including depression, perhaps even suicide (Bender & Lösel, 2011; Loeber & Hay, 1997; Moffitt & Caspi, 2001, Nagin & Tremblay, 1999, Parker & Asher, 1987; Roff, 1984; Rubin, 1985, Rubin, Burgess, &

Coplin, 2002, Valois, MacDonald, Bretous, & Fischer, 2002).

Shure and Spivack learned something interesting from the solutions given by socially adjusted and behaviorally competent children as well as those who were not. It might, at first, appear that the solution "Wait 'til he's not looking and then take it," is an aggressive one, based on the content, "take it." Or, it might appear to be a solution that an inhibited child would give because, as one might conjecture, "The child doesn't have to confront anyone, and there's no conflict." It turned out that neither was the case; that it was the socially *adjusted* children (those displaying neither aggressive nor inhibited behaviors) who were most likely to give that solution. After having thought about why this was the case, Shure and Spivack came upon two possibilities. First, socially adjusted youngsters were likely to give more, different, relevant solutions to the presented interpersonal problems, and "Wait 'til he's not looking and then take it" was only one of several solutions offered. Therefore, a child who gave this solution was not stuck on one or two ways to solve a problem. Second, the cognitive components of this solution include a non-impulsive thought, "Wait…" and thinking of the best time to do something—"when he's not looking." However rudimentary, this could be the precursor to a more sophisticated problem-solving skill found related to behavioral adjustment in the preteen years, a skill called *means–ends thinking*—planning sequenced steps toward a goal (e.g., making friends), anticipating potential obstacles that could interfere with carrying out that plan (the kids don't like him), and recognizing that time and timing, that is, recognizing a good time to act and/or appreciating that goals are not always reached immediately (Spivack & Shure, 1982). Another solution that made Spivack and Shure recognize that it may be *how*, not what children think that guides behavior is "Say 'I'm sorry'" for having broken mommy's flower pot or other act of property damage. While one may think that it would have been the adjusted children who gave that solution, a socially appropriate one, it turned out that while those youngsters could offer that one, inhibited children got stuck

on that solution for nearly every stimulus presented (broke a flower pot, scratched a table, tore a hole in a book, etc.).

Given that perhaps the *process* of solving a problem, rather than the content per se, can guide behavior, Shure, Spivack, and Jaeger (1971) tested children for other skills that could both distinguish good from poor problem solvers and skills that would relate to measures of social adjustment and interpersonal competence. As measured by the What Happens Next Game (WHNG) (Shure & Spivack, 1990), the ability to anticipate what might happen next if an act were carried out or *consequential thinking* emerged as a significant mediator of behavior as well. For example, when asked, "What might happen next" if a child grabbed a toy from another (Shure, 2003), poor problem solvers more likely gave responses such as, "He'll grab it back," "He'll hit him," or, "He'll tell the teacher." Good problem solvers could also think of these, but added responses such as, "It might break," "He'll lose a friend," or, as one very creative boy said, "He'll eat marshmallows in front of him and then when he wants one, he'll say no 'cause you took my truck.'" When asked what might happen next if, for example, a child takes something from an adult without first asking, poor problem solvers were not only more likely to think of fewer consequences, but much less empathic ones. Over and over, impulsive and inhibited youngsters were more likely to give consequences directed toward themselves, such as "He'll get whooped," "He'll have to go to his room," or "Mom will take away his toys." Adjusted youngsters who could also think of those possibilities were also more likely to think of empathic possibilities. Responding to a fictitious child having taken an umbrella without her mom knowing it, one adjusted child said, "When it rains, she won't have an umbrella, and she'll get wet, and she'll catch a cold."

Having identified alternative solution and consequential thinking skills as associated with social adjustment and interpersonal competence in 4- to 6-year-olds, and sequenced planning, or means–ends thinking as an additional, more complex skill beginning about age 8, Spivack and Shure then asked why better problem solvers are more socially adjusted and interpersonally competent than their peers and with adults as rated by teachers as well as peers and independent observers (Shure, 1993). Do ICPS skills precede healthy adjustment or vice versa? Are children who are socially adjusted and interpersonally competent because they have good problem-solving skills, or do children have good problem-solving skills because they are socially adjusted and interpersonally competent? It seems reasonable to assume that children who get along with others, are not aggressive, and not socially inhibited have more opportunity to relate to others and more opportunity to practice social cognitive skills. It seems equally logical that an individual who becomes preoccupied with the end goal of a motivated act rather than how to obtain it, who is not adept at thinking through ways to solve a typical interpersonal problem, or does not consider consequences and the possibility of alternate routes to the goal is an individual who might make impulsive mistakes, become frustrated and aggressive, or evade the problem entirely by withdrawing. In any case, his initial needs remain unsatisfied, and, if such behaviors occur repeatedly, intense unpleasant affect will be aroused, interpersonal relationships can suffer, and varying degrees of maladaptive behavior and symptoms can ensue. On the other hand, an individual with means-ends thinking, a habit of thinking in terms of alternate possible solutions and an appreciation of consequences, should more effectively evaluate and choose from a variety of options when faced with a problem, turn to a different (more effective) solution in the case of actual failure, experience less frustration, be successful in interpersonal affairs, and be less likely to exhibit psychological dysfunction. Although there is no doubt an interaction of both premises, it seems reasonable to assume that youngsters like Zachary and Sara are likely, with their ICPS competence, to experience less frustration and failure than youngsters who cannot bounce back if their first ideas should elude them.

An implicit assumption of Spivack's theoretical position (Spivack & Shure, 1982) is that the availability of ICPS thinking is an antecedent condition for interpersonal adjustment and psychological health. This notion of mediating

impact of ICPS upon behavior was put to the test via intervention created to investigate a linkage between ICPS ability and behavioral adjustment by experimentally altering ICPS skills, and then observing changes in the child's display of behaviors naturally associated with ICPS skills. If ICPS ability were found to mediate such behaviors, Spivack and Shure would be able to identify those ICPS skills that play the most significant role in adjustment, which would form the basis for a new approach to prevention of high-risk behaviors in children.

From Theory to Training Program

In the early 1970s, Shure and Spivack began systematic intervention to enhance ICPS skills with inner-city 4-year-olds. Based on Spivack's theoretical position and the content of solutions given by children when we tested them, the approach was to teach children *how*, not what to think, in ways that would help them successfully resolve everyday interpersonal problems. Originally called Interpersonal Cognitive Problem Solving (ICPS), now called I Can Problem Solve (also ICPS), the training manuals for preschool and for kindergarten and the primary grades (Shure, 1992a, 1992b) consist of sequenced games and dialogues, including prerequisite language skills, feeling word concepts, and the final alternative solution and consequential thinking skills to be learned.

ICPS Word Pairs

Word pairs such as is/is not, same/different, before/after, might/maybe, and some/all are first used in game form because when children learn to associate particular words with play, they are more likely to use them when it's time to settle disputes. In nonstressful situations, children first have fun thinking about what an object in the room is and is not (e.g., "This *is* a table, it is *not* a chair, a balloon, a ceiling"), then to name something in the room that is the *same*, and something *different*, whether they pointed to the table *before* or *after* they pointed to the floor, and what thing Mom *might* point to next. Children can have fun talking about how Mom *is* the *same* as Dad, and how Mom is *not* the *same,* is *different* from Dad, what games they like to play that are *different* from games their sister likes to play, and whether it rained *before* or *after* they played outside. Children also like to play with the words *now* and *later,* and make up situations such as, "I am eating breakfast *now.* I will eat dinner *later."* The words *some* and *all* have been used in a phrase, to think, for example, that "I like to play with my new truck *some* of the time, but *not all* of the time. I can let my brother play with my truck *some* of the time too." It's fun for children to make up their own ways of using these words, ways that later help them think about how to solve conflicts that come up at home and at school. Applying these word pairs to real life, for example, a child can respond to the question, "Is your idea a good one or *not* a good one," in light of what *might* happen next, and is the child able to think about what happened before a fight began with questions such as, "Did he hit you *before* or *after* you hit him?" The words *is* and *is not* are also incorporated into phrases that help the child think about good times and *not* good times to do things, such as when a child is interrupting someone. The child can be asked, "Is this a good time or *not* a good time to talk to me?" Children enjoy thinking about the question, "Can you think of a *different* way to tell your brother what you want," and they're more willing to wait until later when they recognize the word *later* from their play games.

The second phase of the ICPS training program helps children identify feelings, not only of others, but their own. Children learn that it is possible to learn that different people can feel different ways about the same thing—that feelings change, and there are ways to determine this by watching, listening, and asking. After learning games to put words to people's feelings, children learn to think about what makes other people feel the way they do. Children who do not care if, for example, a child hits them while grabbing a truck may have become immune to their own, albeit temporary pain to get what they want. Once feeling words are identified and children think about what makes people feel the way they do, they are ready for games and dialogues that teach

solution and consequential thinking skills, in light of their own and other's feelings—and that if one solution doesn't work, or is thought to not be a good idea—it is possible to try a *different* way.

Beginning about age 8, children in the intermediate elementary grades (Shure, 1992c) are exposed to age-appropriate problem situations to think of feelings, solutions, and consequences, as well as more sophisticated skills of thinking: How a person can have more than one feeling about the same thing at the same time (mixed emotions), understanding that there is more than one explanation why people do what they do ("Maybe he didn't wave because he's mad at me," or, "Maybe he just didn't see me"), and ability to engage in the sequenced planning, or the means-ends thinking skill described above.

In addition to the ICPS programs for use in schools from preschool through grade six, ICPS has been developed for use by parents. With the *Raising a Thinking Child Workbook* (Shure, 2000), and its Spanish edition Enseñando a Nuestros Niños a Pensar (Shure, 2005) based on *Raising a Thinking Child* (Shure, 1996) and *Raising a Thinking Preteen* (Shure, 2001), the same ICPS approach was adapted for use at home.

Shure and Spivack learned that in addition to teaching prerequisite and problem-solving skills to children, application of newly acquired ICPS skills to real life can be key to actual behavior change. Using the concepts described, the trainer, whomever that may be, learns to help children associate *how* they think with what they do through a process Shure calls "ICPS dialoguing." Replacing negative punishment, demands, or threats, such as often humiliating time-out or yelling, or even the more positive approaches of suggesting what to do (e.g., "Ask your brother for what you want"; "share your toys"), and explaining and reasoning (e.g., "If you hit your brother, you might hurt him"), ICPS trainers ask questions that guide children to *think* about what they do in light of how they and others might feel, what might happen next, and if needed, to think of a different way to solve the problem. Here is how one mother used the ICPS dialoguing approach with her preschool child, Sean, who complained, "Mommy, Tommy hit me."

Mom: What's the problem? What's the matter?

Sean: Tommy hit me.

Mom: What happened *before* he hit you?

Sean: I hit him first.

Mom: What for?

Sean: He won't let me have any clay.

Mom: How do you think Tommy feels when you hit him?

Sean: Mad.

Mom: And then what happened *after* you hit him?

Sean: He hit me.

Mom: And how did that make *you* feel?

Sean: Mad.

Mom: Can you think of a *different* way to get Sean to let you have some clay so you both won't be mad and he won't hit you?

Sean: I could tell him I'll help him make a dog.

Sean felt less threatened when asked "What happened *before* he hit you?" than he would have from the more threatening question, "*Why* did you hit him!?" Associating the word *before* with his ICPS word games, Sean felt safe to tell his mom what really happened. When this mother discovered that her child hit first, she didn't offer advice or lecture the pros and cons of hitting. Instead, she continued the ICPS dialogue by encouraging her child to think about his own and Tommy's feelings, and the original problem (wanting the clay). Then she helped him look for alternative ways to solve the problem and consider what might happen as a result of those solutions. Now active participants, not passive recipients, children who are engaged to think about what they do are much more likely to carry out their own ideas than those demanded, suggested, or even explained by an adult. By sending a covert message, "I care how you feel, I care what you think, and I want you to care too," children are also more likely to care about other people too.

Evidence of Impact with Adjusted and High-Risk Children

What did ICPS training do for the thinking and behavior of the children? When trained by teachers, not only did ICPS skills and behavior

of youngsters trained as early as preschool and kindergarten improve more than comparable controls, but as measured 1 and 2 (Shure & Spivack 1982), and up to 4 years later (Shure, 1993), the impact was maintained. In only 3 months time, and regardless of IQ, impulsive children became less impatient and less likely to explode when faced with frustration. Socially withdrawn youngsters became more outgoing, more able to express their feelings, and less fearful. Tanya, for example, who played onlooker day after day before training and shied away when her teacher tried to help her into a group, made a dramatic move during the 11th week of the program. She told a group in the doll corner, "If you need a fireman, I'm right here." One of the children who previously ignored her then happened to notice a pretend fire.

Not only did the behaviors of the trained group as a whole improve (also replicated by others, e, g., Allen, 1978; Boyle & Hassett-Walker, 2008; Feis & Simons, 1985; Kumpfer, Alvarado, Tait, & Turner, 2002; Santos Elias, Marturano, Ameida Motta., & Giurlani, 2003; Weddle & Williams, 1993; Wowkenech, personal communication, August 26, 1978), but those who most improved in the trained problem-solving skills were the same children whose behavior most improved (Shure & Spivack, 1980), suggesting a direct link and support for Spivack's theory that the trained ICPS skills played a significant role in mediating behavior. Importantly, youngsters showing behavioral adjustment and social competence in preschool were less likely than controls to begin showing behavioral aberrance in kindergarten, suggesting that ICPS serves as a primary prevention program as well as one that reduces already existing high-risk behaviors. In the Feis and Simons (1985) study, trained preschoolers in rural Michigan, compared to comparable controls, decreased negative behaviors, especially anxious/fearful and hyperactive/distractable behaviors as measured by the Behar and Stringfield (1974) teacher rating scale, outcomes also found by Aberson, Albury, Gutting, Mann, and Trushin (1986). Behavioral changes were associated with an improved ability to problem solve. Importantly, trained children also received fewer referrals to mental health services than controls. In the Wowkenech (1978) study, behavioral impact was not only greater for ICPS-trained 5-year-olds than for age-mates trained in modeling-reinforcement groups, but as soon as the training was over, ICPS-trained youngsters continued to try other ways to resolve a conflict, while modeling-reinforcement-trained youngsters were more likely to revert to their old (often ineffective) ways of handling conflict.

A form of aggression that provokes conflicts among peers that has recently been noticed by researchers is what Crick (1996) has coined *relational aggression*, aggression that "involves harming others through purposeful manipulation or damage to their peer relationships" (e.g., using social exclusion as a form of retaliation) p. 2317. This form of aggression includes spreading rumors and telling lies about someone so others won't play with that child, talking about a party in front of a child who is not invited, being told there is no room at the cafeteria table when there are several empty seats, etc. Relational aggression is more common in girls than in boys (Ostrov & Crick, 2007), who are more relationship-oriented than boys. Being the victim of relational aggression can be more hurtful than being kicked in the shins because it lasts longer, the victim begins to wonder why no one likes her, and soon doesn't want to come to school. Victims of relational aggression often experience psychological distress including depression and anxiety, peer rejection, and loneliness (Crick & Bigbee, 1998; Crick & Grotpeter, 1995). While this type of aggression begins in about the third grade, there are precursors as early as preschool Ostrov, Woods, Jansen, Casas, and Crick (2004). Crick, Casas, and Mosher (1997) found that among 3- to 5-year-olds, children who say they won't invite a peer to a birthday party if they can't have their way, won't let a classmate into their play group, won't listen to someone or may cover their ears are more likely to experience social-psychological maladjustment than peers not engaged in these kinds of behaviors. And, as Ostrov (2010) has found, even as early as preschool, victims of relational aggression are likely to engage in later relational aggression just as victims of physical

aggression are likely to engage in later physical aggression. Victims of aggression may suffer in misery beyond their years in school. In fact, Smith, Singer, Hoel, and Cooper (2003) found that youngsters who were threatened, humiliated, belittled, or otherwise picked on in school—especially those who did not, and still don't have coping strategies—may continue to be victimized years later in the workplace.

It seems reasonable to assume that both the perpetrator and the victim of relational aggression would benefit by ability to solve interpersonal problems, by finding other ways to treat peers they don't like or who they feel betrayed them, and by finding ways to cope with being treated with such behaviors. Boyle and Hassett-Walker (2008), who implemented ICPS with kindergarten and first-grade children, found significant gains in positive prosocial behaviors, but also significant reductions in both physical and relational aggression, suggesting that trained children did find alternative ways to react to peers who upset them or made them feel angry. While no known research to date has studied the victims of relational aggression exposed to ICPS, Shelly, age 4, was told there was no room in the art corner for her when there was plenty of space. Before ICPS, Shelly would have walked away and sulked. This time she said, "I'll make you a ticket to the zoo," and the girl laughed and let her sit next to her. Shelly cut a "ticket" out of construction paper, gave it to her and the two girls played together the rest of the free play period. Shelly was no longer rejected, or lonely.

For fifth and sixth graders, first trained in the ICPS approach, the content of particular problems and what adults say and do can differ, but the extent to which an adult encourages the child to think does not change as a child gets older or because he or she is a member of a particular socioeconomic level. Although it did take somewhat longer to achieve the same behavioral impact as with younger children, the positive prosocial behaviors increased in the same 3-month time period in grade five, while the negative behaviors decreased after a second exposure, in grade six (Shure & Healey, 1993). Although it is possible that the delayed impact on negative behaviors can be a result of less intense training due to academic demands (3 times weekly vs. daily for the younger children), it is also reasonable to assume that perhaps aberrant behaviors are simply more habitual in older than in younger children and therefore more resistant to change. Given that ICPS and behaviors in older children are still correlated phenomena, more intense or extensive ICPS intervention appears logical to pursue. The evidence suggests, however, that even though it may take somewhat longer to affect negative behaviors in older children, for those not trained earlier in life, grades five and six are not too late. Importantly, standardized achievement test scores improved among ICPS-trained children, especially social studies, reading, and math, suggesting that children whose behavior improved could better focus on the task-oriented demands of the classroom, and subsequently, do better in school. Returning to Brooks and Goldstein's (2001) analysis that resilience involves "hardships and obstacles as challenges to confront rather than as stressors to avoid," it is important to note that Elias et al. (1986) have shown that fifth graders who learn problem-solving skills experience less stress during their transition from elementary to middle school. In addition to the logistics of transferring to a new school and coping with peer pressure, these stresses included adjusting to more stringent academic requirements. The youngsters in the Elias et al. study stayed on-task and performed better academically in school.

It may be important here to underscore the importance of the ICPS dialoguing in effecting behavior change. Weissberg and his colleagues developed social problem-solving programs for elementary school-age children and found that compared to their first attempts, Weissberg et al. (1981) attribute improved behavioral gains in both urban and suburban second to fourth graders to methodological research improvements (e.g., better-matched controls, less teacher rating bias), more motivated, responsible teachers, and more closely monitored training, supervision, and consultation efforts. They also attribute behavioral gains to a curriculum that might better have met the needs of urban as well as suburban teachers

and students, which had been started earlier in the year, and, very importantly, to newly emphasized dialoguing to help children apply newly acquired cognitive problem-solving skills to everyday interpersonal problems. In fact, Weissberg and Gesten (1982) report that the incorporation of dialoguing into the curriculum may "be a key teaching approach to facilitating children's independent problem solving efforts" (p. 59).

In addition to relational aggression, another area of research receiving recent attention is that of school bonding. Blum (2002) found that adolescents who feel connected to school, that teachers care about them and treat them fairly, feel a part of the school, and importantly, feel safe are less likely to engage in violence, substance abuse, and other serious outcomes. It turned out that the most important factor contributing to a feeling of connectedness was school climate, including teachers who encouraged students to be actively involved in classroom management, where students treat each other with respect, get along well with the teacher, are engaged in academic lessons, etc. These are all features that ICPS fosters, and recognition of bonding as a contributor to resiliency can add important insight into why behaviors of ICPS-trained youngsters improve. In 6- to 8-year-olds, Kumpfer, Alvarado, Tait, and Turner (2002) found that a similar feeling of belongingness to school increased significantly in ICPS-trained youngsters compared to controls, youngsters whose self-regulation also improved, suggesting the link between a feeling of school bonding and behaviors at a very early age.

Are parents able to be effective ICPS mediators? Shure and Spivack (1979) found that inner-city, African-American preschoolers trained by their mothers, like those trained by their teachers, significantly improved more than controls in solution and consequential thinking and in impulsive and inhibited behaviors as observed in school, suggesting that ICPS skills learned at home generalized to a different setting—the school. Mothers who improved their own problem-solving skills and applied ICPS dialogues when handling real problems at home had children who most improved in the trained ICPS skills and behaviors. Importantly, it was the mothers who best learned to solve problems between a hypothetical mother and her child (e.g., her child has been saying "no" a lot lately) who were also most likely to apply the ICPS dialogues when real problems would arise, partly, we believe, because they learned to solve a problem one step at a time, to recognize and circumvent potential obstacles, to appreciate that problems cannot always be solved immediately (means-ends thinking), as well as to understand, or, at least accept their child's point of view. When first trained in kindergarten by their teachers, and in first grade by their mothers (Shure, 1993), children whose mothers best applied the ICPS dialogues were still maintaining their gains 3 years later, at the end of grade four.

From Training Adjusted and High-Risk Children to Clinical Applications

So far we have addressed ways that ICPS can be used to help children solve the more typical, everyday problems, such as hitting siblings or classmates and sharing. Although fewer studies have been conducted with children with clinical diagnoses, Shure and Spivack (1972) found social problem-solving deficiencies in 8- to 12-year-old youngsters attending a school for the emotionally disturbed compared to age-mates in public schools, and Lochman and Dodge (1994) confirm that severely violent preadolescents and adolescents tend to be more deficient in a wide range of social cognitive processes, including social problem-solving skills, than their moderately aggressive or nonaggressive peers. Similarly, Dodge (1993) cites research within his cognitive model of information processing that suggests that both aggressive and depressed youngsters who view their interpersonal worlds with anger or hopelessness are deficient in social problem-solving skills, and "demonstrate deviant response accessing patterns that indicate a dearth of competent behavioral responses" (p. 569). Consistent with Dodge, depressed 9- to 11-year-olds were, compared to nondepressed peers, significantly more deficient in the measured ICPS skill of means-ends thinking (Sacco & Graves, 1984). Interestingly, Higgens and Thies (1981) found that even within

a group of institutionalized emotionally disturbed boys, the more socially isolated were more deficient in measured ICPS skills than those who were less isolated.

Although training of depressed children specifically with ICPS has not, to date, been conducted, severely antisocial, often isolated children can benefit from ICPS training alone or when combined with other forms of cognitive-behavior therapy. Small and Schinke (1983) applied a problem-solving approach at a residential treatment center for 7- to 13-year-old emotionally troubled boys of normal intelligence, referred because of hyperactivity, impulsivity, extreme acting-out, delinquency, learning difficulties, and minimal neurological dysfunction. Conducted in six 60-min training sessions over 2 weeks, the impact of an adapted ICPS curriculum was compared to a combined ICPS/social skills training, where leaders modeled use of effective gestures, expressions, and verbal statements, and group members acted as protagonists, antagonists, coaches, and feedback sources during practice role play. When combined, the boys tried new styles of problem-solving and interpersonal communication, gave one another social praise for displaying adaptive behavior, and planned how to exercise their learning when faced with problems. Compared to a time-comparable discussion-only group, in which the boys merely discussed problems but did not learn ICPS or social skills, and a test-only condition, the ICPS-adapted group combined with social skills training had the most impact on decreasing classroom teacher-rated behaviors as measured by the Devereax Elementary School Behavior (DESB) rating scale (Spivack & Swift, 1967), including classroom disturbance, impatience, disrespect-defiance, and external blame. With teachers blind to experimental conditions, it is notable that ICPS alone and social skills training alone still had significantly more impact than groups with no problem-solving or social skills training, offering hope that "troubled young people can learn to think and act responsibly in social situations" (p. 12).

In a study with 7- to 13-year-old male outpatients in a psychiatric clinic, (Yu, Harris, Solovitz, & Franklin, 1985) children, mostly from the working class, single-parent (divorced) families, received the Rochester Social Problem Solving curriculum (Weissberg, Gesten, Liebenstein, Doherty-Schmid, & Hutton, 1979)—a program that, like ICPS, teaches social problem-solving (called SPS) and thinking skills. Over a 20-week period, twice a week, children were trained in groups by clinic staff members, and, in addition, concurrent group parent sessions were held. Parents were informed about the concepts their children were learning and encouraged to implement the principles at home, and group discussions included a variety of parent issues. Compared to control groups, who received generally eclectic clinical services ranging from individual to family therapy, trained children improved in both SPS skills and parent-rated behaviors, including greater social competence and less externalizing symptomatology (e.g., delinquent or aggressive behaviors). Parents who attended the most sessions also had children who exhibited less internalizing (e.g., depressed or uncommunicative behaviors). Although not compared to training by the clinical staff alone, it is important to note that among diagnostically disturbed children, SPS group training with added parent training can have more impact than non-ICPS treatment, which consisted of a variety of therapeutic treatment variables assumed to be ameliorative of the manifest psychopathology.

Over a 6-month period, DeFranco-Nierenberg and Givner (1998) found that severely emotionally disturbed low-income kindergarten to second graders trained by their counselors significantly improved compared to comparable non-trained youngsters on PIPS solution scores (Shure and Spivack, 1974a, 1974b). They also showed increased prosocial behaviors and decreased inhibited, internalizing behaviors as measured by the Hahnemann Preschool Behavior Rating Scale (Spivack & Shure, undated) and the Achenbach and Edelbrock teacher report form (1983). When the teacher worked together with the counselor, externalizing, impulsive behaviors also decreased. While training was longer than for normal children (6 months) and in smaller groups (6 children per group), it is important to note that ICPS can have significant impact on the problem-solving

skills and behavioral adjustment in this population.

In a sample of psychiatric inpatient 7- to 13-year-olds hospitalized for treatment of antisocial child behavior, Kazdin, Esveldt-Dawson, French, and Unis (1987) found that 20, 45-min sessions, 3–4 times a week of treatment modeled after ICPS had greater impact than nondirective relational therapy or no treatment at all. The cognitive problem-solving-trained youngsters showed "significantly greater decreases in externalizing and aggressive behaviors in overall behavior problems at home and at school, and to increases in prosocial behaviors and in overall adjustment" (p. 76), and the impact was seen at the 1-year follow-up. As measured by the Achenbach and Edelbrock (1983) rating scale, prosocial behaviors of problem-solving-trained children improved to the point of falling within the normative range; the majority did, however, remain outside the normative range for deviant behaviors. The finding, with respect to prosocial behaviors, is interesting in that with normal but high-risk children within the same general age range, studied by Shure and Healey (1993) and described above, it was the prosocial behaviors that improved first as well. A later combination of problem-solving with a behavioral parent-management component (in which the parent reinforced the child's behavior with privileges, activities, and prizes) did increase the number of deviant behaviors to fall within the normal range (Kazdin, Siegel, & Bass, 1992).

Although ICPS-like training for severely antisocial children did not transform most of the youngsters studied by Kazdin et al. into normally behaving youngsters, the decreases in externalizing and aggressive behaviors were significantly greater than those exposed to a therapy in which children were guided to express feelings, shown empathy and unconditional positive warmth, but not trained to solve problems directly. This finding is important because ICPS intervention is based on the premise that empathy, recognition, and open discussion about feelings are prerequisite to behavior change. They generate a greater repertoire of solutions, but the solution and consequential thinking most directly mediate behavior.

If, for example, a withdrawn child is aware that something she did made someone angry—a step ahead of not being sensitive to that outcome—her anxiety about that person's anger won't be relieved unless she knows what to do to allay that anger. Whether the population is within the normative or the clinical behavior range, knowing what to do is a result of the final problem-solving solution, consequential and sequenced planning skills of ICPS.

We now turn our attention to how the second author (Aberson) helped three children with multiple neurological and clinical disorders develop characteristics associated with resilience as a result of training in ICPS. All three demonstrated characteristics of attention deficit hyperactivity disorder (ADHD). Patricia also had comorbid conditions of anxiety and depression, and Jimmy, of impulsivity and oppositional defiance. The third child, Jorge, developed posttraumatic stress disorder (PTSD) following a serious accident 1 year after the initial treatment, and returned to Aberson for help. These children (whose names have been changed to protect confidentiality) received training from their parents who participated in small-group family training or in family therapy.

Patricia's Story

A child of British origin, Patricia demonstrated characteristics of (ADHD) inattentive type when she was in kindergarten (as reported in Aberson, 1996; Aberson & Ardila, 2000). Her mother, a single parent, attended 6 weekly small-group parenting classes when Patricia was in second grade. By that time ratings on the Behavior Assessment System for Children (BASC) (Reynolds & Kamphaus, 1992) by her teacher, her mother, and herself suggested that she was also experiencing symptoms of depression and anxiety in addition to attention problems. Patricia was not doing her work at home or at school, despite average intelligence and achievement levels. Her grades were below average. She had only one friend at school, who was able to bully her by telling her she would not be her friend if she did not do what she wanted. Her relationship with her mother, whose

ratings on the Parenting Stress Inventory (Abidin, 1990) indicated significantly high levels of stress related to parenting Patricia, was usually confrontational and punitive with specific difficulties related to getting ready for school in the mornings and doing homework. These factors resulted in destruction of the parent–child relationship, despite the fact that Patricia was regressed in her behavior and very dependent on her mother.

Aberson, who was at that time a school psychologist assigned to Patricia's school, explained to Patricia that her mother would be learning some games to play with her and would be asking her questions to help her learn how to solve problems. Patricia agreed that this would be a good idea.

To help Patricia think about her dawdling in the morning, her mother learned to ask ICPS dialogue questions as, "How do you feel when you come to school on time?" (recognizing child's feelings), "How do you think your teacher feels when you're late?" (recognizing the other person's feelings), "How do you feel when everybody's yelling at each other in the morning?" and, in time, "What can you do to solve this problem?" Her mother aided Patricia in solving the problem by breaking the solution down into smaller steps, with questions as: (1) "What can you do the night before to make it easier to get ready in the morning?" (2) "Can you make a list of the different things that you have to do to get ready?" (3) "What would you do first, second, third?" (applying sequenced steps of means-ends thinking) as a way to help her get her tasks in order, and (4) "Can you think of a way to mark each task after doing it so you'll know it's complete?" After 6 weeks of ICPS training, these steps were no longer necessary. Patricia's mother reported that although at first ICPS dialoguing with her daughter involved lengthy conversations due to Patricia's oppositional responses, eventually it did take hold and their relationship improved. Patricia was able to plan what she was going to wear to school the night before and also independently plan how she could get ready on time in the morning.

To help Patricia complete her work in school, as well as her homework, which she often refused to do, her mother shifted from arguing about it to asking questions such as, "What do you want to do when you finish your homework?" (a way of empowering, instead of overpowering her child). Her teacher reported that her effort and work completion in school improved, and battles over homework gradually ended, with Patricia's becoming able to do her homework independently with only occasional help from her mother.

Although Patricia continued to have difficulty making friends, her peer relationships did improve when playing with children at home. Instead of going to her mother and crying when she was having difficulty getting along with a playmate, she began to think of alternative ideas of what to do when her friend wanted to play with different things.

Because Patricia was struggling due to a mild learning problem in math and was less mature than her peers, she, together with her mother, decided that she should repeat the fifth grade, despite the fact that retention was not recommended by the school. Patricia was happy with this decision, which she played a part in making, and told her peers that she felt she needed more time before going to middle school. Several years later, in the tenth grade, Patricia was earning As and Bs, even in math. She had friends and continued to enjoy a close relationship with her mother. Her resilience was demonstrated by the fact that she benefited from retention in the fifth grade. Although this outcome is not consistent with research on the effect of retention (Dawson, Raforth, & Carey, 1990), her success might be attributed to the relationship of mutual respect between Patricia and her mother and use of the problem-solving approach in making this decision.

In Patricia's case, the immediate benefit of the ICPS dialoguing was the improvement in her relationship with her mother, followed by improvement in school and eventually improved peer relationships. Four years after the parent-training sessions, Patricia was, as again measured by ratings from teachers, her mother, and by herself, free of symptoms of depression and anxiety, although mild attention problems remained. Never medicated from the start, she continued to be unmedicated and remained in a regular school program.

Jimmy's Story

Jimmy, of Southeast Asian descent, was adopted as an infant. His parents learned ICPS in a parent-training group, followed by family therapy, when Jimmy was in the second grade. At that time, Jimmy was impulsive, oppositional, and defiant in school and at home. Before ICPS, his physical education (PE) teacher told his parents that he was just a "mean kid." When asked how he felt about being left out of PE, Jimmy answered, "Sad." Using an ICPS vocabulary word, he was asked, "What happened *before* your teacher told you that you couldn't play?" He responded that he was fooling around and would kick the ball into another kid. When asked what he could do so that wouldn't happen, Jimmy answered that he could say to himself, "Don't fool around, and make sure my hands and feet are quiet." On the next report card Jimmy earned an A in conduct in PE. Before ICPS, Jimmy often did not bring home report cards because they resulted in punishment and lectures. Now Jimmy and his parents agreed to use a report card in a new way. The teachers rated Jimmy in four different areas, on a scale of 1–5, including doing his work in class, homework, getting along with peers, and following rules. His parents agreed to respond to the report by asking three questions, written on the bottom of the report card: first, "What makes you feel happy about this report?" second, "Does anything make you feel sad or frustrated?" "What?" and third, "What can you do tomorrow to make it better?" After only 2 weeks, Jimmy was earning the highest ratings in all four areas. He felt proud because he now knew that he had the power to make things better. After ten sessions, Jimmy became a better student and had more friends.

Jimmy's relationship with his parents became closer, and having been helped to think about his own and other's feelings, including how someone feels when he shouts at them, he was able to demonstrate empathy toward his younger, handicapped brother. On one occasion when his mother became frustrated with his brother shouted at him, Jimmy asked, "How do you think Steven feels when you speak to him like that?" Mom was surprised at how Jimmy had used an ICPS question she had previously learned to ask of him. When Jimmy was asked, "What did you learn from ICPS?" he answered, "I learned that the *same* solution will not work in every situation." Because of the increased academic demands 3 years later, in the fifth grade Jimmy and his mother decided that his test grades might improve with stimulant medication. And in middle school, Jimmy was on the honor roll.

Jorge's Story

Jorge, a child diagnosed with the ADHD-combined type, was in second grade in a self-contained gifted program when his parents entered into family therapy. He was, at that time, taking stimulant medication. This family is middle-class Cuban American with a second male child, who at that time was in preschool. Jorge, although gifted, was experiencing conflict with his parents primarily with regard to doing homework and fighting with his younger brother. His parents used both punitive techniques and rewards in dealing with family problems. With neither of these having the desired effect, both parents and their children were becoming increasingly frustrated.

Jorge and his family became acquainted with ICPS when they attended a brief presentation at Jorge's school. It was Jorge's idea for a family to attend sessions to learn how to problem solve. After the family learned the objectives of the program and specific goals for the family were outlined, feeling games were introduced, and each member listened to the other nonjudgmentally. During that time, Jorge's parents learned that he felt sad when they shouted at him. As a result, his parents held family meetings each week to play ICPS games and problem solve instead of shouting. Jorge also had a problem in school. He was unable to concentrate on his work because he kept talking with his friends.

During the problem-solving sessions, Jorge thought of ways he could solve this problem. He asked his teacher if he could sit alone in a quiet place when doing seat work and then return to his seat next to his friends. He also planned a homework schedule with his mother and took over the responsibility for doing his homework. He and his younger brother worked out a plan so that his younger brother, who acted out for Jorge's attention, would be able to wait for Jorge to finish his homework before playing with him. Jorge used the ICPS phrase, "This is *not a good time*. I will play with you when I finish my homework." Feeling that the family's stress level was significantly reduced, therapy was terminated after 10 weeks.

A year later, an unfortunate setback occurred. On a family trip, the SUV rolled over several times and Jorge, able to exit the car, witnessed his fathers' close call with death. This accident resulted in the entire family experiencing posttraumatic stress disorder as well as physical injuries to both parents. At first, the parents did not apply the techniques of ICPS, and Jorge's behavior and school performance deteriorated. With the combination of PTSD and ADHD, Jorge was very anxious and angry and afraid to be alone in his room. At times, he became belligerent toward his mother.

Because of the traumatic accident and its resultant stress, Jorge and his parents returned to therapy for support. Learning to adapt the vocabulary and principles of ICPS to the new situation, Jorge was guided to think of different things he could visualize or say to himself when he experienced panic. He was also taught slow, deep breathing as an additional tool for coping with panic. These new visualization and slow, deep-breathing skills, skills specific to anxiety disorder, could now provide additional options from which to choose when Jorge was faced with this new type of problem.

Jorge's parents agreed to apply ICPS dialogues rather than shouting when they became frustrated with their son. His father, who struggled with a low frustration tolerance due to his injuries, thought of things different from shouting that he could do when he became frustrated or angry. In addition, Jorge's teacher was advised about these family changes and thought of ways she could help Jorge when he began to panic, such as allowing him to see the counselor. After a few months, the family had returned close to their functioning before the accident. After 6 months Jorge's father returned to his former responsibilities at work as well. In grade 6, Jorge earned good grades at school, continued to mature, and took on more responsibility. Occasionally he, like many children with ADHD, didn't study for a test or began a project late, resulting in a low grade. However, he learned from his mistakes, studied and planned earlier the next time. He was no longer afraid to be alone. Jorge and his parents learned how to share and solve problems together, paving the way for a close, positive relationship that had strengthened the family bonding in ways that hadn't existed before. Jorge observed with pride that other families didn't listen to each other and problem solve the way his family does.

Comments on the Efficacy of Clinical Cases

Each of the children described above displayed symptoms of ADHD, and two of them also experienced at least one initial comorbid disorder, not uncommon for children with ADHD (Hinshaw, 2000). Research suggests that there is significant comorbidity between attention deficit disorder with disorders of mood, anxiety, and conduct (Biederman, Newcorn, and Sprich, 1991). Despite existing literature that suggests that training is based on the ICPS model has little or no impact on guiding interpersonal behaviors in real-life situations with children with ADHD (Abikoff, 1991), including parents may provide some clues for its success. In discussing interventions with children with ADHD, Hinshaw (2000) reports several studies that demonstrate that cognitive-behavioral therapies, including problem-solving, are typically conducted with the child, either individually or in small group formats. The premise of potentially greater impact by including parents can be supported by the one study reported by Abikoff that did have a positive impact. Kirby (1984) incorporated social problem-solving as

one component of a 7-week summer program with unmedicated ADHD youngsters involved parents, and it was those parents who participated in the program who rated their children as most improved in self-control.

Abikoff and Gittelman (1985) also concluded that social problem-solving training yielded no significant impact on academic, behavioral, or cognitive measures in children with ADHD, nor did it facilitate withdrawal of medication. In this study, parents attended two training sessions and were instructed to encourage and praise a systematic and reflective approach to schoolwork. In addition, children were rewarded points in exchange for toys and games for "working hard and trying your best" to encourage the child's participation in the program. This would not be effective unless the child had the skills to do that. Jorge's way of "working hard" and "trying his best" was in *his* deciding to ask his teacher if he could sit away from the other children to avoid distractions while doing class work. The outcome of Jorge's making this decision was very different from what it would have been had the teacher made the decision for him. Unlike dispensing points in exchange for toys and games to try hard (external rewards), Jorge's newly acquired problem-solving skills nourished a genuine desire to succeed (internal rewards). Unlike Abikoff and Gittelmans' subjects, for whom cognitive training did not help discontinue medication, intensive ICPS dialoguing by his parents may have contributed to Jorge's becoming medication free.

More than the fact that parents were intimately involved in the therapeutic process may be *how* they were involved. Referring to clinicians who employ cognitive-behavioral (CB) strategies, Braswell and Kendall (2001) point out, "the CB clinician must strive to be sensitive to the parents' beliefs about the causes of the child's difficulties; otherwise, it may be difficult for the parents to fully endorse or enthusiastically participate in a treatment plan that is not consistent with the parents' understanding of the problem" (p. 257). In this regard, the effect of the children's neurological condition on their behavior was explained. Consistent with Braswell and Kendall's (1988) recommendation, difficulties at school and at home were viewed as "problems to be solved rather than the inevitable outcome of a specific disease process or family circumstance" (p. 176). The parents were asked what solutions they had attempted in the past and then were asked if they were ready to try a new approach. The difference between the problem-solving approach and other methods of handling problems was explained, such as commands, demands, punishing, and also, how it differed from commonly used positive approaches such as suggesting what and what not to do and why. Beginning with a very simple problem, such as the child interrupts the parent, the parent practiced the different ways of talking with their child about this. They came to see that what they were doing was *one* way, not a bad way, but that ICPS is a *different* way. These parents were excited to try something new. The transfer of the relationship of mutual respect that developed between the therapist and the parents during the sessions to their relationship with their children may have played a key role in the success of the intervention.

To help parents understand their children's behavior, some cognitive-behavior therapists help parents reframe what their children are doing. For example, a parent who views his or her child's shoving of others as innately destructive can be helped to reinterpret that behavior with statements as, "I notice he is most likely to shove other children when the classroom is very crowded and the children are expected to share a small number of supplies" (Braswell & Kendall, 2001, p. 258). Although reframing can set the stage for the parent to understand their child's behavior in a new light and "encourage constructive efforts to cope with the problem at hand," ICPS training gives the parent tools to teach their children specific skills to do that.

In addition to the parents' understanding of their children's behavior and their beliefs being in accord with the intervention they are receiving, Whalen and Henker (1991) report that "consideration of children's preferences may be a practical means of enhancing clinical outcomes" (p. 135). They continue, "Soliciting and considering the child's view when selecting and evaluating therapies conveys a positive message about the child's

competence and worth, recruits the child as a partner in the therapeutic process, and provides the child opportunities to learn how to make, evaluate, and modify personally relevant decisions." In each of the case studies described above, the children were consulted regarding their family's participation in the program to which they agreed. In fact, it was Jorge himself who requested the family therapy using ICPS.

The Issue of Generalization

It may have been the therapist's approach to the parents with whom she worked that helped their children generalize their social cognitive skills from the setting in which they were learned, to another setting—an effect that Whalen and Henker (1991) report rarely occurs with children with ADHD. These authors propose two types of generalization one might look for when evaluating a program: (1) transfer of treatment-related gains in nontarget domains and nontreatment settings including academic and social skills and (2) positive ripples as improved likeability, perceived self-efficacy, willingness to take risks or accept challenges, improved frustration tolerance, and attitudes toward studying and learning. Jimmy and Jorge were helped to transfer their attitudes toward studying and learning through a home-school report card developed by the therapist which was responded to with ICPS dialoguing techniques rather than external (often negative) consequences. Patricia's teacher at the time of parent training was aware of the intervention and, although not trained in ICPS, was more sensitive to her feelings than before.

Braswell and Kendall (1988) note that "overlap between training tasks and generalization targets is necessary for obtaining optimal gains. Training in applying the new skills to a variety of tasks provides the child with opportunities to learn how the strategies can be adapted to an as yet unexperienced situation" (p. 203). Not only did these children learn how to think in ways they could successfully resolve problems in a variety of settings and for a variety of problems, but the generalization across settings and time may have occurred because of the continued parent–child dialoguing and enhanced feelings of empowerment of the parents as well as the children.

It might be proposed that the ripple effects of the treatment, namely, increased feelings of self-efficacy, resulted in an increased motivation in school and increased frustration tolerance in these children. Additionally, the process of problem-solving, that is, thinking of different solutions, evaluating their potential consequences, including how they and others feel or might feel, may have been internalized by the children rather than believing that one particular solution is best for any one particular problem that may arise in their lives. As noted by D'Zurilla and Nezu (2001), " 'Problem solving' refers to the process of *finding* solutions to specific problems, whereas 'solution implementation' refers to the process of *carrying out* those solutions to actual problematic situations" (p. 213). Not teaching specific solutions to solve specific problems plus the encouragement to implement solutions offered by the child that are predicted to have positive consequences (through ICPS dialoguing) may contribute to these children's ability to carry out their newly acquired ICPS skills in settings other than where they were first learned. In the arena of social behaviors and interpersonal competence, we saw earlier with nonclinical but high-risk children that parent-trained children were able to generalize their learned ICPS skills from the setting in which they were trained (the home) to a different setting (the school). Although socialization skills were never a problem for Jorge, improvement in the ability to solve interpersonal problems and empathize with others appears to have contributed to the improved socialization skills in Patricia and Jimmy.

The Comorbid Conditions

In all three cases, follow-up suggested the comorbid diagnoses no longer existed and the children were compensating adequately with the symptoms of ADHD. Patricia no longer experienced depression or anxiety. In fact, she tried out for the school soccer team and enjoyed attending school in England during the summer. She still had attention problems but was functioning well due to her compensating for the problem because of her high level of motivation and increased self-confidence. Jimmy had replaced impulsivity and oppositional/defiant behavior with the use of effective problem-solving strategies and continued to have positive peer relationships when observed 4 years later. Stimulant medication was introduced (in grade five), not for interpersonal behaviors, but for attention to schoolwork. And Jorge, who did not have a comorbid condition diagnosis until the automobile accident, which at that time was so severe that PTSD became primary, no longer experienced these symptoms and again was compensating for symptoms of ADHD and functioning well.

Although ICPS intervention does not cure ADHD's core symptoms of hyperactivity and the ability to stay focused, Braswell and Kendall (2001) conclude from the research they cite that cognitive problem-solving approaches can be suitable "for treatment of adjunctive issues (such as parent–child conflict), and for treatment of coexisting concerns (including aggressive behavior, anxiety, and depression)" (pp. 276–277), the very comorbid behaviors exhibited by Patricia and Jimmy. Although improvement can, at least in part, be due to improved executive functioning problems common to ADHD, such as planning and use of verbal mediation to self-regulate behavior, these three children learned the very skills that Whalen and Henker (1991) argue must be acquired before cognitive-behavior therapy can be effective—"sufficient foresight and verbal dexterity to plan, guide, and evaluate their behaviors" (p. 131). ICPS may also provide the structure and mode of interaction in the family that increases the necessary structured environment that ADHD children need.

Amount of Training

Despite the above advantages to advance impact of ICPS, one might question how behavioral changes can occur and remain after only 6–10 family therapy or parent-training sessions. With regard to cognitive-behavior therapy (CBT), Goldstein and Goldstein (1998) concluded that "When cognitive behavior therapy is dealing with conditions that are 'hard wired' or neurologically based as appears to be the case with ADHD, it may be the case that CBT applications have not been implemented with the intensity that matches the true treatment needs of the clients" (as cited by Braswell & Kendall, 2001, p. 276). Despite the relatively few treatment sessions, the parents of children described in these case studies provided intensive treatment to their children on a daily basis through playing the ICPS games and dialoguing with their children about problems that came up at home and at school. In addition, the lasting effect of the treatment was also fostered through supportive telephone communication every 3 or 4 months over several years with the therapist—a form of informal booster shots.

Asperger's Syndrome

In addition to ADHD, exemplified by Patricia, Jimmy, and Jorge, ICPS can have a significant impact on children diagnosed with Asperger's syndrome. Children with Asperger's syndrome are often hyper verbose about what interests them, and their conversations are often one-sided and egocentric. They do not pay attention to the needs and interests of others, or how they react to what the child is saying. They also have difficulty noticing behavioral cues in others, and once they start talking about what interests them, they have difficulty shifting to a new topic (Klin, Volkmar, & Sparrow, 2000). Klin et al. note that executive functioning deficits are evident across the entire autistic spectrum, including those with Asperger's syndrome. The American Psychiatric Association's Diagnostic and Statistical Manual of Mental Disorders (DSM IV TR, 2009) notes that children with Asperger's have difficulty maintaining peer relations, display repetitive movements, and have a narrow range of interests.

Aberson, who has worked with children with Asperger's syndrome, has found that they not only have difficulty shifting to a new topic, but also in shifting behaviors. She adds that they have

poor self-regulation and are often rigid and stubborn, lacking flexibility in their thinking. As a result, they are often rejected by their peers. They are offended without cause and are not offended when there is a cause. Continuous peer rejection may lead to unexpected aggressive responses on their part. When their parents and/or teachers teach them interpersonal problem-solving skills, they learn to think more flexibly and to better regulate their behavior. As a result, they function better at home and at school.

Billy, a very bright 4-year-old with Asperger's syndrome, was rejected by his peers at preschool due to his rigid behaviors and poor self-regulation, behavior which was also displayed at home. Because his parents didn't understand why he was behaving this way, they put him in time-out, which made the situation worse. ICPS was able to help Billy modify his behavior.

Billy's Story

Billy has twin brothers who were, at the time of treatment, under 1 year of age. Both of his parents were becoming increasingly more frustrated because of his aggressive and inappropriate behaviors at home and at school. The situation came to a head when he was asked to leave his preschool for aggressively behaving like the class police officer with the other children. Additionally, he frequently hit his baby brothers. When told to go to time-out he hit or kicked his parents or brothers on the way there or afterwards.

Billy's parents sought help with the above problems and received parent training with the ICPS approach. Additionally, Billy's mother participated in ICPS games with her son in the psychologist's office. Treatment lasted for approximately 10 weeks. After 1 month changes were noticed at home. For example, 1 day after Billy was playing video games and was forced to stop for dinner, he demanded that he be given the ketchup. His mother asked him, "What is a *different* way you might ask for the ketchup?" He responded, "May I please have the ketchup?" Using ICPS words, he asked, "Can I finish my video game *after* dinner?" He also learned to understand that his mother could play with him *some of the time* but *not all of the time*. He also learned to recognize *good times* and *not good times* for him to play with his mother.

After 10 weeks Billy became more cooperative at home and his aggressive behavior ceased. In first grade he was placed in a full day gifted program with accommodations where he remained with the same friends throughout the fifth grade. He is currently in a magnet program as well as gifted classes in middle school. He is an empathic high functioning student and enjoys positive relationships with teachers, parents, peers, and siblings. Most importantly, his bonding with his parents is so close that he openly problem solves with them whenever needed.

In addition to the intensity of training and the increased bonding between parent and child, the questions of ICPS dialoguing, the goal of which is to stimulate and enrich the ICPS skills of the child, help children take over tasks independently. Additionally, children become aware of the natural consequences of their behavior and how they and others feel when they don't live up to their end of the responsibility or hurt others physically or emotionally. The repeated association of ICPS dialogue questions redirecting behaviors and in planning tasks with the fun games of ICPS may, as it did for Patricia, Jimmy, Jorge, and Billy, result in children's being more attentive to their parents—and in more positive interactions with them.

Qualifying Considerations for ICPS Impact on Behavior

There are many variations of CBT (summarized in Braswell & Kendall, 1988, 2001) that may have a significant impact on how a child's thinking affects his or her behavior. No claim is made that ICPS is the most efficacious way to go about doing that, but rather, it is presented as a different way. However, a comprehensive meta-analysis of school-based social and emotional learning programs, of which ICPS is one, has shown that these kinds of programs have significant impact on behaviors that predict later, more serious

outcomes as discussed in this chapter, and also, on academic achievement in normal and high-risk, but not clinically diagnosed youngsters from kindergarten through high school (Durlak, Weissberg, Dymnicki, & Taylor, Schellinger, 2011).

Regarding impact of ICPS with children diagnosed with ADHD and Asperger's syndrome such as those described here is clearly encouraging, it should also be noted that these children were not referred. In fact, their parents initiated the therapy, and, as noted, one of them at her child's request, and were at least of average intelligence. Although Jorge and his parents did suffer a trauma, it was temporary.

For parents who have their own chronic psychological disturbances to deal with, ICPS may not, indeed, be enough. In this regard, however, Baydar, Jamila Reid, and Webster-Stratton (2003) found that mothers of nonclinical Head Start children with mental health risk factors of depression, anger, history of abuse as a child, and substance abuse were engaged in, and benefited from, a program based on the problem-solving model at levels comparable to mothers not experiencing these risk factors. With their training adapted to meet the needs of the parents (e.g., transportation, child care), trained parents with mental health risk factors, compared to controls, significantly reduced harsh/negative and inconsistent/ineffective parenting and increased supportive positive parenting. This finding is encouraging because the need to train parents with these kinds of maladaptive behaviors becomes evident with Cataldo (1997) finding that maltreating (child abusing) mothers, compared to non-maltreating mothers, were not only deficient in the ability to think of solutions to problems that come up with their children, but were deficient in solving-problems in general (e.g., wanting her friend to go with her to a movie). Not only were the maltreating mothers poor problem solvers, but the children of abused parents are similarly deficient in problem-solving skills (Haskett, 1990). The positive impact of training of parents with maladaptive behaviors as shown by Baydar et al. research notwithstanding, with respect to the specific behaviors of the children described here, more systematic empirical research comparing ICPS with other CBT techniques, such as cognitive restructuring and/or attribution training, and in combination with behavioral ones (e.g., rewards) is needed, as well as comparing the impact of these when implemented by diagnostically disturbed and nonclinical samples of parents. It would also be useful to compare training of peers and teachers as well as parents, a combination that Braswell and Kendall (1988) suggest might maximize generalization. Before concluding, however, that even ICPS and ICPS-like interventions alone cannot succeed with children with ADHD and Asperger's, we believe the clinical evidence presented by the four case studies described, the impact of ICPS on severely emotionally disturbed teacher- and counselor-trained youngsters, and the decreased behavioral dysfunction in non-clinical ICPS teacher-trained youngsters in the studies mentioned earlier provides sufficient justification for more systematic empirical research that actively engages parents together with their children, research that may provide further understanding of what it takes to have an impact with these particular populations at home and at school.

Final Thoughts

As Kumpfer and Alvarado (2003) have noted, "The probability of a youth acquiring developmental problems increases rapidly as risk factors such as family conflict, lack of parent–child bonding, disorganization, ineffective parenting, stressors, parental depression, and others increase in comparison with protective or resilience factors. Hence, family protective mechanisms and individual resilience processes should be addressed in addition to reducing family risk factors" (p. 458). The parent–child bonding that developed and endured into adolescence in cases documented over time by Aberson and Ardila (2000) provides the ongoing communication that helps children develop goals and confidence in confronting new challenges as well as peer pressure. These children have learned that no matter how difficult situations may be in other settings, the family will provide a sanctuary where everyone is heard and accepted

and problems can be solved. It is the open and accepting communication fostered by ICPS that increases the bonding and feelings of empowerment that problems can, indeed, be solved. As one parent stated, "I learned that I as a parent can be part of the solution for my child rather than adding to the problem. Before using this approach I was trying to take power and felt powerless. Now we solve the problem together." When the parents described in Aberson and Ardila were asked 2 or more years after training how often they dialogue with their children, they often believed, as one parent explicitly said, "I can't tell you that. That's just our way of life. But honestly, we don't have to dialogue very much because our children solve problems for themselves." Children who have lived in environments using the ICPS program develop the abilities associated with resilience as they learn to think for themselves and cope with the challenges of an unpredictable world.

References

Aberson, B. (1996). *An intervention for improving executive functioning and social/emotional adjustment of ADHD children: Three single case design studies.* Unpublished doctoral dissertation, Miami Institution of Psychology, Miami, FL.

Aberson, B., Albury, C., Gutting, S., Mann, F., & Trushin, B. (1986). *I can problem solve (ICPS): A cognitive training program for kindergarten children.* Unpublished manuscript, Report to the Bureau of Education, Miami, FL: Dade County Public Schools.

Aberson, B., & Ardila, A. (2000). *An intervention for improving executive functioning and social/emotional adjustment of three ADHD children. A four-year-follow-up.* Unpublished manuscript.

Abidin, R. (1990). *Parenting stress index-short form.* Charlottesville, VA: Pediatric Psychology Press.

Abikoff, H. (1991). Cognitive training in ADHD children: Less to it than meets the eye. *Journal of Learning Disabilities, 24,* 205–209.

Abikoff, H., & Gittelman, R. (1985). Hyperactive children treated with stimulants: Is cognitive training a useful adjunct? *Archives of General Psychiatry, 42,* 953–961.

Achenbach, T. M., & Edelbrock, C. S. (1983). *Manual for the child behavior checklist and revised child behavior profile.* Burlington, VT: University Association in Psychiatry.

Allen, R. J. (1978). An investigatory study of the effects of a cognitive approach to interpersonal problem solving on the behavior of emotionally upset psychosocially deprived preschool children. Unpublished doctoral dissertation, Center for Minority Studies, Brooking Institute, Union Graduate School, Washington, DC.

American Psychiatric Association. (2009). *Diagnostic and statistical manual of mental disorders (DSM IV TR)*. Washington, DC: APA.

Arend, G., Gove, F. L., & Sroufe, L. A. (1979). Continuity of individual adaptation from infancy to kindergarten: A predictive study of ego-resiliency and curiosity in preschoolers. *Child Development, 50*, 950–959.

Baydar, N., Jamila Reid, M., & Webster-Stratton, C. (2003). The role of mental health factors and program engagement in the effectiveness of a preventive parenting program for Head Start mothers. *Child Development, 74*, 1433–1453.

Behar, L., & Stringfield, S. (1974). A behavior rating scale for the preschool child. *Developmental Psychology, 10*, 601–610.

Bender, D., & Lösel, F. (2011). Bullying at school as a predictor of delinquency, violence, and other antisocial beahviour in adulthood. *Criminal Behavior and Mental Health, 21*, 99–106.

Biederman, J., Newcorn, J., & Sprich, S. (1991). Comorbidity of attention deficit hyperactivity disorder with conduct, depressive, anxiety and other disorders. *American Journal of Psychiatry, 148*, 564–577.

Blum, R. (2002, July). *Promoting student connectedness to school: Evidence from the national longitudinal study of adolescent health*. Paper presented at the National Technical Assistance Meeting, Washington, DC.

Boyle, D., & Hassett-Walker, C. (2008). Reducing overt and relational aggression among young children: The results of a two-year-outcome evaluation. *Journal of School Violence, 7*, 27–42.

Braswell, L., & Kendall, P. C. (1988). Cognitive-behavioral methods with children. In K. S. Dobson (Ed.), *Handbook of cognitive-behavioral therapies* (pp. 167–213). New York: Guilford.

Braswell, L., & Kendall, P. C. (2001). Cognitive-behavioral therapy with youth. In K. S. Dobson (Ed.), *Handbook of cognitive-behavioral therapies* (2nd ed., pp. 246–294). New York: Guilford.

Brooks, R., & Goldstein, S. (2001). *Raising resilient children: Fostering strength, hope and optimism in your child*. New York: Contemporary Books.

Cataldo, R. (1997). *Social problem solving skills in maltreating and comparison mothers*. Unpublished doctoral dissertation, Philadelphia, PA: Allegheny University of the Health Sciences.

Crick, N. R. (1996). The role of overt aggression, relational aggression, and prosocial behavior in the prediction of children's future social adjustment. *Child Development, 67*, 2317–2327.

Crick, N. R., & Bigbee, M. A. (1998). Relational and overt forms of peer victimization: A multiinformant approach. *Journal of Consulting and Clinical Psychology, 66*, 337–347.

Crick, N. R., Casas, J. F., & Mosher, M. (1997). Relational and overt aggression in preschool. *Developmental Psychology, 33*, 579–588.

Crick, N. R., & Grotpeter, J. K. (1995). Relational aggression, gender, and social-psychological adjustment. *Child Development, 66*, 710–722.

D'Zurilla, T. J., & Nezu, A. M. (2001). Problem solving therapies. In K. S. Dobson (Ed.), *Handbook of cognitive-behavioral therapies* (2nd ed., pp. 211–245). New York: Guilford.

Dawson, M., Raforth, M. A., & Carey, K. (1990). Best practices in assisting with promotion and retention decisions. In A. Thomas & J. Grimes (Eds.), *Best practices in school psychology II* (pp. 137–145). Washington, DC: National Association of School Psychologists.

DeFranco-Nierenberg, K., & Givner. A. (1998, August). *Effects of an interpersonal cognitive problem-solving curriculum with seriously emotionally disturbed children, grades K-2*. Paper presented at the annual meeting of the American Psychological Association, San Francisco, CA.

Dodge, K. (1993). Social-cognitive mechanisms in the development of conduct disorder and depression. *Annual Review of Psychology, 44*, 559–584.

Durlak, J. A., Weissberg, R. P., Dymnicki, A., & Taylor, R. D., & Schellinger (2011). The impact of enhancing students' social and emotional learning: A meta-analysis of school-based universal interventions. *Child Development, 82*, 405–432.

Elias, M. J., Gara, M., Ubriaco, M., Rothman, P. A., Clabby, J. F., & Schuyler, T. (1986). Impact of a preventive social problem solving intervention on children's coping with middle-school stressors. *American Journal of Community Psychology, 14*, 259–276.

Feis, C. L., & Simons, C. (1985). Training preschool children in interpersonal cognitive problem-solving skills: A replication. *Prevention in Human Services, 14*, 59–70.

Goldstein, S., & Goldstein, M. (1998). *Understanding and managing attention deficit hyperactivity disorder* (2nd ed.). New York, NY: Wiley.

Haskett, M. E. (1990). Social problem-solving skills of young physically abused children. *Child Psychiatry and Human Development., 2*, 109–118.

Higgens, J. P., & Thies, A. P. (1981). Problem solving and social position among emotionally disturbed boys. *American Journal of Orthopsychiatry, 51*, 356–358.

Hinshaw, S. P. (2000). Attention-deficit/hyperactivity disorder: The search for viable treatment. In P. C. Kendall (Ed.), *Child and adolescent therapy: Cognitive-behavioral procedure* (2nd ed., pp. 88–128). New York: Guilford.

Kazdin, A. E., Esveldt-Dawson, K., French, N. H., & Unis, A. S. (1987). Problem-solving skills training and relationship therapy in the treatment of antisocial child behavior. *Journal of Consulting and Clinical Psychology, 55*, 76–85.

Kazdin, A. E., Siegel, T. C., & Bass, D. (1992). Cognitive problem-solving skills training and parent management training in the treatment of antisocial behavior in children. *Journal of Consulting and Clinical Psychology, 60*, 733–747.

Kirby, E. A. (1984, August). *Durable and generalized effects of cognitive behavior modification with attention deficit disorder children.* Paper presented at the annual meeting of the American Psychological Association, Toronto, ON, Canada.

Klin, A., Volkmar, F. R., & Sparrow, S. S. (2000). *Asperger's syndrome.* New York: Guilford.

Kumpfer, K. L., & Alvarado, R. (2003). Family-strengthening approaches for the prevention of youth problem behaviors. *American Psychologist, 58,* 457–465.

Kumpfer, K. L., Alvarado, R., Tait, C., & Turner, C. (2002). Effectiveness of school-based family and children's skills training for substance abuse prevention among 6-8-year-old rural children. *Psychology of addictive behaviors, 16,* S65–S71.

Lochman, J. E., & Dodge, K. A. (1994). Social-cognitive processes of severely violent, moderately aggressive, and nonaggressive boys. *Journal of Consulting and Clinical Psychology, 62,* 366–374.

Loeber, R., & Hay, D. (1997). Key issues in the development of aggression and violence from childhood to early adulthood. *Annual Review of Psychology, 48,* 371–410.

Moffitt, T. E., & Caspi, A. (2001). Childhood predictors differentiate life-course persistent and adolescent-limited antisocial pathways among males and females. *Development and Psychopathology, 13,* 355–375.

Nagin, D. S., & Tremblay, R. (1999). Trajectories of boys' physical aggression, opposition, and hyperactivity on the path to physically violent and nonviolent juvenile delinquency. *Child Development, 79,* 1181–1196.

Ostrov, J. M. (2010). Prospective associations between peer victimization and aggression. *Child Development, 81,* 1670–1677.

Ostrov, J. M., & Crick, N. R. (2007). Forms and functions of aggression during early childhood: A short-term longitudinal study. *School Psychology Review, 36,* 22–43.

Ostrov, J. M., Woods, K. E., Jansen, E. A., Casas, J. F., & Crick, N. R. (2004). An observational study of delivered and received aggression, gender, and social psychological adjustment in preschool: "This white crayon doesn't work…". *Early Childhood Research Quarterly, 19,* 355–371.

Parker, J. G., & Asher, S. R. (1987). Peer relations and later personal adjustment: Are low-accepted children "at risk"? *Psychological Bulletin, 102,* 357–389.

Reynolds, C. R., & Kamphaus, R. W. (1992). *Behavior assessment system for children.* Circle Pines, MI: American Guidance Service.

Roff, J. D. (1984). Childhood aggression and social adjustment as antecedents of delinquency. *Journal of Abnormal Child Psychology, 12,* 111–126.

Rubin, K. H. (1985). Socially withdrawn children: An "at risk" population? In B. H. Schneider, K. H. Rubin, & J. E. Ledingham (Eds.), *Children's peer relations: Issues in assessment and intervention* (pp. 125–139). New York: Springer.

Rubin, K. H., Burgess, K. B., & Coplin, R. J. (2002). Social inhibition and withdrawl in childhood. In: P. K. Smith & C. H. Hart (Eds.). *Blackwell handbook of childhood social development.* Malden, MA: Blackwell, pp. 329–352.

Sacco, W. P., & Graves, D. J. (1984). Childhood depression, interpersonal problem-solving, and self-ratings of performance. *Journal of Clinical Child Psychology, 13,* 10–15.

Santos Elias, L. C., Marturano, E. M., Ameida Motta, A. M., & Giurlani, A. G. (2003). Treating boys with low school achievement and behavior problems: Comparison of two kinds of intervention. *Psychological Reports, 92,* 105–116.

Shure, M. B. (1992a). *I can problem solve (ICPS): An interpersonal cognitive problem solving program for children [preschool].* Champaign, IL: Research Press.

Shure, M. B. (1992b). *I can problem solve (ICPS): An interpersonal cognitive problem solving program for children [kindergarten/primary grades].* Champaign, IL: Research Press.

Shure, M. B. (1992c). *I can problem solve (ICPS): An interpersonal cognitive problem solving program for children [intermediate elementary grades].* Champaign, IL: Research Press.

Shure, M. B. (1993). *Interpersonal problem solving and prevention. A comprehensive report of research and training: A five-year-longitudinal study* (Report# MH-40801). Washington, DC: National Institute of Mental Health.

Shure, M. B. (1996). *Raising a thinking child: Help your young child resolve everyday conflict and get along with others.* New York: Pocket Books.

Shure, M. B. (2000). *Raising a thinking child workbook.* Champaign, IL: Research Press.

Shure, M. B. (2001). *Raising a thinking preteen. The I can problem solve program for 8- to 12-year-olds.* New York: Owl/Holt.

Shure, M. B. (2003). A problem solving approach to preventing early high-risk behaviors in children and preteen. In D. Romer (Ed.), *Preventing adolescent risk* (pp. 85–92). Thousand Oaks, CA: Sage.

Shure, M. B. (2005). *Enseñando a Nuestros Niños a Pensar.* Champaign, IL: Research Press.

Shure, M. B., & Healey, K. N. (1993, August). *Interpersonal problem solving and prevention in urban 5th- and 6th- graders.* Paper presented at the meeting of the American Psychology Association, Toronto, ON, Canada.

Shure, M. B., & Spivack, G. (1972). Means-end thinking, adjustment, and social class among elementary-school-aged children. *Journal of Consulting and Clinical Psychology, 38,* 348–353.

Shure, M. B., & Spivack, G. (1974a). *Preschool interpersonal problem solving (PIPS) test.* Philadelphia, PA: Hahnemann University.

Shure, M. B., & Spivack, G. (1974b). Interpersonal problem solving thinking and adjustment in the mother-child dyad. In M. W. Kent & J. E. Rolf (Eds.), *Primary prevention of psychopathology* (Social competence in children, Vol. III, pp. 201–219). Hanover, NH: University Press of New England.

Shure, M. B., & Spivack, G. (1980). Interpersonal problem solving as a mediator of behavioral adjustment in preschool and kindergarten children. *Journal of Applied Developmental Psychology, 1,* 29–44.

Shure, M. B., & Spivack, G. (1982). Interpersonal problem solving in young children: A cognitive approach to prevention. *American Journal of Community psychology, 10,* 341–356.

Shure, M. B., & Spivack, G. (1990). *What happens the next game (WHNG)* (2nd ed.). Philadelphia: Hahnemann University.

Shure, M. B., Spivack, G., & Jaeger, M. A. (1971). Problem-solving thinking and adjustment among disadvantaged preschool children. *Child Development, 42,* 1791–1803.

Simmons, R. (2002). *Odd girl out: The hidden culture of aggression in girls.* New York: Harcourt Books.

Small, R. W., & Schinke, S. P. (1983). Teaching competence in residential group care: Cognitive problem solving and interpersonal skills training with emotionally disturbed preadolescents. *Journal of Social Service Research, 7,* 1–16.

Smith, P., Singer, M., Hoel, H., & Cooper, C. L. (2003). Victimization in the school and the workplace: Are there any links? *British Journal of Psychology, 94,* 175–188.

Spivack, G., & Shure, M. B. (undated). *Hahnemann PreSchool Behavior rating scale.* Philadelphia, PA: Hahnemann University.

Spivack, G., & Shure, M. B. (1982). Interpersonal cognitive problem-solving and clinical theory. In B. Lahey & A. E. Kazdin (Eds.), *Advances in child clinical psychology* (Vol. 5, pp. 323–372). New York: Plenum.

Spivack, G., & Swift, M. (1967). *Devereux Elementary School Behavior (DESB) rating scale manual.* Devon, PA: Devereux Foundation.

Valois, R. R., MacDonald, J. M., Bretous, L., & Fischer, M. A. (2002). Risk factors and behaviors associated with adolescent violence and aggression. *American Journal of Orthopsychiatry, 40,* 454–464.

Weddle, K. D., & Williams, F. (1993). *Implementing and assessing the effectiveness of the interpersonal cognitive problem solving (ICPS) curriculum in four experimental and four control classrooms.* Memphis State University: Unpublished manuscript.

Weissberg, R. P., & Gesten, E. L. (1982). Consideration for developing effective school-based social problem-solving (SPS) training programs. *School Psychology Review, 11,* 56–63.

Weissberg, R. P., Gesten, E. L., Carnrike, Cl, Toro, P. A., Rapkin, B. D., Davidson, B., et al. (1981). Social problem solving skills training: A competence- building intervention with second- to fourth-grade children. *American Journal of Community Psychology, 9,* 411–423.

Weissberg, R. P., Gesten, E. L., Liebenstein, N. L., Doherty-Schmid, K. D., & Hutton, H. (1979). *The Rochester social problem solving (SPS) program. A training manual for teachers of 2nd-4th grade children.* Rochester, NY: Center for Community Study, University of Rochester.

Whalen, C. K., & Henker, B. (1991). Therapies for hyperactive children: Comparison, combinations, and compromises. *Journal of Consulting and Clinical Psychology, 59,* 129–137.

Wiseman, R. (2002). *Queen Bees and Wannabes: Helping your daughter survive cliques, gossip, boyfriends, and the new realities of girl world.* New York: Crown.

Yu, P., Harris, G., Solovitz, B., & Franklin, J. (1985). *A preventive intervention program for children at high risk for later psychopathology.* Austin, TX: Texas Department of Mental Health and Mental Retardation. Unpublished report.

Part VII

Conclusions

The Future of Children Today

29

Sam Goldstein and Robert B. Brooks

How do we go about predicting the future of children today? What statistics should be examined? What outcomes should be measured? What formulas computed? There are no definitive or precise answers. In the second edition volume, we have attempted to expand upon and address these issues through the study and clinical application of resilience and resilience processes. We have sought to address which variables and through which processes within the child, immediate family, and extended community interact to offset the negative effects of adversity, thereby increasing the probability of our survival. Some of these processes may serve to protect the negative effects of specific stressors while others simply act to enhance development. In the truest sense, the study of resilience as an outcome phenomenon gathers knowledge that hopefully can be used to shape and change the future for the better.

What is the future of children today? In 2002, The National Center for Children in Poverty suggested that approximately one in six children in the United States lives in poverty (NCCP, 2002). However, the official poverty measure provides

only part of the story. It is widely suggested that on average families needed income about twice the federal poverty level to make ends meet. Children living in families with incomes below this level in 2006, for example, represented 39% of the nation's children, more than 28 million (Douglas-Hall & Chu, 2007). These statistics are higher in third world countries. Poverty is associated with multiple risk factors and long-term stressors that threaten development, ranging from exposure to violence, lack of appropriate medical, educational, psychological care and poor nutrition (Garbarino, 1995). As multiple authors in this volume have demonstrated, stress during all stages of children's development increases risk for a wide range of adverse outcomes, including those related to education, vocation, psychological, and emotional adjustment. These have a long-term effect well into the adult years (Shore, 1997). Further, the younger the child the greater is the risk and vulnerability (Fantuzzo, McWayne, & Bulotsky, 2003). For example, 20% of children under age 6 live at or below the poverty level (Fantuzzo et al.). Multiple barriers for change exist, including a continued lack of understanding of those forces or phenomena that protect vulnerable youth as well as access to those services that have been deemed effective for those at risk (National Advisory Mental Health Councils Workgroup on Child and Adolescent Mental Health Intervention, Development and Deployment, 2001; National Institute of Health and Mental Health, 1998). A report by the Surgeon General (U.S. Department

S. Goldstein (✉)
Neurology, Learning and Behavior Center,
Salt Lake City, UT 84102, USA
e-mail: info@samgoldstein.com

R.B. Brooks
Department of Psychology, McLean Hospital and
Harvard Medical School, 60 Oak Knoll Terrace,
Needham, MA 02498, USA
e-mail: contact@drrobertbrooks.com

S. Goldstein and R.B. Brooks (eds.), *Handbook of Resilience in Children*,
DOI 10.1007/978-1-4614-3661-4_29, © Springer Science+Business Media New York 2013

of Health and Human Services, 1999) set forth priorities to reduce stigma and increase access to assessment and treatment services, take advantage of resources available in the community, and foster partnerships among professionals.

These reports and the data they summarize raise grave concerns about the future of children based upon assessment of their functioning today. Yet our knowledge of those factors that protect and insulate continues to grow. We know more about how to help vulnerable children or for that matter all children transition successfully into adult life than ever before. As the authors in this second edition have attested, we have begun the work to further our understanding and create an applied science; a model that embraces the "whole-child perspective" focusing upon competence, context, and contributors to children's physical and mental health. As Fantuzzo et al. (2003) note, "competencies of the whole child not disorders or deficiencies are core to this developmental perspective" (p. 17). As such, a model of resilience must focus on children by examining the tasks they must perform and master at each age as they prepare to transition into adulthood. As we better understand these tasks and the forces that nurture mastery we become better prepared to foster resilience in all children. Such a model at its core focuses upon assets and abilities rather than diagnoses and disabilities. In this model, the interaction of the child and the environment form the context in which development takes place. Such a model also focuses on adults in the child's world capable of contributing to healthy development and resilience. Finally, such a model focuses on competencies of the child rather than deficiencies measured based upon an a priori list of abnormal behaviors.

A recently published study (Ungar, 2008) reports on a 14 site evaluation of over 1,500 youth globally. These findings support four propositions underlying a culturally and contextually embedded understanding of resilience:

1. There are global as well as culturally contextually specific aspects to young people's lives that contribute to their resilience.
2. Aspects of resilience exert differing amounts of influence on a child's life depending on a specific culture and context in which resilience is operating.
3. Aspects of children's lives that contribute to resilience are related to one another in patterns that reflect a child's culture and context.
4. Tensions between individuals and their cultures and contexts are resolved in ways that reflect highly specific relationships between aspects of resilience. As Ungar points out, resilience as a phenomenon may be far more complex than originally theorized. Interventions to seek to bolster aspects of resilience among culturally diverse populations of at-risk children and youth only succeed if these phenomena are better understood.

To gaze into the future of our species is but to gaze into the eyes of children. Our future is determined by the success or failure of our efforts to prepare children to become happy, healthy, functional, and contributing members of society in their adult lives. But the task of raising children and preparing a generation to take our place has become increasingly more difficult. Perhaps it is the complexity of our culture that brings with it the increased risks and vulnerabilities that have fueled the statistics of adversity for youth—delinquency, mental health problems, academic difficulty. These reflect our increasing difficulty instilling in children the qualities necessary for health, happiness, and success. It is within this framework that the fields of medicine, mental health, and education jointly arrive at the crossroads. This path reflects a conscious effort to help all children develop and become proficient in ways of thinking, feeling, and behaving, which can and will insulate them from the many adversities they are likely to face in our world. The many accomplished and gifted authors contributing to this volume represent as Wright and Masten (2004) point out, the third wave of resilience research, representing an effort to bring scientific theory and hypothesis into clinical practice. The breadth, depth, scope, and quality of the work in this volume offer great promise that, as Bell (2001) points out, resilience can be cultivated and strengthened in all youth.

As this second edition attests, there is an increasing body of research focusing on understanding the means and manner by which some youth overcome adversities that are overwhelming to many others. For example, although estimates of the incidence of a range of psychiatric disorders in children of depressed mothers are high, a sizable proportion of children of depressed mothers eventually achieve acceptable levels of psychosocial functioning (Downey & Coyne, 1990). How do these children, despite exposure to a significant adversity, manage to achieve positive adaptation? One approach to examining resilient outcomes in the face of adversity has been to measure protective factors that may interact with risks as well as "resource factors" that may have positive effects on both high- and low-risk groups (Conrad & Hammen, 1993). In their study, Brennan, Le Brocque, and Hammen (2003) examined parent–child relationships in detail as predictors of resilient outcomes in children of depressed mothers. Depressed mothers have been found to display less optimal parenting qualities than nondepressed mothers (Goodman & Gotlib, 1999). Brennan et al. (2003) followed over 800 15-year-old teenagers and their parents drawn from a large longitudinal study. They demonstrated that positive parent–child relationship qualities acted as protective factors for adolescent children of mothers with a history of depression. High levels of perceived maternal warmth and acceptance and low levels of perceived maternal psychological control and emotional over involvement were associated with higher levels of resilient outcomes in these youth. These results are consistent with findings of others (Belsky, 2001; DePanfilis, 2006). It is likely that these qualities too act as resource factors even for children of mothers who are not depressed. In fact, the parenting qualities these authors assessed had the same direction of effect for children of depressed and nondepressed mothers.

Can these findings be applied to create an applied science of resilience? In 1998, Olds, Pettit, Robinson, and Henderson demonstrated they could. This group identified risk factors for disruptive and aggressive behavior in children. They provided a program of prenatal and early childhood home visitation for groups of mothers who were then followed through their children's 15th birthday. Many of these were mothers 18-years-old or younger at the start of the study. This program reduced three domains of risk for the development of problem behaviors in children. The effects of the program included a reduction in maternal substance abuse during pregnancy, a reduction in child maltreatment, and a reduction in family size, closely spaced pregnancies, and chronic-welfare dependents. Thus, a comprehensive prenatal and early childhood visitation program was able to affect risks that likely contribute to adversity, increasing resilience among children and youth born into at-risk families. Even since the publication of the first edition of this volume, there has been a significant increase in scientific research as well as trade and educational programs under the umbrella of resilience (Olds et al., 1998).

As Fraser and Galinsky (1997) hypothesize, we will eventually collect and integrate sufficient research to create a resilience-based model of practice. Such a practice, these authors suggest, provides a framework for conceptualizing psychological, emotional, and behavioral conditions in childhood well beyond symptom and impairment descriptions. Such a model provides markers, correlates, and possible causes classified ecologically as broad environmental conditions, family, school, and neighborhood conditions and individual psychosocial and biological conditions. Such a model appreciates that some risk factors contribute uniquely to particular problems and some protective factors may insulate certain problems but may also act in an affirmative way for even unaffected youth. With such a model, clinicians would choose the best course of "treatment" for each affected individual by taking advantage of protective factors, seeking to reduce risks, and as needed, providing direct intervention to the affected child. As these authors point out, this perspective is "based on the idea that childhood problems are multidetermined. That is, they develop as the result of many causes whether at the level of the individual, the family or community or the broader environment" (p. 267). For such a model to be utilized effectively, certain thresholds of knowledge must be crossed by clinicians. These include:

Basic knowledge of risk and protection,

- Specific knowledge of risk and protective factors for specific problems or disorders.
- Specific knowledge of risk and protective factors in a local community.
- Knowledge of interventive research so that effective change strategies can be used to reduce the influence of risk.
- Knowledge of interventive research so that effective change strategies can be used to strengthen protective mechanisms (Fraser & Galinsky, 1997).

An article "Prevention that Works for Children and Youth" by Weissberg, Kumpfer, and Seligman (2003) in an issue of the *American Psychologist* reflects the growing interest in applying resilience processes through a preventive model. Yet, there is much work to be done to systematically evaluate the myriad of variables within children, their families, and in the environment that may contribute to, mediate, and moderate adult outcome. Much additional research remains to be completed to understand how to best disseminate and promote this knowledge so that it becomes an integral part of raising and educating children and fostering their mental health. It is hoped that the clinical application of resilience processes will lead to a primary prevention model which, as Weissberg, Kumpfer, and Seligman (2003) note, "is a sound investment in society's future" (p. 425).

References

Bell, C. C. (2001). Cultivating resiliency in youth. *Journal of Adolescent Health, 29,* 375–381.

Belsky, J. (2001). Emanuel Miller lecture developmental risks (still) associated with early child care. *Journal of Child Psychology and Psychiatry, 42*(7), 845–859.

Brennan, P. A., Le Brocque, R., & Hammen, C. (2003). Maternal depression, parent-child relationships, and resilient outcomes in adolescence. *Journal of the American Academy of Child and Adolescent Psychiatry, 42,* 1469–1477.

Conrad, M., & Hammen, C. (1993). Protective and resource factors in high- and low-risk children: A comparison of children with unipolar, bipolar, medically ill, and normal mothers. *Developmental Psychopathology, 5,* 593–607.

DePanfilis, D. (2006). *Child neglect: A guide for prevention assessment and intervention.* Washington, DC:

U.S. Department of Health and Human Services Administration for Children and Families.

Douglas-Hall, A., & Chu, N. M. (2007). *Basic facts about low income children, birth to age 18.* New York: National Center for Children in Poverty, Mailman School of Public Health, Columbia University.

Downey, G., & Coyne, J. C. (1990). Children of depressed parents: An integrative review. *Psychology Bulletin, 108,* 50–76.

Fantuzzo, J., McWayne, C., & Bulotsky, R. (2003). Forging strategic partnerships to advance mental health science and practice for vulnerable children. *School Psychology Quarterly, 32*(1), 17–37.

Fraser, M. W., & Galinsky, M. J. (1997). Toward a resilience-based model of practice. In M. W. Fraser (Ed.), *Risk and resilience in childhood: An ecological perspective.* Washington, DC: National Association of Social Workers Press.

Garbarino, J. (1995). *Raising children in a socially toxic environment.* San Francisco, CA: Josey-Bass.

Goodman, S., & Gotlib, I. (1999). Risk for psychopathology in the children of depressed mothers: A developmental model for understanding mechanisms of transmission. *Psychology Bulletin, 106,* 458–490.

National Advisory Mental Health Council's Workgroup on Child and Adolescent Mental Health Intervention, Development and Deployment. (2001). *Blueprint for change: Research on child and adolescent mental health.* Rockville, MD: National Institute of Mental Health.

National Center for Children in Poverty (2002, March). *Child poverty fact sheet: Low-income children in the United States: A brief demographic profile.* New York: National Center for Children in Poverty, Mailman School of Public Health, Columbia University.

National Institute of Health and National Institute Mental Health. (1998). *Bridging science and service. A report by the National Advisory Mental Health Council's Clinical Treatment and Services Research Workgroup.* Washington, DC: National Institute of Mental Health.

Olds, D., Pettit, L., Robinson, J., & Henderson, C. (1998). Reducing risks for antisocial behavior with a program of prenatal and early childhood home visitation. *Journal of Community Psychology, 26,* 65–83.

Shore, R. (1997). *Re-thinking the brain: New insights into early development.* New York, NY: Families and Work Institute.

U.S Department of Health and Human Services. (1999). *Mental health: A report by the surgeon general.* Rockville, MD: USDHHS.

Ungar, M. (2008). Resilience across cultures. *British Journal of Social Work, 38,* 218–235.

Weissberg, R. P., Kumpfer, K. L., & Seligman, M. E. P. (2003). Prevention that works for children and youth. *American Psychologist, 58,* 425–432.

Wright, M. D., & Masten, A. S. (2004). Resilience processes in development: Fostering positive adaptation in the context of adversity. In S. Goldstein & R. Brooks (Eds.), *Handbook of resilience in children.* New York, NY: Kluwer.

Index

A

ACTH. *See* Adrenocorticotropin (ACTH)
Adaptation
  adult, 94, 95
  adversity, 19
  children, 22, 83, 99, 143
  context-specific, 24
  dysfunctional/deviant, 46
  and human development, 39
  human system, 8
  individuals, 119
  life crisis, 41
  measurement, 4
  mutual, 5
  outcomes, 106, 107
  personal adjustment and ecological, 298
  positive (*see* Positive adaptation)
  protective factors, 4
  public health
    adversities, 460, 464
    community, 470
    mental health and social difficulties, 460
    process, 464
  quality, 94, 95
  resilient, 24–26
  service of, 298
  socioemotional, 109
  stress, life, 39
ADHD. *See* Attention deficit hyperactivity disorder
    (ADHD)
Adolescents
  adaptation, 108
  ADHD, 189
  African Americans, 7
  and children, 15, 65
  children, depression (*see* Depression, youth)
  children of mothers, depression, 509
  children, resiliency scales (*see* Resiliency Scales for
    Children and Adolescents (RSCA))
  coping problems, 25

depression, 83, 193
hyperactivity, 225
indicated prevention programs, 465
lives, 96
Mexican descent, 47
modern, 82
neuroticism, 59
poverty, 110
PTSD (*see* Posttraumatic stress disorder (PTSD))
PYD (*see* Positive youth development (PYD))
recruitment, Lord's Resistance Army (LRA), 310
resilient, 41
sickle cell disease, 45
suicides, 7
thriving indicators
  definition, 436
  developmental stages, 436
  Search Institute, 436
  violence, 435
young girls, 82
Adrenocorticotropin (ACTH)
  PTSD, 169
  release, pituitary, 164–165
  stress reactivity, adult rats, 166–167
Adversity. *See also* Positive adaptation
  ABC model, 205–206
  childhood, 90, 99
  classrooms, 407
  competent youth, 9
  development, children, 6
  distribution, individual adolescents and context
    relations, 294, 301, 304
  emotional reactivity, 276
  family, 63
  major life events approach, 242
  nurturing resilience, 443
  Personal Resiliency Profiles, 282–283
  poverty/neighborhood, 11
  prediction, resilience, 3
  prenatal and early childhood visitation program, 509